Sing Us One of the Old Songs

Millie Lindon. Reproduced by kind permission of the British
Music Hall Society.

Sing us one of the old songs, George,
One of the songs we know;
Try, old man, do what you can,
And we'll let the chorus go.
We can't forget what you used to be,
In the days when life was new;
Sing us a song,
And if you go wrong,
We'll help to pull you through.

W. B. Kelly and J. H. Woodhouse (1900)

Sing Us One of the Old Songs

A Guide to Popular Song 1860–1920

compiled by
Michael Kilgarriff

OXFORD UNIVERSITY PRESS

1998

Oxford University Press, Great Clarendon Street, Oxford OX2 6DP

Oxford New York

Athens Auckland Bangkok Bogota Buenos Aires Calcutta
Cape Town Chennai Dar es Salaam Delhi Florence Hong Kong Istanbul
Karachi Kuala Lumpur Madras Madrid Melbourne Mexico City Mumbai
Nairobi Paris Saõ Paulo Singapore Taipei Tokyo Toronto Warsaw
and associated companies in
Berlin Ibadan

Oxford is a registered trade mark of Oxford University Press

Published in the United States
by Oxford University Press Inc., New York

British Library Cataloguing in Publication Data
Data available

Library of Congress Cataloging in Publication Data
Kilgarriff, Michael.
Sing us one of the old songs: a guide to popular song 1860–1920 /
compiled by Michael Kilgarriff.
p. cm.
Includes bibliographical references and title index.
Contents: Core song-list—Artistes' repertoires—Lyricists and
composers—Date-list—Show songs.
1. Popular music—Great Britain—Bibliography. I. Title.
ML128.P63K55 1998 782.42164′0941—dc21 98–30286
ISBN 0-19-816657-5

1 3 5 7 9 10 8 6 4 2

Typeset by Best-set Typesetter Ltd., Hong Kong
Printed in Great Britain
on acid-free paper by
Biddles Ltd.,
Guildford & King's Lynn

PREFACE

'OH, if you want a book like that you'll have to do it yourself.'

The regularity with which archivists and librarians and Music Hall historians rolled out this response made me realize that if I wanted hard information on songs popular in Britain from 1860 to 1920 I would indeed have to do it myself. In *Sing Us One of the Old Songs* therefore lie the answers to the questions which excite Music Hall buffs more than anything in life: who wrote what and when and who sang it?

There are six principal sections:

1. CORE SONG-LIST: full details of some 1,250 songs and ballads most likely to be found in today's 'Old Time' shows.

2. ARTISTES' REPERTOIRES: some 18,000 titles under nearly 1,700 names.

3. LYRICISTS AND COMPOSERS: some 6,000 titles under more than 1,750 names.

4. DATE-LIST: titles for each year with significant artistes.

5. SHOW SONGS: shows from which songs originated.

6. INDEX OF SONG AND SKETCH TITLES

US popular music became rapidly more influential in Britain after the turn of the century and I have listed therefore many titles from Broadway and vaudeville which found a ready welcome on this side of the Atlantic. Having included the songs I felt it would be churlish to exclude the singers and tunesmiths so they are here too.

The criteria for a song's inclusion are popularity, topicality, and significance in the career of its singer. Also targeted for inclusion are titles still remembered and performed, for it is to today's Music Hall performers and producers that these checklists are primarily aimed. The non-active enthusiast and the casual enquirer will also find much of value herein if only because the information offered is not readily available. Many specialist libraries and collections are not open to the public; my intent is to bring much previously inaccessible material within general reach.

It is a pound to a penny I have missed out your granny's favourite, in which case I apologize to you both, though not too humbly. This compilation may have its shortcomings, but as The Great Macdermott used to sing, It's Better Than Nothing At All.

Michael Kilgarriff

Ealing
September 1998

Acknowledgements

KIND and willing assistance from the following is gratefully acknowledged:

John Adrian (Grand Order of Water Rats), Leslie Baker, Tony Barker, Katie Barnes, Mick Booth (Campbell Connelly), Geoffrey Brawn (Players' Theatre), Robert J. Bruce (Bodleian Library, Music Section), Peter Charlton, Clyde Clayton, Graeme Cruickshank (Palace Theatre), Hubert W. David, Johnny Dennis, Michael Diamond, Ruth Edge (EMI Archives, Hayes), John Foreman, English Folk Dance & Song Society, John M. Garrett, J. H. Garrod, the late Joe Ging, Frank Ginnett, Michael Goater, Catherine Haill (The Theatre Museum), Edward Hayward, Tudor Henson (National Library of Wales), Malcolm S. Higgins (Guildhall School of Music and Drama), Tony Locantro, Terry Lomas (British Music Hall Society), Richard Mangan and Alison Paine (Mander & Mitchenson Theatre Collection), Chantel Morel (Institut Français du Royaume-Uni), Bob Parker (British Library, Music Department), Charles Pemberton, Jane Pettit (Boosey & Hawkes), Al and Dave Sealey ('Cosmotheka'), Sir Donald Sinden CBE FRSA, Len Thorpe (Warner Chappell Music Ltd.), Max Tyler (British Music Hall Society), Ian Wallace (The Music Alliance), John Whitehorn (EMI Music Publishing), and John Williams (British Actors' Equity Association).

I should also like to mention the help and advice freely given by the staffs of the National Sound Archive, the Public Record Office, and the United States Information Service Reference Center.

Any errors are of course entirely my own responsibility.

M.K.

Contents

Principal Popular Song Publishers

————•◆•————

Publishing house changes of name, mergers, reassignments, acquisitions, takeovers, and the sub-publishing of American songs represent a very thorny thicket for the researcher, and though I have included many original publishers, most titles in the Core Song-List are now available either from Chappell's or EMI.

EMI Music Publishing Ltd. (Francis Day & Hunter, B. Feldman & Co., Charles Sheard, Reynold's Music, Keith Prowse Music, Darewski, Paxton, Lawrence Wright, etc.) distributes though International Music Publications (IMP), Unit 15–16, Southend Road, Woodford Green, Essex IG8 8HN (0181-551 6131). Out-of-print songs may be obtainable from Express Music, 10 Denmark Street, London WC2H 8LS (0171-836 2505).

Chappell Music Ltd. (Ascherberg, Hopwood & Crew, Howard & Co., etc.) is a subsidiary of Warner Chappell International Ltd., 129 Park Street, London W1Y 3FA (0171-629 7600) and also distributes through IMP.

Hard-to-find songs may be tracked down via The Music Alliance (formerly The Performing Right Society Ltd.), 29 Berners Street, London W1P 4AA (0171-580 5544). Contact their Works Registration department with the exact title and ask for details of the current publisher/copyright holder.

Within the European Union copyright protection for songs as with other intellectual property lasts for seventy years after the death of the writer and composer, after which period the work passes into the public domain. A publisher's own edition or reprint, however, may still be protected, especially if it is included in a recent compilation.

AFF	Affiliated Music	Est. 1957 by amalgamation of FD&H and ROB. Bought by EMI 1972
AHC	Ascherberg, Hopwood & Crew	Est. 1906, London. Bought by CHA 1969. Eugene Ascherberg died 1908
AMS	Amsco	NY based. FDH/EMI
ASC	E. Ascherberg & Co.	Est. 1877, London. Acquired HOW 1899, BLO 1906. Merged with H&C 1907
ASH	Edwin Ashdown	Est. 1860, London, as Ashdown & Black. H. Black retired in 1882 and died in 1888. From 1883 the company was named Edwin Ashdown. Acquired Hatzfeld 1903, Enoch 1927, LAR 1929. List includes Harry Clifton, Arthur Lloyd, Harry Sydney, and A. G. Vance. Bought by MSL 1982

BAT	J. Bath	Est. *c*.1865–1901 London. List includes George Gros smith sen. and Corney Grain
BAY	Bayley & Ferguson	London, but originated in Glasgow, 1884
BER	Irving Berlin Inc.	FDH/EMI
BLO	John Blockley	Est. London, 1853, by John Blockley (1800–82). Acquired Morison Kyle 1864. Songs of Sam Cowell, Harry Liston, etc. Bought by ASC 1906
BMC	Broadway Music Corp.	FDH
BOO	Thomas Boosey & Co.	Est. *c*.1792, London. Became Boosey & Hawkes 1930. Published Bellini, Claribel, Donizetti, Stanford, Verdi
BOS	Bosworth	Est. 1889, Leipzig
BOW	Bowerman & Co.	fl. 1887–1919. Published songs for News of the World
CAS	Cassell & Co.	fl. 1858–70 London
CCC	Campbell, Connelly & Co.	Est. 1925, London. Bought by MSL 1982
CHA	Chappell Music Ltd.	Est. 1810, London. Works by Gilbert & Sullivan, Leslie Stuart, Paul Rubens, Lionel Monckton, Ivan Caryll, Sidney Jones, Franz Lehár. Acquired AHC 1969. Subsidiary of Warner Chappell International Ltd. since 1988
CKH	Charles K. Harris	US based. FDH/EMI
CRA	J. B. Cramer & Co. Ltd.	Est. 1824, London. Songs of Herbert Campbell, J. L. Toole. Johann Baptist Cramer d. 1858. Acquired MET 1934
CUR	J. Curwen & Son Ltd.	Est. 1863. John Curwen was the pioneer of the Tonic Sol Fa system of notation
DAC	D'Almaine & Co.	fl. 1834–66. See G&D and SHE. Published 'Musical Bijou' series from 1830
DAL	Henri D'Alcorn	fl. 1855–82 London. List included Arthur Lloyd. From 1868–72 D'Alcorn & Black. Henri D'Alcorn (1828–1905) retired 1879. Some songs bought by H&C. See G&D
DAR	Herman Darewski Music Pub. Co.	Est. 1916, London. Acquired SHE 1918. Bought by FEL 1929
DAS	Dash Music Co. Ltd.	Acquired by CCC in late 1930s
DAV	Davidson's	Est. George Henry Davidson 1840, London. Output included 'Musical Treasury' series. From 1860 to 1881 known as Music Publishing Co. List included Sam Cowell and the songwriter J. Caulfield.
DEA	Frank Dean & Co.	Est. Henry Decker (1860–1922), better known as songwriter Harry Dacre, and fl. 1895–1905. FEL
DOV	Dover Publications Inc.	Distributes in UK through Constable & Co. Ltd.
DUF	Duff, Stewart & Co.	fl. 1831–1930, London. John Duff d. 1867; F. C. Stewart was his nephew
EBM	Edward B. Marks Music Corp.	NY based. FDH/EMI

EMI	EMI Music Pub. Ltd.	Acquired KPM 1969. FDH/AFF 1972. See IMP
EMP	Empire Music	Issued by Hart & Co.
F&D	Francis Bros & Day	Est. 1877, London, brothers James (1840–86) and William (1845–1907) Francis with David G. Day (1850–1929). Name soon changed to Francis & Day. Issued Comic Song Annuals 1882–1958. See FDH
FAM	F. A. Mills	NY based. EMI
FDH	Francis, Day & Hunter	Est. 1891 after death of James Francis when Harry Hunter (1841–1906) became a partner. See F&D. Acquired FEL 1953 and ROB 1957. See AFF. Bought by EMI 1972. Hunter sold out 1903
FEI	Leo Feist	NY based. FDH/EMI
FEL	B. Feldman & Co. Ltd.	Est. 1895, London. Issued Comic Song Annuals c.1896–1952. Acquired STA 1922, DAR 1929. Sold to FDH 1953. See AFF
FRH	Frederick Harris	NY
G&D	Goulding & D'Almaine	FDH. Goulding est. 1786, D'Almaine joined 1798, but Goulding & D'Almaine not est. till 1823. D'Almaine went independent 1834, the stock being sold in 1867 after his death the previous year
GAY	Noel Gay Publishing Co.	Est. 1938. CCC
GEM	Gus Edwards Music Publishing Co.	NY based
GUE	John Guest	fl. 1875–1904, London
H&C	Hopwood & Crew	Est. 1860, London. William Hopwood (1831–74) and George Crew (retired 1875). Acquired much of DAL's list at auction 1879. Songs of Harry Clifton, George Leybourne, Jolly John Nash, G. H. Macdermott, Alfred Vance. Merged with ASC 1907
HAR	J. Harms Inc.	CHA. See TBH
HHC	Howley, Haviland & Co.	DAR/EMI
HHD	Howley, Haviland & Dresser	FEL/EMI
HOW	Howard & Co.	Est. 1874. Songs of Marie Lloyd, George Robey, Gus Elen, Charles Chaplin sen., Sam Torr. Bought by H&C 1899
HVT	Harry von Tilzer Music Co. Ltd.	EMI
IMP	International Music Publications	Publishes for, amongst others, EMI and CHA (see above)
KBM	Kendis-Brockman Music Co. Inc.	FEL
KPM	Keith, Prowse Music Publishing Co. Ltd.	Est. London Robert Keith 1815; joined by Thomas Prowse 1829. Acquired REY 1962. Bought by EMI 1969. Robert Keith d. 1846, Thomas Prowse 1886

KYL	Morison Kyle	fl. 1858–80, Glasgow. Sam Cowell's songs bought by BLO 1864. Also published songs for Christy Minstrels
LAR	J. H. Larway	fl. 1891–1950, London. Bought by ASH 1929
LMP	London Music Publishing Co.	fl. 1883–94. List incl. Bantock, Benedict, MacFarren
MAR	R. March & Cowri	PAX
MAU	Peter Maurice Music Co. Ltd.	FDH/EMI
MAY	R. Maynard	London
MET	Metzler & Co.	fl. 1833–1933. Originally Metzler & Son. List included Howard Paul, also works of Gounod and Bizet. Bought by CRA 1934
MIL	Jack Mills Music Inc.	NY based. FEL/EMI
MOC	B. Mocatta & Co.	fl. 1888–96, London. Some copyrights bought 1896 by RAW
MSL	Music Sales Ltd.	Est. USA 1935, British presence from 1970. Acquired ASH and CCC 1982, NOV 1993
Music Publishing Co. *see* DAV		
'Musical Bouquet'		Series 1–78 issued *c.*1845 by James Bingley and William Strange, and from 1855 to *c.*1889 by Charles Sheard (1826–1918). Over 8,000 songs were published in the series. See SHE
'Musical Treasury' *see* DAV		
NOV	Novello	Est. 1829 Joseph Alfred Novello (1810–96) with his father Vincent (1781–1861). List included Elgar and Mendelssohn. Acquired PAX 1971. Bought by MSL 1993
NOW	News of the World	Published songs on licence from FDH. Also see BOW
OAK	Oak Publications Ltd.	NY based. Distributes through MSL
OLI	Oliver Ditson & Co.	Est. 1835, Boston, Mass.
P&H	Pace & Handy Music Co.	NY based. FDH
PAX	W. Paxton & Co.	fl. *c.*1855–1970, London. Bought by Novello 1971. MSL
PIG	Pigott & Co.	fl. *c.*1827–1960, Dublin. Samuel Pigott d. 1853
RAW	Reeder & Walsh	fl. 1896–1950. Bought some Mocatta copyrights 1896. Selling agents: FEL. See AFF
REM	Jerome H. Remick & Co. (Remick Music Corporation)	NY based. SHE/FEL/EMI
REY	Reynold's Music	Est. 1887, London. Bought by KPM 1962. Albert Chevalier songs and concert party material
RIC	G. Ricordi & Co.	Est. 1808, Florence; London, 1875. UK agents: BOO
ROB	Robbins Music	Est. 1927, NY. Joined FDH 1957; see AFF

ROS	Harold Rossiter Music Co.	Est. 1891, Chicago. FEL
SHA	Shapiro Bernstein & Co.	NY based. CCC
SHE	Sheard, Charles & Co.	Est. 1851, London. Took over D'Almaine's 'Musical Bijou' series (see DAC) and 'Musical Bouquet' series, q.v. List included operatic arias, Henry Russell and Henry Bishop ballads. Bought by DAR 1918 the year of Sheard's death at the age of 92
SIL	L. Silberma(n)n & Grock	Est. c.1920, London. CCC
SNY	Ted Snyder & Co.	Est. 1908, NY. FDH/EMI
STA	Star Music Publishing	Bought by FEL 29 Sept. 1922
STE	Joseph W. Stern	EBM/FDH/EMI
SUN	Sun Music Publishing	FDH
TBH	T. B. Harms & Co.	Est. 1881, NY. UK distributors FDH till 1920 (on and off) then CHA. List included Jerome Kern and George Gershwin
TRB	T. R. Broom	FDH/EMI
WBS	Waterson, Berlin & Snyder	NY based. FEL/EMI
WES	West & Co. Ltd.	EMI
WIL	Joseph Williams Ltd.	Est. 1818, London. List included Harry Clifton, Corney Grain, Mr & Mrs T. German Reed, H. G. Pélissier, etc. Joseph W. Williams d. 1883; his son Joseph B. Williams d. 1923
WIT	M. Witmark & Sons	Est. NY 1885. M. Witmark (1833–1910). Bought by Warner Bros 1929. FEL/EMI
WLY	Willey & Co.	fl. 1869–87, London
WRI	Lawrence Wright Music Co. Ltd.	Bought by EMI 1987

ABBREVIATIONS

a.k.a.	also known as
attr.	attributed to
div.	divorced
Fr.	French
int.	interpolated into
k.a.	known as
k.i.a.	killed in action
m	music by
m.	married
mon.	monologue
prod.	production
sk.	sketch
trad.	traditional
var.	various
w	words (lyrics) by
w.	with

CORE SONG-LIST

As well as the scores of thousands of songs written specifically for the variety stage, many operatic arias, musical comedy hits, and parlour ballads found their way on to the Halls, the most popular of which are listed below. The Gilbert and Sullivan canon is excluded, as are folk songs, which, like G&S, sit uneasily in a Music Hall programme. Some traditional airs and operatic arias are listed.

After the song title lyricists and composers are given in brackets with lyricists to the left of the colon. A single name in brackets indicates the writer of both lyrics and music. Joint lyricists and/or composers are linked by an ampersand. The three-letter code which follows indicates the earliest recorded and/or current publishers (see the list on pp. xi–xv).

Dates indicate either a song's initial appearance or its first publication, whichever is known to be the earlier.

After dates original and/or significant performers are listed in alphabetical order. Where no performer is given the song was free to be sung by everybody and not strongly associated with any individual artiste.

Unless otherwise stated theatres are in London.

ABA DABA HONEYMOON (Fields: Donovan) FEI 1914

Elizabeth Brice & Charles King, Jack Lee & Billy Delaney, Ruby Raymond & Fred Heider, Ruth Roye, The Two Bobs, The Two Rascals & Jacobson. Music often wrongly attributed to Walter Donaldson.

ABDUL ABULBUL AMIR (P. French, rev. Crumit) CAR/AHC/FDH 1927

Frank Crumit, Percy French, A. Grock, Al Jolson. Percy French performed the original version (Abdalla-Bulbul Ameer) in 1877 at a smoking concert for his fellow Trinity College Dublin students.

A-BE MY BOY (Rule & McGhee: Grock & Silbermann) SIL 1919

Daisy Wood. Partly composed by the great Swiss clown Grock, who also recorded the song with Lily Morris.

ABIDE WITH ME (Lyte: Monk)   var.   1847

The Revd Henry Francis Lyte's words were pounced upon by many composers; only William Henry Monk's familiar setting has survived, although in 1896 Samuel Liddle's setting enjoyed a vogue, being sung by Clara Butt in concert halls and Lilian Doreen in Music Halls.

ABSENT-MINDED BEGGAR, THE (Kipling: Sullivan)   Enoch & Sons   1899

John Coates, Ian Colquhoun, Ada Reeve. Kipling's poem without Sullivan's music was also recited on the Halls by, amongst others, Billie Burke, Mrs Brown Potter, and Mrs (Beerbohm) Tree.

ACROSS THE BRIDGE (Bowyer: G. Le Brunn)   FDH   1888

Charles Godfrey.

ACT ON THE SQUARE, BOYS (Lee, Alfred)   SHE?   1866

Harry Sydney, Alfred Vance. A ladies' version was sung by Alice Dunning.

AFTER THE BALL (Charles K. Harris)   FDH   1892

May Irwin, Richard Jose, George Lashwood, J. Aldrich Libbey, Helene Mora, Horace Wheatley. Int. *A Trip To Chinatown*, Madison Square, and Hoyt's, NY. London: Toole's, 1894.

Vesta Tilley sang an 1893 rewrite by Fred Bowyer & Orlando Powell, with new music for the verses and adapted words throughout; in 1894 they also wrote a parody for Arthur Roberts. The song was also burlesqued by Walter Munroe, by G. W. Hunter of the Mohawk Minstrels, and adapted by Harrington & George Le Brunn for Charles Godfrey. All were published but the version remembered today is the original, first sung, or so the story goes, by one Sam Doctor, an amateur who forgot the words and retired in confusion. But according to Harris himself After The Ball was first sung by Ann Whitney with the Clarke Burlesquers though later popularized by J. Aldrich Libbey, who received an inducement of $500 and a cut of the royalties. (See **TAKE BACK YOUR GOLD** for similar venality.) The song was also given a tremendous boost by May Irwin, the first to sing it in vaudeville. Yet another parody entitled After the Cinderella was performed by G. Wallis Arthur. (Charles K. Harris, *How to Write a Popular Song*; Bernard Sobel, *Burleycue*, 66; Ian Whitcomb, *After the Ball*.)

AFTER YOU'VE GONE (Creamer: Layton)   FDH   1918

Al Jolson, Sophie Tucker.

AH! SWEET MYSTERY OF LIFE (Rida J. Young: V. Herbert)   FEL   1910

Orville Harrold. From *Naughty Marietta*, New York, NY.

AIN' IT NICE? (Weston & B. Lee: Harris-Weston)   FDH   1923

Daisy Dormer.

AIN'T I NO USE MISTER JACKSON? (C. W. Murphy & Lipton) SHE 1905
Victoria Monks.

AIN'T IT GRAND TO BE BLOOMIN' WELL DEAD? (Sarony) CCC 1932
George Jackley, Leslie Sarony.

ALABAMA JUBILEE (Yellen: G. Cobb) REM/FDH 1915
Elizabeth Murray.

ALBERT AND THE LION *see* **LION AND ALBERT, THE**

ALEXANDER'S RAG-TIME BAND (Berlin) SNY/FEL 1911
The Two Bobs, Emma Carus, Arthur Collins, Byron G. Harlan, Al Jolson, Ethel
Levey, Clarice Mayne, Billy Murray, Ellaline Terriss, Maud Tiffany. In 1916 The
Two Bobs were claiming to have introduced this song 'to the London public'.

ALGERNON, GO H'ON! (W. David & B. Lee) FEL 1914
Florrie Forde.

ALGY'S ABSOLUTELY FULL OF TACT (Chester) REY 1927
Fred Chester.

ALGY, THE PICCADILLY JOHNNY WITH THE LITTLE GLASS EYE
(H. Norris) FDH 1895
Vesta Tilley.

ALICE BLUE GOWN (McCarthy: Tierney) FEI 1919
Edith Day. From *Irene*, Empire.

ALICE, WHERE ART THOU? (Guernsey: Ascher) FDH 1861
Words usually attributed to Alfred Bunn.

ALL COONS LOOK ALIKE TO ME (R. Morton: Hogan) WIT/SHE 1896
Marie Dressler, Ernest Hogan, May Irwin, Emerald Sisters, Eugene Stratton, Billy
Williams.

ALL DOWN PICCADILLY (Wimperis & Monckton: Monckton) CHA 1909
Dan Rolyat. From *The Arcadians*, Shaftesbury.

ALL HANDS ON DECK (C. W. Murphy & Lipton) FDH 1909
George Lashwood.

ALL IN A DAY *see* **BID ME GOODBYE FOR EVER**

ALL ROUND MY HAT (Hansett: Valentine)   Dale Cockerill & Co.   1834
Parody of All Round my Hat I Wears a Green Willer, a Gloucester folk ballad.

ALL'S WELL (T. J. Dibdin: Braham)   Joseph Williams/var.   1803
John Braham & Charles Incledon, Patrick A. Corri & James Davis. From *The English Fleet in 1342*, Covent Garden.

ALL THAT I ASK OF YOU IS LOVE (Selden: Ingraham)   SHA/FEL   1905
Frank Morrell, Frank Mullane, Violet Romaine, Bessie Wynn.

ALL THAT I WANT IS YOU (Goodwin: Monaco)   SHA   1920

ALL THE GIRLS ARE LOVELY BY THE SEASIDE
   (W. David & B. Lee: Fragson)   FEL   1913
Harry Carlton, Harry Fragson, Ella Retford. From *Eightpence a Mile*, Alhambra.

ALL THE LITTLE DUCKS WENT QUACK! QUACK! QUACK! (Watkins)
   FDH   1904
Mark Sheridan.

ALL THE NICE GIRLS LOVE A SAILOR (SHIP AHOY!) (Mills: B. Scott)
   STA/FEL   1909
Hetty King, Ella Retford.

ALL THRO' STICKING TO A SOLDIER (Wincott)   MAY   *c.*1905
Louie Freear, Jenny Hill, Ada Lundberg.

ALL THROUGH RIDING ON A MOTOR (Murray)   FDH   1903
Vesta Victoria.

ALOHA OE (FAREWELL TO THEE) (Liliuokalani: Wilmott)   FDH   1878
Alma Gluck.

ALONZO THE BRAVE (Cowell: arr. Harroway)   DAL   *c.*1850
Sam Cowell. The title comes from a poem in *The Monk*, the spine-tingling Gothic novel of 1796 by M. G. Lewis which remained a favourite subject for burlesque for decades; E. L. Blanchard also wrote a version. The music is a succession of brief quotations from current popular melodies.

AMATEUR WHITEWASHER, THE (F. Murray: F. Leigh)   AHC   1896
Frank Seeley.

AMOROUS GOLDFISH, THE (Greenbank: S. Jones)   H&C   1896
Marie Tempest. From *The Geisha*, Daly's.

ANCHOR'S WEIGH'D, THE (S. J. Arnold: J. Braham)
  Goulding D'Almaine/BOO   1811
John Braham, Evan Williams. From *The Americans*, Lyceum. Also sung on the
Halls by, amongst many others, Bessie Bonehill and George Leybourne.

AND HER GOLDEN HAIR WAS HANGING DOWN HER BACK
  (McGlennon: Rosenfeld)   FDH   1894
Yvette Guilbert (see also below). Interpolated into *The Shop Girl*, Gaiety, in which
Seymour Hicks sang revised words by Adrian Ross. The original version, despite
being aired on both sides of the Atlantic by such fine talents as Lottie Gilson,
Eunice Vance, and Alice Leamar, was not particularly successful. One source says
that McGlennon composed the music, which was only arranged by Rosenfeld.

AND THE BAND PLAYED ON *see* **BAND PLAYED ON, THE**

AND THE GREAT BIG SAW CAME NEARER AND NEARER
  (R. H. Weston & B. Lee: Harris-Weston)   FDH   1936
Leslie Sarony.

AND THE LEAVES BEGAN TO FALL (Harrington: G. Le Brunn)   FDH   1904
Marie Lloyd.

AND THE PARROT SAID (W. David & O. Powell)   FDH   1907
Daisy Jerome, Marie Lloyd.

ANNIE LAURIE (W. Douglas)   var.   *c.*1700
Revised by Lady John Douglass Scott 1835.

ANONA (V. Grey)   FEI   1903
Florrie Forde, Maidie Scott.

ANOTHER LITTLE DRINK (F. C. Grey: Ayer)   FEL   1916
Frank Lester & Violet Loraine & George Robey. From *The Bing Boys Are Here*,
Alhambra.

ANY DIRTY WORK TODAY? (R. H. Weston & B. Lee)   FDH   1922
George Carney.

ANY OLD IRON? (Charles Collins & Sheppard: F. Terry)   SHE/FEL   1911
Harry Champion.

ANY TIME'S KISSING TIME (Asche: F. Norton)   KPM   1916
Aileen D'Orme, Violet Essex & Courtice Pounds. From *Chu Chin Chow*, His
Majesty's.

APPLES OR ORANGES, BILLS OF THE PLAY (Merion)   DUF   1867
Annie Adams.

ARCHIBALD, CERTAINLY NOT! (Robey & St John: A. Glover)   FDH   1909
George Robey.

ARE WE DOWNHEARTED? NO! (W. David: L. Wright)   WRI   1914
Florrie Forde, Charles Bignell, Shaun Glenville, Harrison Latimer. A 1906 song of
the same title by George Robins was sung by Will Edwards and Paul Mill.

ARE WE TO PART LIKE THIS, BILL? (Castling & Charles Collins)
   NOW/FEL   1903
Kate Carney.

ARE YOU FROM DIXIE? (Yellen: G. L. Cobb)   FEL   1913
The Two Rascals & Jacobson.

'ARF A PINT OF ALE (Tempest)   SHE/DAR   1905
Gus Elen.

ARMY OF TODAY'S ALL RIGHT, THE (F. Leigh: Lyle)   FDH   1914
Vesta Tilley. Gave Vesta Tilley the soubriquet 'England's Greatest Recruiting
Sergeant'.

'ARRY (E. V. Page)   WIL/REY   1882
Jenny Hill.

'ARRY 'ARRY 'ARRY (F. Leigh & F. Murray: G. Le Brunn)   SHE/DAR   1902
Fred T. Daniels, Alec Hurley.

ART IS CALLING FOR ME (I WANT TO BE A PRIMA DONNA)
   (H. B. Smith: V. Herbert)   WIT   1911
Louise Bliss. From *The Enchantress*, New York, NY. Not to be confused with I
Want to be a Prima Donna (Edgar Malone: Tom Sherman *WIT*, 1909), sung by
Maggie Cline.

ASK A P'LICEMAN (E. W. Rogers: Durandeau)   F&D   *c.*1885
James Fawn.

ASLEEP IN THE DEEP (Lamb: Petrie)   PET/SHE   1897
Norman Allin, G. H. Chirgwin, Peter Dawson, Signor Foli.

AS THEY MARCHED THROUGH THE TOWN *see* **CAPTAIN WITH HIS
WHISKERS, THE**

As Your Hair Grows Whiter (Dacre) DEA/FEL 1897
Rosie Eaton.

At A Minute To Seven Last Night (David: Mayo) FDH 1906
Sam Mayo.

At My Time O' Life (Connor) FDH *c.*1888
Herbert Campbell.

At The Bottom Of The Deep Blue Sea (Lamb: Petrie) PET 1899
Peter Dawson.

(At) The Darktown Strutters' Ball (S. Brooks) FDH 1917
Original Dixieland Jazz Band, Blossom Seeley, Sophie Tucker, The Versatile Three (Haston, Mills & Tuck).

At The Vicar's Fancy Ball (David & B. Lee) FDH 1915
Ernest Shand.

At Trinity Church I Met My Doom (F. Gilbert) FDH 1894
Tom Costello.

Auld Lang Syne (trad.) var. 1793
Although there is little doubt that Robert Burns substantially reworked the words, he claimed only to have taken the song down 'from an old man's singing'; this 1793 version is the one familiar to us today. The air, which Burns regarded as 'mediocre', is a.k.a. I Fee'd a Lass at Martinmas but its origins are much older. See Fuld, *The Book of World-Famous Music*, 115–16.

Automatic Battery, The (Maraville: J. S. Baker) F&D *c.*1888
Harry Randall.

Awake! (A Moving Love Song) (P. Edgar: Pether) FDH 1917
Joseph Cheetham, John Coates.

Ayesha, My Sweet Egyptian (C. Johnson & Burley: M. Scott) STA 1908
Evelyn Taylor.

Baby On The Shore, The (Grossmith sen.) BAT/REY 1898
George Grossmith sen.

Baby's Name, The (C. W. Murphy & A. S. Hall) FDH 1900
Charles Bignell.

BACHELOR GAY, A (C. Harris & Valentine: J. W. Tate)   AHC   1916
Thorpe Bates. From *The Maid of the Mountains*, Daly's (1917) after Manchester try-out.

BACIO, IL (THE KISS) (Aldieghieri: Arditi)   Cramer Beale & Chappell   1860
Marietta Piccolomini.

BACK ANSWERS (Coverdale)   REY   1923
Robb Wilton.

BACK TO TENNESSEE (Shannon)   Grinnell Bros, Detroit   1911
Clark & Adler.

BACON AND GREENS (Cowell: air, Haste To The Wedding)   KYL   1859
Sam Cowell, Arthur Lloyd.

BALLAD OF SAM HALL, THE (trad.)   var.   *c.*1840
W. G. Ross. Based on a ballad of at least a century earlier. A version is in Peter Davison's *The British Music Hall* (see Sources and Bibliography: Published Song Collections).

BALLIN' THE JACK (Burris: C. Smith & Europe)   STE/EMI   *c.*1909
Donald Brian, Fanny Brice, Lillian Lorraine, Elsie Janis & Basil Hallam. Popularized in *Ziegfeld Follies of 1913*, New Amsterdam. Int. *The Girl From Utah*, 1914, Knickerbocker, NY (originally Adelphi, London, 1913). London: included in *The Passing Show of 1915*, Empire. The meaning of the song's title is disputed.

BANDOLERO, THE (Stuart)   CHA   1894
Norman Allin, Peter Dawson, Signor Foli.

BAND PLAYED ON, THE (J. F. Palmer)   DAR/FEL   1895
Tony Pastor, Lillian Russell. Originally known as The Strawberry Blonde. This song has been wrongly attributed to Chas. B. Ward and should not be confused with next entry.

BAND PLAYED ON, THE (V. Grey: Naish)   REY   1916
Clifford Grey, Archie Naish. Not to be confused with previous entry.

BANG WENT THE CHANCE OF A LIFETIME (Robey & Rohmer)   FDH   1908
George Robey.

BARMAID, THE *or* **THE IDOL OF THE ROSE & CROWN** (Rogers)   FDH   1894
Marie Lloyd.

BATHING (Harrington: Le Brunn)   FDH   1898
Marie Lloyd.

BATTLE HYMN OF THE REPUBLIC, THE
   (Julia Ward Howe: trad./Steffe?)   var.   1861
Hutchinson Family. *See* **JOHN BROWN'S BODY**.

BAY OF BISCAY, THE (Cherry: Davy)   var.   1805
John Braham. From *Spanish Dollars*, Covent Garden.

BEAUTIFUL DREAMER (Foster)   var.   1864
Christy Minstrels. Stephen C. Foster's last song.

BECAUSE (Teschemacher: D'Hardelot)   CHA   1902
Dalton Baker, Thorpe Bates, Enrico Caruso, John Harrison, John McCormack, Ernest Pike, Denham Price, Maggie Teyte.

BEDELIA (Jerome: Schwartz)   FDH   1903
Emma Carus, Moses Gumble, Lloyd Morgan, Blanche Ring. From *The Jersey Lily*, Victoria, NY. Int. *The Orchid*, Gaiety, and sung to his own words by George Grossmith jun.

BEEFEATER, THE (THE TOWER OF LONDON) (Darnley)   FDH   1898
Dan Leno.

BEER, GLORIOUS BEER *see* **GLORIOUS BEER**

BELGIUM PUT THE 'KIBOSH' ON THE KAISER (Ellerton)   FDH   1914
Mark Sheridan.

BELLA WAS A BARMAID (Harrington: Le Brunn)   FDH   1902

BELLE OF THE BALL, THE (Hunt)   H&C   1873
George Leybourne.

BELLS ARE RINGING, THE *see* **FOR ME AND MY GAL**

BE MY LITTLE BABY BUMBLE BEE (S. Murphy: H. I. Marshall)
   REM/FEL   1911
Elizabeth Brice & Charles King, Ada Jones & Billy Murray, Elizabeth Spencer & Walter Van Blunt. From *Ziegfeld Follies of 1911*, Jardin de Paris, and interpolated into *A Winsome Widow* (a revision of *A Trip To Chinatown*, Madison Square, 1892) at the Moulin Rouge 1912, all NY. Int. *The Grass Widow*, Apollo (London) and Liberty, NY, 1917.

BESIDE THE SEASIDE *see* **I DO LIKE TO BE BESIDE THE SEASIDE**

BETTER LAND, THE (Hemans: Cowen)   BOO   *c.*1880
Antoinette Sterling.

BID ME GOODBYE FOR EVER (ALL IN A DAY) (Tabrar)   FDH   1898
Vesta Victoria.

BIGGEST ASPIDISTRA IN THE WORLD, THE
  (Harper & Haines & Connor)   CCC   1938
Gracie Fields.

BILL BAILEY, WON'T YOU PLEASE COME HOME? (Cannon)   FEL   1902
Carroll Johnson, Victoria Monks, Fanny St Clair.

BILLY (FOR WHEN I WALK) (Goodwin: Kendis & Paley)   FDH   1911
Ada Jones, Beth Tate, Madge Temple.

BILLY BARLOW (Purday, arr. Saunders)   Catnatch/var.   *c.*1830
Sam Cowell, W. G. Ross, J. L. Toole. There were many variations on this song
throughout the century.

BILLY MUGGINS (Ridgwell)   FDH   1897
Charles R. Whittle.

BILLY'S ROSE (George R. Sims)   Fuller   1879
From the *Dagonet Ballads* series of poetic recitations mostly written for *The
Referee*, a Sunday newspaper. Other poems by Sims were published under the title
Ballads Of Babylon (J. P. Fuller, 1880). The original Dagonet was supposedly King
Arthur's knighted fool.

BIRD IN A GILDED CAGE, A (Lamb: Von Tilzer)   FEL   1899
May A. Bell, Emma Carus, Florrie Forde, Marie Kendall, James Norrie.

BIRD ON NELLIE'S HAT, THE (Lamb: Solman)   STE/PAX/FEL   1906
Janet Allen, Maidie Scott, Anona Winn.

BLACK SHEEP OF THE FAMILY, THE (Barnes)   FDH   1909
Fred Barnes. A.k.a. The Scapegrace of the Family.

BLAYDON RACES (Ridley: air, Brighton)   var.   1862
George Ridley. See C. E. Catchside-Warrington (Sources and Bibliography: Published Song Collections).

BLESS THIS HOUSE (H. Taylor: Brahe) BOO 1927
Peter Dawson, Gracie Fields, John McCormack.

'BLIGE A LADY (Harrington: Powell) FDH 1890
Charles Godfrey.

BLIND BOY, THE (R. Lee: G. W. Moore) FDH 1871
G. H. Chirgwin, Tom Chirgwin, Little Willie (Moore & Burgess Minstrels). Not to be confused with Colley Cibber's 1738 poem 'Blind Boy', set to music by over a dozen composers.

BLOOM IS ON THE RYE, THE *see* **MY PRETTY JANE**

BLUE BELL (Madden & Dolly Morse: Theo Morse) HHC 1898
Anna Driver, Haydn Quartet, Hamilton Hill.

BLUE BELL OF SCOTLAND, THE (Jordan) var. 1800
Mrs Jordan.

'BOBBIES' OF THE QUEEN, THE (E. Turner: Santley) HOW 1897
Maud Santley.

BOBBIN' AROUND (W. F. Florence, arr. Tully) DAL/FEL *c.*1856
Mrs Caulfield, Christy Minstrels, Sam Cowell, Mrs W. J. Florence.

BOBBING UP AND DOWN LIKE THIS (W. David: Reeve) FDH 1899
Austin Rudd.

BOERS HAVE GOT MY DADDY, THE (Mills & Castling) FDH 1900
Tom Costello, Charles Foster, Arthur Reece.

BOILED BEEF AND CARROTS (Collins & Murray) FEL 1909
Harry Champion.

BOIS ÉPAIS (SOMBRE WOODS) (Lully: Marzials) BOO 1892
Plunkett Greene.

BOLD GENDARMES, THE *see* **GENDARMES' DUET**

BOND STREET TEA-WALK, THE (Harrington: Le Brunn) FDH 1902
Marie Lloyd.

BOOTS (Kipling: McCall) Swan 1928
Peter Dawson. Kipling's poem was originally published in the *Scots Observer* in

1890 and included in the first series (1892) of his *Barrack-Room Ballads*. J. P. McCall was a pseudonym of the singer Peter Dawson. There were several other settings, including one by J. P. H. Sousa.

BOOZE IS THERE (Haydon: Redfern)   MAY   *c.*1890
Sam Redfern.

BOWERY, THE (Hoyt: Gaunt)   FDH   1891
Ada Blanche, Harry Conor. From *A Trip To Chinatown*, Madison Square and Hoyt's, NY. In the 1894 London version at Toole's the words were rewritten as **BRIGHTON**. The music is based on La Spagnola, traditional Neapolitan.

BOY IN THE GALLERY, THE (Ware)   H&C   *c.*1881
Dot Hetherington, Jenny Hill, Marie Lloyd, Louie Pounds, Nellie Power.

BOY'S BEST FRIEND IS HIS MOTHER, A (Miller: Skelly)   FDH   1883
Brothers Bohee (Haverly's Minstrels), J. Fuller (Mohawk Minstrels), Harry Hunter (Mohawk Minstrels), Nellie Wallace.

BOYS OF THE CHELSEA SCHOOL (Carter & R. P. Weston)   FDH   1902
George Leyton.

BOYS OF THE OLD BRIGADE *see* **OLD BRIGADE, THE**

BRADSHAW'S GUIDE (H. S. Leigh: Cave)   WLY/DAL   1876
Fred Albert, J. A. Cave.

BRAHN BOOTS (Weston & Lee: Weston)   FDH   1935
Stanley Holloway. Not published until 1941.

BRAVO, DUBLIN FUSILIERS! (Wheeler)   FDH   1899
Leo Dryden, Pat Rafferty, Marie Tyler. Leo Dryden was the composer's stage name.

BREAK THE NEWS TO MOTHER (Chas. K. Harris)   DAR/FEL   1897
Norman Blair, Florence Chester, Ella Dean, Charles Foster, Alfred Hurley, Elsie Janis, Arthur Reece.

BRIGHT EYES (H. B. Smith: Motzan & M. K. Jerome)   MIL   1920
Nellie Wigley.

BRIGHTON (Morton & Gilbert: Gaunt)   FDH   1894
R. G. Knowles. From *A Trip To Chinatown*, Toole's. See also **BOWERY, THE**.

BRIGHTON (Rubens & Wimperis: Rubens) CHA 1911
Connie Ediss. Also known as **TAKE ME ON THE BOAT TO BRIGHTON**. From *The Sunshine Girl*, Gaiety.

BRINDISI (Piave: Verdi) var. 1856
Lizzie Pearce & Russell Grover, Marietta Piccolomini & C. A. Zolari. From *La Traviata* (Fenice, Venice 1853) based on the younger Dumas' novel and play *La Dame aux Camélias*. Brindisi is Italian for a toast and has become a generic term for this type of carousing song found in many operas. The *Traviata* Brindisi is often sung as a soprano solo.

BROKEN DOLL, A (F. C. Harris: Tate) FDH 1915
Al Jolson, Clarice Mayne, Ida René. From *Samples*, Playhouse. In January 1916 moved to the Vaudeville, finally transferring to the Comedy in October of that year.

BROWN BIRD SINGING, A (Barrie: Haydn Wood) CHA 1922
Dora Labbette, John McCormack, Stella Power.

BROWN BOOTS *see* **BRAHN BOOTS**

BROWN THE TRAGEDIAN (G. W. Hunt) DAL 1870
Arthur Lloyd.

BURGLAR BILL (Anstey) Bradbury, Agnew & Co 1888
From *The Young Reciter*, twelve burlesque recitations. Reissued with *Model Music-Hall* (Methuen & Co. Ltd., 1931).

BURLINGTON BERTIE (Norris) DEA 1900
Vesta Tilley.

BURLINGTON BERTIE FROM BOW (Hargreaves) WRI 1914
Ella Shields. William Hargreaves and Ella Shields were later married and subsequently divorced.

BUTTERCUP, THE (Burnand: Sullivan) BAY/CRA 1867
George Du Maurier & Harold Power, George Du Maurier & Quintin Twist. From *Cox & Box*, a musical adapted from J. Maddison Morton's farce *Box & Cox* (Lyceum, 1847). The initial public performance (there had been two private domestic showings in November 1866 and April 1867) was for a charity matinee at the Adelphi; at the show's first full-scale professional airing in 1869 the duet was sung by Arthur Cecil and T. German Reed at the Gallery of Illustration, Regent Street. It is also published as The Dicky Bird And The Owl for soprano and baritone with words by Margaret A. Sinclair (*BOO c.*1896).

BUY ME SOME ALMOND ROCK (Tabrar)   H&C   1893
Marie Lloyd.

BY THE BEAUTIFUL SEA (Atteridge: Carroll)   FDH   1914
Ada Jones, Bessie Wynn. Included in second edition of *Hullo, Tango!*, Hippodrome, and sung by Shirley Kellogg.

BY THE LIGHT OF THE SILVERY MOON (Madden: Edwards)   FEL   1909
Al Jolson, Lillian Lorraine, Georgie Price, Ella Retford. From *Ziegfeld Follies of 1909*, Jardin de Paris, NY.

BY THE SAD SEA WAVES (Bunn: Benedict)   CHA   1844
Jenny Lind. From *The Brides Of Venice*, Drury Lane.

BY THE SAD SEA WAVES (L. Barrett: L. Thomas)   FDH   1894
Lester Barrett, Vesta Tilley. The composer is better remembered as Leslie Stuart. The lyricist is his brother and one of the song's original performers.

BY THE SEA (Glover Kind)   FEL   1910
Ernest Shand, Mark Sheridan.

BY THE SIDE OF THE ZUYDER ZEE (Mills: B. Scott)   FEL   1906
Maudi Darrell, Happy Fanny Fields, May Moore Duprez, Annie Purcell.

CA-BAGES, CA-BEANS AND CAR-ROTS (W. Stanley & A. Allen)   WRI   1919
George Bass.

CAKE WALK, THE (Stuart)   FDH   1898
Eugene Stratton.

CALLER HERRIN' (Nairne: air, trad. Scots)   var./FDH   *c.*1823
G. H. Chirgwin (parody), Antoinette Sterling.

CALL ROUND ANY OLD TIME (E. W. Rogers: Moore)   FEL   1908
Victoria Monks.

CAMPTOWN RACES, THE (S. C. Foster)   var.   1850
Sundry Minstrel troupes.

CAN-CAN, THE   var.   1867
Clodoche Troupe, Colonna Troupe, Mlle Finette, Mlle Rigolboche, Mlle Sara (Sarah Wright). The can-can was first performed in London by the all-male Clodoche quartet at the Princess's in the summer of 1866, being interpolated into

Watts Phillips's melodrama *The Huguenot Captain*. The 1867 Christmas pantomime at the Lyceum (*Cock Robin*) riskily included the notorious dance, led with uproarious success by Mlle Finette; the following April her energetic art was further exercised in a ballet at the Alhambra called *Mabille in London*. It was not until 1871 that the authorities decided London had been outraged enough and the Colonna Troupe's high-kicking abandon in the ballet *The Two Nations* lost the Alhambra its music hall licence, making Leicester Square 'a hideous, howling wilderness'. (Hibbert's *Playgoer's Memories*; Soldene's *Recollections*, 95; *The Era* 13 Dec. 1874, p. 11.)

CAN LONDON DO WITHOUT ME? (Hargreaves)   FEL   1902
Tom E. Hughes.

CAN'T STOP! CAN'T STOP!! CAN'T STOP!!! (Wincott)   AHC   1895
Harry Freeman.

CAPTAIN CALLED THE MATE, THE (A. West)   F&D   1888
Alexandra Dagmar, Harry Freeman, Arthur West.

CAPTAIN GINJAH, O. T. (Leigh & Bastow)   FDH   1910
George Bastow.

CAPTAIN JINKS OF THE HORSE MARINES (Maclagan: Rickards)   MET   1862
Tom Maclagan, Harry Rickards, W. Lingard.

CAPTAIN MAC' (O'Reilly: Sanderson)   BOO   1914
Foster Richardson.

CAPTAIN WITH HIS WHISKERS, THE (Bayly: Mullen)   EW Allen/F&D   1869
Mrs W. J. Florence, Jenny Hill, Emma J. Nichols. Original music and words Sidney Nelson *c.*1838 as Oh! They March'd Thro' The Town and sung by Lucy Vestris. Alfred Mullen's popular 1869 version entitled As They Marched Through The Town substantially altered both music and words of the refrain.

CAROLINA IN THE MORNING (Kahn: Donaldson)   FDH   1922
Al Jolson, Dorothy Ward.

CASEY JONES (Seibert: Newton)   FDH   1909
The Two Bobs, Billy Murray, Albert Whelan. The real Casey Jones died heroically at the controls of the Cannon Ball Express on 30 April 1900, trying to save his train. (*Erie Railroad Magazine*, 24/2, Apr. 1928.)

CHALK FARM TO CAMBERWELL GREEN (Monckton)   CHA   1915
Gertie Millar. From *Bric-a-Brac*, Palace.

CHAMPAGNE CHARLIE (Leybourne: A. Lee)   SHE/FEL   1866

George Leybourne. A ladies' version was sung by Louie Sherrington; a parody ('Captain Crosstree Is My Name . . .') was sung by Fred Dewar in F. C. Burnand's burlesque of *Black-Eye'd Susan* at the Royalty for over a year. The prototype Champagne Charlie was the fourth Marquess of Hastings, a notorious gambler, high-liver, and spendthrift.

CHARLIE DILKE UPSET THE MILK (F. Gilbert)   SHE   1885
G. H. Macdermott.

CHARLIE ON THE MASH (Murray & Fred W. Leigh)   FDH   1898
Florrie Forde.

CHARMING YOUNG WIDOW I MET IN THE TRAIN, THE (Cove)
    BOW/DAL   *c.*1863
Fred Albert, W. Randall. Originally titled 'I Live In North Wales'.

CHEER, BOYS, CHEER! (Mackay: Russell)   var.   1852
Henry Russell.

CHEER UP, BULLER! (St Clair)   FDH   1901
F. V. St Clair, Harriett Vernon.

CHERRY RIPE (Herrick: Horn)   var.   1824
Charles Edward Horn, John Orlando Parry, Lucy Vestris. Included in *Paul Pry*, Haymarket.

CHICKALEARY COVE, THE (Bain(e) & Ernèe Clarke)   SHE   *c.*1870
Alfred Vance.

CHINATOWN, MY CHINATOWN (Jerome: Schwartz)   FDH   1910
Gwendoline Brogden, Edwin Foy (Eddie Foy sen.), Shirley Kellogg. From *Up and Down Broadway*, Casino, NY. London: included in *Push And Go*, Hippodrome.

CIRIBIRIBIN (Thaler: Pestalozza; English *w* T. Taylor, *MIL* 1909)   var.   1898
Lucrezia Bori.

CITY WAIF, THE (Harrington: Le Brunn)   F&D   1889
Jenny Hill.

CLEMENTINE *see* **OH! MY DARLING CLEMENTINE**

CLICQUOT (F. W. Green: Rivière)   H&C   1867
Alfred Vance.

CLOSE THE SHUTTERS, WILLIE'S DEAD (J. E. Stewart, arr. Martyn)
    FDH/var.   *c.*1875
Christy Minstrels, Sydney Herbert (Moore & Burgess Minstrels).

COAL-BLACK MAMMY (Cliff & St Helier)   FDH   1921
Marie Blanche & Ivy St Clair, Laddie Cliff, Stanley Holloway, Jack Hulbert.

COBBLER'S SONG, THE (Asche: Norton)   KPM   1916
Peter Dawson. From *Chu Chin Chow*, His Majesty's.

COCKLES AND MUSSELS (Yorkston, based on trad.?)   F&D   1882

COFFEE SHOP AT PIMLICO, THE (Bell)   P. Watts   1864
Frank Bell.

COLONEL BOGEY MARCH (Alford)   Hawkes   1913
Sundry bands. 'Kenneth J. Alford' was (Major) Frederick J. Ricketts, bandmaster of the 2nd Battalion, the Argyll & Sutherland Highlanders (93rd).

COME AND PUT YOUR ARMS AROUND ME, GEORGIE DO (Mills: B. Scott)
    STA/FEL   1909
Jessie Templeton.

COME BACK TO ERIN (Claribel)   FDH   1866
Louise Kirkby Lunn, Carlotta Patti, Charlotte Sainton-Dolby.

COME, COME, I LOVE YOU ONLY *see* **MY HERO**

COME DOWN AND OPEN THE DOOR (Cotes: B. Scott)   FEL   1921
Sisters Wood. One of the Sisters Wood also worked this song solo as Rosie Lloyd. Based on Come Down and Open the Door, Love (A. Sutherd: Slade Murray, arr. Edmund Forman) F&D 1884 sung by Slade Murray.

COME DOWN MA EVENING STAR (R. H. Smith: Stromberg)   FEL   1902
Lillian Russell. From *Twirly Whirly*, Weber & Fields' Music Hall, NY, and interpolated into *Hokey Pokey* at the same theatre in 1912.

COME HOME, FATHER (Russell: Work)   H&C/SHE/EMI   1858
Alabama Barnstormers, Horace Norman (Christy Minstrels). Featured in William W. Pratt's legendary prohibitionist drama *Ten Nights in a Bar-Room*, first performed on 23 August 1858 at the National Theatre, Washington DC.

COME IN AND CUT YOURSELF A PIECE OF CAKE (Kendal)   FEL   1911
Jack Pleasants.

COME INTO THE GARDEN, MAUD (Tennyson: Balfe)   BOO   1856
Joseph Cheetham, John Coates, John Harrison, John McCormack, J. W. Raynor,
Jim Sipple, Miss Bertie Stokes. Composed for J. Sims Reeves, the greatest English
tenor of his generation. Despite Tennyson's reservations, Balfe's setting is the only
one of some seventeen efforts to have survived. The poem was written in 1855 and
revised in 1859, also in 1865.

COME JOSEPHINE IN MY FLYING MACHINE (Bryan: F. Fisher)   SHA   1910
Blanche Ring, Harry Tally.

COME OVER THE GARDEN WALL (Macdonald: Tate)   FRL   1920
Clarice Mayne.

COME TO ME MY MELANCHOLY BABY *see* **MY MELANCHOLY BABY**

COME TO THE BALL (Ross: Monckton)   CHA   1910
Gertie Millar, Helen Trix. From *The Quaker Girl*, Adelphi.

COME TO THE FAIR (H. Taylor: Easthope Martin)   Enoch & Sons   1917
Foster Richardson, Herbert Thorpe. From *Three More Songs of the Fair*.

COME TO YOUR MARTHA (Vance)   SHE   1868
Alfred Vance.

COME WHERE MY LOVE LIES DREAMING (S. C. Foster)   var.   1855
Christy Minstrels.

COME WHERE THE BOOZE IS CHEAPER (E. W. Rogers: Durandeau)
  MOC/R&W/MAY   *c.*1890
Charles Coborn. This song is often attributed to (Sir) George Dance but my copy
gives Rogers: Durandeau. There is no copy in the British or Bodleian Libraries and
Coborn's autobiography gives no clues.

COME WITH ME DOWN REGENT STREET (W. Norton & C. W. Murphy)
  FDH   1910
Daisy James, Winifred Ward.

COMRADES (McGlennon)   FDH   1887
Tom Costello, Helene Mora.

CONSCIENTIOUS OBJECTOR'S LAMENT, THE (Burnaby & Rice)   DAR   1917
Alfred Lester. From *Round the Map*, Alhambra.

CONUNDRUMS (I'M A PHILOSOPHER) (C. Osborne) FDH 1895
T. E. Dunville. Musical comedy version interpolated into *The Belle of New York*, Shaftesbury, 1898.

CORSICAN MAID, THE (Fearnley: Saker) FDH 1909
Evie Greene.

COSTER GIRL IN PARIS, THE (F. W. Leigh: Powell) FDH 1912
Marie Lloyd.

COSTER'S MUVVER, THE (M. Arnold: Le Brunn) FDH 1894
Gus Elen.

COSTER'S SERENADE, THE (Chevalier: Crook) REY 1890
Albert Chevalier.

COSTER'S WEDDING, THE *see* **WEDDING MARCH!, THE**

COULD YOU BE TRUE TO EYES OF BLUE? (Cobb: Edwards) MIL/AHC 1899
Lilian Doreen, Lottie Gilson, Hamilton Hill. From *A Chinese Honeymoon*, Theatre Royal Hanley.

COVENT GARDEN IN THE MORNING (Graydon: Coote) DAL 1873
George Leybourne, Alfred Vance.

COVER IT OVER QUICK JEMIMA (Collins & Sheppard) DAR 1911
Harry Champion.

COWSLIP AND THE COW, THE (Leo) FEL 1905
Wilkie Bard, Albert Whelan.

CRICKETER, THE (Bullock) Simpson & Co 1869
Tom Maclagan, Howard Paul.

CROSSING THE BAR (Tennyson: Behrend) BOO 1893
Antoinette Sterling. The poem was written by Tennyson on his deathbed and is known to have attracted over eighty settings.

CRUEL MARY HOLDER (Lloyd arr. Bicknell) DAL 1866
Arthur Lloyd.

CUCUMBER SONG, THE *see* **LITTLE BIT OF CUCUMBER, A**

CURFEW SHALL NOT RING TONIGHT, THE (Horr: Himan) SHE 1882
Mohawk Minstrels.

CURSE OF AN ACHING HEART, THE (Fink: Piantadosi)   FEI/AHC   1913
Joe Burns, Emma Carus, Will Oakland, Manuel Romain.

CUSHIE BUTTERFIELD (Ridley: Clifton)   H&C/var.   *c*.1863
George Ridley. Geordie words to Harry Clifton's earlier **POLLY PERKINS OF PADDINGTON GREEN**. A version is in Peter Davison's *The British Music Hall* (see Bibliography: Published Song Collections).

CZARDAS (Eng. *w* Aïdé: J. Strauss II)   BOO   1876
Mlle C. Cabella, Constance Drever, Marie Geistinger. From *Die Fledermaus*, an der Wien, Vienna 1874. London: Alhambra.

DADDY'S ON THE ENGINE (Snape & A. Albert: Potter)   SHE   1895
Arthur Albert.

DADDY WOULDN'T BUY ME A BOW WOW (Tabrar)   FDH   1892
Arthur Roberts, Vesta Victoria.

DAISY BELL (Dacre)   FDH   1892
Florrie Forde, Katie Lawrence. In 1894 Harry Dacre wrote a sequel entitled Fare You Well, Daisy Bell which was sung by a number of artistes but not, it would seem, No either Miss Forde or Miss Lawrence.

DANCE WITH YOUR UNCLE JOSEPH (Hargreaves & Lipton)   FEL   1915
Charles R. Whittle.

DANCING ON THE STREETS (J. Blake & Lawlor)   FDH   1894
Kate Carney. British version of **SIDEWALKS OF NEW YORK**.

DANDY COLOURED COON, THE (R. Morton: G. Le Brunn)   FDH   1893
Eugene Stratton.

DANNY BOY (Weatherly: trad., Londonderry Air)   BOO   1912
John McCormack, Edna Thornton.

DARBY AND JOAN (Weatherly: Molloy)   BOO   1878
Antoinette Sterling. Sundry writers have sought to capture the legendary devotion of Mr Darby and his wife Joan; they flourished in their affection in the mid-eighteenth century and were first celebrated musically by Henry Woodfall, who had enjoyed their kindness.

DARK GIRL DRESS'D IN BLUE, THE (Clifton)   FEL   1862
Harry Clifton, George Leybourne. See also **I'M THE DARK GIRL DRESS'D IN BLUE**, one of many spin-offs, including The Young Chap Dressed in Blue, sung by A. G. Vance.

DARLING MABEL (Mills: B. Scott) FDH 1896
Leonard Barry.

DEAR (GREEN) LITTLE SHAMROCK, THE (W. Cherry: W. Jackson) var. 1806
Violet Essex. Revised *c.*1870 possibly by J. W. Cherry, a descendant of the *orig.* lyricist.

DEAR 'LIZA *see* **FUTURE MRS 'AWKINS, THE**

DEAR OLD PALS (G. W. Hunt) H&C 1877
Charles Chaplin sen., G. H. Macdermott.

DEAR OLD SHEPHERD'S BUSH (F. C. Grey: Ayer) FEL 1916
Frank Lester. From *The Bing Boys are Here*, Alhambra.

DEATH OF NELSON, THE (S. J. Arnold: Braham)
Goulding D'Almaine/BOO 1811
John Braham, Ian Colquhoun, Sims Reeves, Evan Williams. From *The Americans*, Lyceum.

DELANEY'S DONKEY (Hargreaves) FDH 1921
Mooney & Holbein.

DID YOUR FIRST WIFE EVER DO THAT? (Castling) EMI 1932
Marie Kendall. From the film *Say It with Flowers*. Published in *Great Comedy Songs*, Book 2 (*EMI* 1987).

DINGLE DONGLE DELL *see* **IN THE DINGLE DONGLE DELL**

DIVER, THE (G. W. Thompson: Loder) DUF/HOW 1890
Norman Allin, Signor Foli, T. F. Kinniburgh.

DIXIE or **DIXIE'S LAND** *see* **I WISH I WAS IN DIXIE**

DOES THIS SHOP STOCK SHOT SOCKS? (De Pinna) FDH 1912
George Graves, Archie Pitt.

DO IT AGAIN (Dixon: Grock & Thurban & Silbermann) SIL 1917
Fred Barnes, Irene Bordoni.

DOLLY'S LAMENT (Schayer: C. D. Arnold) OLI 1894
Lydia Yeamans-Titus.

DOLLY VARDEN (F. W. Green: Alf Lee) SHE 1872
Alfred Vance.

DON'T BE CROSS *see* **MILLER'S DAUGHTER, THE**

DON'T DILLY DALLY (Collins & Leigh)   FEL   1919
Marie Lloyd, Marie Lloyd jun.

DON'T GIVE ME DIAMONDS, ALL I WANT IS YOU (Chas. K. Harris)
   FEL   1910
Gertie Gitana.

DON'T GO DOWN IN THE MINE, DAD (Donelly: Geddes)   WRI   1910
Frank Boyce, J. H. Greener.

DON'T GO OUT TONIGHT, DEAR FATHER (Golding: W. L. Thompson)
   SHE   1889
Elsa Lanchester, sundry Minstrel troupes.

DON'T HAVE ANY MORE, MRS MOORE (Castling & Walsh)   FEL   1926
Lily Morris. According to Eileen Hellicar (see Sources and Bibliography) the
original Mrs Moore was her grandmother Georgina Moore (1877–1963), who after
having seven children was given the eponymous advice by her brother, known as
Arthur Le Clerq. Inspired by his own wit, he then wrote the song. In fact Le Clerq
had no hand in the song at all; other erroneous statements and dubious assertions
by Hellicar render the whole story unreliable.

DON'T MAKE A NOISE OR ELSE YOU'LL WAKE THE BABY (G. W. Hunt)
   AHC   1876
George Leybourne.

DON'T SING THE CHORUS (Castling & Collins)   WIT   1911
Vesta Victoria.

DON'T STOP MY 'ARF A PINT O' BEER (Pratt: Moore)   SHA/HVT 1911
Gus Elen.

DOROTHY DEAN (Dacre)   DEA/FEL   1894
Marie Kendall.

DOWN AT THE FARM-YARD GATE (McGlennon)   SHE   1893
Katie Lawrence.

DOWN AT THE OLD BULL AND BUSH (Krone & Hunting & Sterling:
   Von Tilzer)   HVT/FEL   1903
Florrie Forde. Adapted from Under the Anheuser Bush (Sterling: Von Tilzer).

DOWN AT THE WELSH HARP WHICH IS HENDON WAY *see* **COSTER'S SERENADE, THE**

DOWN BY THE OLD MILL STREAM (T. Taylor)   FEL   1910
Frank Morrell. John Read's 1885 song of the same title was sung by Fred Coyne (1) but is now forgotten.

DOWN FELL THE PONY IN A FIT (Wincott & Leighton, arr. Baker)
   RAW   1897
Harry Champion.

DOWN ON THE FARM *see* **I WANT TO GO BACK TO MICHIGAN**

DOWN THE DIALS (Wincott: Elen)   MAY   1893
Gus Elen.

DOWN THE ROAD (F. Gilbert)   FDH   1893
Gus Elen. Parodies were sing by G. Wallis Arthur and George Beauchamp.

DOWN WENT THE CAPTAIN (Bowyer: Royle, arr. Ison)   H&C   1887
G. H. Macdermott, Kate Royle.

DOWN WHERE THE WURZBURGER FLOWS (Bryan: Von Tilzer)   HVT   1902
Norah Bayes, Arthur Collins. After introducing it at the Orpheum Theatre, Brooklyn, Nora Bayes became so identified with the song that for a time she was known as 'The Wurzburger Girl'. With new words the song was launched in Britain as **RIDING ON TOP OF THE CAR**.

DRAKE GOES WEST (O'Reilly: Sanderson)   BOO   1910
Ivor Foster, Robert Radford.

DRAKE'S DRUM (Newbolt: Stanford)   Stainer   1905
Peter Dawson, Plunkett Greene. From *Songs of the Sea*.

DRINK TO ME ONLY WITH THINE EYES (Jonson: anon.)   var.   *c.*1777

DUTCHMAN'S COURTSHIP, THE (Clifton)   H&C   *c.*1875
Harry Clifton.

'E CAN'T TAKE THE ROIZE OUT OF OI (Chevalier)   REY   1896
Albert Chevalier.

'E DUNNO WHERE 'E ARE (Wright: Eplett)   HOW   1890
Gus Elen. Parodied as There Goes The Bloke Who Dunno Where 'E Are in an 1894 version by Alec Hurley and sung by Marie Lloyd in *Pretty Bo-Peep* at the

Shakespeare, Liverpool. Yet another parody entitled 'E's Found Out Where 'E Are had words by G. Wallis Arthur (who was also the performer) and music by Fred Eplett. Jack Jones's Reply was sung by Arthur Rigby.

END OF MY OLD CIGAR, THE (R. P. Weston & David)   FDH   1914
Harry Champion.

END OF THE ROAD, THE (Lauder & Dillon)   FDH   1924
Harry Lauder.

ENGLISH SPEAKING RACE AGAINST THE WORLD, THE
   (A. Hall & O. Powell)   SHE   1898
Charles Godfrey.

ERISKAY LOVE LILT, AN (Macleod: trad., arr. Kennedy Fraser)
   BOO/var.   1909

Margaret Kennedy & Marjory Kennedy Fraser, Louise Kirkby Lunn. Published in *Songs of the Hebrides*.

ESAU TAKE ME ON THE SEESAW (Murphy & Lipton)   FDH   1908
Madge Temple.

ETON BOATING SONG (Adew i.e. W. J. Cory: A. Drummond)
KPM/FDH   1878
Transcribed by T. L. Mitchell-Innes, arr. Evelyn Woodhouse.

EVERYBODY'S DOIN' IT NOW (Berlin)   WBS/BER/FEL   1911
Ida Barr, Lydia Barry, Ida Crispi & Fred Farren, Ida Crispi & Robert Hale, Ethel Levey, Ruby Raymond, Maud Tiffany. Included in *Everybody's Doing It*, the Empire revue of 1912.

EVERYBODY WORKS BUT FATHER (Havez)   Helf & Hager/DOV   1905
Arthur Collins, Lew Dockstader, Maidie Scott.

EVERY LITTLE MOVEMENT HAS A MEANING OF ITS OWN
   (Cliffe: J. C. Moore)   FEL   1910
Marie Lloyd. See next entry.

EVERY LITTLE MOVEMENT HAS A MEANING OF ITS OWN
   (Harbach: Hoschna)   WIT   1910
Lina Abarbanell. Interpolated into *Madame Sherry*, New Amsterdam, NY. The NY version was substantially different from the original European and London (Apollo, 1903) productions. Witmark's refused permission for this song to be per-

formed in British Music Halls; Marie Lloyd therefore sang a totally different song with the same title—then as now, titles could not be copyrighted.

EVERYTHING IN THE GARDEN'S LOVELY (Harrington: Le Brunn) FDH 1898
Marie Lloyd.

EVERYTHING IS PEACHES DOWN IN GEORGIA (G. Clarke: Ager & Meyer)
FEI 1918
American Quartet, Al Jolson, Lee White.

EV'RYBODY KNOWS ME IN MY OLD BROWN HAT (Collins & Leigh)
FDH 1920
Harry Champion

EV'RYBODY'S AWFULLY GOOD TO ME (Rubens) CHA 1901
George Grossmith jun. From *The Toreador*, Gaiety.

EV'RY LITTLE WHILE (F. C. Harris: Tate) FDH 1916
Clarice Mayne, Lee White. From *Some*, Vaudeville. This title was used by at least five other composers, including Rudolf Friml in 1928 and Jerome Kern in 1932.

EXCELSIOR! (Longfellow: Balfe) BAY/CRA 1857
Hubert Eisdell & Norman Allen, John Harrison & Robert Radford, Herbert Thorpe & Foster Richardson, Ernest Pike & Peter Dawson.

EXCURSION TRAIN, THE (W. F. Vendevell, arr. Willem Vendevell)
WIL *c.*1875
Edward Marshall.

FALLEN STAR, A (Chevalier: Alfred H. West) REY 1898
Albert Chevalier.

FALL IN AND FOLLOW ME (Mills: B. Scott) FEL 1910
Whit Cunliffe, Charles R. Whittle.

FAREWELL MY LITTLE YO-SAN! (Mills: B. Scott) FDH 1904
Tom Costello.

FARMER GILES *see* **VARMER GILES**

FATAL WEDDING, THE *see* **THOSE WEDDING BELLS SHALL NOT RING OUT**

FATHER DEAR FATHER *see* **COME HOME, FATHER**

FATHER O'FLYNN (Graves: Stanford) BOO   1882
Norman Allin, Signor Foli, Plunkett Greene, R. Watkin Mills, Robert Radford,
Charles Santley.

FATHER'S GOT THE SACK FROM THE WATERWORKS (C. Collins: T. Sullivan)
    FDH   1915
Maidie Scott.

FEDERATION DAY (H. Heath: H. Hyde) MAR   1906
Written to mark the founding of the Variety Artistes' Federation. See also **LET'S
ALL GO TO THE MUSIC HALL.**

FIACRE, LE (Xanrof; Eng. *w* B. Gray) MAU   1892
Yvette Guilbert, Jean Sablon.

FILL 'EM UP (Rule & Walsh & McGhee: Silbermann) SIL   1920
Hetty King.

FINE OLD ENGLISH GENTLEMAN, A (arr. Purday) FDH   1826
Henry Russell. Arranged Charles H. Purday from The Old and New Courtier
(trad.). The music is said to resemble a hymn tune by Martin Luther.

FIREMAN IN THE AMATEUR BRIGADE, THE (Boden: T. Barrett) F&D   1886
T. W. Barrett.

FIRST LOVE—LAST LOVE—BEST LOVE (C. Grey: Ayer) FEL   1918
George Robey & Clara Evelyn, George Robey & Violet Loraine. From *The Bing
Boys on Broadway*, Alhambra.

FISHERMEN OF ENGLAND, THE (Dodson: M. F. Phillips) CHA   1921
Thorpe Bates, Peter Dawson.

FLANAGAN (Murphy & Letters) F&D   1910
Florrie Forde.

(FLOATING WITH) MY BOATING GIRL (T. Sullivan) FEL   1911
Fred Barnes.

FLORAL DANCE, THE (Moss: air, trad. Cornish, arr. Moss) CHA   1911
Peter Dawson.

FLOWER, THE (Ross: Schubert adap. & arr. Clutsam) CHA   1922
Clara Butterworth & Courtice Pounds. From *Lilac Time*, Lyric. Freely adapted
from *Das Dreimädlerhaus* (Raimundtheater, Vienna, 1916), a celebration of Franz

Schubert's life and works based on the novel *Schwammerl* by R. H. Bartsch. The NY version was known as *Blossom Time* (Ambassador, 1921), music arranged by Sigmund Romberg.

FLOWER SONG (Bizet)   MET/CRA   1875
Italo Campanini. From *Carmen*, Opéra-Comique, Paris. London: Her Majesty's, 1878. Libretto by Henri Meilhac & Ludovic Halévy, based on the story by Prosper Mérimée. The first English version was by Henry Hersee.

FLYING TRAPEZE, (THE DARING YOUNG MAN ON) THE
   (Leybourne: A. Lee)   FEL   1868
George Leybourne, Tony Pastor.

FOLKESTONE FOR THE DAY (Bateman: Le Brunn)   FDH   1900
Marie Lloyd.

FOLLOWING IN FATHER'S FOOTSTEPS (E. W. Rogers)   FDH   1892
Vesta Tilley.

FOR HE'S A JOLLY GOOD FELLOW (Planché: arr. Reed)   var.   ?
The music enjoys a notoriously confused genesis, and although often stated as having been inspired by the martial exploits of the Duke of Marlborough ('Malbrouk') it is much older, possibly based upon a medieval French cradle song. Today's familiar English words by J. R. Planché were arranged by T. German Reed 'from an old English burthen'.

FOR ME AND MY GAL (THE BELLS ARE RINGING)
   (Goetz, Leslie, & Meyer)   WBS/MIL   1917
Elizabeth Brice & Charles King, Al Jolson, Van & Schenck.

FOR ME! FOR ME! (Wincott)   H&C/FEL   1895
Fred Earle.

FOR MONTHS AND MONTHS AND MONTHS (Tabrar)   FDH   1909
Jack Norworth, Jack Smiles.

FOR OLD TIMES' SAKE (Osborne)   FDH   1898
Florrie Forde, Al Jolson, Millie Lindon, Harry Taylor.

FOR TONIGHT *see* **WALTZ SONG**

FOR YOU ALONE (O'Reilly: Geehl)   Gould & Bottler   1909
Enrico Caruso.

FOUR-AND-NINE (W. David: B. Lee & Bobs)   FDH   1915
The Two Bobs.

FOUR-'OSS SHARRYBANG, THE (Grain)   BAT/REY   *c.* 1885
Corney Grain.

FOU THE NOO (Grafton: Lauder)   FDH   1905
Harry Lauder.

FRANKIE AND JOHNNY (trad., arr. Leighton Bros. & Shields)   var.   1912
Leighton Brothers, Frank Crumit, Mama Lou. A 1904 version, He Done Me
Wrong, was claimed by Hughie (Bill Bailey Won't You Please Come Home) Can-
non, though the song was common along the Mississippi River in the 1880s.

FRESH, FRESH AS THE MORNING (Fred Gilbert)   FDH   1896
Bilton Sisters. Belle Bilton also sang this song solo as Lady Dunlo after her forced
but temporary separation from the Earl of Clancarty's heir.

FRIEND O' MINE (Weatherly: Sanderson)   BOO   1913
Norman Williams.

FROM MARBLE ARCH TO LEICESTER SQUARE (Knight: Lyle)   HOW   1914
Vesta Tilley.

FROM POVERTY STREET TO GOLDEN SQUARE (Pelham & Rule: Rule)
    FEL   1908
Kate Carney, Florrie Forde.

FUNICULI FUNICULA (Denza)   RIC   1880
Beniamino Gigli, John McCormack.

FUNNY WITHOUT BEING VULGAR (Brett: Ingle)   REY   1891
Albert Chevalier.

FUTURE MRS 'AWKINS, THE (Chevalier)   REY   1892
Albert Chevalier.

GABY GLIDE, THE (Pilcer: Hirsch)   CHA   1911
Gaby Deslys & Harry Pilcer, The Three Rascals. Interpolated into NY version of
Vera Violetta, Winter Garden (original production, music by E. Eysler, an der
Wien, Vienna, 1907). Also in NY interpolated into *The Whirl of Society*, (Winter
Garden, 1912) and *The Little Parisienne* (theatre not known, 1913). London: inter-
polated into *Hullo, Rag-time!*, Hippodrome, 1912.

GALLOPING MAJOR, THE (Leigh: Bastow) FDH 1906
George Bastow.

G'ARN AWAY! WHAT D'YER TAKE ME FOR? (Rogers) FDH 1892
Marie Lloyd.

GAY BOHEMI-AH (H. Greenbank: Jones) H&C 1895
Maurice Farkoa. From *An Artist's Model*, Daly's.

GENDARMES' DUET (Farnie: Offenbach) BOO 1871
Felix Bury & Edward Marshall. From *Geneviève de Brabant*, des Bouffes-Parisiens, Paris 1859. London: Philharmonic, Islington. In march time the music is also known as the US Marines' hymn From the Halls of Montezuma, to the Shores of Tripoli (*c.*1917, *w* anon.).

GEORGIE TOOK ME WALKING IN THE PARK
 (MacDonald: Meher & J. W. Tate) STE/FEL 1908
Clarice Mayne.

GET OUT AND GET UNDER (Clarke & Leslie: Abrahams) FDH 1913
Gerald Kirby, The Three Rascals. Interpolated into *Hullo, Tango!*, Hippodrome.

GET YOUR HAIR CUT *see* **GIT YOUR 'AIR CUT**

GHOST OF BENJAMIN BINNS, THE (Dacre) DEA 1884
Harry Randall.

GHOST OF SHERLOCK HOLMES, THE (R. Morton: Barry) FDH 1894
H. C. Barry.

GIDDY LITTLE GIRL SAID 'NO!', THE (Harrington: O. Powell) HOW 1894
Harry Freeman.

GILBERT, THE FILBERT (Wimperis: Finck) FDH 1914
Basil Hallam. From *The Passing Show*, Palace.

GINGER, YOU'RE BALMY (Murray) FDH 1910
Harry Champion.

GIPSY'S WARNING, THE (Goard) PAX/FDH 1864
Christy Minstrels, Ernest Pike.

GIRL ON THE RAN-DAN-DAN, THE (Stuart) FDH 1896
Lottie Collins, Marie Lloyd.

GIRLS FROM BRYANT'S & MAY, THE (Bateman: Le Brunn)   FDH   1901
Kate Carney, Bella Lloyd.

GIRLS, STUDY YOUR COOKERY BOOK (Murley: M. Scott)   FEL   1908
Florrie Forde.

GIRL THAT I M.A.R.R.Y., THE (Trevelyan)   SHE   1902
James Norrie.

GIT YOUR 'AIR CUT (Beauchamp & Osborne: Eplett)   SHE   1892
George Beauchamp.

GIVE ME A COSY PARLOUR (Gifford & Lawrance & Mellor)   RAW   1907
Victoria Monks.

GIVE ME A LITTLE COSY CORNER (F. C. Harris: Tate)   FDH   1918
Clarice Mayne.

GIVE ME A TICKET TO HEAVEN (Harrison & Elton)   FDH   1902
Denham Harrison, Herbert Payne.

GIVE ME THE MOONLIGHT (L. Brown: A. Von Tilzer)   BMC/FDH   1917
Fred Barnes, Elsie Janis, Randolph Sutton. Included in *Hullo! America*, Palace,
1918.

GIVE MY REGARDS TO BROADWAY (Cohan)   FAM/FEL   1904
George M. Cohan, Billy Murray. From *Little Johnny Jones*, Liberty, NY.

GIVE MY REGARDS TO LEICESTER SQUARE (Hargreaves)   FEL   1905
Victoria Monks.

GLORIOUS BEER (Leggett: Godwin)   FDH   1895
Harry Anderson.

GLORIOUS DEVON (Boulton: German)   BOO   1905
Dalton Baker, Peter Dawson, R. Watkin Mills, Robert Radford, H. Lane Wilson.

GLOW-WORM, THE (Eng. *w* Cayley-Robinson: Lincke)   STE/DOV   1902
Mills Brothers, May Naudain, Ellaline Terriss. From *Lysistrata*, Apollo, Berlin.
Interpolated into US production of *The Girl Behind the Counter*, Herald Square,
NY, 1907. A revised version of the show under the title *Step This Way* was pre-
sented at the Oxford in 1916.

GOD BLESS THE PRINCE OF WALES (Linley: Richards)   var.   1862
Sims Reeves. The original Welsh words by Ceiriog (John Ceiriog Hughes) under the title Ar Dywysog Gwlad y Bryniau.

GOD SAVE THE KING (anon.—possibly Henry Carey or John Bull)
   var.   *c.*1743
The circumstances surrounding the composition and first performance of this song remain a matter of learned debate.

GOING TO THE DERBY IN A DONKEY CART (A. Lloyd)   DAL   1880
Edwin Boyde, Arthur Lloyd, J. W. Rowley, Alfred Vance.

GOLDEN DUSTMAN, THE (E. Graham: Le Brunn)   FDH   1897
Gus Elen.

GOLDEN WEDDING, THE (Adams: Godfrey)   FDH   1886
Charles Godfrey.

GOLD! GOLD! GOLD! (G. W. Hunt)   H&C   1875
George Leybourne.

GOOD-BYE! (Whyte-Melville: Tosti)   RIC   1880
Enrico Caruso, Violet Cameron, Kate Cove.

GOOD-BYE, DOLLY GRAY (Cobb: P. Barnes)   HHC/DAR/FEL   1898
Tom Costello, Harry Ellis (Primrose & Dockstader Minstrels), Hamilton Hill, Harry MacDonough, Leo Stormont. Inspired by Spanish-American War February–August 1898. A 1902 sequel by John Read entitled 'A Letter from the Front' was also sung by Hamilton Hill.

GOOD-BYE-EE (Weston & Lee)   FDH   1917
Florrie Forde, Harry Tate, Charles R. Whittle, Daisy Wood.

GOODBYE, LITTLE YELLOW BIRD *see* **LITTLE YELLOW-BIRD**

GOODBYE, MY LADY LOVE (J. Howard)   TBH/FDH   1904
Ida Emerson & Joe Howard, Blanche Ring.

GOOD MAN IS HARD TO FIND, A (Eddie Green)   P&H/FDH   1918
Jack Norworth, Sophie Tucker, Lee White.

GOOD MORNING, MR POSTMAN (Pelham & Rule)   FDH   1908
Kate Carney.

GORGONZOLA CHEESE *see* **THAT GORGONZOLA CHEESE**

GRANDFATHER'S CLOCK, (MY) (Work) var. 1876
Sundry Minstrel troupes, John Read, Henry Russell.

GRANDMAMMA (Ross: Monckton) CHA 1906
Gertie Millar. From *The New Aladdin*, Gaiety.

GRASS WIDOWER, THE (Woodhouse) SHE 1891
Dan Leno.

GREAT EXPECTATIONS *see* **IT'S ONLY A FALSE ALARM**

GREEN EYE OF THE LITTLE YELLOW GOD, THE (Hayes: Clarke)
REY 1911
Milton Hayes, Bransby Williams. Parodied by Billy Bennett as The Green Tie on the Little Yellow Dog (see **MY MOTHER DOESN'T KNOW I'M ON THE STAGE**); also by Reginald Purdell in his 1940 sketch *Pukka Sahib* (Reynold's) from *Up And Doing* at the Saville starring Stanley Holloway as the reciter with Leslie Henson and Cyril Ritchard as the interrupting Indian Army Officers. A two-handed version in which the reciter is sabotaged by an 'assistant' standing behind him and illustrating the story with not always appropriate gestures is included in the present writer's *Make 'Em Roar*, vol. 1 (Samuel French, 1980).

GREEN HILLS O' SOMERSET (Weatherly: Coates) CHA 1909
Margaret Cooper, Peter Dawson.

GREEN TREES WHISPERED LOW AND MILD, THE (Longfellow: Balfe)
BOO 1856
Charlotte Sainton-Dolby.

GRIZZLY BEAR, (DANCE OF) THE (Botsford: Berlin) FEL 1910
Fanny Brice, Vernon & Irene Castle, Sophie Tucker. From *Ziegfeld Follies of 1910*, Jardin de Paris, NY.

GYPSY WARNED ME, THE (Weston & B. Lee) FDH 1920
Violet Loraine. From *The Whirligig*, Palace.

HAIL, CALEDONIA! (Ogilvie: Stroud) FDH 1912
Peter Hope, Alma Jones.

HAIL! HAIL! THE GANG'S ALL HERE (D. Morse: T. Morse & Sullivan)
FEI 1917
The tune of the chorus is based on Come Friends Who Plough the Sea from Arthur Sullivan's *Pirates of Penzance* (copyright performance given at the Bijou, Paignton, 1879; later that year presented at the Fifth Avenue Theatre, NY, finally

reaching London in 1880 at the Opera Comique). Sullivan's music is itself a burlesque of the Anvil Chorus from Verdi's *Il Trovatore* (1853).

HALF-PAST NINE (Pink: Le Brunn)   FDH   1893
Charles Godfrey, Nellie Wallace.

HALF-PAST TWO (Greenbank & Wimperis: Talbot)   CHA   1909
Phyllis Dare & Harry Welchman. From *The Arcadians*, Shaftesbury. Cut from NY
production but interpolated into *The Girl from Montmartre* (1912) and sung by
Richard Carle & Hattie Williams.

HAMPSTEAD IS THE PLACE TO RURALIZE (W. Williams)   DAL   1861
Annie Adams, Albert Steele.

HAPPY BIRTHDAY TO YOU (P. S. Hill: M. J. Hill)   KPM   1934
Music originally composed in 1893 as Good Morning To All.

HAPPY ELIZA AND CONVERTED JANE (Oliver, arr. L. Field)
    Alphonse Bertini   1881
Sisters Cuthburt, Sisters Jonghmans.

HARD TIMES COME AGAIN NO MORE (S. C. Foster)   FDH   1858
Christy Minstrels.

HARD TIMES, COME AGAIN NO MORE (Tabrar)   H&C   1888
Johnny Danvers, Harry Rickards.

HAS ANYBODY HERE SEEN KELLY? (Murphy & Letters)   FDH   1909
Nora Bayes, Emma Carus, Florrie Forde, Charles R. Whittle. Interpolated into
The Jolly Bachelors, Broadway, NY (1910).

HAS ANYBODY SEEN MY TIDDLER? (Carter & Mills)   FEL   1910
Millie Payne.

HAS ANYONE SEEN A GERMAN BAND? (Mills: B. Scott)   STA/FEL   1907
Florrie Forde, Ella Retford.

HEARTS AND FLOWERS (Brine: *m* arr. Moses-Tobani)
    Carl Fischer/PAX/BOS   1891
Anona Winn. Music derived from Alphons Czibulka's 1891 original in *Winter
Stories*.

HEAVEN WILL PROTECT AN HONEST GIRL (Weston & Lee: R. H. Weston)
    FDH   1933
Gracie Fields.

HEAVEN WILL PROTECT THE WORKING GIRL (E. Smith: Sloane)
CKH   1910
Marie Dressler. From *Tillie's Nightmare*, Herald Square, NY.

HEAVY SWELL OF THE SEA, THE (BIG) (Clay: Lee)   SHE   1879
George Leybourne.

HE CALLS ME HIS OWN GRACE DARLING (Barclay)   FDH   1898
Vesta Victoria.

HE'D HAVE TO GET UNDER *see* **GET OUT AND GET UNDER**

HE LED ME UP THE GARDEN (Gibson: Searson)   REY   1929
Edith Faulkner.

HELLO, CENTRAL GIVE ME HEAVEN (Charles K. Harris)   CKH   1901
Baby Lund, Byron G. Harlan, J. Aldrich Libbey.

HELLO! HELLO! HELLO! *see* **IT'S A DIFFERENT GIRL AGAIN!**

HELLO! HELLO! WHO'S YOUR LADY FRIEND? (David & B. Lee: Fragson)
FEL   1913
Harry Fragson, Mark Sheridan.

HELLO! MA BABY (Emerson: J. Howard)   TBH/FDH   1899
Marguerite Cornille, Ida Emerson & Joe Howard, Millie Legarde, Julie Mackey.

HELLO! SUSIE GREEN (Barrett: Darewski)   FDH   1911
G. H. Elliott, Ella Retford.

HELLO! THERE, FLANAGAN (Godfrey & Mills & Scott)   STA   1909
Florrie Forde.

HEN WLAD FY NHADAU (LAND OF MY FATHERS)
(E. James: air, Rosin The Beau, arr. J. James)   var.   1856
English translation by Owain Alaw (bardic name of John Owen), another by Eben
Fardd (Ebenezer Thomas). English version sung by Signor Foli. (*The National
Library of Wales Journal*, 8 (1953), 244–57.)

HER CHRISTIAN NAME WAS MARY (Tom Graham)   SHE   1895
Walter Kino.

HERE STANDS A POST (C. W. Scott: W. C. Levey)   London   1878
Bessie Bonehill, Marie Compton, W. C. Levey, Nellie Moon. There were various
versions of this song, which was also known as Waiting for the Signal.

Here's To Love And Laughter (Wimperis: Rubens) CHA 1911
Violet Essex. From *The Sunshine Girl*, Gaiety.

Here We Are Again (Godfrey & B. Williams) FDH 1911
Billy Williams.

Here We Are! Here We Are!! Here We Are Again!!! (Knight & Lyle)
FDH 1914
Mark Sheridan.

He's All Right When You Know Him (Coborn) FDH 1887
Charles Coborn.

He's Been A Long Time Gorn (R. P. Weston) FDH 1904
Stewart Morton.

He's Going There Every Night (Murray & Lee: Le Brunn) FDH 1898
Marie Loftus.

He's Going To Marry Mary Ann (Tabrar) FDH 1885
Bessie Bellwood.

He's Only A Working Man *see* **Only A Working Man**

Hildebrandt Montrose (Harrigan: Lee & Harrigan) DAL 1876
Nellie Farren, Arthur Lloyd, G. H. Macdermott.

His Lordship Winked At The Counsel (Dance: Conroy) AHC 1887
Harry Rickards.

His Own Mother Wouldn't Know Him Now (Connor, arr. Baker)
FDH 1893
J. R. Rowley.

Hitchy-Koo (L. Wolfe Gilbert: Abrahams & Muir) FDH 1912
Lew Hearn & Bonita, American Ragtime Octette, The Three Rascals. Int. *Hullo, Rag-time!*, Hippodrome.

Hobnailed Boots That Farver Wore, The
(R. P. Weston & F. J. Barnes) FDH 1907
Billy Williams.

Hold Your Hand Out, Naughty Boy (Murphy & David) FDH 1913
Florrie Forde, Ella Retford, Ted Yorke.

HOLY CITY, THE (Weatherly: Adams)   BOO   1892
Herbert Cave, Peter Dawson, Edward Lloyd, Michael Maybrick (a.k.a. Stephen Adams, the song's composer), Helen Mora.

HOME! SWEET HOME! (Payne: Bishop)   G&D/FDH   1823
Anna Maria Tree *et al.* Originally one of Henry Bishop's Sicilian Airs and included in *Clari, or The Maid of Milan*, Covent Garden. The song was an especial favourite of Adelina Patti, who would delight her fans and outrage the purists by inserting it into the most unlikely operas at the most unsuitable moments.

HONEYSUCKLE AND THE BEE, THE (Fitz: Penn)   FDH   1901
Maud Courtney, Clifford Essex, Ellaline Terriss. From *Prima Donna*, Herald Square, NY (not Victor Herbert's 1908 musical of the same name). London: interpolated into *Bluebell in Fairyland*, Vaudeville.

HOP LIGHT HOO (Ware)   H&C   *c.*1860
E. W. Mackney. D. D. Emmett wrote a song with the same title *c.*1844 of which the music is lost but the words indicate a quite different rhythm and story-line from Ware's.

HOT CODLINS (C. Dibdin jun.: Whitaker)   DAL/PAX   1819
Sam Cowell, Joseph Grimaldi, Tom Matthews. Int. revival of *The Talking Bird* or *Harlequin Perizade*, Sadler's Wells.

HOT TIME IN THE OLD TOWN, A (Hayden: Metz)   EBM   1896
R. G. Knowles, Mama Lou, Josephine Sabel.

HOW ARE YER? (Judge & H. Williams)   FEL   1913
Florrie Forde.

HOW CAN A LITTLE GIRL BE GOOD? (Bay: Tabbush)   FDH   1919
Maidie Scott.

HOW COULD RED RIDING HOOD? (arr. R. D. Whichard)   WRI   1922
Sophie Tucker.

HOW DARE YOU! (Boden & Keith & Merson: Eplett)   RAW   1906
Harry Ford.

HOW'D'YA LIKE TO SPOON WITH ME? (Laska: Kern)   FDH   1905
Georgia Caine, Millie Legarde. Int. US production of *The Earl and the Girl*, NY Casino. Also int. *The Rich Mr Hoggenheimer*, Wallack's, NY and the 1914 Aldwych revival.

How'ya Gonna Keep 'Em Down On The Farm?
(S. Lewis & J. Young: Donaldson)   FEL   1919
Eddie Cantor, Sophie Tucker, Dorothy Ward.

Hullo! Tu-Tu (M. Scott-Gatty: C. Scott-Gatty)   CHA   1909
Margaret Cooper.

Hush! The Bogie! (Pettitt & Sims: Lutz)   H&C   1890
E. J. Lonnen, G. H. Macdermott, Ted Snow (Mohawk Minstrels), Horace Wheatley. London version of **Whist! The Bogie Man** featured in *Carmen Up-to-Data*, Gaiety.

I Ain't A-Going To Tell (Pink: Tempest)   FDH   1896
Alec Hurley. Based on an American song (Ellis & Parker, 1893).

I Ain't 'Arf A Lucky Kid (C. Hayes: B. Hayes)   REY   1914
Kathleen Burchell.

I Ain't Nobody In Perticuler (MacKenzie: Fred Leigh)   FDH   1907
Alec Hurley.

I 'Aven't Told 'Im (Murray & Leigh: Le Brunn)   FDH   1898
Alec Hurley.

I Belong To Glasgow (Fyffe)   FDH   *c.* 1920
Will Fyffe. Will Fyffe jun. states that his father 'probably performed it in 1920 and certainly in 1921. It is possible that he sang the song during the First World War.'

I Can Say 'Truly Rural' (David & Arthurs)   STA/FEL   1909
Wilkie Bard, Herbert Rule.

I Can't Do My Bally Bottom Button Up (J. P. Long)   FEL   1916
Ernie Mayne.

I Can't Forget 'Auld Reekie' (Lambe)   FDH   1907
Jessie Preston.

I Can't Forget The Days When I Was Young (Mayo: W. David)
DAR/FEL   1919
Marie Lloyd.

I Can't Reach That Top Note (David & Arthurs)   STA   1909
Wilkie Bard, Herbert Rule.

I Can't Take My Eyes Off You (Rida J. Young: Rubens)   CHA   1904
Constance Windom. Interpolated into US production *Three Little Maids*, Daly's, NY.

I Can't Tell Why I Love You But I Do (Cobb: G. Edwards)
   HHC/DAR/FEL   1900
Emma Carus, Lil Hawthorne, Julie Mackey, Harry MacDonough, Clarice Vance.

I Couldn't Exert Myself (Cotes: Robey)   H&C   1902
George Robey.

Ida! Sweet As Apple Cider (Leonard: Munson)   STE   1903
Eddie Leonard.

I Didn't Raise My Boy To Be A Soldier (Bryan: Piantadosi)   FEI   1915
Gene Greene.

I'd Like To Live In Paris All The Time *see* **Coster Girl In Paris, The**

I Do Like An Egg For My Tea (Leo)   FDH   1919
Bert Coote. Included in *Back Again*, Ambassadors'.

I Do Like A S'Nice S'Mince S'Pie (David & B. Lee)   FEL   1914
Jay Laurier.

I Do Like To Be Beside The Seaside (Glover Kind)   FEL   1909
Mark Sheridan.

I Do Like You Susie In Your Pretty Little Sunday Clothes
   (Murphy & David)   FDH   1912
Daisy Dormer.

I Don't Care What Becomes Of Me (Mills: B. Scott)   FEL   1911
Sam Mayo. A 1910 HVT song of the same title (Worton David & George Campbell: Fred Mayo) was also sung by Sam Mayo. Which of the two was sung by Fred Earle is not known.

I Don't Seem To Want You When You're With Me
   (Rubens)   CHA   1904
Margaret Cooper. From *Lady Madcap*, Prince of Wales's.

I Don't Want To Fight (Pettitt: V. Davies)   SHE   1878
Herbert Campbell. Celebrated parody of **Macdermott's War Song**.

I Don't Want To Play In Your Yard (Wingate: Petrie) FEL 1894
Jenny Clare & Madeline Majilton, Julie Mackey, The Tiny Websters.

I'd Rather Lather Father, Than Father Lather Me
(Hunter: Redmond) AHC 1876
G. H. Macdermott, Mohawk Minstrels.

I Dream Of Jeanie *see* **Jeanie With The Light Brown Hair**

I Dreamt That I Dwelt In Marble Halls (The Dream)
(Bunn: Balfe) CHA 1843
Louisa Pyne, Elizabeth Rainforth. From *The Bohemian Girl*, Drury Lane. See also
Yes, We Have No Bananas.

I Felt So Awfully Shy (Burley & H. Bull) FDH 1914
Jack Pleasants.

If I Could Only Make You Care (Dempsey: Schmid) REM/FDH 1913
The Zigeuner Quartet.

If I Had A Girl As Nice As You (Murphy & Lipton) FDH 1904
Alfred Gordon, Herbert Payne, Ernest Pike.

If I Only Knew The Way (H. Greenbank: Talbot) AHC 1896
Venie Belfry. From *Monte Carlo*, Avenue.

If I Should Plant A Tiny Seed Of Love (Macdonald: Tate) FEL 1908
Dora Lyric, Clarice Mayne, Maude Mortimer.

If It Wasn't For The 'Ouses In Between (Bateman: Le Brunn)
FDH 1894
Gus Elen

If I Were On The Stage (Kiss Me Again) (Blossom: Herbert) FEL 1905
Fritzi Scheff. From *Mdlle Modiste*, Knickerbocker, NY.

If The Managers Only Thought The Same As Mother
(Berlin: Snyder) FEL 1910
Maidie Scott. From *The Jolly Bachelors*, Broadway, NY.

If The Man In The Moon Were A Coon (Fischer) FDH 1905
G. H. Elliott.

If The Missus Wants To Go Let Her Drown (Ray) FDH 1902
Phil Ray.

IF THE WIND HAD ONLY BLOWN THE OTHER WAY
(E. Williams & Wynn: Williams)   STE   1909
Maidie Scott, Bessie Wynn.

IF THE WORLD WERE RULED BY GIRLS (Arthurs & Murphy)   FDH   1905
Whit Cunliffe, Ada Reeve.

IF THOSE LIPS COULD ONLY SPEAK (Ridgewell & Godwin)   FDH   1905
Will Godwin.

IF YOU CAN'T DO ANY GOOD DON'T DO ANY HARM (Bedford)
FHD   1902
Kate Carney.

IF YOU CAN'T GET A GIRL IN THE SUMMERTIME (Kalmar: Tierney)
MIL   1915
Lou Lockett & Jack Waldron, Harry Tierney.

IF YOU COULD CARE (FOR ME) (Wimperis: Dareswki)   DAR   1918
Irene Bordoni, Alice Delysia. From *As You Were*, London Pavilion. Adapted from
Plus ça Change by Rip (Georges Thenon).

IF YOU'RE IRISH COME INTO THE PARLOUR (Glenville: Miller)   FEL   1919
Shaun Glenville.

IF YOU WANT TO HAVE A ROW WAIT TILL THE SUN SHINES
(Hargreaves)   FEL   1904
Victoria Monks.

IF YOU WERE THE ONLY GIRL IN THE WORLD (Grey: Ayer)   FEL   1916
George Robey & Violet Loraine. From *The Bing Boys are Here*, Alhambra.

I GOTTER MOTTER *see* **MY MOTTER**

I HEAR YOU CALLING ME (Harford: Marshall)   BOO   1908
Lucrezia Bori, John Coates, Charles W. Harrison. This ballad is particularly associated with John McCormack for whom it was said to have been composed.

I JUST CAN'T MAKE MY EYES BEHAVE
(Cobb & H. B. Smith: Gus Edwards)   GEM   1906
Anna Held, Ada Jones. From *A Parisian Model*, Broadway, NY.

I LIFT UP MY FINGER AND I SAY 'TWEET TWEET' (Sarony)   FDH   1929
Stanley Lupino, Leslie Sarony.

I Like London (Wimperis: Talbot) CHA 1909
May Kinder. From *The Arcadians*, Shaftesbury.

I Like You In Velvet (Rubens) CHA 1904
Maurice Farkoa. From *Lady Madcap*, Prince of Wales's.

I Like Your Apron And Your Bonnet (Harrington: Lawrance)
FEL 1911
Mabel Green, Ella Retford.

I Like Your Old French Bonnet (Mellor & Lawrance & Gifford)
FEL 1909
Daisy Dormer.

I Like Your Town (Bedford & R. P. Weston) FDH 1915
Harry Bedford.

I Live In Trafalgar Square (Murphy) FDH 1902
Morny Cash.

I'll Be With You In Apple Blossom Time (Fleeson: A. Von Tilzer)
FDH 1920
Nora Bayes.

I'll Be Your Sweetheart or **Bluebells** (H. Dacre) DEA/FEL 1899
Lil Hawthorne, Marie Kendall.

I'll Make A Man Of You (Wimperis: Finck) FDH 1914
Clara Beck, Gwendoline Brogden. Included in *The Passing Show*, Palace. Written five months *before* the outbreak of World War I and not intended, as is often stated, as a recruiting song. (Herman Finck, *My Melodious Memories*, 68.)

I'll Meet You At The Bodega (Rogers) FEL 1905
Maude Mortimer.

I'll Place It In The Hands Of My Solicitor (F. Gilbert) AHC 1887
Arthur Lloyd.

I'll Sing Thee Songs Of Araby (Wills: F. Clay) CHA 1877
Ben Davies, Ruby Helder, Edward Lloyd, Sims Reeves. From the cantata *Lalla Rookh*, derived from Thomas Moore's 1817 poem. Set by some forty other composers.

I'll Take You Home Again Kathleen (Westendorf)   var.   1876
John McCormack.

I'll Walk Beside You (Lockton: A. Murray)   CHA   1936
John McCormack.

I Love A Lassie (Lauder & Grafton: Lauder)   FDH   1905
Harry Lauder. Subtitled Ma Scotch Bluebell.

I Love A Piano (Berlin)   CHA   1915
Harry Fox, Ethel Levey. From *Stop! Look! Listen!*, Globe, NY. London: retitled
Follow the Crowd, Empire.

I Love The Moon (Rubens)   CHA   1911
Phyllis Dare, Maggie Teyte. From *The Sunshine Girl*, Gaiety.

I Love To Go Swimmin' With Women (MacDonald: Romberg)
   WIT   1921
Pat Rooney. From *Love Birds*, Apollo, NY, but cut before opening.

I'm Afraid To Come Home In The Dark
   (H. H. Williams: Van Alstyne)   FDH   1906
May A. Bell, Della Fox, May Irwin, Hetty King, Elizabeth Murray, Ella Retford,
Maisie Scott, May Vokes. From *A Knight for a Day*, Wallack's, NY—revised ver-
sion of *Mamselle Sallie*, Grand Opera House and New York, NY (1906).

I'm a Little Too Young To Know (Reeves: Venton)   FDH   1889
Ada Reeve.

I'm Alone Because I Love You (Joe Young)   FEL   1931
Bud & Joe Billings.

I'm Always Chasing Rainbows (McCarthy & Carroll)   FDH   1918
Harry Fox & The Dolly Sisters. From *Oh, Look!*, Vanderbilt, NY. Music based on
Chopin's Fantasie Impromptu, op. 66.

I'm A Man That's Done Wrong To My Parents (trad.)   CRA   1889
From *English County Songs*, ed. Lucy Broadwood.

I May Be Crazy But I Love You (Stuart)   FDH   1902
Eugene Stratton.

I'm Falling In Love With Someone (Rida J. Young: V. Herbert)
   FEL   1910
Orville Harrold. From *Naughty Marietta*, New York, NY.

I'M FOREVER BLOWING BUBBLES (Kenbrovin & Kellette)
    KBM/REM/FEL   1918
Fred Barnes, Albert Campbell, Charles Hart, Elsie Janis. Interpolated into *The Passing Show of 1918*, Winter Garden, NY.

I'M GETTING READY FOR MY MOTHER-IN-LAW (Wincott)   RAW   1896
Harry Champion.

I'M GLAD I TOOK MY MOTHER'S ADVICE (Not known)   *c.*1915
Maidie Scott. Seemingly unpublished, but recorded by Scott on HMV B568 in 1915. Note this is not T. E. Dunville's 1895 Mother's Advice song, which had words and music by Charles Osborne but was quite different.

I'M GOING BACK TO HIMAZAS (F. Austin)   WRI   1927
Harry Gordon.

I'M GOING TO GET MARRIED TODAY—HOORAY! (B. Scott & Cotes)
    FDH   1899
Maggie Duggan.

I'M HENERY THE EIGHTH, I AM (Murray & R. P. Weston)   FDH   1910
Harry Champion.

I MIGHT LEARN TO LOVE HIM LATER ON (Weston & Lee)   FDH   1921
Violet Loraine. From *London, Paris and New York*, London Pavilion.

I'M JUST WILD ABOUT HARRY (Sissle: E. Blake)   WIT/SHE/FEL   1921
Lottie Gee, Florence Mills. From *Shuffle Along*, 63rd Street, NY.

I'M LOOKING FOR MR WRIGHT (Weston & Murphy & Darewski)
    FDH   1909
Madge Temple.

IMMENSEIKOFF (Lloyd)   H&C   1873
Arthur Lloyd.

I'M NINETY-FOUR THIS MORNIN' (Fyffe)   FDH   1922
Will Fyffe.

I'M NOT PARTICULAR (Leigh & Murray)   AHC   1898
George Beauchamp.

I'm One Of The Boys *see* **One Of The Boys**

I'm Selling Up The 'Appy 'Appy 'Ome (Boden)   SHE   1889
Harry Champion.

I'm Shy, Mary Ellen, I'm Shy (Ridgewell & Stevens)   FDH   1910
Jack Pleasants, Jack Smiles.

I'm The Bosom Friend Of Albert, Prince Of Wales
   (Horowitz: Bower)   WIT/SHE   1891

I'm The Dark Girl Dress'd In Blue (W. Williams)   WIL   1863
Kate Harley. See also **The Dark Girl Dress'd in Blue.**

I'm Twenty-One Today (Kendal)   FEL   1911
Stanley Kirkby, Jack Pleasants, Albert Whelan.

I Must Go Home Tonight *see* **Oh, I Must Go Home Tonight**

I'm Waiting Here For Kate (David & Arthurs)   FDH   1909
Wilkie Bard.

In A Monastery Garden (Ketelbey)   LAR   1915
Peter Dawson.

I Never Cried So Much In All My Life (Haines & Harper & Castling)
   CCC   1936
Gracie Fields.

In Olden Spain (C. Lalo: E. Lalo)   Edwin Ashdown Ltd.   1888
Julie De Savigny. From *Le Roi d'Ys*, Opéra-Comique, Paris.

In Other Words (C. Grey: Ayer)   FEL   1916
George Robey. From *The Bing Boys are Here*, Alhambra.

In The Baggage Coach Ahead (G. L. Davis)   HHD/DOV   1896
Imogene Comer.

In The Dingle Dongle Dell (Kummer)   STE   1904
Margaret Cooper.

In the Gloamin' (Orred: Lady A. Hill)   Gould & Bottler   1877
Signor Campobello, Will Oakland, Carlotta Patti.

IN THE GOOD OLD SUMMERTIME (Shields: George Evans)
 HHD/DAR/FEL   1902
Julie Mackey, Blanche Ring, Stewart & Gillen. Interpolated into *The Defender*,
Herald Square, NY.

IN THESE HARD TIMES (R. P. Weston & Fred J. Barnes)   FDH   1915
Whit Cunliffe.

IN THE SHADE OF THE OLD APPLE TREE (Williams: Van Alstyne)
 FDH   1905
Nora Bayes, Lillian Rosewood.

IN THE STRAND (I WISH I WAS WITH NANCY) (F. Hall)   1861
E. W. Mackney. Air, **I WISH I WAS IN DIXIE** but no acknowledgement to D. D.
Emmett on Foster & L'Enfant's song sheet.

IN THE TWI-TWI-TWILIGHT (Wilmot: Darewski)   FDH   1907
George Lashwood.

IN THE VALLEY OF GOLDEN DREAMS (Murphy & David)   FDH   1913
Florrie Forde, Gertie Gitana.

I PARTED MY HAIR IN THE MIDDLE (David & Murphy)   FDH   1913
George Formby.

I PUT ON MY COAT AND WENT HOME (J. & W. Hargreaves)   FEL   1910
George Formby.

I REALLY CAN'T STOP DANCING (Tich: Ison)   SHE   1893
Little Tich.

IS ANYBODY LOOKING FOR A WIDOW? (Gifford)   REM/SHE   1908
Vesta Victoria.

I STOPPED, I LOOKED, AND I LISTENED (Ayer)   FEL   1916
George Robey. From *The Bing Boys are Here*, Alhambra.

IS YOUR MOTHER IN MOLLY MALONE? (Mills: Everard)   FDH   1903
Walter Munroe.

IT AIN'T ALL LAVENDER (Tabrar)   SHE/FEL   1894
Harry Randall, George Robey.

I THINK I'LL BUY PICCADILLY (Waite)   WRI   1926
J. R. Rickaby.

IT'S A BIT OF A RUIN THAT CROMWELL KNOCKED ABOUT A BIT
(Bedford & Sullivan: Bedford)   FEL   1912
Marie Lloyd, Marie Lloyd jun.

IT'S A DIFFERENT GIRL AGAIN! (Arthurs: B. Scott)   FDH   1906
Whit Cunliffe.

**IT'S A GREAT BIG SHAME (I'M BLOWED IF 'E CAN CALL 'ISSELF
'IS OWN)** (Bateman: Le Brunn)   FDH   1894
Gus Elen.

IT'S ALL RIGHT IN THE SUMMER TIME (Everard & Murray)   FDH   1902
Vesta Victoria.

IT'S A LONG, LONG WAY TO TIPPERARY (Judge & Williams)   FEL   1912
Florrie Forde, Jack Judge, Maude Mortimer. In 1933 Jack Judge stated that he had
given Harry Williams a share of the royalties in all his published songs in return for
past financial assistance, but that Williams did not write one single word or note
of Tipperary or any other song bearing their names. The Williams family still
strongly disputes this assertion. (J. B. Booth, *A Pink 'Un Remembers*, 121–2; *The
Independent Magazine* 'Back Bites' column of 18 Sept. 1993.)

IT'S A PITY TO WASTE THE CAKE (Harrington: O. Powell)   FEL   1909
George Lashwood.

IT'S A SAD SAD STORY (Lidden)   SHE   1907
Kate Butler.

IT'S LOVELY TO BE IN LOVE (F. C. Harris: Tate)   FDH   1915
Clarice Mayne.

IT'S MY BATH NIGHT TONIGHT (Weston & Lee)   FDH   1922
Jack Pleasants.

IT'S NICE TO GET UP IN THE MORNING (Lauder)   FDH   1913
Harry Lauder.

IT'S NICE TO HAVE A HOME OF YOUR OWN (A. E. Lawrence & Lester)
FDH   1900
Harry Anderson.

IT'S NO USE YOU CALLING 'HANNAH!' (C. Collins & F. J. Barnes: Collins)
FDH   1907
Kate Carney.

IT'S ONLY A FALSE ALARM (GREAT EXPECTATIONS) (Pink: Randall)
FDH 1889
Harry Randall.

IT'S PART OF A P'LICEMAN'S DUTY (E. W. Rogers) FDH 1906
Vesta Tilley.

IT'S THE POOR THAT HELP THE POOR (Mills & Castling) FDH 1904
Millie Denham, Florrie Gallimore.

I USED TO SIGH FOR THE SILVERY MOON (Barrett: Darewski) FDH 1909
G. H. Elliott, Daisy Wood.

I'VE GOT MY EYE ON YOU (Leigh & Arthurs) FDH 1913
Clarice Mayne. Not Cole Porter's 1940 song I've Got my Eyes on You.

I'VE GOT RINGS ON MY FINGERS (R. P. Weston & F. J. Barnes: M. Scott)
FDH 1909
Ellaline Terriss. Included in *Captain Kidd*, Wyndham's. In NY int. *The Midnight
Sons* (Broadway, 1910) for Blanche Ring, who also sang it in *The Yankee Girl*
(Herald Square, 1910), *When Claudia Smiles* (39th St., 1914) and *Right this Way*
(46th St., 1938).

I'VE GOT THE OOPERZOOTIC (Hunter: Foreman) FDH 1896
Johnny Danvers (Mohawk Minstrels).

I'VE NEVER LOST MY LAST TRAIN YET (Rollit: Le Brunn) BOW *c.* 1906
Marie Lloyd.

I WANT A GIRL JUST LIKE THE GIRL WHO MARRIED DEAR OLD DAD
(Dillon: Von Tilzer) FDH 1911
American Quartet, Al Jolson, Dorothy Ward.

I WANT TO BE A LIDY (Dance: Malbert) AHC 1899
Louie Freear, Alma Jones, Hilda Trevelyan. From *A Chinese Honeymoon*, Theatre
Royal, Hanley.

I WANT TO BE A MILITARY MAN (Clement: Stuart) FDH 1899
Louis Bradfield. From *Florodora*, Lyric.

I WANT TO BE A PRIMA DONNA *see* **ART IS CALLING FOR ME**

I WANT TO BE IN DIXIE (Berlin & Snyder) FEL 1911
American Ragtime Octette, Arthur Collins, Byron G. Harlan, May Irwin, Jen
Latona, Ella Retford, Willie Solar, The Three Rascals. From *She Knows Better*

Now, Plymouth, Chicago. Interpolated into *The Whirl of Society*, Winter Garden, NY. Included in *Hullo, Rag-time!*, Hippodrome.

I WANT TO GO BACK TO MICHIGAN (Berlin)   FEL   1914

Daisy James, Frank Mullane, Rae Samuels, Daisy Wood. Interpolated into Aldwych revival of *The Earl and the Girl* as Down on the Farm with new words J. P. Long & Ernie Mayne; also interpolated into *5064 Gerrard*, the 1915 Alhambra revue in which it was sung in its original form (as Back to the Farm) by Beatrice Lillie.

I WANT TO GO TO IDAHO (Gifford & Lawrance & Mellor)   FDH   1908

G. H. Elliott.

I WANT TO MEET A GOOD YOUNG MAN (J. Cooke jun.)   EMP   1885

Nellie L'Estrange.

I WANT TO PLAY WITH LITTLE DICK (Will J. Godwin)   FDH   1897

Vesta Victoria.

I WANT TO SING IN OPERA (David & Arthurs)   FDH   1910

Wilkie Bard.

I WANT TO TAKE A YOUNG MAN IN AND DO FOR HIM (Wilcock)
   REY/FEL   1931

Nora Blakemore.

I WAS A GOOD LITTLE GIRL TILL I MET YOU (F. C. Harris: Tate)
   FDH   1914

Clarice Mayne, Ella Retford. From *This and That*, Comedy.

I WAS ONE OF THE RUINS THAT CROMWELL KNOCKED ABOUT A BIT *see* **IT'S A BIT OF A RUIN THAT CROMWELL KNOCKED ABOUT A BIT**

I WAS STANDING AT THE CORNER OF THE STREET
   (Formby & J. Hunt: Formby)   FEL   1910

George Formby, Harry Randall.

I WISH I'D BOUGHT DUCKS (Leo)   FDH   1900

Wilkie Bard.

I WISH I WAS IN DIXIE (D. D. Emmett)   FDH/FEL   1859

Bryant's Minstrels (which included Emmett), Buckley's Serenaders. First performed as an ensemble walk-round by Bryant's Minstrels at the Mechanics' Hall, 472 Broadway, NY, on Monday, 4 April 1859. See also **IN THE STRAND**.

I Wonder If The Girl I'm Thinking Of Is Thinking Of Me?
(Castling: Neat)   FEL   1906
Maude Mortimer.

I Wonder If You Miss Me Sometimes (Mills: B. Scott)   FEL   *c.*1910
Lily Morris, Ella Retford.

I Wonder What It Feels Like To Be Poor?
(Murphy & Lipton & Magine)   WRI   1913
Tom E. Hughes.

I Wonder Who's Kissing Her Now? (Hough & F. R. Adams: Orlob)
CKH/FEL   1909
Ada Reeve, Harry Woodruff. From *The Prince of Tonight*, Princess, Chicago.
Though he had no hand in its composition Joseph E. Howard was for years cred-
ited with the music. Only after a protracted court case was the true composer,
Harry Orlob, acknowledged and compensated.

I Won't Be A Nun (Countess of W-N-K, arr. Smart)
Brewer/TRB   early 19th c.
Published by Sheard's 1874 *Musical Bouquet* (3903) and 'dedicated to Father
Ignatius'.

I Would—If I Could—But I Can't—So I Won't
(Parsons & Relsie: Tracey)   REY   1922
Margaret Bannerman.

I Wouldn't Leave My Little Wooden Hut For You
(Collins & Mellor)   FDH   1896
Daisy Dormer, Clarissa Talbot.

Jeanie With The Light Brown Hair (S. C. Foster)   var.   1854
Christy Minstrels, Mohawk Minstrels, John McCormack. Inspired by Stephen
Foster's wife, Jane. Alas, their marriage was a stormy one and he died alone and
penniless at the age of 38.

Jere-Jeremiah (David & Murphy)   FDH   1913
Florrie Forde, Clarice Mayne.

Jerusalem (W. Blake: Parry)   CUR   1916
Peter Dawson.

Jerusalem's Dead, The (Daly: Crook)   FDH   1895
Albert Chevalier. Cockney rhyming slang, i.e. Jerusalem = Jerusalem Artichoke =

moke. The song is a paean of regret for the death of the singer's donkey, which in the lyrics (but not the title) is called a *Jee*rusalem.

JESSIE'S DREAM (Campbell: Blockley)   CHA   1858
Charlotte Russell.

JESSIE THE BELLE AT THE (RAILWAY) BAR (Ware)   SHE   1867
Annie Adams, Henri Clark, Fred French, George Leybourne, Harry Liston, Mrs F. R. Phillips, Alfred Vance, George Ware, Mrs George Ware.

JINGLE BELLS (Pierpoint)   var.   1859
Christy Minstrels.

JINGO SONG, THE *see* **MACDERMOTT'S WAR SONG**

JOHN BROWN'S BODY   var.   1861
Hutchinson Family. American Civil War Unionist marching song. Words anonymous (though there are sundry claimants) and the music partly inspired by William Steffe's 1858 Methodist hymn Say Brothers Will You Meet Us. The original John Brown was an Army sergeant at Fort Warren. See also **BATTLE HYMN OF THE REPUBLIC**.

JOHN, GO AND PUT YOUR TROUSERS ON! (Williams)   FDH   1907
Billy Williams.

JOHNNIE (Mayo)   DAR   1923
Sam Mayo.

JOHNNIE AT THE GAIETY (Grossmith)   BAT   1895
George Grossmith jun.

JOHNNY GET YOUR GUN (Belasco; Eng. *w* T. L. Clay)   TBH/SHA/FDH   1886
Gus Garrick, 'Funny' Little Thomas (Mohawk Minstrels), Moore & Burgess Minstrels, Nellie Richards. Sundry folk melodies are said to be the inspiration for this song, including Johnny Get Your Hair Cut and The Arkansas Traveller.

JOHNNY JONES *see* **WHAT'S THAT FOR, EH?**

JOHNNY JONES AND HIS SISTER SUE *see* **LITTLE PEACH IN AN ORCHARD GREW, A**

JOHNNY MORGAN'S SISTER (Hyde)   FEL   1907
Maidie Scott.

John Willie, Come On (Formby)   FDH   1908
George Formby.

Jolly Dogs *see* **Slap Bang! Here We Are Again!**

Jolly Good Luck To The Girl Who Loves A Soldier
   (Leigh: Lyle)   FDH   1906
Vesta Tilley.

Jolly Little Polly On Her Gee-Gee-Gee (Dacre)   DEA   1895
Fannie Leslie.

Joshu-Ah (B. Lee & Arthurs)   FDH   1906
Clarice Mayne.

Juanita (Hon. Mrs Norton: air, Handel's Lascia Ch'io Pianga)   FDH   1850
Christy Minstrels.

(Jump) Jim Crow (anon., arr. Blewitt)   Charles Jeffries/DAL   *c.*1829
John Dunn, T. D. Rice.

Just A Little Bit Of String *see* **Simple Little String, A**

Just A Song At Twilight *see* **Love's Old Sweet Song**

Just A-Wearyin' For You (Stanton: Jacobs-Bond)   FDH   1916
Jessie Bartlett Davis.

Just Before The Battle, Mother (Root)   var.   1863
Charles Bernard (Moore & Burgess Minstrels), Will Oakland.

Just Like The Ivy (Castling & Mills)   FDH   1902
Marie Kendall.

Just Touch The Harp Gently (S. Mitchell: Blamphin)   H&C   1870
William Leslie, sundry Minstrel troupes.

Just Try To Picture Me Back Home In Tennessee
   (Jerome: Donaldson)   WBS   1915
Dainty Doris, G. H. Elliott, Herbert Payne, Two Rascals & Jacobson.

Kashmiri Song (Pale Hands I Loved) (Hope: Woodforde-Finden)
   BOO   1902
Clara Butt, Peter Dawson, Ivor Foster, John McCormack. One of the four Indian
Love Lyrics extracted from Laurence Hope's *The Garden of Kama*.

KATHLEEN MAVOURNEEN (Crawford: Crouch) var. 1836

David Bispham, Clara Butt, Joseph A. Cave, John McCormack, Mme Patey-Whittock.

KEEMO KIMO (J. Allen: trad.) DAL/SHE 1840

Mrs Caulfield, Mrs W. J. Florence, Christy Serenaders. A version published in 1854 has words by Geo. P. Christy and music by Woods. Geo. P. Christy is a misprint either for Edwin (Ned) P. Christy or for Geo. N. Christy, the name adopted by George N. Harrington as a co-founder with Ned of the original Christy Serenaders/Minstrels.

KEEP OFF THE GRASS (Monckton) CHA 1901

Gertie Millar. From *The Toreador*, Gaiety.

KEEP RIGHT ON TO THE END OF THE ROAD *see* **END OF THE ROAD, THE**

KEEP THE HOME FIRES BURNING (TILL THE BOYS COME HOME)
(Guilbert: Novello) AHC 1914

Fred Barnes, Stanley Kirkby, Sybil Vane.

KEEP YOR FEET STILL GEORDIE HINNEY (Wilson: air, Nellie Gray) *c.*1870

Joe Wilson. Wilson's songs were mostly written and published in Newcastle-on-Tyne between 1864 and 1874 by Wilson himself and from 1872 also published by Thomas Allen. See C. E. Catchside-Warrington (Sources and Bibliography: Published Song Collections).

KERRY DANCE, THE (Molloy) BOO/var. 1879

Peter Dawson, John McCormack, Mme Louie Sherrington, Charles Tree. Derived from The Cuckoo, music and words by Margaret Casson *c.*1790.

KEYS OF HEAVEN, THE (trad. Cheshire air arr. H. W. Greaves)
CRA/var. 1893

Clara Butt & Kennerley Rumford, Yvette Guilbert, Dora Labette & Hubert Eisdell.

KILLALOE! (R. Martin: Morelli) J. A. Lafleur & Son 1887

E. J. Lonnen. From *Miss Esmerelda*, Gaiety.

KILLARNEY (Falconer: Balfe) ASC/FEL 1861

Ian Colquhoun, John McCormack. From *Peep o' Day*, Lyceum.

KISS ME AGAIN *see* **IF I WERE ON THE STAGE**

KISS THE GIRL IF YOU'RE GOING TO (Barnes & R. P. Weston) FDH 1907

Marie Kendall.

KITTY, THE TELEPHONE GIRL (Gifford & Lawrance & Mellor & Trevor)
  FDH   1912

Jack Norworth. Interpolated into second edition of *Hullo, Tango!*, Hippodrome (1913) and *5064 Gerrard*, Alhambra (1915).

K-K-K-KATY (O'Hara) FEI/DAR   1918

Marie Brett & A. Frank Varney, Walter Williams. Interpolated into *Buzz-Buzz*, Vaudeville.

KNEES UP, MOTHER BROWN! (B. Lee & Harris Weston & I. Taylor)
  MAU   1938

Elsie & Doris Waters. Though this song dates back at least to 1918 (in his 1941 novel *Random Harvest* James Hilton wrote 'in some curious telepathic way it sprang up all over London on Armistice Night, in countless squares, streets and pubs'), the Lee, Harris Weston, & Taylor version would seem the first to be published.

KNOCKED 'EM IN THE OLD KENT ROAD *see* **WOT CHER!**

KNOCK THE TWO ROOMS INTO ONE (Mills & B. Scott) DEA   1900
Ethel Haydon.

LAMBETH WALK, THE (Rogers) FDH   1899
Alec Hurley.

LAMBETH WALK, THE (Rose & Furber: Gay)
  Cinephonic Music Co. Ltd./CCC   1937
Teddie St Denis & Lupino Lane. From *Me and my Girl*, Victoria Palace.

LAND OF HOPE AND GLORY (A. C. Benson: Elgar) BOO   1902
Clara Butt. The title of the five marches which comprise *Pomp And Circumstance* is from *Othello* III. iii: 'pride, pomp and circumstance of glorious war'. Number 1 (a trio) was composed in 1901 and the words, after adjustment also to the music, were added the following year for the coronation of King Edward VII.

LAND OF MY FATHERS *see* **HEN WLAD FY NHADAU**

LARK IN THE CLEAR AIR, THE (Ferguson: air, An Tailliuir) FDH   *c.*1850

LAST ROSE OF SUMMER, THE *see* **'TIS THE LAST ROSE OF SUMMER**

LAUGHING SONG, THE (Eng. *w* Aïdé: J. Strauss II) BOO   1876
Miss E. Chambers, Marie Geistinger. From *Die Fledermaus*, an der Wien, Vienna, 1874. London: Alhambra.

LEAVE A LITTLE BIT FOR YOUR TUTOR (Harrington: Le Brunn)   FDH   1901
Harry Freeman.

LET ME CALL YOU DADDY (Rogers)   FDH   1904

LET ME CALL YOU SWEETHEART (Whitson: Friedman)   ROS/FEL   1910
Maude Galbraith, Peerless Quartet.

LET'S ALL GO DOWN THE STRAND (Castling & C. W. Murphy)   FDH   1908
Charles R. Whittle.

LET'S ALL GO TO THE MUSIC HALL (Butler & Tilsley: Nicholls)   WRI   1934
Kate Carney, Harry Claff. Anthem of the Variety Artistes' Federation. See also
FEDERATION DAY.

LET'S HAVE FREE TRADE AMONGST THE GIRLS (Castling: Glover Kind)
    FEL   1911
Whit Cunliffe.

LET'S WAIT AND SEE THE PICTURES (Carter & Glover Kind)   FEL   1910
Tom Clarke, Arthur Lennard.

LET THE GREAT BIG WORLD KEEP TURNING (Grey: Ayer)   FEL   1917
Laddie Cliff & Violet Loraine. From *The Bing Girls are There*, Alhambra.

LET THE REST OF THE WORLD GO BY (Brennan: Ball)   FEL   1919
Ernest R. Ball, Albert Campbell, Charles Hart.

LIFE ON THE OCEAN WAVE, A (Arnold & Sargent: H. Russell)   var.   1838
Henry Russell.

LILY OF LAGUNA, THE (Stuart)   FDH   1898
Eugene Stratton, G. H. Elliott.

LINDEN LEA (Barnes: Vaughan-Williams)   BOO   1902
John Coates, Louise Kirkby Lunn.

LINGER LONGER LOO (Younge: S. Jones)   ASC   1893
Millie Hylton, Cissie Loftus, Ellaline Terriss, May Yohé. Yvette Guilbert also performed an immensely popular impersonation of Millie Hylton's performance of
this song. Int. *Don Juan*, the last Gaiety burlesque. See also **THE LONGER YOU
LINGER**.

LION AND ALBERT, THE (Edgar)   FDH   1932
Marriott Edgar, Stanley Holloway.

LISTEN TO THE MOCKING BIRD (Hawthorne: Winner)
Winner & Shuster, Phil   1855
Alma Gluck, sundry Minstrel troupes.

LITTLE ANNIE ROONEY (Nolan)   FDH   1889
Lottie Gilson, Michael Nolan. Nolan also wrote and sang a follow-up number
called Today I've Made Sweet Annie Rooney my Wife. Vesta Tilley's version was
entitled Annie Body's Rooney and Jessie McNally performed a companion song
entitled Every Sunday Afternoon.

LITTLE BIT OF CUCUMBER, A (Connor)   FDH   1915
Harry Champion.

LITTLE BIT OFF THE TOP, A (Murray & Leigh)   FDH   1898
Harry Bedford.

LITTLE BIT OF HEAVEN FELL, A (Brennan: Ball)   FEL   1914
Ernest R. Ball, Chauncey Olcott. From *The Heart of Paddywhack*, which did not
reach Broadway.

LITTLE BROWN JUG (Nash: J. E. Winner)   Winner/Ditson   1867
Jolly John Nash, Ted Snow (Mohawk Minstrels), James Francis (Mohawks).

LITTLE DAMOZEL, THE (Weatherly: Novello)   BOO   1912
Lucrezia Bori, Evangeline Florence.

LITTLE DOLLY DAYDREAM (Stuart)   FDH   1897
Eugene Stratton.

LITTLE GREY HOME IN THE WEST (Eardley-Wilmot: Lohr)   CHA   1911
Thorpe Bates, Peter Dawson, Alma Gluck, Charles W. Harrison, John
McCormack, Maggie Teyte.

LITTLE OF WHAT YOU FANCY DOES YOU GOOD, A (Leigh & Arthurs)
FDH   1915
Marie Lloyd.

LITTLE PEACH IN AN ORCHARD GREW, A (H. T. Smith & Wye)   FDH   1889
Christy Minstrels, Johnny Danvers (Mohawk Minstrels), D. G. Longworth &
Marie Stuart, E. J. Lonnen. A parody was sung by Charles Danby & Letty Lind in
Ruy Blas and the Blasé Roué (Gaiety) under the title Johnny Jones and his Sister
Sue, a version of which was also performed by Nellie Farren & Fred Leslie. A fur-
ther parody was sung by Billy Richardson of Sam Hague's Minstrels as Little Pair
Of Whiskers.

LITTLE YELLOW BIRD (Murphy: Hargreaves)   FDH   1903
Flo De Vere, Minnie Jeffs, Ellaline Terriss. Interpolated into *The Cherry Girl*,
Vaudeville.

'LIZA HAD HOLD OF MY HAND (Kendal)   FEL   1910
Jack Pleasants.

LIZA JOHNSON (Bateman: Le Brunn)   FDH   1901
Kate Carney. Subtitled The Ragtime Coster.

LOCH LOMOND (Lady J. D. Scott, arr. Finlay)
Paterson & Sons Edinburgh   *c.*1845

LONGER YOU LINGER, THE (G. Maurice)   MOC   1903
Harry Champion. Parody of **LINGER LONGER LOO.**

LOOK WHAT PERCY'S PICKED UP IN THE PARK (Burley: Castling)
   FDH   1912
Dolly Harmer. Vesta Victoria, NB. Recorded as See what Percy's Picked up in
the Park by Ella Retford in April 1912, four months before Vesta Victoria's first
recording.

LORD LOVEL (anon.: trad.)   DAL   *c.*1842
Sam Cowell, J. W. Sharp. Originally a ballad, perhaps fifteenth century, remembered now mainly for its early Victorian parody.

LORD MAYOR'S COACHMAN, THE (Hunter: D. Day)   FDH   1881
Will Freeman (Mohawk Minstrels), H. P. Matthews.

LOST CHILD, THE (T. Hood: arr. G. Ford)   DAL   1834
Sam Cowell.

LOST CHORD, THE (Procter: Sullivan)   BOO   1877
Clara Butt, Enrico Caruso, Peter Dawson, Alma Gluck (w. Efrem Zimbalist),
Louise Kirkby Lunn, John McCormack, Antoinette Sterling. Adelaide A. Procter's
poem was set by Sullivan as his much-loved brother lay dying. It had been sent to
him by Antoinette Sterling, who subsequently gave the first public performance.
She also cut herself in on a sheet-music royalty.

LOST, STOLEN OR STRAYED (Mills: B. Scott)   FDH   1897
Millie Lindon, Sisters Lloyd. A parody was sung by Ted Cowan. A song of the same
title by Henry Pontet was published 1883. Mrs Lewis Waller (Florrie West) performed a sketch also with this title.

Love, Goodbye (Lehár)   CHA   1911
Lily Elsie. From *The Count of Luxembourg*, an der Wien, Vienna 1909. London: Daly's.

Love Or Gold (Rogers, arr. J. Neat)   FEL   1900
Vesta Tilley.

Love's Garden Of Roses (Rutherford: H. Wood)   CHA   1914
Ben Davies, Hubert Eisdell.

Love's Old Sweet Song (Bingham: Molloy)   BOO   1884
Clara Butt, Antoinette Sterling.

Love Will Find A Way (H. Graham: Fraser-Simson)   AHC   1916
José Collins. From *The Maid of the Mountains*, Daly's (1917) after Manchester try-out.

Lowther Arcade, The *see* **Tin Gee-Gee, The**

Lucky Jim (How I Envy Him) (Howitz: Bowers)   WIT/SHE   1896
G. H. Chirgwin, Harry Davenport. London: interpolated into *The Belle of New York*, Shaftesbury.

Macdermott's War Song (G. W. Hunt)   H&C   1877
G. H. Macdermott. According to the eminent choirmaster and musical scholar Sir Richard Terry (1865–1938) the melody is a pasticcio of the Kyrie in Mozart's Twelfth Mass and the Scottish ballad Castles in the Air. See **I Don't Want to Fight** for parody.

Macnamara's Band (Stamford: O'Connor)   LAR/AHC   1889
W. J. Ashcroft. A later edition gives words by Terence O'Shaughnessy although they are identical with Stamford's.

Ma Blushin' Rosie (Edgar Smith: Stromberg)   WIT/SHE   1900
Fay Templeton. From *Fiddle-Dee-Dee*, Weber & Fields' Music Hall, NY.

Ma Curly-Headed Babby (Clutsam)   Stanley Lucas, etc.   1897
Maggie Teyte.

Macushla (J. V. Rowe: MacMurrough)   BOO   1910
John McCormack, Chauncey Olcott. Not to be confused with 'Macushla Asthore' (Shannon: Ball 1920).

Mademoiselle From Armenteers (Hinky-Dinky Parlez-Vous?)
var.   *c.*1915
Shaun Glenville and Harry Carlton sang a version by Carlton & J. A. Tunbridge

(FEL 1919), though Harry Wincott later declared himself to be the original writer. Another claimant was the Canadian Gitz Rice, with lyrical assistance from a British soldier called Edward 'Red' Rowland. This seems to have been one of those songs that was in the air—cf. In Eleven More Months And Ten More Days I'll Be Out Of The Calaboose—though all versions derive from The Landlady's Little Daughter a.k.a. Three German (or Prussian) Officers Crossed The Line, a German song with words by Johann Ludwig Uhland to a traditional air.

MAGGIE MURPHY'S HOME (Harrigan: Braham)   FDH   1890

Jenny Hill. Jenny Hill sang her own version of Harrigan's words.

MAIDEN'S PRAYER, THE (var.: Bądarzewska-Baranowska)   PAX   1856

Despite worldwide popularity (it was issued by more than eighty publishers) this melody resisted all efforts by lyricists to turn it into a ballad—the execrable words in my own copy are unattributed. The piece is dismissed by *Grove* as possessing 'no artistic merit, being a salon composition of a type common in the 19th century'.

MAID OF ATHENS (Byron: Gounod)   Goddard & Co.   1873

Byron's poem dates from 1810—the maid was said to have been the 12-year-old daughter of the deceased British vice-consul in Athens.

MAISIE (IS A DAISY) (Mayne: Monckton)   CHA   1900

Rosie Boote, Gertie Millar. From *The Messenger Boy*, Gaiety. It was Gertie Millar's performance of this song in a provincial production that prompted the composer to persuade George Edwardes to give her the lead in *The Toreador*, thus launching her glittering career at the Gaiety. Later she married Monckton, after his death becoming the Countess of Derby. The first singer of the song, Rosie Boote, despite her defiantly plebian name, did even better by marrying the Marquess of Headfort.

MAJOR-GENERAL WORTHINGTON (Waite)   WRI   1916

J. W. Rickaby.

MAN ON THE FLYING TRAPEZE, THE (DARING YOUNG) *see* **FLYING TRAPEZE, THE**

MANSION OF ACHING HEARTS, THE (Lamb: Von Tilzer)   FEL   1902

Florrie Forde.

MAN THAT BROKE THE BANK AT MONTE CARLO, THE (Gilbert)
FDH   1891

Charles Coborn. Charles De Ville Wells claimed to have broken Monaco Casino's cash reserves six times over three days in July 1891, winning £40,000 at roulette.

Later he lost the lot, went to jail, and died penniless in 1926. Other names have been suggested as Fred Gilbert's inspiration but Charles Coborn firmly identifies the source as Wells. Maggie Duggan inserted the song into *Cinder-Ellen up too Late* at the Gaiety in 1892, while parodies and 'answer' songs were performed by many performers, including W. P. Dempsey, Leo Dryden, Nellie L'Estrange, Marie Lloyd, Harry Pleon, the Tilley Sisters, and Tom Woottwell. In the USA the song was notably performed by William Hooey.

M'APPARI TUTT'AMOR (ACH! SO FROMM/AH! SO PURE)   1846

Enrico Caruso, Beniamino Gigli, Mario. Although usually given as from Flotow's *Martha* (1847) this aria was intended for his *L'âme en peine* (Paris Opéra 1846) and was not interpolated into *Martha* until an 1865 production at the Lyrique, Paris; it has stayed ever since.

MARCHING THROUGH GEORGIA (Work)   var.   1865

MARGIE (Davis: Conrad & Robinson)   WBS   1919
Eddie Cantor, Original Dixieland Jazz Band.

MARRIED TO A MERMAID (A.L.C.: M. Watson)   DAL/ASH/FDH   1866
Arthur Lloyd.

MARROW SONG, THE (Siebert)   WRI   1952
Billy Cotton.

MARSEILLAISE, LA (De Lisle)   var.   1792
Originally entitled War Song of the Army of the Rhine, the composer being a captain of engineers. Its markedly enthusiastic adoption by *bataillons* from Marseilles led to the more familiar name.

MARTHA SPANKS THE GRAND PIANNA (Dance: Talbot)   AHC   1899
Louie Freear, Alma Jones, Hilda Trevelyan. From *A Chinese Honeymoon*, Theatre Royal Hanley.

MARY ANN SHE'S AFTER ME (Fred E. Leigh)   FDH   1911
George Bastow.

MARY ANN'S REFUSED ME (Darnley, arr. Eplett)   SHE   1895
Dan Leno.

MARY LLEWELLYN (E. W. Rogers)   FDH   1906
Lovedon Plass.

MARY'S A GRAND OLD NAME (Cohan)   FAM/FEL   1905
George M. Cohan, Lil Hawthorne, Fay Templeton. From *Forty Five Minutes from Broadway*, New Amsterdam, NY.

MARY'S GHOST (T. Hood: Blewitt)   T. Hudson   *c.*1840
Jonathan Blewitt.

MARY'S TICKET (J. P. Long: G. Wells)   RAW   1909
Florrie Forde.

MARY WAS A HOUSEMAID (Risque: Lambelet)   BOO   1899
Claire Romaine, Yvette Guilbert. From *Pot-Pourri*, Avenue.

MASKS AND FACES (Harrington: Le Brunn)   F&D   1888
Jenny Hill.

MATINEE HAT, THE (Kent)   Essex & Crammeyer   1897

MATTINATA ('TIS THE DAY) (Teschemacher: Leoncavallo)   RIC   1904
Enrico Caruso, John Coates, Ben Davies, Beniamino Gigli, John Harrison.

MAYBE IT'S BECAUSE I'M A LONDONER (Gregg)   SUN   1947
Bud Flanagan. From *Together Again*, Victoria Palace—the first post-War Crazy Gang show.

MEET ME IN ST LOUIS, LOUIS (Sterling: K. Mills)   SUN   1904
Nora Bayes, Lew Dockstader, Lottie Gilson, Ethel Levey, Billy Murray, Bonnie Thornton, Gus Williams. Promotional song for the St Louis Exposition.

MEET ME TONIGHT IN DREAMLAND (Whitson: Friedman)   FDH   1909
Reine Davies, Ernest Pike.

MEMORIES (Kahn: Van Alstyne)   REM   1915
The Versatile Three.

MERRIEST GIRL THAT'S OUT, THE (Merion, arr. Minsai)   MET   *c.*1865
Annie Adams.

MERRY WIDOW WALTZ (B. Hood: Lehár)   CHA   1907
Joe Coyne & (*a*) Lily Elsie, (*b*) Constance Drever, Mizzi Gunther & Louis Treumann. From *The Merry Widow*, Daly's. Originally *Die lustige Witwe* (an der Wien, Vienna 1905) adapted from Henri Meilhac's play *L'Attaché d'ambassade*.

MIDNIGHT SON, THE (Rogers)   STE   1897
Vesta Tilley.

MIGHTY LAK' A ROSE (Stanton: Nevin) BOO 1901
Ada Crossley.

MILLER'S DAUGHTER, THE (Carroll: Zeller) Bosworth 1894
Alexander Girardi. Originally Sei Nicht Bös from *Der Obersteiger* (*The Mine Foreman*), an der Wien, Vienna. Briefly Interpolated into *An Artist's Model* at the Gaiety where, to words by Adrian Ross, it was sung as a duet by Marie Tempest and Haydn Coffin. Often known as Don't Be Cross. Written as tenor solo but after the popular recordings by Elisabeth Schumann and Elisabeth Schwarzkopf now usually sung by sopranos. Not to be confused with The Miller's Daughter from Paul Rubens' 1902 musical comedy *Three Little Maids*, Apollo.

MILLIE! (FROM PICCADILLY) (Harrington: Le Brunn) SHE/DAR 1901
Marie Lloyd.

MINER'S DREAM OF HOME, THE (Dryden & Godwin) FDH 1891
Leo Dryden. A 'reply' called Going Home *or* The Miner's Return was also sung by Dryden, while the original was parodied by, amongst others, Herbert Campbell.

MINSTREL BOY, THE (Moore: air, The Moreen, arr. Bunting) var. 1807
Emily Soldene, John McCormack.

MISS JULIA (WERY PEKOOLIER) (Beulah: Blewitt) CHA 1826
Jonathan Blewitt.

MISTER BEAR (R. F. Johnson: Blaney) CHA 1913
Norah Blaney, Margaret Cooper.

MOLLY O'MORGAN (Godfrey & Letters) FEL 1909
Nora Emerald, Ella Retford.

MOON HAS RAISED HER LAMP ABOVE, THE (Oxenford: Benedict)
CAS 1862
Ivor Foster & Herbert Cave, Charles Santley & William Harrison. From *The Lily Of Killarney*, Covent Garden, based on Dion Boucicault's play *The Colleen Bawn* (Adelphi, 1860), itself adapted a dramatization of *The Collegians*, an 1829 three-volume novel by Gerald Griffin.

MOONLIGHT BAY, (ON) (Madden: Wenrich) REM/FEL 1912
Dolly Connolly, Herbert Payne, Esta Stella.

MOONLIGHT BLOSSOMS (Rogers) FEL 1899
Vesta Tilley.

MOONSTRUCK (Monckton) CHA   1909
Gertie Millar. From *Our Miss Gibbs*, Gaiety.

MORE WORK FOR THE UNDERTAKER (Leigh) FDH   1895
Charles Bignell.

MOTHER MACHREE (Rida J. Young: Olcott & Ball) FEL   1910
Ernest R. Ball, Beniamino Gigli, Charles W. Harrison, John McCormack, Will
Oakland, Chauncey Olcott. From *Barry of Ballymore*, which premiered in Kansas,
reaching Broadway in 1911 (theatre not known). Int. *Isle o' Dreams*, Grand Opera
House, NY (1913). John McCormack's theme tune.

MOTHER O' MINE (Kipling: Tours) CHA   1903
Hayden Coffin, Ben Davies, John McCormack. Words adapted from the dedica-
tion to Kipling's 1890 novel *The Light that Failed*. Some eighteen composers are
known to have set the poem.

MOTHER'S ADVICE *see* **I'M GLAD I TOOK MY MOTHER'S ADVICE**

MOTHER'S SITTING KNITTING LITTLE MITTENS FOR THE NAVY
 (R. P. Weston: Darewski) FDH   1915
Nora Bayes, Al Jolson, Jack Norworth.

MOTHER TONGUE, THE (A. Hall: Le Brunn) FDH   1899
Tom Costello.

MOTHER WAS A LADY (IF JACK WERE ONLY HERE) (Marks: Stern)
 STE/EBM   1896
Meyer Cohen, Lottie Gilson, Burt Shepard.

MOUNTAINS OF MOURNE (P. French: air, Bendemeer's Stream) var.   1896
Percy French, John McCormack.

MR GALLAGHER & MR SHEAN (Gallagher & Shean: Foy) MIL/WRI   *c.*1920
Gallagher & Shean. Included in *Ziegfeld Follies of 1922*, New Amsterdam, NY.

MRS CARTER (C. W. Murphy & Bateman: Murphy) FDH   1900
Gus Elen.

MUFFIN MAN, THE (Harry King) F&D   1889
Dan Leno.

MURDERS (Henty & Rihill) REY   *c.*1914
George Grossmith jun., Leslie Henson, Dick Henty, Louis Rihill. Interpolated into
Tonight's the Night, Gaiety, 1916.

MY ACTOR MAN (F. C. Harris: Tate) FDH 1913
Marie Lloyd.

MY AESTHETIC LOVE (Lonsdale: Eaton) SHE 1881
Alfred Vance.

MY AIN FOLK (W. Mills: Lemon) BOO 1904
Clara Butt, Maggie Teyte, Edna Thornton.

MY BEAUTIFUL LADY (H. Morton: Caryll) CHA 1911
Hazel Dawn. From *The Pink Lady*, Globe.

MY BLUSHING ROSIE *see* **MA BLUSHIN' ROSIE**

MY BOY'S A SAILOR MAN (Mills & B. Scott) STA 1909
Daisy Dormer.

MY BRUDDA, SYLVEST' (Lasky & Stern: F. Fisher) FEL 1908
Mabel Hite & Mike Donlin, Sam Stern.

MY CASTLE IN SPAIN (Mellor: Lawrance & Gifford) FDH 1906
Lil Hawthorne.

MY COSEY CORNER GIRL (C. N. Douglas: Bratton) WIT 1903
Agnes Fraser & Henry Lytton, Edna May & George Grossmith jun., Harry MacDonough. Int. *The School Girl* (Prince of Wales's) and *The Earl and the Girl* (Adelphi). Music based on traditional air, In a Cosy Corner.

MY CRICKET GIRL (Leo) FDH 1903
Sable Fern.

MYFANWY (Mynyddog: J. Parry) I. Jones, Treherbert 1880
Carmen Hill. English words (under the title Arabella) by Cuhelyn.

MY FIDDLE IS MY SWEETHEART (Hunter: Chirgwin) FDH 1895
G. H. Chirgwin.

MY FIRST CIGAR (Law: Grain) BAT 1890
Louis Bradfield, Corney Grain.

MY FLO FROM PIMLICO (Knox) FDH 1901
Paul Knox, Maude Mortimer.

MY GAL IS A HIGH BORN LADY (Fagan)   FEL   1896
Charles Ernest (Haverly's Minstrels), Barney Fagan, Yvette Guilbert, Sisters
Hawthorne, Clara Wieland.

MY GAL SAL (Dresser)   Larrabee Pubs., NY   1905
Louise Dresser.

MY GIRL'S A YORKSHIRE GIRL (Lipton & Murphy)   FDH   1908
Florrie Gallimore, Charles R. Whittle.

MY GRANDFATHER'S CLOCK *see* **GRANDFATHER'S CLOCK**

MY HAT'S A BROWN 'UN (Rogers, arr. Lamont)   Marshalls   1891
George Robey.

MY HEART IS WITH YOU TONIGHT (Mills: B. Scott)   STA/FEL   1912
Nellie Wigley.

MY HERO (Stange: Straus)   FEL   1910
Constance Drever, Olga Petrova. From *The Chocolate Soldier* (*Der Tapfer Soldat*),
an der Wien, Vienna (1908) based on Bernard Shaw's play *Arms and the Man*
(Avenue, 1894). First produced in English at the Lyric, NY 1909 and first seen in
London the following year at the Lyric.

MY LEETLE ROSA (anon.: Longstaffe)   REY   1927
Violet Field.

MY MAMMY (Lewis & Young: Donaldson)   BER/DAR   1921
Al Jolson. Interpolated into *Sinbad*, Winter Garden, NY, late in the run.

MY MEATLESS DAY (Weston & Lee)   FDH   1917
Ernie Mayne.

MY MELANCHOLY BABY (G. A. Norton & M. B. Watson: E. M. Burnett)
FDH   1912
Tommy Lyman. Originally entitled Melancholy (1911). Ernie Burnett copyrighted
the song but there is some doubt over his claim to be the composer.

MY MOTHER DOESN'T KNOW I'M ON THE STAGE (Connor)   1929
Billy Bennett. Unpublished but recorded on Columbia 5719. Although Bennett
wrote a good deal of his own material, many of his most memorable poems and
monologues were the work of T. W. Connor. Much of both men's output was
published by PAX in *Four Burlesque Monologues* (1927) and in the *Billy Bennett's
Budget* series, (1929–38).

My Mother Was A Lady *see* **Mother Was A Lady**

My Motter (Wimperis: Monckton)   CHA   1909
Alfred Lester. From *The Arcadians*, Shaftesbury.

My Nellie's Blue Eyes (Scanlon: air, Vieni Sul Mar arr. Forman)
  SHE/FDH   1883
Tom Costello, J. Fuller (Mohawk Minstrels), William Scanlon (Christy Minstrels).
Vieni Sul Mar is a Venetian ballad, famously recorded by Caruso. See also **Two
Lovely Black Eyes.**

My Next-Door Neighbour's Gardin (Bateman & Elen: Le Brunn)
  FDH   1900
Herbert Darnley, Gus Elen.

My Old Dutch (Chevalier: Ingle)   REY   1892
Albert Chevalier.

My Old Kentucky Home (S. C. Foster)   var.   1853
Alma Gluck.

My Old Man's A Dustman *see* **What D'yer Think Of That?**

My Old Pal Joe (Bateman: M. Scott)   FDH   1906
Tom Costello.

My Own Little Girl (P. Greenbank: Monckton)   CHA   1902
Hayden Coffin. From *The Country Girl*, Daly's.

My Pretty Jane (The Bloom Is On The Rye) (Fitzball: Bishop)
  BOO   1831
Ben Davies, E. W. Mackney, Sims Reeves, Lydia Yeamans.

My Son! My Son! (My Only Son) (Rogers: Le Brunn)   FDH   1890
Charles Godfrey.

Mystery Of A Hansom Cab, The (Rogers: Durandeau)   FDH   1888
Walter Munroe. Words a burlesque of Fergus W. Hume's novel of the same name,
dramatized most successfully by Arthur Law at the Princess's.

My Sweetheart's The Man In The Moon (Thornton)   AMS/ROB   1892
Bonnie Thornton.

My Wife's First Husband (Clifford)   FDH   1898
Nat Clifford, Ernie Mayne.

MY WIFE'S GONE TO THE COUNTRY (Whiting: Snyder & Berlin)
SNY/FEL   1909
Arthur Collins, Byron G. Harlan, Mabel Hite, Phil Parsons.

MY WILD IRISH ROSE (Olcott)   WIT   1899
Chauncey Olcott.

MY WORD YOU DO LOOK QUEER (Weston & Lee)   FDH   1922
Ernest Hastings, Stanley Holloway.

MY YIDDISHER MOMME (Yellen: Pollack)   WRI   1925
Belle Baker, Sophie Tucker.

NANCY LEE (Weatherly: Adams)   BOO   1876
Marie Compton, Peter Dawson, John McCormack, Michael Maybrick (a.k.a. Stephen Adams, the song's composer).

NARRAGANSETT (ON THE BEACH AT) (H. Morton: Kerker)   TBH/A&C   1897
Dan Daly. From *The Belle of New York*, NY Casino.

NATURE'S MADE A BIG MISTAKE (Ellerton & David: Ellerton)   FDH   1910
Gus Elen.

NAUGHTY! NAUGHTY! NAUGHTY! (Harrington: Le Brunn)   H&C   1904
Marie Lloyd.

NELLIE DEAN (B. Clarke: H. Armstrong)   FEL   1905
Gertie Gitana.

NEVER DESERT A FRIEND (Hunter: C. Coote jun.)   H&C   1876
W(illiam) Randall.

NEVER INTRODUCE YER DONAH TO A PAL
(A. Durandeau & Ellis: Durandeau)   SHE   1891
Gus Elen.

NEVER MIND! (Dent & Goldburn)   FDH   1913
Gertie Gitana, Eric Marshall, Clarice Mayne.

NEVER SHARE YOUR LODGINGS WITH A PAL (Pink: Eplett)   MAY   c.1895
Arthur Tinsley.

NEXT HORSE I RIDE ON, THE (Everard & Murray)   FDH   1905
Vesta Victoria.

Nice Quiet Day, A (A Postman's Holiday) (Bateman & Baynes: M. Scott)
    FDH   1901
Gus Elen.

Night I Appeared As Macbeth, The (Hargreaves)   WRI   1919
Billy Merson.

Nirvana (Weatherly: Adams)   BOO   1900
Ben Davies, Edward Lloyd.

Nix My Dolly Pals (Rodwell)   DAC   1839
Mrs Keeley & Paul Bedford. From J. B. Buckstone's adaption of Harrison Ainsworth's novel *Jack Sheppard*, Adelphi.

No, 'Arry, Don't Ask Me To Marry (Castling: Le Brunn)   FDH   1893
Marie Lloyd.

Nobody Knows You When You're Down And Out (J. Cox)
MCA Inc.   1923
Jimmie Cox.

Nobody Loves A Fairy When She's Forty (Le Clerq)   WRI   1934
Tessie O'Shea (unentered).

Nobody Noticed Me (Grey & B. Lee)   FDH   1917
Jack Pleasants.

Nonsense! Yes! By Jove! (H. Nicholls: O. Barrett)   FDH   1881
George Barrett & J. L. Shine, Robert Brough & Harry Nicholls, Herbert Campbell & Charles Grosse, Fred Stimson & Fawcett Lomax. From *Whittington and His Cat*, Gaiety.

Nora Malone (Call Me By Phone) (McCree: A. Von Tilzer)   FDH   1909
Hedges Brothers & Jacobson, Herbert Payne, Blanche Ring. Interpolated into *The Yankee Girl*, Herald Square, NY.

No Rose In All The World *see* **Until**

'Norrible Tale, A (Blanchard, arr. M. Hobson)   AHC   1865
Sam Cowell, J. L. Toole. Also sung by Alfred Vance in version by H. J. Whymark.

Not For Joseph (A. Lloyd)   DAL/ASH   1866
Arthur Lloyd. Lloyd also wrote a companion song entitled Just The Thing for Frank, and a ladies' version—Not For Flo'—which was sung by Kate Santley.

Now I Have To Call Him Father (Collins & Godfrey)   REM/FDH   1908
Vesta Victoria.

Now Is The Hour (Haere Ra) (Kaihau: C. Scott)   KPM   ?
Gracie Fields. The only copy in the British Library was received in 1928 and gives
words and music Maewa Kaihau. No publisher is given. My copy also has words by
Maewa Kaihau but gives music by Clement Scott; the copyright date is 1913 (W.
H. Paling & Co. Ltd., Sydney, Australia) and there are substantial differences
between the two in both words and music. Some sources also give credit for this
song to one Dorothy Stewart, or Dorothy Scott. To add to the confusion, the original music would seem to have been a Swiss cradle song, so this 'Maori Song
of Farewell' may be altogether bogus. The New Zealand High Commission in
London could shed no light on the matter.

Now You've Got Yer Khaki On (Collins & Leigh)   STA   1915
Marie Lloyd.

Nursie-Nursie (W. David & B. Lee)   FDH   1910
Clarice Mayne.

Off To Philadelphia (Temple: air, Irish trad. arr. Battison Haynes)
    BOO   1889
Ian Colquhoun, Plunkett Greene.

Oft In The Stilly Night (Moore: trad. or Sir John Stevenson)   var.   1815

Oh, Bleriot! (Weston & Barnes & Bedford)   FDH   1909
Harry Bedford.

Oh, Dem Golden Slippers (Bland)   FDH   1879
James Bland, Haverly's Minstrels, G. W. 'Pony' Moore (Moore & Burgess
Minstrels).

Oh, Flo! (Why Do You Go?) (Dacre)   DEA   1901
Harry Dacre, Harry Taylor.

Oh, Fred! Tell Them To Stop (Meen)   DIT/SHE/FEL   1880
Fred Coyne (1), George Leybourne, Tony Pastor.

Oh! How Rude! (B. Scott: Cotes)   HOW   1899
Arthur Lennard, George Robey.

Oh, I Must Go Home Tonight (W. Hargreaves)   FEL   1909
Billy Williams.

OH! IT'S A LOVELY WAR (Long & M. Scott) FEL 1917
Ella Shields.

OH! IT'S A WINDY NIGHT TONIGHT (Chapman) FEL ?
S. W. Wyndham.

OH! JACK, YOU ARE A HANDY MAN (Clifford) FDH 1901
Katie Lawrence.

OH! LONDON, WHERE ARE YOUR GIRLS TONIGHT? (Weston & Lee)
FDH 1918
Vesta Tilley.

OH! MR PORTER (T. Le Brunn: G. Le Brunn) HOW/AHC 1892
Norah Blaney, Marie Lloyd.

OH! MY DARLING CLEMENTINE (Percy Montrose? Barker Bradford?)
var. 1884
Walter Howard (Mohawk Minstrels). Emerging from the American gold-rush communities, this song's precise provenance will probably never be determined.

OH! OH! ANTONIO (Murphy & Lipton) FDH 1908
Edith Fink, Florrie Forde.

OH! THE BLACK LIST (B. Scott) FDH 1903
Tom Costello, Ella Dean, Charles Gardener, Ryder Slone, George Robey, J. W. Rowley, Mark Sheridan, and Harry Tate as well as the following unlisted names: Madge Daly, Albert Le Fre, and Johnny Worman. The title referred to a hare-brained scheme to have persistent drunkards black-listed from their pubs and for their photographs to be displayed.

OH, THE FAIRIES! (Lonsdale: Eaton) SHE 1878
George Leybourne.

OH, WHAT A BEAUTY! *see* **MARROW SONG, THE**

OH, WHAT A WICKED YOUNG MAN YOU ARE (Stamford, arr. Forman)
F&D *c.*1882
Ethel Victor.

OH WHERE, OH WHERE, HAS MY LITTLE DOG GONE? (S. Winner)
Septimus Winner, Philadelphia/var. 1864
A. W. Young. Also known as Der Deitches Dog. Air, Lauterbach, German

traditional, though some claim the music as medieval English. The version sung by Young was interpolated into John Brougham's burlesque *La Belle Sauvage* at the St James's in 1869.

OH! WOODMAN, SPARE THAT TREE (Morris: Russell)   J. Lawson   1837
Henry Russell.

OH, YOU BEAUTIFUL DOLL (A. Seymour Brown & Ayer)   RMC/FEL   1910
American Ragtime Octette, Ida Barr, Gene Greene, Clarice Mayne, Billy Murray. Originally sung by the writers as Ayer & Brown.

OH, YOU LITTLE DARLING (Tabrar)   AHC   1882
Nellie L'Estrange, Kate Vaughan. Interpolated into *Whittington & His Cat*, Gaiety.

OLD-AGE PENSION, THE (Weston & Bedford)   FDH   1908
Harry Bedford.

OLD BRIGADE, THE (Weatherly: Barri)   KPM/EMI   1881
Norman Allin, Peter Dawson, Maud Distin, Ian Colquhoun, Signor Foli.

OLD DICKY BIRD (Connor, arr. Eplett)   FDH   1901
George Lashwood.

OLD FATHER THAMES (Wallace: O'Hogan)   WRI   1933
Thorpe Bates, Norman Blair, Peter Dawson, Roy Henderson, Stanley Holloway.

OLD FOLKS AT HOME (WAY DOWN UPON THE SWANEE RIVER)
  (S. C. Foster)   var.   1851
Christy Minstrels, Alma Gluck (with Efrem Zimbalist), Christine Nilsson, Emma Thursby.

OLD MAN'S DARLING, AN (Murray & Everard)   H&C   1903
Vesta Victoria. A less remembered song of the same title by Albert Hall: Orlando Powell (1895) was sung by George Lashwood.

OLD RUSTIC BRIDGE BY THE MILL, THE (Skelly)   PAX/FDH   1881
C. Chivers (Mohawk Minstrels), Walter Glynne.

OLD SAM (SAM, PICK OOP THA' MUSKET)
  (Holloway: Wolseley Charles)   FDH   1930
Stanley Holloway. The composer was Holloway's accompanist.

OLD SOLDIERS NEVER DIE (Foley)   DAR/FEL   1920

OLD SUPERB, THE (Newbolt: Stanford) BOO   1904
Dalton Baker, Peter Dawson, Stewart Gardner, Plunkett Greene.

OLD TIN CAN, THE (Mayo & H. Leighton: Mayo) SHE/DAR   1905
Sam Mayo.

OLGA PULLOFFSKI THE BEAUTIFUL SPY (Weston & Lee: Harris-Weston)
   FDH   1935
Jack Hylton's Band.

ON A SUNDAY AFTERNOON (Sterling: H. Von Tilzer) ROB   1902
Leonard Barry, Florrie Forde, J. Aldrich Libbey, Baby Lund, Julie Mackey.

ONAWAY, AWAKE, BELOVED! (Longfellow: Cowen) MET/DIT   1892
Robert Radford, Evan Williams. From Longfellow's poem *Hiawatha*.

ONE OF 'THE BOYS' (R. P. Weston & F. J. Barnes: M. Scott) FDH   1907
George Formby.

ONE OF THE SHABBY GENTEEL (Castling) FDH   1902
Harry Bedford.

ONE TOUCH OF NATURE MAKES THE WHOLE WORLD KIN (McGlennon)
   FDH   1897
Marie Loftus, Helene Mora.

ONLY A GLASS OF CHAMPAGNE (Wimperis: Gay)   Noel Gay/CCC   1939
Evelyn Laye. Included in *Lights Up*, Savoy (1940).

ONLY A 'ITTLE DIRLY DIRL (Andrews) OLI   *c.*1880

ONLY A PANSY BLOSSOM (Rexford: F. Howard) TRB/SHE   1883
Mohawk Minstrels, Will Oakland (Moore & Burgess Minstrels).

ONLY A WORKING MAN (Rule & Holt) DAR/FEL   1923
Lily Morris.

ON MOONLIGHT BAY *see* **MOONLIGHT BAY**

ON MOTHER KELLY'S DOORSTEP (Stevens) FDH   1925
Fred Barnes, Randolph Sutton.

ON THE BANKS OF THE WABASH FAR AWAY (Dresser)   HHC/FEL   1891
James Norrie, Billy Rice Minstrels.

ON THE GOOD SHIP 'YACKI HICKI DOO LA' (Merson)   FDH   1917
Billy Merson.

ON THE MARGATE BOAT (Mills & B. Scott)   FDH   1899
Herbert Darnley, Charles Foster, Lillie Langtry, Harry Taylor. This Lillie Langtry
is not the Jersey Lily but a young Music Hall artiste who cheekily(?) enterpris-
ingly(?) used the same famous name.

ON THE ROAD TO MANDALAY (Kipling: Speaks)   BOO   1907
Peter Dawson, Lawrence Tibbett. Kipling's poem 'Mandalay' was first published in
the *Scots Observer* in 1890 and included in the first series (1892) of his *Barrack-
Room Ballads*. Only Oley Speaks's setting has survived out of a dozen or more published attempts.

OOH! 'ER! (THE SLAVEY) (Wynne)   REY   1927
Wish Wynne.

O SOLE MIO (Capurro: Di Capua)   RIC   1898
Enrico Caruso.

OUR 'ARMONIC CLUB (Chevalier)   Chas. Fox   1887
Albert Chevalier.

OUR HANDS HAVE MET BUT NOT OUR HEARTS (THE FALSE FRIEND)
   (Hood: Wallace)   AHC   1846
Lucy Clarke, Maud Distin.

OUR LODGER'S SUCH A NICE YOUNG MAN (Barclay & Murray)   FDH   1897
Vesta Victoria.

OURS IS A NICE 'OUSE, OURS IS (Rule: Holt)   FEL   1921
Alfred Lester.

OUR THREEPENNY HOP (Castling)   FDH   1901
Kate Carney.

OUT WHERE THE BLUE BEGINS (Graff & McHugh: F. B. Grant)
   Jack Mills   1923
Florrie Forde.

OVER THERE! (Cohan)   FEI/CHA   1917
Nora Bayes, Enrico Caruso.

'Ow I 'Ate Women (P. Greenbank: Fraser-Simson) AHC 1924
A. W. Baskcomb, Hugh E. Wright. From *The Street Singer*, Lyric.

'Ow's This For A Start? (R. P. Weston & F. W. Leigh: Le Brunn)
FDH 1899
Alec Hurley.

Pack Up Your Troubles In Your Old Kitbag (Asaf: Powell)
FDH 1915
Florrie Forde, Adele Rowland. Interpolated into *Her Soldier Boy*, Astor, NY 1916.
Not included in the London production, Apollo 1918 (retitled *Soldier Boy*).

Paddle Your Own Canoe (Clifton, arr. Hobson) AHC 1866
Harry Clifton, Fred French.

Paddy McGinty's Goat (Weston & Lee & Two Bobs) FDH 1917
The Two Bobs.

Pale Hands I Loved *see* **Kashmiri Song**

Panama Hat, The (Leo) DEA 1902

Pansy Faces (H. B. Smith: Penn) FDH 1902
Irene Bentley, Leila McIntyre, Ellaline Terriss. From *Mother Goose*, Drury Lane,
and int. *The Girl from Dixie*, Madison Square, NY.

Paradise For Two, A (C. Harris & Valentine: J. W. Tate) AHC 1916
José Collins & Thorpe Bates. From *The Maid of the Mountains*, Daly's (1917) after
Manchester try-out.

Parted (Weatherly: Tosti) RIC 1899
Peter Dawson, Edgar Granville, Hubert Eisdell.

Patchwork Garden, The (Bateman & P. Mill: Dix) FDH 1902
Paul Mill. Int. *The Earl and the Girl* (Adelphi) for Florence Lloyd & Walter
Passmore. The song was also performed by the author of *The Earl and the Girl*,
Seymour Hicks.

P.C. 49 (Hargreaves) FEL 1913
J. W. Rickaby.

Peggy O'Neil (Dodge & Nelson & Pease) FDH 1921
Dorothy Ward.

Peg O' My Heart (Bryan: F. Fisher) AHC/FEI 1913
José Collins, Evie Greene, Laurette Taylor. From *Ziegfeld Follies of 1913*, New

Amsterdam, NY. Inspired by J. Hartley Manners's sentimental straight play *Peg o' my Heart* (Cort, NY, 1912). The 1922 musical version (*Peg o' my Dreams*) was short-lived.

PERCY FROM PIMLICO (Leamore)   HOW/AHC   1898
Tom Leamore.

PERFECT CURE, THE (Perry: Blewitt)   DAL   1861
J. H. Stead. The music is Blewitt's The Monkey and the Nuts.

PERFECT DAY, A (Jacobs-Bond)   FRH   1910
David Bispham, Alma Gluck.

PHILOSOPHY (A BEE ONCE LIGHTED ON A FLOWER) (anon.: Emmell)
    Lublin   1904
Margaret Cooper, Maurice Farkoa.

PHIL THE FLUTER'S BALL (P. French)   PIG   1889
Peter Dawson, Percy French, Albert Whelan.

PHOTO OF THE GIRL I LEFT BEHIND, THE (Merson)   FDH   1911
Billy Merson.

PIANO TUNER, THE (Cotes)   NOW/BOW   *c.*1906
George Robey.

PICCADILLY (W. Williams & Sievier: Morande)   unpub.   1921
Hetty King. EMI have a copy in manuscript.

PICCADILLY TROT (Arthurs: David)   FDH   1912
Marie Lloyd.

PICKING ALL THE BEST ONES OUT (Wincott & Leighton)   FDH   1900
Dan Crawley.

PICTURE THAT IS TURNED TO THE WALL, THE (C. Graham)
    WIT/PAX   1891
Andrew Mack, Julius P. Witmark.

PIGTAIL OF LI FANG FU, THE (Rohmer, arr. Thurban)   REY   1919
Bransby Williams.

PINK PETTY FROM PETER, A (Rubens)   CHA   1907
Grace Leigh. From *Miss Hook of Holland*, Prince of Wales's.

Pipes Of Pan, The (Wimperis: Monckton)   CHA   1909
Florence Smithson. From *The Arcadians*, Shaftesbury.

Play A Simple Melody (Berlin)   CHA   1914
Elsie Baker & Billy Murray, Sallie Fisher & Charles King, Ethel Levey & Blanche
Tomlin. From *Watch your Step*, New Amsterdam, NY; London: Empire, 1915.

Playing The Game In The West (Formby & Kendal)   FEL   1910
George Formby.

Please Sell No More Drink To My Father (F. B. Pratt: C. A. White)
   SHE/DAR   1884
From *The Temperance Vocalist*, a collection of edifyingly sober songs. Recorded by
Elsa Lanchester in 1926.

Please Will You Hold The Baby, Sir? (Bays)   LMP   1898
Percy Beaufoi.

Polka And The Choirboy, The (Grain)   BAT   1889
Corney Grain.

Polly Perkins Of Paddington Green (Clifton)   H&C   *c.*1863
Harry Clifton. Air based on Nightingales Sing, traditional. See **Cushie
Butterfield**. An American version called Polly Perkins Of Washington Square
was sung by Tony Pastor.

Poor Butterfly (Golden: Hubbell)   FDH   1916
Regine Flory. From *The Big Show*, Hippodrome, NY.

Poor John (Leigh: Pether)   FDH   1906
Ada Jones, Vesta Victoria.

Poor Old Cock *see* **Old Dicky Bird**

Pop Goes The Weasel (Sloman: anon.)   FEL   1833
Charles Sloman.

Popsy Wopsy (Mills: B. Scott)   STA/FEL   1913
Daisy Dormer, Molly McCarthy, Ella Retford, Lilian Shelley.

Postman's Holiday, A *see* **Nice Quiet Day, A**

Preacher And The Bear, The (Arzonia)   AMS/FDH   1903
Albert Whelan.

PRETTY BABY (Kahn: Van Alstyne & T. Jackson)   FDH   1916
Al Jolson. From *A World of Pleasure*, Winter Garden, NY.

PRETTY GIRL IS LIKE A MELODY, A (Berlin)   BER/CHA   1919
John Steel. From *Ziegfeld Follies of 1919*, New Amsterdam, NY.

PRETTY LIPS (Lloyd)   H&C   1872
Arthur Lloyd.

PRETTY LITTLE GIRL FROM NOWHERE, THE (E. R. Rogers: Neat)
  FEL   1909
Edith Fink, Florrie Forde, Ella Retford.

PRIVATE TOMMY ATKINS (Hamilton: Potter)   H&C   1893
Charles Arnold, Hayden Coffin. First sung by Arnold in a military sketch, then by
Coffin in *A Gaiety Girl* (Prince of Wales's). With new topical verses also int. *San
Toy* (Daly's) during the Boer War and again sung by Coffin.

PULLING HARD AGAINST THE STREAM (Clifton)   H&C   1867
Harry Clifton.

PUSHING YOUNG MAN, THE (Mayo)   SHA/HVT   1906
Sam Mayo.

PUT A BIT OF TREACLE ON MY PUDDEN, MARY ANN
  (F. W. Leigh & Champion)   DAR   1922
Harry Champion.

PUT A LITTLE BIT AWAY FOR A RAINY DAY (C. W. Murphy & Lipton)
  FDH   1905
Carlotta Levey, Ella Retford.

PUT ME AMONGST THE GIRLS (C. Murphy & Lipton)   FEL   1907
Charles R. Whittle.

PUT ME UPON AN ISLAND WHERE THE GIRLS ARE FEW (Letters)
  National Music   1908
Wilkie Bard, Will Letters.

PUT ON YOUR OLD GRAY BONNET (S. Murphy: Wenrich)   REM/FEL   1909
Dolly Connolly, Hayden Quartet.

PUT ON YOUR SLIPPERS (Harrington: O. Powell)   FDH   1911
Marie Lloyd.

PUT ON YOUR TAT-TA, LITTLE GIRLIE (Leigh) FDH   1910
Clarice Mayne.

PUT YOUR ARMS AROUND ME HONEY (McCree: A. Von Tilzer) WIT   1910
Lina Abarbanell, Elizabeth Murray. Interpolated into *Madame Sherry*, New Amsterdam, NY.

QUEEN OF MY HEART (Stephenson & Cellier) CHA   1886
Hayden Coffin. Originally entitled Old Dreams, Sarah Doudney's words were rewritten by B. C. Stephenson to provide Hayden Coffin with an additional song in *Dorothy* (Gaiety). Interpolated on 15 October 1886 three weeks after opening night, it sensationally boosted the show's fortunes and provided Coffin with the hit of his career.

QUEEN OF THE CANNIBAL ISLE (Pelham & Rule) HVT   1909
Gertie Gitana.

RAGTIME COWBOY JOE (Clarke: Muir & Abrahams) FAM   1912
Daisy Dormer, Gene Greene, Hedges Brothers & Jacobson, The Three Rascals.

RATCATCHER'S DAUGHTER, THE (Bradley: Cowell or anon.)
   DAV/DAL/var.   *c.*1852
Ernest Butcher & Muriel George, Sam Cowell. A version pub. DAV *c.*1860 contained extra verses by Charles Sloman.

RED WING (Chattaway: K. Mills) FEL   1905
Harry MacDonough, Herbert Payne. Music based on Robert Schumann's piano piece The Merry Peasant.

REST OF THE DAY'S YOUR OWN, THE (David & Long) FDH   1915
Jack Lane.

RIDING ON A LOAD OF HAY (Arden: Birch) LMP/SHE   1877
Harry Birch.

RIDING ON TOP OF THE CAR (Leigh & Bryan: Von Tilzer) HVT/FDH   1905
George Lashwood. See also **DOWN WHERE THE WURZBURGER FLOWS.**

RIGHT ON MY DOO-DAH (Leighton & Wincott) FEL   1900
Harry Champion.

RILEY'S COWSHED (Damerell & R. Hargreaves) WRI   1924
George Bass.

RING DOWN THE CURTAIN (Brennen: Story)   FEL   1902
J. K. Emmett, Herbert Payne.

RING THE BELL SOFTLY, THERE'S CRAPE ON THE DOOR
    (D. Smith: Catlin)   GUE   1876
Christy Minstrels.

RING THE BELL, WATCHMAN (Root)   WLY   1872
Christy Minstrels.

ROAD TO THE ISLES, THE (Macleod: M. Kennedy Fraser)   BOO   1915
Margaret Kennedy & Marjory Kennedy Fraser. Music written at Marjory Kennedy
Fraser's request for 'a tramping song for the Scots lads "somewhere in France"' (*A
Life Of Song*, 150).

ROAMIN' IN THE GLOAMIN' (Lauder)   FDH   1911
Harry Lauder.

ROCK-A-BYE YOUR BABY WITH A DIXIE MELODY
    (Lewis & Young: Schwartz)   FEL   1918
Al Jolson. Interpolated into *Sinbad*, Winter Garden, NY.

ROCKED IN THE CRADLE OF THE DEEP (Millard: J. P. Knight)   FDH   1839
Norman Allin, Peter Dawson, Harry Lauder, Robert Radford.

ROSARY, THE (Rogers: Nevin)   Boston Music Co./BOO   1898
Beniamino Gigli, Alma Gluck, John Harrison, John McCormack, Charles Santley.

ROSE OF TRALEE (?)   var.   *c.* 1850
John McCormack. Soodlum's *Irish Ballad Book* (Oak, 1982) credits the song to one
William P. Mulchinock but both FDH and FEL credit the words to E. Mordaunt
Spencer and the music to Charles W. Glover.

ROSES OF PICARDY (Weatherly: H. Wood)   CHA   1916
Joseph Cheetham, Peter Dawson, Hubert Eisdell, Ernest Pike, Florence
Smithson.

ROSIE'S YOUNG MAN (F. W. Leigh & Pether)   FDH   1908
Eileen Douglas.

ROSIE, YOU ARE MY POSY *see* **MA BLUSIN' ROSIE**

ROWDY DOWDY BOYS, THE (McGlennon & Conley: McGlennon)
FDH   1891

Millie Hylton. Int. *Cinder-Ellen up too Late*, Gaiety, sung by Maggie Duggan.

Row, Row, Row (Jerome: Monaco) FDH   1912
Bonita, Daisy Jerome, Shirley Kellogg, Lillian Lorraine. Int. *Ziegfeld Follies of 1912*, Moulin Rouge, NY. London: included in *Hullo, Rag-time!*, Hippodrome.

Rule, Britannia! (James Thomson or David Mallet: Arne) var.   1741
Thomas Lowe.

Rum-Tiddley-Um-Tum-Tay (F. W. Leigh: O. Powell) FDH   1908
Marie Lloyd. Chorus music adapted from Non, Je Ne Marche Pas by A. Mas & J. Taillefer.

Runcorn Ferry, The (Edgar) FDH   1933
Marriott Edgar, Stanley Holloway. A.k.a. Tuppence Per Person Per Trip.

Saftest O' The Family, The (Lauder & Beaton: Lauder) FDH   1904
Harry Lauder.

Sailing (G. Marks) Reid Bros.   1886
George Formby.

Sailors Don't Care (Rudd) FEL   1918
Austin Rudd.

St Louis Blues, The (Handy) P&H/FDH   1914
Sophie Tucker, W. C. Handy.

Salute My Bicycle (Harrington: Le Brunn) FDH   1895
Marie Lloyd.

Sam, Pick Oop Tha' Musket *see* **Old Sam**

Santa Lucia (English *w* Cleather: Cottrau) RIC   1850
Enrico Caruso.

Sarah (Sitting In The Shoe Shine Shop)
  (McHugh & J. G. Gilbert & Conley & Macey) WRI   1919
Jack Hylton's Band.

Say Au Revoir But Not Goodbye (H. Kennedy) H. Kennedy NY   1893
Julie Mackey, John McCormack, James Norrie.

SCAMP, THE *or* **THEY CAN'T HOLD A CANDLE TO ME**
  (Pettitt: Major)   London   1873
G. H. Macdermott, Will Riley.

SCAPEGRACE OF THE FAMILY, THE *see* **BLACK SHEEP OF THE FAMILY, THE**

SEASIDE GIRL, THE (R. P. Weston)   FDH   1903

SEASIDE GIRLS (Norris)   DEA   1899
Vesta Tilley.

SEASIDE HOLIDAY AT HOME, A (Bowyer: Laye)   FDH   1903
Herbert Campbell.

SEASIDE POSTERS ROUND THE HOME (Bateman: Pether)   FDH   1919
Ernest Hastings.

SEAWEED (Earle)   FDH   1905
Fred Earle.

SECOND-HAND ROSE (G. Clarke: Hanley)   KPM   1921
Fanny Brice. From *Ziegfeld Follies of 1921*, Globe, NY.

SEE ME DANCE THE POLKA (Grossmith sen.)   REY   1886
Billie Barlow, George Grossmith sen., Jolly John Nash.

SEE THAT MY GRAVE'S KEPT GREEN (G. Williams)   SHE   1878
Moore & Burgess Minstrels.

SEE WHAT PERCY'S PICKED UP IN THE PARK *see* **LOOK WHAT PERCY'S PICKED UP IN THE PARK**

SEVENTH ROYAL FUSILIERS, THE (**A STORY OF INKERMAN**)
  (Pink: Le Brunn)   FDH   1891
Charles Godfrey. A parody was sung by Fred Harvey.

SHADE OF THE PALM (Stuart)   FDH   1899
Sydney Barraclough, Melville Stewart. From *Florodora*, Lyric.

SHALL I BE AN ANGEL, DADDY? (Collins & F. J. Barnes)   FDH   1897
George D'Albert.

SHE COST ME SEVEN AND SIXPENCE (J. Hargreaves & Mayo)   FDH   1904
Sam Mayo, Wilkie Bard. Based on traditional air, Early in the Morning.

SHE'D A BROTHER IN THE NAVY (G. Thorn: Redmond) F&D 1877
James Francis (Mohawk Minstrels), Howard Paul.

SHE'D NEVER HAD A LESSON IN HER LIFE, (AND)
  (Murray: Powell) SHE/FEL 1903
Marie Lloyd.

SHE DOES THE FANDANGO ALL OVER THE PLACE (G. W. Hunt)
  H&C 1883
Henri Clark.

SHEENY COON, THE (Castling) FDH 1898
Tom Costello.

SHE GLORIES IN A THING LIKE THAT (Everard) H&C 1899
Ada Reeve.

SHEIK OF ARABY, THE (H. B. Smith & Wheeler: Snyder) WBS 1921
Fred Barnes, Dorothy Ward.

SHE IS FAR FROM THE LAND (Moore: Lambert) CHA 1897
John McCormack. Thomas Moore's poem was set by many composers; only Lambert's version has lasted.

SHE IS MORE TO BE PITIED THAN CENSURED (William B. Gray)
  ROB/AHC 1894
Charles Falke, Harry Taft, Milner Verren.

SHE IS THE BELLE OF NEW YORK (H. Morton: Kerker) TBH/A&C 1897
Harry Davenport, Frank Lawton. From *The Belle of New York*, NY Casino; London, Shaftesbury 1898.

SHE MAY HAVE SEEN BETTER DAYS (Thornton) TBH 1894
Rose Elliott, Bonnie Thornton, W. H. Wyndham (Primrose & West Minstrels).

SHE PUSHED ME INTO THE PARLOUR (Ellerton: Mayne) FDH 1912
Ernie Mayne.

SHE'S A LASSIE FROM LANCASHIRE (Lipton & Murphy & Neat) FEL 1907
Florrie Forde, Ella Retford.

SHE'S BEEN A GOOD WIFE TO ME (W. David: O. Powell) FDH 1907
Alec Hurley.

SHE SELLS SEA-SHELLS (Sullivan: Gifford) FDH   1908
Wilkie Bard, Sam Mayo. First sung by Wilkie Bard in *Dick Whittington*, Drury Lane.

SHE'S ONLY A WORKING GIRL (J. T. Kelly) WIT/SHE   1895
Florrie Forde, Charles Foster.

SHE'S PROUD AND SHE'S BEAUTIFUL (F. W. Leigh & Bastow) FDH   1906
George Bastow.

SHE TOLD ME TO MEET HER AT THE GATE (Castling & Collins) FEL   1923
S. W. Wyndham.

SHE WAS ONE OF THE EARLY BIRDS (Connor) FDH   1895
George Beauchamp.

SHE WAS POOR BUT SHE WAS HONEST (anon.)   *c.*1901
A version is published in *Bawdy Ballads* (MSL) and another in *Twenty-four Folk Songs* (ROB). Weston & Lee also wrote a version described as 'based on traditional' which was recorded by Billy Bennett in 1930 on Columbia DB-164 and on Regal MR-147. There is no evidence for the claim that the author was George R. Sims. M. Willson Disher declared the original unprintable though not without literary merit, and that his memories of the song 'belong to the Grey Brigade of London volunteers after the South African War' (*Victorian Song*, 46).

SHE WAS! SHE WAS!! SHE WAS!!! (Day) FDH   1885
Slade Murray.

SHINE ON HARVEST MOON (Norworth: Bayes-Norworth & Norworth)
FDH   1908
Nora Bayes & Jack Norworth, Olive Lenton. From *Ziegfeld Follies of 1908*, Jardin de Paris, NY. Int. *Hullo, London!*, Empire, 1910.

SHIP AHOY! *see* **ALL THE NICE GIRLS LOVE A SAILOR**

SHIP I LOVE, THE (McGlennon) SHE/FEL   1898
Tom Costello.

SHIPMATES O' MINE (Teschemacher: Sanderson) BOO   1913
Peter Dawson, Ivor Foster, Robert Radford, Norman Williams.

SHIP WENT DOWN, THE (Tabrar) H&C   1898
Harry Rickards.

Shooting Of Dan McGrew, The (Service: Clarke) REY   1917
Bransby Williams. From *Songs of a Sourdough*.

Show Me The Way To Go Home (I. King) CCC   1925
Ella Shields.

Side By Side (H. Woods) WRI   1927
Florrie Forde.

Sidewalks Of New York, The (J. Blake & Lawlor) DAR   1894
Lottie Gilson, Charles B. Lawlor. See also **Dancing On The Streets.**

Signalman On The Line, The (B. Daly: B. Andrews) FDH   1893
Frank Celli.

Silver Bell (Madden: Wenrich) FEL   1910
Gertie Gitana.

Silver Threads Among The Gold (Rexford: Danks)
    TRB/PAX/FDH   1873
Sundry Minstrel troupes, Will Oakland, Emily Soldene.

Simon The Cellarer (Bellamy: Hatton) F&D   1847
Peter Dawson, Charles Santley.

Simple Little Maid In The Corner, The (Duffy & J. M. Harrison)
    FDH   1896
Kitty Dee.

Simple Little String, A (Monckton) CHA   1896
Ellaline Terriss. From *The Circus Girl*, Gaiety. Interpolated into *Bluebell in Fairy-land*, Vaudeville, 1901.

Since I Became A Married Man (W. P. Keen) FDH   1907
G. W. Hunter.

Since I Came To London Town (R. Morton: Costa) RIC   1900
Armand 'Ary, Letty Lind. Adapted from P. M. Costa's A Frangesa.

Since I Walked Out With A Soldier (Davenport: Pelissier) WIL   1909
H. G. Pelissier.

Sing Sing Sing (Damerell & Rutland) FEL   1910
Damerell & Rutland.

SING US ONE OF THE OLD SONGS (Kelly & Woodhouse)　FDH　　　1900
Millie Lindon.

SISTER MARY WALKED LIKE THAT (Levaine: Massage)　FDH　　　1886
Jolly John Nash.

SISTER 'RIA (Mills: Lennard)　FDH　　　1895
Lizzie Fletcher.

SISTER SUSIE'S SEWING SHIRTS FOR SOLDIERS (Weston: Darewski)
　FDH　　　1913
Harry Cove, Al Jolson, Jack Norworth. From *Hullo, Tango!*, Hippodrome.

SKYE BOAT SONG (Boulton: A. C. Macleod)　CRA　　　1884
R. Watkin Mills. Based on what is variously described as a traditional 'chanty' or 'Highland rowing measure' or 'Jacobite song'.

SKYLARK! SKYLARK! (E. W. Rogers)　FDH　　　1901
Arthur Lennard.

SLAP BANG! HERE WE ARE AGAIN! (Copeland)　DAL/ASH　　　1865
Frank Hall, Tom Maclagan, Alfred Vance.

SMILES (Callahan: Lee S. Roberts)　FDH　　　1917
Nell Carrington, Elsie Janis, Clarice Mayne, Millie Lindon, Blossom Seeley. Included in *The Passing Show of 1918*, Winter Garden, NY. Not to be confused with next entry.

SMILES! (McGlennon)　FDH　　　1890
Little Tich. Not to be confused with previous entry.

SMILIN' THRU'/THROUGH (Penn)　FEL　　　1918
Jane Cowl, Walter Glynne, John McCormack.

SMITH, JONES, ROBINSON AND BROWN (Harrington & Mayo: Mayo)
　DAR　　　1910
Lily Morris, Ella Retford, Ella Shields, Daisy Wood.

SO HER SISTER SAYS (Harrington: Le Brunn)　H&C　　　1894
Jenny Valmore

SOLDIERS IN THE PARK (Hopwood & Greenbank: Monckton)　CHA　　　1898
George Baker, Ethel Haydon, Grace Palotta, Florence Smithson. From *A Runaway Girl*, Gaiety.

SOLDIERS OF THE QUEEN (Stuart) FDH 1891

Albert Christian, Hayden Coffin. Interpolated into *An Artist's Model*, Daly's (1895). One edition boasts that Jay Laurier also sang the song; he was an eccentric comedian so it is likely that his version was a parody.

SOMEBODY'S COMING TO TEA (Clay Smith & Weston & B. Lee) FDH 1917

Kirkby & Hudson, Lee White.

SOMEBODY WOULD SHOUT OUT 'SHOP!' (Weston & Lee) FDH 1915

Stanley Kirkby & Harry Hudson.

SOME OF THESE DAYS (S. Brooks) FDH 1910

Shirley Kellogg, Ethel Levey, Ella Retford, Sophie Tucker. Included in second edition of *Hullo, Tango!*, Hippodrome (1914).

SOMEWHERE A VOICE IS CALLING (Newton: A. F. Tate) LAR/FDH 1911

Frances Alda, John Coates, Peter Dawson, Hubert Eisdell, John McCormack.

SONG OF THE SHIRT, THE (Hood: Blewitt, arr. Tully) 1843

Henry Russell. Thomas Hood's poem was originally published anonymously in *Punch* and *The Times*. It was set by many composers, including Arthur Behrend— the eminent soprano Antoinette Sterling's preferred setting.

SONG OF THE THRUSH, THE (Hastings: G. Le Brunn) FDH 1897

Jenny Hill, Peggy Pryde. Pryde was Hill's daughter.

SONGS MY MOTHER TAUGHT ME (Heyduk, transcr. N. Macfarren: Dvořák)
    N. Simrock/A. Lengnick 1880

Edward Lloyd, Ernest Pike, Maggie Teyte, Evan Williams. From *Zigeunermelodien*, op. 155 no. 4.

SONG THAT REACHED MY HEART, THE (Jordan) FDH 1887

T. Campbell (Mohawk Minstrels), Julian Jordan.

SONS OF THE SEA (McGlennon) SHE/FEL 1897

Ian Colquhoun, Arthur Reece.

SOPHY (B. Lee: T. C. Sterndale Bennett) REY 1913

T. C. Sterndale Bennett.

SORRENTO (Aveling: De Curtis) RIC 1911

SPANIARD THAT BLIGHTED MY LIFE, THE (Merson) FDH 1909

Al Jolson, Billy Merson. Originally sung as a duet by Billy Merson with Beatrice

Allen in *Dick Whittington* at Brighton and performed as such in the second edition of *Hullo, Rag-time!* (Hippodrome, 1913) by him with Dorothy Minto (also with Ida Valli).

SPIDER AND THE FLY, THE (Hudson: anon.)   DAL/HAR   *c.*1835
Kate Castleton, Thomas Hudson, Henry Russell. It is possible that Russell composed the tune.

STAR OF BETHLEHEM (Weatherly: Adams)   BOO   *c.*1886
Ben Davies, Ruth Helder, John Harrison, Edward Lloyd, John McCormack, Michael Maybrick (a.k.a. Stephen Adams, the song's composer).

STEAMBOAT BILL (Shields: Leighton Bros.)   FDH   1910
Leighton Bros.

STOP YER TICKLIN', JOCK (Lauder & Folloy: Lauder)   FDH   1904
Harry Lauder, Jay Laurier.

SUNSHINE OF PARADISE ALLEY, THE (Ford: Bratton)   WIT   1895
Lottie Gilson, Sisters Levey, Julius P. Witmark.

SUNSHINE OF YOUR SMILE, THE (Cooke: L. Ray)   FDH   1913
Norman Blair, John Coates, Olga & Elgar & Eli Hudson, John McCormack.

SUSSEX BY THE SEA (Ward-Higgs)   DAR/FEL   1907

SWALLOWS, THE (Bingham: Cowen)   BOO   1895
Alma Gluck.

SWANEE (Caesar: Gershwin)   TBH/FDH   1919
Laddie Cliff, Al Jolson. Interpolated into *Sinbad*, Winter Garden, NY. London: included in *Jig-Saw!*, Hippodrome.

SWEET ADELINE *see* **YOU'RE THE FLOWER OF MY HEART**

SWEET AND LOW (Tennyson: Barnby)   Foster & King   1863
Charles Santley. From Tennyson's 'The Princess, a medley', a poem 'respectfully perverted' by W. S. Gilbert for *The Princess* (1870), itself the basis of his and Arthur Sullivan's comic opera *Princess Ida* (Savoy, 1884). Over forty other musical settings of the poem are known.

SWEET GENEVIEVE (Cooper: Tucker)   LMP/PAX/FDH   1869
Belle Cole, John McCormack, Mohawk Minstrels, Will Oakland, Peerless Quartet. Words from George Cooper's poem in memory of his beloved wife, who died

shortly after their marriage. Henry Tucker's music was added some fifteen years later.

SWEETHEART MAY (Stuart)   FDH   1894
Vesta Tilley.

SWEETHEARTS STILL (E. W. Rogers)   FEL   1902
James Merrylees, Vesta Tilley.

SWEET LITTLE ROSE OF PERSIA (F. J. Barnes & Collins: Collins)   FDH   1900
Tom Leamore. Perhaps prompted by Arthur L. Sullivan's and Basil Hood's comic opera *The Rose of Persia*, Savoy, 1899.

SWEET ROSIE O'GRADY (Nugent)   FEL   1890
Annie Hart, Lil Hawthorne, Marie Kendall, Walter Munroe, Maude Nugent, Pat Rafferty. Nugent's claim to the words and music has been questioned.

SWEET VIOLETS (SWEETER THAN ALL THE ROSES) (Emmet)   HOW   1883
J. Fuller (Mohawk Minstrels), Jenny Hill.

SWIMMING MASTER, THE (Darnley)   BOW   *c.*1904
Dan Leno, Max Miller.

SWIM, SAM! SWIM! (Weston & Lee)   FDH   1916
Jay Laurier.

SWING ME HIGHER, OBADIAH! (Rick: M. Scott)   FEL   1907
Florrie Forde, Lily Lena.

SWING SONG, THE (Eldée & P. Greenbank: Messager)   CHA   1904
Mariette Sully & Jean Perier, Ruth Vincent & Lawrence Rea. From *Véronique*, des Bouffes-Parisiens, Paris, 1898. First London production (in French), Coronet, 1903; first in English, Apollo, 1904.

TAKE A LOOK AT ME NOW (Sterling: Von Tilzer)   FDH   1911
Ella Retford, Beth Tate.

TAKE BACK YOUR GOLD (Pritzkow: Rosenfeld)   STE/EBM/DOV   1897
Emma Carus, Imogene Comer, Louis W. Pritzkow (Primrose & West Minstrels). Although Pritzkow is credited with the words they were in fact by Rosenfeld, who offered Pritzkow the kudos (probably backed up with a cash inducement) to help popularize the song. See also **AFTER THE BALL**.

TAKE ME BACK TO DEAR OLD BLIGHTY (Mills & Godfrey & B. Scott)
   FEL   1916

Ouida Macdermott, Lily Morris, Ella Retford, Dorothy Ward, Daisy Wood.

TAKE ME IN A TAXI, JOE (Mills: B. Scott) STA   1913

May Moore Duprez, Vesta Victoria.

TAKE ME OUT TO THE BALL GAME (Norworth: A. Von Tilzer)
   York Music/DOV   1908

Nora Bayes, Henry Fink, Billy Murray.

TALE OF ACKMED KURD, THE (*or* **HASHISH**) (Forbes: Crispen)
   REY   1925

Kit Keen.

TALE OF THE SKIRT, THE (Leigh: Le Brunn) FDH   1904

Marie Lloyd.

TA-RA-RA-BOOM-DE-AY (?) SHE/FDH   1891

José Collins, Lottie Collins, Alice Leamar. Originally published in the USA as Ta-Ra-Ra Boom-Der-É in a version by Henry J. Sayers, who stated that he first heard it sung at the piano by one Mama Lou in The Castle, a brothel run by Babe Connors in St Louis in the late 1880s. The song only became popular after Lottie Collins (who on a visit to the USA in 1891 had acquired the British rights) electrified London with her energetic dancing first at the Tivoli, then in *Dick Whittington* at the Islington Grand and concurrently in *Cinder-Ellen up too Late* at the Gaiety. The sheet cover of her version reads 'written by Richard Morton, music arranged Angelo A. Asher on a melody composed by Alfred Moor-King'. Or, as some maintain, was the tune composed by Theodore T. Metz? Did it derive from a Tyrolean folk song? A further complication is the claim by the minor British composer Alfred Gilbert (1828–1902) that he wrote the tune some twenty years earlier and that Sayers plagiarized it for his show *Tuxedo*. There may have been merit in Gilbert's assertion for he was awarded £250 in the High Court as a share of royalties. Parodies and 'answer' songs were performed, amongst many others, by George Beauchamp, Charles Bignell, Marie Collins, W. P. Dempsey, Katie Lawrence, Julie Mackey, Harry Randall, J. C. Rich, Harry Pleon, and (for the Mohawk Minstrels) Johnny Danvers and Johnny Schofield. (Fuld; Gammond, *Oxford Companion to Popular Music*; Whitcomb, *Irving Berlin and Ragtime America*, 106; for the Alfred Gilbert information see Short and Compton-Rickett, *Ring up the Curtain*, 200.)

TEDDY BEARS' PICNIC, THE (Bratton: Kennedy) FEL   1930

Val Rosing (with Henry Hall's Orchestra). Music composed in 1907 as a tribute to US President Theodore Roosevelt. Jimmy Kennedy's words added in 1930 at the request of the publisher for use in a Manchester pantomime. Val Rosing's celebrated recording, made in 1932, was nominated by the 1933 International Radio Convention as ideal for testing broadcasting equipment.

TELL ME, DEAR FLOWER *see* **FLOWER, THE**

TELL ME, PRETTY MAIDEN (E. Boyd Jones & Rubens: Stuart)   FDH   1899
Sextet. From *Florodora*, Lyric.

TEMPLE BELL, THE (Wimperis: Monckton)   CHA   1911
Florence Smithson. From *The Mousmé*, Shaftesbury.

TENOR AND BARITONE (A. B. Black: H. L. Wilson)   RAW   1896
Ernest Pike & Stanley Kirkby.

THAT GORGONZOLA CHEESE (F. W. Leigh: Champion)   AHC   1894
Harry Champion.

THAT IS LOVE! (McGlennon)   FDH   1891
Marie Loftus. A parody written and performed by G. W. Hunter and R. G. Knowles was published by FDH in 1892.

THAT OLD ROCKING CHAIR (Osborne)   TBH/FDH   1902
Millie Lindon.

THAT'S AN IRISH LULLABY (TOO-RA-LOO-RA-LOO-RAL) (Shannon)
   WIT   1913
Chauncey Olcott. From *Shameen Dhu*, USA (theatre not known).

THAT'S THE REASON NOO I WEAR A KILT (Lauder)   FDH   1906
Harry Lauder.

THAT'S WHAT GOD MADE MOTHERS FOR (L. Wood)   FDH   1924
The Two Rascals.

THEN WE HAD A NICE QUIET DAY *see* **POSTMAN'S HOLIDAY, THE**

THEN YOU'LL REMEMBER ME (Bunn: Balfe)   PAX/CHA   1843
Beniamino Gigli, William Harrison, Edward Lloyd. From *The Bohemian Girl*, Drury Lane.

THEN YOU WINK THE OTHER EYE (WHEN THE WINKLE MAN GOES BY)
   (Lytton: Le Brunn)   Marshall's   1890
Marie Lloyd.

THERE ALWAYS WILL BE FAIRIES (St Clair: Clarke)   FDH   1898
F. V. St Clair.

THERE ARE FAIRIES AT THE BOTTOM OF OUR GARDEN (Fyleman: Lehmann)
    CHA   1907
Dora Labette, Beatrice Lillie.

THERE ARE NICE GIRLS EVERYWHERE (R. P. Weston)   FDH   1909
Whit Cunliffe.

THERE'LL BE A HOT TIME IN THE OLD TOWN TONIGHT *see* **HOT TIME**
etc., **A**

THERE'S A LONG, LONG TRAIL A-WINDING (King & Elliott)   WES   1913
Ernest Pike, Ada Reeve.

THERE'S DANGER ON THE LINE (THE GREAT SEMAPHORE SONG)
    (G. P. Norman)   H&C   *c.*1885
G. H. Macdermott. Arthur Lennard sang a song *c.*1911 by Leigh, Collins, and
Murray with the same title.

THERE'S SOMETHING ABOUT A SOLDIER (O. Powell)   *c.*1910

THERE THEY ARE—THE TWO OF THEM ON THEIR OWN (Murray & Leigh:
    Adapted by Le Brunn from Ethelbert Nevin's Narcissus)
    FDH   1898
Marie Lloyd.

THEY ALL HAVE A MATE BUT ME (Geoghegan)   H&C   1870
Sam Torr.

THEY ALL WALK THE WIBBLY WOBBLY WALK
    (Long: Pelham)   STA/FEL   1912
Mark Sheridan.

THEY ALWAYS PICK ON ME (S. Murphy: H. Von Tilzer)   HVT/FEL   1911
Ada Jones.

THEY BUILT PICCADILLY FOR ME (Hargreaves)   FEL   1913
J. W. Rickaby.

THEY CAN'T GET THE BETTER OF ME (F. Wood)   FDH   1909
Will Bentley.

THEY DIDN'T BELIEVE ME (Rourke: Kern)   FDH   1914

Donald Brian & Julia Sanderson, George Grossmith jun. & (a) Adrienne Brune, (b) Haidée de Rance, (c) Madge Sanders. Int. NY version of *The Girl from Utah*, Knickerbocker. London: included in *Tonight's the Night*, Gaiety, 1915.

THEY'RE ALL SINGLE BY THE SEASIDE (W. David & F. W. Murphy)
    FDH   1911

Florrie Forde, Ella Retford.

THEY'RE ALL VERY FINE AND LARGE (Bowyer)   FDH   1885

Herbert Campbell.

THORA (Weatherly: Adams)   BOO   1905

Joseph Cheetham, Ivor Foster, Ruby Helder, John McCormack.

THOSE WEDDING BELLS SHALL NOT RING OUT (Rosenfeld: Jonghman)
    DOV   1893

Leonard Barrie, Gus Edwards, Helene Mora, Arthur Reece, William H. Windom. Based on The Fatal Wedding by Gussie L. Davis.

THOUGH ALL YOUR FRIENDS MAY LEAVE YOU (Castling)   FDH   1903

Kate Carney.

THREE FISHERS WENT SAILING (Kingsley: Hullah)
    Addison, Hollier & Lucas   1857

Louise Kirkby Lunn, Charlotte Sainton-Dolby, Antoinette Sterling.

THREE O'CLOCK IN THE MORNING (Theodora Morse: Robledo)
    WES/FEL   1921

Paul Whiteman Band.

THREE POTS A SHILLING *see* **WHEN THE SUMMER COMES AGAIN**

THREE TREES, THE (D. Powell)   FEL   1910

Tom McNaughton, Albert Whelan, Mark Sheridan. Interpolated into *The Spring Maid* (*Die Sprudelfee*), Liberty, NY.

TICHBORNE TRIAL (F. W. Green: Alf Lee)   SHE   1872

Alfred Vance.

TICKLE ME, TIMOTHY, DO! (F. Barnes & R. P. Weston)   FDH   1907

Billy Williams.

TIDDLEY-OM-POM (F. W. Leigh: O. Powell)   FDH   1907
Marie Lloyd.

TILL THE BOYS COME HOME *see* **KEEP THE HOME FIRES BURNING**

TILL THE SANDS OF THE DESERT GROW COLD (Graff: Ball)   FEL   1911
Ernest R. Ball, Peter Dawson, Robert Howe.

TIN GEE-GEE, THE (Cape)   FDH   1891
Fanny Wentworth. His own version was sung by Mel B. Spurr.

TING, TING, THAT'S HOW THE BELL GOES (Tabrar)   FDH   1883
George Leybourne.

TIPPITIWITCHET *see* **TYPITYWITCHET**

'TIS THE DAY *see* **MATTINATA**

'TIS THE LAST ROSE OF SUMMER (T. Moore: Milliken, adap. Moore)
   FDH   1807
Catherine Hayes, Christine Nilsson, Adelina Patti, Emma Thursby. From Thomas
Moore's *Irish Melodies*, the air based on Richard A. Milliken's 1790 song
The Groves of Blarney (also Castle Hyde). Used to great effect by Friedrich von
Flotow in his light opera *Martha* (see **M'APPARI**). Music also arranged by
Beethoven.

TO CHEER HIM UP AND HELP HIM ON HIS WAY (Kendal)   FEL   1912
Jack Pleasants.

TOMMY (Kipling: Carmichael)   SHE   1892
Charles Coborn. Kipling's poem is from the first series of his *Barrack-Room
Ballads*.

TOMMY DODD (E. Clarke & E. Webb)   CKH   1868
Sydney Barnes, Ernèe Clarke.

TOMMY MAKE ROOM FOR YOUR UNCLE (Lonsdale)   H&C   1876
W. B. Fair, Tony Pastor.

TOO-RA-LI-OO-RA-LI-AY (Montagu)   FDH   1906
Ernest Shand.

Too-Ra-Loo-Ra-Loo-Ral *see* **That's An Irish Lullaby**

Touch Of The Master's Hand, The (Welch: Longstaffe) REY 1936
Nosmo King.

Trail Of The Lonesome Pine, The (MacDonald: Carroll) FDH 1913
'Edna Brown' & James Harrison, Hedges Brothers & Jacobson, Laurel & Hardy, Molly McCarthy, The Two Bobs.

Tramp, Tramp, Tramp, The Boys Are Marching (Root) FDH 1864
Christy Minstrels, Hutchinson Family. Sung by Pat Carey under the title The Life of a Soldier. See also **Work, Boys, Work**.

Tricky Little Trilby (Harrington: Le Brunn) FDH 1895
Marie Lloyd.

Trixie Of Upper Tooting (Reeve: Rubens) H&C 1896
George Grossmith jun., Lionel Mackinder, Ada Reeve.

Trot Here And There (Eldée & P. Greenbank: Messager) CHA 1904
Mariette Sully & Jean Perier, Ruth Vincent & Laurence Rea. From *Véronique*; see **Swing Song** for details.

Trottin' To The Fair (Graves: trad., arr. Stanford) BOO 1901
Plunkett Greene. From *Songs of Erin*.

Trumpeter, The (Barron: Dix) BOO 1904
Peter Dawson, Ivor Foster, Charles Knowles, Robert Radford, Watkin Mills.

Tuner's Oppor-Tuner-Ty (H. Adams: Fred Coyne) HOW 1879
Fred Coyne.

Tuppence Per Person Per Trip *see* **Runcorn Ferry, The**

Turkey(s) In Yhe Straw *see* **Zip Coon**

Turned Up (Castling & Rule) FEL 1924
Florrie Forde, Lily Morris.

Turn Off The Gas At The Meter (Stamford) H&C 1878
G. H. Macdermott.

Twiddley Bits, The (Dance & J. Adams: E. Woodville) H&C 1901
Louie Freear, Alma Jones, Hilda Trevelyan. Interpolated into *A Chinese Honey-*

moon, Strand. The composer is variously listed as Ernest Woodhouse and Ernee Woodville; the published vocal score gives Ernie Woodville.

TWIDDLY WINK (Leigh: O. Powell)   FDH   1912
Marie Lloyd.

TWIGGY VOO? (Harrington: Le Brunn)   FDH   1892
Marie Lloyd.

TWO LITTLE BOYS *see* **WHEN WE WERE TWO LITTLE BOYS**

TWO LITTLE GIRLS IN BLUE (Chas. Graham)   FDH   1892
Lily Burnand, Marie Kendall, James Norrie, Horace Wheatley.

TWO LITTLE SAUSAGES (Monckton)   CHA   1907
Gertie Millar & Edmund Payne. From *The Girls of Gottenburg*, Gaiety.

TWO LOVELY BLACK EYES (Coborn)   FDH   1886
Charles Coborn. See also **MY NELLIE'S BLUE EYES**.

TWO OBADIAHS, THE (Lyste)   H&C   1876
J. L. Toole, G. H. Macdermott.

TWO SWEETHEARTS (Barrett)   FDH   1892
Lester Barrett.

TYPITYWITCHET (C. Dibdin jun.: W. Reeve?)   DAL   1810
Sam Cowell, Joseph Grimaldi, Tom Matthews. From *Bang-Up!* or *Harlequin Prime*, Aquatic (Sadler's Wells).

UNDERNEATH THE ARCHES (Flanagan—additional words McCarthy)
  CCC   1932
Flanagan & Allen.

UNDER THE BED (Castling)   EMI   1929
Nellie Wallace. Unpublished, but a transcription from the record (HMV B-3034) is available from EMI.

UNDER THE DEODAR (Ross: Monckton)   CHA   1902
Aileen D'Orme, Evie Greene, Maggie May. From *A Country Girl*, Daly's.

UNTIL (Teschemacher: Sanderson)   BOO   1910
Ivor Foster, Dick Henderson, Maggie Teyte.

UP FROM SOMERSET (Weatherly: Sanderson) BOO 1913
Peter Dawson.

UP IN A BALLOON (G. W. Hunt) H&C 1868
George Leybourne. A ladies' version written for Nellie Power by her mother was also sung by Annie Adams, Alice Dunning, and Louie Sherrington. Yet a third set of words was written for the US market by H. B. Farnie. No connection with the 1908 song of the same title by Ren Shields: Percy Wenrich.

UP THE ALMA'S HEIGHT (Colomb) CRA 1854
Emily Soldene. Another musical celebration of British and French military prowess in the Crimean War was T. Walker's and J. Harroway's On Alma's Heights sung by Tommy Farrant.

UP WENT THE PRICE (Ware) H&C 1882
G. H. Macdermott.

VARMER GILES (Robson & Wells) FDH 1902
George Bastow. Air, **VILLIKINS AND HIS DINAH**.

VEEPIN' VILLER, THE *see* **WEEPIN' WILLER, THE**

VICAR AND I WILL BE THERE, THE (Grey: Ayer) REY 1919
Clifford Grey.

VIEWING THE BABY (Weston & Lee) FDH 1926
Clarice Mayne.

VILIA (Ross: Lehár) CHA 1907
Constance Drever, Lily Elsie, Mizzi Gunther. From *The Merry Widow*; see **MERRY WIDOW WALTZ** for details.

VILLAGE BLACKSMITH, THE (Longfellow: Balfe) BOO 1855
Harry Cavendish, Hayden Coffin, William Scanlon (Christy's Minstrels). Also sung very successfully to his own setting by W. H. Weiss.

VILLIKINS AND HIS DINAH (anon.) DAV/PAX/AHC *c.*1836
Sam Cowell, Frederick Robson, J. L. Toole. Revived *c.*1930 by Ernest Butcher & Muriel George. First sung in the printed version by Frederick Robson in *The Wandering Minstrel* at the Olympic, 1853, though the origins of this song remain obscure. (Sands: *Robson of the Olympic*, App. 3.)

VOLUNTEER ORGANIST, THE (W. B. Gray: H. Lamb) LMP/PAX 1893
Peter Dawson, William Glenroy, Arthur Reeves. William B. Gray was a pseudonym of William Glenroy.

VOT A GAME! OI! OI! (Aiston & Thurban) FDH   1912
Arthur Aiston.

WAGGLE O' THE KILT, THE (Lauder) FDH   1918
Harry Lauder.

WAIATA POI (Alfred Hill) CHA   1908
Peter Dawson, Kennerley Rumford.

WAIT FOR THE TURN OF THE TIDE (Clifton: Coote) H&C   1868
Harry Clifton.

WAITING (Flagg: Millard) Ashdown & Parry/var.   1867
Alexandra Dagmar.

WAITING AT THE CHURCH (Leigh: Pether) FDH   1906
Vesta Victoria.

WAITING FOR THE ROBERT E. LEE (L. Wolfe Gilbert & Muir) FDH   1912
American Ragtime Octette, Peter Bernard, The Two Bobs, Fanny Brice, Dolly
Connolly, Al Jolson. Interpolated into *The Honeymoon Express*, Winter Garden,
NY.

WAITING FOR THE TRAIN *see* **CHARMING YOUNG WIDOW I MET IN THE
TRAIN, THE**

WAIT TILL THE CLOUDS ROLL BY (J. T. Wood: Fulmer) HOW/FDH   1881
Mohawk Minstrels, Moore & Burgess Minstrels, Will Oakland.

WAIT TILL THE SUN SHINES, NELLIE (Sterling: Von Tilzer) HVT/FEL   1905
Winona Banks, Emma Carus, Gladys Fisher, Byron G. Harlan, Harry Talley.

WAIT TILL THE WORK COMES ROUND (Cornell & T. Leybourne: Elen)
FEL   1906
Gus Elen.

WALKING HOME WITH ANGELINE (G. Totten Smith: Roundbach)
CHA/FDH   1902
Eily Helene, Stanley Kirkby. From *Kitty Grey*, Apollo.

WALTER! WALTER! LEAD ME TO THE ALTAR (Haines & Harper & Forrester)
CCC   1937
Gracie Fields.

WALTZING MATILDA (Paterson: Barr, arr. Cowan)
Allan & Co., Melbourne/AHC 1895

Peter Dawson. Despite the title the song is in 4/4 time. As well as being based on James Barr's Craigielea, the music may have a second source— The Bold Fusilier, a seventeenth-century English marching song.

WALTZ ME AROUND AGAIN, WILLIE (G. Cobb: Shields)
FAM/FEL/DOV 1906

Margaret Cooper, Florrie Forde, George Grossmith jun., Blanche Ring. Originally from the short-lived *His Honor the Mayor*, but then included in *Miss Dolly Dollars*, 14th Street, both NY. London: included in *The New Aladdin*, Gaiety.

WALTZ SONG (FOR TONIGHT) (Chas. H. Taylor: German) CHA 1907

Ruth Vincent. From *Tom Jones*, Apollo.

WATCHING THE TRAINS COME IN (Leo) FEL 1916

Jack Pleasants.

WATCHING THE TRAINS GO OUT (Hargreaves) FEL 1912

Jack Pleasants.

WATCHMAN! WHAT OF THE NIGHT? (anon.: Sarjeant) BOO/CRA 1905

Ivor Foster & Herbert Cave, John Harrison & Robert Radford.

WAY DOWN UPON THE SWANEE RIVER *see* **OLD FOLKS AT HOME, THE**

WE ALL CAME IN THE WORLD WITH NOTHING (Collins & Wallis)
FEL 1907

Tennyson & Wallis. Billy Williams sang a parody.

WE ALL GO THE SAME WAY HOME (Castling & Murphy) FDH 1911

Charles R. Whittle.

WE ALL GO TO WORK BUT FATHER (Reed) FDH 1891

J. C. Heffron, Leslie Reed.

WE ALL WENT UP UP UP THE MOUNTAIN (Box & Cox & Butler)
KPM 1933

George Jackley, The Midnight Minstrels.

WEDDING MARCH!, THE *or* **THE COSTER'S WEDDING** (Harrington: Le Brunn)
FDH 1902

Marie Lloyd, Marie Lloyd jun.

WE DON'T WANT TO FIGHT (BUT BY JINGO! IF WE DO) *see* **MACDERMOTT'S WAR SONG**

WE DON'T WANT TO LOSE YOU *see* **YOUR KING AND YOUR COUNTRY**

WEE DEOCH-AN-DORIS, (JUST) A (Lauder & Cunliffe & Grafton)   FEL   1910
Harry Lauder.

WEEPIN' WILLER, THE or **THE MILLER'S DAUGHTER** (Clifton)   H&C   1865
Harry Clifton.

WE'LL KEEP A WELCOME (Joshua & Harper: M. Jones)   Edward Cox   1940
Mai Jones. According to the South Wales *Western Mail* of 5 January 1988 this song
was first broadcast on 24 September 1940 but had been 'devised' by Bill (later
James or Jimmy) Harper some ten years previously.

WE PARTED ON THE SHORE (Lauder)   FDH   1906
Harry Lauder.

WE REALLY HAD A MOST DELIGHTFUL EVENING (David & Lee)
FEL   1911
Ernest Shand.

WE USED TO GATHER AT THE OLD DUN COW (Connor)   STA/FEL   1918
Ernie Mayne.

WE'VE ALL BEEN HAVING A GO AT IT (Leighton & Wincott)   FEL   1896
Harry Champion.

WHACKY WHACKY WHACK! (Ware)   H&C   1892
Marie Lloyd.

WHAT A MOUTH! (Weston)   FDH   1906
Harry Champion.

WHAT CHEER, 'RIA! (Bellwood: Herbert)   H&C   1885
Bessie Bellwood, Nellie Farren.

WHAT DID SHE KNOW ABOUT RAILWAYS? (Cotes: B. Scott)   FDH   1897
Marie Lloyd, Marie Lloyd jun. Note: 'Railways' was slang for women's red stock-
ings, hence the joke in the last line of the third verse.

WHAT DO I CARE? (R. Morton: Venton)   FDH   1892
Ada Reeve.

WHAT DO YOU THINK OF THE IRISH NOW? (A. Hall & Castling)
FDH 1900
Pat Rafferty.

WHAT DO YOU WANT TO MAKE THOSE EYES AT ME FOR? (H. Johnson & McCarthy: Monaco) DAR 1916
Emma Carus, Walter Jeffries. From *Follow Me*, Casino, NY. London: Interpolated into *A Better 'Ole*, Oxford.

WHAT D'YER THINK OF THAT? (MY OLD MAN'S A DUSTMAN) (J. P. Long)
WRI 1922
Ernie Mayne.

WHATEVER YOU DO KEEP FIT (Cliffe & Formby & Gifford) FEL 1937
George Formby.

WHAT HO, SHE BUMPS! (Castling & A. J. Mills) SHE/FDH 1899
Charles Bignell. Not to be confused with J. W. Rickaby's song of the same title, words by Willie Stern and music by Cuthbert Collins (SHE 1899). The title was a catch-phrase meaning 'that's splendid!'.

WHAT IS THE USE OF LOVING A GIRL IF THE GIRL DON'T LOVE YOU?
(Leo) FDH 1902
Sable Fern.

WHAT I WANT IS A PROPER CUP OF COFFEE (Weston & Lee) FDH 1926
Ernie Mayne, Johnny Schofield.

WHAT'S THAT FOR, EH? (JOHNNY JONES *or* I KNOW NOW) (Harrington: Le Brunn) FEL 1892
Marie Lloyd.

WHAT WILL THE NEIGHBOURS SAY? (Harrington: Le Brunn) FDH 1900
Lily Marney.

WHEN A FELLAH HAS TURNED SIXTEEN (Rogers) FDH 1894
Vesta Tilley.

WHEN A FELLOW IS TWENTY-ONE (Mills & B. Scott) SHE 1904
Hetty King.

WHEN ARE YOU GOING TO LEAD ME TO THE ALTAR, WALTER?
(Dore: Desmond) FDH 1933
Randolph Sutton.

WHEN FATHER LAID THE CARPET ON THE STAIRS (Jackson)　REY　　　1912
Nelson Jackson, Burt Shepard.

WHEN FATHER PAPERED THE PARLOUR (Weston & F. Barnes)　FDH　　1909
Billy Williams.

WHEN I DISCOVERED YOU (Berlin & Goetz)　BER　　　　　　　　1914
Vernon & Irene Castle, Joseph Coyne & Ethel Levey. From *Watch Your Step*, New Amsterdam, NY. London: Empire, 1915.

WHEN I LEAVE THE WORLD BEHIND (Berlin)　FEL　　　　　　　1915
Belle Baker, Gertie Gitana, Emilie Hayes, Al Jolson, Fritzi Scheff.

WHEN I MARRY AMELIA (Ross: Monckton)　CHA　　　　　　　　1901
Henry Lytton, Fred Wright jun. From *The Toreador*, Gaiety.

WHEN IRISH EYES ARE SMILING (Graff & Olcott: Ball)　WIT/FEL　　1913
Ernest R. Ball, Norah Delaney, Chauncey Olcott, John McCormack. From *Isle o' Dreams*, Grand Opera House, NY.

WHEN I TAKE MY MORNING PROMENADE (Mills: B. Scott)　FEL　　1910
Marie Lloyd.

WHEN JOHNNY COMES MARCHING HOME (Gilmore)　Trayhearne/var.　1863
G. W. Moore (Christy Minstrels). Parodied by, amongst many others, Tom Bass, Harry Liston, and George Beauchamp.

WHEN OTHER LIPS *see* **THEN YOU'LL REMEMBER ME**

WHEN SHE WALKS (Boden: Skerry & H. Ford)　RAW　　　　　　1906
Harry Ford.

WHEN THERE ISN'T A GIRL ABOUT (Castling & Collins)　FEL　　　1906
Arthur Reece, Billy Williams.

WHEN THE SUMMER COMES AGAIN (THREE POTS A SHILLING) (Bedford)
　FDH　　　　　　　　　　　　　　　　　　　　　　　　　　1895
Kate Carney, Fred Mason.

WHEN THE WAR IS OVER MOTHER DEAR (Mills & Long & B. Scott)
　STA　　　　　　　　　　　　　　　　　　　　　　　　　　1915
George Baker.

WHEN WE WERE TWO LITTLE BOYS (Madden: Morse, arr. Braden)
HHD/DAR/SHE   1903

WHEN YOU AND I WERE YOUNG, MAGGIE (Johnson: Butterfield)
FDH   1866
Christy Minstrels, Harry MacDonough, Will Oakland. Maggie was Maggie Clark
to whom George W. Johnson wrote the poem as a love tribute. Alas, she died
within a twelvemonth of their wedding.

WHEN YOU LIVE OPPOSITE TO ME (Murphy & Lipton)   FDH   1911
Daisy Dormer.

(WHEN YOU'RE) ALL DRESSED UP AND NO PLACE TO GO (Burt: Hein)
FDH   1913
Raymond Hitchcock. From *The Beauty Shop* (*Mr Manhattan*), Astor, NY.

WHEN YOU WERE SWEET SIXTEEN (Thornton)   WIT/SHE   1898
Hamilton Hill, Bonnie Thornton, Julius P. Witmark.

WHEN YOU WORE A TULIP AND I WORE A BIG RED ROSE (Mahoney: Wenrich)   FEI   1914
Dolly Connolly.

WHERE ARE THE LADS OF THE VILLAGE TONIGHT? (Weston: Darewski)
FDH   1914
Harry Cove, George Lashwood.

**WHERE DID ROBINSON CRUSOE GO WITH FRIDAY ON
SATURDAY NIGHT?** (Lewis & Joe Young: Meyer)   FEL   1916
Al Jolson, Ethel Levey. From *Robinson Crusoe, Jr.*, Winter Garden, NY. London:
int. *Follow the Crowd*, Empire.

WHERE DID YOU GET THAT HAT? (Rolmaz)   FDH   1888
J. C. Heffron, Millie Hylton, Joseph J. Sullivan. The US edition (J. Harding, New
York, 1888) credits words and music to the American comic singer Joseph J. Sullivan. Who pirated whom is unclear though the sequel (A New Hat Now!) is attributed only to Rolmaz.

WHERE DO FLIES GO IN THE WINTERTIME? (Leo & Mayo)   DAR   1919
Ernie Mayne, Jack Pleasants, Bert Weston.

WHERE MY CARAVAN HAS RESTED (Teschemacher & Cleveland: Lohr)
CHA   1909
Hubert Eisdell, Kennerley Rumford.

WHERE OH WHERE HAS MY LITTLE DOG GONE? *see* **OH WHERE, OH WHERE,** etc.

WHERE'S THE GOOD? (Boden: Brantford)   FDH   1911
Harry Ford.

WHERE THERE'S A GIRL THERE'S A BOY (Arthurs: Penso)   FDH   1919
Gina Palerme & Andrew Randall. From *The Girl for the Boy*, Duke of York's, a musical version of Paul Gavault's play *La Petite Chocolatière* (Théâtre des Alliés, Paris) of which, under the title *Tantalising Tommy*, a translation had been seen at the Playhouse in 1910.

WHERE WAS MOSES WHEN THE LIGHTS WENT OUT? (Stamford)
H&C   1878
G. H. Macdermott. Not to be confused with Vincent P. Bryan and Harry Von Tilzer's 1901 song of the same title, whose second edition shows extensive revisions to the verses and Andrew Sterling paired with Bryan as lyricist. The title is from a joke first recorded *c.*1821 in *Riddles*:
Q: Where was Moses when the light went out?
A: In the dark.

WHICH SWITCH IS THE SWITCH, MISS, FOR IPSWICH?
(David & Barnett & Darewski)   FDH   1915
Jack Norworth. From *Rosy Rapture*, Duke of York's.

WHIFFENPOOF SONG, THE (Kipling & others: Scull, adap. Galloway)
FDH   1909
Rudy Vallee, The Whiffenpoofs. Yale student song whose words (Meade Minnigerode and Guy S. Pomeroy) were a part-parody of Rudyard Kipling's 1892 'Gentlemen-Rankers' (from his *Barrack Room Ballads*); Guy H. Scull's 1893 music adapted by Tod B. Galloway. The Whiffenpoof was an imaginary fish from Victor Herbert's 1908 operetta *Little Nemo*. (*Yale Alumni Magazine* (Oct. 1950), 4.)

WHILE LONDON'S FAST ASLEEP (Dacre)   DEA   1896
Marie Tyler.

WHILE STROLLING THRU THE PARK ONE DAY (Haley: Keiser)   ROB/FDH
1880
Du Rell Twin Brothers, Tom Howard & Patsy Barrett.

WHIST! THE BOGIE MAN (Harrigan: D. Braham)   H&C   1880
Christy Minstrels, Harrigan & Hart, Mohawk Minstrels. From *The Mulligan Guards' Surprise*, Theater Comique, NY. See **HUSH! THE BOGIE!** for British version.

WHITE DOVE, THE (C. Grey: Lehár) CHA 1912
Robert Michaelis, Lawrence Tibbett. From *Zigeunerliebe*, Carltheater, Vienna 1910. London: Daly's.

WHITE WINGS (B. Winter) F&D 1870
Peter Dawson, Mohawk Minstrels, Will Oakland, Manuel Romain, Moore & Burgess Minstrels, Banks Winter (Thatcher Primrose & West Minstrels). The official song of the Young Women's Christian Association. Some say that Banks Winter did not in fact write this song but purchased it from singer Joseph Gulick for $20.

WHOA! BACK-PEDAL (W. David: Pether) FDH 1900
T. E. Dunville.

WHOA, EMMA! (Lonsdale) 1880
Fred Coyne, George Leybourne. Bessie Bellwood and Kate Carney also sang a song of this title which may have been Lonsdale's. In 1878, however, Herbert Daykin had also written a song of the same title (a current catch-phrase meaning 'be careful'); who sang which is unclear.

WHOLE HOG OR NONE, THE (Ware: Mackney, arr. H. Howard) SHE 1855
E. W. Mackney. Not to be confused with next entry.

WHOLE HOG OR NONE, THE (Sloman: Moore, adap. Westrop) SHE 1862
Charles Sloman, Marcus Wilkinson. Music from Thomas Moore's Love's Young Dream. Not to be confused with previous entry.

WHO'LL CARE FOR THE CHILDREN? (Osborne) SHE 1899
Arthur Lennard, Arthur Reece.

WHO'LL HAVE ME? (G. Hodson) DAL 1851
Miss Poole.

WHO PAID THE RENT FOR MRS RIP VAN WINKLE WHEN RIP VAN WINKLE WENT AWAY? (Bryan: F. Fisher) FEI 1914
Sam Bernard, Al Jolson, Marie Lloyd, Ella Retford, Sophie Tucker. Int. *The Belle from Bond Street*, Shubert, NY (adapted from *The Girl from Kay's*, Apollo, 1902 and Herald Square, NY, 1903) and *The Honeymoon Express*, Winter Garden, NY.

WHO PUT THE BRICKS IN BRIXTON? (Rule) WRI 1920
Syd Walker, Dorothy Ward & Shaun Glenville.

Who's Coming Up In The Gallery? (B. Scott)   SHE   1894
Katie Lawrence.

Who Threw The Overalls In Mistress Murphy's Chowder?
   (Giefer, arr. Forey)   Mullen/EBM   1898
Annie Hart.

Who Were You With Last Night? (Godfrey & Sheridan)   FEL   1912
Mark Sheridan.

Why Am I Always The Bridesmaid? (Collins & Leigh)   FDH   1917
Lily Morris.

Why Did I Leave My Little Back Room In Bloomsbury?
   (Carter & Mills)   FDH   1898
Alf Chester.

Why Did You Make Me Care? (Maguire: Solman)   WRI   1912
Manuel Romain.

Why Do The Men Run After Me? (T. W. Connor)   F&D   1912
'Dame' Dan Crawley.

Why Do They Always Pick On Me? *see* **They Always Pick On Me**

Why Do They Call Me A Gibson Girl? (Stiles: Stuart)   FDH   1906
Camille Clifford. Int. *The Belle of Mayfair*, Daly's, NY.

Wild Wild Women, The (A. Wilson & Piantadosi)   FDH   1917
Al Lewis, The Versatile Three. From *Doing our Bit*, Winter Garden, NY.

William, James And 'Enry (Crampton)   AHC   1908

Willow Pattern Plate, The (Stuart)   FDH   1896
Sisters Hawthorne.

Will You Love Me In December As You Do In May? (Walker: Ball)
   WIT/DOV   1905
Janet Allen, American Quartet, Ernest R. Ball, Norman Blair, Haydn Quartet. The
lyricist, James J. Walker, was Mayor of New York 1925–32. Janet Allen was his first
wife.

Will You Walk Into My Parlour? *see* **Spider And The Fly, The**

Wink The Other Eye *see* **Then You Wink The Other Eye**

Wire In, My Lads! (Godwin: Leigh) FDH   1906
George Bastow. An expression meaning to set to with a will, current among mid-nineteenth-century London athletes.

With Her Head Tucked Underneath Her Arm
  (Weston & Lee: Harris Weston) FDH   1934
Stanley Holloway.

With My Little Wigger Wagger In My Hand
  (Earle & Carter & Wells) HVT/FEL   1909
Fred Earle.

With This Hat On (F. J. Barnes: R. P. Weston) FDH   1911
Tom Woottwell.

Wolf, The (Shield) Preston   1820
Charles Incledon, Charles Sloman.

W.O.M.A.N. (F. W. Leigh) FDH   1902
George Lashwood.

Won't You Buy My Pretty Flowers? (A. W. French: Persley)
  SHE/PAX/FDH   1876
George Clare (Mohawk Minstrels).

Won't You Play A Simple Melody? *see* **Play A Simple Melody**

Woodman, Woodman, Spare That Tree
Irving Berlin wrote a song of this title for the *Ziegfeld Follies of 1911*; for the Henry Russell ballad see **Oh, Woodman Spare That Tree**.

Work, Boys, Work (Clifton: Root) HOW   1867
Harry Clifton, Fred French. Though not acknowledged by Clifton on the song sheet the music is G. F. Root's American Civil War song **Tramp, Tramp, Tramp, the Boys are Marching**.

Wor Nanny's A Mazer (Armstrong) var.   *c.*1880
Tommy Armstrong.

Wot Cher! (Chevalier: Ingle) REY   1891
Albert Chevalier.

Wotcher, 'Ria *see* **What Cheer 'Ria**

WOT'S THE GOOD OF HANYFINK? WHY, NUFFINK! (Chevalier: Ingle)
REY   1894
Albert Chevalier.

YANKEE DOODLE BOY, THE (Cohan)   FEL   1904
George M. Cohan, Billy Murray. From *Little Johnny Jones*, Liberty, NY. Music inspired by Yankee Doodle, anon. *c.*1740.

YARN OF THE NANCY BELL, THE (W. S. Gilbert)   John Camden Hotten 1869
Originally published in *Fun* and collected in *The 'Bab' Ballads*. Alfred Plumpton composed a piano accompaniment which, frankly, is no help at all.

YES! LET ME LIKE A SOLDIER FALL (Fitzball: W. V. Wallace)   CRA   1845
William Harrison. From *Maritana*, Drury Lane.

YES, WE HAVE NO BANANAS (Silver: I. Cohn)   WRI   1923
Eddie Cantor, Florrie Forde. Int. *Make it Snappy*, Winter Garden, NY. The chorus opens with a quote from the Hallelujah Chorus, continues with a few bars of **I DREAMT THAT I DWELT IN MARBLE HALLS**, and ends with the last line of My Bonnie Lies Over The Ocean.

YES YOU ARE (A. West)   FDH   1891
Jenny Valmore.

YIDDLE ON YOUR FIDDLE PLAY SOME RAG-TIME (Berlin)   SNY   1909
Fanny Brice, Sam Stern.

YIP-I-ADDY-I-AY (Cobb: J. H. Flynn)   CHA   1908
George Grossmith jun., Blanche Ring. From *The Merry Widow and the Devil* (burlesque of *The Merry Widow*), Weber & Fields' Music Hall, NY. London: interpolated into *Our Miss Gibbs*, Gaiety (1909).

YOU AIN'T ASHAMED OF ME, ARE YOU, BILL? (Harrington: Le Brunn)
FDH   1895
Alec Hurley, Rosie Lloyd.

YOU AIN'T HEARD NOTHING YET (Kahn & Jolson: DeSylva)   FEL   *c.*1919
Al Jolson.

YOU ASK ME WHY I LOVE YOU (C. W. Murphy)   SHE   1902
Julie Mackey.

YOU CAN DO A LOT OF THINGS AT THE SEASIDE THAT YOU CAN'T DO IN TOWN (Ridgewell & Stevens)   FDH   1911
Mark Sheridan, Vesta Victoria.

You Can't Do That There 'ere (Wallace: Rolls) MAU   1935
Jack Payne & Band, Mrs Jack Hylton (Ennis Parkes).

You Can't Do Without A Bit Of Love (A. Allen & B. Lee) FDH   1916
Kirkby & Hudson.

You Can't Get Many Pimples On A Pound Of Pickled Pork (Terry)
   FDH   1914
Ernie Mayne.

You Do Soon Change Your Mind (Boden: Brantford) RAW   1903
Harry Ford.

You'll Have To Marry Me Now (Brighton) SHE   1895
Charles Brighton.

You Made Me Love You (McCarthy: Monaco) BMC/FDH   1913
Al Jolson, Grace La Rue, Ella Retford, Florence Smithson, Beth Tate, Lee White.
Int. *Keep Smiling*, Alhambra.

You May Pet Me As Much As You Please (G. Cooper: H. Millard)
   SHE   1880

You Naughty, Naughty Men (Kennick: Bicknell) Dodsworth   1866
Nellie Cavendish, Mrs F. R. Phillips. From *The Black Crook*, Niblo's Gardens, NY.

Young Man Who Worked At The Milk Shop, The (Mills & Carter)
   FDH   1901
Marie Kendall.

Young Men Taken In And Done For (H. King: Le Brunn) FDH   1888
Dan Leno.

Your Baby 'As Gorn Dahn The Plug-'Ole (Spade) DAS/CCC   1944
Elsa Lanchester. From *Ditties from the Ditty Box*. 'Jack Spade' is a composite
pseudonym of Elton Box, Desmond Cox, and Lewis Ilda, the last-named being the
publisher Irwin Dash. It seems likely that this song is a burlesque with no authen-
tic traditional origin. It was recorded by Elsa Lanchester in 1951. The US version,
Your Baby Has Gone Down The Drainpipe, is by Morey Amsterdam: Kay Patrick
(FEI/DFH, 1946).

You're A Thing Of The Past Old Dear (Harrington: Le Brunn)
   FDH   1905
Marie Lloyd.

You're The Flower Of My Heart (Sweet Adeline) (Husch: Armstrong)
WIT/DOV 1903

George Donaldson (Symphony Quartet), Hayden Quartet, William R. Moore (Haverly's Minstrels), Peerless Quartet, Quaker City Four, Leo Stormont. Originally Down Home In Old New England, 1896.

Your King And Your Country (Rubens) CHA 1914

Alice Delysia, Maggie Teyte, Edna Thornton.

You Splash Me And I'll Splash You (Lamb: Solman) STE 1907

Alice Lloyd.

Zazel (G. W. Hunt) SHE 1878

George Leybourne. Zazel, née Rosa M. Richter (1860–1937), achieved celebrity as the first 'human cannonball'.

Zip Coon (Dixon & Farrell or perhaps George Nicholls) var. *c.*1828

Christy Minstrels, G. W. Dixon & Bob Farrell, D. D. Emmett, Joseph Sweeney. First published by J. L. Hewitt & Co. in NY 1832; in London 1836. From 1834 a.k.a. Turkey(s) in the Straw.

Artistes' Repertoires

A title against a name indicates a recognized association, not that the artiste necessarily had exclusive rights to the song or sang it first. Sometimes the writer/composer was in a strong enough position to retain the rights to a song rather than sell it outright, in which case it could be Sung by Everybody.

A song could be hijacked, as in the famous case of Marie Lloyd, who sang Nelly Power's The Boy In The Gallery without permission; it might be sold or released to another artiste—Harry Clifton, a seminal figure in the 1860s, made no great mark with his own Shabby Genteel though it later earned Victor Liston great esteem.

While not totally comprehensive—a virtually impossible undertaking—the lists in this section are widely representative of performers' outputs. Titles are included for their historical or social interest, for their popularity, or because they were a significant influence upon the singers' careers. I have been wary of discographies. Prior to the Great War, for instance, Ben Albert and Harry Champion each made well over one hundred gramophone recordings; Will Evans's and Harry Lauder's pressings numbered over two hundred, Albert Whelan's three hundred, Florrie Forde's four hundred, and in a short career Billy Williams's total was well in excess of five hundred. Often these were no more than opportunistic cover versions of songs popularized by others and were not therefore characteristic of their stage repertoires.

The repertoires of artistes who continued to flourish after 1920 only includes numbers which have become hallowed by custom and usage as honorary Music Hall songs, such as Don't Have Any More, Missus Moore (Lily Morris, 1926) and The Marrow Song—Oh, What A Beauty! (Billy Cotton, 1952).

Though they disdained to appear on the Halls, a few society entertainers whose material has survived, such as Clifford Harrison, Corney Grain, and George Grossmith sen., are listed in this section, together with some eminent opera and concert singers identifiable with those popular arias and parlour or shop ballads which reached (and are still heard on) the variety stage. Emily Soldene often sang Home! Sweet Home! at the original Empire and Harry Lauder sometimes surprised his admirers by giving them Rock'd In The Cradle Of The Deep. The Anchor's Weigh'd was sung occasionally by George Leybourne and regularly by

Bessie Bonehill, and even Dan Leno attempted Oft In The Stilly Night, though only in his early days and it must be admitted not with any great success.

Also listed are the principal Minstrel companies which courted the carriage trade by largely confining their performances to concert halls; by the beginning of the twentieth century an increasing degree of cross-over ensured that artistes and songs were becoming familiar from all genres of popular entertainment, including the heady new excitements of revue and musical comedy.

Although this volume is primarily a song guide, such worthy monologuist/ reciters as R. A. Roberts and Bransby Williams could not be ignored; similarly, comedy sketch troupes which enjoyed an immense vogue on the Halls from the 1890s onwards are represented by such eminent professors as Will Evans, George Gray, and Fred Karno. Dramatic sketches—or more properly one-act plays— performed by leading luminaries of the legitimate theatre are also listed because of their widespread popularity after the introduction of double licensing in 1911.

Speciality acts are excluded, also ballet which apart from the larger West End venues was not seen in Music Halls to any great extent until the 1920s. Nor, though they did undertake provincial tours, could the likes of Maud Allan, De Dio, Isadora Duncan, My Fancy, Loie Fuller, Florence Hewitt, La Pia, or Lady Constance Stewart Richardson be considered staple Music Hall fare. The only dancers listed therefore are Topsy Sinden (who was occasionally known to sing), Irene & Castle Vernon, whose ballroom-style dancing popularized many songs, The Tiller Girls, and those associated with the Can-Can.

Names in capital letters have their own entries. °denotes an entry in the Lyricists and Composers section. Only a selection of the titles in this section is included in the Core Song-List.

ABARBANELL, Lina 1879–1963
Every Little Movement Has A
  Meaning Of Its Own (Harbach:
  Hoscha)
Put Your Arms Around Me Honey
Toy Monkey, The

ADAMS, Annie 1843–1905; m. Harry
WALL°
Apples Or Oranges, Bills Of The Play
Are You Gazing On This Little
  Beauty?
Barber, The
Do You Want Apartments?
English Girls
Farewell, Mary Jane
Gaslight Green
Go Ahead

Goodbye, I'm Going To March Away
Hampstead Is The Place To Ruralize
He Played On The Indian Drum
He Was An Officer And A Gentleman
I Knew That I Was Dreaming (ladies'
  version)
It's Enough To Make A Girl Go Mad
Jessie The Belle At The Bar
Johnny Came A-Courting Me
Johnny The Engine Driver
Let's Enjoy Life While We Can
Look At The Clock
Man With The Indian Drum, The
Merriest Girl That's Out, The
Mona (From Barcelona)
Oh! Voulez Vous
Oh, Wouldn't You Like To Know
Once He Was A Gay Young Sailor

Pretty Carolina *or* Chow Chow
    Chopstick
Speak Up Like A Man
Susan, Susan, Pity My Confusion
Three To One—Bar One
Up In A Balloon (ladies' version)
Upon The Grand Parade
When The Band Begins To Play
Why Am I Left Single?

ADAMS, Emily
    Butcher Boy, The
    Never Say Die
    Stage-Struck Nell
    Tramway Car, The

ADAMS, J. W.°
    Aggie Astore
    Funny Little Nigger, The
    Girl With The Glossy Hair, The
    My Girl Sarah
    Thespian Hero, The

ADESON, Claire formerly Clara
Bernard; m. Martin ADESON
    Doctor Maud's First Patient (sk.) (w.
        Martin ADESON)

ADESON, Martin d. 18 Jan 1936; m.
Claire ADESON
    Doctor Maud's First Patient (sk.) (w.
        Claire ADESON)
    I Never Enjoyed Myself So Much
        Before
    Outside Eliza
    Plumbers, The (sk.) (w. Harry
        GRATTAN)
    Spoiled

ADYE, Oscar 1858–1914
    Between The Nightfall And The Light
        (sk.) (w. Lillie LANGTRY (1))

AETHIOPIAN VOCALISTS *see*
HUTCHINSON FAMILY

AGUTTER, Percy
    Good Evening, Mr Green
    I Didn't Let It Upset Me

AISTON, Arthur° d. 31 May 1919
    Shift Up A Little Bit Farther
    Vot A Game! Oi! Oi!

ALBANI, Dame Emma *c.*1847–1930
    Angels Ever Bright And Fair
    Annie Laurie
    Down In The Forest
    Home! Sweet Home!
    In A Persian Garden (w. David
        BISPHAM & Ben DAVIES & Hilda
        WILSON)
    Robin Adair
    'Tis The Last Rose Of Summer

ALBERT, Arthur° 1872–1930
    Daddy's On The Engine
    Highly Colored Tie, The
    I Want A Girl That's Lonely
    Life In The West End Of London
    Mother Of The Girl I Love, The
    That's Why I Enlisted For A Soldier
    Where One Goes, We All Go
    Will You Dance With Me, Marie?

ALBERT, Ben 1876–1925
    All I Want
    Ancient Lights
    Artful Alliterations
    Country Life
    End Of The Chapter, The
    First Time I Ever Went Burgling, The
    Ha, Ha, Ha! He, He, He!
    His Whiskers!
    Hurray For A Country Life
    I Am The Cook Who Cooks
    I Don't Mind If It Amuses You
    It's A Fat Lot
    Leave 'Em Alone And They'll Play For
        Hours
    Logic
    My Inquisitive Kiddy
    My Inventive Kiddy
    Non Stops
    Nuts And Fruit
    Oh, What An Exhibition!

On The Day King Edward Gets His
  Crown On
Pop Goes—
Puzzles
Seven Ages Of Man, The
She Ain't A Bit Like The Other Gals
So Long As I Know What You're
  Doing
Three Blind Mice
Trade Names
Tra-La-La *or* Scraps
Was That A Knock?
What Is It—Likes So Much?
What's The Good Of Sighing?
What The Suffragettes Will Bring Us
  To
Whistle And Shut Your Eyes
Why Go Abroad?
Women And Men
Work
You Thought I Was Going To Say

ALBERT, Fred* 1844–86; claimed to
sing only his own songs
  Adam And Eve
  Bradshaw's Guide
  Brave Captain Webb
  Charming Young Widow I Met In The
    Train, The
  Cheer For Plimsoll, A
  Cribbage
  Game Of Nap, A
  Give Me The Girl That Is Tender And
    True
  Grocer's Boy
  Hundred To One About That, A
  I Knew That I Was Dreaming
  Mad Butcher, The
  Man Can't Be Always At Business, A
  Mary, The Pride Of The Dairy
  Muddled Maxims
  My Wife Has Joined The Shakers
  Our Tuppenny Philosophy
  Perverted Proverbs *or* Proverbs
    Upside Down
  Playing On The Same Old String
  Prince Of Wales In India, The

Proper Sort Of Girl
Same Old Thing, The
Sentimental Songs
Take Care Of The Pence
Talk Of The Town
That's What Astonishes Me
Turkey And The Bear, The
Was That A Knock?
We Mean To Keep Our Empire In
  The East
We Will Beat Back The Russians
What Old Father Christmas Said
Wheel Of Life, The
World Turned Upside Down, The
You Can't Have Too Much Of A Jolly
  Good Thing

ALBINI, Jessie
  I'm A Flirt
  It Wasn't That
  Keep Straight On
  Mary's Canary
  My Diary
  Not There!
  Right Side Up, With Care

ALDA, Frances 1883–1952
  Somewhere A Voice Is Calling

ALDRIDGE, Arthur 1879–1929
  Let Me Return To Dreamland
  Nirvana
  Sandy Boy (Hooch Aye)
  The Trumpeter
  You Shall Not Call In Vain

ALEXANDER, Sir George 1858–1918
  Howard And Son (sk.)
  Social Success, A (sk.)

ALEXANDER & MOSE est. 1930; black-
faced cross-talk act. The first Alexander
was James CAREW and the second Albert
WHELAN. Mose was Billy BENNETT.
  B(l)ack Chat
  Black Draughts
  Cost Of *Not* Living, The
  Propaganda

ALLANDALE, Fred 1866–1921; m. Maie
ASH

Britannia's Lullaby
Busy Day, A (sk.) (w. Maie ASH)
Eyes
He'd Have To Salute
My Honey Dear
Soldier And The Girl, The (sk.) (w. ASH)
Ten Little Bridesmaids (w. ASH)
War Time

ALLEN, Beatrice

Spaniard That Blighted My Life, The (w. Billy MERSON)

ALLEN, Janet 1889–? m. James J. Walker°

Bird On Nellie's Hat, The
Will You Love Me In December (As You Do In May)?

ALLIN, Norman 1884–1973

Asleep In The Deep
Bandalero, The
Battle Eve, The (w. Hubert EISDELL)
Diver, The
Erl King, The
Excelsior! (w. EISDELL)
Father O'Flynn
Midshipmite, The
Old Brigade, The
Passing By
Rocked In The Cradle Of The Deep
Song Of The Flea, The
Wolf, The

AMERICAN QUARTET

Everything Is Peaches Down In Georgia
I Want A Girl Just Like The Girl Who Married Dear Old Dad
Rebecca Of Sunnybrook Farm
Will You Love Me In December (As You Do In May)?

AMERICAN RAGTIME OCTETTE est. Lewis F. Muir° & Albert de Courville

1912. A.k.a. The Famous Original American Ragtime Octette: Nat D. Ayer° (see AYER & BROWN), Peter Bernard° (c.1888–1960), George Britt, Harry Bloom, H. Tinner, Jack Butler, N. Coster, William Woods, and from 1913 Charles Reid (pianist) replacing Melville GIDEON. Names against song titles indicate soloists

Ghost Of A Violin (Harry Bloom)
Hitchy-Koo (Peter Bernard)
I'll Take You To The Rag-Time Dance
I Want To Be In Dixie
My Little Lovin' Sugar Babe
Oh, You Beautiful Doll
Ragging The Baby To Sleep (George Britt)
Ragtime Jockey (Peter Bernard)
That Hypnotizing Man
Waiting For The Robert E. Lee (Jack Butler & Britt)

ANDERSON, Harry 1857–1918

All The Harm I Wish You
Bit Coming In Every Week, A
Cheer, Boys, Cheer!
Cheer Up, Mother! Cheer Up Dad!
Confound His Enemies, Long May He Reign
Drink Up Boys
D. T. Fund, The
Fairy Queen, The
Fishing Club, The
Folies-Bergère, The
Glorious Beer
Good Health, Old Boy
He Talked In His Sleep
His Particular Pal
Idolizer, The
I Like My Glass Of Foaming Beer
It's Nice To Have A Home Of Your Own
I Want A Wife Not An Ornament
I Won't Desert You Captain (w. Winnie DERSON)
Join Our Goose-Club

Jolly Company *or* Boys Of The Old
    Old School
Keyhole And The Key, The
Lap! Lap!! Lap!!!
Little Band Of Redcoats That Every
    Nation Fears, The
Man! Man! You Think You're Cock Of
    The Walk
Merrie Merrie England
My New Pal *or* She's A Jolly Good
    Fellow
Oh! The Lady Guide
Oh! The Night Birds
Oh, 'Tit Bits'
One Of The Best
On The Same Old Spot Once More
Order Of Dear Old Pals, The
Our Rulers
Out! On The Hi Ti Hi!
Roaming Romeo, A
Same Old Spot, The
She Is A Different Sort Of Angel Now
She May Not Be A Lady
Sue, Sue, My Pretty Little Sue
There You Are, There You Are, There
    You Ain't
This Is A Chorus Song
Top Of The Class
Up He Went Like A Rocket
Way To Live, The
We'd A Nice Little Parlour When We
    Started
We'll Not Desert Our Captain
We're All Right
We Will Make A Night Of It
When The Prince Of Wales Is King
When The Wine Is Out
When We're Up In Town
Woman Without A Tongue, A
World Will Still Go Rolling Merrily
    On, The
You Know The Boys That I Mean

ANDERSON, Reddick 1871–1907
    Another Little Patch Of Red
    Bang Up To Date Young Lady, The

Kicking Up A Row Like That
My Old 'Oss And I
My Own Sweet Nell
Queen, The
Seven Edwards, The (scena)
Young Lady, The

ANSON, G. W. 1848–1920
    Captain Puffity Puff
    King Of The Strand, The
    Moods And Tenses (A Grammatical
        Absurd-Ditty)
    Nabuchodonosor Jones!

ANSON, Myles
    My Mary, The Hielan' Fishwife (sk.)
        (w. Decima **MOORE**)

ANTHONY, Mark*
    Don't Ask Me Where!
    Little Gold Mine, The
    Oh, I, Oh, I, Oh!
    Pick 'Em Out Where You Like

ARCHER, Alice *see* **LENA**, Lily

ARCHER, Frederick
    A. B. C.
    Great Sensation Song, The
    I'm Sister To The Cure
    Uncle Sam

ARCHER, Joe
    At The Seaside
    Before I Get Married Again
    Don't Take Me Away From The Girls!
    Hi! Johnny, Who's Your Tailor?
    Hold Me Tight A Little Longer, Joe
    House That Jack Built, The
    If There Were No Men
    I Have
    I Leave
    I'm Coming In With You
    In The Days Of Adam And Eve
    I Put My Umbrella Up
    I Saw, He Saw, They Saw
    I Shall Have To
    It Belongs To Somebody Else

It's A Mad Mad World
Join In The Chorus
Keep On Jogging Along
Kelly's Gone To Kingdom Come
Little Things And What They Lead To
McNab, McDuff, McPherson And Me
Matrimonial Bliss
Money, Mr Mooney
My Wife's Upset Me
Never Fall In Love
Oh, 'Enery
Out With My Barrow
Patsy Hennessey
Tell Your Mother You've Lost It
That's Another Little Thing Wants
   Seeing To
There's A Jack For Every Jill
Things That A Man Can't Do
This Is The Way We Do The Trick
To Help Me On My Journey Lend Me
   Half A Crown
Try, Try, Try Again
What A Conjure! What A Cop!
What Do You Think I Saw Today?
What Has Become Of Our Songs?
When Father Put His New Suit On
Where Are You Going To, Charlie?
While You're Sleeping
Yankee Doodle Mixtures
You Can Always Find A Way
You Look All Wrong Because You're
   Bandy
You're Wearing The Hat Your Father
   Wore
You Stop Where You Are

ARMSTRONG, Barney 1870–1921; a.k.a.
Bernard Armstrong
   Another Champion
   Cupid, The Cause Of It All
   Don't It Tantalize You?
   Funny Stories
   He's Gone
   If I, If I, If I, If I, If I, If I Do
   Next Time
   Parapher-Paraphernalia

This Is No Place For Me
Tooral-Oo

ARMSTRONG, Tommy° 1848–1920
   Th'Row Between Th'Caiges
   Trimdown Grange Explosion
   Wor Nanny's A Mazer

ARNOLD, Charles 1855–1905
   Private Tommy Atkins

ARNOLD, Henry C. d. 12 Nov. 1920
   Quite English, You Know
   There's Room For Some Improvement
      There
   They Don't Do That In Polite Society

ARTHUR, G. Wallis°
   After The Cinderella (parody of After
      The Ball)
   All Through A Dear Little Lady
   Always More Or Less
   Arabella
   As Long As The World Goes Round
   Calculations
   Down The Road (parody)
   Drinks
   'E's Found Out Where 'E Are
   Giddy Little Polka, The
   Good Night, Little Babe
   Hello! Little Girl, Hello!
   Home Chatter
   Life's Beautiful Dreams
   Marionette's Courtship, The
   Matrimonial Agency, The
   Millie, The Millie-ner
   Snapshots
   That's His Girl
   Tittle Tattle
   Triple Conspiracy, A
   Winkle And The Pin, The
   Zee Boxes And Mosso

ARUNDALE, Sybil 1882–1965; orig. w.
sister Grace as Sisters Arundale
   Fisher Maid Of Old St Malo, The
   Hippopotamus
   In A Waltz, Waltz, Waltz

Little Contrary Mary
My Cinnamon Tree
On A Vanguard
Tom-Tit Song, The
Tooral Looral
Ward In Chancery, A (sk.)

ASH, Maie 1888–1923; m. Fred
ALLANDALE
Blighty
Busy Day, A (sk.) (w. Fred
    ALLANDALE)
Good-Bye, Butterfly
Send Him A Cheerful Letter
Soldier And The Girl, The (sk.) (w.
    ALLANDALE)
Take Your Girlie Where The Band Is
    Playing
Ten Little Bridesmaids (w.
    ALLANDALE)
When Summer Flowers Are Blooming
    I'll Return

ASHCROFT, W. J. (Billy) Barney (?)
1845–1918
Crockery Ware, The
I Haven't Been Home This Morning
Just To Pay Our Respects To
    Maguiness
McGinty The Swell Of The Sea
MacNamara's Band
Man That Struck O'Hara, The
Norah Kearney
Quarter To Two, A
Swimming Match, The
There Goes Muldoon The Solid Man
We Had Half A Day
Wreck Of The Ragamuffin

ASHLYN, Quenton°
Bassoon, The
Just At That Critical Moment
Ladies, The
Ladies In Parliament
Marriage À La Mandoline
Quite Full
Very Embarrassing Very

ASHTON, Margaret
Don't Forget, Mignonette
Flo, You Are The Only Girl I Know
His Country, King And Girl
My Little Redbreast
Right Away My Nell, I'm Going
Summer
Winter Girl, The
You're Not The Only Rosebud In A
    Garden Fair

ASHWELL, Lena 1872–1957
Debt, The (sk.)
Man In The Stalls, The (sk.)

ASTOR, Adelaide d. 24 May 1951; sister
of Millie HYLTON, q.v. for other sisters;
cousin of Millie LINDON; m. George
GROSSMITH jun.
Dorothy Flop

ATCHISON-ELY, Edgar
All I Want Is My Black Baby Back
I Love Nobody But You
Polka Is The Dance For Me, The
Reggy The Reigning Rage
When Miss Marie Johnson Marries
    Me

ATHERTON, Alice 1846–99; m. Willie
EDOUIN
Babies On Our Block *or* Sally
    Waters
Cabin Where I Was Born, The
Eyes Of English Blue
I've Been To Gay Paree
Laughing Song (not from *Die
    Fledermaus*)
Mamie, Come Kiss Yo' Honey Boy
My Anneliza
No, No, No! I Cannot!
Sweetest Eyes

ATHOL, L. B.
Kingdom Of Home Sweet Home, The
Sausages In The Pan
That Is Home!

True As The Evergreen Our
    Friendship Shall Be
Two Little Paper Roses

ATKINS, Will
How Can I Break The News?
I Went With Him *or* My Pal Jack
Last Roll Call, The
Milly Clare
My Boy's Birthday
Silent Smithy, The

ATWILL, Lionel 1884–1946
Between The Nightfall And The Light
    (sk.) (w. Lillie LANGTRY (1))
Rivals For Rosamund (sk.)

AUSTA, Amber 1883–1910
Any Windows To Mend?
Coal (Have You Got Your Coals In For
    The Winter, Mrs Johnson?)
Come Down, Joanna Brown, Come
    Down!
Don't Tell Me Funny Stories
Good-Night, Mr Brown! I'm Out!
Oysters And Clams
Scoot!
You're Always Spring Cleaning

AUSTIN, Charles° 1877–1944
Coronation Walk, The
Discharged From The Force (sk.)
I'm Silly I Am
It's A Bright Look Out
I've Only Been Married A Week
Kind Friends
Look At Me Looking At You
My Face
Oh, The Poison
Parker Captures The K—r (sk.)
Parker On The Panel (sk.)
Parker, P. C. (sk.)
Parker's Burglary (sk.)
Parker's Progress (sk.)
Pretty Peggy
Silly Billy
Stage Struck Waifs (sk.)

AYER & BROWN fl.1910–12; Nat D.
Ayer° (1887–1952) and A. Seymour
Brown° (1885–1947). In 1912 Ayer came
to the UK w. AMERICAN RAGTIME
OCTETTE
Don't Mention My Name
Gee, I Like The Music With My Meals
If You Talk In Your Sleep
Oh, You Beautiful Doll

AYLWYN, Jean 1885–1963
He's Awfu' Guid Tae Me
Mary Marmalade

BABINGTON, Barbara
Mr Smith From Aberystwyth
That Mysterious Rag
Why Do I Ask If You Love Me?

BAGNALL, Sam° 1836–85
All Among The Clover
Beautiful Lily, Queen Of The Valley
Evening Star Is Brightly Shining, The
Flirting With Nell
Granny Dear
Magic Circle, The
Marble Arch
Midnight Ranger, The
Night After The Battle, The
On The Banks Of The Beautiful
    Severn
Poor Little Sweep
She's As Bright As The Morning Star
She's A Wink And A Smile That
    Charms Me
Starry Night For A Ramble, A *or* Kiss
    And Never Tell
Strolling Home With Rosey Posy
Wait For Me Love Through The
    Winter
Welcome Little Robin

BAKER, Belle 1895–1957; m. Maurice
Abrahams°
All Of Me
Blue Skies
Cohen Owes Me $97
Eli Eli

Lovey Joe (1910)
My Yiddishe Momme
Put It On, Take It Off, Wrap It Up
    And Take It Home
When I Leave The World Behind

BAKER, Chris at one time w. Fred
KARNO
    Copper They Copped In The Copper,
        The
    Doh, Ray, Me
    I Sent My Sister To Assist 'Er
    I Was Looking Back To See
    Noise Annoys An Oyster, A
    Rhoda Rode To Ryde
    They Can All Come To My House At
        Ryehouse
    Why Did The Fly-Fly Fly?
    Woking Waker Of Working Men, The

BAKER, Dalton 1879–?
    Beauty's Eyes
    Because
    Chorus, Gentlemen!
    Glorious Devon
    Lanagan's Logg
    Maire, My Girl
    Messmates
    Old Shield, The
    Old Superb, The
    She Is Far From The Land

BAKER, Elsie 1893–1971; a.k.a. Edna
BROWN
    Play A Simple Melody (w. Billy
        MURRAY)

BAKER, George 1885–1976; recorded
under sundry aliases incl. Walter
JEFFRIES
    Death Or Liberty
    Demon's Song
    Gipsy Song (*Gipsy Love*)
    Give A Man A Horse He Can Ride
    Hear The Bugles Calling
    Love And Wine
    Soldiers In The Park
    Three For Jack

When The Great Red Dawn Is
    Shining
When The War Is Over, Mother Dear

BALL, Ernest R.° 1878–1927
    Fighting For Liberty
    Gold, Gold, Gold
    Kathleen Aroon
    Let The Rest Of The World Go By
    Little Bit Of Heaven Fell, A
    Mother Machree
    Till The Sands Of The Desert Grow
        Cold
    When Irish Eyes Are Smiling
    Will You Love Me In December (As
        You Do In May)?

BALL, Harry° 1841–88; father of Vesta
TILLEY
    I'm Mourning For Jemima
    Katie Trips The Dell
    What In The Name Of Goodness Is
        England Coming To Today?

BANDON, Sid°
    Baby
    11th Hussars, The
    Mary And The Butcher
    Millionaire, A
    Says I To Myself Says I
    Tales Of London Life

BANKS, Walter
    Squeezed
    They're Few And Far Between
    Trysting Tree, The

BANNERMAN, Margaret 1896–1976
    I Would If I Could But I Can't So I
        Won't

BARCLAY, Lawrence° d. 16 Dec. 1949;
uncle of Vesta VICTORIA
    Bricks And Mortar
    I Keep Popping In And Having 'Em
        (Popping In And Out)
    I Suffer From The Same Complaint
    Last Of The Dandies, The (Barnes:
        Collins)

Look What She's Done For Willie
Mary's Gone Away
Mother Took Me
Oh! It's Beautiful
Oh! Ria, What Have You Done For
Me?
Oh! The Cottage By The Sea
One More River
Our 'Andy Man
Sandwich Man, The

BARCLAY & PERKINS George Barclay°
(1868–1944), m. Kate CARNEY, and
Walter Perkins (Bentley)
Katie McGinty
Mary Ann
Two Squires, The
What D'Ye Think Of Hoolihan?

BARD, Wilkie 1874–1944; m. Nellie
STRATTON
A B C D (The Singing Master)
All Becos 'E's Minding A 'Ouse
All Change For Llanfairfechan!
All Day
Allowed To Be Drunk On The
Premises
Am I In The Way?
Barmaid, The
Barman, The
Bath Chair Man, The
Beauty Parlour, The
Bootshop, The (sk.)
Bruvver Jim The Horfis Boy
Can I Come In?
Can't You Go Further Than That?
Chrysanthemums
Cleaner, The
Come To My Garden Of Parsnips
Come Up In My Balloon
Cowslip And The Cow, The
Doctor Nevill
Doorman At Frightley's, The
Do You Know Any More Funny
Stories?
Do You See The Idea? I See (w. John
HUMPHRIES)

'E Ain't The Bloke I Took Him For At
All
Hail, Smilin' Morn
Has Anyone Been Asking For Me?
Has Anyone Seen Our Cat?
He Was More Like A Friend Than A
Husband
Hurrah For The Sea!
I Can Say 'Truly Rural'
I'd Like To Go Halves In That
I Don't Want To Cause Any Trouble
I Fell Off The Bus
I Felt Quite Out Of Place
If The Shooting Suit Should Suit
If You're Doing That For Me You Can
Stop
I'm Bursting To Tell You This
I'm Glad I Went Up In The Bar
I'm Here, If I'm Wanted (The
Policeman)
I'm Not Such A Goose As I Look
I'm Waiting Here For Kate
I.O.M. (I Owe 'Em)
I Really Can't Reach That Top Note
Isn't It A Pity I've To Die?
Is There Anything Else You'd Like?
It Gets On Your Nerves Does The
Chorus
I Think I'd Better Shift This Scene
I Think I Shall Stop Here A Bit
I Think We Shall Have Some Rain
I Thought There Was Something The
Matter
It's Been A Nice Day
It Was A Sad, Sad Day For Me
It Was Beautiful
I Want An Idea For A Song
I Want To Sing In Opera
I Want You To Notice My Leggings
I Wish I'd Bought Ducks
I Wonder What He's Going To Do
Next
Leith Police, The
Let Me Sing
Limerick Mad
Little Nipper, The

Moo-Cow
Murder Bureau, The (sk.)
My Little Deitcher Girl
Never Have A Lodger For A Pal
Night Watchman, The (sk.)
Not A Single Man Said No
One And A Penny A Day
O, O, Capital O
Our Dramatic Club
Park Keeper, The
Pennyworth Of Winkles
Plumber, The
Put Me Upon An Island Where The
    Girls Are Few
Scrub Woman, The (sk.) (w. Nellie
    STRATTON)
Shall I Save You An Almanac?
She Cost Me Seven-and-Sixpence
She Sells Sea-Shells On The Seashore
Sing My Lads Yeave Ho!
Stewed Prunes And Prisms
That's Where She Sits All Day
There's A Home For You With Me,
    Love
There's An Idea For A Song
There's An Idea Gone Wrong
There's A Peculiar Thing
They're Copper-Bottoming Them,
    Mum
Tongue-Twisting Tango Tune, The
Troubles!
Truth, The
Turkish Bath Attendant, The
Turn Over Leaf
Waltz, Waltz, Waltz!
Watching The People Pop In!
What Is Your Sweetheart's Name?
What's The Matter With England?
What Will Be Will Be
What Will You Have Next?
When The Bugle Calls
When You See Me Dance The
    Minuet
Will You Sing This Glee With Me?
Wriggley Rag, The
You Are My Girl-Ski

You Do Keep Popping In And Out!
You've Got To Sing In Ragtime
You! You! You!

BARKER, George° 1812–76
Empty Cradle, The
Irish Emigrant, The
Mary Blane
White Squall, The

BARKER, Harley Granville *see*
GRANVILLE-BARKER, Harley

BARLOW, Billie 1865–1937
All In A Row
Away On The Continong
Band, The
Caprice
Chong Chong, Chow Chow
Do Buy Me That Mamma Dear
Hands Across The Sea
If I Like It
I'm Not Supposed To Know
I Want To Look As Well As You
John Bull's Put On His Thinking Cap
    At Last
Lady Barber, The
Latest Piece Of Scandal, The
Marching Girl, The
Marry Me Marjorie Moore
Mashing The Band
No English Need Apply
On My Bicy-Icy-Bicycle
Pinky Panky Ping Pang Pong
Quite English, You Know
Save A Nice One For Me
See Me Dance The Polka
Tol, Lol, Lol
Way To Sing A Song, The
You Don't Have To Marry The Girl

BARNES, Fred° 1884–1938; not to be
confused with Fred J. BARNES
Adam 'Ad 'Em
All The Girls Loved Bertie When He
    Had A Motor-Car
At The Mississippi Cabaret
Au Revoir Paree

Black Sheep Of The Family, The
Boys In Khaki, Boys In Blue
Cherry Lips
Curly Head
Do It Again
Down Home In Tennessee
Down Where Red Poppies Bloom
Down Where The Swanee River
    Flows
Drink To The Health Of Father
Girl With Paint And Powder, A
Give Me A Million Beautiful Girls
Give Me The Moonlight
Hallo! Here Comes A Jolly Sailor
Have You Seen The Wise Old Owl?
Hello Hawaii! How Are You?
He Used To Sing In His Sleep
Horsey, Keep Your Tail Up
I'll Make You Want Me
I Love The Ladies
I'm A-Goin' To Get There
I'm Forever Blowing Bubbles
I've Tried To Be Good
Lead Me To That Beautiful Band
Let's Have A Little Bit Of Sunshine
Lover's Lane
My Boating Girl (Floating With)
My Mother's Rosary
Oh, What A Pal Was Mary
On Mother Kelly's Doorstep
On Our Happy Wedding Day
On These Dark Nights
Ragtime Violin
Raise Your Hat To The Lady
Sally, The Sunshine Of Our Alley
Same Old Park, The
Samoa
Shake That Shimmy
Sheik Of Araby, The
So We All Went Walking Round
There's A Friend In Every Milestone
There's A Little Bit Of Devil In Every
    Angel (w. Jen LATONA)
They All Did The Goose-Step Home
They're All After A Girl
Thuthi! (Susie)

Till The Boys Come Home
Two Little Dirty Hands
Wedding Bells Ringing For Sammy
What's The Matter With London
    Town?
What You've Never Had You Never
    Miss
When I Met You
Where Did Robinson Crusoe Go With
    Friday On Saturday Night?
Who Is The Girl You're Going To
    Meet Tonight?
You Can't Fool Around With The
    Women
You've Got Me And I've Got You
You Were The First One

BARNES, Fred J.* d. 3 Jan. 1918; not to
be confused with Fred **BARNES**
    Four Suits Of Cards, The

BARNES, Sydney* d. 1889; sometimes
spelled Sidney
    After Dark
    Any Chairs To Mend?
    Cherry Lips
    I'll Have Your Hat
    Just Down The Lane (w. **MOHAWK**
        MINSTRELS)
    Nancy Had A Fancy For Botany
    Pet Of The Argyle, The
    Polly Pink, The Dyer's Daughter
    Pretty Barmaid, The
    Riding To Hampton With Beautiful
        Bella
    Tommy Dodd
    West End Style, The

BARR, Ida 1882–1967; orig. k.a. Maud
Laverne; m. Gus **HARRIS** (div.)
    Everybody's Doin' It Now
    I Don't Care If I Never Get Home
    Oh, You Beautiful Doll
    Stop Stop Stop
    Tramp, The *or* You're Up Today And
        Down To-Morrow
    You Used To Be A Friend To Me

BARRACLOUGH, Sydney *c.*1870–1930
Devout Lover, The
Land Of My Home
Shade Of The Palm, The

BARRETT, George 1849–94
Nonsense! Yes! By Jove! (w. J. L.
SHINE)

BARRETT, Lester° d. 14 Sept. 1924;
brother of Leslie Stuart°; from 1899 on
staff of Francis, Day & Hunter
Ada's Serenade
After All We've Done For Him
All For Me
All For The Sake Of Finnigan
Bang Goes The Bell! Ting! Ting!
Beautiful Mona
By The Sad Sea Waves (Barrett:
Thomas)
Come Along Boys
Dance With Me
Delaney's Chicken
Did I Go? *or* My Old Pal Jones
Down By The Sea
Fairy Tales
Ga-Ga-Ga-Ga-Good-Bye
Give Him My Kind Regards
He Couldn't Take The Two Of Us
Hilarity
Hooligan's Mule
How Did I Know?
I Changed My Mind
I Didn't Know Till Afterwards
I Know Where To Find 'Em
I'll Make You Up A Bottle
I'm Prepared For Her
In A Cottage By The Sea
In The Meantime
In The Summer
It's Not Cooked Yet
Kelly The Carman
Kicking Up A Row Like That
Looking For A Job
Love To All
McGinnis's 'At Home'
Milligan's Motor Car

Never To Return Again
On Sunday Night It Was Barney
McHugh
Pious Polly Payne
Sally Ran Away And Left Me
Still The Same
Take 'Em Off
That Was Enough For Me
They All Came Back
They're All At Home
They're All Fine Girls
Two Sweethearts
We Saved It For The Lodger
You Can't Think Of Everything

BARRETT, Medley° d. 1 Oct. 1937
Baden Powell's Scout
Coronation Walk, The
Half-Day Holiday Boys, The
Home-Made Motor Car, The
I Want My Little Gollywog!
Little Tommy's Christmas Pudding
My Bruvver
Navy Of The King, The
That's Why The British Loved The
King
Up Jumps The Ghost Of Sarah Porter
Why Do The British Love Their
King?

BARRETT, Patsy 1877–1915
While Strolling Thru The Park One
Day (w. Tom HOWARD)

BARRETT, T. W.° 1851–1935
As Jolly As A Sandboy
Bells Of London, (Oh!) The
Blow Me Up An Apple Tree
Could You Lend My Mother A
Saucepan?
Crackpot In The City, The
Fireman In The Amateur Brigade,
The
Gal Went 'C'st', The
Gutta-Percha Girl, The
He's Got 'Em On
I Cried Copper

I Don't Like London
I Got Across A Gee-Gee
I'll Have A Separation
I'm Not Its Father
I Took It On
It's All Up With Poor Tommy Now
It's The Queerest Thing I've Heard In All My Life
I've Been And Got Married Today
Jenny Johnson
John The Masher
Jolly As A Sandboy
Josser Huntsman, The
Marquis Of Camberwell Green, The
Nobleman's Son, A
On The Spa At Scarborough
Peg Leg Polly
That's The Way To The Zoo
Up To Dick
We Are A Merry Family
We've All Joined The Blue Riband Army
What A Fool I Must Have Been To Marry Jane

BARRINGTON, Rutland° 1852–1922
Check To The Queen! (sk.)
Moody Mariner, The
Tramp, The

BARRY, H. C.° d. 28 Jan. 1909
Alas! My Poor Brother!
De Big Black Coon
Dotty On The Ditties
Ghost Of Sherlock Holmes, The
Julie-Ooley
Junior Job-Lot Club, The
Only Way, The
Through The Telephone

BARRY, Leonard
All Doing Something For Baby
Bachelor's Club, The
Call Again
Darling Mabel
Fatal Wedding, The
Fish 'E 'Asn't Caught, The

Gay Boulogne
Girl With The Straw-Coloured Hair, The
If This Should Meet The Eye
I Shall Never Make The Missis Like My Ma
It's Just Like Money Frown Away
I've Been Down To The Races
Job Like That, A
Little Miss Nobody
Moucher, The (The Moocher's Walk)
Nice Little Room Upon The Second Floor
Oh, Be Careful, My Friends
Old Oak Tree, An
On A Sunday Afternoon
Out All Night
Pet Of The Crew, The
Rambling Up And Down
She Was A Fisherman's Daughter
She Was A Stranger In London
Soldier's Parade, The
That's My Rival
Think I'd Marry A Girl!
Tickets, Please
Two Can Live Cheaper Than One

BARRY, Lydia 1876–1932
Chances That He's Had, The
Everybody's Doin' It Now

BARRY, W. H. d. 6 Sept. 1893
Now Is The Time To Try

BARWICK, Edwin 1857–1928; orig. k.a.
E. R. Barwick; see Fred WILLIAMS
Chances That He's Had, The
Cornet Player, The
Country Cottage, A
Curate, The *or* I'm So Glad I Came
He's Altered His Opinion
Irving On The Brain (Oh! Mr Irving)
Limelight Man, The
Mary *or* She's Been A Sunday School Teacher
Two Entries
Work And Be Contented (parody)

BASKCOMB, A. W. 1880–1939; at one
time w. Fred KARNO
  'Ow I 'Ate Women

BASS, George 1888–1928
  Ca-bages, Ca-beans And Car-rots
  I've Never Wronged An Onion
  Riley's Cowshed
  Tony The Swiss Mountaineer
  When I Get My Bolshevik Blood Up

BASS, Tom° 1852–1913
  As I Walks Along My Beat
  Bill-Poster, The *or* Stick 'Em Up, Bill
  Every Little Doggy Has His Day
  Forester's Fete At The Palace, The
  If It Wasn't For The Lotion
  I'm A Member Of The County
    Council
  In The Days Of Old Lang Syne
  Last Man, The
  Model From Madame Tussaud's, A
  Mrs Pratt, The Monthly Nurse
  Nothing
  Policeman On His Beat, A
  Rich (Man And The Poor) Man's
    Storycum, The
  Stage-Struck Wife, The *or* Just Fancy
    The Missus In Tights!
  That Would Be A Novelty
  There's Bigger Fools Than Me In The
    Army!
  Vanishing Lady, The
  When Johnny Comes Marching Home
    (parody)

BASTOW, George° 1871–1914; m. Ruth
LYTTON
  And So The Poor Dog Had None
  At Work—At Play
  Captain Ginjah, O.T.
  Don't Forget Your Poor Old Farver
  Galloping Major, The
  I Didn't Know What To Do
  Jimmy Brown Essays
  Jocular Judge, The
  Jolly Jarge

Let Us Pause
Mary Ann, She's After Me
Muvver's Nursery Rhymes
My Husband Left Me Again!
Nott-Schott Duel, The
One Long Round Of Pleasure
Ragtime Yokel, The
She's A Dear Old Girl
She Said She Would
She's Proud And She's Beautiful
She Was Such A Nice Young Gal
Story Of A Tin Tack, The
Take Your Uncle Tim
That Cat
That's Their Idea Of A Lady
They Won't Know Oi Coom From The
  Coontry
Varmer Giles
When We Were Twenty-One
Who Is It? 'Man!' Said The Woman
Why Are You Waiting Here?
Wire In, My Lads! *or* The Oldest
  Inhabitant

BATES, Thorpe 1883–1958
  Admiral's Broom, The
  Bachelor Gay, A
  Because
  Deathless Army, The
  Fishermen Of England, The
  Little Grey Home In The West
  Love Is My Life (w. José COLLINS)
  Old Father Thames
  Paradise For Two, A (w. COLLINS)
  When You're In Love (w. COLLINS)

BAWN, Harry 1872–1928; m. Mae Rose
Bawn k.a. My Fancy
  Day The Nostrils Won, The
  'E Do Know Where He Is
  'E's Making A Great Mistake
  I Felt As If We'd Been Pals For Years
    And Years
  Oh! Won't The Missus Be Delighted
  Polly Ain't An Angel
  Thirst For Gold, The

BAYES, Nora* *c*.1880–1928; while m. to
Jack NORWORTH (her second husband
of five) wrote as Nora Bayes-Norworth
 Dirty Hands
 Down Where The Wurzburger Flows
 Has Anybody Here Seen Kelly?
 I'll Be With You In Apple Blossom
  Time
 In The Shade Of The Old Apple Tree
 Japanese Sandman, The
 Just Like A Gypsy
 Meet Me In St Louis, Louis
 Mother's Sitting Knitting Little
  Mittens For The Navy
 Over There
 Shine On Harvest Moon (w. Jack
  NORWORTH)
 Take Me Out To The Ball Game
 When John McCormack Sings A Song
 When Miss Patricia Salome Did Her
  Funny Little Oo La Palome

BEAUCHAMP, George* 1863–1901; m.
Nellie LINGARD
 All On The Fidgety Fudge
 All On The Nod
 Among My Knick-Knacks
 Born Unlucky
 Clever, Ain't You?
 'E'd Come A Long Way To Oblige
 Faces
 Five O'Clock Tea
 Git Your 'Air Cut!
 Goose And The Golden Eggs, The
 Go 'Way Widdi Widdiway
 Has Anybody Seen Our Cat?
 Having A 'Liker'
 He's Got To Keep A-Movin'
 House That Colonel North Built, The
  (parody)
 How De-Do-De?
 I Can't Change It
 If I Hadn't Ha' Been So Shy
 I'll Give Him Ta-Ra-Ra Boom-De-Ay
 I'm Not Particular
 I'm One Of The Jays

 I'm The Little Bit O' Sweet Stuff
 In Our Backyard Last Night
 It's All Over
 It Wasn't Mine
 I've Been Trying
 Johnny Is A Good Boy—Now *or* The
  Four Johnnies
 Josser Fighting Man, The
 Just Before The Battle, Mother
  (parody)
 Leicester Square
 Let's Be Jubilant!
 Men
 Monte Carlo Boys, The
 Naval Exhibition!, The
 Now We Shan't Be Long
 Oh! Billy Cumming, Can It Really Be
  The Truth?
 One Of The Family
 One Of The Jays
 On The Green (parody of The Wearin'
  Of The Green)
 Our Side
 Phew! Dem Golden Kippers (parody)
 Puss! Puss! Puss!
 Rolling Stone, The *or* She Was
  Gathering The Moss
 Send 'Em Up
 She's The Boss, I'm The Slavey
 She Was A Respectable Lady
 She Was One Of The Early Birds And
  I Was One Of The—
 Soap!
 Svengali!
 That Is My One
 That's The Time To Catch 'Em
 Then We Parted
 They're All Getting It Up For Me
 They're Coming On Again
 Trade Marks
 Trying It On
 Up The Road (parody of Down The
  Road)
 We Did Have A Lively Time
 We've Been Touching 'Em Up A Bit
 What Ho! There's Hair!

When Johnny Comes Marching Home
  (parody)
Where Has He Mizzled To Now?
  (parody of The Mistletoe Bough)
Yew-Ra-Li-Arty

BEAUDET, Louise 1861–1947
Chic
De Little Coon Outside
I Could Give Him Away But I Won't
I'm A Gay Soubrette
London By The Sea
M'Sieu Le Millionaire!

BEAUFOI, Percy
Laundryman, The
Please Will You Hold The Baby, Sir?

BECK, Clara b. 1860?
Biddy, My Irish Widdy!
I'll Make A Man Of You
You Taught Me How To Love You

BEDFORD, Harry° 1873–1939
All The Girls'll Follow You
Always On The Dream
Broken-Down Sportsman, The
Brown Broke And Breezy
Cooking The Cock Of The North
Crossed In Love Was Chrissie
Fancy You've Got All You Fancy
Flop 'Em Out
Germans Are Coming, So They Say,
  The
Good Old Moore
Half-Day Holiday Boys, The
How Are The People At Home? *or* I
  Believe In Owing It
I Believe You My Boy
I Like Your Town
I've Been Digging For The Gold
I Was Getting My Monkey Up!
I Will Have A Flower In My Coat
I Wouldn't Grumble Any More
Little Bit Off The Top, A
Little Bit Of Sugar On The Top, A
Live A Day At A Time

My Artificial Rose
My Midnight Watch
Oh, Blériot!
Oh, My! What Can The Matter Be?
Old-Age Pension, The
One Of The Shabby Genteel
On The March
Plenty Of Water
Quacks And Cheap Jacks
Ri-To-Looral-Looral-Laddy Oh!
Salome (The Sheep's-Head And The
  Tin Tack)
Second-Hand Aristocrat, The
Stammering Sam
Stopping Up All The Holes
Tale Of The Old Iron Pot, The
That Cat
They're The Sort Of Girls That I
  Like
Village Wedding, The
Walk Round Eliza!
We Always Have Our Little Bit At
  Home
When I Breathe
When I Get Some Money, When—
  W—W—W
Where Do You Think I Found Her?
Who Got 'Em?
Yer Comes The Foreigner

BEDFORD, Paul (John) 1792–1871
Nix My Dolly Pals (w. Mrs **KELLEY**)
Paul-y-Toole-y-Technic, The (w. J. L.
  TOOLE)

BELFORT, May 1872–1929
Foreign Land, The
Lazy Maisy Daisy
Sucker And The Shark, The
Tickle Me

BELFRY SISTERS May and **VENIE**
Sisters Gelatine

BELFRY, Venie *c.*1876–1910
College Boys, The
Daisy (On The Great Big Wheel)

If Only I Knew The Way
Love By Wire

BELL, Frank° *c*.1830–82
Coffee Shop At Pimlico, The
Sewing Machine, The

BELL, May A.
Bird In A Gilded Cage, A
I'm Afraid To Come Home In The
Dark
My Lady Hottentot

BELLA & BIJOU fl.1880s–1911; Bijou
was Peter Cannon (1873–1914), his first
partner being Bella Fothergill, sister of
his wife Florence (1871–1911); from
1905 'Bella' was Florence herself. See
FOTHERGILL FAMILY
Betting Man, The
Britannia And The Jap
Broken Vows
Earl And The Serio, The
Lawyer And Client, The
Mother

BELLEW, Kyrle 1885/7–1948; Violet
Marian Bellew (not actor H. Kyrle
Bellew (1855–1911)); m. Arthur
BOURCHIER
Sacrament Of Judas, The (sk.)
(w. Arthur BOURCHIER)

BELLWOOD, Bessie° 1857–96
Alphonso The Fancy Man
Aubrey Plantagenet (The Penny
Novelette)
Bravo! Bravo! Bravo! Mary Ann!
Buck Up, Me Boys
Cabman, The
Come To The Cookshop, Come My
Bride
Come Under My Parasol
Detectivess, The
Duchess Of Petticoat Lane, The
Folly
Good Old Boss, He's All Right
Has Anyone Seen My Mary Ann?

Hero Of A Penny Novelette
He's Going To Marry Mary Ann
Hi Diddle Diddle Um
If You Love The Girl
I'm A Lady Who Has Seen Better
Days
It's All Right
It's Bound To Come To Her
My Day Out
Organ Grinding Girl, The
Pro's Coachman, The
Rosey Posey
She Sits Among The Cabbages And
Peas
What Cheer, Ria!
Whoa, Emma! (H. Daykin?)

BENNETT, Billy 1887–1942; specialist
in comic monologues and burlesque
parodic recitations. Most of his
material written by himself and T. W.
Connor°
Black And White Cargo
Bookmaker's Daughter, The
Bugle Calls (Rat-A-Tat Plonk! Plonk!),
The
Call Of The Yukon, The
Cecil The Copper
Christmas Day In The Cookhouse
Cucumber's Race!
Dampmoor Express, The
Do As You'd Be Done By
Doctor Goosegrease
Don't Send My Boy To Prison
Father Come Home
Fire At The North Pole, The
Foreign Legion, The
Gambler, The
Green Tie On The Little Yellow Dog,
The
Infernal Triangle, The
League Of Nations, The
Lights Of London, The
Limehouse Liz
Me And A Spade
Miser, The

My Mother Doesn't Know I'm On The
   Stage
Napoleon
Nell
Ogul Mogul
One Of The Rank And Vile
One Over The Eight
Only Girl I Ever Loved, The
Poor Hard-Working Man (By
   Himself), The
Postman, The
Prodigal Son, The *or* The Morning
   After
Road To Mandalay, The (parody)
Sailor, The
Sailor Comes Home—With The
   Washing, The
Sailor's Farewell To His Horse, A
Scotch Express From Ireland, The
Sergeant's Overcoat, The *or* The
   P'liceman That Nearly Got Caught
Shamus O'Brien—Oy! Oy!
She's Mine
She Was Happier When She Was Poor
She Was Poor But She Was Honest
   (song)
Shooting Of Dan McGrew, The
   (parody)
Sobstuff Sister
Soldier's Soliloquy, A
Street Of A Thousand Lanterns, The
Tale Of The Rockies, A
Tight Brigade, The
Tightest Man I Know, The
Travellers, The ('Twas A Dark And
   Stormy Night)
Trumpeter, The (parody)
Wedding That Wasn't, The

BENNETT, T. C. Sterndale° 1882–1944;
grandson of Sir William Sterndale
Bennett°
   Come To Town, Miss Brown
   I'm Courtin' Sairey Green
   In My Museum
   My Bungalow In Bond Street

My Word! Jones Of The Lancers
On The Banks Of The Serpentine
Sammy, The Dashing Dragoon
Sophy
Swankers By The Sea (sk.)
   (w. Courtice & Louie POUNDS)

BENSON, Sir Frank 1858–1939
   Shakespeare's War Cry (compilation of
   speeches)

BENSON, Jennie 1852/62–?; of King &
Benson
   If You Want To Be Popular, Girls
   In Cherry Blossom Land
   Lonely Soul, A
   Smoke Clouds
   Take Advice From One Who Knows
   That Dancing Melody

BENSON, Maggie *c.*1890–?; daughter-
in-law of Kate CARNEY
   Terry, My Blue-Eyed Irish Boy

BENTLEY, Irene 1870–1940
   Pansy Faces

BENTLEY, Will b. 1873
   Because It's The Fashion To Do So
   Can't You See I'm Thinking?
   Don't Refuse Her
   Don't You Think He's Mad?
   Down Where The Breezes Blow
   I Altered My Mind
   I Felt A Little Awkward
   If I Had Only Slept Another
      Wink/Minute
   My Matrimonial Magazine
   My Wife's Cake
   Our Wedding
   Summer Holidays
   There's Nothing So Bad But It Might
      Have Been Worse
   They Can't Get The Better Of Me
   They Do Things So Different Abroad
   This Isn't A Song With A Chorus
   What Would A Gentleman Do?
   Would You Mind Doing That Again?

BERESFORD, Kitty
Ordered South
Won't You Teach Me? (w. Ethel
HAYDON)

BERGMAN, Henry
Always (w. Gladys CLARK)

BERMOND, Beatrice fl. 1860s–?;
possibly a.k.a. Bessie BERMOND
Beneath The Mistletoe
Man That Played The Harp, The
Naughty Men
Strolling Through The Barley With
Harry

BERMOND, Bessie 1840–late 1920s?; see
previous entry
Dumb Wife, The
He Kissed Me Once
Old Brown's Daughter
Only A Penny

BERNARD, Charles W.
Just Before The Battle Mother
(w. MOORE & BURGESS)
Rock'd Upon The Billow
Sir Marmaduke
Sweethearts And Wives
Tom Bowling (w. MOORE & BURGESS)
When I Beheld The Anchor Weighed
Yes, We Must Part!

BERNARD, Peter c.1888–1960
Issy! Issy! Is He Getting Busy?
Waiting For The Robert E. Lee

BERNHARDT, Sarah 1844–1923; all
sketches or excerpts from classic dramas
Aiglon, L'
Cathédrales, Les (solo recitation)
Dame Aux Camélias, La
Du Théâtre Au Champ D'Honneur
Elizabeth, Reine D'Angleterre
Fédora
Hamlet
Lucrèce Borgia
Phèdre

Samaritane, La
Soldier Of France, A
Tosca, La

BERRY, W. H. 1870–1951; m. Kitty
Hanson (c.1871–1947)
Ballymoney Conversazione, The
Bassoon, The
Gentlemen's Gentleman, The
In The Springtime
It Isn't My Fault (w. Marie BLANCHE)
It's A Kind Of A Sort Of A Feeling
Our Beano
Our Farm
Soap Soap Soap
Souvenirs

BEULAH, Jacob° d. 1873; sometimes
spelled Beuler
Lord High Admiral King And The
Sailor, The

BIGNELL, Charles° 1866–1935
After The Squall
Are We Downhearted? No! (David:
Wright)
Baby's Name Is Kitchener, The
Because I Happened To Be There
Billy Robinson's Gone
Bravo, CIVs!
Break It Gently
Chicago Exhibition, The
Cock O' The Walk
Come Along 'Liza
Coronation Day
Death Of The Bogie Man, The
Different Kinds Of Girls
Don't You Feel Peculiar?
Dotty-Otty
Drink! Drink!! Drink!!!
Empty Chair, The
For A Thousand Years You've Served
Us *or* Old John Bull & Co
For Me
I Couldn't Get In!
I Don't Suppose You Have
I Got Married This Morning

I Know You Know—And I Know
I'll Give Him Dolly Daydream
In The Rand
I Persuaded Him
I Remembered! So Never Never
     More
I've Done It
I've Got A Lot Of Them At Home
I've Had Some, Thanks!
Johnson's Evening Party
Keep Your Eye On 'Em
Khaki Pantomime, The
Lady And The Gent And The Other
     One, The
Looking After
Lor' Me
Minstrel Boy, The (parody)
More Work For The Undertaker
Now What Will Become Of Old
     Ireland? or Charlie Parlie
Ology, Ossity, Oddity
Right In The Middle Of The Road
Settled!
Shall I Ever?
Superstitious Wife, The
Susie Sighed For Cider
Ta-Ra-Ra Boom (parody)
That Concluded His Little
     Entertainment
That's Impossible
That's Mine When You've Done With
     It
That's When You Feel All Wrong
That's Where You Feel It The Most
There'll Be No Beano There
There's Only One Thing Stops Me
They're All Beautiful
Things Were Very Very Lively
Toodle-Loodle-Lay
Too Long A Lingering!
Too, Too, Too, Too Strong
To The Right And Left Of Yer
Twinkle Twinkle Little Star
Up To Date
We All Went Home In A Cab

We Shall Be Angels In The Sweet
     Bye-And-Bye
What-Ho! She Bumps! (Castling &
     Mills)
What Makes You Turn Your Nose Up,
     Sally?
What Will The Poor Little Girls Do
     Then?
When The Winkle Man Goes By
     (parody of Then You Wink The
     Other Eye)
When, Where, Why And How

BILLINGS, Bud & Joe
I'm Alone Because I Love You

BILTON, Belle 1868–1906; a.k.a. Vis-
countess (or Lady) Dunlo; see BILTON
SISTERS
Fresh, Fresh As The Morning (also w.
     Flo BILTON)
They're After Me

BILTON SISTERS fl. 1881–8; BELLE
and her sister Florence, Mrs Seymour
(c.1871–?), who went solo from 1888
Are You Aware He's Moved?
Fresh, Fresh As The Morning (also
     sung solo by Belle BILTON)
Meet Me Tonight
Oh Dear! Oh Dear!! Oh Dear!!!

BINT, Will* 1851–1913; a.k.a. Billie
Beau Bint; m. (1) Kate of LEAMAR
SISTERS (dec'd); (2) unknown; (3)
Fanny Robins
Always Smile
Brown—Upside Down
Don't They Love Us!
He Hasn't A Feather To Fly With
I Bought Her A Sealskin Jacket
I'll Tell Your Mother What You've
     Done
I Tell Them My Father's A Marquis
I Will If You Will
Let It Go
My Father Was Never A Marquis

Not There, Not There, My Child
So Was Mine
There's Another Jolly Row Downstairs
Turn It Up, Tiddly Um
Wake 'Em Up!
Where Are Those Boys?
Where Are Those Girls?
Whistling Song, The

BIRCH, Harry
Riding On A Load Of Hay

BIRCHMORE, Tom
Great Cake Walk, The (w. MOORE & BURGESS)
His Sweet Capacious Smile (w. MOORE & BURGESS)
We All On De Road (w. MOHAWKS)
Why Did Yer Slope Wid De Yaller Man, Susie? (w. MOORE & BURGESS)

BISPHAM, David S. 1857–1921
Drink To Me Only With Thine Eyes
Hanging Of Danny Deever, The
In A Persian Garden (w. Emma ALBANI & Ben DAVIES & Hilda WILSON)
Kathleen Mavourneen
O That We Two Were Maying (Gounoud)
Perfect Day, A

BLACK, Broughton° d. 1905
Irish Courtship

BLAIR, Norman
Break The News To Mother
Old Father Thames
Sunshine Of Your Smile, The
Will You Love Me In December (As You Do In May)?

BLAKE, Harry b. 1866
Hiawatha
Man From The Moon, The
Peer, The

BLAKEMORE, Nora
I Want To Take A Young Man In And Do For Him

BLANCHARD, John 1831–74
Alonzo The Brave
Belle Of Belgrave Square, The
Dance Of Tullochgorum
Little Fat Grey Man, The
Lo, The Factotum
Matilda Toots
Miss Dorothy Lean
Nose Out Of Joint, The
Rose Of Castile

BLANCHE, Ada 1862–1953; daughter of Sam Adams (1837–93), Music Hall manager
Bowery, The
Diamond King, The
Gentlemen From London, The
Honey, Love Me Do
I Take After My Papa
I Work A Telephone
My Best Girl
Soldier Boy's Motto, A

BLANCHE, Marie b. 1893
Coal-Black Mammy (w. Ivy ST HELIER)
It Isn't My Fault (w. W. H. BERRY)
Little Bit Of Coaxing, A
When I Leave The World Behind

BLAND, James A.° c.1850–1911
Carry Me Back To Old Virginny
In The Evening By The Moonlight
Oh, Dem Golden Slippers

BLAND, Louis
Be Mine *or* Won't You Be My Sweetheart?
Dolly's Lullaby
Old Farm House, The

BLAND(E), Edith 1858–1923; m. Austin Brereton (1862–1922)

Princess And The Recruit, The (w.
   Fannie LESLIE)
Why Wasn't I Born A Boy?

BLANEY, Norah° 1894–1984
   It Ain't Gonna Rain No Mo' (w. Gwen
      FARRAR)
   Mister Bear
   Oh! Mr Porter
   Our Little Garden Subbub (w.
      FARRAR)
   Percy's Posh Plus-Fours Are Priceless
      (w. FARRAR)
   Ukulele Lady (w. FARRAR)

BLEWITT, Jonathan° 1782–1853;
sometimes spelled Blewett; wrote all his
own songs
   Adieu, My Moustache
   (Little) Merry Grey Fat Man, The
   Mary's Ghost
   Merry Little Woman, The
   Monkey And The Nuts, The
   Perfect Cure, The
   Tho' Fifty I Am Still A Beau
   Useful Young Man, The

BLISS, Louise
   Art Is Calling For Me (I Want To Be A
      Prima Donna) (Smith: Herbert)

BLUNT, Arthur C. *see* CECIL, Arthur

BLYTHE, Marie
   Another Little Girl In Your Eye
   Can't You Find A Sweetheart Of Your
      Own?
   Don't Put Your Umbrella Up Before It
      Starts To Rain
   My Sweet Italian Maid
   Nell Of Old Drury
   Same Girl On Sunday, The

BLYTHE, Vernon *see* CASTLE, Vernon

BLYTHE, Coralie 1880/1–1928; m.
Lawrence GROSSMITH; sister of Vernon
CASTLE
   If I Were A Girl Instead

Ping Pong (w. Louis BRADFIELD)
Tup-ny Show, The

BOBS, THE TWO° Bob Adams
(1874–1948) and Bob Alden (1882–1932)
   Aba Daba Honeymoon
   Alexander's Ragtime Band
   At The Fox-Trot Ball, That's All
   Barber's Ball, The
   Belle Of The Barber's Ball
   Big Brown Boo-Hoo Eyes
   Casey Jones
   Dicky Bird!
   Dooley's Farm
   Four-And-Nine
   Ginty's Gramophone
   Goodbye, London Town
   He's A Rag Picker
   If You Want To Please Suzannah
   I'm On My Way To Dublin Town
   Indianapolis
   In My Harem
   I'se A-Looking For A Job (For My
      Poor Dear Wife)
   I Want To Catch The Two To Two To
      Tooting
   Muldoon's Big Bassoon
   My Cosy Little Bungalow
   My Girl From Boston Town
   Oh! Darling, Do Say Yes!
   Old Man Brown
   On The Five Fifteen
   Our Village
   Paddy McGinty's Goat
   Pennsylvani-ah
   Ring Out Those Bells
   She Wants To Marry Me
   That Ragtime, Dinner-Time Band
   That Syncopated Music-Teacher Man
   There's A Girl In Havana
   Trail Of The Lonesome Pine, The
   Waiting For The Robert E. Lee
   We Go Like This—We Go Like That
   When Paderewski Plays

BOGANNYS, THE fl. 1900–43; a.k.a. JOE
BOGANNY'S COMEDIANS; est. Joe

(Clifton) Boganny (1873–1943) and his brothers; formerly The Three Brothers Clifton. Troupe later included Joe's son Sam Linfield (b. 1898), Bob Cook (b. 1905), Bertram (Wimpey) Miles (b. 1915), Etty (d. 31 Oct. 1948), and Christopher Sheen (b. 1908)
> Five Minutes In China Town (The Opium Fiends)
> Lunatic Bakers, The *or* Fun In A Bakehouse

BOHEE, BROTHERS George B. Bohee (b. 1857) and James Douglas Bohee (1844–97), performers with HAVERLY'S MINSTRELS and from 1880 proprietors of their own troupe.
> Boy's Best Friend Is His Mother, A (George Bohee solo)
> Good-Bye, Honey, I Am Gone

BOISSETS, THE fl. 1870s–1900s; orig. Jean Boisset and his wife in the 1860s. The celebrated family mime (sketch) troupe (known in 1873 as The Comets) incl. their sons Fred (1863–95) and Hugo. Later personnel incl. Alfred (1870–1943), Frank, Willie (d. 1899?) who m. Ida RENÉ. Non-family Boissets incl. Welch(?) (1867–1901), Bert Olrac, Lou Romali (d. 20 Nov. 1918)
> Adventure In The Wild West, An
> Bricklayers, The
> Dock Strike, The
> Evening Party, The
> Melomania
> Trip To The Continent, A
> Up The River

BOND, Jessie 1853–1942
> Deep, Deep Sea, The
> Mechanical Sailor, The
> She Wore A Wreath Of Roses

BONEHILL, Bessie 1855–1902; m. Lew Abrahams, manager of Queen's Poplar
> Anchor's Weigh'd, The
> British Tar, The

Buttercups And Daisies
Chink Chink Chink
Cutting Part Of The Play, The
Dermott's Dream
Gallant Blue Jackets Of England, The
Girls Of Today, The
God Save Our King
Good Old-Fashioned Days, The
Here Stands A Post (Waiting For The Signal)
He's A Jolly Good Fellow *or* When You're Up In The World
In The Days Of Gay King Charlie
It Suited Her Just As Well!
Katie Brown
Ladies I've Been Told, The
Life Of A Jolly Sailor, The
Money
Night Owls
Playmates Of Mine
Scapegrace Brother Jack
Shoulder To Shoulder
So Much The Better For You
Sweet Nell Of Old Drury
That's The Cutting Part
That's When You Learn To Love Them More And More
Two Hundred Years Ago
Waiting For The Signal (Here Stands A Post)
What A Popular Man You Are
When You're Up In The World *or* He's A Jolly Good Fellow
Where Should We Be Without Her?
Women Of Tomorrow, The

BONITA b. 1885/6; a.k.a. Pauline Hall; m. Lew HEARN (div.)
> Hitchy-Koo (w. Lew HEARN)
> My Lady Hottentot
> Row, Row, Row
> Snookey-Ookums (w. HEARN)
> You're My Baby (w. HEARN)

BOOTE, Rosie 1878–1958
> Maisie (Is A Daisy)

BORDONI, Irene 1893–1953; m. (1)
Edgar Becman (d. 20 Apr. 1919); (2) E.
Ray Goetz° (div.)
  Do It Again
  If You Could Care For Me
  I Won't Say I Will But I Won't Say I
    Won't
  So This Is Love

BORI, Lucrezia 1887–1960
  Bacio, Il (Arditi)
  Ciribiribin
  Danza, La (Tarantella) (Rossini)
  I Hear You Calling Me
  Little Damozel, The
  Paloma, La

BOSTOCK, N. C. 1850–1916
  We Were Lads Together (w. J. W.
    HALL)

BOURCHIER, Arthur 1863–1927; m. (1)
Violet VANBURGH (div.); (2) Kyrle (Violet
Marion) BELLEW
  sketches:
  Arm Of The Law, The
  Divorce While You Wait (w. Violet
    VANBRUGH)
  Doctor Johnson
  Eleventh Hour, The (w. VANBRUGH)
  Find The Woman (w. VANBRUGH)
  Knife, The (w. VANBRUGH)
  Man In The Case, A (w. VANBRUGH)
  Marriage Has Been Arranged, A (w.
    VANBRUGH)
  Pair Of Knickerbockers, A
  Pearls (w. VANBRUGH)
  Prayer Of The Sword, The
  Sacrament Of Judas, The (w. Kyrle
    BELLEW)
  Woman And The Law, The ('serial-
    play', each act being performed on
    successive weeks; w. VANBRUGH)

BOWLER, Chris
  Down In The Valley
  Gold Gold
  If I Had The Power

BOYCE, Frank 1863–1919
  Don't Go Down In The Mine, Dad
  In Your Gown Of Grenadine (You're
    My Best Girl)

BOYDE, Edwin 1870–1909; son of J. W.
ROWLEY
  Football Referee Song
  Going To The Derby In A Donkey
    Cart (solo and w. J. W. ROWLEY)
  Molly Riley
  Oh! The Black List
  Old Woman, The
  Still His Whiskers Grew
  Three Months' Hard
  Ting-A-Ling-A-Ling
  What Ho! There's Hair!
  Where Was Johnny When The
    Scotchman Came?
  Whoa, Alice! Where Art Thou?

BRADFIELD, W. Louis 1866–1919
  Detrimental Man, The
  Fun On A Motor
  Galloping (w. Kate CUTLER)
  I Don't Care
  I Want To Be A Military Man
  Looking For A Needle In A Haystack
  Mariah
  My First Cigar
  Phrenology
  Ping Pong (w. Coralie BLYTHE)
  Polka And The Choir Boy, The
  Poor Pierrot
  Semi-Detachment (w. CUTLER)
  She Didn't Know Enough About The
    Game
  Sort Of A—, Kind Of A—, A
  That's All

BRAHAM, Harry 1874–1923
  All Bad! Very Very Bad!
  Burnaby The Brave
  Hundreds And Thousands
  I'm A Lawyer And My Name Is Marks
  Kiss When You Can
  Lock Him Up

Nobody Knows Who Done It
Remarkable Fellah!, A
Sir Garnet Will Show Them The Way
Something Like This!
Tommy's In The Cupboard
What's The World Coming To
What With Yours And What With
  Mine

BRAHAM, John° 1772/4–1856
All's Well (w. Charles INCLEDON)
Anchor's Weigh'd, The
Bay Of Biscay, The
Death Of Nelson, The
Jolly Young Waterman, The
Love's Young Dream
Then Farewell, My Trim-Built Wherry
When Thy Bosom Heaves The Sigh
  (w. Catherine STEPHENS)

BRAHAM, Marie
Bookie Up To Date
Mamm's Only Boy
Steering To Those We Love

BRAITHWAITE, Dame Lilian
1873–1948
sketches:
Five Birds In A Cage
Odd Woman, The
Sunbeam
Tag, Der

BRANTFORD, Bert° brother of Harry
FORD
He Doesn't Mean Any Harm
I Can't Understand It
My Dinah Is My Dinner
So Am I
Testimonials
They're Always Pulling My Leg
Wait For Your Old Age Pension
Work (Poor, Proud And Particular)
You'd Better Call Round Again

BRENNIR, Albert
Out With My Gun In The Morning
Ready When Wanted

True Man Of My Word, A
When My Ship Comes Home Boys

BRENNAN, Mrs R.
Speak Out Like A Man
Winking At Me

BRETT, Harry° sometime chairman at
Metropolitan Music Hall
All Right, Thanks!
Chips Off The Old Block
Courting A Widow
Mounsey
Poor Old Uncle Jones
You Put On The Trousers

BRETT, Marie
K-K-K-Katy (w. Frank VARNEY)

BRIAN, Donald 1877–1948
Ballin' The Jack
They Didn't Believe Me (w. Julia
  SANDERSON)

BRIAN, J. F.° m. Mrs J. F. BRIAN
Dancing Mad
Drum Major, The

BRIAN, Mrs J. F. m. J. F. BRIAN
Aunt Sally
Delicate Nerves
Do, Dear
He Asked For My Hand
Hokey Pokey Chief
Hurdy Gurdy Child
Kitty Patterson
Lady Dundreary
Sarah Ridley
So Early In The Morning

BRICE, Elizabeth c.1885–1965; no rela-
tion to Fanny BRICE
Aba Daba Honeymoon (w. Charles
  KING)
Be My Little Baby Bumble Bee (w.
  KING)
Elephant Skid (w. KING)
For Me And My Gal (w. KING)

Greatest Thing I Ever Did, The (Was
    To Fall In Love With You)
Lovey Joe (1911)

BRICE, Fanny 1891–1951; no relation to
Elizabeth BRICE; 'Baby Snooks'—
numerous monologues and sketches
from 1934
    Ballin' The Jack
    Becky Is Back In The Ballet (and
        sundry other 'Becky Cohen'
        routines)
    Dance Of The Grizzly Bear, The
    Fol De Rol Dol Dol
    I Don't Know Whether To Do It Or
        Not
    If We Could Only Take Their Word
    Lovey Joe (1910)
    My Man
    Rose Of Washington Square (her
        theme song)
    Sadie Salome, Go Home (and sundry
        other 'Sadie' songs)
    Second-Hand Rose
    Song Of The Sewing Machine, The
    Waiting For The Robert E. Lee
        (solo and w. Al JOLSON)
    Yiddle On Your Fiddle Play Some
        Rag-Time

BRIGHTON, Charles* 1867–96
    Accident'ly Done
    All You Want Is A Penn'orth Of
        Paint
    I Chanced It!
    In The Morning On The Brain *or*
        Ev'rything They Did Was *In The*
        Morning
    That's The Girl Who Was Given Away
        With Half-A-Pound Of Tea
    When Enoch, He Knocked, She
        Knocked Enoch
    You'll Have To Marry Me Now

BRITTON, Hutin 1876–1965; m.
Matheson LANG
    Westward Ho!

BROADFOOTE, Marguerite d. 1915
    Boys Of London Town, The
    Comin' Through The Rye
    Could I But Shape The Children's
        Dreams
    It's A Grand Old World We Live In
    I Wonder What We'd Do Without Our
        Girls
    Little Starlight Sue
    Maggie Lauder
    My Daddy's A Gentleman
    Of A' The Airts
    Where The Kye Came Hame

BROCKBANK, Harrison 1867–1947; see
also KARNO, Fred
    Absent-Minded Beggar, The
    Always True To You
    Far O'er The Sea
    Gentleman Of France, A
    Here's A Health Unto His Majesty
    Joy Of My Doting Heart
    Troopship, The

BROGDEN, Gwendoline b. 1891
    Chinatown, My Chinatown
    I'll Make A Man Of You

BROOKS, George* 1867–1947
    Alice
    All You've Got To Do
    And His Day's Work Was Done
    Don't Touch Me There
    Good-Night, Nurse
    Grandfather Green
    Happy Land
    He's Got The Job
    I Am The Catch Of The Season
    It Seems To Me
    I've Turned Against It Now!
    Jack Of All Trades
    My Father's Jokes
    Runaway Mounted Foot, The
    Sage And The Onion, The
    Story Tellers' Club, The
    Testimonials
    That's Another Funny Thing He Had
        To Tell

That's What They Told To Me
There's Another One Out Of Work
Turn On The Water! *or* Fireman's
  Tales
When Father's Done With 'Em
Would You Mind Passing The Salt?
Yarns *or* The Captain Told The Mate
You Can't Beat The Old-Time Girl

BROUGH, Lionel 1837–1909; a.k.a. Lal
Brough
  Awful Little Scrub, An
  Deutscher, The
  Muddle-Puddle Porter, The
  Oh! Ain't It Pe-Cu-Li-Ar?
  Put It In The Bag
  Sapper Brigade, The
  Ye Baron Of Ye Rhine

BROUGH, Robert 1857–1907
  Never Mind!
  Nonsense! Yes! By Jove! (w. Harry
    NICHOLLS)

BROWN, Edna recording alias of Elsie
BAKER
  Mysterious Moon
  Trail Of The Lonesome Pine, The
    (w. James HARRISON)

BROWN, NEWLAND, & LE CLERQ orig.
BROWN, NEWLAND, & WALLACE;
sketch comics; Ben Brown (1848–1926),
James Newland (1843–1931), and
George Le Clerq (1848–1911) whose
sons were k.a. Gus McNaughton of
THE MCNAUGHTONS and Arthur Le
Clerq°
  Black Justice
  Coffee Can Brothers, The
  Dark Night Before Us, A (BROWN &
    LE CLERQ only)
  Go As You Please
  He Would Be An Actor
  House Of Commons, The
  Killing Indians
  Thompson's Dead

BROWN, NEWLAND, & WALLACE
Charles Wallace (1849–1903); see also
BROWN, NEWLAND, & LE CLERQ
  Slocum's Dog (sk.)

BRUCE, Ernest
  Eccentricity
  Smile Your Sweetest Smile Again *or*
    Don't Be Angry With Me Darling
    (w. CHRISTY MINSTRELS)
  Spelling Bee, The

BRUNE, Adrienne 1892/7–?
  They Didn't Believe Me (w. George
    GROSSMITH jun.)

BRUTON, James° 1806/12–67
  Boy Wot Visits The Palace, The
  General Tom Thumb
  Railway Mania
  Singing For The Million

BRUTON, John chairman at the Coal
Hole Song & Supper Rooms
  Cattle Show, The

BRYAN, Mrs *see* BRIAN, Mrs

BRYANT'S MINSTRELS fl. 1856–70s; est.
Dan (1833–75), Jerry (1838–61) and
Neil Bryant (1835–1902). From 1858 to
1866 the troupe included Daniel D.
EMMETT
  Black Brigade
  Dixie's Land *see* I Wish I Was In Dixie
  Down In Alabam' (Ain't I Glad I Got
    Out De Wilderness)
  Finnegan's Wake
  How Are You, Greenbacks?
  I Ain't Got Time To Tarry *or* The Land
    Of Freedom
  I Wish I Was In Dixie (w. Daniel D.
    EMMETT)
  Jonny Roach
  Lannigan's Ball
  Little Dan
  Wide Awake *or* Dar's A Donkey in De
    Tent

BUCKLAND, George 1820–84
Blighted Hopes
Do You Think It Fair?
Good Little Boy, The
Hannah Sophia McWhopper
Little Mr Binks
Maniac, The
My Memory Is So Bad
My Old Wife Is A Good Old Cratur
Naughty Little Boy, The
Tittle Tattle

BUCKLEY, Fred *see* BUCKLEY'S
SERENADERS
Somebody's Courting Somebody

BUCKLEY, George *see* BUCKLEY'S
SERENADERS

**BUCKLEY'S (NEW ORLEANS) SERE-
NADERS** formerly The Congo Melodists;
est. 1843 by James Buckley (1803–72)
and his sons Frederick* (1833–64),
R. Bishop (1826–67), and George Swaine
Buckley (1829–79). Disbanded during
Civil War. Names in brackets are soloists
Bring Thy Shattering Heart To Me
Dere's Someone In De House Wid
Dinah
Father James
Heigho! Heigho!
Hen Convention
I'd Choose To Be A Daisy (Fred
BUCKLEY)
I Wish I Was In Dixie's Land
Katy Dean
Kiss Me Quick And Go My Honey
Laughing Song, The (George
BUCKLEY)
Old Bob Ridley
Once More Upon The Sea
Say A Kind Word When You Can

BUDD, John
Boys In Blue
By The Light Of Your Eyes
Meet Me In Daffodil Time
Nita Carita

BULLEN, Julia d. 1891; m. George
Lewis
Colonel Crusher
Halloa! There
I'm So Fly
Oh, You Girls!
Tiddy-Fol-Lol!

BURCHELL, Kathleen
I Ain't 'Arf A Lucky Kid

BURGE, Bella 1877–1962; Mrs Dick
Burge (née Leah Belle Orchard), Marie
Lloyd's dresser-companion, a.k.a. Bella
LLOYD. Performed w. Rosie WOOD as
the SISTERS LLOYD; in 1889 k.a. Ella
LANE, a name resumed after her hus-
band's imprisonment

BURKE, Billie 1885–1970; daughter of
Billy BURKE; second wife of Florenz
Ziegfeld jun.
Absent-Minded Beggar, The
(recitation)
First Post In The Morning, The
Molly Molyneux
My Little Canoe
My Otaheitee Lady
Pine Girl, The

BURKE, Billy (W. E.) 1843–1906; father
of Billie BURKE
Brannigan's Band
Clara Nolan's Ball
Dance With The Girl With The Hole
In Her Stocking
Paddy Duffy's Cart

BURNABY, Davy* 1881–1949
Archibald Vere De Vere
Dear Old Pal Of Mine
DSO And VAD
Ogo Pogo, The

BURNAND, Lily* b. 7 Dec. 1865; m. (1)
Will (W. H. Doris) Kendall (1854–92)
(dec'd); (2) Michel Kirschen
Dear Little Nobody's Darling
Don't Blame Me

Don't Care For Rosie
Don' You Wish You Could?
Fair Lady Mine
Flour
Funicular
Goodbye, Sis
Harum Scarum Girl
Hi Ti Hi Ti
I'll Never Grow Tired Of You
In The Park
I Say, Mary, By The Way
Lady Slavey, The *see* 'Tis Hard To
    Love
Lady With A Past, A
Leg Of Mutton Sleeves
Man
Mary's Tricky Nicknacks
Mashers, The
Molly MacIntyre
My Baby May
My Lucy Loo
Now She's Got Her Picture On The
    Postcard
Out On The Ran-Dan
Pretty Polly MacIntyre
Rather!
Riding On Daddy's Shoulder
Ringing Cheer For The Kharki And
    Red
She Was A Perfect Lady
Sparkling Wine
Stowaway, The
Such A Nobby Lad
'Tis Hard To Love And Say Farewell
    or The Lady Slavey
Two Little Girls In Blue
Under The Lilac Tree
Up We'll Go
What Is The Reason Of That?
You Ain't Like You Used To Be
You, You, You!
Zanzi-Zanzibar!

BURTON, Jesse
Brave Old Commodore, The
Didn't We Fight In Days Gone By?

Mac And I
Nancy, You're My Fancy
You Might Want Him Again

BURY, Felix
Gendarmes' Duet (w. Edward
    MARSHALL)

BUTCHER, Ernest 1885–1965; m. (1)
Muriel GEORGE (div.); (2) Edna Brough;
w. Muriel George specialized in folk and
early Music Hall songs
Boots
Grinder John
I Married A Wife

BUTT, Dame Clara 1873–1936;
m. Kennerley RUMFORD
Abide With Me (by Monk and by
    Liddle)
Birthday, A
Deep River
Fairy Pipers, The
Fairy Went A-Marketing, A
For Love Of You
Harvest Moon, The
How Pansies Grow
Husheen
Kashmiri Song
Kathleen Mavourneen
Land Of Hope And Glory
Leaves And The Wind, The
Lost Chord, The
Love's Old Sweet Song
My Ain Folk
My Dear Soul
My Son
Noel
Oh Divine Redeemer
On Guard (The Sentinel's Song)
Put Your Head On My Shoulder,
    Daddy
Rosary, The
Roses By Summer Forsaken
Sea Pictures (Elgar)
Song Of Thanksgiving, A
There Is No Death

There's A Land
War Song, A
Wee Small Bird
Yonder

BUTTERWORTH, Clara
Country Night Song
Enchanted Forest, The
Flower, The (*Lilac Time*)
    (w. Courtice POUNDS)
Heigh Ho! The Sunshine
Sing, Joyous Bird
Soul Of The Spring
Were I A Moth

BYFORD, George 1852–1932
Broken-Down Masher, The (parody of
    The Masher King)
I Am Getting Naughty—I Am
Only A Ha'penny
Simple Maiden

CABELLA, Mlle
Czardas (*Die Fledermaus*)

CAHILL, Marie 1870–1933
Absinthe Frappé
Congo Love Song
Nancy Brown
Under The Bamboo Tree
When I First Began To Marry, Years
    Ago
Why Little Boy Was Blue

CAINE, Georgia 1876–1964
How'D'Ya Like To Spoon With Me?
    (w. Victor MORLEY)

CALLAGHAN, T. C. (Tom) 1852–1917
Get It Over
Me Too! Me Too! Me Too!
Only One Girl In The World For Me
    (parody)
Song Pirate's Lament, The
Years And Years Ago

CALVÉ, Emma 1858–1942
Invocation (Guy D'Hardelot)
Sans Toi

CAMERON, Violet 1863–1919; cousin of
Florence LLOYD, Violet LLOYD, and
Lydia THOMPSON
Good-Bye (Tosti)
Gretna Green
My Soul Is An Enchanted Boat
Somebody That I Like Better
Up To Date (*Faust Up To Date*)
Yea Or Nay

CAMP, Jack (J. E.) 1866–1907
All Have A Dinner With Me
Fond Words My Dear Mother Said,
    The
Hanging Mother's Picture On The
    Wall

CAMPANINI, Italo 1845–96
Flower Song (*Carmen*)

CAMPBELL, Albert
I'm Forever Blowing Bubbles
Let The Rest Of The World Go By

CAMPBELL, Herbert 1844–1944
All Blowin' All A-Growin'
All Outside
All The Latest Improvements
Anything For Peace And Quietness
At My Time O' Life
Be Prepared!
But That's The Wust O' Gals
Chin Music
Cockney In France, The
Comin' Thro' The Dye (parody)
Commemoration Day
Cowardy Cowardy Custard
Cupid's A Dodger
Dada's Baby Boy
Did You Ever Hear A Girl Say No?
Domestic Pets
Do You Think So? Yes, I Think So
    (w. Harry NICHOLLS)
England For The English (Bowyer:
    Baker)
Everybody Ought To Come To My
    Happy Land
Exhibition Lodger

Father Dear Father The Brokers Are In (parody)

Fish?

Fly And The Treacle Pot, The

Forbidden Fruit

Good Job Too! Serve Him Right, A

Good Old Joe

Greatest Show On Earth, The

Great McNoodle Went On Town, The

Growing Up Children's Games

Have You Noticed It?

He's A Very Nice Man To Know

I Can't Stand Mrs Green's Mother

I Don't Think It's Ever Been Done

I Don't Want To Fight (parody of Macdermott's War Song)

I Kissed Her Under The Parlor Stairs

I'll Never Go Home Any More

I'm Another

I'm Coming

I'm Getting A Big Boy Now

I'm Going To Make Other Arrangements

I'm In It

Im-Pe-Cu-Ni-Os-I-Ty (w. Fannie LESLIE & G. H. MACDERMOTT)

Impudent Parney (parody—words only)

I'm So Dry or The Bona Fide Traveller

In Her Own Back Yard

In My Fust 'Usband's Time

Invalid Chair, The

I Should Like To Drop Across One

It Is Not True

It Made No Difference—Not A Bit Of Difference

It's Enough To Make A Parson Swear

It's Hard At First

It's Nothing To Do With You (w. Dan LENO)

It's The Seasoning Wot Does It

I Wonder How Long It Will Last

I Wonder What Next They Will Do

I Wouldn't Lend You Much On That Job Lot, A

Josser's Cricket Club, The

Keep It Dark

Keep The Pot A-Boiling

Laugh At Your Uncle John

Little Tommy Topweight

Lot Of Wet, A

Major!, The

Mama's Darling Boy

Marry Come Up (w. NICHOLLS)

Matrimonial News, The

Milkman, The

Miner's Dream Of Home, The (parody)

Mixture As Before, The

Modern Sweeney Todd, The

Mother Will Be Pleased

My Daughter

My Inventive Pal

My Wife's Out Of Town

Naughty Johnny Morgan

Naughty! Naughty! Naughty! (Le Brunn)

Never Empty Cradle, The

New Boy, The

No Class

Nonsense! Yes! By Jove! (w. Charles GROSSE)

No Show Tonight

Not Much

Not Really (w. NICHOLLS)

Not So Much Of The Father

Now We're Busy

Now We Shan't Be Long

Now You're Married I Wish You Joy

Oh! Isn't It Awful!

Oh, What A Mug!

Oil Shop (Soap, Starch And Candles), The

Ole Clo!

On The Sly

Oompah, The

Oppotuny-Opperty, The

Patching Up The Seats Of The Mighty

P.C., The

Pew Opener, The

Pirate 'Bus, The

Pity To Waste It, A
Pop Went The Weasel
Quiet Lodgings
Run For The Doctor
Seaside Holiday At Home, The
Serve Him Right! *or* A Good Job Too
Shall I Be An Angel, Daddy?
Shout Hurrah! Shout Hurray!
    (w. LENO)
Six Months' Hard
So And So—Such And Such
    (w. LENO)
(Taking) The Whisper
That's A Woman All Over
That's My Baby
That's The Time To Go
That's The Worst Of Gals, (But)
There Never Was Such Times
    (w. NICHOLLS)
There's No Deception There
They Ain't Got No Class
They Call Me The Poor Little
    Stowaway
They Don't Make Them Like That
    Now
They're All Very Fine And Large
They Were A Lovely Pair
Things Are Very Quiet Just Now
Things That Don't Concern Me
Three Girls In A Boat
Three Small Crows
Tricks Of The Trade, The
Triplets, The
12 O'Clock M.P.
Up I Came With My Little Lot
Variety Is Charming
Wages
Wanted: A Lady Help
We'll Never Go Back No More
We're All On The Job
What A Blessing!
What Can A Man Do Now?
What Do They Do With The Old
    'Uns?
What's The Odds?
What To Sing Nowadays?

When Noah Hung Out In The Ark
When The 'Gee-Gees' Run Again
When The Tart Is Young
When You Come To Think Of It
Who Wants To Back 'Em?
Wrong 'Uns
You Can Tell Where He's Been
You'll Never Be An Angel, Daddy

CAMPBELL, Mrs Patrick 1865–1940
    Dawn Of The World (prologue to film)
    Law Of The Sands, The (sk.)
    Pro Patria (sk.)
    Sorceress, The (sk.)

CAMPOBELLO, Enrico b. 1839; pseud.
of Henry M. Martin
    In The Gloamin'
    In The Moonlight
    Song Of The Old Bell
    Stormfiend!, The

CANTOR, Eddie 1892–1964
    How'Ya Gonna Keep 'Em Down On
        The Farm?
    If You Knew Susie
    Ma, He's Making Eyes At Me
    Makin' Whoopee
    Margie
    They're All Sweeties
    Yes, Sir, That's My Baby
    Yes, We Have No Bananas

CAREW, James 1872–1938; third husband of Dame Ellen Terry GBE
(1847–1928); from 1930–1 w. Billy
BENNETT as Alexander of the black-face
cross-talk act ALEXANDER & MOSE
    all sketches:
    Case Of John Walker, The
    Moments Before
    Odd Number, The
    Westerner, The
    Zanfwills

CAREY, Pat 1856–1910; m. Lizzie
Howard (1864–1901)
    Callaghan Does It For Me
    Dublin Car Man, The

Easy To Tell He Was Irish
Hurrah For The Life Of A Sailor
Irish Are Always In Front, The
Life Of A Soldier (Tramp, Tramp,
    Tramp, The Boys Are Marching)
My Native Land So Green
Pass The Word To Calligan
Where Are All The Irishmen?
With The Help Of McCarthy And
    Magee

CARLE, Richard 1872–1941
Half-Past Two (w. Hattie WILLIAMS)

CARLOS, Frederick° d. 25 Nov. 1904
Around The Christmas Tree
Brown Up The Flue
It Goes In At One Ear And Out Of
    The Other
Yankee Boy, The

CARLTON, The Great (Arthur)
1880–1942
Hanki-Homey Showman, The (sk.)

CARLTON, Harry° d. 1961?
All The Girls Are Lovely By The
    Seaside
And His Day's Work Was Done
Goodbye, Olga
Mademoiselle From Armenteers
My Bungalow In Bond Street
Snookey-Ookums
So What's The Use
We Really Had A Most Delightful
    Evening
When Silence Can Be Heard

CARLYLE, Vi
Come Along, My Little Daisy
My Pretty Little Mountain Maid
Oh, For Shame!
Sad Good-Bye

CARNEY, Alice b. 1877; sister of Kate
CARNEY
Bermondsey Flo
Billy And I
Drink Once More

Liza Liza
My Little Birds Can Tell
Mother's Old Arm Chair
O What A Change In Sarah
There's A Nice Little Home A-Waiting

CARNEY, George 1887–1947; at one
time w. Fred KARNO
Almost Human
Any Dirty Work Today?
Fool Of The Force, The (sk.)
I Live In Leicester Square
Now She's Looking For Mademoiselle
    From Armentieres
Stage Door Keeper, The
What Was The Tale The Colonel Told
    The Adjutant?

CARNEY, Kate 1868–1950; until 1889
k.a. Kate PATTINSON (her real name);
may also have used the name Kate
Raynard. Sister of Alice CARNEY; m.
George Barclay (Shea) of BARCLAY &
PERKINS; mother-in-law of Maggie
BENSON
Absent Minded Bounder, The
Alice's 'Ouse
Are We To Part Like This, Bill?
Baked Potato Can, The
Bill's Mouth Organ
Casey, Oh Casey
Cockney Rag, The
Coster's Banquet, The
Dancing On The Streets (orig.
    Sidewalks Of New York)
Donkey Cart Built For Two, A *or*
    Sarah
Don't Forget To Call Me In The
    Morning
Down At Hampton Court
Duchess Of Drury Lane, The
From Poverty Street To Golden
    Square
Girls From Bryant's And May, The
Good Morning, Mr Postman
Has Anyone Seen My Yiddisher Boy?
He Can't Act The Gentleman

He Pushed Me On His Barra
Here's My Love To Ould Ireland
Hi Hiddley
I Am A Romany
If You Can't Do Any Good, Don't Do
  Any Harm
I Got My Money Back Because It
  Wouldn't Bump
I'll Give Him 'Strolling In The
  Garden'
I'll Look After You
I'll Sell The Flowers
I Loved You In The Sunshine
I'm A Regular (Popular?) Lady Now
I'm Coming Back, Love
It's No Use You Calling 'Hannah'!
Janey Delaney
Let's All Go Round To Alice's House
Let's All Go To The Music Hall
'Liza Johnson
Maggie Maguire!
Marriage Races, The
Martha, Martha, Why Won't You
  Name The Day?
Mother-In-Law
Mouth Organ Brigade, The
Oh, Charlotte
Oh! Kate Carney (answer to When
  The Summer Comes Again)
Oh, Please, Sea!
Oh! Sally I Loves Yer
Only A Bugler Boy
On The Brighton Promenade
Our Laundry (musical) (sk.)
Our Threepenny Hop
Our Village Home In The East
Out Where The Blue Begins
Oyster Stall, The
Picture Album, The
Polly Brown
Rachel, My Girl
Regular Lady, A
Sarah or A Donkey Cart Built For Two
Somewhere In France, Dear Mother
So Now I Can Work For You
Sweet Rosie

Ten Days' Leave
That's Good Enough For Me
That's How They Say Goodbye
Though All Your Pals May Leave
  You
Though Her Head Is Bent With Age
Tuppenny Tube, The
Up In A Music-Hall Gallery
Wait Till Bill Gets Hold Of 'Em
What's The Matter With You Single
  Men?
When The Snowflakes Gently Fall
When The Stars Are Peeping
When The Summer Comes Again
  (Three Pots A Shilling)
Where Does The Profit Come In?
Whoa, Emma! (H. Daykin?)
Why Should A Man Remain Single?
Wouldn't You Like To Know?
You Don't Want Me or The Girl You
  Cast Aside
You Must Be Doing Some Overtime
You Toast The Muffins And Crumpets

CARNEY, Tom 1859–1911
Down By The Old Village Well
Father's Phonograph
Kate O'Grady
Little Nellie Green
Masked Ball, The
Sailor Boy's Watch, The
Saying Good-Night At The Door
Welcome The Exile Home

CARR, Percy 1865–1926
Down At Shepherd's Bush
Gibraltar (w. Kitty TIMMS)
Sailor's Birthday Presents, The

CARRICK, Tom 1868–1913
Before—And After
Left Us
Long Story Short, A
My Customers

CARRINGTON, Nell 1895–1963
Smiles (Callahan: Roberts)

CARTER, Dave
Ireland, The Land Of The Shamrock
Love Me, And The World Is Mine
On The Day You Sang 'Come Back To
Erin'
Sweet Bells Of Shandon
When They Ask You What Your Name
Is
Won't You Give Me A Sprig Of
Shamrock?
You Never Know

CARUS, Emma 1879–1927
Alexander's Rag-Time Band
Bedelia
Bird In A Gilded Cage, A
Curse Of An Aching Heart, The
Does True Love Ever Run Smooth?
Down In Bom-Bombay
Has Anybody Here Seen Kelly?
I Can't Tell Why I Love You But I
Do
I'm Not Pretty But I'm Good To My
Folks
I Think I Could Be Awfully Good To
You
Melinda's Wedding Day
'Mid The Green Fields Of Virginia
Mrs Carter, You're A Tartar
Remember She's A Girl
Siam
Take Back Your Gold
That's How I Need You
Then I'll Stop Loving You
Violet And The Rose And You, The
Wait Till The Sun Shines, Nellie
What Do You Want To Make Those
Eyes At Me For?
When Charlie Plays The Slide
Trombone In The Silver Cornet
Band
Wops! My Dear

CARUSO, Enrico 1873–1921
Because
For You Alone
Good-Bye (Tosti)

Lost Chord, The
M'Appari Tutt'Amor
Mattinata
O Sole Mio
Over There
Santa Lucia
Vieni Sul Mar

CASEY'S COURT fl. 1906–50s; orig.
Casey's Circus; sketch troupe founded
by Will **MURRAY** (b. 1877) which
featured many famous comedians, also
son Roy Leo and eventually grandson
Roy jun.

CASH, Morny 1872–1938; brother of
Harry Dalton
All Of A Doo-Dah
Beautiful Beautiful Bed
(Eh! Dear Me!) It's A Fine Place
Paree
Eh! What A Fool I Was To Go To The
Isle Of Man
Have A Banana
He Did The Cake Walk
Hooray! Hooray! I'm Going To Be
Married Today!
How Are They Going To Get To
London?
I Live In Trafalgar Square
I'm Having The Time Of My Life
I'm Taking The Open-Air Treatment
Let Me Put My Clogs On Do!
Married A Year Today
My Ninepence
My Wench Is A Factory Wench
Our Village (I Do Have A Lovely
Time)
Out He Went At Seven in The
Morning
Poor Mamma
Shirts
Stick To My Hand Penelope
Where Did The Cruel Bullet Strike
You?
You Must Hear All, And You Must Say
Nowt

CASS, Frank d. 14 May 1927
  I Lost My Train Again
  Jones!
  'Tis A Faded Picture

CASTLE, Vernon & Irene fl.
1912–*c*.1918; Vernon Blythe
(1887–1918) and his wife Irene Foote
(1893–1969); primarily ballroom dancers.
Vernon's sister was Coralie BLYTHE
  Castle Walk, The
  Dance Of The Grizzly Bear
  Hesitation Waltz
  Texas Tommy
  Turkey Trot
  When I Discovered You

CASTLETON, Kate 1857–92
  For Goodness' Sake Don't Say I Told
    You
  Will You Walk Into My Parlour? Said
    The Spider To The Fly

CAULFIELD, Mrs J. 1822–70; née Matt-
ley; m. John Caulfield sen.° (1809–65);
mother of John Caulfield jun.° (d. 25
Apr. 1879) and Lennox Grey
  Bobbin' Around
  Captain With His Whiskers, The
  Fare You Well, My Own Mary Anne
  Keemo Kimo
  Little Dorrit
  My Heart Is Like A Silent Lute
  Postman's Knock, The
  Queen's Letter, The
  Ring Out, Ring Out, Ye Merry Bells
  There's Peace In The Valley

CAVE, Herbert
  Holy City, The
  Moon Has Raised Her Lamp Above,
    The (w. Ivor FOSTER)
  Watchman, What Of The Night?
    (w. FOSTER)

CAVE, J. Arnold° 1823–1912
  All The Dogs Went Bow-Wow-Wow
  Bradshaw's Guide

  Carry Me Back To Ole Virginny
  Dearest May
  Dramatic Maniac, The
  England For The English (Cave:
    Dagonet)
  Factotum, The
  God Bless Victoria! Albion's Queen (?)
  Gwine Ober De Mountains
  I'm Afloat
  I'm Ninety-Five
  Kathleen Mavourneen
  Mother He's Going Away
  Old Joe Sat At De Garden Gate
  Sigh Of The Slave, The
  Sneeze, The
  Somebody In De House Wid Dinah
  Statty Fair, The
  Villikins And His Dinah
  While The World Goes Merrily Round

CAVENDISH, Harry d. 1888; celebrated
chairman of the Royal Holborn and the
London Pavilion Music Halls
  Village Blacksmith, The

CECIL, Arthur 1844–96; a.k.a. Arthur
Blunt
  Buttercup, The (w. German REED
    Co)

CELLI, Frank H. 1842–1904
  Beat Of The Drum, The
  Give It A Name
  Guards' National Song, The
  Here's A Health Unto His Majesty
  Midshipmite, The
  Ordered Abroad ('a scenic recitation')
  Parson And A Man, A
  Signalman On The Line, The
  Tomorrow Will Be Friday

CERITO, Ada 1877–1944
  All He Left Was A Pair Of Trousers
  Boys And Girls
  Canoodle Round The Corner, A
  D-I-A-B-O-L-O ('Cos He Can't Do
    That And Catch It)
  Gay Parisienne, The

Granny's Advice
I Want Another Old Man To Begin
My Second Husband (sk.)
One Of The Kids
Pets Of The Bois Boulogne
When Father Backs A Winner

CHAMBERS, Emma
Laughing Song, The (*Die Fledermaus*)
Slippery Sarah

CHAMBERS, McCall
'E Didn't Ought To Do It
Fine Old/Ould Irish Gintleman, The
I Burst Out Laughing
Mother, Father And I
My Moke
Nationality
Tips For The General Election
Waltzing As She Is Waltzed
We'd Never Met Before
Whoi-a! Wot-O!

CHAMPION, Harry° 1865–1942; until
1887 k.a. Will Conray
All The Dogs Went Bow-Wow-Wow
All Wobberlee
And I'm Selling Up The Happy
Home
Any Old Iron
Any Old Rags?
Any Old Thing Will Do!
Are You Sure You've Had Enough
As Large As Life In The Harem
Baked Sheep's Heart Stuffed With
Sage And Onions
Belinda The Barber-ous
Blowing 'Em Out
Boiled Beef And Carrots
Cover It Over Quick, Jemima
Cut Yourself A Bit Of Cake
Daisy, What Daisy Roots!
Don't Do It Again, Matilda
Down Came The Blind
Down Fell The Pony In A Fit
Dr Shelley
End Of My Old Cigar, The

Ev'rybody Knows Me In My Old
Brown Hat
Father Did Look Funny
Funny Little Bunny Sonny Had, The
Ginger, You're Balmy!
Good Old Yorkshire Pudden
Grow Some Taters
Hangin' 'Em Out To Dry
Have A Drop Of Gin, Joe
Have You Paid The Rent?
Have You Seen Her?
Here Comes Old Beaver
Home-Made Soup
Hot Meat Pies, Saveloys And Trotters
Hot Tripe And Onions
I Did It But Never Again
I Didn't Get A Wink All Night
I'm Getting Ready For My Mother-
In-Law
I'm Henery The Eighth, I Am!
I'm Proud I'm A Cockney
I'm Proud Of My Old Bald Head
I'm Selling Up The 'Appy 'Appy
'Ome
In 'The World Turned Upside Down'
In Training
I See You've Got The Old Brown Hat
On
I Skedaddled
It's A Pretty Little Place Inside
It's A Very Bad Job About Me
It Won't Last Very Very Long
I Was Holding My Cocoanut
I Was Out In Half A Tick
Just As I Was Taking It
Keep On! Keep On!! Keep On!!!
Ku Klux Klan
Let 'Em All Go
Let Me Alone, I'm Busy
Let's Have A Basin Of Soup
Let's Have A Ditty From Brown
Little Bit Of Cucumber, A
Longer You Linger, The
Mr Knick Knock
Music Goes Round And Round, The
My Diary

My Heart's Good But My Feet Won't
  Let Me
My Old Ham-Bone
My Old Iron Cross
My Poor Heart Went 'Pitter-Patter'
My Ragtime Missus
My Wife's Sister's Cat
Never Let Your Braces Dangle
Not Much
Old Dun Cow, The
Old High Hat I Got Married In, The
Old Red Lion, The
On The Mediterranean
On Top!
Out Went The Gas
P.C. Green (They Never Interfere
  With Me)
Peace! Peace! Peace!
Ping-Ping-Pong
Pip-Ip
Put A Bit O' Treacle On My Pudden,
  Mary Ann!
Ragtime Ragshop
Right On My Doo-Dah
Robin Redbreast
Saturday
Sit On 'Em And Keep 'Em Warm
Standard Bread
Stick To Me Tight
Such A Nice Young Man
Take Your Umbrella With You, John!
Tally-Owe, The Tallyman!
That Funny Little Bobtail Coat
That Gorgonzola Cheese
They're All Gone
They Won't Move At All
Thirsty Man, The
Three Meals A Day
Two, Two, Tooty-Two
We've All Been Having A Go At It
We've Got The Lodgers In And We
  Can't Get 'Em Out
What A Mouth!
When Are You Going To Stop?
When Do I Begin?
When The Old Dun Cow Caught Fire

Where's My Pianner?
While I Was Licking My Stamp
Who Says London Ain't The Country?
William The Conqueror
Work Boys Work
Wot Cheer, Me Old Brown Son
Yer 'At Don't Fit Yer Very Well!
Yorkshire Pudden
You Can't Help Laughing, Can Yer?
You Don't Want To Keep On Shewing
  It

CHAPLIN, Charles sen.° 1864–1901;
m. Lily HARLEY; father of Charles
CHAPLIN jun.
  As The Church Bells Chime
  Dear Old Pals *or* Pals That Time
    Cannot Alter
  Eh! Boys?
  Every-Day Life
  Girl Was Young And Pretty, The
  Hi Diddle Diddle!
  Oui! Tray Bong! (My Pal Jones)
  She Must Be Witty, She Must Be
    Pretty
  Wanderer's Return, The
  We All Of Us Know What That Means
  Yesterday

CHAPLIN, Charles jun. 1889–1977;
son of Charles CHAPLIN sen. and Lily
HARLEY; half-brother of Sydney
CHAPLIN
  Football Match, The (Fred Karno sk.)
  Jimmy The Fearless (Fred Karno sk.)
  Mumming Birds (Fred Karno sk.)

CHAPLIN, Sydney 1884–1965; son of
Sydney Hawkes and Lily HARLEY;
half-brother of Charles CHAPLIN
jun.
  Football Match, The (Fred Karno sk.)

CHAPMAN, Ella
  He Wanted Some More
  I Tell My Banjo All
  Tom, Dick And Harry And Another

CHARD, Doris *see* DORIS, Dainty

CHARD, Kate 1861–1942
Drink Of The Golden Cup
Polly Up A Plum Tree
Robin Hood Up To Date

CHEETHAM, Joseph 1875–1932
Awake! (A Moving Love Song)
Come Into The Garden Maud
Roses Of Picardy
Thora

CHESTER, Alf d. 20 Oct. 1925
And The Peas Were Lovely
Baby's Father
D'You Mean It?
Faded Leaves
Fireman's Story, The
Forgotten *or* He Was One Of The
   Light Brigade
Golden Reef, The (sk.)
He Was One Of The Light Brigade
I Want To See The Wheels Go Round
I Went Like This To The Lady
I Wonder If The Sergeant Knows
I Woo-Oo
Last Time, The
Little Thing Like This Is Very Handy,
   A
Lost For Ever
Love Came First
Musical Mechanic, The
On Duty: A Tale Of The Crimea
On Her Majesty's Service
Only A Year Ago/To Go(?)
Postman's Story, The
Queen's Pardon, The
Quite Right
Sailing Merrily Home
Tale Of The 95th, A
Up Came Brown With A Lot Like
   Mine
Warder's Story, The (Waiting For The
   Verdict)
Why Did I Leave My Little Back
   Room?

With 'Our' Money
Wreck Of The Lifeboat, The

CHESTER, Florence possibly one of the
SISTERS CHESTER
Break The News To Mother
Man To Suit This Child, The

CHESTER, Frederick°
Algy's Absolutely Full Of Tact

CHESTER, SISTERS (fl. 1892–1907) orig.
Florrie Chester w. sisters Grace and
Laura; later w. Maud(e) Graham and
Mab Ottoway. Another combination was
Florrie, Maude, and Edith. See
CHESTER, Florence
What's The Use Of An Old Log-Cabin
   To Me?

CHEVALIER, Albert° 1861–1923; m.
Florrie (1878–1931) daughter of George
LEYBOURNE shortly after her divorce
from Herbert Clayton (1875–1931);
wrote all his own words and some music
Ahn's Page Ten
Alice
'Andle To My Name, An
'Anky Panky *or* the Quickness of The
   'And Deceives The Eye
'Appy 'Ampstead *or* Oh! 'Ampstead
'Arry And 'Arriett
'Ave A Glass Along O' Me
Birdcatcher, The
Black's De Colour
Blue Ribbon Jane
Buvons Sec (Vive Le Vigneron)
Candid Man, The
Centenarian, The (mon.)
Chips Of The Good Old Block
Christmas Chimes Across The Snow
Christmas Night's Dream, A
Christmas Song, A
Cockney Tragedian, The
Cosmopolitan Courtship
Coster's Courtship, The (Yuss)
Coster's Honeymoon, The
Coster's Serenade, The

Critic, The
Dolly's Advice
Dotty Poet, The
'E Can't Take The Roize Out Of Oi
Everflowing Brook, The
Fallen Star, A (mon.)
Fiévre Militaire, La
Funny Without Being Vulgar
Future Mrs 'Awkins, The
Goody Goody Time, The
Goose With The Golden Eggs, The
   (sk.)
Great Man Of Wardle, The (mon.)
'Hecho', The
He J. Hann
He Knew It!
Hemmer (mon.)
Her Coster Boy In Khaki
Herr Schwollenhedt
Hif Not, Why Not? (mon.)
How?
How Soon We All Forget These Little
   Things
Hunting
If I'd A Bloomin' Throne To Call My
   Own
In The Good Old Days
I Shouldn't Do It If I Were You
'Is Mind's A Puffick Blank
It Ain't So Much The Things 'E Sez
It Gits Me Talked Abaht
I've Got 'Er 'At
Jerusalem's Dead, The
Johnnie's Serenade, The
Laces
Ladies' Bazaar, The (mon.)
Lag's Lament, The
Lonely Lamp Post, The
Mafekin' Night
Man With A Tear In His Voice, The
M. Armand Thibault (mon.)
Mistake!, A
My Country Cousin
My Old Dutch
Nasty Way 'E Sez It, The

Nellie Mine
Nipper's Lullaby, The
Not A Bit Of Good
Not Me! Taint Likely, Would You?
Oh! 'Ampstead *or* 'Appy 'Ampstead
Oh! The Langwidge!
Old Bachelor, An (mon.)
Our 'Armonic Club
Our Bazaar
Our Court Ball
Our Little Nipper ('E Only Stands
   About So High)
Our Restorong
Peculiar
Pierrot Coster
Poet, The (Dotty) (mon.)
Racecourse Sharper, The
Right As Ninepence
Rose Of Our Alley, The
She Was High, I Was Low
Sich A Nice Man Too
Tick! Tock!
Toymaker's Tragedy, The
Village Constable, The (mon.)
Villains At The Vic, The
Vive Le Vigneron (Buvons Sec)
Waxwork Show, The
We Did 'Ave A Time
Who'll Buy?
Wings Of Memory
Wipe Dat Head
With Me
Workhouse Man, The (mon.)
Wot Cher! (Knock'd 'Em In The Old
   Kent Road)
Wot's The Good Of Hanythink? Why,
   Nuffink!
Wot Vor Do 'E Luv Oi? (mon.)
Yankee In London, The (mon.)
Yer Never Ask'd/Aks'd 'Im For It
You Are A Tasty Lot!
You Can't 'Elp Likin' 'Im
You Oughter
Yours Etc
Yuss (The Coster's Courtship)

CHIP, 'Little' Sam 1881–1917
Don't Tell My Wife
I'll Do It, Do It, Do It, If I Bust!
Nipper's Reply, The
Oh! Flossie! Pretty Little Flossie!
Since My Wife's Been Away

CHIRGWIN, G. H.° 1854–1922; orig. w.
Chirgwinnie Family incl. father Edward
Chirgwin (1810–82) and brother John
(d. 19 Mar. 1882); later worked double
act w. brother Tom CHIRGWIN; solo
from 1876
All In His Sunday Clothes
All Scotch
All The Time (I've Got A New Girl
Now)
Asleep In The Deep
Black And White
Blind Boy, The
Blind Coon, The
Caller Herrin' (parody)
Charmer
Cockney Coon, The
Cockney Coon's Sweetheart, The
Cockney Linnets, The
Cockney Piccaninnies' Serenade,
The
Come Home, Father
Comin' Thro' The Rye (parody)
Comparisons Are Melodious
Don't Sing A Coon Song Please
Girl Upstairs, The
Good Old London Town Girl, A
Half A Pint Of Mild And Bitter
He's Been A Good Old Pal
I'd Take Her To The Aquarium, I'd
Take Her To The Zoo
In A Farmhouse Near To Regent
Circle
Italiana Multimagarnacan
It Could Never Happen Here
Je-hos-so-phat
Jester, The
Jocular Joker, The

Music Professor, The (sk.) (w. Tom
CHIRGWIN)
My Fiddle Is My Sweetheart
My Fiddle Was My Sweetheart
Naughty Boy, The
Night Of The Party, The
Norah Dear
Not The Baby But The Bicycle!
Old Nigger Ben
Rag-Time Coon, The
Second Floor, The
Spoony Coon, The
Swanker, The
Sweet Louise
Very Nearly
Village Blacksmith, The (parody)
Will You Gang Awa, Jimmie?
Would-Be Coon, The

CHIRGWIN, Tom d. 1881; brother of
G. H. CHIRGWIN
Blind Boy, The
Music Professor, The (sk.) (w. G. H.
CHIRGWIN)

CHRISTIAN, Albert d. 16 June 1915
Britishers Together
Little Anglo-Saxon Every Time, The
Mynheer Van Dunck
Ould Plaid Shawl, The
Soldiers Of The Queen, The
There's A Little Flag On High
Wearing Of The Green, The

CHRISTIE, Nellie
Cannibal Nigger, The
Chloe
Dandy Coon's Sweetheart, The
De Lamb From Alabam'!
Real Susie Tusie, The

CHRISTY MINSTRELS *or* **SERENADERS**
fl. 1842/3–54; est. Edwin (Ned) P.
Christy (*c.*1815–62), George N. Harrington (1827/8–68) later k.a. George
Christy°, and Tom Vaughn. An early
member was T. Christian (1810–67);

others were H. Montague (d. Feb. 1888) and, in 1845, Richard M. Hooley (1822–93). Revived 1857 in London as Raynor & Pierce's Christy Company. After death of Earl H. Pierce (1823–59) disbanded in 1860 by J. W. RAYNOR, who returned to the USA, leaving any number of 'original' Christy troupes such as Christy's Coloured Comedians (fl. 1863/4), Cooper's Female Christys (fl. 1870s—proprietor Mrs F. J. Cooper), ANDY MERRILEES' ARMOUR-CLAD FEMALE CHRISTYS, and MOORE & BURGESS to proliferate. See Ernest BRUCE; Charles ERNEST; Walter WALTER; William LESLIE; John RAWLINSON. Names in brackets are soloists

Ah, He Kissed Me When He Left Me
Amber Tresses Tied In Blue
Angels Whisper Sweet Goodnight
Annie Lisle (G. J. Wilsom)
Beautiful Star
Belle Mahone's Reply
Beneath The Snow
Be Our Love Like The Ivy
Bobbin' Around
Brown Eyes Has That Little Maiden
Carry Me Back To Old Virginny
Close The Shutters, Willie's Dead
Come Where My Love Lies Dreaming
Cottage By The Sea, The
Day Our Mother Died, The
Day When You'll Forget Me
Days When I Was Young, The
Don't Forget To Dream Of Me
Down By The Gate
Down South Where The Sugar Cane Grows
Dreaming Of Home And Of Mother
Drifting With The Tide
Driven From Home
Eileen's Answer
Ella Ree
Emancipation Day
Empty Cradle, The
Father, Bring Home Your Money Tonight
Fire In The Grate, The
Gathering Shells By The Sea
Gentle Annie
Gently Down The Stream
Gipsy's Warning, The
Girl In The Grate, The
Golden Hours
Grandfather's Clock
Hard Times Come Again No More
Have I Not Been Kind To Thee?
Hoop De Dooden Do (Earl H. Pierce)
Hunting Eyes
I'd Choose To Be
I Do Not Ask Dame Fortune's Smile
I Knew I'd Get A Letter
I'll Ne'er Forget The Kiss You Gave Me
I Stand On Memory's Golden Shore
It Seems Like A Dream (G. W. Winterhaigh)
Jingle Bells
John Brown's Body
Juanita
Keemo Kimo
Keep One Little Kiss For Me
Kind Words Can Never Die
Little Blue Eyes Sweet And True
Little Ones At Home, The
Little Peach In An Orchard Grew, A
Lucy Long (George Harrington/Christy)
Minnie Clyde
Mocking Bird, The
Mother Would Comfort Me (Wilsom)
Must We Then Meet As Strangers?
My Home On The Old Ohio
Nelly Bly
Nelly Of The Hazel Dell
Nobody's Darling But Mine
Old Cottage Gate, The
Old Dog Tray
Only A Face At The Window
Only A Flower Then
Only A Sweet Little Letter

Only Speak Kindly To Me
On The Sands!
Poor Old Tramp, The
Pretty As A Picture
Put It Down To Me (S. Hall)
Put My Little Shoes Away
Ring The Bell Softly, There's Crape
  On The Door
Ring The Bell, Watchman
Rock Me To Sleep Mother
Rosa Dear
Rosa Lee *or* Don't Be Foolish Joe
Roses Underneath The Snow
Say A Kind Word If You Can
Sea Shells
See That My Grave's Kept Green
She's A Rosey, She's A Posey
Silver Threads Among The Gold
Still Watch Over Me Little Star
  (Mr Winterhaigh)
Time May Steal The Rose, Darling
Toll The Bell
Tramp, Tramp, Tramp, The Boys Are
  Marching
Under The Willow She's Sleeping
U-Pi-Dee
Victoria's Black Hussars
Virginia Rosebud
We Are Coming, Sister Mary
We Shall All Meet The Little Ones
  There
When You And I Were Young,
  Maggie
Whist! The Bogie Man
Zip Coon (Turkey In The Straw)
STEPHEN FOSTER songs: Beautiful
  Dreamer, Camptown Races,
  Kentucky Home, Luleana, Massa's
  In The Cold Cold Ground, Oh!
  Susanna, Old Folks At Home, Ring
  De Banjo, Willie We Have Missed
  You, etc.

CHURCHILL, Billy 1863–1949; orig. w.
father J. W. Churchill (1842–93)? as
Churchill & Peter

Girls Wouldn't Be Wanted At All
I Am As Well Here As I Am
My Hundred Pound Motor Car
Stand Up, Stand Up

CLAFF, Harry 1880–1943
Cavalier
Fighting Rajah, The
Let's All Go To The Music Hall
Till We Meet Again

CLARE, George w. MOHAWK
MINSTRELS
Silver Threads Among The Gold
Sweet Little Girl With The 'Jersey'
  On, The
Wait Till The Clouds Roll By
Won't You Buy My Pretty Flowers?

CLARE, Jenny
Creep-Mouse (w. Madeline
  MAJILTON)
I Don't Want To Play In Your Yard
  (w. MAJILTON)

CLARE, Tom 1876–1946
Absolutely Wrong
Angel And The Child, The
Awfully Chap, The
Beautiful Girlie Girls
Britannia's Lullaby
Cohen On The Telephone (and sundry
  other 'Cohen' routines)
Come With Me To The Sea
Cynthia
Do It Now
Familiarity
German At The Telephone, The
Girl In Chintz, The
Green Grass Grew All Round
Ideal Home, The
If You'd Only Told Me
I Had A Little Garden
Is It Done In Suburbia?
Is It Likely?
It's Refined
I've Seen It On The Pictures

My Beastly Eyeglass
Night When The Old Cow Died, The
Percy Was Painfully Pale
Seven Years Hard
Silly Ass!
Souvenirs
Sybil
Waltzing Willie
We Ought To Be Thankful For That
What Did You Do In The Great War,
　Daddy?

CLARK, Gladys
Always (w. Henry BERGMAN)

CLARK, H. Donald
Choir Boy, The
Orthodox Curate, The

CLARK, Henri° 1840–1905; sometimes
spelled Clarke
Amatory Frenchman, The
Awistoquatic Actaw, The
Belinda B or The Walking Dictionary
Breach Of Promise Case, The
Custom Of The Country, The
Dolly Dot
Down Among The Coals
Ephraim Fox
Fairy Queen, The
Fellow That Looks Like Me, The
Frenchman, The or Tra La La Bon
Frenchman's Tabby Tom Cat, The
Goblins In The Churchyard, The
Grocer's Boy, The
I Don't Think You're In It, Old Man
I'm Not Such A Saint As I Look
It's My Turn Next! or The Pretty
　Milliner
I Won Her Heart At Billiards
Jessie The Belle At The Bar
Just As You Are For Ninepence or The
　Art Photographer
Let Go The Anchor Boys
L. S. D. or 'Tis Money Makes The
　Mare Go
Mad Butcher, The

Made In Germany
Mercenary Matilda
Moral Young Man, The or This
　Wicked World
Nautical Swell, The
Peculiar People
Peter Pimple
Pirate Bus, The
Poor Chinee, The
Poor Washerwoman, The
Railway Porter Dan
Rolling On The Grass
She Does The Fandango All Over The
　Place
Some Of The Ghosts
Something In The City
Sweet Mrs Tickle
Tra La La Bon Bon
Ulster Wrapper, The
Wait Till You Get It
We're All Scotch
When Parnell's The King Of Old
　Ireland
When She Says She Will, She Does!

CLARK, Herbert
Chinee And The Coon, The
I Could Do With A Penny For A Share

CLARKE, Dorothy
Come Over The Garden Wall

CLARKE, Emilie A.°
I'm Coming Home To You
Sincerity—My Friend

Clarke, Ernèe° 1836–98; sometimes
spelled Ernie
Tommy Dodd

CLARKE, George 1887–1947
They Go Wild, Simply Wild, Over Me

CLARKE, Lucy
Our Hands Have Met But Not Our
　Hearts

CLARKE, Tom 1884–1957
Let's Wait And See The Pictures

CLEVERE, Amy
Ain't You Got A Big Black Moon?
Black Belle
Don't Be Angry, Mr Bee
Don't Forget, Mignonette
Down By The Ferry
Girlie With The Baby Stare, The
I'm Sorry But I Can't Come Out!
Leaf Of Shamrock, A
Lily, I Am Longing, Love, For You
Ma Brown-Eyed Babe
Milly Burne (same as next entry?)
Milly And The Millionaire (previous
   entry?)
My Paleface Queen
Old Oak Tree, The
Pearl
You Tell Me That You're Going To
   Wed A White Man

CLIFF, Laddie° 1891–1937; formerly
Boy Perry; son of Cliff RYLAND; m.
Phyllis MONKMAN
Coal-Black Mammy
Let The Great Big World Keep
   Turning (w. Violet LORAINE)
Swanee
We'll Go To Church On Sunday
   (w. Phyllis MONKMAN)
You Made Me Love You

CLIFFORD, Camille 1885–1971
I'm A Duchess
Matinée Girl, The
Miss Sylvia
Why Do They Call Me A Gibson Girl?

CLIFFORD, Charles d. 22 Jan. 1943
Grandfather's Clock
Leave It Alone!
Sitting In The Chimney Corner

CLIFFORD, Harry 1871–1947
Blow For Old England's Fame, A
Gold! Gold! Gold! (Medley Barrett)
Just One Redeeming Feature
My Bruvver
Old Home's The Best After All, The

That's When Lovely Woman's At Her
   Best
Who'll Mind Us When You're Gone,
   Daddy?

CLIFFORD, Nat°
Crazy Millionaire, The
Dartmoor
Didn't We Fight For England—In
   The Future?
Don't Sing A Coon Song Please
Engine Driver's Story, The
Fancy Meeting You!
He Didn't Know Me
I'll Never Leave The Dear Old Home
I Thought My Luck Was In
John Bull's Little Khaki Coon
My Wife's Husband
Oh! That Chicken
Oh, The Beautiful Spring
Silver Spoon In His Mouth, A
Someday
That's How I Saved My Life
Tramps
Will You Know Me Mother Dear?

CLIFTON, Harry° 1832–72; m. Fanny
EDWARDS; wrote much of his own
material
Adventures Of Robinson Crusoe, The
Agreeable Young Man, The or Never
   Say Yes When You Mean To Say No
Always Do As I Do
As Long As The World Goes Round
As Welcome As The Flowers In May
Awfully Jolly
Barclay's Beer
Bear It Like A Man
Bit Of My Mind, A
Broken Down
Calico Printer's Clerk, The
Charity Crow
Christmas Party
Commercial Man, The or Sold Again
Could I Live My Time Over Again
Cupid In The Kitchen (w. Fanny
   EDWARDS)

Darby Maguire
Dark Girl Dress'd In Blue, The
Don't Be After Ten
Dutchman's Courtship, The
Elderly Beau, The
Faithless Maria *or* The Land Of Green
   Ginger
Family Man, The
Folly And Fashion (w. EDWARDS)
Good Old Days, The
Good Tempered Man
Grass Grows Greener
Happy Policeman, The (w. EDWARDS)
Hardware Line, The
Have You Seen The Ghost?
He Must Have A Thousand A Year
I Am One Of The Olden Time
I'll Go And Enlist For A Soldier
I'm Only Bridesmaid After All
Innocence
Isabella, The Barber's Daughter
   (She'd A Gingham Umbrella)
Island Of Green, The
It's Better To Laugh Than To Cry
It's Not The Miles We Travel
Jemima Brown
Jolly Old Country Squire, A
Jones's Musical Party
Lannigan's Ball
Let Your Motto Be 'Up And Doing'
Look Always On The Sunnyside
Look Before Leaping
Love And Pride (w. EDWARDS)
Mail Train Driver, The
Mary Ann *or* The Roving Gardener
Mary Bun Of Camden Town
Merry Old Uncle Joe
Michaelmas Day
Modern Times *or* Past And Present
Mother-In-Law, The
Motto For Every Man, A
Musical Missis
My Mother In Law
My Old Wife And I
My Rattling Mare And I
Never Look Behind

Old Man's Advice, An
On Board Of The Kangaroo
Paddle Your Own Canoe
Particular Friend, A
Polly Patterson
Polly Perkins Of Paddington Green
Poor Old Mike
Pull Back, The
Pulling Hard Against The Stream
Purely A Matter Of Taste
Put The Brake On When You're Going
   Down The Hill
Railway Bell(e), The
Rocky Road To Dublin, The
Sailor Sinbad, The
Schoolboy, The
Seventy Two And As Hard As Steel
Shabby Genteel
Shelling Green Peas
(Tell Me) What's A Married Man To
   Do
Ten Minutes Too Late
There's A Smile Waiting For Me At
   Home (w. EDWARDS)
There's Nothing Succeeds Like
   Success
There's Room In The World For All
Trifles Light As Air
Trying To Get Thin *or* Mr Double
   Stout
Try To Be Happy And Gay, My Boys
Up A Tree
Up With The Lark In The Morning
Very Suspicious *or* Family Jars (w.
   EDWARDS)
Wait For The Turn Of The Tide
Waste Not, Want Not
Water Cresses *or* The Watercress Girl
Waterford Boys
Way To Be Happy, The
Weepin' Willer, The *or* The Miller's
   Daughter
Where The Grass Grows Green
Where There's A Will There's A Way
Work, Boys, Work
Would You Be Surprised?

Young Man On The Railway, The *or*
  The Mail Train Driver

CLINE, Maggie 1857–1934
Arrah, Go On, You're Only Fooling
Come Down McGinnis
Down Went McGinty
I'm On Agen With Monaghan
I Want To Be A Prima Donna
  (Malone: Sherman)
McNulty Carved The Duck
Nothing's Too Good For The Irish
Stop That Noise
Throw Him Down, McCloskey

CLINE, Peggy
I Met Her At Mooney's
Oh, Where Is My Wandering Boy
  Tonight?
Pop

CLODOCHE
Can-Can

COATES, John 1865–1941
Absent-Minded Beggar, The
At The Mid Hour Of Night
Awake! (A Moving Love Song)
Come Into The Garden Maud
Diaphina
Eleanore
Green Grow The Rashes O!
I Hear You Calling Me
Linden Lea
Ninetta
Since First I Saw Your Face
Somewhere A Voice Is Calling
Sound An Alarm
Sunshine Of Your Smile, The
'Tis The Day (Mattinata)
Watchman's Scene, The

COBORN, Charles° 1852–1945
Absence Makes The Heart Grow
  Fonder—Of Somebody Else
All By Myself And Without Any Help

Another Kind Of Love
Bertie The Pet Of The Girls
Bloke With A Moke, A
Borrow! Borrow! Borrow!
Bounders' Football Club, The
But It Ain't
Buvons Sec
Chairman Of The Friendly Lead, The
Chapter Of Proverbs, A
Chap Wot Sings Outside The Pubs,
  The
Cheek, Beautiful Cheek
Come Where The Booze Is Cheaper
Coster's Friendly Lead, The *or* The
  Benefit Of Our Pal Jim
Don't Make A Stranger Of Me
Don't Marree (parody of Sweet
  Marie)
Do Ra Mi Fa *or* The Music Master
Drop To Square The Missus, A
English As She Is Spoke
'E Was A Perfect Gentleman
Excellent Advice
Four Fingers And A Thumb
Fudge, The Q. C.
Goo-Goo-Goo *or* The Dutchman's
  Baby
He Knows The Werry Number On
  Your Door
Here's Another Kind Of Love
He's All Right When You Know Him
  (Bill Sloggins)
Hextry Special
House Won't Let, The
How They Nurse The Baby
Hush! Hush! Here Comes The
  Broker's Man!
I Don't Care A Button Who Knows It
I'll Go Where I'm Respected
I'm A Swell With Toothpick And
  Crutch
I'm Bound To Be Guided By May
I'm Rather Too Old For It Now
I Shan't Try It On Any More
I've Escaped The Vaccination Act
Johnny, My Lad

Just As I Thought
Let Somebody Else Have A Go
Life-Boat Crew, The
London Cabby, The
Man That Broke The Bank At Monte
    Carlo, The
Me And The Prince Of Wales
My Wonderful Song
Naughty Schoolboy, The
Nobby Coster-Bloke, The
Not Before We Wanted To
Off She Goes Again
Oh! The Jubilee (1887)
Oh! What An Alteration
Our 'Armonic Club
Pierrot Inquisitive *or* What Is It?
Poor Little Darlings Are Not To
    Blame, The
Pretty Little Girl That I Know, The
Put Them In The Lord Mayor's Show
Rather More
Secret Signs
Should Husbands Work?
Silent Maiden, A
Something Rather Dangerous,
    Something Rather Nice *or* My
    Definition Of A Kiss
So They All Came
'Taint The Way To Make Life Sweeter
Tar's Farewell, The
Tell It To The Marines
That's The Way The World Goes
    Round
That's Why The British Loved The
    King
Time! Gentlemen Please
Tommy
Tree And The Lover, The
Truly Rural
Two Lovely Black Eyes
We Don't Want 'Im Down Our Way
What Did Your Mother Say, Johnny,
    My Lad?
What's The Matter With—? He's All
    Right
Why Do The British Love Their King?

Yes! Pa, Yes! Ma
Young Man Who Used To Live Over
    The Way, The

COFFIN, C. Hayden 1862–1935
Beneath The Skies
Boys Of The Household Brigade, The
Dover Patrol, The
Farewell Waltz, The (w. Marie
    TEMPEST)
Forgive (w. **TEMPEST**)
Four Horsemen Of The Apocalypse,
    The (film shown at the Palace
    Theatre, London, to which Coffin
    spoke the prologue)
Hands Off
Hybrias The Cretan
In Bondage
In The King's Name—Stand!
Is Love A Dream?
Jack's The Boy
Kathleen Mavourneen
Land Where The Best Man Wins, The
Look With Thine Eyes Into Mine
Lorraine, Lorraine, Loree
Love, Could I Only Tell Thee
Mine At Last
Motherland
Mother O' Mine
My First, My Last
My Lady's Bower
Nobby VC (sk.)
Old Brigade, The
Old Garden, An
O That We Two Were Maying
Prince Ivan's Song
Private Tommy Atkins
Queen Of My Heart
Queen Of The Earth And Sea
She Is Far From The Land
Soldiers Of The Queen, The
Sons Of The Motherland
Star Of My Soul
Sunshine Above
To Anthea
Village Blacksmith, The

West Country Lad
Who Sings Of England?

COHAN, Charles b. 1886
Jingle Of The Gold, The
My Little Eva
When My Rachel Smiles

COHAN, George M.° 1878–1942; m.
Ethel LEVEY (div.)
Give My Regards To Broadway
Harrigan
Mary's A Grand Old Name
Why Did Nellie Leave Her Home?
Yankee Doodle Boy, The

COHEN, Meyer
My Mother Was A Lady
Take A Seat Old Lady

COLE, Lieut. (Walter)
Wouldn't You Like To Go?

COLE, Belle 1845–1905
Don't Cry
Harbour Way, The
Killarney
Lost Chord, The
Scent Of The Roses, The
Sweet Genevieve
Vale Of Arklow, The
Wandering In Dreamland
What Are You Thinking Of?

COLE & JOHNSON Tommy Cole
(1909–33) & n.k.
Congo Love-Story, The
Lazy Moon, The
Maiden With The Dreamy Eyes, The
Under The Bamboo Tree

COLEMAN, Bessie
Missing Word, The
Oh, Mr Pearson
Riding On The District Railway

COLLETTE, Charles 1842/3–1924
Colorado Beetle Collared At Last, The
Company Promoter, The

Gilhooley
Hard Luck (mon.)
Home Rule (w. MOHAWK
    MINSTRELS)
I Felt That I Was Justified In Doing It
Lot To Do Today, A
Skibbereen
Something Gone Wrong With My
    Brain
Thirteen Club, The
Tipperary Christening, The
What An Afternoon
What Happened To Jones
You Have To

COLLIER, Beatrice
Apache Dance, The (w. Fred FARREN)

COLLINS, Arthur 1865–1932
Alexander's Rag-Time Band
Down Where The Wurzburger Flows
Everybody Works But Father
I'd Leave My Happy Home For You
I Want To Be In Dixie
My Wife's Gone To The Country
Preacher And The Bear, The

COLLINS, George d. 28 Mar. 1940
Fellows Call Me Jam
I Wish I Was
Laughable Times (parody of Comin'
    Thro' The Rye)
Mr N Peck
What A Friend, What A Sport

COLLINS, José 1887–1958; daughter of
Lottie COLLINS; step-daughter of James
W. TATE
Always
Bajou *or* Bayou
Dark Grows The Sky
In Cherry-Blossom Time In Japan
I've Built A Bamboo Bungalow For
    You
I Want To Be More Than A Friend
Just You And I And The Moon
Little Love, A Little Kiss, A

Little Maid Of Brittany
Looking For The Limelight
Love Is My Life (w. Thorpe BATES)
Love's Cigarette
Love Will Find A Way
My Cuban Girl
Oh, For A Night In Bohemia
Paradise For Two, A (w. BATES)
Peg O' My Heart
Rebecca Of Sunnybrook Farm
Sunray
Ta-Ra-Ra Boom-De-Ré (see Lottie
    COLLINS for UK version)
Wait For Me, Fritzy Dear
When You're In Love (w. BATES)

COLLINS, Lottie 1866–1910; orig. w.
younger sisters Marie COLLINS and
Lizzie as The Three Sisters Collins;
mother of José COLLINS; third husband
James W. TATE
Bicycle Marriage, A
Carrie From Camden Town
Circus Girl, The
Coachman's Wife, The
Donna Señora Of Gay Seville, The
Gertie, The Gaiety Girl
Girl On The Ran-Dan-Dan, The
Goodbye, Mr Williams
He Was Whistling This Tune All The
    Day (The Whistling Coon)
If That Apple Could Have Spoken
I Never Saw A Girl Like That
I Went To Paris With Papa
Just On The Tip Of My Tongue
Kitty Clar
Leader Of Society, A
Little Widow, The
Marguerite
Millie And The Motor
Night Out, A
Oh! The River (You Know The Sort Of
    Girl I Mean)
Quakeress Ruth
Queen Of Gay Paree
Something More Than That

Sunray
Ta-Ra-Ra-Boom-De-Ay (British
    version; see José COLLINS for orig.
    US version)

COLLINS, Marie d. 22 Jan. 1918; orig.
w. sisters Lizzie and Lottie COLLINS as
The Three Sisters Collins; solo from age
17
Be On Your Guard Boys
Boom Ta-Ra-Rum Girls, The
Boys Of The Empire
Come Home Again
Drink, Boys
Face The Music, Boys
Just Another Month Or So
Just A Sprig Of Holly
Leave Them Alone, Boys
Nothing Shall Part Us Now!
Real Good Boys
Take It On, Boys
What Are We Here For?
When The Day Begins To Dawn
When We've Got The Ships

COLLINS, Sam 1827–65
Billy O'Rourke
Dan Of Dublin
Day That Paddy Was Breech'd, The
Donnybrook Fair
Fiddler's Wife, The
Gooseberry Bush
House That Jack Built, The
Irish Boy
Irish Wedding, The
Judy Foy
Limerick Races
Long And The Short Of It
No Irish Need Apply
Paddy Connor's Wedding
Paddy Don't Care
Paddy Of Age
Paddy's Dream
Pat Murphy (I'm An Irish Boy)
Pat Of Mullingar
Pity The Downfall Of Uncle Sam
Rocky Road To Dublin, The

Sprig Of Shillelagh, The
Twig Of The Shannon, The

COLONNA TROUPE est. *c*.1870; Mme
Colonna (née Newham) a.k.a. Leona
Dare
    Can-Can, The (as The Colonna
      Quadrille)

COLQUHOUN, Ian
    Absent-Minded Beggar, The
    Auld Lang Syne
    Death Of Nelson, The
    Fighting Téméraire, The
    For King And Sireland
    If You Meet A Vessel In Distress
    Killarney
    Off To Philadelphia
    Old Brigade, The
    Sons Of The Sea
    Tom Bowling
    Under The Same Old Flag

COLVERD, 'Jovial' Joe d. 7 Feb. 1903;
father of Arthur REECE
    John Bull
    Over The Hills And Far Away

COMBES, Arthur 1855–1941
    Angels Are Hovering Round
    Business Man In London, The
    Cabby Knows His Fare
    Called To The Bar
    Carriage Waits M'Lord
    City Swell, The
    Harum Scarum
    I Saw 'Er Steal 'Er Apron To 'Er Eye
    It Takes A Girl To Do It
    Kimberley
    Old Old Tale, The
    She Stoops To Conquer
    That's What The Wild Waves Say
    Those Tassels On The Boots
    Up Go The Fireworks
    Young Country Squire, The

COMER, Imogene
    Baby's Prayer

In The Baggage Coach Ahead
She Was Bred In Old Kentucky
She Was Waiting For Her Absent
    Boy
Take Back Your Gold

COMPTON, Fay 1894–1978; m. H. G.
PÉLISSIER
    Harbury Pearls, The (sk.)
    Innocent And Annabel (sk.) (w.
      Stanley LOGAN)

COMPTON, Marie
    Barney O'Hay
    Here Stands A Post
    Love Lane
    Nancy Lee

CONNOLLY, Dolly 1887?–1965; m.
Percy Wenrich°
    By The Camp Fire
    Moonlight Bay
    Put On Your Old Gray Bonnet
    Red Rose Rag, The
    Waiting For The Robert E. Lee
    When You Wore A Tulip And I Wore
      A Big Red Rose

CONOR, Harry *c*.1856–1931
    Bowery, The

CONROY, Dan d. 27 Feb. 1940
    Biscuits In Bed
    Cassidy's Barber Shop
    In The Middle Of The Night
    Who Is It?

CONWAY, Alice
    I'm Going To Be Married Next
      Sunday
    Tasty! Very! Very, Very Tasty!

COOMBES, Arthur *see* COMBES

COOPER, Florrie
    Coming Back Home Again
    My Little Baby Boy
    Right At The Top
    Stars Are Angel Faces, The

COOPER, Dame Gladys 1888–1971
Bridal Suite, The (sk.) (w. Seymour
 HICKS)
Half-An-Hour (sk.)
Papa's Wife (sk.) (w. HICKS)

COOPER, Margaret° 1877–1922; m.
Arthur Humble-Crofts° (d. 1918)
Agatha Green
Beautiful Country Of Dreams
Bobby Dear
Bon Jour, Marie
Catch Me
Chimney Sweep, The
Clovelly
Come To Town, Miss Brown
Daddy And Baby
Dougal Was A Scotchman
English Rose, An
Fairy-Land
Gathering Nuts In May
Green Hills O' Somerset
Hello! Martha
He Met Her On The Stairs
His Dusky Maid
His Little Teddy Bear
Hullo! Tu-Tu
I Don't Seem To Want You When
 You're With Me
I'm A Ripping Sort Of Girl
In The Dingle Dongle Dell
I Want Somebody To Love Me
Janie
Jest Her Way
Last Year, Sweetheart
Let Us Waltz Around Together
Li'l Cannibal Coon
Little Black Dog, The
Little Crimson Rose
Love Is Meant To Make Us Glad
Ma Dusky Maid
Mammy's Prayer
Maria's Diary
Master And Man
Mister Bear
Mother's Darling

My Bungalow In Bond Street
My Heart's At Your Feet
My Moon
My Sunday Best
Old Chap
Paper Fan
Peter
Philosophy (anon: Emmell)
Skinny Piccaninny
Sweep
Touchin' Fings
Visitors
Waltz Me Around Again, Willie
When You Meet Your Girl
Won't You Go Off To The Zoo?
You'll Get Heaps O' Lickins
Ypsilanti

COOTE, Bert° 1868–1938; son of Robert
COOTE
I Do Like An Egg For My Tea
Lamb On Wall Street, The (sk.)
Look At The Buildings We Are
 Building

COOTE, Robert° 1834–88; father of
Bert COOTE
Blighted Barber, The *or* Fe, Fi, Fo,
 Fum
Hundred Years Ago, A
Jolly Christening Party
Little Maid, The *or* The Gay Deceiver
Master (Tommy) Wattle And The Big
 Blue Bottle
Merry And Wise
Oh! I Wish Your Mother Would Come
Pic-nic Party, The
Show Me The Man
Swells Of The Ocean
'Tis Really Very Unpleasant

CORNEILLE, Marguerite *see*
CORNILLE, Marguerite

CORNEY, Arthur°
Ask Yourself The Question
Cupid And The Dice Box
Don't, Brethren, Don't

For A Week Or Two
Gently Does The Trick
I Don't Want It
I Know What You Mean
Illustration
It Came Off
It Doesn't Improve Your Appearance
I Took It
It's Another Colour Now
Near It
Nobody Knows It But Me
No Room
Oh! Take Care Of It
Something Went Wrong With The
   Works
There Is No Room For Me
There's Nothing In It
Up Comes Jones
Very Good Guess, A
Young Country Squire, The

CORNILLE, Marguerite Empire debut
1897; sometimes spelled Corneille
   Come Back, Love
   Conversation Guide, The
   Dolly's Doctor
   Farewell Song, The
   Hello! Ma Baby
   L.C.C., The
   Ma Charmeuse
   Nightingale Song, The
   Shine On!

CORVAN, Ned° 1831–65
   Cat-Gut Jim
   £4.10, *or* The Sailor's Strike
   Oot O' Wark; *or* The Year '62

COSTELLO, Tom° 1863–1943
   All Round The Town
   All Through A Little Piece Of Bacon
   All Through 'Ta-ra-ra-boom-de-ay'
   Archie, The Catch Of The Season
   At Trinity Church I Met My Doom
   Blow Winds Gently
   Boers Have Got My Daddy, The
   Boys That Do The Fighting, The

Bridget The Spaniard
Burglar Coon, The
Bus, The *or* Mary McIntyre
Buy A Bicycle
Circus Girl, The
Club Raid Upside Down, The
Come Down, Mrs Brown! Come
   Down!
Comrades
Convict And The Bird, The
Dandy Yiddisher Coon, The
Dawn Of Freedom, The
Died Like A True Irish Soldier
Does It Hurt You Very Much?
Don't Be Angry, Daddy
Down Our Street
Duchess Of Deansgate, The
Eliza Brown *or* A Big Screwdriver
Fair Trade
Faithful *or* A Simple Soldier's Song
Farewell My Little Yo-San!
Father's Come Home With His Money
   All Right
Fed Up
Fighting Ships Of England, The
   (Nelson's Return)
For Auld Lang Syne (My Home Is Far
   Away)
Gate, The (Here I'm Waiting)
Goodbye, Dear Old London Town
Happy Hibernian, The
Have Me On A Three Months' Lease
He'll Never See His Mother Any
   More
He's In Regular Employment Now
He's In The Asylum Now
His Funeral's Tomorrow
Homeland—Good-bye!
If You'll Be True To Me
I Gave The Missus A Brace Of Kisses
I'll Forgive Him
I'm Giving Up My Job To The Kaiser
I'm Going Home
I'm Going To Ride A Bicycle
I Promised
Irish Jew, The

It Don't Go Well With Scroggs
I've Been Sleeping On The Floor All Night
I've Come Back To Town Once Again
I've Got The Girl I've Got The Ring
I've Got To Prove It
I've Made Up My Mind To Sail Away
I've Worked Eight Hours This Day
Laughing Madman, The
Lavender, The Howler (Ain't He A Delicate Creature?)
Mad Willie (Ding-Dong, Bell!)
Martin Sprague, The Gallant Fireman
Mary Devine
Mashah Up To Datah, The
Mermaids
Motherland (Australia Will Be There)
Mother Tongue, The
Mrs Gottem
Music Sweet Music a.k.a. Music At Home(?)
My Home Is Far Away
My Nellie's Blue Eyes
My Old Comrade
My Old Pal Joe (The Ten-Bob Rise)
My Ould Woman
Nellie Brown
Nelson From His Monument
Never Knock At Her Door Now, My Boy
Norah, My Wife
Oh! Maria, If You Love Me
Oh! The Black List
Old Clown, The
Once More I Sent The Needful 18 Stamps
One-Legged Family, The
One Of The Racing Boys
One, Two, Three
On Monday I Met Him
Piccadilly Circus Girl, The
Place I Was Lodging In Last, The
Playmates In Schooldays Were We
Poor Old Bunker
Quiet Little Corner Down In Kent, A
Ready!

Sail Away
Sailing Home
Sales's On Now, The
She Comes Home Tight On Saturday Night
She'd Changed Her Mind
She Don't Want A Maid To Dress Her Hair
Sheeny Coon, The
She Makes Me Do The Cakewalk
She's Too Good For Me
Ship I Love, The
Skipper In The Mercantile Marine, The
Society Actor, The (The Pet Of The Bankruptcy Court)
Somebody's Eyes Are Glistening
Song That Will Live Forever, The
Stay At Home Brigade, The
Still Growing
Strolling In The Garden
Such A Lamb
Sunday Afternoon
Take Me On A Three Years' Lease
Temperance Brigade, The
Ten Pound Note, The
Theosophee or Oh! Mrs B, Can It Be Really True?
There She Was Again
There's No-One To Say Good-Bye
They Bloom In The Summer
They Discharged Him Because He Was Old
Till Pay Day Comes Again
Two Angels
Unemployed Reserve Man, The
What Ho! There's Hair!
What I Say I Do Do, I Do Do
What's In A Name?
When The Old Church Bells Are Ringing
When You Hear The Bugle Calling
When You Hear Your Country Calling
Who's Going To Mash Me Tonight?
Why Did You Go To War?

Why Don't You Speak And Let Me
Go?
Will You Go?
Working Man's Sunday At Home, The
Wreck Of The Serpent, The
You're Still One of The Boys
Zanana! (A Romance of The
Backwoods)

COTTON, Billy (& HIS BAND)
1899–1969
Hokey Cokey *or* Cokey Cokey
Marrow Song, The

COURT, Dorothy m. Haydn Wood°
Bird Of Love Divine
Love's Garden Of Roses
Oh! Flower Divine
Wings Of Morning

COURTNEIDGE, Dame Cicely
1893–1980; m. Jack HULBERT
Dear Little Jappy Girls
Good-Bye, Kid!
I Like London
Little Japanese Mamma
Right Man, The
Why Has A Cow Got Four Legs? (w.
Wilson HALLET)

COURTNEY, 'Baron' 1835–1901
Take It, Bob

COURTNEY, Maud 1884–1959
Didn't We, Jim? (mon.)
Honeysuckle And The Bee, The

COVE, Harry
Sister Susie's Sewing Shirts For
Soldiers
Where Are The Lads Of The Village
Tonight?
You're My Baby

COVE, Kate
Dear Heart
For Ever And Ever (Tosti)
Good-bye (Tosti)
Little Bird, So Sweetly Singing

May Morning, A
Oh Dry Those Tears

COVENEY, Harriett 1827–92
Didn't He Seem To Like It?
Polly Patterson
Sensation

COWAN, Ted 1877–1960, brother of Sam
MAYO
Coward, The (sk.)
I Jumped On A 'Bus
Just A Little Ray Of Sunshine
Lost, Stolen Or Strayed (parody)
When I Am MP
When We Get Married

COWELL, Sam° 1820–64
Alonzo The Brave
Artful Dodger, The
As I Was A-Walking Beside The
Seaside
Bacon And Greens
Billy Barlow
Billy Taylor
Black Your Boots
Bobbin' Around
Broomstick
Cheesemonger's Daughter, The
Cork Leg, The
Crinoline
Dodger's Return, The
Faust And Monsieur Diable (w. F.
JONGHMANS)
Forty Thieves, The
Giles Scroggin's Ghost
Grocer And The Bluebottle, The
Hamlet (parody)
Hero's Life I Sing, A
Hot Codlins
House That Jack Built, The
Jemima Took Me Down A Peg
Keemo! Kimo!
Life And Death Of Bad Macbeth, The
Little Red Riding Hood
Lively Flea, The (Ivy Green
parody)

Lord Lovel (parody)
Lord Tom Noddy
Lost Child, The
Miss Julia (Wery Pekoolier)
Monster Statue, The
'Norrible Tale, A
O, My Love's Dead
Othello (parody)
Pantomime, The
Railway Porter, The
Ratcatcher's Daughter, The
Reuben Wright And Phoebe Brown
Richard III (parody)
Saint George And The Dragon
Sandy Hollar, The
Skying A Copper
Typitywichet
Villikins And His Dinah
Warbling Wagoner, The
Wedlock Is A Ticklish Thing
Wery Pekoolier (Miss Julia)
Who's Your Father?
Widow Glib And Sir Steeple
Workhouse Boy, The

COWL, Jane 1884–1950; a.k.a. Jane
COWLES
Honeysuckle And The Bee, The

Cox, Jimmie b. 1882
Nobody Knows You When You're
Down And Out

Cox, Lizzie *see* THORNTON, Bonnie
Smilin' Through

COYLE, Edgar
At My Lady's Feet (Lady Molly)
Dear Home Land
Down The Vale
Eileen Alannah
Little Silver Ring, A

COYLE, John E. 1868–1909
Don't Be Silly
Don't You Think He Ought To See A

Doctor?
I'll Give Him Dolly Daydream
She *Must* Have Known!
What Do You Think She Did?
You Don't Mean To Say That's
Wisdom?

COYNE, Frank 1854–82
Minstrel Boy's Medley Up To Date,
The
New Jerusalem *or* Cruel Jane Jemima
Oh! Polly *or* Bob's Birthday

COYNE, Frank 1875–1906; né Josiah
Jones; committed suicide by cutting his
throat in the bath; discovered by his wife
Carrie Joe
Animals, The (Whoa)
Below! Below! Below!
Boxing Kangaroo, The
Come And Have A Tiddley At The
Fountain
Doing My Duty
Have It Over Your Side, Lucy
He's Making Up For Lost Time Now
Horse The Missus Dries The Clothes
On, The
I Can't Get Rid Of 'Em
I Don't Know What I'm Going To Do
I Know 'Em All
I Know Where They Are
I'll Oblige
I'm Doing That Job Now
I'm Looking At Yer
I'm Ninety-Five And I'm Still Alive
I'm Very Well Known Round There
It's Just Beginning To Grow
Just As I Was Getting Into Bed
Let's Go Round There Now
Love For Dinner
Next Door To Me
Not Now
Puzzling Proverbs
Real Man's Josiah Harris
Save Your Money
Shift Up A Little Bit Farther

Sleeping In The Old Back Yard
So I'll Never Ride Again
Susie Anna *or* Seven Shillings And A
    Tanner
Terrible Night, A
That Pudding
That's What He Bought With His
    Wages
Then The Girl Said Oh!
There's No Room
They're Getting Larger
Tick! Tick!
Tiddly At The 'Fountain', The
Too Hard
Treat Her Very Careful
Watching The Stars As They Fall
We're Making Up For Lost Time Now
What's The Good Of A Pair Of Kilts?
Whoa! The Animals
Yes, We Did
You'd Better Come Down At Once
You've Got A Long Way To Go

COYNE, Fred° (1) 1845–86; né Sterling
As Good As They Make 'Em (The
    Best of Old Pals)
Bank Holiday *or* A Twopenny Ride On
    A Tramcar
Barber's Daughter, The *or* I'll Throw
    Myself Off London Bridge
Billy Johnson's Ball
Bugle's Sounding, The
Chink-Chink-Chink
Down By The Old Mill Stream (John
    Read)
Drink Up Old Fellow
Full Inside (Who'll Oblige A Lady?)
Gallant Blue Jackets Of England, The
G. P. O., The
Here's Another Kind Of Love
Here There And Everywhere *or* The
    Lunatic Traveller
Her Heart Was True To Me
He Taught Her To Sing Tra-La-La
Hurrah For Beaconsfield!

I Bought Her A Sealskin Jacket
I Don't Know You
I'd Tell You If I Were A Little Fly
I Fancy I've Seen You Before
If We Could Only See Through The
    Keyhole
If You Love Me Tell Me Tottie
It's Funny When You Feel That Way
It's Nice
I Want To Go Home To Mama
Jacob Schmidt
Known To The Police
Let Her Apply To Me
Luncheon Bar, The
New Electric Light, The
Oh, 'Ain't I Having A Day!
Oh, Fred Don't Be Frivolous
Oh, Fred! Tell Them To Stop
Oh, Julia
Oh, Nicodemus
Oh, Very Well, Mary Ann, I'll Tell
    Your Ma
Oh, What It Would Be To Be There
Passing The Time Away
Piano Girl, The
Poor, But A Gentleman Still
Raspberry Tart In A Little Poke
    Bonnet, A
Round The Corner (Courting On The
    Sly)
Sir Anthony Nash
Somebody Wanted The Doctor
Squire And Maria, The
Stop As Long As You Used To
Stop It!
Swell Upon The Stock Exchange, The
That's What Puzzles The Quaker
Then To My Love I'll Prove Untrue
There You Are Emma
Three Nice Old Ladies Went To The
    Aquarium
Tuner's Oppor-tunerty, The
Turn The Mangle, Joe
Under The British Flag
Velocipede, The (New)

Wait Till His Ship Comes Home
We Can't Do Without It
What Do You Take Me For?
What Will Sarah Say?
When I Took Our Nance To Church
When They're Making Me A King
Where's The Cat?
Where The Good Ship's Going
Whoa, Emma! (Lonsdale)
Who'll Oblige A Lady? *or* Full Inside
Why Part With Jumbo?
Will A Monkey Climb A Tree?
Yellow Coin, The
You're Getting It Up For Me
Zoedone

COYNE, Fred (2) 1871–1943
Six Thousand Miles Of Sea

COYNE, Joseph 1867–1941
Do You Like Me? (w. Violet LORAINE)
I'm A Married Man
Merry Widow Waltz (w. Lily ELSIE
    and also w. Constance DREVER)
What's The Use Of Going To Bed?
When I Discovered You (w. Ethel
    LEVEY)

CRAGGS, THE acrobatic sketch troupe
est. J. W. ('Pa') Cragg (1846–1931) w.
variously his wife Mary, their daughters,
sons, and others. In 1915 the act con-
sisted of Cragg and his five sons incl.
Billy (1872–1918) and James Henry
Pullen Cragg (1871–1931)
Billy The New Steward
Laughter Land
Territorials, The *or* England's Last
    Hope

CRAMPTON, Ernest d. 24 June 1941
Flicker Of The Firelight, The
Great-Grandmamma
When Love Calls

CRAVEN, Elise
Jellico And The Fairy (sk.) (w. Cyril
    MAUDE)

CRAVEN, TOM (d. 5 Aug. 1919) m.
MOXON, Constance
Down Our Alley
Heads And Tails

CRAWLEY, Dan 1872–1912; m. Lilian
Bishop. Later in his career specialized in
portrayal of elderly ladies, and so k.a.
'Dame' Dan Crawley
Ain't It All Right, Eh?
Anywhere Does For Me!
Awful Dad, An
Bit Too Young, A
Do As You Like With Me
Father Keeps On Doing It
Fiddle-De-Dee
He's A Pal
I Finish 'Em Off
I Got The Best Of It After All
I Know How To Settle It!
I'm A Bit Too Young And Tender
I'm A-Goin' To be Married On Sunday
I'm Much Better Off Where I Am
I'm Round There Tonight!
I Never Do
In My Trousers Pocket
It Doesn't Belong To Me
It's So Simple
I've Got Something To Be Thankful
    For
I Was Werry Busy
John The Tailor
Like Mine
Look Here, Loo—That Won't Do!
More Trouble In Our Native Land
Not In These Trousers
Now You're Married I Wish You Joy!
Picking All The Best Ones Out
Sailing Merrily On
She's Gone And Left Me
So Does Father
Te-Um-Te-Iddley-Ay!
There's A Nice How-d'ye-do!
They Can't Diddle Me
Tootle-Toot!
Trouble In Your Native Land

We All Went Home Again
Wedding Anniversary, The
We've All Been Doing A Bit
What Are We Going To Do?
When I Got Up This Morning
Why Do The Men Run After Me?

CREAMER & LAYTON Henry Creamer°
(1879–1930) and Turner Layton°
(1894–1978)
    After You've Gone
    Way Down Yonder In New Orleans

CRISPI, Ida d. 14 Feb. 1955
    Everybody's Doin' It Now (w. Fred
    FARREN and w. Robert HALE)

CRITCHFIELD, W. T. orig. k.a. Billy
Critchfield
    Age Of Reformation, The
    Chandler's Shop, The
    Cookshop Man, The
    Freedom Of Opinion
    Half-Pay Naval Captain, A
    Hard-Up Poet
    Jolly John Bull
    Merry Laughing Fellow, A
    Miser's Daughter, The
    Old Sarah Walker
    Sayings And Doings
    Soft Place In His Head
    So Said Mr Johnson

CROCKER, Joseph P. *see also* MOORE &
BURGESS MINSTRELS
    Old Bob Ridley

CROSSLEY, Ada 1874–1929
    Caro Mio Ben
    Easter Hymn (Frank Bridge)
    Fairy Waters
    Friends Again I Long To Love
    Hame
    Life's Gifts
    Life's Hope
    Love The Pedlar
    Magdalen At Michael's Gate
    Mighty Lak' A Rose

My Gentle Child
O That We Two Were Maying (Nevin)
Sink, Red Sun
Song For Women
There's Only One England
Through Love To Light

CROUCH, F. Nicholls° 1808–96
    Kathleen Mavourneen

CRUIKSHANK, (Alfred) 1875–1956
    H-O-M-E
    Old Brass Bottle, The

CRUMIT, Frank° 1889–1943; third husband of Julia Sanderson (1887–1975)
    Abdul Abulbul Amir
    Dapper Dan
    Frankie And Johnny
    Granny's Old Armchair
    Oh, Me! Oh, My!
    Pig Got Up And Slowly Walked Away,
      The
    Prune Song, The
    Some Sort Of Girl

CUNLIFFE, Whit° 1876–1966
    All Around The Clock
    All For The Ladies, All For The Girls
    And Here's Another Thing
    And So We Go On
    Any Complaints? No!
    As Soon As A Girl Begins To Know
    Beware! Beware!
    Blame It On To Poor Old Lloyd
      George
    Book Of Popular Songs, (Whit
      Cunliffe's)
    Breakfast Table Problems
    Business As Usual
    Buying A Stamp
    Caddie, The
    Charabanc
    Do You Believe In Women's Rights?
    D'You Follow Me?
    Economise
    Ev'ry Girl Is Doing Her Bit
    Eyes

Fair, Fat And Forty
Fall In And Follow Me
Girls, Girls, Girls!
Here's Another Thing
Here's To The . . . (Toasts To The
    Untoasted)
I'd Like To Be
I Followed Her Here, I Followed Her
    There
If The World Were Ruled By Girls
I'll Come Back When You're Not So
    Busy
I'm Back In Town
In These Hard Times
It's A Different Girl Again! (Hello!
    Hello! Hello!)
It's A Sure Sure Sign
It's In A Good Cause And It's Got To
    Be Done
I Want To Mingle With The Girls
I Would, I Would
Keep On Carrying On
Knocking At Every Door
Let's Have Free Trade Amongst The
    Girls
Let's Start All Over Again
Matrimonial Handicap, The
Mr Cupid
Night Off, A
Nobody's Satisfied
Now, Are We All Here? Yes!
Now That The Lights Are Low
Now We're Civilized
Oh, It's A Game!
Oh, The Steamer! Oh, The Sea!
Old Days And The New
Paree! That's The Place For Me
Poor Old Father (Women Get The
    Best Of It)
Profiteering Profiteers, The
Same Old Tale, The
Seven-And-Six
She's Not The Only
Tax The Bachelors
There Are Nice Girls Everywhere
There's A Catch In It Somewhere

There's Something In The
    Atmosphere Of Gay Paree
There's Something In The Seaside Air
They All Lived Happily Afterwards
Tight Skirts Have Got To Go
Up She Goes
Very First Girl I See, The
We'll All Have A Holiday In The
    Summer Time
What Would The Seaside Be Without
    The Ladies?
Whit Cunliffe's Book Of Popular
    Songs
You Can't Do As You Like With A
    Girl
You'll Get On In England If You're
    Not An Englishman
You're Never Too Old To Love A Girl
You're Well Dressed If You're Wearing
    A Smile

CUNNINGHAM, Minnie 1870–1954
Art Of Making Love, The
Bridget And Mike
Did You Ever See A Feather In A
    Tom-Cat's Tail?
Don't Make A Mountain Out Of A
    Molehill
Give Us A Wag Of Your Tail, Old Dog
He Lives In A World Of His Own
Hurdy Gurdy Girl, The
If New Friends Are Silver, Old
    Friends Are Gold
It's Not The Hen That Cackles The
    Most
It Takes a Dirty Hand To Make A
    Clean Hearth-Stone
I've Got A Beau!
Just A Girl!
Little Maiden All Forlorn
Looking At The Pictures
Moon, Die Away
Motor Car Marriage, The
My Own Nigger Boy
That's Where The Man Comes In
Totty, The Nobleman's Daughter

You Can't Judge Cigars By The Picture
 On The Box
You'll Have To Pay

CURRAN, Fred
Bring Your Own Bread And Butter
 (Come To The Wedding)
Come On Steve
Good-Bye, Rachael
I'm On Strike
Money And Misery
Watson's Walnut Watteay What-Not

CURZON, Alma
Fairy Mary
Sixty Years!
What Did The Others Say?

CUTHBURT, SISTERS
Happy Eliza And Converted Jane

CUTLER, Kate 1870–1955; m. Sydney
Ellison (1869–1930)
Duchess's Diamonds, The (sk.)
Fellow Who Did, The
Fellow Who Might, The
Galloping (w. Louis BRADFIELD)
Lucifer And His Angel (sk.)
Pink Nightgown, A (sk.)
Semi-Detachment (w. BRADFIELD)
Somebody (w. Melville STEWART)
Willie Was A Gay Boy

DACRE, Harry° 1860–1922
Bring Your Concertina, John
Model England
Oh, Flo! (Why Do You Go?)

DAGMAR, Alexandra c.1860–?; a.k.a.
Miss Grant Washington
All Alone In Old Cologne
Goodbye, Dolly Gray (parody)
Hey, Ho, Can't You Hear The
 Steamer?
Hiawatha
King And A Gentleman, The
My Zulu Lu
Phoebe
Waiting (Millard)

When The Band Played 'Men Of
 Harlech'
Won't You Be My Sweetheart?
Yarns *or* The Captain Told The Mate

DAINTON, Marie 1880–1938
À La Girl, The
Game Of Life, The (w. Eugene
 STRATTON)
Little Lieutenant, The (sk.)
Mary Was A Housemaid

D'ALBERG, Rosie
As His Father Did Before Him
Don't Send Me Back
Flower Girl, The
Obadiah Walked Behind The Drum
That's Where I'm Off To Now

D'ALBERT, George 1870–1949; orig.
boy soprano w. MOHAWK MINSTRELS;
solo act 1884; returned to Mohawks; solo
again from 1897
Ah, Why Did I Deny My Love?
Be British!
Bravo! Good Old Bobs!
Canoodle In My Canoe
Choose Her In The Morning
Christmas Boxes
Circumstances Alter Cases
Consolations
Don't Do Away With The Peers
 (Piers)
He Comes From Barcelona Where
 The Nuts Come From
Hiding The Button
His Charity Covers His Sin
If I Can't Come Round To Your House
If We Had Only Known
I'm All Right
I Shall Never Forget Her
Isn't It Lovely To Be In Love?
I've Gone And Lost That Darned Old
 Train Again!
John Bull's Traveller
La-La-La-La, Sing This Chorus With
 Me

Living Pictures Wanted (w. MOHAWKS)
Mary Mason *or* Why Did She Ask Me
    To Tie Up Her Shoe?
Misthress Biddy Was A Giddy Little
    Widdy
My Daddy's A Gentleman
Only One Girl At A Time
Ordered South
Peace
Peculiar Julia!
Philadelphia
Quaint
Ring On The Telephone, The
See-Saw Sue
Shall I Be An Angel, Daddy?
She Looked At Me Over Her Shoulder
    (w. MOHAWKS)
Thanking You All The Same
Top Of The 'Bus
Truth, Or A Lie?, The
Wait Till I Return
Wanted—A Lady
When Shall It Be?
When The Cock Begins To Crow
Will My Dream Come True?
You Can't Blame Me For That
You Must Call The Lady 'Mother'
Your Dear Old Dad Was Irish (Your
    Mother Came From Wales)
You're Not Going Like That!

DALLAS, J. J. 1847–1915; a.k.a. John
Dallas
Brother
Cold, Cold Coffee Stall, The
Dear Me, Is That Possible?
Doge With An E, The
Fifteen Puzzle, The
He Knew It!
His Majesty The Baby
I Am So Cold
In My Late Husband's Time
It's A Little Bit Of Sugar For The Bird
It's The Only Bit Of Comfort That I've
    Got
It Tickled Me Most Immensely

I Was There As Well!
Just My Luck
Made In England
Nervous Man, The
Now And Then
Phosphorescent Crew, The
Put Away
Soldier Born, A
Something's Sure To Happen After
    That
Sometimes! Generally! Always! (w.
    Arthur WILLIAMS)
What I've Suffered There Nobody
    Knows
When We Were Young (w. Arthur
    ROBERTS)

D'ALMAINE, Ernest°
Boys Of The Thin Red Line, The
Midshipman, The
My Heart Is Yours If Your Heart's
    Mine
Nelson (A Hundred Years Ago)
When Your Love Grows Cold

D'ALTON, Curtis 1857–1911
England, Home And Victory
Lads Of Merry England, The
Last Of The Boys, The
Longshoreman, The
Our Jack's Come Home Today (w.
    MOORE & BURGESS)
Sons Of England
Sons Of The Brave
That Awful Yeo-Ho!
Under The Same Old Flag

DALTON, Will
Abode Of Love, The
Bring 'Em To Me
Bringing Home The Sunday's Dinner
Buy! Buy! Buy! *or* The Cheesemonger
Father Coaxed Her In
Have A Bit Of Hokey-Pokey
Hero, The
I Don't Care—Let 'Em Laugh

If A Girl Says She Won't, She Won't
I'm About Here, I Am!
It'll Take A Bit Of Wearing Out
I Want To Go Home Again
Just As Good As New
Lottery Of Marriage, The
Medical Man, The
Oh! Girls, If He Wants To Kiss You!
Oh, Mister Noah! (A Tale Of An Ark)
Right Over It
Steeplejack, The
That's The Girl For me
Town Crier, The
Two Rooms To Let
We Do Travel On Our Line
What Ho! There's Hair!
When Another Ten Years Roll By
When I Go Out In The Garden

DALY, Dan 1858–1905
And Then He Woke Up
He Got Plenty
Narragansett (On The Beach At)

DALY, John 'Dutch' 1848–1924; impersonator, especially of the concertina
Love (mon.)

DANBY, Charles 1859–1906; m. Florence Levey (*c.*1865–?)
Around The Town (w. Arthur ROBERTS)
I'm The Big Boss Dude From O-Hi-O
Johnny Jones And His Sister Sue (w. Letty LIND)
Lump Came In My Throat, A
Razzle Dazzle (w. Nellie FARREN & Fred LESLIE)
Sammy, My Old Friend Sam
Tears Rolled Down His Cheek, The

DANIELS, Fred T.
'Arry, 'Arry, 'Arry
Come, Come, Caroline
Cook Who Cooks

DANVERS, Billy 1884–1964
Kiss Me Goodnight
Why Did I Marry My Wife?

DANVERS, Johnny 1860–1939; uncle of Dan LENO; w. MOHAWK MINSTRELS 1886–*c.*1905 and Palladium Minstrels during World War I
Beautiful Spring Onion, The
Clara Nolan's Ball
De Golden Bees Are Buzzin'
Ducks And Quacks (sk.) (w. Walter PASSMORE)
Echo, The (w. Johnny SCHOFIELD)
Good Old Aby Linkum
Handy Dandy Band, The
Hard Times Come Again No More
Her Father's Boot
Hip-I-Addy-I-Ay (parody of Yip-I-Addi-I-Ay)
If The Missis Says It's Black
I Had No Luck That Day
I Know A Gal Dat Lubs A Coon
I'll Send You Down A Letter From The Sky
It's Little Things Like These That Make Me Hate Him
I've Got The Ooperzootic
Lily Of My Life, The
Little Peach In An Orchard Grew, A (A Tale Of Woe)
McFadden Learning To Waltz
Merry King Of Mafeking, The
Nobody Knows The Words
Obadiah And Maria (w. SCHOFIELD)
Ping Pang Poo
Queer Fish (sk.) (w. Agnes FRASER & PASSMORE)
Same Old Lunatic, The
Sisters Gee-Up, The (w. SCHOFIELD)
Soldiers' Mess, The (sk.) (w. PASSMORE)
Sweet Williams (sk.) (w. PASSMORE)
Ta-Ra-Ra Boom-Der-É *or* Pop Goes The Question (w. SCHOFIELD)
Two Johnnies In Love (w. SCHOFIELD)
Uncle Jupe Lubs Chicken Soup
Where The Flow'rets Grow
Why Didn't You Come Before, John?

Why Don't You Leave It Alone?
Wild Man From Borneo, The (w.
    Little THOMAS)
You Give Yourself Away Matilda

DARE, Phyllis 1890–1975; sister of Zena
DARE
    Au Revoir, Little Hyacinth
    Charming Weather (w. Harry
      WELCHMAN)
    Girl With A Brogue, The
    Good-bye, Pierrette!
    Half-Past Two (w. WELCHMAN)
    Hazel Eyes
    I'll Wait For You, Little Girlie
    I Love The Moon
    I Want No Other Little Girl But You
    Mitislaw *or* The Love Match (w.
      Maurice FARKOA)
    Model And The Man, The (sk.) (w. Ivy
      ST HELIER)
    Moon-Bats, The
    My Silent Sweetheart
    One Hour Of Love With You
    Papa's Wife (sk.) (w. Seymour HICKS)
    Rainbow
    Somewhere In France With You
    Violin Song
    Where You Go, Will I Go
    Why Did I Ever Love You?

DARE, Zena 1887–1975; sister of Phyllis
DARE
    I'll Be A Good Little Girl
    Molly O'Halloran
    Papa's Wife (sk.) (w. Seymour HICKS)
    Suppose (w. HICKS)
    Tuppenny Tube, The (w. Farren
      SOUTAR)

DARNLEY, Albert d. 12 Nov. 1944; see
also DARNLEY BROTHERS
    Robbin' Hood

DARNLEY Herbert° 1871–1946; see
also DARNLEY BROTHERS
    Captain Potts (The Messenger Boy)

CIVs
Dashing Militaire, The (The Old
    Guard)
Dolly
John McLauchlan, Hero
Moving In (sk.)
My Next Door Neighbour's Garden
My Old Clay Pipe
Sandow Girl, The (sk.)
Skirmishers, The (sk.)
Smoke, Smoke, Smoke (Fumed In
    Oak)
That's How We've Made Our Name
Typewriter Song, The
Youngest Son, The

DARNLEY BROTHERS Herbert DARN-
LEY and perhaps Albert DARNLEY
    Over The Sea
    You've Got To Come To England

DARRELL, Maudi 1883–1910; daughter
of the agent Hugh J. Didcott (1836–
1909); m. Ian Bullough, as did Lily
ELSIE
    By The Side Of The Zuyder Zee
    Rosalie, I Want You So!

D'AUBAN FAMILY, THE included John
D'AUBAN, w. sisters Emma & Marietta;
see also D'AUBAN & WARDE TROUPE
    Black & White (sk.)
    War Talk (sk.)

D'AUBAN, John & Emma Emma (d. 13
Oct. 1910), sister of John (1841–1922).
See also D'AUBAN FAMILY; John &
Emma WARDE; D'AUBAN & WARDE
TROUPE
    Ain't She Werry Shy?
    Happiest Pair That's Out, The

D'AUBAN & WARDE TROUPE sketch
artistes, ballet dancers, and pan-
tomimists; see also John & Emma
D'AUBAN; John & Emma WARDE.
Emma D'Auban m. John Warde and

Emma Warde m. John D'Auban
 Biter Bit, The
 Deux Blanchiseuses, Les
 I'm A Married Man Myself
 Love In A Muddle
 Where's The Police? (w. Fred & Mrs
  Evans)

DAVENPORT, Harry 1866–1943
 Oh, Lucky Jim (How I Envy Him)
 She Is The Belle Of New York

DAVIES, Ben 1858–1943
 Drink To Me Only
 I'll Sing Thee Songs Of Araby
 In A Persian Garden (w. Emma
  ALBANI & David **BISPHAM** & Hilda
  WILSON)
 In Sympathy
 Lend Me Your Aid
 Love's Garden Of Roses
 Mother O' Mine
 My Dreams
 My Pretty Jane
 Nirvana
 Sing To Me
 So Fare Thee Well
 Star Of Bethlehem
 That Victor Love
 'Tis The Day (Mattinata)
 To Mary (Oh Mary Dear, That You
  Were Here)
 Willow, The

DAVIES, Mary 1855–1930
 Come And Rest
 In Early Spring
 Miller And The Maid, The
 Summer Shower, A
 Twickenham Ferry

DAVIES, Reine d. 2 Apr. 1938
 Meet Me Tonight In Dreamland

DAVIES, Vincent
 Courting In The Rain
 Missus Is Missing
 Pat-A-Cake, Pat-A-Cake

DAVIS, Jessie Bartlett 1860–1905
 I Love You Truly
 I Only Know I Love You
 I Wonder If 'Twas Very Wrong?
 Just A-Wearyin' For You
 Oh, Promise Me
 One Thought Of You
 When Love's Dream Was In Bloom

DAWES, Fred *see* **EVANS** & **LUXMORE**

DAWN, Hazel 1894–1988
 My Beautiful Lady

DAWSON, Peter 1882–1961; also
recorded as Frank Danby, Leonard Daw-
son, Will Strong, and at least nine other
aliases, including Hector **GRANT** under
which name Dawson also worked the
Halls; composed songs as J. P. McCall°
 Asleep In The Deep
 At The Bottom Of The Deep Blue Sea
 Australia
 Bandolero
 Bless This House
 Boots
 Cobbler's Song, The
 Down By The Salley Gardens
 Drake's Drum
 Drink To Me Only With Thine Eyes
 Drum Major, The
 Eleanor
 Excelsior! (w. Ernest **PIKE**)
 Fishermen Of England, The
 Floral Dance, The
 For All Eternity
 Glorious Devon
 Green Hills O' Somerset
 Holy City, The
 Hybrias The Cretan
 I Travel The Road
 Jerusalem
 Jovial Monk Am I, A (*La Poupée*)
 Kashmiri Song
 Kerry Dance, The
 Largo Al Factotum
 Little Brown Jug

Little Grey Home In The West
Lost Chord, The
My Old Shako
Navajo *or* Navaho
Old Brigade, The
Old Father Thames
Old Superb, The
On The Road To Mandalay
O Ruddier Than The Cherry
O Star Of Eve
Parted (Tosti)
Phil The Fluter's Ball
Rocked In The Cradle Of The Deep
Roses Of Picardy
Route Marchin'
Sergeant Of The Line
Shipmates O' Mine
Sincerity
Singer Was Irish, The
Somewhere A Voice Is Calling
Till The Sands Of The Desert Grow
    Cold
'Tis I
Trumpeter, The
Up From Somerset
Volunteer Organist, The
Waiata Poi
Waltzing Matilda
White Wings
Wolf, The
Yeomen Of England, The (*Merrie
    England*)

DAY, Edith 1896–1971
Alice Blue Gown
Irene O'Dare
Kiss In The Dark, A

DEAN, Ella
Child's Dream, A
Grandad's Tales Of Glory
Little Hero
Looking Back
My Mountain Daisy
Never To Meet Again *or* The Bold
    Dragoon
Oh! The Black List

On The Banks Of Bantry Bay (w. J. W.
    ROWLEY)
Stowaway, The
White Squall, The
Willow Tree, The
Wreck Of The Serpent, The

DEANE, Charles 1866–1910
Academy Artist, The
All Have A Drink With Me
All In A Row
All Night Tram, The
All The Way
Anything Wet
Band Struck Up, The
Beautiful Grub
Beautiful Home 'On Hire'
Belle Of The Bar, The
Champs Elysées, Les
Chap Who's In The Know, The
Come Along With Me
Day I Backed A Winner, The
Elephant And Castle, The
Father Of The Boys
Follow The Girls
Four And Twenty Of Us (Last Night)
Four Englishmen In Paree
Four In Hand The Jolly Racing Boys
Garden Gate, The
Grub, Beautiful Grub
'Johnny Walker' Walk, The
Jonah And The Whale
Kick, Boys, Kick
King Cash
King Of The Pier, The
K-N-O-W-I-N-G
Left! Right!
Lovely Woman
Meet Me Tonight
Night Out, A
Now We Shan't Be Long
Oh! The Sea
Oh, What Mugs The Poor Men Are!
One Man, One Vote
One Of The Boys
One Or Two Half O' Pints

One's Enough
On The March
Patsy, The Billingsgate Porter
Pretty Poll
She Wouldn't Dance With Me
Ship Went Up And The Ship Went
　Down, The
Strolling Round The Town
Summoned To An Inquest
Then We Went
They're All Coming Home In The
　Morning
To Your Girl, My Girl
Trafalgar Square
Under The Red Robe
[Up And Down] We Sang A Song
Up To Date Swell, The
What Do You Do With Your Money?
What Ho! There's Hair!
What Makes You Turn Your Nose Up,
　Sally?
When They All Go Out To Work
When They Go To Bye-Bye
When You Find 'Em On The
　Pavement
When You Wake Up In The Morning
Whoa! The Gee Gees
Will You Dance With Me?
Wobberly Walk, The

DEARING, Rose
Artful Maiden, The
I Want A Little Dolly
That's All
That's The Way To Keep A Man At
　Home

DEARTH, Harry 1876–1933
Corporal's Ditty, The
Drinking Song (Sullivan's *The Rose of
　Persia*)
Dumbledum Day
Jack Briton
Lighterman Tom
Mother England's Brewing
My Old Shako
Old Farmer John

Sea Road, The
Sergeant Of The Line, The
Stonecracker John
World's All Right—Keep Smiling, The
Young England

DE BATHE, Lady *see* LANGTRY, Lillie
(1)

DEE, Kitty
Simple Little Maid In The Corner, A

DELANEY, Jack
Aba Daba Honeymoon (w. Jack LEE)
Back Home In Tennessee
Everybody's Jazzing Now
John Peel Rag, The
Oh! Oh! Oh! For The Sight Of A
　Girl
Oh, You Do A Lot Of Funny Things
　You Do
Put On The Searchlight
Something's Always Happening By
　The Seaside
When Irish Eyes Are Smiling

DELANY, Nora sometimes spelled
Norah Delaney; m. Prince Littler
(1901–73) whose sister Blanche m.
George ROBEY
Don't Forget There's Someone In
　Australia
Everybody's Jazzing Now
I Must Be Hame On New Year's Day
Take Me Back Back Back To Inverary
Yaaka Hula Hickey Dula

DELYSIA, Alice 1889–1979
If You Could Care For Me
Live For All You're Worth
Oh, God Bless You, Damn You,
　Clicquot, You Make The World Go
　Round
Poor Little Rich Girl
Rêve Passé, Le
You'd Be Surprised
Your King And Your Country (We
　Don't Want To Lose You)

DEMPSEY, W. P.
Any Amount Of Bites!
Bank That Broke The Man At Monte
    Carlo, The
Bow-Wow On The Brain
Cricket—After Grace
Fifteen Of 'Em On The Parlour Floor
Girl He Left Behind Him, The
Here's To Me Donkey And Me
    Barrow
House To Let
Jacob In Search Of A Father
Man Who Carries The Boards, The
Man Who Wrote Ta-Ra-Ra Boom-
    De-Ay!, The
Mistaken My Vocation
Oh! Take Me There
Once Aboard The Lugger *or* The
    Operatic Villain
Out Of Work
Reuben Glue (With A Little Bunch Of
    Whiskers On His Chin)
Second-Hand Clothes
Since The Old Man Went To Work
There Ain't A Bit O' Pride About Me
They're All Like Life
Usual Morning Performance, The
We'd Any Amount Of Bites
When You Ride On Your Motor Car
Whoa! The Humming Birds
Work And Be Contented (parody)
You Mustn't Do A Thing Like That

DENHAM, Millie
Find A Dear Little Girl
It's The Poor That Help The Poor
Lady Like You, A

DE RANCE, Haidée also a 'violiniste'
Lonely
They Didn't Believe Me (w. George
    GROSSMITH jun.)

DERSON, Winnie
Great March King, The
I Won't Desert You Captain (w. Harry
    ANDERSON)

Only Good-Night, Not Good-Bye
Till Her Boy Comes Home

DE SILVA, Nina 1868–1949; m. Sir John
MARTIN-HARVEY
Aurora's Captive (sk.)

DESLYS, Gaby 1881–1920; m. Harry
PILCER
Come Back To Me (Reviens)
Dance of The Grizzly Bear, The (w.
    Harry PILCER)
Dear Little Johnny (w. PILCER)
Diabolo
English Language, The
Everything In America Is Ragtime
Gaby Glide, The (w. PILCER)
Gaby Trot, The
Just Once Again (w. PILCER)
Mademoiselle Chic (sk.)
Night-Club Girl, The (w. PILCER)
Parisienne, La
Philomene
Sur La Plage
Tout En Rose

DE VERE, Florence
Little Yellow Bird
Miller's Daughter, A (Rubens)
Paper Fan, A
What Is A Maid To Do?

DE VOY, Albert 1836–1915
Dolly
I Like To Smoke My Pipe By My Own
    Fireside
While I Am Away Love Think Of Jolly
    Jack

DEWAR, Frederick 1831–78
Captain Crosstree Is My Name
    (parody of Champagne Charlie)

DICKSON, Dorothy 1893–1995
Look For The Silver Lining (w.
    Gregory STROUD)
Wild Rose

DISTIN, Maud
Monarch Of The Woods

Old Brigade, The
Our Hands Have Met But Not Our
   Hearts

DIXEY, Henry E. 1859–1943
David Garrick (sk.)
Fiji Baby, The

DIXON, George W. 1795–1861
Fireman's Call, The
Zip Coon (Turkey In The Straw) (w.
   Bob FARRELL)

DOCKSTADER, Lew 1856–1924; & his
Great Minstrel Company est. 1886; see
also PRIMROSE & DOCKSTADER
MINSTRELS
Belle Of The Boulevard, The
Coon Coon Coon
Everybody Works But Father
Every Race Has A Flag But The Coon
It Ain't No Lie
I Want My Lulu
Lord! Have Mercy On A Married Man
Meet Me In St Louis, Louis
Nit-Nit-Nit
Oh! What A Beautiful Ocean
Since Mary Harris Went To Paris
There's A Man Coming With A Bundle
What Would The Congregation Say?
You Get All Dat's Comin' To You

DOLBY, Charlotte *see* SAINTON-
DOLBY, Charlotte

DOLLY SISTERS Jennie a.k.a. Yansci
(1892–1941) m. Harry FOX (US) and
Rosie a.k.a. Roszika (1892–1970)
I'm Always Chasing Rainbows (w.
   Harry FOX)
Keep On Humming

DONALDSON, George
You're The Flower Of My Heart
   (Sweet Adeline) (w. SYMPHONY
   QUARTETTE)

DONLIN, Mike 1877–1933
My Brudda, Sylvest' (w. Mabel HITE)

DOREEN, Lilian
Abide With Me (Liddle)
Beyond
Could You Be True To Eyes Of Blue?
Queen Of Love
Queen Of Old Samara
When The Right One Comes Along

DORIS, Dainty 1897–1936; m. Albert
WHELAN
Baby, You're The Sweetest Baby I
   Know
By And By
In The Valley Of The Moon
Just Try To Picture Me Back Home In
   Tennessee
Snow-Time In Switzerland

D'ORME, Aileen 1877–1939
Any Time's Kissing Time
Hush! Little Girl Don't Cry
Under The Deodar
Vie, La

DORMER, Daisy 1883–1947; m. Albert
Jee (of THE EGBERT BROTHERS)
Ain' It Nice?
Anywhere Will Do
Back Home In Tennessee
Beautiful Baby Doll
Buffalo
Can't You Take The Baby Over There
   With You?
Colombo
Don't Call On Friday
Don't Go Back To Carolina
D, O, U, With A G, H, Spells Dough
Everybody Loves Their L'il Old Home
Fares, Please!
Gee! That Ragtime Step!
Girl In The Clogs And Shawl, The
Good-Night, Mr Brown! I'm Out!
Hey, Ho Can't You Hear The
   Steamer?
I Do Like You Susie In Your Sunday
   Clothes
I Like Your Old French Bonnet

I'm Goin', I'm Goin'—I'm Gone
I'm Wait-Wait-Waiting, All I Want Is A
   Man
I've Been Dreaming
I Want A Girl
I Wish I Lived Next Door To You
I Wish I Were You
I Wouldn't Leave My Little Wooden
   Hut For You
Kiss Me Goodbye, My Little Soldier
   Boy
Little Lancashire Rose
Mac! Mac! Mac! Are You Coming
   Back-Back-Back?
Make Your Mind Up, Maggie
   Mackenzie
Marco Pizzicato
Mister Johnson *or* You Told Me To Go
My Boy's A Sailorman
My Man's A Bad Man
My Tennessee, Is That You Calling
   Me?
On The Way To Home Sweet Home
Popsy Wopsy
Ragtime Cowboy Joe
Roses Round My Door
Same Girl On Sunday
Scoot!
Taffy's Got His Jennie In Glamorgan
Take Your Greedy Eyes Off My Little
   Girl!
There's A Great Big Puff-Puff
   Steaming Along To Me
There's A Little Lane Without A
   Turning
Tired Of Me
Underneath The Japanese Moon
Waiting For A Girl
Wedding Bells Won't Ring For You
   And Me, The
What You've Got Look After
When I Live Opposite To You
When I See You Fishing
When The Roses Bid Summer Good-
   Bye
When Will The Sun Shine For Me?

When You Live Opposite To Me
When You're A Long Way From
   Home
When You're Going Back To Dixieland
Wherever The Girls Are You'll Find A
   Jack Tar
Where've You Been While The Sun's
   Been Shining?
Why Don't You Come Around And
   See Me?
Why Don't You Go To Lancashire?
You Shan't Come In My Pretty Cage
You Were The First One

DOUGLAS, Mr
   Unknown Quantity, The (w. Belle
   ELMORE)

DOUGLAS, Eileen
   Miss Lollipop
   Musical Comedy Girl, The
   Rosie's Young Man
   She Taught Him A Thing Or Two,
   Too!

DOWNES, W. H. 1855–1941; sometimes
spelled Downs
   What Will Your Answer Be?
   When Is Daddy Coming Home?

DREDGE, Robert w. MOHAWK
MINSTRELS
   Beautiful Mona
   He Gave His Life For England
   Tears Are Blessings
   Tennessee's My Home

DRESSER, Louise 1882–1965
   My Gal Sal

DRESSLER, Marie 1869–1934
   All Coons Look Alike To Me
   Every Race Has A Flag But The Coon
   Great Big Girl Like Me, A
   Heaven Will Protect The Working Girl
   When Charlie Plays The Slide
   Trombone In The Silver Cornet
   Band
   Why Adam Sinned

DREVER, Constance 1880–1948
  Czardas (*Die Fledermaus*)
  Merry Widow Waltz, The (w. Joseph
    COYNE)
  My Hero (*The Chocolate Soldier*)
  Vilia
  You—Just You

DRIVER, Anna 1876–1915
  Blue Bell

DRUM & MAJOR fl. 1900s–1920s; Tom
Major (1879–1962) a.k.a. Tom Ball or
Tom Major-Ball w. his wife Kitty Grant
(1874–1928). His younger son by his
second wife Gwen (Coates) Glen
(1905–70) is John Major, Prime
Minister of Great Britain 1990–7
  After The Overture (sk.)
  Broker's Man, A (sk.)
  Rose Of Palestine (sk.)

DRYDEN, Leo* 1863–1939; m. (1) Amy
FENTON (div.); (2) Marie TYLER (dec'd);
(3) Ada Colley
  Actor And A Man, An
  As The Years Roll By
  Boys Of The Rank And File
  Bravo, Dublin Fusiliers (Ireland's
    Reply)
  Breach Of Promise Case, The (sk.)
  Britannia (sk.) (w. Amy FENTON)
  Call Us And We'll Soon Be There
  Christmas Bells
  Come Back—Forgive And Forget
  David Garrick (sk.)
  Desert, The
  Everyday Life
  False Gods
  Falsely Accused (mon.)
  Father Of The Boys (John Bull Up To
    Date)
  Fiscal Joe
  Flag Of Liberty, The
  For Freedom And Japan (sk.)—also a
    song
  Free Again

  Gallant Gordon Highlanders
  God Bless And Keep Victoria
  Going Home *or* The Miner's Return
  Great White Mother, The
  Health, Wealth, Women And Wine
  House Of Temperley, The
  How India Kept Her Word
  Icebound
  I'm Going Back To My Home Again
  India's Reply
  Jack Crawford *or* He Nailed Our
    Colors To The Mast
  Jack Is A Jolly Good Fellow
  Josephine
  Lifeboat Crew, The
  Love And Duty
  Love Is The Magnet
  Lucie Manette (sk.)
  Masher And Barmaid
  Mercia (sk.)
  Mice And Men
  Military Blunder, A (mon.)
  Miner's Dream Of Home, The
  Miner's Return, The (Going Home)
  Napoleon's Son (sk.)
  Only Way, The
  Planter's Reverie, The
  Pull Boys Together
  Romance Versus Reality
  Rumfoozlers' Club, The
  Sailor's Light, The
  Skipper's Daughter, The
  Sole Survivor, The
  Take No Notice
  They Cop The English Off At Monte
    Carlo
  Trafalgar's Day
  'Twixt Love And Duty
  What Britishers Are Made Of
  White Man, A (sk.)

DUGGAN, Maggie 1860–1919
  All In A Row
  All Together
  Do! Do! My Huckleberry, Do!
  For A Nosegay

Girl With The Golden Hair, The
Give It A Wink
He Didn't Know Ge-Og-Ra-Phy!
I'm Going To Get Married Today,
    Hooray!
I'm The Airy Fairy
In Her Hair She Wore A White
    Camelia
K-N-O-W-I-N-G
Leave 'Em Alone, They'll Come
    Home In The Morning
Look At The Weather We've Had
Made In England
Making The Time Fly
Man That Broke The Bank At Monte
    Carlo, The
Mary Ann MaGinty (Little Miss
    Muffet)
Not Dead Yet
Oh, Mr Soldier Man
Oh! The Music
She Never Comes Home Till
    Morning
There's Something About 'Er As
    Fetches Yer

DU MAURIER, George 1834–96
Buttercup, The (w. Quintin TWISS)

DUNBAR, 'Merry' Annie
Gentleman Scamp, The (sk.)
He Thought Of His Home Sweet
    Home
I Don't Care
It Is Just To Please The Ladies
Look At Isabella!
Romping In The Park
That's Where The Money Goes

DUNBAR, E. C.° 1841–1900
Assassination Of Mr C. Robin, The
Bear It And Grin

DUNCAN, Minnie m. Arthur Godfrey (d.
16 May 1934)
Bit Too Soon, A
Coster's Christening, The (w. Arthur
    Godfrey)

I'll Be Your Daily Mail
When Big Ben Strikes

DUNLO, Viscountess *see* **BILTON**, Belle

DUNN, James W.°
Cosy Little Home, A
Don't Leave Your Father, Boy
Fauntleroy Jones
Jack's As Good As Gold
John Bull And His Three Little
    Brothers
Jovial Miller Joe
Love's Jubilee

DUNN, John 1812–75
Jump Jim Crow
Sich A Gittin' Upstairs

DUNNING, Alice 1847–97; m. Horace
LINGARD
Act On The Square (ladies' version)
As Good As Gold (ladies' version)
Funny Crazy Man, The
Up In A Balloon (ladies' version)

DUNVILLE, T. E. 1868–1924; m. Millie
LINDON (div.)
Accidents (Up To The Moon He
    Bunked)
Actions Speak Louder Than Words
Adam Had An Adder
All In A Row
All One Price
And The Verdict Was
Angels Have Called Him Home, The
Babies
Bad Language
Bunk-A-Doodle I Do
Con-Stant-I-No-P-L-E
Conundrums (I'm A Philosopher)
Couldn't Help It, Had To!
Did He?
Dinky Doo, Twenty-Two
Fire Was Burning Hot, The
Fish I Caught At Brighton, The
Funny Man, Ha, Ha!, The
Getting To The Bottom Of It

He Felt A Draught
He Stopped (air: Grandfather's Clock)
How's That For A Snap-Shot?
Hypochondriac, The
I Didn't Get A Look At 'Em At All
I'm A Philosopher (Conundrums)
Ingenious Man
In Our Backyard Last Night
It Hurts!
It's Only Once A Year
Just For Curiosity
Just My Luck
Kick Off!
Lighthouse Keeper, The
Lively On And Lively Off
Love
Man Of The Wide Wide World, The
Mixtures *or* That Finishes The First
 Verse
Mother's Advice (Osborne)
Mumps The Memory Man
Naval Scarecrow
Never Twice Alike
Night Duty
Noses
Not Yet
Nuff Said
Nurse Procter
One Night Only
One Thing Brought Up Another
Packed Ev'ry Night
Phonetic Family, The
Pop-Pop-Popperty-Pop
Postponed
Punctured
Remedies
Riley Did It!
Scientific Man, The
Sentry, The
Sherlock Holmes
Signs
Somebody's Mother
Sour Apple Tree, The
'Special Scotch'-Man, The
Still I Breathe
Stormy Winds Did Blow, The

Telegraph Boy
That'll Doodle Doodle Doodle Doodle
 Do
That Reminds Me! Ever Heard This?
Then We Had Another One
There Must Be Another One
 Somewhere
There Yet *or* I Can't Get Rid Of 'Em
They Were Very Very Good To Me
'Twas A Dark And Stormy Night
Two Little Boys In Blue (parody)
Umpi-Doodle-Um
War Correspondent At The Front,
 The
Washerwoman, The
Washie Wishie Man
Well Caught!
We're Another Man Short In Our
 Force
What Can I Do For You Now?
What Price That For A Quick
 Change?
Whoa! Back-Pedal!
Wishee Washee Man, The

DUPREZ, May Moore 1885–1946
Beautiful Brittany
Bonnie Scotland
By The Side Of The Zuyder Zee
Coax Me
Dutch Police Girl, The
Gretchen
Hans Across The Sea
Hey Lassie, Hae Ye Got A Sister?
If A Rooster Can Love So Many
 Chickens Can't A Man Love More
 Than One?
Jeremiah
Leetle Meester Baggy Breeches
Louisa Schmidt
Making Eyes
Nora From Norway
Sing A Hielan' Melody
Take Me In A Taxi, Joe
Under The Hebrew Moon
What's The Use Of Moonlight

When There's No-One Round
To Love?

DU RELL TWIN BROTHERS
Fountain In The Park, The
While Strolling Thru The Park

DURIAH, F.° w. MOHAWK MINSTRELS
B.R.O.W.N.
There's Going To Be A Wedding

DU VAL, Charles H.° 1846–89
Bright Sparkling Wine
Green Shores Of Erin, The
Leaning On A Balcony
My Beaux or I Can't Make Up My
Mind

DWYER, Johnny c.1853–1926
Cock Of The South
Grinding Up The Golden Corn
In My Hand (I Wish There Were No
Prisons)
Luny Bill
She's Worth Her Weight In Gold

EARLE, Fred° 1877–1915; son of Joseph
Tabrar°
Birdseed
But I Can't Remember Now
Charley's Aunt
Do, Do, Be Always On The 'Do'!
Don't Stick It Out Like That
For Me! For Me!
For My Corn Began To Shoot
His Room's To Let
I Don't Care What Becomes Of Me
I Looked Out Of The Window
In The Dark
I Take 'Em Home To Father Every
Night
I've Been Laying On The Field
John! John! John! (Time's Going On)
Jones You're Wanted
Landlady's Daughter, The
Let 'Em See You've Got One Father
Like This

Little Dummy Teat My Mother Gave
Me
Meat! Meat!
Oh! Sally O!
Oh! The Harbour Lights
Only Think Of It (Half A Dollar)
On The March
Pom Tiddly Om Pom or That's Not
Good Enough For Me
Seaweed
She Was A Girl Who Knew A Bit
Take Pity On A Starving Man
Te-Hi-Aye or The First Time I—
That'll Be The Time
They All Come Back To Me
They're All In Mourning
Trilby's Rival
Trust Him Now
Warm Today!
We've All Got To Go And See The
Doctor
Whack-Fol-The-Diddle-Ol-The-Di-
Do-Day!
When They Found I Was A Soldier
With My Little Wigger-Wagger In My
Hand

EDGAR, Marriott° 1880–1951; wrote all
his own material; half-brother of Edgar
Wallace°
Genial Duchess, The
I Never Never Never Never Saw Such
A Thing Before
Let's Swap
Lion And Albert, The
Man In Red, The
Marksman Sam
Monday
Out In The Open
Return Of Albert, The
Runcorn Ferry, The

EDGAR, Ralph
Happy England
It's Only For Life
John Bull
Pothouse Politician, A

EDGE, Jack b. 18 Oct. 1891
Could Lloyd George Do it?
I'm Going To Be Married In June

EDISS, Connie 1871–1934
Advertisements
Brighton (Rubens)
Class Class!
Fancy Dress Song
Good Behaviour
I Did It Very Well
I Don't Know But I Guess
I Love Society
In The Wash
I've Been To The Durbar
Lady Tom (When My Hubby Is Sir Tom)
Little Girl From Paris
Painting
Pity
Riding (w. Willie EDOUIN)
Rosie Rosie (I Ride To Win)
She'd Never Done A Thing Like That Before
She's A Lady Without Education
Way To Treat A Lady, The
What Could A Poor Girl Do?
When I Marry A Millionaire
When I Was In The Chorus Of The Gaiety

EDOUIN, Willie 1841/6–1908; m. Alice ATHERTON
Riding (w. Connie EDISS)
When We Are On The Stage (w. Florence ST JOHN)
You Fly Sky High

EDWARDS, Fanny 1843–1908; m. Harry CLIFTON
Beautiful Moon
Cupid In The Kitchen (w. Harry CLIFTON)
Folly And Fashion (w. CLIFTON)
Happy Policeman, The (w. CLIFTON)
He Must Have A Thousand A Year
I'm Only Bridesmaid After All

Laura! Laura! Frederick's Come
Love And Pride (w. CLIFTON)
There's A Smile Waiting For Me At Home (w. CLIFTON)
Very Suspicious or Family Jars (w. CLIFTON)

EDWARDS, Gus* 1879–1945
I Am Crazy To Go On The Stage
Military Man, The
Take Me To My Louisiana Home
Those Wedding Bells Shall Not Ring Out

EDWARDS, Will E. d. 28 Apr. 1940?
All Change
Are We Downhearted? No! (Robins)
Don't Let It Go Any Farther
Don't You Know A Different Game To That?
Father!
He Started In A Very Small Way
Is There Anything More I Can Show You?
It Grows On Yer
Little Tommy's Christmas Pudding
Our Beano
Queries or Nobody Seems To Know
Wake Of Patsy Callaghan, The
Why, Of Course! (w. Paul MILL)

EGBERT BROTHERS, THE Albert Jee (1878–1942) who m. Daisy DORMER and his brother Seth (1878–1944)
All The Winners
Happy Dustmen, The

EGERTON, Frank*
My Name It Is John Barleycorn
Nellie or Ten Past Nine
Sing To Me, Johnnie

EISDELL, Hubert 1874–1948
Battle Eve, The (w. Norman ALLIN)
Excelsior!
Keys Of Heaven, The (w. Dora LABETTE)
Love's Garden Of Roses

Parted (Tosti)
Roses Of Picardy
Somewhere A Voice Is Calling
Where My Caravan Has Rested

ELEN, Gus° 1862–1940
'Allays In Jail
All By Myself
'Arf A Pint Of Ale
Bang Went The Copper
Boom-De-Ay Ta-Ra-Ra
Bore O' Bef'nal Green, The
Buffalo Bill
But That's Nothing
Cabby, The
Catch 'Em Alive Oh! (The Fly Paper
   Man)
Cockney Cabby, The
Coster's Mansion, The
Coster's Muvver, The
Coster's Nightmare, The
Coster's Pony, The
Cove What's Lived In London All 'Is
   Life, A
Dick Whittington—A Parody (You
   Have Made A Nice Old Mess
   Of It)
Don't Stop My 'Arf A Pint O' Beer
Down By The Icebergs
Down The Dials
Down The Road
'E 'As My Symperfy
'E 'As The As-Er-Dacity To Grumble
'E Dunno Where 'E Are
'E Grumbles
'E's A Reg'lar Barney Tomato
'E Talks Like A Picture Book
Faithful Coster, The
Faithless Donah, The
Finest Flow O' Langwidge Ever 'Eard,
   The
Flying Man, The (Baldwin's Rival)
Funny Little Thing Is A Baby, A
Golden Dustman, The
Go Like This
Good Riddance

Great Spink Pearls, The
Haunted By 'Daisy Bell'
Haunted Idiot, The
I Couldn't Get Out
If It Wasn't For The 'Ouses In
   Between
If I Was King Of England
I Helped Myself
I'm Going To Settle Down In England
I'm Happy
I'm Very Unkind To My Wife
Inky
I Shall Never Find Anuvver Pal Like
   Bill
It's A Great Big Shame! or I'm Blowed
   If 'E Can Call 'Isself 'Is Own
It's A Marvel How 'E Doos It But 'E
   Do!
It's A Sprahtin or The Coster's
   Moustache
It's Naughty
It Sounds So Werry Pretty
It Was Gone
Jilted Shoeblack, The
Just Because She's Got An 'Andle To
   Her Name
King Of The Castle, The
Life's Worth Living After All
Lucky Treasure Seeker, The
Me And 'Er And 'Er And Me
Men You Meet In A Pub
Meriah
Mrs Carter (Murphy)
My Next-Door Neighbour's Gardin
Myrtle
Nature's Made A Big Mistake
Never Introduce Your Donah To A Pal
New Cut Coon, The
New Perjarma Hat, The
Nice Quiet Day, A (A Postman's
   Holiday)
Nixie In Your Ski
Not Tonight
Old Granny Gladdy or Teetotallers By
   Act Of Parliament
'Oo Could Be Happier Than Me?

Our Pretty Little Willa Down At
  Barkin'
Our Tyke
Pavement Artist, The
Postman's Holiday, A (A Nice Quiet
  Day)
Publican, The
Seven Dials
Skipper In The Mercantile Marine,
  The
Some O' Yer Do Git Abaht
Sometimes
Star Of Captain Coe, The
There Ain't No Gitting Rid Of 'Im At
  All
Thoughtful Thinking Man, The
'Tis A Lady
Unemployed Question, The (scena)
Wag Of The Dog's Tail, The
Wait Till The Work Comes Round
What A Garden
Who's That A-Squalling?
Wrong Un', The (sk.)
You 'Ave Made A Nice Old Mess Of It
  see Dick Whittington
You Can Almost Shut Your Eyes And
  'Ear Them Grow
You Could See As 'Ow 'E Didn't Feel
  At 'Ome
You've Only Got To Stop Just Where
  You Are
You Wouldn't 'It An Old 'Un Would
  Yer!

ELLIOTT, G. H. 1884–1962; m. (1)
Emilie HAYES (dec'd); (2) Florence
May Franey k.a. June (1907–96)
  Anyone
  Baby Lucy
  By The Blue Lagoon
  Caroo
  Cinnamon Sue
  Dinah
  Don't Go Back To Carolina
  Good-bye For Ever
  Hello! Susie Green

Here Comes The Chocolate Major
He's My Military Man
How D'You Do, My Baby?
If It Means Love
If The Man In The Moon Were A
  Coon
If You're Going Back To Dixie
If You Should See A Dandy Coon
In Arizona
In That Little Home Built For Two
I'se A-Waitin' For Yer Josie
I Used To Sigh For The Silvery Moon
I've Had My Fortune Told
I Want To Go To Idaho
I Want You To See My Girl
Just Try To Picture Me Back Home In
  Tennessee
Kate, Won't You Roller Skate?
Lazy Maisie
Lily Of Laguna, The
Little Dolly Daydream
Lonely Bachelor Coon, A
Lovelight
Ma Havanah Queen
Maisie Lou
Mamie May
Mammy's Mississippi Home
Mandy From Tonypandy (Yaaki-
  Daaki-Yaaki-Dah)
Mister Owl
Moon, Moon, Moon
Mr Golliwog, Good Night
My Californian Girl (w. Emilie
  HAYES)
My Orange Girl
My Southern Maid
My Venice Girl
Only Coon Without A Gal, The
Rastus Brown
Ride A Cock Horse To Town
Sadie, You're So Condescending
Sue, Sue, Sue
Sunny Skies
Susie 'Oo!
There's A Little Black Cupid In The
  Moon

Vera
Waiting
What Is Your Name?
When The Midnight Choo Choo
    Leaves For Alabam'
Why Can't A Coon Wed A Young
    White Girl?
Yaaki-Daaki-Yaaki Dah (Mandy From
    Tonypandy)
You'd Never Know That Old Home
    Town Of Mine

ELLIOTT, Gertrude 1874–1950; m. Sir
Johnston FORBES-ROBERTSON
    Happy Prince, The (mon.)
    My Cousin Caruso (sk.)
    Rose Of The Ghetto, The (sk.)

ELLIOTT, Leslie b. 1893
    Oh Cecil, I Shall Have To Call The
        Guard
    Sing Hey! For The Life Of An Actress
    You Really Needn't Bother Any More

ELLIOTT, Lottie
    Bow-Wow On The Brain
    Stroke Of The Pen, A
    Velvet And Rags The World Over

ELLIOTT, Rose
    If You Love Her And She Loves You
    I Will Love You Just The Same
    She May Have Seen Better Days
    She's A Woman Still or Don't Be Hard
        On Her
    What's The Good Of Worrying,
        Father?
    When My Ship Is Sailing
    While The Bells Were Ringing

ELLIOTT-SAVONAS, THE James B.
Elliott (d. 22 May 1906), May (d. 5 July
1929), Ralph (1841–1909), Thomas
(1870–1929)
    Garden Of Harmony, The (sk.)
    Palace Of Orpheus, The (sk.)

ELLIS, Madge
    He Only Did It Once

Kiss Your Goosie Woosie
Little, You Know, So So, A
Midway In The Moon, The
Modern Country Maid, The
Only A Little Yaller Coon
Somehow Or Anyhow
You Show Me Your Slate

ELLISON, J. W.
    All Through A Gee-Gee-Gee
    Our British Girls
    Sweetest Sign Of All, The

ELMORE, Belle 1873–1910; poisoned
and dismembered by her husband 'Dr'
Hawley Harvey Crippen (1862–1910)
    Down Lovers' Walk
    Major, The
    She Never Went Further Than That
    Sister Mary Ann
    Unknown Quantity, The (w. Mr
        DOUGLAS)

ELSIE, Lily 1883/6–1962; m. Ian
Bullough, widower of Maudi DARRELL
    Dollar Princess, The
    Merry Widow Waltz (w. Joe COYNE)
    Vilia

ELTON, Fred° d. 1960
    Butterfly And The Rose, The
    Don't Forget, Mignonette
    Kate or One Little Name That's
        Impressed On My Memory
    Knickerbockers
    Little Maid Of Monte Carlo
    One Flag, One Fleet, One Throne
    Sea Sights (parody)
    Sons Of England, Sons Of Wales
    Tra La La Mixtures
    When The Leaves Are Tinged With
        Gold (The 100 Guineas Song)

ELVIN, Joe° (& Co.) 1862–1935; sketch
troupe; see also KEEGAN & ELVIN
    Ally Sloper's Birthday
    'Appy 'Ampstead (Le Brunn)
    Another Winner

Billy's Money Box
Bookie, The
Clock, The
Confidence Trick, The
Day's Sport, A
Deaf
Dreadful Tragedy, A
Duffy's Dining Rooms
Fares, Please
Hansom Cabby, The
Holy Friar, The
Jockey, The
Joke, The
King O' The Castle
Life's Little Troubles (At The Dentist)
Lively Figure, A
Money For Nothing
Mother's New Husband
My Lot
Obedient Billy
One Of The Boys
On The Flat
Out All Night
Over The Sticks
Paying The Bill
Poor Joe
Riding To Orders
Rocket, The
Sailor Lad
Squeaker, The
Sunny Seaside, The (song)
Taxi, The
Tight Rein, A
Tinker's Holiday, The
Toffo's Trotter
Tonight's The Night
Touched
Trespassers Beware!
Two Nights Out
Uncle Izzy
Under Cross Examination
Village Maiden, The
What's In A Name? (song)
Whines And Spirits
Who Sez So?
Wrong House, The

EMERALD, Connie 1891–1959; m. Stanley LUPINO; see also SISTERS EMERALD
  Love Me While The Lovin' Is Good

EMERALD, Nell b. 1878; m. Will H. Fox (1858–1929); see also SISTERS EMERALD
  Come And Make Love To Me
  I'd Rather Polka Than Waltz, Bill
  Love
  You Are A Little White Girl

EMERALD, Nora 1869–1964; m. Will EVANS; see also SISTERS EMERALD,
  Molly O'Morgan

EMERALD, SISTERS Connie, Nora, & Nell
  Ain't They Nobby?
  All Coons Look Alike To Me
  Do As We Do
  Mammy
  Milkmaid, The
  Money Isn't Everything
  Simple Little Maidens
  Two Modest Little Maidens

EMERSON, Billy 1845–1902
  Big Sun Flower
  Melissa
  Pretty As A Picture
  Sociation Ball

EMERSON, Ida° m. Joseph E. HOWARD
  Goodbye, My Lady Love (w. Joseph E. HOWARD)
  Hello! Ma Baby Love (w. HOWARD)

EMERY, Winifred 1863–1924; m. Cyril MAUDE
  Playwright, The (sk.) (w. Cyril MAUDE)

EMMET, Joseph K.° 1841–91; m. Lottie GILSON
  Bells Are Ringing
  Kiss Me
  Peek-A-Boo
  Ring Down The Curtain

EMMETT, Daniel Decatur° 1815–1904;
sometimes spelled Emmit or Emitt;
wrote most of his own material; see also
BRYANT'S MINSTRELS and VIRGINIA
MINSTRELS
  Fine Old Color'd Gemman
  I Wish I Was In Dixie (w. BRYANT'S
    MINSTRELS)
  Jordan Is A Hard Road To Travel
  My Old Aunt Sally
  Old Dan Tucker
  Rocky Road (I'm Going Home To
    Dixey)
  Way Down Louisiana
  Yes, I Will, By Jingo
  Zip Coon (Turkey In The Straw)

EMNEY, Fred 1865–1917; sketch comic;
nephew of Arthur and Fred WILLIAMS
  Arrival Of A Rival, The
  Mrs Le Browning (w. Sydney
    FAIRBROTHER)
  Plumbers, The (w. Harry GRATTAN)
  Sister To Assist 'Er, A (w.
    FAIRBROTHER)

ERNEST, Charles
  Come O'er The Stream Jessie (w.
    CHRISTY MINSTRELS)
  Come Sing To Me Again (w. CHRISTY
    MINSTRELS)
  Little Maggie May (w. Christy
    MINSTRELS)
  My Gal Is A High Born Lady (w.
    HAVERLY'S MINSTRELS)

ERROL, Bert 1883–1949; brother-in-law
of Cliff RYLAND
  Blue Eyes
  I Want You, Want You, Want You
  My Sahara Rose

ESMOND, Maud
  I'd Like To Call You Sweetheart
  Joan! Joan! Joan! Come Home!
  Kind Mr Postman
  Mother's Message
  You Can't Stop The Sun From Shining

ESSEX, Clifford
  Caterpillar And The Rose, The
  Honeysuckle And The Bee
  My Cinderella Sue
  Pierrot's Song, The
  Rain, Rain, Go Away

ESSEX, Violet 1892–1941
  Any Time's Kissing Time (w. Courtice
    POUNDS)
  Dear Little Shamrock, The
  Granny's Song At Twilight
  Here's To Love And Laughter

ETHIOPIAN SERENADERS est. 1846
Francis G. Germon, Moody G.
Stanwood, George A. Harrington, G.
William White, G. W. Pell
  Aunt Sally
  Buffalo Gals
  Come Darkies Sing
  Dandy Broadway Swell, The
  De Boatman's Dance
  De Boatman's Daughter
  De Coloured Fancy Ball
  De Spring Ob De Year Hab Come At
    Last
  I'll Tell Thee A Tale
  I Wish I Was In Old Virginny
  Locumloshos Jimjam
  Lucy Neal
  Mary Blane
  My Skiff Is On The Shore
  Oh, Susannah
  Old Dan Tucker
  Old Joe
  Rosa Lee or Don't Be Foolish Joe
  Rose Of Alabama
  Who's Dat Knocking At De Door?

EVANS, George 'Honey Boy'
1870–1915
  I'll Be True To My Honey Boy
  Willie The Weeper

EVANS & LUXMORE see also EVANS, Will
  Musical Pub, The or After Hours (sk.)
    (w. Fred Dawes)

Evans, May d. 25 Feb. 1911; sister of
Will Evans and Harry Evans (w. Fred
Karno)

Do Unto Mother As She Has Done To
You
'E Means No 'Arm
For Baby's Sake
He Takes Me Up In The Gallery
Mary Ann Made A Mistake
Oh, Nancy!
Oh! That Slavey!
One Of The Proudest Moments Of
His Life
Sweetest Flower Dies, The
We Both Loved Kate

Evans, Will° 1872–1931; sketch comic;
brother of May Evans and Harry Evans
(w. Fred Karno); teamed w. Barry
Lupino (1882–1962) as Lupino & Evans;
m. (1) Ada Luxmore (d. 13 May 1897) w.
whom k.a. Evans & Luxmore; (2) Nora
Emerald

A To Z (song)
Barmaid's Lament, The
Breach Of Promise Case
Building The Chicken House
Cowcaddens (song)
Derby Winner, The
Developing A Photograph
Down At The Garden Gate (song)
Englishman, The (song)
Harnessing The Horse
Hidden Treasure
I Do Love Myself, Don't I? (song)
If I Had A Thousand A Year (song)
Jim! (song)
Jockey, The
(K)night In Armour
Lady Godiva
Laying A Carpet
Lucinda Wriggle (song)
Mermaid, The (song)
Missing Verse, The (song)
Mothers And Daughters
Papering A House

Plain Mrs Dripping
Police Court Justice
Railway Station Sandwich, The (song)
Robinson Crusoe
Salome (Weston)
Sharp Tin Tacks (song)
Snowstorm, The
Suffragette, The (song)
That's Dangerous (song)
White-Washing A Ceiling
Yachting
You Don't Know, They Don't Know,
And I Don't Know (song)
You Put Me In Mind Of Me (song)

Evelyn, Clara 1886–1980
First Love—Last Love—Best Love (w.
George Robey)
Lulu Von Linden
You, Just You

Everard, Dan
There'll Be No War!
Yuss, I Don't Fink

Fair, W. B. 1850–1909
Hot Member
John Bull's Handerkerchief
May Be!
More R Than F
That'll Pull 'Em Round
Tommy Make Room For Your Uncle
What Will You Have To Take?

Fairbrother, Sydney 1873–1941
I Wants A Man Like Romeo
Mrs Le Browning (sk.) (w. Fred
Emney)
Sister To Assist 'Er, A (sk.) (w. Emney)

Fairburn, George d. 15 May 1918
Each One Got The Wrong 'Un
Gentlemen Of The Jury
I Haven't Told The Missus Up To Now
It's Coming Home Tonight
Not One!
Old Man Laughed With A Ha! Ha!
Ha!, The

Pro's Political Palaver, The
She Did
So Do I, Ha! Ha! Ha! Ha!
They All Bobbed Up And Down

FALKE, Charles
She Is More To Be Pitied Than
  Censured
She Was Bred In Old Kentucky

FANCOURT, Tom° d. 7 Aug. 1940
Charming Young Girl, The
Come And Have A Tid'ly Round The
  Corner
Farmer's Son, The
Herr Von Clarinette
I Caught It
Ticket Of Leave Man, The
Try Another One!
We All Went Following On

FANE, Sydney P.
My 'Little Mary'
Ping Pong Courtship
Rhymes And Reasons

FANNIN, Paddy 1840–88
Inlightened Car Man, The
Irish Jaunting Car, The
Irish Volunteer, The
Jude Foy
Private Still, The
Sports Of Dublin, The

FARKOA, Maurice c.1864–1916
Chic Parisien, Le
Do I Like Love?
English Mees, The
Fair Exchange, A
Gay Bohemi-ah
Grammatical Grievances
I Like You In Velvet
I Never Flirt
Laughing Song, The
Little Story, A
Military Masher, The
Mitislaw or The Love Match (w. Zena
  DARE)

Mrs 'Enery 'Awkins (in French)
Philosophy (anon: Emmell)
Say Yes
There Little Girl Don't Cry
Trilby Will Be True
Two Dirty Little Hands
Who'll Marry Me?
Why Won't You?

FARRANT, Tommy
England's Queen To England's Heroes
Midshipmite, The
On Alma's Heights
Shadows Of Memory
Spring
Three Ages Of Love, The
Willie, We Have Missed You

FARRAR, Gwen 1899–1944
Dangerous Men
It Ain't Gonna Rain No Mo' (w. Norah
  BLANEY)
Our Little Garden Subbub (w.
  BLANEY)
Percy's Posh Plus-Fours Are Priceless
  (w. BLANEY)
Ukulele Lady (w. BLANEY)
Where Are They?

FARRELL, Bob°
Zip Coon (Turkey In The Straw) (w.
  George W. DIXON)

FARRELL, Nellie 1859–89; m. Pat
FEENEY
As True As The Stars That Are Shining
Dear Old Paddy's Land
Harbour Lights, The
Her Lad In The Scotch Brigade
Irish Girl's Opinion, An
My Boy's Birthday
My Heart Has Gone With A Sailor
One Black Sheep Will Never Spoil A
  Flock
Staunch To The Red White And Blue
Tim McGee or We're Going To be
  Married In The Morning

Wanderer, The
Where The Sweet Green Shamrock
Grows

FARREN, Fred d. 8 May 1956
Apache Dance, The (w. Beatrice
COLLIER)
Everybody's Doin' It Now (w. Ida
CRISPI)

FARREN, Nellie 1848–1904; m. Robert
SOUTAR; mother of Farren SOUTAR
Chucked Again
Continong, The (w. Edward TERRY &
Kate VAUGHAN)
Crutch And Toothpick
Don't Know So Much About That (I)
(w. Fred LESLIE)
En Garçon *or* The Bachelor's Ballad
Far By And Bye, The
Five Ages (w. LESLIE)
Hildebrandt Montrose
How Do You Like London?
I Am Such A Silly Little Thing
If She Told Me To Go To Jericho
I'm A Jolly Little Chap All Round
I'm Glad To Be Back Again
I'm Ninety-Five
Inside
It Mayn't Be Yet
It's a Funny Little Way I've Got
It's Nice
I've Just Had A Wire To Say So (w.
LESLIE)
Jack's Alive-O!
Johnny Jones And His Sister Sue (w.
LESLIE)
Lover's Alphabet, The (w. W. E.
ROYCE & TERRY)
Ma's Advice (w. LESLIE)
My Boy
Nice Boy
One Of The Boys
Polite Pilot, The
Pretty Little Poll Of Plymouth
Razzle Dazzle (w. Charles & Leslie
DANBY)

Ship Goes Up, Up, Up
Street-Boy's Life, A (Street Arab)
Thimble Jack The Newspaper Boy
Toddy-Fol-Lol
What Cheer, Ria!
What Price That?
When Noah Hung Out In The Ark
Whistling Song, The (w. TERRY)
Young Cock Cackles As The Old Cock
Crows, The

FAULKNER, Edith
He Led Me Up The Garden
Men

FAWN, James 1850–1923
Ah! Ah!
Ain't You Glad You Didn't?
(And) Then The Band Played
Another Glass Round
Answers To Correspondents
'Arf A Mo!
As If I Didn't Know!
Ask A P'liceman
Beautiful Girls
Beware Of The Dress That's Full Of
Girl
Blackwall Dock
Briton, The
Brown Caught A Gudgeon
But However
By And By (w. Arthur ROBERTS)
Can It Be Done?
Chicago
Cobbler, The
Copy Your Uncle Joe
Copy Your Uncle John
Daddy Long Legs
Deception
Don't Say That You Heard It From
Me
Don't Tell The Missus
Dream Of The Albert Hall, A
Drum Solo, The *or* Rum Tiddely Um
Tum
Exchange And Mart
Fine And Fresh And Blooming

Four Jolly Good Fellows
Funny! Very Funny! (w. Arthur
    ROBERTS)
Girls At The Top Of Our Street *see*
    Those Girls etc.
Goodness Gracious (w. ROBERTS)
Good Old London
Half A Mo'!
Handy Man, The
Have Another
He Did It
He Isn't A Marrying Man
Hello! Where Are You Coming To?
He Wanted Me To Have Some
Hurrah For The Ribbon Of Yellow
Hush! Mum's The Word
I Borrowed It
I Did It!
I Dropped It
I Haven't Quite Made Up My Mind
I'll Tell Your Mother What You've
    Done
Instinct
Is It Likely? Oh, Dear No
It Makes A Fellow Think A Bit
It Must Have Been The Lobster
It's Silly To Wait
It Was Mine
I've Joined 'Em *or* Yea Yea Yea
Ju-Jah!
Just In Time
Keep Your Eye On 'Em (ladies'
    version)
Kisses (I've Done It Before And I'll
    Do It Again)
Last Bus, The
Magistrate, The *or* Up Before The
    Beak
Man At The Door, The
Man Mighty Man
Man's Not Required
Masonry
Matrimonial Agent, The
Mind The Baby
Mine You Know
Missis, The

Money Matters
Musical Wife, The *or* Nursery
    Rhymes
National Harmonic Club, The
Never Again In Love
No More
Not Wanted
Obedient Miss, An
Off To America
Oh! Can It Be Love?
Oh, Caroline
Oh Do Elizabeth
Oh, The Popsy Wopsy
Oh, The Weather
Once Or Twice
Only One (Hall)
On My Own
Our Fishing Match
Play's The Thing For Me, The
Postman, The *or* I'd Like To Be In
    The 'Know', You Know
Publican, The *or* Brother Bung
Right Before The Missis Too!
Sanitary Inspector, The
Saving Them All For Mary
Second Sight
Selina, *or* The Duchess of Rosemary
    Lane
She Trotted Me Off To Church
She Wasn't Far Off It
Ship Went Down To The Bottom Of
    The Sea, The
Single Gentleman, The
Soldier, The
Squire And Maria, The
Tablets
There Ain't A Word
They Never Do It Now
They're All Going Off
Thick
(This Is) The House That Jerry Built
This'll Do! This'll Do!
Those Girls At The School At The
    End Of The Street
Turned Up
We Are Four Jolly Good Fellows

We're Expecting 'Em
We're Moving
We're Taking It In Turns
We Won't Go Home Till Morning And
  Then We Won't Go Home
What A Bit Of Luck
What Do They Care About That?
What's It To Do With Me?
Why Should London Wait?
Wibbly Wobbly Club
Will You Split One With Me?
Woman, Lovely Woman
Wrong Way, The
Yellow Ribbon Army, The
You Can't Get 'Em
You Couldn't Tell T'Other From
  Which
You're Another

FEATHERSTONE, Bessie 1880–1907
Aladdin's Lamp
Language Of The Penny Novelette,
  The
Latest London Betting, The

FEENEY, Pat 1850–89; m. Nellie
FARRELL
Dan Murphy's Running Dog
How Paddy Stole The Rope
Man With One Eye, The
Mary Ann
Michael Murphy
Shaughraun, The

FEMALE CHRISTYS *see* CHRISTY
MINSTRELS; MERRILEES, Andy

FENTON, Amy m. Leo DRYDEN (div.)
Britannia (sk.) (w. Leo DRYDEN)

FERN, Sable 1876–1942; m. Frank LEO;
orig. k.a. Little Sable
Always Give And Take A Little Bit
Arcade Johnnie, The *or* Once Upon A
  Time
Be Prepared
Boy Scout, The *or* Teach The Rising
  Generation

Can't You See I Want You To Be My
  Girl?
Don't Go Without Your Sunshade
Don't Hang Your Trouble On Me
Echo Of An Old Old Tale, The
Iona Of Arizona
It's A Grand Sight To See Them Going
  Away
It's Not The Cage I'm After It's The
  Bird
Keep Whistling
May, My May
My Cricket Girl
My Lily Of The Valley
No Coon Am Pining For Me
Oh, Mother Eve!
Put Your Trust In Me Little Girl
Read Between The Lines
Rising Son, The
Sixpenny-A'penny Tie
That's Why I Love Her So
There Are Good Fish Still In The Sea
There Can Only Be One Queen Bee
  In A Hive
What Is The Use Of Loving A Girl?
Where Is The Heart?
You Can't Stop The Sun From Shining

FIELD, Violet
My Leetle Rosa

FIELDHOUSE, Will°
Baby's Sweetheart
Conductor Of The Tramway, The
Hero, The
I Don't Think!
I Looked And I Looked
I Ne'er Thought It On Him
In My Mind
It Doesn't Matter
Kitty Nolan
Little Dora Donough
Little Nancy Newlove
Mamie, I Wants A Lady
No Flies On Him
Old Church Gate, The
One Of The Nuts

Ping Pong On The Brain
Pretty May Day
Rosie Lee
Wait For Your Old Age Pension

FIELDING, Ben 1849–93
Beautiful Kent
Clara, Clara, Will You Come Out
    Tonight?
Don't Go Like That Darling
Howling, Yowling Boys
Little Mary
Little Mud-Cabin, The
Love Be True To Me
Mother England
Stay With Me, Johnnie
Yes, You Shall Be A Sailor

FIELDS, Arthur 1888–1953; recorded
under at least nine other names incl.
Donald Baker, Vel Veteran, and Mr X
    Along Came Ruth
    When I Send You A Picture Of Berlin

FIELDS, 'Happy' Fanny 1881–1961
By The Side Of The Zuyder Zee
Den He Blow Blow Blow
England And Germany
Ev'ry Little Bit Helps
Send Me A Picture Postcard
Suffragette, The
When Schultz Fights The Drum

FIELDS, Dame Gracie 1898–1979; m.
(1) Archie PITT (div.); (2) Monty Banks
(Mario Bianchi (1897–1950)) (dec'd); (3)
Boris Alperovici
Biggest Aspidistra In The World, The
Bless This House
Heaven Will Protect An Honest Girl
I Never Cried So Much In All My Life
Little Old Lady
My Blue Heaven
Now Is The Hour (Haere Ra)
Ramona
Sally
Walter! Walter! (Lead Me To The
    Altar)

What Can You Give A Nudist On His
    Birthday?

FINETTE, Mlle née Josephine Durwend
Can-Can, The (w. her troupe fl.
    c.1865)

FINGLASS, Thomas E.
Black Sheep, The
Coon From Ohio, The
Idaho
It's A Long, Long Way To My Home
    In Kentucky
Kaloolah
Ma Little White Flower
Ma Lucy Anna From Alabama
On The Farm Down At Old
    Pensacola
Rose Of Alabam (w. Alice REGAN)
Say Good-Bye, Ma Lady-Love!
She's My Only Gal
That Mysterious Moon
That Mysterious Rag
Tomorrow Morning Wedding Bells
    Will Ring
Yaaka Hula

FINK, Edith
I Don't Want To Go On The Flip-Flap
No, Ebernezer! No
Oh! Oh! Antonio
Only A Thin Chalk Line
Rosiére, La

FINK, Henry 1893–1963
Ghetto Glide, The (w. Blossom
    SEELEY)
Take Me Out To The Ball Game

FISHER, Sallie 1881–1950
Play A Simple Melody (w. Charles
    KING)

FISK JUBILEE SINGERS fl. 1871–8;
est. George L. White, University of
Tennessee, Nashville
Deep River
Didn't My Lord Deliver Daniel
Nobody Knows The Trouble I See

Sometimes I Feel Like A Motherless
  Child
Steal Away
Swing Low, Sweet Chariot

FITZHENRY, Miss pseud. of Emily
SOLDENE
  Happy Be Thy Dreams
  Memory Of The Past, The

FLANAGAN & ALLEN° fl. 1924–45; Bud
FLANAGAN and Chesney Allen
(1894–1982)
  Umbrella Man, The
  Underneath The Arches

FLANAGAN, Bud 1896–1968; see also
FLANAGAN & ALLEN
  If You Want To Be Somebody
  Maybe It's Because I'm A Londoner
  Music, Maestro, Please
  Strollin'

FLETCHER, Lizzie d. 21 Sept. 1915
  He Doesn't Mention Everything
  If I Meet The Girl With The Golden
    Hair
  Sister 'Ria

FLORENCE, Mrs W. J. 1831–1906
  Bobbing Around
  Captain With His Whiskers, The
  Emmer Jane
  Grecian Bend, The
  Keemo, Kimo! (Polly Won't You Try
    Me, Oh?)
  Ridin' In A Railroad Keer

FLORENCE, Evangeline 1873–1928
  April Morn
  Carnival Time
  Little Damozel, The
  Slumber Tree

FLORY, Regine 1894–1926
  Poor Butterfly
  Some Sort Of Somebody (w. Nelson
    KEYS)
  Tanko, The

FOLI, Signor 1835–99; né Allen James
Foley; m. Mme R. Foli°
  Asleep In The Deep
  Bandolero, The
  Bedouin Love Song
  Comrades (Jaxone: Benedict)
  Diver, The
  Down Among The Dead Men
  Father O'Flynn
  Father Time
  Gage D'Amour
  Heart Of Oak
  Hybrias The Cretan
  I Am A Friar Of Orders Grey
  I Fear No Foe
  In Cellar Cool
  Land Of My Fathers
  Old Brigade, The
  Old Organist, The
  Old Soldier, The
  O Ruddier Than The Cherry
  Queen Of Lassies
  Shadow Of The Cross
  Star Of Hope, The
  Three Jolly Tars
  Vicar Of Bray, The
  Wolf, The

FOLLIES, THE fl. 1897–1913; est. H. G.
PÉLISSIER
  Tiddle-y-pom

FOOTE, F. Barrington 1855–1911
  Ask Nothing More
  Eastern Lament, An
  Three Beggars, The
  Three Merry Men
  Yes, I Love You

FORBES-ROBERTSON, Sir
Johnston 1853–1937; m. Gertrude
ELLIOTT
  Passing of the Third Floor Back, The
    (sk. version)

FORD, George 1812?–72?
  Big Ben

Crystal Palace Comic Programme,
  The
Lost Child, The
St James And St Giles

FORD, Harry° 1877–1955; orig. k.a.
Young Ford; brother of Bert
BRANTFORD
  After That My Time Is All My Own
  Bertie In Love
  Can't You Make Your Mind Up?
  Can't You Take My Word?
  Cupid
  Day That I Became A Millionaire, The
  Did He?
  Don't Apologize
  Don't Blame Me
  Don't Mind Me
  Don't Say It Like That, Please
  Everyone Notices Me
  Fancy I'm Off The Earth
  Get On My Back! I'll Carry You
    About!
  Have Mine!
  He Doesn't Mean Any Harm
  How Dare You!
  I Always Like To Do Things Nice And
    Friendly
  I Can't Understand It
  I Didn't Know What To Say
  I Didn't Like To
  I Don't Want To
  I Fancy You're Looking For Me
  If I Did
  If I'm Poor I'm Proud And I'm
    Particular (Work)
  If I Were You
  I Have To Make It Last Me All The
    Week
  Imagination
  Is It Necessary?
  I Thought You Knew
  It's A Shame
  It's Nice To Know People Who Are
    Kind
  I Wonder

I Wouldn't Mind Taking His Place
Language (Does Oo Love Oo's Dear
  Ickle Oosems?)
Let It Go
Money I Shall Never Get, The
Must You?
My Aunt's Will
Never Again
Night Watchman, The
Oh! Her Face
Oh! Tomorrow
Proverbs
Railway Porter, The
Sandwich Walk, The
Shan't Take You Out Any More
Sights Of London, The
So Am I
Such A Thing Is Impossible Really
Surely Not!
That's Enough
Value For Money
Watching 'Em
We've All Been There
What A Face!
What A Nice Little Thing
What A Silly I Must Have Been
What Did I Do?
What Does He Want It For?
What Oh! Time To Go
What's The Good?
When Is It My Turn?
When She Walks
Where?
Where's The Good?
While You Wait
Why Can't He Take My Word?
Will He?
Work (see If I'm Poor etc.)
Wouldn't You?
You Do Soon Change Your Mind

FORD, Maude see FORDE, Maude

FORDE, Florrie 1876–1940; sister of
Nan Tiltman (1874–1912)
  After You With The Girl
  Algernon, Go H'on!

All Aboard For Margate
Anona
Any Old Place Where The Sun Shines
Anything To Take Me Home
Anywhere In Manxland
Are We Downhearted? No! (David: Wright)
Back To My Home Once More
Banquet In Misery Hall
Bird In A Gilded Cage, A
Brixton Girl, The
Can't You See I'm Lonely?
Charlie, Charlie
Charlie On The Mash
Come And Do The Kelly Two-Step
Come Into The Parlour, Charley!
Dainty Little Dame From Chicago
Daisy Bell
Day By Day
Don't Go Jane
Down At Rosherville
Down At The Old Bull And Bush
Do You Know Mr Donahue?
Dream Your Troubles Away
Easy Street
Ever And Ever
Flanagan
Float Me, Charlie!
Follies Of Youthity, The
For Old Times' Sake
For She's Good Enough For Me
From Poverty Street To Golden Square
Girls And Boys
Girls, Study Your Cookery Book
Good-bye-ee!
Good-bye, London Town
Has Anybody Here Seen Kelly?
Has Anyone Seen A German Band?
He Kissed Me When He Left Me And Told Me I Had To Be Brave
Hello! There, Flanagan
He Used To Sing In His Sleep
Hold Your Hand Out, Naughty Boy!
How Are Yer?
I Don't Care If The Mormons Come

If She'd Only Been A Poor Girl
I'll Take Her To Jamaica
I Love My Little Polly
In The Sunny Summertime
In The Valley Of Golden Dreams
It's A Long Long Way To Tipperary
I Wouldn't Care To Change You For A New Wife Now
Jack, Jack, Jack
Jere-Jeremiah
Jolly Good Luck To Everyone
Just Across The Bridge Of Gold
Kelly's Come Back To The Isle Of Man
Last Good-Bye, The
Last Waltz, The
Let's All Go Into The Ballroom
Let's All Harmonize
Like A Good Little Wife Should Do
Little Cotton Dolly
Looping The Loop With Lucy
Lotus And The Lily, The
Mansion Of Aching Hearts, The
Mariar
Mary's Ticket
My Bugler Boy
My Little Love Bird
Not An M-U-G
Oh, Charley, Take It Away
Oh, Flo, Did You But Know!
Oh! Oh! Antonio
Oh, Please, See!
Oh, The Scenery Was Absolutely Grand!
Oh What A Pal Was Mary
On A Holiday
On A Sunday Afternoon
Out Where The Blue Begins
Pack Up Your Troubles In Your Old Kit-bag
Pal Of Mine
Pasadena
Picture No Artist Can Paint, A
Pretty Little Girl From Nowhere, The
Remember Where You Come From
Riding Home On A Load Of Hay

Right-Ho! I'm On My Way
Rip Van Winkle
Sailing In My Balloon, (Come Go)
She's A Lassie From Lancashire
She's A Plain, Homely Girl
She's Only A Working Girl
She Wears No Crown Of Gold
Side By Side (Woods)
Sing! Sing! Why Shouldn't We Sing?
So Let It Go, Boys
Somewhere The Sun Is Shining
Sue, My Sue
Suzannah's Long Stocking
Swing Me Higher, Obadiah!
Take Me Back To Dear Old Blighty
Take Me To Hear The Band Play
There's Something About A Soldier
   (O. Powell)
They Do Like Their Little Bit Of Red
They're All Right In The Moonlight
They're All Single By The Seaside
Tinker, Tailor, Soldier, Sailor
'Tis A Faded Picture
Turned Up
'Twas The Last, Last Kiss!
Up To One Of Your Tricks Again
Waltz Me Around Again, Willie
Water Chute, The
We All Come Fra Lancashire
When The Sweet Magnolias Bloom
Won't You Waltz The Merry Widow
   Waltz With Me?
Yes, We Have No Bananas
You Are Queen Of My Submarine
You'd Better Beware! Beware!

FORDE, Hal *c*.1877–1955
As The World It Goes Round And
   Round
Come Along To London Town
Down At Shepherd's Bush
Every Fellow's In Love With A Girl
It's My Night Out Tonight
Wrestling Wife, The

FORDE, J. George 1830–73
Lost Child, The (parody of Thomas

Hood's 'The Lost Heir')
Trades And Callings
We've Still Got The Lads In Red

FORDE, Maude
Mammy's An Angel
Wax Lights, Sir? (as Little Maude)

FORMBY, George° 1877–1921
Animal Language *or* Said The Pig
Bert The Bad Bolshevik
Bits Fra' Wigan
Come Away
Did You See The Crowd In Piccadilly?
Don't Fall Out With Your Husband
Every Day In The Week
Fireman Like Me, A
Gathering Nuts In May
Gee Up!
Heigh-oh! That's All I Know
I Began To Run
I Don't Know Where I'm Going
I Lifted The Latch And Walked In
I'm Such A Hit With The Girls
I'm Taking My Father's Tea
I Parted My Hair In The Middle
I Put On My Coat And Went Home
I Sobbed And I Cried Like A Child
I've Lost My Wife
I Was Standing At The Corner Of The
   Street
John Willie, Come On!
John Willie's Ragtime Band
Lancashire Scotchman, The
Looking For Mugs In The Strand
Lucky Jim
Man From Lancashire, The
Man Was A Stranger To Me, The
Me, Me, Me
My Mother Said
Not Quite So Daft As I Look
No Wonder I Look Jolly
One Of 'The Boys'
One, Two, Three, Four, Five
Playing The Game In The West
Plink Plonk (The Skin Of A Spanish
   Onion)

Sailing
Since I Had A Go At My Dumb-Bells
Then We All Went Marching In
Those Happy Days
To Let
Twice Nightly
Walker Walked Away
We All Went Home In A Cab
We All Went To Leicester Square
We're All Old Pals Together

FORREST, Arthur 1850–1908
Daddy Wouldn't Buy Me A
Sweetheart
He Bunged It On To Me
It's Only Artificial After All
Long Ago
Me And My Old Pal Brown
My Cousin

FOSTER, Charles 1854–1913; a.k.a. Burt
SHEPARD
Boers Have Got My Daddy, The
Break The News To Mother
Coronation Day
I'm The Plumber
On The Margate Boat
She's Only A Working Girl

FOSTER, Fred 1850–80
Duchess Of Devonshire, The
Girl Of The Period, The

FOSTER, George 1864–1946
Bury Me In The Gutter
Duck Foot Sue
I Haven't Got Over The Feeling
Law Courts In The Strand, The

FOSTER, Ivor b. 1870
Drake Goes West
Gwenny
If I Might Come To You
In An Old Fashioned Town
Jolly Old Cavalier, A
Kashmiri Song
Moon Has Raised Her Lamp Above,
The (w. Herbert CAVE)
Shipmates O' Mine

Song Of All The Ages, The
Thora
Trumpeter, The
Until
Up From Somerset
Watchman, What Of The Night? (w.
CAVE)

FOTHERGILL FAMILY fl. 1880s–1910s;
comic sketch troupe est. Fred Fothergill
(1839–1903) w. sundry combinations of
his daughters incl. Bella, Emily,
Florence, Rose. Bella m. Will Kellino in
1915 and Florence m. Peter Cannon
(**BELLA & BIJOU**)
Donnybrook Fair
Killarney
Trafalgar

Fox, Della 1871/2–1913
Good-Bye, Maggie May
I'm Afraid To Come Home In The
Dark

Fox, Harry (UK) 1817–76; legendary
chairman at The Middlesex, Drury Lane
Harvest Home, The
I Likes A Drop Of Good Beer
Jolly Nose
Warbling Waggoner, The

Fox, Harry (USA) 1882–1959; origin-
ator of the foxtrot; m. Jennie **DOLLY**
Girl On The Magazine Cover, The
I Love A Piano
I'm Just Wild About Harry (w. **DOLLY**
SISTERS)

FOY, Edwin 1856–1928; a.k.a. Eddie
Foy sen.
Chinatown, My Chinatown
Ghost That Never Walked
He Goes To Church On Sundays
I'm Tired

FOY, Tom 1879–1917
Ah'm Disguised
Ah'm Excited

Ah've Been To A Wedding
All Through T'Black Horse
Amateur Theatricals
Aye, Ah'm Upset
Early Wedded
First Of April, The (The Donkey
     (sk.))
Fool Of The Family, The
I Reckon He'll Be Much Obliged To
     Me
I've Been To America
I've Been To China
I've Had Some Money Left Me
My Bunker Bump
Scouting
Yorkshire Man In London, A (sk.)

FRAGSON, Harry° 1869–1913;
sometimes billed solely as FRAGSON
All The Girls Are Lovely By The
     Seaside
Amour Qui Rit, L'
Band Box Girl, The
Beautiful Baby, The *or* Doctor Ridge's
     Food
Billy Brown Of London Town
Employment Bureau, The
Father's Safety Razor
Hello! Hello! Who's Your Lady
     Friend?
If We All Went Out On Strike
In Gay Paree
John Bull's Budget
My Chin Chin Lu
Oh! I Say!
On Your Honeymoon
Other Department, Please! The
Paper Bag Cookery
Petite Femme Du Métro, La
Since Sister Mary Went To Gay Paree
Songs And Operas In Rag Time
Statues On The Spree
Those Attractive Posters
Tom Tom The Piper's Son (own
     version)
Whispers Of Love

FRAME, W. F. 1848–1919
Angus McIndoe
Bonnie Hoose O' Ivy
Dinna Man, Donal
Hielan' King O' France, The
Hielan' Rory
Hooch Aye
It's A Braw Bricht Moonlicht Nicht
Lassie Needs A Pairtner When The
     Nichts Grow Cauld, A
Maister Duncan McIntosh
Oh, Peter
Vegetarian, The

FRANCIS, Harry also w. MOHAWK
MINSTRELS
Co-Operation
Corkscrew And A Candle, A
Dat Gal's Mouth
Dickory Dink
Down The Area (Mashing Mary Ann)
She Was A Cut Above Me
Winkle's Wedding, The

FRANCIS, James 1840–86; co-founder
1867 of MOHAWK MINSTRELS; est.
music publishers Francis Bros & Day
1877
Chinese Grin, The
Cupid's A Dodger
Emancipation Day (Harry Hunter)
Father Dear Father The Brokers Are
     In (parody)
Go And Put Your Bonnet On, Betsy
Harry Hunter's 'Spelling B' Song
Little Brown Jug
Lucindah At The Windah
Lucy Cocket
Manders's Menagerie
Matilda Gorger *or* Mulligatawny Soup,
     A Mackerel And A Sole
Miss Jenny Ap-Thomas Ap Shenkin
     Ap Jones
Miss Mary Grundy
Mother-In-Law Brigade, The
Mother's Love Can Never Die, A
Mrs Brown And Her Luggage

Mulligan Guards, The
On Monday I Met Mary Ann
On The Banks Of The Silvery Thames
Rinking Rose *or* She Said She'd Be
My Bride
St Patrick's Day Parade
Sammy Stammers
She'd A Brother In The Navy
She Doesn't Like The Men
They Ought To Have A Muzzle On
Victoria's Black Hussars
Will You Be My Hollyhock?
Will You Marry William Harry?
Wonderful Musician, The
Wonderful Octopus, The

FRANKLIN, Jennie°
Don't It Make Him Look A Fool!
I Met A Lubly Gal
Ladies' Orchestra, The
Wickedest Girl At School, The
Yawning
Yodelling Song (I Kept On Mit Mine
Cry)

FRANKS, Sydney *c.*1842–1900
B.R.O.W.N.
Helen's Babies
Mrs Brown's Tea Fight
Peter Piper
She's Just About The Age
Younger Son, The

FRASER, Agnes 1878–1968; m. Walter
PASSMORE
In Zanzibar (w. Walter PASSMORE)
My Cosey Corner Girl (w. Henry
LYTTON)

FRASER, Robert *c.*1833–78?
Brown From Abyssinia
I Don't Believe They Do
It Hasn't Happened Yet
Joey Ladle

FRASER, Marjory Kennedy°
1857–1930; sister of Margaret KENNEDY
Eriskay Love Lilt, The (*Songs of the
Hebrides*)

Road To The Isles, The (*Songs of the
Hebrides*)

FREEAR, Louie 1873–1939; sister of
WILLIE and Albert Freear
All Thro' Sticking To A Soldier
Betsy Barlow
Blowed If Father Ain't Commenced
To Work
It's Painfully True (w. Robb
HARWOOD)
I Want To Be A Lidy
Martha Spanks The Grand Piano
My First Young Man
Not What 'Ria Wanted
Oh, Susannah!
She Just Walks On
Sister Mary Jane's High Kick
Sister Mary Jane's Top Note
Such A Nice Gal Too
That's A Bit Of Comfort To A Poor
Old Maid
Tooraladdie
Twiddley Bits
Won't Nobody Employ Me?

FREEAR, Willie° d. 28 Dec. 1889?; a.k.a.
Billy Freear and Little WILLIE; brother
of Louie and Albert Freear
Absent Minded Rooster, The
Mrs Isaac Newton Moon
Sucking Cider Through A Straw (w.
MOORE & BURGESS)

FREEMAN, Harry 1858–1922; member
No. 1 of the Grand Order of Water Rats
All The Lot For A Quid
Always Handy, Very Handy
Another Rocket
Aren't They Pretty? Aren't They Nice?
Automatic Gas, The
Beautiful Man Like Me, A
Boozing
But Oh! She Said She Was A Country
Girl
Can't Stop! Can't Stop!! Can't Stop!!!
Cheer, Boys, Cheer!

Cobbler Got The Wax, The
Di-Di-Diddly-Di!
Don't You Worry Over Me
Driver Of An All Night Tram, The
English Champions
Fol The Riddle I Do Day
Four-p'ny-a-p'ny Banquet
Friend Of The Family A
Giddy Little Girl Said 'No!', The
Glorious Beer
Having A Jolly Good Holiday
(He's A) Friend Of The Familee *or*
    One Of The Familee
He's A Rider
He Went
How's That?
Husband Number Four
I'd Better Call Again Next Week
If You Don't Trouble Trouble
I Haven't Made Any Enquiries Up To
    Now
I'm Giving 'Em All A Turn
I'm Looking For The Owner
I'm Not A-Going To Move
I'm Off To Klondyke
I'm Often On The Job Round There
I'm Still In It!
I Nab'd 'Em—For A Change
In Darkest London
Indian Exhibition
I Shall Be There
It Isn't The First Time
It Never Troubles Me
It's A Nice Night Tonight!
It's Rising, Rapidly Rising
I Was There With Mine
I Wouldn't Mind Having A Try
Keep On Doing It
La-Didily-Idily-Umti-Umti-Ay *or*
    Jones's Wedding
Leave A Little Bit For Your Tutor
Leicester Square
Little Bit Of Luck, A
Lord Mayor's Coachman, The
Madame La Sharty (Biddy The Belle
    Of The Ballet)

Many A Time
Mesmerist, The
My Missis Thinks She Trilby
Nice Night Tonight, A
Nice Thing For A Man Like Me!
Night In, A
Not The Only One
Oh! Mr Robinson
Old Maids And Young Maids
One Of The Familee *or* He's A Friend
    etc.
Only Sometimes
Over The Sticks
Political Jockeys
Princess May And The Duke Of York,
    The
Regular Flipity Flop!, A
Right! Right!
She Said She Was A Country Girl
She Stood Behind The Parlour Door
Stand Up
That's All Rum-Fum-Foozle-Up
That's Him! That's Him! That's Him!
That's The Stuff To Give 'Em
That Was Enough For Me
Then The Music Started
There Is No Such Luck For Me
There Was I As Large As Life
They're After Me
They Went To The Usual Place Again
They Were All Occupied
Too-Tah-Too
Went
We've Both Been Going There Before
What A Good Job I Wasn't There
What A Little Bit Of Luck
What Can You Expect For Your
    Money?
What Cheer, Trilby
While There's A Woman
You Look After Me Old Boy
You've Got To Have A Lot More Yet
You've Made A Big Mistake

FREEMAN, Will W. MOHAWK
MINSTRELS

Boys Of The Queen's Navee
I Drove My Mare To Banbury Fair
'If' And 'Suppose' *or* Shouldn't We
  Think It Strange?
Lay Of The Last Lunatic Minstrel,
  The
Lord Mayor's Coachman, The
Man Who Knew How To Drive, The
Over The Garden Wall
Quips The Quaker

FRENCH, Alfred W.
I Couldn't Get Away From It
Not Always!
Only Us Two
On Principle
Punctuation
That's Why He Loves Me
'Twas Only A Little Love Token

FRENCH, Fred° 1830–99
Abyssinian Gold (She Was Such A
  Nice Young Girl)
Advertisements
Angelina Brown
Away Down Holborn Hill
Come Along, Do, Now Don't Be
  Bashful
Destitute Orphans, The
Friend In Need Is A Friend Indeed, A
Hanki-Panki *or* The Girl From China
Jemmy Riddle
Jessie The Belle At The Bar
Joe The Cabby
Mad Barber, The
Martha The Milkman's Daughter
Mincemeat (Her Mincemeat Knife
  Went Chop Chop Chop)
Oh! That's The Style For Me
Paddle Your Own Canoe
Rustic Young Beauty, The
Second Thoughts Are Best
She Was Fat, Fair, And Forty
Skidamalinska Of Delhi
Take Care Of The Pence And The
  Pounds Will Take Care Of

Themselves
Things That Take Place In Our
  Street
Very Fine Girl Of Her Age, A
When These Old Clothes Were New
Work, Boys, Work And Be Contented
Wreck Off London Bridge, The

FRENCH, George d. 25 July 1938
Covent Gardeners, The
What Ho! She's Never Going To
  Bump Any More

FRENCH, Percy° 1854–1920
Abdalla-Bulbul Ameer
Are Ye Right There, Michael?
Eileen Oge
Mountains Of Mourne
Phil The Fluter's Ball
Slattery's Mounted Foot

FYFFE, Will° 1885–1947; wrote all his
own material
Come And See The Baby
Daft Sandy
Engineer, The
I Belong To Glasgow
I'm Ninety-Four This Mornin'
Sailing Up The Clyde
Sandy's Holiday
Twelve And A Tanner A Bottle

GALBRAITH, Maude 1891–1962
Let Me Call You Sweetheart

GALLAGHER & SHEAN° fl. 1910–25; Ed
Gallagher (*c.*1873–1929) and Al Shean
(1868–1949), who was uncle to the SIX
MASCOTS
Mr Gallagher & Mr Shean

GALLIMORE, Florrie 1867–1944; sister
of Arthur Kenyon; m. Florian Fratelli
Always Look After Number One
Belle Of Barcelona, The
Dear Little Tyrolese
Debt You Can Never Repay, A
Don't Put My Papa's Portrait Up For
  Sale (as child)

Don't Start To Worry If The Sun Don't
  Shine
Don't You Do It?
Everytime (Uncle Joe)
Flower That I Plucked From Mother's
  Grave, The
Girls Are A Match For The Men,
  The
Go To Sleep, Baby
How Can I Leave You?
How Could I Tell?
Humanity (sk.) (see LAWSON, John)
Hush, Little Baby
Ida From Devonshire
I Dreamt My Little Boy Of Thee (as a
  child)
If You Want To Come In, Come In
I'll Give Him Writing To Mignonette
I'll Go Right Back To Ohio
I Love You, Yes I Do
It's The Poor That Help The Poor
I've Got Three Letters Of The
  Alphabet
I Wish You Luck
Jones!
Lady From Madrid, The
Little Green Leaf From The Bible,
  The
Mary Kissed The Captain
Mountain Home
My Girl's A Yorkshire Girl
My Japanese Charmer
Norah Norah (Come Back To The
  Pole!)
Old Brass Locket, An
Old Calabar
Once We Were Sweethearts
Picture From Nature, A
Queen Of The Drapery
Remember Me To Mother Dear
Round The Bandstand In The Park
Sammy Played The Saxophone
Shop Girl, The
Somebody Else's Baby
Things A Woman Observes
Uncle Joe Can Find 'Em Every Time

We Are All Stars
Widow Doolin'
You May Want A Friend Some Day
You Might Be A White Man's Wife
You Wonder Why I Love You

GAMMON, Barclay 1867–1915; wrote
most of his own material
  Adverts Of Modern Medicine Makers
    (Shocks)
  Do Have Pity On The Moon
  Down By The Koo-La-Loo
  Nursery Rhymes In Ragtime
  Shocks see Adverts etc.
  Suffragette's Anthem, The
  Who Killed Ragtime?
  Who Smashed Bill Kaiser?

GANNON, Nellie c.1855–1926; m. Harry
Wright°
  Boy Pirate (or Buccaneer), A
  I Traced Her Little Footsteps In The
    Snow
  Just As The Sun Went Down
  Lady Auctioneer
  Lady Cricketer, The
  Lady Jockey, The
  Nelson
  Only A Few Miles Of Water
  Since Mary Ann Has Learnt To Ride A
    Bicycle
  Wait Till The Summer Sun Shines
  While Leaning On The Arm Of
    Charley
  Wishing The Boys Farewell

GANTHONY, Nellie°
  Khaki
  Little Liz
  My Mandoline

GANTHONY, Robert° 1849–1931
  Half Back's Farewell, The
  Hey Down Derry
  In The Twilight
  Pierrot Inquisition, The
  Sambo's Serenade
  Venice In London

GANTY, Little
Falling In And Falling Out
I'm Beginning To Like The Job
I've Only Been There A Week

GARDENER, Charles
And He Tootles
Courting
Dear One, No One
How I Mesmerise 'Em
Johnny, Get A Van
Maggie Murphy's Grace
Marching!
Oh! The Black List
Oh! What A Surprise I Got
Our Neighbourhood
That Was Before We Were Married
Treasures Of Home (Relics Of Liza)

GARDNER, Stewart
Danny Deever
Devout Lover, The
Old Garden, An
Old Superb, The

GARDNER, Will 1879–1910
Apologies
Drill Sergeant, The
Family Lullaby, The
Football Spectator, The
Her Showed Oi The Way
I Was With The Mater
Music Hall Shakespeare, The
Polyglot Speech, The
Saccaboni
Wheezes

GARRICK, Gus c.1870–?
Down Went McGinty
Dr Bogie
I Can't Now
I'd Never Noticed It Before
I Had A Good Home And I Left
I'm Fond Of What I Like
Johnny Get Your Gun
More Than Likely
(Music Hall) Tit Bits
No Flies On Him

Our Neighbourhood
Silence Is Golden
Sloan-Broke Bookie, The
Ti-Ol-The-Diddle-Ol-The Day
You've Never Seen These Before

GEE, Lottie
I'm Just Wild About Harry

GEISTINGER, Marie 1833–1903
Laughing Song, The (*Die Fledermaus*)

GEORGE, Marie 1879–1955
Fol-Lol-The-Diddle-Ol-The-Day!
Hello, You Fellows!
I Don't Want To Be A Lady
Look Out, Mr Man
My Little Irish Canary

GEORGE, Muriel & BUTCHER, Ernest
fl. 1920s–c.1943; specialists in folk and
early Music Hall songs. Muriel George
(1883–1965) m. (1) Arthur Davenport;
(2) Ernest BUTCHER (1885–1965) (div.)
Allonette
Blue Muselin, The
Bulls Won't Bellow, The
Cicely Sweet
If Every Star
Me And My Jane
Mistress Of The Master
Moon My Moon (solo Muriel
    GEORGE)
Mother's Darling (solo GEORGE)
Oh No John
On Ilkla Moor B'at 'At
Parson And Me
Ratcatcher's Daughter, The
Sweet Nightingale
Top Of The Hill
Tree In The Wood, The
Villikens And His Dinah

GERRARD, Teddie 1890–1942; often
misspelled Gerard
Glad To See You're Back
Limehouse Blues
Naughty, Naughty, One Gerrard

Night-Club Girl, The (w. Harry
    PILCER)
Pass Along
She'd A Hole In Her Stocking

GIBSON, Alf 1860–1920
All Of A Sudden He Stopped
Beautiful Work Of Art, A
Frozen Meat
He Only Did It Once
How Will I Do?
I Couldn't Let It Stop Down There
I Got The Sack
I Never Let It Upset Me
I Shall Never Let It Upset Me
It Wasn't Long Before I Shifted
I've Got To Get Back To Work
Popping 'Em Into Me
Take It In
They Soon Made An Angel Of Him
    There
You Can't Get Away—There It Is

GIDEON, Melville° 1884–1933; see also
AMERICAN RAGTIME OCTETTE
I'm In Love With A Girl In A
    Crinoline Gown
I'm Tickled To Death I'm Single

GIFFORD, Harry° d. 1960
Don't You Know A Different Game To
    That?
What A Shame
You Don't Stay In One Place Long

GIGLI, Beniamino 1890–1957
Caro Mio Ben
Funiculi Funicula
Mama
M'Appari Tutt'Amor (Ach! So
    Fromm/Ah! So Pure)
Mattinata
Mother Machree
O Sole Mio
Rosary, The
Santa Lucia
Then You'll Remember Me (When
    Other Lips)

GILBERT, Bert b. 1873; m. Ada REEVE
(div.)
Covent Garden Ball, The
I Want Yer Ma Honey
Poacher, The
There's A Girl Inside

GILBERT, Fred° 1849–1903
Dreaming Of Thy Gentle Face
Long Lost Boy, The
Under The May Bush

GILBEY, George
Ain't You Happy?
Did You?
Goalkeeper, The (Spouty)
I Was Laughing All Over My Face
Lawyer, The
Oh! The Sea, Blow The Sea! or Kelly
    The Captain
Thing Like That Might Get About,
    A
What'll?
Why?

GILL, Basil 1876–1955
Julius Caesar (Shakespeare—tent
    scene)
Man Who Was, The (sk.)

GILSON, Lottie 1869?–1912; m. Joseph
K. EMMET
And Her Golden Hair Was Hanging
    Down Her Back
Caprice
Could You Be True To Eyes Of Blue?
Don't Wear Your Heart On Your
    Sleeve
Games We Used To Play
Henrietta
His Last Thoughts Were Of You
I Don't Blame You, Tom
I Love You Both
In Good Old New York Town
Isabelle She Is A Belle
La-Didily-Idily-Umti-Umti-Ay or
    Jones's Wedding
Let Bygones Be Bygones

Little Annie Rooney
Little Lost Child, The (A Passing
    Policeman)
Little Willie, He Knew A Thing Or
    Two
Lulu
Mary And John
Meet Me In St Louis, Louis
Military Mollie
Mother Was A Lady, (My)
Mr Captain Stop The Ship
My Best Girl's A New Yorker
No One Ever Loved You More Than I
Oh, What A Difference In The
    Morning
Old Sexton, The
Old Turnkey, The
Pretty Jenny Slattery
She's Such A Nice Girl Too
Sidewalks Of New York, The
Sunshine Of Paradise Alley, The
Sweet Melodies And Memories Of
    Home
What Do You Think?
When They Play God Save The King
Where The Silv'ry Colorady Wends Its
    Way
White Squall, The
You're Not The Only Pebble On The
    Beach

GINNETT, Fred E. 1859–1924
    Claude Duval (equestrian sk.)
    Dick Turpin's Ride To York (sk.)
    Rejected Remounts (sk.)

GIRARDI, Alexander 1850–1918
    If Only I Could Fly With You Through
        Life
    Kissing Is No Sin
    Roses In The Tyrol
    Sei Nicht Bös (Miller's Daughter—
        Don't Be Cross)
    Take Your Time
    When My Grandpa Was Twenty
    Yes, Writing And Reading

GITANA, Gertie 1887–1957
    Dinna Forget
    Dolly At Home (as Little Gitana)
    Don't Give Me Diamonds, All I Want
        Is You
    I'm Sorry I Make You Sad
    I Never Knew What Sweetheart
        Meant Till I Met You
    I Think Of You
    I Want You, My Honey, I Do
    Kitty Dear
    Lola Lee
    Meet Me In Moon-Time Mary
    Meet Me Jennie
    Molly McClory
    Morning Star!
    My Devon Girl
    My Indian Maid
    My Rose Of Surrey
    Nellie Dean
    Never Mind
    Nobody Else But You
    Old Dutch Bonnet
    Once Upon A Time
    Queen Of The Cannibal Isle
    Schoolgirl's Holiday, A
    Silver Bell
    Strolling With My Mary Down The
        Lane
    Sweet Caroline
    Sweet Jessie Dear
    There'll Always Be A Corner By The
        Fire For You
    There's A Cottage In Ballymahone
    There's Silver In Your Hair (But
        There's Gold In Your Heart)
    Under Southern Skies
    When I Leave The World Behind
    When I See The Lovelight Gleaming
    When The Corn Is Yellow On The
        Hillside
    When The Harvest Moon Is Shining
    When The Summer Days Are O'er,
        Anna Gray
    Yesterday You Called Me Sweetheart
    You Made Me Happy For A While

You Were Coming Thro' The Corn,
Molly Dear

GLANVILLE, Alfred *see* VANCE, Alfred

GLENROY, William° *c.*1868–1932;
pseud. of W. B. Gray°
Volunteer Organist, The

GLENN, Hope
Angel Faces
Don't Cry
Hark! Hark! The Dogs Do Bark
I Dream'd A Dream
Love Abides

GLENVILLE, Shaun° 1884–1968; m.
Dorothy WARD; began as one of the SIX
BROTHERS LUCK
Are We Downhearted? No! (David:
Wright)
Art Of Deception, The (sk.)
He's A Credit To Ould Ireland Now
Hogmanay
If You Come From Yorkshire
If You're Irish Come Into The Parlour
I'm A Good Girl Now
Mademoiselle From Armenteers
Mickey Rooney's Ragtime Band
Rouken Glen
Something In The Irish After All
When An Irishman Goes Fighting
Who Put The Bricks In Brixton? (w.
Dorothy WARD)

GLINDON, Robert° *c.*1799–1866
Biddy, The Basket Woman
Black Bottle Imp
Dog's Meat Man, The
Jack Robinson
Literary Dustman, The
My Skiff Is On De Shore
Rose Lee
Walker The Twopenny Postman

GLUCK, Alma 1884–1938; m. Efrem
ZIMBALIST
Aloha Oe (Farewell To Thee)
Brindisi (*La Traviata*)

Brook, The
Carry Me Back To Old Virginny (w.
Efrem ZIMBALIST, violin obbligato)
Chanson Hébraïque (w. ZIMBALIST)
Have You Seen But A Whyte Lily
Grow?
Land Of The Sky-Blue Water, The
Lass With The Delicate Air, The
Listen To The Mocking Bird
Little Grey Home In The West
Lo! Here The Gentle Lark
Long Ago
Lost Chord, The (w. ZIMBALIST)
My Little Grey Home In The West
My Old Kentucky Home
Old Black Joe
Old Folks At Home (w. ZIMBALIST)
Perfect Day, A
Rosary, The
Swallows, The

GLYDER, Hilda m. Harry WELDON
If You Want To Get On In Revue
I Love You
Ma, He's Making Eyes At Me
Oh! I Don't Care For A Lot Of It!
Stop It, John!

GLYNNE, Walter
English Rose, The
Just Because The Violets
Old Rustic Bridge By The Mill, The
Smilin' Through

GODDEN, Jimmy 1879–1955
Business Guide, The
History
My Advice
My Luck
Why Should England Worry?

GODFREY, Charles° 1851–1900
Across The Bridge (The Bridge At
Midnight)
Advance, Australia! England Number
Two
After The Ball (Le Brunn)
Armada, The

At Constantinople
Balaclava, (A Story Of) (sk.) *or* On
   Guard
Biography
Blessings Of Marriage, The
'Blige A Lady
Blind Collier, The
Dancing Round The Apple Tree
Dear Old Uncle Charlie
Donniest Don Of The Day, The
Do This!
Dreaming *or* I Thought I Was There
Dusky Warrior, The
England In Danger?
English Speaking Race Against The
   World, The
Flipperty Flop Young Man, The
Gay Paree
Giddy Little Curate, The
Gigantic Wheel, The
Girl In The Pinafore Dress, The
Golden Wedding, The
Good Old Santa Claus
Good Old Times, The
Grand-dad's Birthday *or* What A Time,
   What A Time That Was!
Grandmother's Cat (parody of
   Grandfather's Clock)
Half-Past Nine
Hanky Panky
Here Upon Guard Am I
Hi-Tiddley-Hi-Ti!
Hold On, Johnny, Hold On, Jack
Homage To Colonel Burnaby
How D'Ye Do, Dear Boy?
I'm In The Chair
I Never Felt Like It Before
Inkerman, (A Story Of) *or* The 7th
   Royal Fusiliers
I Said I Would Buy Her A Cage-I-Ty
It's All Over Now With The Ladies
Jacob Strauss
John Bull In The China Shop
Johnny Bull's Concert Hall
Just A Little
Last Shot, The

Life, Love And Death
Little Stowaway, The
Lobster And The Whale, The
Lost Daughter, The
Maiden's Prayer, The
Masher King, The
Master And Man
Merrie Merrie Egland
Midnight Train, The
Miser, The
Mister Brown And The Venetian Blind
Moonbeams
My Birthday
My Lost Darlings!
My Pal Jim
My Shadow Is My Only Pal
My Son! My Son!
My Willie
Nelson (song and sk.)
Never Mind The Moon, John
Night Alarm, The (sk.)
Oh, Ain't It Pe-cu-li-ar?
Oh! Don't It Tickle You?
Oh! For The Jubilee
Oh Love! Beautiful Love!
Oh! The Popsy Wopsy
Oh, What A Happy Land Is England
Old England And The New
Old Joe Blake
On Guard—A Story Of Balaclava (sk.)
Original Bogie Man, The
Our Mary Ann
Our Stuck-Up Little Square
Pair Of Dark Blue Eyes, A
Parley Vous Français?—Eh, Madame?
Poor Old Benjamin The Workhouse
   Man
Poor Old Jones
Pretty Maid Was Young And Fair, The
Primrose Song, The
Regent Street
Rickety Rackety Crew, The
Road To Ruin, The
Sago Fun
Sailor And His Lass, A
Sailor's Been To Sea (See), The

Sawdust Chest, The
Seeing Life
Seven Ages Of Man, The
7th Royal Fusiliers, The *or* A Story Of
    Inkerman
Siberia
Soldier And A Man, A
Squire, The *or* Far From The
    Madding Crowd
Story Of A Kiss, The
Such A Don, Don't You Know!
Such A Very Very Fine Old Man
Tale Of The Mile End Road, A
That's When You Cheer, Boys, Cheer!
Their Heads Nestled Closer Together
They All Look Alike In The Dark
Tinkle, Tinkle, Tum
Tone To Soci-e-tee!, A
'Twas Just Down Chelsea Way
Two Little Dimpled Cheeks
Walking Wedding, The
When A Chap Is Single
When A Child
When The Missis Is Out
Why Don't You Be Steady, Maria?
Will You Be Mine, Pretty Bird?
Wreck Off London Bridge, The
You Know The Girl I Mean

GODWIN, Will° d. 25 Apr. 1913
Broken Vow, The
Hand Of Justice, The
He Was Only A Cabin Boy
Hurrah For The Horse And Hound
If Those Lips Could Only Speak!
Let's Have A Jolly Good Chorus
Lights Of Home, The
Nineteenth Century Boys, The
    (Godwin: Powell)
Severed *or* The Broken Pledge
Some Mother Will Lose A Son
That's Why I Enlisted For A Soldier
There's A Silvery Lining To Ev'ry
    Cloud
Toast Those Who Are Absent
Twenty Years Ago (A Mother's Letter)

Unity Of Nations
What Would I Give To Be Home
    Again
Wishing The Boys Farewell

GOLDEN, George Fuller 1868–1912;
founder (1900) of the White Rats of
America; w. Cliff RYLAND as Ryland &
Golden (fl. 1892–9)
Paris Day By Day
Rootie-Tootie

GORDON, Alf 1875–1915; recording alias
of Will TERRY
All The Little Ducks Went Quack!
    Quack! Quack!
If I Had A Girl As Nice As You
Riding On Top Of The Car
Seaweed

GORDON, Ernest w. MOHAWK
MINSTRELS
Bells And Drums
I Gave My Love A Breast Knot
Keep A Loving Heart For Me

GORDON, Harry 1893–1957
I'm Going Back To Himazas

GORDON, Kitty 1878–1974
Alma, Where Do You Live?
Dreaming
Love At The Door

GORDON, Marjorie b. 1893
If You Look In Her Eyes (w. Evelyn
    LAYE)

GRAHAM, Tom° *c.*1869–97
Baby Language
Facts And Figures
I Took It Off
I've Got The Five-Pound Note
Newsboy, The
Pa, Ma, And Paris
Quips And Cranks
Short And Sweet
Storyettes
That's All

GRAHAME, Gracie d. 13 Dec. 1945
Bells Are Ringing In The Steeple
Bicycle Who Loved The Fiddle, The
Charlie
Fishing
Parasol, The
Please, Mr Man In The Moon!
Please, Mr Soldier!
Reclaimed *or* The World, The Flesh
  And The Devil

GRAIN, Richard Corney° 1845–95;
wrote almost all his own material; from
1870 w. GERMAN REED COMPANY
Actor And The Bishop, The
At The Seaside
Banjo Mania
Cautious Lover, The
Children's Voices
De Ole Umbrella
Detective's Song, The
Four 'Oss Sharrybang, The
Girton Girl
Grandma's Song
He Did It And He Didn't Know Why!
He's On The Move
I'm A Chappie
Jarge's Jubilee
Johnnie! Me And You!!
Kicklebury Brown
Masher King Of Piccadilly, The
Merry Merry Waiter's Thumb, The
Moan Of The Muzzled, The
My First Cigar
My Old Clay Pipe
My Old Dress Suit
Noah's Story
Old Couple's Polka, The
Old Pilot Jim
Old Trombone, The
Ole Black 'Oss, The
Our Servants' Ball
Our Threepenny Hop
Owls And The Mice
Photography Mania
Polka And The Choirboy, The

Recipe For Comic Songs, A
Tilda Banks (The Slavey's Lament)
Village Beadle, The

GRANT, Hector alias of Peter DAWSON
Lassie, Dinna Sigh For Me
Sandy, You're A Dandy

GRANT, Miss Norman°
At A Football Match
Bertie, The Catch Of The Year
Dear Little Seaside Girl
Did You?
Fairy Queen In The Pantomime, The
How To Capture Your Prince (mon.)
I'm A Dolly, Just A Dolly
Just Smile (mon.)
Orphan, The (mon.)
Ping Went The String
That Wasn't Being Untrue (mon.)
There's A Girl You All Know
They Did Not Know (mon.)
When Father Took To Writing Songs
You Never Can Tell

GRANVILLE, Edgar 1855–1909
Down Our Way
(Just) One More
Parted (Tosti)
Up And Down

GRANVILLE-BARKER, Harley
1877–1946; m. Lillah MCCARTHY (div.)
Ask No Questions And You'll Hear No
  Stories (sk.) (w. Nigel PLAYFAIR)
Farewell Supper, A (sk.) (w. Lillah
  MCCARTHY and PLAYFAIR)
Wedding Morning, The (sk.) (w.
  PLAYFAIR)

GRATTAN, Harry° 1867–1951; sketch
comic
Buying A Gun (w. G. P. HUNTLEY)
Careless Lassie, A
Chorus Girl, A
Curious
Heart Case, A
Her Ladyship

It's Been In The Family For Years
On Duty
Packing Up
Plumbers, The (w. Martin ADESON;
    also w. Fred EMNEY)

GRAVES, George 1872–1946
All Clear Out Of The Park
Does This Shop Stock Shot Socks
    With Spots?
He Knew She Never Blamed Him
I Sent My Sister To Assist 'Er
Key Of The Flat, The (sk.)
Koffo Of Bond Street (sk.)
What A Lady

GRAY, George * c.1863–c.1940
Breaches Of Promise
Colonel With The Slouching Hat, The
    (mon.)
Don't Forget Your Mother (Road To
    Ruin)
Fighting Parson, The (sk.)
Fool Of The Family, The
Good-Night, Nurse (also a song)
Lover's Walk, The
Love That Kills, The (also a song)
My Shadow Is My Only Pal
Night Alarm, The (sk.)
Parson Grey V.C. (sk.)
People's King, The (sk.)
Road To Ruin, The (sk.)
Something In Between
Till A Woman Comes Between
Yer Can't 'It 'Im, Can Yer?

GRAY, Ruby
Pink Petty From Peter, A

GREEN, Gene 1881–1930; sometimes
spelled Greene
I Didn't Raise My Boy To Be A Soldier
King Of The Bungaloos
Oh, You Beautiful Doll
Ragtime Cowboy Joe

GREEN, Marion 1890–1956
English Maids

Lightly Lightly (w. Maggie TEYTE)
Red Rose
Under The Moon
What Are The Names? (w. TEYTE)

GREENE, Evie 1876–1917
Arrah Be Aisy
Corsican Maid, A
Experience
I Shall Never Cease To Love You
Molly The Marchioness
Not The Little Boy She Knew
Peg O' My Heart
Powder Puff
Puzzled
Queen Of The Philippine Islands, The
Rose, A Kiss, A Ring, A
She Lived In The Friendly Isles
Star Of Eve
That Was The End Of My Dream
Try Again, Johnnie
Under The Deodar
When Love Creeps In Your Heart

GREENE, Gene see GREEN, Gene

GREENE, H. Plunkett 1865–1936
Bois Épais (Sombre Woods)
Drake's Drum
Erl King, The
Fairy Lough, The
Father O'Flynn
Infinite Love
King Charles
Maire, My Girl
Molly Brannigan
Off To Philadelphia
Old Navy, The
Old Superb, The
On The Way To Kew
O Ye Dead
Quick, We Have But A Second
Sands Of Dee, The (Clay)
Trottin' To The Fair

GREENE, Mabel
I Like Your Apron And Your Bonnet
In The Merry Month Of May

GREENER, J. H.
Broken Home, The
Don't Go Down In The Mine, Dad
Down In The Pit

GREY, Clifford° 1887–1941
Band Played On, The (Grey:Naish)
My Motor Bike
Vicar And I Will Be There, The (?)

GRIFFITHS, Brothers fl. 1876–1937;
Freddie G. Delaney (1856–1940) and
Joe Ridgeway (d. 1901). Ridgeway was
replaced by Fred jun. (Fred Victor
Delaney) whose sister Lutie (d. 17 Oct.
1945) also occasionally worked in the act,
regularly after their father retired. See
also HANLON-LEES, THE.
Bill And The Buffalo
Blondin Donkey, The
Pogo The Performing Horse
Strong Man, The
Wrestlers, The
Wrestling Lion, The

GRIMALDI, Joseph 1779–1837
Clown's Bazaar, The
Dog Tray
Frog He Would A-Wooing Go, A
Hot Codlins
London Now Is Out Of Town
Massena's Retreat *or* The Grapes Are
Sour
Me And My Neddy
Oyster Cross'd In Love, An
Peep At Turkey, A
Poor Putty
Typitywitchet

GROCK° 1880–1959; Charles Adrien
Wettach, 'The World's Greatest Clown';
made instrumental recordings w. sundry
partners
Abdul Abulbul Amir
A-Be, My Boy (recorded 1919 w. Lily
MORRIS)
Once More Give Me Your Smile (w.
'partner')

GROSSE, Charles
Nonsense! Yes! By Jove! (w. Herbert
CAMPBELL)

GROSSMITH, George sen.° 1847–1912;
orig. k.a. 'junior'; brother of Weedon
GROSSMITH; father of GEORGE jun. and
Lawrence GROSSMITH. Wrote virtually
all his own material
American Girl, The
Automatic Gardener, The
Awful Little Scrub, An
Baby On The Shore, The
Bus Conductor's Song, The
Carrottina (sk.)
Castle Bang (sk.)
Christmas Party, The
Cockney's Life For Me, A
Dicky Birds Are Singing In The Tree
Do Not Spoil Your Children
Duke Of Seven Dials, The
Eighteen And Three
Happy Little Fatherland, The
Happy Old Days At Peckham, The
He, She And The Postman
How I Became An Actor
Human Oddities (sk.)
I Am A Respectable Spectre
Ibsenite Drama, The
In The Stalls (sk.)
I've Loved Another Girl Since Then
Johnnie At The Gaiety
Keep The Baby Warm, Mother
Lords And Commons Are Getting
Mixed!, The
Lost Key, The
Mother And Her Child Were There,
The
Muddle-Puddle Porter, The
My Janet
Noisy Johnnie, The
Off We Go To The Gaiety
Oh! I Wish I Were Some Other
Fellah!
On The Sands
Paderewski Craze, The

Parrot And The Cage, The
Paul Pry
Rhymers That Don't Rhyme
See Me Dance The Polka
See Me Reverse
Seven Ages Of Song
Silver Wedding, The
Society Nigger, The
Speaker's Eye, The
That Dreadful Piano
That Everlasting Coon
That Summer Quarter's Rent
They Tell Me I Am A Most Horrible
    Bore
Thou Of My Thou
Tinkle-Tootle-Tum
Trials Of An Entertainer, The
Truth Or Something Near It, The

GROSSMITH, George jun.* 1874–1935;
m. Adelaide ASTOR; son of George
GROSSMITH sen.; brother of Lawrence
GROSSMITH; nephew of Weedon
GROSSMITH

    Angelina
    Beautiful, Bountiful Bertie
    Bedelia
    Bertie The Bounder
    Carrie
    Ev'rybody's Awfully Good To Me
    Gay Lothario, The
    Girls All Call Me Otto, The (Otto Of
        Roses)
    He Was A Careful Man
    He Was A Careless Man
    He Went To A Party
    I Am So Volatile
    I'm Fond Of Any Blonde
    Leader Of The Labour Party, The
    Mister Dooley
    Murders
    My Cosey Corner Girl (w. Edna MAY)
    Photographer, The
    Rosalie
    Sunday Afternoon
    They Didn't Believe Me (w. Haidée

DE RANCE; also w. Adriene BRUNE
    and w. Madge SANDERS)
Tommy Will You Teach Me How To
    Tango?
Too Slow
Trixie Of Upper Tooting
Waltz Me Around Again, Willie
Yip-I-Addy-I-Ay

GROSSMITH, Lawrence 1877–1944; m.
Coralie BLYTHE; brother of George
GROSSMITH jun.; nephew of Weedon
GROSSMITH; son of George GROSSMITH
sen.

    Cupid's Telephone
    Hullo, People!
    Loose End, A (sk.)
    Man In The Stalls, The (sk.)

GROSSMITH, Weedon 1852–1919;
brother of George GROSSMITH sen.;
uncle of George jun. and Lawrence
GROSSMITH

    Pantomime Rehearsal, A

GROVER, Russell
    Brindisi (*La Traviata*) (w. Lizzie
        PEARCE)
    Charming Sarah Peel
    Enchanted Hash, The
    Kiss, The
    Laugh And Grow Fat
    Muleteer, The
    Nothing More
    She Was Sister To The Angels
    Those Bright Blue Eyes
    Three Topers, The *or* Smith, Brown
        And Jones
    Under A Hedge

GUERRERO, Rosario
    Cauchemar, Le (The Nightmare) (sk.)
    Daughter Of the Mountain, The (sk.)
    Gitana, La (sk.)

GUILBERT, Yvette 1865–1944
    À La Villette

And Her Golden Hair Was Hanging
    Down Her Back (McGlennon)
Cloche D'Ys, La (Les Cloches De
    Nantes)
Comin' Through The Rye
Conscrit Morphinée, Le
Curé De Pomponné, Le
Demoiselles De Pensionnat, Les
Dumb Wife Cured, The
Fée Carabosse, La
Femme À Narcisse, La
Fiacre, Le
Glu, La
Grand'mère, La
Hôtel Du No 3, L'
Houssards De La Garde, Les
I'm Seventeen Come Sunday
I Want Yer, Ma Honey
Keys Of Heaven, The
Linger Longer Loo
Maîtresse D'Acteur
Mary Was A Housemaid
Ma Tête
My Gal Is A High Born Lady
Pierreuse, La
Pocharde, La
Promise, La
Quat'z' Étudiants, Les
Sainte Galette
Soûlarde, La
Sur Le Scène
Très Bien
Vierges, Les
With My Holyday Gown

GUMBLE, Moses 1876–1947; m. Clarice
VANCE (div.)
    Bedelia
    In A Spanish Town

GÜNTHER, Mizzi 1879–1961
    Merry Widow Waltz (w. Louis
        TREUMANN)
    Vilia

GWENN, Edmund 1876–1959
    Bogey From Scotland Yard, The

Half-An-Hour (sk.) (w. Violet
    VANBRUGH)
Twelve Pound Look, The (w.
    VANBRUGH)

GWYNNE, Nell 1869–1903
    I'm An Observationizer
    My New Young Man
    Trust A Woman To Guess

HAGUE'S MINSTRELS, Sam est. Sam
Hague (d. 7 Jan. 1901). See also
RICHARDSON, Billy. Names in brackets
are soloists
    Agricultural Show, The (Harry Price)
    Old England, Home And King! (Sam
        Richards° d. 24 Oct. 1936)
    Please Give Me A Penny, Sir (Sydney
        Herbert)

HAINES, Will E.° d. 1958
    Mr Nobody From Nowhere
    They All Had To Get Out In Their
        Nighties

HALE, Robert 1873–1963
    Everybody's Doin' It Now (w. Ida
        CRISPI)

HALL, Frank° 1836–98; a.k.a. Herbert
Stewart
    Did You Ever Feel That Way?
    Dog Show
    Down In Piccadilly
    Exhibition Of 1862, The
    Johnny Don't Care
    Kleptomania (I Really Couldn't Help
        It)
    Life Is Like A Game Of Cricket
    Polly Compton
    Properest Thing To Do, The
    Railway Station, The
    Sewing Machine, The
    Yankee Fix, The

HALL, J. W.°
    All Doing A Little Bit
    All Through Winking At A
        Magistrate

Chap Who Came To Serenade My
  Sister, The
Does Anybody Want To Buy A
  Bicycle?
Ever Since The Baby Came
Football Referee, The *or* I Was The
  M.U.G.
Ghost Of Patsy Finnigan's Cock-A-
  Doodle-Doo, The
Girl Next Door To Me, The
He Thinks He's Gone To Bed
I Fished All Day And I Fished All
  Night
I'll Go Home And Fancy I'm Dead
It's Only Silly Tommy
I Was Surprised!
John James 'Enery Irving Wilson
  Barrett Baggs
Just Because I Wouldn't Let Her Wear
  A Crinoline
Looking For A House To Let
Mouse Ran Under The Bed, The
My First Wife
My Sweetheart Jane
On Monday She Sings 'Molly Riley
  O'
Our Ruth Ann (They Call Her
  'Monkey Brand')
Place Where Thy Make Mud Pies,
  The
She Thinks She's Wilson Barrett
Street Where They Never Clean The
  Windows, The
Up And Down The Streets I'm
  Running
We Didn't Get Her Out Till Morning
Welcome At Home, The
We Were Lads Together

HALL, Tatten d. 21 July 1945; H. C.
Tatten-Hall
  Cockney In Kilts, The
  Dandy, The

HALL, Wendell W.* 1896–1969
  It Ain't Gonna Rain No Mo'

HALLAM, Basil 1889–1916; k.i.a.;
engaged to Elsie JANIS
  Ballin' The Jack (w. Elsie JANIS)
  Constant Lover, The
  Gilbert, The Filbert
  Goodbye, Girls, I'm Through
  I've Got Everything I Want But You
    (w. JANIS)
  You're Here And I'm Here (w. JANIS)

HALLETT, Wilson 1881–1943
  Any Rags
  His Old Familiar Tune
  I'm Tired
  Nigger Laughing Song, A
  Why Has A Cow Got Four Legs? (w.
    Cicely COURTNEIDGE)

HAMILTON, Rose 1874–97; orig. w.
Hamilton & Clark; m. Tom LEAMORE
  All Have A Drink With Me
  Below! Below! Below!
  Have You Noticed It?
  It's Goodbye To Mandie
  Mary's Gone Back To The Country
    Again
  My Honey Baby
  My Johnny
  Nod Your Head
  Poor Little Girl Wanted Looking After,
    The
  Rose Of Mayo, The
  Smartest Boy On Earth, The
  Strike Up The Band
  That's How They Do It In London
  That's Where You See An Alteration
  Why Don't You Do It Now?
  Young Student

HANDY, W. C. 1873–1958
  Beale St Blues
  Memphis Blues, The
  St Louis Blues, The

HANLEY, Ted 1868–1927; brother of
Alec HURLEY
  'Ow's This For A Start?
  They've All Gone In For 'Em

HANLON-LEES, The est. *c.*1860; acrobatic troupe of brothers trained by 'Professor' John Lees (d. 1855): Frederick (1845–66), Alfred (d. 1887), George (1839–1926), William (1844–1923), Thomas (1836–68), and Edward (1854–1931). In 1876 'the arena of Gymnastic and Acrobatic art' was abandoned for sketches. Other 'Hanlons' were Robert (Little Bob) (1861–1907) and Dick (d. 17 Oct. 1905); also Joe Ridgeway of the BROTHERS GRIFFITHS.
>   Devil's Waterfall, The
>   Do-Mi-Sol-Do
>   Gymnase Paz, Le
>   Nights Of Fun
>   Soirée En Habit Noir, Une
>   Trip To Switzerland, A (Voyage En Suisse)
>   Village Barber, The

HANSON, Edwin member of QUAKER CITY FOUR/QUARTETTE
>   Dear Old Tennessee (w. PRIMROSE & DOCKSTADER'S)

HARDING, Evelyn
>   Down Vauxhall Way
>   Gretna Green

HARDING, Lyn 1867–1952
>   Honour Is Satisfied (sk.)

HARDING, Muriel *see* PETROVA, Olga

HARE, Gilbert 1869–1951
>   I Pagliacci (as a one-act sk.) (w. Mrs Brown POTTER)

HARE, Sir John 1844–1921
>   Mario, The (sk.)
>   Quiet Rubber, A (sk.)

HARE, Winifred b. 1875
>   Banish Sorrow Till Tomorrow
>   Britain's Sons Shall Rule The World
>   Come Down Lover's Lane

>   Four-And-Twenty Little Men
>   Glimpse-impse-impse, A
>   Hello! Hello! Hello!
>   Honey Boy
>   I Can Offer You A Cosy Little Flat
>   It's Better Than Being A Carnegie
>   Just 'Cause The Bee Loves Honey
>   My Silent Sweetheart
>   One Little Lonely Star
>   Poor Little Fly
>   Princess And The Troubador, The (sk.) (w. Topsy SINDEN)
>   She's His Sunday Girl
>   Sleep, Little Brown Dove
>   When I Gaze In Those Dear Dreamy Eyes
>   Why Do The Girls Love Charlie?
>   You Are A White Little Girl

HARLAN, Byron G.
>   Alexander's Rag-Time Band
>   Cheer Up, Mary
>   Hello Central, Give Me Heaven
>   I Want To Be In Dixie
>   Mother Hasn't Spoken To Father Since
>   My Wife's Gone To The Country
>   Wait Till The Sun Shines, Nellie

HARLEY, Kate
>   Aunt Sally
>   Away Down Holborn Hill
>   Colleen Bawn, The
>   Form, Girls, Form
>   Granny Snow
>   I'll Never Get Married I Vow
>   I'm A Happy Little Wife And I Don't Care
>   [I'm] The Dark Girl Dress'd In Blue
>   I Really Couldn't See It
>   I Should Like To Know The Reason *or* Any Other Girl
>   Kiss In The Railway Train, The
>   Ladies' Darling, The
>   Lords Of Their Own Creation

Making A Sensation
Old Sarah Walker
Thames Embankment, The

HARLEY, Lily 1865–1928; née Hannah
Hill; m. Charles CHAPLIN sen.; a.k.a.
Lily Chaplin, mother of Charles jun. and
Sydney CHAPLIN
    Opportunity

HARMER, Dolly 1867–1956; see also
KARNO, Fred
    Down Quality Street
    'E Dunno Why 'E Do It, But 'E Do
    Helping Mother
    Hupper Ten, The
    I'm Absolutely Bustin' To Be Just Like
      That
    Look What Percy's Picked Up In The
      Park
    One Little Cottage All Our Own
    Polly And Her Poodle
    Proposals
    She Didn't Go Far Upon The Journey

HARNEY, Ben R.° 1871–1938
    Mister Johnson Turn Me Loose
    You've Been A Good Old Wagon But
      You've Done Broke Down

HAROLD, Lily
    Dennah Dinah Do
    He Wanted A Girl
    Honey, Come An' Listen To Me
    It's A Good Thing—Push It Along
    John Bull's Picture Gallery
    Little Pug-Dog Wobbled Close
      Behind, The
    Little Yo San
    My Pearl Is The Queen Of Girls
    Snowflakes

HARRADEN, Herbert°
    Afternoon At Home, The
    Captain And The Mermaid, The
    Chloe
    Fly And The Spider, The
    Good-Bye, Honey

I Pity Him So (Poor Old Jo!)
Parents, The
Photographic Fiend, The
Present Generation, The
Sneezing Serenade, A

HARRIGAN, Ed° 1844–1911; see also
HARRIGAN & HART
    Babies On Our Block, The

HARRIGAN & HART Ed HARRIGAN and
Anthony (Tony) Hart (1855–91)
    St Patrick's Day Parade
    Salvation Army, Oh
    Sam Johnson's Colored Cakewalk
    Skidmore Fancy Ball (and sundry
      other Skidmore songs)
    Whist! The Bogie Man

HARRIS, Gus m. Ida BARR (div.)
    Everybody Calls Me Chu Chin
      Chow
    Gentile And Jew
    God Save Our Sailor King
    Hi, Hi, Hi, I'm Learning The Way To
      Fly
    I'm The Only Yiddisher Scotsman In
      The Irish Fusiliers
    Show Me A Train That Goes To
      London
    Whoops, Let's Do It Again

HARRIS, Leslie°
    Dream Of An 'At Home', A
    Human Nature
    Ladies' Penny Paper, The
    Serial Story, The
    That Fatal Wink
    Up With The Banns And Take Her
    When The Minister Comes To Tea
    Wiggley Waggley Japanese, The
    William White
    Woman Who Shops, The

HARRISON, Charles W. 1885?–1945?
    I Hear You Calling Me
    Little Grey Home In The West
    Mother Machree

HARRISON, Clifford 1850–1904;
elocutionist; son of William **HARRISON**
Allegro, L'
Brook, The
Cane-Bottom'd Chair, The
Christmas Carol, A
Cloud, The
Crossing The Bar (Lockton?)
Dream Of Eugene Aram, The
Fall Of Corinth, The
Henry V At Agincourt
Isles Of Greece, The
Last Minstrel, The
Lochinvar
Lost And Found
Lotus Eaters, The
Marsyas
Ode To The West Wind
Paul Revere's Ride
Pied Piper, The
Raven, The
Richard ll
Silas Marner's Comforters

HARRISON, Denham d. 1945
Another Little Patch Of Red
Give Me A Ticket To Heaven
It Must End Up Happily
Namouna

HARRISON, James
Trail Of The Lonesome Pine, The (w.
Edna **BROWN**)

HARRISON, John 1867–1929
Because
Blue Alsatian Mountains, The
Come Into The Garden Maud
Excelsior! (w. Robert **RADFORD**)
Larboard Watch (w. **RADFORD**)
Mattinata
Rosary, The
Watchman, What Of The Night? (w.
RADFORD)

HARRISON, William 1813–68; father of
Clifford **HARRISON**
Glorious Wine

Gold Rules The World
Heart's First Dream Of Love, The
Lullaby, The (Benedict)
Moon Has Raised Her Lamp Above,
The (w. Charles **SANTLEY**)
Once More Upon The Path Of Life
Then You'll Remember Me (When
Other Lips)
Though Born In Woods
Yes! Let Me Like A Soldier Fall

HARROLD, Orville 1878–1933
Ah! Sweet Mystery Of Life

HART, Annie c.1860–1947
Pride Of Shanty-Town!, The
Sweet Rosie O'Grady
Who Threw The Overalls In Mistress
Murphy's Chowder?

HART, Anthony see **HARRIGAN & HART**

HART, Charles d. 20 Feb. 1916
I'm Forever Blowing Bubbles
Let The Rest Of The World Go By

HART, E. A.
Dear Little Nellie Who Lives By The
Sea
Fireman, The
I Love To Flirt With The Girls
Our Noble Fire Brigades

HARVEY, Fred 1856–95
Bookmakers, The (What Do You Want
To Back?)
Buggins, He Ought To Know You
Know
Dearly Beloved Brethren, Isn't It A
Sin?
Edge
In
Inky-man or The Seventh Royal
Booziliers
Interval, The
It Was Me
It Wasn't Me
Makes You Feel Uneasy

Muggins He Ought To Know, You
  Know
Night I Played Richard The Third,
  The
Our Flat
Our Society
Out
That's The Cause Of It
That Was Me

HARVEY, 'Bonnie' Kate
Able Seaman, An
Bonnie Boy In Blue, A
Did 'Em, Did 'Em, Do It?
Gallant 93rd, The
Little Bit Of Red, The
Oh! Mother Eve
Oh, What A Delusion
Pet And Pride Of The Dairy, The
Promenading On A Frosty Night
Shamrock, The Thistle And The Rose,
  The
Sligo *or* Thy Land's My Land!
Some Do! Some Don't!
You Fancy Yourselves, You Do!
You Know That You've All Done The
  Same
You Lay Your Snares
Young Country Squire, The
You See I'm But A Simple Country
  Maid

HARVEY, Martin *see* MARTIN-HARVEY,
Sir John

HARVEY, Mrs Martin *see* DE SILVA,
Nina

HARVEY, Rose d. 7 Oct. 1899
Do Drop In At The Dew Drop Inn
Farewell, My Little Yo-San
Good-Bye, Tilly
Lot 99
Mary Kino
Mary's Learning Something Every
  Day
There's Something Missing

HARWOOD, Frank
Come Down Lover's Lane
Dear Little 'Yellow Boy'!
Every Little Picture Tells A Story
My Pipe
Rowing To Hampton Court
Which Is The Key To Your Heart?
Wit, Woman And Wine

HARWOOD, Robb 1869–1910
It's Painfully True (w. Louie FREEAR)

HASTINGS, Ernest°
And Yet—I Don't Know!
Ballads Ragged And Martialized
Bolshevik, The
Bow Bells
Ever Since He Pelmanized
Exemptions And Otherwise
Foods Of All Nations (Eating)
Future Variety Show, The
Gerrard Six Four
Happiest Christmas Of All, The
I Might Marry You
Lights Out
Lord Luv 'Im!
Love Limited
Matilda
Military Representative, The
Mother Always Sends The Very Thing
Muldoon's Ball
My Word, You Do Look Queer!
Oh, Dear, What Can The Matter Be?
Profiteer's Ball, The
Rumours
Seaside Posters Round The Home,
  The
Song Of The Ford, The
Special Constable, The
Syncopated Village Blacksmith, The
Three Ages of Man, The

HASTINGS, Florrie 1872?–1972?
Possibly d. 7 July 1949
Just Because She Didn't Know The
  Way
Like A Lady

HASTINGS, Fred°
Can I Be Of Any Assistance?
Cruise Of The Ancient Lights, The
End Of The Pier, The
Fishing
See-Saw
Song Without A Name, The
Subject To Slight Alteration

HASTON, MILLS & TUCK *see* VERSA-
TILE THREE, THE

HATTON, John L.° 1809–86
Simon The Cellarer
To Anthea

**HAVERLY'S (AMERICAN UNITED)
MASTODON MINSTRELS** fl. 1875–85; est.
Christopher k.a. Jack H. Haverly
(1837–1901); see ERNEST, Charles;
KNOWLES, R. G.; RICHARDS, Nellie;
STRATTON, Eugene. Names in brackets
indicate soloists
Billy's Appeal (Billy RICE)
Boy's Best Friend Is His Mother, A
(BOHEE BROS.)
My Gal Is A High Born Lady (Charles
ERNEST)
Oh, Dem Golden Slippers (William R.
MOORE)
Sweet Adeline (MOORE)

HAVERLY'S COLOURED MINSTRELS fl.
*c.*1881; troupe incl. Richard Little;
Wallace KING

HAWTHORNE, Lil d. 1926; orig. w.
HAWTHORNE, THREE SISTERS
Don't Cry, Little Girl!
Give It To The Baby
I Can't Tell Why I Love You, But I Do
If A Girl Like You Loved A Boy Like
Me
I'll Be Your Sweetheart *or* Bluebells
I'm A Gal O' Tennessee
Kitty Mahone *or* Do Have Some Pity,
Kitty (?)
Little Molly Igo

Little Tam O'Shanter, The
Love Steals In
Lucy Loo
Mah Ellaline
Mamie May
Mary's A Grand Old Name
My Castle In Spain
My Cosy Caravan
Nicest Little Dolly In The Shop, The
Spring-Time Is Ring-Time
Sunray
Sweetest Girl In Illinois, The
Sweet Rosie O'Grady
Sweet Suzanne
Tell Me True
Tessie, You Are The Only Only Only
That's What The Daisy Said
There's Not Another Girlie
Whose Little Girl Are You?

HAWTHORNE, THREE SISTERS fl.
1893–8; Lil, Lola, and Nellie; see also
HAWTHORNE, Lil
Climb De Golden Fence
Courting On A Wheel
Gay Vivandière, The
My Gal Is A High Born Lady
Polly Pretty Polly
She's The Daughter Of Officer Porter
Sleighing
Story Of Jack And Jill, The
Sunday Night In Lovers' Lane
Sunshine Of Paradise Alley, The
Willow Pattern Plate, The

HAWTREY, Sir Charles 1858–1923 (all
sketches)
Compleat Angler, The
Elegant Edward
Haunted Husband, The
Her Wedding Night
Little Fowl Play, A
Q
Time Is Money (w. Lottie VENNE)
Waiting At The Church

HAY, Will 1888–1949; in 1920s w. Fred
KARNO

Find The Beetle (sk.)
Moonstruck (sk.)
Nosey Nose (sk.)

HAYDEN-CLARENDON, J.°
Just To Take The Chill Off
Practical Impossibilities
Question Of Time, A

HAYD(E)N QUARTET fl. 1907–14; incl.
Billy MURRAY
Blue Bell
Put On Your Old Gray Bonnet
Will You Love Me In December (As
You Do In May)?
You're The Flower Of My Heart
(Sweet Adeline)

HAYDON, Ethel 1877–1954; m. George
Robey (div.)
Circus Girl, A
Cuckoo, The
Follow The Man From Cook's (octet
from *A Runaway Girl*)
Home That's Home For Me, The
Knock The Two Rooms Into One
Let Me But Hope
My Heart Is Your Heart
Rose Of My Heart, The
Soldiers In The Park
When I Dreamed I Was Santa Claus
Won't You Teach Me? (w. Kitty
BERESFORD)

HAYES, Emilie 1887–1940; sometimes
spelled Emily; m. G. H. ELLIOTT
My Californian Girl (w. G. H.
ELLIOTT)
Put On Your Best Kimona
Thank God For Victory
That Little Quaker Meeting House
When I Leave The World Behind
You Used To Tell Me I Had Baby
Eyes

HAYES, Catherine 1820/5–81
Always With Me
Charlie, Ye Are Welcome

Harp That Once Through Tara's Halls,
The
Kathleen Mavourneen
Those Happy Days Are Gone
'Tis The Last Rose Of Summer

HAYES, J. Milton° 1884–1940; mon-
ologues; wrote his own material
Babette
Back O' Beyond
Billy's Biograph
Bubbles
By The Yukon Trail
Cherry Tree Lane
Dream Ring Of The Desert
Foreign Legion, The
Green Eye Of The Little Yellow God,
The
If I'd My Way
Meanderings Of Monty, The (series)
Mebbe So
One, Two, Three
Social Scale, The
Whitest Man I Know, The
Yukon Trail, The

HAYNES, Joe *c*.1850–1909; chairman
and manager of Bedford, Camden Town
11th Hussars, The
Nellie And I Go Strolling

HAZEL, Agnes 1867–1913; sister of Jim
SIPPLE
Canoodle Round The Corner, A
Don't You Heed What The Young
Men Tell You
Little Girl Over The Way, The

HEARN, Lew b. 1882; m. (1) BONITA
(div.); (2) Catherine Wiley
Hitchy-Koo (w. BONITA)
Snookey-Ookums (w. BONITA)
You're My Baby (w. BONITA)

HEATH, Rosée
Little Cherry Blossom, Will You Love
Me?
My Dainty Little Darling

She's The Only Girl I Love
Who'll Buy My Shrimps?

HEATHCOTE, Ernest
Puffs
Walking In My Sleep
What A Friend We Have In Mother

HEBDEN, Will 1863–1919
Irishman, The
Sailors Of Her Majesty Victoria
Soldiers Of Her Majesty Victoria

HEDGES BROTHERS & JACOBSON
Freddie (d. 28 Feb. 1920) & Elven
(1889–1931) Hedges w. Jesse JACOBSON
I Don't Know Where You Live
If I Had The Lamp Of Aladdin
Nora Malone
Oh! Charley, Take It Away
On San Francisco Bay
Ragtime Cowboy Joe
There'll Come A Time
Trail Of The Lonesome Pine, The

HEFFRON, J. C. 1857–1934
Do As I Tell You
New Hat Now!, A
We All Go To Work But Father
Where Did You Get That Hat?

HEIDER, Fred
Aba Daba Honeymoon (w. Ruby
RAYMOND)

HEIGHT, Amy d. 21 Mar. 1913
De Tennessee Christ-nin'
He's Jest Too Sweet For Anything
I'm In Love With A Dandy Colored
Coon
Topsy (Ma Popsy Wopsy)
Walk Up And See De Show

HELD, Anna 1873–1915; first wife of
Florenz Ziegfeld jun. (1867–1932)
Bashful Betsy Brown
I Have Such A Nice Little Way With
Me
I Just Can't Make My Eyes Behave

It's Delightful To Be Married
I've Lost My Teddy Bear
Kewpie Doll
Maiden With The Dreamy Eyes, The
Music Hall Girl, The
Pretty Little Mollie Shannon
Pretty Little Tonkin Girl
Something More Than That
Won't You Come And Play With Me?

HELDER, Ruby b. 1891; 'Lady Tenor'
Dear Love
Eleanore
I'll Sing Thee Songs Of Araby
Last Watch, The
M'Appari Tutt'Amor
Mountain Lovers
My Dreams
My Queen
Once Again
Remember Me
Star Of Bethlehem
Thora

HELF, J. Fred 1871–1915
If Money Talks, It Ain't On Speaking
Terms With Me
When The Spring-Time Brings The
Roses, Jessie Dear
When The Whip-Poo-Will Sings,
Marguerite
When You Know You're Not
Forgotten By The Girl You Can't
Forget

HEMSLEY, Harry May b. 1877
Child-Life

HENDERSON, Dick 1891–1958
Little White Rose
Pal Of My Cradle Days
Tiptoe Through The Tulips
Until

HENDERSON, May 1884–1937
Caroline Brown Of Chinatown
My Black Daisy
Nobody Loves Me

HENDERSON, Roy b. 1899
Old Father Thames
Simon The Cellarer

HENESIER, Mme *see* WARE, Mrs
George W.

HENLEY, Josephine
Denny Murphy's Daughter Nell
Girl Can't Do Everything, A
They're At It Again

HENRY, Roland°
Amateur Mesmerist, The
Language Failed Him
When Daddy Comes Home Tonight

HENSON, Leslie 1891–1957; m. Madge
SAUNDERS
Carry On The Good Work
I'd Like To Bring My Mother
In The Trenches (sk.)
It'll All Be The Same A Hundred
Years From Now
Jones Of The Lancers (My Word!)
Murders
Pukka Sahib (Green Eye Of The Little
Yellow God) (sk.)

HENTY, Dick°
Murders

HERMAN, Phil
Hooligan's Canary
Jane Magee
Last Grip, The
Little Baby Patsy
Oh! Bess, My Darling Bess

HETHERINGTON, Dot
Boy In The Gallery, The

HICKS, Sir Seymour° 1871–1949; m.
Ellaline TERRISS
After The Honeymoon (sk.) (w.
Ellaline TERRISS; also w.
VALLI-VALLI)
And Her Golden Hair Was Hanging

Down Her Back (Adrian Ross
lyrics)
Bridal Suite, The (sk.) (w. Gladys
COOPER, also w. TERRISS)
Cook's Man (sk.) (w. TERRISS)
Elsie From Chelsea
Fly-By-Night, The (sk.) (w. TERRISS)
Garrick (sk.) (w. TERRISS)
Hampton Club, The (sk.)
King Richard III (Shakespeare,
abridged)
Little Mad'moiselle, The
Oh! Mr Chamberlain
Papa's Wife (sk.) (w. TERRISS; also w.
COOPER and w. Zena DARE)
Patchwork Garden, The
Quaint Old Bird, A
Rip Van Winkle Was A Lucky Man
Scrooge (sk.)
Sleeping Partners (sk.) (w. Madge
LESSING; also w. TERRISS)
Slum Angel, A (sk.) (w. TERRISS)
Suppose (w. DARE)
What Could The Poor Girl Do?
Winner, The (sk.)

HILL, Carmen
Annie Laurie
Coolan Dhu
Crooning Water
Down In The Forest
Forethought
Gray Days
Happy Song
If I Might Come To You
It Is Only A Tiny Garden (My Garden)
Lochleven
Myfanwy
My Message
O My Garden Full Of Roses
Poppies For Forgetting
Reason
Rose In The Bud
Rose Of My Heart, The
Roses Of Forgiveness
Thoughts Have Wings

'Tis The Hour Of Farewell
Wait

HILL, Hamilton 1874–1910
Baby In Dreamland
Bedelia
Beresford, We Wish You Had Been
    There
Beyond The Gates Of Paradise
Blue Bell
Could You Be True To Eyes Of Blue?
Don't Cry Sister Jane
Farewell, My Little Yo-San
Fireman's Song, The
For The Empire And England's Glory
Good-Bye, Dolly Gray
Good Luck, Japan!
I'll Be With You When The Roses
    Bloom Again
I Want To Be A Soldier!
Letter From The Front, A
Little Boy Called Taps, A
Love Me The Same As In Days Gone
    By
Mignon, To You Returning
Queen Of Love
Sailing Home
Sammy
Sun Is Always Shining, The
Sweet Eileen
There Goes My Soldier Boy
There's A Man In Manitoba
There's Music In The Sound Of Home
When My Ship Is Sailing
When We Meet
When You Were Sweet Sixteen
Which Sailor Boy Do *You* Want?

HILL, Jenny 1849/50–96; m. John
William Woodley (1839–90) k.a. Johnny
or Jean Pasta (separated). Mother of
Letty Pasta later k.a. Peggy PRYDE and
Jenny Hill Davidson (1876–1952). Some
sources state erroneously that agent
Edward Turnbull became her second
husband

'Arriet's Answer
'Arry
Bai Jove! (The Modern Swell)
Balradour
Beautiful Star
Betrayed Virgin, The
Bold Soldier Boy
Bother The Men *or* A Fig For The
    Men
Boy About Town, The
Boy In The Gallery, The
Captain With His Whiskers, The
City Waif, The *or* The Streets Of
    London Town
Coffee-Shop Gal, The
Dear Old Ned
Early One Morning
East End Girl, The
Every Pub We Saw, We Went Inside
    Of It
Four Ale Sal
Good Old London Bill (That's Bill)
He's Out On The Fuddle
He Was Her Only Son
If I Only Bossed The Show
I'm A Woman Of Very Few Words
I'm Determined No Longer To Stand
    It
I Mean To Have A Legal Separation
I'm So Fly
I See You've Got 'Em On
It's A Funny Little Way We've Got In
    England
It Wants A Bit Of Doing
I've Been A Good Woman To You
Jack *or* You Mustn't Tell My Mother
Keep Your Eyes Off My Chap
Life's Highway
Little Gyp (sk.)
Little Stowaway, The (The Thrush)
    (sk.)
Little Vagabond Boy, The
Lodging House Drudge, The
Maggie Murphy's Home
Masks And Faces
Modern Swell, The *see* Bai Jove!

Monday Was The Day
Old Brown's Daughter (parody)
On The Continong
Opinion Of Sarah, The
Pretty Little Dimple Chin
Ps And Qs
Sally's Wedding Day
Shadows Of St Pauls (sk.)
Song Of The Thrush
Southend Picnic, The
Star Upon Star
Sweet Violets
That's Bill (Good Old London Bill)
That's How He Carries On
Thereby Hangs A Tale
Tricky
Where Does The Laugh Come In?
You Don't Get Over Sal

HILL, Reuben
Beauty And The Beast
Come Along, Little Girl
Daddy Is Near
Empty Frame, The
In The Years That Are To Come
Jack Still Knows How To Fight
Last Bus Home At Night, The
Music Teacher, The
People You Meet In The Strand
Sparkling Polly

HILLIER, James 1840–74
Brigham Young
Dolly Varden
Fie For Shame! *or* What Would
    Mamma Say?
Mine Own Susan Jane
Nice Cup Of Tea, A
Oh I Wish Your Mother Would Come
Pat A Cake
Rosherville
Sourkraut's Farewell
Sourkraut's Return
Tickle In The Tunnel, A
Timid Lover, The
Turn It Up

HITCHCOCK, Raymond 1874–1929
Rest Goes Home To My Wife, The
So What's The Use?
They Give Me A Medal For That
'Twas In September
When You're All Dressed Up And No
    Place To Go

HITE, Mabel 1885–1912
My Brudda, Sylvest' (w. Mike
    DONLIN)
My Wife's Gone To The Country
Stupid Mr Cupid

HOBBS, Billy d. 1917; see also **MOHAWK
MINSTRELS**
I'm Not A Love-Sick Coon
Ma Honey Isn't Jam
Meet Me Half-Way Susie
Nobody
Rosalie *or* My Lady Love Ain't There
She Ain't A Bit Like The Other Girls
She Loves Me
Stand And Deliver, Isabella Brown
When Daffney Holds Her Finger Up

HOBBS, John W.° 1799–1877
Phillis Is My Only Joy

HODSON, Miss G. A. b. 1830?
Kentish Gipsies, The (w. J. W. **SHARP**)
Matrimonial Sweets (w. **SHARP**)
What Are The Men About?
When My Ship Comes Home

HODSON, George A.° 1798–1863
Dan Of Dublin
Galway Meg
He Knew She Never Blamed Him
O Give Me But My Arab Steed
Parting, The
Tell Me Mary How To Woo
    Thee

HOGAN, Ernest° *c.*1865–1909
All Coons Look Alike To Me

HOLLINGSWORTH, A. B. 1829–65
Chilly Man, The
Colleen Bawn, The
Go It While You're Young
Man With The Carpet Bag, The
Mysterious Tailor, The
Oh I Can Get No One To Love Me
Special Bobby, The (To Keep The
Peace)

HOLLOWAY, Stanley° 1890–1982
And Yet—I Don't Know
Brahn Boots (mon.)
Coal-Black Mammy
Dark Girl Dress'd In Blue, The
Lion And Albert, The (mon.)
My Word You Do Look Queer
Old Father Thames
Old Sam (Sam, Pick Oop Tha'
Musket) (mon.)
With Her Head Tucked Underneath
Her Arm

HONEY, George 1864–1905
It's Doubtful, Very Doubtful
My Little Girl *or* When The Curtain's
Down
Only A Little Paper Parcel
Right Across The Bridge

HONRI, Percy 1874–1953; as an adult a
noted concertina virtuoso
Death Of Nelson, The (as a boy
'tenor')
Fisherman's Child, The (as a boy
'tenor')
God Be With You
Hello, Little Box Of Soldiers (*1915
revue*)
If I Were A Man (as a boy 'tenor')
Judgement Day, The
Vesper Bells (*1915 revue*)

HOOD, Marion 1853–1912
Flower Song (*Ruy Blas* burlesque)
Song Of My Heart
They Call Me The Belle Of Dollis
Hill

HOPKINS, Ted d. 31 Mar. 1937
Charge Of The Welsh Brigade, The
Treorchy Fair

HORN, Charles Edward° 1786–1849
Cherry Ripe
Deep, Deep Sea, The

HORTON, Priscilla 1818–95; m. T. Ger-
man REED; see also REED Co., German
Murmur Of The Shell, The
Musing On Days Gone By
Song Of All Nations, The
White Squall, The

HOWARD, Gus *see* McNAUGHTONS,
THE

HOWARD, Joseph E.° 1878–1961; m.
Ida EMERSON
Goodbye, My Lady Love (w. Ida
EMERSON)
Hello! Ma Baby Love (w. EMERSON)

HOWARD, Lizzie 1874–1903
As A Mother Would Cherish Her Baby
Baby And I
Family Scapegrace, The
God Bless And Keep Victoria
Golden Years *or* Never Again
Union Jack, The
Vanity Fair

HOWARD, Milly
Croquet
Girl In Advance Of The Times, The
Horse Guards Blue

HOWARD, Tom
While Strolling Thru The Park One
Day (w. Patsy BARRETT)

HOWARD, Walter° 1842–1905; all w.
MOORE & BURGESS MINSTRELS except
where indicated
And The Nightingale Sang Of Love (w.
MOHAWK MINSTRELS)
Do You Know Where Nowhere Is?
Heigho! Says The Sailor's Wife
His Name Was Joshu-a

How That Poor Girl Suffered For Me
I Very Often Do
Josephus Orange Blossom
Lodger And Mary Ann, The
Look At The Price Of Coals!
Love, 'Tis A Very Funny Thing
Magpie Said 'Come In', The
Oh My Darling Clementine (w.
    MOHAWKS)
Oh, What Nose My Lodger's Got
Peculiar Man, The
Poor Thing
Quaker's Daughter, The (Yea, Verily!
    Verily, Yea!)
Riding In A Pullman Car
Royal Wild Beast Show, The (w.
    CHRISTY MINSTRELS)
Sir Rufus The Run
Song Of Songs, The
They've Both Got The Beautiful
    Hump
Thousand A Year And A Liver
    Complaint, A
Unfortunate Man, The
Villain Still Pursued Her, The
Virgin Only Nineteen Years Old, The
    (w. CHRISTYS)
Wax-Work Show, The (w. CHRISTYS)
What's The (H)odds?
When She Comes Home With The
    Milk In The Morning
When The Sun Shines Bright On A
    Moonlight Night

HOWELL, Henry
Dog's Meat Man, The
Jack Robinson
Walker, The Twopenny Postman

HOWES, Milly
Jolly Little Butcher Boy, The
Pretty As A Picture
Tripping O'er The Hills

HUDSON, Harry *see* KIRKBY & HUDSON

HUDSON, Olga & Elgar & Eli Olga
was the soprano Eleanor JONES-HUDSON

(d. 2 Aug. 1945); her husband Eli (1877–
1919) was an excellent flautist and
conductor. 'Elgar' was their daughter
Winifred, a 'piccolist' (d. 4 Nov. 1940)
    Angels Guard Thee
    Beloved
    Just A Little Love (Un Peur D'Amour)
    Sunshine Of Your Smile, The
    When You Are Near
    Youth And Love

HUDSON, Thomas° 1791–1844
Dog's Meat Man, The
Ghost Of Kitty Maggs, The
I Never Says Nothing To Nobody
Jack Robinson
Lively Flea, The (parody of Ivy
    Green)
Poor Robinson Crusoe
Singing Made Easy
Spider And The Fly, The
Walker, The Tuppenny Postman

HUGHES, Tom E. *c.*1880–1938
Can London Do Without Me?
I Can Sleep In Oxford Street
I Don't Think I'm So Busy After All
I Don't Think She Treats Me Fair
I Wonder What It Feels Like To Be
    Poor?
Leicester Square
One Of The Upper Ten

HULBERT, Jack° 1892–1978; m. Dame
Cicely COURTNEIDGE
Awfully Chap, The
Coal-Black Mammy
Have You Forgotten? (w. Phyllis
    MONKMAN)
I Did Feel A Dreadfully Ass
On The River Cam
Rag-Time Craze, The
Reckless Reggie Of The Regent Palace
Wusky Woozle, The

HUMPHRIES, Griffith°
Bazaar And Fancy Fair, The
Drama Up-To-Date

8 Bars Rest
Give A Little Cough
How *Dear* Thou Art
It Wouldn't Be A Bad Idea
Mingle Your Eyebrows With Mine,
    Love

HUMPHRIES, John *c.*1864–1927
Do You See The Idea? I See (w.
    Wilkie BARD)

HUNTER, G. W.* 1851–1936; wrote
much of his own material
After The Fall (parody of After The
    Ball)
All The Comforts Of A Home
Amateurs' Show, The
As Pretty As A Picture
Bald Bull-Dog, The
Bald Headed Swell, The
Because She Ain't Built That Way
Christening, The ('Twas Down In That
    Place Tipperary)
Courtship
Did He Get There?
Doctor Jeremiah Jones
Don't Swear
Down By The Garden Gate
Duck Foot Sue
Funny Things They Do Upon The Sly
'General' Up To Date, The
Give What You Can To Those In
    Distress For The Poor Working Girl
    Hasn't Any
Gone Before
Gone Wrong
Haul Me Back Again
He Never Smiled Again
Hezekiah Brown
Hungry Man From Clapham, The
I Remember
It's All Right Now
Just To Show There Is No Ill Feeling
Kissing
Logical Conclusions
Lovely Woman, Charming Woman
McGilligan's Wedding

Maggie Murphy's Flat (parody)
Married Life
Modern Country Maid, The
Nobody Knows What Trouble Was
    There
Oh! Dear Me, What's The Matter
O 'Lizer Para-Lizer
Only To See That Face Again
Riding On (The) Top Of An Omnibus
Scarlet Fever Jane
Since I Became A Married Man
Sitting Down To Tea
Solomon's Proverbs
Song That Broke My Heart, The
Table Etiquette
Take My Advice, If You Don't You
    Ought
Thanks! Thanks! Thanks!
That Is Love (parody)
That's Another Story
There Are Moments When One Wants
    To Be Alone
They Never Will Invite You Any More
They Wanted To Take My Photograph
Things 'Tis Better Not To Dwell On
Trilby On The Brain
Various Topics Old And New
Wedded Bliss
What Funny Things Are Done Upon
    The Sly
Wherever I May Go
Word-lets, Gag-lets, and Yarn-lets

HUNTER, Harry* 1841–1906; wrote
mostly for the MOHAWK MINSTRELS
from 1874. Joined Francis & Day music
publishers 1886; retired 1903
Boy's Best Friend Is His Mother
Contented Duffer, The
Dinah Duck
Doctor Says I'm Not To Be Worried
Do Your Duty Well
If You See Lucy Let Me Know
I'm A Ship Without A Rudder
I Saw Esau Kissing Kate (Country
    Cousin)

Johnny Will You Come Along Now?
Just Behind The Battle Mother
    (parody)
Lindy, I'm Coming Back To You
Little Joe
Lord Mayor's Coachman, The
Man Who Leads A Wretched Life,
    The
Mazy Dance, The
Never Give In
Peter Perfect
Say So Saucy Sue
Tears Are Blessings
Victoria's Jubilee

HUNTING, Russell° 'Michael Casey'
monologues
    At A Fight
    At A Wake
    At The Dentist
    Courting His Girl
    Motoring To Brighton
    Taking The Census

HUNTLEY, G. P. 1868–1927
    Algy's Simply Awf'lly Good At Algebra
    Arms And The Girl (sk.)
    Belinda
    Buying A Gun (sk.) (w. Harry
        GRATTAN)
    Curios (w. GRATTAN)
    Fairy Glen Laundry, The (w.
        GRATTAN)
    Looking For A Needle In A Haystack
    Ode, An
    Oh! Lor!
    Queen Of Wheels
    Since My Old Dutch Pegged Out

HURLEY, Alec 1871–1913; second
husband of Marie LLOYD; brother of Ted
HANLEY
    About The Matter I Ain't Got Nothin'
        To Say
    'Addick Smoker's Daughter, The
    After Twelve

(And) She Wears A Little Bonnet
'Arry, 'Arry, 'Arry
At Our Outing
Baby Boy (The Ostler's Love Song)
Barmaid, The or She Was A Nice
    Little Innocent Thing
Best Little Woman In The World, The
Boy Is Only Seven Years Of Age, The
(But) 'E Can't Make Up 'Is Mind
Coat 'Urts Me Underneath The Arm,
    The
Cockneys In Japan
Cockney Sportsman, The
Cockney's Travels, The
Coster's Banquee-et, The
Coster's Beanfeast, The
Coster's Family Tree, The
Coster's Friendly Lead, The (scena)
Coster's Sister, The
Down At Berm-On-Sea
'E's Takin' A Mean Advantage
Every Blessed Bit As Good As You
Gentleman Bug-gu-lar, The
Getting About
Girl Who Sloshed The Lather, The
Good-Bye, Lizzie
He Is Ignorant
He's A Dear Old Friend
He's A Good Old Moke
His Nibs—My Son
I Ain't A-Goin' To Tell
I Ain't Nobody In Perticuler
I 'Aven't Told 'Im
I Don't Know What To Say
I'm Going Home To The Wife And
    Nipper
I Never Work Upon A Monday
I Should Drive It In The Lord Mayor's
    Show
'Is Old Man's 'At Won't Fit 'Im
It's All Clobber That He Thinks About
It's Money Well Laid Out
It's Not The One Who's Richest Who
    Has Got The Biggest Heart
It's The Strangest Co-In-Ci-Dence
    I've Ever Seen

I've Been A Little Distance On The
Way
Jeremiah
Lambeth Walk, The (E. W. Rogers)
Little Gussie
Little Mother, The
Little Tommy Tompkins
Many Can Help One, Where One
Can't Help Many
Mary And Her Lamb
My Boy Jimmy
My London Country Lane
My Pretty Little Bunch Of Flowers
Never Let Your Donah Go Upon The
Stage
Nobody's Little Daughter
No More Up At Covent Garden—Jack
Jones Esq
Not Exactly
Oh, Polly! Pretty Little Polly
'Old Yer Row!
Our 'Ouse Is Our Own
'Ow Abaht The Ahtin'?
'Ow's This For A Start?
Pick-a-ninny, The
Poetical Fellow, The
Ragtime Navvy
Ria Brown
Rosy (Whoa! The Crackling On The
Pork)
Round And Round
Round The Corner
See Him At Home
She's Been A Good Wife To Me or My
Old Pipe
She Wears A Little Bonnet
Since Bill's Been Crossed In Love
Sleeping Beauty, The
Strongest Man On Earth, The
Sweet Little Liza May
Thanks, Beg Your Pardon For My
Mistake
That's 'Ow We Doos It In The Mile
End Road!
They're All Coming Down Tomorrow
Morning

Toy
We're All Pals Together
What A Kid 'E Is
When We 'As A Row, Oh! It Is A Row
Where Have I Seen That Face?
Wide
You Ain't Ashamed O'Me, Are You,
Bill?
You Can Get A Sweetheart Any Day
You Can't Do This And You Can't Do
That
You're My Gal—You're My Donah

HURLEY, Alfred
Break The News To Mother
Daddy
Dolly My Darling I Love You
My Own Little Lily Of Killarney

HURST, J. H. d. 20 Apr. 1905?; initials
variously printed as J. P. and J. W.
After Tonight Say Good-Bye
Birthday Presents
My Pipe
She'd A Dark And A Rolling Eye
Studying The Face
They Say I'm Too Old To Go To War
This Is Bliss or Love À La Mode
What Do People Marry For?
When He's 'So-So'

HUTCHINSON FAMILY fl. 1839 onwards;
US family troupe of thirteen siblings
orig. k.a. The Aethiopian Vocalists,
the most prominent being Jesse jun.
(1813–53) who was also their manager,
Judson (1817–59), John (1821–1908),
Asa (1823–84), and Abby (1829–92).
The last-named four (a.k.a. The Hutchin-
son Quartette) came to Britain with Jesse
in 1845. Names in brackets indicate
soloists
All's Well
Angel's Invitation To The Pilgrim, The
Battle Hymn Of The Republic
Blow Ye Trumpet, Blow!
Bridge Of Sighs, The

Clear The Track For Emancipation
Come Let Us Part (Abby & John)
Cottage Of My Mother, The
Cot Where We Were Born, The
Crows In A Cornfield
Grave Of Napoleon, The
I'm To Be Queen Of The May, Mother
Indian Hunter, The
Irish Emigrant's Lament, The
John Brown's Body
Kind Words Can Never Die (Abby)
King Alcohol
Land Of Canaan, The
Lincoln And Victory
Maniac, The (John)
Matrimonial Sweets
Ohio Boatman, The
Old Granite State, The
O Liberate The Bondsman
Rally Round The Flag Boys
Slave's Appeal, The (Jesse)
Snowstorm, The
Song Of The Shirt, The (Russell)
Star-Spangled Banner, The
Tenting On The Old Camp Ground
There's A Good Time Coming
Tramp, Tramp, Tramp, The Boys Are
   Marching
We Wait Beneath The Furnace Blast
Yankee Doodle

HUTH, Maud 1861–1927
   I'd Rather Be A Nigger Than A Poor
      White Man
   Mule Let Fly, The
   That'll Be All Right Baby
   What Yer Gwine To Do In De Winter?

HUXLEY, Gladys
   If You Feel Lonely Send Around For
      Me
   It's Not So Much The Waltz As Her
      Dreamy Eyes
   I've Got A Spooney-Ooney Feeling
   Won't You Go With Me To Go-Go?

HYAMS, Reuben
   Birthplace Of Freedom, The

Boy In Blue, The
Now Poland Strives For Liberty
Sergeant And The Recruit, The
Tom Bowling

HYLTON, Jack (& His Band) 1892–1965;
see also **HYLTON**, Mrs Jack
   I've Never Seen A Straight Banana
   More We Are Together, The
   Mucking About The Garden (w.
      Tommy **HANDLEY** & Leslie
      SARONY)
   Olga Pulloffski The Beautiful Spy
   Sarah (Sitting In The Shoe Shine
      Shop)

HYLTON, Mrs Jack c.1882–1957; a.k.a.
Ennis **PARKES**
   You Can't Do That There 'Ere

HYLTON, Millie 1868–1920; sister of
Adelaide **ASTOR** and Letty **LIND**; also of
Fanny Dango (1876–1972) and Lydia
Flopp; cousin of Mille **LINDON**
   As In A Looking-Glass
   Ballooning or Up Amongst The Stars
   Belle's Parade, The
   Boys Shall Love The Girls, The
   Charlie From Aldershot
   Come Along Do!
   Comme Ça!
   Could You Love A Little Man Named
      Carney?
   Crooning On De Cotton Farm 'Way
      Down West
   Crooning To The Baby
   Dairy Mary
   Days Of Tom And Jerry, The
   Dear Old Boy
   Dick Turpin
   Ding-Dong!
   Faithful Woman, A
   Girl At The A.B.C., The
   Henley Romance, A or Little Lucy
      Was Her Name
   If I Hadn't Been Ladylike
   If Your Hair Were Not So Curly

I Mean To Be A Lady
Ladies' School, The
Last Of The Dandies, The
   (Harrington: Le Brunn)
Life's High Road
Linger Longer Loo
Little Goody Two-Shoes
Ma Jeanette And Marguerite
Mary's A Fairy
No English Need Apply
Not In Those Trousers
Now, Don't Be Bashful
Oh! The Coronation
Oh! The Rhino
Old Church Bells
Pretty Little Maid Of Norway
Puff! Puff! Out Went The Moon
Queen's Own Little Box Of Soldiers,
   The
Red, White And Blue
Regular Rosey Red, A
Ringle Jingle Boys, The
Rowdy-Dowdy Boys, The
Sailing Through The Air
Shipmates In Safety, Shipmates In
   Danger
Sister Martha's Birthday
Something Sweet
There's Nothing So Lovely As Woman
Till Six O'Clock In The Morning
Toddle Away
Where Did You Get That Hat?

INCLEDON, Charles 1763–1826
   All's Well (w. John **BRAHAM**)
   Arethusa, The
   Black-Ey'd Susan
   Lass Of Richmond Hill, The
   Storm, The (G. A. Stevens)
   Wolf, The

IRVING, Ethel 1870–1963
   Dolly's Little Bills (sk.)
   My Lady Busy
   Rhoda Ran A Pagoda

IRVING, H. B. 1870–1919; brother of
Laurence **IRVING**

Story Of Waterloo, A (sk.)
Van Dyck, The (sk.)

IRVING, Laurence° 1872–1914; brother
of H. B. **IRVING**
   King And The Vagabond, The
   (Gringoire) (sk.)
   Peg Woffington (sk.)

IRWIN, Flo(ra) c.1859–1930; 1875–83
worked w. sister **MAY** as Irwin Sisters
   Mammy's Little, Piccaninny Boy
   Mollie (A Dainty Bit Of Jolly)
   You're Alright But You Don't Get In

IRWIN, May 1862–1938; 1875–83
worked w. sister **FLO** as Irwin
Sisters
   After The Ball
   Albany
   All Coons Look Alike To me
   Bully Song, The
   Champagne Song
   De New Bully
   Frog Song, The
   He Cert'ny Was Good To Me
   Hot Tamale Alley
   I Can't Give Up My Rough And
     Rowdish Ways
   I Couldn't Stand To See My Baby
     Lose
   I Love My Honey, Yes I Do
   I'm Afraid To Come Home In The
     Dark
   I've Worked Eight Hours This Day
   I Want To Be In Dixie
   Mamie Come Kiss Your Honey Boy
   Ma Onliest One
   Mary Ellen Simpkins' Bike
   Mis-Fits
   Mister Johnson Turn Me Loose
   Moonshine
   Mrs Peckham's Carouse (sk.)
   My Babe From Boston Town
   Syncopated Sandy (May Irwin's Great
     'Rag-Time' Song)
   Todelo Tune

When You Ain't Got No Money, Well,
You Needn't Come Round

JACK & EVELYN fl. 1903–23; Jack
O'Connor (1886–1923) and sister Evelyn
(b. 1888)
Book Of Life, The
Cigarette Papers
Come Into The Office
Dream Book, The
Fairy, The
Growing Older Every Day
Introductions
Napoleon
Picture Postcards
Sherlock Holmes
Take Me Somewhere With You,
Johnny (On The Pier)
Trilby Up To Date

JACKLEY, George 1884–1950
Ain't It Grand To Be Blooming Well
Dead?
Doh *or* Tonic Dol-Fa
We All Went Up Up Up The
Mountain

JACKSON, Nelson° b. 24 Sept. 1879
Ballymoney Conversazione, The
Bargains
Father's Photographs
French We Speak At Home, The
He Followed The Directions Of The
Book
Hints For Emergencies
Hints For Inventors
In 1950
In The Future
In The Glorious Days Gone By
Inverary Mary
Irish Sandow School, The
Killarney Trip To Paris, The
Killjoys, The
Let's Have A Song About Father
New Roundabout Papers, The
No!
Nothing To Worry About

Nursery Rhymes Grown Up
Our Curate
Our New Flat
Photographing The Baby
Picture Postcards
Pinkerton's Purple Pills
Poor Old Cassidy
Sandy McCluskey
Santy Klors
Since Angelina Joined A Cooking
Class
Society Snapshots
Special Constable, The
This Wonderful England Of Ours
Three Ages Of Man, The
When Father Carved A Duck
When Father Laid The Carpet On
The Stairs
When Father Tried To Put The Twins
To Bed
When Richard The First Sat On The
Throne
When Uncle Sings The Only Song He
Knows

JACOBSEN, Hilda
Cairo
Cigarette
In The Blue Alsatian Mountains (My
Brave Mountaineer)
It's A Certainty That You're In Love
You Shall Live In A Chalet

JACOBSON, Jess pianist w. (1) **HEDGES
BROTHERS & JACOBSON**; (2) **RASCALS &
JACOBSON, THE TWO**

JAMES, Daisy *c.*1885–1940; formerly
Daisy Martin, m. Harry Villiers (d. 7 Jan.
1906)
Barmaid, The *or* She Was A Nice
Little Innocent Thing
Come With Me Down Regent Street
Daisy Don't Want You
Dat's Me
Dolly Song, The
Gaiety Girl, A
Gibson Girl, The (sk.)

Go Easy!
Her Eyes That Shine Like Diamonds
I Want To Go Back To Michigan
Jack Shepherd
Mine's A Better One Than Yours
My Fellow's A Hero
Oh, Hamlet, What Have You Done To
   Me?
Oui Oui
Popitty Popitty Pop
Snookey-Ookums
That Dancing Jubilee
There's A Good Time Coming By And
   By
Tramway Tickets
When The Golden Corn is Waving
Who's The Girl You're Going To Meet
   Tonight?
Won't You Tell Me The Lady's Name?
Would You Like To Come And Make
   A Fuss Of Me?
You Must Come Round On Saturday
Young Men Specially Invited

JAMES, Katie d. 1913
   Come And See The Cows, Boys
   Coons Are All A-Dreaming, The
   De Cabin By De Ohio
   Drummer Lad, The
   Gaiety Girl, A
   Girl With A Flea In Her Stocking, The
   Go To Sleep My Honey
   Kitchen Company
   Ladies' Club, The
   Make The Best Of It
   Mamie, My Darling
   Petite Parisienne, La
   Pray Excuse My Speaking
   Simple Maiden, Tell Me Why
   Skating At Niagara
   Some
   So You Are (w. Fred LESLIE)
   Sportsman's Young Wife Up To Date,
      The
   World Turned Inside Out (Penetrating
      Photo-Rays)

JAMES, Wilson b. 1872
   Beauty Spot, The
   Calculatas The Memory Man
   Do You Remember?
   Since Then I've Used No Other

JANIS, Elsie 1889–1956; engaged to
Basil HALLAM (k.i.a.); as a child k.a.
Little Elsie
   Ballin' The Jack (w. Basil HALLAM)
   Break The News To Mother
   Florrie The Flapper
   Give Me The Moonlight
   I Love Them All Just A Little Bit
   I'm Forever Blowing Bubbles
   I've Got Everything I Want But You
      (w. HALLAM)
   Jazz Band, The
   Smiles (Callahan: Roberts)
   Will You?
   You're Here And I'm Here (w.
      HALLAM)

JEFFRIES, Walter recording alias of
George BAKER
   What Do You Want To Make Those
      Eyes At Me For?

JEFFS, Minnie
   Little Yellow Bird
   My Cosey Corner Girl
   Somebody's Sailor Boy

JEROME, Daisy b. 1881; sister of Sadie
JEROME
   And The Parrot Said
   Clarice, Come Over To Paris
   Dairyman's Daughter, The
   D, O, U With A G, H, Spells Dough
   Ellen Esmeralda
   Little Pat Of Butter, A
   Mother
   My Lady Vi
   Poor Man Never Gets A Chance, The
   Press, The Pupil And The Petticoat,
      The
   Row, Row, Row

Smart
Starlight Sue

JEROME, Sadie 1876–1950; sister of
Daisy JEROME
Lalage Potts, That's Me!
Lay Your Hand Upon My Heart
Mammy's Black Coon
Man In The Moon, The

JESSICA, THE BEAUTIFUL 1873–1908;
née Jessica Grace; m. Joe O'GORMAN
That's How He Shows His Love

JOHNSON, Carroll b. 1851
Bill Bailey, Won't You Please Come
Home?
Just Come Up And Take Your Presents
Back

JOHNSON, Winifred E. c.1871–1931; m.
R. G. KNOWLES
Cat That Came Back, The

JOLSON, Al° 1886–1950
After You've Gone
Alexander's Rag-Time Band
Anniversary Song, The
April Showers
Avalon
Broken Doll, A
By The Light Of The Silvery Moon
California Here I Come
Down Among The Sheltering Palms
Everything Is Peaches Down In
Georgia
For Me And My Gal
For Old Times' Sake
If You Knew Susie
I Want A Girl Just Like The Girl Who
Married Dear Old Dad
I Wish I Had A Girl
Me And My Shadow
Mother's Sitting Knitting Little
Mittens For The Navy
My Mammy
Pretty Baby

Ragging The Baby To Sleep
Rock-A-Bye Your Baby With A Dixie
Melody
Sister Susie's Sewing Shirts For
Soldiers
Sonny Boy
Spaniard That Blighted My Life, The
Swanee
There's A Rainbow Round My
Shoulder
Toot, Toot, Tootsie!
Waiting For The Robert E. Lee (solo
and w. Fanny BRICE)
When I Leave The World Behind
Where Did Robinson Crusoe Go With
Friday On Saturday Night?
Where The Black Ey'd Susans Grow
Who Paid The Rent For Mrs Rip Van
Winkle?
Yoo-Hoo
You Ain't Heard Nothin' Yet
You Made Me Love You

JONES, Ada d. 2 May 1922
Be My Little Baby Bumble Bee (w.
Billy MURRAY)
Billy (For When I Walk)
By The Beautiful Sea
Cuddle Up A Little Closer (w.
MURRAY)
He Lost Her In The Subway
Hottentot Love Song, The
I Am Looking For A Sweetheart (w.
MURRAY)
I Just Can't Make My Eyes Behave
Little Cherub
Mary Went Round And Round And
Round
Moon Has Got His Eye On You
Poor John
Ring Ting-A-Ling
They Always Pick On Me

JONES, Alma
Hail, Caledonia
I Want To Be A Lidy

I Want Yer, Ma Honey
Little Curl, A
Martha Spanks The Grand Piano
Twiddley Bits

JONES, Mai 1899–1960
We'll Keep A Welcome

JONES, Paul
Drummer Boy, The
He's Gone
I Did Laugh
I Did Run
Miner, The
Somnambulist, The
Very Soon

JONES-HUDSON, Mrs Eleanor d. 2 Aug.
1945; see also HUDSON, Olga, & Elgar &
Eli
Ariosi
My Heart Is With You Tonight
My Honeylulu Honey Lou
Take Me Back To The Garden Of
Love

JONGHMANS, Ferdinand 1822–87;
father of SISTERS JONGHMANS
Captain Matthew Webb *or* Swimming
From England To France
Delhi
Faust And Monsieur Diable (w. Sam
COWELL)
Gallants Of England, The
Largo Al Factotum
Let Brotherly Love Continue
Life Is Too Short To Be Sad So Be
Jolly
Name Of England, The
One More Glass Before We Part
Pif Paf
Queen At Sea, The
Rule Britannia
Wreck Of The Hesperus

JONGHMANS, SISTERS Josie d. 21
Oct. 1932; daughters of Ferdinand
JONGHMANS (the other n.k.)

Back Among The Old Folks Once
Again
Happy Eliza And Converted Jane

JORDAN, Mrs° 1762–1816; née Dorothy
Bland, mistress of HRH the Duke of
Clarence later King William IV
Auld Robin Gray
Blue Bell Of Scotland, The

JORDAN, Julian° 1850–1927
Song That Reached My Heart, The

JOSE, Richard 1872–1941
After The Ball (Harris)
With All Her Faults I Love Her Still

JUDGE, Jack° 1878–1938
Have You Heard Of Michael O'Leary?
How Are Yer?
It's A Long, Long Way To Tipperary
It's A Long Way No Longer

KARNO, Fred° 1866–1941; Knockabout
comedian, sketch writer, and producer.
Orig. Leonaro in acrobatic act k.a.
Alvene (or Olvene) and Leonaro. Some
Karno 'Speechless Comedians' were:
Chris BAKER; A. W. BASKCOMB; Charlie
Bell (1871–1930); Harrison BROCKBANK;
Albert Bruno; George CARNEY; Charles
CHAPLIN jun.; Syd CHAPLIN; Leslie
Crowther (1933–96); Harry Evans
(1865–1905); Bud FLANAGAN; Archie
Glen (b. 1889); Dolly HARMER; Will
HAY; Fred KITCHEN; Stan LAUREL;
Jay LAURIER; Barry LUPINO; Gus
MCNAUGHTON (of THE
MCNAUGHTONS); Ernest Mack; W. E.
Matthews (1884–1947)?; Jack Melville
(d. 1977); Jimmy Nervo (1897–1975);
Cossie Noel (also w. THE LEOPOLDS);
Billie REEVES; Dan ROLYAT; Harry
WELDON; Harold Wellesley (also w.
Fred KITCHEN). See next entry
All Women
Bailiff, The

Blunders
Casuals, The
Dandy Thieves, The (short version of
   His Majesty's Guests, revised as
   Sergeant Lightning)
Diving Birds, The
Doss House, The
Early Birds, The
Flats
Football Match, The
GPO, The
Hilarity
His Majesty's Guests (*see* Dandy
   Thieves, The)
Home From Home
Hot And Cold
Hydro, The
Imperial Yeomen, The
Jail Birds
Jimmy The Fearless
London-Suburbia
Love In A Tub (w. Tom LEAMORE)
Moonstruck
Moses And Son
Mr Justice Perkins
Mumming Birds, The (orig. Twice
   Nightly; in the USA k.a. A Night In
   An English Music Hall)
New Women's Club, The
Nosey Nose
Parlez-Vous Français?
Perkins, M.P.
Perkins The Hunter
Portland (Karno Trio)
Saturday To Monday
Sergeant Lightning *see* Dandy Thieves
Smoking Concert, The
Thirsty First, The
Three Bites
Ticket Of Leave Man
Tragedy Of Errors, A
Travellers' Rest, The (Karno Trio)
Twice Nightly *or* A Stage Upon A
   Stage *see* Mumming Birds
Wakes Week
Week End, A

Who's Who
Wontdetainia
Yap-Yaps, The (Karno Trio)

KARNO, Ted (& Co.) whether related to
Fred **KARNO** is not known; d. 25 May
1922
   Hotel De Quick

KEEGAN & ELVIN fl. 1873–1901; sketch
comics a.k.a. Keegan & Little Elvin;
Matthew (Joseph) Keegan (1841–1901)
& son Joe **ELVIN**
   Bookie, The
   Boots At The Swan, The (as Keegan &
      Young Joe)
   Broker's Man, The
   Clock, The
   Dreadful Tragedy, A (w. Annie Leonie)
   I Ain't Barmy
   Joke, The
   Over The Sticks
   Toffo's Trotter
   Village Maiden, The

KEELEY, Mrs 1806–99
   Nix My Dolly Pals (w. Paul **BEDFORD**)
   Poor Louise

KEEN, Kit d. 9 June 1947; a.k.a. Gus
Lind, coon singer
   My Hindoo Queen
   Tale Of Achmed Kurd, The (mon.)

KELLOGG, Shirley b.1888; m. Albert de
Courville (1887–1960) (div.)
   Beware Of Chu-Chin-Chow
   By And By You Will Miss Me (w.
      George **ROBEY**)
   By The Beautiful Sea
   Chinatown, My Chinatown
   Come On, My Baby! (w. Billy
      MERSON)
   Good-Bye, Khaki!
   Hello, New York Town
   Hindustan
   In Tulip Time
   Little Girl

Maid-O'-The-Mist
Oh, Isn't It Funny What The
   Searchlight Can Do?
Over There
Ragtime Soldier Man
Roseway
Row, Row, Row
Somebody Knows—Somebody Cares
Some Of These Days
Wedding Glide, The (w. Gerald
   KIRBY)
Who's The Lady Now?
You'll Always Be The Same Sweet
   Baby

KENDALL, Marie 1873–1964; formerly
Baby Chester; m. Steve MCCARTHY
   Always Wear A Flower In Your Coat
   Bird In A Gilded Cage, A
   Can't You Wait A Minute, Liza?
   Come Away
   Dark Night Before Yer, A
   Did Your First Wife Ever Do That?
   Don't We Like To Hear Of Victory?
   Dorothy Dean
   'E Ain't Got Nuffin' To Tell
   England Is Good Enough For Me
   'E's Allus Got A Cert
   Faith, Hope And Charity
   Going Home To Baby
   How Do We Go Now?
   If I Could See This For 1s 6d What
      Could I See For A Quid?
   I'll Ask Mr Santa Claus
   I'll Be Your Sweetheart *or* Bluebells
   I'm One Of The Girls
   Johnny Without His Trousers
   Just Like The Ivy
   Kiss The Girl If You're Going To
   Little Yankee Masher, A
   My Old Man Is One Of The Boys And
      I Am One Of The Girls
   Oh! Said The Judge, Be Careful
   Oh! The Decorations
   Pretty Polly MacIntyre
   Put That In Your Pipe And Smoke It

She Went Down To Richmond
Starry Night And A Beautiful Girl, A
Sweet Rosie O'Grady
That's What I Shall Buy With Mine
That's When You Love Them The Best
Three Boys
Two Little Girls In Blue
We've Got Quite Enough Of Our Own
What Ho! She Bounces!
When Liza Got On The Donkey
Why Don't You Marry The Girl?
Woman, You're A Travelling
   Menagerie
You Do Get Something For Your
   Money
You Mustn't Take Any Away!
Young Man Who Worked At The Milk
   Shop
You're Looking Remarkably Well,
   Considering!

KENDIS & PALEY
   Cheer Up, Mary!
   If I Had A Thousand Hearts
   On A Crocodile

KENNEDY, Kool w. MOHAWK
MINSTRELS
   Gimme Your Handy Pandy
   Tiddley-Umty-Iso
   Why Jane

KENNEDY, Margaret sister of Marjory
Kennedy FRASER
   Songs Of The Hebrides

KENNEDY-FRASER, Marjory *see*
FRASER, Marjory Kennedy

KENNEY, Horace 1890–1955
   Trial Turn, The (sk.)

KENT, Edward°
   Harmony Hall (musical sk.)
   Love's Garden
   Minnie The Manicurist
   Pop
   Rage Of Rag Time, The

Ruby Do Be Mine
They Can't Mean What They Sing!
Waif And The Wizard, The
Way Down The Regent's Canal
Why Did They Call Him Watt?
Would You Mind Playing A Tune?

KENYON, Neil 1873–1946
Caddie, The
Elder Of The Kirk, The
Hielan' Bargee, The
Making A Will
Men Who Paved The Way, The (mon.)
Ne'er Dae Well, The
Postmaster Of Dunrobin, The (mon.)
Stationmaster, The (mon.)

KERRIDGE, Emma* c.1845–?
Flying Scud, The
Kiss In The Railway Train, The
Oh, Didn't He Seem To Like It?
(ladies' version)
Ticket On The Shawl, The

KEYS, Nelson 1886–1939
Back Your Fancy
Red, White And Blue
Some Sort Of Somebody (w. Regine
FLORY)

KING, Charles 1889–1944
Aba Daba Honeymoon (w. Elizabeth
BRICE)
Be My Little Baby Bumble Bee (w.
BRICE)
Cough John Cough And Make The
Baby Laugh
Elephant Skid (w. BRICE)
For Me And My Gal (w. BRICE)
Play A Simple Melody (w. Sallie
FISHER)

KING, Hetty 1883–1972; m. Ernie
LOTINGA (div.)
Captain Reginald D'Arcy Of The
Guards
Cheer Up, Molly
Dragoon Guard

Edinboro' Toon
Fill 'Em Up
Follow The Tram-lines
Good-Bye, Jenny
Hold My Hand And Look Into My
Eyes
I Can't Keep My Eyes Off The Girls
I Do Make A Hit With The Ladies
I'm Afraid To Come Home In The
Dark
I'm Afraid You'll Have To Come Along
O' Me!
I'm Going Away
I Suppose She Knows
I've Been Out With Johnny Walker
I've Got The Time, The Place, But
Not The Girl
I Want A Gibson Girl
Kiss Me, My Honey
Love 'Em And Leave 'Em Alone
My English Sailor Man
My Pals Are The Lamp Posts
Oh! The Birds In The Birdcage Walk
Oh! Those Girls (Those Saucy Seaside
Girls)
Oh, You Do Remind Me Of Your
Father
Piccadilly
Poppy Show, The
Queen Of My English Home
Rain, Rain, Go Away (My Ladybird's
Waiting For Me)
Ship Ahoy! (All The Nice Girls Love A
Sailor)
Tommy, Tommy, Tommy
When A Fellow Is Twenty One or
When A Fellow Becomes Of Age
When I Get Back To Piccadilly

KING, Katty 1852–1891; daughter of
T. C. King (1825–93); m. Arthur LLOYD;
also see LLOYD TRIO, Arthur
Katie's Letter
Whistling Thief, The
Wicked Squire, The (sk.) (w. Arthur
LLOYD)

KING, Lovett
My Zither
Oddities
Rejected
So Did The General Too!
Tips For The General Election

KING, Nosmo 1886–1949; pseud. of
Vernon WATSON
Touch Of The Master's Hand, The

KING, Walter 1866–1911
Poor Old Jim The Jockey
They Can All Laugh At Me

KINNIBURGH, T. F. b. 1887
Annie Laurie
Bonnie Dundee
Deathless Army, The
Diver, The
Hurray For The Highlands
Lea Rig, The
March Of The Cameron Men
Scotland Yet
Scots Wha Hae Wi' Wallace Bled

KINO, Walter° 1867–1902
All In A Row
At The Garrison Ball
Beautiful Story Of Love, A
Belinda Played In Pantomime
Down Rotten Row
Give It A Miss In Baulk
Hello! Hello!! Hello!!! (Scott & Mills)
Her Christian Name Was Mary But
   She Took The R Away
I Changed A Five Pound Note
If Only The Stars Could Speak
Jack Loves The Girls
Marble Arch, The
Mary Ought To Know, You Know
Oh! Jemima Mary Jane
Oh! The Nursemaid
Our Sally
Our Sal's In The Pantomime
Our Sal's Vocation
Rose Rose, Pretty Rose
Strolling Down The Strandity

Um-Ta-Ra-Ra
What Will Mother Say?

KIRBY, Gerald
He'd Have To Get Under
R-R-R-Rip That Melody
Wedding Glide (w. Shirley KELLOGG)

KIRKBY, Stanley c.1880–1949; recorded
prolifically under sundry aliases incl.
Murray Johnson; see also KIRKBY &
HUDSON
Be British
Come Back To Ballinasloe
Tenor And Baritone (w. Ernest PIKE)
'Tis A Story That Shall Live For
   Ever
Walking Home With Angeline

KIRKBY & HUDSON fl. 1916–25; Stanley
KIRKBY and Harry Hudson (d. 27 July
1969)
At Finnigan's Ball
Body In The Bag, The
Dixie Wedding, The
Eeh! By Gum, It Were A Real Fine
   Do
Epitaphs
I'm Twenty-One Today
On The 'Nancy Lee'
Order, Please
Pop Goes The Major!
Prize Fight In Ballinasloe, The
Sally, The Sunshine Of Our Alley
She's Got To Come From Devon
Somebody's Coming To Tea
Somebody Would Shout Out 'Shop!'
Ten Little Fingers, Ten Little Toes
That's What Girls Are For
You Can Sing Of Your Tennessee
You Can't Do Without A Bit Of Love

KIRKBY-LUNN, Louise see LUNN,
Louise Kirkby

KITCHEN, Fred° 1872–1950; sketch
comic formerly w. Fred KARNO. Troupe
incl. Harold Wellesley

All Eyes
All Nonsense
Bailiff(s), The (for Fred KARNO)
Bungler's Luck
GPO, The (for KARNO)
His Majesty's Guests (for KARNO)
Hotch Potch (song)
How To Cook A Sausage (song)
If The Cap Fits (song)
It's All Square
Moses And Son (for KARNO)
Number 90
Oh, Happy Married Life (song)
Perkins MP (for KARNO)
Persevering Potts
Pinkie
Potts In Port
Private Potts
Saturday To Monday (for KARNO)
Sundowner, The
What's He Doing?
Winning Ways

KNOWLES, R. G. ° 1858–1919; at one
time w. HAVERLY'S MASTODONS; m.
Winifred E. JOHNSON
Adam Missed It
After That
All The Girls Are Lov-er-ly Ov-er-ly
Bang Went His Chance Of Paradise
Breach Of Promise Case, The
Brighton (The Bowery)
Christopher Columbus Up-To-Date
Dreamy Eyes
Every Little Bit Added To What
   You've Got Makes Just A Little Bit
   More
Funny Stories
Get It Over!
Girl, The Woman And The Widow,
   The
Girl Wanted!
Girly-Girly
Goodbye, Omnibus: The Tuppeny
   Tube For Me
Hey Up!! It's Coming

Hot Time In The Old Town (Tonight),
   A
House, The Flat And The Bungalow,
   The
I Counted Forty First!
If That's Your Game I'm Going
If You Want To Choose A Wife
In The Broad Daylight
It's One Of Those Things That's Got
   To Be Done
I Want You To Be My Only-Only
Just To Take The Chill Off
Love, Marriage And Divorce
LSD
Man v Woman
Never Again
Not Me
Oh! Dear No
Oh, The Daylight Bill
Once Upon A Time
Only To See
On The Benches In The Park
Perhaps—P'raps Not!
Philosophy (Wilmott: Leigh)
Pins
Practical Impossibilities
Results!
Silence Reigned Supreme
Since 'Trilby' Came To Town
Snap-Shots!
Some Things Are Better Left Unsaid
Stopped It!
Tableaux Vivants
That Is Love (parody)
There's An Exhibition
Time Is Money
Tour Round London, A
Trip To Paris, A
Tuppenny Tube, The
What Happened To Jones?

KNOX, Paul°
I'll Ne'er Forget The Girl That Loves
   Me
My Flo From Pimlico
She's My Jo

Tale The Roses Told, The
What The Sunbeam Whispered To
The Lily

LABETTE, Dora b. 1898
Brown Bird Singing, A
Keys Of Heaven, The (w. Hubert
EISDELL)
Lass With The Delicate Air, The
Love's Philosophy
There Are Fairies At The Bottom Of
Our Garden
Were I A Butterfly

LABURNUM, Walter b. 1847; sometimes
misspelled Laburnam
Bengal Cheroots
Cod Liver Oil
Fashionable Fred
Have You Seen The Shah, Boys?
Hookey Walker
If I Only Had My Way
It's Very Strange To Me
Justice In England
Music Hall Snob, A
Music Master, The
Straight Tip, The
Swell Without Money, A
There's Nothing Of That About Me
Two Thousand A Year
Unlimited Loo
Up I Came With My Little Lot
Waiting For Nelly At The Temple Bar

LAKE, Lew (& Co.) Lew Lake
(c.1874–1939) w. Bob Morris
(1866–1945), sketch artistes. His com-
pany included at various times Rich
Beamish, Jock Cochrane, and Eddie
Molony
Bloomsbury Burglars, The (Nobbler &
Jerry)
Cohen And Son
Daylight Robbery, A
Five Years Later
In The Bullrushes

King Nobbler
My Pal Jerry
Old Chinas In China
Pimple
Rib-Nosed Baboon, The

LA MARR, Chummie d. 22 Aug 1945;
sometimes spelled La or Le Mara; first
name Barbara (not Barbara La Marr
(1896–1926))
Heroes Of The Transvaal War, The
Mary Jane And The Motor Car
My Little Treasure
Peaceful Coronation, A
Shadows

LANCHESTER, Elsa 1902–86
Don't Go Out Tonight Dear Father
Don't Tell My Mother I'm Living In
Sin
I've Danced With A Man
Please Sell No More Drink To My
Father
She Was Poor But She Was Honest
When The Old Dun Cow Caught
Fire
Your Baby 'As Gorn Dahn The
Plug-'Ole

LANE, Ella 1877–1962; a.k.a. Bella
BURGE and Bella LLOYD
Don't Make Those Wicked Eyes At
Me!
Why Do The Boys Run After The
Girls?

LANE, Horace b. 1880; m. Violet
LLOYD
Merry Buskers, The (sk.) (w. Violet
LLOYD)

LANE, Jack 1879–1953
Day At The Zoo, A
I Shear Sheep In The Sheep-Shearing
Season
Oh, Dear, What Can The Matter Be?
Rest Of The Day's Your Own, The
Some Girls Are Nicer Than Others

Where Does The Rhinososorus Get
His R.H.I.N.O?

LANE, Lupino 'Nipper' 1892–1959;
nephew of Stanley LUPINO; see
LUPINOS, THE
Lambeth Walk, The (Noel Gay) (w.
Teddie ST DENIS)
Love, Or Something Like It (w.
Blanche TOMLIN)

LANG, Matheson 1879–1948; m. Hutin
BRITTON
House On The Heath, The (sk.)
Westward Ho! (sk.) (w. Hutin
BRITTON)

LANGTRY, Mrs 1853–1929; 'The Jersey
Lily'; after her second marriage some-
times billed as Lady de Bathe. Not to be
confused with Lillie LANGTRY (see next
entry). All sketches
Ashes (w. Alfred LUNT)
Between The Nightfall And The Light
(w. Oscar ADYE; also w. Lionel
ATWILL)
Blame The Cinema
Helping The Cause
Right Sort, The

LANGTRY, Lillie 1877–1965; sometimes
spelled Lily. Not to be confused with
Mrs LANGTRY (see previous entry)
Auntie Green
Barnet Fair, The
Cheap Excursion Train, The
Day At The Zoo, A
It's My Night Out
On Good Old 'Ampstead 'Eath
On The Margate Boat
Romping In The Playground

LA RUE, Grace 1881–1956
Highland Mary
It's Your Money Not Your Heart
Peu D'Amour, Un
Sands Of The Desert
Tango Dream, A

When A Girl Leads The Band
You Made Me Love You

LASHWOOD, George 1863–1942; m.
Lottie Fink (Williams)
After All The Shouting
After The Ball
Alexander's Bagpipe Band
All Alone
All Hands On Deck (Lipton)
Babby's Parade, The
Beresford
Billy's Letter To The Queen
Cabman's Story, The
Captain La-Di-Da
Dear Mr Admiral
Death Or Glory Boys, The (A Story Of
The 17th Lancers)
Don't Forget Tonight
Every Cloud Has A Silver Lining
Farewell For Ever
Fire! Fire!! Fire!!!
Fireman's Dream, The
Fol-The-Rol-Lol
Friend And Wife
Gallant Twenty-First, The
Gentlemen Of My Day, The
Georgie From Georgia
Girls All Love A Soldier Bold, The
Girls, Beware Of The Serpentine
Go, Go
Good-Bye, Dolly Gray
Goodnight, Number One!
Hang Out The Front-Door Key
If It's A Lady
I Forgot The Number Of My House
If You'll Be My Girl
I'm Coming Home To You
In The Twi-Twi-Twilight
It's A Pity To Waste The Cake
It's The Best World We've Ever Seen
It's The Custom Over There
It Would Take A Lot Of That To Upset
Me
I've Been Out With Charlie Brown
I Was The Only Gentleman There

I Wish I Was There Again
Jo'burg Joe
Last Bullet, The
Long Long Walk, A
Lottery Of Marriage, The
Love And Honour
Lovetime
Motherland! *or* Australia Will Be
    There
Mumbles Head *or* The Three
    Heroines
My Latch Key
My Old Short Clay
My Poll
Nicolo, Nicolo, Play On Your Piccolo
Not At All The Silly Girl You Took Me
    For
Number On The Door, The
Nursery Rhymes
Oh! Blow The Scenery On The
    Railway!
Oh! For A Night In The West
Oh, Girls! What Am I To Do With It?
Oh, I Wish I Was There Again!
Oh! The Merry Widow
Old Dicky Bird
Old Man's Darling, An (Hall: Powell)
Once A Soldier, Always A Soldier
Only Girl I Ever Loved, The
On The Prom-Tiddley-Om-Pom-Pom!
O-Oh! That Rag-time Sea!
Oui! Oui! Oui!
Pa, Ma And Paris
Policeman's Honeymoon, The
Riding On Top Of The Car
Rory O'More, The Toreador
Saturday Afteroon
Saturday-Aturday
Sea, Sea, Sea
Send For A P'liceman
Shall I Meet You On The Bois De
    Boulogne?
She Never Does That To Me
She's My Best Girl
Snoozle-Oozle-Oo
Something To Remember You By

Susie's Sousa Mad
There's A Girl Wanted There
There's Another Fellow Looks Like
    Me
They Bunged Him Into My Growler
Three Women To Every Man
Topical Tipster, The *or* The Old Firm
Trafalgar Square, The
Twenty Girls, Thirty Girls
Up The West, West, West
Victoria, The Mother Of Our Nation
What A Lovely Lot They Are!
When There Isn't A Light At All
When You Have Lots Of Feathers
Where Are The Lads Of The Village
    Tonight?
White Man, A
Whoa! The Girls
Why Can't Every Man Have Three
    Wives?
Why Don't They Do It?
W.O.M.A.N. *or* Whoa, Man, Whoa!
You All Want Something To Cuddle

LATIMER, Harrison
    Are We Downhearted? No! (David:
        Wright)

LATONA, Jen 1881–1955; orig. k.a.
Jennie Gabrielle; from 1900 to 1910
appeared with husband Frank
(1856–1930) as Frank & Jen Latona
    Always True
    Because I'm Married Now
    Can't You Love Me True?
    Down In D-I-X-I-E
    Ev'rybody's Doing It At The Seaside
    Ev'ry Day Is One Day Nearer
    He Was Thinking!
    Hush, Here Comes The Dream-Man
    I'm Glad My Boy Grew Up To Be A
        Soldier
    I'm Going Back To Bonnie, Bonnie
        Scotland
    I'm Going Back To Dixie
    In My Airship
    I Remember You

I Used To Be Afraid To Go Home In
  The Dark
I've Got Rings On My Fingers
I Want To Be In Dixie
Keep On Swinging Me Charlie
Land Of I Dunno Where
Maggie McLaren
Maria
Nation's Soldier Sons!, The
Oliver (You Make Me Go All Of A
  Twist)
R-R-R-Rip That Melody
Rum-Tum-Tiddle
Sergeant Daddy VC
S.W.E.E.T.H.E.A.R.T.
That Li'l Old Home
There's A Little Bit Of Devil In Every
  Angel (w. Fred BARNES)
Wedding In Fairy Land
We've All Come Home From Ireland
When The Wedding Bells Go Ding-
  Dong
Why Do You Keep Laughing At Me?
You Can't Blame The Suffragettes For
  That
You've Got To Be Cute As Well As
  Beautiful

LAUDER, Sir Harry° 1870–1950
At The Sign Of The Bluebell Inn
Auld Brig Of Ayr, The
Aye, Wakin' O
Bella McGraw
Bella, The Belle O' Dunoon
Blarney Stone, The
Bonnie Hielan' Mary
Bonnie Leezy Lindsay
Bonnie Wee Annie
Breakfast In My Bed On Sunday
  Morning
Callig(h)an—Call Again!
Camlachie Scout, The or I'm The Man
  They Left Behind
Charlie Macneil
Don't Let Us Sing Any More About
  War, Just Let us Sing Of Love

Down In Johnson's
Drinking
Early In The Morning
End Of The Road, The
Ev'ry Laddie Loves A Lassie or
  Picnic
Flower O' The Heather
Fou The Noo
Gilt-Edged Bertie
He Was Very Kind To Me
Hey Donal
I'd Love To Be A Sailor
If I Were In The LCC
I Got Spooney On Mary
I Know A Lassie Out In Ohio
I'll Love You Tomorrow As I Love You
  Today
I Love A Lassie or Ma Scotch
  Bluebell
I Love My Jean
I Love You
I'm Going To Marry-arry
Inverary
Inverary Harriers, The
Is That You, MacAllister?
I Think I'll Get Wed In The Summer-
  Time
I Took Him Up To Take Him Down
It's A Fine Thing To Sing
It's Just Like Bein' At Hame
It's Nice To Get Up In The Morning
It's Nice When You Love A Wee
  Lassie
I've Loved Her Ever Since She Was A
  Baby
I've Something In The Bottle For The
  Morning
I Wish I Had Somebody To Love Me
I Wish You A Happy New Year
I Wish You Were Here Again
Jean M'Neil
Jerry-Co
(Keep Right On To) The End Of The
  Road
Killiecrankie
Kilty Lads, The

Laddies Who Fought And Won, The
Lads Who Have Fought And Died,
   The
Last Of The Sandies, The
Love Makes The World A Merry-Go-
   Round
Message Boy, The
Mr John Mackie
Mrs Jean McFarlane
My Bonnie Bonnie Jean
Nanny
O'er The Hill To Ardentinny
Ohio
Picnic or Ev'ry Laddie Loves A Lassie
Piper MacFarlane
Portobello Lassie, The
Queen Amang The Heather
Referee, The
Roamin' In The Gloamin'
Rocked In The Cradle Of The Deep
Saftest O' The Family, The
Same As His Faither Did Before Him,
   The
She Is Ma Daisy
She Is My Rosie
Should I?
Shouther To Shouther
Some Folks Do And Other People
   Don't
Soosie Maclean
Sound Advice
South Pole, The or The Bounding
   Bounder
Stop Yer Ticklin', Jock
Sunshine O' A Bonnie Lass's Smile
Swanee
Ta-Ta, My Bonnie Maggie Darling
That's The Reason Noo I Wear A Kilt
There's Somebody Waiting For Me
Tobermory
To Jericho
Waggle O' The Kilt, The
We 'A Go Hame The Same Way
Wedding O' Lauchie McGraw, The
Wedding O' Sandy Macnab, The
Wee Deoch-An-Doris, (Just) A

Wee Hoose 'Mang The Heather
Wee Jean MacGregor
Wee Nellie McKie Frae Skye
We Parted On The Shore
When I Get Back Again Tae Bonnie
   Scotland
When I Was Twenty-One
While The British Bulldog's Watching
   At The Door

LAUREL, Stan 1890–1965
   Jimmy The Fearless (Fred **KARNO** sk.)

LAURI TROUPE, THE sketch comics
incl. Charles Lauri sen. (1823–89),
Charles jun. (1848–1904), Ted (d. 28
Feb. 1893), Little Dick Pedro (d. 20
Feb. 1894), Edward (d. 9 Jan. 1919)
   Cook Of The Kitchen, The or The
      Mischievous Cat
   Enfant Prodigue, L' (full-length play)
   Gelert, The Faithful Hound
   Ki, Ki
   On The Roofs
   Puss, Puss
   Satan Junior
   Sculptor And The Poodle, The
   Sioux, The
   Tit For Tat
   Tot, Tot
   Voyage En Suisse
   White Cat

LAURIER, Jay° 1879–1969; at one time
w. Fred **KARNO**
   Blo-ay-ters
   Bread! Bread! Bread!
   Bye-Lo
   Cut Me Off A Little Bit Of Roly Poly
   Emilina Brown
   Ev'ry Fellow's Got To Take His
      Sweetheart
   Fat And Artful
   Get Away—You're Kidding!
   Give Me A Little Blanc-mange
   He Cats And She Cats

I Do Like A S'Nice S'Mince S'Pie
I Do Like Nice Bright Lights At
   Night
I'm Always Doing Something Silly
I Saw Six Short Soldiers
It Quite Upset Oi For The Day
I Want Something To Practise On
Nobody Loves Me
Play Me A Trickley-Tickle-y Tune
Ring-O-Roses
Shall Us? Let's!
Silly Billy Brown
Six Short Soldiers
Sneezing
Soldiers Of The Queen (parody?)
Sticks And Stones May Break My
   Bones
Stop Yer Ticklin', Jock
S'What's S'Nicer Than A S'Nice S'Ice
   S'Ice?
Swim, Sam! Swim!
They All Think The World Of Me
Treacly-Eacly Pudden
Wait Till I've Finished My Orange
What Are Little Girls Made Of?
Why Is Cecil Selling Sea Shells?

LAW, Fred 1845–1902
Allow Me To See You Home
Blue-Eyed Mary Ann
Bombardment Of Alexandria, The
Carroty Joe
Don't Tell The Missus
Drummer, The
Electric Light, The
Peaceful Abode, A
Pet Of The Hunting Field, The
Ten Thousand A Year

LAWLOR, Charles B. 1852–1925
Best Man In The House, The
Daisy McIntyre
Irish Jubilee, The
Mick Who Threw The Brick, The
Pretty Jenny Slattery
Sidewalks Of New York, The

LAWRENCE, Mrs b. 1834
Gay Coquette, The
Willie, Why Not Speak Your Mind?
Yankee Girl, The

LAWRENCE, Joe 1849–1909; father of
Vesta **VICTORIA**
Ev'ry Saturday Afternoon
Her Daddy's Been And Bought Her A
   Bow-Wow (Bull-Dog)
If Only I Was Long Enough
I'm A-Waiting Here For Ju-li-a
Mary Jane

LAWRENCE, Katie 1870–1913; m. (1)
George Fuller (dec'd); (2) ? Gervase
All Night Tram, The
Butcher Kept His Eye On 'Liza, The
Change For A 'Quid'
Come Back To The Old Folks At
   Home
Daddy's Gone To London
Daisy Bell
Daisy May
Darling Lulu
Don't You Believe It
Down At The Farm-Yard Gate
Do You Think They Would?
Everybody's Darling
Gipsy Maid, The
He Never Cares To Wander From His
   Own Fireside
His Little Wife Was With Him All The
   Time
Humpy Umpy Ay
I Can't Find 'Em
In A Snug Little Home Of Your Own
I've Gone Out For The Day
I've Got Troubles Of My Own
I Want A Partner In The Firm
Johnny Met Her On A Steamer
Katie, My Own
Keep Your Nose Out Of My Bonnet
Laugh And The World Laughs With
   You
Lizer 'Awkins

Mankind And Womankind

Mary Jane *or* A Wonderful Game Of Love

Mary Met The Milkman At The Corner

Mary's Tambourine

Molly, The Rose Of Mayo

My English Belle

My Old Man!

Oh, Charlie, Come To Me

Oh, I Wonder What They're Doing Now?

Oh! Jack, You Are A Handy Man

Oh! Mister Morgan

Oh, Monte Carlo

Oh! The Soldiers Of The Queen

Oh, Uncle John!

Old Butterfly

On The Beach

Poke Bonnet, The

Rose Of Mayo, The

Say Nothing

She Looked A Perfect Lady

She's My Little Ray Of Sunshine

She Tells You The Tale So Nicely

Ship That Belongs To A Lady, The

Stick To Me And The Kids

Sunshine And Showers

Sweet Little Rosie-Posey

Ta-Ra-Ra Lament, The

They're The Best Friends Of All

Thinking Of The Lad Who Went Away

Tommy Jack And Joe

Two Little Brandies And Sodas

Universal Peace

Up With The Angels Now

Visitors Are Requested Not To Touch

We Had The Usual At The Gate

We Like Them Just A Little

What A Lady

Whipsy Whopsy

Who's Coming Up In The Gallery?

Why Can't I Be A Pal Of Yours?

Why Shouldn't We Fight For Our Own?

Widow's Plea For Her Son, The

Wot Yer Sally

You Know The Kind Of Girl I Mean

Young Country Squire, The

LAWSON, Cissie *see* LAWSON, Mrs John

LAWSON, John 1865–1920; see also LAWSON, Mrs John

dramatic sketches:

Affinity, The

Baker Street Mystery, The

Bride For A Living, A

Call To Arms, The

Disraeli

Ghetto, The

Humanity (*see* GALLIMORE, Florrie)

Keep To The Bible

Key To The Bible, The

King Of Palestine, The

King Of The Jews, The

King's Minister, The

Kissed To Death

Living In

Man Against Motor

Men Must Work And Women Must Weep

Miracle, The

Monkey's Paw, The (mon.)

Mormon's Wife, The

Mr Todd Of London

Only A Jew (sung in *Humanity*)

Open Door, The

Our 'Appy 'Ome (sung in *The Ruling Passion*)

Pigs In Clover

Ruling Passion, The

Sally In Our Alley

Sherlock Holmes

Shield Of David, The

Siberia

Thaumaturgy

Unripe Fruit

Unwritten Law, The

Vanderdecken-Todd

Wages Of Hell, The

Who's Calling? (song)

Who's That Calling (parody on
  previous title)

LAWSON, Mrs John née Russell; m.
John LAWSON, with whom she often
appeared but also a headliner in her
own right, sometimes billed as Cissie
Lawson
  dramatic sketches:
  Again A Woman
  Bride For A Living, A
  Devil's Sunday, The
  Woman In The Case, The

LAWSON, Warren w. MOHAWK
MINSTRELS
  Absent Dear Ones
  Come Into The Meadow
  My Dream, My Joy, My Love For
    Aye
  'Tis Only In Dreams

LAWTON, Frank M. d. 1914; father-
in-law of Evelyn LAYE
  She Is The Belle Of New York
  Whistling Bowery Boy

LAYE, Evelyn 1900–96; daughter of
Gilbert Laye°; daughter-in-law of Frank
M. LAWTON
  Guard's Brigade, The
  If You Look In Her Eyes
  I'm The Smartest Girl In Greece
  Only A Glass Of Champagne
  When I Grow Too Old To Dream

LEA, Lilian
  Bells Of Remembrance
  By The Blue Lagoon
  Dream Of Love, A
  Peggy Machree
  Way Down The Old Canal

LEACH, Au(gus)tus° d. 17 Aug. 1903
  Bishopsgate Park
  Ding Dong
  Luncheon Bar, The
  Petticoat Lane
  Tell Me John Bull's All Right

LEAMAR, Alice 1869–1950; unrelated to
SISTERS LEAMAR
  And Her Golden Hair Was Hanging
    Down Her Back (McGlennon's orig.
    version)
  For The Sake Of Old Times
  He's Sailing On The Briny Ocean
  In The Vegetable Line Is Bill
  Jack's Farewell
  Just In The Old Sweet Way
  Just The Same
  Lose 'Im, Liza, Lose 'Im
  Mary And Her Fido
  Musical Society
  Story Of Adam And Eve, The
  Susian-I-Oh-I-Oh!
  Ta-Ra-Ra Boom-De-Ay
  Then You Grasp The Situation In A
    Minute
  Young Country Squire, The

LEAMAR, (DASHING) SISTERS fl.
1870s–93; sisters Kate (d. 26 May 1893)
who m. Billy BINT, and Nellie (d. 5 July
1938). Kate sometimes worked solo. Not
related to Alice LEAMAR
  Belles Of The Beach
  Don't They Love Us?
  Go And Inform Your Father
  Harem, The
  Love Laughs At Locksmiths
  Not Tonight!
  One Kiss More
  Paradise In The Strand
  Romano's, Italiano's
  Two Girls Of Good Society
  We Are Not So Young As You Think
  We've Just Escaped From The Harem
  Why Is The Whole World So Gay
    Today?

LEAMORE, Tom° 1866–1939; m. Rose
HAMILTON
  Baden Powell Scout, The
  Broker's Man, The
  Cat's Meat Man, The
  Don't Cry, Daddy!

Fair Old Beano, A
Gallant Deeds
Gold! Gold! Gold! (Miser's Song)
Hi Hi Hi
Hiring System, The
Hundreds Of Inches From Home
I'll Never Leave Home Any More
I'm A Dandy
I'm Taking 'Em In
I Never Hear From Them
Innocent Worm, The
I Thought She Was So Shy
It's Alright In The Summer
I Used To Be Poor Myself
I've Been Left In Charge
I've Dodged The Undertakers Up Till
   Now!
Last Night or The Policeman's Story
Lifeboatman's Story, The
Love In A Tub (sk.) (w. Fred KARNO)
Mary Ann
My Intended
My Lovely Susie-Sue!
Never Get Married To A Thing They
   Call A Man
Oh! Let Me Have Another, Georgie
Only A Picture
Out For A Fair Old Beano
Percy From Pimlico
Place They Call The 'Lump', The
Postman's Rat-Tat, The
Private Tec, The
Rip Van Winkle
Sad Story, The
Sandwich Man, The
Sarah From The Bone Yard
Serving 'Em All Alike
She's My Daughter
Shipwrecked Captain, The
Sweet Little Rose Of Persia
Tally Ho!
Terrible Things The Papers Say, The
Volunteer, The
We We
What A Friend, What A Sport
What A Funeral

Window Cleaner, The
You Stick To The Ship, My Lads

LE BLANC, Marie d. 29 July 1924
And So He Said 'My Dear Maid, Will
   You Marry Me?'
Baby's Shoes
East And West
First-Class Boy, The
Friends Were Saying Goodbye
Good Boy
I Do Love You
I'm A Wrong 'Un
John Bull's Letter Bag
No English Need Apply
Oh! I Say
Scotch Brigade, The
They Like You All The Better If You
   Do
They Wouldn't Do That In London
Three Blind Mice And The Farmer's
   Lass
Three Little Words (I Love You)
When His Mother-In-Law's At Home
Would You Do It? So Would I!
Yes And No
You Know A Thing Or Two!

LE CLERQ, Augustus see THE
MCNAUGHTONS

LE CLERQ, George see BROWN,
NEWLAND & LE CLERQ

LEE, Haidée orig. w. Lee & Kingston
King Baby
Melinda Loo
My Daddy's Coming Home

LEE, Jack
Aba Daba Honeymoon (w. Billy
   DELANEY)

LE FRE, Albert 1870–1970; also
comic sketches w. Le Fre Trio: brothers
James (d. 7 Aug. 1932) and Sydney (d.
16 May 1919), and at one time Fred
Zola

Dancing Family, The (sk.)
End Of The Journey, The
Gentleman Scamp, The (sk.)
He Belonged To My Lodge
Oh, The Black List
Professor, The (sk.)
That's What You See In The Halls
Tip-Top Topper, The

LEGARDE, Millie
Hello! Ma Baby
Hey Ho!
How'D'Ya Like To Spoon With Me?
My Coal Black Lady
Nurseryettes

LEIGH, Grace 1875–1950; m. Lionel
MACKINDER
Pink Petty From Peter, A

LEIGHTON BROTHERS°
Frankie And Johnny
Steamboat Bill

LEIGHTON, Queenie 1872–1943; a.k.a.
Lillie Leighton
All Girls Are Angels
Automobile Honeymoon, The
Crackling Of The Pork, The
Cruise Of The Great Britain, The
Friday Afternoon
Heart Of Gold
Is London Like It Used To Be?
Love's Gramophone
Lu Lu Mine
Mary Had A Little Lamb
Mr Wood, Mrs Wood, And All The
    Little Splinters
My Silent Sweetheart
There's A Little Bit Of Good In The
    Worst Of Us

LE MARA, Chummie see **LA MARR,**
Chummie

LEMORE, Harry° d. 1 Sept. 1898
For A Woman's Sake
Jim And His Partner Joe
Little Gussie
Styles Of Proposing

LENA, Lily b. 17 July 1877; née Alice
Archer; cousin of Marie **LLOYD**; see also
SISTERS LENA
And The Poor Little Bird Fell Dead
Don't I Wish It Was Me
Have You Another Little Girl At
    Home Like Mary?
In The Drawing Room I Often Met
    Him
Ivy
Johnny O'Morgan On His Little
    Mouth Organ Playing 'Home Sweet
    Home'
Oh, Be Careful Joe
Ruby
Swing Me Higher, Obadiah
Waltz Me Right Up To The Altar,
    Walter
White Silk Dress, The
You Can't Be Sure You've Married The
    Man Till You've Been On
    Honeymoon
You Can't Tell A Sailor How To Make
    Love

LENA, SISTERS fl. 1893–6; Rosie **WOOD**
and Lily **LENA**
Trip To Paris, A

LENNARD, Arthur° 1867–1954
After The Show
All Doing Something For Baby
All Through The Motor-Car
And So The Poor Dog Had None
At Waterloo
Babs
Baby Gone To Sleep
Bad As You Are
Beautiful Rose
Big Ben Struck One
Boy And The Eagle, The
Butterfly
Catchemaliveograph
Cheap Today
Chirp Of The London Sparrow, The
Clementina Brown

Cockney Conversation
Collier's Child, The
Courting—Married
Dear Hearts Are Waiting
Dear Little Lambs (Baa, Baa, Baa)
Doesn't It Get Dark Soon?
Fine Weather
Flower And The Weed, The
Fly Little Fish, The
Give Him The Moon To Play With
Gordon Highlanders, The
Great Big Wheel, The
Greetings
Heroes
He's A Handy Man
He's A Jolly Good Fellow
He's Only A Little 'Un
How He Received The News
How Would You Like To Be A Baby?
I Do Love You And You Love Me
If I Had Been Born A Girl
If I Meet The Girl With The Golden
   Hair
I'm A-Going To Stop Outside
In Dreamland
I Think Three Makes Jolly Good
   Company
It's Hard To Say Good-bye
I've Only One Little Flower
I Was The Honeysuckle—Mary Was
   The Bee
Jack And Jill
Just A Little
Kerbstone Millionaire, The
Language Of London Town, The
Language Of Love, The
Let's Wait And See The Pictures
Life Of A Soldier, The
Little Golden Hair (parody)
Little Rosie Dean
Louisa's Lovers
Love Has No Need For Words
M.A.D.A.M.
Man Without A Woman
Maria Martin's Bogie
Moon, Moon, Moon!

Mother
Number Nine (Love Dove Lane)
Occupations
Oh, How Rude!
Old Fisher's Story, An
Old Harmonium—Yum-Yum
Old Potts And Young Potts
Old Toll Gate, The
One Of The Brave Old Guards
One Of The Sights Of London
Only A Broken Toy
Only A Month Ago
Only A Voice From Dreamland
Our Johnny
Pardners
Pass By!
Phonograph, The
Play That Melody Again
Put It There
Put Me A Girl Inside
Rolling Round The Wheel
Same Two Birds In The Same Old
   Cage, The
Seeing The New Year In
Shadow On The Blind, The
She's Beautiful To Me
She's His Mother
She's My Wife
She Was One Of The Forty Thieves
Sing Me A Ballad In Ragtime
Skylark! Skylark!
Somebody Else's Baby
So Was I
Sparrow And The Mustard, The
Storm And Calm
Sweet Seventy-Two
Telling The Same Old Story
Tell Me, Daddy, Do Dreams Come
   True?
That's A Bit Of Acting Off The Stage
That's The Kind Of Man James Is
That's What I'm Weeping For
That Was My Happiest Time
There's A Lump In Your Throat And A
   Tear In Your Eye
There's A Tear In Mother's Eye

There's Danger On The Line (Leigh &
    Collins & Murray)
They Can't Do More Than That
They Were After Her Gladstone Bag
This Is No Place For A Sailor!
Three Brass Balls, The
Three Makes Jolly Fine Company
Timothy Tubbs And All The Tubbs
Upsey-Daisy-Baby!
Visiting Day
We Only Miss The Old Folks When
    They're Gone
When The Baby Started To Talk
When The Summer Breezes Blow
When You Get A Bit Of Something In
    Your Eye
Which Would You Like To Spare?
Who'll Care For The Children While
    I'm Away?
Wives (Beautiful Wives)
You're At Your Old Game

LENNOX, Lottie b. 1886
Ain't It Grand To Be A Father?
Boys Of The Brave Reserve, The
Donah's Wedding, The
Good-Bye, Polly *or* I Might Come
    Back Saloon
Good-bye, Tommy Atkins
Ground He Walks Upon, The
How Should I Know You Love Me,
    Joe?
I Feel So Lonely
I Must Take The Old Dad Home
In The Army
Is The Old Home In The Same Place?
Look Out Boys There's A Girl About
Mary Married A Marquis
Maude
Mother's Found Another Father
Old Love Is The Gold Love, The
Only A Factory Girl
Our Motor-Moke
Out With My Barrow
Pretty Little Sweet, Sweet Dickey
    Bird

Put On Your Old Green Bonnet
Send Along A Wire
Six Little Kiddies To Keep
Sweet Nell Of Old Brewery
There'll Be No War!
What's The Good Of A Jam-Pot, Boys?
Where Was Mabel When The Band
    Struck Up?
You're A Very Lucky Fellow, Mister
    Brown

LENO, Dan° 1860–1904; nephew of
Johnny DANVERS; m. Lydia Reynolds
All Through A Little Piece Of Bacon
As Hot As I Can Make It
Barrister, The
Beefeater, The (The Tower Of
    London)
Boot Man, The
Bow Street (The Usher)
Buying A House
Cavalier, The (Charles I)
Clever Mr Green
Courting The Widow
Dear Old Mike
Detective Camera
Diamond Ring, The
Doctor, (I'm) The
Down Where The Red Poppies Grow
Forty Thieves, The
Going Out Of Town
Going To Buy Milk For The Twins
Going To The Races
Grass Widower, The (Oh! What A Day
    I'm Going To Have Tomorrow)
Great D.T., The
Hard-Boiled Egg And The Wasp, The
Has Anyone Seen A Moving Job?
Heighho! What Might Have Been!
Her Mother's At The Bottom Of It All
Horseshoe On The Door, The
Huntsman, The
Ice Cream Man, The
I'm Queen Of The Tarts Tonight
I'm Waiting For Him Tonight (parody
    of Queen Of My Heart)

Irish Harvestman, The
Italian Boy, The
It's Nothing To Do With You (w.
 Herbert CAMPBELL)
Jap, The
Lecturer, The
Lucky Horseshoe, The
McGlochell's Men
Mary Ann's Refused Me
May-Day Fireman, The
Midnight March, The
Milk For The Twins
Minstrel Boy, The
Mocking Bird, The (mon.)
Mother's Washing Day
Mrs Kelly (I'll Marry Him)
Mr Wix Of Wickham (revue)
Muffin Man, The
My Old Man
My Sweet Face
My Wife's Mother's Gone Away
My Wife's Relations
Never More
No More Fancy Balls For Me
North Pole, The
Orlando Dando (song and revue)
Our Stores Ltd
Pity The Poor Italian
Professor Of Anatomy
Railway Guard, The
Recruiting Sergeant, The
Red Poppies, The
Robin, The
Salvage Man, The
She Sleeps In The Valley
Shopwalker, The *or* Walk This Way!
 Step This Way!
Shout Hurrah! Shout Hurray! (w.
 CAMPBELL)
So And So—Such And Such (w.
 CAMPBELL)
Spiritualism
Swimming Master, The
That's How It's Done
Tower Of London, The (The
 Beefeater)

Waiter, The
Wait Till I'm His Father
When Rafferty Raffled His Watch
When The Heart Was Young
Where Are You Going To My Pretty
 Maid?
Who Does The House Belong To?
Young Men Taken In And Done For

LENTON, Olive
 Shine On Harvest Moon

LEO, Frank° d. 30 Oct. 1940; m. Sable
FERN
 ABC
 'Arry And The Family At The Zoo
 (scena)
 Her Smiles Are For Me
 Love
 Ma Coon's Got Lots Of Money
 My Lily Of The Valley
 My, My, My
 She Ain't A Bit Like The Other Girls

LEONARD, Bob & Jenny Bob Leonard
(1855–1932) and his wife Jenny
 Jones's Parlour Floor
 Molly Owen
 My Fairy, Mary Green
 Paris Up To Date

LEONI, Henri
 Just A Tiny Cottage
 Linette
 My Dreamy Lou
 Susie
 Two Eyes Of Blue
 When Angelus Is Ringing

LEOPOLDS, THE (ORIGINAL) fl.
*c.*1870–1900s; comic sketch troupe est.
William Kelly (d. 1888) w. brother John;
joined *c.*1872 by brothers Frederick (d.
1902) and Willie, and in 1880 by brother
Harry a.k.a Henri (d. 1904). Other
troupers were Ernest and Joseph.
Non-family 'Leopolds' include Queenie

Bronte, Amy Hall, Val Kimm, Fred
Ingram, Herbert Lewis, Cossie Noel
(also with Fred KARNO), and Lillie
Trownsell
    Bear, Baron And Sentinel
    Belle France, La
    Eagle's Nest, The
    Frivolity
    Merry Monks, The
    Music Hath Charms
    Those Terrible Boys!

LESLIE, Fannie 1858–1935;
granddaughter of Theodore Hook
(1788–1841); orig. k.a. Frances Leslie;
m. (1) Walter Gooch° (div.); (2)
Broughton Wilson
    Analytical Kissing
    At The Ball
    At The Corner Of The Street
    Bal Masqué, The
    Between The Lines
    Boys Of London Town, The
    Buy A Box Of Lights, Sir
    Chiko Chiko Chikkori
    Dancing Up To Date
    Dashing Little Soldier, The
    Favorite, The
    Genuine Thoughts
    Head Over Heels In The Morning
    How They Do It!
    Husband, Wife And Child
    Im-Pe-Cu-Ni-Os-I-Ty (w. Herbert
        CAMPBELL & G. H.
        MACDERMOTT)
    In The Morning
    I Saw A Ship Go Sailing By
    It's Money Makes The Mare Go
    It's Surprising How They Alter
    I Want My Money Back
    Jolly Hard Lines
    Jolly Little Polly On Her
        Gee-Gee-Gee
    Lately Bye And Bye
    Little Pirate Of The Nore, The

Living Pictures Without The Gilded
    Frame
Love's Tyrant (sk.)
Muzzling (The Marquis De Leuville's
    Plea For The Dogs)
My Lady Fair
Nineteenth Century Boys, The
    (Godwin: Powell)
Oh, Look At Her Crinoline
Oh, What A Difference In The
    Morning
On The Benches In The Park
On The QUIET
On The Railway
Picture Without The Golden Frame
Pling-Plong For Breakfast
Polish Girl's The Girl For Me, A
Princess And The Recruit, The (w.
    Edith BLANDE)
Run Up The Flag
She Always Dressed In Black
Sweet Italy
That Is A Woman's Way
That Shape Won't Suit Me
That's One Of Your Girls
That's When You See The Man
They Don't Speak To One Another
    Now
Think Of The Wives And Children
Topical Cookery Book, The
Waiting For A Drink On Sunday
    Morning
White Blossoms

LESLIE, Fred 1855–92; a.k.a. A. C.
Torr°
    Bright Little Glass
    Don't Know
    Five Ages (w. Nellie FARREN)
    I'm In Love With The Man In The
        Moon (w. Letty LIND)
    I've Just Had A Wire To Say So (w.
        FARREN)
    Je Suis Un Grand Détective
    Johnny Jones And His Sister Sue (w.

FARREN)
Love In The Lowther
Love In The Orchestra
Ma's Advice (w. FARREN)
Razzle Dazzle (w. Charles & Farren
    DANBY)
Romance Of The Looking Glass, The
So You Are (w. Katie JAMES)
Stick To The Whiskey You're Used
    To!
Sworn In
Very Extraordinary, Isn't It?

LESLIE-STUART, May 1894–1956;
daughter of Leslie Stuart°; her repertoire
seems to have consisted entirely of her
father's songs
Heligoland
Sweetheart May

LESLIE, William
Just Touch The Harp Gently (w.
    CHRISTY MINSTRELS)
Sing Dearest Sing (w. MOORE &
    BURGESS MINSTRELS)
'Twas Like A Spirit's Sigh (w.
    CHRISTYS)
Wake Us At Dawn, Mother (w.
    CHRISTYS)
Wish Me Goodnight Once More (w.
    CHRISTYS)

LESSING, Madge m. George B.
McClellan (1866–1932)
Evolution Of Rag Time, The
Good-bye, Little Girl, Good-bye
Henry Klein
I Am An Actor
I Hear The Pipers Calling, Jenny
    Mine!
Little Boy Called Taps, A
Lutie
My Irish Molly O
My Irish Rose
Rose Ana

Sleeping Partners (sk.) (w. Seymour
    HICKS)
Witches, The

LESTER, Alfred 1872–1925
Amateur Hairdresser, The (sk.)
Another Little Drink (w. Violet
    LORAINE & George ROBEY)
Broker's Man, The (sk.)
Conscientious Objector's Lament, The
Hamlet (burlesque mon.)
Labour Candidate, A (sk.)
Longshoreman Bill (sk.)
Married And Settled
My Motter
Night Porter, The
Ours Is A Nice 'Ouse Ours Is
Property Man, The
Restaurant Episode, A (sk.)
Scene-Shifter's Lament, The (mon.)
Simpson's Stores (sk.)
Village Fire Brigade, The (mon.)

LESTER, Frank
Dear Old Shepherd's Bush

LESTER, George°
Back Again
I Was Underneath
Whiskers Round The Bottom Of His
    Trousers

LESTER, Harry
Girls Have The Best Of It, The
I Was Underneath
Man Of The World, A
Plenty Of Room

L'ESTRANGE, Nellie m. John Cooke°
Beforehand
Below! Below!! Below!!!
Dear Old Chums
Do You Take Me For A Pillar?
Girls And The Boys, The *or* Nice
    Enough For Anything
Hardly! What Say You?
Here Floats The Flag!

I'll Take It Home To Sarah's
It's Nice
I Want To Meet A Good Young Man
Jack's The Lad
Johnnie Is An Angel Now
Just Like You
Just To Oblige
Martha Jane
No Fear
No You Don't
Oh! Mr Nobody
Oh! You Great Big Darling
Oh, You Little Angel
Oh, You Little Darling (I Love You)
Poor Gal Didn't Know, You Know, The
Rather!
She Broke The Richest Man In Monte
   Carlo
Shoo-Fly
That Was You
Two Little Maids In Blue (parody)
Very Quietly
What A Wonderful Diff'rence It
   Makes
You Can't Believe The Men
You May Whistle For It
Young Country Squire, The

LETTERS, Will° 1877–1910
   Put Me Upon An Island Where The
      Girls Are Few
   Something Seems To Tell Me You'll
      Forget Me

LEVEY, Adele debut 1887; from 1910
worked solo as a 'raconteuse'; see also
LEVEY SISTERS
   Cheer O!
   Criticise
   Don't Worry

LEVEY, Carlotta debut 1887; see also
LEVEY SISTERS
   British Boys
   Do A Good Turn When You Are Able
   Don't Tell The World Your Troubles
   Gambling Man, The

Heart Full Of Love And A Pocket Full
   Of Money, A
He Was One Of The Boys
Honolulu Lulu
I'm Going To Try My Luck In London
I'm Happy When I'm By My Baby's
   Side
Lazy Man, The
Maggie Ryan From Dublin Town
Money Don't Make Happiness
My Boy
Put A Little Bit Away For A Rainy
   Day!
Stella
Telephone Me, Baby
Under The Golden Laburnum Tree
What's The Good Of Living?
Who Says A Coon Can't Love?

LEVEY, Ethel 1880–1955; m. George M.
COHAN (div.)
   Alexander's Rag-Time Band
   Bacchanale Rag, The
   Down In Jungle Town
   Everybody's Doin' It Now
   Hannah's A Hummer
   Hitchy-Koo
   How Do You Do, Miss Ragtime?
   I Guess I'll Have To Telegraph My
      Baby
   I Love A Piano
   I Was Born In Virginia (Ethel Levey's
      Virginia Song)
   Meet Me In St Louis, Louis
   Melinda's Wedding Day
   Minstrel Parade, The
   Miss Musical Numbers
   My Tango Girl
   Pride Of The Prairie, Mary
   Queen Of Morning-Land
   San Francisco Sadie
   Show Us How To Do The Fox Trot
   Simple Melody, (Play) A (w. Blanche
      TOMLIN)
   Somehow, Sometime, Some Place
   Some Of These Days

Take Me To That Swanee Shore
Telephone Me, Baby
That Haunting Melody
That Rag-Time Suffragettte
When I Discovered You (w. Joseph
COYNE)
Where Did Robinson Crusoe Go With
Friday On Saturday Night?

LEVEY, (THREE) SISTERS fl. 1887–1910;
CARLOTTA, May-Lilian, and ADELE
(Del). After May retired on marriage
Carlotta and Adele worked as a double
Beautiful Brigade, The
Doris
Factory Girl, The
Latest Girl In Town, The (Carlotta &
Adele)
Laugh, Boys
Nineteenth Century Boys, The (Lamb:
Peters)
Saucy Seventh, The (Adele & May-
Lilian)
Soldiers, Sailors And Marines, The
Sporting Girls
Sunshine Of Paradise Alley, The

LEVEY, W. C. 1837–94
Fig For The Vicar, A
Geraldine
Here Stands A Post

LEWIS, Al 1901–67
Wild Wild Women, The

LEWIS, Eric
I'm A Judge Of The Modern Society
Sort
In The Good Old Days
Never Recognise Your Ma-In-Law At
All

LEWIS, 'Jolly Little' (George W.) d. 6
July 1893; w. MOHAWK MINSTRELS; m.
Adelaide Downing
Cows Won't Milk, The Bulls Won't
Roar, The
Girl Who Stands No Nonsense, The
Handsome Page, The

Hush! Mum's The Word
I Traced Her Little Footmarks In The
Snow
Keep Smiling
On The Banks Of The Silvery
Thames
Poor Old Stable Jem

LEYBOURNE, George° 1842–84;
father-in-law of Albert CHEVALIER
After Me
After The Opera
Alas, Poor Ghost!
Anchor's Weigh'd, The
Artful Joe
Awfully Clever
Barber's Apprentice Boy, The
Basket Of Onions, The
Belle Of The Ball, The
Belle Of The Rink, The
Blighted Gardener, The
Bloomsbury Square
Bold Fisherman, The
Bom! Bom! Bom! (The Tragedy Of
Pretty Polly Pringle)
Brass
Broken-Hearted Shepherd, The
Cackle, Cackle, Cackle
Captain Cuffs Of The Glorious Buffs
Captain De Wellington Boots
Chalk It Up
Champagne
Champagne Charlie
Chang The Chinese Giant
Charlie Baker
Chisel, Chisel
Come Fill Me A Tankard
Comet Of The West, The (Stand
Aside)
Cool Burgundy Ben
Darling Mary Jane
Dear Me! Is That Possible?
Do Everybody
Donkey Rifle Corps, The
Don't Make A Noise Or Else You'll
Wake The Baby

Down In A Diving Bell
Dryland Sailor, The
Eel-Pie Shop, The
Encore!
Fair Girl Dress'd In Check, The
Fairy Queen, The
Farmyard Conversation
Father Says I May
Fifty Miles Under The Sea
Fizz
Flying Trapeze, The (Daring Young Man On The)
Galloping Snob Of Rotten Row, The
Gay Masquerade
Give A Man A Chance
Give Over George
Gold! Gold! Gold! (Hunt)
Good-bye, Polly
Gymnastic Wife, The
Hallelujah Band, The
Handsome Postman, The
Have You Seen Ruth?
Heavy Swell Of The Sea, The
He Is The Man For Me, My Boys
Holland's Barmaid Show
I Always Was A Swell
I Am A Millionaire
I Am The Man For The Ladies
I Feel Like A Fish Out Of Water
If Ever I Cease To Love
Ikey George
I Knew That I Was Dreaming
I'll Have Your Hat
I'm A Member Of The Rollicking Rams
I'm On The Teetotal
I Say Cabby!
I Should Like To Be An Alligator
It Don't Suit Charley Baker
It's Only The Major
I've Lost My Bow-Wow
I Wish That I Could Fly
I Won't Believe It's True
Jessie The Belle At The (Railway) Bar

Jumping Noises
Kiss Behind The Door or Where's Rosina Gone?
Knifeboard Of An Omnibus, The
Lancashire Lass, The
Last Bus, The
Lemonade And Sherry
Little Flora Stands Behind The Bar
Lounging In The Aq
Love Song a.k.a. Leybourne's Love Song
Man In The Moon Is Looking, Love, The
Moet And Shandon
Moggy Dooral
Mother Says I Mustn't
Mother Wouldn't Let Me
Mouse-Trap Man, The
Music Mad
My Lancashire Lass
My Name It Is John Barleycorn
My Pretty Yorkshire Lass
My Wife Has Joined The Mormons
Not Today, Baker
Oh, Fred! Tell Them To Stop
Oh! George
Oh, Mr Edison
Oh, The Fairies!
On Tops Of Trees
Parisian 'Arry or The Cockney Abroad
Polly, Put The Kettle On
Poor Pill Garlic
Pop! Pop! Pop! or Sparkling Wine
Pretty Little Flora
Pretty Little Sarah
Pride Of Petticoat Lane, The
Punch And Judy Man
Put Away For A Rainy Day
Real Jam or Sweeter Than Marmalade
Riding On A Donkey
Rocked In The Cradle Of The Deep
Rock The Cradle John
Rollicking Rams, The
Rolling Home In The Morning

Rosemary Lane
Scrumptious Love
She Danced Like A Fairy *or* She
   Doated On Leybourne
She Was A Spark
She Was The Belle Of The Ball
Showman, The
Sparkling Piper Heidsieck
Susan Sweet
Sweet Isabella
Sweet Margaret, The Belle Of
   Battersea
Tailor And The Crow, The
Take Me In Your Arms, Love
Telegraph Girl, The
That's Where You Make The Mistake
There's Nothing New Under The
   Sun
They All Do It
Tichborne Trial, The
Ting, Ting, That's How The Bell Goes
'Tis There You Have Made A Mistake
Turkey Rhubarb
Under The Sea
Up In A Balloon
Up In The Monument
Upper Ten (Thousand), The
Vive La Bacchanale
Wait Till My Ship Comes Home
Watching The Mill Go Round
We Cards In The Guards
What Are You Up To, Jane?
When I Was Prince Of Paradise
When You're Married You'll Find Out
When You've Got The Money You're
   A Brick, Brick, Brick
Where's My Dolly Gone?
While The Gas Is Burning
Whoa, Emma! (Lonsdale)
Who's Coming Out For A Spree
   Tonight?
Why Did She Leave Her Jeremiah?
Will, Oh!
Woman And Wine
Young Carpenter, The

You Should See Them Dance At The
   Gay Mabille
Zazel

LEYTON, George 1864–1948
All For A Lady Fair
All Hands On Deck (Lipton)
Always Ready!
Angel Of My Home
Back From The War
Bar Lambs
Battery No VII
Best Of Friends Must Part, The
Boys Of The Chelsea School
Britannia's Babes
Deserter, The *or* He's Not Guilty
Different Styles Of Singing
Emigrant Ship, The
Every Man At His Post (dedicated to
   the crew of the SS Titanic)
Face Of An English Girl, The
Five Georges, The
Forgotten (He Was One Of The Light
   Brigade)
Good-Bye, Mother! Good-Bye, Dad!
How Shall I Break The News?
Hurrah For The Road
I Do Like To Be Where Girls Are
Idol Of London Town, The
Last Muster, The
Longing To Meet
Modern Melody, A *or* The Musical
   Barmaid
My Post Is Here!
Off To The War
Pair Of Spectacles, A
Parted (Gabriel)
Saying Farewell To England
Somnambulist
Still I Am Ready
Take Me Down Bond Street
Three Musketeers
Toasts
Wellington At Waterloo
Woman's Revenge, A

Wreck Of The Birkenhead, The
You Can't Do Without A Girl
You Know The Girl I Mean
You Know The Man I Mean

LIBBEY, J. Aldrich c.1872–1925
After The Ball
Comrades Still
Don't Listen
Hello Central, Give Me Heaven
My Little Sweetheart Jess
Nellie To Me Is A Queen
Old Man's Story, The
On A Sunday Afternoon
Rosie, Sweet Rosabel
Take Him To Your Heart Again

LILBURN, Charles
All The Days Of The Week
I Haven't Been So Happy For A Long
    Long Time!
Oh! Mr Turncock
Poor Old Man
That's Nice!
They're The Sort
What For?
What Will Become Of England?
Whether You Like It Or Not
Why Are The Girls So Fond Of Me?
You're The Girl I've Been Looking For

LILLEY, A. C. 1842–1916
Drummed Out (sk.)

LILLIE, Beatrice 1894–1989
Girls Of The Old Brigade, The
Go To L, O, N, D, O, N
I Want To Go Back To Michigan (Back
    To The Farm)
March With Me
Now's The Time
There Are Fairies At The Bottom Of
    Our Garden
There's Life In The Old Girl Yet
When I Am With Her Again
When I Said Goodbye To You
Where The Black Eye'd Susans
    Grow

LINCOLN, Fred
All Bran' New!
If Only I Had A Stiver For A Stamp
Matrimonial Case, A
Oh! Ain't It A Gift!
That's The Job For Me
There Was 'Two Legs' Sitting On
    'Three Legs'
They Saved It Specially For Me
Wriggling

LIND, Jenny 1820–87
By The Sad Sea Waves (Benedict)
Comin' Through The Rye
Home! Sweet Home!
Swiss Echo Song

LIND, Letty 1862–1923; orig. k.a. La
Petite Letitia; sister of Millie HYLTON
q.v. for other sisters; cousin of Millie
LINDON
Chinee Dolly
Chon Kina
Di, Di, Di
Dom-Dom-Domino
Dutch Girl, The or Her Father Keeps
    A Brewery
Farmyard, The
Gaiety Girl And The Soldier, The
Gay Tom-Tit, The
I Am A Naughty Girl
I'm In Love With The Man In The
    Moon (w. Fred LESLIE)
Interfering Parrot, The
I Wonder Why
Johnny Jones And His Sister Sue (w.
    Charles DANBY)
Little Daisy With The Dimple or I
    Wonder Why
Marguerite Of Monte Carlo
Oyuchasan
Peer Of The Realm, The
Since I Came To London Town
Toy Monkey, The

LINDON, Millie b. 1877; m. (1) T. E.
DUNVILLE (div.); (2) Sir Edward Hulton

(d. 23 May 1925); cousin of Adelaide
ASTOR and Letty LIND
  Angel Of My Dreams, The
  Binks' Wife (Leave Her To Me)
  Days Of The Ruffle And The Patch,
    The
  Dear Marguerite Good-Bye
  Enjoyment
  For My Lady's Bright Blue Eyes
  For Old Times' Sake
  If Only Your Heart Could Speak
  In Barcelona
  Last Farewell, The
  Lost, Stolen Or Strayed (Mills: Scott)
  Maisey! My Maisey!
  Mary—She Kept A Dairy
  Mimosa
  My Little Pal
  Old Pals Up-To-Date
  Old Plaid Shawl, An
  Old Rocking Chair, That
  Postman, The
  Pussy Had Another Sardine
  Rain Came Pitter-Patter Down, The
  Say Goodbye, Maisey
  She Came To Town To See The Plum
    Tree
  Simple Milliner, The
  Sing Us One Of The Old Songs
  Skeleton In The Cupboard, The
  Smiles (Callahan: Roberts)
  So Did Eve!
  Sometimes
  Song Of The Kettle, The
  Sweethearts
  That Old Fashioned Habit Called
    Love
  That Old Rocking Chair
  Wearers Of The Little Grey Cloak,
    The
  What Is A Gentleman?
  What Is A Lady?

LINDON, SISTERS Isobel (d. 26 Apr.
1897) and Agnes (d. Feb. 1886)
  Gallant Blue Jackets Of England, The

  Heroes Of The Wave
  What Has Free-Trade Done For
    England?
  Yachting Off The Isle Of Wight

LINGARD, NELLIE 1868–99; m. George
BEAUCHAMP
  Rosie Gray
  T.R.I.C.K.Y

LINGARD, William H.° 1838–1927;
a.k.a. Horace LINGARD; m. Alice
DUNNING
  Belle Of Belgrave Square, The
  Captain Jinks Of The Horse Marines
  Grecian Bend, The
  Italian Guinea Pig Boy
  Leading Actor, The
  Lucy Gray or The Ugly Donkey
    Card
  Man Who Played The Bass, The
  On The Beach At Brighton
  Sal And Methusalem
  Statues
  Upper Ten, The

LINN, Harry° 1846–90
  Fattest Man In The Forty-Twa', The
  Get A Little Table
  Going Down The Hill
  Help One Another Boys
  Jim The Carter Lad
  Keep To The Right
  Never Be Downhearted Boys
  Never Dip Your Oar Too Deep
  Never Push A Man When He's Going
    Down
  Pull Slow And Steady Boys
  Wake Up, Johnny
  When The Cock Begins To Crow
  Where There's Life There's Hope
  Y'Heave Oh!
  You Never Miss The Water Till The
    Well Runs Dry

LISTER, Frank 1868–1917
  No 99 (sk.)
  Sundowner, The (sk.)

LISTON, Harry* 1843–1929
Any Vinders To Mend?
Baronet, The
Blighted Gardener, The (Cabbages And Turniptops)
Blindman's Buff
Chang The Fychow Giant
Convict, The
Dancing Rose
Dancing To The Organ
Dare-Devil Dick
Days To Come, The
Day We Went To Ramsgate, Oh!, The
Faithless Rose I Shall Never More Be Jolly
Fancy Goes A Very Long Way
Flunkey, The
Fwightful Dilemma, A
Ginger! Ginger!
Handsome Page Of Raspberry Jam, The
Happy Jack
Have You Seen My Polly?
I Love The Verdant Fields
It's All Over, Dolly's Gone Dancing
It's Really A Dreadful Affair
Jessie The Belle At The Bar
Kilkenny Boy, The
London Lions
Merry Moments
Naughty Mary Ann
Naughty Naked Cupid
Nobody's Child
Notting Hill
Peter Simple!!!
Ride A Cock Horse
Rustic Damsel, The
Them Three Acres Of Land And A Cow
Tin-Pot Band, The
West End Girls, The
When Johnny Comes Marching Home (parody)
Why Didn't You Say So Before?

LISTON, Victor 1838–1913
Auctioneer's Daughter, The
Bad Ballet Girl
Captain's Daughter, The (Minnie Bell)
Charming Arabella
It's Bad But It Might Have Been Worse
Mangling Done Here
Of Course It's No Business Of Mine
Polly Darling
Shabby Genteel
Shilling Or Two, A

LLOYD, Alice fl. 1870s; 'Female Tenor' not to be confused with Marie Lloyd's sister; see following entry
Good-Bye At The Door, The
Hearts Of Oak
Monarch Of The Woods, The
Village Blacksmith, The
White Squall, The

LLOYD, Alice 1873–1949; a.k.a. Alice WOOD; sister of Gracie LLOYD, Daisy WOOD, Marie LLOYD, and Rosie WOOD; see also LLOYD SISTERS; m. Tom MCNAUGHTON
Baby Calls Her Ma, The
Bandy Legs
Bloke That Wrote 'The Sheik', The
Boudoir Secrets
Class Will Tell
Come Along, Let's Make It Up
Cook's Excursion Trip, A (w. Tom MCNAUGHTON)
Coster Rag
Father And Mother's Out
Girl Who Thought She Would!, The
Good Old Iron
Higher Up
I Didn't Go Home At All
If You Go—Then This Will Bring You Back
I've Got The Riding Habit
I Wish I Had A Pal Like You

Little Church Around The Corner,
The
Louie Didn't Know!
Many Happy Returns Of The Day
Mary Green
May
Meet Me, Jenny, When The Sun Goes
Down
'Mongst The Poppies And The Corn
Nancy Brown
Never Introduce Your Bloke To Your
Lady Friend
No Thanks, Mr Octopus
Oh, That Conductor!
Queen Of Old Samara
Rosy's Cosy Bungalow
So Original
Story Of A Clothes Line, The
That's A Man
There's Room In My Heart For You
Three Ages Of Woman, The
Tourist And The Maid, The
Waterfall
When The Right One Comes Along
Who You Lookin' At, Eh?
Wise Virgin And The Foolish, The
You Don't Know You're Alive
Young Men Lodgers, The
You Splash Me And I'll Splash You
Yum! Yum! (I Can See The Lovelight
In Your Eyes)

LLOYD, Arthur* 1840–1904; m. Katty
KING; see LLOYD TRIO, Arthur. Godson
of T. D. RICE. Wrote much though not
all of his own material; claimed to have
written over 1,000 songs
Acting Mad
All Through Obliging A Lady
American Beef
American Drinks
And That's Why I've Not Got 'Em On
Arthur And Martha
At It Again
Baby Show, The

Bacon And Greens
Ballet Girl, The
Bandy-Legged Borachio *or* The Roley
Poley Eye
Barbara Allen The Cruel
Beautiful Strong Cup Of Tea, A
(parody of Beautiful Isle Of The
Sea)
Beautiful Young Widow Brown
Beauty Of Brixton, The
Beef, Pork And Mutton, Will You
Buy? (The Butcher)
Beware Of The Widows (sk.)
Bird Whistle Man, The
Bit Of My Mind, A
Blighted Barber, Ye (Fe, Fi, Fo, Fum)
Bloated Young Aristocrat, The
Brewer's Daughter, The
Brown The Tragedian
Bundle Rolled Into An Apron, A
But Of Course It's No Business Of
Mine
Captain Cuffs Of The Glorious Buffs
Captain La-di-dar-di-doo
Chillingowerllabadorie
Circus Master
Clang Clang His Cymbals Went
Amidst The Millingtary Band
Clarionet Player
Constantinople (*see* Seringapatam)
Continental Swell, The
Cow And Three Acres, A
Cruel Mary Holder
Dada
Dancing Swell, The
Diddle Diddle Dumpling My Son
John
Dirty Dicks And Matilda Hicks
Dobb's Visit To Paris
Doctor Gregory Bolas Squill
Don't Ask Me To Give Up Flo
Drink And Let's Have Another
Dutch Clock Man, (Song Of) The
Etcetera
Farmer Fenn

For Goodness' Sake Don't Say I Told
    You
Funny Mrs Jones
Gallant 93rd., The
German Band, A
Getaway
Going To The Derby In My Little
    Donkey Cart
Good-Bye John
Happiest Day Of My Life, The
Happy Thought
Hildebrandt Montrose
How Did You Leave The Pigs?
I Couldn't
I Fancy I Can See Her Now
I Like To Be A Swell
I'll Place It In The Hands Of My
    Solicitor
I'll Strike You With A Feather
Ill Used Organ Man, The
Immenseikoff (The Shoreditch Toff)
Ipecacu-anha, The Doctor's Daughter
I Sigh For Her In Vain
Isn't It A Beauty?
I Think It Looks Very Much Like It
It Makes Me So Awfully Wild
It's A Sort Of Thing We Read About
    But Very Seldom See
It's Naughty But It's Nice
It's Wonderful How We Do It But We
    Do
I Vow'd That I Never Would Leave
    Her
I Would I Were Lord Mayor
Johnny Go Into The Garden
Just By The Angel At Islington
Just One Little Polka
Just The Thing For Frank
Just To Show There's No Ill-Feeling
Ka-Fooze-Lum
Languid Swell, The
Last Bus, The
Little Charlie or The Twin Sisters (sk.)
Madame Rachel
Marquis And The Beggars, The
Married To A Mermaid

Massacre Of The MacPherson, The
Mrs Mary Plucker Sparrowtail
My Story It Is True
My Wife's Relations
Not For Joseph
Nursery Rhymes
Off To The Derby
Oh, Angelina Was Always Fond Of
    Soldiers
Oh! Marigold
Old Clothes Man, The
Old Woman And Her Pig, An
One More Polka
Organ Grinder, The
Our Party (sk.)
Pardonnez Moi
Pepper's Ghost
Piano Organ Man, The
Pity A Poor Foreigner
Policeman 92X
Pollee-Wollee-Hama, The Jolly
    Japanese
Postman, The
Pretty Lips
Pretty Little Mary—Chuck! Chuck!
    Chuck!
Promenade Elastique, The
Putney Bus, The
Railway Guard, The
Railway Porter, The
Reflecting On The Past
Rick Ma Tick
Riding On Top Of An Omnibus
Robber Of The Rhine, The
Roman Fall, The
Run For The Bus, A
St George's And St James'
Schoolmaster, The
Sea Sarpint, The
Seringapatam (companion to
    Constantinople)
Sharps And Flats
She'd Kept Them All For Me
Signor Macstinger—The Baritone
    Singer
Silly Billy

Somebody's Luggage
Some Lady's Dropt Her Chignon
Song Of (Many) Songs, The (medley)
Sophia Phia! Phia!
Street Musician, The
Sugar Shop, The
Take It, Bob (Song Of The Mill)
Takes The Cake
Take Your Time, Don't Hurry
Ten To One On The Lodger!
There Are Many Worse Off Than You
Thomas' Sewing Machine
Three Acres And A Cow
Tichborne Case, The
Tipperary Rose
Twin Brothers, The
Unfortunate Young Man, The
Upon My Soul I Couldn't
Ups And Downs
Watling's Pork Pie
Wedding Day
What A Wonderful Scholar Was He
Where Are You? There You Are!
Who'll Buy My Curiosities?
Who'll Shut The Door?
Who's For The Bank?
Wicked Squire, The (sk.) (w. Katty
    KING)
You Know What I Mean
You May Look But You Mustn't Touch
You Understand

LLOYD, Bella 1877–1962; a.k.a. Bella
BURGE and Ella LANE; also see SISTERS
LLOYD a.k.a. WOOD SISTERS
    Girls From Bryant's And May, The
    Girl You Leave Behind You, The
    Language Of Popular Songs, The

LLOYD, Edward 1845–1927
    Alice, Where Art Thou?
    Blue Alsatian Mountains, The
    Down The Vale
    Good Company
    Holy City, The
    I'll Sing Thee Songs Of Araby
    In The Old-Fashioned Way

Is It Yes?
Island Of Dreams
Last Watch, The
Love In Her Eyes
Nirvana
Romany Lass, The
Songs My Mother Taught Me
Star Of Bethlehem
Sweethearts
Then You'll Remember Me (When
    Other Lips)
There Was Once A Time My Darling
Thou And I
When In The Early Morn

LLOYD FAMILY, THE ALICE, DAISY
(WOOD), and ROSIE, sisters of Marie
LLOYD, later joined by her daughter
Marie LLOYD jun.

LLOYD, Florence b. 25 Mar. 1876; sister
of Violet LLOYD; cousin of Violet
CAMERON and Lydia THOMPSON
    Dear Little Girl Of Mine
    Patchwork Garden, The (w. Walter
        PASSMORE)

LLOYD, Gracie 1875–1961; sisters:
ALICE, DAISY (WOOD), MARIE, and
ROSIE (WOOD); see LLOYD SISTERS

LLOYD, Marie 1870–1922; m. (1) Percy
Court(e)nay (div.); (2) Alec HURLEY
(dec'd); (3) Bernard Dillon (judicial
separation); mother of Marie LLOYD jun.
(by Percy Court(e)nay); eldest sister of
ALICE, DAISY (WOOD), GRACIE, and
ROSIE (WOOD). Marie's two youngest
siblings also appeared briefly on the
Halls as Sid & Maudie (Sydney b. 1 Jan.
1885; Maud b. 25 Sept. 1890). Another
younger brother Johnny (b. 7 Dec. 1871)
m. Ouida MACDERMOTT
    A. B. C. Girl, The (Flossie The
        Frivolous) (sk.)
    Actions Speak Louder Than Words
    After The Pantomime's Over
    Among My Knick-Knacks

And The Leaves Began To Fall
And The Parrot Said
Are You Looking For A Girl Like Me?
'Arriet's Reply
As If She Didn't Know
Barmaid, The (The Idol Of The Rose
    And Crown)
Bathing
Beauty And The Looking Glass
Bird In The Hand, A
Bond Street Tea-Walk, The (song and
    sk.)
Boy In The Gallery, The
Buy Me Some Almond Rock
Chance Your Luck
Charity Bazaar (All For Sweet Charity)
Chili Widow, The
Clever, Ain't You?
Come Along, Let's Make It Up
Cosmopolitan Girl, The
Coster Girl In Paris, The
Coster's Christening, The
Coster's Wedding, The (Wedding
    March)
Customs Of The Country
Directoire Girl, The
Don't Dilly Dally (The Cock Linnet
    Song)
Don't Grumble At Women Any More
Don't Laugh!
Do They Do These Things In
    London?
Eh? What! What! What!
End Of A Perfect Day, The
Everybody Wondered How He Knew
Every Little Movement Has A
    Meaning Of Its Own (Cliffe:
    Moore)
Everything In The Garden's Lovely!
Feminine Moods And Tenses
Folkestone For The Day
French Lady's Maid, The
Gal Wot Lost Her Bloke At Monte
    Carlo, The
G'arn Away! What D'yer Take Me
    For?

Geisha, The (Le Brunn)
Girl In The Khaki Dress, The
Girl On The Ran-Dan-Dan, The
Good Old Iron
Harry's A Soldier
He Knows A Good Thing When He
    Sees It
He's All Behind (as Bella Delmere)
Hi-Ti-Tiddley-Um or The Song From
    London
How Can A Girl Refuse?
How Dare You Come To London?
Hulloa! Hulloa!! Hulloa!!!
I Can't Forget The Days When I Was
    Young
I'd Have Liked To
I'd Like To Live In Paris All The Time
    (The Coster Girl In Paris)
I Don't Know How To Tell Yer How I
    Lubs Yer
If You Want To Get On In Revue
I Know Now or Johnny Jones or
    What's That For, Eh?
I Like You, And You Like Me
I Live In Hopes
I'll Show You Where The Elephant Is
    Hiding
I'm A Good Girl Now
I'm A Lonely Little Petunia In An
    Onion Patch
I'm Satisfied If You Are
In The Good Old Times (as Bella
    Delmere)
In The Language Of The Eye
I Say
It Didn't Come Off After All
It's a Bit Of A Ruin That Cromwell
    Knocked About A Bit
It's A Jolly Fine Game Played Slow
I've Never Lost My Last Train Yet
I Was Slapped
Johnny Jones (What's That For, Eh? or
    I Know Now)
Keep Off The Grass
Lady Jane
Let's All Go Round To Mary Ann's

Listen With The Right Ear
Little Bit Of Lovin', A
Little Of What You Fancy, A
Madam Duvan
Maid Of London, 'Ere We Part
Millie From Piccadilly
Mischief
My Actor Man
My Harry's A Sailor
My Soldier Laddie (as Bella Delmere)
Naughty Continong, The (You Should Go To France)
Naughty! Naughty! Naughty! (Le Brunn)
Near Thing
Never Let A Chance Go By
No, 'Arry, Don't Ask Me To Marry
Not For Bill!
Not For The Best Man Breathing
Now You've Got Yer Khaki On
Of Course!
Oh! George
Oh, Jeremiah, Don't You Go To Sea!
Oh! Mister What's-Er-Name
Oh, Mr Porter
One Thing Leads To Another
Piccadilly Trot, The
Poor Thing
P'r'aps You've Seen The Pictures?
Put On Your Slippers
Red And The White And The Blue, The
Rich Girl And The Poor, The
Rosie Had A Very Rosy Time
Rum-Tiddley-Um-Tum-Tay!
Salute My Bicycle!
Same Thing, The
Saturday To Monday
Saucy Bit O' Crackling, A
She Didn't Like To Tell Him What She Wanted
She'd Never Had A Lesson In Her Life, (And)
She Doesn't Know That I Know What I Know
She Has A Sailor For A Lover

She Lisped When She Said Yes
She Wore A Little Safety Pin Behind
Shop Girl, The
Silly Fool!
Sleep! Sleep! He's Always Got His Eyes Shut
Something On His Mind
Spanish Señora, The
Sure To Fetch Them (as Bella Delmere)
Tale Of The Skirt, The
Talk About A Big Responsibility
That Accounts For It
That's How The Little Girl Got On
That's Where The Young Man Smiles
That Was A Bloomer
That Was Before My Time, You Know
Then You Wink The Other Eye
There Goes The Bloke Who Dunno Where 'E Are
There They Are—The Two Of Them On Their Own
There Was Something On His Mind
Three Ages Of Woman (Woman's Opinion Of Man)
Three Women To Every Man
Tiddley-Om-Pom!
Time Is Flying (as Bella Delmere)
Ting-A-Ling-Ling-Tay
Tricky Little Trilby
Trumpet Call, The
Twiddly Wink, The
Twiggy Voo?
Vat Ze English Call Ze—Zat Was It
Very Nice, Too
Wedding March, The (Coster's Wedding)
Whacky Whacky Whack!
What Did She Know About Railways?
What Do You Take Me For? (G'arn Away!)
What's That For, Eh? (Johnny Jones or I Know Now)
What What!
When I Take My Morning Promenade
When She's In Town

Who Are You Getting At, Eh?
Who Paid The Rent For Mrs Rip Van
Winkle?
William 'Enery Sarnders
Wink The Other Eye *see* Then You
Wink The Other Eye
Woman's Opinion Of Man (Three
Ages Of Woman)
Wrong Girl, The
Wrong Man, The
You Ain't Ashamed O' Me, Are You,
Bill?
You Can't Stop A Girl From Thinking
You Needn't Wink—I Know
Young Country Squire, The
You're A Thing Of The Past, Old Dear
You Should Go To France (first as
Bella Delmere)

LLOYD, Marie jun. 1888–1967; née
Myria Matilda Victoria (a.k.a. Maudie)
Courtenay; daughter of Marie LLOYD;
see also LLOYD FAMILY, THE. Sang only
her mother's repertoire including:
Don't Dilly Dally (The Cock Linnet
Song)
It's A Bit Of A Ruin That Cromwell
Knocked About A Bit
Little Of What You Fancy Does You
Good, A
Wedding March!, The (The Coster's
Wedding)
What Did She Know About Railways?

LLOYD, Rosie 1879–1944; a.k.a. Rosie
WOOD; m. Will Poluski jun. (of THE
POLUSKIS); see LENA SISTERS, also
SISTERS LLOYD a.k.a. WOOD SISTERS
'Cause I Don't Want You
Come Down And Open The Door
(solo, also w. Bella BURGE—see
SISTERS LLOYD)
Cuckoo? What Cuckoo!, The
'Ere's Yer Fine Water-Creases!
I Still Love You, My Lou!
Joan! Joan! Joan! Come Home!
Lady Doctor, The

Let's Have A Bit Of A Do
Oh! Star Of Eve
Poor Old Liza Perkins
Sailing In My Balloon (Come Go)
She Didn't Come From Borneo
Sun Is Always Shining, The
Sunshine After Rain
When It's Moonlight On The Prairie
Who's Going To Take Me For A Walk
Tonight?
Will You Remember Me?
Won't You Drop Me Just One Line?
You Ain't Ashamed O' Me, Are You,
Bill?

LLOYD SISTERS Alice LLOYD and
Gracie LLOYD; not to be confused with
the SISTERS LLOYD
Cinderella Up-To-Date
Quarrelling

LLOYD, SISTERS fl. *c*.1890; Rosie LLOYD
and Bella LLOYD a.k.a. WOOD SISTERS;
not to be confused with the LLOYD
SISTERS
Come Down And Open The Door
Dancing In The Moonbeams
Lost, Stolen Or Strayed (Mills: Scott)
Ma Jeanette And Marguerite
Sunshine After Rain

LLOYD TRIO, Arthur Arthur, Lilli, and
Dulcie, children of Arthur LLOYD and
Katty KING. Other children who joined
their father on the Halls from time to
time were Annie, Katty jun., and Harry,
all sometimes k.a. King-Lloyd
Twin Sisters, The *or* Little Charlie
Who'll Shut The Door?

LLOYD, Violet b. 1879; sister of Flo-
rence LLOYD and cousin to Violet
CAMERON and Lydia THOMPSON; m.
Horace LANE
If Ever I Marry (w. Edmund PAYNE)
Merry Buskers, The (w. Horace LANE)
Punch And Judy (w. PAYNE)

Trixie
Visitors

LOCKETT, Lou 1893–1964
If You Can't Get A Girl In The
   Summertime (w. Jack WALDRON)

LOFTUS, Cissie 1876–1943; daughter of
Marie LOFTUS
Brigadier Bing Bong
Diamond Express, The (sk.)
Linger Longer Loo
'Twas At A Sing-Song

LOFTUS, Kitty 1867–1927
Dainty Dora
English Boy, An
My Girl (w. Arthur NELSTONE)
Only One The Poor Girl Had, The
Trombone Man, The

LOFTUS, Marie 1857–1940; mother of
Cissie LOFTUS
(And) She Lisped When She Said 'Yes'
Be Home When The Clock Strikes
   Ten
Cantineer Of The Irish Brigade, A
Dad's Dialects, The
Don't You Believe It, Dear Boys
Go On!
He Kissed I Once
He Pushed It Right Along
He's Going There Every Night (He'd
   Never Been There Before)
Hullo! I've Been Looking For You!
I'm So Shy
It Didn't Take Too Long To Do
John Bull's Letter Bag
Kilkenny Kate
Man In The Dirty Coat, The
Marie's Lovers
No English Need Apply
Oh, Mr Shakespeare, What Have You
   Done For Me?
One At A Time
One Touch Of Nature Makes The
   Whole World Kin
Sally's A-Coming—Hurrah! Hurrah!

She'd Never Been There Before (She's
   Going There Every Night)
She Went Right Past Her Junction
She Wore A Little Safety-Pin Behind
Shop Girl, The
Singers Past And Present (mon.)
Sister Mary Wants To Know
Story Of A Shilling, The
That Is Love
That's How She Answers Yes
That Shows What A Woman Can Do
That Was The Soldier's Song
There's A Nice Warm Welcome
   Waiting For Him
Thing You Can't Buy With Gold, A
To Err Is Human, To Forgive Divine
Two Little Drummer Boys
Vulgar Boy, The
Zat Was What He Said

LOMAX, Fawcett 1883–1958
Nonsense! Yes! By Jove! (w. Fred
   STIMSON)

LONGWORTH, D. G.
Little Peach In An Orchard Grew, A
   (w. Marie STUART)

LONNEN, E. J. 1860–1901
Any Time You Pass
'Arry On The Steamboat
'Ave A Glass Won't Yer?
Ballyhooley
Coster's Wedding, The
Devil And The Lawyer, The
Dispensary Doctor, The
Donegal
Enniscorthy
How To Mesmerise 'Em!
Hush! The Bogie!
I Raise An Objection To That
I Shall Have 'Em By And Bye
It Will Cause Unpleasantness (w.
   Arthur WILLIAMS)
Jolly Boys' Club, The
Killaloe!
Killymablanagan
Little Peach In An Orchard Grew, A

McCarthy's Widow
Mullingar
My Feyther Be A Farmer
Nummy Num Num (w. May YOHÉ)
Odd-Ditty, An
On Parade
Rumpty Tumpty Tiddely Umpti
She Was A Fairy
Simple Days Of Long Ago, The
Socialistic Club Of Tipperary, The
Wake Of Mulligan's Wife, The
Wanted
Well, I Said So
What Will You Have To Drink?

LOPEZ, Vincent & His Band 1894–1975

In A Little Spanish Town
Nola

LORAINE, Violet 1887–1956
All Clear Out Of The Park
All The World Will Be Jealous Of Me
Another Little Drink (w. Alfred
  LESTER & George ROBEY)
Brave Women Who Wait
Bulldog's Bark, The
Dear Old Saturday Night
Do You Like Me? (w. Joseph COYNE)
First Love—Last Love—Best Love (w.
  ROBEY)
Gipsy Warned Me, The
He Misses His Missis's Kisses
Here Comes Tootsie
How'd You Like To Float With Me?
Hullo! Little Boy!
If You Were The Only Girl In The
  World (w. ROBEY)
I'll Make You Want Me
I Might Learn To Love Him Later On
I Want A Girl With The 'Glad' Eye
Japanese Sandman, The
Kipling Walk, The
Let The Great Big World Keep
  Turning (w. Laddie CLIFF)
Oh, By Jingo! Oh, By Gee!
Some Girl Has Got To Darn His Socks
When Millie Tied Her Shoe Up In

The Strand
Where The Black Eye'd Susans
  Grow

LORIMER, Jack 1883–1920; father of
Max Wall (1908–90)
Ching-A-Ling
Doing The Seaside Promenade
If All The Girls Wore Kilts
I've Just Come Up For The Day
Jeanie McGregor
McCluskey
My Highland Laddie, Oh
PC McWheeler
Three Jolly Scotchmen
When We Went To London

LORRAINE, Lillian 1892–1955
Ballin' The Jack
By The Light Of The Silvery Moon
Daddy Has A Sweetheart And Mother
  Is Her Name
Nothing But A Bubble
Row, Row, Row
Some Boy
Swing Me High, Swing Me Low
Up Up Up In My Aeroplane

LOSEBINI, Mme Elizabeth 1819–88;
mother of Constance LOSEBY
Fair Exchange (w. Constance LOSEBY)
Gathering Flowers (with LOSEBY)
Hashed Opera (with LOSEBY)
I Never Shall See Thee More

LOSEBY, Constance 1851–1906; m.
John Caulfield jun.°; daughter of Mme
LOSEBINI
Fair Exchange (w. Mme LOSEBINI)
Gathering Flowers (w. LOSEBINI)
Hashed Opera (w. LOSEBINI)
Little Jehu, The
Nil Desperandum
Pretty Flowers
Sally In Our Alley
Slave Ship, The
Stonewall Jackson
Tell Me My Heart
Thou Art So Near And Yet So Far

LOTINGA, Ernie 1876–1951; m. Hetty
KING (div.); sketch comic; from 1899 to
1909 one of the SIX BROTHERS LUCK
Bluebottles
Drinkwater's Matrimonial Agency
Jimmy Josser
Millions
Pepper's Detective Agency

LOU, Mama
Bully Song, The
Frankie And Johnny
Hot Time In The Old Town (Tonight),
A
Ta-Ra-Ra-Boom-De-Ay
Who Stole The Lock On The Hen
House Door?

LOVE, Mabel 1874–1953
Cook's Excursion Trip, A (w. Eugene
STRATTON)
Funny Little Man, The (w. Little
TICH)
Silly Old Man In The Moon, The

LOWE, Rachel 1876–c.1930
Any Rags?
Cat's Meat Man, The
Lucky Duck, The
My Boy Bill
Take Me Down To Blackpool
They All Go To Church On Sunday
Up With Woman And Down With
Man
What's The Use Of That, Huh?

LUCK, SIX BROTHERS fl. 1890s–1900s;
sketch comics; see also GLENVILLE,
Shaun; LOTINGA, Ernie; LUPINO,
Stanley
Demon Of The Cellar, The
Hermit, The
HMS Perhaps
Hotel Grande, The
New Slavey, The

LUND, Baby
Hello Central! Give Me Heaven
Just Next Door
On A Sunday Afternoon

LUNDBERG, Ada 1850–99; m. Tom L.
Everard (d. 26 Oct. 1896); mother of
George Everard°; aunt of Ruth
LYTTON
All Through Sticking To A Soldier
Betsy Barlow
Coster's Night Out, The
Good Old Mother-In-Law
He Loves Me!
I'm All Right Up Till Now
My First Young Man
Poor Old Maid, A
Sarah Of The Fried Fish Shop
Sich A Nice Gal Too
That's A Bit Of Comfort To A Poor
Old Maid
Tooraladdie
Walker, London

LUNN, Louise Kirkby 1873–1930
Auld Robin Gray
Come Back To Erin
Country Night Song
Daddy
Deep In The Heart Of A Rose
Eriskay Love Lilt, An
For Thee
I Know Where I'm Going
Linden Lea
Lost Chord, The
One Spring Morning
On The Banks Of Allan Water
O Peaceful England
O That We Two Were Maying
(Nevin)
Pretty Creature, The
Three Fishers Went Sailing
Violets
When The Stars Were Young

LUNT, Alfred 1892–1977
Ashes (sk.) (w. Mrs LANGTRY)

LUPINO, BROTHERS Arthur (1864–1908)
and Harry (1865–1925), uncles of
Stanley LUPINO and grand-uncles of
Lupino LANE. Arthur was the orig. Nana

in J. M. Barrie's *Peter Pan*; see also
LUPINOS, THE
    Fiddler And His Dog, The

LUPINO, Stanley 1894–1942; m. Connie
EMERALD; nephew of BROTHERS
LUPINO; uncle of Lupino LANE; at one
time w. SIX BROTHERS LUCK. See also
LUPINOS, THE
    Could Lloyd George Do It?
    I Lift Up My Finger And I Say 'Tweet!
      Tweet!'
    I'm On The Staff
    Midnight Revels

LUPINOS, THE fl. since *c*.1600; noted
performing family incl. Harry (1)
(1827–96), George sen. (1820–1903)
and sons Arthur and Harry (2) (see
LUPINO, BROTHERS) and George jun.
(1852–1932) who m. Florence Ann
Webster (1860–99). George jun.'s sons
were Barry (see EVANS, Will and
KARNO, Fred) and Stanley LUPINO.
Other Lupinos were Mark (1894–1930),
Wallace (1897–1961), and Lupino LANE.
Barry (1882–1962) m. Gertie Latchford,
widow of Bert SINDEN
    The Wreckers

LUXMORE, Ada *see* EVANS, Will

LYMAN, Tommy 1894–1964
    My Blue Heaven
    My Melancholy Baby

LYNNE, Frank° 1863–1916; sometimes
spelled Lynn
    Business Suspended
    Do What You Can For Ninepence
    Father's Box Of Tools
    Holding Each Other Up
    I Can't Make It Out—Can You?
    I Didn't Mind It
    My Daddy's As Good As Yours
    My Inquisitive Kiddy
    Oom-Pom-Pom
    Our Sally
    Schoolmaster, The *or* Sit Down

    Sensations
    That's What He Bought With His
      Wages
    Trifling Occurrences
    Twelve Hundred Years Ago
    When Father Took The Baby Out

LYRIC, Dora 1879–1962
    All That Glitters Isn't Gold
    Coax Me
    Fine Feathers Made Fine Birds
    Goodbye, Baby
    If At First You Don't Succeed
    If I Should Plant A Tiny Seed Of Love
    I'll Tell Tilly On The Telephone
    I'm Leaving Monte Carlo
    I've Enough And A Little To Spare
    I Want A Boy Who'll Be My Only Boy
    Lame Dog And The Stile, The
    Never Put Off Until Tomorrow
    Soldier And A Man, A
    Song The Kettle Is Singing, The
    There's No Place Like Home, Tommy
    There's Someone Wants You
    What's The Use Of Knocking At An
      Empty House?
    When The Lilac Blooms In
      Springtime
    When You're In Rome

LYSTER, Amy
    Charley's Aunt
    Do, Dear, Do
    Your Brother Ain't Got What My
      Brother's Got
    Zig! Zig! Zig!

LYTTON, Sir Henry 1865–1936
    My Cosey Corner Girl (w. Agnes
      FRASER)
    My Ellaline
    O Peaceful England
    When I Marry Amelia
    Yeomen Of England, The (*Merrie
      England*)

LYTTON, Ruth m. George BASTOW;
niece of Ada LUNDBERG

Cameron Highlander, The *or* Your Jamie Will Be Coming Home
Her Name Is Annie Laurie
Look At The Kiltie Boys—Hooch Aye!
What A Thing It Is To Be A Boy

MACCABE, Frederic* 1830–1904
Don't Stay Out Too Late At Night
Early In The Morning Merrily Oh!
Fascinating Fellow
It Serves You Right
My Galloping Horse
My Love Is On The Sea
Obstinate Man, An
Patent Medicines
Shamrock Of Old Ireland
Willie Has Gone For A Soldier

McCARTHY, Dennis J.
Bar, The (mon.)
Because We Love Our Queen
Boys Of The Four-In-Hand, The
Boys Will Be Boys
British Boys
Captain Said 'I'll Stick To My Ship', The
Carrie Gray
Cousin Charlie (mon.)
Diamond King, The
Friends Were Saying 'Good-bye'
I Was Wanted
Jack Was A Hero
Jameson's Ride (mon.)
Napoleon (mon.)
Oh! It Do Give Me The Needle
Sixty Years A Soldier
Sweetest Words, The
That's Bill (mon.)
Unbeliever, The (mon.)
Under A Burning Sun
Under The Same Old Flag
When A Soldier Says Farewell

McCARTHY, Lillah 1875–1960; m. Harley GRANVILLE-BARKER (div.)
Annajanska, The Wild Grand Duchess (sk.)

Farewell Supper, A (sk.) (w. Harley GRANVILLE-BARKER and Nigel PLAYFAIR)
Fourth Act, The (w. Ben WEBSTER)

McCARTHY, Molly d. 9 Oct. 1944
Popsy Wopsy
Trail Of The Lonesome Pine, The

McCARTHY, Steve d. 3 Apr. 1944; m. Marie KENDALL
I've Got Her Wooden Leg
That Cat
We've Got Quite Enough Of Our Own
When Are You Going To War?

McCORMACK, Harry*
Alone I Did It
Little Tommy Tit-Bit *or* I've Only Got To Look At 'Em
Mistaken Identity
My May Queen
Obadiah Binks *or* If You See That Man
Ringing The Changes

McCORMACK, Count John 1884–1945
Ah, Moon Of My Delight
Ballymure Ballad, A (Next Market Day)
Bantry Bay
Believe Me If All Those Endearing Young Charms
Bless This House
Brown Bird Singing, A
Come Into The Garden Maud
Come Where My Love Lies Dreaming
Danny Boy
Funiculi Funicula
Green Bushes, The
Has Sorrow Thy Young Days Shaded
I Hear You Calling Me
I'll Take You Home Again Kathleen
I'll Walk Beside You
Jeanie With The Light Brown Hair
Kashmiri Song
Kathleen Mavourneen
Kerry Dance, The

Killarney
Little Grey Home In The West
Lost Chord, The
Macushla
Maire, My Girl
Minstrel Boy, The
Molly Bawn
Mother Machree
Mother O' Mine
Mountain Lovers
Mountains Of Mourne
Nancy Lee
Nirvana
Non E Ver
Rosary, The
Rose Of Tralee
Roses
Say 'Au Revoir', But Not 'Goodbye'
She Is Far From The Land (E. Frank
    Lambert)
Smilin' Through
Snowy Breasted Pearl, The
Somewhere A Voice Is Calling
Star Of Bethlehem
Sunshine Of Your Smile, The
Sweet Genevieve
Take, Oh Take Those Lips Away
Terence's Farewell To Kathleen
Thora
Venetian Song (Tosti)
When Irish Eyes Are Smiling

MACDERMOTT, G. H.° 1845–1901;
m. Annie Milburn, daughter of
J. H. MILBURN; father of Ouida
MACDERMOTT
    Always The Same
    Another Fellah's
    At Half Past Seventeen We Dine
    Beaten By A Head
    Beatin' Of My Own 'Art, The
    Can You Wonder When Trade's So
        Bad
    Captain Criterion
    Charlie Dilke Upset The Milk
    Cockalorum

Dear Old Pals
Did You Ever Catch A Weasel Asleep?
Ditto Repeato Over Again
Don't Run Old England Down
Down At Westminster
Down Went The Captain
Envy Of The World Down At
    Westminster, The
Fire Escape, The (Charlie Parnell's
    Naughty Shape)
Fishing For Truth In A Well
Give Me A Grip Of Your Hand
Going Going Going
Gone To Smash
Half-Past Twelve
Hear! Hear!
He Isn't A Marrying Man
Hi Cockalorum, Jig Jig Jig
Hi Hi Hoopla
Hildebrandt Montrose
How Did You Lose Your Arm?
How Does He Do It?
Hush A Bee Bo
I'd Rather Lather Father, Than Father
    Lather Me
I'll Strike You With A Feather
Im-Pe-Cu-Ni-Os-I-Ty (w. Herbert
    CAMPBELL & Fannie LESLIE)
I'm The Idol Of The Hall
In A Very Different Place
Influenza, The
Isn't That A Dainty Dish?
Is The Guv'nor In?
It All Depends On Randy
It Is A Famous Story
It's A Little Bit Too Hot
It's All Codoirum
I've No Use For It
Jacks And Jills
Jeremiah Blow The Fire
Jingo Song, The a.k.a. Macdermott's
    War Song
Jubilation Day (air, Le Père de
    Victoire)
Just Fancy You've Heard It Before
King Kalulu

Little Miss Muffet Sat On A Tuffet
Lodger's Come, The
Lots Of Love For Breakfast
Macdermott's War Song (The Jingo Song)
Maid And The Magpie, The
Major K.N. Pepper
Matilda's Up To Snuff
Millie's Cigar Divan
Mind The Paint
More Than Ever
M'Yes
My Landlady's Daughter
Never Court A Girl Who's A Dove Dove Dove
Not Much (It's Better Than Nothing At All)
Not Too Much But Just Enough
Oh The Miller
Oh! The Pretty Creature
Oh! The Sea! The Beautiful Sea!
Oh Verily
Oh, We Are A Getting On
Old Familiar Faces, The
On 'Change
On The Strict Q.T.
O Tobacco, Fragrant Weed
Our Lads In Red (sk.)
Pa And Ma (Of Course He Did)
Parcels Post, The
Parson And The Clerk, The
Quite English, You Know
Rap, Rap, Rap (I'm Married To A Medium)
Remarkably Loose
Says Aaron To Moses
Scamp, The (They Can't Hold A Candle To Me)
Sea Sarpint, The
She Wanted To Be A Fairy
Snob, The
So It Was!
So Long As The World Goes Round
Speak To My Wife
Speak Up My Darlings
Standard Of The Blue, The

Sweethearts And Wives
There's Danger On The Line (The Great Semaphore Song) (G. P. Norman)
There's Only One In It, That's Me
They All Do It
They've All Got 'Em
Three Young Men Who Never Went Astray
Too Late To Save Our Gordon
True Blues, Stand By Your Guns
Turn Off The Gas At The Meter
Two Obadiahs, The
Up Went The Captain
Up Went The Price
Very Different Place, A
Volunteer, The
Waiting For The Signal (new Jingo Song)
We Don't Want To Fight *see* The Jingo Song
W. E. G.
We Have Men, We Have Money
We'll All Get Jolly As The Night Wears On
We're Much Better Off As We Are
What Would You Do, Love?
When The Bells Of The Village Go Ring, Ding, Dong
Where Was Moses When The Light Went Out?
Where Will You Find Such Another?
Whist! The Bogie Man
Why Part With Jumbo (The Pet Of The Zoo)
Widow And The Bachelor, The
Wild, Wild West Of London, The
Willing Chap, The
You Are Always Sure To Fetch Them With Wst, Wst, Wst
You Should See Us On The Strict Q. T.
You've Guessed It In One

MACDERMOTT, Ouida 1889–1980; daughter of G. H. MACDERMOTT; m.

Johnny Wood (b. 7 Dec. 1871) (div.)
who was brother of Marie LLOYD
    Down On The Farm
    Just Like The Dear Old Swing
    My Heart Is With You Tonight
    My Pretty Little Piece Of Dresden
      China
    Sweet Little Sunbonnet Lady
    Take Me Back To Dear Old Blighty

MacDONOUGH, Harry 1870–1943
    Garden Of Dreams, The
    Good-Bye, Dolly Gray
    I Can't Tell Why I Love You, But I Do
    My Cosey Corner Girl
    Nancy Brown
    Red Wing
    When You And I Were Young,
      Maggie

MacEACHERN, Malcolm 1883–1945;
Jetsam of 'Flotsam & Jetsam' (w. B. C.
Hilliam)
    Deathless Army, The
    Desert, The
    Devonshire Wedding, A
    Hear The Pipers Calling, Jennie Mine
    Hybrias The Cretan
    In Cellar Cool
    Mighty Deep, The
    My Old Shako
    Roadways Song Of The Waggoner
    Tom O' Devon

MACKAY, Julia *see* MACKEY, Julie

MACKENZIE, Scott
    Dear Old Melodies
    Don't You Want A Boy To Love You?
    Girls And Boys
    Love Coon
    Sammy Dear
    Zulieeo!

MACKEY, Julie b. 1893; sometimes misspelled Julia Mackay
    Adieu But Not Farewell
    As Your Hair Grows Whiter

Baby Loo
Cat Came Back, The
Caterpillar And The Rose, The
De Piccaninny's Dream
Don't You Leave Me Honey
Ev'ry Little Bit Helps
Fisherman's Bride, The
Goodbye, Ma Lady Love
Hello! Ma Baby
Her Memory Brings Me No Regret
His Parents Haven't Seen Him Since
Honey, You'se Ma Lady Love
I Can't Tell Why I Love You, But I Do
I Can't Think Ob Nuthin' Else But
    You
I Don't Want To Play In Your Yard
In The Good Old Summertime
Juliana
Just One Girl
Little Piece Of Orange Peel, A
My Black Daisy
My Coal Black Lady
My Daddy's As Good As Yours
On A Sunday Afternoon
Only A Lead
Only Just Because You're You
Pebbles Of The Beach, The
Queen Of The Earth
Rosalie
Say 'Au Revoir', But Not 'Goodbye'
Stories Mother Told
Sweet Annie Moore
Terah-Rah-Hool-Ey-Ah!
There's A Little Star Shining For You
Under The Bamboo Tree
Way Down Where De Coons Come
    From
Why Can't It Always Be Christmas?
Woman's Little Kingdom, A
World's Full Of Girls, The
You Ask Me Why I Love You
You'll Be With Me All The While

MACKINDER, Lionel 1869–1915 k.i.a.;
m. Grace LEIGH
    Girl Next Door But One, The

Little Willie
One Of The Boys
Trixie Of Upper Tooting

McIntyre, Leila 1882–1953
Pansy Faces

McIvor, Will
Don't Give Way, Lizzie Lee!
Other Side Of The Curtain, The
Some Day You'll Know

Maclagan, Tom° 1827–1902
Bitter Beer
Bould Sojer Boy, The
Captain Jinks Of The Horse Marines
Cricketer, The
Doing The Grand *or* I Wish I'd Had A
    Dicky
Don't You Do It Again
Easy Come, Easy Go
Gal From Pennsylvania, The (Sam's
    Sally)
Girl With A Blue Dress On
Happy Quako
Hoop A Doodle Dum (I Want A
    Wife)
How's Your Poor Old Feet?
I'm Saucy Sam, Heigh-Ho!
Jeames
Married On Wednesday (Polly Bluck)
Musical Age
Old Brigade, The
Pity The Downfall Of Uncle Sam
Ramoni, The Queen's Violinist (next
    entry?)
Sensation Fiddler, The
Slap Bang, Here We Are Again (Jolly
    Dogs)
Tom Tandem
Uncle Sam
Wanted A Wife
White Squall, The

MacNally Jessie 1867–1903; m. W. H.
McCarthy
Daisy Carey

Every Sunday Afternoon
Kathleen Asthore
Norah Brady

McNaughton, Tom 1867–1923; m.
Alice **Lloyd**; see **McNaughtons**, The
Cook's Excursion Trip, A (w. Alice
    Lloyd)
Three Trees, The

McNaughtons, The fl. 1889–*c*.1920;
M'**Naughtons**, **The** a.k.a. The Two
McNaughtons (orig. The Brothers
Parker). Tom **McNaughton** and Fred
(1869–1920), brother-in-law of Jessie
Preston. In 1909 Tom was succeeded
by Augustus Howard (1884–1969) a.k.a.
Gus McNaughton also k.a. Augustus Le
Clerq who m. Lottie Govett (see
Poluskis, The). Son of George and
brother of Arthur Le Clerq°, Gus was
also w. Fred **Karno**
Prompter, The

McNeil, Dave
At The Railway Station
Garden Of Eden, The

Mackney, E. W.° 1825–1909
Betsy Blossom
Clementine Coults
Come Along You Blacks
Darkies' Christmas Day
De Nigger Fancy Fair
De Nigger Hamlet
Garret Near The Sky, The (parody of
    Cottage By The Sea)
Hoop De Dooden Do
Hop Light Hoo
I'm Dry Sweet Tart
In The Strand (I Wish I Was With
    Nancy)
I Wish I Was A Baby a.k.a. I'd Choose
    To Be A Baby
Ladies, Won't You Marry?
Little Dog's Tail, The
Married On Wednesday (Polly Bluck)
Mingo's Wide Awake

My Garret Near The Sky
My Mary Jane
My Pretty Jane
My Rosa On My Arm
Nigger's Birthday
Nothing More
Oh! Don't I Love My Billy
Oh! Fie, Miss Smart, Oh! Fie (parody
    of Good-Bye, Sweetheart,
    Good-Bye)
Old Bob
Old Grey Goose, The
Old Nigger Ben
One Night While Wandering The
    Other Side Of Jordan
Only Ten Of Us
Over There!
Oxford Street
Peter Gray
Polly Crow
Ram Jam Jerusalem
Rosa Tanner
Runaway Jack
Sally, Come Up
Sambo's Apparition (A Nigger's
    Holiday)
She'd A Black And A Rolling Eye
Sich A Gittin' Upstairs
Sly Young Coon, The
Some Folks
Victim Of Love, The
When We Were Pals Together
Whole Hog Or None, The (Mackney)
Who'll See Me Over De Mountain?
Who'll Stop De Fight?
Young Carpenter, The

MACS, THE TWO fl. *c.*1880–93; Frederick Michael (1854–94) and brother
Patrick Joseph (1863–93) Maccabe who
m. Alice MAYDUE. Orig k.a. Hilton &
Curly. In 1881 John Patrick McNally and
John William Young 'Maccabe' also
called themselves The Two Macs. The
brothers sued and lost but the bogus
Macs soon dropped out of sight. At one

time one of the 'genuine' Macs was Dan
Kennedy
    Comical Vanishing Lady, The
    It's A Good Thing McCarthy Wasn't
        There
    Rowdy-Dowdy Boys, The
    Sisters Dimple
    Talkative Man From Galway (Borneo),
        The
    Tapping A Man For Beer
    Wait Till The Fog Rolls By (parody)
    Wild Man Of Borneo (Poplar), The

MACE, Minnie
    I'll Be Your Dew Drop
    Moontime Is Spoontime
    My Prairie Girl

MACK, Andrew 1863–1931
    Broken Hearts
    Flowery Courtship
    Man That Left The Town With
        Coxey's Army, The
    Man That Stole My Luncheon, The
    Picture That Is Turned To The Wall,
        The

MAJILTON, Madeleine
    Creep-mouse (w. Jenny CLARE)
    I Don't Want To Play In Your Yard (w.
        CLARE)

MALIBRAN, Maria 1808–36
    Deep, Deep Sea, The
    Eloisa
    Merry Spring, The
    Oh, Shall We Go A-Sailing?

MANLEY, Edith
    Silver And The Gold
    When Daddy Returns

MANSFIELD, Harry
    Give Me A Nice Little Four-Roomed
        House
    Real Good Wife, A
    When The Children Have Gone To
        Bed

MAPLE, George
Always Look On The Bright Side
Cot By Killarney, The
Georgina On The Pier
I Treasure You More Today
Johnnies
Lucky Sixpence, The
Maids I've Loved, The
Sambo
Sexton And The Ghost, The
Sweetheart Rose
When The Setting Sun Lights Up The
    Western Sky

MARIO, Signor 1809–84; Don Giovanni
Matteo, Marchese di Candia; m. Giulia
Grisi (1811–69)
Good-bye, Sweetheart, Good-bye
M'Appari Tutt'Amor (Ach! So
    Fromm/Ah! So Pure)
Signora

MARIO, Minnie 1858–1905; orig. w.
sister Dot (d. 23 Jan. 1898) as Sisters
Mario
Baby's Box Of Soldiers
Kerry Wedding, The
Little Vagabond Boy
Ring, The (sk.)

MARIUS, Monsieur (Claude) 1850–96;
m. Florence ST JOHN (div.)
I Love My Love, My Love Loves Me
Sa-Ha-Carte-Tierce-Circle, Octave-
    Prinz-Quinz
Strawberries And Cream
Where Shall I Take My Bride?

MARNEY, Lily
All The 'O's Were There
Arrah, Go On!
Be Aisy
He Doesn't Go There Now
He Lies Asleep
Hold Yer Head Up Patsy McGann
I'm Going To Be Married In The
    Morning
Indian Prince, The

John James Callaghan
John James Murphy
Keep Yer 'Air On!
McCarthy's Boarding House
Macra-Mac-Menac-Menac-McCann
Oh! The Sandals
Only A Saturday Soldier
What Will The Neighbours Say?

MARS, Annie
Home Again, My Cherry Blossom!
Pansy

MARS, Gwennie w. The Follies
I Love The Yankees

MARS, May
Esau Wood
I'll Make You Want Me
In The Fire, Fire Glow
I Want Molly And She Wants Me
Let Me Think I'm Someone
Love Me As You Used To Love Me
My Boy
Oh! George, Tell Them To Stop The
    Flip Flap
Pretty Maid Of The Pyrenees
Waltz Me In Ragtime
We'll Fight Till We Win Or Die
You Shall Have A Shalimar

MARSHALL, Edward 1824–1904
Adolphus Brown
Enchanted Hash, The (sk. and mon.)
Excursion Train, The
Gendarmes' Duet (w. Felix BURY)
I'm Sister To The Cure
In The Park (parody of In The
    Strand)
John Bull—They Don't Bamboozle
    Me
Last Man In Town, The
London Dundreary
Mayfair Policeman, The
Selina Sly

MARTIN-HARVEY, Sir John 1863–1944
Conspiracy, The (sk.)

Rouget De L'Isle (sk.)
Taming Of The Shrew, The
(condensed)

MARTIN-HARVEY, Lady *see* DE SILVA,
Nina

MARTINETTIS, THE fl. 1875–*c.*1910;
Paul (1851–1924/5), Pauline
(1845–1927), Albert (1865–98), Clare (d.
1945), Julien (1821–84); also Alf,
Desiree, Philippe. Family sketch troupe
not to be confused with the earlier Mar-
tinettes. Personnel incl. Charles Wilford
(Dukes) (1845–87)
    After A Masquerade Ball
    Duel In The Snow
    Keyhole, The
    Magic Flute, The
    Night Of Terror, A
    Paris By Night
    Remorse
    Robert Macaire
    Village Schoolmaster, The

MARX BROTHERS, THE (FOUR/THREE)
Chico (Leonard: 1886–1961), Harpo
(Adolph: 1888–1964), Groucho (Julius:
1890–1977), Gummo (Milton:
1893–1977), Zeppo (Herbert: 1901–79).
See also MASCOTS, THE SIX (MUSICAL)
    Fun In Hi Skule (School Days) (sk.)
    Home Alone (sk.)

MASCOTS, THE SIX (MUSICAL) fl.
*c.*1907–10 a.k.a. The Three (Four)
    Nightingales. Est. Minnie Marx
    (1864–1929) w. sister Hannah and
    various sons later k.a. The
    (Four/Three) MARX BROTHERS.
    Minnie's brother was Al Shean° of
    GALLAGHER & SHEAN. Unrelated
    Nightingales included Lou Levey
    and Janie O'Riley; a non-family
    Mascot was Paul Yale. Gummo left
    the act 1918 and Zeppo in the late
    1930s
    Darling Nellie Gray

How'd You Like To Be My Little
    Sweetheart?
Mandy Lane
Peasie Weasie

MASON, Alf° 1865–1948
    Castles In The Air
    She Couldn't Swallow Me
    Street Minstrel, The

MASON, Fred 1865–95
    Down Petticoat Lane
    I Tickled Her Under The Chin
    It Makes You Careful, Doesn't It?
    It's Rather Early, Isn't It?
    Married And Settled
    Whoa, Polly

MATTHEWS, H. P.
    Charming Man, The
    Dear Me, Is That Possible?
    Fancy Yourself In His Place
    Forgetful Man, The
    Ha! Ha! Ha! (Scott-Gatty)
    I Never Do
    It's My Turn Next
    Leave It To Me
    Lord Mayor's Coachman, The (The
        Man Who Knew How To Drive)
    Policeman B
    Tam O'Shanter Hat, The
    What Shall We Do With Cyprus?
    When She Says She Will, She Does!
    Wonderful Musician

MATTHEWS, Tom 1805–89
    Hot Codlins
    Life Of A Clown, The
    Typitywitchet

MAUDE, Cyril 1862–1951; m. Winifred
EMERY
    French As He Is Spoke (sk.)
    Jellicoe And The Fairy (sk.) (w. Elise
        CRAVEN)
    Playwright, The (sk.) (w. Winifred
        EMERY)
    Sairey Gamp (sk.)

MAUDE, Little *see* **FORDE**, Maude

MAVIUS, Gladys
Another Little Girl In Your Eye
Boy Blue
By The Old Fireside
Coon Ambassador, The
D'You Know My Girl?
England's The Place For Me
I Never Reply
It's No Use You Hanging Up Your Hat
Round Here!
Jeannie McGregor
Just A Sprig Of Holly
Kiss Your Own Scotch Laddie
Let's Go Home Together!
Mr No One From No Where
My Little Prairie Flower!
One Little Girl To Love Me
Primrose Time
Rose, With Her Sunday Smile
Sailing Home On My Schooner
What's The Use Of An Old Log-Cabin
To Me?
When The Leaves Are Falling
Why Shouldn't I Love My Little
Girl?
Why Should We Wait Till We're Old?
Will You Be My Eskimo?
Won't They Be Glad To See Me!

MAY, Daisy
As On Their Wedding Day
I Do It For Him Now
When Bill Can't Graft

MAY, Edna 1878–1948
Call Round Again
Clytie
Come To St George's
Cupid And the Maiden
Daughters Of The Guard, The
Dear Little Baby
Follow On, Follow On
In Gay Mayfair
In Montezuma
Mamie, I've A Little Canoe

My Cosey Corner Girl (w. George
GROSSMITH jun.)
Purity Brigade, The
They All Follow Me

MAYBRICK, Michael 1844–1913; a.k.a.
Stephen Adams°
Holy City, The
Little Hero
Midshipmite, The
Miller's Daughter, The
Nancy Lee
Sailor's Dance, The
Sir Brian The Bold
Sprung A Leak
True Blue
Warrior Bold, A

MAYDUE, Alice° *c.*1870–?; m. (Patrick)
Joe Maccabe of THE TWO MACS
Girl I Love, The
I Don't Know
Katie Molloy
Little Annie Rooney
My Bride
No English Need Apply
Old Dock Gate
Queen He Swore To Serve, The
Rorty 'Ria Brown
Sandy Boy (Hooch Aye)
She's Not A Princess
Stowaway, The (The Little Hero)
Strike Me With A Baby In My Arms
Thereby Hangs A Tale
Umble-Tay
Woman's Revenge, A
You're Always Welcome

MAYER, Daisy
Ain't You Gwine To Let Me Say
'Good-Bye'?
I Don't Love A-Nobody
I'll Be True To My Honey Boy
In My Dear Old Home Tonight
Pretty Coloured Picture
Red Hot Member, A (Oh! Dem
Colored Ladies)

MAYNARD, Harry
Down By The Beautiful Sea
Fighting For The Red White And
Blue
Gallant Little Bugler
I Had A Wife
My Wife
You Don't Catch Me, Daddy

MAYNE, Clarice (and 'THAT')
1886–1966; orig. k.a. Clarice Mabelle; m.
(1) James W. TATE, k.a. 'THAT' (dec'd);
(2) Teddy Knox (1896–1974) of Nervo &
Knox
Ain't We Got Fun?
Alexander's Rag-Time Band
All O' The Time
All Round The Clock
Anywhere In The World With You
Blushing Moon
Broken Doll, A
Come And Cuddle Me
Come Over The Garden Wall
Dearie Mine
Ev'ry Little While
Faces
From One Till Two I Dream Of You
Georgie Took Me Walking In The
Park
Give Me A Little Cosy Corner
I Love You
I'm Longing For Someone To Love
Me
Incidents
In The Days Of Good Queen Bess
It's Lovely To Be In Love
I've Got My Eye On You
I Was A Good Little Girl Till I Met
You
Jenny MacGregor
Jere-Jeremiah
Joan! Joan! Joan! Come Home!
Joshu-ah
Mr & Mrs Smith
My Water Lily

Never Mind
Nursie-Nursie
Oh, Those Naughty Eyes
Oh, You Beautiful Doll
Parasol For Two, A (parody of A
Paradise For Two)
Poppy
Pretty Patty's Proud Of Her Pink Print
Petticoat
Put On Your Tat-Ta, Little Girlie!
Queen Of The Orchard
Sadie
She Didn't Come From Borneo
Smiles (Callahan: Roberts)
Somewhere In France With You
Tale Of A Hat, The
Viewing The Baby
When Mr Smith Was In And Mrs
Smith Was Out
When The Midnight Choo Choo
Leaves For Alabam'
Will He Answer 'Goo Goo'?
Will You Promenade With Me?
You've Grown Tired Spooning With
Me

MAYNE, Ernie* 1871–1937
And The Fog Grew Thicker And
Thicker
Back Home In Tennessee (parody)
Breakfast, Dinner And Tea
Chip And Fish
Cupid
Doubles (And That Went Down)
Down On The Farm (parody of I
Want To Go Back To Michigan)
Eat Less Bread
Everyone Calls Me Tarzan
Goosey, Goosey, Gander
I Can't Do My Bally Bottom Button
Up
I Do Like A Little Bit Of Turkey At
Christmas Time
I Like A C'Hup Of Co'Hocoa
I've Never Wronged An Onion

Lloyd George's Beer
Love! Love!! Love!!!
My Mary
My Meatless Day
My Wife's A Luxury
My Wife's First Husband
My Wife's My Wife
Nobody Loves A Fat Man
Oh, I'm So Simple
Oh, The Kharki!
Peep-a-bo!
Plenty Of Pudden
She Pushed Me Into The Parlour
Ten Little Fingers, Ten Little Toes
There Are Millions Of People
We Used To Gather At The Old Dun
   Cow
What D'Yer Think Of That? (My Old
   Man's A Dustman)
What I Want Is A Proper Cup Of
   Coffee
Where Do Flies Go In The Winter-
   Time?
Wireless On The Brain
You Can't Get Many Pimples On A
   Pound Of Pickled Pork

MAYO, Sam° 1875–1938; brother of Ted
COWAN
   At A Minute To Seven Last Night
   Baby, Baby
   Bom! Bom! Bom! Zim! Zim! Zim!
   Chinaman, The
   Ching Chang Wing Wang
   Clap Hands, Daddy's Coming Home
   Didn't I? Wasn't I?
   Doctor's Advice (I Do Like A Blow On
      The Sea)
   Doh, Ray, Me, Fah, Soh, Lah, Te, Doh
   Eskimo, The
   Fiddle-De-Diddle-De-De
   Fireman, The
   Futurist Pictures
   Gone Where They Don't Play Billiards
   I Don't Care What Becomes Of Me

   (Campbell & David: Mayo)
   I Don't Care What Becomes Of Me
      (Mills: Scott)
   I Feel Very Very Bad
   I'm Going To Sing A Song
   I'm Here, If I'm Wanted
   Incidents And Accidents
   I Never Stopped Running Till I Got
      Home
   I Played My Concertina
   I've Only Come Down For The Day
   I Went To Sleep Again
   Johnnie *or* Johnny
   Kind Friends
   Listen To Me And I'll Prove That I'm
      Right
   Little By Little And Bit By Bit
   Lost Of Littles Make A Lot
   Most Miserable Man On Earth, The
   My Little Dog Was With Me All The
      While
   Night Watchman
   Old Tin Can, The
   One-Man Band, The
   Oof! Oof! Oof! Oof! Oof!
   Policeman, The (I'm Here If I'm
      Wanted)
   Programmes!
   Pushing Young Man, The
   She Cost Me Seven-and-Sixpence
   Stop! Stop! Stop!
   Tally Ho
   Then The Night Began To Fall
   Ting-A-Ling-Ting
   Toreador, The
   Trumpet Song, The
   When I Woke Up This Morning
   Widow, The
   Would You Like To Know The
      Reason?

MELBA, Dame Nellie 1861–1931
   Banks Of Allan Water, The
   Dawn, The
   Down In The Forest

Home! Sweet Home!
Invitation
Lo! Here The Gentle Lark
O For The Wings Of A Dove (Hear
   My Prayer)
Sing, Sweet Bird
Softly Awakes My Heart

MELFORD, Mark° (& Co.) 1851–1914;
sketch troupe
   Best Man Wins
   Between The Acts
   Blackberries
   Bottled Bequest, The
   Coming Clown, The
   Desperation
   Frantic Fanatic, A
   Frivolity
   Hampshire Hog, The (Never Say
      Die)
   Jim's Little Joke
   Kleptomania
   Midnight Charge, A
   Militant Crusader, A
   Millionaire For A Minute
   My Wife Won't Let Me
   Non-Suited
   Once A Year
   Ransomed
   Ratts [sic]
   Rope Merchant, The
   Secrets Of The Police
   Tale Of A Tigress
   Turned Up
   What For?
   Young Pretender, The

MELVILLE, Harry d. 1 Oct. 1898
   I'm Going To Be A Professional
   Once More In The Dear Old Land
   Spare The Old Mud Cabin
   Tipperary Christening, The

MELVIN, G. S. 1886–1946; orig. k.a.
Hugh Donovan
   Drowned
   Gladys The Girl Guide

Hussars, The
I Like To Jump Upon A Bike
I'm Happy When I'm Hiking

**MERRILEES' ARMOUR-CLAD FEMALE
CHRISTYS, Andy** fl. 1871–c.1881; prop.
Andy Merrilees (1841–1904)
   Affectionate Tear, The
   Beautiful Nelly
   Erin, The Memory Sweet Of Thee
   Gallant Soldier, The
   I'm Thinking Of Thee Mother
   I Sleep To Dream Again Of Thee
   Lost Claribel
   'Neath The Daisies She Is Sleeping
   Once Again In Dear Old Scotland
   On, Still On
   Song Of Freedom, The
   Sweet Sing The Little Birds
   Victoria, Empress Of India
   Weep Not Mother For Your Darling

MERRITT, James 1850–1908; chairman
and manager of Crowder's Music Hall
   I'd Rather You Than Me
   I Wonder How Long It Will Be
   That's My Firm Opinion

MERRY MACS, THE see **MACS, THE
TWO**

MERRY, Mark°
   Have You Noticed The Paper Today?
   Me!
   No. No. No.
   What Would Be The Use Of Them To
      Me?

MERRYLEES, James 1868–1902
   All Through The Rain
   Captain Of The Dry-Land Tars
   Eliza The Mesmerizer
   Follow Your Leader
   I Can't Remember
   Keep On The Sunny Side
   Naethin' At A'!
   Pilot, The
   Sing A Song To Me, Mother

Sweethearts Still
Where Does True Happiness Lie?

MERSON, Billy° 1881–1947; a.k.a. Ping Pong
Come On, My Baby (w. Shirley **KELLOGG**)
Gay Cavalier, The
I'm Going Away
I'm Setting The Village On Fire
Lighthouse Keeper, The (Merson)
Night I Appeared As Macbeth, The
On The Good Ship 'Yacki Hicki Doo La'
Out On The Prairie
Photo Of The Girl I Left Behind, The
Setting The Village On Fire
Signora
Spaniard That Blighted My Life, The (orig. w. Beatrice **ALLEN**, later w. Dorothy **MINTO** and w. Ida **VALLI**)
Wi-Ki-Walla-Walla-Ooh-Ba-Bay

MICHAELIS, Robert 1884–1965
White Dove, The

MIDNIGHT MINSTRELS
We All Went Up Up Up The Mountain

MIKES, THE TWO
I Lent £10 To Callaghan
You Get There Just The Same

MILBURN, J. H. (Jem) d. March 1923; father-in-law of G. H. **MACDERMOTT**
All Among The Hay
As Good As Gold
At Our House
Autumn Leaves
Barnacles
Chums (My Old Pal Jim)
Come Along Boys, Let's Make A Noise
Croquet
Doolan's Farm
Dora Dene

Home! Sweet Home! Up To Date
How Did You Lose Your Arm?
I Can't Make It Out, Can You?
I Can't Pull It Off
I Feel So Happy Just Now
If You Meet Her
Lay Me On My Little Bed (parody)
Moonlight Walk, The
Mr Funny Face
Old Mulberry Tree, The
One Bright October Morning
On The Banks Of The Beautiful Severn
On The Beach At Brighton
Pull Yourselves Together, Boys
Shan't I Be Glad When Sally Comes Home
Sound Advice *or* What To Eat, Drink, And Avoid
Tripe Topsy
What Is That Without Any Hands?
Women, The

MILL, Paul° 1863–1916
And—There You Are
Are We Downhearted? No! (Robins)
Better Than Going To Work
Bye Bye Betsy
Coster Othello, The
Don't You Remember?
German Bandsman, The
Good For Trade
How Pa And Ma Differ
I Can Never Make Up My Mind
Isn't It Wonderful?
Isn't That Like A Man?
Leo Brown
Maid In The Lowther Arcade, The
Man In Possession, The
Patchwork Garden, The
Penelope
Penny Whistler, The
Poetry *v.* Truth
Sixpenny Pops
That Isn't A Bad Idea (w. Ambrose **THORNE**)

That's How They Spend The Day
Tut-Tut! (Mill)
Village Of Toad-In-The-Hole, The
What's The Matter With Me?
Why, Of Course! (w. Will EDWARDS)
You Never Know
You Will Excuse Me, Won't You?

MILLAR, Gertie 1879–1952; m. (1)
Lionel Monckton° (dec'd); (2) Earl of
Dudley
   Captivating Cora
   Chalk Farm To Camberwell Green
   Come Along With Me To The Zoo
    Dear
   Come To The Ball
   Do You Know Mr Schneider?
   I'm The Fool Of The Family
   I've Come Along To Paris For A
    Change
   Keep Off The Grass
   Little Mary
   Liza Ann
   Maisie (Was A Daisy)
   Moonstruck
   Neville Was A Devil
   Oh! Take Care Of Little Mary
   Quaker Girl, A
   Tony From America
   Toy Town
   Two Little Sausages (w. Edmund
    PAYNE)
   We Never Do That In Yorkshire

MILLARD, Evelyn 1870–1941
   Adventure Of Lady Ursula, The (sk.)
   Madame Butterfly (sk.)
   My Friend Thomas Atkins (sk.)

MILLER, Ruby 1889–1976; m. (1) Lieut.
Philip Samson (k.i.a. 1918), (2) Max
Darewski (1894–1929)
   Between Five And Seven
   Man In The Street, The (sk.)
   Woman Intervenes, The (sk.)

MILLIS, Fred° 1858–1913;
ventriloquist—names are of his dummies

For England! The Colonies' Message
O'Reilly Knows 'Em (Terence
   O'Reilly)
When We're Dead And Gone (Brother
   Zachariah)

MILLS, Florence c.1895–1927
   I'm Just Wild About Harry

MILLS, Horace 1864–1941
   Epitaphs!
   Little Bit Of Something Else, A
   Virtue Rewarded

MILLS, R. Watkin 1849–1930
   Curfew, The
   Father O'Flynn
   Glorious Devon
   Skye Boat Song
   Speed On My Bark
   Trumpeter, The
   Wi' A Hundred Pipers
   Yeoman's Wedding Song, The

MILTON, Mark d. 1923?
   Exchange Is No Robbery
   For Further Evidence
   Have A Game
   I'll Pay You When My Ship Comes
    Home
   Insurance Man Like His Father, The
   Off His On-i-on
   Take Me There

MINTO, Dorothy b. 1893; m. Shiel
Barry jun. (1883–1916) k.i.a.
   Spaniard That Blighted My Life, The
    (w. Billy MERSON)

MOHAWK MINSTRELS fl. 1867–1900;
est. James FRANCIS and brother William
(1844–1908). Fully professional 1873;
from 1874 troupe incl. Harry HUNTER,
as 'Mr Interlocutor' and principal song-
writer. In 1900 merged w. MOORE &
BURGESS MINSTRELS. See also BARNES,
Sydney; BIRCHMORE, Tom; COLLETTE,
Charles; DREDGE, Robert; DURIAH, F.;
FRANCIS, Harry; FRANCIS, James;

GORDON, Ernest; HOWARD, Walter;
LAWSON, Warren; OLIVER, Roland;
RUSSON, F.; SNOW, Ted; THOMAS,
Funny Little. Names in brackets
are soloists
  Alone In The World (Master Freddy
    Bentley)
  Anglo-Saxon, The
  Baby Boy Has Passed Away
  Balaclava
  Believe Me, If All Those Endearing
    Young Charms
  Better Be Good Than Be Great
  Big Six, The
  Boy's Best Friend Is His Mother, A
    (J. Fuller)
  Boys Of The Queen's Navee
  Boys Who Fighting Fell, The
  Charleston Blues, The
  Close The Shutters, Willie's Dead
  Colorado Beetle's Come, The
  Curfew Shall Not Ring Tonight, The
  Day I Marry Lucie, The
  Dear Old 'Bobs'
  Dear Old Shady Lane, The (C.
    Temple)
  Doctor Of The Regiment, The
  Do Not Nurse Your Anger
  Don't Linger Round (Charles Kellen)
  Don't You Cry For Me, Dear Mother
  Dotlet In The I
  Down By The River Side I Stray (J.
    Kavanagh)
  Drum-Major, The (Cyrus Bell)
  Farrier, The
  Fun Of The Fair
  God Protect England
  Grandfather's Clock (My) (J. B.
    Ferrell)
  Grandmother's Cat
  Green Lanes Of England, The
  Harp That Once Through, Tara's
    Halls, The
  How Nice And Fat You Are
  Hurry Little Children
  I'd Rather Lather Father, Than Father

  Lathered Me
  I Have Sent A Loving Message
  In The Old Time, Mary (Charles
    Linwood)
  Jeanie With The Light Brown Hair
  Keep A Movin'
  Kiss Me Goodbye Darling
  Last Little Word That Baby Said
  Lay Of The Last Lunatic Minstrel,
    The
  Let Me Kiss Your Tears Away
  Little Bobby's Dead
  Little Sweetheart Come And Kiss Me
  Minstrel Boy, The
  Molly Mine
  Mother's Tender Love, A
  Mulligan Guards, The
  My Dear Old Cabin Home
  My Nellie's Blue Eyes (Fuller)
  Nein! Nein! Nein! (Will Parker)
  Never Be Ashamed Of Your Mother
    (Bentley)
  Nobody Knows The Words
  Nuffin Hurts Me
  Oh Dem Golden Slippers
  Oh, Let Me Call Thee Mine (George
    Eustace)
  Old Rustic Bridge By The Mill, The
    (C. Chivers)
  Only A Pansy Blossom
  On Monday I Met Mary Ann
  On The Way To Woolloomooloo
  Patty Pan Wants A Nice Young Man
    (Tony Weller)
  Queen Of My Life (Linwood)
  Remember You Have Children Of
    Your Own
  Scotch Lassie Jean (Fuller)
  See That My Grave's Kept Green
  She Deceived Her Johnny
  Sister's Good-Bye, A
  Sit By Me Mother (Last Words)
  Skaters, The
  Somebody Whispered So Sweetly
  Some Of Each
  Someone To Say Good Bye To (Fuller)

Song Of The Little Lame Boy, The
Song That Reached My Heart (T.
   Campbell)
Still I Love Thee
Sweet Genevieve
Sweet Violets (Fuller)
Take It Off! (Fred Lynne)
Taking Out The Baby (Parker)
Tam O' Shanter Hat, The (F. Durian)
Tears Are Blessings, Let Them Flow
There's A Light At The Window
There's Going To Be A Wedding
Thinking Of The Olden Time
Tommy Atkins' Return
Tread Softly The Little One's Sleeping
'Twas Love That Gave Birth To The
   Tear (Frank Elsworth)
Twilight (Elsworth)
Up Dargai's Heights
Victoria's Victory
Waiting With A Welcome (George
   Rendall)
We Cannot See Our Own Fault
We're Growing Old Together
Where's That Nigger, Josey?
Whist! The Bogie Man
White Wings

MONKHOUSE, Harry 1854–1901
   Foolish Flossy
   Henrietta, Have You Met Her?
   I'm Getting A Big Boy Now
   Jimmy On The Chute

MONKMAN, Phyllis 1892–1976; m. Lad-
die CLIFF
   Extra Special Constable, The
   Have You Forgotten? (w. Jack
      HULBERT)
   We'll Go To Church On Sunday (w.
      Laddie CLIFF)

MONKS, Victoria 1885/90–1927
   Ain't I No Use, Mr Jackson?
   Ain't The Old Place Good Enough For
      You?

Ain't Yer Gwine To Say How Do?
All Aboard For London Town
Bill Bailey, Won't You Please Come
   Home?
Bombay
Brown Eyes *or* Eyes Of Blue
Buy Me A Home In London
Call Round Any Old Time
Can't You Hear Me Calling, Mr
   Primrose Brown?
Come Along With Me
Don't Tell Your Pals Your Troubles
Enjoy Yourself
Give Me A Cosy Parlour
Give My Regards To Leicester Square
Hello, Old Man!
Hullo! Miss London
I Ain't A-Going To Leave Home In
   The Rain
I'd Like To Go On A Honeymoon
I Do Feel So Lonely
If I Could Only Say In French What
   I'm Thinking In English
If You Want To Have A Row Wait Till
   The Sun Shines
I Love But Only One And That Is You
   see Love Song
I'm Going Home (*or* I'se Gwine Back)
   To Jacksonville
I'm Going To Get My Own Back
I'm Leaving Home
I Never Lose My Temper
Is London Like It Used To Be?
It's Not So Much The Waltz Dream As
   Her Dreamy Eyes
I Wish I Had A Pal Like You
Judgement Day
Just Because She Made Dem Goo-
   Goo Eyes
Kaiser Bill
Let's Be Merry And Bright
Liberty Hall
Little Bit The Boys Admire, The
Love Song *or* Victoria Monks' Love
   Song *see* I Love But Only One etc.
Meet Me In Rose-Time

Men, Why Live In Lodgings?
Milk O!
Moving Day
My Daddy is Wonderful
My Little Eva
My Sumurun Girl
Never Turn Your Back Upon A Fellow
New York, London Or Paris
Pompeii
Riding In A Motor Car
Sandy Boy
Say Hello, Old Man
Sneezing Song *see* Won't You Come
    Down etc.
Sweet Saturday Night
Take Me Back To London Town
Take Me Back To My Home, Sweet
    Home
That Door Was Made For To Keep
    You Out
That Vicky Glide
There's A Girl In Berlin
There's A Girl Inside
Tickle Me
We've Got A Navy, A British Navy
What Do We Care, We Two?
When Big Ben Strikes (as Little
    Victoria)
When You're Out Of Sight You're Out
    Of Mind
Why Do You Keep Knocking At Dat
    Door?
Will You Come Back To Bom-Bom-
    Bay?
Won't You Come Down And Open
    Dat Door? (A-Chew)
You Ain't Got The Girl Till The Ring
    Is On Her Finger
You Didn't Want To Do It But You
    Did
You Might Shake Hands

MONTAGU, Edward° d. 5 Feb. 1975;
sometimes spelled Montague
    My Best Gal's Gone And Left Me
    On The Dear Old Shore

MONTAGUE, Harold° b. 1874; wrote
most of his own material
    Artful Coon, The
    Castles In Spain
    Country Cousin, The (I Saw Esau
        Kissing Kate)
    Do You Follow Me?
    Handy Little Thing To Have About
        You, A
    Lady And The Dog, The
    Learning To Ride The Byke
    My Beastly Eyeglass
    Never Mind Posers
    Really? Yass. Great Scott!
    Someone Should Speak To Him
        Gently
    Those Nose
    When Maud Put Her New Bathing
        Costume On

MONTAGUE, J. H.
    Beneath The Linden Trees (w. Marie
        WILTON)

MONTROE, Marie
    Br-Oom-De-Doo-Dum
    Oh! Love Is A Passion
    Why Wasn't I Born A Boy?

MOODY, John 1814–52
    Good St Anthony
    Lord Tom Noddy (Seven Ages)

MOON, Nellie d. 2 July 1907
    Boy In Yellow, The
    Girl In The Tight-Fitting Jersey,
        The
    Here Stands A Post
    We Two (w. Topsy VENN)

MOONEY & HOLBEIN Harry(?) Mooney
(1889–1972) & ? Holbein
    Delaney's Donkey

MOORE, Alec
    Curtain Drops, The
    I've Got Room For Another One
    I Will Be There
    Lum Tum Diddley Um

Moral Maiden A
Sleeping In The Air

MOORE, Carrie 1883–1956
Bravo, Territorials
Green Ribbon, The
Sandow Girl, The

MOORE, Decima 1871–1964
Barney In Connemara
Come Apricots On Garden Walls
Goblin And The Fay, The
Honey, Love Me Do
My Mary, The Hielan' Fishwife (sk.)
   (w. Myles ANSON)
White Silk Dress, The

MOORE, G. W. 'Pony'[*] 1820–1909;
father-in-law of Eugene STRATTON. See
also MOORE & BURGESS MINSTRELS
Ada With The Golden Hair
Baby Don't You Cry
Before The Baby Wakes
Comical Ghosts, The
Dress'd In A Dolly Varden
Fannie Fancied A Fancy Man
Grecian Bend, The
High, Low Or Jack Game
Hunky Dorum or She Lived With Her
   Mother In Camden Town
Mixed Up Family, The
My Darling Angelina
Oh, Dem Golden Slippers
Oh, I'd Like To Be A Bird
Oh, Johnny, You're In Luck This
   Morning
Over On The Surrey Side
Patrick, Mind The Baby
Plum Pudding, The
Pretty Little Girl That I Know, The
Shew! Fly or I Feel Like A Morning
   Star
Tapioca
Ten Little Nigger Boys, The
U-Pi-Dee
Valley By The Stream, The
When Johnny Comes Marching Home

MOORE & BURGESS MINSTRELS fl.
1864–1903; orig. Moore & Crocker
Christy Minstrels. Est. G. W. 'Pony'
MOORE w. Frederick Burgess (1826–93)
& Joseph P. Crocker (d. 1869). Became
MOORE & BURGESS MINSTRELS 1871;
c.1873 proclaimed themselves 'Formerly
Original CHRISTY MINSTRELS'; 1900
merged w. MOHAWK MINSTRELS. See
also BIRCHMORE, Tom; LESLIE, William;
DREDGE, Tom; HOWARD, Walter;
OAKLAND, Will; RAEBURN, Sam. Names
in brackets are soloists
After Toiling Cometh Rest
Beautiful Dreamer
Belle Brandon
Beside The Sweet Shannon
Bicycle Belle, A
Blow The Bellows, O!
Boy's Best Friend Is His Mother, A
Brannigan's Band
Break It Gently To My Mother
Buckles On Her Shoes, The
Come Where The Nightingale's
   Trilling
Coon From The Moon, The
Daisies Gently Wave (Her Angel Form
   Reposes)
Daisy Darling
Day When You'll Forget Me
De Comin' Ob De King
Down The Stream
Emancipation Day (Charles Sutton)
Extra! Extra!
Five Little Pigs
Flight Of The Birds, The
Gentle Flowers
Get Up Jack, John Sit Down
Giddy Old Owl, The
Grandfather's Clock
Grogan The Masher
Haunting Eyes
Have I Not Been Kind To Thee
Hello-Bab-by (Dave Braham)
Henrietta Pye
Her Front Name Was Hannah

Honey, Does Yer Love Yer Man
Honey, Love Me Do
I Don't Think I'll Say Any More
I'll Be Waiting For You At The
   Window
I'll Sail The Seas Over For Thee
I'll Speak To You Gladly Again
I'm Going Out To Tea To Tooting
I'm Waiting For A Letter, Love
Johnny Get Your Gun
Josephus Orange Blossom
Kiss Me Mother Ere I Die
Kitty Wells
Last Look, A
Letter That Never Came, The
Lilly Dale
Little Church Round The Corner, The
Little Flo'
Little Maggie May
Little Sunshine
Mamie, Come Kiss Yo' Honey Boy
Mammy's Carolina Twins (Arthur
   Gallimore)
Man That Knows It All, The
Mary My Own (Thomas Campbell)
Might Have Been, The
Molly
Money, The Money For Me, The
Monkey's Courtship, The
Mother's Rustic Rocking Chair
Mother To Her Child, The
Mottoes That Are Frames Upon The
   Wall, The
Mr Dooley's Geese
Mulligan Guards
Must We Then Meet As Strangers
My Coal Black Lady
My Lily
My Own Darling Kate
Off To Brighton
Oh! Gently Breathe The Tender Sigh
Oh! Would I Were A Bird
Old Log Cabin In The Lane, The
Old Settee By The Door
One At Home Who Thinks Of Me
   (Louis Rainford, d. 26 Nov. 1923)

On His Geranium (Walter Norman)
Only A Flower There
Only A Kiss And Goodbye (Campbell)
Only A Pansy Blossom
Orphan Boy, The (Mother, How I
   Love That Name) (Mr Poynter)
Pat And His Little Brown Mare
Patrick, Mind The Baby
Picture 84
Please Give a Penny, Sir
Please God Make Room For A Little
   Child
Please To Put That Down
Remember You Have Children Of
   Your Own
See That My Grave's Kept Green
She Sleeps Beneath The Daisies
Shew! Fly *or* I Feel Like A Morning
   Star
Side by Side The Old Folks Sleep
Silver Threads Among The Gold
Soft Twilight's Here
Song Of The Brotherhood, The
Speak, Only Speak
Sweetest Story Ever Told, The
Sweetheart I Am Coming Home
Sweet Lurline
Sweet, Sunny Smile Of My Darling,
   The
Tenting On The Old Camp Ground
There Are Kisses Waiting For Me
They Come As A Dream
True As The Stars That Are Shining
Under The Daisies
Wait Till The Bus Rolls By, John
   (parody of next entry)
Wait Till The Clouds Roll By
Watching For Pa (Vernon Reed)
When The Tide Comes In
White Wings
Yaller Girl That Winked At Me, The
Yes, Mary, Your Father's Come Home

MOORE, William R. w. HAVERLY'S
MASTODON MINSTRELS
   Sweet Adeline

MOORE-DUPREZ, May *see* DUPREZ, May Moore

MORA, Helene *c.*1861–1903; 'female baritone'
Actions Speak Louder Than Words
After The Ball
Comrades
Don't You Like To Play With Little Baby?
Down Where The Cotton Blossoms Grow
Holy City, The
Kathleen
Little Boy In Green, The
Moth And The Flame, The
One Night In June
One Touch Of Nature Makes The Whole World Kin
Those Lost Happy Days
Those Weddings Bells Shall Not Ring Out

MORGAN, Lloyd 1892–1970
Bedelia
By The Shores Of The Mediterranean
Egypt
Rollicking Rajah, The

MORLEY, Victor 1871–1953
How'D'Ya Like To Spoon With Me? (w. Georgia CAINE)

MORRELL, Frank 1877–1925
All That I Ask Of You Is Love
Down By The Old Mill Stream (Taylor)

MORRIS, Lily 1882–1952
A-Be, My Boy (recorded 1919 w. GROCK)
Dear Old Mr Pom Pom
Don't Have Any More, Missus Moore
Fly Away, Pretty Bird
Getting Married Tomorrow Morning
Have You Seen My Soldier Boy?
Home Again, My Cherry Blossom
I'll Buy A Mangle, Polly
I Love My Motherland
I'm A Poor Little Beggar In England
I Want To Stay Just As I Am
I Was Born With A Spoon In My Mouth
I Wonder If You Miss Me Sometimes (I Wonder If You Care)
Just The Same As Dolly Does
Kiss Me, My Honey
Lardi-Doody-Day
Little Wosie Posie
Major Puff 'Em
Minnetonka
Old Apple Tree, The
Only A Working Man
Ro-me-o And Juliet
See You Later
Sing Us A Song Of Bonnie Scotland
Smith, Jones, Robinson And Brown
Take Me Back To Dear Old Blighty
That's Where The Soldiers Go
That's Why I Love You
There's The Wee White Heather Growing
Truly Rural
Turned Up
Way To Kiss A Girl, The
What Are You Going To Do About Selena?
Who Does The Lady Belong To?
Why Am I Always The Bridesmaid?
Wipe Your Feet Before You Go In
You'll Always Meet A Son O' Bonnie Scotland

MORTIMER, Maude d. Oct. 1922
Colleen Bawn
Daisy Day
Down By The Ferry
Do You Miss Me In The Dear Homeland?
Fairies, Fairies
Good-Bye Little Girl Good-Bye
He Wants Every Girl
Hold Me Just A Little Bit Tighter
If I Should Plant A Tiny Seed Of Love

I'll Meet You At The Bodega
It's A Long, Long Way To Tipperary
It's A Poor Heart That Never Rejoices
I've Made Up My Mind To Sail Away
I Wonder If The Girl I'm Thinking Of
   Is Thinking Of Me
Just As The Brook Flows
La La La
Last Christmas Day
Let's Have A Song About The Boys
My Boys
My Flo From Pimlico
My Little Persian Rose
My Sweetheart And My Wife
Oh, Oh, Oh!
Sunday Morning Band, The
Sweetheart Come Back Again
When The Blue Moon Shines
Why Won't You Let Me Kiss You?
You Can't Stop The Sun From Shining
You Go Your Way

MOSEDALE, E. (Teddy) 1838–1908
My Chestnut 'Orse
My Isabelle
Nancy Fancied A Soldier
Our Bill
Sarah
What Have You Done With Your
   Overtime?

Moss, W. F. 1855–1946
Blind Leading The Blind, The
Football *or* Misery And Mud
I Was On It
Relations
Relic Of Bygone Days, A
Servants' Ball, The
That's Where The Trouble Begins
Too-Roo-Loor-Lay

MOXON, Constance fl. *c*.1890; m.
CRAVEN, Tom
Binks The Actor
By Their Language
For The Crown
George, Dear!

Hands Across The Sea
He Was Born To Be A Gentleman
I'd Like One Like Pa Had Yesterday
I'll Keep It There Till Father Comes
   Home!
It Comes Quite Natural
I Want One Like Pa Had Yesterday
Liberty Hall
Like A Girl
Milk O! *or* The Up-To-Date Yodeller
Mother, Mother, What Am I To Do?
Side By Side (Woods)
Toff For Ten Minutes, A
Twinkle Twinkle Little Star
What Did It Cost To Paint It?
Whistling Bluecoat Boy, The

MOZART, George 1864–1947
Callers
Colonel Nutty Of The Nuts (sk.)
Coney Ragtimer (also sundry other
   'Coney' songs)
Day At The Races, A (sk.)
Derby Day
Family Party, The (sk.)
Flash-Light Express, The
If I, If I, If I, If I, If I, If I Do
Old Hats
Quack Physician, The
Soldier And A Maid, A (sk.)

MULLANE, Frank
All That I Ask Of You Is Love
Dear Old Girl
I Want To Go Back To Michigan

MUNROE, 'Viscount' Walter d. 23 Aug.
1914
After The Ball (parody)
Agricultural Irish Girl, The
Beautiful Language
Best Man, The
Blue Spotted Handkerchief, The
Boys Of The Emerald Isle
Bridget MacCarthy
Colleen Dhu
Connemara

Consequence, The
Earl Of Fife, The
18th Royal Irish Brigade, The
Electric Railway, The
Ennis (When Burke Put Up For
   Mayor)
Famous In Love, Famous In War
Gallant Gordons, The
Gilhooly's Supper Party
Girls Of Our Empire, The
Grandfather's Darling Boy
He Hadn't Been Used To Luxuries
He Left His Old Woman Behind Him
Hennessey's Fancy Ball
How Go, Mike?
How Rafferty Won The Mile
I Love A Dear Little Lady
Irish Italian Organ Grinder, The *or*
   The Irish Mickey
Irishman's Way, An
Irishmen Must Be There
I Saved It Up For Rafferty
Isn't It A Treat To Be Alive?
Is Your Mother In Molly Malone?
Ivanhoe
Kitty Malony
Lady Killer, The
Leave Your Boots On The Mat
Let Them All Come
Let Us Have A Song We Can All Sing
Lost Her Way
Lum Tum Diddley Um
McGinnis's 'At Home'
Man That Struck O'Hara, The
Mary Ann Maginty (Little Miss
   Muffit)
Molly Now Don't Be Teasing
Monkey And The Masher, The
Monte Carlo (parody)
Mystery Of A Hansom Cab, The
New Man, The
Now The Young Folks Are Away
One Of The Old Brigade
One We Loved So Well, The
Only A Dear Old Bicycle
On The Scroll Of Glory

Patsy Brannigan
Piper's Elopement, The
Roller Skating
Same Irish Nature, The
Search The Page Of History
She'll Be Seventeen On Sunday
She's Fair, She's Young
She's My Little Girl
She Was Standing Upon The Quay
Shillelagh, The
Skating At Olympia
Sweet Rosie O'Grady
That's Why I'm An Irishman
Tim Browne's Race
Time Is Coming, The
True Born Irishman, The
Waiting For Me
Welcome Home
We'll Just Have Another Soyez
We Tossed Up Who Should Kill Him
What Will They Say In England? (A
   Story Of The Gallant 21st)
When The Boys Come Home Again
When You're Tired Of Roaming
You, And I, And All Of Us
You're A Jolly Fine Fellow When Then
   Want You

MURRAY, Billy 1877–1954; see also
HAYD(E)N QUARTET and PEERLESS
QUARTET
   Alexander's Rag-Time Band
   And He'd Say 'Oo-La-La-Wee-Wee!'
   Are You Coming Out Tonight, Mary
      Ann?
   Be My Little Baby Bumble Bee (w.
      Ada JONES)
   Casey Jones
   Come Take A Trip In My Air-Ship
   Cuddle Up A Little Closer (w. JONES)
   Give My Regards To Broadway
   I Am Looking For A Sweetheart (w.
      JONES)
   Little Ford Rambled Right Along, The
   Meet Me In St Louis, Louis
   My Little Dutch Colleen

Oh, You Beautiful Doll
Play A Simple Melody
Take Me Out To The Ball Game
Yankee Doodle Boy, The
You're A Grand Old Flag

MURRAY, Charles m. Ethel VICTOR
Young Country Squire, The
You're Another

MURRAY, Elizabeth
Alabama Jubilee
Don't Ever Come In Without
Knocking
I'm Afraid To Come Home In The
Dark
Put Your Arms Around Me Honey

MURRAY, Slade° 1859–1913
Balaclava (Oh 'Tis A Famous Story)
(Elliott: Murray)
Beautiful Language
But—No More
Charge Of The 21st., The
Come Down And Open The Door,
Love
Far, Far Away
For Ever!
Good Old Mary Ann
Good Young Man Who Died, The
Hard To Say!
Hip, Hooray! For Temperance
I Forget
I Haven't For A Long Time Now
It's All Right But It's Awkward
Oh, Love, Will You Be Mine?
Oh, My! Certainly Not
Oh, She Was Such A Beautiful Girl
One We Loved So Well
Over And Over Again
Poor Poet, The
Rootity-Toot, She Plays The Flute
She Was! She Was!! She Was!!!
'Snip' That Never Returned, The
So He Did
That's When You Feel It
Thought Reading On The Brain

Tim Macarthy's Daughter
Too Late (parody of Macdermott's War
Song)
Waiting For Me
Waiting! Waiting!! Waiting!!!
We Don't Do That In Our Days
When You Come Home In The
Morning
Where Are You Going To My Pretty
Maid
You Should Never Never Marry

MURRAY, Will b. 11 Apr 1877; see
CASEY'S COURT. At one time partnered
Arthur WOODVILLE as The Freans

NAISH, Archie° b. 1878
Band Played On, The (Grey: Naish)
Duck Pond, The
Employment Bureau, The
How Many Beans Make Five?
Made In England
Night Light, The
Sybil
Village Pump, The
Why Don't They Knight Charlie
Chaplin?
Won't You Waltz With Me?

NARES, Owen 1889–1943
Boy Comes Home, The (sk.)
Foolery (sk.)
Smith Family, The (sk.)
Willow Tree, The (sk.)

NASH, 'Jolly' John° 1830–1901; father
of Nance Oldfield (1873–1904)
Baa Baa Baa
Belinda The Market Gardener's
Daughter
Blow Your Own Trumpet
Cigar Girl, The
Come, Let Us Be Gay, Boys (men's
version of The Madcap)
Concertina Man, The
Convivial Man, The
Cork Jacket, The
Don't You Believe It

Downy Old Sparrow, The
Dumplings
Dutch Song
Eccentric Man, The
England, Dear Old England
Frenchman And The Englishman, The
Funny Man, The
Gog And Magog
Go To Putney
Happy Go Lucky *or* Never Say Die
Ho Ho Ho—Hee Hee Hee (a.k.a.
    Little Brown Jug)
Horseflesh Banquet At The Langham
    Hotel
I Always Take It Easy
I Care Not How Fortune May Vary
I Couldn't Help Laughing
I'll Never Have Her Back Again
I'm Not Inquisitive
I'm Such A Jolly Man
I'm Such A Very Lucky Man
I Owe Ten Shillings To O'Grady
It's Coming, Boys, It's Coming
It's The Way Of The World, My Boys
It's Very Different Now
It Tickled Me So
Jog Along Boys
Laughing Gas
Learn On Yourself to Rely
Little Brown Jug (Ho Ho Ho—Hee
    Hee Hee)
Little Fat Grey Man, The
London, Chatham And Dover, The
Man That Played The Cornet, The
Merry And Wise
Merry Funny Little Toper, The
Merry Laughing Man, The
Muldoon's Wedding
Never Give In
Never In This Wide Wide World
Never Say Die
Nice Old Maid
Nobody Knows It But Me
Oh, Wouldn't You Like To Know?
One Hundred Years To Come
One Pound One

Phantom Coach, The *or* The Hyde
    Park Ghost
Racketty Jack
See Me Dance The Polka
Shadow On The Door
Sister Mary Walked Like That
So Mote It Be
Squire And Maria, The
Take It Easy, John
That's How The Fiddling Is Done
This Is How He Laughs
Three Topers, The (Smith, Jones And
    Brown)
Tickling Mad
Tinkling Of The Bells
Tompkins
Tom's Father
Who Cut Your Hair?
Wouldn't You Like To Go?
Young Country Squire, The
Young Man Of The Day

NATHAN, Ben d. 9 May 1919
    Ada's Serenade
    Christmas Carol, A (Dickens reading)
    I'm Blowed If I Can Tell
    My Boy! My Boy!
    Not A Return
    Oh, Albert Chevalier!
    Sauerkraut

NAUDAIN, May 1880–1920
    Glow-Worm, The

NAVETTE, Nellie d. 3 Aug. 1938
    Can't Yer Coon Jine
    De Darkies' Dance
    De Risin' Ob De Moon
    English Lady Cricketers
    My Jack's A Sailor

NELSTONE, Arthur 1870–1929
    Animated Doll, The
    As You Were
    Bobby With India Rubber Shoes,
        The
    I'm A Monarch With Original Ideas
    My Girl (w. Kitty **LOFTUS**)

NENO, George
Do They Want More Men?
Drink Boys, And Pass Round The
	Wine
How To Sing Extempore
That's How He Pays His Way

NEVIS, Ben
Lot Were Coming, A
Three Old Flats In Town
What The—What The—What The—
	Shall We Do?
You Must Have A Little Bit More

NICHOLLS, H. could be next entry or
next entry but one
We Insured His Life For Fifty

NICHOLLS, Harry° 1852–1926
Ben Bobstay
Be Prepared!
Do You Think So? Yes, I Think So (w.
	Herbert CAMPBELL)
Marry Come Up (w. CAMPBELL)
Nonsense! Yes! By Jove! (w. Robert
	BROUGH)
Not Really (w. CAMPBELL)
Now I Come To Think Of It
Ould Ireland So Green
Put A Plaster On My Chest
Put Them In The Lord Mayor's Show
Their Customs Are Very Peculiar
There Never Was A Time (w.
	CAMPBELL)
Things I Might Have Said
When You Come To Think Of It

NICHOLLS, Herbert *see also*
NICHOLLS, H.
I Haven't Been Home Since Yesterday
I Put 'Em On

NICHOLS, Emma J.
As They Marched Through The Town
	(The Captain With His Whiskers)

NICHOLSON, G. W.
Adolphus Brown
Broken-Down Tenor, The

German Street Stormers Band, The
Victoria, England's Queen

NIGHTINGALES, THE FOUR *see*
MASCOTS, THE SIX (MUSICAL)

NILSSON, Christine 1843–1921
Auld Robin Grey
Comin' Through The Rye
I'm Alone
Let Me Dream Again
Now Was I Wrong
Old Folks At Home, The
Take Me To The Ball Tonight
'Tis The Last Rose Of Summer

NOLAN, Michael° 1867–1910
As Long As She's Irish She'll Do
Ball Went Rolling Down The Hill,
	The
Brick Came Down, The
Brick Went Up, The
C. M. Maloney, AB
'Come In' Sez Widdy Malone
Dada's Baby Boy
£5 Note They Never Found
Glorious Sprig Of Shamrock For Your
	Coat, A
Grace Conroy
Granny
Has Anybody Here Seen Casey?
How Can They Tell That Oi'm
	Oirish?
I Came Up Smiling
If *That* Comes True
Irish Garçon, The
I Whistle And Wait For Katie
Knock Your Heads Together
Little Annie Rooney
Little Girl Over The Way, The
Logan's Looking-Glass
M'Cormack
Mickey's Visiting Cards
More Than His Job Is Worth
My Irish 'Pet Name' Girl
Myself And Susie Malone
Navy's Motor Ride, The

Next Sunday Morn
Nobody Knows And Nobody Cares
Norah From Killarney (I Don't Want
  An Indian Maid)
Now, Be Aisy, Ma'am
Pat's Performing Bear
Play Us An Old 'Come All Ye'
Proud Of Her Irish Boy
Sez Mary 'No!'
Silver Falls Of Erin
Sing Us An Irish Song
Sullivan Pawned The Donkey
Sweet Ella MacMahon
Sweetest Irish Music, The
There Was Hooligan
There Won't Be Any Annual
They Left No Stone Unturned
Today I've Made Sweet Annie Rooney
  My Wife
Two Eyes To See With
'Twould Be More Than His Job Is
  Worth
Wait Awhile Boys
We All Went Round
We Didn't Have A Funeral After All
We Were All Micks
What Paddy Gave The Drum
What Will Poor Callaghan Do?
You Gave Me A Rose
Your Boy In The Irish Guards
Your Eyes Have Told Me So

NORA, Helene
Those Wedding Bells Shall Not Ring
  Out

NORA, Little
It Wouldn't Do To Let Him Know
Soldier's Request, The *or* The Two
  Comrades

NORMAN, Horace all w. CHRISTY
MINSTRELS
Boyhood Days
Come Home, Father
Far Away
I Am Lonely Tonight

Oh Would I Were A Bird
Slave's Lament, The

NORRIE, James d. Jan. 1913
All That Glitters Is Not Gold
Baby's Dolly
Be Mine Own Again
Bid Me Not Forget The Past
Bird In A Gilded Cage, A
Daddy's Gone To Glory
English Girl, An
Girl I Want To M.A.R.R.Y., The
I Love One Girl—She Loves Me!
Let Bygones By Bygones
Let Us Be Friends As Before
Little Emily
Little May-Queen Darling
Molly Brown
Neighbours—Simply Neighbours
Only One Girl In The World For Me
On Sunday
On The Banks Of The Wabash Far
  Away
Say 'Au Revoir', But Not 'Goodbye'
Sweethearts Once
Terry, My Blue-Eyed Irish Boy
There'll Come A Time Some Day
Two Little Girls In Blue
Venus, My Shining Love
When The Squire Brought Home His
  Bride!
When You Know The Girl You Love—
  Loves You
Whom Do You Love? *or* The Tale Of
  A Penny

NORWORTH, Jack° 1879–1959; m. Nora
BAYES (div.)
Cassidy—Private Michael Cassidy
  VC
For Months And Months And Months
Give Me A Tinkle On The Telephone
Good Man Is Hard To Find, A
He's A Ragpicker
I'm A Nut
Kitty, The Telephone Girl
Molly McCarty

Mother's Sitting Knitting Little
Mittens For The Navy
Naughty Boy
On His First Day Home On Leave
Shine On Harvest Moon (w. Nora
BAYES)
Sister Susie's Sewing Shirts For
Soldiers
Which Switch Is The Switch, Miss,
For Ipswich?

NOTT, Charles E. 1855–1931
Ah, How She Loved Me!
In Old Kent Road (parody)
My Sweet-Hearts When I Was A Boy
Sadder But Wiser Man, A

NOVELLO, Clara 1818–1908; no relation
to Ivor Novello's mother
As Pants The Hart
Beating Of Mine Own Heart, The
Bonnie Prince Charlie
From Mighty Kings
God Save The Queen
Rule Britannia
'Tis The Last Rose Of Summer

NUGENT, Maude° 1874–1958
My Lady Hottentot
Sweet Rosie O'Grady

OAKLAND, Will 1880–1956; w. MOORE
& BURGESS MINSTRELS
Curse Of An Aching Heart, The
In The Gloamin'
Just Before The Battle Mother
Mother Machree
Only A Pansy Blossom
Ring Me Up Heaven, Please Central
Silver Threads Among The Gold
Sweet Genevieve
Wait Till The Clouds Roll By
When You And I Were Young, Maggie
White Wings
With All Her Faults I Love Her Still

O'FARRELL, Talbot 1878–1952
Casey's Charabanc

Ev'ry Day You're Away
God Gave Me Wonderful Dreams
How Can My Heart Forget?
I'd Just Paint The Leaf Of The
Shamrock
If I Could Bring You Back Again
If Winter Comes
Kingdom Within Your Eyes, The
Let's Start All Over Again
Lisp Of A Baby's Prayer, The
Success
Tears Of An Irish Mother
That Old-Fashioned Mother Of Mine
There's Silver In Your Hair
You'll Be Some Wonderful Girl

OGDEN, Alice
Honourable Brown MP, The
On The Silvery Tide
Pleasures Of The Skating Rink, The

OGILVIE, Hugh d. 25 Oct. 1931
Hail Caledonia

O'GORMAN, Joe° 1863–1937; member
no. 1 of the Variety Artists' Federation;
m. (1) Maggie Coleman (1867–98)
(dec'd), mother of his sons Dave & Joe
jun.; (2) Jessica Grace k.a. THE BEAUTI-
FUL JESSICA. See also TENNYSON &
O'GORMAN
Bog Trot, The (An Irish Cake Walk)
Epitaphs
Flanigan Simply Did As He Was Told
Molly O'Malley
My Irish Molly O!
Sez Pat To Himself 'Wow-Wow'!
Three Men Went Out A-Hunting
Top Of The Mornin', Bridget McCue!
What Did Patsy Do?

OLCOTT, Chauncey° 1858–1932
Little Bit Of Heaven Fell, A
Macushla
Mother Machree
My Beautiful Irish Maid
My Wild Irish Rose
Outcast Unknown

That's An Irish Lullaby (Too-Ra-Loo-
Ra-Loo-Ral)
When Irish Eyes Are Smiling

OLIVER, (Martha) Patti 1834–80
I Don't Intend To Wed
Pretty Seeusan Don't Say No

OLIVER, Roland w. MOHAWK
MINSTRELS
How Many Friends Have You Got?
Laurel Crown, The
Life Is A Journey
On To The Front
Romany Rye
Victor And Vanquished

OLIVER, Will° 1852–1916
My Father's Face
Pop! Pop! Pop!
Sailor's Been To Sea (See), The
Wanting To Meet Pretty Mary
Yarmouth On The Sands

OLIVIER, F.
Great Exhibition, The
I Gave Her A Kiss

ORIGINAL DIXIELAND JAZZ (orig. JASS)
BAND fl. 1916–25 & 1936–8; leader and
founder Nick LaRocca° (1889–1961),
cornet; Larry Shields° (1893–1953), clar-
inet; Henry Ragas° (1890–1919), piano;
Eddie Edwards (1891–1963), trombone;
Tony Sbarbaro° (1897–1969), drums. For
the band's 1919 visit to the UK the
pianist was J. Russel Robinson°
(1892–1963) and the trombonist Emile
Christian (1895–1973). The orig. drum-
mer was John Stein; another pianist for a
time was Billy Jones
At The Jazz Band Ball
Bluin' The Blues
Clarinet Marmalade
Dixie Jass Band One-Step
Fidgety Feet
Indiana (Back Home In)
Lazy Daddy

Livery Stable Blues
Margie (You're The Girl I Love)
Oh! Mother I'm Wild!
Original Dixieland One-Step, The
Ostrich Walk
Ramblin' Blues
Sensation Rag
Skeleton Jangle
That Teasin' Rag
Tiger Rag
Toddlin' Blues
When You Hear That Dixieland Jazz
Band Play

ORRIDGE, Ellen 1856–83
At The Ferry
Chain Of Memory, The
Lights Of London, The

OSBORNE, Charles° 1858–1929
Business Will Be Carried On As Usual
Naval Exhibition, The
Old Pals Up-To-Date
Puzzling Proverbs

PALERME, Gina
I'll Take The Lot
Where There's A Girl There's A Boy
(w. Andrew RANDALL)

PALMER, Minnie 1857–1936
My Sweetheart
Only A Little Yaller Coon
Open Up De Golden Gates
Peek-A-Boo

PALOTTA, Grace
Follow The Man From Cook's (octet
from *A Runaway Girl*)
Soldiers In The Park

PAREPA, Mme 1836–74; a.k.a.
Euphrosyne Parepa-Rosa; m. Carl Rosa
(1842–89)
Florentine Flower Girl, The
Lily Bells
Magic Of A Smile, The
Nightingale's Trill
Oh Bright Were My Visions

Sing Birdie Sing
Spirit Of Spring, The
Wood Nymph's Call, The

PARKER, BROTHERS *see*
MCNAUGHTONS, THE

PARKES, Ennis *see* HYLTON, Mrs Jack

PARRY, John Orlando° 1811–79;
from 1860 to 1869 w. GERMAN REED
COMPANY; wrote much of his own
material
ABC Duet, The (Singing Lesson)
Arm, Arm, Ye Brave
Berlin Wool
Bluebeard
Charming Chloe Cole
Charming Woman, The
Cherry Ripe
Country Commissions (sk.)
Don't Be Too Particular
Echoes Of The Past (sk.)
Fair Rosamond
Good Samaritan, The
Goosey Goosey Gander
Inchcape Bell, The
Invisible Prince's Inaudible Waltz,
The
Jenny Jones
Little Ewe Lamb, The
Little Mary Of The Dee
Lords Of Creation
Master And The Pupil, The
Musical Husband, The
Musical Wife, The
Operatic Rehearsal, An
Public Dinner, A (sk.)
Smile Again, My Bonnie Lassie
Take A Bumper And Try
Tell Me, Gentle Stranger
Tenor And The Tintack, The
Wanted A Governess
Wanted A Wife
Wedding Breakfast (sk.)
Whittington And His Cat
Wise And Foolish Virgins, The

PARSONS, Phil
All Through The Wedding March
Here's Another One Off For A Sailor
I Want To Be Introduced, If It's A Girl
Mister Pussyfoot
My Wife's Gone To The Country
Pick Me A Nice One
We're All Happy When The Sun
Shines

PARTRIDGE, James
Blackbird Gay, The
Mistaken Vocation, A
That Simple Minded Man

PASSMORE, Walter° 1867–1946; m.
Agnes FRASER
Chances That He's Had, The
Crocodile, The
Ducks And Quacks (sk.) (w. Johnny
DANVERS)
Fiddler And His Dog, The
Hamlet (travesty sk.)
Me And My Little Brood
Mistress Of The Sea
Patchwork Garden, The (w. Florence
LLOYD)
Queer Fish (sk.) (w. Agnes FRASER
and DANVERS)
Soldier's Mess (sk.) (w. FRASER and
DANVERS)
Sweet Williams (sk.) (w. FRASER and
DANVERS)

PASTOR, Charles d. 11 June 1926
Be In Time
Cold And Frosty Morning, A
Over Here And There
Pretty Girl's Name Was Flo, The
Won't She Be Surprised?

PASTOR, Tony° *c.*1832–1908; 'The
Father of Vaudeville' claimed a reper-
toire of over 2,500 songs
Alabama Claims, The
Awfully Fly
Band Played On, The (The Strawberry
Blonde)

By Instalments
Cat Came Back, The
Civil Service Reform, The
(Daring Young) Man On The Flying
  Trapeze, The
Down In A Coal Mine
Draft, The
Electric Shock, The
Fall Of Lander, The
First She Would And Then She
  Wouldn't
Freemen, Rally
Girl With The Golden Hair, The
Governor Pays The Bills
Great Atlantic Cable, The
Grecian Bend, The
Happiest Darkies Out, The
Hunky Boy Is Yankee Doodle
If Your Foot Is Pretty Show It
I'll Give You A Pointer On That
I'm A Young Man From The Country
  But You Don't Get One Over Me
I'm Off To Philadelphia
Irish Volunteer, The
Lucy Long
Lula, The Beautiful Hebrew Girl
March For The Union
Monitor And The Merrimac, The
My Grandfather Was A Wonderful
  Man
My Matilda Jane
New England Boys, The
Oh, Fred! Tell Them To Stop
Oh, Nicodemus
Old England's Position
On The Beach At Long Branch
Peaceful Battle Of Manassas, The
Polly Perkins Of Washington Square
Sarah's Young Man
Sixty Was The Number
Star-Spangled Banner, The
Stop That Knocking (as a boy)
Sumter, The Shrine Of The Nation
Sweet Kitty O'Neil
They All Do It
They Were All There

Things I Don't Like To See
Tommy Make Room For Your Uncle
Walking Down Broadway
Waterfall, The
We Are Marching To The War
What's The Matter With Hewitt?
When The Cruel War Is Over
Where Tweed Is Gone
Yankee's Escape From Secesh, The
  (mon.)
Ye Sons Of Columbia
Yum Yum Yum

PATERSON, Kate *see* CARNEY, Kate

PATEY, Janet Monach 1842–94; a.k.a.
Mme Patey-Whyttock
  Addio, L' (Mozart)
  Auntie
  Banks Of Allan Water, The
  Forget-Me-Not
  Full Fathom Five
  Gentle Youth
  Kathleen Mavourneen
  Lascia Ch'io Pianga
  Old Harpsichord, The
  Remembrance

PATTI, Adelina 1843–1919; after her
second marriage (to the tenor Ernesto
Nicolini in 1886) a.k.a. Adelina Patti-
Nicolini; sister of Carlotta PATTI
  Bacio D'Addio, Il (On Parting)
    (Byron: Patti)
  Comin' Through The Rye
  For All Eternity
  Home! Sweet Home!
  I Dreamed Of A Beautiful Garden
  Last Farewell, The
  My Darling's Lullaby
  Nightingale's Trill
  Only (Gounod)
  Romance
  Rosebuds
  She Wore A Wreath Of Roses
  Sing Me A Merry Lay
  Swiss Echo Song

'Tis The Last Rose Of Summer
Within A Mile Of Edinboro' Town
Woodland Serenade

PATTI, Carlotta 1840–89; sister of
Adelina PATTI
 Come Back To Erin
 Comin' Through The Rye
 In The Gloamin'
 Swiss Echo Song

PATTINSON, Kate 1869–1950; later k.a.
Kate CARNEY
 Baked Potato Can, The
 Good Morning, Mr Postman!
 When The Snowflakes Gently Fall

PAUL, Howard° 1830–1905; m. Mrs
Howard PAUL
 Absent-Minded Man, The
 Age Of Paper, The
 Bad Lot, A
 Banting
 Betsy Wareing
 Carry Your Friend In Your Pocket
 Cricketer, The
 Faust In Five Minutes
 Fighting Dog, The
 Good Old Days, The
 Good Queen Bess (w. Mrs Howard
  PAUL)
 Here's My Heart And Here's My Hand
 I Am So Volatile
 Impudent Puppy
 I Wish I Had Been Born A Man
 Jeddy Dowkins And His Gal
 Julius Caesar
 Ka-Foozle-Um
 Man Who Knows Everybody, The
 Married On Wednesday (Polly Bluck)
 Mister Noah, He Built An Ark
 Model Cabby, The
 Mr Gorilla
 Music Man, The
 Sandwich Man, The
 Selina Sly
 She'd A Brother In The Navy

Timid Young Man, The
Turkish Land
Twin Brothers, The
Up The Thames To Richmond
Vegetarian, The
Whack Row De Row
What Our Swells Are Coming To
What People Say
Why Did My Sarah Sell Me?

PAUL, Mrs Howard 1833–79; née
Isabella Featherstone; m. Howard PAUL
 Bother The Men!
 Bright Chanticleer (Old Towler)
 Dog And Cat
 Good Queen Bess (w. Howard PAUL)
 If Ever I Should Wed
 Jemimer Lobb
 Pin Money
 Rocks Ahead!
 Sabre Song, The (*Grand Duchess of
  Gerolstein*)
 Star-Spangled Banner, The
 Tom Tandem
 Unprotected Female, The
 When In Spain
 William That Married Susan

PAULINE, Princess 1873–1915?
 Alice, Where Art Thou Going?
 It's Alright But It's Awkward
 I've Got 'Em
 Little Tottie Brown Shoes
 Maggie Ryley
 Sporting Girl, A
 Yankee Girl, A

PAULTON, Dan° m. Rose SYLVESTER
 Coster, The Curate And The Jew, The
 I Give You My Word I'm Going
 Life's Short Span
 New! New! New!
 Pet O' The Pantomime, The

PAULTON, Harry 1841–1917
 Great Nonsense Song
 I Am Music'ly Mad
 I Arrived In Time To Get It

Learned Leviathan, The
Moods And Tenses (A Grammatical
    Absurd-Ditty)
Sammy, My Old Friend, Sam
Shtubborn Leedle Hans
There Are Others
Toiling Tourist, The
Where Can My Little Brother Be?

PAYNE, Edmund 1865–1914
Clowns (w. Katie SEYMOUR)
Follow The Man From Cook's (octet
    from *A Runaway Girl*)
If Ever I Marry (w. Violet LLOYD)
Love On The Japanese Plan (w.
    SEYMOUR)
Mummies (w. SEYMOUR)
Professions (w. SEYMOUR)
Punch And Judy (w. LLOYD)
Sunday Afternoon
Two Little Sausages (w. Gertie
    MILLAR)
Vegetarian, The

PAYNE, Herbert
Give Me A Ticket To Heaven
If I Had A Girl As Nice As You
Just Try To Picture Me Back Home In
    Tennessee
Moonlight Bay
Nora Malone (Call Me By Phone)
Red Wing
Ring Down The Curtain

PAYNE, Jack & His Band 1899–1969
You Can't Do That There 'Ere

PAYNE, Millie *c.*1890–1917
Has Anybody Seen My Tiddler?
I'll Play You At Your Own Game Now
Jenny Jones
Listen To The Humming Bird
Old Log Cabin Down The Lane,
    The
Ring-A-Ding! Puff-Puff!
Silly Sally Oh
This Is The Harem Skirt

PAYNE, W. chairman at Lusby's
Neapolitaine
Our Sailors On The Sea

PEARCE, Albert
By The Side Of The Zuyder Zee
Dreamland
Drinking Song (*The Rose of Persia*)
Peace, Peace
Two Eyes Of Blue
Yeoman Of England, The (*Merrie
    England*)

PEARCE, E. (Lizzie) d. 1890
Betsy Gay
Brindisi (*La Traviata*) (w. Russell
    GROVER)
Buy A Broom
Dashing White Sergeant, The
Irish Love
Launch The Lifeboat
My Dreams
Queen Of The Sea, The
Tell Me My Heart
'Twas Night And All Around Was Still
When The Family Are From Home

PEARCE, William 1838?–64?
Cease Rude Boreas
Hurrah For The Road!
Ship On Fire, The

PEARL, Arthur° 1869–1945
I Pushed The Bassinette
Leaving Home
Oh! Ria (A Cockney's Love Affair)
We Ain't Been Introduced

PEERLESS QUARTET incl. Billy MURRAY
I Can Always Find A Little Sunshine
    In The YMCA
Let Me Call You Sweetheart
Sweet Genevieve
You're The Flower Of My Heart
    (Sweet Adeline)

PELHAM, Paul° d. Apr. 1919
After Many Years

Be British!
Bells Of Fate
Brighton Was The Place
Constantinople At Olympia
Coster's Daughter, The
Dear Old Dad *or* The Son's Return
Gathering Of The Clans, The
He's A Good Old Has-Been
He Said To Me
Horse Came In, The
I Know You, You Know
Interrupted Actor, The
I Put It On
Is Life Worth Living?
I Wonder Where And What Will Be
    The End?
My Stage Struck Familee
Old Father Christmas
One Touch Of Nature
Only A Dream
Proposing
Scandals Are 'Cuming', The (A
    Baccarat Song)
She Was Young And I Was Old
Show Me Another Girl Like Mine
Sweet Nellie's The Girl I Love
Tale The Roses Told, The
They're All Coming Home In The
    Morning
Time To Put The Right Foot Down
T-R-I-C-K-Y
Two Little Vagabonds
Why Did You Go To War?
Work And Wages
Wreck Of The 'Seagull', The

PÉLISSIER, Harry G.° 1874–1913; m.
Fay COMPTON; see also FOLLIES, THE
    Back To The Land
    If It Wasn't For The Likes O' Huss!
    Jane!
    Mein Faderland
    Oh What A Happy Land Is England
    Seven Sleepers Of Ephesus, The
    Tipperary Millionaire, The

PENNIKET, Tom 1814–77
    Soldier Bill
    When These Old Clothes Were New

PENROSE, Charles 1876–1952; recorded
under sundry names including Merry
Andrew, Arty Chuckles, Charles Jolly,
and Charlie Pencaws. Also briefly
appeared with Bille WHITLOCK (2) as
Penrose & Whitlock and recorded with
him as The Jolly Jesters and The Two
Old Sports
    I Couldn't Help Laughing
    Jolly Old Farmer
    Laughing Family, The
    Laughing Husband, The
    Laughing Policeman, The
    Merry Party
    Oh! Who Says So?
    That Contagious Laugh
    They All Laugh Like This
    What Do We Pay Rates For?

PENROSE, Pearl
    Come Back, Sweetheart
    Come, Come To Me, Darling
    Hippity-Hip-Hooray *or* Four O'Clock
        In The Morning
    Keep Away!
    Little Miss D.C.
    Mary's Cheeks Are Rosy
    Sam's Lament
    Shipmates And Messmates

PERIER, Jean 1869–1954
    Swing Song, The (w. Mariette SULLY)
    Trot Here And There (w. SULLY)

PERTWEE, Roland 1885–1963
    Her Wedding Night (w. Violet
        VANBRUCH)

PETROVA, Olga 1886–1977; formerly
Muriel Harding
    My Hero (*The Chocolate Soldier*)
    Shulamite, The (sk.)
    To A Child That Enquires (recitation)

PHILLIPS, Brandon
Curtain Has Fallen Again, The
Old School-House Door, The

PHILLIPS, Mrs F. R.° 1829–99
As They Marched Through The Town
    (The Captain With His Whiskers)
Bit Of My Mind, A
Bob Ridley
Charming Sue
Down The Green Lanes
Elegant Time To Come, The
Ghost Medley, The
Glass With Care
I'll Ask My Mother
I Must Go Out On Sundays
It's Just As Well To Take Things In A
    Quiet Sort Of Way
Jessie The Belle At The Bar
Just As We Please
Lass I Love On England's Shore,
    The
Mrs John Bull
Never Had A Bean
Nice Young Man
No Irish Need Apply (ladies' version)
Oh, You Naughty Naughty Men
Opinions Of The Press, The
Peter Pepper Corn
Recollections Of Islington And
    Sadler's Wells
Shadows On The Wall (ladies'
    version)
When The Pigs Began To Fly

PICCOLOMINI, Marietta 1834–99
Bacio, Il (Arditi)
Brindisi (*La Traviata*) (w. C. A.
    ZOLARI)

PICTON, Sam 1859–93
Going Through The Mill
Rose, Shamrock And Thistle

PIDDOCK, J. C. d. 5 Dec. 1919
Melinda Loo
My Dear Old Coat
Wanted A Wife For a Millionaire

PIKE, Ernest
Bailiff's Daughter Of Islington, The
Because
Excelsior! (w. Peter DAWSON)
Gipsy's Warning, The
If I Had A Girl As Nice As You
Meet Me Tonight In Dreamland
Merry Vagabonds, The (w. Foster
    RICHARDSON)
Roses Of Picardy
Sing Me To Sleep
Songs My Mother Taught Me
Tenor And Baritone (w. Stanley
    KIRKBY)
There's A Long, Long Trail A-Winding

PILCER, Harry° 1885–1960; m. Gaby
DESLYS
Dance Just Once Again (w. Gaby
    DESLYS)
Dear Little Johnny (w. DESLYS)
Gaby Glide, The (w. DESLYS)
Night-Club Girl, The (w. DESLYS, also
    w. Teddie GERRARD)

PIMPLE, Little
I Love Somebody's Wife
I've Got A Girl To Care For
My Heart's Own Queen

PINK, Wal(ter)° c.1862–1922
Gone For Ever
Parrot, The (sk.)
QC, The (sk.)
That's When You Feel All Right
Those Papers (sk.)
Three Individuals

PITT, Archie 1885–1940; m. Dame
Gracie FIELDS (div.)
Does This Shop Stock Shot Socks
    With Spots?
I'm Just Going To Clean Father's
    Boots

PLAYFAIR, Sir Nigel 1874–1934
Ask No Questions And You'll Hear
    No Stories (w. Harley

GRANVILLE-BARKER)
Farewell Supper, A (w. GRANVILLLE-BARKER and Lillah McCARTHY)
Wedding Morning, The (w. GRANVILLE-BARKER)

PLEASANTS, Jack 1874–1924

At Ten O'Clock At Night
Baby Face
Bad Lad Of The Drama, The
Be Careful
Come In And Cut Yourself A Piece Of Cake
Day I Picked Up A Sovereign In The Street, The
Diabolo
Early Bird, The
Feeding The Ducks In The Park
Fourteen And Sixpence A Week
I Deserve A Good Slapping, I Do!
I Didn't Want To Do It But I Did
I Felt So Awfully Shy
I'll Be A Bad Lad, 'Liza Ann!
I'll Be Cross, Arabella, I'll Be Cross
I'll Be Out All Night Tonight
I Love To Go Butterfly Catching
I'm A Dada
I'm Learning A Song For Christmas
I'm Longing To Go Back
I'm Shy, Mary Ellen, I'm Shy
I'm The Black Sheep Of The Flock
I'm Twenty-One Today
I Said 'Good-Bye'
I Shall Get In Such A Row When Martha Knows
I Shall Sulk
I Think I Shall Wash My Neck Tonight
It's My Bath Night Tonight
It's My Golden Wedding
It's The First Time That I've Been In Love
I've Lost All Ambition In Life
I Want To be Pally With Everyone
I Wonder What Mother Will Say
Jack's Come Home Today

Just To Show Who Was Boss Of The House
Let's Play Something That We All Know
Liza Had Hold Of My Hand!
Long Years Ago
Mother (same as next entry?)
Mother's So Particular With Me
Night I Fought Jack Johnson, The
Nobody Noticed Me
Norman The Mormon
Reet Up To T'Mark
Rocking The Baby To Sleep
Ruth! You Know That's Not The Truth
Said I—Said She
She Made Me Do It
She Makes Me Walk In Ragtime
Stand In The Corner And be A Good Boy
To Cheer Him Up And Help Him On His Way
Watching The Trains Come In
Watching The Trains Go Out
We'd A Party At Our House
Where Do Flies Go In The Wintertime?
Why Do They Call Me Archibald?

PLEON, Harry° 1861–1911

Been Had (sk.)
Behind Me
Best Man, The
Day We Reached Pretoria, The
He Would Act (sk.)
I Didn't Break The Bank At Monte Carlo
I Only Stand So High
Mock Melodrama, (Harry Pleon's)
My Queer Old Dutch
Nelson Off His Column
On The Brain (sk.)
On The Day King Edward Gets His Crown On
Peck's Bad Boy (sk.)
Penny All The Way!
Professional Reunion, The

Ta-Ra-Ra-Boom-De-Ay (parody)
Twelve Little Doo-Dah-Doos
Up-To-Date Ta-Ra-Ra-Bomb!, The

PLUMPTON, Joseph
Dcwny Sam
Game Of Speculation, The
Periwinkle Man, The
There's Life In The Old Boy Yet

POLAIRE, Emilie 1880–1959
Visiteur, Le (sk.)

POLUSKI, BROTHERS fl. 1877–1922;
comedy sketch troupe est. Joe (?)
'Poluski' and Will Govett (*c.*1858–1923).
In 1886 Joe was succeeded by Will's
brother Sam (1866–1922). Will m. Nelly
Waite (1859–1932); joining the act from
time to time were their sons George
(1894–1939) and Will jun. a.k.a. Billy
(1887–1929) who m. Rosie WOOD.
Their daughters (k.a. the Sisters Govett)
were Winifred WARD and Lottie
Govett who m. Gus Howard of THE
MCNAUGHTONS. Another 'Poluski'
was Joseph Ford (d. 12 Jan. 1931)
  Black Eel, The a.k.a. Electric Eel, The
  Black Sheep, The
  Bo'sun, The
  I Do Like Your Eyes
  Kalkulating Talking Horse, The
  Late On Parade
  Military Manoeuvres
  Near The Slaughter House (also a
    song)
  Prevaricator, The
  Puffalo Bill
  Schemers, The
  Tally O! The Tallyman!
  Tipster, The
  Trade
  Two Schemers, The
  Village Blacksmith, The
  Wibbles And Wabbles

POOLE, Eliza 1819–1906
Always With Me

Annette And Theodore
As If You Didn't Know
Be Sure You Call As You Pass By
Billet Doux
Don Jose's Ward, Teresa
Effie Sunshine
Fair And Soft And Young And Gay
Happy Heart Could Thy Beating Be
I Love A May Morning
I Only Ask A Home With Thee
Ladies' Darling, The
Oysters, Sir?
Smart Young Bachelors
Somebody Cares For Me
Song Of Charlotte Stanley
Sweet Voices
Two Letters, The
Who'll Have Me?
Words Of Kindness
Young Lady's No, A

POPLAR, Fred m. Kitty WAGER
Brown's Mascots
Isn't He A Nice Pal?
Popular Nursery Rhymes Medley
She Was Fair

POTTER, Mrs (James) Brown
1859–1936; Cora Urquhart Potter
  Absent-Minded Beggar, The
    (recitation)
  Legend Of The Daisies, The
    (recitation)
  Love's Apotheosis (sk.)
  Mary Queen Of Scots (sk.)
  Ordered To The Front (sk.)
  Paglicacci, I (sk.) (w. Gilbert HARE)
  School For Scandal, The (screen
    scene)

POUNDS, Courtice 1862–1927; brother
of Louie POUNDS
  Any Time's Kissing Time (w. Violet
    ESSEX)
  Do You Waltz?
  Flower, The (*Lilac Time*) (w. Clara
    BUTTERWORTH)

Hello! Come Along Girls
Lizette
Never Laugh At Love
Swankers By The Sea (sk.) (w. T. C.
  Sterndale BENNETT & Louie
  POUNDS)
Whether The Weather Is Weather Or
  Not
Woulds't Thou Recall The Past?

POUNDS, Louie c.1873–?; sister of
Courtice POUNDS
  Gertie On The Go-Go
  Lady Of Fashion, A
  Navaho a.k.a. Navajo
  Said I To Myself, Said I
  Sammy
  She Always Does The Right Thing
  Sombrero
  Swankers By The Sea (sk.) (w. T. C.
    Sterndale BENNETT & Courtice
    POUNDS)
  Weeping Willow Wept, (And) The

POWER, Nellie 1854–87
  Boy In The Gallery, The
  City Toff, The or Crutch And
    Toothpick or La-Di-Da!
  Dear Little Flora (Down By The
    Sea)
  Doctor's Apprentice
  Dreaming Eyes Of Long Ago
  Fisherman's Daughter Who Loves
    O'er The Water, The
  I'm Such A Simple Young Man
  I'm The Jockey
  Jack, Jack, Jack
  La-Di-Da! (The City Toff)
  Little Pet Jockey, The
  Merry Savoyard, The
  Nice Looking Girl, The
  Oh I Say! He Does The Heavy In The
    City
  Oh Johnny! (Don't You Go To Sea)
  One Little Kiss
  Penny Paper Collar Joe

Pretty Miss Ricketts
Quack, Quack, Quack
Racketty Jack
Story Of Sindbad The Sailor, The
Such A Mash
Tiddy-Fol-Lol!
Up In A Balloon (ladies' version)
Who'll Buy My Broom?
Why Won't I Change My Name?

PRAEGER, Lou & HIS ORCHESTRA
1908–78; sometimes spelled Preager
  Hokey Cokey or Cokey Cokey

PRESTON, J. B.
  He Did As I Advised Him
  Wife, The
  You'll Tak' His Head

PRESTON, Jessie 1876–1928; orig. w.
sister Georgina as the SISTERS
PRESTON
  All Scotch
  Big Ship Is Waiting!, A
  Bonnie Mary O' Glengary
  Curley
  Daddy Went Upon A Steamer
  I Can't Forget 'Auld Reekie'
  I'm His Daisy
  I Want You To See My Girl
  Mary's Mishaps (Ri-Fol-The-Rol-
    The-Rol)
  Nyomo
  Sandy Boy (Hooch Aye)
  Universal Peace

PRESTON, SISTERS fl. c.1875–c.1900;
sisters JESSIE and Georgina (c.1870–?)
who m. Fred McNaughton[av] of THE
McNAUGHTONS; started their
performing careers as toddlers
  Bal Masqué, The
  Georgie
  Haddon Hall
  I'm Too Much Of A Gentleman
  Love And Kisses
  Oh! You're A Daisy

You Shan't Come And Play In Our
   Yard

PRESTON, Will°
  Australia
  Cousin Sarah
  Nothing Like It
  Shut It!
  We All Went Together

PRICE, Denham
  Because
  Jolly Sailor, The
  Little Irish Girl, The
  Maire, My Girl
  Midshipmite, The
  Old Brigade, The
  To My First Love
  White Squall, The
  You'd Better Ask Me

PRIMROSE & DOCKSTADER MINSTRELS
fl. 1898–1903; see also DOCKSTADER,
Lew; HANSON, Edwin
  Goodbye, Dolly Gray (solo: Harry
    Ellis, d. 1935)

PRIMROSE & WEST MINSTRELS fl.
1877–98; est. George H. Primrose
(1852–1919) and Billy West who m. Fay
TEMPLETON (div.). See also PRIMROSE
& DOCKSTADER MINSTRELS;
THATCHER, PRIMROSE & WEST
MINSTRELS, and also PRITZKOW, Louis
W. ; WINDOM, W. H.; WINTER, Banks
  Jack Gorman (solo: F. W. Oakland)
  Little Lost Child, The (A Passing
    Policeman)

PRITZKOW, Louis W.°
  Take Back Your Gold (w. PRIMROSE &
    WEST MINSTRELS)

PRYDE, Peggy b. 19 July 1869; daughter
of Jenny HILL and Jean Pasta (John
Woodley); as a child k.a. Letty Pasta; m.
(1) George Pearson; (2) George Sinclair
Hamilton (d. 19 Oct. 1899). Sang many
of her mother's songs
  And Lots Of Other Things

Bother The Men
Chips Off The Old Block
He'd Never Been There Before
Italiano Sarah
I've Just Come Out Of Holloway
Lots Of Other Things
Monte Carlo
Night At The Play, A
Oh, Romeo!
Only One Girl In The World For Me
Push Dem Clouds Away
Respect Our Queen
Romeo And Sally's Wedding Day
Shilling A Week And My Tea, A
Sister Mary Jane's Top Note
Song Of The Thrush, The
That's What The World Is In Need Of
  Today
We'll Be There
What Did The Lady Do?
You Fancy Yourselves, You Do!

PURCELL, Annie d. 13 Dec. 1932; a.k.a.
Nan McNamara
  Airship And The Swallow, The
  Baby Strauss
  By The Side Of The Zuyder Zee
  Gertie And The Gramaphone [sic]
  Good-Bye, My Little Flo
  Good-Bye, Olga!
  Hush-A-Bye, Sweetie
  In The Valleys Of Switzerland
  Little Brown Man Of Japan, The
  Moya
  My Little Turtle-Dove
  On The Isle Of Anglesea
  She Didn't Come From Borneo

PYNE, Louisa 1832–1904
  As Torrent Roaming O'er The Height
  Bird Of The Wilderness, The
  Cruiskeen Lawn, The
  I'm Alone
  Inez The Fair
  In My Wild Mountain Valley
  My Childhood's Days
  O Tender Shadow

Power Of Love, The
Sleep, My Darling
Song Of The Nightingale
Sultana Zulema
'Twas He My Only Thought
What Sunshine Bright
Why Throbs This Heart?
Would'st Thou Win Me

QUAKER CITY FOUR *or* **QUARTETTE**
personnel incl. Edwin HANSON
In Dear Old Georgia
You're The Flower Of My Heart
(Sweet Adeline)

RADFORD, Robert 1874–1933
Drake Goes West
Excelsior! (w. John HARRISON)
Father O'Flynn
Glorious Devon
In Cellar Cool
I Would I Were A King
Larboard Watch (w. HARRISON)
Onaway! Awake, Beloved!
Rocked In The Cradle Of The Deep
Shipmates O' Mine
Song Of The Waggoner
Trumpeter, The
Watchman! What Of The Night?
(w. HARRISON)

RAE, Bob
Economy
Imagine It!
Kathleen Muldoon
Ma Conscience
Only One The Poor Girl Had, The
She Danced

RAEBURN, Sam° 1865–90; w. MOORE &
BURGESS MINSTRELS
Ain't It Marvellous!
Boys Together
That Pie! (parody of For You)

RAFFERTY, Pat° 1861–1952
Ain't It Marvellous?
Black Cat, The
Boys Of The Territorial Army, The

Bravo, Dublin Fusiliers (Ireland's
Reply)
Bus, The (Mary MacIntyre!)
Come Back To Erin And Me
Dancing To The Organ In The Mile
End Road
Dear Ould Ireland's The Place For me
Early In The Morning
Every Time The Bell Goes
Floor Gave Way, The
Four Loyal Britons
Fuchsia, My Fairy Flower
Good-Bye, Canada!
Good Night
Good Old Rasper(ree)!
Hand That Rocks The Cradle, The
Have Another Go
He Had A Bit Of It
He Had A Little Drop
He Isn't On The Job Just Now
He'll Never Forget Ould Ireland
He's Very Very Ill Indeed
He Was One Of The Old Brigade
(parody)
Hopping And Popping About
How Do You Do?
I'll Go To Paddy's Lad
I'll Wait For You At The Gate
I Mean To Enjoy Myself
I Met Her At Mooney's
Irish Guards, The
Irish Language, The (As She Is
Spoken)
I Went Out On Strike This Morning
John Bull, Aren't We Loyal Now?
Jokes
Jolly Old Irish Pensioner, The *or* Send
For The Pensioner
Just To Show His Authority
Katie Connor
Kempton Park
Little Irish Postman, The
Little Leaf Of Shamrock
McAnulty's Garden Party
Mammy Is The Captain
Mary Carey From Tipperary

Meeting Of The Clans, The
Mind How You Go, Jemima!
Miss Hooligan's Christmas Cake
Molly Riley, O!, (On Monday She
    Sings)
Murphy's Talking Parrot
My Blind Norah
My Dear Old Irish Mother
My Girl Is Irish With Silvery Hair
My Jaunting Car
My Ould Woman
Nancy Clancy
Norah, My Village Queen
Oh! The Girl I Left Behind Me
Oh! What A Night We Had
Oh, Where Is My Wandering Boy
    Tonight?
One Good Turn Deserves Another,
    John
On The Bonnie Bonnie Banks Of
    Loch Lomond
Paddy's Serenade
Peggy Cline
Poor Mick
Put Yourself In Milligan's Place
Queenstown Harbour
Rivals
She Started Tickling
Still His Whiskers Grew
Sweet Little Womanly Woman
Sweet Rosie O'Grady
Swinging On Riley's Gate
That's Where My Love Lies Dreaming
Then She Started Tickle-ing!
There's An Irishman Up In The
    Moon
Thick-Headed Danny
Though Absent From Home
Three Mothers-In-Law, The
Tickle-ickle-um
We Drew His Club Money This
    Morning
We Had A Little Drop
We're The Same Old Pals Today
We Walked Home
We Won't Talk Of Foreign Invasion

What Do We Want With
    Conscription?
What Do You Think Of The Irish
    Now?
Where Are Your Ten
    Commandments?
Where Does My Love Lie Dreaming?
Whiskey
Why Didn't They Send For Me?
Why Do They Call Them Hooligans?

RAINFORTH, Elizabeth° 1814–77
Ah, Why Do We Love?
I Dreamt That I Dwelt In Marble
    Halls
In Childhood Calm And Sinless Bloom
O To Bound O'er The Bonnie Blue
    Sea
Violet, The
Wi' A Hundred Pipers An' A'

RA-LESLIE, Ethel
I Can See Red Roses Blooming
My Sunny Egyptian
Little Billee Taylor

RANDALL, Andrew
Where There's A Girl There's A Boy
    (w. Gina PALERME)

RANDALL, Harry° 1860–1932
Amateur Detective, The
'Arry The 'Andy Man
Automatic Battery, The
Boarding House, The
Conscience
Cook Who Cooks, The
Dear Me!
Diabolo Mad
Drink! (By One Who's Had Some)
Exchange And Mart
Expecting It Every Tick
For The Sake Of The Little Ones At
    Home
Garden Outside In, The
Ghost Of Benjamin Binns, The
Good Old Annual, The
Ginger In The Gutter

Great Expectations (It's Only A False Alarm)
He Wore A Worried Look
'Homeward Bound', The
Husbands By One Who Has Had Four
I Can't Get At It
I Did Laugh!
I Don't Know Where He Gets His Ideas
I Don't Know Where To Find 'Em
I Forgot It!
I'll Say No More To Mary Ann
I'm Not A Bad Sort, Am I?
I'm Using Sunday Language All The Week
I Mustn't Let Her See Me All At Once
I Picked It Up
I Stood Just So!
It Ain't All Lavender
It Pays So Much Better Than Work
It's A Wonder I'm Alive To Tell The Tale
It's Only A False Alarm (Great Expectations)
I Was In It (Fairly In It)
I Wasn't So Drunk As All That
I Was Standing At The Corner Of The Street
I Wonder Where He Gets His Ideas From?
I Won The Bicycle
Judge, The
Just In A Motherly Way
Later On
Let 'Em All Come
Lightning Results
Little Teddy Brown Down At 'Margit'
Long Long Ago
Love By One Who Knows
Man—By One Who Loathes 'Em
Missing Word, The
Model Dwellings
Mottoes On The Wall
Mr Tootle
My Conscience Wouldn't Let Me
My Wife's A Cook

New Photographee, The
Nightmare, The
Ninepence-Ha'penny An Hour
No Matter!
Oh!!!
Oh! Let It Be Soon
Oh! Mr Jackson
Oh! My Tooth
Oh! The Business!
Oh! The Models
Oh! What A Night It Must Have Been
Old Cracked Basin, The
Only Truly Happy Married Man, The
Ours Is A Happy Little Home
Our Village (Was On The Slow And Dirty Line)
Pass No Rude Remarks
Poor Pa Paid
Right Behind!
Same Old Lie, The
She Practises Tobogganning
She's Changed My Boots For A Set Of Jugs
She Was A Sensible Girl
Shoreditch Handicap, The
Something Occurred
Something Tickled Her Fancy
Something You Wouldn't Know Unless You Knew
Strike A Blow For Liberty And Freedom
Sunday At Home
Tatcho
That Interfering Marm Downstairs
That Touches The Spot
There Isn't Many Wives Like Mine
They All Take After Me
They Made Such A Fuss Of Me!
They Wanted Oiling
Thing You Wouldn't Know Unless You Knew, A
Tobogganing
Toothache Song, The
Tut-Tut-Tut-Tut-Dear Me!
Up To Here!
Up Went The Price Of Girls

We're Moving
We've Had 'Em All Irish, We've Had
  'Em All Scotch (The Model Maid
  Servant)
What D'Yer Think Of Me Now?
What's All This Fuss About
  Finger-Prints?
What To Do In An Emergency
Whistling Wife, The
Who Killed Cock Warren?
Who Killed Ta-Ra-Ra? (parody of
  preceding entry)
You 'Ave To 'Ave 'Em
You Know It's Not Nice

RANDALL, Nellie
Don't Do Like That ???
Just What You Fancy
King Baby

RANDALL, Pollie *c.*1853–1910; m.
Walter Burnot°
  Bridge, The (sk.)
  Fisher Boy, A
  Hero Of The Colours, The (sk.)
  Jane Shore (sk.)
  John Bull's Flags
  Prince Of Pleasure, The
  Sailor Far Away, A

RANDALL, William 1830–98
  All My Eye
  As I Walked By Myself
  Bathing
  Belle Of Belgrave Square, The
  Bill Stickers, Beware!
  Billy
  Bob Fubbs
  Charming Young Lady/Widow I Met
    In The Train, The
  1851 & 1862
  Exhibition Of '62, The
  Ginger In The Gutter
  Goose Club, The
  Great Exhibition, The
  Happy Little Man, The
  Hole In The Shutter, The (Mr Drake's

Dilemma)
I Fancy I See A Ghost
I'm A Timid Nervous Man
I'm A Young Man From The Country
Isabella And Her Gingham Umbrella
Jolly West End Of The Town, The
Jones's Sister
Julia's Crinoline
Lodging House Cat, The
Long And Short Of It, The
Man About Town, The
Matrimonial Swindle, The
Missus Took A Sly Glance At Me, The
Morrison's Patent Pills
Never Desert A Friend
No Irish Need Apply
Not To Be Had In 62
Not Twice
Old Union Jack, The
On The Sands!
Parlour Blind, The
Porter's Knot, The (mon.)
Postman Of Mayfair, The
Properest Thing To Do, The
Rather Too Old To Be True
Sarah's Young Man
Simple Simon
String Of Ballads, The
Take It Quiet
Tell Mama We're Happy
Temperance Band, The
Three Topers, The (Smith, Jones And
  Brown)
Touching That Little Account
Two In The Morning
When I Gits To Be An M.P.

RANDS, Harry°
  She Must Be Handsome
  She's Always The Best In My Dreams
  Strolling Through Fairlight

RASCALS, THE THREE° fl. 1908–27;
Eddie Fields (d. May 1962), Charles
O'Donnell (1886–1962), and unknown.
For a time from 1923 the act incl.
Benjamin Levin k.a. Benny Leven but

from c.1936 k.a. Issy Bonn (1903–77).
See also RASCALS & JACOBSON, THE
TWO
  Banjo Joe
  Gaby Glide, The
  He'd Have To Get Under
  Hitchy-Koo
  I Want To Be In Dixie
  Mickey Rooney's Ragtime Band
  Ragtime Cowboy Joe
  Ragtime Soldier Man
  Ragtime Suffragette, The
  That Beautiful Band
  That Old Sweetheart Of Mine
  Wedding Glide
  When The Midnight Choo Choo
    Leaves For Alabam'

RASCALS, THE TWO see also RASCALS,
THE THREE
  Are You From Dixie?
  Can You Tame Wild Women?
  That's What God Made Mothers For
  When You Wore A Tulip And I Wore
    A Big Red Rose

RASCALS & JACOBSON, THE TWO
recording accompanist Jess JACOBSON;
see also HEDGES BROTHERS & JACOB-
SON; RASCALS, THE THREE
  Aba Daba Honeymoon
  Try To Picture Me Back Home In
    Tennessee
  We Used To Kiss Goodnight
  What'll You Do When You Get
    Married?

RAVENSBURG, Elaine sometimes spelled
Ravensbury
  Daisy Mayflower
  Good-Night, Mamma
  Hush, Ye Night Winds
  I Love Him With All My Heart
  May, Love
  My Princess Zulu Lulu
  Wooloomooloo

RAWLINSON, John w. CHRISTY
MINSTRELS

  Birds Await The Day, The
  Blue Eye'd Nelly
  Break It Gently To My Mother
    (Templeton Minstrels)
  Gabrielle
  I Heard A Spirit Sing
  I'll Meet Then In The Lane
  I'm Thinking Of Thee Dear Mother
  Little Daisy
  Little Robin Tapping On The Pane
  Oh, Would I Were A Bird
  Sail On Silver Cloud
  Valley By The Stream, The
  Yes, I'll Meet Thee Dearest

RAY, Gabrielle 1883/5–1973
  Cupid's Rifle Range
  Pink Pyjama Girl

RAY, Phil° 1872–1918; m. Nellie
WIGLEY
  Brighton Walk, The
  Delusions
  If The Missus Wants To Go Let Her
    Drown
  Just When You Least Expect It
  Mary Used To Go To Sunday School
  Sideways
  That's Enough
  Tramcar
  Walking In My Sleep
  Wow! Wow!

RAYBURN, Kittee sometimes spelled
Kitty
  Anna From Havana
  Bubbles In The Air
  Cock O' The Roost (Men—Men—
    Men)
  Come And Make Love To Me
  'E's A Bloke As I'd Like To Go Out
    With
  He Thought He Wouldn't Venture
    Any London
  I'd Rather Stay In Rodger's Row
  I Should Say So

Love And L. S. D. (w. Gypsy WOOLF)
Marching In The Band
Mugg's Motor Car
My 'Arry And Me
My Dolly And Me
My Soldier Boy's Coming Home
Oh, Willie! We Have Missed You
Raggedy-Taggedy Brigade, The
Sally Wasn't Such A Lady
She Wore A Wreath Of Roses And
  One Or Two Other Little Things
Sun's A-Peeping, The
Two Hearts Made One
Westward Ho! ('Neath The Dear Old
  Union Jack)
Won't You Come To Me In Canada?
Your Soldier Boy's Coming Home

RAYMOND, Ruby
Aba Daba Honeymoon (w. Fred
  HEIDER)
Everybody's Doin' It Now

RAYNOR, J. W.
Come Into The Garden Maud
Nelly Gray (w. CHRISTY
  MINSTRELS)
Tom Bowling

REA, Laurence
Swing Song, The (w. Ruth VINCENT)
Trot Here And There (w. VINCENT)

READ, John° 1839–1920; wrote most of
his own material
All For Her
All Round The Squares
Bill Of Fare, The
Bonny Black Dress
Don't Touch Him
Drink Up, John!
End Of The World, The
Every Inch A Sailor
Give Me A Grip Of Your Hand
Good-Bye, Lovely Lou
Grandfather's Clock
Grandmother's Chair
He Knows How To Do It

How The Shoe Pinches
I Brought Her Up To London
If You Love Me Tell Me Tottie
I'm Going Home To Live Along With
  Mother
I'm In It
It's A Very Silly Thing To Do
It's Nice
Johnny Morgan
Keep It On The Quiet
Lesson From Dad, A
Liza, Do You Love Me?
Naughty! Naughty! Naughty! (Read)
Oh! Polly She's The Girl For Me
Oh, That Brown
Old Arm Chair, The
Old Chums
Old Village School, The
She Cries Her Bloomin' Lavender
Simple Simon (The Boy Who Longed
  For Jam)
Strolling On The Beach
Sweeter Than Jam
Swinging To And Fro
That's How The Poor Have To Live!
Tiddle-A-Wink The Barber
Wake Up England
Wishes

REDFERN, Sam° 1851–1915
Any Excuse For A Booze
Babies
Booze Is There
Down In A Cottage Near A Wood
Good Old Days Of Adam, The
Home! Home!! Home Sweet Home!!!
  (topical parody)
I'll Bet You A Dollar You Don't
In The Moonlight—Lovely Moonlight
On It Like A Bird
Queen Of Nankipoo, The
Sister May Wants To Know
That's The Latest
What Will You Lend On My 'Dolly'?
Woman's In It
Women

REECE, Arthur 1870–1964; son of
'Jovial' Joe COLVERD; m. Rose SULLIVAN
  All Except The Last
  Ballad Monger, The
  Boers Have Got My Daddy, The
  Break The News To Mother
  Britannia's Handy-Man
  Bury Her Picture With Me
  Come With Me To The Races
  Difference Between East And West,
    The
  Follow The Soldiers
  For England's Bit Of Bunting
  Gallant Twenty-First, The
  Girls Who Dote On The Military, The
  Good News From The War
  He Was One Of The Dear Old
    Regiment
  He Was The Light Of Her Life
  His Majesty's Mail
  How Was I To Know?
  How Will The Voyage End? (On! On!
    On!)
  Hundred Years To Come, A
  It's Moonlight Ev'ry Night In London
  It Was Three O'Clock In The Morning
  Jolly Good Health To The Bridal Pair
  Lads In Navy Blue, The
  Making Room For Mighty London
    Town
  Man Came First
  Mother's Gift To Her Country, A
    (Soldiers Seven)
  Now's The Time To Win!
  Oh Girls You Don't Know How I Love
    You
  Oh Joe I Want To Go To The Picture
    Show
  Oh, What A Lovely Game!
  One Of The Boys Who Serve Our
    King
  Price Of Beer, The
  Price Of Peace, The
  Rare Old Time
  Right In The Middle Of Mine
  Send Us A Few More Girls

  Seventh Royal Fusiliers, The
  Somebody's Found A Girl
  Someone To Mind The Children
  Sons Of The Sea
  Story Of The Stars!, The
  There's Always 'Alf-A-Pint Of Beer
    For Him
  They Wanted To Go To Chicago
  Those Wedding Bells Shall Not Ring
    Out
  'Tis A Hundred Years Ago
  To-night! To-night! To-night! (A
    Telephony Story)
  Under The Mistletoe
  We Mean To Keep The Seas
  When There Isn't A Girl About
  When The Troops Come Home
  Who'll Care For The Children While
    I'm Away?
  You're A J-J-J

REED Co., German fl. 1855–95; est. T.
German REED and wife Mrs T. German
REED. Later company members incl. son
Alfred German Reed (1847–95); Arthur
CECIL; Gertrude Chandler; H. Nye
Chart jun. (1868–1934); Avalon Collard;
Susan Galton; Isabelle Girardot; Corney
GRAIN; Fanny Holland (1848–1931) who
m. Arthur Law°; North Home; Mr
MacMoyes; John Orlando PARRY; Annie
Sinclair; Dora Thorne; Kate Tully;
Marion Wardroper; Arthur Wilkinson.
All sketches:
  Back In Town (incl. My Old Dress Suit
    sung by Corney GRAIN)
  Big Bandit, A
  Carnival Time
  Charity Begins At Home
  Foundling, The (Fanny Holland)
  In Cupid's Court
  In Possession
  Killiecrumper
  Melodramania
  Odd Pair, An
  Pantomime Rehearsal, A

Pretty Bequest, A
Tally-Ho!
Treasure Trove (incl. The Sobbing
    Quartet)
Tuppins And Co
Verger, The
Wanted—An Heir

REED, Leslie°
Anything'll Do For Me
He Didn't Go To Work Next
    Morning
He's Never Been Heard Of Since
I Haven't Been Home Since Yesterday
Last Act—Finale
One Of The Old, Old Boys
Our Bill
Our Little Two Year Old
She Is A Fancy Ironer
There Always Will Be Singers
We All Go To Work But Father

REED, Thomas German° 1818–88; m.
Mrs T. German REED; see also REED
Co., German
Buttercup, The (w. Arthur CECIL)
Detective's Song
For He's A Jolly Good Fellow

REED, Mrs T. German 1818–95; née
Priscilla HORTON; see also REED Co.,
German
I Never Does Nothing At All
Mama Won't Bring Me Out

REES, Ernest° d. 9 Mar. 1916
Come Round And Call Me Early In
    The Morning
How Dare I Live!
I'm Farmer Scroggins
Yea, Verily Verily O!

REEVE, Ada° 1874–1966; m. (1) Bert
GILBERT (div.); (2) Wilfred Cotton
Absent-Minded Beggar, The
And Just Then He Fell Out Of Bed
British Institutions
By The Sea And Up In Town

Ça Va Sans Dire
Come Along With Me, Boys
Father's Little Man
Find The Man
Foolish Questions
For A Girl
Goo-Goo Land
He, She And The Weather-Glass
If The World Were Ruled By Girls
I'm A Little Too Young To Know, You
    Know
I'm A Merry Little Devil
Is It Nothing To You?
I Think It Must Be Love
I've An Inkling
I Wonder Who's Kissing Her Now?
Ladies Beware
Little Puritan, The
Lively
Louisiana Lou
Love Me Just A Little, Sue, Do, Do,
    Do
Men
My Otaheitee Lady
My Susie-Anna From Louisiana
Nobody Knows, Nobody Cares
Now Will You Be Good?
Oh! You Men!
Open Your Mouth And Shut Your
    Eyes
Pious Girl, The
She Glories In A Thing Like That
She Was A Clergyman's Daughter
Something Else
Susie 'Oo!
Tact
That Little Word 'Yes'
There's A Long, Long Trail A-Winding
They've Both Changed Their
    Occupations Now
Trixie Of Upper Tooting
What Do I Care?
When I Leave Town
Why?
Women, I Ought To Know Them For
    I'm One Of Them

REEVES, Arthur
Volunteer Organist, The

REEVES, Billie c.1864–1943
Early Birds (w. Fred KARNO)
Mumming Birds (w. KARNO)
New Women's Club, The (w. KARNO)

REEVES, J. Sims 1818–1900
Anchor's Weigh'd, The
Bay Of Biscay
Behold The Morn Is Beaming
Bonny Jean
British Volunteer, The
Come Into The Garden, Maud
Comrades (Jaxone: Benedict)
Death Of Nelson, The
Flag That Brav'd A Thousand Years,
  The
Folded Hands
For Thee, My Love, For Thee
God Bless The Prince Of Wales
Good Night! Good Night! Beloved
I'll Sing Thee Songs Of Araby
In This Old Chair
I Wander By My Dear One's Door
  Each Night
Last Good Night, The
Love's Confession
Margaretta
Mary Of Argyle
Merry Breeze, The
Miller's Daughter, The
My Pretty Jane
My Queen
Oft In The Stilly Night
Once Again
Refrain Thy Voice From Weeping
Rose Of The Morn
Sing Again Ye Happy Children
Then You'll Remember Me
There's None So Fair As She
Tom Bowling
When Thou Wilt Be My Bride?

REGAN, Alice
Rose Of Alabam, The (w. Tom E.
  FINGLASS)

RÉJANE, Mme 1857–1920
Alerte, L' (sk.)
Bet, The (sk.)
Lolotte (sk.)

RENÉ, Ida c.1878–?; m. (1) Willie
Boisset (dec'd)—see BOISSETS; (2)
Arthur Prince (1881–1948)
Before She Had Been With Us A
  Week
Broken Doll, A
Jeremiah The Dyer
Landlady's Daughter, The
Little Lost Coon, The
Maid And The Monk, The
Marriage À La Mode
My Coal Black Lady
Old-Fashioned Cottage, The
Poster On The Wall, The
Rake's Progress, The
Rook And The Crow, The
Smartest Little Woman In A Very
  Smart Set, The
Tommy Don't You Worry
When You Were Sweet And Twenty
  And I Was Twenty-One
Widowette, The

RETFORD, Ella 1886–1962; m. (1) F.
Stanislaus (conductor) (2) Pierce of
Pierce & Monaghan
All The Boys In Khaki Get The Nice
  Girls
All The Girls Are Lovely By The
  Seaside
Be Sure He's Irish
By The Light Of The Silvery Moon
Hannah, Won't You Open The
  Door?
Has Anyone Seen A German Band?
Have You Seen My Chinee Man?
Heartaches
Hello There, Little Tommy Atkins
Here's The Thirty Shillings You Paid
  For My Ring! Good-Day, Mr
  Johnson, Good-Day!

Hey, Ho, Can't You Hear The
  Steamer?
Hi! Hi! Hi! Mister McKie!
Home Sweet Home Ain't Nothing
  Like This
If You Can't Call On Sunday, Mister
  Grundy
If You're Yorkshire You're One Of Us
I Like Your Apron And Your Bonnet
I'm Afraid To Come Home In The
  Dark
I Want To Be In Dixie
I Was A Good Little Girl Till I Met
  You
I Wonder If You Miss Me Sometimes
L'il Liza Jane
Mister Wright—You're Wrong!
Molly Molloy
Molly O'Morgan
My Bungalow In Borneo
Oo-Oo-Marie
Patricia
Play A Little Ragtime On Your Piccolo
Popsy Wopsy
Pretty Little Girl From Nowhere,
  The
Put A Little Bit Away For A Rainy
  Day
Sarah! Come Over Here!
See (Look) What Percy's Picked Up In
  The Park
She's A Girl Up North
She's A Lassie From Lancashire
Smith, Jones, Robinson And Brown
Some Of These Days
So Shi! (Why Are You So Shy?)
Sun Am Shining—Why Don't You Go?
Take A Look At Me Now
Take Ma Finger Tips Melinda
Take Me Back To Dear Old Blighty
Take Me On The Flip-Flap
There's A Girl In Havana
They're All Single By The Seaside
Under The Honey Moon Tree
We're Irish And Proud Of It Too
Who Paid The Rent For Mrs Rip Van

Winkle?
You Made Me Love You

RICE, Billy w. HAVERLY'S MASTODON
MINSTRELS; also ran his own troupe
  Billy's Appeal
  On The Banks Of The Wabash

RICE, T. D. 1808–60; godfather of
Arthur LLOYD
  Gombo (Gumbo) Chaff
  I Do—I Don't Do Nothing!
  Jump Jim Crow
  Sich A Gittin' Upstairs

RICH, J. C. d. Oct. 1928
  Angling Song
  Fellows We Met At The Races, The
  I Dreamt That I Was Dreaming
  I'm Off To Germany
  Just About As Good As We Have
    Got (?)
  Sheeney Man, The
  Three A Penny
  True To My English Rose
  Vindow Man, The
  Who Killed Ta-Ra-Ra?

RICH & RICH° fl. 1897–1915; Harry
Rich (1872–1915) and Charlie Rich
(d. 2 Nov. 1938)—the two were not
related
  Best Of Everything, The
  Charley Take Hold Of My Arm
  Jenny, My Own True Love
  King Of Karactacus, The
  Loch Lomond (parody)
  Starting Out With Nothing In Your
    Pocket
  They Still Stand Saying Goodnight
  We Don't Want A Girl
  We Should Like A Girl
  Wishing

RICHARDS, Nellie 1864–1932; orig. w.
HAVERLY MINSTRELS
  Alabama Coon, The (Little)

At The Garrison Ball (Un Tour De Valse)
Babies On Our Block, The
Baby Eyes
Beat Of The Drum, The
By-Bye, My Honey
Climbing Up The River Mighty Slow
Coon From The Moon, The
De Order Of De Golden Key
Ding-Dong Bell
Dream Of Glory, A
England And America
Garrison Ball
Hard Times Come Again No More (Foster)
Home At Last
How 'Bout Dat Baby
I Long To See The Girl I Left Behind
I'm So Lonely
In England Now
Johnny Get Your Gun
Kiss Me, Daffy
Life's Story
Little Alabama Coon, The
Louisiana Lou
Loving Parents At Home
On De Injine
Push Dem Clouds Away
St James's Park
Vagabond, The

RICHARDSON, Billy w. SAM HAGUE'S MINSTRELS
Little Pair Of Whiskers, A
Shout Out, Little Children

RICHARDSON, Ernest°
How You Show It
In Duplicate
Super's Lament, The

RICHARDSON, Foster 1891–1942
Captain Mac'
Come To The Fair
Excelsior! (w. Herbert THORPE)
Merry Vagabonds, The (w. Ernest PIKE)

RICHMOND, SISTERS Josie (1862–1930) and Lulu (d. 29 June 1927)
Collar And Cuffs
Come On
Cruise Of The Hot Cross Bun, The
Drink
Farmer's Boy, The
Give Me A Pony And Trap
Just To Show Our Respects To McGuinness
Pretty As A Butterfly

RICKABY, J. W. *c.*1869–1929; brother of Ted WAITE
First I Went And Won The D.C.M.
Hokey-Pokey
I'm A Bobby
I'm Always Thinking Of Her
I'm An Airman
I May Be Right, I May Be Wrong
I'm Not So Young As I Used To Be
I'm Spending The Legacy Papa Left To Me
I'm The Biggest Guy On Broadway
I Think I'll Buy Piccadilly
It's Absolutely Beautiful Outside
I've Been Driven From Home
I've Brought The Coal
Just As The Sun Goes Down
Major General Worthington
Mountaineer, The
Napoleon's White Horse
Not In These Boots
Not So Much Of The Father
Now We're Busy
P.C. 49
Ragtime Navvy, The
Rajah Of The Nincompoo Islands, The
Society Outcast, The
There's A Good Time Coming
They Built Piccadilly For Me (Silk-Hat Tony)
What-Ho! She Bumps (Stern: Collins, C.)
Why Can't It Always Be Saturday?

RICKARDS, Harry° 1841–1911; m.
Carrie Tudor (*c.*1840–79) (div.)
Ain't You Coming Out Tonight?
All For The Sake Of Sarah
Alpine Hat, The (The Swell With The)
Ask Me Another
Captain Jinks Of The Horse Marines
Cerulea Was Beautiful
De Lubsick Coon
Doctor Compus Mentis
Fair English Girls
Faithless Su-Si-An
Hammersmith Belle, The
Happy Days Of Childhood, The
Happy Go Bill
Hard Times Come Again No More
    (Tabrar)
His Lordship Winked At The Counsel
If She Told Me To Go To Jericho
I'll Stand Sam For Today And I'm
    Twenty-One
I'll Tell Your Wife
In England Now
I Never Go East Of Temple Bar
I Say, Peter! Don't You Lose Your
    Temper!
It's Nice To Be A Father
I Wish I Was A Fish (Sweet Polly
    Primrose)
I Wonder When She'll Let Mama
    Come Out
Lardy Dardy Do
Lost In The Snow
Mugby Junction
Not In These Boots
Only A Penny
Ou-Ah! Ou-Ah! That's What The Girl
    Would Say
Oxford Joe
Pharaoh And Sarah
Promenade The Spa
Ship Went Down To The Bottom Of
    The Sea, The
Slate And Pencil Man, The
Stout And Bitter
Strolling By The Stream By Moonlight
Strolling In The Burlington
Swell With The Alpine Hat, The
That's The Sort Of Men We Want In
    England Here Today
That's What The Country Wants To
    Know
That's When You Feel It
They All Do It
They All Say They Love Me
They Call Me The God Of Wine
Ti! Hi! Tiddelly Hi!
Virgin Only Nineteen Years Old, The
Walking In The Starlight
We Meet Each Night As The Clock
    Strikes Nine
We're Not Dead Yet
Where Is My Nancy?
Wroughty Tom

RICKS, P. J.
Doolan The Millionaire
Haven't We Fought For You?
Where, Oh Where Is My Norah?

RIDGWELL, Charles° d. 1916
Couldn't Make The Old Girl Hear
Our Lodger

RIDLEY, George° 1834–64
Blaydon Races, The
Bobby Cure, The
Cushie Butterfield
Johnny Luik-Up The Bellman

RIGHTON, Edward d. 1 Jan. 1899
Cock A Doodle Do
Private And Confidential
Sneeze, The (Dundreary's Brother
    Sam)

RIGOLBOCHE b. 1842; née Marguerite
Badel
Can-Can, The (dance)

RIGBY, Arthur W. 1865–1944
18
(For) He Was A Married Man
How To Manage A Husband

I Knew
I'm The Plumber
I'm Throwing Myself Away
Is England Still In Danger?
Isn't It Hard To Find
It May Be So
Jack Jones Esq. Late Covent Garden
  Porter (Jack Jones' Reply)
John James 'Enery Irving Wilson
  Barrett Baggs
Judge Let Him Off, The
Little Bits Of Blue
Liza's Tootsies
March Of The Married Men, The
Mary's Ankles
Oh, The Pallis *or* Crystal Palace—
  Bank Holiday
Oh Trilby, What Have You Done For
  Me?
Oh! What A Silly Thing To Do
Oh, What A Wicked World We Live In
Oo-Diddley-Oo!
Our Happy Happy Evenings For The
  Poor
Overcoats
Pom Tiddley Om Pom Pom
Scraps From Popular Songs
Something I Shall Never See Again
Song From The Heart, A
Therein Lurks Unseen Danger
They Never Do That To Me
What They Showed Me In Paree
Women's Rights (sk.)
You've Got To Be, You Shall Be
  Happy

RIHILL, Louis° 1879–1931
Murders

RILEY, Fred 1853–1909
He's Never Been Heard Of Since
Ladies, The
Monarch Of All Good Wine, The
Only One Of The Rank And File
Soldier's Request, The *or* The Two
  Comrades
Sweet Little Norah Malone

There's My Little Missus In The Old
  Arm Chair
Under The Shadow Of St Paul's

RILEY, Will 1845–97
Blow The Candle Out
Broken Hearted Tradesman, A
Certainly Not!
Human Nature
I Hope I Didn't Intrude
It Tickles The Ladies
Not So Much Of It
Oh, You Ridiculous Man
Scamp, The (They Can't Hold A
  Candle To Me)
Tattler, The
Will A Monkey Climb A Tree?

RING, Arthur b. 1865
I Was One Of 'Em
Lotion, The
Monte Carlo
Romance And Reality
Still The Game Goes On
They Notice It So
You Must Go

RING, Blanche *c*.1876–1961
Bedelia
Belle Of Avenue A, The
Claudie
Come Josephine In My Flying
  Machine
Goodbye, My Lady Love
I'd Leave My Happy Home For You
In The Good Old Summertime
I've Got Rings On My Fingers
My Irish Molly, O
Nora Malone (Call Me By Phone)
Tipperary Nora
Waltz Me Around Again, Willie
Yip-I-Addy-I-Ay

RIPON, George
Fellow Who Played The Drum, The
Football Match, The
I Have! I Have!
Irishman In France

Never Never Never No More!
Now When You Take A Wife
Squeeze My Little Finger
Tra-La-La-La Brigade, The
We've All Had 'Em
Where I Am Lodging Now
World's Machinery, The

RIVERS, Alf 1866–1955
Beautiful Dora
Cock A Doodle Doo
I've Got Something Else To Shout
  About

ROBERTO, SISTERS fl. 1870s–80s
I'm A Virgin
There Is No Harm In Kissing
Two Hearts In One

ROBERTS, Arthur* 1852–1933
Accent On, The
After The Ball (Bowyer & Powell
  parody)
After You With That
All *That* Sort Of Thing Don't Cher
  Know?
And So Say All Of Us
Another London
Are You Going Far This Evening?
Are You Going To The Ball This
  Evening?
Around The Town (w. Charles
  DANBY)
Artful As A Waggon-Load Of Monkeys
Auctioneer's Story, The
Broken Down Tragedian, The
Brother
Canneaux
Come, Come, Caroline
Coo-Ee-Oo
Co-Operation
Counterfeits Among The Gold
  (parody)
Crutch And Toothpick
Daddy Wouldn't Buy Me A Bow-Wow!
Daisy Bell (parody)
Dashing Militaire, The

Dick Turpin
Do Not Trust Him (The Spoofer's
  Nanny)
Don't Know So Much About That
Don't Take Any Notice, It's Only The
  Boy
Dotlet Of My Eye, The
Faint Heart Never Won Fair Lady
Farmer's Daughter, The
For Thee, My Love, For Thee
Funny! Very Funny (w. James FAWN)
General Of The Umtiadioos
Girl Who Lost Her Honeymoon, The
  (sk.)
Girl Who Took The Wrong Towing-
  Path, The (sk.)
Good Business
Good, Damn (or Darned) Good
Goodness Gracious
Good Young Man Who Died, The
Great Trickoli, The (sk.)
Great Tutor Song, The
Guessing At The Ball
HMS Robertus (sk.)
I Am A Respectable Singer
If I Was Only Long Enough
If I Were To Do Such A Thing
If Mary Jones Would Only Marry Me
I Found It!
I Know All About It Now
I'm A Regular Randy Pandy O!
I'm Going To Do Without 'Em
I'm Living With Mother Now
In My 'Ansom
In Parenthesis
Isn't It Lovely?
It Came With The Merry May, Love
It Don't Belong To Me
It's A Kind Of A Sort Of A Feeling
It's All Explained In This
It's Been In The Family For Years
It Touched Me Up A Little
It Was Just On The Tip Of My
  Tongue
I Wanted To Go On The Stage
I Was Never More Surprised

I Went To Find Emin *or* We Went To
   Find Emin
Jack Has A Wife In Every Port
Jack The Dandy Oh
Jolly Old Bachelor, The
Just The Same As Dolly Does
Lord Mayor's Banquet, The
Mabel, Sweet Mabel
Mad Actor, A
More Or Less
My Katty Kiss'em
1901
No, No, Fathead!
Nothing Coming In
Off! Very Much Off!
Old Soldiers
Or Words To That Effect
Pink Dominos
Pretty Souls
Previous Notice Of The Question
Put It To The Vote
Question Of Time, A
Quite Sufficient
Roberts On Billiards
Round The Town
She'd Never Been In Pantomime
   Before
She May Not Be That Sort Of Girl
She Wanted Something To Play With
S'm Other Ev'ning
Some Girls Do And Some Girls
   Don't
Sort Of A Kind Of A—, A
So Shy
Stand Me A Cab Fare, Duckie
Tain't Natural
Talking Waltz, The
Tee Ru Tum Ba
That Beautiful Smile
That's How You Parley-Voo!
There's Very Little In It
There Was A Little Maid
There You Are, Don't You Know
Three Weeks' Courtship
Tidings Of Comfort And Joy
Tipperary Rose

Topsy Turvy
Tut Tut Tut Who'd Have Thought It?
'Twas Only A Year Ago, Love
Waltzing Round The Water-Butt
We Are! We Are! We Are!
Wedding Bells (Take Him Home)
Wedding Of The Monkey And The
   Cat, The
We're Not So Chummy As That
We Went To Find Emin (I Went To
   Find Emin)
What Are You Going To Have, My
   Friends?
What A Wonderful Thing Is Life
What Do *You* Think?
What Shall We Do With Cyprus?
When We Were Young (w. J. J.
   DALLAS)
Where Do I Come In?
Where's The Count?
Whether You Want It Or Not
Who's That A'Calling?
Wicked Vicar Song, The
Winkle And The Whale, The
Wo-oh! Emma
You Can't Do It!
You'll All Be Wanted
You're Another

ROBERTS, R. A.° 1866–1932; 'Protean'
(i.e. quick-change) artiste
   Because I Look A Fool (song)
   Change Will Do You Good, A (song)
   Cruel Coppinger
   Dick Turpin
   Duel By Proxy
   It Pleased The Children So
   Little Johnny Porter
   Lucinda's Elopement
   Old Friends And Old Times
   Ringing The Changes
   Three Nice Girls (song)

ROBEY, Sir George° 1869–1954; m. (1)
Ethel HAYDON (div.); (2) Blanche Littler
(1899–1981), whose brother Prince m.
Nora DELANY

A, B, ab-
All For Her
All That I Could Spare
And That's That!
And Very Nice, Too
Another Little Drink (w. Alfred
    LESTER & Violet LORAINE)
Archibald, Certainly Not!
Artist, The
As A Friend
Auctioneer, The
Bang Went The Chance Of A Lifetime
Barrister, The
Be A Man!
Been There Ever Since
Bride, The
Burglar Jim
By And By You Will Miss Me (w.
    Shirley KELLOGG)
Caretaker, The
Charity Bazaar (All For Sweet Charity)
Charles II
Chinese Laundry Man, The
Clarence, The Last Of The Dandies
    (Idol Of Society)
Come Along With Me
Come Away
Could You Tell Me?
Cupid
Daisy Dillwater, District Nurse
Dear Kind Doctor
Did We?
Editress, The
Fact Is—, The
Fancy That!
Fine
First Love—Last Love—Best Love (w.
    Clara EVELYN and w. LORAINE)
Five Minutes Late
German Hotel Manager, The
German Musician, The
Girl Wanted
Give It A Wink
Gladiator, The
Good Queen Bess (The Days Of

Elizabeth)
He'll Get It Where He's Gone To Now
Henry VIII
He Was Never Used To Luxuries
How Rude!
I Couldn't Exert Myself
I'd Bow To Superior Knowledge
Idea, The
Idol Of Society, The (Clarence, The
    Last Of The Dandies)
I Do Love You
If You Were The Only Girl In The
    World (w. LORAINE)
I Had To Be Cruel To Be Kind
I Like To Do Things My Own Way
I Live Underneath
I'll Get My Own Back
I'm Amazed
I'm Dodging It
I'm Dotty
I Mean Ter Say!
I Naturally Resented The Intrusion
In Other Words
(In) The Subbubs
I Shall Sleep Well Tonight
I Simply Go And Do It And It's Done
Is That You?
I Stopped, I Looked And I Listened
It Ain't All Lavender
I Think That Will Do For Today
It's A Lie
It's A Long Time To Wait
It's A Very Deserving Case
It's Fine
It's The First Time I've Ever Done
    That
It Suddenly Dawned On Me
I've Done 'Em
I Wasn't Sure
Kindly Note The Change In His
    Address
Kindness Rewarded
Lost-Luggage Man, The
Louisa
Manager Of The Splitz Hotel, The

Maurice, I Prithee, Cease!
Mayor Of Muckemdyke, The
Meet Me By Moonlight Alone
Mere Detail, A
More In Sorrow Than In Anger
Mormon's Song, The
Mrs Blobbs (You Never Miss The
   Things You've Never Had)
My Hat's A Brown 'Un
Never As Long As I Live
Norah Dear
Now I Should Think He's Sorry
Now Laugh!
Now We Can Both Laugh Together
Oh, How Rude
Oh! The Black List
Oliver Cromwell
Once
One-Legged Family, The
Only Me
Piano Tuner, The
Pinky Ponky Poo
Poor Thing
Prehistoric Man, The
Pro's Landlady, The
Raleigh
Reductions For Taking A Quantity
Remedies
Richard Coeur De Lion
Riddle-Me-Ree
Same Moon Is Shining In The Sky,
   The
Say No More About It
'Scuse Me! Must Go
Settled
Shakespeare
She Spoke To Me First
She Was A Stranger In London
Shurr-Up!
Simple Pimple, The
Slight Mistake On The Part Of My
   Valet
Society Doc, The
Solid, Substantial, And Thick
Staring Me In The Face

Sticking It Out
Sweet Marie
Take These
Tale Of Woe
Tempt Me Not
That's What I Call Plucky
That's Where They Found Me
That's Work!
Then I Understood
Then We Parted
They're Always Taking Me For
   Someone Else!
They Wanted Me
Thing He Had Never Done Before, A
Too Soon
Touching That Little Affair
Up-To-Date Servant, The
We Did
Weekly Chronic, The
We Haven't Spoken Since
What A (Funny) Game!
What Funny Things You See When
   You Haven't Got A Gun
What I Have I'll Hold
What Is One Among So Many?
What Was There Was Good
Widow Of Colonel De Tracey, The
Without A Word
Worm's Eye View, A
Wow-Wow
Yes! That's It
You Feel Disappointed, Don't You?

ROBINA, Fanny 1861–1927; sister of
Florrie ROBINA
   All The Boys In Our Choir
   Coming Back Home Again
   Dear Mother I've Come Home To Die
   I Wooed My Love
   King Of The Boys
   My Little Baby Boy

ROBINA, Florrie 1867–1953; m. T. Reed
Pinaud (d. 10 Feb. 1925); sister of Fanny
ROBINA
   Britain's Marketing

English Rose, The
Esmerelda
I Know What You Mean
I Love The Rowdy Dowdy Boys
Ma Dusky Rose
Marguerite
Not In England
Prince Tiptoe
Sweet Annie Moore
Sweetest Flower That Grows
Teddy O'Neale
Timothy Winks (The Winking Man)
Two Little Hearts Made One
Two Maiden Aunts
We Put Him In A Cab And Sent Him
   Home

ROBINSON, Bill 'Bojangles' 1878–1949
Doing The New Low Down

ROBSON, Frederick 1821–64
Alonzo The Brave
As I Was A-Walking Beside The
   Seaside
Invasion Song
Porter's Knot, The (mon.)
Statty Fair, The
Undaunted Female, The
Villikins And His Dinah

ROLYAT, Dan 1872–1927; m. Florence
SMITHSON (div.); see also KARNO,
Fred
All Down Piccadilly
Simplicitas

ROMAIN, Manuel 1870–1926
Always Think Of Mother
Curse Of An Aching Heart, The
White Wings
Why Did You Make Me Care?

ROMAINE, Claire 1873–1964; daughter
of Edward Solomon°; m. Edgar
ROMAINE
I *Do* Know!
I'm So Careful
I Would Woo Thee

Mary Was A Housemaid
Maud
Oh, Sally! *or* The Coachman Tells Me
   So
Pennies
They Don't Mind Me
Wouldn't You Like To Know?

ROMAINE, Edgar m. Claire ROMAINE
Jolly Bohemian Boys

ROMAINE, Violet
All I Remember
All That I Ask Of You Is Love
Take The Path Where The
   Honeysuckle Grows

ROME, Fred° b. 1874; wrote all his own
material
Adverts Of Modern Medicine Makers
   (Shocks)
Burlesque Ballads
Business Guide, The
Calculatas The Memory Man
Evolution
Explained
Girls
Gone To Lunch
Ha! Ha! Ha!
I Was Had!
Longshoreman Bill
Moving The Piano
Non Stops
Pleasures
Reasons
Shocks (Adverts etc.)

ROONEY, Pat sen.° 1847–92; father of
Pat ROONEY jun.
Are You The O'Reilly? (orig. Is That
   Mr Reilly?)
Biddy The Ballet Girl (Madame La
   Sharty)
Day I Played Baseball, The
His Old High Hat
Is That Mr Reilly? (*see* Are You The
   O'Reilly?)
Katy Is A Rogue

Old Dinner-Pail, The
Owen Riley
Pretty Peggy
Sound Democrat, The

ROONEY, Pat jun. 1880–1962; son of
Pat ROONEY sen.
I Love To Go Swimmin' With Women

ROSE, Julian 1879–1935
Levinsky (mon.)

ROSEWOOD, Lillian
In The Shade Of The Old Apple
Tree

ROSING, Val 1890–1963
Teddy Bears' Picnic, The

ROSS, W. G. *c*.1813–*c*.1882
Alonzo The Brave
Ballad Of Sam Hall, The
Billy Barlow (own version)
Black Lecture On Phrenology
Going Home With The Milk In The
Morning
Hamlet Ye Dane
Jack Rag
Life And Death Of Bad Macbeth
Lively Flea, The (parody of Ivy Green)
Lover's Leap *or* A Romance Of The
Times
Mrs Johnson
Othello, Ye Moore Of Venice
Pat's Leather Breeches
Poor Married Man, A
Richard The Third
What Is A Man Like?

ROUSE, Willie* 1877–1928
Ah, Dearie Me
Crystal Gazing
Do You Remember?
Gags
Happenings
I Was There
Knowledge
Lady Wanted Washing, The
Mock Turtle

My Motor Bike
Pipe Lights
Servants
Silver Sea, The

ROWLAND, Adele 1883–1971
Lily Of The Valley
Mammy O' Mine
Pack Up Your Troubles
That Soothing Serenade

ROWLAND, Frank
I Tried It On
Then The Show Begins
Wives

ROWLEY, J. W. 1847–1924; father of
Edwin BOYDE
Almighty Dollar, The
As Welcome As The Flowers In May
(The Jolly Miller)
Biddy The Belle Of The Ballet
(Madame La Sharty/Shortie)
Birds Upon The Trees, The
British Isles
Call Him In
Captain Of The Lifeboat Crew, The
Carving Up Of The Turkey, The
Costermonger's Wife, A
Dear Old Pals (provincial rights only)
Down By The Old Abbey Ruins
Down In A Coal Mine
Eggs For Your Breakfast In The
Morning
England Is England Still
Gallant 24th., The *see* Noble 24th.,
The
Gladstone (The Tide's On The Turn)
Going To Hampstead In A Van *see*
Joe's Birthday
Going To The Derby In A Donkey
Cart (solo and w. Edwin BOYDE)
Hang Up Your Hat Behind The Door
He's Not Dead Yet
His Own Mother Wouldn't Know Him
Now
I Love The Verdant Fields
I'm A Dad Dad Dad!

I Must Have A Day Off For That
Irishman's Home Sweet Home
I Should Like To
It Always Comes Round To Me
It's Only Once A Year
It's The Same Old Thing
It Was Only The Way It Was Done On
The Stage
Jeremiah, Blow The Fire! (provincial
rights only)
Joe's Birthday *or* Did You Ever Go To
Hampstead In A Van?
Johanna Magee
Life In The East Of London
Life Is Like A Game Of See-Saw
Madame La Sharty (Biddy The Belle
Of The Ballet)
Matilda Gorger *or* Mulligatawny Soup,
A Mackerel And A Sole
More! More! Give Me Some More
My Sairey Ann
Naughty Biddy Macarthy
Noble 24th., The (Vanquished Not
Disgraced)
Not Dead Yet
Oh, How Different Now!
Oh! The Black List
Old 'Un, The
Only Fancy
Only Once A Year
On Monday She Sings 'Molly Riley O!'
On The Banks Of Bantry Bay (w. Ella
DEAN)
Our Ruth Ann
Our Wedding Jubilee
Patsy Brannigan
Pretty Girl! Rather!
Pull Down The Blind
Quite Another Thing
Rather Too Old For Me
Riley Did It!
Roley-Poley Over
See-Saw Margery Daw
She's As Sweet As A Lump Of
Obadiah Rock
Spank The Grand Piano Matilda

Starry Night And A Beautiful Girl, A
There's Bound To Be A Row
They All Belong To Mary
They're All Good
Tipperary Christening, The
True British Hearts
We Drew His Club Money This
Morning
Welcome At Home, The
What Do You Think?
What Shall We Do With Cyprus?
When You Wash A Nigger White
Where Was Johnny When The
Scotchman Came?
Why Should I Leave Old England?
Widow Doolin'
Will And The Way, The
Will You Be My Hollyhock?

ROXBY, Wilfred
Are You There, Moriarty?
Down In The Daisy Dell
Girl I Love On England's Shore, The
Marrying The Farmer's Daughter
Of Course It Means Nothing To Me
Where Are Your Friends When Your
Money Is Gone?

ROYCE, Sid
Lover's Alphabet, The (w. Nellie
FARREN and Edward TERRY)
Oh, It's Dangerous
She Was Right
Then The Show Begins

ROYE, Ruby 1895–1960
Aba Daba Honeymoon

ROZE, Lelia
Dandy Gay Conductor Of The Band,
A
My Banjo Loo
She Is My Girlie

RUDD, Austin° 1869–1929
Bobbing Up And Down Like This!
Body's Upstairs, The
Come Out!

Do You Mind Getting Up A Little
  Farther?
Eiffel Tower, The
Gallery And Boxes
He Hadn't Much Left
How Pleasant
I Didn't Know
I'm The Lodger
I Put It Somewhere Else
I Saw Him Home
I Was Off
Leave The Old One
Making The Ladies Laugh
Miles Away From Land, Miles Away
  From Sea
Music Hall Chant
Oh! The Difference
Pretty Little Maid Said 'Oui
  Monsieur', The
Pro's Supper, The
Red Lights, Danger
Sailors Don't Care
She Was In My Class
Suppose You Haven't Got It
They Found Me
This Is The Way You Go
We Had To Part

RULE, Herbert* 1884–1927
  Her Coo-Coo Eyes
  I Can Say 'Truly Rural'
  I'd Like To Be An Actress
  I Really Can't Reach That Top Note
  It's Easy To Pick Up The Chorus
  La-La-La-La, Sing This Chorus With
    Me
  Minutes
  Other Yacht, The
  Peter Piper Picked A Peck Of Pickling
    Peppercorns
  Wooloomooloo

RUMFORD, Kennerley 1870–1957; m.
Dame Clara BUTT
  Keys Of Heaven, The (w. Clara BUTT)
  King Charles
  Myrra

Old Grey Fox, The
O Peaceful England
Songs From The Turkish Hills
Three Little Songs (M. V. White)
Waiata Poi
Where My Caravan Has Rested
Yeomen Of England

RUSSELL, Bernard 1876–1910
  Advice For Beginners
  Anatomy
  Are You A Mason?
  First Act And The Last, The
  Fishing
  Have You Got A Cigarette Picture?
  Hold Your Hand Out!
  How They Argue The Point
  I Keep On Walking
  I'm Wanted On The Phone
  I Should Like To Be A—
  I Was Shaving Myself At The Time
  Oh, Chantecler
  Potted Poetry
  Press Cuttings
  Sad Are The Tidings I Bring
  See-Saw
  Verdicts
  Where Did I Put My Hat?

RUSSELL, Bijou
  Bilbao
  It's No Use You A-Knocking At The
    Door
  Pack Your Trunk Tonight
  What You Goin' To Do When The
    Rent Comes Round?

RUSSELL, Charles 1863–1948
  Coster Politician, The
  '54 (Charles Russell's Great Scena)
  Gutter Hotel
  I'll Take Orf My 'At To 'Is Name
  John Bull
  Oh, Tonight!
  On Duty
  Penny On The Can
  Soldier's Letter, The

When The Camp-Fire's Burning
   Brightly

RUSSELL, Charlotte 1837–1901
Jessie's Dream

RUSSELL, Gurney
Argumentative Man, The
Chiropodist, The
It's Wery 'Ard

RUSSELL, Henry° 1812–1900; father of
Sir Landon Ronald°
African Village, The
Ben Battle (Nelly Gray)
Chase—Set Every Inch Of Canvas,
   The
Cheer, Boys, Cheer!
Come Home, Father
Eva's Farewell
Fine Old English Gentleman, A
Flag Of The Free, The
Grandfather's Clock (My)
Ivy Green, The
Land Of St Patrick (The Irish Hurrah)
Life On The Ocean Wave, A
Maniac, The
(Oh!) Woodman, Spare That Tree
   (The Old Oak Tree)
Old Arm Chair, The
Ship On Fire, The
Slave Sale, The (Come, Who Bids?)
Song Of The Shirt, The
Spider And The Fly, The
There's A Good Time Coming, Boys
Wery Pekooliar (Miss Julia)

RUSSELL, Kate
Jolly Young Middy, A
Marching Through The Park
Vivandière, A

RUSSELL, Lillian 1861–1922; m. (1)
the conductor Harry Braham (div.);
(2) the composer Edward Solomon°
(annulled); there were two further
husbands
Alice

All On Account Of Liza
Come Down Ma Evening Star
In The North Sea Lived A Whale
Letter Song, The (*La Perichole*)
Napoli
Oh, How I Love The Military
Sabre Song, The (*Grand Duchess of
   Gerolstein*)
Somebody's Sweetheart I Want To Be
Song Of Thanksgiving, A
Your Kiss

RUSSON, F. w. MOHAWK MINSTRELS
Barney Take Me Home
Bring Back My Fisher Boy
Father's Loving Smile, A
Love Untold, The

RYLAND, Cliff 1856–1930; father of
Laddie CLIFF; brother-in-law of Bert
ERROL; orig. w. George Fuller GOLDEN
as Ryland & Fuller, then w. John J.
Sweeney as SWEENEY & RYLAND; solo
from 1899
Face
Man Of Eccentric Notions, The
Millionaire, A
Mrs Phelan's Child
Night We Let The Gorgonzola Loose,
   The
Nothing
Pen'orths
Round The Corner
Sing Tra-La-La-La
Sing Us A Song Of Nonsense
Somebody's Mother
There's Mischief Brewing

SABEL, Josephine 1866–1945
Bit O' Blarney, A
Ella, Come Under My Umbrella
Faded Leaf Of Shamrock, A
Hot Time In The Old Town (Tonight),
   A
Remus Takes The Cake
Sabel's Sparkling Champagne Song
Somebody Loves Me (Hattie Starr)

St Aubyn, Mr
Baker, The Quaker And The
Undertaker, The
Call Her Back And Kiss Her
Don't Hit Him When He's Down

St Clair, Fanny of Howard & St
Clair
Bill Bailey, Won't You Please Come
Home?
Lucy's Black Coon
Ma Coon Am A Millionaire

St Clair, F. V.° 1860–1922
All Through A Little Piece Of Bacon
Busy
Carving Up Of The Turkey, The
Cheer Up, Buller
Chums (My Old Pal Jim)
Down In The Mine
Down With The Old Free Trade
European Dance, The
Fireman Jim
Follow The Drum
Girl With The Golden Hair, The
Gladstone Is The Captain Of The Ship
John Bull
In London
Is The Same Old London There?
John Bull's Letter Bag
John Bull's Railway Station
Kitchener! Gone But Not Forgotten
Kitchener! Stand By Him
Leave 'Em Alone, They'll Come
Home In The Morning
Little Jap Horner
Loss Of The Drummond Castle, The
Made In England
Mary Jane And The Motor Car
Oh! Cerulia
Oh! Mister Morgan
Oh, Mr Lloyd
Oh! The Music
Railway Guard, The
Ring Up Britain *or* John Bull's
Telephone
Road To India, The

Salisbury And Gladstone
Show Me The Girl With The Golden
Hair
Stand By The Flag
Success To Her Majesty! (Long May
She Reign)
Tailor Tried To Catch Her, The
That's Where Mary's Gone
There Always Will Be Fairies
They Can't Do It
When We All Begin To Fly
Wreck Of The Serpent, The

St Denis, Teddie
Lambeth Walk, The (Noel Gay) (w.
Lupino Lane)

St Helier, Ivy° 1890–1971
Coal-Black Mammy (w. Marie
Blanche)
Lis(z)t To The Rhapsody Rag
Mary From Tipperary
Model And The Man, The (sk.) (w.
Zena Dare)
My Affinity
There's A Little Bit Of Bad In Every
Good Little Girl

St John, Florence 1854–1912; made
her Music Hall debut as Florence Leslie
though principally a musical comedy
artiste; m. (1) Lieut. R. N. St John
(dec'd); (2) unknown; (3) Monsieur
Marius (div.); (4) Arthur Cohen
Artless Thing, The
Ask Me To Marry
At Midnight On My Pillow Lying
Blindman's Holiday
British Barmaid, The
Carmen's Diary
Dear Mother, In Dreams I See Thee
Dreamless Rest
Eyes Of English Blue
Fie! Fie! Fie!
Fond Heart, Oh, Tell Me Why
For You
He Loves Me He Loves Me Not

How Awfully, Awfully Nice
I'm Such A Pretty Girl
Island Of Love, The
I've Been Hoo-dooed
Letter Song, The (*La Perichole*)
Love Me For Ever!
Maid With A Wink In Her Eye, The
Meet Me Once Again
My Mother Sent Me To The Vines
Novice, The
Only An Orange Girl
Sighing Swain, The
Simple Little Maid, A
Such A Don
When Love Is Young
When We Are On The Stage (w. Willie
     EDOUIN)
Why We Must Say Goodbye
Within The Maze Of Dreams

SAINTON-DOLBY, Charlotte° 1821–85;
k.a. Charlotte Dolby until her marriage
to Prosper Sainton in 1860
     Angels' Home, The
     Beloved One
     Bonnie Dundee
     Come Back To Erin
     Estelle
     First Violet, The
     Five Months Ago
     Green Trees Whispered Low And
          Mild, The
     I Stood On The Beach
     Lady Of The Lea
     Many A Time, And Oft
     My Love He Stands Upon The Quay
     Rainy Day, The
     Regret
     Self-Banished, The
     Swiss Echo Song
     Teddington Lock
     Those Dear Old Times
     Three Fishers Went Sailing
     When We Are Old And Grey
     White Cockade, The
     You Needn't Say A Word

SAMUELS, Rae sometimes spelled Ray
     Down In Dear Old New Orleans
     It Takes A Long Tall Brown-Skin Gal
          To Make A Preacher Lay His Bible
          Down
     I Want To Go Back To Michigan

SANDERS, Laura
     But A Lady Can't Propose
     Do—Dear
     R. R. Esq
     Underground Railway, The

SANDERS, Scott 1888–1956
     On The Road To Anywhere

SANDERSON, Julia 1887–1975
     They Didn't Believe Me (w. Donald
          BRIAN)

SANSOM, C.
     Alphabet Of Sweethearts
     One, Two, Buckle My Shoe, That's
          What I Did For Anna
     She's As Sweet As Sugar Candy, Oh
     True To The Core
     Who Stole The Donkey?

SANTLEY, Sir Charles 1834–1922;
composed songs as Ralph Betterton
     Colleen Bawn, The
     Erl King, The
     Even Bravest Heart May Swell
     Exile's Dream, The
     Fairy Lough, The
     Father O'Flynn
     Gipsy John
     Guard Our Homes
     Heart Of Oak
     Joconde
     Leather Bottèl, The
     Let Me Love Thee
     Lowly Peasant Girl, A
     Moon Has Raised Her Lamp Above,
          The (solo and w. William
          HARRISON)
     Morning Star, The
     Mountebank, The

My Queen
O Moon Of Night
Owl, The
Quaker Cousin
Queen's Shilling, The
Rosary, The
Scout, The
Simon The Cellarer
Stroller's Song, The
Sweet And Low
To Anthea (Hatton)
Trottin' To The Fair
Vagabond, The
Vulcan's Song
Wolf, The
Yeoman's Wedding Song, The

SANTLEY, Kate 1837–1923; m. Arthur
w. **WYNDHAM**
Awfully Awful
Bell Goes A-Ringing For Sa-i-rah,
    The
Cupid
Do—Dear
Girl Of The Period, The
I Sha'n't, I Won't
My Love He Likes A Soldier Bold
Nobody Knows As I Know
Not For Flo' (ladies' version of Not
    For Joseph)
Peter Gray
Polly Patterson
Sparkling Wine
Stranger . . . Stranger Than Ever, The
We Follow
You Are A Very Handsome Man

SANTLEY, Maud°
'Bobbies' Of The Queen, The

SARA, Mlle *see* **WRIGHT**, Sarah

SARONY, Leslie° 1897–1985
Ain't It Grand To Be Bloomin' Well
    Dead?
And The Great Big Saw Came Nearer
    And Nearer

I Lift Up My Finger And I Say 'Tweet-
    Tweet'

SAUNDERS, Madge 1894–1967; m.
Leslie **HENSON**
I'd Like To Bring My Mother (w.
    Leslie **HENSON**)
They Didn't Believe Me (w. George
    GROSSMITH jun.)

SCANLON, William J.° 1856–98
My Nellie's Blue Eyes (w. **CHRISTY**
    MINSTRELS)
Village Blacksmith, The (w. **CHRISTY**
    MINSTRELS)

SCHEFF, Fritzi 1880–1954
Be Kind To Poor Pierrot
If I Were On The Stage (Kiss Me
    Again)
When I Leave The World Behind
When The Fairest Flowers Are
    Blooming

SCHNEIDER, Hortense 1837–1920
Dites-Lui (Tell Him)
Letter Song, The (*La Perichole*)
Sabre Song, The (*Grand Duchess of
    Gerolstein*)

SCHOFIELD, Johnny w. **MOHAWK**
MINSTRELS
Coon That Can't Remember, The
Echo, The (w. Johnny **DANVERS**)
If I Were The Man In The Moon
Kind Sort Of A Something, A
Little Bit Of String, A
Mary Jane McCarty
Mother And Child Are Doing Well
Obadiah And Maria (w. **DANVERS**)
Sally Snow
She Danced At The Alhambra
Sisters Gee-Up, The (w. **DANVERS**)
Ta-Ra-Ra Boom-Der-É *or* Pop Goes
    The Question (w. **DANVERS**)
Two Johnnies In Love (w. **DANVERS**)
What I Want Is A Proper Cup Of
    Coffee

When Mary Had A Puncture In Her
   Tyre
You're Certain To Get Married If Your
   Nose Turns Up

SCOTT, Maidie *c*.1887–1966
Anona
Baby Brother
Bird On Nellie's Hat, The
But Father . . .?
Dear, Kind Poppa
Everybody Works But Father
Father Keep The Home Fire Burning
Father's Got A Job
Father's Got The Sack From The
   Waterworks
Green Apple Pain
Happy Jappy Soldier Man
How Can A Little Girl Be Good?
If I'd Had My Mother There To Guide
   Me
If The Managers Only Thought The
   Same As Mother
If The Wind Had Only Blown The
   Other Way
I Had To Chalk A Cross Upon My
   Slate
I Hope It Keeps Fine For Mother
I'm Afraid To Come Home In The
   Dark
I'm Glad I Took My Mother's Advice
Johnny Morgan's Sister
Kiss Me, My Honey
Mother Is The Leader Of Society
Mother Put A Card In The Window
Once Again The Curate Preaches
One, Two, Three
Won't You Listen To That Big Brass
   Band?

SCOTT, Malcolm 1872–1929; brother of
Admiral Sir Percy Scott Bt.; mons.
After You With The Soap, Dear
Boadicea
Chemist, The
Cuba Chloe

Directoire Girl, The
Encyclopaedia Britannica
Fiscal Policy
Geography
Grammar
I Lubsher
I Want A Gibson Girl
Katherine Parr
Kiss Me, My Honey (song)
Mariana
Mrs John Bull
Nell Gwynne
One, Two, Three Polka Song, The
Salome (Weston)
Sports
Stepping Stones To General
   Knowledge
Very Likely
What Does A Billiard Ball Do When It
   Stops Rolling?
Yip-I-Addy-I-Ay (song)
You Never Know Your Luck (song)

SEEL, Charles° d. 20 Dec 1903
Coster's Linnet, The
Dreaming
Four Flights Up And Four Flights
   Down
John The Blooming Toff
What Are You Laughing At?
Who Gives This Woman Away?

SEELEY, Blossom 1892–1974
Darktown Strutters' Ball, The
Ghetto Glide, The (w. Henry FINK)
Mammy's Little Coal Black Rose
San Francisco Guide
Smiles (Callahan: Roberts)
Somebody Loves Me
Toddling The Todalo
Turkey Trot
Way Down Yonder In New Orleans

SEELEY, Frank d. 11 Mar. 1913; orig.
half of Seeley & West
All Over Me
Amateur Whitewasher, The

Anywhere There Will Do
As Soon As I Go To Bed
Balmy Family, The
Clap Hands, Daddy's Come Home
Coming In—Going Out
Ding Dong
Electrical Man, The
Father's Got A Job
Father's Got 'Em
Fluttering In The Breeze
I Could Do With A Lot More Like
  'Em
I Didn't Want Asking Twice
I Don't Want To Go Any Farther
I'll Never Forget The Day
I'm A P'liceman
I'm Going Home To My Mother
In Beautiful Working Order
In Our Locality
In Training
It's Homely! So Homely!
It's Windy
Kicked Out
Let Go, Eliza
Little Bit Further Down, A
Louisa Brought Him Home Last
  Sunday
Me No Likee, Likee
More Than Ever
Mother Went Out To Find One
On Top Of The Garden Wall
Our New Father
Pass 'Em Over
Running Up And Down Our Stairs
Sold Again
Spring Cleaning
Take 'Em Away!
They All Came Round On Sunday
We All Had A Finger In The Pie
Wide, Wide World, The
Windy

SEWELL, J. W.° a.k.a. James Sewell
Bogey From Scotland Yard, The
Bond Street Mash-ah, The
End Of The Country Girl

Mackenzie (That Devil Of A Daddy)
New Photographee, The
Only A Week Away
So Now We Shan't Be Long
Woman After This

SEYMOUR, Katie 1870–1903
Clowns (w. Edmund **PAYNE**)
Follow The Man From Cooks (octet
  from *A Runaway Girl*)
Love On The Japanese Plan (from *A
  Runaway Girl*)
Mummies (w. **PAYNE**)
Professions (w. **PAYNE**)

SHAND, Ernest° 1868–1924
Agitator, The
At The Seaside
At The Vicar's Fancy Ball
Bachelors
Belinda
Bootman, The
By Kind Permission Of The Daily Mail
By The Sea
Consequences
Don't Mention It, Please
Eve! Eve! Eve!
Everything's An Extra In The Season
Gone! Like That
He Put The Idea In My Head
Hi! There! Whoa!
Hope For The Best
I Can't Oblige Today
In A Case Like That Don't Wait
In Other Lands
I Popped Inside To Buy One
I Really Only Meant To Be Polite
I Want To Meeet The Kaiser
La Diddley Diddleyum
Last Pub, The
Lest We Forget
Little Bo Peep
Little Mary
Lloyd Jarge
Look At The Weather We're Having
More Trouble In Store For Someone
New Insurance, The

Nobody Knows And Nobody Cares
(Oh) Dearly Beloved Brethren
Oh! Isn't It Singular?
Palmist, The
Paris Exhibition, The
Poor Noah
Put The Idea In My Head
Ragtime Curate, The
Rooty Tooty
Short Stories (La-Diddle-Diddley-Um)
Taffy's At His Old Old Game, John Bull
That's All!
Through The Telephone
Toodle-oodle-oodle-oddle-oo
Too-Ra-Li-Oo-Ra-Li-Ay
Waiter, The
We Really Had A Most Delightful Evening
What Are You Doing It For?
What Would The Congregation Say?
What Would You Do?
When Juggins Was Twenty-One
When Tommy Came Marching Home
Why Does A Lady?
Wide, Wide World, The

SHARP(E), John W. 1818–56
Billy Taylor
Bloomer Costume, The
Bottle, The
Box And Cox
Cab! Cab!! Cabby!!!
Cadger's Ball, The
Cockney Tourist, The
Dainty Plant Is The Cabbage Green, A
Electric Light, The
Jenny Lind
Kentish Gipsies, The (w. Miss G. A. HODSON)
Lamentations Of Punch, The *or* Pity The Downfall Of Poor Punch And Judy
Lively Flea, The (parody of Ivy Green)

Lord Lovel (parody)
Matrimonial Sweets (w. HODSON)
Modern Swell's Diary, The
Monster Statue, The
Mrs Caudle's Curtain Lectures
Pity The Downfall etc. *see* Lamentations Of Punch, The
Polkamania
Queen Victoria's Visit To Ireland
Royal Visit To The Coal Exchange, The
There's A Good Time Coming
Who'll Buy My Images?

SHEAN, Al *see* **GALLAGHER & SHEAN**

SHELLEY, Herbert° 1870–1921
Colours We Love, The
Dan The Dandy
Hi-Diddle-Diddle!
His Old Straw Hat
I Always Wears An Orchid Next Me 'Eart
Old Oak Well, The
Smoke, Smoke, Smoke (Fumed In Oak)
That Old Sunny Window
Workhouse Gate, The

SHEPARD, Burt 1854–1913; a.k.a.
Charles **FOSTER**
In The Shade Of The Old Apple Tree (parody)
Laughing Song, The
Potted Poetry
So Did Eve
That's Why I Left My Home
When Father Laid The Carpet On The Stairs
When The Gentle Breezes Blow!
Whistling Coon, The

SHERIDAN, Mark° 1867–1918
All The Little Ducks Went Quack! Quack! Quack!
And Other Things Too Numerous To Mention

And The Villain Still Pursued Her
At The Football Match Last Saturday
Belgium Put The 'Kibosh' On The
    Kaiser
By The Sea
Colonel Knut
England's Contemptible Little Army
Fancy Meeting You At The Isle Of
    Man
Fresh And Lovely
Hear What The Crowd Say!
Hello! Hello! Who's Your Lady
    Friend?
Here We Are! Here We Are!! Here
    We Are Again!!!
High Street Promenade, The
I Do Like To Be Beside The Seaside
I Don't Want To Be Beside The
    Seaside
I Felt Quite Sorry For The Fellow
I Looked Into The Book
Inventor, The
It's Suspicious
It's Very Very Warm Round There
I Wanted A Wife
Josser Football Team, The
Leave Off Aggravating
Let's Go Home Together!
Let The Good Work Go On
Limerickitis (Trying To Find A Strong
    Last Line)
Mr Bottomley—John Bull
Nature
Nursery Rhymes (Oh! Be Careful)
Oh! The Black List
On A Bright Summer's Day
One Of The B'hoys
One Of The Soldiers
On My Own
Perambulator Promenade, The
Poor Old Insurance Bill
Take A Nice Stroll Through The Park
That Was Years And Years And Years
    And Years Ago
There Ain't Going To Be Any Ragtime
There's No Harm In Kissing A Lady

There! There! There! (The Three
    Trees)
They All Walk The Wibbly Wobbly
    Walk
Tom! Tom! Tom! (Mr Tommy Atkins)
Top-Hat Every Time
Tut, Tut! That's A Bygone
We All Went Marching Home Again
We Shall All Do The Goose-Step
What A Fine Old Game You're Having
What A Game It Is! Wow! Wow!
When A Woman Says No!
When The Lads Come Home
When They Do! They *Do*!
When We've Wound Up The Watch
    On The Rhine
Where Have You Left The Girls?
Who Were You With Last Night?
You Can Do A Lot Of Things At The
    Seaside That You Can't Do In
    Town

SHERRINGTON, Louie
Beautiful Bill
Blind Boy, The (J. Lemmens)
Call Him Back Before Too Late
Champagne Charlie Was His Name
    (ladies' version)
Houp-La
In The Centre Row Of Covent Garden
    Market
I Should Like To Be A Fairy (Paper
    Wings)
Kerry Dance, The
Music Man
My Johnny Love Is A Soldier
Spinning
Up In A Balloon (ladies' version)
Upper Ten
Wait Till The Moonlight Falls On The
    Waters
Walking In The Zoo
Where's Peter?

SHIELDS, Ella 1879–1952; m. William
Hargreaves° (div.)

Adeline
Alexandra
Archie, PC
Bravo, Territorials!
Burlington Bertie From Bow
Dat's All
Do You Want Any Coal?
Girl In White, The
If You Knew Susie
I'm Cuthbert
I'm Going Back To Yarrawonga
I'm Not All There
In The Army (I Don't Admire The
    Girl In White)
Just One Kiss And Then—Another
    One
King's Navee, The (sk.)
Lady Said 'Oui, Oui', The
Millionaire, The
Oh! It's A Lovely War
Oh, The Baa-Baa-Lambs!
She Loves Me
Show Me The Way To Go Home
Smith, Jones, Robinson And Brown
Sun Am Shining—Why Don't You
    Go?, The
Waltz Time
Waxwork Show, The
What's The Use Of An Old Log-Cabin
    To Me?
When You've Got No Money In Your
    Pocket
Why Did I Kiss That Girl?
Why Don't You Go?
Wide Awake Walter From Wimbledon
    Way
You'll Stick To London Town
You're A Dangerous Girl

SHIELDS, Sammy 1872–1933
Bonnie Mary
Cricket A.B.C., The
Football A.B.C., The
Football Spectator, The
Pass The Ball
Play The Game

SHINE, J. L. 1854–1930
Less Said About It The Better, The
New Home Rule
Nonsense! Yes! By Jove! (w. George
    BARRETT)

SIDNEY, Harry *see* SYDNEY, Harry

SIM, William
Farewell, Alanna
Give Me My Heart Back Again
Golden Love
Softly Smiles Love's Golden Summer

SINDEN, Bert 1877–1911; brother of
Topsy SINDEN; m. Gertie Latchford (d.
26 Oct. 1946) who after his death m.
Barry Lupino (see LUPINOS, THE)
Frolic Of The Breeze, The
Where Do You Come From, My
    Pretty Maid? (w. Topsy SINDEN)

SINDEN, Topsy 1878–1951; née Harriet
Augusta Sinden; sister of Bert SINDEN
Armenia (sk.)
Blue Hussar, The (sk.)
Land Of I-Dunno-Where, The
Princess And The Troubador, The (sk.)
    (w. Winifred HARE)
Quaker Maid, The
Where Do You Come From, My
    Pretty Maid? (w. Bert SINDEN)

SIPPLE, Jim brother of Agnes HAZEL
Beautiful Leaves
Come Into The Garden Maud
Kathleen Mavourneen
McGregor's Gathering
Margaretta
Sally In Our Alley
Sweet Spirit Hear My Prayer

SKETCHLEY, Arthur° 1818–82; 1868–81
wrote and performed some thirty topical
sketches around the character of Mrs
Brown

SLOMAN, Charles° 1808–70
Artful Dodger, The

Barber's The Go, A
Batchelor's Inventory, The
Chandler's Shop, The
Charming Sue
City Of Silence, The
Core Reg'lar, The
Daughter Of Israel, The
Daughters Of Salem
Dream Of The Hebrew Maiden, The
Furniture On Hire
I Don't Stand Upon Ceremony
Israel's Fatherland
Jephtha
Jew Hath The Heart Of A Man, A
Jewish Captives In Babylon, The
Jew's A Man For All That, A
Jew's Lovely Daughter, The
Maid Of Judah, The
Original Beautiful Boy, The
Ostler Joe
Pop Goes The Weasel
Rose Of Raby
Shaving Shop, The
Smoakers's Medley, The
Streams Of Jordan, The
Tablets Of Sinai, The
Tune Me A Minstrel Lay
Who Am I?
Whole Hog Or None, The (Westrop)
Wolf, The

SLONE, Ryder d. 19 Apr. 1925
Are Yer 'Sleep?
Don't Go Back To Sing-Sing
I'm Nobody
It's Our Silver Wedding (The Night
    Watchman)
Nobody Waiting There To Greet Me
Oh! Poor Glasgow!
Oh! The Black List
One She'll Love The Best
Waiting For Further Evidence
You Wish You Were A Girl

SMILES, Jack
Fish Sauce
He's Done It Again

(I Don't Suppose He'll Do It Again)
    For Months And Months And
    Months
I'm Shy, Mary Ellen, I'm Shy
Jack Smiles' Popular Laughing Song

SMITH, (Henry) Clay b. 12 Feb. 1885;
m. Lee WHITE
    If It's In 'John Bull' It *Is* So

SMITHERS, Florence 1857–1927; all
sketches
    Dandy Doctor, The
    Done Brown
    Hard Lines
    In Charge
    Matrimony
    Paddington Pet, The

SMITHSON, Florence 1885–1936; m.
Dan ROLYAT (div.)
    Angel Of My Heart
    Arcady Is Ever Young
    Dance Along With Me
    Dance With A Song
    Dream Of Delight, A
    Fun Of The Fair, The
    I Found You
    In Your Crinoline You're Charming
    I Want To Be Somebody's Baby
    Just For Tonight
    Little Blue Moon
    Night And Day (I'll Watch And Pray)
    Pipes Of Pan, The
    Roses Have Made Me Remember,
        The
    Roses Of Picardy
    Singing Maiden
    Soldiers In The Park
    Star Of The Night
    Sweet Johnny Blossom
    Temple Bell
    Wyoming Lullaby
    You Can Have An Irish Name (But
        You Can't Wear The Shamrock)
    You Made Me Love You
    Your Eyes Of Blue

SMITHSON, Georgina d. 15 May 1899
  Buy A Broom
  Cupid
  Factory Girl
  Fun Of The Fair, The
  Gay Coquette, The
  German Brown Girl, The
  Sarah Ridley
  Stage-Struck Girl
  Sweet Johnny Blossom
  Volunteer, The
  Young Man From The Country,
    The

SNAZELLE, G. H. 1848–1912
  Australian Yarn, An (mon.)
  How Bill Adams Won The Battle Of
    Waterloo (mon.)
  Whistling Stammerer, The (mon.)

SNOW, Ted w. MOHAWK MINSTRELS
  Hurrah For The Life Of A Farmer
  Hush! The Bogie Man
  I Love To Think Of The Days When I
    Was Young
  Johnny Was A Piper
  Little Brown Jug
  Nancy Goodman
  Old Log Cabin In The Lane, The
  Slavery Days

SOLAR, Willie 1891–1956
  I'm Going Back To Dixie
  You Made Me Love You

SOLDENE, Emily 1844–1912; orig. k.a.
Miss FITZHENRY
  Happy Be Thy Dreams
  Home! Sweet Home!
  I Love Him So
  Launch The Lifeboat
  Marriage Bells, The
  Minstrel Boy, The
  Sabre Song, The (*Grand Duchess of
    Gerolstein*)
  Silver Threads Among The Gold
  Sleep
  Up The Alma's Height

SOTHERN, E. A. 1826–81
  Lord Bateman
  Oh! S-S-Sam Is A F-F-Fella That You
    Never Can Find

SOUTAR, (Joe) Farren 1874–1962; son
of Nellie FARREN and Robert SOUTAR
  So Did Eve!
  Tuppenny Tube, The (w. Zena DARE)
  What Makes The Woman?

SOUTAR, Robert 1827–1908; m. Nellie
FARREN; father of Farren SOUTAR
  Nice Girl, A

SPARK, The Little
  Alice In Wonderland
  Back To Town
  Dear Little Dancing Doll, The
  Don't Cry, Mama
  Has Anybody Seen My Dolly?
  Mammy, When I'm A Man!
  Red Riding-Hood

SPENCER, Elizabeth
  Be My Little Baby Bumble Bee (w.
    Walter VAN BLUNT)

SPRY, A. G.
  How Do I Go?
  Maud (parody)
  Where's My Two Bob Gone?

SPURR, Mel B. ° 1852–1904; the pre-
eminent society entertainer at the piano,
he wrote much but by no means all of his
own material
  Advance And Retreat
  After Dinner
  And I Don't Blame Him
  And So Did I
  'Arriet's Appeal
  Barnaby Phee, KC
  Betsy And I Are Out (mon.)
  Bounder, The
  Christmas Pantomime, A (sk.)
  Christmas Party, A
  Dinah
  Do It Thoroughly

Don't Forget The Porter
Extras
For A Very Very Long Long Time
Girl For Me, The
Girl From College, The
Good Night
Groom's Story, The (mon.) (Conan Doyle)
Hamlet Up-To-Date
Has It Ever Occurred To You?
His Only Joke
How We Laugh
How We Propose
How We Sing
In An Oven With Jerrybim (Lijer Goff) (mon.)
I Pause For A Reply
It Does Go
It Makes You Think
Jones's Musical Party
Mrs Brown At The Play (mon.)
Muddle-Puddle Porter, The
Not Understood
Oh! Be Careful
Oldest Inhabitant, The
Over The Hill To The Poor-House (mon.)
Quick Work
Settler's Story, The (mon.)
Silver Wedding
Tin Gee-Gee, The (The Lowther Arcade)
Tin-Tack On The Floor
Waif And The Wizard, The
What A Fool You Would Be To Believe Her!
What Is A Gentleman?
When I Was A Boy At School
Why Did The Night Owl 'Owl?
World Went Very Well Then, The

SQUIRE, Tom d. 1981
Bang Went The Door
Dancing Deacon
Fishing
I Can Tell It By Your Bumps

In The Future
I Should Like To Be A Soldier
Modern Mephistopheles, The
Special Constable, The
Time Will Show
Up! Up!! Up!!! And Down! Down!! Down!!!

STANHOPE, Erroll° 'England's Lady Whistler'
Dinah An' Me
My Honey Dear
Oh, Mary Ann!
One, Two, Three Polka Song, The

STANLEY, Walter
Can't We Take A Few Home, Father?
I'll Ask My Mother And Let You Know Next Sunday Afternoon
I'm One Of The Simple Sort
La Di Do De
Let Me Get Out And Walk
Look At The Time You Save!
Oh! The Motor-Car
Poor Old Shirt Was Short
Songs I Left Behind Me, The

STEAD, J. H. 1827–86
Ain't You Sorry You Dressed Yourself?
Angelina's Got A Baby
Aunt Sally
Belle Of Belgrave Square, The
Betsy Bangle
Dancing To The Organ
Diana Kitty Annie Maria, The Pride Of Clerkenwell
Did 'Em Like Muffins For Tea?
Didn't She Seem To Like It?
Grand Masquerade, The
Great Exhibition, The
Great Sensation Song, The (The Perfect Cure)
Here He Goes
Here There And Everywhere
If A Body Meets A Bobby
I'm As Happy As A King (I'm So Jolly Happy)

I've Joined The Teetotal Society
Julia Anna Maria Jane Matilda
Love's Perfect Cure
Matilda Toots
Oh My Oh Dear I Feel So Queer
Oh, Wouldn't You Like To Be Me?
Perfect Cure, The
Reg'lar Cure, The
She Gently Pressed My Hand
Susan's Sunday Out
Take It Quiet
That Blessed Baby
Tom Richard's Wedding
Up To The Knocker

STEEL, John 1900–71
Pretty Girl Is Like A Melody, A

STEELE, Albert 1836–88
Be Sure You Say I'm Out
Curly Little Bow-Wow, The
Hampstead Is The Place To Ruralize
Have You Seen Her Lately?
Lavender Girl
Things That Ought Not To Be

STELLA, Esta
Dear Old Crinoline
Honey Don't Leave Me
Moonlight Bay
Your Number's Up

STEPHENS, Catherine 1794–1882
Alice Gray (?)
Are You Angry, Mother?
Auld Robin Gray
Bantry Bay
Here Like The Gem That Ocean
  Hides
I'd Be A Butterfly
Lo! Here The Gentle Lark
When Thy Bosom Heaves The Sigh
  (w. John BRAHAM)

STEPHENS, Fred W.
After The Tin-Gee-Gee

Boney Mary Of Argyle (parody)
Burglar's Serenade, The
Coster Othello, The
Coster's Minuet, The
He Wasn't Even Satisfied
Irish Punter, The (A Tale Of The Turf)
Story Of A Musical Bee, The
That's His Girl
Tips For The General Election
Toy Lovers, The
Trilby, The French-Irish Girl
Whoi-A! Wot-O!

STERLING, Antoinette 1843–1904
Better Land, The
Caller Herrin'
Children Asleep
Chorister, The
Crossing The Bar
Daddy
Darby And Joan
Dear Wife, A
Gift, The
Home, Dearie, Home
Home! Sweet Home!
Lost Chord, The
Love Comes To All
Love's Old Sweet Song
Loyal Lovers
Reaper And The Flowers, The
Sands Of Dee, The (Clay)
Song Of The Shirt, The (Behrend)
Sunshine And Rain
Three Fishers Went Sailing
Voices
We're A Noddin'
When The Tide Comes In

STERN, Sam° b. 1883
Bravo Antonio
Cohen Owes Me Ninety-Seven
  Dollars
I'm Just Nobody
My Brudda, Sylvest'
My Rachel Myer From Hawaii
My Rachel's Beautiful Eyes
Solomon's Trombone

Vere Vas Moses Ven The Light Vent
Out?
When That Yiddisher Band Played
That Irish Tune
Yiddle On Your Fiddle Play Some
Rag-Time

STERNDALE-BENNETT, T. C. *see*
BENNETT, T. C. Sterndale

STEVENS, Charles E. 1854–1910
Guinea Hamper, The
If I'd A Bloomin' Throne To Call My
Own
Oh! Take Me There
Phrenology
Work And Be Contented (parody)

STEVENS, Victor *c.*1853–1925
Bundle 'Em Off At Once
In Public! In Private!
No! Yes! Well, You Ought To Know
Old Granny Gladdy (Teetotallers By
Act Of Parliament)
Then He Died

STEWART, Melville 1869–1915
Millionaire, The
Phrenology
Shade Of The Palm, The
Somebody (w. Kate CUTLER)

STEWART & GILLEN
In The Good Old Summer Time

STIMSON, Fred 1857–84
Nonsense! Yes! By Jove! (w. Fawcett
LOMAX)
What Could You Wish For More?

STOCKWELL, Walter
Boys Together
Dear Old Friendly Faces
Don't It Make You Wild?
'E Do Know Where He Is
Fairly Knocked The Yankees In
Chicago
Give Me The Girl In The Plain Cotton
Dress

Giving The Game Away
Great Millionaire, The
Grip Of The Hand, A
They Call Us Darby And Joan
Waiting To Welcome Him Home
We Didn't Get Home For A Week
Where Have The Girls All Gone To?

STOKES, Miss Bertie 'female tenor'
Anchor's Weigh'd, The
Come Into The Garden Maud
Slave Mother, The
White Squall, The

STOREY, Fred 1856–1917
By Arrangement (sk.)
Merchant Of Venice, The ('tabloid'
version)

STORMONT, Leo
Cruiser Jack
Fighting Man, The
God Bless Victoria
Goodbye, Dolly Gray
I Wonder If He Loves Me
Lifeboat Crew, The
Queen Of The Earth
Sailors Of Our Fleet
Sons Of Our Empire
Sweet Adeline
What Is Our Own We'll Hold
Young British Soldier, The

STRATTON, Charles 1832–83; better
known as General Tom Thumb
Yankee Doodle

STRATTON, Eugene 1861–1918; m.
Bella Moore (1867–1955) daughter of
George 'Pony' MOORE; came to UK w.
HAVERLY'S MASTODONS
All Coons Look Alike To Me
Aunt Mandy
Banshee, The
Black's De Colour
Cake Walk, The
Cane Brake Song, The
Can't Lose Me, Charlie!

Coloured Chloe
Coloured Millionaire, The
Come And Kiss Your Honey On The
Lip!
Cook's Excursion Trip, A (w. Mabel
LOVE)
Cool!
Coon Drum-Major, The
Coon That Never Told A Lie, The
Dandy Coloured Coon, The
Darkies' Jubilee, The
Dat Little Gal Of Johnson's
Dear Boy—Ta-Ta
De Baby Am A-Crying, Mommer,
Come!
De L'il Meetin' House
Game Of Life, The (w. Marie
DAINTON)
Hoodoo, The
Hot-Footed Bee, The
Idler, The
I Don't Know Nobody
I Lub A Lubbly Girl, I Do
I May Be Crazy (But I Love You) (A
Mexican Romance)
I'm The Father Of A Little Black
Coon
Is Yer Mammie Always With Yer?
Jes' So
Keep Yer Big Feet Movin'
Lazy Daisy
Lily Of Laguna, The
Little Dolly Daydream
Lovely Annie Lisle
Love Me Little, Love Me Long
Lubly Girl's Reply, The
Lucy, Tell Me I'se Yer Beau
Ma Little Sister Sue
Millionaire, The
My Cute Maluma Girl
My Gal Is A High-Born Lady
My Little Black Pearl
My Little Octoroon
My Second Time On Earth
One Hundred Yards In Rear
Sheelah Magee

She's Mine! I'm Hers!
Susie Tusie
Syncopated Dandy
There's Nothing Like Your First Love
After All
Thousand Yards In Rear, A
Trilby Will Be True
Uncle Jasper
Waitress' Love Letter, The
When De Golden Sun Went Down
Whistling Coon, The
Whistling Susanna
Whistling Yaller/Yellow Girl, The
Won't You Love Me? Won't You?
You Can't Lose Me, Charlie

STRATTON, Nellie 1875–1947; m. Wilkie
BARD
Eagle, The
Give Us A Bit Of Your Kilt
In An Old Sedan Chair
Little Wild Rose, I'm Leaving You
Shy Widow, The
Where's The Gold Of London?

STROUD, Gregory b. 1892
Look For The Silver Lining (w.
Dorothy DICKSON)

STUART, Childie d. 8 May 1923
Chase Me, Charlie

STUART, Marie c.1871–1912
Little Peach In An Orchard Grew, A
(w. D. G. LONGWORTH)

STUART, May see LESLIE-STUART, May

STUART, Tom 1878–1933
Mick Magilligan's Daughter, Mary
Anne
Nation Once Again, A

STUDHOLME, Marie 1875–1930
Grow, Little Mushroom, Grow!
Honeymoon Girl, The
Tom Tit
When The Boys Come Home Once
More

SULLIVAN, J.°
I'm Lively Pompey Jones

SULLIVAN, Joseph J.° 1817–1917
Where Did You Get That Hat?

SULLIVAN, Rose 1863–95; m. Arthur
REECE
Boys Across The Sea
Brothers Maloney, The
Danny M'Call
I Do Not Sigh For Wealth
Mickey's Trousers
My Brother Jack
Ould Oireland
Paddy M'Grah The Marvellous
    Fighting Man
Side By Side (J. M. Harrison)
We've Lived Together, We've Died
    Together
You'll Have To Name The Day

SULLY, Mariette b. 1878
Swing Song, The (w. Jean PERIER)
Trot Here And There (w. PERIER)

SUTTON, Randolph 1888–1969
All By Yourself In The Moonlight
Bushes At The Bottom Of The
    Garden, The
Jollity Farm
On Mother Kelly's Doorstep
Over The Garden Wall
When Are You Going To Lead Me To
    The Altar, Walter?

SWEENEY, Joseph d. 26 Oct. 1900?; see
also VIRGINIA MINSTRELS
Jenny Get Your Hoe Cake Done
Lucy Long
Zip Coon (Turkey In The Straw)

SWEENEY & RYLAND fl. 1880–92; John
J. Sweeney (1847–92) and Cliff RYLAND
Down Went McGinty
I'd Fifty Shillings On My Inside
    Pocket
Irish Dukes, The
Irish Jubilee, The

Mary Is Mashed On Me
Mine Did
Norah Delaney

SYDNEY, Harry° 1825–70; or Sidney;
claimed to sing only his own songs
A. B. C. (Signs Of The Times)
Act On The Square, Boys
As We Journey On The Road
Boat Race Day Of 1866, The
Building Castles In The Air
Coaching Days *or* Forty Years Ago
Country Cousins
Do The Best You Can
Farmer's Son, The
Fifty One And Sixty Two
Flag Of Old England, The
Free And Easy
Good Evening
Hornsey Wood (I Really Think She
    Did)
I'm A Young Man From The Country
    But You Don't Get One Over Me
I Mean To Be Jolly
In A Quiet Sort of Way
I Stand It Like A Lamb
It's Just As Well To Take Things In A
    Quiet Sort Of Way
It Very Much Depends Upon The
    Style In Which It's Done
Jemima
Jones's Sister
Keep On Never Minding
Let The World Jog Along
Little Red Riding Hood
Meet Me In The Phil When The
    Clock Strikes Nine
Missus Took A Sly Glance At Me, The
My Christmas Song
My Sporting Old Grey Mare
My Uncle
Night In A Workhouse, A
Not Good Enough For Me
Old John Bull
Oxford And Cambridge Boat Race
Pat Of Mullingar

Plodding Through The Rain
Political ABC, The
Quiet Sort Of Man, A
Rolling Stone Was Never Known To
Gain Much Moss, A
Royal Baby, The
Sally In Our Alley (parody)
Shadows On The Wall
Signs Of The Times In The ABC, The
Sly Glance, A
Song Of The Fight, The
Speculation
Sweetest Eyes
Take A Lesson From Me
That's What I Want To Know
There's Life In The Old Boy Yet
There's Nothing Beats Trying But
Doing
Turns
University Boat Race, The
What Will I Do Now?
Whisky In The Jar
Why I Fill My Pipe Again
Wolf, The
Young Man Up From The Country, A

SYLVESTER, Rose m. Dan PAULTON
Coster And The Curate And The Jew,
The
Mister Man
Pet O' The Pantomime, The

SYMPHONY QUARTETTE *see* DONALD-
SON, George

TAFT, Harry 1876–1939
She Is More To Be Pitied Than
Censured

TALBOT, Clarissa
I Wouldn't Leave My Little Wooden
Hut For You
Just A Little
Servant Question, The (By One Who
Knows)

TALLY, Harry 1866–1939
Come Josephine In My Flying
Machine

Mandy, Won't You Let Me Be Your
Beau?
Sadie Moore
Wait Till The Sun Shines, Nellie

TANGUAY, Eva 1878–1948
America I Love You
Egotistical Eva
Give An Imitation Of Me
Go As Far As You Like, Kid
I Can't Help It
I Don't Care, I Don't Care
I Love To Be Lazy
It's All Been Done Before But Not
The Way I Do It
I Want Someone To Go Wild With
Me
My Sambo
Nothing Bothers Me
Salome Dance (parody of Maud
Allen's notorious exhibition)
Shinny On Your Own Side
Tanguay Rag, The
What Money Can't Buy
Whistle And Help Me Along

TARRI, Suzette 1881–1955
Red Sails In The Sunset

TATE, Beth b. 1890
All Alone
Billy (For When I Walk)
Everybody Two-Step
I Don't Want To
Innocent Bessie Brown
Leave The Rest To Me
Someone I love
Sorry, Good-Night
Take A Little Bit Off If You Want To
Get On
Take A Look At Me Now
They're Wearing 'Em Higher In
Hawaii
Twinkling Star, The
What Happened In The
Summer-Time
You Made Me Love You

TATE, Harry[*] (& Co.) 1872–1940; sketch troupe incl. (inter alia) Harry Beasley, Tom Tweedly, and Tate's son Ronald Hutchison (b. 1902) k.a. Harry Tate jun.

Billiards
Business As Usual
Cabbies' Lament, The (song)
Contempt Of Court
Fishing
Flying
Fortifying The Garden (Gardening)
Golfing
Good-bye-ee (song)
How's Your Father? (song)
Joyland
Motoring
Number Seven
Oh! The Black List (song)
Peacehaven
Push And Go
Selling A Car
There's More To Follow (song)
Ward In Chancery, A
Where Shall We Go To? (song)

TATE, James W.[*] 1876–1922; brother of Dame Maggie **TEYTE**; m. (1) Lottie **COLLINS** (dec'd), a union which brought Tate three step-daughters incl. José **COLLINS**; (2) Clarice **MAYNE**, to whom he was accompanist and song-writer; always billed after her as 'THAT'

TATTEN-HALL, H. C. *see* HALL, Tatten

TAYLOR, Evelyn
Ayesha, My Sweet Egyptian
Cheer Up! Nobody's Girl
Come Right Back To Your Home Again
Fireman Jim
We Can't All Live In Easy Street
When Mister Poverty Comes Knocking At Your Door

TAYLOR, Harry b. 1889?
Bally Bulldog, The

Duty Of A Wife, The
For Old Times' Sake
Oh, Flo! (Why Do You Go?)
On The Margate Boat
Quips The Quaker
Welcome, CIVs!

TAYLOR, James G. 1838–95
Calais Packet, The
Chilly Man, The
I'm The Lying Dutchman Gay
Old Sarah Walker
Seven Ages Of Man
She's A Daisy
Simple Simon

TAYLOR, Laurette 1884–1946
Peg O' My Heart

TEMPEST, Dame Marie 1864–1942
Amorous Goldfish, The
Bid You Good Morrow
Bonjour, Pierrot
Dear Mother, In Dreams I See Thee
Farewell Waltz, The (w. Hayden COFFIN)
Forgive (w. COFFIN)
Give Me Love
Golden Isle, The
I Love Him Only
I Want To Be Popular
Jewel Of Asia, The
O Mimosa San
On Y Revient Toujours
Shearing Of Samson, The (sk.)
Speak But One Word
Tout Passé
Welcome Bonnie Charlie
Who's For This Flag?

TEMPLE, Madge d. 8 Dec. 1943
Billy (For When I Walk)
By The Side Of The Silvery Sea
Come, Be My Rainbow
Esau, Take Me On The Seesaw
He's A Very Old Friend Of Mine
I'm Looking For Mr Wright
In Daisy Dreamland

Joan! Joan! Joan! Come Home!
Kitty Brady
Little Golden Daffodil
On The Silvery Sands
Pansy
Wouldn't You Like To Be The
    Bridegroom?

TEMPLETON, Fay 1865–1939; m. Billy
West of PRIMROSE & WEST'S
MINSTRELS (div.)
    45 Minutes From Broadway
    I'm A Respectable Working Girl
    Ma Blushin' Rosie
    Mary's A Grand Old Name
    So Long, Mary
    What You Want And What You Get
    Woodchuck Song, The

TEMPLETON, Jessie
    Come And Put Your Arms Around
        Me, Georgie Do

TENNYSON & O'GORMAN fl. 1881–1901;
Joe Tennyson (1858–1926) and Joe
O'GORMAN; see also TENNYSON &
WALLIS
    Talkative Man From Galway/Poplar,
        The
    When They Get Old
    Wild Man Of Borneo/Poplar, The

TENNYSON & WALLIS, fl. 1902–15; Joe
Tennyson (1858–1926) and William H.
Wallis (d. 9 May 1949); see also TEN-
NYSON & O'GORMAN
    Paragraphs
    Put Off Your Troubles Till Tomorrow
    We All Came In The World With
        Nothing
    When They Get Old
    You Can't Take It With You When You
        Die

TERRISS, Ellaline 1871–1971; m. Sir
Seymour HICKS
    After The Honeymoon (sk.) (w.
        Seymour HICKS)

Alexander's Rag-Time Band
Always Tell Your Wife (sk.)
Anytime, Anywhere, If I'm With
    You
Au Revoir, My Little Hyacinth
Boy Guessed Right, The
Bridal Suite, The (sk.) (w. HICKS)
Cash On Delivery (sk.)
Caterpillar And The Rose, The
Cheyenne (Shy Ann)
Cook's Man (sk.) (w. HICKS)
Fly-By-Night, The (sk.) (w. HICKS)
Garrick (sk.) (w. HICKS)
Glow, Glow, Little Glowworm
'Gobbl'ums' Will Get You, The
Had I But Known
Honeysuckle And The Bee, The
I Love You, My Love, I Do
I've Got Rings On My Fingers
I Want Yer, Ma Honey
Joan Of Arc (sk.)
Lady At Large, A (sk.)
Linger Longer Lou
Little Yellow Bird
Lousiana Loo
Ma Chère
My Indiana Anna
My Little Buttercup
My Old Doll
Navaho a.k.a. Navajo
Pansy Faces
Papa's Wife (sk.) (w. HICKS)
Pink Of Perfection, The (sk.)
Simple Little String, A
Sleeping Partners (sk.) (w. HICKS)
Slum Angel, A (sk.) (w. HICKS)
Song Of The Shop, The
Streets Of Cairo, The
Sunflower And The Sun, The
Teasing
Umpty Umpty Ay
We're Really Proud Of You

TERRY, Edward° 1843–1912
    Complaints *or* The Ills Of Life With
        Their Remedies

Continong, The (w. Nellie FARREN
and Kate VAUGHAN)
H'Angelina!
Language Of Love, The
Lover's Alphabet, The (w. FARREN and
Sid ROYCE)
Mashers, The
Melting Moments
Mixed
Quack's Song, The
Song Of A Genius, The
Weights And Measures
Whistling Song, The (w. FARREN)

TERRY, Dame Ellen 1847–1928
Merchant Of Venice, The (excerpts)
Merry Wives Of Windsor, The
(excerpts)
Romeo And Juliet (excerpts)

TERRY, Will° 1875–1915; recording
alias: Alf GORDON
Alphonse Dupon (mon.)
Beautiful Girls
Commercial Traveller, The (mon.)
Crime, A (mon.)
Fugitive, The (mon.)
Growing The Prize Sweet Pea
He'll Be Quite All Right In A Bit
I'm His Daisy
I Turned Up My Trousers And Ran
(mon.)
I Want A Nice Girl
Jock McGrau
Lucky Cat, The
Ma Grannie, Ma Mither And Mysel'
More 'Excelsior' Varied
Mr Schmidt Learns To Swim (mon.)
Mr Schmidt Plays Billiards (mon.)
My Landlady's At It Again (mon.)
Mystery, A (mon.)
Our Fire Brigade (mon.)
Pavement Artist's Story, The (mon.)
Right Away
Showman's Story, The (mon.)
Sir Robert Gazeuppard's New Comet
Sports (mon.)

Truthful Ballad, A (mon.)
'Twas (mon.)

TEYTE, Dame Maggie 1888–1976;
sister of James W. TATE
Because
Curly-Headed Babby
Gods Are Come Again, The
I Love The Moon
Lightly Lightly (w. Marion GREEN)
Little Grey Home In The West
My Ain Folk
Philomel
Songs My Mother Taught Me
Until
What Are The Names? (w. GREEN)
Your King And Your Country (We
Don't Want To Lose You)

'THAT' see TATE, James W. and MAYNE,
Clarice

THATCHER, George 1844–1913; see
also PRIMROSE & WEST MINSTRELS
Willie Montrose

**THATCHER, PRIMROSE & WEST
MINSTRELS** see PRIMROSE & WEST
MINSTRELS, also WINTER, Banks

THOMAS, Arthur° 1863–1919; son of
Funny Little THOMAS
Fiscal Fight, A
Khaki Night And Day
Pom-Per-Ra-Ra-Pom-Pom
Runaway Motor Car, The

THOMAS, Brandon° 1857–1914
Beside De Cabin Door
Don't You Come And Bodder Me
I Lub A Lubbly Gal, I Do
Sing Along Sambo!
Soapy Soap
Tabby's Catastrophe
Thickening Of The Tympanum, The
Tommy Atkins

THOMAS, Funny Little (Joseph)
1839/40–1920; w. MOHAWK MINSTRELS

1879–1904 and w. Palladium Minstrels
c.1913; father of Arthur THOMAS
   Betsy The Butterman's Daughter
   Brickbats Never Shall Be Slaves
   Catherine And Caroline
   E-Lec-Tric-I-Ty
   Fair Weather Friends
   Good-Bye Emily Jane
   He Like A Soldier Fell (parody)
   I Believe It, For My Mother Told Me
      So (parody)
   I Can't Stand Mrs Green's Mother
   I Carry My Sunshine With Me
   I Don't Want No Tellin'
   I'm Sorry For The Poor Rich Young
      Man
   I Shall Never Go Courting Annie
      Moore Any More
   Johnny Get Your Gun
   Khaki Night And Day
   Man's Best Friend Is His Pocket, A
      (parody)
   Mother In Law's Lament, The
   Nobody Knows, Nobody Cares
   Pom-Per-Ra-Ra Pom-Pom
   Put Me Some Jam Roll By, Jenny
      (parody)
   Runaway Motor Car, The
   Scientific Simpleton, The
   Silliest Coon In Town, The
   Song That Reached My Heart, The
      (parody)
   There Is No Place Like Home
   There We Lay! Ill All Day
   Tom Bowling (parody)
   Under The Chestnut Tree
   Waltzing Round The Water Butt
   We Are All Humbugs
   Wedding In The Crow Family, A
   We Two
   We've All Got A Lot To Be Thankful
      For
   White Wings (parody)
   Wild Man From Borneo, The (w.
      Johnny DANVERS)
   You Never Know Your Luck

   Young Man Who Used To Live Over
      The Way, The

THOMPSON, Lydia 1866–1908; cousin of
Florence LLOYD and Violet LLOYD; m.
Walter TILBURY
   Brannigan's Band
   Come Down, Darling Do
   I've Been Photographed Like This
   Oh How Delightful
   Pretty Darkie Don't Say No
   Velocipede Song

THORNE, Ambrose d. 26 Aug. 1936
   Conversations
   Girl I Want, The
   I Come From Gay Paree
   I Hope They Won't Put A Tax On Girls
   Meet Me Under The Clock
   Mixed Relations
   My Novelette
   Oh, Leave Me With The Ladies!
   Picture Postcard Girls, The
   Practical Tactical Nautical Man, The
   That Isn't A Bad Idea (w. Paul MILL)
   When We Want A Change In The
      Government

THORNE, Mabel
   Coalman, The
   Oh, De Wet!
   Swing Me Higher, Obadiah
   Teddy

THORNTON, Miss fl. 1860s
   I Dare No Longer Stay
   Minnie Clyde
   Pretty Bird
   Riding In A Railway Train
   Sweet Love Arise
   Wapping Old Stairs

THORNTON, Bonnie c.1871–1920; a.k.a.
Lizzie Cox; m. Jim Thornton
   Caprice
   Dear Good Mr Best, The
   Della Lee, You're Fooling Me
   Down In Poverty Row

Jack, How I Envy You
Lucky Jim
Meet Me In St Louis, Louis
My Little Circus Queen
My Sweetheart's The Man In The
    Moon
She May Have Seen Better Days
Streets Of Cairo (The Poor Little
    Country Maid)
When You Were Sweet Sixteen

THORNTON, Edna 1875–1958
Believe Me If All Those Endearing
    Young Charms
Danny Boy
God's Garden
Hame
Kiss In The Railway Train, The
Love's Coronation
Love's Old Sweet Song
My Ain Folk
Night Has A Thousand Eyes
Oh Dry Those Tears
Softly Awakes My Heart
Your King And Your Country

THORPE, Herbert
Come To The Fair
Excelsior! (w. Foster RICHARDSON)

THUMB, General Tom pseud. of
Charles STRATTON

THURSBY, Emma 1845–1931
Home! Sweet Home!
Old Folks At Home, The
'Tis The Last Rose Of Summer

TIBBETT, Lawrence 1896–1960
On The Road To Mandalay
White Dove, The

TICH, Little° 1867–1928
All Over The Shop
Armlets
Ballerina, The (Little Miss
    Turpentine)
Barber, The
Best Man, The

Boxer, The
Chinese General, The
Close, Very Close Indeed
Curiosity
Dentist, The
Don Of The Don Juans, The
Don't Go Any Further
Farthest North Gamekeeper, The
Funny Little Man, The (w. Mabel
    LOVE)
Gamekeeper, The
Gas Inspector, The
General, The
Girl Got Off At Clapham, The
How I Climbed The Pole
I Could Do, Could Do, Could Do,
    Could Do, Could Do With A Bit!
Idiosyncracies
I Do, Doodle-Oodle-oo
I'm An Inspector Of The Metropolitan
    Police
I'm Lord Tom Noddy
I Really Can't Stop Dancing
It Was Close, Very Close Indeed
It Went—Went Quick!
Jockey, The
King Ki-Ki
Kitchener's Karol
Lamplighter, The
Lifeguardsman, The
Little Miss Turpentine (The Ballerina)
One Of The Deathless Army (The
    Territorial)
Park Keeper, The
Pirate, The
Police Inspector, The *see* I'm An
    Inspector etc.
Popularity
Puzzles
Right! Right! Right!
Risky Thing To Do, A
Sale, The
Sergeant-Major, The
Serpentine Dancer, The
Skylark, The
Smiles! (McGlennon)

Steeplejack, The
Sweet Simplicity
Tally O! The Tallyman!
Tax-Collector, The
Territorial, The (One Of The
    Deathless Army)
There's A Silly Thing To Ask A
    Policeman
Toreador, The
Twenty-Third, The
Waiter, The
Was I Afraid?
Weather, The
We've Got To Put Up With It Now
What Will The Cock-A-Doodle Do?
When She Sees Me In My Sunday
    Suit
You Can Tell What They've Been Up
    To
You Do See And You Don't See
Zoo Keeper, The

TIERNEY, Harry° 1890–1965
If You Can't Get A Girl In The
    Summertime

TIETJENS, Therese 1831–77
Bird That Came In Spring, The
Gentle Shade
It Was A Dream
Ocean, Thou Mighty Monster (Weber)
Of Love They Say
Promise Of Life, The
'Tis The Last Rose Of Summer

TIFFANY, Maud(e) disappeared 1914
Alexander's Rag-Time Band
Everybody's Doin' It Now
While They Were Dancing Around

TILBURY, Walter° 1868–1942; m. Lydia
THOMPSON
Come Back Home To Ireland
Eton Boy On The Continong, The
Forget The Past
Jack The Handyman
Land Of The Free, The
Lazy

Queen And The Shamrock, The
Respect Our Queen
Rook And The Crow, The
Sweet Seventeen
Tommy Don't You Worry

TILLER GIRLS, THE fl. 1890–1960s;
est. John Tiller (1854–1925) 1890 as
Les Jolies Petites (four juveniles); first
adult troupe est. 1891 as The Tiller
Quartette (Annie Johnson, Patti Bell,
Madge Vernon, Amy Knott). Troupes
were billed under many names; John's
son Lawrence Tiller ran similar all-girl
troupes
Little Gypsies, The (Les Jolies Petites)
Magic Hotel, The (sk.)
Mamma's Babee (Les Jolies Petites)
Mystic Hussars, The
Quaint Old Village of Honeysuckle
    Hollow, The
That Whistling Band
When The Boys Come Back

TILLEY SISTERS Amy and Nellie
Dinkey Arno (parody of The Man
    That Broke The Bank At Monte
    Carlo)
Oh! Mr P'Liceman, Oh! Oh! Oh!

TILLEY, Vesta 1864–1952; daughter
of Harry **BALL** & Matilda Powles
(1842–1901); orig. k.a. The Great
Little Tilley
Afternoon Parade, The
After The Ball (adap. Bowyer &
    Powell)
Ah, Dear Heart (Let Me Hold You
    Like This For Ever)
Algy, The Piccadilly Johnny With The
    Little Glass Eye
All Right, Mary Ann
All Right, Papa!
And The Band On The Pier Starts
    Playing!
Angels Without Wings

Anglo-Saxon Language, The
Annie Body's Rooney
Army Of Today's All Right, The
At The Races
Aunt Matilda
Bachelors
Bazaar Maids, The
Bit Of A Blighty One, A
Bold Militiaman, The
Bonita
Boys Of The Racketty Club, The
Boys That Mind The Shop, The
Brand New Millionaire, The
Brave Little Dummer Boy, The
Burlington Bertie
By The Sad Sea Waves (Thomas)
Can You Wonder That The Moon
    Turned Pale?
Charge Of The Light Brigade, The
Clamber Closer Clara
Come Along Home, Papa
Coronation Dude, The
Cuckoo, Little Cuckoo
Daily Male, The
Dandy River Boy, The
Daughters (What Shall We Do With
    Our)
Do, Da
Doesn't Anybody Want The Curate?
Don't It Do Your Eyesight Good?
Eighteen Round The Waist
End Of The Song, The
England Is Ready
'Ere The Lamps Are Lit
Evening Star, The
Fairly Knocked The Yankees In
    Chicago
Fellows In The Royal Artilley, The
First She Would And Then She
    Wouldn't
Fisherman's Child, The (as a juvenile)
Following A Fellah With A Face Like
    Me
Following In Father's Footsteps
For A Day Or Two
For The Honour Of Old England

For The Sake Of The Dear Little
    Girls
For The Week End
Friends Of My Youthful Days
From Marble Arch To Leicester
    Square
Ga-Ga-Ga-Ga-Good-Bye
German Prince, The
Giddy Little Isle Of Man, The
Girls I've Left Behind Me, The
Girl Who Loves A Soldier, The
Girl With The Roses Red, The
Give It To Father
Give Me A Chance
Half Past Nine
Happy Hampton
He's Going In For This Dance Now
He's Going To Meet His Girl
Hi, Boys! Hi, Boys! or Uncle Joe's
    Spree
Home, That's Home For Me
Hystery Of England, A or
    Chronological Crammers
If The Girl Doesn't Mind
I Know My Business (The Messenger
    Boy)
I'll Show You Around Gay Paree
I'm A Bachelor
I'm Going To Be A Nut
I'm Looking For Trilby
I'm Obliging Brother Bertie
I'm The Idol Of The Girls
In A Cottage By The Sea
In Dear Old England's Name
In London
In The Days Of The Cavalier
In The Pale Moonlight
In The Royal Artillery
In The Summer
Introduce Me To The Lady
Isabella
Is Marriage A Failure?
It Isn't The Isle Of Man Any Longer
It's Part Of A P'liceman's Duty
I Want To Have A Chinese
    Honeymoon

Jolly Good Luck To The Girl Who
   Loves A Soldier
King Baby
Lady Who Parlez-Vous's, The
Latest Chap On Earth, The
Let Me Hold You Like This For Ever
Let's Make A Night Of It
Limelight Man, The *see* Oh! Venus
   etc.
Little Mad'moiselle, The
London In France
Love Or Gold
Love's Language
Man Who Broke The Brokers, The
Mary And John
May Queen Victoria Reign
Midnight Son, The
Midnight Son's Farewell, The
Military Medal, The
Minding It For Uncle
Monty From Monte Carlo
Moonlight Blossoms, The
My Friend, My Flag
My Friend The Major
Naughty Boy! (Sydney's Holidays)
Naval And Military Bazaar, The
Near The Workhouse Door (Poor Jo)
New Policeman, The
Nice Quiet Week, A
No English Need Apply
Obliging Brother Bertie
Oh Caroline
Oh! London, Where Are Your Girls
   Tonight?
Oh! Venus, Let Me Call You Sal *or*
   The Song Of The Limelight Man
Oh! You Girls!
150 Years Ago
On Furlough
Only A Brave Little Drummer Boy
Only A Pair Of Shoes
Only Girl On The Pier, The
Oofless Duke, The
Order For The Play, An
Our Drive
Our Sea Trip

Parrot And The Parson, The
Pet Of Rotten Row, The
Piccadilly Crawl, The
Piccadilly Johnny With The Little
   Glass Eye, The *see* Algy etc.
Please Sir, I've Lost My Way
Pomponette
Poor Little Ned
Pretty Boy
Pretty Little Maiden's Sea-Trip, The
Prodigal Son, The
(Quite A Toff In My) Newmarket Coat
Quite Right Too
Racketty Club, The
Ragged Robin And The Rose
Right Kind Of Girl, The
Rosie May
Scotch And Polly
Seaside Girls
Seaside Sultan, The
Sea-Trip, The
September
Showing Aunt Matilda Round The
   Town
Simple Maiden, A
Sisters!
Six Days' Leave
Smile, The
Somebody's Darling
Some Danced The Lancers
Something To Play With
Squeeze Her Gently
Strolling Along With Nancy
Strolling With Norah
S-U-N-D-A-Y
Sunshine And Shadow
Supposing—
Sweetheart May
Sweethearts Still
Sydney's Holidays Are In September
   (Naughty Boy)
Tablet Of Fame, The
Tell Them I'm All Right
That's Pa!
That's The Time A Fellah Wants His
   Ma

There's A Good Time Coming For The Ladies
Three Chapters
To See If It Was Fit For Father
Wedding Day, The
Welcome, CIVs! (City Imperial Volunteers)
What A Nut!
What Shall We Do With Our Daughters? (Chatterton)
What Would The Seaside Be Without The Ladies?
When A Fellah Has Turned Sixteen
When I Was Young
When The Right Girl Comes Along
When Will Old England Be Herself Once More?
When You're A Married Man
Where Are The Girls Of The Old Brigade?
Who Said 'Girls'?
Wise Old Owl, A

TIMMS, Kitty
Gibraltar (w. Percy CARR)

TINSLEY, Arthur 1865–94
Across The Way
As You Were Before
Don't Be Sure Of It
Never Share Your Lodgings With A Pal
We Did Have A Lively Time
Will You Come Across The Way?
You're A Liar-ty

TINSLEY, Tom 1853–1910; celebrated Gatti's chairman and manager
All Among The Apples And Pairs
Big Boss Eye, A (parody)
Countryman's Simple Idea, A
Doodah Up To Date

TITIENS, Therese see TIETJENS, Therese

TOMLIN, Blanche b. 1889
Dearest, I Bring You Daffodils

Just My Love—I'll Never Let Him Go
Love, Or Something Like It (w. Lupino LANE)
Morning In The Highlands
Simple Melody, (Play) A (w. Ethel LEVEY)

TOOLE, J. L. 1830–1906
Billy Barlow
Bob Simmons' Courtship
Evergreen Chappie, The or What's The Odds So Long As You're Happy?
Grasp Of An Honest Hand, The
He Always Came Home Late To Tea
He, She, And The Postman
Honest Man
Jack's Present
Madame Tussaud's or Waxworks
Matilda D—
'Norrible Tale, A (The Suicidal Family)
Paul-y-Toole-y-Technic, The (w. Paul BEDFORD)
Speaker's Eye, The
Still I Am Not Happy
Trip To Margate, A
Two Obadiahs, The
Uncle Dick's Darling
Villikins And His Dinah

TORR, Sam 1846–99
Baby's Got A Tooth
Barber, A
Bit Of 'All Right!', A
Bulls Won't Bellow, The
Diddle Diddle Dumpling My Son John
Don't Say Who Gave You The Tip
Draw Near The Fire
Forgive And Forget
Frolics Of Parliament
Go And Blab That!
I'm Looking At You Now
It's Just To Please The Boy
It's The Same Old Game

It Wants Running Over A Time Or
Two
Joyful, Joyful, Oh Won't It Be Joyful?
Little Bit Of All Right
May Every Good Fellow Become An
Oddfellow
M.O.N.E.Y
My Son John
Oddfellows, The
Oh, Won't It Be Joyful?
Old Adam Was Father Of Them All
On The Back Of Daddy-Oh!
Same Old Game, The
Second Same Old Game, A
She Was In My Class
Sir Garnet Will Show Them The
Way
Something Dropped On Me
Spelling Bee, The
There's No Parting
There's Nothing In It
They All Have A Mate But Me
Things You'll Never See
To Be There
We Boys of The Pelican Club
We're A Lot Of Jolly Boys At The
Club
You're More Than Seven

TRAVERS, Hyram 1850–1922
Bank Holiday
Bradlaugh
Don't Take My Children From Me
I Cannot Make It Out
I. O. U.
More In The Cupboard If Wanted
Old Mulberry Tree, The
Rather Too Old For Me
Showman, The
Whitechapel Boy, The
Yes! Yes! Yes!

TRAVERS, Nat
Coster's Home Sweet Home, The
Does Mother Ever Speak About Your
Daddy?
Ginger's Friendly Lead

He's Moved In A Bigger House Now
Look What Eddication's Done For
Bob
My Gee-Gee Wears A Bonnet
Retired Coaley, The
Ugly Nipper, The
You Won't Always 'Ave It

TREE, Mrs (Lady) 1863–1937; née
Helen Holt; m. Sir Herbert Beerbohm
TREE
Absent-Minded Beggar, The
(recitation)
Handyman, The (recitation)
Soldier Soldier (recitation)

TREE, Anna Maria 1801–62
Home! Sweet Home!

TREE, Charles 1868–1940
Cap'n John
Crocodile, The (English County
Songs)
Dumbledum Day
Giles
Kerry Dance, The
Kitchener's Boys
No, John, No
Somerset Farmer, The
Up From Somerset
Widdicombe Fair
Young Tom O' Devon

TREE, Sir Herbert Beerbohm
1853–1917; m. Mrs **TREE**
Macbeth (sleep-walking scene) (w.
Violet **VANBURGH**)
Man Who Was, The (sk.)
Trilby (abridged play)

TRENTINI, Emma 1878–1959
Giannina Mia
Italian Street Song
Love Is Like A Firefly
Naughty Marietta

TREUMANN, Louis 1872–1942
Merry Widow Waltz (w. Mizzi
GUNTHER)

TREVELYAN, Hilda 1880–1959
  Gate Of Dreams, The (sk.)
  Martha Spanks The Grand Piano
  Twiddley Bits, The

TRIX, Helen° 1892–1951; see also TRIX,
Helen & Josephine
  Ain't Got Nothin', Never Had Nothin',
    Don't Want Nothin' But You
  Come To The Ball
  Follow Me
  I Always Think Of Someone That I
    Love
  If You Mallee Me (Chinese Song)
  It's Making Me Love You All The
    More
  Kiss Your Minstrel Boy Good-Bye
  Love (We Need It, Eh, Honey?)
  Perhaps And Perhaps Not
  Sam
  So What's The Use?

TRIX, Helen & Josephine see also
TRIX, Helen
  Dapper Dan
  Dixie Highway

TUBB, Carrie 1876–1976
  Autumn
  Be Still, Blackbird
  Break O' Day
  Green Cornfield, A
  Hello! Little Stranger
  Love's Greeting
  Music When Soft Voices Die
  Nightingale Of June
  O For The Wings Of A Dove
  Soul Of The Spring
  Valley Of Laughter, The
  What Shall I Say?

TUCKER, Sophie 1884–1966
  After You've Gone
  All The World Will Be Jealous Of
    Me
  Angle Worm Wiggle
  But He Only Stayed Till Sunday
  Darktown Strutters' Ball, (At) The

Dat Lovin' Rag
Ev'rybody Shimmies Now
Good Man Is Hard To Find, A
Grizzly Bear, The
He Hadn't Up Till Yesterday
How'Ya Gonna Keep 'Em Down On
  The Farm?
I Ain't Got Nobody
I Don't Want To Get Thin
If You Can't See Mama Every Night
  You Can't See Mama At All
I Just Couldn't Make My Feelings
  Behave
It's All Your Fault
It's Moving Day Way Down South
Life Begins At Forty
Moving Day In Jungle Town
My Yiddishe Momme
Nobody Loves A Fat Girl
River Stay 'Way From My Door
St Louis Blues
Some Of These Days
When You Want 'Em You Can't Get
  'Em
Who Paid The Rent For Mrs Rip Van
  Winkle?
Wrong Church But The Right Pew,
  The
Yiddisher Rag, The

TURNER, Harry
  I've Had A Winning Day
  Nellie *or* Ten Past Nine
  Once More Harry
  Sing To Me Johnnie
  They're Just The Girls That Would
  Yarmouth On The Sands
  You've Still Got The Same Old Walk

TWIST, Quintin
  Buttercup, The (w. George DU
    MAURIER)

TYLER, Marie 1875–1905; second wife
of Leo DRYDEN
  Baked-Potato Can, The

Bravo, Dublin Fusiliers! *or* Ireland's
  Reply
Break O' Day Boys, The
Drummer's Letter, The
If The Thames Could Only Speak
London City *or* It Was Never Built
  For Me
My Baked-Potato Can
Only Friend 'E 'Ad, The
Rose Of Mayo, The
Sculler's Song, The
Twenty Years Ago (A Mother's Letter)
Uncle's Trombone
While London's Fast Asleep

UNSWORTH, James 1821–75
  Am I Right Or Any Other Man?
  Oh, Mary Jane

VALLEE, Rudy 1901–86
  Whiffenpoof Song, The

VALLI, Ida
  Spaniard That Blighted My Life, The
    (w. Billy MERSON)

VALLI-VALLI 1882–1927
  After The Honeymoon (sk.)
    (w. Seymour HICKS)
  I Never Flirt
  Petite Parisienne, La

VALMORE, Jenny *c.*1865–?
  Bicycle Will Not Do, A
  Daisy's Answer
  Don't Lay The Blame Upon The
    Ladies
  Early Bird's Reply, The
  He's Single, He's Married
  I Don't Know
  It Makes A Good Impression
  Rose In Her Sunday Clothes
  So Her Sister Says
  Stars Didn't Happen To Be Shining,
    The
  Twelve Little Maids
  When The Wintry Winds Begin To
    Blow

Wouldn't You Like To? No—Yes, You
  Would
Yes, I Did
Yes, You Are!
Yes, You Did
You Will, Wouldn't You?

VALROSE, Lizzie
  In The Silence Of The Night
  Oh, You Girls
  Très Bien

VAN & SCHENCK Gus Van (1888–1968)
and Joe Schenck (1892–1930)
  For Me And My Gal
  Honey Man
  If I Could Peep Through The
    Windows Tonight
  Mandy
  Midnight In Dreamy Spain
  My Old Log Cabin Home
  Oh, How She Can Sing
  Who's Sorry Now?

VAN BIENE, Auguste° (& Co.)
1850–1913; dramatic musical sketches
  Broken Melody, The
  Karl's Luck
  Master Musician, The
  Phantom Melody, The

VAN BLUNT, Walter
  Be My Little Baby Bumble Bee (w.
    Elizabeth SPENCER)

VANBRUGH, Dame Irene 1872–1949;
sister of Violet VANBRUGH; all sketches
  Half-An-Hour (w. Edmund GWENN)
  Pistols For Two
  Rosalind
  Tag, Der
  Twelve Pound Look, The (w. GWENN)

VANBRUGH, Violet 1867–1942; sister of
Irene VANBRUGH; m. Arthur
BOURCHIER (div.); all sketches
  Divorce While You Wait (w. Arthur
    BOURCHIER)
  Eleventh Hour, The (w. BOURCHIER)

Find The Woman (w. BOURCHIER)
Great Aunt Elizabeth
Her Wedding Night (w. Roland
    PERTWEE)
Knife, The (w. BOURCHIER)
Macbeth (sleep-walking scene) (w.
    Herbert TREE)
Man In The Case, A (w. BOURCHIER)
Marriage Has Been Arranged, A (w.
    BOURCHIER)
Pearls (w. BOURCHIER)
Woman And The Law, The ('serial-
    play' with each act played at weekly
    intervals) (w. BOURCHIER)
Woman In The Case, The

VANCE, Alfred° 1838–88; a.k.a. Alfred
Glanville; see also Eunice VANCE
    Act On The Square, Boys
    Afternoon Crawl, The
    À La Française
    Always Gay And Free
    Always Make The Best Of It
    Anastatia, The Angel Of Holloway
    Be Always Up And Doing, Boys!
    Beau Of Baden-Baden, The
    Beautiful Columbine
    Beautiful Girls
    Beautiful Nell
    Beer
    Belgravia
    Belle De Mabille, La
    Belle Of Camberwell, The
    Belle Of Eaton Square, The
    Billiard Bob
    Blighted Husband (Poor Married
        Man)
    Bon-Bon Beau, The
    Brokin 'Earted Butler, The
    Carrie The Belle Of The Ballet
    Chickaleary Cove, The
    Clementina
    Cliquot! Cliquot!
    Come To Your Martha, Come, Come,
        Come
    Continental Swell, The

Converted Cracksman, The
Costermonger Joe
Country Life For Me, A (The Squire's
    Son)
Covent Garden In The Morning
Dancing Swell, The
Dancing To The Organ
Dick Murphy Of T.C.D.
Doing The Academy
Dolly Varden
Don Of The Club, The
Don't Tell Jones
Eaton Square
Exhausted Swell, The
Fair Girl Dress'd In Check, The
Fitz-Jones The M.P.
Galloping Snob Of Rotten Row, The
Girl What I Calls Mine, The
Girl With The Golden Hair, The
Glitter
Going To The Derby In A Donkey
    Cart
Happy Go Bill
Have You Seen Her?
Have You Seen The Shah?
Here Stands A Young Man Who Wants
    A Sweetheart
Hornsey Wood
How Do You Like London?
Howling Swell, The
Hunky Chunk
Hurrah, Boys, Hurrah!
Husbands' Boat, The
I Am One Of The Old True Blues
Idol Of The Day, The
I'll Never Never Leave Her
I'm Her Pa
I Never Was Meant For The Sea
In The B-u-r-l-i-n-g-t-o-n (Burlington)
Is He Guilty? (sk.)
Jessie The Belle At The Bar
Jolly Dogs (Slap Bang! Here We Are
    Again)
Julius Cornelius
Kerreck Kard (The Great Event)
King Of Trumps, The

Languid Swell, The
Late Lamented Jones, The
London Society
Lord Swoon
Mabel Fair
Master Greedy
Matilda Baker (The Lifeguardsman)
May The Present Moment Be The
    Worst Of Your Lives
Maze At Hampton Court, The
Money Was Made To Spend
Mrs Jones
Mr Spriggs The Grocer
My Aesthetic Love
My Dear Boys
My Friend The Major
My Nancy Fair
My Pretty Nell, The Flower Of Pall
    Mall
Nancy Green or A Trip To Kew
Naughty Young Man, The
'Norrible Tale, A
O Jemima
Old Brown's Daughter
Our Glorious English Beer
Pal O' Mine
Par Excellence
Perambulator, The (Matilda's Young
    Guard)
Peter Potts The Peeler
Pickles
Polly Put The Kettle On
Poor Married Man (Blighted
    Husband)
Pretty Polly If You Love Me Do Say
    Yes
Pretty See-u-san, Don't Say No
Pride Of Notting Hill
Pull Together
Push Along, Keep Moving
Quite Au Fait
Roaring Boys, The
Roman Fall, The
Secret Still
Serjeant Sharp Of Lincoln's Inn

She Lodges At A Sugar Shop
Sir Robert De Beard
Sir William Hyde-Parker
Slap Bang! Here We Are Again (Jolly
    Dogs)
So Are We All, Dear Boys
Soda And B—
So Did I
Sold Everywhere
Sparkling Moselle
Style, By Jove! The
Sweet Jenny
Taking My Ease
That's The Style For Me, Boys
Thoroughbred Swell
Tick! Tick! Tick!
Ticket Of Leave Man, The
Toothpick And Crutch
Touches Of The Times
Vance's Yorkshire Chap see A Country
    Life For Me
Walking In The Zoo
What'll Mith Robinthon Thay?
What's The Verdict(?)
Widow Jones
You Never Can Tell
Young Chap Dressed In Blue
Young Man Of The Day, The
Your Mother Won't Know

VANCE, Clarice d. 24 Aug. 1961; m.
Moses GUMBLE (div.)
    I Can't Tell Why I Love You But I
        Do
    Salome (Harrington & Powell)

VANCE, Eunice a protégée of but not
related to Alfred VANCE; sang many of
her mentor's songs (marked V)
    Act On The Square, Boys (V)
    And Her Golden Hair Was Hanging
        Down Her Back
    Costermonger Joe (V)
    Ginger
    I Can't Resist You, Sir
    Late And Early Club, The

Oh! We've Got A Lot Of 'Em
Pal O' Mine (V)
Slap Bang! Here We Are Again (Jolly
   Dogs) (V)
So Did I (V)
There's A Good Time Coming

VANE, Sybil b. 1893
   Carnival Time
   Keep The Home Fires Burning (Till
      The Boys Come Home)

VARNEY, Frank
   K-K-K-Katy (w. Marie BRETT)

VAUGHAN, Kate 1855–1903; orig. w.
sister Susie (1853–1950) as the Sisters
Vaughan
   Continong, The (w. Nellie FARREN
      and Edward TERRY)
   Is There Any Harm In That?
   Oh, You Little Darling (I Love You)

VENN, Topsy
   We Two (w. Nellie MOON)

VENNE, Lottie 1852–1928
   At The Garrison Ball
   Cat And The Governess, The (sk.)
   Dado Song, The
   Harness Belt, The
   High-Class Chaperone, The
   I Saw My Chance And Took It
   Lady Wasn't Going That Way, The
   Mrs Justice Drake (sk.)
   Time Is Money (sk.) (w. Charles
      HAWTREY)

VERDI, Lena
   I'm Going Back To The Fatherland
   I Never Kiss Any Boys Round Here
   I Want To Be Among The Boys
   Mrs Carter (Gus Elen impersonation)
   When, When, When Is Your Ship
      Coming Home?

VERDI, Ruby d. 17 Dec. 1918
   Over A Cup Of Tea

Same Thing—Not Quite
There You Are—That's A Girl

VERNO & VOYCE fl. 1890s–1910s;
orig. Sydney Verno (d. 17 Jan. 1897)
and brother Albert Voyce (b. 1870);
Sydney replaced by Barney Stuart
   Britannia's School
   Butcher And The Baker, The (sk.)
   Courting And Reporting
   Daddy Shall Be Your Trainer
   For Old Love's Sake *or* He Took The
      Blame
   German Jockey, The (sk.)
   Ha'porth Of Gold
   It's Not The Bird In The Gilded
      Cage
   John Bull At Home (sk.)
   King Of The Clouds (sk.)
   Maid Of The Moon, The (sk.)
   Man And Master (sk.)
   Oh, My Lulu
   Outward Bound (sk.)
   Prodigal Son, The (sk.)
   Somebody's Mother (sung by Albert
      Voyce)

VERNON, Harriett 1852–1923
   Blood Is Thicker Than Water
   Cheer Up And Let's Be Jolly!
   Cheer Up, Buller!
   Chicago (The World's Fair)
   Cleopatra
   Don Giovanni
   Dream Of The Days Of Old, A
   Duchess Of Devonshire
   Emblems
   Forget-Me-Not
   Gay Musketeers, The
   Goodwood Raciness
   Grand Old British Lion, The
   Half-Way House, The
   If She'd Only Dance With Me
   In The Pale Moonlight
   Joan Of Arc (sk.)
   Karama

Keep To The Right
Legend Of Champagne, The
Lilac Girl, The
Mark Antony
My Mountain Maid
Nelson
No English Need Apply
Pierrot's Dream
Pong! Pinga! Pong!
Sailor Jack
Sappho
Slumber Song
Sunshine And Shadow
Take Care, Beware
Tick! Tick! Tock! (The Lady Telegraph
    Clerk)
Ting-A-Ling Ting-Tay
Two Strings To Your Bow
Waifs Of The Street
Wait For Me, Pretty Fairy
Young King Neptune

VERNON, Jessie *c.*1870–?
Britannia
I Am One Of The Girls That Do
    Know
Oh, You Fellows
What We See In London

VERREN, Milner d. 29 July 1908
As I Love You
Give Me Your Answer Do
Kiss Baby Before You Go
My Heart Is Your Heart
Only The Stars To Peep
She Is More To Be Pitied Than
    Censured
She's Good Enough For My Wife
Think Of The Days That Have Passed,
    Love

VERSATILE THREE, The a.k.a. HASTON,
MILLS & TUCK; variously A. A. Haston,
C. W. Mills, A. Tuck, and Julius Coving-
ton (1892–1927)
Any Time, Any Day, Anywhere
Baby

Darktown Strutters' Ball, (At) The
Don't You Remember The Time?
Georgia
I Don't Want To Get Well
I Want A Doll
Ja-Da
Jazz Band Concert
Just To Amuse The Baby
Land Of Golden Dreams, The
Memories
Monkey Doodle Harem
My House Is Haunted By The Ghost
    Of A Beautiful Girl
Oh, Joe, With Your Fiddle And Bow
    (as The Versatile Four)
Oogie Oogie Wa Wa
Stumbling
Them Sighing Crying Dying Blues
They're Calling Me In Tennessee
What Did It Cost King Solomon To
    Keep 600 Wives?
When I Get Back To My Hometown
    (as Versatile Four)
Why Don't My Dreams Come True?
Wild Wild Women, The

VESTRIS, Lucy 1797–1856
Bavarian Girl's Song, The (Buy A
    Broom)
Buy My Images
Cherries Red
Cherry Ripe
Come Live With Me And Be My Love
    (Bishop)
Flower Girl, The
Love From The Heart (Yes I Will
    Leave My Father's Halls)
Lover's Mistake, The
My Heart's True Blue
Oh! They March'd Thro' The Town

VICTOR, Ethel 1858–1903; m. Charles
MURRAY
Ducky Darling
Is There Any Harm In That?
Kisses We Steal Are The Sweetest,
    The

Not Too Much Mother But Just
  Mother Enough
Oh, What A Wicked Young Man You
  Are
Only One (sk.)
They Say I Am Pretty
What A Nice Place To Be In!

VICTORIA, Vesta 1874–1951; daughter
of Joe LAWRENCE; niece of Lawrence
BARCLAY; first k.a. Baby Victoria, then
Little Victoria
  A B C D E F G
  'Ackney With The 'Ouses Took Away
  All She Gets From The Iceman Is Ice
  All Right, Mr Irving
  All The Best
  All Through Riding On A Motor
  Always Leave Them Wanting
  And He Blames My Dreamy Eyes
  Baby With Men's Ways, A
  Battersea Park
  Bid Me Goodbye For Ever (All In A
    Day)
  Billy Green
  Captain Sparrowstarver
  Carlo
  Chanticleer Song, The
  Ching, Ching, Chinaman
  Come Along Up In The Flip Flap
  Come Back And Be As You Used To
    Be
  Coming Through The Rye, Jenny
    Mine
  Daddy Wouldn't Buy Me A Bow-Wow!
  Don't Get Married Any More, Ma!
  Don't Get Older, If You Please, Ma
  Don't Sing The Chorus
  Double Dutch
  Dutch Girl, The
  'E Ain't Got The Pluck To Come
    Round
  Father, Mother And An Apple
  Father Wants The Cradle Back
  Flower Serenade, The
  Getting Spliced

Girl He Left Behind Him, The
Golliwog, The
Good-bye, Daddy
Good-For-Nothing Nan
Go To Sleep, Baby
Gramaphone Song, The
He Calls Me His Own Grace Darling
He Had All The Best Of Me
He Was A Good Kind Husband
His Lordship
I Can't Get Nobody To Love Me
I Don't Know Where I'm Going But
  I'm On My Way
If That Ain't Love, What Is?
I'll Give Him Stopping Out All Night
I'll Never Ride Any More On A Bike
I'm A Little Turkey Girl
I'm A Slop
I'm Looking For A Don Juan
I Never Had A Father Or A Mother
Is Anybody Looking For A Widow?
It Ain't All Honey And It Ain't All
  Jam
It Didn't Take Long To Come Off
It May Be A Lovely Game (The Lady
  . Golfer)
It's All Right In The Summertime
It's Easy To Be A Lady If You Try
I've Got Husbands In Both Places
I've Got My Mother's Husband And
  She's Got Mine
I've Told His Missus All About Him
I Want To Play With Little Dick
John At The Wishing Well
Just Because They Put Him In
  Trousers
Keep It Dark
Kitty O'Grady
Lady Railway Guard, The
Landlady, The
Lass Who Loved A Sailor, The
Leading The Simple Life (Arcady)
Left Luggage
Little Willie *or* He Knew A Thing Or
  Two
Look What Percy's Picked Up In The

Park *or* See What Percy's Picked Up In The Park
Love's Sweet Dream
Lunnon's Beautiful (The Country Girl)
Man! Man!! Man!!!
Mary Ann, Mary Ann, Come In
Mary, Queen Of Scots
Mary Took The Calves To The Dairy Show
Molly Malone
Mother Hasn't Spoken To Father Since
Mother's Had A Row With Father
Mother's Made It Up With Father
Mountain Guide, The
My Bloke
My Mariuccia Take A Steamboat
My Old Man!
Naughty Little Spider Spied Her, The
Never Never Never No More
Next Horse I Ride On, The
No, Thanks, Not For Me
Now I Have To Call Him Father
Nurse Girl, The
Oh, Amelia
Oh Charlie Don't Leave Your Mary Ann
Oh, Girls, Never Trust A Policeman
Oh! If Mama Only Knew
Oh! Ma, I'll Never Do It Again
Old Man's Darling, An (Murray & Everard)
Old Tin Kettle
'Oliday On One Pound Ten, A
On The Same Place Everytime
Our Lodger's Such A Nice Young Man
Out With His Pals
Over The Garden Wall
Picked Me Up—Sat Me Down
Poor John
Poor Old Adam Was My Father
Pride Of The Ballet
Pull The String
Queen Of The Jujah Islands

Sarah Stubbs
See What Percy's Picked Up *see* Look What Percy's etc.
Some Would Marry Anything With Trousers On
Streaks Of Sunshine
Summer Blouses
Take A Cake Home For The Baby
Take Me In A Taxi, Joe
Take Me There
That'll Never Do For Me
That's What He's Done For Me!
Two-To-Two To Tooting, The
Uncle Billy Was A Fireman
Waiting At The Church
Waiting For Me
Wait Till I'm A Woman
Waltzing Round 'Is Bloomin' Self
Wedding Bells
What's Good Enough For Father
When Tommy Comes Home Again
Who Robbed Poor Cock-A-Doodle-Do
Will He Answer 'Goo Goo'?
Willie's Got Another Girl Now
Willie Wallie Winkham
Wing Tee Wee
You Can Do A Lot Of Things At The Seaside That You Can't Do In Town
You've Taken Her Away

VINCENT, Charles
Coals
Faithless Sally 'Opkins
Nuggets
Since You've Taken To The Name Of Maud St Clair

VINCENT, Ruth 1877–1955
Fat Little Feller Wih His Mammy's Eyes, A
Land Of The Long Ago
Moon Blossom
Swing Song, The (w. Laurence REA)
Trot Here And There (w. REA)

Waltz Song (For Tonight) (*Tom Jones*)
Who's For This Flag?

VIRGINIA MINSTRELS fl. Jan.–July 1843; very first minstrel group: Dick Pelham (1815–76), Dan Emmett (1815–1904), Frank Brower (b. 1823), and Billy WHITLOCK (1). Revived in Dublin Apr.–May 1844 with Whitlock replaced by Joseph SWEENEY
    Alabama Joe
    Gumbo Chaff
    I Wish I Was In Dixie's Land
    Jim Crack Corn (The Blue Tail Fly)
    Jim Crow
    Lubly Fan
    Lucy Long
    Lucy Neal
    Old Dan Tucker
    Ring, Boys, Ring

VOKES, George* 1852–95
    D'You Know? I Don't Like London
    Play Up At Them, They're All Milky

WADE, Dion d. 28 Feb. 1919
    I'll Call When You're Not So Busy
    What D'Yer Want To Talk About It For?
    What's The Idea Of That?
    Wouldn't You Be Better In A Home?

WAGER, Kitty m. Fred POPLAR
    Dear Little Girl You Love, The
    Do Me A Favour Harry
    Everybody Gives You Good Advice
    Ev'ryone Must Have A Start In Life
    Girls At The Penny Bazaar, The
    Katey
    Though You May Marry Another
    Up The Pole

WALTE, Ted* d. 7 Apr. 1971; brother of J. W. RICKABY
    Night I Fought Jack Johnson, The

WAKEFIELD, J. H.
    North Of Fifty Three

Oh, Beautiful Marriage
Who Discovered Dixie?

WALDEN, Harry 1887–1955
    And Only Me Knows Why
    I See You've Come Back With The Wood

WALDRON, Jack
    Black Sal And Dusty Bob
    British Lion, The
    Lady-Like Young Man
    Life In Quashibungo
    Man's Perfidy
    Mr Timm's Unfortunate Attachment
    Oh Come With Me To The Fountain
    Seven Dials Tragedy, The
    Up The Thames To Richmond
    Vegetarian, The
    Whatever Makes Them Do It
    Woman's Rights
    Young Folks At Home

WALKER, Syd 1887–1945
    Any Rags, Bottles Or Bones?
    For Nights And Nights And Nights
    Who Put The Bricks In Brixton?

WALKER, Whimsical 1850–1934
    Captain Hamilton VC (sk.)

WALKER & WILLIAMS *see* WILLIAMS & WALKER

WALL, Harry b. 1838; m. Annie ADAMS
    As Good And A Great Deal Better
    Dose Of Physic, The
    Isabella
    St James & St Giles
    Timid Man, The
    Underground Railway, The

WALLACE, Charles *see* BROWN, NEWLAND & WALLACE

WALLACE, Nellie 1870–1948; orig. one of The Three Sisters Wallace
    Blasted Oak, The
    Boy's Best Friend Is His Mother, A
    Catherine Parr

Down By The Riverside
Finesse
Geranium
Half-Past Nine
He's A Dear Old Man
I Can't Go To Sleep
I Lost Georgie In The Park
I Lost George In Trafalgar Square
In The Cottage With The Roses At
   The Door
Isn't It A Cruel World?
I've Been Jilted By The Baker, Mr
   White
I Was Born On A Friday
I Was The Early Birdie After The
   Early Worm
Meet Me (The Sniff Song)
My Mother's Pie Crust
Oh, The 'Obble
Tally Ho
Three Cheers For The Red White
   And Blue
Till My True Love Returns
Under The Bed (My Mother Said)
Where Are You Going To, My Pretty
   Maid?

WALLER, Lewis 1860–1915; m. Mrs
Lewis WALLER
   Ballad Of The 'Clampherdown', The
      (recitation)
   Fortune's Fool (mon.)
   Forum Scene (*Julius Caesar*)
   How We Beat The Favourite
      (recitation)

WALLER, Mrs Lewis 1862–1912; a.k.a.
Florrie WEST
   Lost, Stolen Or Strayed (sk.)
   Zaza (sk. version)

WALLIS, Bertram 1874–1952
   There's A King In The Land Today

WALLIS, Walter
   Coon's Lullaby, The
   Fancy Telling Me That!

He's Got It To Come
Mr & Mrs Wallis
Our Football Supper
Whipper-In, The

WALMER, Cassie b. 1888
   Always Add A Little
   Always Leave Them Wanting
   Anna Maria
   Araminta, MP
   Better To Give Than Receive
   Come Down, Joanna Brown, Come
      Down
   Good-bye, Ebenezer
   Mr Opportunity
   Persevere
   Selina Snow

WALMSLEY, Fred 1879–1943
   Seven Years With The Wrong Woman
   You Don't Take A Sandwich To A
      Picnic

WALSH, Sam 1877–1920
   Gentleman Of France, A (mon.)
   Two Little Girls And A Lad (mon.)

WARD, Artemus° 1834–67; pseud. of
Charles Farrar Browne, celebrated
American humorous lecturer and writer;
pub. songbook 1866 including some
standards

WARD, Dorothy 1890–1987; m. Shaun
GLENVILLE
   Blue Eyes
   California Here I Come
   Carolina In The Morning
   Ev'rywhere I Go I'll Leave My Heart
      With You
   Good-Bye, Everybody's Girlie!
   How'Ya Gonna Keep 'Em Down On
      The Farm?
   I Am Thinking Of You, Bonnie Mary
   I Want A Girl Just Like The Girl Who
      Married Dear Old Dad
   Just A Memory
   Just Like A Thief

Lonesome And Sorry
Mademoiselle From The Maginot
   Line
Mary Jane
Only A Few Broken Toys
Peggy O'Neil
Roses Have Made Me Remember,
   The
Shanty In Old Shanty Town, A
Sheik Of Araby, The
Shufflin' Along
Somebody Else
Somebody's Baby
Some Night, Some Waltz, Some Girl
Take Me Back To Dear Old Blighty
Take Me Back To Your Heart
Till We Meet Again
We've Got To Put Up With It Now
When Life's Sun Is Setting
Who Put The Bricks In Brixton? (w.
   Shaun GLENVILLE)
You'll Always Be Fancying The Same
   Sweet Baby
You'll Miss Your Mother's Love
You Planted A Rose
You've Got To Do It

WARD, E. D.
Gift Of Repartee, The
Merlin The Prophet
They Don't Do That Sort Of Thing
   Now

WARD, Harry d. 20 Jan. 1920?
Clergyman's Daughter
I Doat On My Louisa
Selling Ice Cream
What A Jolly Day

WARD, Winifred c.1880–1975; daughter
of Will POLUSKI sen. At one time w. sis-
ter Lottie as the Sisters Govett
Come With Me Down Regent Street
Oh, Lizette, Don't Forget Your British
   Soldier Boy
Ready Every Time
Red Of The Rosebud

Salterello (violin piece by Papini)
Sporty Boy-ee
They All Do The Goose Step

WARDE, John & Emma John d. 23 June
1892; sister Emma's dates unknown;
their father was William Warde
(1811–59); they m. John & Emma
D'AUBAN
Dixey's Land (parody)
Love Charm
Proverbs

WARE, George[*] 1829–95; m. Mrs
George WARE
Coutts
English, Irish, And Scotchman
House That Jack Built, The
How The World Goes Round
Jessie, The Belle At The Railway Bar
My Lovely And Accomplished Jenny
Squire And Maria, The

WARE, Mrs George W. c.1834–?; a.k.a.
Mme Henesier; m. George WARE
Any Other Man
Girl That Can't Keep Still, The
Homeward Bound
Jessie The Belle At The Bar
Little Men Before Tall Ones For Me
Rifle Song, The
Young Girl From The Country, A

WARNER, Charles 1846–1909; per-
formed these sketches in USA only
At The Telephone
Devil Montague
Drink0 (condensed version)

WATERFIELD, Charles
I'll Hit You In A Minute
Let's Have A Song With A Chorus
She Hadn't A Word To Say
We All Had One

WATERS, Elsie & Doris fl. 1923–70s;
Elsie (c.1895–1990) sister of Doris
(c.1904–78)
Knees Up Mother Brown

WATSON, George
  Behind The Veil
  Good Old Barnum
  Lights Of Home, The

WATSON, Vernon 1886–1949; see also
Nosmo KING
  When The War Is Over

WAY, Owen
  Directions
  Do You Remember?
  Excuses
  Left Us
  Only A Week Away
  Potted Poetry
  When Mother Cooked The Pancake

WEBER & FIELDS fl. 1877–1912; Joseph
'Mike' Weber (1867–1942) and Lewis
Maurice 'Mayer' Shanfields (1867–1941)
  Here We Are A Jolly Pair

WEBSTER, Ben (1864–1947)
  Fourth Act, The (w. Lillah
    McCARTHY)

WEBSTERS, THE TINY Cissie and Ada
  I Don't Want To Play In Your Yard

WEISS, W. H.° 1820–47
  Martin The Man At Arms
  Village Blacksmith, The

WELCHMAN, Harry 1886–1966
  As Soon As They Heard My Voice
  Charming Weather (w. Phyllis DARE)
  Half-Past Two (w. DARE)

WELDON, Harry 1881–1930; m. Hilda
GLYDER
  British Bulldogs
  Bullfighter, The
  Dick Turpin's Brother
  Father
  Fearless McGirkin
  Football Match, The (Fred KARNO sk.
    featuring Weldon's famous character
    Stiffy the Goalkeeper)

I Get More Like A 'Pro' Every Day
I'm Going Back Back Back To Alabam
I See You've Come Back With The
  Wood
It's A Bird
I Want To Be Somebody's Baby Boy
Jack Sheppard
Joe, The Crossing Sweeper (sk.)
Love! Love!! Love!!!
Matador, The (sk.)
On The Road To Ruin
Police'll Have Me Before Long, The
S'No Use
Stiffy The Goalkeeper (song)—see
  Football Match, The
S'Too Old
White Hope, The (Tell 'Em What I
  Did To Colin Bell) (sk. and song)

WENTWORTH, Bessie 1873–1901
  Alabama Coon, The
  Consequential Coon, The
  Convict's Story, The (recitation)
  Coon's Serenade, The
  Daddy's Gwine To Bring You
    Something Nice
  Dancin' For De Cake!
  Darkey Aristocrat, The
  Darkies' Dear Old 'Home Sweet
    Home', The
  Darkie's Wedding, The
  De Missis Ob De House
  Dey Loved Each Other All De While
  Dinner-Time!
  Down In Carolina
  Farewell, Regions Of Gold
  Fashionable Coon, The
  Going Home!
  Good Old Uncle Brown
  Happy 'Cos Dey Foun' Dis Coon
  Hide Yer Pretty Face Behind Yer Fan
  Honey, Does Yer Love Yer Man?
  I Ain't A-Goin' To Throw Myself Away
  Looking For A Coon Like Me,
    (They're)

Love Keeps Dem Always Young
Love Me, Love Me, Lou
Military Coon, The
Mona's The Donah For Me
My Boy!
My Gal *or* My Sweetheart's My
    Mammy
My Gal, She's Got Eyes Like
    Diamonds
My Gardenful Of Love
My Lady Loo
My Whistling Gal
Not While De Coons Am About,
    Sammy
Oh, Dinah, Dear! *or* The Faithless
    Octoroon
Old Madrid
One Of The Dandy Fifth
Only One Girl In The World For Me
Piccaninny Hush-A-Bye
Sambo's Confession
Santy Claus Is Comin' 'Fore De
    Mornin'
She's My Love (Why Wasn't I A
    Different Colour?)
She Won't Make Up Her Mind
Somethin' Dat You Can't Describe
Uncle Tom
Victoria Cross, The
Yankee Dude, The

WENTWORTH, Fanny° *c.*1849–1934
Coster's Confession, The
Dolly's Mistake, The
Goo-Goo Song, The
Hippopotamus And The Flea, The
Looks Well On The Boards
Monkey On A Stick, A
Tin Gee-Gee, The (The Lowther
    Arcade)
Up-To-Date At Home, An
What A Beautiful World This Would
    Be!

WENTWORTH, Reg d. 7 May 1932
Ding! Dong! There It Goes Again

I Must Get Married By Twelve
    O'Clock To-Night
My Lovesome Cuddlesome Girl
Willie, What Would Piccadilly Say?

WEST, Arthur° *c.*1864–94
Captain Called The Mate, The
Copy Your Uncle Tom
Earl Of Fife, The
Gentlemen Of The Jury
Johnny Bull's Concert Hall
Let's Have Another
Paris Exhibition, The
Three Months' Hard

WEST, Charles
Scapegrace, The
Skipper's Farewell, The (Never
    Returned To Port)

WEST, Florrie 1862–1912; a.k.a. Mrs
Lewis **WALLER**
I Cannot Find My Little Pussy Cat
John James O'Reilly
Mamie, Come Kiss Your Honey Boy
Who Stole My Pug-Wug-Wug?

WEST, Mae 1888–1980
All I Want Is Just A Little Lovin'
And Then—
Any Kind Of A Man
Cave Girl, The
Ev'rybody Shimmies Now
Good Night, Nurse
I've Got A Style All My Own
Philadelphia Drag, The
They Are Irish

WEST, W. H. C.° 1817–1876
Act Unto Your Brother As You'd Have
    Him Act To Thee
Am I Right Or Any Other Man?
Billy Barlow
Irish Love Letters
Jenny Lind Mania, The
Jumbo Jim
Man With The Carpet Bag, The

O My Love's Dead
Southerly Wind And A Cloudy Sky, A

WESTON, Bert 1884?–1930?
At The Play
On A Holiday
Where Do Flies Go In The
Wintertime?

WESTON, Julia 1840?–1905?
Being An Actress
Female Rifle Corps, The
Lady Whose Nerves Are Affected, The
Lass Who Loves A Sailor, The
Sally Scrags

WHEATLEY, Horace° 1850–1923
After The Ball
Bogie Man, The
Harrigan
I'll Be A Soldier Too
Me Too! Me Too! Me Too!
Oyster Supper, The
'Twas In Trafalgar Square (parody)
Two Little Girls In Blue
When You Wear Your Old Knee-
Breeches!
Would You Mind Playing A Tune?

WHELAN, Albert 1875–1962; m. (1)
Florrie McRae (dec'd); (2) Dainty **DORIS**
(dec'd); (3) Renée ?; from 1931 also as
Mose w. Billy **BENNETT** in black-face
cross-talk act **ALEXANDER** & **MOSE**
Butterfly And The Bee, The
Casey Jones
Cowslip And The Cow, The
Have A Drop Of Gin, Old Dear
Hello, Sunshine Hello
I'm A Business Man
I'm Twenty-One Today
Jolly Brothers, The (Die Lustige
Brüder—Whelan's whistled
signature tune)
Old Top Hat, The
Phil The Fluter's Ball
Preacher And The Bear, The
She's Only Been With Us A Week

Three Trees, The
Why Do We Love Our King?
Won't You Tell Me The Lady's Name?
You Can't Understand The Ladies

WHIFFENPOOFS, THE 1909–; Yale
University student singing group est.
Meade Minnigerode° (1887–1967), Guy
S. Pomeroy° (b. 1880), James Howard,
Carl Lohman, and Denton Fowler to be
joined by Robert Mallory, Richard
Holsford, and (in 1910) Ted Guest.
The group is now limited to fourteen
seniors
Mavourneen
Shall I Wasting In Despair?
Whiffenpoof Song, The

WHITE, Alec
Santy Klors
Tale Of A Pig, The
United Evermore—The Thistle,
Shamrock, Rose!

WHITE, Lee 1886–1927; m. Clay
SMITH
All Alone By The Telephone
Everybody's Charlie Chaplin Mad
Every Little While
Everything Is Peaches Down In
Georgia
Good Man Is Hard To Find, A
High Cost Of Living, The
Humpty Dumpty
I've Got The Sweetest Girl Of All
Margo Magee
Pullman Porters On Parade
Somebody's Coming To Tea
Ten Million Germans
Topical Acrostic, The
Where Did That One Go?
You Made Me Love You

WHITEFORD, Jock
By The Banks Of Allan Water
Keep On Doing It, Sandy!
My Bonnie Jessie
Waitin' For Me Bonnie Jean

WHITEMAN, Paul (& Band) 1890–1967
Japanese Sandman
Limehouse Blues
Three O'Clock In The Morning
Whispering

WHITLOCK, Billy° (1) b. 1813; a.k.a.
William M. Whitlock; see also VIRGINIA
MINSTRELS and WHITLOCK'S
MINSTRELS
Lucy Long

WHITLOCK, Billy° (2) 1874–1951;
recorded as Dudley Roy, Madame Paula,
R. White, R. Humphreys, etc., also
briefly appeared with Charles PENROSE
as Penrose & Whitlock and recorded
with him as The Jolly Jesters and The
Two Old Sports
All I Said Was 'Ha! Ha! Ha!'
Always Jolly
Come Under My New Gamp
I Had To Laugh At Once
Laughing All The Day
Laughing Friar, The
Merriest Man Alive, The
Nice Old Maid, A
Scotch Hot (revived 1950 as The Hop
   Scotch Polka)
Sunny Jim

WHITLOCK'S MINSTREL'S see also
WHITLOCK, Billy (1)
Cudjos Wild Hunt
Dandy Jim From Carolina
De New York Gals
De Old Grey Goose
Get Away Home, My Yaller Gal
In De Wild Racoon Track
Mary Blane
Oh Wake Up In The Morning
What's That Knockin' At The Door?

WHITNEY, Ann with the Clarke
Burlesquers
After The Ball

WHITTLE, Charles T. 1874–1947
Billy Muggins

Come And Have A Drink With Me
Connemara
Cressie Leonard
Dance With Your Uncle Joseph
Factory Lass
Fall In And Follow Me
Follow The Blind Man
Follow The Footprints In The Snow
Girl In The Clogs And Shawl, The
Good-bye-ee
Has Anybody Here Seen Kelly?
Have Another One
Have You Heard John James O'Hara?
He's A Naughty Naughty Boy!
I Don't Care If There's A Girl There
If She Comes Fra' Lancashire
I'm Dunn—Mister Dunn
I've Got My Hands Up—Don't Shoot
I've Got To Get The Nine Train
   Back
I've Said Good-bye To The Dear Old
   Strand
I Want You To See My Girl
I Was Out Late Last Night
I Wonder What The Girls Did Then
Keep Your Hands Off—That's Mine
Let Me Wait For Daddy
Let's All Go Down The Strand
Let's Have The Lights Up In London
London Lass Is Lucy, A
Molly O'Morgan
Moon! Shine Again
Mother's Boy
My Girl's A Yorkshire Girl
Nicey-Nicey
Nothing Like This In America
Now Are We All Here?
Oh, That Goodnight At The Door
Put Me Amongst The Girls
Take It Nice And Easy
Take Your Little Percy To The
   Pantomime
There's Something In The Seaside Air
They Like A Good Old Married Man!
They're All Right In The Moonlight
Toddling Home

Tommy Trouble
Up The Gravel Path—Sailing
We All Go Home In Ragtime
We All Go The Same Way Home
We'll All Do The Same As The
  Children Do!
What You Can't Get You Can Always
  Do Without
When The Lights Are Low
When You've Got A Lady Near You
Why Hasn't Daddy Come Home?
You Might Do Worse That Marry A
  Factory Lass

WIELAND, Clara
Every Inch A Soldier And A Man
I Will Not Marry The Corporal
Little Gay Parisienne, The
Mad'moiselle Pom-Pom
Militaire, The
My Gal Is A High Born Lady
Sweet Little Lady!
Thank You Kindly

WIELAND, W. H.° 1831–66
Black Cook, The
Handsome Nigger Joe
I Am The Girl Called Nancy (answer
  to In The Strand)
Musical Shoeblack, The
Titles And Distinctions

WIGLEY, Nellie m. Phil RAY
Bright Eyes
My Heart Is With You Tonight

WILKINSON BROTHERS
Dublin's New Policemen
Irish Boys, The
Paddy's Land

WILKINSON, Marcus 1827–92
Detached Villa
Didn't She Seem To Like It?
Muffins For Tea
Underground Railway, The
Whole Hog Or None, The (Westrop)

WILKINSON, Matt
Any Time You Are Passing Our Way
Once Or Twice (?)
Really Kind Of Him
Registry Office, The

WILLIAMS, Arthur 1845–1915; brother
of Fred WILLIAMS; uncle of Fred
EMNEY sen.
How To Mesmerise 'Em!
I Didn't, I Couldn't, I Wouldn't
I Haven't Been Kissed For Weeks
It Will Cause Unpleasantness (w. E. J.
  LONNEN)
Just In The Old Sweet Way
Mistaken My Vocation
Never Empty Cradle, The
Oh, What A Pity
Sometimes! Generally! Always! (w. J. J.
  DALLAS)
What Has Become Of The Door?

WILLIAMS, Bert° 1874–1922; see also
WILLIAMS & WALKER
Dark-Town Poker Club, The
Ghost Of A Coon, The
Jonah Man, A
Let It Alone
My Castle On The Nile
Nobody
Play That Barbershop Chord
That's A-Plenty
Voodoo Man, The
When It's All Goin' Out And Nothin'
  Comin' In
Woodman, Woodman, Spare That
  Tree (Berlin)
You Ain't So Warm
You Can't Make Your Shimmy Shake
  On Tea
You Got The Right Church But The
  Wrong Pew

WILLIAMS, Billy° 1877–1915
All Coons Look Alike To Me
Cohen
Come Into The Garden, John

Give My Love To Scotland, Maggie
Here Comes Oxo!
Here We Are Again (Williams:
   Godfrey)
He Used To Play On The Oboe
Hobnailed Boots That Farver Wore,
   The
In The Land Where There Are No
   Girls
I Used To Play On The Oboe
I Wish It Were Sunday Night
   Tonight
Jean, Jean From Aber-Aberdeen
Jean Loves All The Jockeys
John, Go And Put Your Trousers On!
Kangaroo Hop, The
Let's All Go Mad
Let's Go Where The Crowd Goes
Let's Have A Song Upon The
   Gramophone
Little Willie's Wild Woodbines
My Girl From London Town
Oh, I Must Go Home Tonight
Oh, Mister MacPherson
Oh! The Girls Of Gottenberg
Old Grey Coat
Only Bit Of English, The
Put A Bit Of Powder On It, Father!
Ragtime Wedding
Save A Little One For Me
Serves You Right!
Since Poor Father Joined The
   Territorials
Taximeter Car, The
That We've Got
Tickle Me, Timothy, Do!
Waiting Till The Moon Went In
We All Came In The World With
   Nothing (parody)
We All Say Too-Ra-Loo-Ral-Addie!
We Don't Want Any More Daylight
We're All Waiting For A Girl
When Father Papered The Parlour
When Poor Old Father Tried To Kill
   The Cock-A-Doodle-Oo
When There Isn't A Girl About

Where Does Daddy Go When He
   Goes Out?
Where! Oh, Where!
Why Can't We Have The Sea In
   London?

WILLIAMS, Bransby 1870–1961; mons.,
also speeches and scenes from Shake-
speare inc. *Hamlet*, *Henry V*, and *The
Merchant of Venice*; renowned as a
Dickens delineator
   Bagshot, Major Joe (*Dombey & Son*)
   Billy's Biograph
   Buzfuz, Serjeant (*Pickwick Papers*)
   Caretaker, The
   Carton, Sydney (*A Tale Of Two Cities*;
      also see Noble Deed, The)
   Chadband (*Bleak House*)
   Chimney Seat, The
   Chuzzlewit, Jonas (*Martin Chuzzlewit*)
   Clean Sweep, A
   Coward, The
   Cuttle, Captain (*Dombey & Son*)
   Devil-May-Care
   Dismal Jimmie
   Fagin (*Oliver Twist*)
   Fallen Star, The
   For A Woman's Sake
   Fra Giacomo
   Furniture Mover, The
   Gamp, Mrs Sarah (*Martin Chuzzlewit*)
   Grandfather (*The Old Curiosity Shop*)
   Green Eye Of The Little Yellow God,
      The
   Heep, Uriah (*David Copperfield*)
   Hindoo's Paradise, The
   How We Saved The Barge
   'Is Pipe
   Jack
   Jim Bludso
   Jingle, Alfred (*Pickwick Papers*)
   Last Of His Race,The (sk.)
   Lounger, The
   Micawber, Wilkins (*David
      Copperfield*)
   Noble Deed, The (sk.) (*A Tale Of*

Two Cities; also see 'Carton,
 Sydney')
Old Time Actor
Orange Blossom
Pecksniff (*Martin Chuzzlewit*)
Peggotty, Dan'l (*David Copperfield*)
Penny Showman, The
Pigtail Of Li Fang Fu, The
Portrait, The
Proposals
Quilp, Daniel (*The Old Curiosity
 Shop*)
Rake Windermere
Scrooge (*A Christmas Carol*)
Seven Ages Of Man, The
Sheep And The Goats, The
Shooting Of Dan McGrew, The
Sikes, Bill (*Oliver Twist*)
Squeers, Wackford (*Nicholas
 Nickleby*)
Stage Door Keeper, The
Street Watchman, The
Student, The
Tigg, Montague (*Martin Chuzzlewit*)
Uncle Tom's Cabin
Veteran's Birthday, The
Vicar's Christmas Eve, The
Voyage Of Disaster, A
We Drew His Club Money This
 Morning
Whitest Man I Know, The
Who Killed Cock Robin? (one-man
 revue)
Yogi's Curse, The

WILLIAMS, Charlie° 1853–80
Christmas Cheer
Cleopatra's Needle
European Congress, The
Fight In The Menagerie, The
Funny Little Man
I Leave It Entirely To You
I Love To Flirt With The Girls
Jolly Lot Of Friends, A
Quarrel In The Menagerie, The
Spelling B.

That's Another Topic From The
 Telegraph Wire
Union Jack Of Old England, The
What A Funny Little Man You Are
What An Englishman Is Made Of
What Victoria Is Made Of

WILLIAMS, Evan 1867–1918
All Through The Night
Anchor's Weigh'd, The
Annie Laurie
Bay Of Biscay, The
Beauty's Eyes
Death Of Nelson, The
Lass Of Richmond Hill
Love's A-Biding
Onaway! Awake, Beloved!
Songs My Mother Taught Me

WILLIAMS, Fred (& Co.) 1861–1916;
comic (sk.) troupe; brother of Arthur
WILLIAMS; uncle of Fred EMNEY sen.;
regular partner Edwin BARWICK
Aladdin And The Teapot
Bluebeard
Devil Bird, The
Drudge, The
Jubilee Teapot
Little Marguerite
Showman's Ledger, The (song)
Susan
Will Tell

WILLIAMS, George *see* BROWN, NEW-
LAND & LE CLERQ

WILLIAMS, Gus° *c.*1847–1915
Meet Me In St Louis, Louis

WILLIAMS, Hattie 1870–1942
Half-Past Two (w. Richard CARLE)

WILLIAMS, Norman 1881–1938
Friend O' Mine
Shipmates O' Mine

WILLIAMS & WALKER fl. 1893–1909;
George W. Walker° (1873–1911) and
Bert WILLIAMS, sometimes billed as
Walker & Williams

Black Four Hundred's Ball, The
Coon's Trade-Mark, The
Every Race Has A Flag But This Coon
Good Morning, Carrie
Look Out Dar Down Below!
Oh, I Don't Know, You're Not So
    Warm

WILLIAMS, Walter° 1887–1940
Don't Speak All At Once, Little Girls
Keep Quite Close To The Railings
K-K-K-Katy
Make Me The King Of Your Heart

WILLIE, Little later W. FREEAR
(brother of Louie FREEAR) whose three
younger brothers succeeded him as
'Little Willie': Albert (1865–1905), Fred
(1864–89), and Walter
Blind Boy, The (w. MOORE &
    BURGESS MINSTRELS)

WILSON, Frank 1859–1918?
'Bond St' Masher, The
Butterfly

WILSON, Hilda 1860–1918; sister of H.
Lane WILSON
In A Persian Garden (w. Emma
    ALBANI & David BISPHAM & Ben
    DAVIES)

WILSON, H. Lane° c.1864–1937;
brother of Hilda WILSON
Border Ballad, The
Glorious Devon
Ho! Jolly Jenkin
Old Brigade, The
Tinker's Song, The
Yeoman's Wedding Song

WILSON, Joe 1841–75
Aa Hope Ye'll Be Kind To Me Dowtor
Affected Bella
Aw Wish Yor Muther Wad Cum
Ben Battle (Nelly Gray)
Cockney's Lament, The
Cum, Geordy, Haud The Bairn
Draper's Appeal, The

Flog'd In Jail!
Glorious Vote Be Ballot
I'm Leaving Thee In Sorrow, Annie
In Memory Of The Hartley
    Catastrophe
Keep Yor Feet Still Geordie Hinney
Lads Upon The Wear, The
Maw Bonny Gyetside Lass
Maw Bonny Injineer
Meun-Leet Flit, The
Nelly Gray (Ben Battle)
Pork Shop Lass, The
Prepare For What's Te Cum
She's Gyen Te Place At Jarrow
That Factory Lass
Tom Broon
Varry Canny
What Gud Can Sweerin De?

WILSON, Lizzie
British Volunteer, The
Don't Be Angry With Me, Darling
Fancy Ball, A
Give Me The Man Of Honest Heart
Little Sweetheart Come And Kiss Me

WILSON, May
Frog Who Went A-Wooing, The
It's The Pixieman
Jus' You
Ma Little Lu-Lu
Minne-Ha-Ha
My Plain Little Every-day Girl
Since The World Began
Wingey, Wangey, Woo

WILSON, Nellie d. 24 May 1932
All Through Winking At A Magistrate
Boys Of The Royal Navee, The
Jolly Frivolity Boys, The
One After The Other

WILTON, Marie fl. 1900s; not Lady
(Squire) Bancroft (1838–1921)
Beneath The Linden Trees (w. J. H.
    MONTAGUE)
Good-Bye And God Bless You Jack
If I Could Meet You

I Love Poll And Poll Loves Me
Old Love Mem'ries
Take This Locket, My Darling
When We Grow Older

WILTON, Robb 1881–1957
Back Answers (recitation)
Fire Station, The (sk.)
His Journey's End (sk.)
Magistrate, The (sk.)
Police Station, The (sk.)
Prison Governor, The (sk.)

WINDLEY, Harry°
And The Missis Popped Up At The
 Time
Brickbats Never Shall Be Slaves
Gordon, The Hero Of Khartoum
I'd Like It All Over Again
Laughing Man, The
Nein! Nein! Nein!
She Boxed My Ears With The
 Frying-Pan
What Will The Neighbours Say? (Oh
 Dear!)

WINDOM, Constance
I Can't Take My Eyes Off You

WINDOM, William H. sometimes
spelled Wyndham
Fatal Wedding, The
She May Have Seen Better Days (w.
 PRIMROSE & WEST MINSTRELS)

WINGETT, Harry 1845–1905
If You Want A Double Shuffle I Can
 Do A Bit Yet
I Never Walk When I Can Ride Upon
 My Father's Shoulders
Same Old Face, The

WINN, Anona 1908–1994
Bird On Nellie's Hat, The
Hearts And Flowers

WINTER, Banks° 1857–1936
White Wings (w. THATCHER,
 PRIMROSE & WEST MINSTRELS)

WITMARK, Julius P. 1870–1929
Her Eyes Don't Shine Like Diamonds
Mammy's Little Pumpkin Colored
 Coons
Only Me
Only One Girl In The World For Me
Picture That Is Turned To The Wall,
 The
Sunshine Of Paradise Alley, The
When You Were Sweet Sixteen

WOOD, Daisy 1877–1961; sisters Alice,
Grace, Marie, and Rosie LLOYD (WOOD)
A-Be, My Boy
Come Again Through Lover's Lane
Cupid
Diamond Queen, The
Down On The Farm (I Want To Go
 Back To Michigan)
Duchess Of Pas De Quatre, The
Everybody Loves Their L'il Old Home
Get That Girl!
Good-bye-ee
Hello, Hawaii, How Are You?
Holding Hands
Hop It!
How'd You Like To Float With Me?
Hurry Up, There!
I Like You, And You Like Me
I Used To Sigh For The Silvery Moon
I Want To Go Back To Michigan
 (Down On The Farm)
Lover's Lane
Mary, My Mary
My Diamond Queen
Never Mind The Rain
Number One, London Town
Oh! George, Tell Them To Stop The
 Flip Flap
Old Pair Of Shoes, An
One Day She Helped Herself To
 Father
Saturday Afternoon Till Sunday
 Morning
Seaside On The Bran
See Where I Throw My Cigarette

She Was A Fisherman's Daughter
Smith, Jones, Robinson And Brown
Splash Me *see* You Splash Me etc.
Take Me Back To Dear Old Blighty
There's A Girl For Every Soldier
They'll Never Know Me In Old
   Dahomey
When You Come Near Me—I'm All
   Of A Ooh
Will You Be My Valentine?
You Splash Me And I'll Splash You

WOOD, Frank* 1844–1919
Father's Whiskers
Hey-Ho, We're Going With Uncle
   Joe
She Follows Me Everywhere I Go-o-
   o-o!
They Can't Get The Better Of Me
Where The Wild Waves Roar

WOOD, Rosie 1879–1944; a.k.a. Rosie
LLOYD; m. Will Poluski jun. (of THE
POLUSKI BROTHERS). Sisters Alice,
Gracie, Marie, and Daisy (WOOD);
see also SISTERS LENA, SISTERS
LLOYD, WOOD SISTERS
Sun Is Always Shining, The

WOOD SISTERS a.k.a. SISTERS LLOYD
(Bella BURGE & Rosie LLOYD)
Come Down And Open The Door
   (also solo by Rosie LLOYD)

WOODRUFF, Harry 1870–1916
I Wonder Who's Kissing Her Now?

WOODVILLE, Arthur at one time part-
nered Will MURRAY as The Freans
Any Old Port In A Storm
I've Been Out With The Man In The
   Moon
Joe, I Want To Go To The Football
   Match With You
You Can't Beat London For The Girls

WOOLF, Gypsy
De Player Ob De Big, Big Drum
Don't Tell Ma Mammie, Please

Love And L. S. D. (w. Kittee
   RAYBURN)
Twinkling Star
You're De Only Coon I Fancy

WORMAN, Johnny
Good-For-Nothing
If I Hadn't Been A Sunday School
   Teacher
Oh! The Black List

WOOTTWELL, Tom* 1865–1941; often
misspelled Wootwell
Anything To Sell My Papers
Blowed If I Didn't Wake Up
Coloured We Cost 2d
Faces
Have An Arf O' Gin, Old Dear
He Left The Earth Behind Him!
Hello, Old Dear
I Ain't Got No Farver
I Know Nothing About It
I'll Tell You What I Did The Other
   Day
In My First Time On Earth
It Must Have Been Years Ago
I Wonder Why?
Lady That He Met At Monte Carlo,
   The
Little Boy Blue (The Discontented
   Copper)
Little Shirt My Mother Made For Me,
   The
Lock Of My Grandmother's Hair, A
Man With The Bullet Proof Coat, The
Matrimony
Now Here's An Important Case
Only A Man
'Owd Yer Rah (What D'Ye Say?)
Sadness Of Her Sadness, The
Scandal Says
That's How I Diddle 'Em
Then We Went A-Hunting
To-Morrow
Wait A Minute
Water Walker, The
What Do I Want With A Man?

What D'Ye Say? Ow'd Yer Row
Wife, The Lodger And I, The
With This Hat On
You're Next

WRIGGLESWORTH, Mr
Beadle Of The Parish, The
London's A Comical Place
Margate Hoy, The

WRIGHT, Fred jun. 1871–1928; son of
Fred Wright (1826–1911); brother of
Huntley WRIGHT and Haidée Wright
(1867–1943)
Dear Little Daisy
I'm Tired Of Being Respectable
When I Marry Amelia

WRIGHT, Hal
Let's Have A Song About Rhubarb
Take Back The Heart That You Gave
Me
Then You'll Be Sorry For Me

WRIGHT, Hugh E.° 1879–1940
Idiosyncracies
In Your X-Ray Gown
'Ow I 'Ate Women
Wine Woman And Song

WRIGHT, Huntley 1872–1943; son of
Fred Wright (1826–1911); brother of
Fred WRIGHT jun. and Haidée Wright
(1867–1943)
Chin-Chin Chinaman
I'm Not Well
Mrs Brown

WRIGHT, Sarah c.1855–?; a.k.a. Mlle
SARA ('Wiry Sal'); m. 'Long John', a
ticket attendant at the Opera Comique,
Strand
Can-Can, The

WYNDHAM, Arthur W. 1841–88; m.
Kate SANTLEY
Life Boat Crew, The (sk.)

WYNDHAM, Sir Charles 1837–1919;
scenes from

Merchant Of Venice, The
Merry Wives Of Windsor, The

WYNDHAM, S. W.
Dicky-Bird
Fourpence-Ha'p'ny Change
Has Anyone Got A Corkscrew?
I'd Like To Live To Ninety Nine
I Like A Doughnut
I'm Going To Be There
It Wasn't What I Done For Mrs
Murphy
Let's Have An Animal Chorus
Let's Have A Quiet Time Tonight
Me-ow-wow
Milkman, The
Oh, For A Roly-Poly!
Oh! It's A Windy Night Tonight
Oh! To-Morrow Night
'Sbeen A Terrible Night Tonight
She Told Me To Meet Her At The
Gate
What Do You Want To Live To
Ninety-Nine For?

WYNDHAM, William H. see WINDOM,
William H.

WYNN, Bessie° 1876–1968
All That I Ask Of You Is Love
By The Beautiful Sea
I Don't Want Another Sister
If The Wind Had Only Blown The
Other Way

WYNNE, Edith
Bessie Hope
Colinette
Little Footsteps Tripping
Looking Forward
Maiden's Dream, The
Our Love Of Early Years
You Said You Wouldn't But You Did

WYNNE, Wish° 1882–1931
Country Girl, The
'Er Upstairs
Exit Muriel

Ooh! 'Er! (The Slavey)
Our Kiddie
Servant Girl, A (mon.)
We Were So Happy When We Were
    Poor

YEAMANS, Lydia 1866–1929; after
marrying her accompanist F. J. Titus
k.a. Lydia Titus-Yeamans
December And May
Dolly's Lament
I Guess I'll Have To Telegraph My
    Baby
I Loves Ye In The Same Ole Way
I Wish I Had A Baby To Dandle On
    My Knee
Maniac, The
My Pretty Jane
Sally Of Our Alley
Who's That Calling So Sweet?

YOHÉ, May 1869–1938
De Days Ob Long Ago
English Lass, The
Gordon Boys, The
Kiss Me To Sleep
Land Of Love, The
Lazily Drowsily
Linger Longer Loo
Many And Many A Weary Mile
No Coon Am Pining For Me
Nummy Num Num (w. E. J. **LONNEN**)
Oh Come My Love To Me
Oh Honey My Honey
Postilion Of Love
'Tis Hard To Love And Say Farewell
What's A Poor Girl To Do?

YORKE & ADAMS
Fortune Teller, The

Insurance Act, The
Under The Hebrew Moon
Wedding Of Becky Strauss, The

YORKE, Harry c.1852–1923
Benjamin Buff
Here I Am, Lucinda
Lord Knows Who!
Sailor's Been To Sea (See), The
Wilhelmina Wimple

YORKE, Tom
Cutting Down Expenses
Don't Rob The Children Of The
    Sunshine
Do You Want Me Or Do You
    Don't?
Harmony Court
Ups And Downs
William

YOUNG, A. W.
Oh Where, Oh Where, Has My Little
    Dog Gone?

YOUNG, Ted d. 17 May 1921
Farewell, Pretty Selina
Keep It Up
Oh! Black-Eyed Susan
Simple Mary Brown

ZIGEUNER QUARTET
If I Could Only Make You Care

ZIMBALIST, Efrem 1889–1985
Old Folks At Home (violin
    obbligato—Dvořák's Humoreske—
    to soprano of wife Alma **GLUCK**)

ZOLARI, C. A.
Brindisi (*La Traviata*) (w. Maria
    PICCOLOMINI)

LYRICISTS AND COMPOSERS

ALTHOUGH many artistes feature on song sheets as part-author or composer their actual contributions were sometimes minimal. Albert Chevalier, Harry Lauder, and Al Jolson were notorious for cutting themselves in on royalties by changing a word here and a note there or refusing to sing the song unless given a co-writer credit.

Spellings of names and wording of titles sometimes vary from edition to edition and not infrequently from page to page. Arbitrary decisions have therefore had to be made from time to time, and alternative titles indicated.

As with Artistes' Repertoires I have only included titles which are still performed, which were popular in their day, or which have some historical significance. The well-remarked prolificity of Music Hall tunesmiths resulted in a Himalayan mountain of 'popular' songs, 99.9 per cent of which remain in well-deserved oblivion. G. W. 'Jingo' Hunt ('I write songs by the yard, the dozen and the bushel') claimed to have written 7,000 songs, not more than a handful of which are remembered today, while Joseph Tabrar ('Richard Wagner? I could put him to bed and he wouldn't know he'd been alive!') reckoned his total at over 17,000—words, music, and band parts—thirty of which were allegedly written in a single day!

Sketch-writers are represented by the likes of Harry Grattan and Wal Pink; it is perhaps surprising to learn that Shaw, Barrie, and Granville-Barker wrote for the Halls also.

Names given in brackets after song titles are co-writers. *w* indicates the writer(s) of the words (the lyricists or lyrists) and *m* the composer(s) of the music. In the case of multiple authorship I have followed convention by putting the lyricist(s) first, before the colon, and the composer(s) after. An ampersand indicates that words and/or music were written jointly. Full names are given only for the first entry in a joint authorship list.

Dates are generally of first publication though where ascertainable the year of original performance is given.

Only a selection of the titles in this section is included in the Core Song-List. * denotes an entry in the Artistes' Repertoires section.

AARONS, Sam
Fiddle-De-Diddle-De-De (Sam MAYO &
Harry LEIGHTON & Arthur RICKS, arr.
AARONS) 1906
Have An Arf O' Gin Old Dear (Tom
WOOTTWELL & J. P. HARRINGTON,
arr. AARONS) 1906

ABRAHAMS, Henry
I Want To Be A Bloomer (m William H.
MONTGOMERY) 1851

ABRAHAMS, Maurice 1883–1931; m.
Belle Baker°
He'd Have To Get Under (Get Out And
Get Under) (w Grant CLARKE &
Edgar LESLIE) 1913
Hitchy-Koo (L. Wolfe GILBERT: &
Lewis F. MUIR) 1912
Ragtime Cowboy Joe (GILBERT: &
MUIR) 1912

A. H. *see* HUTCHINSON, Abby

A. L. pseudonym of Mrs Rudolf
Lehmann, mother of Liza LEHMANN
Bois Épais (Sombre Woods) (Théo
MARZIALS: Jean B. LULLY, arr. A. L.)
1892

A. L. C. reputed pseudonym of William
Makepeace THACKERAY
Married To A Mermaid (m William
Michael WATSON) 1866

ADAMS, Frank R. 1883–1963
I Wonder Who's Kissing Her Now? (&
William HOUGH: Harry ORLOB &
Joseph E. HOWARD) 1909

ADAMS, Harry
As If I Didn't Know (m E. JONGHMANS)
1884
Crutch and Toothpick (m JONGHMANS)
1880
Golden Wedding, The (m Charles
GODFREY) 1886
Here Upon Guard Am I (m
JONGHMANS) 1881

How D'Ye Do, Dear Boy? (m GODFREY)
1886
Hush Hush Hush! (Dolly Song) (m E.
Denham HARRISON) 1899
Jacks And Jills 1882
Masher King, The (m JONGHMANS)
1884
Shoulder To Shoulder (m JONGHMANS)
1882
Side By Side (m J. M. HARRISON, arr.
John S. BAKER) 1891
Tuner's Oppor-Tuner-Ty, The (& Fred
COYNE: COYNE) 1879
Wedding Bells (Take Him Home) (m
JONGHMANS) 1881

ADAMS, J.
Twiddley Bits (& George DANCE: Ernie
WOODVILLE) 1901

ADAMS, J. W. °
Aggie Astore 1865
Funny Little Nigger, The
Girl With The Glossy Hair, The
My Girl Sarah

ADAMS, Stephen 1844–1913;
pseudonym of Michael MAYBRICK°
Blue Alsatian Mountains, The (w
CLARIBEL) c.1880
Holy City, The (w Fred E. WEATHERLY)
1892
Midshipmite, The 1875
Nancy Lee (w WEATHERLY) 1876
Nirvana (w WEATHERLY) 1900
Roses (w WEATHERLY) 1905
Sprung A Leak (w Arthur MATTHISON)
1883
Star Of Bethlehem (w WEATHERLY)
1887
Tar's Farewell c.1880
They All Love Jack (w WEATHERLY)
1886
Thora (w WEATHERLY) 1905
When I Was One-And-Twenty (w A. E.
HOUSMAN (1896)) 1904
Also set by Arthur SOMERVELL and some
thirty-two others.

ADEW *see* CORY, W. J.; DRUMMOND, A.;
MITCHELL-INNES, T. L.; WOODHOUSE,
Evelyn

ADDISON, R. B.
Don't Cry (*w* W. RILEY) 1892

AGER, Milton 1893–1979
Ain't She Sweet? (*w* Jack YELLEN) 1927
Everything Is Peaches Down In Georgia
  (Grant CLARKE: & George W.
  MEYER) 1918
Happy Feet (*w* YELLEN) 1930
Hard-Hearted Hannah (*w* YELLEN)
  1929

AHRENS, Cora B.
Paddy From Cork 1911

AÏDÉ, C. Hamilton 1826–1906
Czardas (*Die Fledermaus*) (*m* Johann
  STRAUSS II) 1876
Forsaken, The (*m* Virginia GABRIEL)
  1861
Laughing Song, The (*Die Fledermaus*)
  (*m* STRAUSS II) 1876

AINGER, Alfred C. 1837–1904
Victoria, Our Queen (*m* Joseph BARNBY)
  1888

AISTON, Arthur° 1868–1924
Shift Up A Little Bit Farther (& Fred W.
  LEIGH) 1903
Vot A Game! Oi! Oi! (& T. W. THURBAN)
  1912

ALAW, Owain 1821–83; pseudonym of
John Owen
Land Of My Fathers (Hen Wlad Fy
  Nhadau) (Evan JAMES: James JAMES.
  English transl. ALAW) 1856
  See also Eben FARDD.
Yr Hen Lange (The Old Bachelor) (*w&m*
  TALHAIARN, arr. ALAW) 1862

ALBERT, Arthur° 1872–1930
Daddy's On The Engine (& P. H. SNAPE:
  Sam POTTER); also attr. Charles
  GRAHAM 1895

ALBERT, Fred° 1845–86; much never
published; wrote for himself and others
Bradshaw's Guide (*w* Henry S. LEIGH)
  1876
Brave Captain Webb 1875
Cheer For Plimsoll, A 1876
Cribbage
Game Of Nap, A 1881
I Knew That I Was Dreaming (*w* A. J.
  BIRTCHNELL) *c*.1875
Isn't That A Peculiar Thing?
Mad Butcher, The
Man Can't Be Always At Business, A
  c.1886
Mary, The Pride Of The Dairy 1874
Muddled Maxims 1886
Perverted Proverbs 1878
Proper Sort Of Girl
Riding On The Tramway
Sailor's Return, The
Singing Machine, The
Take Care Of The Pence
That's What Astonishes Me
Turkey And The Bear, The 1877
Welsh Miners, The 1877
We Will Beat Back The Russians *c*.1878
What Old Father Christmas Said
Wroughty Tom
You Can't Have Too Much Of A Jolly
  Good Thing 1878

ALDIGHIERI, Gottardo 1824–1906
Bacio, Il (The Kiss) (*m* Luigi ARDITI)
  1860

ALFORD, Kenneth J. 1881–1945;
pseudonym of Major Frederick Joseph
Ricketts
Colonel Bogey March 1913

ALLANDALE, Fred° 1866–1921
My Honey Dear (*m* Erroll STANHOPE)
  1898

ALLEN, Andrew d. 1950
Ca-bages, Ca-beans And Car-rots (&
  Wynn STANLEY) 1919
Dear Old Mother (& STANLEY) 1920

Let's Have A Song About Rhubarb (&
STANLEY) 1922
You Can't Do Without A Bit Of Love (&
Bert LEE) 1916

ALLEN, J.
Keemo Kimo! (*m* trad.) 1840
See Edwin P. CHRISTY for later version.

ALLEN, Oswald
Three Acres And A Cow (*m* Alfred LEE)
1885

ALLINGHAM, William 1824–89
Robin Redbreast (*m* CLARIBEL) 1865

ALLITSEN, Mary 1849–1912; pseudo-
nym of Frances Bumpus
England My England (*w* William Ernest
HENLEY) 1900
Prince Ivan's Song (*w* Marie CORELLI)
1902
Song Of Thanksgiving, A (*w* J.
THOMSON) 1897
There's A Land (*w* Charles MACKAY)
1896

ALLSOPP, Fred 1869–1942
They All Had To Get Out In Their
Nighties (*m* Will E. HAINES) 1907

AMSTERDAM, Morey 1909–96
Your Baby Has Gone Down The
Drainpipe (*m* Kay PATRICK; US
version of Your Baby 'As Gorn Dahn
The Plug-'Ole, Elton BOX & Desmond
COX & Lewis ILDA) 1946

ANDERSON, Arthur d. 1942
Land Where The Best Man Wins, The
(*m* Howard TALBOT) 1906
Joggin' Along The Highway (*m* Harold
SAMUEL) 1917

ANDREWS, A. F. 1857–1924
Only A 'Ittle Dirly Dirl 1880

ANDREWS, J. Charles Bond 1857–99
Alice (*w* Albert CHEVALIER) *c.*1899
Nipper's Holiday (*w* Mel B. SPURR) 1893
Oh! The Langwidge! (*w* CHEVALIER)
1895

Pierrot Coster (*w* CHEVALIER) 1895
Signalman On The Line, The (*w* Brian
DALY) 1893
Uncle John (The Lay Of The Hopeful
Nephew) (*w* CHEVALIER & DALY)
1894

ANSTEY, F. 1857–1934; pseudonym of
Thomas Anstey Guthrie
Burglar Bill 1888

ANTHONY, A.
Bear It And Grin (*m* E. C. DUNBAR)
1877

ANTHONY, George
Far, Far Away (*m* David DAY)
It's The Queerest Thing I've Heard
In All My Life (*m* T. W. BARRETT)
*c.*1885

ARCHBOLD, W. A.
Mr Captain Stop The Ship (*m*
McGLENNON) 1894

ARCHER, Eveline
Give Her A Vote, Papa (*m* Myrtle
JACKSON) 1908

ARDEN, Hope
Riding On A Load Of Hay (*m* Harry
BIRCH) 1877

ARDITI, Luigi 1822–1903
Bacio, Il (The Kiss) (*w* Gottardo
ALDIGHIERI) 1860

ARMSTRONG, A. E.
Sailor's Farewell (*w* J. GODDARD) 1879

ARMSTRONG, Harry 1879–1951
Nellie Dean (*w* Billy CLARKE) 1916
You're The Flower Of My Heart (Sweet
Adeline) (*w* R. Husch GERARD; orig.
Down Home In Old New England,
1896) 1903

ARMSTRONG, Tommy° 1848–1920
Th'Row Between Th'Caiges (air, Robin
Thomson's Smiddy O) *c.*1880

Trimdown Grange Explosion (air,
    Go And Leave Me If You Wish It)
    1882
Wor Nanny's A Mazer (air, trad.) *c*.1880

ARNDT, Felix 1889–1918
Nola (*w* added 1924 James F. BURNS)
    1915

ARNE, Thomas 1710–78
Rule, Britannia! (*w* David MALLETT or
    James THOMSON) *c*.1741

ARNOLD, Clarence D.
Dolly's Lament (*w* Julia SCHAYER) 1894

ARNOLD, Malcolm
Coster's Muvver, The (*m* George LE
    BRUNN) 1894
Faithless Donah, The (*m* Tom ARTHUR)
    1896
Good Night, Little Babe (& W. ARTHUR)
    1901
My Best Gal's Gone And Left Me (*m* Ed
    MONTAGU) 1900

ARNOLD, S. J. 1774–1852
Anchor's Weigh'd, The (*m* John
    BRAHAM) 1811
Death Of Nelson, The (*m* BRAHAM)
    1811
Life On The Ocean Wave, A (& Epes
    SARGENT: Henry RUSSELL) 1838

ARTHUR, F.
Courtship (*w* G. W. HUNTER & Charles
    WILMOTT) 1890

ARTHUR, Tom
Faithless Donah, The (*w* Malcolm
    ARNOLD) 1896

ARTHUR, G. Wallis°
After The Cinderella (parody of After
    The Ball) 1901
Arabella (*m* W. ARTHUR) 1908
Calculations 1901
'E's Found Out Where 'E Are (*m* Fred
    EPLETT)
That's His Girl 1893

ARTHUR, W.
Arabella (*w* G. Wallis ARTHUR) 1908
Good Night, Little Babe (& Malcolm
    ARNOLD) 1901

ARTHURS, George 1875–1944
Amateur Anarchist, An (sk.) 1912
Boudoir Secrets (& Orlando POWELL)
    1907
Building The Chicken House (sk.) (*w*
    Will EVANS) 1913
Caddie, The (The Links of Life?) 1914
Cowcaddens 1906
Don't Tempt Me (sk.) 1915
Girl Who Thought She Would
    (& POWELL) 1907
I Can Say 'Truly Rural' (& Worton
    DAVID) 1909
I Can't Reach That Top Note (& DAVID)
    1909
If The World Were Ruled By Girls
    (& C. W. MURPHY) 1905
I'm Waiting Here For Kate (& DAVID)
    1909
It's A Different Girl Again! (*m* Bennett
    SCOTT) 1906
I've Got The Riding Habit (& POWELL)
    1907
I Want To Sing In Opera (& DAVID)
    1910
Joshu-ah (& Bert LEE) 1906
Key Of The Situation, The (sk.) 1912
Links Of Life, The (The Caddie?) 1914
Little Of What You Fancy, A (& Fred
    W. LEIGH) 1915
My Bungalow In Bond Street (*m* T. C.
    Sterndale BENNETT) 1910
Ne'er-Dae-Well
On The Banks Of The Serpentine (*m*
    BENNETT) 1910
On The Road To Tipperary (*m* Leslie
    STUART) 1907
Our Laundry (sk.) (& Harry CASTLING;
    m arr. LE BRUNN) 1904
Piccadilly Trot, The (*m* DAVID) 1912
Three Ages Of Woman, The

(Woman's Opinion Of Man)
(w POWELL) 1907
Where There's A Girl There's A Boy (m
R. PENSO) 1919
White Knight, The (sk.) 1912
Who's The Lady Now? (& Lou HIRSCH)
1914
Wriggley Rag, The (& DAVID) 1912
You Are My Girl-Ski (& DAVID) 1910

ARUNDALE, Claude
Question Of Time, A (w J. HAYDEN-
CLARENDON) 1897

ARZONIA, Joe 1881–1953; pseudonym of
Arthur Longbrake
Preacher And The Bear, The 1903

ASAF, George 1880–1951; pseudonym
of George Powell
Pack Up Your Troubles In Your Old Kit-
Bag (m Felix POWELL) 1915

ASCHE, Oscar 1871–1936
Any Time's Kissing Time (m Frederic
NORTON) 1916
Cobbler's Song, The (m NORTON)
1916

ASCHER, Joseph 1828–69
Alice, Where Art Thou? (w Wellington
GUERNSEY) 1861

ASHER, Angelo A. b. 1860
Ask Yourself The Question (w&m Arthur
CORNEY, arr. ASHER) 1890
Diamond Ring, The (w&m Herbert
DARNLEY, arr. ASHER) c.1900
Gone For Ever (Wal PINK: Frank
ALYMER, arr. ASHER) 1888
Good Old Days Of Adam, The (George
THORN: Sam REDFERN, arr. ASHER)
1893
Mounsey (w Albert CHEVALIER) 1894
Ta-Ra-Ra-Boom-De-Ay (Richard
MORTON: Alfred MOOR-KING, arr.
ASHER) 1891
See also Henry J. SAYERS and CORE SONG-
LIST.

ASHLYN, Quenton°
Bassoon, The 1900
Ladies, The 1900
Mother's Wedding Ring (& Charles
WILLIAMS (2)) 1897

ATKINS, Norton 1862–1902
Fighting For The Flag They Love (m
George LE BRUNN) 1896
No More Fancy Balls For Me (&
Herbert DARNLEY) 1895
Oh, Sally (m Fred EPLETT) 1895
Oui! Tray Bong! (My Pal Jones) 1893
Three Makes Jolly Fine Company (E. W.
ROGERS & H. C. HUDSON: & Charles
COLLINS) 1903
Tribute To The Memory Of W. E.
Gladstone, A (& Charles WILLIAMS
(2)) 1898
Who Gives This Woman Away? (m
Charles SEEL) 1890

ATTERIDGE, Harold R. 1886–1938
By The Beautiful Sea (m Harry
CARROLL) 1914

AUSTIN, Charles° 1877–1944
Discharged From The Force (sk.) 1909
Parker, P.C. (& Charles RIDGWELL)
1908

AUSTIN, Fred 1872–1952
I'm Going Back To Himazas 1927

AVELING, Claude b. 1869
Sorrento (m Ernesto DE CURTIS) 1911

AYER, Nat D.° 1887–1952
Another Little Drink (w F. Clifford
GREY) 1916
Dear Old Shepherd's Bush (w GREY)
1916
Fact Is, The (w GREY) 1918
First Love—Last Love—Best Love (w
GREY) 1918
If You Were The Only Girl In The World
(w GREY) 1916
In Other Words (w GREY) 1916

I Stopped, I Looked, And I Listened (&
  GREY: AYER) 1916
Let The Great Big World Keep Turning
  (w GREY) 1917
Moving Day In Jungle Town (w A.
  Seymour BROWN) 1909
Nobody Noticed Me (& Bert LEE) 1918
Oh! You Beautiful Doll (w BROWN) 1910
Shufflin' Along (w Ralph STANLEY)
  1922
Ten Million Germans 1914
That Rag-Time Suffragette (& Harry
  WILLIAMS) 1913
Vicar And I Will Be There, The
  (w GREY) 1919

AYLMER, Frank
Gone For Ever (Wal PINK: AYLMER, arr.
  Angelo ASHER) 1888
Our Village (w PINK) 1889
That's When You Feel All Right (PINK:
  AYLMER arr. E. FORMAN) 1889
Three Individuals (w PINK) 1890

AYLWARD, Florence 1862–1950
Beloved, It Is Morn (w anon.) 1896
Love's Coronation (w W. SUTCLIFFE)
  1902

BĄDARZEWSKA-BARANOWSKA, Tekla
1834–61
Maiden's Prayer, The (a famous melody
  but bereft of lasting lyrics) 1856

BAGNELL, Sam° 1836–85
Starry Night And A Beautiful Girl, A

BAILLIE, Joanna 1762–1851
Chough And Crow To Roost Are Gone,
  The (*Fugitive Verses*, 1790: Henry R.
  BISHOP) 1816

BAIN(E), W. d. 1895?
Chickaleary Cove, The (w Ernee
  CLARKE) c.1870

BAKER, John S. possibly a.k.a. John J.
STAMFORD
Automatic Battery, The (w George
  MARAVILLE) c.1888

Below! Below! Below! (Geo
  HORNCASTLE: J. COOK, jun., arr.
  BAKER) 1888
Bill's Mouth Organ (w&m Harry
  BEDFORD, arr. BAKER) 1894
Bond Street Mash-ah, The (w&m James
  W. SEWELL, arr. BAKER) 1889
Couldn't Make The Old Girl Hear
  (w&m George LESTER, arr. BAKER)
  1897
Down Fell The Pony In A Fit (w Harry
  WINCOTT & Harry LEIGHTON) 1897
England For The English (w Fred
  BOWYER) 1888
  Note 1854 song of same title J. A. CAVE:
  DAGONET.
Fairly Knocked The Yankees In Chicago
  (w&m James WALSH (1), arr. BAKER)
  1893
Floor Gave Way, The (Albert HALL: Pat
  RAFFERTY, arr. BAKER) 1893
For The Sake Of The Old Times (w&m
  Oswald STOLL, arr. BAKER) 1890
He's Very Very Ill Indeed (Sam MAYO:
  RAFFERTY, arr. BAKER) 1890
His Own Mother Wouldn't Know Him
  (w&m T. W. CONNOR, arr. BAKER)
  1893
If I Only Bossed The Show (w BOWYER)
  1889
Little Bit Of Luck, A (w&m Carl
  HOWARD, arr. BAKER) 1897
McAnulty's Garden Party (w&m
  RAFFERTY, arr. BAKER) 1890
Mackenzie (That Devil Of A Daddy)
  (w&m J. W. SEWELL, arr. BAKER)
New Hat Now!, A (w&m James
  ROLMAZ, arr. BAKER)
Popular Nursery Rhymes Medley (w&m
  Carl HOWARD, arr. BAKER) 1893
Side By Side (Harry ADAMS: J. M.
  HARRISON, arr. BAKER) 1891
That's Where The Trouble Begins (w&m
  Wal PINK, arr. BAKER) 1891
Thereby Hangs A Tale (w BOWYER)
  1889
Treasures Of Home (Relics Of Liza)

(*w&m* Harry CASTLING, arr. BAKER)
1891

Wake 'Em Up (*w&m* William BINT, arr.
BAKER) 1890

Who'll Care For The Children? (*w&m*
Charles OSBORNE, arr. BAKER) 1899

Word-Lets, Gag-Lets, And Yarn-Lets
(Richard MORTON: Johann STRAUSS
II, arr. BAKER) 1893

BALDWIN, Charles sketch writer
Bungler's Luck (& Fred KITCHEN) 1913
Clicked Again 1919
First Night (& G. PAYNE) 1907
Mumming Birds (Twice Nightly) 1904
Persevering Potts (& KITCHEN) 1911
Saturday To Monday (& Fred KARNO &
KITCHEN) 1903
Year Dot, The 1905

BALFE, Michael W. 1808–70; grandfather of A. H. BEHREND

Come Into The Garden, Maud (*w* Alfred
TENNYSON) 1855

Cottage Near Rochelle, The (*w* E.
FITZBALL) 1835

Excelsior (*w* Henry W. LONGFELLOW)
1857

Good Night! Good Night! Beloved (*w*
LONGFELLOW) 1856

Green Trees Whispered Low And Mild,
The (*w* Longfellow) 1856

I Dreamt That I Dwelt In Marble Halls
(*w* Alfred BUNN) 1843

I Shot An Arrow Into The Air (*w*
LONGFELLOW) 1859

Killarney (*w* Edmund FALCONER)
1861

Light Of Other Days, The (*w* BUNN)
1836

Sands Of Dee, The (*w* Charles
KINGSLEY); see Fred CLAY

Then You'll Remember Me (*w* BUNN)
1843

Village Blacksmith, The (*w*
LONGFELLOW) 1855
See also W. H. WEISS.

BALL, Ernest R.° 1878–1922
Door Of Hope, The (*w* Dave REED)
1907

Fighting For Liberty (& J. Sutton
PATEMAN: Will HYDE) 1897

Let The Rest Of The World Go By (*w* J.
Keirn BRENNAN) 1919

Little Bit Of Heaven Fell, A (*w*
BRENNAN) 1914

Mother Machree (Rida Johnson YOUNG:
& Chauncey OLCOTT) 1910

She's So Much Like You, Mother (*w* B. J.
GILBERT) 1906

Till The Sands Of The Desert Grow
Cold (*w* George GRAFF) 1911

When Irish Eyes Are Smiling (*w* GRAFF
& OLCOTT) 1912

Will You Love Me In December As You
Do In May? (*w* James J. WALKER)
1905

BALL, H. T.
Good Old English Ale, The (*m* George F.
KEMP) 1854

BALL, Harry° 1841–88
Don't Say Who Gave You The Tip
Friends Of My Youthful Days (*w*
Herbert COLE) 1886

Now It's All Over For Ever (*w* Harry
CLEMENT: BALL, arr. F. W.
HUMPHRIES) 1881

Oh, Caroline 1882

(Quite A Toff In My) Newmarket Coat
(arr. HUMPHRIES) 1882

Sir Garnet Will Show Them The Way (*w*
George HORNCASTLE)

BANDON, Sid
Mary And The Butcher (& J. MURPHY:
W. T. WEBB) 1894

BANTA, Frank
Pretty Jennie Slattery (J. W. BLAKE &
Charles B. LAWLOR *m* arr. BANTA)
1895

BANTOCK, Sir Granville *see* GRABAN

BARBER, J.
Invocation (Heinrich HEINE adap.
  BARBER: Guy D'HARDELOT) 1894

BARCLAY, George° 1868–1944; m. Kate
Carney°
He Pushed Me On His Barra
Let's All Go Round To Alice's Place

BARCLAY, Lawrence+° d. 16 Dec.
1949; uncle of Vesta Victoria°
He Calls Me His Own Grace Darling
  1898
I Suffer From The Same Complaint
Oh! Ria, What Have You Done For Me?
  (& Mark LORNE) c.1910
Our Lodger's Such A Nice Young Man
  (& Fred MURRAY) 1897

BARINCOTT?, Reg. S.
Maiden In Grey, The (w Mrs G.
  HUBI-NEWCOMBE) 1912

BARKER, George A.° 1812–76
Empty Cradle, The (w W. B. B.
  STEVENS) 1869
Irish Emigrant, The (w Lady DUFFERIN)
  1846
Mary Blane (w Wellington GUERNSEY)
  1846
Shall I Wasting In Despair? (w George
  WITHER) 1861
White Squall, The (w Richard JOHNS)
  1835

BARKER, Harley Granville see
GRANVILLE-BARKER, Harley

BARNBY, Sir Joseph 1838–96
Beggar Maid, The (w Alfred TENNYSON)
  1880
Sweet And Low (w TENNYSON) 1863
Victoria, Our Queen (w Alfred C.
  AINGER) 1888

BARNES, Fred° 1884–1938
Raise Your Hat To The Lady (w Will
  HYDE) 1907
Scapegrace Of The Family, The (or

Black Sheep Of The Family, The)
  1909
Till The Boys Come Home

BARNES, Fred J.° d. 3 Jan 1918
Fancy You've Got All You Fancy (&
  Harry BEDFORD & R. P. WESTON)
  1908
Four Suits Of Cards, The 1898
Germans Are Coming So They Say, The
  (& BEDFORD & WESTON) c.1914
Hobnailed Boots That Farver Wore, The
  (& WESTON) 1907
I'm The Black Sheep Of The Flock, Baa!
  Baa! (& WESTON) 1912
In These Hard Times (& WESTON)
  1915
It's No Use You Calling 'Hannah!' (&
  Charles COLLINS: COLLINS) 1907
I've Got Rings On My Fingers (&
  WESTON: Maurice SCOTT) 1909
Kiss The Girl If You're Going To (&
  WESTON) 1907
Last Of The Dandies, The (m COLLINS)
  see HARRINGTON: G. LE BRUNN 1901
My Rachel's Eyes (& SCOTT & WESTON)
  c.1912
Oh, Bleriot! (& WESTON) 1909
One Of The Boys (& WESTON: SCOTT)
  1907
Play That Melody Again (m COLLINS)
  1900
Salome (& Harry BEDFORD & R. P.
  WESTON) 1908
  See also Orlando POWELL.
Shall I Be An Angel, Daddy? (m
  COLLINS) 1897
Studying The Face (m J. H. HURST)
  1897
Sweet Little Rose Of Persia (&
  COLLINS: COLLINS) 1900
Tickle Me, Timothy, Do! (& WESTON)
  1907
Tra-La-La! (& WESTON) 1906
What A Conjure! What A Cop! (&
  WESTON) 1907

When Father Papered The Parlour (&
WESTON) 1909
With This Hat On (*m* WESTON) 1911

BARNES, Paul *c.*1864–1922
Goodbye, Dolly Gray (*w* Will D. COBB)
1898

BARNES, Sydney° d. 1889
Nancy Had A Fancy For Botany (*w* Tom
HAINES)

BARNES, William 1801–86
Linden Lea (*m* Ralph VAUGHAN
WILLIAMS) 1902

BARNETT, Eugene
Rhoda Rode A Roadster (*w* Willie
YOUNGE) 1896

BARNETT, Harry V.
Tick! Tock! (*m* Alfred H. WEST) 1894

BARNETT, J.
Which Switch Is The Switch, Miss, For
Ipswich? (& Worton DAVID &
Herman DAREWSKI) 1915

BARNETT, John 1802–90
Love's Review 1832
Rise, Gentle Moon (*w* J. R. PLANCHÉ)
1828

BARR, James 1779–1860
Waltzing Matilda (Andrew B. PATERSON:
BARR, arr. Marie COWAN) 1895
See Andrew B. PATERSON for sources.

BARRETT, Lester° d. 1924; brother of
Leslie STUART
Ada's Serenade 1890
After All We've Done For Him 1892
All For The Sake Of Finnigan 1899
Beautiful Mona 1890
By The Sad Sea Waves (*m* Lester
THOMAS) 1894
See also Julius BENEDICT.
Come Along Boys 1891
Dance With Me (arr. Edmund FORMAN)
1890
Delaney's Chicken (& P. SWEENEY) 1896
Down By The Sea 1891

Fairy Tales 1905
Ga-Ga-Ga-Ga-Good-Bye (& SWEENEY)
1894
Give Him My Kind Regards 1890
Hello! Susie Green (*m* Herman
DAREWSKI) 1911
Hooligan's Mule 1897
How Did I Know? 1893
I'll Make You Up A Bottle 1891
In The Meantime 1893
I Used To Sigh For The Silvery Moon (*m*
DAREWSKI) 1909
Looking For A Job (& P. SWEENEY)
1899
Love To All 1897
Mamie May (*m* DAREWSKI) 1911
My Brown-Eyed Loo (*m* DAREWSKI)
1914
Never To Return Again 1890
Pious Polly Payne 1890
Some Danced The Lancers (*m* THOMAS)
1894
Sue, Sue, Sue (*m* DAREWSKI) 1908
Take 'Em Off 1890
They're All Fine Girls (& SWEENEY:
THOMAS) 1895
Two Sweethearts 1892
We Saved It For The Lodger (*m* Felix
McGLENNON) 1889

BARRETT, Medley° d. 1 Oct. 1937
Baden Powell's Scout 1908
Coronation Walk, The 1903
Gold! Gold! Gold! 1903
Half-Day Holiday Boys, The 1905
His Nibs—My Son 1907
Home-Made Motor Car, The 1904
Hystery Of England (Chronological
Crammers) 1905
It's A Great Big Shame No Longer (*w*
Edgar BATEMAN) 1919
I Want My Little Gollywog! (& Nat
CLIFFORD) 1906
Maria And Her Motor 1904
My Bruvver 1904
Navy Of The King, The 1904

That's Why The British Loved The King
(& Charles COBORN) 1910
Up Jumps The Ghost Of Sarah Porter (&
T. F. ROBSON) 1903
Why Do The British Love Their King?

BARRETT, Oscar c.1846–1941
I'm Getting A Big Boy Now (w Harry
NICHOLLS) 1880
Nonsense! Yes! By Jove! (w NICHOLLS)
1881

BARRETT, T. W.° 1851–1935
Fireman In The Amateur Brigade, The
(w Harry BODEN) 1886
It's The Queerest Thing I've Heard In
All My Life (w Geo. ANTHONY) c.1885
I've Been And Got Married Today 1884

BARRETT, Thomas Augustine see
STUART, Leslie and THOMAS, Lester

BARRI, Odoardo 1844–1920; pseudo-
nym of Edward Slater
At Peace But Still On Guard (w Fred E.
WEATHERLY) 1876
Happy Day, A (w WEATHERLY) 1878
Lady Doctor's Husband, The (w John B.
LAWREEN & John OXENFORD)
Old Brigade, The (w WEATHERLY) 1881
Patchwork (w H. L. D'Arcy JAXONE)
Saved From The Storm (w WEATHERLY)
1876
Shadow, A (w Adelaide Anne PROCTER)
1876
Song Of The Gout (w LAWREEN &
OXENFORD) 1879
Star Of Hope, The (w Mme A. FOLI)
1878

BARRIE, Sir James 1860–1937; all
sketches
Half An Hour 1913
New Word, The 1915
Old Lady Shows Her Medals, The 1917
Pantaloon 1905
Rosalind 1912
Seven Women 1917

Slice Of Life, A 1910
Tag, Der 1914
Twelve Pound Look, The (orig. entitled
Success) 1910
Will, The 1913

BARRIE, Royden d. 14 Apr. 1948;
pseudonym of Rodney Bennet
Brown Bird Singing, A (m Haydn
WOOD) 1922

BARRINGTON, Rutland° 1852–1922
Check To The Queen (sk.) (& Philip
CUNNINGHAM) 1912

BARRON, J. Francis 1870–1940
My Old Shako (m Henri TROTÈRE) 1907
Trumpeter, The (m J. Airlie DIX) 1904

BARRY, H. C.° d. 28 Jan. 1909
Alas! My Poor Brother! (w Colin
MACKAY) 1900
Ghost Of Sherlock Holmes, The (w
Richard MORTON) 1894
Junior Job-Lot Club, The (w G. P.
HUNTLEY) 1896
Kitchener's Karol (& Colin MACKAY:
BARRY) 1899
Since My Old Dutch Pegged Out (w
George H. GRAY & HUNTLEY) 1897

BARTHOLOMEW, William 1793–1867
Dream, The (m Michael COSTA) 1858
O For The Wings Of A Dove (Hear My
Prayer) (m Felix MENDELSSOHN)
1844

BARWICK, Edwin° 1858–1928
Chances That He's Had, The (m Walter
PASSMORE) 1896
Curate, The (m PASSMORE) 1894

BASS, Tom° 1852–1913
Bill-Poster, The (& George
HORNCASTLE; m arr. Alfred LEE)
1892
Copy Your Uncle John 1887
I'm A Member Of The County Council
1889

Model From Madame Tussaud, A
Rich (Man's And The Poor) Man's
Storycum, The 1899

BASTOW, George° 1872–1914
Captain Ginjah, O. T. (& Fred W.
LEIGH) 1910
Galloping Major, The (*w* LEIGH) 1906
I Don't Know What To Do (& Carl
HOWARD) 1903
She's Proud And She's Beautiful (&
LEIGH) 1906
She Was Such A Nice Young Gal (&
HOWARD) 1903

BATCHELDER, James
Charming Young Girl, The (Fred PERRY:
Tom FANCOURT, arr. BATCHELDER)
1868

BATCHELOR, B. M. d. 10 Apr. 1941
Ta-Ra-Ra-Boom-De-Ay (English *w* B. M.
BATCHELOR: Angelo A. ASHER) 1891
See also Henry J. SAYERS and CORE SONG-
LIST.

BATEMAN, Edgar 1860–1946; on music
staff of Francis, Day & Hunter
Folkestone For The Day (*m* George LE
BRUNN) 1900
Girls From Bryant's And May, The (*m* LE
BRUNN) 1901
Haunted Idiot, The
If It Wasn't For The 'Ouses In Between
(*m* LE BRUNN) 1894
Ipecacuanha (& J. P. LONG) 1917
It's A Great Big Shame! (I'm Blowed If
'E Can Call 'Isself 'Is Own) (*m* LE
BRUNN) 1894
It's A Great Big Shame No Longer (*m*
Medley BARRETT) 1919
Lightning Results (*m* Harry RANDALL)
1897
'Liza Johnson (*m* LE BRUNN) 1901
Mrs Carter (& C. W. MURPHY:
MURPHY); sung by Gus Elen 1900
My London Country Lane (& Albert
PERRY) 1900

My Next Door Neighbour's Gardin (&
Gus ELEN: LE BRUNN) 1900
My Old Pal Joe (*m* SCOTT) 1906
Nice Quiet Day, A (Postman's Holiday)
(& Eustace BAYNES: Maurice SCOTT)
1901
Oh, The Daylight Bill (& T. W. DOWN:
Herman E. DAREWSKI jun.) 1908
Patchwork Garden, The (& Paul MILL:
J. Airlie DIX) 1902
Seaside Posters Round The Home, The
(*m* Henry E. PETHER) 1919

BATES, Charles
Hard Hearted Hannah (& Bob
BIGELOW & Jack YELLEN) 1924

BAY
How Can A Little Girl Be Good? (*m*
Reginald TABBUSH) 1919

BAYES-NORWORTH, Nora° 1880–1928;
m. Jack NORWORTH (div.)
Shine On Harvest Moon (Jack
NORWORTH: & NORWORTH) 1908

BAYLY, Thomas Haynes 1795–1839;
a.k.a. Philip Mortimer
Adieu, My Moustachios (*m* Jonathan
BLEWITT) 1837
Captain With His Whiskers, The *see* Oh!
They March'd Thro' The Town
Come Dwell With Me (*m* Alexander
LEE) 1830
He Knew She Never Blamed Him (*m*
George HODSON) 1834
I'd Be A Butterfly 1829
Long Long Ago (rev. 1942 as Don't Sit
Under The Apple Tree) *c*.1835
Mistletoe Bough, The (*m* arr. Henry
BISHOP; *w&m* from trad.) 1840
Oh! They March'd Thro' The Town (The
Captain With His Whiskers) (*m* Sidney
NELSON) *c*.1838
See also CORE SONG-LIST.
Pilot, The (*m* NELSON) *c*.1825
She Wore A Wreath Of Roses (*m* Joseph
P. KNIGHT) 1840

Soldier's Tear, The (*m* Alexander LEE)
   c.1833
Welcome Me Home 1829

BAYMAN, James
Mother Bear Me To The Window 1874
Music Mad (*w* George LEYBOURNE)

BAYNES, Eustace
Nice Quiet Day, A (Postman's Holiday)
   (& Edgar BATEMAN: Maurice SCOTT)
   1901

BAYS, R. E.
Please Will You Hold The Baby, Sir?
   1898

BEAUCHAMP, George° 1863–1939
Git Your 'Air Cut (& Chas. OSBORNE &
   Fred EPLETT) 1892

BEATON, Bob
Saftest O' The Family, The (& Harry
   LAUDER: LAUDER) 1904

BEDDOE, Alfred 1847–92
Quite English, You Know 1887

BEDFORD, Harry° 1873–1939
Always On The Dream (& A. J. MILLS)
   1898
Bill's Mouth Organ (arr. John S. BAKER)
   1894
Broken-Down Sportsman, The (& R. P.
   WESTON) 1907
Brown, Broke And Breezy (& WESTON)
   1910
Cooking The Cock Of The North (&
   WESTON) 1911
Fancy You've Got All You Fancy (& F. J.
   BARNES & WESTON) 1908
Germans Are Coming So They Say, The
   (& BARNES & WESTON) *c*.1914
If You Can't Do Any Good Don't Do Any
   Harm 1902
I Like Your Town (& WESTON) 1915
It's A Bit Of A Ruin That Cromwell
   Knocked About A Bit (& Terry
   SULLIVAN: BEDFORD) 1912

Old-Age Pension, The (& WESTON)
   1908
Salome (& BARNES & WESTON) 1908
   See also Orlando POWELL.
When The Summer Comes Again (Three
   Pots A Shilling) 1895

BEHREND, Arthur H. 1853–1935;
grandson of Michael W. BALFE
Auntie (*w* Fred E. WEATHERLY)
   c.1880
Crossing The Bar (*w* Alfred TENNYSON)
   1893
   Also set by Edward G. LOCKTON and
   Hubert PARRY, amongst others.
Daddy (*w* Mary Mark LEMON) 1880
Song Of The Shirt, The (*w* Thomas
   HOOD 1843) 1879
   See also Mrs F. A. DAVIDSON; Jonathan
   BLEWITT; Henry RUSSELL.
Toddles (*w* Eugene FIELD) 1907

BELASCO, Frederick 1861–1920;
pseudonym of Monroe H. ROSENFELD
Johnny Get Your Gun (British *w* T. L.
   CLAY) 1886

BELL, Frank° *c*.1830–82
Coffee Shop At Pimlico, The 1864
Telegraph, The 1866

BELLAMY, W. H. 1800–66
Simon The Cellarer (*m* J. L. HATTON)
   1847

BELLWOOD, Bessie° 1857–96
What Cheer Ria (*m* Will HERBERT) 1885

BENEDICT, Sir Julius 1804–85
By The Sad Sea Waves (*w* Alfred BUNN)
   1844
   See also Lester THOMAS.
Comrades (*w* H. L. D'Arcy JAXONE)
   1883
Lullaby, The (*w* John OXENFORD) 1862
Moon Has Raised Her Lamp Above, The
   (*w* OXENFORD) 1862
Rock Me To Sleep Mother 1865

BENNETT, Billy° 1887–1942 *see* entry in
ARTISTES' REPERTOIRES

BENNETT, T. C. Sterndale° 1882–1944;
grandson of Sir William Sterndale
BENNETT
I'm Courtin' Sairey Green (*w* Clifford
GREY) 1914
In My Museum (*w* GREY) 1914
Leanin' (*w* Hugh E. WRIGHT) 1926
My Bungalow In Bond Street (*w* George
ARTHURS) 1910
My Word! Jones Of The Lancers (*w* Guy
M. EDEN) 1911
On The Banks Of The Serpentine (*w*
ARTHURS) 1910
Sammy The Dashing Dragoon (*w* GREY)
1914
Sophy (*w* Herbert LEE) 1913
Swankers By The Sea (sk.) (*w* Willie
ROUSE) 1914

BENNETT, Sir William Sterndale
1816–75; grandfather of T. C. Sterndale
BENNETT
Come To Town, Miss Brown

BENSON, Arthur C. 1862–1925
Land Of Hope And Glory (*m* Edward
ELGAR) 1902

BENTEEN, Fred D. d. 1864
Jim Crack Corn (De Blue Tail Fly) 1845

BERLIN, Irving 1888–1990
Alexander's Rag-Time Band 1911
Always 1925
Blue Skies 1926
Dance Of The Grizzly Bear (*w* George
BOTSFORD) 1910
Discoveries (When I Discovered You)
(& E. Ray GOETZ) 1914
Everybody's Doin' It Now 1911
He's A Ragpicker 1914
If The Managers Only Thought The
Same As Mother (*m* Ted SNYDER)
1910
I Love A Piano 1915

I'm Going Back To Dixie (& SNYDER)
1911
I Want To Go Back To Michigan (Down
On The Farm) 1914
Kiss Me My Honey (*m* SNYDER) 1910
Marie From Sunny Italy (*m* Nick
NICHOLSON—first pub. song) 1907
My Wife's Gone To The Country (&
George WHITING: SNYDER) 1909
(Play A) Simple Melody 1914
Pretty Girl Is Like A Melody, A 1919
Sadie Salome, Go Home 1909
Snookey Ookums 1913
That Mysterious Rag (*m* SNYDER) 1912
When I Discovered You (Discoveries)
(& GOETZ) 1914
When I Leave The World Behind 1915
When I Lost You (prompted by the
death of his wife, Dorothy Goetz)
1912
When The Midnight Choo-Choo Leaves
For Alabam' 1912
Woodman, Woodman, Spare That Tree
(parody on ballad by Henry RUSSELL)
1911
Yiddle On Your Fiddle Play Some Rag-
Time 1909

BERNARD, Peter *c.*1888–1960; see also
American Ragtime Octette°
Effa-Saffa-Laffa-Daffa-Dil (& MAGINI)
1919

BERNOTT, W.
Waiter, The (& A Boy JONES: G. LE
BRUNN) 1892

BERRY, Joseph
Same Old Lie, The (*m* Harry RANDALL)
1890

BESLY, Edward M.
Boy Scout Song, The 1910
Come Roller Skating 1910
North Pole Song, The 1910

BESSO, M.
Only A Jew (& John LAWSON) 1896

BEULER, Jacob 1796–1873; sometimes spelled Beulah
Miss Julia (Wery Pekoolier) (*m* Jonathan BLEWITT) 1826
Lord High Admiral King And The Sailor, The *c*.1851
Nervous Family, The

BEVERLEY, M.
Go Pretty Rose (*m* Théo MARZIALS) 1886

BICKNELL, G.
Cruel Mary Holder (*w&m* Arthur LLOYD, arr. BICKNELL) 1866
You Naughty, Naughty Men (*w* T. KENNICK) 1865

BIGELOW, Robert W. 1890–1965
Hard Hearted Hannah (& Charles BATES & Jack YELLEN) 1924

BIGNELL, Charles° *c*.1866–1935
Cock-O'-The-Walk (& J. P. HARRINGTON: George LE BRUNN) 1898
Things Were Very, Very Lively (& T. BROWN & J. W. DAWSON) 1894
We Shall Be Angels In The Sweet Bye-And-Bye 1888

BINGHAM, G. Clifton 1859–1913
Ask Not (*m* Maude V. WHITE) 1905
Boys Are Marching, The (*m* Theo BONHEUR) 1899
Brow Of The Hill, The (*m* Henri TROTÈRE) 1897
Dear Heart (*m* Tito MATTEI 1874) 1888
Dear Home-Land, The (*m* Walter SLAUGHTER) 1892
In Old Madrid (*m* TROTÈRE) 1889
Love, Could I Only Tell Thee (*m* John Mais CAPEL)
Lovers Still (*m* Leslie MAYNE) 1889
Love's Old Sweet Song (*m* J. L. MOLLOY) 1884
Merry Vagabonds, The (*m* Stanley GORDON) 1906

Promise Of Life, The (*m* Frederich M. COWEN) 1893
Scent Of The Mignonette, The (*m* Hope TEMPLE) 1897
Swallows (*m* COWEN) 1895

BINT, William° *c*.1850–1913
I'll Tell Your Mother What You've Done 1881
I Tell Them My Father's A Marquis (arr. George ISON) 1884
I Will If You Will 1887
My Father Was A Marquis (*w* Walter HASTINGS) 1887
So Was Mine (HASTINGS: BINT, arr. Warwick WILLIAMS) 1889
Wake 'Em Up (arr. John S. BAKER) 1890
Where Are Those Girls? *c*.1900
Whistling Song, The 1887

BIRCH, Harry
Riding On A Load Of Hay (*w* Hope ARDEN) 1877

BIRTCHNELL, A. J.
I Know That I Was Dreaming (*m* Fred ALBERT) 1875

BISHOP, Sir Henry R. 1786–1855
Buy A Broom (*w* James R. PLANCHÉ) 1825
Chough And Crow To Roost Are Gone, The (*w* Joanna BAILLIE) 1816
Come Live With Me And Be My Love (*w* Christopher MARLOWE) 1819
Home! Sweet Home! (*w* John Howard PAYNE) 1823
Lo! Here The Gentle Lark (*w* William SHAKESPEARE) 1819
Mistletoe Bough, The (*w* Thomas Haynes BAYLY; *w&m* from trad.) 1840
My Pretty Jane (The Bloom Is On The Rye) (*w* Edward FITZBALL) *c*.1830

BIZET, Georges 1838–75
Flower Song, The (*Carmen*) (*w* Henri

MEILHAC & L. HALÉVY; orig. Eng. transl. Henry HERSEE (1878)) 1875
Habanera (*Carmen*) (*w* MEILHAC & HALÉVY; orig. Eng. transl. HERSEE) 1875
Toreador Song (*Carmen*) (*w* MEILHAC & HALÉVY; orig. Eng. transl. HERSEE) 1875

BLACK, H. Broughton° d. 1905
Irish Courtship (*m* John W. IVIMEY) 1898
Tenor And Baritone (*m* H. Lane WILSON) 1896

BLAKE, Eubie 1883–1983; a.k.a. J. Hubert Blake
I'm Just Wild About Harry (*w* Noble SISSLE) 1921

BLAKE, James W. 1862–1935
Pretty Jennie Slattery (& Charles B. LAWLOR *m* arr. Frank BANTA) 1895
Sidewalks Of New York, The *or* Dancing On The Streets (& LAWLOR) 1894

BLAKE, William 1757–1827
Jerusalem (*m* Hubert PARRY) 1916

BLAMPHIN, Charles 1830/1–95; harpist with Templeton's Minstrels and the Christy Minstrels°
Beautiful Gal O' Mine
Death Of Stonewall Jackson, The
Double-Handed Gridiron
I'd Rather Be A Rose 1865
I'm Lively Pompey Jones (*m* J. SULLIVAN) 1873
Just Touch The Harp Gently (*w* Samuel N. MITCHELL) 1870
Nigger General

BLANCHARD, E. L. 1820–89
Alonzo The Brave (*m* ?) *c*.1850
See also Sam COWELL & J. HARROWAY.
'Norrible Tale, A (The Suicidal Family) (*m* arr. M. HOBSON) 1865
See also H. J. WHYMARK.

BLAND, Dorothy *see* JORDAN, Mrs

BLAND, James A.° 1854–1911
Carry Me Back To Old Virginny 1878
In The Evening By The Moonlight 1880
Oh, Dem Golden Slippers 1879

BLANEY, Norah° 1896–1986
Mister Bear (*w* Roy Frank JOHNSON) 1913
Skinny Piccaninny (*w* JOHNSON) 1917

BLEWITT, Jonathan° *c*.1781–1853; sometimes spelled Blewett
Adieu, My Moustachios (*w* Haynes BAYLY) 1837
Ben Battle (Nelly Gray) (*w* Thomas HOOD) 1829; set by at least 5 others
Cork Leg, The *c*.1835
Cure, The *see* The Perfect Cure
Jump Jim Crow (trad. US, arr. BLEWITT) 1837
Mary's Ghost (*w* Thomas HOOD) *c*.1840
See also Maude Valérie WHITE.
Merry Little Grey Fat Man, The 1845
Merry Little Woman, The
Miss Julia (Wery Pekoolier) (*w* Jacob BEULER) 1826
New Police Act, The (*w* J. BRETON) 1840
Paddy Carey *c*.1835
Perfect Cure, The (Frederick C. PERRY: air BLEWITT's 'The Monkey And The Nuts') 1861
Reg'lar Cure, The (Charles SLOMAN: air as previous entry)
Song Of The Shirt (*w* Thomas HOOD) 1843
See also Arthur H. BEHREND; Mrs F. A. DAVIDSON; Henry RUSSELL.
Tho' Fifty I Am Still A Beau
Useful Young Man, The

BLOCKLEY, John 1800–82
Arab's Farewell To His Favourite Steed, The (*w* Hon Mrs NORTON) 1869
Charge Of The Light Brigade, The (*w* Alfred TENNYSON) 1855

Jessie's Dream (*w* Grace CAMPBELL) 1858

Listening Angels (*w* Adelaide A. PROCTER) 1860

Many Happy Returns Of The Day (*w* Eliza COOK) 1850

Old Clock On The Stairs, The (*w* Henry W. LONGFELLOW) 1857

Shake Of The Hand, The (*w* TALHAIARN) 1857

BLOCKSIDGE, W.
Token, The (*m* W. H. SQUIRE) 1909

BLOOM, Sol 1870–1949; a.k.a. Albert H. FITZ
Hootchy Kootchy Dance 1893
In Dahomey 1902

BLOSSOM, Henry 1866–1919
If I Were On The Stage (Kiss Me Again) (*m* Victor HERBERT) 1905

BOBS, The Two° fl. *c*.1905–27; Bob Adams (1876–1948) and Bob Alden (1882–1932)
Four-And-Nine (Worton DAVID: & Bert LEE) 1915
Paddy McGinty's Goat (& R. P. WESTON & LEE) 1917
When Paderewski Plays (& WESTON & LEE) 1916

BODEN, Harry d. 23 Nov. 1925
Another Winner (*w* Wal PINK) (sk.) 1912
Every-Day Life (*m* Charles CHAPLIN) 1891
Fireman In The Amateur Brigade, The (*m* T. BARRETT) 1886
How Dare You! (& KEITH, ? & Billy MERSON: Fred EPLETT) 1906
I'm Selling Up The 'Appy 'Appy 'Ome (& Harry CHAMPION) 1889
Marquis Of Camberwell Green, The (*m* E. R. SHROSBERRY) 1884
Sandwich Man, The (*m* Bert BRANTFORD) 1904

There You Are, There You Are, There You Ain't 1888

When She Walks (*m* W. SKERRY & Harry FORD) 1906

Where's The Good? (*m* BRANTFORD) 1911

You Do Soon Change Your Mind (*m* BRANTFORD) 1903

BOGETTI, Edwin
Gladstone Is The Captain Of The Ship John Bull (*w* F. V. ST CLAIR) 1881

BONHEUR, Theodore pseudonym of Charles Arthur Rawlings
Battle Eve, The (*w* G. W. SOUTHEY) 1898
Boys Are Marching, The (*w* G. Clifton BINGHAM) 1899
King's Own, The (*w* Herbert K. CROFTS) *c*.1895
True To Jack (*w* L. LENNOX) 1892

BOOSEY, William 1864–1933
Come To Me (*m* Luigi DENZA) 1885

BOOTH, Frank
Santy Klors (*m* Nelson JACKSON) 1902

BOOTH, T. G.
Lucy Long (*m* William M. WHITLOCK) 1838

BOTSFORD, George d. 1949
Black And White Rag (piano piece) 1907
Dance Of The Grizzly Bear (*m* Irving BERLIN) 1910

BOUGHTON, Rutland 1878–1960
Black Monk, The 1910
Immortal Hour, The (*w* from plays & poems of Fiona MACLEOD) 1920

BOULTON, Sir Harold 1859–1935
Glorious Devon (*m* Edward GERMAN) 1905
Skye Boat Song, The (*m* A. C. MACLEOD) 1884

BOWERS, E. 1827–65
Dear Mother I've Come Home To Die
(*m* H. TUCKER) 1863

BOWERS, F. V. 1874–1961
I'm The Bosom Friend Of Albert, Prince
Of Wales (*w* Charles HORWITZ) 1891
Oh, Lucky Jim (*w* HORWITZ) 1896
Pig Got Up And Slowly Walked Away,
The (*w* Benjamin Hapgood BURT)
1896

BOWMAN, Euday Louis 1887–1949
12th Street Rag 1914

BOWMER, Harriett°
Nice Looking Girl, The (*m* G. W. HUNT)
1865

BOWYER, Fred 1849–1936
Across The Bridge (*m* G. LE BRUNN)
1889
After The Ball (& Orlando POWELL)—a
version for Vesta Tilley° 1893
After The Ball (& POWELL)—a parody
for Arthur Roberts° 1894
See also CORE SONG-LIST.
Cabby Knows His Fare (*m* LE BRUNN)
1889
Down Went The Captain (*m* Kate
ROYLE, arr. George ISON) 1887
England For The English (*m* John S.
BAKER) 1888
For 1854 song of the same title see J. A.
CAVE: DAGONET.
If I Only Bossed The Show (*m* BAKER)
1889
I'm Going To Do Without 'Em (*m*
William George EATON) 1882
It's A Little Bit Of Sugar For The Bird
(& W. E. SPRANGE: John CROOK)
1895
Little Stowaway (sk.)
Seaside Holiday At Home, A (*m* Gilbert
LAYE) 1903
Shadows Of St Paul's (sk.)
Thereby Hangs A Tale (*m* BAKER) 1889
They're All Very Fine And Large 1885

True British Swell, The (*m* EATON) 1881
We Follow (*m* Georges JACOBI) 1887
Wrap Me Up In My Tarpaulin Jacket
(*w&m* G. J. WHYTE-MELVILLE *w* rev.
BOWYER *m* arr. E. J. SYMONS) 1884

Box, Elton (Harold) d. 11 Nov. 1981
See Jack SPADE
In The Quartermaster's Store (adap. with
Desmond COX & Dave REED) 1940
We All Went Up Up Up The Mountain
(& COX & Ralph BUTLER) 1933

BOYCE, William 1711–79
Heart Of Oak (*w* David GARRICK) 1759

BOYD JONES, Ernest *see* JONES, Ernest
Boyd

BOYER, De Lucien
Yahama! (*m* Karl HOSCHNA) 1909

BOYLE, Marcus
John The Masher (arr. E. FOREMAN)
1884

BRADEN, Alan
When We Were Two Little Boys
(Edward MADDEN: T. F. MORSE, arr.
BRADEN) 1903

BRADFORD, Barker?
Oh! My Darling Clementine (or Percy
MONTROSE?) (*w* 1863 *m* 1884)

BRADLEY, Revd Edward 1827–89;
a.k.a. Cuthbert Bede
Ratcatcher's Daughter, The (*m* Sam
COWELL or perhaps anon.) *c*.1852
See CORE SONG-LIST.

BRAHAM, David 1838–1905
Maggie Murphy's Home 1890
Whist! The Bogie Man (*w* HARRIGAN)
1880
British version Henry PETTITT &
George R. SIMS: Meyer LUTZ, arr.
Edmund FORMAN 1890.

BRAHAM, John° 1772/4–1856
All's Well (*w* Thomas J. DIBDIN) 1803

Anchor's Weigh'd, The (*w* S. J. ARNOLD)
1811

Death Of Nelson, The 1811
See George THORN for parody.

Queen Mab (*w* Percy Bysshe SHELLEY)
1813

When Thy Bosom Heaves The Sigh (*w*
Charles Armitage BROWN) 1814

BRAHAM, Philip 1882–1934
Limehouse Blues (*w* D. FURBER) 1922

BRAHE, May H. d. 14 Aug. 1956
Bless This House (*w* Helen TAYLOR)
1927

BRANTFORD, Bert°
Sandwich Man, The (*w* Harry BODEN)
1904

Where's The Good? (*w* BODEN) 1911

You Do Soon Change Your Mind (*w*
BODEN) 1903

BRATTON, John W. 1867–1947
My Cosey Corner Girl (*w* Charles Noel
DOUGLAS) 1903

Sunshine Of Paradise Alley, The (*w*
Walter H. FORD) 1895

Teddy Bears' Picnic, The (*w* added
Jimmy KENNEDY 1930) 1907

BRENNAN, J. Keirn 1873–1948
Let The Rest Of The World Go By (*m*
Ernest R. BALL) 1919

Little Bit Of Heaven Fell, A (*m* BALL)
1914

BRENNEN, Robert H.
Ring Down The Curtain (*m* Pauline B.
STORY) 1902

She's A Singer, But A Lady, Just The
Same (*m* STORY) 1902

BRETON, J.
New Police Act, The (*m* Jonathan
BLEWITT) 1840

BRENTON, H. E.
Girl From College, The (*w* Mel B.
SPURR) 1894

BRETT, Harry
All Right, Thanks! (arr. Edward J.
HENSON)

Courting A Widow 1895

Funny Without Being Vulgar (*m* Charles
INGLE) 1891

Hunting (*m* INGLE) 1892

Poor Old Uncle Jones! (BRETT: BRETT,
arr. HENSON) 1895

You Put On The Trousers (& Carlile
VERNON) 1896

BRICE, Annie *see* HERBERT, Annie
Brice

BRIDGE, Frank 1879–1941
Ballad Of The 'Clampherdown', The (*w*
Rudyard KIPLING) 1899

Easter Hymn (Eng. *w* H. WAGEMAN)
1912

E'en As A Lonely Flower (*w* K. F.
KROCKER after Heinrich HEINE)
1905

BRIGHTON, Charles° 1867–96
You'll Have To Marry Me Now 1895

BRINE, Mary D.
Hearts And Flowers (from *Winter
Stories*, Alphons CZIBULKA, *m* adap.
Theodore MOSES-TOBANI) 1899

BRINKWORTH, W. H.
Young Man On The Railway, The (*w*
Harry CLIFTON) 1865

BROADWOOD, Lucy C. 1858–1929
I'm A Man That's Done Wrong To My
Parents (trad. ed. Laye BROADWOOD)
1889

BROOKS, George° 1867–1947
I've Turned Against It Now! 1891

BROOKS, Shelton 1886–1975
Darktown Strutters' Ball, (At) The 1917

Some Of These Days 1910

There'll Come A Time 1911

When You Hear That Dixieland Jazz
Band Play 1918

BROUGH, Barnabus
Sigh Of The Slave, The (*m* J. A. CAVE)
1853

BROWN, A. Seymour° 1885–1947
Moving Day In Jungle Town (*m* Nat D.
AYER) 1909
Oh! You Beautiful Doll (*m* AYER) 1910

BROWN, Charles Armitage 1786–1842
When Thy Bosom Heaves The Sigh (*m*
John BRAHAM) 1814

BROWN, J. Conway
Fashionable Fred (*w* Walter BURNOT)
c.1868

BROWN, Lew 1893–1958
Give Me The Moonlight (*m* Al VON
TILZER) 1917
That Hypnotizing Man (*m* VON TILZER)
1911

BROWN, T. d. 20 June 1919
Things Were Very, Very Lively (&
Charles BIGNELL & J. W. DAWSON)
1894

BROWNE, Charles Farrar *see* WARD,
Artemus

BROWNE, P.
Something Went Wrong With The Works
(*m* Arthur CORNEY) 1887

BROWNE, Raymond E.
Mormon Coon, The (*m* Clay SMITH)
1905

BROWNING, Robert 1812–89
King Charles (*m* Maude Valérie WHITE)
1898; and 11 other settings

BRUTON, James° 1806–68
Boy Wot Visits The Palace, The (arr.
Henry GIFFON) *c*.1840
Railway Mania 1846

BRYAN, Alfred 1871–1958
Come Josephine In My Flying Machine
(*m* Fred FIS(C)HER) 1910

I Didn't Raise My Boy To Be A Soldier
(*m* Al PIANTADOSI) 1915
Peg O' My Heart (*m* FIS(C)HER 1913
Who Paid The Rent For Mrs Rip Van
Winkle When Rip Van Winkle Went
Away? (*m* FIS(C)HER) 1914

BRUCE, George
Jim And His Partner Joe (& Harry
LEMORE: F. W. VENTON) 1892

BRYAN, Vincent P. 1883–1937
Down Where The Wurzburger Flows (*m*
Harry VON TILZER; British *w* Fred W.
LEIGH as Riding On Top Of The Car)
1902
In My Merry Oldsmobile (*m* Gus
EDWARDS) 1905
In The Sweet Bye And Bye (*m* VON
TILZER) 1902
Riding On Top Of The Car (& LEIGH:
VON TILZER) 1902
Where Was Moses When The Light
Went Out? (*m* VON TILZER); rev.
version lyrics with Andrew B.
STERLING 1901
See John J. STAMFORD for earlier identical
title.

BRYANT, Edward E.
Felix Kept On Walking (*m* Hubert W.
DAVID) 1923

BUCALOSSI, Procida 1831–1918
On The Rialto 1901
Their Customs Are Very Peculiar (*w*
Harry NICHOLLS) *c*.1885

BUCK, Gene 1885–1957
Daddy Has A Sweetheart And Mother
Is Her Name (*m* Dave STAMPER)
1911
Some Boy (*m* STAMPER) 1911

BUCKLEY, F. Bishop 1833–64
I'd Choose To Be A Daisy If I Could Be
A Flower 1860
Wait For The Wagon *c*.1850

BUDIK, Franz
Jolly Brothers, The (Die Lustige Brüder)
  1872
  Utilized by Albert Whelan° as the first(?)
  signature tune.

BULL, Harry
I Felt So Awfully Shy (& Joe BURLEY)
  1914

BULL, Dr John 1562–1628
God Save The King (?) (or Henry
  CAREY, or anon.) c.1743

BULLOCK, W. J.
Cricketer, The 1869

BUNN, Alfred c.1797–1860
By The Sad Sea Waves (m Julius
  BENEDICT) 1844
  See also Lester THOMAS.
I Dreamt That I Dwelt In Marble
  Halls (m Michael William BALFE)
  1843
Light Of Other Days, The (m BALFE)
  1836
Scenes That Are Brightest (m W. Vincent
  WALLACE) 1845
Then You'll Remember Me (m BALFE)
  1843

BUNTING, Edward 1773–1843
Minstrel Boy, The (Thomas MOORE:
  trad. (Welsh) The Moreen, arr.
  BUNTING) 1807

BURKE, Charles A. 1822?–54?
On The Piers At Night (m Frank
  SADDLER) 1897

BURLEY, Joe
Always Look After Number One (&
  Frank W. CARTER) 1907
Ayesha, My Sweet Egyptian (& Cecil
  JOHNSON: Maurice SCOTT) 1908
Girls, Study Your Cookery Book (m
  SCOTT) 1908
Hot Meat Pies, Saveloys And Trotters (&
  Charles COLLINS) 1913

I Felt So Awfully Shy (& Harry BULL)
  1914
I Got Married To A Widow (& Maurice
  SCOTT) 1908
Look (or See) What Percy's Picked Up In
  The Park (m Harry CASTLING) 1912
Man! Man! You Think You're Cock Of
  The Walk (& CARTER)
We're Not All Lilies Of The Valley (&
  CARTER) 1907

BURNABY, Davy° 1881–1949
Conscientious Objector's Lament, The
  (& Gitz RICE) 1917
DSO and VAD (& RICE) 1917

BURNAND, Sir Francis C. 1836–1917
Buttercup, The (m Arthur L. SULLIVAN)
  1867
He Always Came Home To Tea (m W.
  Meyer LUTZ) 1877
Little Street Arab, The (m LUTZ) 1881

BURNAND, Lily° b. 7 Dec 1865
My Baby May 1899

BURNETT, Ernest M. 1884–1959
My Melancholy Baby (w George A.
  NORTON & Maybelle E. WATSON)
  1912

BURNOT, Walter d. 14 May 1905; m.
Pollie Randall
De Coon Ob 1999 (m George LE
  BRUNN) 1898
Fashionable Fred (m J. Conway BROWN)
  c.1868

BURNS, James F. 1898–1960
Nola (m Felix ARNDT 1915) BURNS's w
  1924

BURNS, Robert 1759–96
Ae Fond Kiss (air, Rory Dall's Port)
  1787
Afton Water (sung to sundry airs,
  including Away In A Manger) 1786
Auld Lang Syne (w&m trad., adap.
  BURNS) 1793

Banks O' Doon, The (air, The
  Caledonian Hunt's Delight) 1785
Comin' Through The Rye 1794
Green Grow The Rashes O! 1784
Highland Lassie O 1786
John Anderson, My Jo 1790
My Heart's In The Highlands (air, Failte
  Na Miosg) 1790
My Love, She's But A Lassie Yet 1790
(O My Luve's Like) A Red, Red Rose
  (air, Low Down He's A Broom)
  1794
O Whistle, And I'll Come To Ye, My Lad
  1793
Scots, Wha Hae' Wi' Wallace Bled (air,
  Hey Tutti Taitie) 1793
Ye Banks And Braes O' Bonnie Doon (m
  attr. Charles MILLER, adap. Lost Is
  My Quiet For Ever) 1788

BURRIS, Roy
Ballin' The Jack (m Chris SMITH &
  James Reese EUROPE) 1913

BURT, Benjamin H. 1875–1950
Pig Got Up And Slowly Walked Away,
  The (m F. V. BOWERS) 1896
When You're All Dressed Up And No
  Place To Go (m Silvio HEIN) 1913

BUTLER, E. G. see FORRESTER, Noel

BUTLER, Ralph 1887–1969
Let's All Go To The Music Hall (& Harry
  TILSLEY: Horatio NICHOLLS) 1934
We All Went Up Up Up The Mountain
  (& Elton BOX & Desmond COX) 1933

BUTLER, Richard see HENRY, RICHARD

BUTTERFIELD, J. A. 1837–91
When You And I Were Young, Maggie
  (w George W. JOHNSON) 1866

BYASS, Gilbert
After Dinner (w Mel B. SPURR) 1895

BYFORD, George* 1852–1932
Broken Down Masher, The (m E.
  JONGHMANS) 1887

BYRON, A. F.
'Bus Conductor, The (m Leopold
  JORDAN) c.1880

BYRON, George, Lord 1788–1824
Maid Of Athens (m Charles GONOUD)
  1873

BYRON, H. J. 1834–84
Mr Gorilla (m F. MUSGRAVE) c.1870

CAESAR, Irving 1895–1996
Swanee (m George GERSHWIN) 1919

CALLAHAN, J. Will 1874–1946
Smiles (m Lee S. ROBERTS) 1918

CAMPBELL, George
I Don't Care What Becomes Of Me (&
  Worton DAVID: Fred MAYO) 1910

CAMPBELL, Grace pseudonym of Benjamin Britten
Jessie's Dream (m John BLOCKLEY)
  1858

CAMPBELL, Jimmy 1903–67
Show Me The Way To Go Home (& Reg
  CONNELLY) 1925
  NB. Campbell & Connelly wrote jointly as
  Irving KING.

CAMPBELL, Thomas 1777–1844
Hybrias The Cretan (transl. CAMPBELL:
  J. W. ELLIOTT) 1855

CANNON, Hughie 1877–1912
Bill Bailey, Won't You Please Come
  Home? 1902

CAPE, Fred 1849–93
Tin Gee-Gee, The (The Lowther
  Arcade) 1891

CAPEL, John Mais 1862–c.1930
Lorraine, Lorraine, Loree (w. Charles
  KINGSLEY) 1897
Love, Could I Only Tell Thee (w. Clifton
  BINGHAM) 1896

CAPURRO, Giovanni 1859–1920
O Sole Mio (m Edoardo DI CAPUA) 1898

CAREY, Henry 1687–1743
God Save The King (?) (or Dr John
    BULL or anon.) c.1743
Sally In Our Alley (air, The Country
    Lass) 1715

CARLETON, Will 1838–85
Betsy And I Are Out (mon.)
Over The Hill To The Poor-House
    (mon.)
Settler's Story, The (mon.)

CARLOS, Frederick° d. 25 Nov. 1904
Around The Christmas Tree 1886
Dragoon Guards, The (& H. SUMMERS)
    1878
Father, What Have You Got For Us?
    1881
He'll Be Back Bye And Bye (arr.
    Edmund FORMAN) 1885
He's Got 'Em On 1879

CARLTON, Harry° d. 8 Dec. 1961
Mademoiselle From Armenteers
    (version with J. A. TUNBRIDGE) 1919
    See also Gitz RICE and CORE SONG-
    LIST.
Oh! The Birds In The Birdcage Walk (&
    Frank W. CARTER)

CARMICHAEL, Mary Grant 1851–1935
Tommy (w Rudyard KIPLING) 1892

CAROLAN, Tom d. May 1935
We Buried Him Yesterday 1889
We Drew His Club Money This Morning
    (arr. Orlando POWELL) 1889

CARPENTER, Alfred
Let's Swap (w Marriott EDGAR) 1910

CARPENTER, J. E. 1813–70
Abraham Lincoln (m P. RATHBONE)
    1863
What Are The Wild Waves Saying? (m
    Stephen Ralph GLOVER) 1850

CARR, Lynn
Swell Upon The Stock Exchange, The
    1876

CARR, Thomas 1789–1849
Star-Spangled Banner, The (Francis
    Scott KEY: John Stafford SMITH, ed.
    CARR; air based on Smith's Anacreon
    In Heaven) c.1814

CARROLL, Harry 1892–1962
By The Beautiful Sea (w Harold R.
    ATTERIDGE) 1914
I'm Always Chasing Rainbows (& Joseph
    MCCARTHY) 1918
I'm Going Down To Tennessee (&
    Arthur FIELDS) 1914
On The Mississippi (Ballard
    MACDONALD: CARROLL, arr.
    FIELDS) 1912
Trail Of The Lonesome Pine, The (w
    MACDONALD) 1913
Yiddisher Turkey Trot (& FIELDS) 1912

CARROLL, Johnnie d. 1916?
I Will Love You To The Last 1899
Let Me Shake The Hand That Shook
    The Hand Of Sullivan! c.1889
When We Were Happy, You And I
    1896

CARROLL, Peter
Miller's Daughter, The (Don't Be Cross)
    (m Karl ZELLER) 1894

CARTER, Frank W. d. 13 Mar. 1955
Always Look After Number One (& Joe
    BURLEY) 1907
Boys Of The Chelsea School (& R. P.
    WESTON) 1902
Good-Bye, Canada! (& Pat RAFFERTY)
    1912
Has Anybody Seen My Tiddler? (& A. J.
    MILLS) 1910
Let's Wait And See The Pictures (& John
    A. Glover KIND) 1910
Love! Love!! Love!!! (& Gilbert WELLS)
    1913
Man! Man! You Think You're Cock Of
    The Walk (& BURLEY) 1909
My Girl Is Irish With Silvery Hair (&
    RAFFERTY) 1909

Oh! The Birds In The Birdcage Walk (& Harry CARLTON)

Right In The Middle Of The Road (& MILLS) 1900

We're Not All Lilies Of The Valley (& BURLEY) 1907

Why Did I Leave My Little Back Room In Bloomsbury? (& MILLS) 1898

With My Little Wigger-Wagger In My Hand (& Fred EARLE & Gilbert WELLS) 1909

Young Man Who Worked At The Milk Shop, The (& MILLS) 1891

You've Got A Long Way To Go (& MILLS) 1898

CARTER, T.

Trying To Get Thin *or* Mr Double Stout (*w* Harry CLIFTON) *c*.1865

CARYLL, Ivan 1861–1921 pseudonym of Felix Tilkins (a.k.a. John Tilkin)

Kiss Me To Sleep (*w* Fred E. WEATHERLY) 1894

Lazily, Drowsily 1893

Look In Mine Eyes My Beautiful Lady (*w* Hugh MORTON) 1911

Look With Thine Eyes Into Mine (*w* WEATHERLY) 1891

Oh Honey, My Honey (*w* George R. SIMS) 1893

CASSIDY, James *see* MERION, Charles M.

CASTLING, Harry 1865–1933 a.k.a. Nat Maceo and S. V. Fordykern

All That Glitters Isn't Gold (*m* Bennett SCOTT) 1906

Are We To Part Like This? (& Chas. COLLINS) 1903

Boers Have Got My Daddy, The (& A. J. MILLS) 1900

Don't Have Any More, Missus Moore (& James WALSH (2)) 1926

Don't Sing A Song About The War 1901

Don't Sing The Chorus (& COLLINS) 1911

Girl In The Clogs And Shawl, The (*m* C. W. MURPHY) 1909

He's A Dear Old Friend (*m* Fred E. VENTON) 1891

I Know Where The Flies Go (& William HARGREAVES) 1920

I'm The Man Who Buried Ta-Ra-Ra-Boom-De-Ay (*w&m* CASTLING, arr. Fred EPLETT) 1893

In A Cheap Excursion Train (& Fred GODFREY) 1908

I Never Cried So Much In All My Life (& Will E. HAINES & Jimmy HARPER) *c*.1936

It's The Poor That Help The Poor (& MILLS) 1904

I've Got Her Wooden Leg 1898

I Wonder If The Girl I'm Thinking Of Is Thinking Of Me (*m* John NEAT) 1906

Just Like The Ivy (& MILLS) 1902

Let's All Go Down The Strand (& MURPHY) 1908

Let's Have Free Trade Amongst The Ladies (*m* John A. Glover KIND) 1911

Look (or See) What Percy's Picked Up In The Park (*w* Joe BURLEY) 1912

No, 'Arry, Don't Ask Me To Marry (& George LE BRUNN) 1893

One Of The Shabby Genteel 1902

Our Laundry (sk.) (& George ARTHURS *m* arr. LE BRUNN) 1904

Our Threepenny Hop 1901

Sheeny Coon, The 1908

She Told Me To Meet Her At The Gate (& COLLINS) 1923

Singer Was Irish, The (& MURPHY) 1904

Strolling Round The Town 1893

That Was A Bloomer (*m* LE BRUNN) 1896

(Though) All Your Friends May Leave You 1903

Treasures Of Home (Relics Of Liza) (arr. John S. BAKER) 1891

Turned Up (& Herbert RULE) 1924

Under The Bed (?)

Up To Date Swell, The (*w* Charles DEANE) 1895

We All Go The Same Way Home (& MURPHY) 1911

What Do You Think Of The Irish Now? (& Albert HALL) 1900

What-Ho, She Bumps! (& MILLS); see Willie STERN: Cuthbert COLLINS 1899

When There Isn't A Girl About (& COLLINS) 1906

CATLIN, E. L.
Ring The Bell Softly, There's Crape On The Door (*w* Dexter SMITH) 1876

CAULFIELD, John sen. *c*.1809–65
Bill Stickers Beware (*m* John CAULFIELD jun.) 1861
On The Sands! (*m* CAULFIELD jun.) 1861
Selina Sly (*m* CAULFIELD jun.) 1861

CAULFIELD, John jun. d. 25 Apr. 1879
Bill Stickers Beware (*w* John CAULFIELD sen.) 1861
Old Union Jack, The (arr. T. WESTROP) 1874
On The Sands! (*w* CAULFIELD) 1861
Selina Sly (*w* CAULFIELD) 1861

CAVE, J. Arnold° 1823–1912
England For The English (*m* DAGONET) 1854
  For 1888 song of the same title see Fred BOWYER: John S. BAKER.
Sigh Of The Slave, The (*w* Barnabus BROUGH) 1853

CAYLEY-ROBINSON, Lilla d. 1928
Glow-Worm, The (*m* Paul LINCKE) 1902

CEIRIOG 1832–87; bardic name of John Ceiriog Hughes
Ar Dywysog Gwlad Y Bryniau (God Bless The Prince Of Wales) (*m* Brinley RICHARDS; Eng. *w* George LINLEY) 1862

CELLIER, Alfred 1844–91
Queen Of My Heart (*w* B. C. STEPHENSON; orig. Old Dreams *w* Sarah DOUDNEY) 1886

CHAMPION, Harry° 1865–1942
I'm Selling Up The 'Appy 'Appy 'Ome (& Harry BODEN) 1893
My Wife's Sister's Cat (*m* Robert GORMAN) 1907
Put A Bit O' Treacle On My Pudden, Mary Ann! (& Fred W. LEIGH) 1922
That Funny Little Bobtail Coat (& Robert GORMAN & Tom LOWEN) 1907
That Gorgonzola Cheese (*w* LEIGH) 1894
While I Was Licking My Stamp (*w* Willie WYE) 1913

CHAPIN, Harold 1886–1915
Innocent And Annabel (sk.)

CHAPLIN, Charles sen.° 1864–1901
Every-Day Life (*w* Harry BODEN) 1891
Girl Was Young And Pretty, The

CHAPMAN, W. E.
Oh! It's A Windy Night Tonight

CHARLES, Frederick *c*.1829–1904?
Turn Off The Gas At The Meter (*w&m* John J. STAMFORD, arr. CHARLES) 1878

CHARLES, Thomas W. 1843–95
Cupid's Almanack
Horse Guards Blue, The 1873
What Is Love?

CHARLES, Wolseley d. 28 Nov. 1962
Old Sam (Sam, Pick Oop Tha' Musket) (*w* Stanley HOLLOWAY) 1930
Runcorn Ferry, The (*w* Marriott EDGAR) 1933
Wine Women And Song (*w* Hugh E. WRIGHT) 1913

CHATTAWAY, Thurland
Red Wing (*m* Kerry MILLS) 1905

CHERRY, Andrew 1762–1812
Bay Of Biscay, The (*m* John DAVY) 1805
Dear (Green) Little Shamrock, The (*m* orig. William JACKSON but rev. J. W. CHERRY? *c*.1870) 1806
Paddy Carey's Fortune (*m* John WHITAKER) *c*.1809

CHERRY, J. W. 1824–89
Dear Little Shamrock, The (*w* Andrew CHERRY: *m* orig. William JACKSON, but rev. J. W. CHERRY? *c*.1870) 1806
I'm A Timid Nervous Man
Tom Richard's Wedding 1870

CHESTER, Frederick°
Algy's Absolutely Full Of Tact 1927

CHESTERFIELD, Harry
All Hands On Deck (*m* William SIM) 1878
See also C. W. MURPHY and Dan LIPTON

CHEVALIER, Albert° 1861–1923; full name: Albert Onésime Britannicos Gwathveoyd Louis Chevalier; brother of Charles INGLE
Alice (*m* Bond ANDREWS) *c*.1899
'Andle To My Name, An *c*.1900
'Appy 'Ampstead (*m* John CROOK) 1893
See Wal PINK: George LE BRUNN for sketch of same name.
Blue Ribbon Jane (*m* Charles INGLE) 1894
Candid Man,The (*m* Edward JONES) 1893
Centenarian, The (*m* Alfred H. WEST) *c*.1900
Cockney Tragedian, The (*m* JONES) 1891
Come Back To Me (*m* Auguste VAN BIENE) 1890
Cosmopolitan Courtship (*m* WEST) *c*.1896
Coster's Courtship, The 1888
Coster's Serenade, The (*m* CROOK) 1890
Dolly's Advice (*m* WEST) 1896
Dotty Poet, The 1891

'E Can't Take The Roize Out Of Oi (*m* WEST) 1896
Everflowing Brook, The 1891
Fallen Star, A (*m* WEST) 1898
Future Mrs 'Awkins, The 1892
Great Man Of Wardle, The (*m* WEST) *c*.1900
He Knew It! (*m* INGLE) 1889
Hemmer (*m* WEST) *c*.1900
Herr Schwollenhedt (*m* WEST) 1895
How Soon We All Forget These Little Things 1897
In The Good Old Days (*m* INGLE) 1891
It Gits Me Talked About (*m* WEST) 1900
I've Got 'Er 'At (*m* INGLE) 1899
Mafekin' Night (*m* WEST) 1900
Mistake!, A 1891
Mounsey (*m* Angelo A. ASHER) 1894
My Country Cousin (*m* WEST) 1894
My Old Dutch (*m* INGLE) 1892
Nasty Way 'E Sez It, The (*m* INGLE) 1892
Oh! 'Ampstead (orig k.a. 'Appy 'Ampstead) 1895
Oh! The Langwidge! (*m* ANDREWS) 1895
Old Bachelor, An (*m* WEST) *c*.1900
Our 'Armonic Club 1887
Our Little Nipper ('E Only Stands About So 'Igh) (*m* INGLE) 1892
Peculiar (*m* INGLE) 1891
Pierrot Coster (*m* ANDREWS) 1895
Race Course Sharper, The (*m* WEST) 1896
Right As Ninepence (*m* Julian EDWARDS) 1910
Rose Of Our Alley, The (*m* Sam TUTE, arr. INGLE) 1892
Sich A Nice Man Too (*m* INGLE) 1892
Suit The Action To The Word (*m* VAN BIENE) 1889
Uncle John (The Lay Of The Hopeful Nephew) (& Brian DALY: ANDREWS) 1894
Veteran, The (*m* WEST) *c*.1900
Village Constable, The (*m* WEST) *c*.1900
Villains At The Vic (*m* INGLE) 1893

Waxwork Show, The (*m* JONES) 1891
We Did 'Ave A Time (*m* INGLE) 1896
Who'll Buy? (*m* CROOK) 1893
Workhouse Man, The (*m* WEST) *c*.1900
Wot Cher! (*m* INGLE) 1891
Wot's The Good Of Hanythink? Why,
    Nuffink! (*m* INGLE) 1894
Wot Ver Do 'Ee Luv Oi? (*m* WEST)
    c.1900
Yankee In London, The (*m* WEST)
    c.1900
You Are A Tasty Lot (*w* WEST) 1897
You Can't 'Elp Likin' 'Im (*m* INGLE)
    1892
Yours Etc (*m* CROOK) 1892

CHIRGWIN, G. H.° 1854–1922
Comparisons Are Melodious (Harry
    HUNTER: CHIRGWIN, arr. Warwick
    WILLIAMS) 1888
My Fiddle Is My Sweetheart (*w*
    HUNTER) 1895
My Fiddle Was My Sweetheart (*w*
    Charles OSBORNE) 1896

CHRISTY, Edwin P.° 1815–62
Keemo Kimo (*m* trad.) 1854
    See J. ALLEN for earlier version.

CLARE, Sidney 1892–1972
Miss Annabelle Lee (& Lew POLLACK &
    Harry RICHMAN) 1927
On The Good Ship Lollipop (*m* Richard
    A. WHITING) 1934

CLARIBEL 1830–69 pseudonym of
Charlotte Alington Pye (Mrs Charles
Cary Barnard)
All Along The Valley (*w* Alfred
    TENNYSON) *c*.1865
Blue Alsatian Mountains, The (*m*
    Stephen ADAMS) *c*.1880
Come Back To Erin 1866
Five O'Clock In The Morning *c*.1860
Golden Days (*w* Mrs G. R. GIFFORD)
    1865
I Cannot Sing The Old Songs 1865
Only A Year To Go/Ago? (*w* G. J.

WHYTE-MELVILLE) 1865
Robin Redbreast (*w* W. ALLINGHAM)
    1912
Strangers Yet (*w* Lord HOUGHTON)
    1867
Take Back The Heart (*w* GIFFORD) 1865
When I Was Young And Fair (*w*
    GIFFORD) *c*.1865

CLARK, H. Donald
Choir Boy, The 1908
Orthodox Curate, The 1908

CLARK, Henri° 1840–1905
I Don't Think You're In It Old Man (*m* P.
    SCHUTER)

CLARKE, Billy
Nellie Dean (*m* Harry ARMSTRONG)
    1916

CLARKE, Cuthbert 1869–1953; also
wrote as Elsie Olsen
Anchorsmith (*w* P. J. O'REILLY) 1911
Furniture Remover, The (*w* Clifford
    GREY) 1922
Green Eye Of The Little Yellow God,
    The (*w* J. Milton HAYES) 1911
Shooting Of Dan McGrew, The (*w*
    Robert SERVICE) 1917
There Always Will Be Fairies (*w* F. V. ST
    CLAIR) 1898
Voice Of The Storm, The (*w* T. WALLIS)
    1909
When Our Good King George Is
    Crowned (*w* R. C. THARP) 1911

CLARKE, Emilie A.°
Sincerity—My Friend 1903

CLARKE, Ernèe° *c*.1836–98; sometimes
spelled Ernie Clarke
Chickaleary Cove, The (*m* W. BAIN(E))
    c.1870
Tommy Dodd (& Edmund WEBB) 1868

CLARKE, Grant 1891–1931
Everything Is Peaches Down In Georgia
    (*m* Milton AGER & George W.
    MEYER) 1918

Goodbye, Virginia (m Jean SCHWARTZ) 1915

He'd Have To Get Under (Get Out And Get Under) (& Edgar LESLIE: Maurice ABRAHAMS) 1913

I Love The Ladies (m SCHWARTZ) 1914

Ragtime Cowboy Joe (m Maurice ABRAHAMS & Lewis F. MUIR) 1912

Second-Hand Rose (m James HANLEY) 1921

CLAY, Frederic 1838–89

I'll Sing Thee Songs Of Araby (w W. G. WILLS) 1877
There were some forty other settings.

Nobody Knows As I Know (w J. & H. PAULTON) 1875

Sands Of Dee, The (w Charles KINGSLEY) 1874
See also Michael BALFE.

CLAY, Henry see WORK, Henry Clay

CLAY, T. L. 1850–92

Brass (m Alfred LEE) 1879

Heavy Swell Of The Sea, The (Big) (m LEE) c.1870

Johnny Get Your Gun (w&m Frederick BELASCO; Eng. w CLAY) 1886

Lounging In The Aq (m LEE) 1874

Toothpick And Crutch (m LEE) 1879

CLEATHER, Brenda

Santa Lucia (m Teodoro COTTRAU) 1850

CLEMENT, Frank

I Want To Be A Military Man (m Leslie STUART) 1899

CLEMENT, Harry

Now It's All Over For Ever (m Harry BALL, arr. F. W. HUMPHRIES) 1881

CLEMENTS, J.

I'd Like It All Over Again (w Harry WINDLEY) 1881

CLEVE, Joseph H.

Heroes Of The Transvaal War, The (w F. V. ST CLAIR) 1900

King Of The Boys (w C. ST LEONARDS & James MANHILL) 1893

CLEVELAND, D.

Where My Caravan Has Rested (& E. TESCHEMACHER: Hermann LÖHR) 1909

CLIFF, Laddie° 1891–1937

Coal-Black Mammy (& Ivy ST HELIER) 1921

CLIFFE, Fred 1885–1957

Every Little Movement Has A Meaning Of Its Own (m J. Charles MOORE) 1910
Sung by Marie Lloyd. For Lina Abarbanell's song with same title see Otto HARBACH: Karl HOSCHNA.

CLIFFORD, Nat°

Didn't We Fight For England—In The Future? 1899

Different Kinds Of Girls (m Fred EPLETT) 1899

Engine Driver's Story, The 1898

Fancy Meeting You! 1897

I'm Very Unkind To My Wife

I Want My Little Gollywog! (& Medley BARRETT) 1906

My Wife's First Husband 1898

Oh! Jack, You Are A Handy Man 1901

Silver Spoon In His Mouth, A 1898

CLIFTON, Harry° 1824–72

Adventures Of Robinson Crusoe, The (arr. Martin HOBSON)

Agreeable Young Man, The (arr. HOBSON) 1867

Always Do As I Do

As Long As The World Goes Round

As Welcome As The Flowers In May

Barclay's Beer 1866

Bear It Like A Man (arr. HOBSON) c.1865

Bit Of My Mind, A

Calico Printer's Clerk, The

Charity Crow

Commercial Man, The *or* Sold Again
    1865
Could I Live My Time Over Again ???
Cupid In The Kitchen
Darby Maguire
Dark Girl Dress'd In Blue, The 1862
Don't Be After Ten
Dutchman's Courtship, The *c*.1865
Faithless Maria *or* The Land Of Green
    Ginger
Family Man, The *c*.1870
Folly And Fashion
Good Tempered Man, The
Happy Policeman, The (adap. & arr.
    HOBSON)
Hardware Line, The *c*.1865
Have You Seen The Ghost?
He Must Have A Thousand A Year
I'll Go And Enlist For A Sailor
I'm Only Bridesmaid After All
Isabella, The Barber's Daughter (She'd A
    Gingham Umbrella) 1864
Island Of Green, The
Jemima Brown *or* The Queen Of The
    Sewing Machine 1865
Jolly Old Country Squire, A
Jones's Musical Party (arr. HOBSON)
    1864
Lannigan's Ball
Look Always On The Sunny Side
    c.1865
Love And Pride
Mail Train Driver, The
Mary Ann *or* The Roving Gardener
    1865
Merry Old Uncle Joe
Michaelmas Day 1866
Modern Times *or* Past And Present
Motto For Every Man, A (*m* Charles
    COOTE jun., arr. HOBSON) *c*.1865
My Mother In Law 1860?
My Old Wife And I
My Rattling Mare And I
On Board Of The Kangaroo
Paddle Your Own Canoe (arr. HOBSON)
    1866

Polly Perkins Of Paddington Green (air,
    Nightingales Sing) *c*.1863
Poor Old Mike 1863
Pull Back, The
Pulling Hard Against The Stream 1867
Purely A Matter Of Taste
Put The Brake On When You're Going
    Down The Hill (*m* Vincent SMITH)
    1869
Railway Bell(e) 1866
Rocky Road To Dublin
Shabby Genteel (*w* Henry S. LEIGH)
    1868
Shelling Green Peas (arr. HOBSON)
    1866
Ten Minutes Too Late
There's A Smile Waiting For Me At
    Home (*w&m* CLIFTON, arr. HOBSON)
    1860
Trifles Light As Air
Trying To Get Thin *or* Mr Double Stout
    (*m* CARTER) *c*.1865
Try To Be Happy And Gay, My Boys
Up A Tree
Up With The Lark In The Morning
Wait For The Turn Of The Tide (*m*
    COOTE) 1868
Water Cresses *or* Watercress Girl, The
    1863
Waterford Boys
Weepin' Willer, The *or* The Miller's
    Daughter 1865
Where There's A Will There's A Way
Work, Boys, Work (& J. WILLIAMS) 1867
Young Man On The Railway, The (*m*
    W. H. BRINKWORTH) 1865

CLOSS, William F.
Not What 'Ria Wanted (& Harry PLEON)
    1898

CLUTSAM, G. H. 1866–1951
Flower, The (Adrian ROSS: Franz
    SCHUBERT, arr. CLUTSAM) 1922
I Know Of Two Bright Eyes (Myrra)
    1901
Ma Curly Headed Babby 1897

COATES, Eric 1886–1957
Green Hills O' Somerset (*w* Fred E.
  WEATHERLY) 1909
Stonecracker John (*w* WEATHERLY)
  1909

COBB, George Leo 1886–1942
Alabama Jubilee (*w* Jack YELLEN) 1915
Are You From Dixie? ('Cos I'm From
  Dixie Too) (*w* YELLEN) 1913
Russian Rag 1918

COBB, Gerard F.
Gunga Din (*w* Rudyard KIPLING) 1892

COBB, Will D. 1876–1930
Could You Be True To Eyes Of Blue? (*m*
  Gus EDWARDS) 1901
Goodbye, Dolly Gray (*m* Paul BARNES)
  1898
Goodbye, Little Girl, Goodbye (*m*
  EDWARDS) 1904
I Can't Tell Why I Love You But I Do (*m*
  EDWARDS) 1900
I Just Can't Make My Eyes Behave (&
  Harry B. SMITH: EDWARDS) 1906
Johnny Jones's Sister Sue (*m* EDWARDS)
  1902
Somebody's Sweetheart I Want To Be (*m*
  EDWARDS) 1905
Waltz Me Around Again, Willie (*m* Ren
  SHIELDS) 1906
When Tommy Atkins Marries Dolly Gray
  (*m* EDWARDS) 1906
Yip-I-Addy-I-Ay (*m* John H. FLYNN;
  Eng. *w* George GROSSMITH jun.)
  London 1908

COBORN, Charles° 1852–1945
'E Was A Perfect Gentleman 1897
He's All Right When You Know Him
  1887
I Shan't Try It On Any More 1886
Life-Boat Crew, The 1894
That's Why The British Loved The King
  (& Medley BARRETT) 1910
Two Lovely Black Eyes (arr. Edmund
  FORMAN) 1886

COBURN, Richard 1886–1952; pseudo-
nym of Frank De Long
Whispering (& Vincent ROSE: John
  SCHONBERGER) 1920

COHAN, George M.° 1878–1942; son of
Jerry J. COHAN
Give My Regards To Broadway 1904
I Guess I'll Have To Telegraph 1898
I Was Born In Virginia (Ethel Levey's
  Virginia Song) 1906
Mary's A Grand Old Name 1905
Nelly Kelly, I Love You 1922
Over There 1917
So Long Mary 1906
Why Did Nellie Leave Her Home?
  (Cohan's first *pub*. song; *w* rewritten
  Walter H. FORD) 1894
Yankee Doodle Boy, The 1904
You're A Grand Old Flag 1906

COHAN, Jerry J. 1848–1917; father of
George M. COHAN
Girly-Girly (*w* Richard MORTON)
  c.1890

COHN, Irving 1898–1961
Yes, We Have No Bananas (*w* Frank
  SILVER) 1923

COLE, Herbert
All Right, Mary-Ann (arr. Fred EPLETT)
  1884
Favorite, The [*sic*]
Friends Of My Youthful Days (*m* Harry
  BALL) 1886
I Can't Get At It (*m* Harry RANDALL)
  c.1886
You Have My Answer Now 1899

COLE, Robert A. (Bob) 1863–1911
Cupid's Ramble (& James Weldon
  JOHNSON: J. Rosamund JOHNSON)
  1903
I'll Keep A Warm Spot In My Heart For
  You (as for previous entry) 1906
Under The Bamboo Tree (as for previous
  entry) 1902

COLERIDGE-TAYLOR, S. 1875–1912
Eleanore (*w* Eric MACKAY) 1899
Onaway! Awake, Beloved! (*w* Henry W. LONGFELLOW) 1898

COLLINS, Charles 1874–1923
All Round The Squares (*w* John READ)
Any Old Iron? (& E. A. SHEPPARD: Fred TERRY) 1911
Are We To Part Like This? (& Harry CASTLING) 1903
Boiled Beef And Carrots (& Fred MURRAY) 1909
Cover It Over Quick, Jemima (& SHEPPARD) 1911
Daddy, I'm Going To Bye-Bye
Don't Dilly Dally (& Fred W. LEIGH) 1919
Don't Sing The Chorus (& CASTLING) 1911
Ev'rybody Knows Me In My Old Brown Hat (& LEIGH) 1920
Father's Got The Sack From The Waterworks (& Terry SULLIVAN) 1915
Hot Meat Pies, Saveloys And Trotters (& Joe BURLEY) 1913
I Ask No Vow
I'm Coming In With You 1905
It's No Use You Calling 'Hannah!' (& Fred J. BARNES: COLLINS) 1907
I've Got My Eye On You (& LEIGH) 1913
I Wouldn't Leave My Little Wooden Hut For You (& Tom MELLOR) 1896
Last Of The Dandies (*w* BARNES) 1901
See also HARRINGTON: George LE BRUNN.
Let Go Eliza (& LEIGH) 1902
Mr N Peck (& Charles OSBORNE) 1908
Now I Have To Call Him Father (& Fred GODFREY) 1908
Now You've Got Yer Khaki On (& LEIGH) 1915
Oh! Kate Carney 1896

Play That Melody Again (*w* BARNES) 1900
Shall I Be An Angel, Daddy? (*w* BARNES) 1897
She Told Me To Meet Her At The Gate (& CASTLING) 1923
Sweet Little Rose Of Persia (& BARNES: COLLINS) 1900
There's Danger On The Line (& LEIGH & MURRAY) *c*.1911
See also George P. NORMAN.
Three Makes Jolly Fine Company (E. W. ROGERS & H. C. HUDSON: & Norton ATKINS) 1903
We All Came In The World With Nothing (& W. H. WALLIS) 1907
When There Isn't A Girl About (& CASTLING) 1906
Why Am I Always The Bridesmaid? (& LEIGH) 1917
Wouldn't You Like To Know? 1898
You Be My Gee Gee, Daddy 1902
You Can't Punch My Ticket Again 1897

COLLINS, Cuthbert
What-Ho, She Bumps! (*w* Willie STERN) 1899
See another song with the same title by Harry CASTLING: A. J. MILLS.

COLLISSON, W. Houston 1865–1920
Are Ye Right There, Michael? (*w* Percy FRENCH) 1902
Eileen Oge (*w* FRENCH) 1908

COLOMB, Captain George T. 1808–74
Up The Alma's Height 1854

COLUM, Padraic 1881–1972
She Moved Through The Fair (*m* trad., arr. Herbert HUGHES) 1913

CONLEY, Steve
Sarah (Sitting In The Shoe Shine Shop) (& J. G. GILBERT & Joe MACEY & Jimmy McHUGH) 1919

CONLEY, Tom 1872–1903
He Was One Of The Old Brigade (*m* Pat
 RAFFERTY) 1898
Rowdy-Dowdy Boys, The (& Felix
 MCGLENNON: MCGLENNON) 1891

CONNELLY, Michael d. 1911
Run Up The Flag (*w* Clement W.
 SCOTT) 1884

CONNELLY, Reg 1898–1963
Show Me The Way To Go Home (&
 Jimmy CAMPBELL) 1925
 Note: Campbell and Connelly wrote jointly
 as Irving King.

CONNOR, T. W. d. 24 Jan. 1936; see also
Billy BENNETT in CORE SONG-LIST
All Over The Shop 1895
And His Day's Work Was Done 1903
At My Time Of Life *c*.1888
Beautiful Home 'On Hire' 1901
Fire Was Burning Hot, The
Good Old Annual, The
His Own Mother Wouldn't Know Him
 Now (arr. John S. BAKER) 1893
I'm A Merry Little Devil
I Must Have A Day Off For That 1900
Little Bit Of Cucumber, A 1915
Lively
Man Was A Stranger To Me, The 1919
My Mother Doesn't Know I'm On The
 Stage 1929
Old Dicky Bird (arr. Fred EPLETT) 1901
She Was One Of The Early Birds 1895
We Used To Gather At The Old Dun
 Cow 1918
Why Do The Men Run After Me? 1912

CONNOR, Tommie 1904–93
Biggest Aspidistra In The World, The (&
 Will E. HAINES & Jimmy HARPER)
 1938

CONRAD, Con 1891–1938
Ma, He's Making Eyes At Me 1921
Margie (Benny DAVIS: & J. Russel
 ROBINSON) 1919

Sarah! Come Over Here! (*w* Eddie
 NELSON) 1918

CONROY, Peter
Agricultural Irish Girl, The (*w&m* J. F.
 MITCHELL, arr. CONROY) 1885
Good Young Man, The (Albert HALL:
 Felix MCGLENNON, arr. CONROY)
 1896
His Lordship Winked At The Counsel (*w*
 George DANCE) 1887

COOK, Eliza 1818–89
Eliza, The Slave Mother (*m* Henry
 RUSSELL) 1855
Eva's Farewell (*m* RUSSELL) 1855
Flag Of The Free (*m* RUSSELL) 1855
Little Topsy (*m* RUSSELL) 1855
Many Happy Returns Of The Day (*m*
 John BLOCKLEY) 1850
Old Arm Chair, The (*m* RUSSELL) 1836

COOK, Will Marion 1869–1944
I'm A Jonah Man 1903
I Want To Be A Real Lady 1903
On Emancipation Day 1903

COOKE, John jun. *c*.1860–1900
Angels Are Hovering Round (*w* J. S.
 EVALO) 1889
Below! Below!! Below!!! (*w* George
 HORNCASTLE) 1888
Funny Things They Do Upon The Sly
 (& G. W. HUNTER: HUNTER) 1885
I Want To Meet A Good Young Man
 1885
Married Life (*m* HUNTER) 1885
Millie's Cigar Divan 1884
So It Was! (*w* HORNCASTLE) 1887
What A Blessing 1885
When The Old Man Came Home Sober

COOKE, Leonard d. 25 May 1919
Sunshine Of Your Smile (*m* Lilian RAY)
 1913

COOKE, Thomas Simpson 1782–1848
Love And War *c*.1829
Love's Ritornella *or* Gentle Zitella (*w&m*
 J. R. PLANCHÉ, arr. COOKE) 1829

COOLEY, ?
Bully Song, The (*w&m* COOLEY from trad., arr. Charles E. TREVATHAN) 1895
Frog Song, The (*w&m* COOLEY from trad., arr. TREVATHAN) 1896

COOPER, GEORGE
Beautiful Isle Of The Sea (*m* John Rogers THOMAS) 1865

COOPER, George 1838–1927
Old Chimney Corner Where Grandfather Smiled, The (*m* W. H. RIEGER) 1880
Sweet Genevieve (You're The Flower Of My Heart) (*m* Henry TUCKER) 1869
Strolling On The Brooklyn Bridge (& Joseph P. SKELLY) 1883
You May Pet Me As Much As You Please (*m* H. Millard) 1880

COOPER, Margaret° 1877–1922; m. Arthur HUMBLE-CROFTS
Agatha Green (*w* A. HUMBLE-CROFTS) 1911

COOTE, Bert° 1868–1938; son of Robert COOTE
Lamb On Wall Street, A (sk.) 1912

COOTE, Charles jun. 1831–1916; managing director of Hopwood & Crew
I Won Her Heart At Billiards (*w* George P. NORMAN) 1876
Motto For Every Man, A (*w* Harry CLIFTON)
Never Desert A Friend (*w* Harry HUNTER) 1876
Wait For The Turn Of The Tide (*w* CLIFTON) 1868

COOTE, Robert° 1834–88 father of Bert COOTE
Bandy Legg'd Borachio *or* The Roley Poley Eye 1873
Blighted Barber, Ye *or* Fe, Fi, Fo, Fum (*w* Frank W. GREEN) 1873

Covent Garden In The Morning (*w* J. L. GRAYDON) 1873
Floating With The Tide (*w* GREEN) 1874
Master (Tommy) Wattle And The Big Blue Bottle 1870

COPELAND, Harry d. 1865
Slap Bang, Here We Are Again! (The School Of Jolly Dogs) *c.*1865

COPPOCK, Beatrice Maude
Wax Lights, Sir? (*w* Harriet COPPOCK) 1895

COPPOCK, Harriet
Wax Lights, Sir? (*m* Beatrice Maude COPPOCK) 1895

CORELLI, Marie 1855–1924
Prince Ivan's Song (*m* Mary ALLITSEN)

CORNELL, Charles
Some O' Yer Do Git Abaht (*m* Gus EPLETT) 1894
Wait Till The Work Comes Round (& T. LEYBOURNE: Gus ELEN) 1906

CORNEY, Arthur°
Ask Yourself The Question (arr. Angelo ASHER) 1890
For A Week Or Two 1887
I Took It (arr. George ISON) 1888
Near It (arr. Edmund FORMAN) 1887
Something Went Wrong With The Works (*w* P. BROWNE) 1887
Up Comes Jones 1887
Very Good Guess, A 1890

CORNWALL, Barry 1787–1874 pseudonym of Bryan Waller Procter, father of Adelaide A. PROCTER
Dream, Baby, Dream (*m* Virginia GABRIEL) 1862

CORVAN, Ned° 1831–65
Cat-Gut Jim
Cullercoats Fish-Lass, The (air, Lilla's A Lady)
Fire Upon The Knee, The
£4.10, *or* The Sailor's Strike

Oot O' Wark *or* The Year '62 1862
Soop Kitchen, The
Stage Struck Keelman, The
Toon Improvement Bill, The (air, Na
    Good Luck About The House) *c*.1850

CORY, Adela Florence 1865–1904
a.k.a. Laurence HOPE

CORY, W. J. d. 1910
Eton Boating Song (A. DRUMMOND,
    transc. T. L. MITCHELL-INNES, arr.
    Evelyn WOODHOUSE) 1878

COSTA, Sir Michael 1806–84
Dream, The (*w* William
    BARTHOLOMEW) 1858
Eloisa 1875

COSTA, P. Mario
Since I Came To London Town (*m*
    Richard MORTON) 1900

COSTELLO, Tom° 1863–1943
All Through A Little Piece Of Bacon (&
    F. V. ST CLAIR: George LE BRUNN)
    c.1895
Blow Winds Gently 1898
Fed Up (& Fred LEIGH) 1918
I'm Giving Up My Job To The Kaiser (&
    LEIGH) 1915
I've Come Back To Town Once Again (&
    LEIGH) 1918
Madame Duvan (Joseph TABRAR:
    COSTELLO, arr. Alfred LAMONT) 1891
Mary Devine (& LEIGH) 1915
Nellie Brown (& LEIGH) 1919
When You Hear Your Country Calling (&
    LEIGH) 1913

COTES, C. G. 1874–1905
Auctioneer, The (*m* George ROBEY)
    1903
Chase Me Charlie (*m* Bennett SCOTT)
    1899
Come Down And Open The Door
    (SCOTT, rev. of 1884 orig. A.
    SUTHERD: Slade MURRAY, arr.
    Edmund FORMAN) 1898

Fancy That! (*m* ROBEY) 1900
Good-bye, Tilly (*m* SCOTT) 1899
I Couldn't Exert Myself (*m* ROBEY) 1902
I'm Going To Get Married Today—
    Hooray! (*m* SCOTT) 1899
In The Park (*m* Tom GRAHAM) 1896
Lot 99 (*m* GRAHAM) 1898
Oh! How Rude! (*m* GRAHAM) 1899
Piano Tuner, The
Prehistoric Man (*m* Richard TEMPLE
    jun.) 1902
That'll Never Do For Me (*m* SCOTT)
    1899
Two Little Brandies And Soda (*m*
    SCOTT) 1899
What Did She Know About Railways? (*m*
    SCOTT) 1897
You Know The Man I Mean 1899

COTTRAU, Teodoro 1827–79
Santa Lucia (Eng. *w* Brenda CLEATHER)
    1850

COURTNEY, Clement
Fair Lady Mine (*w* Will HYDE &
    Percival LANGLEY) 1899

COVE, W. H.
Charming Young Widow I Met In The
    Train, The *c*.1878

COVERDALE, Charlie
Back Answers 1923

COWAN, Marie d. 1919
Waltzing Matilda (Andrew B. PATERSON:
    James BARR, arr. COWAN) 1895
See Andrew B. PATERSON for sources.

COWAN, Samuel K.
My Old Clay Pipe (*m* Corney GRAIN)
    c.1880

COWELL, Sam° 1820–64
Alonzo The Brave (*m* arr. J. HARROWAY)
    c.1850
See also E. L. BLANCHARD.
Artful Dodger (& Charles SLOMAN:
    anon.)

Bacon And Greens 1858
Ratcatcher's Daughter, The (*w* Revd
  Edward BRADLEY: *m* perhaps anon.)
  1852
  See Core SONG-LIST.

COWEN, Sir Frederich M. 1852–1935
Better Land, The (*w* Felicia Dorothea
  HEMANS) *c*.1880
Children's Home, The (*w* Fred E.
  WEATHERLY) 1881
Promise Of Life, The (*w* G. Clifton
  BINGHAM) 1893
Swallows (*w* BINGHAM) 1895
Thy Remembrance (*w* Henry W.
  LONGFELLOW) 1892

Cox, Desmond 1903–66; see Jack
SPADE
In The Quartermaster's Store (adap.
  with Elton BOX & Bert REED)
  1940
We All Went Up Up Up The Mountain
  (& Box & Ralph BUTLER) 1933

Cox, Jimmie 1882–1925
Nobody Knows You When You're Down
  And Out 1923

COYNE, Fred° (1) 1846–86
New Jerusalem, The *or* Cruel Jane
  Jemima
Tuner's Oppor-Tuner-ty, The (& Harry
  ADAMS: COYNE) 1879
Under The British Flag (*w* J. VERNON)
  1877

CRAMPTON, Ernest
William, James & 'Enry 1908

CRAWFORD, Josephine V. *see* ROWE,
Josephine V.

CRAWFORD, Mrs Julia *c*.1798–1858
Daughters Of Salem (*m* Charles
  SLOMAN) 1844
Jewish Captives In Babylon, The 1844
Kathleen Mavourneen (*m* F. Nicholls
  CROUCH) 1836
Rose Of Raby (*m* SLOMAN) 1844

CREAMER, Henry° 1879–1930
After You've Gone (*m* Turner LAYTON)
  1918
That's A-Plenty (*m* Bert WILLIAMS) 1909
Way Down Yonder In New Orleans (*m*
  Layton) 1922

CRISPEN, Minnie G.
Tale Of Ackmed Kurd, The (*w* Cedric
  FORBES) 1925

CROAL, George a.k.a. Carlo Zotti
Emigrant's Dream, The 1862
God Bless Our Gracious Queen 1872
Little Sprite, The 1909
March Away (arr. G. A. HODSON) *c*.1834
My Willie 1860
Wedded Flags, The
Zitella 1861

CROFTS, Herbert K.
King's Own, The (*m* Theodore
  BONHEUR) *c*.1895

CROOK, John *c*.1847–1922
'Appy 'Ampstead (*w* Albert CHEVALIER)
  1893
  See Wal PINK: George LE BRUNN for
  sketch of same name.
Coster's Serenade, The (*w* Chevalier)
  1890
It's A Little Bit Of Sugar For The Bird
  (*w* F. BOWYER & W. E. SPRANGE)
  1895
Jerusalem's Dead, The (*w* Brian DALY)
  1895
Oh! 'Ampstead (orig. k.a. 'Appy
  'Ampstead) 1895
Tain't Natural (*w* H. B. FARNIE) 1887
When We Were Young (*m* J. J. DALLAS)
  1888
Who'll Buy? (*w* CHEVALIER) 1893
Yours Etc (*w* CHEVALIER) 1892

CROUCH, F. Nicholls° 1808–96
Kathleen Mavourneen (*w* Julia
  CRAWFORD) 1836
Zephyrs Of Love 1840

CRUMIT, Frank[*] 1889–1943
Abdul Abulbul Amir (from 1877 orig.
Percy FRENCH) 1927

CUHELYN 1829–69; pseudonym of
Thomas Gwallter Price
Arabella (Myfanwy) (*m* Joseph PARRY;
Welsh *w* MYNYDDOG) 1880

CUNLIFFE, Whit[*] 1876–1966
Wee Deoch-An-Doris, (Just) A (&
Gerald GRAFTON & Harry LAUDER)
1910

CUNNINGHAM, Allan 1783–1842
Wet Sheet And A Flowing Sea, A (poem
set by at least thirty composers, the
earliest being Elizabeth MASSON in
1844)

CUNNINGHAM, Minnie[*] 1853–1924
Bridget And Mike (*w* Richard MORTON)
1899
Did You Ever See A Feather In A Tom-
Cat's Tail? (*w* Harry LINN) *c*.1890

CUNNINGHAM, Philip 1865–1928
Check To The Queen (sk.) (& Rutland
BARRINGTON) 1912

CURZON, Amy
Sixty Years! (& George F. HOWLEY:
C. E. HOWELLS) 1897

CURZON, T.
Devonshire Cream And Cider (*m*
Wilfred SANDERSON) 1919

CZIBULKA, Alphons 1842–94
Hearts And Flowers (from *Winter
Stories*, 1891; Mary D. BRINE: adap.
Theodore MOSES-TOBANI) 1899

DACRE, Harry[*] 1860–1922; a.k.a. Frank
Dean, publisher; real name Henry
Decker
As Your Hair Grows Whiter 1897
Chicago 1890
Daisy Bell 1892
Dorothy Dean 1894
Elsie From Chelsea 1896

Empire And The Tivoli, The 1899
Fare You Well, Daisy Bell 1894
Ghost Of Benjamin Binns, The 1884
He's A Good Old Has-Been 1890
I'll Be Your Sweetheart 1899
Jolly Little Polly On Her Gee-gee-gee
1895
Katie Connor 1891
Lads In Navy Blue, The 1899
London City 1899
Never More (arr. George LE BRUNN)
c.1895
Nightmare, The 1889
Oh, Flo! (Why Do You Go?) 1901
Playmates 1890
She Is A Sensible Girl 1899
Shipmates In Safety, Shipmates In
Danger 1892
Sweet Little Rosey-Posey 1895
Very Nearly 1884
While London's Fast Asleep 1896
You See I'm But A Simple Country Maid
1888

DACRE, Louie
Back From The War 1900

DAGONET pseudonym of J. A.
HARDWICK, also of George R. SIMS
England For The English (J. A. CAVE:
HARDWICK) 1854
For 1888 song of same title see Fred
BOWYER: John S. BAKER.

DALLAS, J. J.[*] 1847–1915
When We Were Young (*m* John CROOK)
1888

D'ALMAINE, Ernest
Midshipman, The (*w* Sidney
MIDDLETON) 1893

DALTON, Will
Just Because She's Got An 'Andle To Her
Name (*w* Worton DAVID) 1901

DALY, Brian 1863–1923
Jerusalem's Dead, The (*m* John CROOK)
1895

Signalman On The Line, The (*m* Bond ANDREWS) 1893

Toymaker's Tragedy, The (*m* Charles INGLE) 1896

Uncle John (The Lay Of The Hopeful Nephew) (& Albert CHEVALIER: ANDREWS) 1894

Yer Never Aks'd 'Im For It (*m* INGLE) 1893

DAMERELL, Stanley J.° d. 12 Dec. 1951; pseudonym of Jack Stevens

Riley's Cowshed (& Robert HARGREAVES) 1924

Sing! Sing! Sing! (& ? (John)? RUTLAND) 1910

DAMROSCH, Walter 1862–1950

Hanging Of Danny Deever, The (*w* Rudyard KIPLING) 1897

Looking Glass, The (*w* KIPLING) 1916

DANCE, Sir George 1865–1932; note: did *not* write Come Where The Booze Is Cheaper; see also ROGERS, E. W.: DURANDEAU, A. E.

Angels Without Wings (arr. George LE BRUNN) 1887

English As She Is Spoke (arr. Jean PAULUS) 1880

His Lordship Winked At The Counsel (*m* Peter CONROY) 1887

I Want To Be A Lidy (*m* A. Ward MALBERT) 1901

Martha Spanks The Grand Piano (*m* Howard TALBOT) 1901

May Queen Victoria Reign 1887

Twiddley Bits (& J. ADAMS: Ernie WOODVILLE) 1901

DANIEL, George 1789–1864

Widow Glib & Sir Steeple (air, A Frog He Would A-Wooing Go) *c*.1855

DANIELS, Joe

Dinah Duck (*w* Harry HUNTER)

DANKS, H. P. 1834–1903

Silver Threads Among The Gold (*w* E. E. REXFORD) 1873

DANVERS, Johnny° 1861–1939

Lily Of My Life, The 1901

Where The Flow'rets Grow (*m* Tom RICHARDS 1886

DARE, Coleti

Always Wears An Orchid Next Me 'Eart (*w* Herbert SHELLEY) 1897

DAREWSKI, Herman E. jun.

1883–1947; sometimes spelled Hermann; m. Ruby MILLER°

Au Revoir, My Little Hyacinth (*w* A. E. Sidney DAVIES) 1906

Dear Old Saturday Night (& Albert DE COURVILLE & Ernest RANDELL) 1915

Hello! Susie Green (*w* Lester BARRETT) 1911

If You Could Care For Me (*w* Arthur WIMPERIS) 1918

I'm Looking For Mr Wright (R. P. WESTON: & C. W. MURPHY) 1909

In Cherry Blossom Time In Japan (Leslie STILES: & Gitz RICE) 1917

In The Twi-Twi-Twilight (*w* Charles WILMOTT) 1907

I Used To Sigh For The Silvery Moon (*w* BARRETT) 1909

Make Me The King Of Your Heart (*w* Huntley TREVOR) 1914

Mamie May (*w* BARRETT) 1911

Mary From Tipperary (*w* F. W. MARK) 1908

Mother's Sitting Knitting Little Mittens For The Navy (*w* WESTON) 1915

My Brown-Eyed Loo (*w* BARRETT) 1914

Now Are We All Here? Yes! (*w* TREVOR) 1914

Oh, The Daylight Bill (*w* Edgar BATEMAN & T. W. DOWN) 1908

Sister Susie's Marrying Tommy Atkins (*w* WESTON) 1915

Sister Susie's Sewing Shirts For Soldiers (*w* WESTON) 1913

Somebody's Somebody (*w* Adrian ROSS) 1917

Sue, Sue, Sue (*w* BARRETT) 1908

Where Are The Lads Of The Village Tonight? (*w* WESTON) 1914

Which Switch Is The Switch, Miss, For Ipswich? (& Worton DAVID & J. BARNETT) 1915

You Are A Little White Girl (*w* Hannen SWAFFER) 1904

DARNLEY, J. Herbert 1872–1947; pseudonym of Herbert McCarthy

As I Love You 1901

Beefeater, The (The Tower Of London) 1898

Blowed If Father Ain't Commenced To Work 1897

British Boys

Buying A House (*w* Dan LENO) *c.*1901

Courting The Widow 1895

Diamond Ring, The (arr. Angelo A. ASHER) *c.*1900

Dolly

Don't Forget Your Poor Old Farver! 1905

Do You Like Me? 1917

Father Of Ninety (& Wal PINK) (sk.) 1902

Going To The Races (& LENO) *c.*1899

His Majesty's Guests (sk.) 1902

If We Had Only Known 1898

I'm Coming Home To You 1903

(In) The Subbubs (*w* PINK) 1898

Kimberley 1894

Lazy Daisy 1896

Love Came First 1898

Mary Ann's Refused Me (arr. Fred EPLETT) 1895

Mary Ought To Know You Know 1894

Message Home, The 1909

Mocking Bird, The (*w* LENO) *c.*1900

Mrs Kelly (& LENO) *c.*1899

Mumbles Head 1895

My Sweet Face 1893

No More Fancy Balls For Me (& Norton ATKINS) 1895

Oh! It Do Give Me The Needle 1894

Old Home's The Best After All 1897

On De Injine 1894

Robbin' Hood 1894

Sailing Home 1894

Salvage Man, The (& LENO: DARNLEY) *c.*1899

Sticking It Out (*w* PINK) 1897

Swimming Master, The *c.*1899

That's How We've Made Our Name 1898

Tower Of London, The (The Beefeater) 1898

Typewriter Song, The

Youngest Son, The 1895

You've Got To Come To England 1896

DARRELL, Millie

Birdie, You Must Never Tell 1876

Love's Chidings 1876

There Is No Harm In Kissing

DASH, Irwin d. 18 Mar. 1984 a.k.a. Lewis ILDA, q.v.

DAVENPORT, Arthur d. 1941

I Want Somebody To Love Me (& H. G. PÉLISSIER: PÉLISSIER) *c.*1905

My Moon (*m* PÉLISSIER) 1908

Since I Walked Out With A Soldier (*m* PÉLISSIER) 1909

Ypsilanti (*m* PÉLISSIER) 1908

DAVENPORT, G. Beadle

Twenty Years Ago (A Mother's Letter) (& Will GODWIN: GODWIN) 1897

DAVID, Hubert W. b. 1904; son of Worton DAVID

Felix Kept On Walking (*w* Edward E. BRYANT) 1923

DAVID, Worton 1874–1940; father of Hubert W. DAVID; a.k.a. Wynn STANLEY

Algernon, Go H'On! (& Bert LEE) 1914

All The Girls Are Lovely By The Seaside (& LEE: Harry FRAGSON) 1913

And The Parrot Said (*m* Orlando
POWELL) 1907

Are We Downhearted—No! (*m*
Lawrence WRIGHT) 1914

At A Minute To Seven Last Night (*m*
Sam MAYO) 1906

At The Vicar's Fancy Ball (& LEE) 1915

Bobbing Up And Down Like This (*m*
Norman REEVE) 1899

Chinaman, The (*m* MAYO) 1906

Come And Be One Of The Midnight
Sons (*m* Kenneth LYLE) 1909

Come With Me Down Regent Street (&
C. W. MURPHY) 1910

Eh! Dear Me! It's A Fine Place, Paree!
(& MURPHY) 1914

End Of My Old Cigar, The (& R. P.
WESTON) 1914

Four-And-Nine (*m* LEE & BOBS, THE
TWO) 1915

Hello! Hello! Who's Your Lady Friend!
(& LEE: FRAGSON) 1913

Hold Your Hand Out! (*m* R. Linton
NEVETT) 1909

Hold Your Hand Out, Naughty Boy! (&
MURPHY) 1913

I Can Say 'Truly Rural' (& George
ARTHURS) 1909

I Can't Forget The Days When I Was
Young (*w* Sam MAYO) 1919

I Can't Reach That Top Note (&
ARTHURS) 1909

I Do Like A S'Nice S'Mince S'Pie (&
LEE) 1914

I Do Like You Susie In Your Pretty Little
Sunday Clothes (& MURPHY) 1912

I Don't Care What Becomes Of Me (&
George CAMPBELL: Fred MAYO) 1910

I'm Going To Sing A Song To You This
Evening (*m* F. V. ST CLAIR) 1906

I'm Here If I'm Wanted *see* The
Policeman

I'm Waiting Here For Kate (&
ARTHURS) 1909

In The Valley Of Golden Dreams (&
MURPHY) 1913

I Parted My Hair In The Middle (&
MURPHY) 1913

I Shall Get In Such A Row When Martha
Knows (& MURPHY) 1913

I Want To Sing In Opera (& ARTHURS)
1910

Jere-Jeremiah (& MURPHY) 1913

Just Because She's Got An 'Andle To Her
Name (*m* Will DALTON) 1901

Mickey Rooney's Ragtime Band (&
MURPHY) 1913

Nature's Made A Big Mistake (& Alf
ELLERTON: ELLERTON) 1910

Nobody Else But You (& Ralph PENSO)
1914

Nursie-Nursie (& LEE) 1910

Piccadilly Trot, The (*w* ARTHURS) 1912

Policeman, The (I'm Here If I'm Wanted
(*m* ST CLAIR) 1907

Pushing Young Man, The (*m* MAYO)
1906

Rest Of The Day's Your Own, The (& J.
P. LONG) 1915

She's Been A Good Wife To Me (*m*
Orlando POWELL) 1907

That Old-Fashioned Mother Of Mine (*m*
Horatio NICHOLLS) 1919

They're All Single By The Seaside (&
MURPHY) 1911

We Really Had A Most Delightful
Evening (& LEE) 1910

When That Yiddisher Band Played That
Irish Tune (& MURPHY) 1912

Which Switch Is The Switch, Miss, For
Ipswich? (& J. BARNETT & Herman
DAREWSKI) 1915

Whoa! Back-Pedal (*m* Henry E.
PETHER) 1900

Wriggley Rag, The (& ARTHURS) 1912

Yiddisher-Irish Baby, The (& Fred
GODFREY & WRIGHT) 1915

You Are My Girl-Ski (& ARTHURS) 1910

DAVIDSON, Mrs F. A.
Song Of The Shirt, The (*m* Henry
RUSSELL); prompted by Thomas

Hood's 1843 poem in *Punch* and *The Times*) 1860
See also Arthur H. Behrend; Jonathan Blewitt.

Davidson, W.
Band Box Girl, The (& A. Wimperis: Harry Fragson) 1907

Davies, A. E. Sidney
Au Revoir, My Little Hyacincth (*m* H. Darewski) 1906

Davies, Richard *see* Mynyddog

Davies, T. Vincent
Baa Baa Baa (*w* Walter Greenaway) 1882
City Toff, The *or* Crutch And Toothpick *or* La-Di-Da! (*w* Edwin V. Page) 1879
Country Cousin, The (I Saw Esau Kissing Kate) (*w* Harry Hunter) 1870
Cowardy Cowardy Custard (*w* Page) 1878
Croquet (*w* John B. Lawreen) 1871
I Don't Want To Fight (*w* Henry Pettitt) 1878
If You See Lucy Let Me Know (*w* Hunter) 1874
Johnny Will You Come Along Now (*w* Hunter) 1876
Just Behind The Battle Mother (Hunter: Davies arr. W. Vandervell) 1877
Keep It Dark (*w* Page) 1862
Little Joe (*w* Hunter) 1877
Mazy Dance, The (*w* Hunter) 1870
Moonlight Walk, The (*w* Frank Elton)
Peter Perfect (*w*. Harry Hunter) 1870
Rap, Rap, Rap, I'm Married To A Medium (*w* G. H. Macdermott)
That's The Sort Of Men We Want In England Here Today (*w* John S. Haydon) 1887
Tickling Mad (*w&m* Page, arr. Davies) 1880
Wanted: A Lady Help (*w* Page) 1876

What Shall We Do With Cyprus? (*w* Page) 1879
Who'll Oblige A Lady? (*w* Page)

Davis, Benny 1894–1959
Margie (*m* Con Conrad & J. Russel Robinson) 1919

Davis, Chris
Day At The Races, A
Derby Day *c.*1898
Family Album/Party, The
Fighting Parson, The (& George Gray) 1903
Soldier And A Maid, A

Davis, Dolly *see* Temple, Hope

Davis, Gussie L. 1863–99
Down In Poverty Row (*m* Arthur Trevelyan) 1896
Fatal Wedding, The (arr. as Those Wedding Bells Shall Not Ring Out, Monroe H. Rosenfeld & E. Jonghman) 1893
In The Baggage Coach Ahead (Mother's Body Is Lying) 1896
Picture 84 (*w* Chas. B. Ward) 1894

Davy, John 1763–1824
Bay Of Biscay, The (*w* Andrew Cherry) 1805

Dawes, William 1840–97 *see* Goff, Lijer

Dawson, Forbes
Cockalorum (*m* W. F. Frame) 1896

Dawson, J. W.
Things Were Very, Very Lively (& Charles Bignell & T. Brown) 1894

Dawson, Peter 1882–1961; a.k.a. J. P. McCall

Day, David G. 1850–1929; of Francis Bros & Day (see Publishers section); father of Frederick Day
And The Missis Popped Up At The Time (*w* Harry Windley) *c.*1888

Be Always Up And Doing, Boys! (*w* R.
HARRISON)
Captain Matthew Webb (*w* Harry
HUNTER) 1875
Far, Far Away (*w* George ANTHONY)
Lord Mayor's Coachman, The (*w*
HUNTER) 1881
She Was! She Was!! She Was!!! 1885

DAY, Frederick E. M. 1878–1975;
a.k.a. Edward MONTAGU; son of David
G. DAY; chairman of Francis, Day &
Hunter
Take Your Girlie Where The Band Is
Playing 1910
Why Little Boy Was Blue 1910

DAYKIN, Herbert
Britannia's Got The Needle 1878
That's Nice 1878
Whoa, Emma 1878
   See T. S. LONSDALE for similar title, also
   Charles DEANE.

DEANE, Charles° 1866–1910
All Through A Little Game At Billiards
(& Charles RIDGWELL) 1909
Beautiful Grub 1896
Father Of The Boys (John Bull Up To
Date) (& Leo DRYDEN) 1895
Gal Wot Lost Her Bloke At Monte Carlo,
The (*m* George LE BRUNN) 1892
I'm One Of The Girls 1893
Trafalgar Square (*m* Edward
JONGHMANS) 1899
Up To Date Swell, The (*w* Harry
CASTLING) 1895
Whoa, Emma(?)
   Possibly sung by Kate Carney; for similar
   titles see Herbert DAYKIN and T. S.
   LONSDALE.

DE COURVILLE, Albert 1888–1960
Dear Old Saturday Night (& Ernest
RANDELL & Herman DAREWSKI)
1915

DE CURTIS, Ernesto 1875–1937
Sorrento (Eng. *w* Claud AVELING) 1911

DE FRECE, Sir Walter 1871–1935
At The Races 1890
Brand New Millionaire (& William
JEROME: D. FITZGIBBON) 1894
German Prince, The 1896
Our Drive 1894
Shop-Walker, The (*m* George LE
BRUNN) *c.*1895

DE LISLE, C. Rouget 1760–1836
Marseillaise, La 1792

DEL RIEGO, Teresa 1876–1968
Little Brown Bird (*w* H. M.
NIGHTINGALE) 1912
Oh, Dry Those Tears (Les Larmes) (Fr.
w E. HÉROS; Eng. *w* DEL RIEGO)
1904

DEMPSEY, J. E. 1876–1918
Beautiful Garden Of Roses (*m* Johann C.
SCHMID) 1900
If I Could Only Make You Care (*m*
SCHMID) 1913

DENT, Harry
Never Mind (& Tom GOLDBURN) 1913

DENZA, Luigi 1846–1922
Come To Me (*w* W. BOOSEY) 1885
Funiculi Funicula 1880

DE PINNA, Herbert
Does This Shop Stock Shot Socks With
Spots? 1912

DESMOND, Billy
When Are You Going To Lead Me To
The Altar, Walter? (*w* Walter DORE)
1933

DESYLVA, Buddy 1895–1950
April Showers (*m* Louis SILVERS) 1921
California, Here I Come (& Al JOLSON
& Joseph MEYER) 1924
Kiss In The Dark, A (*m* Victor
HERBERT) 1922
Look For The Silver Lining (*m* Jerome
KERN) 1920

You Ain't Heard Nothin' Yet (& JOLSON & Gus KAHN) 1919

DE WENZEL, Leopold
Tra-La-La *or* Scraps (*w* Edwin V. PAGE) *c*.1881

DE ZULUETA, Pedro
We're Really Proud Of You (*w* Arthur WIMPERIS) 1914

D'HARDELOT, Guy 1858–1936; pseudonym of Helen Rhodes
Because (*w* Edward TESCHEMACHER) 1902
Invocation
My Garden (*w* Edward G. LOCKTON) 1914
Say Yes (*w* Heinrich HEINE Eng. adap. J. BARBER) 1894
Three Green Bonnets (*w* W. H. HARRIS) 1901

DIBDIN, Charles sen. 1745–1814; father of Thomas J. DIBDIN
Ben Backstay 1789
Lass That Loves A Sailor, The 1811
Then Farewell, My Trim-Built Wherry 1774
Tom Bowling 1790

DIBDIN, Charles jun. 1768–1833
Hot Codlins (*m* John WHITAKER) 1819
Scroggin's Ghost (*m* William REEVE) 1804
Tray (*m* WHITAKER) 1801
Typitywitchet (*m* REEVE) 1810

DIBDIN, Thomas J. 1771–1841; a.k.a. Thomas Dibdin Pitt; son of Charles DIBDIN sen.
All's Well (*m* John BRAHAM) 1803
Darby Kelly (*m* John WHITAKER) *c*.1820
God Bless Victoria! Albion's Queen (*m* Tommaso E. G. ROVEDINO) 1837
Snug/Tight Little Island, The (air, 'The Rogue's March')

DI CAPUA, Edoardo 1864–1917
O Sole Mio (*w* Giovanni CAPURRO) 1898

DICKENS, Charles 1812–70; many monologues and sketches were extracted from the novels and performed by Clifford Harrison°, Ben Nathan°, and most notably Bransby Williams°
Ivy Green, The (*m* Henry RUSSELL) *Pickwick Papers* 1837

DICKSON, J. Bernard
Boarding House, The (*m* Harry RANDALL) 1904
Drink! By One Who's Had Some (*m* RANDALL) 1900
Little Teddy Brown Down At Margit 1895
Love By One Who Knows (*m* RANDALL) 1900
Man—By One Who Loathes 'Em (*m* Randall) 1902

DIEHL, Louis d. 1911
Jack's Yarn (*w* George R. SIMS)
Lights Of London Town, The (*w* SIMS) 1880

DILLON, Will
I Want A Girl Just Like The Girl Who Married Dear Old Dad (*m* Harry VON TILZER) 1911

DILLON, William 1877–1966
End Of The Road, The (& Harry LAUDER) 1924

DIX, J. Airlie d. 7 Dec. 1911
Patchwork Garden, The (*w* Edgar BATEMAN & Paul MILL) 1902
That's How I Found The Pole (*w* E. A. SEARSON) 1909
Trumpeter, The (*w* F. Francis BARRON) 1904
Village Of Toad-In-The Hole, The (*w* SEARSON & Paul MILL) 1907

DIXON, George Washington°?
Zip Coon (Turkey In The Straw) (& Bob FARRELL?) *c*.1828

DIXON, Mason

All For Her Country's Sake (Nurse Cavell memorial song) (& L. SILBERMAN) *c*.1915

Back To Dear Old Tennessee (*m* A. GROCK & SILBERMAN) 1916

Crocodile Crawl, The (& Will E. HAINES & Donovan MEHER) 1915

Do It Again (*m* GROCK & SILBERMAN & T. W. THURBAN) 1917

My Colordado Sue (*m* GROCK & 'partner'—SILBERMAN?) 1918

Yaaki-Daaki Yaaki Dah (Mandy From Tonypandy) (*m* SILBERMAN & GROCK) 1917

DODGE, Gilbert

Peggy O'Neil (& Harry PEASE & Ed G. NELSON) 1921

DODSON, Gerald 1884–1956

Fishermen Of England, The (*m* Montague F. PHILLIPS) 1921

DODSWORTH, T.

Fizz (arr. W. G. EASTON) 1878

Fwightful Dilemma, A (*m* & Harry LISTON) 1873

Rustic Young Damsel, The *c*.1880

Susan Sweet 1876

DOLBY, Charlotte 1821–85; after marrying Prosper Sainton in 1860 k.a. Charlotte SAINTON-DOLBY

Oh, Bay Of Dublin (Lady DUFFERIN: DOLBY, arr. DUFFERIN) 1854

When We Are Old And Grey (*w* Fred E. WEATHERLY) 1872

DONALDSON, Walter 1893–1947; *see* DONOVAN, Walter for Aba Daba Honeymoon

Carolina In The Morning (*w* Gus KAHN) 1922

How'Ya Gonna Deep 'Em Down On The Farm? (*w* Sam M. LEWIS & Joe YOUNG) 1919

Just Try To Picture Me Back Home In Tennessee (*w* W. M. JEROME) 1915

My Mammy (*w* LEWIS & YOUNG) 1921

DONNELLY, Robert

Are There Any Little Angels Blind Like Me? (*m* Lawrence WRIGHT) 1910

Don't Go Down In The Mine, Dad (*m* Will GEDDES) 1910

DONOVAN, Walter 1889–1964

Aba Daba Honeymoon (*w* Arthur FIELDS); *m* often wrongly attr. Walter DONALDSON 1914

DORE, Walter

When Are You Going To Lead Me To The Altar, Walter? (*m* Billy Desmond) 1933

DOUDNEY, Sarah

Old Dreams (*m* Alfred CELLIER; with new *w* by B. C. STEPHENSON interpolated into *Dorothy* as Queen Of My Heart) 1879

DOUGLAS, Charles N. 1863–1920

My Cosey Corner Girl (*m* John W. Bratton) 1903

DOUGLAS, William ?–1753?

Annie Laurie (rev. Lady John Douglass SCOTT 1835) *c*.1700

DOUGLASS, Arthur D.

Only One (*w* Edwin V. PAGE) 1887

DOWN, T. W.

Oh, The Daylight Bill (& Edgar BATEMAN: Herman E. DAREWSKI jun.) 1908

DRESSER, Paul 1857–1906

Blue And The Gray, The 1900

Convict And The Bird, The 1888

Here Lies An Actor 1889

Her Tears Drifted Out With The Tide 1891

In Good Old New York Town 1899

I Wonder Where She Is Tonight 1899

Just Tell Them That You Saw Me 1895

Letter That Never Came, The 1885
My Gal Sal 1905
On The Banks Of The Wabash 1891
Pardon Came Too Late, The 1891
We Fight Tomorrow Mother 1898
Where Are The Friends Of Other Days?
1903

DRISLANE, Jack
You Taught Me How To Love You (m
George W. MEYER) 1919

DRUMMOND, Algernon
Eton Boating Song (W. J. CORY:
DRUMMOND, transc. T. L. MITCHELL-
INNES, arr. Evelyn WOODHOUSE)
1878

DRYDEN, Leo° 1863–1939; stage name
of George D. WHEELER
Father Of The Boys (John Bull Up To
Date) (& Charles DEANE) 1895
Going Home (The Miner's Return)
(w J. P. HARRINGTON, arr. F. W.
VENTON) c.1892
Miner's Dream Of Home, The (& Will
GODWIN) 1891

DUFFERIN, Baroness 1807–67; Helen
Selina Blackwood, Countess of Gifford;
grand-daughter of Richard Brinsley
Sheridan and sister of The Hon Mrs
Caroline NORTON
Irish Emigrant, The (m George Arthur
BARKER) 1846
Oh, Bay Of Dublin (DUFFERIN: DOLBY,
arr. DUFFERIN) 1854

DUFFY, H. A.
Last Bullet, The (m George LE BRUNN)
1889
On The Banks Of Bantry Bay (m J. M.
HARRISON) 1894
Simple Little Maid In The Corner, The
(m HARRISON) 1896

DUMAS, Felix
'E Do Know Where He Is (w Harry
WINCOTT) 1894

Young Country Squire, The (w George
WARE) 1891

DUNBAR, E. C.° 1841–1900
Bear It And Grin (w A. ANTHONY)
1877

DUNN, Charles
Oh, Fred! Tell Them To Stop (w&m
George MEEN rev. DUNN) 1880

DUNN, J. W.°
Don't Leave Your Father, Boy (w Harry
WINDLEY) 1889
Fauntleroy Jones
Jack's As Good As Gold
John Bull And His Three Little
Brothers
Love's Jubilee 1887
She Boxed My Ears With The Frying
Pan (w WINDLEY) c.1888
What Will The Neighbours Say? (Oh
Dear!) (w WINDLEY) 1886

DUNN, Will
Shut It! 1890
Yes, You Shall Be A Sailor 1890

D'URFEY, Tom 1653–1723
Within A Mile Of Edinbro' Town (m
James HOOK) 1780

DURANDEAU, Augustus E. 1848–93
Ask A P'liceman (w E. W. ROGERS)
c.1885
Come Where The Booze Is Cheaper (w
ROGERS)° c.1890
Giddy Little Curate, The (w ROGERS)
1891
Mystery Of A Hansom Cab, The (w
ROGERS) 1888
Never Introduce Yer Donah To A Pal (&
Albert E. ELLIS: DURANDEAU) 1891
Pair Of Spectacles, A (& George
HORNCASTLE) 1891
That Was Me (w&m Charles OSBORNE,
arr. DURANDEAU) 1890
Woman, Lovely Woman (w&m Felix
McGLENNON, arr. DURANDEAU) 1886

DURIAH, F.°
There's Going To Be A Wedding

DU VAL, Charles H.° 1846–89
Bright Sparkling Wine
Green Shores Of Erin, The
My Beaux *or* I Can't Make Up My Mind
   1873
My Whisk-aws

DVOŘÁK, Antonin 1841–1904
Humoreske op. 101 no. 7 1897
Songs My Mother Taught Me (from
   Zigeunerlieder, op. 55; *w* Adolph
   HEYDUK; transl. Natalie
   MACFARREN) 1880

EARDLEY-WILMOT, D. 1883–1970
Hello, Martha (& Vere SMITH: SMITH)
   1908
Little Grey Home In The West (*m*
   Hermann LÖHR) 1911

EARLE, Fred° 1877–1915; son of Joseph
TABRAR
On The March 1896
Seaweed 1905
Where Did You Get That Boko, Uncle?
   c.1905
With My Little Wigger-Wagger In My
   Hand (& Frank CARTER & Gilbert
   WELLS) 1909

EATON, William G.
Boy About Town, The (*w* Edwin V.
   PAGE) 1885
Cosy Little Cottage, A 1884
Fizz (*w&m* J. DODSWORTH, arr. EATON)
   1878
Her Name Is Norah 1883
Highly Respectable Singer, The (*w* Wal
   PINK) 1887
I'm Going To Do Without 'Em (*w* Fred
   BOWYER) 1882
Man In The Moon Is Looking, Love,
   The (*w* T. S. LONSDALE) 1877
My Aesthetic Love (*w* LONSDALE)
   1881
Oh, The Fairies (*w* LONSDALE) 1878

Some Girls Do And Some Girls Don't (*w*
   LONSDALE)
This Is The House That Jerry Built (*w*
   LONSDALE) 1887
True British Swell, The (*w* BOWYER)
   1881
You'll All Be Wanted (*w* LONSDALE)
   1878

ECKERT, Carl Anton F. 1820–79
Swiss Echo Song (He Loves But Me/Er
   Liebt Nur Mich from *Deutscher
   Lieder und Romanzen*, op. 12; Eng. *w*
   1873 S. A. WILLIAMS) 1859

EDEN, Guy M. d. 5 Dec. 1954
My Word! Jones Of The Lancers (*m* T.
   C. Sterndale BENNETT) 1911

EDGAR, Marriott° 1880–1951 Half-
brother of Edgar WALLACE
Let's Swap (*m* Alfred CARPENTER) 1910
Lion And Albert, The 1932
Marksman Sam *c*.1932
Return Of Albert, The 1933
Runcorn Ferry, The (*m* Wolseley
   CHARLES) 1933

EDGAR, Percy d. 10 Jan. 1948
Awake! (*m* Henry E. PETHER) 1917
Butterfly And The Rose, The (& Gilbert
   WELLS: Fred ELTON) 1909
Pack Up Your Trunk And Go (& Ralph
   PENSO) 1908
Thank God For Victory (*m* L.
   SILBERMAN) 1919

EDWARDS, Gus° 1879–1945
By The Light Of The Silvery Moon (*w*
   Ed MADDEN) 1909
Could You Be True To Eyes Of Blue? (*w*
   Will D. COBB) 1901
Good-bye, Little Girl, Good-bye (*w*
   COBB) 1904
I Can't Tell Why I Love You But I Do (*w*
   COBB) 1900
I Just Can't Make My Eyes Behave (*w*
   COBB & H. B. SMITH) 1906

In My Merry Oldsmobile (*w* Vincent P. BRYAN) 1905
Johnny Jones's Sister Sue (*w* COBB) 1902
Somebody's Sweetheart I Want To Be (*w* COBB) 1905
When Tommy Atkins Marries Dolly Gray (*w* COBB) 1906

EDWARDS, Julian° 1855–1910
Right As Ninepence (*w* Albert CHEVALIER) 1910

EGAN, Raymond B. 1890–1952
Japanese Sandman, The (*m* Richard A. WHITING) 1921
Till We Meet Again (*m* WHITING) 1918

EGERTON, Frank W.°
Captain Cuffs Of The Glorious Buffs
Captain Dasher 1883
Don't Take My Children From Me 1883
My Name It Is John Barleycorn 1870
Nellie *or* Ten Past Nine
Out On The Ran-Dan *c*.1883
Rambling Through The Town
Sing To Me Johnnie 1882

ELDÉE, Lilian 1870–1904
Swing Song (& Percy GREENBANK: André MESSAGER) 1904
Trot Here And There (& GREENBANK: MESSAGER) 1904

ELEN, Gus° 1862–1940
Down The Dials (*w* Harry WINCOTT) 1893
Flying Man, The (& Albert E. ELLIS) 1888
I Couldn't Get Out 1888
I Helped Myself (& ELLIS) 1888
It Was Gone! 1887
My Next Door Neighbour's Gardin (& Edgar BATEMAN: G. LE BRUNN) 1900
Wait Till The Work Comes Round (*w* C. CORNELL & T. LEYBOURNE) 1906
Who's That A-Squalling? 1888

ELGAR, Sir Edward 1857–1934
Land Of Hope And Glory (*w* Arthur C. BENSON) 1902
War Song, A (*w* C. Flavell HAYWARD) 1903

ELLERTON, Alf
Belgium Put The 'Kibosh' On The Kaiser 1914
Nature's Made A Big Mistake (& Worton DAVID: ELLERTON) 1910
She Pushed Me Into The Parlour (*m* Will MAYNE) 1912

ELLIOTT, G. H.° 1884–1962
How D'You Do, My Baby? (& Arthur LAWRANCE) 1909

ELLIOTT, James W. 1833–1915
Hybrias The Cretan (*w* Thomas CAMPBELL) 1855

ELLIOTT, John Arthur
Balaclava (Oh, 'Tis A Famous Story) (*m* Slade MURRAY, arr. Edmund FORMAN) 1884

ELLIOTT, Zo (Alonzo) 1891–1964
There's A Long, Long Trail A-Winding (& Stoddard KING) 1913

ELLIS, Albert E.
Flying Man, The (& Gus ELEN) 1888
I Ain't A-Going To Tell (& Walter C. PARKER); British version Wal PINK: arr. H. TEMPEST) 1896
I Helped Myself (& ELEN) 1888
My Missis Thinks She's Trilby (*m* Alan MACEY) 1895
Never Introduce Yer Donah To A Pal (& A. E. DURANDEAU: DURANDEAU) 1891

ELTON, Frank 1881–1954
Moonlight Walk, The (*m* Vincent DAVIES)

ELTON, Fred°
Butterfly And The Rose, The (*w* Percy EDGAR & Gilbert WELLS) 1909

Wee Hoose 'Mang The Heather, The
(& Harry LAUDER: & WELLS) 1913

ELTON, Richard d. 1943
Give Me A Ticket To Heaven
(& Denham HARRISON) 1903

ELVIN, Joe° 1862–1935
Tinker's Holiday, The (sk.) c.1885

EMERSON, Ida°
Hello! Ma Baby (m Joseph H. HOWARD)
1899

EMMELL, David
Philosophy (m anon.) 1904

EMMET, Joseph K.° 1841–91
Bells Are Ringing 1879
Kiss Me 1882
Peek-A-Boo 1880
Sweet Violets (Sweeter Than All The
Roses) 1883

EMMETT, Daniel Decatur° 1815–1904;
sometimes spelled Emmitt, among other
variations
Black Brigade, The 1862
De Boatmen's Dance (arr. from trad.)
1843
De Fine Old Colored Gemman 1868
De Wild Goose-Nation (air, Gumbo
Chaff) 1844
I Ain't Got Time To Tarry (The Land Of
Freedom) 1858
I'm Going Home To Dixey (Rocky Road)
(air, I Ain't Got Time To Tarry)
1861
I Wish I Was In Dixie (see HALL, Frank,
In The Strand) 1859
Jo(h)nny Roach 1859
Jordan Is A Hard Road To Travel
(w perhaps anon.) 1853
My Old Aunt Sally (based on Peggy
Perkins by C. DIBDIN jun., 1790)
c.1843
Old Dan Tucker (m anon. arr. EMMETT)
c.1840
Way Down Louisiana

Wide Awake or Dere's A Donkey in
De Tent 1859
Yes, I Will, By Jingo

ENGLISH, Thomas Dunn 1819–1902
Ben Bolt (m Nelson KNEASS) 1848

EPLETT, Fred 1858–1915
All Right, Mary-Ann (w&m Herbert
COLE, arr. EPLETT) 1884
Blind Leading The Blind, The (w A. R.
MARSHALL) 1901
Bore O' Bef'nal Green, The (w W. E.
IMESON) 1899
Cab Man's Story, The
Different Kinds Of Girls (w Nat
CLIFFORD) 1899
'E Dunno Where 'E Are see Jack Jones
'E Found Out Where 'E Are (w
G. Wallis ARTHUR)
Empty Chair, The (w J. P. HARRINGTON)
c.1895
Ev'ry Home Is Fairyland (w Fred W.
LEIGH) 1900
Faithful or A Simple Soldier's Song
(w Fred GILBERT) 1899
Git Your 'Air Cut (& George
BEAUCHAMP & Charles OSBORNE)
1892
Grass Widower, The (w&m J. H.
WOODHOUSE, arr. EPLETT) 1891
How Dare You! (w Harry BODEN & ?
KEITH & Billy MERSON) 1906
Huntsman, The (w Albert PERRY &
George A. STEVENS) 1900
I Do, Doodle-Oodle-Oo (w Richard
MORTON) 1903
I'm The Man Who Buried Ta-Ra-Ra-
Boom-De-Ay (w&m Harry CASTLING,
arr. EPLETT) 1893
In (w&m OSBORNE, arr. EPLETT) 1891
It's A Sprahtin' or The Coster's
Moustache (w MARSHALL) 1897
It Was Only Done In Play (w LEIGH)
1901
Jack Jones ('E Dunno Where 'E Are)
(m Harry WRIGHT) 1894

Jones's Parlour Floor (*w* Bob LEONARD) 1899

Lindy, I'm Coming Back To You (*w* Harry HUNTER) 1904

Mary Ann's Refused Me (*w&m* Herbert DARNLEY, arr. EPLETT) 1895

Never Share Your Lodgings With A Pal (*w* Wal PINK) *c*.1895

Oh, Sally! (*m* Norton ATKINS) 1895

Oh, The Scenery Was Absolutely Grand! (*w* LEIGH) 1900

Old Dicky Bird (*w&m* T. W. CONNOR, arr. EPLETT) 1901

Our Society (*w* Charles WILMOTT)

Our Stores Ltd (*w* WRIGHT) *c*.1895

Out (*w* WILMOTT) 1891

Rag-Time Nursery Rhymes (*w&m* Sam RICHARDS, arr. EPLETT) 1901

Recruiting Sergeant (*w* WRIGHT) *c*.1895

She's The Boss, I'm The Slavey (*w&m* James ROLMAZ, arr. EPLETT) 1888

Some O' Yer Do Git Abaht (*w* Charles CORNELL) 1894

Sullivan Pawned The Donkey 1896

Theosophee (*w* WILMOTT) 1891

EUROPE, James Reese 1881–1919
Ballin' The Jack (Roy BURRIS: & Chris SMITH) 1913

EVALO, J. S. one-time partner of Griff
Angels Are Hovering Round (*m* John COOKE jun.) 1889

Doctor Jeremiah Jones (*m* G. W. HUNTER) 1899

Fine And Fresh And Blooming (*m* Henry E. PETHER) 1894

Hezekiah Brown (*m* HUNTER) 1892

Oh The Weather! (*m* PETHER) 1894

EVANS, George 'Honey Boy'°
1870–1915
I'll Be True To My Honey Boy 1894
In The Good Old Summertime (*w* Ren SHIELDS) 1902

EVANS, Will° 1873–1931
Building The Chicken House (sk.) (*m* George ARTHURS) 1913

Down At The Garden Gate

Laying A Carpet (sk.) 1918

Missing Verse, The

Mothers And Daughters (sk.) 1914

EVERARD, George 1873–1907; son of Ada Lundberg°
How Dare I Live! (*w* Ernest REES) 1902

Is Your Mother In, Molly Malone? (*w* A. J. MILLS) 1903

It's All Right In The Summertime (& Alan MURRAY) 1902

Next Horse I Ride On, The (& MURRAY) 1905

Old Man's Darling, An (& MURRAY) 1903
See Albert HALL: Orlando POWELL for song of same title.

Parapher-Paraphernalia (& Carl HOWARD) 1898

She Glories In A Thing Like That 1899

Wanted—A Lady (& HOWARD) 1899

EWING, Montague 1889–1957
Policeman's Holiday, A 1911

FAGAN, Barney° fl. 1890–1927
English Toff, The (*w* J. P. KEAN)
My Gal Is A High Born Lady 1896

FALCONER, Edmund 1814–79; pseudonym of Edmund O'Rouke
Killarney (*m* Michael William BALFE) 1861

FALKLAND, Arthur
Koffo Of Bond Street (*m* Herbert FINCK) 1910

FANCOURT, Tom° d. 7 Aug. 1940
Charming Young Girl, The (Fred PERRY: FANCOURT, arr. J. BATCHELDER) 1868

Ticket Of Leave Man, The (*m* Watkyn WILLIAMS) 1873

FANE, Sydney P.°
Ping Pong Courtship 1902
Rhymes And Reasons 1905

FANE, V.
For Ever And Ever (*m* F. Paolo TOSTI)
1879

FARDD, Eben 1802–63; pseudonym of
Ebenezer Thomas
Land Of My Fathers (Hen Wlad Fy
Nhadau) (Evan JAMES: James JAMES;
Eng. transl. FARDD) 1856
See also Owain ALAW.

FARNIE, Henry B. 1820–89
Gendarmes' Duet (*m* Jacques
OFFENBACH) 1859
Tain't Natural (*m* John CROOK) 1887
Up In A Balloon (US *w*—orig. *w&m*
G. W. HUNT) 1869
Watch On The Rhine, The (*m* Carl
WILHELM (1854)) 1870

FARQUHARSON, Stewart d. 1890
Annie And Ronald (*m* E. L. J. HIME)
1849
I'll Dream Of Thee (*m* HIME) 1849
I'm Lonely In The Old House Now
(*m* HIME) 1850
Look Always On The Bright Side
(*m* HIME) 1849

FARRELL, Bob?
Zip Coon (Turkey In The Straw)
(& George Washington DIXON?)
c.1828

FAWN, Harriet daughter of James
Fawn°?
Another Glass Round (*w* George
HORNCASTLE) 1888
It Makes A Fellow Think A Bit
(*w* HORNCASTLE) 1894
It Must Have Been The Lobster (*w* A. R.
MARSHALL, arr. Fred HOLLIDAY)
1894
She Wasn't Far Off It (*w* HORNCASTLE)
1889

Single Gentleman, The
(*w* HORNCASTLE) 1894
There Ain't A Word (*w* HORNCASTLE)
1892
Wrong Way, The (*w* HORNCASTLE)
1888

FEARNLEY, George
Corsican Maid, The (*m* George M.
SAKER) 1909

FERGUSON, Sir Samuel 1810–86
Lark In The Clear Air, The (air, trad.)
c.1850

FERRIS, N.
Irish Fusilier, The (*m* W. H. SQUIRE)
1911

FIELD, Eugene 1850–95
Listen To My Tale Of Woe (*w* Hubbard
T. SMITH) 1884
Toddles (*m* Arthur BEHREND) 1907

FIELD, L.
Happy Eliza And Converted Jane (*w&m*
Will OLIVER, arr. FIELD) 1888

FIELDHOUSE, Will°
Hero, The 1911
I Looked And I Looked 1907
Kitty Nolan 1893
Little Dora Donough 1897
Little Nancy Newlove 1899
Old Church Gate, The 1897
One Of The Nuts 1898
Ping Pong On The Brain 1902
Pretty May Day 1896
Rosie Lee 1897
Wait For Your Old Age Pension 1909

FIELDS, Arthur 1888–1953
Aba Daba Honeymoon (*m* Walter
DONOVAN) 1914
I'm Going Down To Tennessee (& Harry
CARROLL) 1914
On The Mississippi (Ballard
MACDONALD: CARROLL, arr. FIELDS)
1912

Yiddisher Turkey Trot (& CARROLL) 1912

FINCK, Herman 1872–1939
Florrie The Flapper (*w* Arthur WIMPERIS) 1914
Gilbert, The Filbert (*w* WIMPERIS) 1914
I'll Make A Man Of You (*w* WIMPERIS) 1914
In The Shadows (instrumental work but US *w* added 1911 by E. Ray GOETZ) 1910
Koffo Of Bond Street (*w* FALKLAND, ARTHUR) 1910
London And Paris (*w* George GRAY) *c*.1895
You Could Hardly Notice It At All (*w* J. Hickory WOOD) 1903

FINK, Harry 1893–1963
Curse Of An Aching Heart, The (*m* Al PIANTADOSI) 1913

FINLAY, Dun
Loch Lomond (*w&m* Lady John Douglass SCOTT, arr. FINLAY) *c*.1845

FIS(C)HER, Fred 1875–1942
Come Josephine In My Flying Machine (*w* Alfred BRYAN) 1910
If The Man In The Moon Were A Coon 1905
My Brudda, Sylvest' (*w* Jesse LASKY & Sam STERN) 1908
Peg O' My Heart (*w* BRYAN) 1913
They Go Wild, Simply Wild, Over Me (*w* Joe MCCARTHY) 1917
Who Paid The Rent For Mrs Rip Van Winkle When Rip Van Winkle Went Away? (*w* BRYAN) 1914

FITCHETT, H. W. 1836–77
Ding Dong (*w&m* Gus LEACH, arr. FITCHETT) 1877
Poor, But A Gentleman Still (*w&m* John STAMFORD, arr. FITCHETT) 1875

FITZ, Albert H. 1870–1949 pseudonym of Sol BLOOM

Honeysuckle And The Bee, The (*m* William H. PENN) 1901

FITZBALL, Edward 1792–1873
Cottage Near Rochelle, The (*m* Michael William BALFE) 1835
My Pretty Jane (The Bloom Is On The Rye) (*m* Henry R. BISHOP) *c*.1830
Yes, Let Me Like A Soldier Fall (*m* W. Vincent WALLACE) 1845

FITZGERALD, Edward 1809–83
In A Persian Garden (*m* Liza LEHMANN) 1896

FITZGERALD, John 1838–1912
Old England And Our Queen (*w* George R. SIMS) *c*.1875

FITZGIBBON, Dave
Brand New Millionaire (*w* William JEROME & Walter DE FRECE) 1894
Man Who Broke The Brokers Down In Wall Street, The (*w* JEROME) 1894

FLAGG, Ellen H.
Waiting (*m* Harrison MILLARD) 1867

FLANAGAN, Bud° 1896–1968
Underneath The Arches (*w&m* FLANAGAN, additional *w* Joseph MCCARTHY) 1926

FLEESON, Neville 1887–1945
I'll Be With You In Apple Blossom Time (& Albert VON TILZER) 1920
Say It With Flowers (& VON TILZER) 1919

FLETCHER, R.
Carol Of The English Race, A (*m* Frank ISITT) 1894

FLORENCE, W. J. 1831–91
Bobbin' Around (arr. J. H. TULLY) *c*.1856
Emmer Jane 1862
Ridin' In A Railroad Keer 1862

FLOTOW, Friedrich von 1812–83
M'Appari Tutt'Amor (orig. Ach! So
   Fromm; Eng. Ah! So Pure) 1846
   See also CORE SONG-LIST.

FLYNN, John H. 1869–1926
Yip-I-Addy-I-Ay (w Will D. COBB; Eng.
   w George GROSSMITH jun.) London
   1909

FOLEY, Jack d. 20 Apr. 1973?
Old Soldiers Never Die (based on Kind
   Words Can Never Die; w&m Abby
   HUTCHINSON) 1920

FOLI, Madame R. m. Signor Foli°
Love Must Come (m Tito MATTEI)
   1883
Oh, Oh, Hear The Wild Wind Blow
   (m MATTEI) 1872
Star Of Hope, The (m Odoardi BARRI)
   1878
Three Jolly Tars (m Meyer LUTZ) 1876

FOLLOY, Frank
Stop Yer Tickling, Jock! (& Harry
   LAUDER: LAUDER) 1904

FORBES, Cedric
Tale Of Ackmed Kurd, The (m Minnie
   G. CRISPEN) 1925

FORD, George
Lost Child, The (Thomas HOOD: ? arr.
   FORD) 1834

FORD, Harry° 1873–1955
When She Walks (Harry BODEN: & W.
   SKERRY) 1906

FORD, Murray see LE BRETON, John

FORD, Lena Guilbert d. 1918
Keep The Home Fires Burning (orig. Till
   The Boys Come Home) (m Ivor
   NOVELLO) 1914

FORD, Walter H.
Sunshine Of Paradise Alley, The (m John
   W. BRATTON) 1895
Why Did Nellie Leave Her Home?

(w&m George M. COHAN but w
   rewritten FORD) 1894

FOREY, Ed A.
Who Threw The Overalls In Mistress
   Murphy's Chowder? (w&m George L.
   GIEFER, arr. FOREY) 1898

FORMAN, Edmund
Bachelors (w&m Oswald STOLL, arr.
   FORMAN) 1889
Balaclava (Oh, 'Tis A Famous Story)
   (John Arthur ELLIOTT: Slade
   MURRAY, arr. FORMAN) 1884
Cockles And Mussels (w&m James
   YORKSTON, arr. FORMAN) 1884
Come Down And Open The Door, Love
   (A. SUTHERD: Slade MURRAY, arr.
   FORMAN, rev. 1898 C. G. COTES:
   Bennett SCOTT) 1884
Cricket (w H. G. L. MILLS) 1889
Dance With Me (w&m Lester BARRETT,
   arr. FORMAN) 1890
Dear Old Bobs (w Harry HUNTER) 1900
He'll Be Back Bye And Bye (w&m
   Frederick CARLOS, arr. FORMAN)
   1885
I've Got The Ooperzootic (w&m
   CARLOS, arr. FORMAN) 1896
John The Masher (w&m Marcus BOYLE,
   arr. FORMAN) 1884
My Nellie's Blue Eyes (m Venetian air:
   Vieni Sul Mar; parodied by Charles
   COBORN in Two Lovely Black Eyes,
   1886)
Near It (w&m Arthur CORNEY, arr.
   FORMAN) 1887
Oh, What A Wicked Young Man You Are
   (w&m J. STAMFORD, arr. FORMAN)
   c.1882
Pong! Pinga! Pong!
Talkative Man From Poplar, The (w&m
   James McEVOY, arr. FORMAN) 1886
That's When You Feel All Right (Wal
   PINK: Frank P. ALYMER, arr. FORMAN)
   1889
Victoria's Victory (w HUNTER) 1897

Whist! The Bogie Man (British version—
see David BRAHAM) 1890
Who Killed Cock Warren? (*w&m*
Geoffrey THORN; *m* arr. FORMAN)

FORMBY, George° 1877–1921
Did You See The Crowd In Piccadilly?
(& Fred LEIGH & Dan LIPTON)
1905
I Was Standing At The Corner Of The
Street (& J. HUNT: FORMBY) 1910
John Willie, Come On 1908
Playing The Game In The West (& Alec
KENDAL) 1910

FORRESTER, Noel d. 1941 pseudonym
of E. G. Butler
Walter! Walter! Lead Me To The Altar
(& Will E. HAINES & Jimmy HARPER)
1937

FOSTER, Stephen Collins 1826–64
Beautiful Dreamer 1864
Camptown Races, The 1850
Come Where My Love Lies Dreaming
1855
Gentle Annie 1856
Hard Times Come Again No More 1854
Jeanie With The Light Brown Hair 1854
Luleana
Massa's In De Cold, Cold Ground 1852
My Baby
My Old Kentucky Home 1853
Nelly Bly 1850
Nelly Was A Lady 1849
Oh! Susanna 1848
Old Black Joe 1860
Old Dog Tray 1853
Old Folks At Home (Way Down Upon
The Swanee River) 1851
Old Uncle Ned 1848
Open Thy Lattice, Love 1842
Ring De Banjo 1853
Some Folks Do 1855
Willie We Have Missed You 1855

Fox, G. D. (George?) 1848?–1902?
Bye Bye Betsy (*w* Paul MILL) 1896

Lucindah At The Windah (*w* Harry
HUNTER) 1884
Oh, The Kharki! 1900
Over The Garden Wall (*w* HUNTER)
1880
Peg Leg Polly (*w* HUNTER)
Penny Whistler, The (*w* MILL) 1896

Foy, Bryan 1894–1977
Mr Gallagher & Mr Shean (*m* Ed
GALLAGHER & Al SHEAN) *c*.1920

FRAGSON, Harry° 1869–1913
All The Girls Are Lovely By The
Seaside (*w* Worton DAVID & Bert
LEE) 1913
Band Box Girl, The (*w* W. DAVIDSON &
A. WIMPERIS) 1907
Hello! Hello! Who's Your Lady Friend?
(*w* DAVID & LEE) 1913

FRAME, W. F.° 1848–1919
Cockalorum (*w* Forbes DAWSON) 1896

FRANKLIN, Jennie°
Artful Maiden, The 1893
Don't It Make Him Look A Fool! 1892
I Met A Lubly Gal 1892
Ladies' Orchestra, The 1894
Wickedest Girl At School, The
Yawning 1892
Yodelling Song (I Keep On Mit Mine
Cry) 1892

FRASER, Marjorie Kennedy°
1857–1930
Eriskay Love Lilt, An (Kenneth
MACLEOD: trad., arr. FRASER) 1909
Road To The Isles, The (*w* MACLEOD)
1915

FRASER-SIMSON, H. 1873–1944
Love Will Find A Way (*w* Harry
GRAHAM) 1916
'Ow I 'Ate Women (*w* Percy
GREENBANK) 1924

FREEAR, Willie° d. 28 Dec. 1889?
Absent Minded Rooster, The 1897

Mrs Isaac Walton Moon (*w* Alf WOOD) 1896

FRENCH, Arthur W.
Barney Take Me Home Again (*m* G. W. PERSLEY) 1889
Won't You Buy My Pretty Flowers? (*m* G. W. PERSLEY) 1876

FRENCH, Fred° 1830–99
Advertisements (*w* H. J. WHYMARK) 1871
Destitute Orphans, The (*w* W. W. THORNTON) 1893
When These Old Clothes Were New (*w* Fred PERRY) 1867

FRENCH, Percy° 1854–1920
Abdalla-Bulbul Ameer (rev. Frank CRUMIT 1927) 1877
Are Ye Right There, Michael? (*m* W. Houston COLLISSON) 1902
Eileen Oge (*m* COLLISSON) 1908
Mountains Of Mourne, The (air, Bendemeer's Stream) 1896
Phil The Fluter's Ball 1889
Slattery's Mounted Foot *c*.1914

FRIEDMAN, Jake 1867–d. 4 Aug 1965?
Strawberries In Cream 1902

FRIEDMAN, Leo 1869–1927
Let Me Call You Sweetheart (*w* Beth Slater WHITSON) 1910
Meet Me Tonight In Dreamland (*w* WHITSON) 1909

FULMER, H. J. 1841–1902 a.k.a. Charles E. PRATT
Wait Till The Clouds Roll By (*w* J. T. WOOD) 1881

FURBER, Douglas 1886–1961
Lambeth Walk, The (& L. Arthur ROSS: Noel GAY) 1937
Limehouse Blues (*m* Philip BRAHAM) 1922

FYFFE, Will° 1885–1947
Come And See The Baby (inspired by the birth of Will Fyffe jun.) 1927
Daft Sandy *c*.1917
Engineer, The *c*.1917
I Belong To Glasgow (see CORE SONG-LIST) *c*.1920
I'm 94 This Mornin' *c*.1921
Mrs McKie (Ah'm Fear'd For) *c*.1930
Sailing Up The Clyde *c*.1927
Sandy's Holiday *c*.1920

FYLEMAN, Rose 1877–1957
There Are Fairies At The Bottom Of Our Garden (*m* Liza LEHMANN) 1907

GABRIEL, Virginia 1825–77; later known as Mary Ann Virginia March
Dream, Baby, Dream (*w* B. CORNWALL) 1862
Far Away In The West (*w* Meta ORRED) 1876
Forsaken, The (*w* Hamilton AÏDÉ) 1861
My Secret (*w* H. MERIVALE) 1870
Nightfall At Sea (*w* A. MATTHISON) 1865
Parted (*w* Russell GRAY) 1873
Sacred Vows (*w* GRAY) 1865
Somebody's Darling *c*.1875
Voices Calling (*w* GRAY) 1869

GALLAGHER, Ed°
Mr Gallagher & Mr Shean (Bryan FOY: & Al SHEAN) *c*.1920

GALLOWAY, Tod B. 1863–1935
Whiffenpoof Song, The (Rudyard KIPLING & others: Guy S. SKULL, adap. GALLOWAY) *c*.1909
See CORE SONG-LIST.

GANTHONY, Nellie
Khaki (*w* Arthur A. SYKES) 1900

GANTHONY, Robert° 1849–1931
Half Back's Farewell, The 1893
Hey Down Derry 1894

In The Twilight 1893
Pierrot Inquisition, The 1893
Sambo's Serenade 1893
Venice In London 1892

GANZ, Wilhelm 1833–1914
Murmuring Sea, The (*w* ZEILA) 1859
Nightingale's Trill, The (*w* ZEILA) 1866
Sing Birdie Sing (*w* ZEILA) 1859
Sing, Sweet Bird (*w* L. W. THORNTON)
1872

GARRICK, David 1717–79
Heart Of Oak (*m* William BOYCE) 1759

GARRICK, Gus°
Dr Bogie (& Mark LORNE)

GATTY, Alfred Scott *see* SCOTT-GATTY,
Sir Alfred

GAUNT, Percy 1852–96
Bowery, The (Charles HOYT: GAUNT
adap. La Spagnola, Neapolitan air)
1891
See Fred GILBERT for UK version known
as Brighton.

GAY, Noel 1898–1954; pseudonym of
Richard Armitage
Lambeth Walk, The (*w* Douglas FURBER
& L. Arthur ROSE) 1937
Me And My Girl (*w* FURBER & ROSE)
1937
Only A Glass Of Champagne (*w* Arthur
WIMPERIS) 1939

GEDDES, Will
Don't Go Down In The Mine, Dad
(*w* Robert DONNELLY) 1910

GEEHL, Henry E. 1881–1947
For You Alone (*w* P. J. O'REILLY) 1909

GEOGHEGAN, Joseph B. d. Jan. 1889
England Is England Still 1886
Frenchman, The 1878
It's Really A Dreadful Affair (*m* Harry
LISTON)

Roger Ruff *or* A Drop Of Good Beer
1860
They All Have A Mate But Me 1870

GEORGE, G. H.
Oh! Don't I Love My Billy (*m* E. W.
MACKNEY) *c*.1862
Sambo's Apparition (*m* MACKNEY)
c.1862

GERARD, R. Husch 1876–1948
You're The Flower Of My Heart
(Sweet Adeline) (*m* Harry
ARMSTRONG) 1903

GERMAN, Sir Edward 1862–1936
English Rose, The (*w* Basil HOOD)
1902
Glorious Devon (*w* Harold BOULTON)
1905
Have You News Of My Boy Jack?
(*w* Rudyard KIPLING) 1914
O Peaceful England (*w* HOOD) 1902
Waltz Song (For Tonight) (*Tom Jones*) (*w*
Charles H. TAYLOR) 1907
Yeomen Of England (*w* HOOD) 1902

GERSHWIN, George 1898–1937
Swanee (*w* Irving CAESAR) 1919
When You Want 'Em You Can't Get 'Em
1916

GIBSON, Fred d. 30 May 1955
He Led Me Up The Garden (*w* E. A.
SEARSON) 1929

GIDEON, Melville° 1884–1933
I'm Tickled To Death I'm Single
I'm In Love With A Girl In A Crinoline
Gown

GIEFER, George L.
Who Threw The Overalls In Mistress
Murphy's Chowder? (arr. Ed A.
FOREY) 1898

GIFFON, Henry
Boy Wot Visits The Palace, The (*w&m*
James BRUTON, arr. GIFFON) *c*.1840

GIFFORD, Hon. Mrs G. R. *c*.1830–71
Golden Days (*m* CLARIBEL) 1865
Take Back The Heart (*m* CLARIBEL) 1865
When I Was Young And Fair (*m* CLARIBEL) *c*.1865

GIFFORD, Harry° d. 8 Jan. 1960
Give Me A Cosy Parlour (& Alf J. LAWRANCE & Tom MELLOR) 1907
Hey! Ho! Can't You Hear The Steamer? (*m* Fred GODFREY) *c*.1913
I Like Your Old French Bonnet (& LAWRANCE & MELLOR) 1909
Is Anybody Looking For A Widow? 1908
I Want To Go To Idaho (& LAWRANCE & MELLOR) 1908
Kitty, The Telephone Girl (& LAWRANCE & MELLOR & Huntley TREVOR) 1912
My Castle In Spain (MELLOR: & LAWRANCE) 1906
She Sells Sea-Shells (*w* Terry SULLIVAN) 1908
We're Irish And Proud Of It Too (& GODFREY & MELLOR) 1914
What A Game It Is! Wow! Wow! (& GODFREY) 1913

GILBERT, B. J.
She's So Much Like You, Mother (*m* Ernest R. BALL) 1906

GILBERT, Frederick 1849–1903
At Trinity Church I Met My Doom 1894
Brighton (*w* Richard MORTON & GILBERT, adap. The Bowery (1891); orig. Charles H. HOYT: Percy GAUNT) 1894
Charlie Dilke Upset The Milk 1885
Down The Road 1893
Dreaming Of Thy Gentle Face 1895
Escaped From The Harem
Faithful *or* A Simple Soldier's Song (*m* Fred EPLETT) 1899
First She Would And Then She Wouldn't 1894
Fresh, Fresh As The Morning 1895

Go And Inform Your Father
Here We Are Again 1911
I'll Place It In The Hands Of My Solicitor 1887
Little Willie's Grave 1874
Long Lost Boy, The 1895
Man That Broke The Bank At Monte Carlo, The 1890
Midnight March, The *c*.1895
Under The May Bush 1874

GILBERT, Joseph Geo. d. 1973
Sarah (Sitting In The Shoe Shine Shop) (& Steve CONLEY & J. G. McHUGH & Joe MACEY) 1919

GILBERT, L. Wolfe 1886–1970
Hitchy-Koo (*m* Lewis F. MUIR & Maurice ABRAHAMS) 1912
Waiting For The Robert E. Lee (*m* MUIR) 1912

GILBERT, Sir William S. 1836–1911
Detective's Song (*m* T. German REED)
Distant Shore, The (*m* Arthur SULLIVAN) 1874
Sweethearts (*m* SULLIVAN) 1875
Yarn Of The Nancy Bell, The *poem* (*m* added Alfred PLUMPTON) 1869

GILL, V. R.
One Of The Deathless Army (& T. W. THURBAN & Will TERRY & Gilbert WELLS) 1910

GILMORE, Patrick S. 1829–92
When Johnny Comes Marching Home 1863

GLENROY, W. B.° pseudonym of William B. GRAY

GLENVILLE, Shaun° 1884–1968
He's A Credit To Ould Ireland Now *c*.1916
If You're Irish Come Into The Parlour (*m* Frank MILLER) 1919

GLINDON, Robert° *c*.1799–1866; all published by John Diprose *c*.1846

Biddy, The Basket Woman
Literary Dustman, The
My Skiff Is On De Shore
Rose Lee

GLOVER, Alfred
Archibald, Certainly Not! (*w* John L. ST
JOHN & George ROBEY) 1909

GLOVER, Charles W. 1806–63
Rose Of Tralee, The (*w* E. Mordaunt
SPENCER) *c*.1850
See William P. MULCHINOCK and CORE
SONG-LIST.

GLOVER, James Mackay 1861–1931
Bai Jove! (*w* H. Chance NEWTON)
1880
Dearie, Dearie 1880
Won't You Join The Army? (*w* George R.
SIMS) 1914

GLOVER, Stephen R. 1812–70
What Are The Wild Waves Saying?
(*w* J. E. CARPENTER) 1850

GLOVER-KIND, John A. *see* KIND, John
A. Glover

GOARD, Henry A.
Gipsy's Warning, The 1864

GODARD, Benjamin L. P. 1849–95
Angels Guard Thee (Berceuse De
Jocelyn) (*w* S. J. REILLY) *c*.1900

GODDARD, J.
Sailor's Farewell (*m* A. E. ARMSTRONG)
1879

GODFREY, Charles° 1852–1900
Golden Wedding, The (*w* Harry ADAMS)
1886
How D'Ye Do, Dear Boy? (*w* ADAMS)

GODFREY, Fred 1880–1953
Bless 'Em All 1916
Hello! There, Flanagan (& A. J. MILLS
& Bennett SCOTT) 1909
Here We Are Again! (& Billy WILLIAMS)
1911

Hey! Ho! Can't You Hear The Steamer?
(*w* Harry GIFFORD) *c*.1913
I Can't Help Loving A Girl Like You
(*w* Dan LIPTON) 1908
In A Cheap Excursion Train (& Harry
CASTLING) 1908
Kangaroo Hop, The (& WILLIAMS) 1912
Molly O'Morgan (& Will LETTERS) 1909
Now I Have To Call Him Father
(& Charles COLLINS) 1908
Take Me Back To Dear Old Blighty
(& MILLS & SCOTT) 1916
They All Look Alike In The Dark
(& MILLS & SCOTT) 1918
We're Irish And Proud Of It (& Tom
MELLOR & Harry GIFFORD) 1914
What A Game It Is! Wow! Wow!
(& GIFFORD) 1913
Who Were You With Last Night?
(& Mark SHERIDAN) 1912
Yiddisher-Irish Baby, The (& Worton
DAVID & Lawrence WRIGHT) 1915

GODWIN, Will J.° 1859–1913
Broken Vow, The 1895
Glorious Beer (*w* Steve LEGGETT) 1895
Hand Of Justice, The (sk.)
Hi Diddle Diddle Um 1893
Hurrah For The Horse And Hound
1898
If Those Lips Could Only Speak!
(& Chas. RIDGWELL) 1905
I Want To Play With Little Dick 1897
Miner's Dream Of Home, The (& Leo
DRYDEN) 1891
Nineteenth Century Boys, The (*m*
Orlando POWELL); sung by Fannie
Leslie and Will Godwin
For song with same title see Arthur
J. LAMB: William Frederick PETERS.
Saved (sk.)
Severed *or* The Broken Pledge 1896
That's Why I Enlisted For A Soldier
1899
Till Six O'Clock In The Morning
(*m* POWELL) 1893

Twenty Years Ago (A Mother's Letter)
(& G. B. DAVENPORT: GODWIN)
1897

What Would I Give To Be Home Again
(w Charles WILMOT) 1908

Wire In, My Lads! (m Fred W. LEIGH)
1906

Wit, Woman And Wine 1907

GOETHE, Johann W. von 1749–1832

Erl King, The (m Franz SCHUBERT);
Carl LOEWE 1815

None But The Lonely Heart (Eng. adap.
A. WESTBROOK: Pyotr TCHAIKOVSKI)
1869

Rose Among The Heather (Eng. transl.
N. MACFARREN: SCHUBERT) 1822

GOETZ, E. Ray 1886–1954; m. Irene
Bordoni° (div.)

For Me And My Gal (& Edgar LESLIE &
George W. MEYER) 1917

In The Shadows (m Herman FINCK
1910) 1911

When I Discovered You (& Irving
BERLIN) 1914

GOFF, Lijer pseudonym of William
DAWES

In An Oven With Jerrybim (monologue
from *The Works of Lijer Goff*) 1878

GOLDBERY, Willie

Aubrey Plantagenet (m George LE
BRUNN)

GOLDBURN, Tom

Never Mind (& Harry DENT) 1913

GOLDEN, John L. 1874–1955

Poor Butterfly (m Raymond HUBBELL)
1916

GOLDING, M. E.

Don't Go Out Tonight, Dear Father
(m W. L. THOMPSON) 1889

GOOCH, Walter m. Fannie Leslie° (div.)

Life 1874

Mystery 1874

GOODWIN, Joe 1889–1943

All That I Want Is You (m Jimmie V.
MONACO) 1920

Billy (For When I Walk) (m James
KENDIS & Herman PALEY) 1911

GORDON, Stanley 1870–1938

Merry Vagabonds, The (w Clifton
BINGHAM) 1906

GORDON-LENNOX, Cosmo 1859–1921

Van Dyck, The (sk.) ('from the French')
1907

GORMAN, Robert

Mary And The Butcher (& E. W.
SELMAN) 1907

My Wife's Sister's Cat (w Harry
CHAMPION) 1907

Robin Redbreast 1909

That Funny Little Bobtail Coat (&
CHAMPION & Tom LOWEN) 1907

GOSTLING, F. M.

Thoughts Have Wings (m Liza
LEHMANN) 1909

GOUNOD, Charles 1818–93

Maid Of Athens (w George, Lord
BYRON) 1873

GOWER, R. Fenton

By The Yukon Trail (m J. Milton HAYES)
1913

Dream Ring Of The Desert, The
(m HAYES) 1912

Whitest Man I Know, The (m HAYES)
1914

GRABAN 1868–1946; pseudonym of Sir
Granville Bantock

A. B. C. Girl, The (w HENRY) 1898

Bicycle Belle, A (w Richard HENRY)
1898

I Certainly Expected Something More
Than That (w HENRY) 1898

GRAFF, George jun. 1887–1973

Till The Sands Of The Desert Grow
Cold (m Ernest R. BALL) 1911

Out Where The Blue Begins (& James
Francis McHugh: Bernard F.
Grant) 1923
When Irish Eyes Are Smiling
(& Chauncey Olcott: Ball) 1912

Grafton, Gerald
Fou The Noo (m Harry Lauder) 1905
I Love A Lassie (& Lauder: Lauder)
1905
Is That You, MacAllister? 1907
Piper MacFarlane (& Lauder: Lauder)
1906
Wee Deoch-An-Doris, (Just) A (& Whit
Cunliffe & Lauder) 1910

Graham, Charles d. 1899
Daddy's On The Engine ? (see P. H.
Snape & A. Albert: Sam Potter)
1895
Picture That Is Turned To The Wall, The
(*not* The Picture With Its Face Turned
To The Wall, J. P. Skelly) 1891
Sweethearts Again 1895
Two Little Girls In Blue 1892

Graham, Eric
Golden Dustman, The (m Le Brunn,
George) 1897

Graham, Harry 1875–1936
Love Will Find A Way (m Harold
Fraser-Simson) 1916

Graham, Tom° 1869–97
Baby Language 1895
Facts And Figures 1895
Her Christian Name Was Mary 1895
In The Park (w C. G. Cotes) 1896
I Took It Off 1897
I've Got The Five-Pound Note 1896
Newsboy, The 1896
Our Sal's In The Pantomime 1896
Plenty Of Room 1896
Quips And Cranks 1896
Storyettes 1895
That's All! 1897

Grain, Richard Corney° 1844–95; all
his songs were published by J. Bath after
1882

Banjo Mania 1889
De Ole Umbrella 1890
First Cigar, The (w Arthur Law) 1890
Four-'Oss Sharrybang, The c.1885
He Did And He Didn't Know Why
c.1885
Jarge's Jubilee c.1885
Kicklebury Brown c.1885
My Old Clay Pipe (w Samuel K. Cowan)
c.1880
My Old Dress Suit 1895
Old Couple's Polka, The 1889
Old Trombone, The c.1885
Ole Black 'Oss, The c.1885
Our Servants' Ball c.1885
Polka And The Choirboy, The 1889
To 'Arry! By The Sea!! 1890

Grant, F. Bernard
Out Where The Blue Begins (w George
Graff jun. & James Francis
McHugh) 1923

Grant, Miss Norman°
Did You? (m Godfrey Mayne) 1904
How To Capture Your Prince (mon.)
1914
I'm A Dolly, Just A Dolly (m Mayne)
1905
Just Smile (mon.) c.1918
Orphan, The (mon.) 1914
Ping Went The String 1915
That Wasn't Being Untrue (mon.) c.1918
They Did Not Know (mon.) 1914
When Father Took To Writing Songs

Grantham, W.
Limerick Races, The 1858

Granville-Barker, Harley
1877–1946; m. Lillah McCarthy° (div.)
Half-An-Hour (sk.)

Grattan, Harry° 1867–1951; all
sketches (dates are of Lord Chamber-
lain's licences)
Buying A Gun 1911
Careless Lassie, A 1913
Chorus Girl, A 1914

Curios 1912
Heart Case, A 1912
Her Ladyship 1912
On Duty
Packing Up 1904
Plumbers, The 1909

GRAVES, Alfred Percival 1846–1931
Daisy Chain (*m* Liza LEHMANN) 1893
Father O'Flynn (*m* Charles Villiers
    STANFORD) 1882
Trottin' To The Fair (*m* trad., arr.
    STANFORD) 1901

GRAY, Barry
Fiacre, Le (Eng. *w* GRAY: *m* & Fr. *w* L.
    XANROF) 1892

GRAY, George *c*.1863–*c*.1939
Fighting Parson, The (& Chris DAVIS)
    (sk.) 1903
London And Paris (*m* Herman FINCK)
    c.1895
Love That Kills, The (sk.) 1907
Parson Grey V.C. (sk.) 1907
People's King, The (sk.) 1912
Road To Ruin, The (sk.) (based on
    William Frith's 1880 series of five
    paintings *The Race for Wealth*) 1902

GRAY, George H.
Since My Old Dutch Pegged Out (& G.
    P. HUNTLEY: H. C. BARRY) 1897

GRAY, Russell
Parted (*m* Virginia GABRIEL) 1873
Sacred Vows (*m* GABRIEL) 1865
Voices Calling (*m* GABRIEL) 1869

GRAY, William B.° *c*.1868–1932; a.k.a.
W. B. Glenroy
Face On The Bar-Room Floor, The
    (*m* Henry LAMB)
She Is More To Be Pitied Than
    Censured 1894
Volunteer Organist, The (*m* LAMB) 1893

GRAYDON, J. L. 1844–1919
Covent Garden In The Morning
    (*m* R. COOTE) 1873

GREAVES, H. W.
Keys Of Heaven, The (arr.) 1893

GREEN, Eddie 1901–50
Good Man Is Hard To Find, A 1918

GREEN, Frank W. d. 1884
Blighted Barber, Ye *or* Fe, Fi, Fo, Fum
    (*m* Robert COOTE) 1873
Captain Webb (*m* Alfred LEE) 1875
Clicquot (*m* J. RIVIÈRE) 1870
Cool Burgundy Ben (*m* LEE) *c*.1868
Dolly Varden (*m* LEE) 1870
Floating With The Tide (*m* COOTE)
    1874
Gainsborough Hat (arr. LEE)
Husbands' Boat, The (*m* LEE) 1869
Late Lamented Jones, The *or* The
    Widow (*m* LEE)
Naughty Young Man, The (*m* Alfred G.
    VANCE) 1876
Ring In The Row (arr. LEE)
Rosherville (*m* LEE) *c*.1870
Strolling In The Burlington (*m* LEE)
Tichborne Trial, The (*m* LEE) 1872
Up In The Monument (*m* LEE) 1870
Velocipede, The (*m* LEE)

GREENAWAY, Walter
Baa Baa Baa (*m* Vincent DAVIES) 1882

GREENBANK, Harry H. 1866–99; a.k.a.
Sydney Carlton; brother of Percy
GREENBANK
Afternoon At Home, An (*m* Herbert
    HARRADEN) 1890
Amorous Goldfish, The (*m* Sidney
    JONES) 1896
Chon Kina (*m* JONES) 1896
Gay Bohemi-ah (*m* JONES) 1895
If I Only Knew The Way (*m* Howard
    TALBOT) 1896
Soldiers In The Park (& A. HOPWOOD:
    L. MONCKTON) 1898
Star Of My Soul (*m* JONES) 1896

GREENBANK, Percy 1878–1968; brother
of Harry H. GREENBANK

Half-Past Two (& Arthur WIMPERIS:
Howard TALBOT) 1909
My Own Little Girl (*m* Lionel
MONCKTON) 1902
'Ow I 'Ate Women (*m* Harold FRASER-
SIMSON) 1924
Swing Song, The (& Lilian ELDÉE:
André MESSAGER) 1904
Trot Here And There (& ELDÉE:
MESSAGER) 1904
When You Are In Love (*m* MONCKTON)
1912

GREGG, Hubert 1914–
Maybe It's Because I'm A Londoner
1947

GREY, F. Clifford° 1887–1941
Another Little Drink (*m* Nat D. AYER)
1916
Band Played On, The (*m* Archie NAISH)
1916
For 'Casey would waltz with a strawberry
blonde, etc.' see J. F. PALMER.
Dear Old Shepherd's Bush (*m* AYER)
1916
Fact Is, The (*m* AYER) 1918
First Love—Last Love—Best Love
(*m* AYER) 1918
Furniture Remover, The (*m* Cuthbert
CLARKE) 1922
If You Were The Only Girl In The World
(*m* AYER) 1916
I'm Courtin' Sairey Green (*m* T. C.
Sterndale BENNETT) 1914
In My Museum (*m* BENNETT) 1914
In Other Words (*m* AYER) 1916
Insurance Dream, An (*m* Willie ROUSE)
1912
I Stopped, I Looked, And I Listened (&
AYER: AYER) 1916
It Doesn't Appeal To Me (*m* Bert LEE)
1914
Let The Great Big World Keep Turning
(*m* AYER) 1917
Married v Single (*m* ROUSE) 1912
Nuggets (*m* ROUSE) 1913

Sammy The Dashing Dragoon
(*m* BENNETT) 1914
Thingummy Bobs (& Leonard POUNDS)
c.1919
Vicar And I Will Be There, The (*m*
AYER)
What A Strain (*m* ROUSE) 1914
White Dove, The (*m* Franz LEHÁR) 1912

GREY, Vivian pseudonym of Mabel
McKinley
Anona (*m* Robert A. KING) 1903

GRIMALDI, W.
D'You Know? I Don't Like London
(*w* George VOKES) *c*.1885

GROCK, A.° 1880–1959; better known
simply as Grock, The World's Greatest
Clown
A-Be My Boy (Thomas McGHEE &
Herbert RULE: & L. SILBERMAN)
1919
Back To Dear Old Tennessee (Mason
DIXON: & SILBERMAN) 1916
Do It Again (DIXON: & SILBERMAN &
T. W. THURBAN) 1917
My Colorado Sue (DIXON: & 'partner'—
probably SILBERMAN, Grock's 1918
partner in a music publishing
business)
Yaaki-Daaki Yaaki Dah (Mandy From
Tonypandy) (as for previous entry)
1917

GROSSMITH, George sen.° 1847–1912;
much of his enormous repertoire was
never published
Awful Little Scrub, An 1881
Baby On The Shore, The 1898
Dismal Dinner Party, The 1894
Happy Fatherland, The 1890
He Was A Careless Man 1881
He Went To A Party 1881
I Am So Volatile (*m*?)
Juvenile Party, A (sk.) 1881
Mother And Her Child Were There, The
1890

Muddle-Puddle Porter, The 1884
See Me Dance The Polka 1886
That Everlasting Coon 1898
Too Slow 1876

GROSSMITH, George jun.° 1874–1935
Bedelia (William JEROME: Jean
SCHWARTZ; Eng. w GROSSMITH)
1903
Johnnie At The Gaiety 1895
Leader Of The Labour Party, The
(m Jerome KERN) 1906
Yip-I-Addy-I-Ay (Will D. COBB: John N.
FLYNN; Eng. w GROSSMITH) 1908

GUERNSEY, Wellington 1817–55
Alice, Where Art Thou? (m Joseph
ASCHER) 1861
Mary Blane (m George A. BAKER) 1846

GUEST, John
British Cheer For Plimsoll, A 1875
Certainly Not! 1876

HAINES, Alfred
No! Yes! Well You Ought To Know
(w&m Victor STEVENS, arr. HAINES)
1887

HAINES, Herbert E. 1879–1923
Through The Telephone (w Charles H.
TAYLOR) 1900

HAINES, Tom
Nancy Had A Fancy For Botany
(m Sydney BARNES)
Slate And Pencil Man, The

HAINES, Will E.° d. 23 Nov. 1958
Biggest Aspidistra In The World, The (&
Tommie CONNOR & Jimmy HARPER)
1938
Crocodile Crawl (& Mason DIXON &
Donovan MEHER) 1915
I Never Cried So Much In All My Life
(& Harry CASTLING & HARPER) 1936
They All Had To Get Out In Their
Nighties (w Fred ALLSOPP) 1907
Walter! Walter! Lead Me To The Altar
(& HARPER & Noel FORRESTER) 1937

HALÉVY, Ludovic 1834–1908
Flower Song, The (Carmen) (& Henri
MEILHAC; orig. Eng. transl. Henry
HERSEE (1878): George BIZET)
1875
Habanera (Carmen) (as for previous
entry) 1875
Toreador Song (Carmen) (as for previous
entry) 1875

HALEY, Ed
While Strolling Thru The Park One Day
(& Robert A. KEISER) 1880

HALL, Albert J. 1864–1907
Baby's Name, The (& C. W. MURPHY:
MURPHY) 1900
Bus or Mary Mac Intyre!, The (& Pat
RAFFERTY: RAFFERTY) 1895
English Speaking Race Against The
World, The (m Orlando POWELL)
1898
Floor Gave Way, The (m RAFFERTY, arr.
John S. BAKER) 1893
Good Young Man, The (m Felix
McGLENNON, arr. Peter CONROY)
1896
I'm Going Home To The Wife And
Nipper (m Albert PERRY) 1897
Mother Tongue, The (m George LE
BRUNN) 1898
New Man, The (m POWELL) 1895
Old Man's Darling, An (m POWELL)
1913
See Alan MURRAY & George EVERARD
for song of same title.
Stars Didn't Happen To Be Shining, The
(m MURPHY)
What Do You Think Of The Irish Now?
(& Harry CASTLING) 1900

HALL, Frank° 1836–98 pseudonym of
Herbert Stewart
Did You Ever Feel That Way? 1869
Down In Piccadilly (arr. P. RATHBONE)
c.1862
In The Strand (I Wish I Was With

Nancy) (air, I Wish I Was In Dixie,
Daniel Decatur EMMETT) 1861
See CORE SONG-LIST.
Kleptomania (I Really Couldn't Help It)
(arr. RATHBONE) 1863
La-di-da c.1865
Life Is Like A Game Of Cricket 1873
Only One c.1865
Polly Bluck or Married On Wednesday
(arr. RATHBONE)
Pretty Jemima
Properest Thing To Do, The 1863
Sally Sly 1863

HALL, J. H.
Ever Since The Baby Came 1894
Home! Home!! Home Sweet Home!!! (&
Sam REDFERN, arr. Walter
HARRISON) 1888
Looking For A House To Let (arr.
HARRISON) 1893

HALL, J. W.°
Football Referee, The or I Was The
M.U.G. 1897
He Thinks He's Gone To Bed 1893
I Fished All Day And I Fished All Night
John James 'Enery Irving Wilson Barrett
Baggs
Mouse Ran Under The Bed, The 1896
On Monday She Sings 'Molly Riley, O!'
1896

HALL, Tatten°
Cockney In Kilts, The (w Tom B.
NEWSOME) 1902
Dandy, The 1902

HALL, Wendell Woods° 1896–1969
It Ain't Gonna Rain No Mo' 1923

HALLIDAY, C.
Come Out! (& Austin RUDD) c.1900
They Found Me (w&m RUDD, arr.
HALLIDAY)

HAMILTON, Henry 1853–1918
Private Tommy Atkins (m S. POTTER)
1893

HANBY, Benjamin R.
Darling Nellie Gray c.1850

HANCOCK, James S. see Jimmy HARPER
(2)

HANDY, W. C. 1873–1958
Beale St Blues 1917
St Louis Blues, The 1914

HANDY, Will pseudonym of James
Weldon JOHNSON and his brother
J. Rosamond JOHNSON
Oh, Didn't He Ramble? 1902

HANLEY, James F. 1892–1942
(Back Home In) Indiana (w Ballard
MACDONALD) 1917
Rose Of Washington Square
(w MACDONALD) 1920
Second-Hand Rose (w Grant CLARKE)
1921

HANLEY, T.
Bulls Won't Bellow, The 1880

HANSETT, I.
All Round My Hat (m John VALENTINE;
parody of trad. ballad) 1834

HARBACH, Otto 1873–1963
Cuddle Up A Little Closer, Honey Mine
(m Karl HOSCHNA) 1908
Every Little Movement Has A
Meaning Of Its Own (m HOSCHNA)
1910
Sung by Lina Abarbanell. For Marie
Lloyd's song with same title see Fred
CLIFFE: J. Charles MOORE.

HARDWICK, J. A. 1815–86 a.k.a.
DAGONET
Bloomer Costume, The c.1851
Children Objected To 1866
Cockney Tourist, The (arr. W. WILSON)
c.1855
International 1862 1862
Making A Night Of It
Monster Statue, The 1846
Night In The Workhouse, A

HARFORD, Harold pseudonym of
Harold Lake
I Hear You Calling Me (*m* Charles
   MARSHALL) 1908

HARGREAVES, James a.k.a. MAGINI;
brother of Robert and William
HARGREAVES
A B C D (The Singing Master) 1914
Here's The Thirty Shillings You Paid For
   My Ring 1905
I Put On My Coat And Went Home
   (& William HARGREAVES) 1910
Isn't It A Pity I've To Die? 1904
She Cost Me Seven-and-Sixpence
   (& Sam MAYO) 1904
We Go Like This, We Go Like That
   (& Robert HARGREAVES) 1916
What's Your Sweetheart's Name? 1904

HARGREAVES, Robert 1893–1934;
brother of James and William
HARGREAVES
Riley's Cowshed (& Stanley J.
   DAMERELL) 1924
We Go Like This, We Go Like That
   (& James HARGREAVES) 1916

HARGREAVES, William 1880–1941;
brother of James and Robert HAR-
GREAVES; m. Ella Shields° (div.)
All In A Day (& J. P. HARRINGTON) 1910
Burlington Bertie From Bow 1914
Can London Do Without Me? 1902
Dance With Your Uncle Joseph (& Dan
   LIPTON) 1915
Delaney's Donkey 1921
Do You Want Any Coal? 1908
Give My Regards To Leicester Square
   1905
Goalkeeper, The (Spouty) 1905
If You Want To Have A Row Wait Till
   The Sun Shines 1904
I Know Where The Flies Go (& Harry
   CASTLING) 1920
I Put On My Coat And Went Home
   (& James HARGREAVES) 1910

I've Brought The Coal 1901
Just As The Sun Goes Down 1913
Little Yellow Bird (& C. W. MURPHY)
   1903
Night I Appeared As Macbeth, The 1919
Oh, I Must Go Home Tonight! 1909
P.C. 49 1913
Sparrow On The Workhouse Wall, The
   1909
They Built Piccadilly For Me (Silk Hat
   Tony) 1913
Watching The Trains Go Out 1912
Why Can't It Always Be Saturday? (*w&m*
   Tom MOY, arr. HARGREAVES) *c*.1900

HARNEY, Ben R.° 1871–1938
Mister Johnson, Turn Me Loose 1896
You've Been A Good Old Wagon But
   You've Done Broke Down 1894

HARPER, J. D.
She Is Ma Daisy (& Harry LAUDER)
   1905

HARPER, James/Jimmy 1904–?;
pseudonym of William Harper
We'll Keep A Welcome (& Lyn JOSHUA:
   Mai JONES) (see CORE SONG-LIST)
   1940

HARPER, Jimmy 1910–?; pseudonym of
James S. Hancock
Biggest Aspidistra In The World, The
   (& Tommie CONNOR & Will E.
   HAINES) 1938
I Never Cried So Much In All My Life
   (& Harry CASTLING & HAINES) 1936
Walter! Walter! Lead Me To The Altar
   (& HAINES & Noel FORRESTER)
   1937

HARPER, William *see* HARPER,
JAMES/JIMMY

HARRADEN, Herbert°
Afternoon At Home, An (*w* Harry H.
   GREENBANK) 1890
Good-Bye, Honey 1892
I Pity Him So (Poor Old Jo!) 1886

Parents, The 1882
Photographic Fiend, The 1890
Present Generation, The 1881

HARRIGAN, Edward° 1845–1911
Hildebrandt Montrose (*w* Alfred LEE &
 HARRIGAN) 1871
Maggie Murphy's Home (*m* David
 BRAHAM) 1890
Whist! The Bogie Man (*m* BRAHAM)
 1880; British version Henry PETTITT
 & G. R. SIMS: Meyer LUTZ, arr.
 FORMAN 1890

HARRINGTON, John P. 1865–1939
After The Ball (*m* George LE BRUNN);
 see also CORE SONG-LIST
All In A Day (& William HARGREAVES)
 1910
All The Girls Are Lovely
Always True (*m* Jen LATONA) 1902
And The Leaves Began To Fall (*m* LE
 BRUNN) 1904
As In A Looking Glass (*m* LE BRUNN)
 1889
Bathing (*m* LE BRUNN) 1898
Bella Was A Barmaid (*m* LE BRUNN)
 1902
'Blige A Lady (*m* Orlando POWELL)
 1890
Bluecoat Boy, The (*m* LE BRUNN)
Bond Street Tea-Walk, The (*m* LE
 BRUNN) 1902
Boys Together (*m* POWELL) 1891
Can't You Love Me True? (*m* LATONA)
 1902
City Waif, The (*m* LE BRUNN) 1889
Cock-O'-The-Walk (& Charles BIGNELL:
 LE BRUNN) 1898
Coster's Christening, The (*m* LE BRUNN)
 1904
Coster's Wedding, The *or* The Wedding
 March! 1902
Customs Of The Country (*m* James W.
 TATE) 1906
Doesn't Anybody Want The Curate?
 (*m* LE BRUNN) 1905

'E Ain't Got Nuffin' To Tell (*m* Bennett
 SCOTT) 1896
Emigrant, The (*m* LE BRUNN) 1889
Empty Chair, The (*m* Fred EPLETT)
 c.1895
Everything In The Garden's Lovely
 (*m* LE BRUNN) 1898
Giddy Little Girl Said 'No!', The
 (*m* POWELL) 1894
Girl You Leave Behind You, The
 (*m* LE BRUNN) 1899
Going Home (The Miner's Return)
 (*m* Leo DRYDEN, arr. F. W. VENTON)
 c.1892
Gone Where They Don't Play Billiards
 (& Sam MAYO: MAYO) 1903
Good-bye And God Bless You Jack
 (*m* SCOTT) 1889
Have An Arf O' Gin Old Dear (Tom
 WOOTTWELL: HARRINGTON, arr. Sam
 AARONS) 1906
He Was Thinking! (*m* LATONA) 1902
I Didn't Break The Bank At Monte Carlo
 c.1890
Idler, The (& Richard MORTON:
 LE BRUNN) 1896
I Know Where The Flies Go On A
 Cold And Frosty Morning (& MAYO)
 1920
I Like Your Apron And Your Bonnet
 (*m* Alf J. LAWRANCE) 1911
I'm Looking For Trilby (*m* LE BRUNN)
 1895
India's Reply (*m* LE BRUNN) 1895
In England Now (*m* LE BRUNN) 1888
It's A Pity To Waste The Cake
 (*m* POWELL) 1909
Last Of The Dandies, The (*m* LE
 BRUNN) 1902
 See also F. J. BARNES: Charles COLLINS.
Leave A Little Bit For Your Tutor (*m* LE
 BRUNN) 1901
Looking For A Coon Like Me (*m* LE
 BRUNN) 1894
Maid Of London, 'Ere We Part (& LE
 BRUNN & Joseph TABRAR) 1896

Masks And Faces (*m* LE BRUNN) 1888

Millie! (*m* LE BRUNN) 1901

My Gal (My Sweetheart's My Mammy) 1894

Nation's Soldier Sons!, The (*m* LATONA) 1902

Naughty Continong, The (*m* LE BRUNN)

Naughty! Naughty! Naughty! (*m* LE BRUNN) 1904

Oh, Isn't It Singular? (*m* LE BRUNN) 1903

Put On Your Slippers (*m* POWELL) 1911

Salome (*m* POWELL); see also R. P. WESTON, etc. 1908

Salute My Bicycle (*m* LE BRUNN) 1895

Seven Ages Of Man (*m* LE BRUNN) 1888

Smith, Jones, Robinson And Brown (& MAYO: MAYO) 1910

So Her Sister Says (*m* LE BRUNN) 1894

There's Something About A Soldier (*m* POWELL) 1910

Tilly The Typress (Mum's The Word) (*m* LE BRUNN) 1902

Tricky Little Trilby (*m* LE BRUNN) 1895

Wedding March!, The *or* The Coster's Wedding (*m* LE BRUNN) 1902

What Britishers Are Made Of (*m* LE BRUNN) 1894

What Will The Neighbours Say? (*m* LE BRUNN) 1900

Why Do The Boys Run After Me? (*m* LE BRUNN) 1904

Wrong Man, The (*m* LE BRUNN) 1890

You Ain't Ashamed O' Me, Are You, Bill? (*m* LE BRUNN) 1904

You're A Thing Of The Past, Old Dear (*m* LE BRUNN) 1905

HARRIS, Sir Augustus 1852–96
Masher's Quadrille, The 1883

HARRIS, Charles K. 1867–1930
After The Ball 1892
See also CORE SONG-LIST.
Break The News To Mother 1897
Don't Give Me Diamonds, All I Want Is You 1910

For Sale, A Baby 1903

Hello Central, Give Me Heaven 1901

Kiss And Let's Make Up 1891

Last Farewell, The 1903

She Has Fallen By The Wayside 1892

There'll Come A Time Some Day 1895

HARRIS, F. Clifford *c.*1875–1949
Bachelor Gay, A (& VALENTINE: James W. TATE) 1916

Broken Doll, A (*m* TATE) 1915

Ev'ry Little While (*m* TATE) 1916

Give Me A Little Cosy Corner (*m* TATE) 1918

Instinct (*m* Liza LEHMANN, adap. TATE) 1904

It's Lovely To Be In Love (*m* TATE) 1915

I Was A Good Little Girl Till I Met You (*m* TATE) 1914

My Actor Man (*m* TATE) 1913

Paradise For Two, A (& VALENTINE: TATE) 1916

Story Of A Clothes Line, The (*m* TATE) 1904

There'll Be Some Dirty Weather Around The Needles 1914

HARRIS, H. L.
Three Green Bonnets (*m* Guy D'HARDELOT) 1901

HARRIS, Leslie°
Dream Of An 'At Home', A (*w* Mel B. SPURR) 1896

Ladies' Penny Paper, The 1898

Wiggley Waggley Japanese, The 1898

HARRIS-WESTON *see* WESTON, R. Harris

HARRISON, Annie F. *see* HILL, Lady Arthur

HARRISON, E. Denham° d. 1945
Give Me A Ticket To Heaven (& Richard ELTON) 1903

Hush Hush Hush! (Dolly Song) (*w* Harry ADAMS) 1899

Lecturer, The (*w* Dan LENO & T. B. SEDGWICK)

HARRISON, J. M.
Only A Few Miles Of Water (*w* Harry WRIGHT) 1895
On The Banks Of Bantry Bay (*w* H. A. DUFFY) 1894
Side By Side (Harry ADAMS: HARRISON, arr. John S. BAKER) 1891
Simple Little Maid In The Corner, The (*w* H. A. DUFFY) 1896

HARRISON, R.
Be Always Up And Doing, Boys! (*m* David G. DAY)

HARRISON, Walter
Home! Home!! Home Sweet Home!!! (J. H. HALL & Sam REDFERN, arr. HARRISON) 1888
Looking For A House To Let (*w&m* HALL, arr. HARRISON) 1893

HARROWAY, J.
Alonzo The Brave (Sam COWELL: arr. HARROWAY) *c*.1850
See also E. L. BLANCHARD.
On Alma's Heights (*w* T. WALKER)

HART,? E. A.?
Love 'Em And Leave 'Em Alone

HART, Geoffrey
Other Side Of The Curtain, The

HASTINGS, Ernest°
Exemptions And Otherwise (*m* R. P. WESTON & Bert LEE) 1916
Hobbies (sk.) (*w* J. Hickory WOOD) 1902
Irish Walk (*w* WOOD) 1903

HASTINGS, Fred°
Can I Be Of Any Assistance? (*w* E. A. SEARSON) 1907
I Was Shaving Myself At The Time 1905
See-Saw 1906

HASTINGS, Walter
Me And 'Er (*m* Geo. LE BRUNN) 1894

My Father Was Never A Marquis (*m* William BINT) 1887
Song Of The Thrush, The (*m* LE BRUNN) 1897
So Was Mine (*m* William BINT, arr. Warwick WILLIAMS) 1889
Where Are Those Boys? (arr. H. MASSEDER) 1889

HATTON, John Liptrot° 1809–86
Shall I Wasting In Despair? (*w* George WITHER) 1869
Simon The Cellarer (*w* W. H. BELLAMY) 1847
To Anthea (*w* Robert HERRICK) 1850
Wreck Of The Hesperus, The (*w* Henry W. LONGFELLOW) 1853

HAVEZ, Jean 1874–1925
Everybody Works But Father 1905

HAWKER, Revd Robert S. 1803–75
Trelawney (Song Of The Western Men) (*m* George Bown MILLETT) 1886

HAWTHORNE, Alice pseudonym of Septimus WINNER
Listen To The Mocking Bird (*m* Richard MILBURN?) 1854

HAYDEN, Joe *c*.1845–1916
Hot Time In The Old Town, A (*m* Theodore M. METZ) 1896

HAYDEN-CLARENDON, J.°
Practical Impossibilities (*m* George LE BRUNN) 1898
Question Of Time, A (*m* Claude ARUNDALE) 1897
Some Things Are Better Left Unsaid (& Charles H. HOYT: Richard STAHL) 1896

HAYDON, John S. 1837–1907
Booze Is There (*m* Sam REDFERN) 1890
I'll Bet You A Dollar You Don't (*m* REDFERN) 1881

That's The Sort Of Men We Want In England Here Today (*m* Vincent DAVIES) 1887

HAYES, Billie
I Ain't 'Arf A Lucky Kid (*w* Charles HAYES) 1914

HAYES, Charles
I Ain't 'Arf A Lucky Kid (*m* Billie HAYES) 1914

HAYES, J. Milton° 1884–1940
By The Yukon Trail (*m* R. Fenton GOWER) 1913
Dream Ring Of The Desert, The (*m* GOWER) 1912
Green Eye Of The Little Yellow God, The (*m* Cuthbert CLARKE) 1911
Meanderings Of Monty, The (series of recitations) from 1927
Whitest Man I Know, The (*m* GOWER)

HAYNES, W. Battison 1859–1900
Off To Philadelphia (rev. & ed. S. TEMPLE: air, trad. Irish, arr. HAYNES) 1889

HAYS, Will S. 1837–1907
Driven From Home 1868

HAYWARD, C. Flavell
War Song, A (*m* Edward ELGAR) 1903

HEATH, Harry
Federation Day (*m* Will HYDE) 1906

HEELAN, Will A.
I'd Leave My Happy Home For You (*m* Harry VON TILZER) 1899

HEIN, Silvio 1879–1928
Moonshine (*w* E. MONTAGU) 1906
When You're All Dressed Up And No Place To Go (*w* Benjamin Hapgood BURT) 1913

HEINE, Heinrich 1797–1856
E'en As A Lonely Flower (K. R. KROCKER after HEINE: Frank BRIDGE) 1905

Invocation (Eng. *w* adap. J. BARBER: Guy D'HARDELOT) 1894
On Wings Of Song (Eng. *w* Delia STUART: Felix MENDELSSOHN) 1834

HEMANS, Felicia D. 1793–1835
Better Land, The (*m* Frederich M. COWEN) *c*.1880
Stately Homes Of England, The (*m* J. C. J. HOBY) 1905

HENDERSON, Gilbert *see* WELLS, Gilbert

HENLEY, William E. 1849–1903
England My England (*m* Mary ALLITSEN) 1900

HENRY, Richard 1854–1931; pseudonym of Richard Butler and H. Chance NEWTON
A.B.C. Girl, The (*m* GRABAN) 1898
Bicycle Belle, A (*m* GRABAN) 1898
I Certainly Expected Something More Than That (*m* GRABAN) 1898

HENRY, Roland°
When Daddy Comes Home Tonight 1896

HENSON, Edward J.
All Right, Thanks! (*w&m* Harry BRETT, arr. HENSON)
Poor Old Uncle Jones! (BRETT: BRETT & HENSON) 1895

HENTY, Dick°
Murders (& Louis RIHILL) *c*.1914
Postman's Knock 1926
Turrible Shy Wi' The Maids 1927

HERBERT, Annie Brice
When The Mists Have Rolled Away (*m* Ira David SANKEY) 1883

HERBERT, Victor 1859–1924
Grandson of Samuel LOVER.
Ah! Sweet Mystery Of Life (*w* Rida Johnson YOUNG) 1910

Art Is Calling For Me (*w* Harry B. SMITH) 1911

If I Were On The Stage (Kiss Me Again) (*w* Henry BLOSSOM) 1905

I'm Falling In Love With Someone (*w* YOUNG) 1910

Kiss In The Dark, A (*w* Buddy DESYLVA) 1922

Kiss Me Again *see* If I Were On The Stage

Woman Is Only A Woman But A Good Cigar Is A Smoke, A (*w* H. B. SMITH) 1905

HERBERT, Will 1844?–96?
What Cheer Ria (*w* Bessie BELLWOOD) 1885

HÉROS, Eugène 1860–1925
Larmes, Les (Oh, Dry Those Tears) (*m* Teresa DEL RIEGO) 1904

HERRICK, Robert 1591–1674
Cherry Ripe (*m* Charles Edward HORN) 1824
To Anthea (*m* J. L. HATTON) 1850

HERSEE, Henry
Flower Song, The (*Carmen*) (Henri MEILHAC & L. HALÉVY (1875); orig. Eng. transl. HERSEE: Georges BIZET) 1878
Habanera (*Carmen*) (as for Flower Song) 1878
Toreador Song (*Carmen*) (as for Flower Song) 1878

HEYDUK, Adolph 1835–1923
Songs My Mother Taught Me (HEYDUK, transl. Natalie MACFARREN: Antonin DVOŘÁK) 1880

HEYWOOD, Thomas *c.*1574–1641
Pack, Clouds, Away (*m* George A. MACFARREN) 1867

HICKMAN, Charles d. 10 Nov. 1935?
Chap Wot Sings Outside The Pubs, The 1889

On A Bright Summer's Day 1902
Scandals Are 'Cuming', The (Baccarat Song) (arr. Warwick WILLIAMS) 1891
They Never Will Invite You Any More (& G. W. HUNTER: HUNTER) 1889

HICKS, Sir Seymour° 1871–1954
'Ackney With The 'Ouses Took Away (*m* Walter SLAUGHTER) 1901
After The Honeymoon (sk.)
Dress Rehearsal, A (sk.) (& A. C. ROBATT) 1907

HILBURY, C. E.
Oh, Amelia (*w* Fred MURRAY) 1906

HILL, Alfred 1870–1960
Waiata Poi 1908

HILL, Lady Arthur 1851–1944; née Annie Fortescue Harrison
In The Gloaming (*w* Meta ORRED) 1877
Let Me Forget Thee (*w* H. L. D'Arcy JAXONE) 1887

HILL, Mildred J. 1859–1916
Happy Birthday To You (*w* Patty Smith HILL) *m* 1893 *w* 1935

HILL, Patty Smith 1868–1916
Happy Birthday To You (*m* Mildred J. HILL) *m* 1893 *w* 1935

HIMAN, Alberto
Curfew Shall Not Ring Tonight, The (*w* G. HORR) 1882

HIME, Edward L. J. 1823–1900
Annie And Ronald (*w* Stewart FARQUHARSON) 1849
I'll Dream Of Thee (*w* FARQUHARSON) 1849
I Met Her On A Monday
I'm Lonely In The Old House Now (*w* FARQUHARSON) 1850
Look Always On The Sunny Side (*w* FARQUHARSON) 1849

HIRSCH, Louis A. 1887–1924
Gaby Glide, The (*w* Harry PILCER) 1911

How Do You Do, Miss Ragtime? 1912

Who's The Lady Now? (& George ARTHURS) 1914

HIRSCH, Walter b. 1891

Horsey, Keep Your Tail Up (& Walter KAPLAN) 1923

HOARE, Florence

All Through The Night (air, trad.)

Greensleeves (trad. attr. Henry VIII, arr. HOARE)

HOBBS, John William 1799–1877

Phillis Is My Only Joy (*w* Charles SEDLEY)

HOBSON, Martin 1833–80

Bear It Like A Man (*w&m* Harry CLIFTON, arr. HOBSON) *c*.1865

Carry Your Friend In Your Pocket 1865

Complaints or The Ills Of Life With Their Remedies (*w&m* Edward TERRY, arr. and partly composed HOBSON) 1869

Grecian Bend, The (*w&m* G. W. MOORE, arr. HOBSON) 1870

Happy Policeman, The (*w&m* CLIFTON, arr. HOBSON)

I Likes A Drop Of Good Beer (anon., arr. HOBSON) 1875

Jones's Musical Party (*w&m* CLIFTON, arr. HOBSON) 1864

Motto For Every Man, A (*w&m* CLIFTON, arr. HOBSON) *c*.1865

Never Push A Man When He's Going Down (*w&m* Harry LINN, arr. HOBSON) 1869

'Norrible Tale, A (The Suicidal Family) (*w&m* E. L. BLANCHARD, arr. HOBSON) 1865

Also adapted by H. J. WHYMARK.

Paddle Your Own Canoe (*w&m* CLIFTON, arr. HOBSON) 1866

Rocky Road To Dublin, The 1865

Shelling Green Peas (*w&m* CLIFTON, arr. HOBSON) 1866

There's A Smile Waiting For Me At Home (*w&m* CLIFTON, arr. HOBSON) 1860

Ticket Of Leave Man, The (*w* Alfred G. VANCE) 1865

Wish, The

HOBY, J. C. J.

Stately Homes Of England, The (*w* Felicia D. HEMANS) 1905

HODDER, G.

Order Of Valour, The (*m* W. H. WEISS) 1857

HODSON, George A.° *c*.1798–1863

He Knew She Never Blamed Him (*w* T. Haynes BAYLY) 1834

March Away (*w&m* George CROAL, arr. HODSON) *c*.1834

O Give Me But My Arab Steed (*w* William McGHIE) 1830

Tell Me Mary How To Woo Thee (*w* F. MORRISON) *c*.1830

Who'll Have Me? 1851

HOGAN, Ernest° *c*.1865–1909

All Coons Look Alike To Me (*w* Richard MORTON) 1896

HOLLIDAY, Fred

It Must Have Been The Lobster (A. R. MARSHALL: Harriet FAWN, arr. HOLLIDAY) 1894

HOLLOWAY, Stanley° 1890–1982

Old Sam (Sam, Pick Oop Tha' Musket) (*m* Wolseley CHARLES) 1930

HOLMANS, G.

Hampstead Is The Place To Ruralize (*w&m* Watkyn WILLIAMS, arr. HOLMANS) 1861

HOLT, Fred d. 5 Dec. 1947

Come On Steve (& Herbert RULE)

Have You Paid The Rent? (& RULE & L. SILBERMAN) 1922

Only A Working Man (& RULE) 1923

Ours Is A Nice 'Ouse (& RULE) 1921

HOOD, Basil 1864–1917
English Rose, The (*m* Edward GERMAN)
1902
Merry Widow Waltz (*m* Franz LEHÁR)
Vienna 1905, London 1907
O Peaceful England (*m* GERMAN)
1902
Orlando Dando (*m* Walter SLAUGHTER)
1898
Yeomen Of England (*m* GERMAN) 1902

HOOD, Thomas 1799–1845
Ben Battle (*m* arr. Jonathan BLEWITT)
c.1840
Words from Hood's poem *Faithless Nelly
Gray*; set by at least five others.
Lost Child, The (*m* ?, arr. George FORD)
1834
Mary's Ghost (*m* BLEWITT)
Also set by Maude Valérie WHITE.
Our Hands Have Met But Not Our
Hearts (The False Friend) (*m* W.
Vincent WALLACE) 1846
Song Of The Shirt (*m* BLEWITT, arr.
J. TULLY) 1843
See also Henry RUSSELL: Arthur
H. BEHREND.

HOOK, James 1746–1827
Lass Of Richmond Hill (*w* Leonard
McNALLY) 1789
Within A Mile Of Edinbro' Town
(*w* partly by Tom D'URFEY) 1780

HOPE, Laurence 1865–1904 pseudo-
nym of Adela Florence Cory
Four Indian Love Lyrics, including
Kashmiri Song a.k.a. Pale Hands I
Loved (extracted from *The Garden of
Kama*) (*m* Amy WOODFORDE-
FINDEN) 1902

HOPWOOD, Aubrey
Soldiers In The Park (& H. GREENBANK:
L. MONCKTON) 1898

HORN, Charles E.° 1786–1849
Cherry Ripe (*w* Robert HERRICK) 1824

Deep, Deep Sea, The (*w* Mrs George
SHARP) 1830

HORNCASTLE, George
Another Glass Round (*m* Harriet AWN)
1888
Below! Below!! Below!!! (*m* John COOKE
jun., arr. John S. BAKER) 1888
Bill-Poster, The (& Tom BASS; *m* arr.
Alfred LEE) 1892
Different Styles Of Singing (Some Sang
High, Some Sang Low) 1891
It Makes A Fellow Think A Bit
(*m* FAWN) 1894
Pair Of Spectacles, A (& A. E.
DURANDEAU) 1891
She Wasn't Far Off It (*m* FAWN) 1889
Single Gentleman, The 1894
Sir Garnet Will Show Them The Way
(*m* Harry BALL)
So It Was! (*m* COOKE) 1887
There Ain't A Word (*m* FAWN) 1892
Wrong Way, The (*m* FAWN) 1888

HORR, G.
Curfew Shall Not Ring Tonight, The
(*m* Alberto HIMAN) 1882

HORWITZ, Charles 1864–1938
I'm The Bosom Friend Of Albert,
Prince Of Wales (*m* F. V. BOWERS)
1891
Oh, Lucky Jim (*m* BOWERS) 1896

HOSCHNA, Karl 1877–1911
Cuddle Up A Little Closer, Honey Mine
(*w* Otto HARBACH) 1908
Every Little Movement Has A Meaning
Of Its Own (*w* HARBACH) 1910
Sung by Lina Abarbanell. For Marie
Lloyd's song with same title see Fred
CLIFFE: J. Charles MOORE.
Yahama! (*w* De Lucien BOYER) 1909

HOUGH, William 1882–1962
I Wonder Who's Kissing Her Now?
(& Frank R. ADAMS: Harry ORLOB
& Joseph H. HOWARD) 1909

HOUGHTON, Lord 1809–85; Richard Monckton Milnes
Strangers Yet (*m* CLARIBEL) 1867
Don' You Wish You Could? 1894

HOUSMAN, A. E. 1859–1936
Loveliest Of Trees (*A Shropshire Lad*) (thirty-four known settings) 1896
When I Was One-And-Twenty (1896) (set to music by Arthur SOMERVELL and Stephen ADAMS (1904); also some thirty-two others)

HOWARD, Carl
Emilina Brown (*w* Jay LAURIER) 1920
Harum Scarum Girl
Hiawatha On The Brain 1904
I Don't Know What To Do (& George BASTOW) 1903
Little Bit Of Luck, A (arr. John S. BAKER) 1897
Oh! Trilby, What Have You Done For Me? 1896
Oh! What A Wicked World We Live In! (& Harry LEIGHTON) 1899
Parapher-Paraphernalia (& George EVERARD) 1898
Popular Nursery Rhymes Medley (arr. BAKER) 1893
She Was Such A Nice Young Girl (& BASTOW) 1903
To Celebrate The Diamond Jubilee 1897
Uncle's Trombone 1894
Usual Morning Performance, The (& LEIGHTON) 1895
Wanted—A Lady (& EVERARD) 1899
What Cheer, Trilby! 1896
While The Bells Were Ringing 1897

HOWARD, Frank 1850–1915
Only A Pansy Blossom (*w* Eben REXFORD) 1883
When The Robins Nest Again 1883

HOWARD, H. H.
Am I Right Or Any Other Man? (*w&m* G. W. HUNT, arr. HOWARD) 1862

Whole Hog Or None, The (George WARE: E. W. MACKNEY, arr. HOWARD) 1855
For a song of the same title see T. WESTROP.

HOWARD, Joseph E.° 1878–1961
Central, Give Me Back My Dime 1905
Goodbye, My Lady Love (arr. Al LA RUE) 1904
Hello! My Baby (*w* Ida EMERSON) 1899
I Wonder Who's Kissing Her Now? (Frank R. ADAMS & William HOUGH: & Harry ORLOB) 1909
Note: although Howard is legally entitled to be credited as co-composer he had no hand in the song's writing.

HOWARD, R.
Ebenezer Tanner
Help One Another Boys
You Never Miss The Water Till The Well Runs Dry

HOWARD, Rowland
When The Cock Begins To Crow (*w* Harry LINN)

HOWARD, Walter° 1847–1905
When The Sun Shines Bright On A Moonlight Night (*w* Harry HUNTER) 1886

HOWE, Julia Ward 1819–1910
Battle Hymn Of The Republic, The (poem 1858: air, adap. Methodist hymn Say Brothers Will You Meet Us, William STEFFE) 1861

HOWELLS, C. E.
Sixty Years! (*w* Alma CURZON & George F. HOWLEY) 1897

HOWLEY, George F.
Sixty Years! (& Alma CURZON: C. E. HOWELLS) 1897

HOYT, Charles H. 1860–1900
Bowery, The (*m* Percy GAUNT, adap. La Spagnola, Neapolitan air) 1891

See also Fred GILBERT.
Some Things Are Better Left Unsaid
(& J. HAYDEN-CLARENDON: Richard
STAHL) 1896

HUBBELL, Raymond 1879–1954
Poor Butterfly (w John L. GOLDEN)
1916

HUBI-NEWCOMBE, Mrs G. 1843–1936
Haven Of Love (m Theodore
PICCOLOMINI) 1897
Maiden In Grey, The (m Reginald S.
BARINCOTT(?)) 1912
Whisper And I Shall Hear (m
PICCOLOMINI) 1897
Within Your Heart (m Henri TROTÈRE)
1901

HUDSON, H. C.
That's The Latest (& Sam REDFERN:
REDFERN) 1888
Three Makes Jolly Fine Company (&
E. W. ROGERS: Norton ATKINS &
Charles COLLINS) 1903

HUDSON, Thomas° 1791–1844; pub-
lished twelve song collections between
1818 and 1831
Arab Steed, The
Back And Belly c.1825
Betsey Baker c.1829
Dainty Plant Is The Cabbage Green, A
Dog's Meat Man, The
Exile's Adieu, The c.1825
Fight To The Breeches, A c.1829
Follow The Drum c.1840
Ghost Of Kitty Maggs, The
Hungry Fish And The Blue-Tailed Fly,
The
I Never Says Nothing To Nobody
Jack Robinson
Lively Flea, The (parody of Ivy Green)
1837
Mousetrap, The
Parson's Clerk, The c.1825
Petticoat And Breeches
Poor Robinson Crusoe 1816

Spider And The Fly, The (m anon., arr.
HUDSON) c.1830
Walker, The Tuppenny Postman

HUGHES, Herbert 1882–1937
Down By The Sally Gardens (W. B.
YEATS (Crossways, 1889): trad., arr.
HUGHES) 1914
Maids of Mourne Shore, The (arr.
HUGHES)
She Moved Through The Fair (Padraic
COLUM: trad., arr. HUGHES) 1913

HUGHES, Jimmy d. 13 Feb. 1973
Bless 'Em All

HUGHES, John Ceiriog see CEIRIOG

HULBERT, Jack° 1892–1978
Awfully Chap, The (m Alan MURRAY)
1914
Rag-Time Craze, The (m MURRAY) 1913
Wusky Woozle, The (m MURRAY) 1913

HULLAH, J. P. 1812–84
Storm, The (w Adelaide A. PROCTER)
1859
Three Fishers Went Sailing, The
(w Charles KINGSLEY) 1857

HUMBLE-CROFTS, Arthur d. 1918;
m. Margaret COOPER
Agatha Green (m Margaret COOPER)
1911

HUMPHRIES, F. W.
Fisherman's Child, The (w&m Harry G.
THOMPSON, arr. HUMPHRIES) 1882
Now It's All Over For Ever (Harry
CLEMENT: H. BALL, arr.
HUMPHRIES) 1881
(Quite A Toff In My) Newmarket Coat
(w&m BALL, arr. HUMPHRIES) 1882

HUMPHRIES, Griffiths°
Bazaar And Fancy Fair, The 1895
Drama Up-To-Date 1898
8 Bars Rest 1896
Give A Little Cough 1896

It Wouldn't Be A Bad Idea 1899
Mingle Your Eyebrows With Mine, Love

HUNT, G. W. *c.*1839–1904
Alpine Hat, The 1870
Am I Right Or Any Other Man? (arr.
　H. H. HOWARD) 1862
Angelina Brown (arr. E. WHITEHOUSE)
　1865
Auctioneer's Daughter, The
Awfully Awful 1877
Awfully Clever
Belle Of The Ball, The 1873
Bell Goes A-Ringing For Sa-i-rah
Billy Johnson's Ball
Blindman's Buff
Bloomsbury Square 1878
Brown The Tragedian 1870
Captain Cuff 1877
Cerula Was Beautiful 1879
Charming Arabella 1869
Cook's Excursion 1873
Custom Of The Country, The 1876
Dear Old Pals 1877
Doctor's Boy 1873
Don't Make A Noise Or Else You'll Wake
　The Baby 1876
Down Among The Coals
Dutch Clock Man, The 1873
Fellow That Looks Like Me 1876
Frenchman, The *or* Tra La La Bon 1873
Gal From Pennsylvania, The (Sam's
　Sally) (*w* Tom LACLAGAN) 1862
German Band, The 1865
Gold! Gold! Gold! 1875
Gone To Smash 1876
Good Job Too! Serve Him Right, A
I Always Take It Easy 1869
Joe's Birthday (Did You Ever Go To
　Hampstead In A Van) 1876
Johnny The Engine Driver 1867
London, Chatham And Dover, The 1865
L. S. D.
Macdermott's War Song (The Jingo
　Song) 1877
Major K. N. Pepper

Nautical Swell, The
Nice Looking Girl, The (*w* Harriett
　BOWMER) 1865
Old Brown's Daughter
On The Continong
Organ Grinder, The 1871
Piano Girl, The 1879
Polly Crow 1866
Polly Darling
Poor Chinee 1876
Rolling On The Grass 1876
She Does The Fandango All Over The
　Place 1883
Soldier's Bride, A
Sourkraut's Return 1872
Sugar Shop
Timid Lover, The 1872
Turn The Mangle, Joe 1877
Up In A Balloon (for ladies' *w* see Mrs A.
　POWER; for US *w* see H. B. FARNIE)
　1868
Wait Till My Ship Comes Home 1879
When The Band Begins To Play 1871
Zazel 1878

HUNT, J.
I Was Standing At The Corner Of The
　Street (& George FORMBY: FORMBY)
　1910

HUNTER, G. W.° 1850–1936
Courtship (& WILMOTT: F. ARTHUR)
　1890
Doctor Jeremiah Jones (*w* J. S. EVALO)
　1899
Down By The Garden Gate 1886
Funny Things They Do Upon The Sly
　(& John COOKE: HUNTER) 1885
Give What You Can To Those In Distress
　1884
Hezekiah Brown (*w* EVALO) 1892
Hungry Man From Clapham, The
　1887
Married Life (*w* J. COOKE jun.) 1885
Riding On (The) Top Of An Omnibus
　1886
Song That Broke My Heart, The (& John

STOCKS: Jordan JULIAN & Michael NOLAN) 1890

That Is Love (parody) (& R. G. KNOWLES: Felix McGELNNON) 1892

They Never Will Invite You Any More (& Charles HICKMAN: HUNTER) 1889

HUNTER, Harry° 1841–1906

Captain Matthew Webb (m David G. DAY) 1875

Comparisons Are Melodious (m G. H. CHIRGWIN, arr. Warwick WILLIAMS) 1888

Contented Duffer, The

Coster Coon, The c.1877

Country Cousin, The (I Saw Esau Kissing Kate) (m T. Vincent DAVIES) 1870

Dear Old Bobs (m Edmund FORMAN) 1906

Dinah Duck (m Joe DANIELS)

Doctor Says I'm Not To Be Worried, The (m Frank VERNON) 1877

Do Your Duty Well (m William WILLIAMS)

Emancipation Day 1878

His Name Was Joshu-a 1877

I Can't Stand Mrs Green's Mother (m Walter REDMOND) 1881

I'd Rather Lather Father, Than Father Lathered Me (m REDMOND) 1876

If You See Lucy Let Me Know (m DAVIES) 1877

I Know A Gal Dat Lubs A Coon c.1877

I'm A Ship Without A Rudder (m VERNON) 1876

I've Got The Ooperzootic (m FORMAN) 1896

Johnny Will You Come Along Now? (m DAVIES) 1874

Just Behind The Battle Mother (m DAVIES, arr. W. VANDERVELL) 1877

Lindy, I'm Coming Back To You (m Fred EPLETT) 1904

Little Joe (m DAVIES) 1877

Look At The Price Of Coal

Lord Mayor's Coachman, The (m DAY) 1881

Lucindah At The Windah (m G. D. FOX) 1884

Madame La Sharty (Biddy The Belle Of The Ballet) (w Sam ROGERS) c.1880

Mazy Dance, The (m DAVIES) 1870

My Fiddle Is My Sweetheart (m G. H. CHIRGWIN) 1895

Nancy Goodman 1880

Never Desert A Friend (m Charles COOTE) 1876

Never Give In (m REDMOND) 1876

Over The Garden Wall (m FOX) c.1880

Peg Leg Polly (m FOX)

Peter Perfect (m DAVIES) 1870

Says So Saucy Sue (m Alfred LEE) 1877

Tam O'Shanter Hat, The (m WILLIAMS) 1881

Tears Are Blessings

There's Another Verse After This

Uncle Jupe Lubs Chicken Soup c.1877

Under The Chestnut Tree 1880

Victoria's Victory (m FORMAN) 1897

When The Sun Shines Bright On A Moonlight Night (m Walter HOWARD) 1886

Woman's Rights

HUNTING, Russell°

Down At The Old Bull And Bush (& Percy KRONE & Andrew B. STERLING: H. VON TILZER). Adap. Under The Anheuser Bush (STERLING: VON TILZER) 1903

HUNTLEY, G. P.° 1868–1927

Junior Job-Lot Club, The (m H. C. BARRY) 1896

Since My Old Dutch Pegged Out (& George H. GRAY: BARRY) 1897

HURRILLE, H.
Moet And Shandon (m George
LEYBOURNE) c.1868

HURST, J. H.° d. 20 Apr. 1905?
Studying The Face (w Fred J. BARNES)
1897

HUTCHINSON, Abby 1829–92; a.k.a.
A. H.
Kind Words Can Never Die (basis for
Old Soldiers Never Die; w&m Jack
FOLEY) 1874

HYDE, Will d. 1941?
Fair Lady Mine (& Percival LANGLEY:
Clement COURTNEY) 1899
Federation Day (w Harry HEATH)
1906
Fighting For Liberty (w Ernest BALL &
J. Sutton PATEMAN) 1897
Johnny Morgan's Sister 1907
Lady Doctor, The (w T. F. ROBSON)
1909
Raise Your Hat To The Lady (m Fred
BARNES) 1907

ILDA, Lewis d. 18 Mar. 1984; see Jack
SPADE

IMESON, W. E.
Bore O' Bef'nal Green, The (m Fred
EPLETT) 1899

INGLE, Charles 1862–1940; pseudonym
of Auguste Chevalier, brother of Albert
CHEVALIER
Blue Ribbon Jane (w Albert CHEVALIER)
1894
Funny Without Being Vulgar (w H.
BRETT) 1891
He Knew It! (w CHEVALIER) 1889
Hunting (w BRETT) 1892
In The Good Old Days (w CHEVALIER)
1891
I've Got 'Er 'At (w CHEVALIER) 1899
My Old Dutch (w CHEVALIER) 1892
Nasty Way 'E Sez It, The
(w CHEVALIER) 1892

Our Little Nipper ('E Only Stands
About So 'Igh) (w CHEVALIER)
1892
Peculiar (w CHEVALIER) 1891
Rose Of Our Alley (CHEVALIER: Sam
TUTE, arr. INGLE) 1893
Sich A Nice Man Too (w CHEVALIER)
1892
Toymaker's Tragedy, The (w Brian
DALY) 1896
Villains At The Vic (w CHEVALIER)
1893
We Did 'Ave A Time (w CHEVALIER)
1896
Wot Cher! (w CHEVALIER) 1891
Wot's The Good Of Hanythink?
Why Nuffink! (w CHEVALIER)
1894
Yer Never Aks'd 'Im For It (w Brian
DALY) 1893
You Can't 'Elp Likin' 'Im (w
CHEVALIER) 1892

INGRAHAM, Herbert 1883–1910
All That I Ask Of You Is Love (w Edgar
SELDEN) 1905
They Don't Speak To One Another Now
(w SELDEN) 1910

IRVING, Laurence 1872–1914
Peg Woffington (one-act play) 1903

ISITT, Frank S. N. 1867–1939
Carol Of The English Race, A (w
R. FLETCHER) 1894
Little Christopher Columbus c.1900
'Tis Hard To Love And Say Farewell or
The Lady Slavey 1894

ISON, George
Down Went The Captain (Fred
BOWYER: Kate ROYLE, arr. ISON)
1887
I Really Can't Stop Dancing (w Little
TICH) 1893
I Tell Them My Father's A Marquis
(w&m William BINT, arr. ISON)
1884

I Took It (*w&m* Arthur CORNEY, arr.
ISON) 1887

IVIMEY, John M.
Irish Courtship (*w* Broughton BLACK)
1898
Just A Little 1901
My Favourite Dance 1906
My Morning Paper 1906
Servant Question (By One Who Knows),
The 1901

JACKSON, Myrtle
Give Her A Vote, Papa (*w* Eveline
ARCHER) 1908

JACKSON, Nelson° b. 24 Sept. 1870
Bargains 1904
In 1950 *c*.1910
In The Future 1913
Inverary Mary 1903
Killjoys, The 1923
Let's Have A Song About Father 1913
Nothing To Worry About 1907
Our Curate
Santy Klors (*w* Frank BOOTH) 1902
Special Constable 1915
This Wonderful England Of Ours
When Father Carved A Duck
When Father Laid The Carpet On The
Stairs 1906

JACKSON, Tony 1876–1921
Pretty Baby (Gus KAHN: Egbert VAN
ALSTYNE) 1916

JACKSON, William 1730–1803
Dear (Green) Little Shamrock, The
(*w* Andrew CHERRY. *m* orig. pub.
JACKSON but later rev. J. W.
CHERRY(?) and pub. J. Blockley
c.1870) 1806

JACOBI, Georges 1840–1906
Toiling Tourist, The (*w* W. PARKE)
c.1885
We Follow (*w* Fred BOWYER) 1887

JACOBS-BOND, Carrie 1863–1947
I Love You Truly 1901

Just A-Wearyin' For You (*w* Frank L.
STANTON) 1916
Perfect Day, A 1910

JAMES, Evan 1809–78; father of James
JAMES
Hen Wlad Fy Nhadau (Land Of My
Fathers) (*m* trad., arr. James JAMES)
1856

JAMES, James 1833–1902; son of Evan
JAMES
Hen Wlad Fy Nhadau (Land Of My
Fathers) (*w* Evan JAMES; Eng. transl.
Owain ALAW: air, trad., arr. James
JAMES) 1856
Another English translation by Eben
FARDD.

JAXONE, H. L. D'Arcy
Comrades (*m* Julius BENEDICT) 1883
Idol Of My Heart, The (*m* Ciro PINSUTI)
1888
Last Milestone, The (*m* Henry PONTET)
1884
Let Me Forget Thee (*m* Lady Arthur
HILL) 1887
Patchwork (*m* Odoardo BARRI)
Queen Of The Earth (Man's Guardian
Angel) (*m* PINSUTI) 1883

JEFFRIES, Charles
Mary Of Argyle (*m* Sidney NELSON)
c.1855

JEROME, M. K.
Bright Eyes (Harry B. SMITH: & Otto
MOTZAN) 1920

JEROME, William 1865–1932
Bedelia (& George GROSSMITH jun.:
Jean SCHWARTZ) 1903
Brand New Millionaire (& Walter
DE FRECE: Dave FITZGIBBON)
1894
Chinatown, My Chinatown (*m*
SCHWARTZ) 1910
Heart Of My Heart (& Andrew MACK)
1899
Just Try To Picture Me Back Home In

Tennessee (*m* Walter DONALDSON)
1915

Man Who Broke The Brokers Down In
Wall Street, The (*m* FITZGIBBON)
1894

Mister Dooley (*m* SCHWARTZ) 1902

My Irish Molly O (*m* SCHWARTZ) 1907

Reuben Glue (& MACK) *c*.1894

Row, Row, Row (*m* Jimmie V. MONACO)
1912

Villain Still Pursued Her, The (*m* Harry
VON TILZER) 1912

JOHNS, Richard 1805–51
White Squall, The (*m* George BARKER)
1835

JOHNSON, Cecil
Ayesha, My Sweet Egyptian (& Joe
BURLEY: Maurice SCOTT) 1908

JOHNSON, George W. 1839–1917
When You And I Were Young, Maggie
(*m* J. A. BUTTERFIELD) 1866

JOHNSON, Howard *c*.1888–1941
Oh! Mother, I'm Wild! (& Harry PEASE
& Eddie NELSON) 1919
What Do You Want To Make Those Eyes
At Me For? (& Joseph MCCARTHY:
Jimmie V. MONACO) 1916

JOHNSON, James Weldon 1871–1938
Congo Love Song (& John Rosamond
JOHNSON) 1903
Cupid's Ramble (& Robert (Bob) A.
COLE: J. R. JOHNSON) 1903
I'll Keep A Warm Spot In My Heart For
You (& J. R. JOHNSON & COLE) 1906
Lift Every Voice And Sing (*m* J. R.
JOHNSON) 1900
Oh, Didn't He Ramble? *see* Will HANDY
1902
Under The Bamboo Tree (& J. R.
JOHNSON & COLE) 1902

JOHNSON, John Rosamond 1873–1954
Congo Love Song (& James Weldon
JOHNSON) 1903

Cupid's Ramble (& Robert (Bob) A.
COLE: J. W. JOHNSON) 1903
I'll Keep A Warm Spot In My Heart For
You (& COLE & J. W. JOHNSON) 1906
Lift Every Voice And Sing (*w* J. W.
JOHNSON) 1900
Oh, Didn't He Ramble? *see* Will HANDY
1902
Under The Bamboo Tree (& COLE &
J. W. JOHNSON) 1902

JOHNSON, Roy Frank
Mister Bear (*m* Norah BLANEY) 1913
Skinny Piccaninny (*m* BLANEY) 1917

JOLSON, Al° 1886–1950
Avalon (& Vincent ROSE) 1920
California, Here I Come (& Buddy
DeSYLVA & J. MEYER) 1924
You Ain't Heard Nothin' Yet (&
DeSYLVA & Gus KAHN) 1919

JONES, A. Boy
It Came Off 1889
Waiter, The (& W. BERNOTT: George LE
BRUNN) 1892

JONES, Edward d. 10 Aug. 1917
Candid Man, The (*w* Albert CHEVALIER)
1893
Cockney Tragedian, The (*w* CHEVALIER)
1891
Waxwork Show, The (*w* CHEVALIER)
1891

JONES, Ernest Boyd 1869–1904
Tell Me, Pretty Maiden (& Paul RUBENS:
Leslie STUART) 1899

JONES, Guy S. 1875–1959
Modest Curate, The (*w* Graham
SQUIERS) 1913

JONES, John *see* TALHAIARN; not the
John Jones (1825–87) known as Idris
Fychan

JONES, Mai° 1899–1960
We'll Keep A Welcome (*w* Lyn JOSHUA
& James HARPER) 1940
See also CORE SONG-LIST.

JONES, Sidney 1861–1946
Amorous Goldfish, The (*w* Harry
    GREENBANK) 1896
Chon Kina (*w* GREENBANK) 1896
Gay Bohemi-ah (*w* GREENBANK) 1895
Linger Longer Loo (*w* Willie YOUNGE)
    1893
Star Of My Soul (*w* GREENBANK) 1896

JONES, Will
I'm Such A Simple Young Man 1885
Oh Johnny! (Don't You Go To Sea) 1884

JONGHMAN(N)S, Edward *c.*1855–1902
As If I Didn't Know (*w* Harry ADAMS)
    1884
Broken Down Masher, The (*w* George
    BYFORD) 1880
Crutch And Toothpick (*w* ADAMS) 1880
Here Upon Guard Am I (*w* ADAMS)
    1881
Masher King, The (*w* ADAMS) 1884
Old Toll-Gate, The (*w* W. ROXBY) 1881
Shoulder To Shoulder (*w* ADAMS) 1882
Those Girls At The School (*w&m*
    Harry NICHOLLS, arr. JONGHMANS)
    1882
Those Wedding Bells Shall Not Ring Out
    (*w* Monroe H. ROSENFELD, rev. The
    Fatal Wedding, Gussie L. DAVIS)
    1893
Trafalgar Square (*w* Charles DEANE)
    1899
We Won't Go Home Till Morning (*w* G.
    WALL) 1881

JONSON, Ben 1574–1637
Drink To Me Only With Thine Eyes
    (from *To Celia*, 1616) (air, trad.,
    sometimes attr. Colonel R. MELLISH)
    1780

JORDAN, Mrs° 1762–1816; a.k.a.
    Dorothy Bland
Blue Bell Of Scotland, The 1800

JORDAN, Joe 1882–1971
That Teasin' Rag 1909

JORDAN, Julian° 1850–1927
Song That Reached My Heart, The
    1887
    Parodied by G. W. HUNTER, etc.

JORDAN, Leopold
'Bus Conductor, The (*w* A. R. BYRON)
    *c.*1880

JOSHUA, Lyn
We'll Keep A Welcome (& James
    HARPER: Mai JONES) 1940

JUDGE, Jack° 1878–1938; see also CORE
SONG-LIST
How Are Yer? (& Harry J. WILLIAMS)
    1913
It's A Long, Long Way To Tipperary
    (& WILLIAMS) 1912
It's A Long Way No Longer 1918
Mona From Barcelona (& WILLIAMS)
    1912
Spookland (& WILLIAMS) 1913
Way The Wind Blows, We'll Go!, The
    (& WILLIAMS) 1913

KAHN, Gus 1886–1941
Carolina In The Morning (*m* Walter
    DONALDSON) 1922
Memories (*m* Egbert VAN ALSTYNE)
    1915
Pretty Baby (*m* Tony JACKSON & VAN
    ALSTYNE) 1916
You Ain't Heard Nothin' Yet (& Buddy
    DeSYLVA & Al JOLSON) 1919

KAIHAU, Maewa
Now Is The Hour (Haere Re/Goodbye)
    (*m* Clement SCOTT; *w&m* adap.
    trad.?) 1913

KALMAN, Bert 1884–1947
If You Can't Get A Girl In The
    Summertime (*m* Harry TIERNEY)
    1915

KAPLAN, Bert
Horsey, Keep Your Tail Up (& Walter
    HIRSCH) 1923

KARNO, Fred° 1866–1941; sketches
Hustle 1899
Saturday To Monday (& Charles
  BALDWIN & Fred KITCHEN) 1903
Who's Who

KEAN, J. P.
English Toff, The (m Barney FAGAN)

KEEN, Walter P.
Since I Became A Married Man 1907

KEISER, Robert A. 1862–1932
While Strolling Thru The Park (& Ed
  HALEY) 1880

KEITH, ?
How Dare You! (& Harry BODEN
  & Billy MERSON: Fred EPLETT)
  1906

KELLETTE, John W. pseudonym of
  James Brockman (1866–1967) &
  Nathaniel Vincent (1889–1979)
I'm Forever Blowing Bubbles (& Jaan
  KENBROVIN) 1918

KELLY, J. T.
(She's) Only A Working Girl 1895

KELLY, W. B.
Sing Us One Of The Old Songs (& J. H.
  WOODHOUSE) 1900

KEMP, George F.
Good Old English Ale, The (w H. T.
  BALL) 1854

KENBROVIN, Jaan 1883–1946;
pseudonym of James KENDIS
I'm Forever Blowing Bubbles (& John
  W. KELLETTE) 1918

KENDAL, Alec d. 2 Aug. 1945
Come In And Cut Yourself A Piece Of
  Cake 1911
I'm Twenty-One Today 1911
Liza Had Hold Of My Hand 1910
Me! (m Mark MURRAY) 1907
Playing The Game In The West
  (& George FORMBY) 1910

To Cheer Him Up And Help Him On
  His Way 1912

KENDALL, A. B.
That's The Reason Noo I Wear A Kilt
  (& Harry LAUDER) 1906

KENDIS, James 1883–1946; see also
Jaan KENBROVIN
Billy (For When I Walk) (Joe GOODWIN:
  & Herman PALEY) 1911
Won't You Fondle Me? (& PALEY) 1904

KENNEDY, Harry
Molly And I And The Baby
Say Au Revoir But Not Good-Bye 1893

KENNEDY, Jimmy 1902–84
Cokey Cokey, The or Hokey Cokey, The
  (m anon.) 1945
Teddy Bears' Picnic, The (m John W.
  Bratton 1907) 1930

KENNEDY-FRASER, Marjory see
FRASER, Marjory Kennedy

KENNEY, Charles Lamb 1821–81
Vagabond, The (m James Lynam
  MOLLOY) 1871

KENNICK, T.
That Blessed Baby
Ticket On The Shawl, The (m Emma
  KERRIDGE)
You Naughty, Naughty Men (m
  G. BICKNELL) 1865

KENT, Edward°
Harmony Hall (musical sk.) 1899
Lively Squire, The 1922
Love's Garden 1899
Matinée Hat, The 1897
Pop 1897
Rage Of Rag Time, The 1903
Ruby Do Be Mine 1905
They Can't Mean What They Sing!
  1910
Waif And The Wizard, The 1898
Way Down The Regent's Canal 1896
Why Did They Call Him Watt? 1911

KERKER, Gustave 1857–1923
Narragansett (On The Beach At)
(w Hugh MORTON) 1897
She Is The Belle Of New York
(w MORTON) 1897
Teach Me How To Kiss (w MORTON)
1897
They All Follow Me (w MORTON)
1897
Wine Woman And Song (w MORTON)
1897

KERN, Jerome 1885–1945
How'D'Ya Like To Spoon With Me?
(w Edward LASKA) 1905
It Isn't My Fault 1916
Leader Of The Labour Party, The
(w George GROSSMITH jun.) 1906
Look For The Silver Lining (w Buddy
DESYLVA) 1920
My Otaheitee Lady (w Charles H.
TAYLOR) 1913
Oh, Mr Chamberlain (w rev. P. G.
WODEHOUSE) 1905
They Didn't Believe Me (w M. E.
ROURKE) 1914

KERRIDGE, Emma° c.1845–?
Ticket On The Shawl, The (w T.
KENNICK)

KETÈLBEY, Albert W. 1875–1959; a.k.a.
Anton Vodorinski
In A Monastery Garden 1915
In A Persian Market 1920
Phantom Melody 1912

KEY, Francis Scott 1779–1843
Star-Spangled Banner, The (m John
Stafford SMITH, ed. Thomas CARR;
air based on Smith's Anacreon In
Heaven) c.1814

KILMER, Joyce 1886–1918
Trees (m Oscar RASBACH) 1922

KIND, John A. Glover 1881–1918
By The Sea (By The Beautiful Silvery
Sea) c.1910

I Do Like To Be Beside The Seaside
1909
Let's Have Free Trade Amongst The
Ladies (m Harry CASTLING) 1911
Let's Wait And See The Pictures (&
Frank W. CARTER) 1910

KING, Harry many of his songs, written
for Dan Leno, remain unpublished
As Hot As I Can Make It (The
Policeman's Song) 1890
Dear Old Mike 1890
Has Anyone Seen A Moving Job?
c.1895
Her Mother's At The Bottom Of It All
(m George LE BRUNN) c.1900
Muffin Man, The 1889
My Old Man (m LE BRUNN) 1890
Young Men Taken In And Done For
(m LE BRUNN) 1888

KING, Robert A. 1862–1932
Anona (w V. GREY) 1903

KING, Stoddard 1889–1933
There's A Long, Long Trail A-Winding
(& Zo ELLIOT) 1913

KINGSLEY, Charles 1819–75
Airly Beacon (m A. M. PARES; other
settings known) 1861
Lorraine, Lorraine, Loree (m John Mais
CAPEL; and 6 others) 1897
O That We Two Were Maying (m
Ethelbert NEVIN; and 15 others) 1902
Sands Of Dee, The (m Frederic CLAY;
plus 14 others and Michael W. BALFE)
1874
Three Fishers Went Sailing, The (m J. P.
HULLAH; and 26 others) 1857

KINO, Walter° 1867–1902
Our Sally 1896
What Will Mother Say? (w A. J. MILLS)
1898

KIPLING, Rudyard 1865–1936
Absent-Minded Beggar, The (m Arthur
L. SULLIVAN) 1899

Ballad Of The 'Clampherdown', The
(*m* Frank BRIDGE) 1899
Boots (*m* J. P. MCCALL) 1928
Poem published 1890; see
Cells (*m* J. P. MCCALL) 1930
Poem published 1892; see CORE SONG-
LIST.
Gentlemen-Rankers 1892
See CORE SONG-LIST, Whiffenpoof Song.
Gunga Din (*m* Gerard F. COBB) 1892
Poem published 1890.
(Hanging Of) Danny Deever, (The)
(*m* W. DAMROSCH) 1897
Poem pub. 1890; 7 other known settings.
(Have You News Of) My Boy Jack?
(*m* Edward GERMAN) 1914
Looking Glass, The (*m* DAMROSCH)
1916
Man Who Was, The (1896 short story
dramatized by F. Kinsey PEILE)
1903
Mother O' Mine (*m* Frank E. TOURS)
1903
Poem published 1890; 18 other known
settings.
(On The Road To) Mandalay (*m* Oley
SPEAKS) 1907
Poem published 1890; 12 other known
settings.
Tommy (*m* Mary CARMICHAEL) 1892

KITCHEN, Fred° 1872–1950; sketches
Bungler's Luck (& Charles BALDWIN)
1913
Number 90 1910?
Persevering Potts (& BALDWIN) 1911
Saturday To Monday (& BALDWIN &
Fred KARNO) 1903

KITTREDGE, Walter 1840–?; a.k.a.
Noggs
Tenting On The Old Camp Ground
1860

KNEASS, Nelson 1825–68
Ben Bolt (*w* Thomas Dunn ENGLISH)
1848

KNIGHT, Charles d. 24 Jan. 1979?
From Marble Arch To Leicester Square
(*m* Kenneth LYLE) 1914
Here We Are! Here We Are! Here We
Are Again! (& LYLE) 1914

KNIGHT, Joseph Philip 1812–87; a.k.a.
Philip Mortimer
Green Trees Whispered Low And Mild,
The (*w* Henry W. LONGFELLOW)
1858
Rocked In The Cradle Of The Deep
(*w* Emma Hart WILLARD) 1839
She Wore A Wreath Of Roses (*w*
Thomas Baynes BAYNES) 1840

KNIGHT, R. A.
Nelson Touch, The (*m* Edward G.
LOCKTON) 1915

KNOWLES, J. W. d. 25 Aug. 1957?
O, O, Capital O 1903

KNOWLES, R. G.° 1858–1919
That Is Love (parody) (& G. W.
HUNTER: Felix MCGLENNON) 1892

KNOX, Paul J.°
My Flo From Pimlico 1901
Tale The Roses Told 1902

KROCKER, K. F.
E'en As A Lonely Flower (KROCKER
after H. HEINE: Frank BRIDGE) 1905

KRONE, Percy
Down At The Old Bull And Bush (&
Russell HUNTING & Andrew B.
STERLING: Harry VON TILZER); from
Under The Anheuser Bush
(STERLING: VON TILZER) 1903

KUMMER, Clare *c.*1873–1958
In The Dingle Dongle Dell 1904

L. L. B.
True Till Death (*m* Alfred SCOTT-
GATTY) 1879

LABERN, John *c.*1815–*c.*1880; song collections published 1842–*c.*1865

Cadger's Ball, The *c*.1840

Electric Light, The

Jenny Lind 1848

Lamentations Of Punch, The *or* Pity The
Downfall Of Poor Punch And Judy
c.1840

Lively Flea, The *c*.1837

Mrs Caudle's Curtain Lectures

Queen Victoria's Visit To Ireland 1849

Royal Visit To The Coal Exchange, The

Useful Knowledge (Listen, Listen All)
(*m* anon.) 1873

Who'll Buy My Images? *c*.1840

LABLACHE, Frederic 1815–87
'Tis I (*m* Ciro PINSUTI) 1876

LAKE, Frank
Bless 'Em All

LALO, Clarence
In Olden Spain (*m* E. LALO) 1888

LALO, Edouard 1823–92
In Olden Spain (*w* C. LALO) 1888

LAMB, Arthur J. 1870–1928
Asleep In The Deep (*m* Henry W.
PETRIE) 1897

At The Bottom Of The Deep Blue Sea
(*m* PETRIE) 1899

Bird In A Gilded Cage, A (*m* Harry VON
TILZER) 1900

Bird On Nellie's Hat, The (*m* Alfred
SOLMAN) 1906

Mansion Of Aching Hearts, The (*m* VON
TILZER) 1902

Nineteenth Century Boys, The (*m*
William Frederick PETERS) 1895
Sung by Sisters Levey—for song of same
title see Will J. GODWIN: Orlando POWELL.

You Splash Me And I'll Splash You
(*m* SOLMAN) 1907

LAMB, Henry
Face On The Bar-Room Floor, The
(*w* William B. GRAY)

Volunteer Organist, The (*w* GRAY) 1893

LAMBE, J. F.
I Can't Forget 'Auld Reekie' 1907

Won't You Give Me A Sprig Of
Shamrock? *c*.1910

LAMBELET, Napoleon 1864–1932
Mary Was A Housemaid (*w* W. H.
RISQUE) 1899

LAMBERT, E. Frank d. 1928; pseudonym of Frederick Psalmon

She Is Far From The Land (*w* Thomas
MOORE, 1807) 1897

Speak But One Word (*w* Edward
TESCHEMACHER) 1896

LAMONT, Alfred
Can't Stop! Can't Stop!! Can't Stop!!!
(*w&m* H. WINCOTT, arr. LAMONT)
1895

Madam Duvan (Joseph TABRAR: Tom
COSTELLO, arr. LAMONT) 1891

My Hat's A Brown 'Un (*w&m* E. W.
ROGERS, arr. LAMONT) 1891

LANE, Edward William 1801–76
Separation (from *Arabian Night's
Entertainment*) (*m* G. A.
MACFARREN) 1867

LANGLEY, Percival
Fair Lady Mine (& Will HYDE: Clement
COURTNEY) 1899

Kitty Dear 1911

LaROCCA, Nick 1889–1961; founder
and leader of the Original Dixieland Jazz
Band° with whom some of the following
titles were jointly devised

At The Jazz Band Ball (& Larry
SHIELDS) 1917

Bluin' The Blues 1917

Clarinet Marmalade (& SHIELDS) 1917

Dixie Jass Band One-Step 1917

Fidgety Feet (& SHIELDS) 1918

Indiana (Back Home In)

Lazy Daddy (& SHIELDS) 1917

Livery Stable Blues (Barnyard Blues)
1917

Original Dixieland One-Step, The 1912
Ostrich Walk 1914
Ramblin' Blues (& SHIELDS) 1920
Sensation Rag 1912
That Teasin' Rag
Tiger Rag (derived from an older
    melody) 1912
Toddlin' Blues
When You Hear That Dixieland Jazz
    Band Play

LA RUE, Al
Goodbye, My Lady Love (w&m Joe
    HOWARD, arr. LA RUE) 1904

LASKA, Edward
Don't You Think I'm Pretty? 1906
How'D'Ya Like To Spoon With Me?
    (m Jerome KERN) 1905
It's Better To Love A Short Man 1907

LASKY, Jesse 1880–1958
My Brudda, Sylvest' (& Sam STERN:
    Fred FIS(C)HER) 1908

LATONA, Jen° 1881–1955
Always True (w John P. HARRINGTON)
    1902
Can't You Love Me True?
    (w HARRINGTON) 1902
Down In D-I-X-I-E c.1918
He Was Thinking! (w HARRINGTON)
    1902
Nation's Soldier Sons, The
    (w HARRINGTON) 1902

LAUDER, Sir Harry° 1870–1950
At The Sign Of The Bluebell Inn (w
    John LINDSAY) 1907
Bella, The Belle O' Dunoon 1922
Blarney Stone (& M. HANNAWAY) 1913
Bonnie Hielan' Mary (& A. MELVILLE:
    LAUDER) 1901
Camlachie Scout, The 1903
Don't Let Us Sing Any More About War
    1918
Down In Johnson's 1900
Early In The Morning 1900

End Of The Road, (Keep Right On To)
    The (& William DILLON) 1924
Fou The Noo (w Gerald GRAFTON) 1905
Hey, Donal 1903
I Love A Lassie (& GRAFTON: LAUDER)
    1905
I Love You 1901
I Think I'll Get Wed In The Summer-
    Time 1919
It's Nice To Get Up In The Morning
    1913
I've Loved Her Ever Since She Was A
    Baby 1909
I Wish You Were Here Again 1919
Killiecrankie 1900
Mr John McKie 1903
O'er The Hill To Ardentinny 1921
Ohio 1921
Piper MacFarlane (& GRAFTON:
    LAUDER) 1906
Queen Amang The Heather (& J.
    MALARKEY) 1909
Roamin' In The Gloamin' 1911
Saftest O' The Family, The (& Bob
    BEATON: LAUDER) 1904
Same As His Faither Did Before Him
    1912
She Is Ma Daisy (& J. D. HARPER)
    1905
Stop Yer Tickling, Jock! (& Frank
    FOLLOY: LAUDER) 1904
Sunshine O' A Bonnie Lass's Smile 1921
Ta-Ta, My Bonnie Maggie Darling 1913
That's The Reason Noo I Wear A Kilt
    (& A. B. KENDALL) 1906
There's Somebody Waiting For Me 1917
Tobermory 1901
Waggle O' The Kilt, The 1918
We 'A Go Hame The Same Way 1916
Wedding O' Sandy McNab 1908
Wee Deoch-An-Doris, (Just) A (& Whit
    CUNLIFFE & GRAFTON) 1910
Wee Hoose 'Mang The Heather, The
    (& Gilbert WELLS: & Fred ELTON)
    1913
We Parted On The Shore 1906

When I Get Back Again Tae Bonnie
   Scotland 1908
When I Was Twenty-One 1918

LAURIER, Jay° 1879–1969
Emilina Brown (*m* Carl HOWARD)
   1920

LAW, Arthur 1843–1913; m. Fanny
Holland (see German Reed Co°)
First Cigar, The (*m* R. Corney GRAIN)

LAWLOR, Charles B. 1852–1925
Best Man In The House, The 1898
Daisy McIntyre 1897
Irish Jubilee, The (& James THORNTON)
   1890
Mick Who Threw The Brick, The 1899
Pretty Jennie Slattery (& James W.
   BLAKE *m* arr. Frank BANTA) 1895
Sidewalks Of New York, The *or*
   Dancing On The Streets (& BLAKE)
   1894

LAWRANCE, Alf J. d. 24 Jan. 1955
Give Me A Cosy Parlour (& Harry
   GIFFORD & Tom MELLOR) 1907
How D'You Do, My Baby? (& G. H.
   ELLIOTT) 1909
I Like Your Apron And Your Bonnet
   (*w* J. P. HARRINGTON) 1911
I Like Your Old French Bonnet (&
   Harry GIFFORD & Tom MELLOR)
   1909
I Want To Go To Idaho (& GIFFORD &
   MELLOR) 1908
Kitty, The Telephone Girl (& GIFFORD
   & MELLOR & Huntley TREVOR)
   1912
My Castle In Spain (MELLOR: &
   GIFFORD) 1906

LAWREEN, John B.
Croquet (*m* Vincent DAVIES) 1871
Lady Doctor's Husband, The (& John
   OXENFORD: Odoardi BARRI)
Song Of The Gout (& OXENFORD:
   BARRI) 1879

LAWRENCE, Albert E.
It's Nice To Have A Home Of Your Own
   (& George LESTER) 1900

LAWSON, John° 1866–1920
Only A Jew (& M. BESSO) 1896

LAYE, Gilbert d. 1925/6?; father of
Evelyn Laye°
Dairy Mary 1905
Seaside Holiday At Home, A (*w* Fred
   BOWYER) 1903

LAYTON, Turner° 1894–1978
After You've Gone (*w* Henry CREAMER)
   1918
Way Down Yonder In New Orleans
   (*w* CREAMER) 1922

LEACH, Au(gus)tus° d. 17 July 1903
Ding Dong (arr. H. W. FITCHETT)
   1877
I'd Tell You If I Were A Little Fly 1877
Luncheon Bar, The
Nancy Fancied A Soldier 1881
You're Getting It Up For Me 1878

LEAMORE, Tom° 1866–1939
It's Alright In The Summer
I Used To Be Poor Myself
Percy From Pimlico 1898

LE BRETON, John d. Jan. 1932; a.k.a.
Thomas Le Breton, pseudonym of
Murray Ford
Sister To Assist 'Er, A (sk.) 1910
Mrs Le Browning *c.*1912

LE BRUNN, George 1863–1905; brother
of Thomas LE BRUNN
Across The Bridge (*w* Fred BOWYER)
   1889
Advance, Australia! England Number
   Two 1897
After The Ball (*w* John P. HARRINGTON)
   (see CORE SONG-LIST)
All That Glitters Is Not Gold (*w* A. J.
   MORRIS) 1896
All Through A Little Piece Of Bacon

(*w* F. V. St Clair & Tom Costello)
c.1895

And The Leaves Began To Fall
(*w* Harrington) 1904

Angels Without Wings (*w&m* George
Dance, arr. G. Le Brunn) 1887

'Appy 'Ampstead (sk.) (*w* Wal Pink)
See Albert Chevalier: John Crook for
song of same name.

'Arry, 'Arry, 'Arry (*w* Fred W. Leigh &
Fred Murray) 1902

Aubrey Plantagenet (*w* William
Goldbery)

Balaclava Charge, The (*w* Pink) 1894

Bathing (*w* Harrington) 1898

Bella Was A Barmaid (*w* Harrington)
1902

Bluecoat Boy, The (*w* Harrington)

Bond Street Tea-Walk, The (*w*
Harrington) 1902

Cabbie's Lament, The (*w* Pink) 1899

Cabby Knows His Fare (*m* Bowyer)
1889

Chance Your Luck (*w* Pink) 1896

City Waif, The (*w* Harrington) 1889

Cock-O'-The-Walk (*w* Charles Bignell
& Harrington) 1898

Come Along, Let's Make It Up
(*w* Thomas Le Brunn) 1901

Cook's Excursion Trip, A (*w* Richard
Morton) 1897

Coster's Christening, The
(*w* Harrington) 1904

Coster's Muvver, The (*w* Malcolm
Arnold) 1894

Coster's Wedding, The *or* Wedding
March! 1902

Dancing In The Moonbeams (*w*
Thomas Le Brunn) 1898

Dandy Coloured Coon, The
(*w* Morton) 1893

De Coon Ob 1999 (*w* Walter Burnot)
1898

Detective Camera (*w* James Newland)
1892

Doctor, The (*w* Morris) 1892

Doesn't Anybody Want The Curate?
(*w* Harrington) 1905

Don't Laugh (*w* Morton) 1891

Emigrant, The (*w* Harrington) 1889

'E Talks Like A Picture Book (*w* A. R.
Marshall) 1893

Everything In The Garden's Lovely
(*w* Harrington) 1898

Fighting For The Flag They Love
(*w* Harrington) 1896

Folkestone For The Day (*w* Edgar
Bateman) 1900

Gal Wot Lost Her Bloke At Monte Carlo,
The (*w* Charles Deane) 1892

Girls From Bryants And May, The
(*w* Bateman) 1901

Girl You Leave Behind You, The
(*w* Harrington) 1899

Golden Dustman, The (*w* Eric Graham)
1897

Good-For-Nothing Nan (*w* Thomas Le
Brunn) 1893

Half-Past Nine (*w* Pink) 1893

Her Mother's At The Bottom Of It All
(*w* Harry King) *c*.1900

He's Going There Every Night (*w* Leigh
& Murray) 1902

Hi-Tiddley-Hi-Ti (*w* Thomas Le Brunn)
1890

I 'Aven't Told 'Im (*w* Leigh & Murray)
1898

Idler, The (*w* Harrington & Morton)
1896

If It Wasn't For The 'Ouses In Between
(*w* Bateman) 1894

I'm Looking For Trilby (*w*
Harrington) 1895

In England Now (*w* Harrington) 1888

It's A Great Big Shame! (I'm Blowed If
'E Can Call 'Isself 'Is Own) (*w*
Bateman) 1894

I've Never Lost My Last Train Yet
(*w* George Rollitt) *c*.1906

Jap, The (*w* Morton) *c*.1895

Last Bullet, The (*w* H. A. Duffy) 1889

Last Of The Dandies, The

(*w* HARRINGTON; see F. J. BARNES:
Charles COLLINS) 1902
Leave A Little Bit For Your Tutor
(*w* HARRINGTON) 1901
'Liza Johnson (*w* BATEMAN) 1901
Lizer 'Awkins (*w* MORRIS) 1892
Looking For A Coon Like Me
(*w* HARRINGTON) 1894
Maid Of London, 'Ere We Part (&
HARRINGTON & Joseph TABRAR)
1896
Masks And Faces (*w* HARRINGTON)
1888
Me And 'Er (*w* Walter HASTINGS) 1894
Millie! (*w* HARRINGTON) 1901
Mischief (*w* Thomas LE BRUNN) 1891
Money For Nothing (sk.) (*w* PINK)
c.1903
Mother Tongue, The (*w* Albert HALL)
1889
My Next Door Neighbour's Gardin
(*w* BATEMAN & Gus ELEN) 1900
My Old Man (*w* Harry KING) 1890
My Son! My Son! My Only Son! (*w* E. W.
ROGERS) 1891
Naughty Continong, The
(*w* HARRINGTON)
Naughty! Naughty! Naughty!
(*w* HARRINGTON) 1904
Never More (*w&m* Harry DACRE, arr.
George LE BRUNN) *c*.1895
No, 'Arry, Don't Ask Me To Marry
(& Harry CASTLING) 1893
Oh! For The Jubilee (*w* A. WEST)
1887
Oh! Mr Porter (*w* Thomas LE BRUNN)
1892
Our Laundry (sk.) (George ARTHURS &
Harry CASTLING *m* arr. George LE
BRUNN) 1904
'Ow's This For A Start? (*w* R. P. WESTON
& LEIGH) 1899
Poor Thing (*w* MORTON) 1891
Price Of Beer, The
Railway Guard, The (*w* ST CLAIR)
c.1895

Salute My Bicycle (*w* HARRINGTON)
1895
Seventh Royal Fusiliers, The (*w* PINK)
1891
Shop-Walker, The (*w* Walter DE FRECE)
1891
So Her Sister Says (*w* HARRINGTON)
1894
Song Of The Thrush, The (*w* HASTINGS)
1897
Such A Don Don't You Know!
(*w* MORTON) 1895
Tale Of The Mile End Road, A
(*w* MORTON) 1891
Tale Of The Skirt, The (*w* LEIGH)
1904
That's The Cause Of It (*w* Charles
WILMOTT) 1893
That Was A Bloomer (*w* Harry
CASTLING) 1896
Then You Wink The Other Eye (*w*. W. T.
LYTTON) 1890
There They Are—The Two Of Them On
Their Own 1898 (LEIGH & Fred
MURRAY: & E. NEVIN)
Tilly The Typress (Mum's The Word)
(*w* HARRINGTON) 1902
Ting Ting, That's How The Bell Goes
1883
Tricky Little Trilby (*w* HARRINGTON)
1895
Twiggy Voo? (*w* MORTON) 1892
Waiter, The (*w* A. Boy JONES & W.
BERNOTT) 1892
We All Went Home In A Cab (*w* Harry
WINCOTT) 1892
Wedding March!, The *or* The Coster's
Wedding (*w* HARRINGTON) 1902
What Britishers Are Made Of
(*w* HARRINGTON) 1894
What's That For, Eh? (Johnny Jones)
(*w* LYTTON) 1892
What Will The Neighbours Say?
(*w* HARRINGTON) 1900
Why Do The Boys Run After Me?
(*w* HARRINGTON) 1904

Wild Man Of Borneo, The (arr. George LE BRUNN) 1890

Wot Cher, Polly! (*w* MORRIS) 1895

Wrong Man, The (*w* HARRINGTON) 1890

You Ain't Ashamed O' Me, Are You, Bill? (*w* HARRINGTON) 1904

You Can Get A Sweetheart Any Day But Not Another Mother 1901

Young Men Taken In And Done For (*w* KING) 1888

You're A Thing Of The Past, Old Dear (*w* HARRINGTON) 1905

LE BRUNN, Thomas 1864–1936; brother of George LE BRUNN

Come Back To Mother And Me 1902

Dancing In The Moonbeams (*m* George LE BRUNN) 1898

Good-For-Nothing Nan (*m* George LE BRUNN) 1893

Heart That Clings To You Still, The 1901

Hi-Tiddley-Hi-Ti (*m* George LE BRUNN) 1893

Mischief (*m* George LE BRUNN) 1891

Mother's Message, The 1904

Oh! Mr Porter (*m* George LE BRUNN) 1892

You're Still The Same To Me 1904

LE CLERQ, Arthur 1891-1976; a.k.a. Arthur Clare, A. W. D. Henley, Peter Henley, Arthur Leigh, and Ralph Milner; son of George Williams°; brother of Gus Howard of The McNaughtons°

Nobody Loves A Fairy When She's Forty 1934

Somewhere In France, Dear Mother (*w* Jack O'CONNOR) 1915

LEE, Alfred d. 14 Apr. 1906

Act On The Square, Boys 1866

Bill-Poster, The (*w&m* Tom BASS & George HORNCASTLE, *m* arr. LEE) 1892

Brass (*w* T. L. CLAY) 1879

Broken-Hearted Shepherd, The (*w* H. J. WHYMARK) *c.*1868

Captain Webb (*w* Frank W. GREEN) 1875

Champagne Charlie (*w* George LEYBOURNE) 1867

Chang The Chinese Giant 1865

Cool Burgundy Ben (*w* GREEN) *c.*1868

Day We Went To Ramsgate, Oh (*w* Harry LISTON) 1868

Dick Murphy Of T.C.D. 1871

Dolly Varden (*w* GREEN) 1870

Eel-Pie Shop, The (*w&m* LEYBOURNE, arr. LEE)

Flying Trapeze, The (Daring Young Man On The) (*w* LEYBOURNE) 1866

Gainsborough Hat (*m&w* GREEN, arr. LEE)

Going To The Derby In A Four-In-Hand 1870

Heavy Swell Of The Sea, The (Big) (*w* CLAY) *c.*1870

Hildebrandt Montrose (Ed HARRIGAN: HARRIGAN & LEE) 1871

Husbands' Boat, The (*w* GREEN) 1869

Idol Of The Day, The (*w* Alfred G. VANCE) 1869

Late Lamented Jones, The *or* The Widow (*w* GREEN)

Lounging In The Aq (*w* CLAY) 1880

May The Present Moment Be The Worst Of Your Lives (*w* VANCE) 1864

Mother Weep Not For Your Boy (*m* NELLA) 1868

Nobody's Child 1872

Not For Joseph (*w* WHYMARK) 1867

Quite Au Fait 1871

Ring In The Row (*w&m* GREEN, arr. LEE)

Roman Fall, The (*w* Hugh Willoughby SWENY) 1870

Rosherville (*w* GREEN) *c.*1870

Says So Saucy Sue (*w* Harry HUNTER) 1877

She Danced Like A Fairy 1875

Sir Robert De Beard

Strolling In The Burlington (*w* GREEN)

Sweet Isabella (*w&m* LEYBOURNE, arr. LEE)

Tichborne Trial, The (*w* GREEN) 1872
Toothpick And Crutch (*w* CLAY) 1879
Uhlan's Farewell, The (*m* NELLA) 1874
Up In The Monument (*w* GREEN) 1870
Velocipede, The (*w* GREEN)
Walking In The Park 1869
Walking In The Zoo (*w* SWENY) 1867

LEE, Bert 1880–1946; a.k.a. B. Lee or
Herbert Lee of the prolific 'Weston &
Lee' song-writing team (fl. 1915–36), the
other being Robert P. WESTON
Ain' It Nice! (& R. P. WESTON: R.
   HARRIS WESTON) 1923
Algernon, Go H'On! (& Worton DAVID)
   1914
All The Girls Are Lovely By The Seaside
   (& DAVID: Harry FRAGSON) 1913
And The Great Big Saw Came Nearer
   And Nearer (& R. P. WESTON: R. H.
   WESTON) 1936
And Yet I Don't Know (& R. P. WESTON)
   1922
Any Dirty Work Today? (& R. P.
   WESTON) 1922
At Finnigan's Ball 1916
At The Vicar's Fancy Ball (& DAVID)
   1915
Beat The Retreat On Thy Drum (& R. P.
   WESTON: R. H. WESTON) 1932
Body In The Bag, The (& R. P. WESTON)
   1921
Bolshevik, The (& R. P. WESTON) 1919
Brahn Boots (& R. P. WESTON: R. H.
   WESTON) 1935
Ever Since He Pelmanized (& R. P.
   WESTON) 1919
Exemptions And Otherwise (& R. P.
   WESTON) 1916
Fares, Please!
Four-And-Nine (DAVID: & The Two
   BOBS) 1915
Good-bye-ee! (& R. P. WESTON) 1917
Gypsy Warned Me, The (& R. P.
   WESTON) 1920
Heaven Will Protect An Honest Girl (&
   R. P. WESTON: R. H. WESTON) 1933

Hello! Hello! Who's Your Lady Friend?
   (& DAVID: FRAGSON) 1913
I Do Like A S'Nice S'Mince S'Pie
   (& DAVID) 1914
If It's In 'John Bull' It *Is* So (& R. P.
   WESTON & Clay SMITH) 1917
I Might Learn To Love Him Later On
   (& R. P. WESTON) 1921
It Doesn't Appeal To Me (*w* Clifford
   GREY) 1914
It's My Bath Night Tonight (& R. P.
   WESTON) 1922
Joshu-ah (& George ARTHURS) 1906
Knees Up, Mother Brown! (& R. H.
   WESTON & I. TAYLOR) 1938
   See also CORE SONG-LIST.
My Meatless Day (& R. P. WESTON)
   1917
My Word You Do Look Queer (& R. P.
   WESTON) 1922
Nobody Noticed Me (& Nat D. AYER)
   1918
Noise Annoys An Oyster, A (& R. P.
   WESTON) 1920
Nursie-Nursie (& DAVID) 1910
Oh! London, Where Are Your Girls
   Tonight? (& R. P. WESTON) 1918
Old Man Brown (& R. P. WESTON)
   1916
Olga Pulloffski (& R. P. WESTON: R. H.
   WESTON) 1935
Only Yiddisher Scotsman etc. *see*
   Sergeant Solomon Isaacstein
Paddy McGinty's Goat (& R. P. WESTON
   & BOBS) 1917
Profiteering Profiteers, The (& R. P.
   WESTON) 1920
Sergeant Solomon Isaacstein (& R. P.
   WESTON) 1916
Shall I Have It Bobbed Or Shingled?
   (& R. P. WESTON) 1924
She Wants To Marry Me (& R. P.
   WESTON) 1915
Somebody's Coming To Tea (& SMITH &
   R. P. WESTON) 1917
Somebody Would Shout Out 'Shop!'
   (& R. P. WESTON) 1915

Sophy (*m* T. C. Sterndale BENNETT) 1913

Swim, Ṣam! Swim! (& R. P. WESTON) 1917

Viewing The Baby (& R. P. WESTON) 1926

We Really Had A Most Delightful Evening (& DAVID) 1910

What I Want Is A Proper Cup Of Coffee (& R. P. WESTON) 1926

When Paderewski Plays (& BOBS & R. P. WESTON) 1916

With Her Head Tucked Underneath Her Arm (& R. P. WESTON: R. H. WESTON) 1934

You Can't Do Without A Bit Of Love (& Andrew ALLEN) 1916

LEE, George Alexander 1802–51

Buy A Broom (Bavarian Girl's Song) (*w* D. A. O'MEARA) 1821

Come Dwell With Me (*w* T. Haynes BAYLY) 1830

Soldier's Tear, The (*w* BAYLY) *c*.1833

LEE, R.

Blind Boy, The (*m* G. W. 'Pony' MOORE) 1871

Not to be confused with Colley Cibber's 1735 poem *Blind Boy*, set by many composers.

LEGGETT, Steve *c*.1868–96

Glorious Beer (*m* Will GODWIN) 1895

LEHÁR, Franz 1870–1948

Love, Goodbye 1909 (Vienna), 1911 (London)

Love, Goodbye Vienna 1909, London 1911

Merry Widow Waltz (*w* Basil HOOD) Vienna 1905, London 1907

Vilia (*w* Adrian ROSS) Vienna 1905, London 1907

White Dove, The (*w* Clifford GREY) 1912

LEHMANN, Liza 1862–1918; daughter of A. L.

Daisy Chain (song cycle) (*w* A. P. GRAVES) 1893

In A Persian Garden (*w* Edward FITZGERALD) 1896

In Memoriam (*w* Alfred TENNYSON) 1899

Also set by over a hundred others.

Instinct (*w* F. C. HARRIS: *m* LEHMANN adap. James W. TATE) 1904

Little Moccasins 1911

There Are Fairies At The Bottom Of Our Garden (*w* Rose FYLEMAN) 1907

Thoughts Have Wings (*w* F. M. GOSTLING) 1909

Young Lochinvar (*Marmion*) (*w* Walter SCOTT) 1898

Also set by many others.

LEIGH, Fred W. 1870–1924; Francis, Day & Hunter's literary editor

All The Dogs Went Bow-Wow-Wow

Amateur Whitewasher, The (& Fred MURRAY) 1896

Army Of Today's All Right, The (*m* Kenneth LYLE) 1914

'Arry, 'Arry, 'Arry (& MURRAY: George LE BRUNN) 1902

Belinda The Barber-ous 1895

Captain Ginjah, O.T. (& George BASTOW) 1910

Charlie On The Mash (& MURRAY) 1898

Cod Liver Oil 1870

Coster Girl In Paris, The (*m* Orlando POWELL) 1912

Dear Mr Admiral 1908

Did You See The Crowd In Piccadilly? (& Geo. FORMBY & Dan LIPTON) 1905

Don't Dilly Dally (& Charles COLLINS) 1919

Ev'rybody Knows Me In My Old Brown Hat (& COLLINS) 1920

Ev'ry Home Is Fairyland (*m* Fred EPLETT) 1900

Fed Up (& Tom COSTELLO) 1918

Fol-The-Rol-Lol (& MURRAY) 1902

Galloping Major, The (*m* BASTOW) 1906

He's Going There Every Night (& MURRAY: LE BRUNN) 1902

He Was A Good Kind Husband (& MURRAY)

Horse The Missus Dries The Clothes On, The (& Henry E. PETHER) 1901

I Ain't Nobody In Perticuler (*w* Scott MACKENZIE) 1907

I 'Aven't Told 'Im (& MURRAY: LE BRUNN) 1898

I'm Giving Up My Job To The Kaiser (& COSTELLO) 1915

I'm Going To Be A Nut (& LYLE) 1915

I'm Not Particular (& MURRAY) 1898

It Was Only Done In Play (*m* EPLETT) 1901

I've Come Back To Town Once Again (& COSTELLO) 1918

I've Got My Eye On You (& COLLINS) 1913

Jolly Good Luck To The Girl Who Loves A Soldier (*m* LYLE) 1906

Last Good-Bye, The (& MURRAY) *c*.1914

Let Go Eliza (& COLLINS) 1902

Little Bit Off The Top, A (& MURRAY) 1898

Little Of What You Fancy, A (& George ARTHURS) 1915

Mary Ann She's After Me 1911

Mary Devine (& COSTELLO) 1915

More Work For The Undertaker 1895

Nellie Brown (& COSTELLO) 1919

Now You've Got Yer Khaki On (& COLLINS) 1915

Oh Girls! (You Don't Know How I Love You) (& MURRAY) 1897

Oh, I Wish I Was There Again 1901

Oh, The Scenery Was Absolutely Grand! (*m* EPLETT) 1900

One Thing Leads To Another (*m* POWELL) 1912

'Ow's This For A Start? (& R. P. WESTON: LE BRUNN) 1899

Oyster Supper, The (& Horace WHEATLEY) 1908

Philosophy (*w* Charles WILMOTT) 1900

Poor John (*m* PETHER) 1906

Put A Bit Of Treacle On My Pudden, Mary Ann (& Harry CHAMPION) 1922

Put On Your Tat-ta, Little Girlie! 1910

Riding On Top Of The Car (*m* Harry VON TILZER) 1905
Original US *w* Vincent P. BRYAN as Down Where The Wurzburger Flows.

Rosie's Young Man (*m* PETHER) 1909

Rum-Tiddley-Um-Tum-Tay (*m* POWELL) 1908

She's Proud And She's Beautiful (& BASTOW) 1906

Shift Up A Little Bit Farther (& Arthur AISTON) 1903

Svengali! (& MURRAY) 1895

That Gorgonzola Cheese (*m* CHAMPION) 1894

There's Danger On The Line (& COLLINS & MURRAY) *c*.1911
See also George P. NORMAN.

There They Are—The Two Of Them On Their Own (& MURRAY: LE BRUNN & E. NEVIN) 1898

They Won't Know Oi Coom From The Coontry 1907

Tiddley-Om-Pom (*m* POWELL) 1906

Twiddly Wink (*m* POWELL) 1912

Waiting At The Church (*m* PETHER) 1906

When You Hear Your Country Calling (& COSTELLO) 1913

Why Am I Always The Bridesmaid? (& COLLINS) 1917

Wire In, My Lads! (*w* Will GODWIN) 1906

W.O.M.A.N. 1902

LEIGH, H. J.
Matilda D—

LEIGH, Henry S. 1837–83
Bradshaw's Guide (*m* Fred ALBERT) 1876

Shabby Genteel (*m* Harry CLIFTON)
1868
Twin Brothers, The 1865

LEIGHTON BROTHERS° Bert 1877–1964
and Frank 1885–1943?
Frankie And Johnny (trad., arr. Ren
SHIELDS & LEIGHTON BROS) 1912
Steamboat Bill (*w* SHIELDS) 1910

LEIGHTON, Harry 1871–1913
Down Fell The Pony In A Fit (& Harry
WINCOTT: John S. BAKER) 1897
Fiddle-De-Diddle-De-De (& Sam MAYO
& Arthur RICKS, arr. Sam AARONS)
1906
In The Rand (& WINCOTT) 1903
Oh! What A Wicked World We Live In
(& Carl HOWARD) 1899
Old Tin Can, The (& Sam MAYO: MAYO)
1905
Picking All The Best Ones Out
(& WINCOTT) 1900
Right On My Doo-Dah (& WINCOTT)
1900
Song Pirate's Lament, The (& WINCOTT)
1902
Usual Morning Performance, The
(& HOWARD) 1895
We've All Been Having A Go At It
(& WINCOTT) 1896

LEMON, Laura G. d. 1924
My Ain Folk (*w* Wilfrid MILLS) 1904

LEMON, Mary Mark
Daddy (*m* Arthur BEHREND) 1880
Memories (*m* Hope TEMPLE) 1883

LEMORE, Harry° d. 1 Sept. 1898
For A Woman's Sake
Jim And His Partner Joe (& George
BRUCE: F. W. VENTON) 1892

LENNARD, Arthur° 1867–1954
Sister 'Ria (*w* A. J. MILLS) 1895

LENNOX, Lindsay
Love's Golden Dream 1895

True To Jack (*m* Theodore BONHEUR)
1892

LENO, Dan° 1870–1904
Buying A House (*m* Herbert DARNLEY)
c.1901
Going To The Races (& DARNLEY)
c.1899
Lecturer, The (& T. B. SEDGWICK:
Denham HARRISON)
Mocking Bird, The (*m* DARNLEY) *c*.1900
Mrs Kelly (& DARNLEY) *c*.1899
Salvage Man, The (& DARNLEY:
DARNLEY) *c*.1899

LEO, Frank° 1874–1940
Can't You Go Further Than That?
Cowslip And The Cow, The 1905
Has Anyone Been Asking For Me? 1902
Her Smiles Are For Me 1903
I Do Like An Egg For My Tea 1919
Is There Anything Else You'd Like? 1899
I've Only Come Down For The Day
I Wish I'd Bought Ducks 1900
I Wonder Where He Gets His Ideas
From?
Keep Whistling (Boy Scout Song) 1910
Mother's Washing Day 1898
Moucher, The 1896
My Cricket Girl 1903
My Lily Of The Valley 1903
No Show Tonight 1899
Oh, Be Careful, My Friends 1900
Oh, Mother Eve! 1908
Panama Hat, The 1902
She Ain't A Bit Like The Other Girls
That's Where She Sits All Day 1900
There Ain't Going To Be Any Ragtime
1903
Turn Over Leaf 1898
Watching The Trains Come In 1916
What Is The Use Of Loving A Girl? 1902
Where Do Flies Go In The Winter
Time? (& Sam MAYO) 1919
Where Is The Heart? 1904
You Can't Get Away—There It Is 1903
You You You 1907

LEON, Harry d. 1970
Sally

LEONARD, Bob
Jones's Parlour Floor (*m* Fred EPLETT)
1899

LEONARD, Eddie 1875–1941
Ida! Sweet As Apple Cider (*m* Eddie
MUNSON) 1903
I've Lost My Mandy 1915
I Want To Go Back To The Land Of
Cotton 1908
I Wish I Was Some Little Girlie's Beau
1914
Oh, Didn't It Rain! 1923
Roll Dem Roly Boly Eyes 1912

LEONCAVALLO, Ruggiero 1858–1919
Mattinata (*w* Edward TESCHEMACHER)
1904
Roseway (*w* Edgar WALLACE) 1913

LESLIE, Edgar 1885–1976
For Me And My Gal (& E. Ray GOETZ
& George W. MEYER) 1917
He'd Have To Get Under (Get Out And
Get Under) (& Grant CLARKE:
Maurice ABRAHAMS) 1913

LESLIE, Fred° 1855–92
Love In The Orchestra (arr. Meyer
LUTZ) 1889

LESTER, George°
Back Again (*w* Frank/Fred THOMAS)
1890
Couldn't Make The Old Girl Hear (arr.
John S. BAKER) 1897
It's Nice To Have A Home Of Your Own
(& Albert E. LAWRENCE) 1900
I Was Underneath (arr. H. E. PETHER)
Whiskers Round The Bottoms Of His
Trousers (*w* A. J. Mills) 1898

LETTERS, Will° 1877–1910
Flanagan (& C. W. MURPHY) 1910
Has Anybody Here Seen Kelly? (&
MURPHY) 1909

Molly O'Morgan (& Fred GODFREY)
1909
Put Me Upon An Island Where The
Girls Are Few (arr. J. Charles MOORE)
1908
Something Seems To Tell Me You'll
Forget Me 1902

LEVAINE, Gus
Sister Mary Walked Like That (*m* A.
MASSAGE) 1886

LEVEY, William Chas. 1837–94
England Has Stood To Her Guns (*w*
Clement W. SCOTT) 1878
Head Over Heels
Here Stands A Post (Waiting For The
Signal) (*w* SCOTT) 1878
There were various versions of this song.
Sweet Italy 1877
White Blossoms *c*.1877

LEWIS, Sam M. 1885–1959
How'Ya Gonna Keep 'Em Down On The
Farm? (& Joe YOUNG: Walter
DONALDSON) 1919
My Mammy (& YOUNG: DONALDSON)
1921
Rock-A-Bye Your Baby With A Dixie
Melody (& YOUNG: Jean SCHWARTZ)
1918
Where Did Robinson Crusoe Go With
Friday On Saturday Night? (& YOUNG:
George W. MEYER) 1916

LEYBOURNE, George° 1842–84
Barber's Apprentice Boy, The 1868
Champagne Charlie (*m* Alfred LEE)
1867
Eel-Pie Shop, The (arr. LEE)
Flying Trapeze, The (Daring Young Man
On The) (*m* LEE) 1866
Moet And Shandon (*w* H. HURRILLE)
c.1868
Music Mad (*m* James BAYMAN)
Sweet Isabella (arr. LEE)
Watching The Mill Go Round 1876

LEYBOURNE, T.
Wait Till The Work Comes Round (&
   C. CORNELL: Gus ELEN) 1906

LIDDEN, Cecil
It's A Sad Sad Story 1907

LIDDLE, Samuel *c.* 1870–*c.* 1940
Abide With Me (*w* Revd Henry Francis
   LYTE) (see CORE SONG-LIST) 1896
Love's Philosophy (*w* Percy Bysshe
   SHELLEY) 1902

LILIUOKALANI, Queen 1838–1917
Aloha Oe (rev. Charles WILLMOTT) 1878

LINCKE, Paul 1866–1946
Glow-Worm, The (Eng. *w* Lilla CAYLEY-
   ROBINSON) 1902

LINDA, Charles
Showman, The (*m* J. WOOLLEY)

LINDO, R. H.
Coster's Confession, The (*m* Fanny
   WENTWORTH) 1895

LINDSAY, John
At The Sign Of The Bluebell Inn (*m*
   Harry LAUDER) 1907

LING, Percy
Street Minstrel, The (*m* Alf MASON)
   1879

LINGARD, William°
Italian Guinea Pig Boy 1866

LINLEY, George 1798–1865
Fox And The Crow, The (LINLEY: adap.
   LINLEY) 1855
God Bless The Prince Of Wales (*m*
   Brinley RICHARDS; orig. Welsh *w*
   CEIRIOG) 1862
Topsy, I's So Wicked 1852

LINN, Harry° 1846–90
Did You Ever See A Feather In A Tom
   Cat's Tail?(*m* Minnie CUNNINGHAM)
   c. 1890
Get A Little Table (arr. W. SIM) 1882
Never Push A Man When He's Going

Down (arr. M. HOBSON) 1869
When The Cock Begins To Crow (*m*
   Rowland HOWARD)

LIPTON, Dan 1873–1935
Ain't I No Use Mister Jackson? (& C. W.
   MURPHY) 1905
All Hands On Deck (& MURPHY)
   1909
See also CHESTERFIELD & SIM.
Dance With Your Uncle Joseph (&
   William HARGREAVES) 1915
Did You See The Crowd In Piccadilly?
   (& Geo. FORMBY & Fred LEIGH)
   1905
Esau, Take Me On The Seesaw (&
   MURPHY) 1908
I Can't Help Loving A Girl Like You
   (*m* Fred GODFREY) 1908
If At First You Don't Succeed (&
   MURPHY) 1906
If I Had A Girl As Nice As You (&
   MURPHY) 1904
I Wonder What It Feels Like To Be
   Poor? (& MURPHY & MAGINI)
   1913
My Girl's A Yorkshire Girl (& MURPHY)
   1908
Oh! Oh! Antonio (& MURPHY) 1908
Put A Little Bit Away For A Rainy Day
   (& MURPHY) 1905
Put Me Amongst The Girls (& MURPHY)
   1907
She's A Lassie From Lancashire (& John
   NEAT & MURPHY) 1907
We Don't Want Any More Daylight (&
   MURPHY) 1908
When You Live Opposite To Me (&
   MURPHY) 1911

LISTON, Harry° 1843–1929(?)
Baronet, The 1867
Days To Come, The 1898
Day We Went To Ramsgate, O (*m* Alfred
   LEE) 1868
Fwightful Dilemma, A (T. DODSWORTH:
   DODSWORTH & LISTON) 1873

I Love The Verdant Fields
It's Really A Dreadful Affair (w J. B.
  GEOGHEGAN)
Merry Moments

LLOYD, Arthur° 1840–1904
All Through Obliging A Lady 1882
American Beef 1878
And That's Why I've Not Got 'Em On
  1891
Arthur And Martha 1882
But Of Course It's No Business Of Mine
  c. 1865
Captain Lardidardidoo 1879
Constantinople c. 1865
Cow And Three Acres, A 1885
Cruel Mary Holder (arr. G. BICKNELL)
  1866
Diddle Diddle Dumpling My Son John
  1882
Don't Ask Me To Give Up Flo 1871
Drink And Let's Have Another 1891
Gallant 93rd., The c. 1883
German Band, A c. 1865
Going To The Derby In A Donkey Cart
  1880
I Couldn't 1887
Immenseikoff 1873
Ipecacu-anha (w W. W. THORNTON)
  1872
I Think It Looks Very Much Like It
It Makes Me So Awfully Wild 1872
It's Naughty But It's Nice 1873
It's Wonderful How We Do It 1865
Just By The Angel Of Islington 1873
Not For Joseph 1866
Of Course It's No Business Of Mine
Oh, Angelina 1867
One More Polka 1887
Pardonnez-moi 1884
Piano Organ Man, The c. 1887
Policeman 92X 1870
Postman, The c. 1867
Pretty Lips 1882
Pretty Little Mary (Chuck! Chuck!
  Chuck!) 1873

Promenade Elastique, The
Roman Fall 1870
St George's And St James' 1873
Signor Macstinger 1881
Silly Billy 1876
Song Of (Many) Songs c. 1864
Sophia Phia! Phia! 1882
Take It Bob (Song Of The Mill) 1873
Take The Cake 1887
Take Your Time, Don't Hurry 1891
Thomas' Sewing Machine 1873
Tichborne Case, The 1873
Twin Brothers, The 1876
Unfortunate Young Man, The
Where Are You? There You Are! 1884
Who'll Shut The Door? 1892
You Know? 1887

LOCKTON, Edward F. 1880–1940 a.k.a.
Edward TESCHEMACHER
Crossing The Bar (w Alfred TENNYSON)
  1915
  Also set by A. H. BEHREND and Hubert
  PARRY and some eighty others.
I'll Walk Beside You (m Alan MURRAY)
  1936
Little Town In Ireland, A (w Edward
  TESCHEMACHER) 1916
My Garden (m Guy D'HARDELOT) 1915
Nelson Touch, The (w R. A. KNIGHT)
  1915
When The Great Red Dawn Is Shining
  (m Evelyn SHARPE) 1917

LODER, E. H.
Diver, The (w G. Douglas THOMPSON)
  1890

LODER, Edward James 1813–65
Barefoot Friar, The (w Walter SCOTT)
  1844

LO(E)HR, Herman(n) 1871–1943
Kitchener's Boys (w Jessie POPE) 1915
Little Grey Home In The West (w
  D. EARDLEY-WILMOT) 1911
Remember Me (w E. TESCHEMACHER)
  1905

Where My Caravan Has Rested (*w*
TESCHEMACHER & D. CLEVELAND)
1909

LOEWE, Carl 1796–1869
Edward (based on trad. Scottish air)
1824
Erl King, The (*w* Johann W. von
GOETHE); see Franz SCHUBERT 1815

LÖHR, Herman(n) *see* LO(E)HR,
Herman(n)

LONG, J. P. d. 29 July 1950
Back At The Farm (& Ernie MAYNE:
Irving BERLIN) 1914
Original *w* BERLIN as I Want To Go Back
To Michigan.
Baden Powell Scout, The 1900
Good Luck, Tommy Atkins! Good Luck,
Jack Tar! 1914
I Can't Do My Bally Bottom Button Up
1916
Ipecacuanha (& Edgar BATEMAN) 1917
It's The First Time I've Ever Done That
(*m* Henry E. PETHER) 1931
John! John! John! Time's Going On (&
Paul PELHAM) 1910
Mary's Ticket (*m* Gilbert WELLS) 1909
Oh! It's A Lovely War (& Maurice
SCOTT) 1917
Rest Of The Day's Your Own, The (&
Worton DAVID) 1915
Ten Little Fingers, Ten Little Toes 1912
They All Walk The Wibbly Wobbly Walk
(*m* PELHAM) 1912
What D'Yer Think Of That? (My Old
Man's A Dustman) 1922
When The War Is Over, Mother Dear (&
A. J. MILLS & Bennett SCOTT) *c.*1915

LONG, Joseph S. 1848–1904
Little Miss Muffet Sat On A Tuffet (*m*
Ernest J. SYMONS) 1882
Not Much (*m* Kate ROYLE arr. Ernest
SYMONS) 1887
She Trotted Me Off To Church (*m* Kate
ROYLE, arr. A. MARTINI) 1883

LONGBRAKE, Arthur *see* ARZONIA, JOE

LONGFELLOW, Henry W. 1807–82
Excelsior (*m* Michael W. BALFE) 1857
Good Night! Good Night! Beloved! (*m*
BALFE) 1856
Green Trees Whispered Low And Mild,
The (*m* BALFE) 1856
I Shot An Arrow Into The Air (*m* BALFE)
1859
Old Clock On The Stairs, The (*m* John
BLOCKLEY) 1857
Onaway! Awake, Beloved! (*m*
S. COLERIDGE-TAYLOR) 1898
Thy Remembrance (*m* Frederich
COWEN) 1892
Village Blacksmith, The (*m* BALFE) 1855
Wreck Of The Hesperus, The (*m* J. L.
HATTON) 1853

LONGSTAFFE, Ernest d. 23 Nov. 1958
My Leetle Rosa (*w* anon.) 1927
Touch Of The Master's Hand, The (*w*
Myra Brooks WELCH) 1936
When The Sergeant-Major's On Parade
1925

LONSDALE, T. S.
But However 1887
Man In The Moon Is Looking, Love,
The (*m* W. G. EATON) 1877
My Aesthetic Love (*m* EATON) 1881
Oh, The Fairies (*m* EATON) 1878
Play Up At Them, They're All Milky!
Run For The Bus, A (*m* Louis RAYNAL)
1884
Some Girls Do And Some Girls Don't (*m*
EATON)
This Is The House That Jerry Built (*m*
EATON) 1887
Thought Reading On The Brain (*m* Slade
MURRAY)
Tommy Make Room For Your Uncle
1876
True Friends Of The Poor 1889
What Do You Take Me For? 1876
Whoa, Emma 1880

See Herbert DAYKIN for a similar title,
also Chas. DEANE.
You'll All Be Wanted (*m* EATON) 1878
You're Another (*m* William SIM) 1877

LORNE, Mark
Dr Bogie (& Gus GARRICK)
Oh! Ria, What Have You Done For Me?
(& Lawrence BARCLAY) *c*.1910
On The Day King Edward Gets His
Crown On (& Harry PLEON) 1902
What's The Matter With Me? 1902

LOVER, Samuel 1797–1868
Grandfather of Victor HERBERT
Bowld Sohjer Boy, The (Songs of Handy
Andy no. 11) 1845
Low Back'd Car, The *c*.1846
Mary Of Tipperary 1857
Molly Bawn 1841
Mother, He's Going Away 1845
Rory O'More 1835
Widow, The 1835

LOWEN, Tom
That Funny Little Bobtail Coat
(& Harry CHAMPION & Robert
GORMAN) 1907

LUCAS, Clarence 1866–1947
Song Of Songs, The (Fr. *w* Maurice
VAUCAIRE; Eng. *w* LUCAS: MOYA)
1914

LULLY, Jean Baptiste 1632–87
Bois Épais (Sombre Woods) (*w* Théo
MARZIALS: *m* arr. A. L.) 1892
From *Amadis*, 1684

LUTZ, W. Meyer 1829–1903
Dreams (*w* T. W. ROBERTSON) 1870
He Always Came Home To Tea (*w*
Francis C. BURNAND) 1877
Hush! The Bogie! (G. R. SIMS & Henry
PETTITT: LUTZ) 1890
Arr. Ed FORMAN; see David BRAHAM.
I Wooed My Love (*w* SIMS) 1889
Little Street Arab, The (*w* BURNAND)
1881

Love In The Orchestra (*w&m* Fred
LESLIE, arr. LUTZ) 1889
Star Of Hope (*w* FOLI) 1876
Three Jolly Tars (*w* Mme R. FOLI) 1876

LYLE, Kenneth
Army Of Today's All Right, The (*w* Fred
W. LEIGH) 1914
Come And Be One Of The Midnight
Sons (*w* Worton DAVID) 1901
From Marble Arch To Leicester Square
(*w* Charles KNIGHT) 1914
Here We Are! Here We Are! Here We
Are Again! (& KNIGHT) 1914
I'm Going To Be A Nut (& LEIGH) 1915
Jolly Good Luck To The Girl Who Loves
A Soldier (*w* Fred W. LEIGH) 1906

LYNNE, Frank° 1863–1916
I Didn't Mind It 1896

LYSTE, H. P.
Two Obadiahs, The 1876

LYTE, Revd Henry Francis 1793–1847
Abide With Me (*m* William Henry
MONK; see also Samuel LIDDLE) 1847

LYTTON, Lord 1803–73; Edward Bul-
wer Lytton
Absent Yet Present (*m* Maude Valerie
WHITE) 1880

LYTTON, W. T.
Then You Wink The Other Eye (*m* LE
BRUNN) 1890
What's That For, Eh? (Johnny Jones) (*m*
George LE BRUNN) 1892

MACCABE, Frederic° 1830–1904
Early In The Morning Merrily Oh! 1866
Fighting Dog, The (*w* Howard PAUL)
1871
Obstinate Man, An 1887
Shamrock, The 1860

McCALL, J. P. pseudonym of Peter
DAWSON
Boots (*w* Rudyard KIPLING) 1928

Cells (*w* KIPLING) 1930

McCARTHY, Joseph 1885–1943
Alice Blue Gown (*m* Harry TIERNEY) 1919
I'm Always Chasing Rainbows (& Harry CARROLL) 1918
Irene O'Dare (*m* TIERNEY) 1919
Rio Rita (*m* TIERNEY) 1927
They Go Wild, Simply Wild, Over Me (*m* Fred FIS(C)HER) 1917
Underneath The Arches (*w&m* Bud FLANAGAN, additional *w* McCARTHY) 1924
What Do You Want To Make Those Eyes At Me For? (& Howard JOHNSON: James V. MONACO) 1916
You Made Me Love You (*m* MONACO) 1913

McCORMACK, Harry°
My May Queen (& T. WILLIAMS: McCORMACK) 1904

McCREE, Junie 1865–1918
Nora Malone (Call My By Phone) (*m* Albert VON TILZER) 1909
Put Your Arms Around Me Honey (*m* VON TILZER) 1910

MACDERMOTT, G. H.° 1845–1901
Rap, Rap, Rap, I'm Married To A Medium (*m* Vincent DAVIES)
We Have Men, We Have Money (& Geoffrey THORN arr. E. J. SYMONS) 1882
Why Part With Jumbo (The Pet of The Zoo)? (*m* SYMONS) 1882

MacDONALD, Ballard 1882–1935
Come Over The Garden Wall (*m* James W. TATE) 1920
Georgie Took Me Walking In The Park (*m* Donovan MEHER & TATE) 1908
If I Should Plant A Tiny Seed Of Love (*m* TATE) 1908
I Love To Go Swimmin' With Women (*m* Sigmund ROMBERG) 1921

Indiana (*m* James F. HANLEY) 1917
On The Mississippi (*m* Harry CARROLL, arr. Arthur FIELDS) 1912
Rose Of Washington Square (*m* HANLEY) 1920
Trail Of The Lonesome Pine, The (*m* CARROLL) 1913

McEVOY, J.
Talkative Man From Poplar, The (arr. Edmund FORMAN) 1886

MACEY, Alan
My Missus Thinks She's Trilby (*w* Albert E. ELLIS) 1895

MACEY, Joe
Sarah (Sitting In The Shoe Shine Shop) (& Steve CONLEY & J. G. GILBERT & Jimmy McHUGH) 1919

MACFARREN, Sir George A. 1813–87
Beating Of My Own Heart, The (*w* R. M. MILNES) 1858
Freya's Gift (*w* Adelaide A. PROCTER) 1869
Pack, Clouds, Away (*w* Thomas HEYWOOD) 1867
Separation (*w* Edward William LANE) 1867
Widow Bird, The (*w* Percy Bysshe SHELLEY) 1867

MACFARREN, Natalie 1828–1916
Rose Among The Heather (Johann W. von GOETHE; Eng. adap. MACFARREN: Franz SCHUBERT) 1894
Songs My Mother Taught Me (Adolph HEYDUK, transl. MACFARREN: Antonin DVOŘÁK) 1880
Watch On The Rhine, The (*m* Carl WILHELM (1854)) 1863

McGHEE, Thomas d. 16 May 1955
A-Be My Boy (& Herbert RULE: L. SILBERMANN & A. GROCK) 1919
Fill 'Em Up (& RULE & James WALSH (2): SILBERMAN)

My Rachel Myer From Hawaii (& RULE
    & Sam STERN) 1917
That's Where The Soldiers Go (&
    WALSH)

McGHIE, William
O Give Me But My Arab Steed (*m*
    George A. HODSON) 1830

McGLENNON, Felix 1856–1943
And Her Golden Hair Was Hanging
    Down Her Back (*m* Monroe H.
    ROSENFELD; see Adrian ROSS)
    1894
Bachelors' Club, The 1895
British Bulldogs 1901
Comrades 1887
Comrades Still 1894
Diggin' Lumps Of Gold 1883
Don't Listen 1895
Down At The Farm-Yard Gate 1893
Englishman's Glory Is Freedom Of
    Speech, An (*w* Henry PRAGER) 1883
For The Sake Of The Dear Little Girls
    1886
Good Young Man, The (Albert HALL:
    McGLENNON arr. Peter CONROY)
    1896
John James Murphy 1898
Leave Me Comrades
Mr Captain Stop The Ship (*w* W. A.
    ARCHBOLD) 1894
One Touch Of Nature Makes The Whole
    World Kin 1897
Rowdy-Dowdy Boys, The (& Tom
    CONLEY: McGLENNON) 1891
Ship Belongs To A Lady, The 1899
Ship I Love, The 1898
Smiles! 1890
Sons Of The Sea 1897
Spare The Old Mud Cabin
That Is Love! 1891
    See G. W. HUNTER & R. G. KNOWLES
    for parody.
To Err Is Human, To Forgive Divine
    1894
We Mean To Keep The Seas

We Saved It For The Lodger (*w* Lester
    BARRETT) 1889
Woman, Lovely Woman (arr. A. E.
    DURANDEAU) 1886

McHUGH, James F. 1896–1967
Out Where The Blue Begins (& George
    GRAFF jun.: F. Bernard GRANT) 1923

McHUGH, Jimmy 1894–1969
Sarah (Sitting In The Shoe Shine Shop)
    (& Steve CONLEY & J. G. GILBERT &
    Joe MACEY) 1919

MACK, Andrew 1863–1931
Heart Of My Heart (& William JEROME)
    1899
Reuben Glue (& JEROME) *c*.1894

MACKAY, Charles 1814–89
Cheer, Boys, Cheer! (*m* Henry RUSSELL)
    1852
Gambler's Wife, The (*m* RUSSELL) 1846
Pauper's Drive, The (*m* RUSSELL) 1876
Ship On Fire, The (*m* RUSSELL)
There's A Good Time Coming, Boys (*m*
    RUSSELL) 1848
There's A Land (*m* Mary ALLITSEN)
    1896
Wind Of The Winter Night (*m* RUSSELL)
    1836

MACKAY, Colin *c*.1876–1905
Alas! My Poor Brother (*m* H. C. BARRY)
    1900
Kitchener's Karol (& BARRY) 1899

MACKAY, Eric 1851–98
Eleanore (*m* Samuel COLERIDGE-
    TAYLOR) 1899

MACKENZIE, Scott
I Ain't Nobody In Perticuler (*m* Fred W.
    LEIGH) 1907

McKINLEY, Mabel *see* GREY, Vivan

MACKNEY, C. H. 1821–86
Kiss In The Railway Train, The (*w*
    Watkins WILLIAMS) 1864

MACKNEY, E. W.° 1825–1909; except
for The Whole Hog Or None all first
published in 1862
Betsy Blossom pub. 1862
Darkies' Christmas Day pub. 1862
Hoop De Dooden Do pub. 1862
Ladies, Won't You Marry? pub. 1862
Little Dog's Tail, The pub. 1862
Mingo's Wide Awake pub. 1862
Oh! Don't I Love My Billy (w G. H.
   GEORGE) pub. 1862
Old Bob Ridley pub. 1862
Old Grey Goose, The pub. 1862
One Night While Wandering pub. 1862
Other Side Of Jordan, The pub. 1862
Peter Gray pub. 1862
Rosa Tanner pub. 1862
Sally, Come Up (w T. RAMSEY) pub.
   1862
Sambo's Apparition (w GEORGE) pub.
   1862
Some Folks pub. 1862
Whole Hog Or None, The (w George
   WARE m arr. H. H. HOWARD) 1855
   For song of same title see T. WESTROP.
Young Carpenter, The c.1862

MACLAGAN, Tom° c.1827–1902
Captain Jinks Of The Horse Marines
   1862
Don't You Do It Again 1863
Gal From Pennsylvania, The (Sam's
   Sally) (w G. W. HUNT) 1862
Hoop A Doodle Dum or I Want A Wife
   1862
Thy Spirit Clings To Me 1864

MACLEOD, A. C. a.k.a. (Lady) Anne
Campbell Wilson
Skye Boat Song, The (w Harold
   BOULTON) 1884
   Some versions have words by Robert
   Louis Stevenson.

MACLEOD, Fiona 1855–1905; pseudonym of William Sharp
Immortal Hour, The (m Rutland

BOUGHTON; w adap. Boughton
from Macleod's plays and poems) 1920

MACLEOD, Kenneth d. 1955
Eriskay Love Lilt, An (m trad., arr.
   Marjory Kennedy FRASER) 1909
Road To The Isles, The (m FRASER)
   1915

MACMURROUGH, Dermot d. 16 May
1943
Macushla (w Josephine V. ROWE) 1910

McNALLY, Leonard 1752–1820
Lass of Richmond Hill (m James HOOK)
   1789

MACNICOLL, J.
Old Tattered Flag, The (arr. J.
   Harrington YOUNG) 1887

MADDEN, Edward 1878–1952
Blue Bell (& Theodora (Dolly) MORSE:
   Theodore F. MORSE) 1898
By The Light Of The Silvery Moon (m
   Gus EDWARDS) 1909
I'd Sooner Be A Lobster Than A Wise
   Guy (m MORSE) 1907
Moonlight Bay (m Percy WENRICH)
   1912
Silver Bell (m WENRICH) 1905
When We Were Two Little Boys (m
   MORSE, arr. Alan BRADEN) 1903

MAGINI pseudonym of James (Jimmy)
HARGREAVES
Effa-Saffa-Laffa-Daffa-Dil (&
   P. BERNARD) 1919
I Wonder What It Feels Like To Be
   Poor? (& Dan LIPTON &
   C. W. MURPHY) 1913

MAGUIRE, Sylvester
Why Did You Make Me Care? (m Alfred
   SOLMAN) 1912

MAHONEY, J. Francis 1882–1945
When You Wore A Tulip And I Wore A
   Big Red Rose (m Percy WENRICH)
   1914

MAHONY, Francis S. 1804–66; a.k.a.
Father Prout
Bells Of Shandon, The (*m* various)
1844

MAJOR, H. Lance 1850–76
Scamp, The *or* They Can't Hold A
Candle To Me (*w* Henry PETTITT)
1873

MALARKEY, J.
Queen Amang The Heather (& Harry
LAUDER) 1909

MALBERT, A. Ward
I Want To Be A Lidy (*w* George DANCE)
1901

MALLETT, David 1705–61
Rule, Britannia! (or James THOMSON:
Thomas ARNE) *c.*1741

MANHILL, James *c.*1848–99
King Of The Boys (& C. ST LEONARDS:
Joseph CLEVE) 1893

MANNING, Robert
When Richard The First Sat On The
Throne 1908

MARAVILLE, George
Automatic Battery, The (*m* John S.
BAKER) *c.*1888

MARCH, Mary Ann Virginia *see*
GABRIEL, Virginia

MARK, F. W. 1868–1938; pseudonym of
E. V. LUCAS
Mary From Tipperary (*m* Herman
DAREWSKI) 1908

MARKS, Edward B. 1865–1945
Caprice (*m* George ROBEY) *c.*1895
December And May (*m* Joe STERN)
Little Lost Child, The (A Passing
Policeman) (*m* STERN) 1894
Mother Was A Lady (*m* STERN) 1896

MARKS, Geoffrey
Sailing 1886

MARLOWE, Christopher 1564–93
Come Live With Me And Be My Love
(*m* Henry R. BISHOP) 1819

MARRYAT, Capt. Frederick 1792–1848
Old Navy, The (*m* Charles Villiers
STANFORD) 1893

MARSHALL, A. R.
Blind Leading The Blind, The (*m* Fred
EPLETT) 1901
Breaches Of Promise 1901
'E Talks Like A Picture Book (*m* George
LE BRUNN) 1893
It Must Have Been The Lobster (*m*
Harriet FAWN arr. Fred HOLLIDAY)
1894
It's A Sprahtin *or* The Coster's
Moustache (*m* EPLETT) 1897
I Won The Bicycle 1884
Under The Red Robe 1897

MARSHALL, Charles *c.*1857–?
I Hear You Calling Me (*w* Harold
HARFORD) 1908

MARSHALL, Edward° 1825–1904
Where There's A Will There's A Way (*m*
Carlo MINSAI) 1881

MARSHALL, Henry I. 1883–1958
Be My Little Baby Bumble Bee (*w*
Stanley MURPHY) 1911

MARTIN, E. A.
I Forgot It (*m* Harry RANDALL) 1888

MARTIN, Easthope 1882–1925
Come To The Fair (*w* Helen TAYLOR)
1917

MARTIN, Horace
Close The Shutters, Willie's Dead
(*w&m* J. E. STEWART, arr. MARTIN)
*c.*1875

MARTIN, Robert
Ballyhooley 1886
I'm A Jolly Little Chap All Round 1887
Irish Fusiliers, The
Killaloe 1887

Mulrooney's Dog (arr. James WEAVER) 1895

MARTINI, A.
She Trotted Me Off To Church (J. S. LONG: Kate ROYLE, arr. MARTINI) 1883

MARZIALS, Théophile 1850–1920
Ask Nothing More (*w* Algernon SWINBURNE) 1883
Bois Épais (*m* Jean Baptiste LULLY, arr. A. L.) 1892
Go Pretty Rose (*w* M. BEVERLEY) 1886
Summer Night, A (*w* Arthur Goring THOMAS)
Twickenham Ferry, The (No. 1 of 'River Ditties') 1878

MASON, Alf°
Street Minstrel, The (*w* Percy LING) 1879

MASSAGE, A.
Sister Mary Walked Like That (*w* Gus LEVAINE) 1886

MASSEDER, H.
Where Are Those Boys? (*m&w* Walter HASTINGS, arr. MASSEDER) 1889

MASSON, Elizabeth *c*.1810–65
Wet Sheet And A Flowing Sea, A. (*w* Allan CUNNINGHAM) 1844
There were at least thirty other settings of Cunningham's poem.

MATTEI, Tito 1841–1914
Dear Heart (*w* Clifton BINGHAM; *m* composed *c*.1874) 1888
Love Must Come (*w* Mme FOLI) 1872
Oh, Oh Hear The Wild Wind Blow (*w* FOLI)

MATTHEWS, E. Cameron; sketch writer
Bustown By The Sea (& Wal PINK) 1907
Chasing Chickweed 1913
Dunmow Flitch, The 1914
His Opportunity 1919

Honeymoon Baby, The 1907
I've Bought A Pub 1913
Last Instalment, The 1917
Mr & Mrs John Bull 1909
No Other Way 1907
Oh! What A Wife! 1919
Photo Fix 1920
Rank Outsider, The 1915
Son Of His Father, The 1913
Star Tip, A 1921
Tale Of Geraniums, A 1913
Thin Red Line, The 1907
When The Clock Went Wrong 1917

MATTHISON, Arthur L. 1826?–83?
Little Hero (*m* Michael MAYBRICK) 1881
Nightfall At Sea (*m* Virginia GABRIEL) 1865
Sprung A Leak (*m* Stephen ADAMS)

MAURICE, George d. 17 June 1903
Longer You Linger, The (parody of Linger Longer Loo, Willie YOUNGE: Sidney JONES) 1893

MAYBRICK, Michael° 1844–1913; a.k.a. Stephen ADAMS
Little Hero (*w* A. MATTHISON) 1881
Warrior Bold, A

MAYER, Nat
Truth, The 1908

MAYNE, Ernie° 1872–1937
Back At The Farm *or* Down On The Farm (& J. P. LONG: Irving BERLIN) 1915
Original *w* BERLIN as I Want To Go Back To Michigan.

MAYNE, Godfrey
Did You? (*w* Norman GRANT) 1904
I'm A Dolly, Just A Dolly (*w* GRANT) 1905

MAYNE, Leslie; pseudonym of Lionel MONCKTON
Lovers Still (*w* C. Clifton BINGHAM) 1889

Maisie (*m* MONCKTON) 1900

MAYNE, Will 1870–1918
She Pushed Me Into The Parlour (*w* Alf
ELLERTON) 1912

Mayo, Fred
I Don't Care What Becomes Of Me (*w*
George CAMPBELL & Worton DAVID)
1910

Mayo, Sam° 1881–1938
At A Minute To Seven Last Night (*w*
Worton DAVID) 1906
Baby
Chinaman, The (*w* DAVID) 1906
Fiddle-De-Diddle-De-De (& Harry
LEIGHTON & Arthur RICKS, arr. Sam
AARONS) 1906
Gone Where They Don't Play Billiards
(& J. P. HARRINGTON: MAYO) 1903
He's Very Very Ill Indeed (*m* Pat
RAFFERTY, arr. John S. BAKER) 1890
I Can't Forget The Days When I Was
Young (*m* DAVID) 1919
If You Want To Get On In Revue *c*.1915
I Know Where The Flies Go On A Cold
And Frosty Morning (&
HARRINGTON) 1920
I'm Here If I'm Wanted *see* The
Policeman 1907
I'm Going To Sing A Song To You This
Evening (*w* DAVID) 1906
Johnnie 1923
Many Happy Returns Of The Day 1919
Old Tin Can, The (& Harry LEIGHTON:
MAYO) 1905
Policeman, The (I'm Here If I'm
Wanted) (*w* DAVID) 1907
Pushing Young Man, The (*w* DAVID)
1906
She Cost Me Seven-and-Sixpence (&
James HARGREAVES) 1904
Smith, Jones, Robinson And Brown (&
HARRINGTON: MAYO) 1910
Tally-Ho 1907
Trumpet Song, The

When I Woke Up This Morning 1904
Where Do Flies Go In The Winter
Time? (& Frank LEO) 1919

MEEN, George 1853–87
Oh, Fred! Tell Them To Stop (rev.
Charles DUNN) 1880

MEHER, Donovan
Crocodile Crawl, The (& Mason DIXON
& Will E. HAINES) 1915
Georgie Took Me Walking In The Park
(Ballard MACDONALD: & James W.
TATE) 1908

MEILHAC, Henri 1831–97
Flower Song, The (*Carmen*) (& Ludovic
HALÉVY; orig. Eng. transl. Henry
HERSEE (1878): Georges BIZET)
1875
Habanera (*Carmen*) (as for Flower Song)
1875
Toreador Song (*Carmen*) (as for Flower
Song) 1875

MELFORD, Mark° 1851–1914; sketches
Best Man Wins, The 1890
Frivolity *c*.1883
Hampshire Hog, The *or* Never Say Die
1899
My Wife Won't Let Me 1917
Non-Suited 1891
Ransomed
Ratts [*sic*]
Rope Merchant, The 1890
Tale Of A Tigress 1907

MELLISH, Colonel R. *see* JONSON, Ben

MELLOR, Tom 1880–1926
Give Me A Cosy Parlour (& Harry
GIFFORD & Alf J. LAWRANCE) 1907
I Like Your Old French Bonnet (&
GIFFORD & LAWRANCE) 1909
I Want To Go To Idaho (& GIFFORD &
LAWRANCE) 1908
I Wouldn't Leave My Little Wooden
Hut For You (& Charles COLLINS)
1896

Kitty, The Telephone Girl (& GIFFORD
& LAWRANCE & Huntley TREVOR)
1912
My Castle In Spain (m LAWRANCE &
GIFFORD) 1906
We're Irish And Proud Of It Too (&
GIFFORD & Fred GODFREY) 1914

MELVIN, Harold E.
Property Man, The (m Arthur WOOD)
1911

MELVILLE, Alexander d. 18 Mar. 1929
Bonnie Hielan' Mary (& Harry LAUDER:
LAUDER) 1901

MENDELSSOHN, Felix 1809–47
O For The Wings Of A Dove (from Hear
My Prayer) (Eng. w William
BARTHOLOMEW) 1844
On Wings Of Song (w Heinrich HEINE;
Eng. w Delia STUART) 1834

MERION, Charles M. d. 28 Mar. 1896;
a.k.a. James Cassidy
Apples Or Oranges, Bills Of The Play
1867
Goodbye Love or The Soldier's Farewell
(m Henry N. WEIPERT) 1873
Let's Enjoy Life While We Can
Merriest Girl That's Out, The (arr. Carlo
MINASI from James Cassidy's
Burlesque Galop) c.1854
Oh! Voulez Vous
Speak Out Like A Man 1873

MERIVALE, Herman 1839–1906
My Secret (m Virginia GABRIEL) 1870

MERRY, Mark
Me! (w Alec KENDAL) 1907

MERRY, Paul
You Put Me In Mind Of Me (w Ernest
REES) 1901

MERSON, Billy° 1881–1947
How Dare You! (& Harry BODEN &
? KEITH: Fred EPLETT) 1906
I'm Setting The Village On Fire 1919

Lighthouse Keeper, The c.1910
On The Good Ship 'Yacki Hicki Doo La'
1917
Photo Of The Girl I Left Behind, The
1911
Spaniard That Blighted My Life, The
1909

MESSAGER, André 1853–1929; m. Hope
TEMPLE
Philomel (w Adrian ROSS) 1919
Swing Song (w Lilian ELDÉE & Percy
GREENBANK) 1905
Trot Here And There (w ELDÉE &
GREENBANK) 1905

METZ, Theodore M. 1848–1936
Hot Time In The Old Town, A (w Joe
HAYDEN) 1896
Ta-Ra-Ra-Boom-De-Ay (see CORE
SONG-LIST) 1891

MEYER, George W. 1884–1959
Everything Is Peaches Down In Georgia
(Grant CLARKE: & Milton AGER) 1918
For Me And My Gal (& E. Ray GOETZ
& Edgar LESLIE) 1917
Where Did Robinson Crusoe Go With
Friday On Saturday Night? (w Sam M.
LEWIS & Joe YOUNG) 1916
You Taught Me How To Love You (w
Jack DRISLANE) 1919

MEYER, Joseph 1894–1987
California, Here I Come (& Buddy
DeSYLVA & Al JOLSON) 1924

MIDDLETON, Sidney
Midshipman, The (m Ernest
D'ALMAINE) 1893

MILBURN, Richard 1845?–1900?
Listen To The Mocking Bird (w Alice
HAWTHORNE) 1854

MILL, Paul° 1863–1916
Bye Bye Betsy (m George D. FOX) 1896
German Bandsman, The 1899
How Ma And Pa Differ

Patchwork Garden, The (& Edgar BATEMAN: J. Airlie DIX) 1902
Penny Whistler, The (*m* FOX) 1896
Tut-Tut! 1897
Village Of Toad-In-The-Hole, The (& E. A. SEARSON: DIX) 1907

MILLARD, Harrison 1830–95
Waiting (*w* Ellen H. FLAGG) 1867
You May Pet Me As Much As You Please (*w* Geo. COOPER) 1880

MILLER, Arthur d. 17 July 1935
Koffo Of Bond Street (sk.)
Key Of The Flat, The (sk.)

MILLER, Charles(?)
Ye Banks And Braes O' Bonnie Doon (*w* Robert BURNS: air, adap. Lost Is My Quiet For Ever) 1788

MILLER, Frank d. 23 Nov. 1970
If You're Irish Come Into The Parlour (*w* Shaun GLENVILLE) 1919

MILLER, Henry 1860?–1926?
Boy's Best Friend Is His Mother, A (*m* J. P. SKELLY) 1883

MILLETT, George Bown
Trelawney (Song Of The Western Men) (*w* Robert Stephen HAWKER) 1886

MILLIKEN, Richard A. d. 1815
'Tis The Last Rose Of Summer (*w* Thomas MOORE: air, The Groves of Blarney (1790)—Castle Hyde, arr. MILLIKEN, adap. MOORE) 1807

MILLS, A. J. 1871–1919
All Round The Town (& Bennett SCOTT & Tom COSTELLO) 1904
All The Nice Girls Love A Sailor (Ship Ahoy!) (*m* SCOTT) 1909
Always On The Dream (& Harry BEDFORD) 1898
Big Ben Struck One (*m* SCOTT) 1907
Boers Have Got My Daddy, The (& Harry CASTLING) 1900
Boys Brigade, The (*m* SCOTT) 1906

Boys In Khaki, Boys In Blue (*m* SCOTT) *c.*1914
By The Side Of The Zuyder Zee (*m* SCOTT) 1906
Come And Put Your Arms Around Me (*m* SCOTT) 1909
Constantinople At Olympia (*m* SCOTT) 1894
Darling Mabel (*m* SCOTT) 1896
Fall In And Follow Me (*m* SCOTT) 1910
Farewell My Little Yo-San! (*m* SCOTT) 1904
Has Anybody Seen My Tiddler? (& Frank W. CARTER) 1910
Has Anyone Seen A German Band? (*m* SCOTT) 1907
Hello! There, Flanagan (& Fred GODFREY & SCOTT) 1909
I Don't Care What Becomes Of Me (*m* SCOTT) 1911
Is Your Mother In, Molly Malone? (*m* George EVERARD) 1903
It's The Poor That Help The Poor (*m* SCOTT) 1904
I've Been Out With Charlie Brown (*m* SCOTT) 1909
I've Made Up My Mind To Sail Away (*m* SCOTT) 1902
I Wonder If You Miss Me Sometimes (*m* SCOTT) *c.*1910
Just Like The Ivy (& CASTLING) 1902
Kiss Me Goodbye, My Little Soldier Boy (*m* SCOTT) 1914
Knock The Two Rooms Into One (*m* SCOTT) 1900
Life Of A Soldier, The (*w&m* MILLS, arr. Albert PERRY) 1895
Lost, Stolen Or Strayed (*m* SCOTT) 1897
See same title by Henry PONTET.
My Boy's A Sailorman (*m* SCOTT) 1909
My Heart Is With You Tonight (*m* SCOTT) 1912
Oh! Ma'm'selle Ju-li-a! 1914
Oliver Cromwell (*m* SCOTT) 1912
On The Margate Boat (*m* SCOTT) 1899
Popsy Wopsy! (*m* SCOTT) 1913

Right In The Middle Of The Road (& CARTER) 1900

Sailing In My Balloon (*m* SCOTT) 1906

Ship Ahoy! (All The Nice Girls Love A Sailor) 1909

Show Me The Way To Your Heart (*m* SCOTT) *c*.1915

Sing Us A Song Of Bonnie Scotland (*m* SCOTT) 1913

Sister 'Ria (*m* Arthur LENNARD) 1895

Slight Mistake On The Part Of My Valet (*w* SCOTT) 1897

Somebody Else (*m* SCOTT) 1912

Take Me Back To Dear Old Blighty (& Fred GODFREY & SCOTT) 1916

Take Me In A Taxi, Joe (*m* SCOTT) 1913

There's A Girl Wanted There (*m* SCOTT) 1903

There's Going To Be A Wedding In The Stars (*m* SCOTT) 1912

They All Look Alike In The Dark (& GODFREY & SCOTT) 1918

What D'Ye Say, Molly Molloy? (*m* SCOTT) 1910

What-Ho, She Bumps! (& CASTLING) *see* W. STERN: Cuthbert COLLINS 1899

What Ho! There's Hair! (1900)

What'll? *c*.1912

What Will Mother Say? (*m* Walter KINO) 1898

When A Fellow Is Twenty-One (*m* SCOTT) 1904

When I Take My Morning Promenade (*m* SCOTT) 1910

When Loves Creeps In Your Heart (*m* SCOTT) *c*.1913

When The War Is Over, Mother Dear (& J. P. LONG & SCOTT) *c*.1915

Whiskers Round The Bottoms Of His Trousers (*m* George LESTER) 1898

Why Did I Leave My Little Back Room In Bloomsbury? (& CARTER) 1898

Wonderful Rose Of Love (*m* SCOTT) *c*.1914

Young Man Who Worked At The Milk Shop, The (& CARTER) 1891

You've Got A Long Way To Go (*m* CARTER) 1898

MILLS, H. G. L.
Cricket (*m* Edmund FORMAN) 1889

MILLS, Ivan
Kaiser Billy! 1916

MILLS, J.
Highly Colored Tie (*m* Fred W. VENTON) 1893

MILLS, Kerry 1869–1948
Meet Me In St Louis, Louis (*w* Andrew B. STERLING) 1904

Red Wing (*w* Thurland CHATTAWAY) 1905

Whistling Rufus 1899

MILLS, Wilfrid
My Ain Folk (*m* Laura G. LEMON) 1904

MILNE, Allan
Adverts Of Modern Medicine Makers (*w* Fred ROME) 1902

MILNES, R. Monckton 1809–85
Beating Of My Own Heart, The (*m* George A. MACFARREN) 1858

MINASI, Carlo
Merriest Girl That's Out, The (*w&m* Charles MERION, arr. MINASI from Jack Cassidy's Burlesque Galop) *c*.1865

Where There's A Will There's A Way (*w* Edward MARSHALL) 1881

MINNIGERODE, Meade° 1887–1967
Whiffenpoof Song, The (Rudyard KIPLING, adap. Guy S. GALLOWAY & MINNIGERODE: Guy H. SKULL adap. Tod B. GALLOWAY) *c*.1909

MITCHELL, J. F. d. 12 Nov. 1888
Agricultural Irish Girl, The (arr. Peter CONROY) 1885

You Should Never Never Marry (*m* Slade
MURRAY) 1884

MITCHELL, Samuel N.
Just Touch The Harp Gently (*m* Charles
BLAMPHIN) 1870

MITCHELL, Sidney D.
Bluin' The Blues (*m* Henry W. RAGAS)
1919

MITCHELL-INNES, T. L.
Eton Boating Song (W. J. CORY: A.
DRUMMOND, transcr. MITCHELL-
INNES, arr. Evelyn WOODHOUSE)
1878

MOLLOY, James Lynam 1838–1909
Bantry Bay 1889
Darby And Joan (*w* Fred E.
WEATHERLY) 1878
Finette (*w* SADIE) 1888
Kerry Dance, The 1879
Love's Old Sweet Song (*w* G. Clifton
BINGHAM) 1884
Oh, How Delightful! (*w* Arthur
SKETCHLEY) 1868
Sailor's Dance, The 1889
Three Beggars, The (*w* WEATHERLY)
*c.*1885
Thursday (*w* WEATHERLY) 1884
Vagabond, The (*w* Charles Lamb
KENNEY) 1871

MONACO, James (Jimmie) V.
1885–1945
All That I Want Is You (*w* Joe
GOODWIN) 1920
Row, Row, Row (*w* William JEROME)
1912
What Do You Want To Make Those Eyes
At Me For? (*w* Howard JOHNSON &
Joseph McCARTHY) 1916
You Made Me Love You (*w* McCARTHY)
1913
You're A Dangerous Girl 1916

MONCKTON, Lionel 1861–1924; a.k.a.
Leslie MAYNE

All Down Piccadilly (Arthur WIMPERIS
& MONCKTON: MONCKTON) 1909
Arcady Is Ever Young 1909
Chalk Farm To Camberwell Green
1915
Charming Weather (*w* WIMPERIS) 1909
Come To The Ball (*w* Adrian ROSS)
1910
Cricket! (*w* B. C. STEPHENSON) 1899
Grandmamma (*w* ROSS) 1906
Half-Past Two (*w* WIMPERIS) 1909
I Love London 1909
I'm A Naughty Girl 1898
I Want To Be A Military Man (*w* Owen
HALL) 1899
Keep Off The Grass 1901
Maisie (*w* Leslie MAYNE) 1900
Moonstruck 1909
My Own Little Girl (*w* Percy
GREENBANK) 1902
Oh! (*w* Fred E. WEATHERLY) 1900
Pipes Of Pan, The (*w* WIMPERIS) 1909
Rhoda Ran A Pagoda 1899
Simple Little String, A 1896
Soldiers In The Park (*w* H. GREENBANK
& A. HOPWOOD: MONCKTON) 1898
Temple Bell, The (*w* WIMPERIS) 1911
Two Little Sausages 1907
Under The Deodar (*w* ROSS) 1902
When I Marry Amelia (*w* ROSS) 1901
When You Are In Love (*w* H.
GREENBANK) 1912

MONK, William Henry 1823–89
Abide With Me (*w* Revd Henry Francis
LYTE) 1847

MONTAGU, Edward° d. 5 Feb. 1975;
sometimes spelled Montague; pseudo-
nym of Frederick E. M. DAY
Molly Molyneux 1907
Moonshine (*m* Silvio HEIN) 1916
My Best Gal's Gone And Left Me (*w*
Malcolm ARNOLD) 1900
My Filipino Baby 1911
My Queen Of Pygmy Land 1911

On The Dear Old Shore 1905
So What's The Use? 1907
Too-Ra-Li-Oo-Ra-Li 1906

MONTAGUE, Harold° b. 1874
Learning To Ride The Byke 1897

MONTGOMERY, William H. d. 1886
I Want To Be A Bloomer (*w* Henry
ABRAHAMS) 1851

MONTROSE, Percy?
Oh! My Darling Clementine (or Barker
BRADFORD?) *w* 1863 *m* 1884

MOOR-KING, Alfred
Ta-Ra-Ra-Boom-De-Ay (see CORE
SONG-LIST) 1891

MOORE, G. W. 'Pony'° 1820–1909
Baby Don't You Cry
Blind Boy, The (*w* R. LEE) 1871
Dress'd In A Dolly Varden 1870
Grecian Bend, The (arr. M. HOBSON)
1869
High, Low Or Jack Game (arr. J.
WILLIAMS) 1866
Hunky Dorum, We Are (Am?) The Boys
(arr. WILLIAMS) 1866
Mixed Up Family, The *c.* 1870
Oh I'd Like To Be A Bird 1870
Pretty Little Girl That I Know
Shew! Fly *or* I Feel Like A Morning
Star
Valley By The Stream, The 1876

MOORE, J. Charles d. 20 Mar 1938
Call Round Any Old Time (*w* E. W.
ROGERS) 1908
Don't Stop My 'Arf A Pint O' Beer (*w*
Cornelius PRATT) 1911
Every Little Movement Has A Meaning
Of Its Own (*w* Fred CLIFFE) 1910
Sung by Marie Lloyd—for Lina
Abarbanell's song with same title see Otto
HARBACH: Karl HOSCHNA.
Put Me Upon An Island Where The
Girls Are Few (*w&m* Will LETTERS,
arr. MOORE) 1908

MOORE, Thomas 1779–1852; *Irish
Melodies* and *National Airs* published in
parts 1807–34
Believe Me If All Those Endearing
Young Charms (air, trad.) 1807
Harp That Once Through Tara's Halls,
The (air, 18th century) 1807
Lesbia Hath A Beaming Eye (*m* trad.?
anon.? arr. Sir John STEVENSON) 1807
Love's Young Dream (arr. STEVENSON)
1807
Meeting Of The Waters, The (air, The
Old Head Of Dennis, arr.
STEVENSON) *c.* 1820
Minstrel Boy, The (air, trad. (Welsh)
The Moreen, arr. Edward BUNTING)
1807
Oft In The Stilly Night (*m* trad.,
sometimes attr. STEVENSON) 1815
She Is Far From The Land (*m* Frank E.
LAMBERT (1897) , also set by many
others) 1807
'Tis The Last Rose Of Summer (air, The
Groves of Blarney (1790)—Castle
Hyde, arr. Richard A. MILLIKEN,
adap. MOORE) 1807

MORANDE, Paul A. d. 22 July 1953
Piccadilly (*w* Bruce SIEVIER & Walter
WILLIAMS) 1921

MORLEY, Joe
Reasons (*w* Fred ROME)

MOROSS, Jerome
Willie The Weeper

MORRIS, A. J. *c.* 1861–1905
All That Glitters Is Not Gold (*m* George
LE BRUNN) 1896
Doctor, The (*m* LE BRUNN) 1892
Lizer 'Awkins (*m* LE BRUNN) 1892
Wot Cher, Polly! (*m* LE BRUNN) 1895

MORRIS, Arthur
Territorial, The (*w* T. WARD) 1908

MORRIS, 'General' George Pope
1802–64

Oh! Woodman, Spare That Tree (*m* Henry RUSSELL) 1837

MORRISON, F.
Tell Me Mary How To Woo Thee (*m* George A. HODSON) *c*.1830

MORSE, Theodora 1890–1953; a.k.a. Dolly TERRISS
Blue Bell (& Edward MADDEN: Theodore F. MORSE) 1898
Three O'Clock In The Morning (*m* Julian ROBLEDO) 1921

MORSE, Theodore F. 1873–1924
Blue Bell (*w* Edward MADDEN & Theodora (Dolly) MORSE) 1898
Bobbin' Up And Down (*w* Dolly TERRISS) 1913
Hail! Hail! The Gang's All Here (TERRISS: & A. L. SULLIVAN) 1917
I'd Sooner Be A Lobster Than A Wise Guy (*w* MADDEN) 1907
When We Were Two Little Boys (MADDEN: MORSE, arr. Alan BRADEN) 1903

MORTON, Hugh 1865–1916 pseudonym of Charles M. S. MCLELLAN
My Beautiful Lady (*m* Ivan CARYLL) 1911
Narragansett (On The Beach At) (*m* Gustave KERKER) 1897
She Is The Belle Of New York (*m* KERKER) 1897
Teach Me How To Kiss (*m* KERKER) 1897
They All Follow Me (*m* KERKER) 1897
Wine Woman And Song (*m* KERKER) 1897

MORTON, Richard d. 13 Jan. 1921
All Coons Look Alike To Me (*m* Ernest HOGAN) 1896
Bridget And Mike (*m* Minnie CUNNINGHAM) 1899
Brighton (orig. The Bowery, Charles H. HOYT: Percy GAUNT 1891; Eng. *w* Richard MORTON & Fred GILBERT) 1894

Cook's Excursion Trip, A (*m* George LE BRUNN) 1897
Dandy Coloured Coon, The (*m* LE BRUNN) 1894
Don't Laugh (*m* LE BRUNN) 1891
Ghost Of Sherlock Holmes, The (*m* H. C. BARRY) 1894
Girly-Girly (*m* Jerry COHAN) *c*.1890
Idler, The (& J. P. HARRINGTON: LE BRUNN) 1896
I Do, Doodle-Oodle-Oo (*m* Fred EPLETT) 1903
Jap, The (*m* LE BRUNN) *c*.1895
La-Didily-Idily, Umti-Umti-Ay (& C. M. RODNEY: RODNEY) 1894
Mock Melodrama (& Harry PLEON: PLEON) 1893
Poor Thing (*m* LE BRUNN) 1891
Regent Street (*m* E. NEVIN)
Since I Came To London Town (*m* P. Mario COSTA) 1900
Such A Don Don't You Know! (*m* LE BRUNN) 1895
Tale Of The Mile End Road, A (*m* LE BRUNN) 1891
Ta-Ra-Ra-Boom-De-Ay (see CORE SONG-LIST) 1891
Twiggy Voo? (*m* LE BRUNN) 1892
What Do I Care? (*m* F. W. VENTON) 1892
Word-Lets, Gag-Lets, And Yarn-Lets (*m* Johann STRAUSS II, arr. John S. BAKER) 1893

MOSES-TOBANI, Theodore 1855–1933
Hearts And Flowers (Mary D. BRINE: adap. MOSES-TOBANI from Winter Stories, Alphons CZIBULKA) 1899

Moss, Katie d. 3 May 1947
Floral Dance, The (air based on trad.) 1911

MOTZAN, Otto 1880–1937
Bright Eyes (Harry B. SMITH: & M. K. JEROME) 1920

Moy, Tom
Why Can't It Always Be Saturday? (arr. William HARGREAVES) c.1900

MOYA d. 1922; pseudonym of Harold Vicars
Song Of Songs, The (Eng. w Clarence LUCAS, Fr. w Maurice VAUCAIRE) 1914

MUIR, Lewis F. 1881–1915
Hitchy-Koo (L. Wolfe GILBERT: & Maurice ABRAHAMS) 1912
Ragtime Cowboy Joe (Grant CLARKE: & ABRAHAMS) 1912
Waiting For The Robert E. Lee (w GILBERT) 1912

MULCHINOCK, William P. 1820–64
Rose Of Tralee, The (see CORE SONG-LIST) c.1850

MULLEN, Alfred d. 1881
As They Marched Through The Town (The Captain With His Whiskers) (Haynes BAYLY: Sidney NELSON adap. MULLEN) (see CORE SONG-LIST) 1869

MUNSON, Eddie
Ida! Sweet As Apple Cider (w Eddie LEONARD) 1903

MURPHY, C. W. 1875–1913
Ain't I No Use Mister Jackson? (& Dan LIPTON) 1905
All Hands On Deck (& LIPTON); see also CHESTERFIELD & SIM 1909
Baby's Name, The (MURPHY & Albert HALL: MURPHY) 1900
Come With Me Down Regent Street (& Worton DAVID) 1910
Dancing To The Organ In The Mile End Road (& Pat RAFFERTY: RAFFERTY) 1893
Eh! Dear Me! It's A Fine Place, Paree! (& DAVID) 1914
Esau, Take Me On The Seesaw (& LIPTON) 1908

Flanagan (& Will LETTERS) 1910
Girl In The Clogs And Shawl, The (w H. CASTLING) 1909
Has Anybody Here Seen Kelly? (& LETTERS) 1909
Hold Your Hand Out, Naughty Boy! (& DAVID) 1913
I Do Like You Susie In Your Pretty Little Sunday Clothes (& DAVID) 1912
If At First You Don't Succeed (& LIPTON) 1906
If I Had A Girl As Nice As You (& LIPTON) 1904
If The World Were Ruled By Girls (& George ARTHURS) 1905
I Live In Trafalgar Square 1902
I'm Looking For Mr Wright (R. P. WESTON: & H. DAREWSKI) 1909
In The Valley Of Golden Dreams (& DAVID) 1913
I Parted My Hair In The Middle (& DAVID) 1913
I Shall Get In Such A Row When Martha Knows (& DAVID) 1913
I Wonder What It Feels Like To Be Poor? (& LIPTON & MAGINI) 1913
Jere-Jeremiah (& DAVID) 1913
Kelly The Carman 1898
Let's All Go Down The Strand (& CASTLING) 1908
Little Yellow Bird (Goodbye) (& W. HARGREAVES) 1903
Mickey Rooney's Ragtime Band (& DAVID) 1913
Milligan's Motor Car 1900
Mrs Carter (& Edgar BATEMAN: MURPHY) 1900
Sung by Gus Elen.
My Girl's A Yorkshire Girl (& LIPTON) 1908
Oh! Oh! Antonio (& LIPTON) 1908
Put A Little Bit Away For A Rainy Day (& LIPTON) 1905
Put Me Amongst The Girls (& LIPTON) 1907

She's A Lassie From Lancashire (&
  LIPTON & John NEAT) 1907
Singer Was Irish, The (& CASTLING)
  1904
Stars Didn't Happen To Be Shining, The
  (w HALL)
They're All Single By The Seaside (&
  DAVID) 1911
Thing He Had Never Done Before, A
We All Go The Same Way Home (&
  CASTLING) 1911
We Don't Want Any More Daylight (&
  LIPTON) 1908
When That Yiddisher Band Played That
  Irish Tune (& DAVID) 1912
When You Live Opposite To Me (&
  LIPTON) 1911
You Ask Me Why I Love You 1902

MURPHY, J.
Mary And The Butcher (& Sid BANDON:
  W. T. WEBB) 1894

MURPHY, Stanley 1875–1919
Be My Little Baby Bumble Bee (m
  Henry I. MARSHALL) 1911
Put On Your Old Gray Bonnet (m
  Stanley WENRICH) 1909
They Always Pick On Me (m Harry VON
  TILZER) 1911

MURRAY, Alan 1890–1952
Awfully Chap, The (w Jack HULBERT)
  1914
I'll Walk Beside You (w Edward G.
  LOCKTON) 1936
On The River Cam 1890
Rag-Time Craze, The (w HULBERT)
  1913
What's The Use? (w Hugh E. WRIGHT)
  1913
Wusky Woozle, The (w WRIGHT)
  1913

MURRAY, Fred d. 11 Jan. 1922
All Through Riding On A Motor 1903

Amateur Whitewasher, The (& Fred W.
  LEIGH) 1896
'Arry, 'Arry, 'Arry (& LEIGH: G. LE
  BRUNN) 1902
Boiled Beef And Carrots (& Charles
  COLLINS) 1909
Charlie On The Mash (& LEIGH) 1898
Fol-The-Rol-Lol (& LEIGH) 1902
Ginger, You're Balmy! 1910
He's Going There Every Night (&
  LEIGH: LE BRUNN) 1902
He Was A Good Kind Husband (&
  LEIGH)
I 'Aven't Told 'Im (& LEIGH: LE BRUNN)
  1898
I'm Henery The Eighth, I Am! (& R. P.
  WESTON) 1910
I'm Not Particular (& LEIGH) 1898
It's All Right In The Summertime (&
  George EVERARD) 1902
Last Good-Bye, The (& LEIGH)
  c.1914
Let's Have A Basin Of Soup 1911
Little Bit Off The Top, A (& LEIGH)
  1898
My Ragtime Missus 1904
Next Horse I Ride On, The (&
  EVERARD) 1905
Oh, Amelia (m C. E. HILBURY) 1906
Oh Girls! (You Don't Know How I Love
  You) (& LEIGH) 1897
Old Man's Darling, An (& EVERARD)
  1903
  See Albert HALL: Orlando POWELL for
  song of same title.
Our Lodger's Such A Nice Young Man
  (& Lawrence BARCLAY) 1897
She'd Never Had A Lesson In Her Life
  (m Orlando POWELL) 1903
Svengali! (& LEIGH) 1895
There's Danger On The Line (&
  COLLINS & LEIGH) c.1911
  See also George P. NORMAN.
There They Are—The Two Of Them On
  Their Own (& LEIGH: LE BRUNN &
  E. NEVIN) 1898

MURRAY, Gaston 1826–89
I Like To Be A Swell

MURRAY, Slade° 1859–1913
Balaclava (Oh, 'Tis A Famous Story)
 (John Arthur ELLIOTT: MURRAY, arr.
 Edmund FORMAN) 1884
Come Down And Open The Door, Love
 (w Arthur SUTHERD, arr. FORMAN,
 rev. 1898 C. G. COTES: Bennett
 SCOTT) 1884
Oh, My! Certainly Not (w SUTHERD)
Thought Reading On The Brain (w T. S.
 LONSDALE)
You Should Never Never Marry (w J. F.
 MITCHELL) 1884

MUSGRAVE, F.
Mr Gorilla (w H. J. BYRON) c.1870

MYNYDDOG 1833–77; pseudonym of
Richard Davies
Myfanwy (m Joseph PARRY; Eng. w (as
 Arabella) CUHELYN) 1880

NAIRN, Ralph
Come And Be A Soldier (w Leslie
 STILES) 1904

NAIRNE, Lady Caroline 1766–1845
Caller Herrin' (air, trad.) c.1823
Hey, Now The Day
Land O' The Leal, The
Wi' A Hundred Pipers An' A' (perhaps &
 Elizabeth RAINFORTH) c.1851

NAISH, Archie° b. 1878
Band Played On, The (w Clifford GREY)
 1916
 For 'Casey would waltz with a strawberry
 blonde, etc.' see J. F. PALMER.
Duck Pond, The 1912
Employment Bureau, The 1906
How Many Beans Make Five? 1914
Made In England 1914
Night Light, The 1916
Sybil
Village Pump, The 1910

Why Don't They Knight Charlie
 Chaplin? 1917
Won't You Waltz With Me? 1910

NASH, 'Jolly' John° 1830–1901
Englishman And Frenchman, The 1896
It's Very Different Now
Laughing Gas
Little Brown Jug (m J. E. WINNER)
 1867
Merry, Funny Little Toper, The 1865
Muldoon's Wedding 1889

NEALE, Revd Dr John 1818–66
Good King Wenceslas (m trad.) 1853

NEAT, John 1876–1949
I Wonder If The Girl I'm Thinking Of Is
 Thinking Of Me (w Harry CASTLING)
 1906
Love Or Gold (w&m E. W. ROGERS, arr.
 NEAT) 1900
Midnight Son's Farewell, The (w&m
 ROGERS, arr. NEAT) 1903
Pretty Little Girl From Nowhere, The
 (w ROGERS) 1909
She's a Lassie From Lancashire (& Dan
 LIPTON & C. W. MURPHY) 1907
Sweethearts Still (w&m ROGERS, arr.
 NEAT) 1902
Thick Ear'd Jim (w&m ROGERS, arr.
 NEAT) 1903
Thick Headed Danny (w&m ROGERS,
 arr. NEAT) 1893

NELLA pseudonym of ?; files and con-
tracts missing from EMI records
Mother Weep Not For Your Boy (m
 Alfred LEE) 1871
Uhlan's Farewell, The (m LEE) 1874

NELSON, Eddie G. 1885–1969
Oh! Mother, I'm Wild! (& Howard
 JOHNSON & Harry PEASE) 1919
Peggy O'Neil (& PEASE & Gilbert
 DODGE) 1921
Sarah! Come Over Here! (m Con
 CONRAD) 1918

NELSON, Sidney 1800–62

Bonnie Dundee (*w* Walter SCOTT) 1855
Also set by many others.

Mary Of Argyle (*w* Charles JEFFREYS)
c.1855

Oh! They March'd Thro' The Town (The
Captain With His Whiskers) (*w*
T. Haynes BAYLY) *c*.1838
See also Alfred MULLEN and CORE SONG-
LIST.

Pilot, The (*w* BAYLY) *c*.1825

NEMO pseudonym of Theodore PIC-
COLOMINI, a.k.a. Henry Theodore
PONTET

I'd Rather Not! (*m* Henry Theodore
PONTET) 1884

NEVETT, R. Linton

Are You A Mason? 1907

Hold Your Hand Out! (*w* Worton DAVID)
1909

NEVIN, E.

Regent Street (*w* Richard MORTON)

There They Are—The Two Of Them
On Their Own (Fred W. LEIGH &
Fred MURRAY: & G. LE BRUNN)
1898

NEVIN, ETHELBERT 1862–1901

Little Boy Blue 1893

Mighty Lak' A Rose (*w* Frank L.
STANTON) 1901

Narcissus (piano instrumental) 1898

O That We Two Were Maying (*w*
Charles KINGSLEY) 1902

Rosary, The (*w* Robert Cameron
ROGERS) 1898

NEWBOLT, Henry 1862–1938

Drake's Drum (*m* Charles Villiers
STANFORD) 1905
Set by eight others.

Old Superb, The (*m* STANFORD) 1904

NEWCOME, Tom B.

Cockney In Kilts, The (*m* Tatten HALL)
1902

NEWLAND, James 1843–1931

Detective Camera (*m* George LE
BRUNN) 1892

NEWMAN, V.

Pinkie (sk.) 1914

NEWTON, Eddie

Casey Jones (*w* T. Lawrence SEIBERT)
1909

NEWTON, Eileen

Somewhere A Voice Is Calling (*m* Arthur
F. TATE) 1911

NEWTON, Ernest d. 29 Jan. 1929; song
editor with Novello & Co.

For Love Of You (*w* Fred E.
WEATHERLY) 1903

Nita Gitana (*w* WEATHERLY) 1893

There Little Girl, Don't Cry (*w* J. W.
RILEY) 1909

NEWTON, H. Chance 1854–1931; a.k.a.
Carados, also Gawain. Wrote lyrics as
Richard HENRY

Bai Jove! (*m* Jimmy GLOVER) 1880

Celestial Bride, The (sk.) 1918

Home From Home (sk.) 1895

How London Lives (*m* Theo WARD)
1898

Wellington (sk.) 1912

NICHOLLS, Harry° 1852–1926

Be Prepared *c*.1890

I'm Getting A Big Boy Now (*m* Oscar
BARRETT) 1880

In My Fust 'Usband's Time (arr. E. J.
SYMONS) 1882

Nonsense! Yes! By Jove! (*m* BARRETT)
1881

Put Them In The Lord Mayor's Show

Their Customs Are Very Peculiar (*m*
Procida BUCALOSSI) *c*.1885

Those Girls At The School (arr.
E. JONGHMANS) 1882

When You Come To Think Of It
1887

NICHOLLS, Horatio 1888–1964;
pseudonym of Lawrence WRIGHT
Let's All Go To The Music Hall
   (w Ralph BUTLER & Harry TILSLEY)
   1934
That Old-Fashioned Mother Of Mine (w
   Worton DAVID) 1919
When The Guards Are On Parade (w
   Leslie SARONY) 1931

NIGHTINGALE, H. M.
Little Brown Bird (m Teresa DEL
   RIEGO) 1912

NOBLE, Gordon
Great White Mother (& G. D.
   WHEELER) 1896

NOLAN, Michael° c.1869–1910
Little Annie Rooney 1889
Song That Broke My Heart, The (G. W.
   HUNTER & John STOCKS: & Julian
   JORDAN) 1890

NORMAN, George P.
I Won Her Heart At Billiards (m Charles
   COOTE jun.) 1876
There's Danger On The Line (The Great
   Semaphore Song) c.1885
   See also Chas. COLLINS & Fred W. LEIGH
   & Fred MURRAY.

NORRIS, Harry B.
Afternoon Parade, The 1897
Algy, The Piccadilly Johnny With The
   Little Glass Eye 1895
Bold Militiaman, The 1896
Burlington Bertie 1900
For The Weekend 1897
Seaside Girls 1899

NORTON, Hon. Mrs Caroline 1808–77;
sister of Lady DUFFERIN and grand-
daughter of Richard Brinsley Sheridan
Arab's Farewell To His Favourite Steed,
   The (m John BLOCKLEY) 1869
Juanita (air, Handel's Lascia Ch'io
   Pianga) 1850
Murmur Of The Shell, The 1861

NORTON, Frederic 1869–1946
Any Time's Kissing Time (w Oscar
   ASCHE) 1916
Cobbler's Song, The (w ASCHE) 1916

NORTON, George A. 1880–1923
My Melancholy Baby (& Maybelle E.
   WATSON: Ernest M. BURNETT) 1912

NORWORTH, Jack° 1879–1959 m. Nora
BAYES-NORWORTH (div.)
Honey Boy 1907
Mr Wu (& R. P. WESTON) 1914
Shine On Harvest Moon (NORWORTH:
   & Nora BAYES-NORWORTH) 1908
Take Me Out To The Ball Game (&
   Albert VON TILZER) 1908

NOVELLO, Ivor 1893–1951
If (w Edward TESCHEMACHER)
Keep The Home Fires Burning (orig. Till
   The Boys Come Home) (w Lena
   Guilbert FORD) 1914
Little Damozel, The (w Fred E.
   WEATHERLY) 1912
Megan (w WEATHERLY) 1914

NUGENT, Maude° 1874–1958
Sweet Rosie O'Grady 1890

O'CONNOR, Jack d. 19 Nov. 1923
Somewhere In France, Dear Mother (m
   Arthur LE CLERQ) 1915

O'CONNOR, Shamus
MacNamara's Band (w John James
   STANFORD) 1889

OFFENBACH, Jacques 1819–80
Can-Can, The 1858
   See CORE SONG-LIST.
Gendarmes' Duet (w H. B. FARNIE)
   1859

OGILVIE, Hugh° d. 25 Oct. 1931
Hail Caledonia! (m Arthur STROUD)
   1912

O'GORMAN, Joe° 1863–1937
Wild Man Of Poplar, The (& Joe
   TENNYSON) 1890

O'HARA, Geoffrey 1882–1967
K-K-K-Katy 1918

O'HOGAN, Betsy pseudonym of
Lawrence WRIGHT
Old Father Thames (*w* Raymond
  WALLACE) 1933

O'KEEFFE, John 1747–1833
I Am A Friar Of Orders Gray (*m* William
  REEVE, from his opera *Merry
  Sherwood*) 1795

OLCOTT, Chauncey° 1858–1932
Mother Machree (Rida Johnson YOUNG:
  & Ernest R. BALL) 1910
My Wild Irish Rose 1899
When Irish Eyes Are Smiling (& George
  GRAFF: BALL) 1912

OLIPHANT, Thomas 1799–1873
Ash Grove, The (Eng. version; air, trad.
  Welsh)
Men Of Harlech

OLIVER, Herbert 1883–1950
Down Vauxhall Way (*Songs Of Old
  London*) (*w* Edward TESCHEMACHER)
  1912
Yonder (*w* TESCHEMACHER) 1920

OLIVER, Will 1852–1916
Happy Eliza And Converted Jane 1881
Waiting To Meet Pretty Mary
Yarmouth On The Sands

OLSEN, Elsie pseudonym of Cuthbert
CLARKE

O'MALLEY, Jack
Coster Rag (*m* J. Royce SHANNON)
  1910

O'MEARA, D. A.
Beauty's Smile (*m* from German trad.)
  1817
Buy A Broom (The Bavarian Girl's Song)
  (*m* Alexander LEE) 1821

O'REILLY, P. J. *c.*1876–1924
Anchorsmith (*m* Cuthbert CLARKE)
  1911

Captain Mac' (*m* Wilfrid SANDERSON)
  1914
Drake Goes West (*m* SANDERSON) 1910
For You Alone (*m* Henry E. GEEHL)
  1919

ORLOB, Harry b. 1885
I Wonder Who's Kissing Her Now? (*w*
  Frank R. ADAMS & William HOUGH:
  & Joseph H. HOWARD) 1909

ORRED, Meta d. 1953
Far Away In The West (*m* Virginia
  GABRIEL) 1876
In The Gloaming (*m* Lady Arthur HILL)
  1877

OSBORN, C.
Don't Leave Your Mother When Her
  Hair Turns Grey (*m* E. J. SYMONS)
  1881

OSBORNE, Charles° 1858–1929
Accidents *or* Up To The Moon He
  Bunked (arr. Henry E. PETHER) 1892
Bunk-A-Doodle I Do (arr. PETHER)
  1893
Conundrums 1895
Forgotten *or* He Was One Of The Old
  Brigade *c.*1889
For Old Times' Sake 1898
Git Your 'Air Cut (& George
  BEAUCHAMP & Fred EPLETT) 1892
Good Old London Town Girl, A
He Was One Of The Light Brigade 1890
  See Pat RAFFERTY for parody.
In (arr. EPLETT) 1891
I Wasn't So Drunk As All That
Jocular Joker, The 1908
Later On 1886
Man With The Bullet Proof Coat, The
  1894
Mother's Advice; *see* CORE SONG-LIST-
  I'm Glad I Took My Mother's Advice
Mr N Peck (& Charles COLLINS) 1908
My Fiddle Was My Sweetheart (*m* G. H.
  CHIRGWIN) 1896
Naval Exhibition, The 1891

Oh! Who Says So? 1906
Old Pals Up To Date
Puzzling Proverbs 1892
Stroke Of The Pen, A 1895
Tableaux Vivants 1894
That Old Rocking Chair 1902
That Was Me (arr. A. E. DURANDEAU) 1890
Umpi-Doodle-Um 1898
War Correspondent, The 1900
Who'll Care For The Children? (arr. John S. BAKER) 1899

OXENFORD, Edward 1846–1929
Teddington Lock (*m* Charlotte SAINTON-DOLBY) 1880

OXENFORD, John 1812–77
I Fear No Foe (*m* Ciro PINSUTI) 1876
Lady Doctor's Husband, The (& John LAWREEN: Odoardo BARRI)
Moon Has Raised Her Lamp Above, The (*m* Julius BENEDICT) 1862
Song Of The Gout (& LAWREEN: BARRI) 1879

OWEN, John *see* Owain ALAW

PAGE, Edwin V. 1847–1925
'Arry 1882
Boy About Town, The (*m* W. G. EATON) 1885
City Toff, The *or* Crutch And Toothpick *or* La-Di-Da! (*m* T. Vincent DAVIES) 1879
Cowardy Cowardy Custard (*m* DAVIES) 1878
If I Were To Do Such A Thing (*m* Arthur ROBERTS) 1878
It Must Have Been The Lobster
Keep It Dark (*m* DAVIES) 1862
Only One (*m* Arthur D. DOUGLASS) 1887
Tickling Mad (arr. DAVIES) 1880
Tiddy-Fol-Lol
Tra-La-La *or* Scraps (*m* Leopold DE WENZEL) *c.* 1881

Wanted: A Lady Help (*m* DAVIES) 1876
What Shall We Do With Cyprus? (*m* DAVIES) 1879
Who'll Oblige A Lady? (*m* DAVIES)
You're Another 1882

PALEY, Herman 1879–1955
Billy (For When I Walk) (Joe GOODWIN: & James KENDIS) 1911
Won't You Fondle Me? (& KENDIS) 1904

PALMER, G.
Tell Me The Sign, John

PALMER, J. F. 1860–1928
Band Played On, The (*w&m* not Charles B. WARD, as often stated; chorus starts: 'Casey would waltz with a strawberry blonde') 1895
See V. GREY: Archie NAISH for 1916 song with same title.

PARES, A. M.
Airly Beacon (*w* Charles KINGSLEY) 1861

PARKE, W.
Toiling Tourist, The (*w* George JACOBI) *c.* 1885

PARKER, Walter C.
I Ain't A-Going To Tell (& Albert E. ELLIS) 1893
British version Wal PINK: *m* arr. H. TEMPEST.
Since Trilby Came To Town 1895

PARKHURST, Mrs E. A.
Father's A Drunkard And Mother Is Dead (& STELLA) 1868

PARRY, Sir Hubert 1848–1918
Crossing The Bar (*w* Alfred TENNYSON) 1903
Also set by A. H. BEHREND and Edward G. LOCKTON and some eighty others.
Jerusalem (*w* William BLAKE) 1916
Proud Maisie (*w* Walter SCOTT) 1899
Set by many others.

PARRY, John Orlando° 1810–79; wrote most of his own material
Charming Chloe Cole 1854
Don't Be Too Particular 1868
Musical Husband, The
Musical Wife, The 1878
Take A Bumper And Try 1874
Wanted A Governess 1870

PARRY, Joseph 1841–1903
Myfanwy (Welsh *w* MYNYDDOG; Eng. *w* (as Arabella) CUHELYN) 1880

PARSONS, Donovan 1888–1980
I Would—If I Could—But I Can't—So I Won't (& Reginald RELSIE: Edward TRACEY) 1922

PASSMORE, Walter° 1867–1946
Chances That He's Had, The (*w* Edwin BARWICK) 1896
Curate, The (*w* BARWICK) 1894
Initials (*w* Eardley TURNER) 1897
Oh, My Late Lamented (*w* TURNER) 1905

PATEMAN, J. Sutton
Fighting For Liberty (& Ernest R. BALL: Will HYDE) 1897

PATERSON, Andrew Barton 'Banjo' 1864–1941
Waltzing Matilda (*m* James BARR, arr. Marie COWAN) 1895
Melody based on Scottish ballad Craigielea and on seventeenth-century English marching song The Bold Fusilier.

PATRICK, Kay
Your Baby Has Gone Down The Drainpipe (*w* Morey AMSTERDAM) 1946
US version of British original Your Baby 'As Gorn Dahn The Plug-'Ole by Elton BOX & Desmond COX & Lewis ILDA).

PAUL, Howard° 1831–1905
Banting 1870

Fighting Dog, The (*m* Fred MACCABE) 1871

PAULTON, Dan
Coster And The Curate And The Jew, The 1897
Life's Short Span (& Gilbert WELLS: PAULTON) 1897
Pet O' The Pantomime, The 1899

PAULTON, Harry° 1842?–1917?
Shtubborn Leedle Hans

PAULTON, J. & H.
Nobody Knows As I Know (*m* Frederic CLAY) 1875

PAULUS, Jean
English As She Is Spoke (*w&m* George DANCE, arr. PAULUS) 1880

PAYNE, John Howard 1791–1852
Home! Sweet Home! (*m* Henry R. BISHOP) 1823

PAYNE, Walter Parker
First Night, The (sk.) (& Charles BALDWIN) 1907

PEARL, Arthur° 1869–1945
I Pushed The Bassinette 1896

PEASE, Harry 1886–1945
My Name Is Kelly (& ?) 1919
Oh! Mother, I'm Wild! (& Howard JOHNSON & Eddie NELSON) 1919
Peggy O'Neil (& Gilbert DODGE & NELSON) 1921

PEILE, F. Kinsey 1861–1934
Man Who Was, The (dramatization of story by Rudyard KIPLING) 1903
Presented in one act at Palace Theatre London 1912.

PELHAM, Paul° d. Apr. 1919; pseudonym of George Young
Be British! (*m* Lawrence WRIGHT) 1912
Bravo! CIVs (*m* Henry E. PETHER) 1900

Confound His Enemies—Long May He
Reign (& Sam RICHARDS) 1901

Don't Forget Your Mother 1902

From Poverty Street To Golden Square
(& Herbert RULE: RULE) 1908

Gathering Of The Clans, The 1899

Good Morning, Mr Postman! (& RULE)
1908

Her Goo Goo Eyes (m RULE) 1908

I'll Sell The Flowers (& RULE) 1908

I Put It On

It's Not The Bird In The Gilded Cage (&
RICHARDS) 1906

John! John! John! Time's Going On (&
J. P. LONG) 1910

Old Father Christmas (& Bennett
SCOTT: PELHAM) 1900

Queen Of The Cannibal Isle (& RULE)
1909

Sweet Nell Of Old Drury (m Valentine
WATSON) 1901

There's Room In My Heart For You (&
RICHARDS) 1902

They All Walk The Wibbly Wobbly Walk
(w LONG) 1912

Woman (& RICHARDS) 1906

PÉLISSIER, H. G.° 1874–1913
If It Wasn't For The Likes O' Huss! 1897
I Want Somebody To Love Me (&
Arthur DAVENPORT: PÉLISSIER)
c.1905
Jane! 1897
My Moon (w DAVENPORT) 1908
Since I Walked Out With A Soldier (w
DAVENPORT) 1909
What A Happy Land Is England (w
Arthur WIMPERIS) 1904
Ypsilanti (w DAVENPORT) 1908

PENN, Arthur A. 1875–1941
Smilin' Through 1918

PENN, William H.
Honeysuckle And The Bee, The (w A. H.
FITZ) 1901
Pansy Faces (w Harry B. SMITH) 1902

PENSO, Ralph
Nobody Else But You (& Worton DAVID)
1914
Pack Up Your Trunk And Go (& Percy
EDGAR) 1908
Scent Of The Violets, The 1907
Where There's A Girl There's A Boy (w
G. ARTHURS) 1919

PERRY, Albert 1880–1941
Huntsman, The (& Geo. A. STEVENS:
Fred EPLETT) 1900
I'm Going Home To The Wife And
Nipper (w Albert HALL) 1897
Life Of A Soldier, The (w&m A. J.
MILLS, arr. PERRY) 1895
My London Country Lane (& Edgar
BATEMAN) 1900
To Keep The Peace (The Special Bobby)
1863

PERRY, Frederick C.
Charming Young Girl, The (m Tom
FANCOURT, arr. James BATCHELDER)
1868
Perfect Cure, The (m J. BLEWITT)
1861
Virgin Only Nineteen Years Old, The (m
Harry RICKARDS) 1869
When These Old Clothes Were New (m
Fred FRENCH) 1867

PERSLEY, George W.
Barney Take Me Home Again (w A. W.
FRENCH) 1889
Won't You Buy My Pretty Flowers? (w
FRENCH) 1876

PESTALOZZA, Alberto
Ciribiribin (Fr. w Rudolf THALER; Eng.
w Tell TAYLOR) 1898

PETERS, W. Frederick
Nineteenth Century Boys, The (w
Arthur J. LAMB) 1895
Sung by Sisters Levey—for song with
same title see Will J. GODWIN: Orlando
POWELL.

PETHER, Henry E. 1867–1932; Francis, Day & Hunter's music editor
Accidents (w&m Charles OSBORNE, arr. PETHER) 1892
Awake! (w Percy EDGAR) 1917
Bravo! CIVs (w Paul PELHAM) 1900
Bunk-A-Doodle I Do (w&m OSBORNE, arr. PETHER) 1893
Fine And Fresh And Blooming (w J. S. EVALO) 1894
Horse The Missus Dries The Clothes On, The (& Fred W. LEIGH) 1901
It's The First Time I've Ever Done That (w J. P. LONG) 1931
I Was Underneath (w&m George LESTER, arr. PETHER)
Oh The Weather! (w EVALO) 1894
Poor John (w LEIGH) 1906
Rosie's Young Man (w LEIGH) 1909
Seaside Posters Round The Home, The (w Edgar BATEMAN) 1919
Waiting At The Church (w LEIGH) 1906
Whoa! Back-Pedal (w Worton DAVID) 1900
With All My Heart c.1910

PETRIE, Henry W. 1857–1925
Asleep In The Deep (w Arthur J. LAMB) 1897
At The Bottom Of The Deep Blue Sea (w LAMB) 1899
Davy Jones's Locker 1901
I Don't Want To Play In Your Yard (w Philip WINGATE) 1894
You Can't Play In Our Yard Anymore (w WINGATE) 1894

PETTITT, Henry 1848–93
Fishing For Truth In A Well (m E. J. SYMONS) 1882
Ginger In The Gutter
Hush! The Bogie! (& G. R. SIMS: Meyer LUTZ, arr. Edmund FORMAN) 1890
See also David BRAHAM.
I Don't Want To Fight (m Vincent DAVIES) 1878
Scamp, The or They Can't Hold A

Candle To Me (m H. Lance MAJOR) 1873
Waiting For The Signal (parody of Macdermott's War Song by G. W. HUNT) 1877
You Are Always Sure To Fetch Them With Wst Wst Wst (w&m PETTITT, arr. E. R. SYMONS) 1882

PHILLIPS, Mrs F. R.° 1829–99
Shadows On The Wall, The (w&m Harry SYDNEY; ladies' version, PHILLIPS)
Troth I Went Out The Other Day (No Irish Need Apply) 1865
Mrs Phillips would seem to have written the lyrics for both men's and ladies' versions. The melody is from The Spider and the Fly.

PHILLIPS, Montague F. 1885–1969
Fishermen Of England, The (w Gerald DODSON) 1921

PHILPOT, Stephen R.
Colours We Love, The (w Herbert SHELLEY) 1902
Dan The Dandy (w SHELLEY) 1907
Hi-Diddle-Diddle! (w SHELLEY) 1901
Little Things That Gold Can't Buy, The (w SHELLEY) 1903
Old Oak Well, The (w SHELLEY) 1906

PIANTADOSI, Al 1884–1955
Curse of An Aching Heart, The (w Harry FINK) 1913
I Didn't Raise My Boy To Be A Soldier (w Alfred BRYAN) 1915
Wild Wild Women, The (w Al WILSON) 1917

PIAVE, F. Mario 1810–76
Brindisi (*La Traviata*) (m Giuseppe VERDI) 1853

PICCOLOMINI, Theodore 1835–1902; a.k.a. Henry PONTET and NEMO
Haven Of Love (w G. HUBI-NEWCOMBE) 1897

Whisper And I Shall Hear (*w* HUBI-
NEWCOMBE) 1897

PIERPOINT, James 1822–93
Jingle Bells 1859

PILCER, Harry° 1885–1960
Gaby Glide, The (*m* Louis A. HIRSCH)
1911

PINERO, Sir Arthur W. 1855–1934
Mr Livermore's Dream (sk.) 1917

PINK, Wal° 1862–1922; the Lord Chamberlain's records from 1900 to 1914 show
that most of Pink's huge output of
sketches was licensed in 1912. The
author of Golfing and Motoring is listed
as Harry TATE, with no mention of Pink,
though he is credited as co-author in the
version of Motoring published by Samuel
French in 1918.
Advance, Australia! England Number
Two (*m* George LE BRUNN) 1897
Another Winner (& Harry BODEN) (sk.)
1912
'Appy 'Ampstead (*m* LE BRUNN)
See Albert CHEVALIER: John CROOK for
song of the same name.
Balaclava (On Guard) 1890
Balaclava Charge, The (*m* LE BRUNN)
1894
Billy's Money Box (sk.) 1912
Bustown By The Sea (sk.) (&
E. Cameron MATTHEWS) 1907
Cabbie's Lament, The (*m* LE BRUNN)
1899
Chance Your Luck (*m* LE BRUNN)
1896
Chips Off The Old Block (sk.) 1913
Fat And Fair (sk.) 1901
Father Of Ninety (sk.) (& Herbert
DARNLEY) 1902
Fishing (sk.) (& Harry TATE) *c.*1910
Gardening (sk.) 1906
Gone For Ever (*m* Frank AYLMER, arr.
Angelo ASHER) 1888
Half-Past Nine (*m* LE BRUNN) 1893

Highly Respectable Singer, The (*m* W. G.
EATON) 1887
I Ain't A-Going To Tell (*m*, arr. H.
TEMPEST; US original Albert E. ELLIS
& Walter C. PARKER) 1893
(In) The Subbubs (*m* DARNLEY) 1898
It's Only A False Alarm (Great
Expectations) (*m* Harry RANDALL)
1889
Money For Nothing (sk.) (*m* LE BRUNN)
*c.*1903
My Brother Jack (*m* Arthur WEST)
1894
Never Share Your Lodgings With A Pal
(*m* Fred EPLETT) *c.*1895
Our Village (*m* ALYMER) 1889
Parrot, The (sk.) 1894
QC, The (sk.) *c.*1899
Seventh Royal Fusiliers, The (*m* LE
BRUNN) 1891
Sticking It Out (*m* DARNLEY) 1897
That's When You Feel All Right (*m*
AYLMER, arr. Ed FORMAN) 1889
That's Where The Trouble Begins (*m*,
arr. John S. BAKER) 1891
Three Individuals (*m* AYLMER) 1890
Under Cross Examination (sk.) 1912
What's In A Name? (sk.) 1912
Who Sez So? (sk.) 1913
Widow's Might
Wrong 'Un, The (sk.) 1895

PINSUTI, Ciro 1829–88
Idol Of My Heart, The (*w* H. L. D'Arcy
JAXONE) 1888
I Fear No Foe (*w* John OXENFORD)
1876
Lifeboat, The (*w* George R. SIMS) 1885
Queen Of The Earth (Man's Guardian
Angel) (*w* JAXONE) 1883
'Tis I (*w* F. LABLACHE) 1876

PLANCHÉ, James R. 1796–1880
Buy A Broom (*m* Henry BISHOP) 1825
For He's A Jolly Good Fellow (*m*
T. German REED) (see CORE SONG-
LIST) 1844

Love's Ritornella *or* Gentle Zitella (*w&m* PLANCHÉ, arr. Tom COOKE) 1829

Rise, Gentle Moon (*m* John BARNETT) 1828

Spring, Gentle Spring (*m* Jules RIVIÈRE) 1873

PLEON, Harry° 1861–1911
Been Had (sk.)
He Would Act (sk.)
Mock Melodrama (& Richard MORTON: PLEON) 1893
Nelson Off His Column (& E. W. ROGERS) 1894
Not What 'Ria Wanted (& William F. CLOSS) 1898
On The Brain (sk.)
On The Day King Edward Gets His Crown On (& Mark LORNE) 1902
Peck's Bad Boy (sk.)
Ta-Ra-Ra-Bomb-De-A 1896

PLUMPTON, Alfred 1840–1902
Launch The Lifeboat 1874
Yarn Of The Nancy Bell, The (*w* William S. GILBERT) 1867

POLLACK, Lew 1896–1946
Miss Annabelle Lee (& Sidney CLARE & Harry RICHMAN) 1927
My Yiddishe Momme (*w* Jack YELLEN) 1925

POLLOCK, Walter Herries 1852–1926
Devout Lover, The (*m* Maude Valérie WHITE) 1883

POMEROY, Guy S.° b. 1888
Whiffenpoof Song, The (Rudyard KIPLING, adap. Minnie MINNIGERODE & Guy A. POMEROY: Guy H. SCULL, adap. Tod B. GALLOWAY) 1909

PONTET, Henry T. 1835–1902; pseudonym of Theodore PICCOLOMINI; a.k.a. NEMO
I'd Rather Not! (*w* NEMO) 1884

Last Milestone, The (*w* H. L. D'Arcy JAXONE) 1884

Lost, Stolen Or Strayed 1883
See same title by A. J. MILLS & Bennett SCOTT.

POPE, Jessie
Kitchener's Boys (*m* Herman LÖHR) 1915

POTTER, S.
Private Tommy Atkins (*m* Henry HAMILTON) 1893

POTTER, Sam
Daddy's On The Engine (*w* Arthur ALBERT & P. H. SNAPE; also attr. Charles GRAHAM) 1895

POUNDS, Leonard
Oh What A Glorious Game! (*m* Willie ROUSE) 1914
Thingummy Bobs (& Clifford GREY) *c.*1919

POWEL, Eldred d. 4 Apr. 1903
Four Fingers And A Thumb 1895
Oh! What A Jubilee 1887
Oh, What An Alteration! 1888

POWELL, Dudley
Three Trees, The 1912

POWELL, Felix 1878–1942
Pack Up Your Troubles In Your Old Kit-Bag (*w* George ASAF) 1915

POWELL, Orlando 1867–1915
After The Ball (& Fred BOWYER)—a version for Vesta Tilley° 1893
After The Ball (& BOWYER)—a parody for Arthur Roberts° 1894
See SONG CORE-LIST.
And The Parrot Said (*w* Worton DAVID) 1907
'Blige A Lady (*w* J. P. HARRINGTON) 1890
Boudoir Secrets (& George ARTHURS) 1907
Boys Together (*w* HARRINGTON) 1891

Coster Girl In Paris, The (*w* Fred W. LEIGH) 1912

Do Buy Me That Mamma Dear (*w* Malcolm ARNOLD) 1894

English Speaking Race Against The World, The (*w* Albert HALL) 1898

Giddy Little Girl Said 'No!', The (*w* HARRINGTON) 1894

Girl Who Thought She Would, The (& ARTHURS) 1907

I Didn't Break The Bank At Monte Carlo (*w* HARRINGTON) *c*.1890

It's A Pity To Waste The Cake (*w* HARRINGTON) 1909

I've Got The Riding Habit (& ARTHURS) 1907

New Man, The (*w* HALL) 1895

Nineteenth Century Boys, The (*w* Will GODWIN)
Sung by Fannie Leslie and Will Godwin—for song with same title see Arthur J. LAMB: William Frederick PETERS.

Old Man's Darling, An (*w* Albert HALL) 1895
See Fred MURRAY & George EVERARD for a song of the same title.

One Thing Leads To Another (*w* LEIGH) 1912

Put On Your Slippers (*w* HARRINGTON) 1911

Rum-Tiddley-Um-Tum-Tay (*w* LEIGH) 1908

Salome (*w* HARRINGTON) 1908
See also R. P. WESTON etc. for the same title.

She'd Never Had A Lesson In Her Life (*w* Fred MURRAY) 1903

She's Been A Good Wife To Me (*w* DAVID) 1907

There's Something About A Soldier (*w* HARRINGTON) 1910

Three Ages Of Woman, The (Woman's Opinion Of Man) (*m* ARTHURS) 1907

Tiddley-Om-Pom! (*w* LEIGH) 1906

Till Six O'Clock In The Morning (*w* GODWIN) 1893

Twiddly Wink (*w* LEIGH) 1912

We Drew His Club Money This Morning (*w&m* T. CAROLAN, arr. POWELL) 1889

POWER, Mrs Agnes d. 1894

Up In A Balloon (ladies' version; orig. *w&m* G. W. HUNT) 1868

PRAGER, Henry

Englishman's Glory Is Freedom Of Speech, An (*m* Felix McGLENNON) 1883

PRATT, Charles E. 1841–1902; a.k.a. H. J. FULMER; may also have been J. T. WOOD

My Bonnie Lies Over The Ocean 1882

PRATT, Cornelius

Don't Stop My 'Arf A Pint O' Beer (*m* J. Charles MOORE) 1911

PRATT, Mrs F. B.

Please Sell No More Drink To My Father (*m* C. A. WHITE) 1884

PRESTON, Will°

Cousin Sarah 1887

Nothing Like It 1891

PRICE, Thomas Gwallter *see* CUHELYN

PRITZKOW, Louis W.°

Take Back Your Gold (*m* Monroe H. ROSENFELD) (see CORE SONG-LIST) 1897

PROCTER, Adelaide Anne 1825–64; often misspelled Proctor; daughter of Barry CORNWALL

Freya's Gift (*m* George A. MACFARREN) 1869

Listening Angels (*m* John BLOCKLEY) 1860

Lost Chord, The (*m* Arthur L. SULLIVAN) 1877

Shadow, A (*m* Odoardo BARRI)

Storm, The (*m* J. P. HULLAH) 1859
Thou Art Weary (*m* SULLIVAN) 1874
Will He Come? (*m* SULLIVAN) 1873

PURDAY, Charles H. 1799–1885
Fine Old English Gentleman (adap. Old
And New Courtier, The trad.) 1826
Watch On The Rhine, The (*m* Carl
WILHELM (1854)) 1870

PURDAY, T. E.
Billy Barlow (arr. G. L. SAUNDERS from
orig. *c.*1830) 1855

RADFORD, Dave b. 1884
It's Tulip Time In Holland (*m* Richard A.
WHITING) 1915
Where The Black-Eyed Susans Grow (*m*
WHITING) 1917

RAEBURN, Sam° 1865–90
Whistling Coon, The 1900

RAFFERTY, Pat° 1861–1952; pseudo-
nym of Henry Browne
Bus *or* Mary Mac Intyre!, The (Albert
HALL & RAFFERTY: RAFFERTY)
1895
Come Back To Erin And Me *c.*1912
Dancing To The Organ In The Mile End
Road (C. W. MURPHY & RAFFERTY:
RAFFERTY) 1893
Floor Gave Way, The (*w* HALL, arr.
BAKER) 1893
Good-Bye, Canada! 1909
He's Very Very Ill Indeed (*w* Sam MAYO,
arr. John S. BAKER) 1890
He Was One Of The Old Brigade (*w*
T. CONLEY) 1898
Parody of He Was One Of The Light
Brigade *w&m* Charles OSBORNE.
I'll Go To Paddy's Lad *c.*1912
I Went Out On Strike This Morning
McAnulty's Garden Party (arr. BAKER)
1890
My Girl Is Irish With Silvery Hair (&
F. W. CARTER) 1912

Why Didn't They Send For Me? (*w*
J. ROLMAZ) 1898

RAGAS, Henry W.° 1890–1919; member
of Original Dixieland Jazz Band°
Bluin' The Blues (*w* Sidney D.
MITCHELL) 1919

RAINFORTH, Elizabeth° 1814–77
Wi' A Hundred Pipers An' A' (possible
collaborator with Lady Caroline
NAIRNE) *c.*1851

RAMSEY, T.
Sally, Come Up (*m* E. W. MACKNEY)
*c.*1862

RANDALL, Harry° 1860–1932
Boarding House, The 1904
Dear Me! *c.*1885
Drink! By One Who's Had Some (*w*
J. Bernard DICKSON) 1900
I Can't Get At It (*w* Herbert COLE)
*c.*1886
I Forgot It (*w* E. A. MARTIN) 1888
It's Only A False Alarm (Great
Expectations) (*w* Wal PINK) 1889
Lightning Results (*w* Edgar BATEMAN)
1897
Love By One Who Knows (*w* DICKSON)
1900
Man—By One Who Loathes 'Em (*w*
DICKSON) 1902
Oh! My Tooth *c.*1886
Same Old Lie, The (*w* Joseph BERRY)
1890

RANDELL, Ernest
Dear Old Saturday Night (& Herman
DAREWSKI & Albert DE COURVILLE)
1915

RANDOLPH, A. P.
How Could Red Riding Hood? (arr.
R. D. WHICHARD) 1922

RANDS, Harry
She Must Be Handsome 1877
She's Always The Best In My Dreams
1876
Strolling Though Fairlight 1877

RASBACH, Oscar 1888–1975
Trees (*w* Joyce KILMER) 1922

RASCALS, THE THREE 1908–27 Eddie
Fields (d. May 1962), Charles O'Donnell
(1886–1962); for third Rascal see
ARTISTES' REPERTOIRES
That Old Sweetheart Of Mine *c*.1913

RATHBONE, P.
Abraham Lincoln (*m* J. E. CARPENTER)
    1863
Down In Piccadilly (*w&m* Frank HALL,
    arr. RATHBONE) 1863
Kleptomania (I Really Couldn't Help
    It) (*w&m* HALL, arr. RATHBONE)
    1863
Polly Bluck *or* Married On Wednesday
    (*w&m* HALL, arr. RATHBONE)

RAY, Lilian d. 20 Dec. 1949
Sunshine Of Your Smile, The (*w*
    Leonard COOKE) 1913

RAY, Phil° 1872–1918
If The Missus Wants To Go *or* Let Her
    Drown 1902

RAYNAL, Louis
Run For The Bus, A (*w* T. S. LONSDALE)
    1884

REACH, Angus B. 1815–84
Slave Chase, The (*m* Henry RUSSELL)
    1855
Slave Sale, The *or* Come, Who Bids (*m*
    RUSSELL) 1835

READ, Ezra
I Haven't Been Home Since Yesterday
    (*m&w* Leslie REED, arr. READ) 1895

READ, John° 1839–1920
All For Her 1878
All Round The Squares (*m* Charles
    COLLINS) 1878
Bank Holiday *or* A Twopenny Ride On A
    Tramcar 1878
Bill Of Fare, The 1882
Don't Touch Him 1878

Down By The Old Mill Stream 1885
Drink Up, John!
End Of The World 1878
Give Me A Grip Of Your Hand 1905
Good-bye, Lovely Lou 1878
Grandmother's Chair 1879
Happy Days Of Childhood, The 1878
How The Shoe Pinches 1901
If You Love Me Tell Me Tottie
I'm In It 1878
It's Nice 1877
Keep It On The Quiet 1873
Letter From The Front, A 1902
Liza, Do You Love Me? 1904
Lost In The Snow 1876
Naughty! Naughty! Naughty! 1878
Oh, Julia 1878
Oh! Polly, She's The Girl For Me 1883
Oh, That Brown
Old Chums 1902
Old Village School, The
Simple Simon *or* The Boy Who Longed
    For Jam 1878
Strolling On The Beach
Sweeter Than Jam 1877
Swinging To And Fro 1879
That's How The Poor Have To Live!
    1884
They All Do It 1876
Tiddle-a-Wink The Barber 1878
Wake Up England 1902
We Meet Each Night As The Clock
    Strikes Nine 1875

REDFERN, Sam° 1851–1915
Booze Is There (*w* J. S. HAYDON) 1890
Good Old Days Of Adam, The (*w*
    George THORN, arr. Angelo ASHER)
    1893
Home! Home!! Home Sweet Home!!!
    (& J. H. HALL, arr. Walter HARRISON)
    1888
I'll Bet You A Dollar You Don't (*w*
    HAYDON) 1881
That's The Latest (*w* H. C. HUDSON)
    1888

REDMOND, Walter
Did You Ever Catch A Weasel Asleep?
(*w* Geoffrey THORN) *c*.1875
I Can't Stand Mrs Green's Mother (*w*
Harry HUNTER) 1881
I'd Rather Lather Father, Than Father
Lathered Me (*w* HUNTER) 1876
Never Give In (*w* HUNTER) 1876
She'd A Brother In The Navy (*w*
THORN) 1877

REED, Dave d. 1946
Door Of Hope, The (*m* Ernest R. BALL)
1907
In The Quartermaster's Store (adap. with
Desmond COX & Elton BOX) 1940

REED, Leslie°
Anything'll Do For Me 1901
He Didn't Go To Work Next Morning
1898
He's Never Been Heard Of Since 1891
I Haven't Been Home Since Yesterday
(arr. Ezra READ) 1895
Last Act—Finale 1901
One Of The Old Old Boys 1892
Our Little Two Year Old 1895
She Is A Fancy Ironer 1895
There Always Will Be Singers 1902
We All Go To Work But Father 1891

REED, T. German° 1817–88
Detective's Song, The (*w* William S.
GILBERT)
For He's A Jolly Good Fellow (*w* J. R.
PLANCHÉ) (see CORE SONG-LIST)
1844

REES, Ernest d. 9 Mar. 1916
Come Round And Call Me Early In The
Morn 1902
How Dare I Like! (*m* George EVERARD)
1902
I'm Farmer Scroggins 1903
You Put Me In Mind Of Me (*m* Paul
MERRY) 1901

REEVE, Ada° 1874–1966; daughter of
Charles REEVES

Trixie Of Upper Tooting (*m* Paul
RUBENS) 1896

REEVES, Charles 1843?–1906; né
Samuel Isaacs; father of Ada REEVE
I'm A Little Too Young To Know (*m* F.
W. VENTON) 1889

REEVE, Norman
Bobbing Up And Down Like This (*w*
Worton DAVID) 1899

REEVE, William 1757–1815
I Am A Friar Of Orders Gray (*w* John
O'KEEFFE) 1795
Scroggin's Ghost 1804
Typitywitchet (*w* Charles DIBDIN jun.)
1810

REILLY, S. J.
Angels Guard Thee (Berceuse De
Jocelyn) (*m* Benjamin L. P. GODARD)
c.1900

RELSIE, Reginald d. 1950
I Would—If I Could—But I Can't—So I
Won't (& Donovan PARSONS: Edward
TRACEY) 1922

REXFORD, Eben E. 1848–1916
Only A Pansy Blossom (*m* Frank
HOWARD) 1883
Silver Threads Among The Gold (*m* H. P.
DANKS) 1873

RHODES, Helen a.k.a. Guy
D'HARDELOT

RICE, Gitz 1891–1947
Conscientious Objector's Lament, The
(& Dave BURNABY) 1917
Dear Old Pal Of Mine (*w* Harold ROBE)
1918
DSO And VAD (& BURNABY) 1917
Goodbye, Helen Of Troy
In Cherry Blossom Time (Leslie STILES:
& Herman DAREWSKI) 1917
I Want To Go Home (*m* anon.) 1915
Mademoiselle From Armenteers (&
Edward 'Red' ROWLAND: RICE)
c.1918

See also Johann Ludwig UHLAND; Harry
CARLTON & J. A. TUNBRIDGE; Harry
WINCOTT; CORE SONG-LIST.

RICH & RICH° Harry Rich (1872–1915)
and the unrelated Charlie Rich (d. 2
Nov. 1938)
King Of Karactacus, The

RICHARDS, Brinley 1817–1885
Ar Dywysog Gwlad Y Bryniau (God Bless
The Prince Of Wales) (*w* CEIRIOG;
Eng. *w* George LINLEY) 1862

RICHARDS, Sam sang with Sam Hague's
Minstrels°
Confound His Enemies—Long May He
Reign (& Paul PELHAM) 1901
For The Empire And England's Glory
1902
It's Not The Bird In The Gilded Cage (&
PELHAM) 1906
My Hundred Pound Motor Car 1901
Old England, Home And King! (arr.
Warwick WILLIAMS) 1902
Rag-Time Nursery Rhymes (*w&m*
RICHARDS, arr. Fred EPLETT) 1901
There's Room In My Heart For You (&
PELHAM) 1902
Woman (& PELHAM) 1906

RICHARDS, Tom d. 1893
Where The Flow'rets Grow (*w* Johnny
DANVERS) 1886

RICHARDS, T.
Is Marriage A Failure? (*w&m* Oswald
STOLL, arr. RICHARDS) 1889

RICHARDSON, Billy
Little Pair Of Whiskers, A 1890
Parody of A Little Peach In An Orchard
Grew by Hubbard T. SMITH & D. A. WYE.
Shout Out Little Children 1891

RICHMAN, Harry
Miss Annabelle Lee (& Sidney CLARE &
Lew POLLACK) 1927

RICK, Alfred E.
Swing Me Higher, Obadiah! (*m* Maurice
SCOTT) 1907

RICKARDS, Harry° 1841–1911
I Wonder When She'll Let Mama Come
Out
Virgin Only Nineteen Years Old, The (*w*
Fred PERRY) 1869

RICKETTS, Major F. J. a.k.a. Kenneth J.
ALFORD

RICKS, Arthur
Fiddle-De-Diddle-De-De (& Harry
LEIGHTON & Sam MAYO, arr. Sam
AARONS) 1906

RIDGWELL, Charles d. 27 May 1916;
sometimes spelled Ridgewell
All Through A Gee-Gee-Gee 1902
All Through A Little Game At Billiards
(& Charles DEANE) 1909
Billy Muggins 1906
If Those Lips Could Only Speak! (& Will
GODWIN) 1905
I Love You Best Of All 1908
I'm All Right (*w* W. H. WALLIS) 1904
I'm Shy, Mary Ellen, I'm Shy (& Geo. A.
STEVENS) 1910
Parker, P.C. (sk.) (& Charles AUSTIN)
1908
You Can Do A Lot Of Things At The
Seaside That You Can't Do In Town
(& STEVENS) 1911

RIDLEY, George° 1834–64
Blaydon Races (air, Brighton) 1862
Bobby Cure, The
Cushie Butterfield (air, Polly Perkins of
Paddington Green, *m* Harry
CLIFTON) *c.*1863
Johnny Luik-Up The Bellman

RIEGER, W. H. d. 1904
Old Chimney Corner Where
Grandfather Smiled, The (*w* George
COOPER) 1880

RIHIL, Louis 1879–1931
Murders (& Dick HENTY) *c*.1914

RILEY, J. W.
There Little Girl, Don't Cry (*m* Ernest NEWTON) 1909

RILEY, W.
Don't Cry (*m* R. B. ADDISON) 1892

RISQUE, W. H. d. 17 Aug. 1916
Mary Was A Housemaid (*w* Napoleon LAMBELET) 1899

RIVIÈRE, Jules 1819–1900
Clicquot (*w* Frank W. GREEN) 1870
Spring, Gentle Spring (*w* James R. PLANCHÉ) 1873

ROBATT, A. C.
Dress Rehearsal, A (sk.) (& Seymour HICKS) 1907

ROBE, Harold
Dear Old Pal Of Mine (*m* Gitz RICE) 1918

ROBERTS, Arthur 1852–1933
If I Were To Do Such A Thing (*w* E. V. PAGE) 1878
Where's The Count? 1904

ROBERTS, Frederick *c*.1850–1930?
I Lent £10 To Callaghan

ROBERTS, Lee S. 1884–1949
Smiles (*w* J. Will CALLAHAN) 1918

ROBERTS, R. A. 1866–1932
Because I Look A Fool 1899
Change Will Do You Good, A 1898
It Pleased The Children So 1896
Little Johnny Porter 1896
That's How You Parlez Vous
Three Nice Girls 1899

ROBERTS, Ralph 1869–1944; sketches
Buffo: The Story Of A Broken Heart 1904
In The Trenches 1916
Woman's Heritage, The 1902

ROBERTSON, J. A.
Bright Little Glass (*w* Bert ROYLE) 1891

ROBERTSON, T. W. 1829–71
Dreams (*m* W. Meyer LUTZ) 1870
Our Lively Neighbours (*m* n.k.)

ROBEY, Sir George 1869–1954
And That's That!
Archibald, Certainly Not! (& J. L. ST JOHN: Alfred GLOVER) 1909
Auctioneer, The (*w* C. G. COTES) 1903
Bang Went The Chance Of A Lifetime (& Sax ROHMER) 1908
Caprice (*w* E. B. MARKS) *c*.1895
Fancy That! (*w* COTES) 1900
I Couldn't Exert Myself (*w* COTES) 1902
It's A Lie (*w* ROHMER) 1909

ROBINS, George
Are We Downhearted? No! 1906

ROBINSON, J. Russel 1892–1963; see also ORIGINAL DIXIELAND JAZZ BAND in ARTISTES' REPERTOIRES
Margie (Benny DAVIS: & Con CONRAD) 1919
Mourni' Blues (*m* A. SBARBARO) *c*.1919

ROBLEDO, Julian 1887–1940
Three O'Clock In The Morning (*w* Dolly TERRISS) 1921

ROBSON, T. F.
Lady Doctor, The (*m* William HYDE) 1909
She Must Be Witty, She Must Be Pretty 1896
Three Old Flats In Town 1897
Up Jumps The Ghost Of Sarah Porter (& Medley BARRETT) 1903
Varmer Giles (& Gilbert WELLS) 1902

RODNEY, C. M.
Ah! Ah! 1895
La-Didily-Idily, Umti-Umti-Ay (*w* Richard MORTON & RODNEY: RODNEY) 1894
Leicester Square

RODWELL, G. Herbert 1801–52
Maid Of All Work
Nix My Dolly Pals 1839
Young Susan Had Lovers

ROECKEL, Joseph L. 1838–1910
Angus MacDonald (*w* Fred E.
   WEATHERLY) 1881
Stormfiend!, The (*w* WEATHERLY) 1881
Woman's Way (*w* WEATHERLY) 1890

ROGERS, Alex C. 1886–1930
I'm A Jonah Man 1903
Let It Alone (& Bert A.WILLIAMS) 1906
Nobody (*m* WILLIAMS) 1905

ROGERS, A. W.
Dangers Of A Patent Safety Cab, The
   1834

ROGERS, E. W. 1863–1913
After The Show 1894
Ask A P'liceman (*m* A. E. DURANDEAU)
   c.1885
Barmaid, The 1894
Best Man, The (McGilligan's Wedding)
   1894
Call Round Any Old Time (*m* J. Charles
   MOORE) 1908
Come Where The Booze Is Cheaper (*m*
   DURANDEAU) *c*.1890
Following In Father's Footsteps 1892
G'arn Away! What D'Yer Take Me For?
   1892
Giddy Little Curate, The (*m*
   DURANDEAU) 1891
I'll Meet You At The Bodega 1905
I'm The Plumber 1898
It's Part Of A P'liceman's Duty 1906
It Suddenly Dawned On Me 1898
Ju-Jah 1893
Lambeth Walk, The 1899
Language Of London Town, The 1898
Latest Chap On Earth, The 1899
Let Me Call You Daddy 1904
Love Or Gold (arr. John NEAT) 1900
Mary Llewellyn 1906
Master And The Man 1892
Midnight Son, The 1897

Midnight Son's Farewell, The (arr.
   NEAT) 1903
Moonlight Blossoms 1899
Mrs Carter, You're A Tarter (sung by
   Emma Carus) 1901
My Hat's A Brown 'Un (arr. Alfred
   LAMONT) 1891
My Son! My Son! My Only Son! (*m*
   George LE BRUNN) 1891
Mystery Of A Hansom Cab, The (*m*
   DURANDEAU) 1888
Nelson Off His Column (& Harry
   PLEON) 1894
New Policeman, The 1896
Oh! The Pallis! (Crystal Palace Bank
   Holiday) 1902
Pretty Little Girl From Nowhere, The
   (*m* NEAT) 1909
Red And The White And The Blue, The
   1900
Sanitary Inspector, The 1894
Simple Pimple, The 1891
Skylark! Skylark! 1901
Sweethearts Still (arr. NEAT) 1902
Thick Ear'd Jim (arr. NEAT) 1903
Thick Headed Danny (arr. NEAT) 1893
Three Makes Jolly Fine Company (&
   H. C. HUDSON: Norton ATKIN &
   Charles COLLINS) 1903
Welcome, CIVs 1900
When A Fellah Has Turned Sixteen 1898

ROGERS, Harry
Russians I'd Fight Like A Turk (*m*
   William SIM) 1877

ROGERS, Robert Cameron 1862–1912
Rosary, The (*m* Ethelbert NEVIN) 1898

ROGERS, Sam
Madame La Sharty (Biddy The Belle Of
   The Ballet) (*m* Harry HUNTER)
   c.1880

ROHMER, Sax *c*.1883–1959; pseudonym
of Arthur Sarsfield Wade or Ward
Bang Went The Chance Of A Lifetime
   (& George ROBEY) 1908
It's A Lie (*m* George ROBEY) 1909

Pigtail Of Li Fang Fu, The (*m* arr. &
transcr. T. W. THURBAN) 1919

ROLLIT, George
Everybody Wondered How He Knew (*m*
Howard TALBOT) 1899
Hulloa! Hulloa! Hulloa! 1899
I've Never Lost My Last Train Yet (*m*
George LE BRUNN) *c*.1906
She'd Never Been In Pantomime Before
1899

ROLLS, Jack d. 1969
You Can't Do That There 'Ere (*w*
Raymond WALLACE) 1935

ROLMAZ, James
New Hat Now!, A (arr. John S. BAKER)
She's The Boss, I'm The Slavey (arr. Fred
EPLETT) 1888
Where Did You Get That Hat? (in the
US version *w&m* attr. Joseph J.
SULLIVAN) 1888
See CORE SONG-LIST.
Why Didn't They Send For Me? (*m* Pat
RAFFERTY) 1898

ROMA, Caro 1866–1937 pseudonym of
Carrie Northey
My Baby 1913

ROMBERG, Sigmund 1887–1951
Auf Wiedersehen 1915
I Love To Go Swimmin' With Women (*w*
B. MACDONALD) 1921

ROME, Fred° b. 1874; much of his
material is unpublished
Adverts Of Modern Medicine Makers (*m*
Allan MILNE) 1902
Gone To Lunch (sk.)
If (*m* Willie ROUSE) 1910
Longshoreman Bill (sk.)
Moving The Piano *c*.1910
Reasons (*m* Joe MORLEY)
Simpson's Stores (sk.) 1915
Snookered (sk.)

RONALD, Sir Landon 1873–1938; son of
Henry RUSSELL
Down In The Forest (from *A Cycle Of*

Life) (*w* Harold SIMPSON) 1915
Sweet June (*w* Edward
TESCHEMACHER) 1902

ROONEY, Pat° 1847–92
Is That Mr Reilly? (adap. 1915 as Are
You The O'Reilly? by Howard
WESLEY) 1883

ROOT, G. F. 1820–95; a.k.a. C. Friedrich
Wurzel
Battle Cry Of Freedom, The 1861
Hazel Dell 1852
Just Before The Battle, Mother 1863
Ring The Bells Of Heaven
Ring The Bell, Watchman 1872
Rosalie The Prairie Flower 1858
Tramp, Tramp, Tramp, The Boys Are
Marching 1864
Vacant Chair, The (*w* Henry S.
WASHBURN) 1861

ROSE, Vincent 1880–1944
Avalon (*w* Al JOLSON) 1920
Whispering (& Richard COBURN: John
SCHONBERGER) 1920

ROSENFELD, Monroe H. 1861–1918;
a.k.a. Frederick BELASCO
And Her Golden Hair Was Hanging
Down Her Back (*w* Felix
MCGLENNON) 1894
See also Adrian ROSS.
Come Along, Sinners 1882
Take Back Your Gold (*w* Louis W.
PRITZKOW) 1897
Those Wedding Bells Shall Not Ring Out
(*m* E. JONGHMANS) 1893
Based on The Fatal Wedding, Gussie L.
DAVIS.
With All Her Faults I Love Her Still
1888

ROSS, Adrian 1859–1933; pseudonym of
Arthur Reed Ropes
And Her Golden Hair Was Hanging
Down Her Back (Felix MCGLENNON,
rev. ROSS: Monroe H. ROSENFELD)
c.1894

Come To The Ball (*m* Lionel
MONCKTON) 1910
Flower, The (*m* Franz SCHUBERT, arr.
G. H. CLUTSAM) London 1922
Grandmamma (*m* MONCKTON) 1906
Philomel (*m* André MESSAGER) 1919
Somebody's Somebody (*m* Herman
DAREWSKI) 1917
Under The Deodar (*m* MONCKTON)
1902
Vilia (*m* Franz LEHÁR) Vienna 1905,
London 1907
When I Marry Amelia (*m* MONCKTON)
1901

Ross, L. Arthur 1888–1958
Lambeth Walk, The (& Douglas
FURBER: Noel GAY) 1937

ROUNDBACH, John E.
Walking Home With Angeline (*w* G.
Totten SMITH) 1902

ROURKE, M.E. 1867–1933; a.k.a. Herbert Reynolds
They Didn't Believe Me (*m* Jerome
KERN) 1914

ROUSE, Willie° 1877–1928
If (*w* Fred ROME) 1910
Insurance Dream, An (*w* Clifford GREY)
1912
Knowledge 1907
Married *v* Single (*w* GREY) 1912
Nuggets (*w* GREY) 1913
Oh! What A Glorious Game (*w* Leonard
POUNDS) 1914
Our Hobbies (*w* Graham SQUIERS)
1911
Swankers By The Sea (sk.) (*m* T. C.
Sterndale BENNETT) 1914
What A Strain (*w* GREY) 1914

ROVEDINO, Tommaso E. G.
God Bless Victoria! Albion's Queen (*w*
Thomas DIBDIN) 1837

ROWE, Josephine V. 1861–1945; a.k.a.
Josephine V. Crawford

Macushla (*m* Dermot MACMURROUGH)
1910

ROWLAND, Edward 'Red' 1882–1955
Mademoiselle From Armenteers (& Gitz
RICE: RICE) *c*.1918
See also Harry CARLTON & J. A.
TUNBRIDGE; CORE SONG-LIST.

ROXBY, Wilfred 1845–87
Old Toll-Gate, The (*m* Edward
JONGHMANS) 1881

ROYLE, Bert
Bright Little Glass (*m* J. A. ROBERTSON)
1891

ROYLE, Kate
Down Went The Captain (Fred
BOWYER: ROYLE, arr. George ISON)
1887
Not Much (*w* Joseph S. LONG: ROYLE,
arr. Ernest J. SYMONS) 1887
She Trotted Me Off To Church (*w*
Joseph S. LONG, arr. A. MARTINI)
1883

RUBENS, Paul A. 1875–1917
Brighton (Take Me On The Boat To) (&
Arthur WIMPERIS: RUBENS) 1911
Ev'rybody's Awfully Good To Me 1901
Here's To Love And Laughter (*w*
WIMPERIS) 1911
I Can't Take My Eyes Off You (*w* Rida
Johnson YOUNG) 1904
I Don't Seem To Want You When You're
With Me 1904
I Like You In Velvet 1904
I Love The Moon 1911
I've An Inkling 1899
Pink Petty From Peter, A 1907
Tell Me, Pretty Maiden (& E. Boyd
JONES: Leslie STUART) 1899
Trixie Of Upper Tooting (*w* Ada REEVE)
1896
When Him Goey La-Di-Da 1901
Your King And Your Country (We Don't
Want To Lose You) 1914

RUDD, Austin° 1869–1929
Come Out! (& C. HALLIDAY) c.1900
I Didn't Know 1892
I've Been Out And Got A Separation
   1894
Music Hall Chant
Pretty Little Maid Said 'Oui, Monsieur',
   The 1895
Sailors Don't Care 1918
She Was A Clergyman's Daughter 1893
She Was In My Class 1894
They Found Me (arr. HALLIDAY)

RULE, Herbert° 1884–1927
A-Be My Boy (& Thomas McGHEE:
   L. SILBERMANN & A. GROCK) 1919
Come On Steve (& Fred HOLT)
Fill 'Em Up (& McGHEE & James
   WALSH (2): L. SILBERMAN)
From Poverty Street To Golden Square
   (& Paul PELHAM: RULE) 1908
Good Morning, Mr Postman! (&
   PELHAM) 1908
Have You Paid The Rent? (& HOLT &
   SILBERMAN) 1922
Her Goo Goo Eyes (w PELHAM) 1908
I'd Like To Be An Actress 1911
I'll Sell The Flowers (& PELHAM) 1908
La-La-La-La, Sing This Chorus With Me
   1910
Minutes (& O. SCHALLER) 1907
My Rachel Myer From Hawaii
   (McGHEE & Sam STERN) 1917
Only A Working Man (& HOLT) 1923
Ours Is A Nice 'Ouse (& HOLT) 1921
Queen Of The Cannibal Isle (& HOLT)
   1909
Turned Up (& Harry CASTLING) 1924
Who Put The Bricks In Brixton? 1920
Woolloomooloo c.1912

RUSSELL, Henry° 1812–1900; father of
Sir Landon RONALD
Buffalo Girls
Cheer, Boys, Cheer! (w Charles
   MACKAY) 1852
Eva's Farewell (w Eliza COOK) 1855

Flag Of The Free, The (w COOK) 1855
Gambler's Wife, The (w COOK) 1846
Ivy Green, The (w Charles DICKSON)
   1837
Land Of St Patrick (The Irish Hurrah)
Life On The Ocean Wave, A (w S. J.
   ARNOLD & Epes SARGENT) 1838
Little Topsy (w COOK) 1855
Maniac, The 1846
Oh! Woodman, Spare That Tree (The
   Old Oak Tree) (w George Pope
   MORRIS) 1837
Old Arm Chair, The (w COOK) 1836
Our Empress Queen 1887
Over The Mountain
Pauper's Drive, The (w MACKAY)
Ship On Fire, The (w MACKAY)
Slave Chase, The (w Angus B. REACH)
   1855
Slave Sale, The or Come, Who Bids (w
   REACH) 1835
Song Of The Shirt, The (w Mrs F. A.
   DAVIDSON, after the poem by
   Thomas HOOD published in *Punch*
   1843) 1860
   See also Arthur H. BEHREND: Jonathan
   BLEWITT; Mrs F. A. DAVIDSON.
There's A Good Time Coming, Boys (w
   MACKAY) 1848
Wind Of The Winter Night (w MACKAY)
Woodman, Spare That Tree *see* Oh!
   Woodman, etc.

RUTHERFORD, Ruth d. 1952
Love's Garden Of Roses (m Haydn
   WOOD) 1900

RUTLAND, (John?)° d. 7 May 1955?
Sing! Sing! Sing! (& Stanley J.
   DAMERELL) 1910

SADDLER, Frank
On The Piers At Night (w Chas. A.
   BURKE) 1897

SADIE 1841–68; pseudonym of Sarah
Williams

Finette (*m* James Lynam MOLLOY)
1888
Also set by others.

ST CLAIR, F. V.° 1860–1922
All Through A Little Piece Of Bacon (&
T. COSTELLO: G. LE BRUNN) *c*.1895
Bradlaugh
Carving Up Of The Turkey, The
Cheer Up, Buller! 1901
Chums *or* My Old Pal Jim 1896
Down With The Old Free Trade
European Dance, The
Fireman Jim
Girl With The Golden Hair, The 1895
Gladstone Is The Captain Of The Ship
John Bull (*m* Edwin BOGETTI) 1881
Heroes Of The Transvaal War, The (*m*
Joseph H. CLEVE) 1900
Ice Cream Man, The
In London
Is The Same Old London There? 1910
John Bull's Letter Bag 1899
John Bull's Railway Station 1903
Kitchener! Gone But Not Forgotten
1916
Kitchener! Stand By Him 1915
Leave 'Em Alone, They'll Come Home
In The Morning
Little Jap Horner 1904
Loss Of The Drummond Castle, The
1897
Oh! Cerulia! (arr. Samuel TUTE) 1897
Oh! Mister Morgan
Oh, Mr Lloyd 1912
Railway Guard, The (*m* LE BRUNN)
c.1895
Ring Up Britain *or* John Bull's Telephone
Road To India, The
Salisbury And Gladstone 1888
Stand By The Flag
Success To Her Majesty! (Long May She
Reign) (arr. TUTE) 1896
That's Where Mary's Gone 1896
There Always Will be Fairies (*m*
Cuthbert CLARKE) 1898

When We All Begin To Fly
When Will Old England Be Herself
Once More?

ST HELIER, Ivy 1890–1971
Coal-Black Mammy (& Laddie CLIFF)
1921

ST JOHN, John L.
Archibald, Certainly Not! (& George
ROBEY: Alfred GLOVER) 1909

ST LEONARDS, C.
King Of The Boys (& James MANHILL:
Joseph CLEVE) 1893

ST QUENTIN, Edward
God Bless Victoria (*w* Clement W.
SCOTT) 1897

SAINTON-DOLBY, Charlotte° 1821–85;
until her marriage in 1860 k.a. Charlotte
DOLBY
Oh, Bay Of Dublin (Lady DUFFERIN:
DOLBY, arr. DUFFERIN) 1854
Teddington Lock (*w* Edward
OXENFORD) 1880
You Needn't Say A Word (*w* Fred E.
WEATHERLY) 1874

SAKER, George M.
Corsican Maid, The (*w* George
FEARNLEY) 1909

SAMUEL, Harold
Joggin' Along The Highway (*w* Arthur
ANDERSON) 1917

SANDERSON, Wilfrid 1878–1935
Captain Mac' (*w* P. J. O'REILLY) 1914
Devonshire Cream And Cider (*w*
T. CURZON) 1919
Drake Goes West (*w* O'REILLY) 1910
Friend O' Mine (*w* Fred E.
WEATHERLY) 1913
Shipmates O' Mine (*w* Edward
TESCHEMACHER) 1913
Until (*w* TESCHEMACHER) 1910

Up From Somerset (*w* WEATHERLY) 1913

SANKEY, Ira David 1840–1908
When The Mists Have Rolled Away (*w* Annie Brice HERBERT) 1883

SANTLEY, Maud°
Bobbies Of The Queen, The (*w* Eardley TURNER) 1897

SARGENT, Epes 1813–80
Life On The Ocean Wave, A (& S. J. ARNOLD: Henry RUSSELL) 1838

SARJEANT, James B. 1850–1936
Watchman, What Of The Night? (*w* anon.) 1905

SARONY, Leslie° 1897–1985
Ain't It Grand To Be Bloomin' Well Dead? 1932
I Lift Up My Finger And I Say 'Tweet Tweet' 1929
Mucking About The Garden (under pseudonym 'Q. Kumber') 1929
When The Guards Are On Parade (*m* Horatio NICHOLLS) 1931

SAUNDERS, G. L.
Billy Barlow (*w&m* T. E. PURDAY, arr. SAUNDERS from orig. *c*.1830) 1855

SBARBARO, A.° 1897–1969; see also ORIGINAL DIXIELAND JAZZ BAND in ARTISTES' REPERTOIRES
Mourni' Blues (*m* J. Russel ROBINSON) *c*.1919

SAYERS, Henry J. 1854–1932
Ta-Ra-Ra Boom-Der-É (*w&m* anon., arr. SAYERS) (see CORE SONG-LIST) 1891

SCANLON, William J.° 1856–98
My Nellie's Blue Eyes (*m* Vieni sul Mar, Venetian ballad) 1883

SCHALLER, O.
Minutes (& Herbert RULE) 1907

SCHAYER, Julia 1840–1928
Dolly's Lament (*m* Clarence D. ARNOLD) 1894

SCHMID, Johann C. 1870–1951
Beautiful Garden Of Roses (*w* J. E. DEMPSEY) 1900
If I Could Only Make You Care (*w* DEMPSEY) 1913

SCHNECKENBURGER, Max 1819–49
Watch On The Rhine, The (*m* Carl WILHELM (1854)) 1840

SCHOFIELD, John
Little Bit Of String, A

SCHONBERGER, John 1892–1959
Whispering (*w* Richard COBURN & Vincent ROSE) 1920
Note: Malvin Schonberger is not now credited with *w*.

SCHUBERT, Franz 1797–1828
Erl King, The (*w* Johann W. von GOETHE) 1815
See also Carl LOEWE.
Flower, The (*w* Adrian ROSS: *m* SCHUBERT, arr. G. H. CLUTSAM) London 1922
Hark Hark The Lark (*w* William SHAKESPEARE) 1826
Rose Among The Heather (*w* GOETHE; Eng. adap. Natalie MACFARREN) 1822
Who Is Sylvia? (*w* SHAKESPEARE) 1826

SCHUTER, P.
I Don't Think You're In It Old Man (*w* Henri CLARK)

SCHWARTZ, Jean 1878–1956
Bedelia (*w* William JEROME & George GROSSMITH jun.) 1903
Chinatown, My Chinatown (*w* JEROME) 1910
Goodbye, Virginia (*w* Grant CLARKE) 1915
I Love The Ladies 1914
Mister Dooley (*w* JEROME) 1902
My Irish Molly O (*w* JEROME) 1907

Rock-A-Bye Your Baby With A Dixie Melody (*w* Sam LEWIS & Joe YOUNG) 1918

SCOLLARD, Clinton 1860–1932
Sylvia (*m* Oley SPEAKS) 1914

SCOTT, Bennett 1875–1930
All That Glitters Isn't Gold (*w* Harry CASTLING) 1906
All The Nice Girls Love A Sailor (Ship Ahoy!) (*w* A. J. MILLS) 1905
Big Ben Struck One (*w* MILLS) 1907
Boys Brigade, The (*w* MILLS) 1906
Boys In Khaki, Boys In Blue (*w* MILLS) *c*.1915
By The Side Of The Zuyder Zee (*w* MILLS) 1906
Chase Me Charlie (*w* C. G. COTES) 1899
Come And Put Your Arms Around Me (*w* MILLS) 1909
Come Down And Open The Door (*w* COTES; rev. of 1884 orig. A. SUTHERD: Slade MURRAY, arr. Edmund FORMAN) 1898
Constantinople At Olympia (*w* MILLS) 1894
Darling Mabel (*w* MILLS) 1896
'E Ain't Got Nuffin' To Tell (*w* J. P. HARRINGTON) 1896
Everybody's Loved By Someone 1901
Fall In And Follow Me (*w* MILLS) 1910
Farewell My Little Yo-San! (*w* MILLS) 1904
Good-bye And God Bless You Jack (*w* HARRINGTON) 1889
Good-bye, Tilly (*w* COTES) 1899
Has Anyone Seen A German Band? (*w* MILLS) 1907
Hello! There, Flanagan (& Fred GODFREY & MILLS) 1909
I Don't Care What Becomes Of Me (*w* MILLS) 1911
I'm Going To Get Married Today— Hooray! (*w* C. G. COTES) 1899
It's A Different Girl Again! (*w* George ARTHURS) 1906

I've Been Out With Charlie Brown (*w* MILLS) 1909
I've Made Up My Mind To Sail Away (*w* MILLS) 1902
I Wonder If You Miss Me Sometimes (*w* MILLS) *c*.1910
Kiss Me Goodbye, My Little Soldier Boy (*w* MILLS) 1914
Knock The Two Rooms Into One (*w* MILLS) 1900
Lost Stolen Or Strayed (*w* MILLS) 1897
See same title by Henry PONTET.
Lot 99 (*w* COTES) 1898
My Boy's A Sailorman (*w* MILLS) 1909
My Heart Is With You Tonight (*w* MILLS) 1912
Oh! How Rude! (*w* COTES) 1899
Oh! Ma'm'selle Ju-Li-a! (*w* MILLS) 1914
Oh! The Black List 1903
Old Father Christmas (& Paul PELHAM: PELHAM) 1900
Oliver Cromwell (*w* MILLS) 1902
On The Margate Boat (*w* MILLS) 1899
Popsy Wopsy! (*w* MILLS) 1913
Sailing In My Balloon (*w* MILLS) 1906
Ship Ahoy! (All The Nice Girls Love A Sailor) 1905
Show Me The Way To Your Heart (*w* MILLS) *c*.1915
Sing Us A Song Of Bonnie Scotland (*w* MILLS) 1913
Slight Mistake On The Part Of My Valet (*w* MILLS) 1897
Somebody Else (*w* MILLS) 1912
Take Me Back To Dear Old Blighty (& Fred GODFREY & MILLS) 1916
Take Me In A Taxi, Joe (*w* MILLS) 1913
That'll Never Do For Me (& COTES) 1899
There's A Girl Wanted There (*w* MILLS) 1903
There's Going To Be A Wedding In The Stars (*w* MILLS)
They All Look Alike In The Dark (& MILLS & GODFREY) 1918

Two Little Brandies And Sodas (*w* COTES) 1899

What Did She Know About Railways? 1897

What D'Ye Say, Molly Molloy? (*w* MILLS) 1910

When A Fellow Is Twenty-One (*w* MILLS) 1904

When I Take My Morning Promenade (*w* MILLS) 1910

When Love Creeps In Your Heart (*w* MILLS) *c*.1913

When The War Is Over, Mother Dear (& J. P. LONG & MILLS) *c*.1915

Who's Coming Up In The Gallery? 1894

Wonderful Rose Of Love (*w* MILLS) *c*.1914

SCOTT, Clement
Now Is The Hour (*w* Maewa KAIHAU; *w&m* adap. trad.?) 1913

SCOTT, Clement W. 1842–1904
England Has Stood To Her Guns (*m* William Charles LEVEY) 1878

God Bless Victoria (*m* Edward ST QUENTIN) 1897

Here Stands A Post (Waiting For The Signal) (*m* LEVEY) 1878
There were various versions of this song.

Run Up The Flag (*m* Michael CONNOLLY) 1884

SCOTT, Lady John Douglass 1810–1900
Annie Laurie (*w&m* William DOUGLAS *c*.1700, rev. SCOTT) 1835

Loch Lomond (arr. Dun FINLAY) *c*.1845

SCOTT, Malcolm° 1872–1929
Mariana (*m* Erroll STANHOPE) 1898

SCOTT, Maurice d. 1933
Ayesha, My Sweet Egyptian (*w* Joe BURLEY & Cecil JOHNSON) 1908

Girls, Study Your Cookery Book (*w* BURLEY) 1908

I Got Married To A Widow (& BURLEY) 1908

I've Got Rings On My Fingers (*w* Fred J. BARNES & R. P. WESTON) 1909

My Old Pal Joe (*w* Edgar BATEMAN) 1906

My Rachel's Eyes (& BARNES & WESTON) *c*.1912

Nice Quiet Day, A (Postman's Holiday) (*w* BATEMAN & Eustace BAYNES) 1901

Oh! It's A Lovely War (& J. P. LONG) 1917

One Of The Boys (*w* BARNES & WESTON) 1907

Swing Me Higher, Obadiah! (*w* Alfred E. RICK) 1907

Tra-La-La! 1906

SCOTT, Sir Walter 1771–1832; all were set by many others
Barefoot Friar, The (*Ivanhoe*) (*m* E. J. LODER) 1844

Bonnie Dundee (*The Doom of Devorgoil*) (*m* Sidney NELSON) 1855

Proud Maisie (*The Heart of Midlothian*) (*m* Charles Hubert PARRY) 1899

Young Lochinvar (*Marmion*) (*m* Liza LEHMANN) 1898

SCOTT-GATTY, Sir Alfred 1847–1918; from 1904 Garter King of Arms
Cricket (*Country House Ditties*, 2) (*w* H. L. TREVOR) 1898

Golf (*Country House Ditties*, 2) 1898

Ha! Ha! Ha! 1879

O Fair Dove, O Fond Dove

True Till Death (*Country House Ditties*, 1) (*w* L. L. B.) 1879

SCOTT-GATTY, Charles
Bobby Dear

Hullo! Tu-Tu (*w* Muriel SCOTT-GATTY) 1909

Janie 1908

Peter (*w* Muriel & Charles SCOTT-GATTY) 1910

SCOTT-GATTY, Muriel
Hullo! Tu-Tu (*m* Charles SCOTT-GATTY)
1909
Peter (& Charles SCOTT-GATTY: Charles
SCOTT-GATTY) 1910

SCULL, Guy H. 1876–1920
Gentlemen-Rankers (*w* Rudyard
KIPLING) 1893
See CORE SONG-LIST—The Whiffenpoof
Song.

SEARSON, Ernest A. 1866–1933
Can I Be Of Any Assistance? (*m* Fred
HASTINGS) 1907
Have A Banana 1918
He Led Me Up The Garden (*m* Fred
GIBSON) 1929
Lost Dog, The (arr. Charles J. WINTER)
1907
Soup 1916
That's How I Found The Pole (*m*
J. Airlie DIX) 1909
Toasts 1904
Village Of Toad-In-The-Hole, The (&
Paul MILL: DIX) 1907
Walks 1919
Wellerisms 1916
Welshman In London, The 1917

SEDGWICK, T. B.
I'm Looking For A Girl Like You *c.*1909
Lecturer, The (& Dan LENO: Denham
HARRISON)

SEDLEY, Sir Charles 1639?–1701
Phillis Is My Only Joy (*m* J. W. HOBBS)
1848

SEEL, Charles° d. 1903
Coster's Linnet, The 1896
Who Gives This Woman Away? (*w*
Norton ATKINS) 1890

SEIBERT, T. Lawrence
Casey Jones (*m* Eddie NEWTON) 1909

SELDEN, Edgar *c.*1868–1924
All That I Ask Of You Is Love (*w*
Herbert INGRAHAM) 1905

They Don't Speak To One Another Now
(*w* INGRAHAM) 1910

SELDON, Arthur
Catch 'Em Alive Oh! *c.*1895
That Was Enough For Me! 1892

SELMAN, E. W.
Mary And The Butcher (& Robert
GORMAN) 1907

SERVICE, Robert 1874–1958
Shooting Of Dan McGrew, The (*m*
Cuthbert CLARKE) 1917

SEWELL, James W.°
Ally Sloper's Party 1888
Bond St Mash-Ah, The (arr. John S.
BAKER) 1889
Mackenzie (That Devil Of A Daddy) (arr.
BAKER)
Only A Week Away

SEYMOUR, Frank d. 1891
My Boy 1873
My Girl 1873

SHAKESPEARE, William 1564–1616
Hark Hark The Lark (*m* Franz
SCHUBERT) 1826
Lo! Here The Gentle Lark (*m* Henry R.
BISHOP) 1819
Who Is Sylvia? (*m* SCHUBERT) 1826
Scenes from or condensed versions (incl.
burlesques) of:
Hamlet
Henry V
Julius Caesar
Macbeth
Merchant Of Venice, The
Merry Wives Of Windsor, The
Othello
Richard II
Richard III
Romeo And Juliet
Taming Of The Shrew, The

SHAND, Ernest° 1868–1924
Lloyd Jarge (*w* Tom WICK) 1914

SHANNON, J. Royce 1881–1946
Back To Tennessee 1911
Coster Rag 1910
That's An Irish Lullaby (Too-Ra-Loo-Ra-Loo-Ral) 1913

SHAPP, Mrs George
Deep, Deep Sea, The (*m* Charles E. HORN) 1830

SHARPE, Evelyn d. 1948
When The Great Red Dawn Is Shining (*w* Edward LOCKTON) 1917

SHAW, Bernard 1856–1950
Annajanska, The Wild Grand Duchess (sk.) 1918
Augustus Does His Bit (sk.)

SHEAN, Al° 1868–1949
Mr Gallagher & Mr Shean (Bryan FOY: & Ed GALLAGHER) *c.*1920

SHELLEY, Herbert°
Colours We Love, The (*m* Stephen R. PHILPOT) 1902
Dan The Dandy (*m* PHILPOT) 1907
Hi-Diddle-Diddle! (*m* PHILPOT) 1901
His Old Straw Hat (*m* Ray WALLACE) 1902
I Always Wears An Orchid Next Me 'Eart (*m* Colet DARE) 1897
Little Things That Gold Can't Buy, The (*m* PHILPOT) 1903
Old Oak Well, The (*m* PHILPOT) 1906

SHELLEY, Percy Bysshe 1792–1822
Love's Philosophy (*m* Samuel LIDDLE) 1902
Set by some 30 others
Widow Bird, The (*m* George A. MacFARREN) 1867

SHEPPARD, E. A.
Any Old Iron? (& Charles COLLINS: Fred TERRY) 1911
Cover It Over Quick, Jemima (& COLLINS) 1911

SHERIDAN, Mark° 1867–1918
Who Were You With Last Night? (& Fred GODFREY) 1912

SHERIDAN, Richard Brinsley
1751–1816
School For Scandal, The (screen scene) 1777

SHIELD, William 1748–1829
Arethusa, The 1804
Bud Of The Rose, The 1786
Ploughboy, The *c.*1788
Thorn, The
Wolf, The 1820

SHIELDS, Larry° 1893–1953
At The Jazz Band Ball (& Nick LaROCCA) 1917
Clarinet Marmalade (& LaROCCA) 1917
Fidgety Feet (& LaROCCA) 1918
Lazy Daddy (& LaROCCA) 1917
Ramblin' Blues (& LaROCCA) 1920

SHIELDS, Ren 1868–1913
Frankie And Johnny (trad., arr. SHIELDS & LEIGHTON BROS) 1912
In The Good Old Summertime (*m* George EVANS) 1902
Steamboat Bill (*m* LEIGHTON BROTHERS) 1910
Waltz Me Around Again, Willie (*w* Will D. COBB) 1906

SHROSBERRY, E. R.
Marquis Of Camberwell Green, The (*w* Harry BODEN) 1884

SIEBERT, Edrich d. 19 Dec. 1984
Marrow Song, The 1952

SIEVIER, Bruce d. 16 Apr. 1953
Piccadilly (& Walter WILLIAMS: Paul MORANDE) 1921

SILBERMAN(N), L.
A-Be My Boy (*w* Herbert RULE & Thomas McGHEE: & A. GROCK) 1919
All For Her Country's Sake (tribute to Nurse Cavell) (& Mason DIXON) *c.*1915
Back To Dear Old Tennessee (DIXON: & GROCK) 1916

Do It Again (DIXON: & GROCK & T. W. THURBAN) 1917
Fill 'Em Up (*w* RULE & McGHEE & James WALSH (2))
Have You Paid The Rent? (& RULE & Fred HOLT) 1922
My Colorado Sue (*m* DIXON: & ? GROCK) 1918
Thank God For Victory (*w* Percy EDGAR) 1919
Yaaki-Daaki Yaaki Dah (Mandy From Tonypandy) (DIXON: & GROCK) 1917

SILVER, Frank 1896–1960
Yes, We Have No Bananas (*m* Irving COHEN) 1923

SILVERS, Louis 1889–1954
April Showers (*w* Buddy DeSYLVA) 1921

SIM, William d. 7 Apr. 1885
All Hands On Deck (*w* Harry CHESTERFIELD) 1878
See also LIPTON & MURPHY.
Cockalorum (*w&m* John J. STAMFORD, arr. SIM) 1878
Get A Little Table (*w&m* Harry LINN, arr. SIM) 1882
Russians I'd Fight Like A Turk (*w* Harry ROGERS) 1877
Where Was Moses When The Light Went Out? (*w&m* STAMFORD, arr. SIM) 1878
See Harry VON TILZER for later identical title.
You're Another (*w* T. S. LONSDALE) 1877

SIMPSON, Harold d. 18 Nov. 1955?
Down In The Forest (from *A Cycle Of Life*) (*m* Landon RONALD) 1915

SIMS, George R. 1847–1922; a.k.a. DAGONET
Billy's Rose (*Dagonet Ballads*) 1881
Hush! The Bogie! (& Henry PETTITT: Meyer LUTZ, arr. Edmund FORMAN) 1890

See also David BRAHAM.
In The Workhouse: Christmas Day (*Dagonet Ballads*) 1881
I Wooed My Love (*m* LUTZ) 1889
Jack's Yarn (*m* Louis DIEHL)
Lifeboat, The (*Dagonet Ballads*) (*m* Ciro PINSUTI, 1885) 1881
Lights Of London Town, The (*Ballads of Babylon*) (*m* DIEHL) 1880
Old England And Our Queen (*m* John FITZGERALD) *c.*1875
Ostler Joe (*Ballads of Babylon*) 1880
Won't You Join The Army? (*m* James Mackay GLOVER) 1914

SINCLAIR, Margaret A.
Dicky Bird And The Owl, The (*m* Arthur SULLIVAN) *c.*1895
Soprano and baritone version of The Buttercup, F. C. BURNAND: SULLIVAN.

SINGER, Dolph 1900–42
Just Around The Corner (*w* Harry VON TILZER) 1925

SISSLE, Noble 1889–1975
I'm Just Wild About Harry (*m* Eubie BLAKE) 1921

SKELLY, Joseph P. fl. 1850–1900
Boy's Best Friend Is His Mother, A (*w* Henry MILLER) 1883
Down By The Old Mill Stream (not Tell Taylor's better-known song) 1874
My Pretty Red Rose 1877
Old Rustic Bridge By The Mill, The 1881
Picture With Its Face Turned To The Wall, The (not The Picture That Is Turned To The Wall, Charles GRAHAM) 1891
Strolling On The Brooklyn Bridge (& Geo. COOPER) 1883

SKERRY, W.
When She Walks (Harry BODEN: & Harry FORD) 1906

SKETCHLEY, Arthur° 1818–82 pseudonym of George Rose; between 1868 and 1881 wrote numerous sks. and mons. around 'Mrs Brown'
Oh, How Delightful! (*m* J. L. MOLLOY) 1868

SLAUGHTER, Walter 1859–1908
'Ackney With The 'Ouses Took Away (*w* Seymour HICKS) 1901
Dear Home-Land, The (*w* Clifton BINGHAM) 1892
Orlando Dando (*w* Basil HOOD) 1898

SLOANE, A. Baldwin 1872–1926
Heaven Will Protect The Working Girl (*w* Edgar SMITH) 1910

SLOMAN, Charles° 1808–70
Artful Dodger, The (& Sam COWELL: anon.)
Charming Sue 1860
Daughter Of Israel 1835
Daughters Of Salem (*w* Julia CRAWFORD) 1844
Dream Of The Hebrew Maiden, The 1859
Jewish Captives In Babylon (*w* CRAWFORD) 1844
Maid Of Judah, The 1830
Pop Goes The Weasel (*m* anon.) 1833
Ratcatcher's Daughter, The (extra verses—see CORE SONG-LIST)
Reg'lar Cure, The (*m* J. BLEWITT)
Rose Of Raby (*w* CRAWFORD) 1844
Social Bricks
Whole Hog Or None, The (*m* arr. T. WESTROP from Love's Young Dream by Thomas MOORE) 1862
For song of same title see E. W. MACKNEY.

SMART, Grenville
I Won't Be A Nun (*w&m* Countess of W-N-K, arr. SMART)

SMITH, Carl
Goo-Goo Song, The (*m* Fanny WENTWORTH) 1900

SMITH, Chris 1879–1949
Ballin' The Jack (Roy BURRIS: & James Reese EUROPE) 1913

SMITH, Henry Clay° b. 12 Feb. 1885?; m. Lee White°
If It's In 'John Bull' It *Is* So (& Bert LEE & R. P. WESTON) 1917
Somebody's Coming To Tea (& LEE & WESTON) 1917

SMITH, Dexter 1839–1909
Ring The Bell Softly, There's Crape On The Door (*m* E. L. CATLIN) 1876

SMITH, Edgar 1858–1938
Heaven Will Protect The Working Girl (*m* A. Baldwin SLOANE) 1910
Ma Blushin' Rosie (*m* John STROMBERG) 1900

SMITH, G. Totten b. 7 Mar. 1871
Walking Home With Angeline (*m* John E. ROUNDBACH) 1902

SMITH, G. Townshend 1813–77
Wanted A Wife *c.*1850

SMITH, Harry B. 1860–1936
Art Is Calling For Me (*m* Victor HERBERT) 1911
Bright Eyes (*m* Otto MOTZAN & M. K. JEROME) 1920
I Just Can't Make My Eyes Behave (& Will D. COBB: Gus EDWARDS) 1906
Pansy Faces (*m* William H. PENN) 1902
Sheik Of Araby, The (& Francis WHEELER: Ted SNYDER) 1921
Woman Is Only A Woman But A Good Cigar Is A Smoke, A (*m* Victor HERBERT) 1905

SMITH, Hubbard, T. *c.*1858–1903
Listen To My Tale Of Woe (*w* Eugene FIELD) 1884
Little Peach In An Orchard Grew, A (& D. A. WYE) 1889

SMITH, John Stafford 1750–1836
Star-Spangled Banner, The (*w* Francis

Scott KEY: SMITH, ed. Thomas CARR)
c.1814
Air based on Smith's Anacreon In Heaven.

SMITH, Robert H. 1875?–1951?
Come Down Ma Evening Star (*m* John
    STROMBERG) 1902

SMITH, Vere 1884–1910
Hello, Martha (*w* W. EARDLEY-WILMOT
    & SMITH) 1908
I'll Be Your Gal 1909
Ma Dusky Maid 1908

SMITH, Vincent
Put The Brake On When You're Going
    Down The Hill (*w* Harry CLIFTON)
    1869

SNAPE, P. H.
Daddy's On The Engine (& Arthur
    ALBERT: Sam POTTER); also attr.
    Charles GRAHAM 1895

SNYDER, Ted 1881–1965
If The Managers Only Thought The
    Same As Mother (*w* BERLIN) 1910
I'm Going Back To Dixie (& Irving
    BERLIN) 1911
Kiss Me My Honey (*w* BERLIN) 1910
My Wife's Gone To The Country (*w*
    BERLIN & George WHITING) 1909
Sheik Of Araby, The (*w* Harry B. SMITH
    & Francis WHEELER) 1921
That Mysterious Rag (*w* BERLIN) 1912
Who's Sorry Now? 1923

SOLMAN, Alfred 1868–1937
Bird On Nellie's Hat, The (*w* Arthur J.
    LAMB) 1906
Why Did You Make Me Care? (*w*
    Sylvester MAGUIRE) 1912
You Splash Me And I'll Splash You (*w*
    LAMB) 1907

SOLOMON, Edward 1853–95;
bigamously m. Lillian Russell°
(annulled)

All On Account Of Liza (*w* H. Pottinger
    STEPHENS) 1881
Good Young Man Who Died (*w*
    STEPHENS) 1881
Old Nigger Ben

SOMERVELL, Arthur 1863–1937
When I Was One-And-Twenty (*m*
    Stephen ADAMS) 1904
This 1896 poem was set by some thirty-
    three other composers.

SOUTHEY, G. W.
Battle Eve, The (*m* Theodore BONHEUR)
    1898

SPADE, Jack composite name of Elton
Box & Desmond COX & 'Ilda LEWIS',
itself a pseudonym of the publisher Irwin
Dash.
Your Baby 'As Gorn Dahn The Plug-'Ole
    1944
    See CORE SONG-LIST.

SPEAKS, Oley 1874–1946
Morning (*w* Frank L. STANTON) 1910
On The Road To Mandalay (*w* Rudyard
    KIPLING) 1907
Sylvia (*w* Clinton SCOLLARD) 1914

SPENCER, E. Mordaunt d. 1888
Rose Of Tralee, The (*m* Charles W.
    GLOVER) *c*.1850
    See also William P. MULCHINOCK and
    CORE SONG-LIST.

SPENCER, J. J.
Curtain Has Fallen Again, The 1899

SPRANGE, W. E.
It's A Little Bit Of Sugar For The Bird
    (& F. BOWYER: John CROOK) 1895

SPURR, Harry brother of Mel B. SPURR
Hamlet Up-To-Date (& Mel B. SPURR)
    1891

SPURR, Mel B.° 1852–1904; brother of
Harry SPURR
And I Don't Blame Him 1903

Christmas Pantomime, A (sk.) 1897

Dinah (*m* Gilbert BYASS) 1895

Do It Thoroughly 1901

Dream Of An 'At Home', A (*m* Leslie HARRIS) 1896

Girl From College, The (*m* H. E. BRENTON) 1894

Hamlet Up-To-Date (& Harry SPURR) 1891

His Only Joke 1897

Nipper's Lullaby (*m* Bond ANDREWS) 1893

Nolan's Science Club 1903

Our Musical Comedy 1901

Small And Early 1902

Why Did The Night Owl 'Owl? 1901

SQUIERS, Graham

Modest Curate, The (*m* Guy S. JONES) 1913

Our Hobbies (*m* Willie ROUSE) 1911

SQUIRE, William H. b. 1871

If I Might Come To You (*w* Fred E. WEATHERLY) 1916

Irish Fusilier, The (*w* F. FERRIS) 1911

Jolly Sailor, The (*w* E. TESCHEMACHER) 1903

Mountain Lovers (*w* WEATHERLY) 1908

Three For Jack (*w* WEATHERLY) 1904

Token, The (*w* W. BLOCKSIDGE) 1909

STAHL, Richard

Some Things Are Better Left Unsaid (*w* J. HAYDEN-CLARENDON & Charles H. HOYT) 1896

STAMFORD, John J. *c*.1840–99; possibly a.k.a. John S. BAKER

Cockalorum (arr. William SIM) 1878

John Bull's Smoking Concert 1891

MacNamara's Band (*m* Shamus O'CONNOR) 1889

Oh, What A Wicked Young Man You Are (arr. Edmund FORMAN) *c*.1882

Poor, But A Gentleman Still (arr. H. W. FITCHETT) 1875

Turn Off The Gas At The Meter (arr. Frederick CHARLES) 1878

Where Was Moses When The Light Went Out? (arr. SIM) 1878
See Harry VON TILZER for later identical title.

STAMPER, Dave 1883–1963

Daddy Has A Sweetheart And Mother Is Her Name (*w* Gene BUCK) 1911

Some Boy (*w* BUCK) 1911

STANFORD, Sir Charles Villiers 1852–1924

Drake's Drum (*w* Henry NEWBOLT) 1905
Set by eight others.

Father O'Flynn (*w* Alfred Perceval GRAVES) 1882

Old Navy, The (*w* Captain Frederick MARRYAT) 1893

Old Superb, The (*w* NEWBOLT) 1904

Trotting To The Fair (GRAVES: *m* trad., arr. STANFORD) 1901

STANGE, Stanislaus 1860–1917

My Hero (*m* Oscar STRAUS) 1910

STANHOPE, Erroll°

Mariana (*w* Malcolm SCOTT) 1898

One, Two, Three Polka Song, The 1897

STANLEY, Erroll

My Honey Dear (*w* Fred ALLANDALE) 1898

STANLEY, Ralph d. 23 Nov 1970

Shufflin' Along (*m* Nat D. AYER) 1922

STANLEY, Wynn 1874–1940 pseudonym of Worton DAVID

Ca-bages, Ca-beans And Car-rots (& Andrew ALLEN) 1919

Dear Old Mother (& ALLEN) 1920

Let's Have A Song About Rhubarb (& ALLEN) 1922

STANTON, Frank L. 1857–1927

Just A-Wearyin' For You (*m* Carrie JACOBS-BOND) 1916

Mighty Lak' A Rose (*m* Ethelbert
 NEVIN) 1901
Morning (*m* Oley SPEAKS) 1910

STARR, Hattie
Hoodoo Coon, A 1898
Laugh, Yo' Little Niggers 1895
Little Alabama Coon 1893
Ma Little Yalla Daisy 1899
Moo-Low! Low-Moo! 1894
Somebody Loves Me 1893

STEFFE, William
Say Brothers Will You Meet Us
 (Methodist hymn used as basis for
 John Brown's Body (*w* anon.) and
 Battle Hymn Of The Republic *w* Julia
 Ward HOWE) 1858

STELLA
Father's A Drunkard And Mother Is
 Dead (& Mrs E. A. PARKHURST)
 1868

STEPHENS, H. Pottinger d. 12 Feb.
1903
All On Account Of Liza (*m* Edward
 SOLOMON) 1880
Good Young Man Who Died, The (*m*
 SOLOMON) 1881

STEPHENSON, B. C. *c*.1840–1906
Cricket! (*m* Lionel MONCKTON) 1899
Let Me Dream Again (*m* Arthur
 SULLIVAN) 1876
Queen Of My Heart (*m* Alfred CELLIER;
 orig. *w* as Old Dreams by Sarah
 DOUDNEY) 1886
Venetian Song, The (*m* F. Paolo TOSTI)
 1889

STERLING, Andrew B. 1874–1955
Down At The Old Bull And Bush (&
 Russell HUNTING & Percy KRONE: H.
 VON TILZER, adap. Under The
 Anheuser Bush, STERLING: VON
 TILZER) 1903
In The Evening By The Moonlight, Dear
 Louise (*m* VON TILZER) 1912

Meet Me In St Louis, Louis (*m* Kerry
 MILLS) 1904
My Old New Hampshire Home (*m* VON
 TILZER) 1898
On A Sunday Afternoon (*m* VON
 TILZER) 1902
Take A Look At Me Now (*m* VON
 TILZER) 1911
Wait Till The Sun Shines, Nellie (*m* VON
 TILZER) 1905
Where The Sweet Magnolias Grow (*m*
 VON TILZER) 1899
Where Was Moses When The Light
 Went Out? (& V. P. BRYAN: VON
 TILZER) 1901
 First version lyrics by Vincent P. BRYAN
 only; see John J. STAMFORD for earlier
 identical title.

STERN, Joe William 1870–1934
December And May (*w* Edward B.
 MARKS)
Little Lost Child, The (A Passing
 Policeman) (*w* MARKS) 1894
Mother Was A Lady (*w* MARKS) 1896

STERN, Sam° b. 1883
My Brudda, Sylvest' (& Jesse LASKY:
 Fred FIS(C)HER) 1908
My Rachel Myer From Hawaii (&
 Thomas McGHEE & Herbert RULE)
 1917

STERN, Willie
What-Ho, She Bumps! (*m* Cuthbert
 COLLINS) 1899
 Not the better-known song of same title by
 A. J. MILLS & Harry CASTLING.

STEVENS, George A. d. 19 Apr. 1954
Huntsman, The (& Albert PERRY: Fred
 EPLETT) 1900
I'm Shy, Mary Ellen, I'm Shy (& Chas.
 RIDGWELL) 1910
On Mother Kelly's Doorstep 1925
You Can Do A Lot Of Things At The
 Seaside That You Can't Do In Town
 (& RIDGWELL) 1911

STEVENS, Victor°
No! Yes! Well, You Ought To Know (arr. Alfred HAINES) 1887

STEVENS, W. B. B.
Empty Cradle, The (*m* George A. BARKER) 1869

STEVENSON, Sir John 1760?–1833
Lesbia Hath A Beaming Eye (Thomas MOORE: anon./trad., arr. STEVENSON) 1807
Love's Young Dream (*w&m* MOORE, arr. STEVENSON) 1807
Meeting Of The Waters, The (*w* MOORE: air, The Old Head of Dennis, arr. STEVENSON) *c*.1820
Oft In The Stilly Night (*w* MOORE; *m* sometimes given as trad.) 1815

STEWART, Herbert *see* HALL, Frank

STEWART, James E. 1820–81
Close The Shutters, Willie's Dead (arr. Horace MARTYN) *c*.1875
Give My Love To All At Home 1874

STILES, Leslie 1876–*c*.1940?; sometimes spelled Styles
Come And Be A Soldier (*m* Ralph NAIRN) 1904
In Cherry Blossom Land In Japan (*m* Herman DAREWSKI & Gitz RICE) 1917
My Oriental Daisy 1906
Tail Of A Comet, The 1907
Why Do They Call Me A Gibson Girl? (*m* Leslie STUART) 1906

STOCKS, John
Song That Broke My Heart, The (& G. W. HUNTER: Julian JORDAN & Michael NOLAN) 1890

STOLL, Sir Oswald 1866–1942
Bachelors (arr. Edmund FORMAN) 1889
Dawn Of Freedom, The *c*.1887
For The Sake Of The Old Times (arr. John S. BAKER) 1890

Is Marriage A Failure? (arr. T. RICHARDS) 1889
Mary And John 1890
Oh, You Girls *c*.1885
Parrot And The Cage, The
Tablet Of Fame, The 1887

STORY, Pauline B.
Ring Down The Curtain (*w* Robert H. BRENNEN) 1902
She's A Singer, But A Lady, Just The Same (*w* BRENNEN) 1902

STRACHEY, H.
I'm A Man That's Done Wrong To My Parents (trad. *w&m* arr. STRACHEY) *c*.1889

STRAUS, Oscar 1870–1954
My Hero (*w* Stanislaus STANGE) 1910

STRAUSS II, Johann 1825–99
Czardas (*Die Fledermaus*) (Eng. *w* C. Hamilton AÏDÉ, 1876) 1874
Laughing Song, The (*Die Fledermaus*) (Eng. *w* AÏDÉ, 1876) 1874
Word-Lets, Gag-Lets, And Yarn-Lets (Richard MORTON: STRAUSS, arr. John S. BAKER) 1893

STROMBERG, John 1853–1902
Come Down Ma Evenin' Star (*w* Robert H. SMITH) 1902
Ma Blushin' Rosie (*w* Edgar SMITH) 1900

STROUD, Arthur d. 23 May 1951
Hail, Caledonia! (*w* Hugh OGILVIE) 1912

STUART, Delia
On Wings Of Song (Felix MENDELSSOHN: Heinrich HEINE, adap. STUART) 1834

STULTS, R. M. 1861–1923
Sweetest Story Ever Told, The 1892

STUART, Leslie 1862–1928; pseudonym of Thomas Augustine Barrett (a.k.a.

Lester THOMAS), who claimed that the
Southport church where he was baptized
burnt down, destroying all records. His
age at death is registered as 66
Bandolero, The 1894
Banshee, The 1900
Cake Walk, The 1898
Coon Drum-Major, The 1899
Coon That Never Told A Lie, The
1903
Girl On The Ran-Dan-Dan, The 1896
I May Be Crazy But I Love You 1902
In The Summer 1897
Is Yer Mammie Always With Ye? 1896
I Want To Be A Military Man (w Frank
A. CLEMENT) 1899
Lily Of Laguna, The 1898
Little Anglo-Saxon Any Time, The 1898
Little Dolly Daydream 1897
Looking For A Needle In A Haystack
1903
Louisiana Lou 1894
Mamie, I've A Little Canoe 1903
Mighty Mother England (w Fred E.
WEATHERLY) 1909
Military Medal, The 1895
My Little Black Pearl 1904
My Little Octoroon 1899
Oh! Venus Let me Call You Sal 1895
Old Shield, The 1907
On The Road To Tipperary (w George
ARTHURS) 1907
Rip Van Winkle 1896
Shade Of The Palm, The 1899
Soldiers Of The Queen, The 1891
Sweetheart May 1894
Tell Me, Pretty Maiden (w E. Boyd
JONES & Paul RUBENS) 1899
There's Nothing Like Your First Love
After All 1906
Trilby Will Be True 1895
Two Little Eyes Of Blue 1901
Vale Of Arklow 1892
Why Do They Call Me A Gibson Girl?
(w L. STILES) 1906
Willow Pattern Plate, The 1896

STYLES, Leslie *see* STILES, Leslie

SULLIVAN, Sir Arthur L. 1842–1900
Absent-Minded Beggar, The (w Rudyard
KIPLING) 1899
Buttercup, The (w F. C. BURNAND;
see The Dicky Bird And The Owl)
1867
Chorister, The (w Fred E. WEATHERLY)
1876
Dicky Bird And The Owl, The (w
Margaret A. SINCLAIR—soprano and
baritone version of The Buttercup)
c.1895
Distant Shore, The (w W. S. GILBERT)
1874
Edward Gray (w Alfred TENNYSON)
1880
Hail! Hail! The Gang's All Here
(D. TERRISS: & T. MORSE) 1917
Let Me Dream Again (w B. C.
STEPHENSON) 1876
Lost Chord, The (w Adelaide
A. PROCTER) 1877
Sweethearts (w GILBERT) 1875
Thou Art Weary (w PROCTER) 1874
Will He Come? (w PROCTER) 1873

SULLIVAN, J.°
I'm Lively Pompey Jones (m Charles
BLAMPHIN) 1873

SULLIVAN, Joseph J.° 1817–1917
Where Did You Get That Hat? (arr.
W. M. LORAINE); see James ROLMAZ
1888

SULLIVAN, Terry d. 11 Dec. 1950
Father's Got The Sack From The
Waterworks (& Charles COLLINS)
1915
(Floating With) My Boating Girl 1911
It's A Bit Of A Ruin That Cromwell
Knocked About A Bit (& Harry
BEDFORD: BEDFORD) 1912
She Sells Sea-Shells (m Harry GIFFORD)
1908

SUTCLIFFE, W.
Love's Coronation (*m* Florence
AYLWARD) 1902

SUTHERD, Arthur
Come Down And Open The Door, Love
(*m* Slade MURRAY, arr. Edmund
FORMAN, rev. 1898 C. G. COTES:
Bennett SCOTT) 1884
Oh, My! Certainly Not (*m* MURRAY)

SWAFFER, Hannen 1879–1962
You Are A Little White Girl (*m* Herman
DAREWSKI jun.) 1904

SWEENEY, P.
Delaney's Chicken (& Lester BARRETT)
1896
Ga-Ga-Ga-Ga-Good-Bye (& BARRETT)
1894
Looking For A Job (& BARRETT) 1899
They're All Fine Girls (& BARRETT:
Lester THOMAS) 1895

SWENY, Hugh W.
Walking In The Zoo (*m* Alfred LEE)
1867

SWINBURNE, Algernon 1837–1909
Ask Nothing More (*m* Théo MARZIALS)
1883

SYDNEY, Harry° 1825–70; little of his
vast output was published; see entry in
ARTISTES' REPERTOIRES
Jones's Sister (My Old Friend Jones)
1865
Little Red Riding Hood 1857
My Mary Jane *c.*1863
My Uncle (*m* J. Harrington YOUNG)
1869
Rolling Stone, A *c.*1860
Shadows On The Wall, The (see Mrs
F. R. PHILLIPS for ladies' version)
Take A Lesson From Me (*m* adap.
YOUNG)
Whisky In The Jar

SYKES, Arthur A.
Khaki (*w* Nellie GANTHONY)

SYMONS, Ernest J.
Dearly Beloved Brethren (*w&m* Joseph
TABRAR, arr. SYMONS) 1881
Don't Leave Your Mother When Her
Hair Turns Grey (*w* C. OSBORN) 1881
Fishing For Truth In A Well (*m* Henry
PETTITT) 1882
In My Fust 'Usband's Time (*w&m* Harry
NICHOLLS, arr. SYMONS) 1882
Little Miss Muffet Sat On A Tuffet (*w*
Joseph S. LONG) 1882
Mind The Paint (*w* N. G. TRAVERS) 1891
Not Much (LONG: Kate ROYLE, arr.
SYMONS) 1887
Sweethearts And Wives (*w* TRAVERS)
1891
We Have Men, We Have Money (G. H.
MACDERMOTT & Geoffrey THORN,
arr. SYMONS) 1882
Why Part With Jumbo (The Pet Of The
Zoo)? (*w* MACDERMOTT) 1882
You Are Always Sure To Fetch Them
With Wst Wst Wst (*w&m* PETTITT,
arr. SYMONS) 1882

TABBUSH, Reginald d. 1973
How Can A Little Girl Be Good (*w* BAY)
1919

TABRAR, Joseph 1857–1931; father of
Fred EARLE°
All In A Day (Bid Me Good-Bye For
Ever) 1898
All The Boys In Our Choir 1893
And Very Nice Too 1912
Bid Me Good-Bye For Ever (All In A
Day) 1898
Buy Me Some Almond Rock 1893
Charley's Aunt 1894
Daddy Wouldn't Buy Me A Bow-Wow
1892
Dear Kind Doctor, A 1895
Dearly Beloved Brethren (arr. Ernest J.
SYMONS) 1881
Dear Me! Is That Possible? 1882
Dear Old Ned 1894
Don't Be So Particular, Dear

For Months And Months And Months
  1909
Goodbye, Goodbye, Goodbye 1887
Hard Times Come Again No More 1888
Have You Seen Her? 1887
He's Going To Marry Mary Ann 1885
He's Sailing On The Briny Ocean 1892
I Love My Little Polly *c.*1900
I Say Cabby! 1882
It Ain't All Lavender 1894
Let Go The Anchor, Boys
Like A Girl 1896
Lock Him Up 1881
Madame Duvan (*m* Tom COSTELLO, arr.
  Alfred LAMONT) 1891
Maid Of London Ere We Part (& J. P.
  HARRINGTON & G. LE BRUNN) 1896
Night Alarm, The (sk.) 1889
Nobody Knows Who Done It 1882
Oh, You Little Darling (I Love You) 1882
Remarkable Fellah!, A 1882
Ro-me-o And Juliet 1896
She Was Fat, Fair, And Forty 1884
Ship Went Down, The 1898
They're All Good 1891
Ti! Hi! Tiddelly Hi! 1888
Ting, Ting, That's How The Bell Goes
  1883
Trilby's Rival 1896
Waiting For Me 1898
We Put Him In A Cab And Sent Him
  Home (*w* Harry WINCOTT) 1895
What's The World Coming To? 1881
What With Yours And What With Mine
  1882
Wilds Of Peckham Rye, The 1882
Winkle's Wedding, The 1894

TALBOT, Howard 1865–1928; pseudo-
nym of Howard Munkittrick
Everybody Wondered How He Knew (*w*
  George ROLLIT) 1899
Half-Past Two (*w* Percy GREENBANK &
  Arthur WIMPERIS) 1909
If Only I Knew The Way (*w* Harry
  GREENBANK) 1896

I Like London (*w* WIMPERIS) 1909
Land Where The Best Man Wins, The
  (*w* Arthur ANDERSON) 1906
Martha Spanks The Grand Piano (*w*
  George DANCE) 1901
My Motter (*w* WIMPERIS) 1909

TALHAIARN 1810–69; bardic name of
John Jones
Shake Of The Hand, The (*m* John
  BLOCKLEY) 1857
Yr Hen Lange (The Old Bachelor) (arr.
  Owain ALAW) 1862

TATE, Arthur F. 1870–1950
Somewhere A Voice Is Calling (*w* Eileen
  NEWTON) 1911

TATE, Harry° 1872–1940
Fishing (& Wal PINK; licensed by Lord
  Chamberlain 1912) *c.*1910
Golfing (& Wal PINK; licensed by Lord
  Chamberlain 1912) *c.*1910
Motoring (& Wal PINK; licensed by Lord
  Chamberlain 1 Feb. 1912) *c.*1905

TATE, James W.° 1875–1922; m. (1)
José Collins° (deceased) (2) Clarice
Mayne°
Bachelor Gay, A (*w* F. Clifford HARRIS &
  VALENTINE) 1916
Broken Doll, A (*w* HARRIS) 1915
Come Over The Garden Wall (*w* Ballard
  MACDONALD) 1920
Customs of The Country (*w* J. P.
  HARRINGTON) 1906
Ev'ry Little While (*w* HARRIS) 1916
Georgie Took Me Walking In The Park
  (MACDONALD: & Donovan MEHER)
  1908
Give Me A Little Cosy Corner (*w*
  HARRIS) 1918
If I Should Plant A Tiny Seed Of Love
  (*w* MACDONALD) 1908
Instinct (*w* HARRIS: Liza LEHMANN,
  adap. TATE) 1904
It's Lovely To Be In Love (*w* HARRIS)
  1915

I Was A Good Little Girl Till I Met You
(*w* HARRIS) 1914
My Actor Man (*w* HARRIS) 1913
Paradise For Two, A (*w* HARRIS &
VALENTINE) 1916
Story Of A Clothes Line, The (*w*
HARRIS) 1904
There'll Be Some Dirty Weather
Around The Needles (*w* HARRIS)
1914
When Life's Sun Is Setting 1911

TAYLOR, Charles H. b. *c.*1860
I Mustn't Let Her See Me All At Once
My Otaheitee Lady (*m* Jerome KERN)
1913
Rally Round The Flag 1917
Through The Telephone (*m* Herbert E.
HAINES) 1900
Up With The Banns 1895
Waltz Song (For Tonight) (*Tom Jones*)
(*m* Edward GERMAN) 1907

TAYLOR, Helen d. 17 Apr. 1943
Bless This House (*m* May H. BRAHE)
1927
Come To The Fair (*m* Easthope
MARTIN) 1917

TAYLOR, Irving 1914–1983
Knees Up, Mother Brown! (& R. Harris
WESTON & Bert LEE) See CORE
SONG-LIST 1938

TAYLOR, Tell 1876–1937
Ciribiribin (Fr. *w* Rudolf THALER; Eng.
w TAYLOR: Alberto PESTALOZZA)
1909
Down By The Old Mill Stream 1910

TCHAIKOVSKY, Pyotr 1840–93
None But The Lonely Heart (op. 6 no. 6)
(*w* Johann W. Von GOETHE; Eng.
trans. A. WESTBROOK) 1869

TEMPEST, Charles
'Arf A Pint Of Ale 1905

TEMPEST, H.
I Ain't A-Going To Tell (*w* Wal PINK: *m*
arr. TEMPEST; US orig. Albert E.
ELLIS & Walter C. PARKER) 1893

TEMPLE, Hope née Dolly Davis; m.
André MESSAGER
Memories (*w* Mary Mark LEMON) 1883
My Lady's Bower (*w* Fred E.
WEATHERLY) 1887
Rory Darlin' (*w* WEATHERLY) 1892
Scent Of The Mignonette, The (*w*
Clifton BINGHAM) 1897

TEMPLE, Richard jun. *c.*1873–1954
Prehistoric Man (*w* C. G. COTES) 1902

TEMPLE, S.
Off To Philadelphia (rev. & ed. TEMPLE:
trad. Irish, arr. W. B. HAYNES) 1889

TENNYSON, Alfred, Lord 1809–92
All Along The Valley (*m* CLARIBEL)
*c.*1865
Beggar Maid, The (*m* Joseph BARNBY)
1880
Brook, The (1855); over 24 settings
Charge Of The Light Brigade, The (*m*
John BLOCKLEY) 1855
Come Into The Garden, Maud (*m*
Michael William BALFE); see also
CORE SONG-LIST 1855
Crossing The Bar (*m* A. H. BEHREND)
1893
Also set by Edward G. LOCKTON and
Hubert PARRY and some 80 others.
Edward Gray (*m* Arthur L. SULLIVAN)
1880
In Memoriam (*m* Liza LEHMANN) and
over 100 other settings 1899
Sweet And Low (*m* BARNBY) and over
40 others 1863

TENNYSON, Joe 1881–1901
Wild Man Of Poplar, The (& Joe
O'GORMAN) 1890

TERRISS, Dolly 1890–1953 a.k.a.
Theodora (Dolly) MORSE
Bobbin' Up And Down (*m* Theodore F.
  MORSE) 1913
Hail! Hail! The Gang's All Here (*m*
  MORSE & Arthur SULLIVAN) 1917

TERRY, Edward° 1843–1912
Complaints *or* The Ills Of Life With
  Their Remedies (*w&m* TERRY, arr.
  and partly composed Martin HOBSON)
  1869

TERRY, Fred E.
Any Old Iron? (*w* Charles COLLINS &
  E. A. SHEPPARD) 1911
You Can't Get Many Pimples On A
  Pound Of Pickled Pork 1914

TERRY, W. a.k.a. T. WARD?
One Of The Deathless Army (& T. W.
  THURBAN & Gilbert WELLS & V. R.
  GILL) 1910

TERRY, Will° 1875–1915
Jock McGrau 1906

TESCHEMACHER, Edward 1876?–1940;
pseudonym of Edward R. LOCKTON
Because (*m* Guy D'HARDELOT) 1902
Down Vauxhall Way (*Songs Of Old
  London*) (*m* Herbert OLIVER) 1912
If (*m* Ivor NOVELLO) 1912
Jolly Sailor, The (*m* W. H. SQUIRE) 1903
Little Town In Ireland, A (*m* Edward
  LOCKTON) 1916
Mattinata (*m* Ruggiero LEONCAVALLO)
  1904
Oh Flower Divine (*m* Haydn WOOD)
  1914
Remember Me (*m* Hermann LOEHR)
  1905
Shipmates O' Mine (*m* Wilfred
  SANDERSON) 1913
Since 1913
Speak But One Word (*m* E. Frank
  LAMBERT) 1896
Sweet June (*m* Landon RONALD) 1902

Until (*m* SANDERSON) 1910
When I Do Wrong 1913
Where My Caravan Has Rested (&
  D. CLEVELAND: LOEHR) 1909
Yonder (*m* OLIVER) 1920

THACKERAY, William M. 1811–63
Married To A Mermaid (A. L. C.: *m* attr.
  William Michael WATSON) 1866
  A. L. C. is reputed to have been
  THACKERAY.

THALER, Rudolf
Ciribiribin (Fr. *w* THALER; Eng. *w* Tell
  TAYLOR: Alberto PESTALOZZA) 1898

THARP, R. C.
When Our Good King George Is
  Crowned (*m* Cuthbert CLARKE) 1911

THAYER, Pati d. 1969
I Travel The Road 1925

THOMAS, Arthur
Runaway Motor Car, The (air, Turkey In
  The Straw) 1898

THOMAS, Arthur G. 1851–92
Summer Night, A (*m* Théo MARZIALS)

THOMAS, Brandon° 1857–1914
Beside De Cabin Door
Don't You Come And Bodder Me
I Lub A Lubbly Girl I Do
Peekin' Froo De Moon 1900
Red Marine, The 1889
Sing Along, Sambo 1884
Soapy Soap!
Tabby's Catastrophe 1884
Thickening Of The Tympanum
Tommy Atkins

THOMAS, Frank (Fred?)
Back Again (*m* George LESTER) 1890

THOMAS, John Rogers 1829–96
Beautiful Isle Of The Sea (*w* G.
  COOPER) 1865
'Tis But A Little Faded Flower 1866

THOMAS, Lester 1862–1928 a.k.a. Leslie
STUART

By The Sad Sea Waves (*w* Lester
  BARRETT); see Julius BENEDICT 1894
Little Mad'Moiselle, The 1895
Louisiana Lou 1894
McGinnis's At Home 1894
Sheelah Magee 1894
Some Danced The Lancers (*w*
  BARRETT) 1894
They're All Fine Girls (*w* BARRETT &
  P. SWEENEY) 1895

THOMAS, William M.
Nice Girl, A 1873

THOMPSON, G. Douglas d. 1927
Diver, The (*m* E. J. LODER) 1890

THOMPSON, Harry G. 1850–1937
Fisherman's Child, The (arr. F. W.
  HUMPHRIES) 1882

THOMPSON, H. S. b. 1825?
Lilly Dale 1852

THOMPSON, Will L. 1847–1909
Don't Go Out Tonight, Dear Father (*w*
  M. E. GOLDING) 1889
Gathering Shells By The Sea 1873
Softly And Tenderly *c*.1900

THOMSON, J.
Song Of Thanksgiving, A (*m* Mary
  ALLITSEN) 1897

THOMSON, James 1700–48
Rule, Britannia! (or David MALLET:
  Thomas ARNE) *c*.1741

THORN, Geoffrey° 1843–1905; pseudo-
nym of Charles TOWNLEY
Did You Ever Catch A Weasel Asleep?
Says Aaron To Moses 1879
She'd A Brother In The Navy (*m* Walter
  REDMOND) 1877
'Twas In Trafalgar Square (*m* John
  BRAHAM) 1888
We Have Men, We Have Money (&
  G. H. MACDERMOTT, arr. E. J.
  SYMONS) 1882

Who Killed Cock Warren? (*m*, arr.
  Edmund FORMAN)

THORN, George
Good Old Days Of Adam, The (*m* Sam
  REDFERN, arr. Angelo ASHER) 1893

THORNTON, James 1861–1938
Irish Jubilee, The (& Charles B.
  LAWLOR) 1890
My Sweetheart's The Man In The Moon
  1892
She May Have Seen Better Days *c*.1890
Streets Of Cairo 1893
When You Were Sweet Sixteen 1898

THORNTON, L. M. d. 8 May 1888
Postman's Knock, The (*m* W. T.
  WRIGHTON) 1855
Sing Sweet Bird! (*m* Wilhelm GANZ)
  1872

THORNTON, W. W.
Destitute Orphans, The (*m* Fred
  FRENCH) 1893
Ipecacu-anha (*m* Arthur LLOYD) 1872

THURBAN, T. W. d. 26 Nov. 1967
Do It Again (Mason DIXON: & A.
  GROCK & L. SILBERMAN) 1917
One Of The Deathless Army (& Gilbert
  WELLS & Will TERRY & V. R. GILL)
  1910
Pigtail Of Li Fang Fu, The (*w&m* Sax
  ROHMER arr. & transcr. THURBAN)
  1919
Vot A Game! Oi! Oi! (& Arthur AISTON)
  1912

TICH, Little° 1867–1929
I Really Can't Stop Dancing (*m* George
  ISON) 1893

TIERNEY, Harry° 1890–1965
Alice Blue Gown (*w* Joseph MCCARTHY)
  1919
If You Can't Get A Girl In The
  Summertime (*w* Bert KALMAR) 1915

Irene O'Dare (*w* McCARTHY) 1919

Rio Rita (*w* McCARTHY) 1927

TILBURY, Walter° m. Lydia THOMPSON (1836–1908)

Jack The Handyman 1900

Land Of The Free, The 1903

Lazy 1897

Queen And The Shamrock, The 1900

Respect Our Queen 1900

TILSLEY, Harry 1897–1934

Let's All Go To The Music Hall (& Ralph BUTLER: Horatio NICHOLLS) 1934

TOBANI, Moses *see* MOSES-TOBANI, Theodore

TORR, A. C. pseudonym of Fred Leslie°

Love In The Orchestra

TOSTI, Sir F. Paolo 1846–1916

Beauty's Eyes (*w* Fred E. WEATHERLY)

For Ever And Ever (*w* V. FANE) 1879

Good-Bye! (*w* G. J. WHYTE-MELVILLE) 1903

Mother (*w* WEATHERLY) 1884

My Dreams (*w* WEATHERLY) 1893

Parted (*w* WEATHERLY) 1901

Venetian Song (*w* B.C. STEPHENSON) 1889

Yesterday (*w* WEATHERLY) 1886

TOURS, Frank E. 1877–1963

Mother O' Mine (*w* Rudyard KIPLING) 1903

TOWNLEY, Charles a.k.a. Geoffrey THORN

Things I Might Have Said, The 1885

TRACEY, Edward

I Would—If I Could—But I Can't—So I Won't (*w* Donovan PARSONS & Reginald RELSIE) 1922

TRAIL, A.

You Needna Come Courting O' Me (*m* W. T. WRIGHTON) 1857

TRAVERS, N. G.

Mind The Paint (*m* Ernest J. SYMONS) 1891

Sweethearts And Wives (*m* SYMONS) 1891

TREVATHAN, Charles E.

Bully Song, The (*w&m* COOLEY, arr. TREVATHAN) 1895

Frog Song, The (*w&m* COOLEY, arr. TREVATHAN) 1896

Lady Tom *c.*1896

TREVELYAN, Arthur

Down In Poverty Row (*w* Gussie L. DAVIS) 1896

Girl That I M.A.R.R.Y., The 1902

TREVOR, H. L.

Cricket (*m* Alfred SCOTT-GATTY) 1898

TREVOR, Huntley 1881–1943; a.k.a. Raymond WALLACE

Kitty, The Telephone Girl (& Harry GIFFORD & Alf J. LAWRANCE & Tom MELLOR) 1912

Make Me The King Of Your Heart (*m* Herman DAREWSKI) 1914

Now Are We All Here? Yes! (*m* DAREWSKI) 1914

TRIX, Helen° 1892–1951

Follow Me 1917

I Always Think Of Someone That I Love 1908

If You Mallee Me (Chinese Song) 1908

It's Making Me Love You All The More 1916

Love (We Need It, Eh, Honey?) 1908

TROTÈRE, Henri 1855–1912; pseudonym of Henry Trotter

Brow Of The Hill, The (*w* G. Clifton BINGHAM) 1897

Deathless Army, The (*w* Fred E. WEATHERLY) 1891

In Old Madrid (*w* BINGHAM) 1889

My Old Shako (*w* Francis BARRON) 1907

Within Your Heart (*w* Mrs G. HUBI-NEWCOMBE) 1901

TRUSSELL, Fred 1858–1923
Queen, God Bless Her, The (The King, God Bless Him) *c.*1900

TUCKER, Henry 1826?–82
Dear Mother I've Come Home To Die (*w* E. BOWERS) 1863
Sweet Genevieve (You're The Flower Of My Heart) (*w* George COOPER) 1869

TULLY, J. H. 1814–68
Bobbin' Around (*w&m* W. J. FLORENCE, arr. TULLY) *c.*1856
Song Of The Shirt (Thomas HOOD: J. BLEWITT, arr. TULLY) 1843

TUNBRIDGE, J. A. 1886–1961
Mademoiselle From Armenteers (rev. with Harry CARLTON) 1919
See also Gitz RICE; Harry WINCOTT; CORE Song-LIST.

TURNER, Eardley d. 23 Jan. 1929
Bobbies Of The Queen, The (*m* Maud SANTLEY) 1897
Initials (*m* Walter PASSMORE) 1897
Oh, My Late Lamented (*m* PASSMORE) 1905
Trot Along In Front 1901

TURNER, Harry
I've Had A Winning Day 1896

TUTE, Samuel
Oh! Cerulia! (*w&m* F. V. ST CLAIR, arr. TUTE) 1897
Rose Of Our Alley, The (Albert CHEVALIER: TUTE, arr. Charles INGLE) 1892
Success To Her Majesty! (*w&m* ST CLAIR, arr. TUTE) 1896

UHLAND, Johann Ludwig 1787–1862
Landlady's Little Daughter, The (Three German Officers Crossed The Rhine) (*m* trad.); see also CORE SONG-LIST

VALDEMAR, A.
Two Beggars, The (*m* H. Lane WILSON) 1879

VALENTINE b. 1876; pseudonym of Archibald Thomas Pechey
Bachelor Gay, A (& Clifford HARRIS: James W. TATE) 1916
Paradise For Two, A (& HARRIS: TATE) 1916

VALENTINE, John
All Round My Hat (*w* I. HANSETT; parody of trad. ballad) 1834

VAN ALSTYNE, Egbert 1878/82–1951
I'm Afraid To Come Home In The Dark (*w* Harry H. WILLIAMS) 1906
In The Shade Of The Old Apple Tree (*w* WILLIAMS) 1905
Memories (*w* Gus KAHN) 1915
Navajo a.k.a. Navaho (*w* WILLIAMS) 1903
Pretty Baby (KAHN: & Tony JACKSON) 1916

VAN BIENE, Auguste° 1845–1913
Broken Melody, The (for cello) 1892
Come Back To Me (*w* Albert CHEVALIER) 1890
Phantom Melody, The (for cello)
Suit The Action To The Word (*w* CHEVALIER) 1889

VANCE, Alfred G.° 1839–88
Come To Your Martha 1868
Fair Girl Dressed In Check 1865
Fitz-Jones The MP 1877
Idol Of The Day (*m* Alfred LEE) 1869
May The Present Moment Be The Worst Of Your Lives (*m* LEE) 1864
My Nancy Fair 1870
Naughty Young Man, The (*w* Frank W. GREEN) 1876
Pal O' Mine *c.*1868
That's The Style For Me 1868
Ticket Of Leave Man, The (*m* M. HOBSON) 1865
Tick! Tick! Tick! 1865
Young Man Of The Day, The

VANDERVELL, Willem

Excursion Train, The (w&m W. F.
   VANDERVELL, arr. VANDERVELL)
   c.1875
Go It While You're Young (w&m W. F.
   VANDERVELL, arr. VANDERVELL)
Just Behind The Battle Mother (Harry
   HUNTER: T. Vincent DAVIES arr.
   VANDERVELL) 1877

VANDERVELL, W. F.

Excursion Train (arr. Willem
   VANDERVELL) c.1875
Go It While You're Young (arr. Willem
   VANDERVELL)

VANE, Bracey

Eaton Square
Have You Seen The Shah? 1873
I'm Not What You'd Call A Good Shot
   1876
I Never Was Meant For The Sea

VAUCAIRE, Maurice

Song Of Songs, The (Eng. w Clarence
   LUCAS; Fr. w VAUCAIRE: MOYA) 1914

VAUGHAN WILLIAMS, Ralph 1872–1958
Linden Lea (w William BARNES) 1902

VENTON, F. W. d. 1918
For A Woman's Sake (w George BRUCE
   & Harry LEMORE)
Going Home (The Miner's Return) (J. P.
   HARRINGTON: Leo DRYDEN arr.
   VENTON) 1893
He's A Dear Old Friend (w Harry
   CASTLING) 1891
Highly Colored Tie (w J. MILLS) 1893
I'm A Little Too Young To Know (w
   Charles REEVES) 1889
Jim And His Partner Joe (w George
   BRUCE & H. LEMORE) 1892
What Do I Care? (w Richard MORTON)
   1892

VERNON, Carlile

You Put On The Trousers (& Harry
   BRETT) 1896

VERNON, Frank 1870–1940
Doctor Says I'm Not To Be Worried, The
   (w Harry HUNTER) 1877
I'm A Ship Without A Rudder (w
   HUNTER) 1876

VERNON, Harry M. 1878–1942?; all
sketches
All Men Are Fools 1912
Canada 1911
Case Of Johnny T. Walker, The 1914
Deputy Sheriff, The 1909
Don't You Believe It 1912
Her Ladyship's Guest 1910
Horse Thief, The 1910
Inspector Wise, CID 1911
Little Johnny Jones 1910
Mountebank, The 1911
Mrs Mason's Alibi 1915
Nevada 1913
Old Old Story, The 1911
Saving Silver City 1913
Silver Medal, The 1909
Ten O'Clock Squad, The 1909
Third Degree, The 1910
Three Thieves, The 1915
Truth About Mr Watson, The 1914
Without Prejudice 1914

VERNON, J.

Under The British Flag (m Fred COYNE)
   1877

VERDI, Giuseppe 1813–1901
Brindisi (*La Traviata*) (w F. Mario
   PIAVE) 1853

VOKES, George° 1852–95
D'You Know? I Don't Like London (m
   W. GRIMALDI) c.1885

VON TILZER, Albert 1878–1956;
brother of Harry VON TILZER
Give Me The Moonlight (w Lew
   BROWN) 1917
Honey Boy (w Jack NORWORTH) 1907
I'll Be With You In Apple Blossom Time
   (w Neville FLEESON) 1920

Nora Malone (Call Me By Phone) (*w* Junie McCREE) 1909

Put Your Arms Around Me Honey (*w* McCREE) 1910

Say It With Flowers (*w* FLEESON) 1919

Take Me Out To The Ball Game (*w* NORWORTH) 1908

That Hypnotizing Man (*w* BROWN) 1911

VON TILZER, Harry 1872–1946; brother of Albert VON TILZER

Bird In A Gilded Cage, A (*w* Arthur J. LAMB) 1900

Down At The Old Bull And Bush (*w* Russell HUNTING & Percy KRONE & Andrew B. STERLING; adap. Under The Anheuser Bush, STERLING: VON TILZER) 1903

Down Where The Wurzburger Flows (*w* Vincent P. BRYAN; British *w* Fred W. LEIGH as Riding On Top Of The Car) 1902

Hands Off 1914

I'd Leave My Happy Home For You (*w* Will A. HEELAN) 1899

I Love You Both 1892

In The Evening By The Moonlight, Dear Louise (*w* STERLING) 1912

In The Sweet Bye And Bye (*w* BRYAN) 1902

I Want A Girl Just Like The Girl Who Married Dear Old Dad (*w* Will DILLON) 1911

I Want To Be An Actor Lady 1903

Just Around The Corner (*w* Dolph SINGER) 1925

Mansion Of Aching Hearts, The (*w* LAMB) 1902

My Old New Hampshire Home (*w* STERLING) 1898

On A Sunday Afternoon (*w* STERLING) 1902

Riding On Top Of The Car (*w* BRYAN & LEIGH: melody Down Where The Wurzburger Flows, orig. VON TILZER; see above) 1902

Take A Look At Me Now (*w* STERLING) 1911

They Always Pick On Me (*w* Stanley MURPHY) 1911

Villain Still Pursued Her, The (*w* William JEROME) 1912

Wait Till The Sun Shines, Nellie (*w* STERLING) 1905

Where The Sweet Magnolias Grow (*w* STERLING) 1899

Where Was Moses When The Light Went Out? (*w* BRYAN & STERLING) 1901
First version lyrics by BRYAN only; see John J. STAMFORD for earlier identical title.

Vox, Valentine

Exhibition Of 1862, The 1862

List To My Prophetic Muse! 1862

W-N-K, Countess of

I Won't Be A Nun (arr. Grenville SMART) early 19th c.

WADE, J. A. 1796–1845

Love Was Once A Little Boy (The Two Houses Of Grenada) *c.*1826

Meet Me By Moonlight Alone 1827

WAGEMAN, H.

Easter Hymn (*m* Frank BRIDGE) 1912

WAITE, Ted° d. 7 Apr. 1971; all written for his brother J. W. Rickaby°

First I Went And Won The DCM 1918

I Think I'll Buy Piccadilly 1926

Major General Worthington 1916

WALKER, George W. d. 1911

Ghost Of A Coon, The (& Bert WILLIAMS) 1900

Look Out Dar Down Below! (& WILLIAMS) 1897

Voodoo Man, The (& WILLIAMS) 1900

When It's All Goin' Out And Nothin' Comin' In (& WILLIAMS) 1902

WALKER, Henry H.°

Awkward Squad, The 1859

Awkward Young Man, The 1860

Betsy Wareing 1859
British Lion, The 1880
Ching Hoti 1857
Damp Troubador, The 1861
Jemima Took Me Down A Peg 1857
Lady-Like Young Man, The 1862
Life In Quashibungo 1858
Man's Perfidy 1858
Mr Timm's Unfortunate Attachment
　1858
Up The Thames To Richmond 1865
Vegetarian, The 1859
Woman's Rights 1859
Young Folks At Home, The 1860

WALKER, James J. 1881–1946
Will You Love Me In December As You
　Do In May? (*m* Ernest R. BALL) 1905

WALKER, T.
On Alma's Heights (*m* J. HARROWAY)

WALL, G.
We Won't Go Home Till Morning (*m*
　Edward JONGHMANS) 1881

WALL, Harry b. 1838; m. Annie
Adams°
Night Porter, The (sk.)
That's The Man For Me 1871

WALLACE, Edgar 1875–1932; half-
brother of Marriott EDGAR
It's A Kind Of A Sort Of Feeling
Roseway (*m* Ruggiero LEONCAVALLO)
　1913

WALLACE, Ray
His Old Straw Hat (*w* Herbert
　SHELLEY) 1902

WALLACE, Raymond 1881–1943;
pseudonym of Huntley TREVOR
Old Father Thames (*m* Betsy O'HOGAN)
　1933
You Can't Do That There 'Ere (*m* Jack
　ROLLS) 1935

WALLACE, W. Vincent 1812–65
Our Hands Have Met But Not Our

Hearts (The False Friend) (*w* Thomas
　HOOD) 1846
Scenes That Are Brightest (*w* Alfred
　BUNN) 1845
Yes! Let Me Like A Soldier Fall (*w*
　Edward FITZBALL) 1845

WALLER, Francis 1809–94
Spinning Wheel, The (*m* trad.) 1884

WALLIS, T.
Voice Of The Storm, The (*m* Cuthbert
　CLARKE) 1909

WALLIS, W. H. d. 9 May 1949
Blacksmith's Lament, The 1897
Cheer, Boys, Cheer! 1895
I'm All Right (*m* Charles RIDGWELL)
　1904
We All Came In The World With
　Nothing (& Charles COLLINS) 1907

WALSH, James (1)
Fairly Knocked The Yankees In Chicago
　(arr. John S. BAKER) 1893

WALSH, James (2) d. 10 Jun. 1955
Don't Have Any More Missus Moore (&
　Harry CASTLING) 1926
Fill 'Em Up (& Thomas McGHEE &
　Herbert RULE: L. SILBERMAN)
That's Where The Soldiers Go (&
　McGHEE)

WARD, Artemus° 1834–67; pseudonym
of Charles Farrar Browne; published
songbook in 1866

WARD, Charles B. 1865–1917
Band Played On, The 1895 *but see*
　J. F. PALMER
Picture 84 (*m* Gussie DAVIS) 1894

WARD, T. a.k.a. W.? TERRY
Territorial, The (*m* Arthur MORRIS)
　1908

WARD, Theo
How London Lives (*w* H. Chance
　NEWTON) 1898

WARD-HIGGS, W. 1866–1936
Sussex By The Sea 1907

WARE, George° 1829–95
Boy In The Gallery, The 1881
English, Irish, And Scotchman, The
Fiddler's Wife, The
He's All Behind 1885
Hop Light Hoo c.1860
House That Jack Built, The
How The World Goes Round
Jessie The Belle At The (Railway) Bar 1867
One Little Kiss 1887
Sir Anthony Nash 1879
Squire And Maria, The 1878
Style, By Jove! The
Up Went The Price 1882
Whacky Whacky Whack! 1892
When They're Making Me A King 1878
Whole Hog Or None, The (m E. W. MACKNEY, arr. H. H. HOWARD) 1855
For song of same title see T. WESTROP.
Woman And Wine
Young Country Squire, The (m Felix DUMAS) 1891
You Should Go To France 1885

WASHBURN, Henry S.
Vacant Chair, The (m G. F. ROOT) 1861

WATKINS, H. M.
All The Little Ducks Went 'Quack! Quack! Quack!' 1904

WATSON, Maybelle E.
My Melancholy Baby (& George A. NORTON: Ernest M. BURNETT) 1912

WATSON, Valentine
Sweet Nell Of Old Drury (w Paul PELHAM) 1901

WATSON, William Michael 1840–89
Married To A Mermaid, The (w A. L. C., reputed pseudonym of William Makepeace THACKERAY: m attr. WATSON) 1866

WEATHERLY, Frederick E. 1848–1929
Angus Macdonald (m Joseph L. ROECKEL) 1881
At Peace But Still On Guard (m Odoardo BARRI)
Auntie (m A. H. BEHREND) c.1880
Beauty's Eyes (m F. Paolo TOSTI)
Children's Home, The (m Frederich M. COWEN) 1881
Chorister, The (m Arthur SULLIVAN) 1876
Danny Boy (air, The Londonderry Air, first pub. 1855) 1912
Darby And Joan (m J. L. MOLLOY) 1878
Deathless Army, The (m Henri TROTÈRE) 1891
For Love Of You (m Ernest NEWTON) 1903
Friend O' Mine (m Wilfrid SANDERSON) 1913
Green Hills O' Somerset (m Eric COATES) 1912
Happy Day, A (m BARRI)
Holy City, The (m Stephen ADAMS) 1892
If I Might Come To You (m W. H. SQUIRE) 1916
Kiss Me To Sleep (m Ivan CARYLL) 1894
Little Damozel, The (m Ivor NOVELLO) 1912
Look With Thine Eyes Into Mine (m CARYLL) 1891
Megan (m NOVELLO) 1914
Midshipmite, The (m ADAMS) 1875
Mighty Mother England (m Leslie STUART) 1909
Mother (m TOSTI) 1884
Mountain Lovers (m SQUIRE) 1908
My Dreams (m TOSTI) 1893
My Lady's Bower (m Hope TEMPLE) 1887
Nancy Lee (m ADAMS) 1876
Nirvana (m ADAMS) 1900
Nita Gitana (m NEWTON) 1893
Oh! (m Lionel MONCKTON) 1900
Old Brigade, The (m BARRI) 1881
Parted (m TOSTI) 1901

Rory Darlin' (*m* TEMPLE) 1892
Roses (*m* ADAMS) 1905
Roses Of Picardy (*m* Haydn WOOD) 1916
Saved From The Storm (*m* BARRI) 1876
Shipmates O' Mine (*m* SANDERSON) 1913
Star Of Bethlehem, The (*m* ADAMS) 1887
Stonecracker John (*m* COATES) 1909
Stormfiend!, The (*w* ROECKEL) 1881
They All Love Jack (*m* ADAMS) 1886
Thora (*m* ADAMS) 1905
Three Beggars, The (*m* MOLLOY) *c.*1885
Three For Jack (*m* SQUIRE) 1904
Thursday (*m* MOLLOY) 1884
Up From Somerset (*m* SANDERSON) 1913
When We Are Old And Grey (*m* Charlotte DOLBY) 1872
Woman's Way (*m* ROECKEL) 1890
Yesterday (*m* TOSTI) 1886
You Needn't Say A Word (*m* Charlotte SAINTON-DOLBY) 1874

WEAVER, James
Mulrooney's Dog (*w&m* Robert MARTIN, arr. WEAVER) 1895

WEBB, Edmund
Tommy Dodd (& Ernèe CLARKE) 1868

WEBB, W. T.
Mary And The Butcher (*w* Sid BANDON & J. MURPHY) 1894

WEIPERT, Henry W.
Goodbye Love *or* The Soldier's Farewell (*w* Charles MERION) 1873

WEISS, W. H.° 1820–67
Village Blacksmith, The (*w* Henry W. LONGFELLOW); see Michael BALFE 1855

WELCH, Myra Brooks
Touch Of The Master's Hand, The (*m* Ernest LONGSTAFFE) 1936

WELLS, Gilbert pseudonym of Gilbert Henderson
Baden-Powell Scout, The (*w* John P. LONG) 1900
Butterfly And The Rose, The (& Percy EDGAR: Fred ELTON) 1909
Life's Short Span (& Dan PAULTON: PAULTON) 1897
Love! Love!! Love!!! (& Frank CARTER) 1913
Mary's Ticket (*w* LONG) 1909
One Of The Deathless Army (& T. W. THURBAN & Will TERRY & V. R. GILL) 1910
Varmer Giles (*m* T. F. ROBSON) 1902
Wee Hoose 'Mang The Heather (& Harry LAUDER: LAUDER & Fred ELTON) 1913
With My Little Wigger-Wagger In My Hand (& CARTER & Fred EARLE) 1909

WENRICH, Percy 1880–1952; m. Dolly Connolly°
Moonlight Bay (*w* Edward MADDEN) 1912
Put On Your Old Gray Bonnet (*w* Stanley MURPHY) 1909
Silver Bell (*w* MADDEN) 1905
When You Wore A Tulip And I Wore A Big Red Rose (*w* Jack MAHONEY) 1914

WENTWORTH, Fanny° *c.*1849–1934
Coster's Confession, The (*w* R. H. LINDO) 1895
Goo-Goo Song, The (*w* Carl SMITH) 1900
Hippopotamus And The Flea, The 1896

WESLEY, Howard
Are You The O'Reilly? *see* Pat ROONEY 1915

WEST, Alfred H. b. *c.*1862; except Tick! Tock! all words by Albert CHEVALIER
Centenarian, The *c.*1900
Cosmopolitan Courtship 1896

Dolly's Advice 1896
'E Can't Take The Roize Out Of Oi 1896
Fallen Star, A 1898
Great Man Of Wardle, The c.1900
Hemmer c.1900
Herr Schwollenhedt 1895
Mafeking Night 1900
My Country Cousin 1894
Old Bachelor, An c.1900
Tick! Tock! (w Harry V. BARNETT) 1894
Veteran, The c.1900
Village Constable, The c.1900
Workhouse Man, The c.1900
Wot Ver Do 'Ee Luv Oi? c.1900
Yankee In London, The c.1900
You Are A Tasty Lot! 1897

WEST, Arthur° c.1864–94
Captain Called The Mate, The 1888
Copy Your Uncle Tom 1894
Drink Up Boys 1890
Earl Of Fife, The 1889
Let's Have Another 1891
Many A Time (We'd Both Been There
  Before) 1888
Money 1885
My Brother Jack (w Wal PINK) 1894
Oh! For The Jubilee (m George LE
  BRUNN) 1887
Paris Exhibition, The 1889
Yes You Are 1891

WEST, Mae° 1888–1980
Cave Girl, The c.1910

WEST, W. H. C.° d. 4 Feb. 1876
Man With The Carpet Bag, The 1862
O My Love's Dead
Southerly Wind And A Cloudy Sky, A
  1845

WESTBROOK, A.
None But The Lonely Heart (Johann W.
  von GOETHE; Eng. transl.
  WESTBROOK: Pyotr TCHAIKOVSKY)
  1869

WESTENDORF, Thomas 1848–1923
I'll Take You Home Again Kathleen 1875

WESTON, R. Harris d. 1978; a.k.a.
Harris-Weston; son of Robert
P. WESTON
Ain' It Nice? (w R. P. WESTON & Bert
  LEE) 1923
And The Great Big Saw Came Nearer
  And Nearer (w WESTON & LEE) 1936
Beat The Retreat On Thy Drum (w
  WESTON & LEE) 1932
Brahn Boots (w WESTON & LEE) 1935
Heaven Will Protect An Honest Girl (w
  WESTON & LEE) 1933
Knees Up, Mother Brown! (& LEE &
  Irving TAYLOR) (see CORE SONG-
  LIST) 1938
Olga Pulloffski (w WESTON & LEE) 1935
With Her Head Tucked Underneath Her
  Arm (w WESTON & LEE) 1934

WESTON, Robert P. 1878–1936; father
of R. Harris WESTON and half of the
prolific Weston & Lee song-writing
team (fl. 1915–36), the other being Bert
LEE
Ain' It Nice! (& Bert LEE: R. H.
  WESTON) 1923
And The Great Big Saw Came Nearer
  And Nearer (& LEE: WESTON) 1936
And Yet I Don't Know (& LEE) 1922
Any Dirty Work Today? (& LEE) 1922
Beat The Retreat On Thy Drum (& LEE:
  WESTON) 1932
Body In The Bag, The (& LEE) 1921
Bolshevik, The (& LEE) 1919
Boys Of The Chelsea School (& Frank
  W. CARTER) 1902
Brahn Boots (& LEE: WESTON) 1935
Do You Believe In Women's Rights?
  1909
End Of My Old Cigar, The (& Worton
  DAVID) 1914
Ever Since He Pelmanized (& LEE) 1919
Exemptions And Otherwise (& LEE)
  1916
Fancy You've Got All You Fancy (& F. J.
  BARNES & Harry BEDFORD) 1908

Germans Are Coming So They Say, The (& BARNES & BEDFORD) *c.*1914

Good-bye-ee! (& LEE) 1917

Gypsy Warned Me, The (& LEE) 1920

Heaven Will Protect An Honest Girl (& LEE: WESTON) 1933

He's Been A Long Time Gorn 1904

Hobnailed Boots That Farver Wore (& BARNES) 1907

If It's In 'John Bull' It *Is* So (& LEE & Clay SMITH) 1917

I Like Your Town (& BEDFORD) 1915

I'm Henery The Eighth, I Am! (& Fred MURRAY) 1910

I Might Learn To Love Him Later On (& LEE) 1921

I'm Looking For Mr Wright (*m* C. W. MURPHY & H. DAREWSKI) 1909

I'm On Agen With Monaghan 1910

I'm The Black Sheep Of The Family (& BARNES) 1912

In These Hard Times (& BARNES) 1915

I've Got Rings On My Fingers (& BARNES: Maurice SCOTT) 1909

It's My Bath Night Tonight (& LEE) 1922

Kiss The Girl If You're Going To (& BARNES) 1907

Little Willie's Woodbines 1908

Mother's Sitting Knitting Little Mittens For The Navy (*m* DAREWSKI) 1915

Mr Wu (& Jack NORWORTH) 1907

My Meatless Day (& LEE) 1917

My Rachel's Eyes (& BARNES & SCOTT) *c.*1912

My Word You Do Look Queer (& LEE) 1922

Noise Annoys An Oyster, A (& LEE) 1920

Oh, Bleriot! (& BARNES) 1909

Oh! London, Where Are Your Girls Tonight? (& LEE) 1918

Old-Age Pension, The (& BEDFORD) 1908

Old Man Brown (& LEE) 1915

Olga Pulloffski (& LEE: WESTON) 1935

One Of The Boys (& BARNES: SCOTT) 1907

Only Yiddisher Scotsman, etc. *see* Sergeant Solomon Isaacstein

'Ow's This For A Start? (& F. W. LEIGH: G. Le BRUNN) 1899

Paddy McGinty's Goat (& LEE & The Two BOBS) 1917

Profiteering Profiteers, The (& LEE) 1920

Salome (& BARNES & BEDFORD) 1908 See also P. J. HARRINGTON: Orlando POWELL for same title.

Seaside Girl, The 1903

Sergeant Solomon Isaacstein (& LEE) 1916

Shall I Have It Bobbed Or Shingled? (& LEE) 1924

She Wants To Marry Me (& LEE) 1916

Sister Susie's Marrying Tommy Atkins (*m* DAREWSKI) 1915

Sister Susie's Sewing Shirts For Soldiers (*m* DAREWSKI) 1913

Somebody's Coming To Tea (& LEE & SMITH) 1917

Somebody Would Shout Out 'Shop!' (& LEE) 1915

Swim, Sam! Swim! 1917

There Are Nice Girls Everywhere 1909

Tickle Me, Timothy, Do! (& BARNES) 1907

Tra-La-La! (& BARNES) 1906

Viewing The Baby (& LEE) 1926

What A Conjure! What A Cop! (& BARNES) 1907

What A Mouth! 1906

What I Want Is A Proper Cup Of Coffee (& LEE) 1926

When Father Papered The Parlour (& BARNES) 1909

When Padereswki Plays (& LEE & BOBS) 1916

Where Are The Lads Of The Village Tonight? (*m* DAREWSKI) 1914

With Her Head Tucked Underneath Her
Arm (& LEE: WESTON) 1934
With This Hat On (*w* BARNES) 1911

WESTROP, T. 1816–81
Old Union Jack, The (*w&m* John
CAULFIELD jun., arr. WESTROP) 1874
Whole Hog Or None, The (*w* Charles
SLOMAN: *m* arr. WESTROP from Love's
Young Dream by Thomas MOORE)
1862
For song of same title see E. W. MACKNEY.

WHEATLEY, Horace* 1850–1923
Oyster Supper, The (& F. W. LEIGH)
1908

WHEELER, Francis
Sheik Of Araby, The (& Harry B. SMITH:
Ted SNYDER) 1921

WHEELER, George D. 1863–1939;
a.k.a. Leo DRYDEN
Bravo, Dublin Fusiliers! (Ireland's Reply)
1899
Great White Mother (& Gordon NOBLE)
1896

WHICHARD, R. D.
How Could Red Riding Hood? (*w&m*
A. P. RANDOLPH, arr. WHICHARD)
1922

WHITAKER, John 1776–1847
Darby Kelly (*w* Thomas DIBDIN) *c*.1820
Hot Codlins (*w* Charles DIBDIN jun.)
1819
Paddy Carey's Fortune (*w* Andrew
CHERRY) 1809
Tray (*w* DIBDIN jun.) 1801

WHITE, C. A. 1832–92
Please Sell No More Drink To My
Father (*w* Mrs F. B. PRATT) 1884

WHITE, Maude Valérie 1855–1937
Absent Yet Present (*w* Lord LYTTON)
1880
Ask Not (*w* Clifton BINGHAM) 1905

Devout Lover, The (*w* Walter Herries
POLLOCK) 1883
King Charles (*w* Robert BROWNING)
1898
Mary's Ghost (*w* Thomas HOOD)1895
Also set by Jonathan BLEWITT.

WHITEHOUSE, E.
Angelina Brown (*w&m* G. W. HUNT, arr.
WHITEHOUSE) 1865

WHITING, George 1884–1943
My Wife's Gone To The Country (&
Irving BERLIN: Ted SNYDER) 1909

WHITING, Richard A. 1891–1938
It's Tulip Time In Holland (*w* Dave
RADFORD) 1915
Japanese Sandman, The (*w* Raymond B.
EGAN) 1920
On The Good Ship Lollipop (*w* Sidney
CLARE) 1934
Till We Meet Again (*w* EGAN) 1918
Where The Black-Eyed Susans Grow (*w*
RADFORD) 1917

WHITLOCK, Billy (1) (William M.)* b.
1813
Lucy Long (*w* T. B. BOOTH) 1838

WHITLOCK, Billy (2)* 1874–1951
Scotch Hot (revived 1949 as Hop Scotch
Polka)

WHITSON, Beth Slater 1879–1930
Let Me Call You Sweetheart (*m* Leo
FRIEDMAN) 1910
Meet Me Tonight In Dreamland (*m*
FRIEDMAN) 1909

WHYMARK, H. J.
Advertisements (*m* Fred FRENCH)
1871
Broken-Hearted Shepherd, The (*m*
Alfred LEE)
'Norrible Tale, A (*w&m* E. L.
BLANCHARD, arr. M. HOBSON; adap.
WHYMARK) 1865
Not For Joseph (*m* LEE) 1867

WHYTE-MELVILLE, G. J. 1821–78
Drink Puppy Drink 1874
Good-Bye! (*m* F. Paolo TOSTI) 1903
Only A Year To Go (*m* CLARIBEL)
    1865
Wrap Me Up In My Tarpaulin Jacket (*w*
    rev. Fred BOWYER: *m* arr. E. J.
    SYMONS) 1884

WICK, Tom
Lloyd Jarge (*m* Ernest SHAND) 1914

WIELAND, W. H.° 1831–66
I Am The Girl Call'd Nancy (*m* D. D.
    EMMETT) 1862
Musical Shoeblack, The
Titles And Distinctions 1862

WILCOCK, Frank
I Want To Take A Young Man In And Do
    For Him 1931

WILHELM, Carl 1815–73
Watch On The Rhine, The (Die Wacht
    Am Rhein) (*w* Max
    SCHNECKENBURGER (1840) 1854
    English words attempted with no lasting
    success by, amongst others, H. B. FARNIE;
    Natalie MACFARREN; Charles H. PURDAY.

WILLARD, Emma Hart 1787–1870
Rocked In The Cradle Of The Deep (*m*
    Joseph P. KNIGHT) 1839

WILLIAMS, Bert A.° 1874–1922
Ghost Of A Coon, The (& George W.
    WALKER) 1900
Let It Alone (& Alex C. ROGERS) 1906
Look Out Dar Down Below! (&
    WALKER) 1897
Nobody (*w* ROGERS) 1905
That's A-Plenty (*w* Henry CREAMER)
    1909
Voodoo Man, The (& WALKER) 1900
When It's All Goin' Out And Nothin'
    Comin' In (& WALKER) 1902

WILLIAMS, Billy° 1878–1915
Give My Love To Scotland, Maggie 1912

Here We Are Again! (& Fred GODFREY)
    1911
John, Go And Put Your Trousers On
    1907
Kangaroo Hop, The (& GODFREY) 1912

WILLIAMS, Bransby° 1870–1961; published selections of his Shakespeare and
Dickens readings plus other recitations
in 1910, 1912, 1913 and 1928 (Reynolds)

WILLIAMS, Charles° (1) 1853–80
Cleopatra's Needle 1878
Fight In The Menagerie, The 1877
Funny Little Man
I Love To Flirt With The Girls
Jolly Lot Of Friends, A 1877
Union Jack Of Old England, The 1872
What An Englishman Is Made Of 1878
What Victoria Is Made Of 1876
Who'll Buy My Pretty Flowers? 1877
You've Said That To Lots Before Me
    1877

WILLIAMS, Charles (2)
Fiscal Showman, The (arr. A. E. WILLS)
    1903
Mother's Wedding Ring (& Norton
    ATKINS) 1897
Tribute To The Memory Of W. E.
    Gladstone, A (& ATKINS) 1898

WILLIAMS, Edna
If The Wind Had Only Blown The Other
    Way (& Bessie WYNN: WILLIAMS)
    1909

WILLIAMS, Gus° c.1847–1915
See That My Grave's Kept Green 1878

WILLIAMS, Harry H. 1874–1922
I'm Afraid To Come Home In The Dark
    (*m* Egbert VAN ALSTYNE) 1906
In The Shade Of The Old Apple Tree (*m*
    VAN ALSTYNE) 1905
Navajo a.k.a. Navaho (*m* VAN ALSTYNE)
    1903
That Rag-Time Suffragette (& Nat D.
    AYER) 1913

WILLIAMS, Harry J. 1858–1924; see
CORE SONG-LIST
How Are Yer? (& Jack JUDGE) 1913
It's A Long, Long Way To Tipperary (&
   JUDGE); see CORE SONG-LIST 1912
Mona From Barcelona (& JUDGE) 1912
Spookland (& JUDGE) 1913
Way The Wind Blows, We'll Go!, The (&
   JUDGE) 1913

WILLIAMS, J.
High, Low Or Jack Game (w&m G. W.
   MOORE, arr. WILLIAMS) 1866
Hunky Dorum, We Are (Am?) The Boys
   (w&m MOORE, arr. WILLIAMS) 1866
Work, Boys, Work And Be Contented (&
   Harry CLIFTON) 1867

WILLIAMS, S. A.
Swiss Echo Song (He Loves But Me/Er
   Liebt Nur Mich) (m Carl Anton
   Florian ECKERT, 1859) 1873

WILLIAMS, T.
My May Queen (& Harry McCORMACK:
   McCORMACK) 1904

WILLIAMS, Walter° 1887–1940
Piccadilly (& Bruce SIEVIER: Paul
   MORANDE) 1921

WILLIAMS, Warwick
Comparisons Are Melodious (Harry
   HUNTER: G. H. CHIRGWIN, arr.
   WILLIAMS) 1888
Old England, Home And King! (w&m
   Sam RICHARDS, arr. WILLIAMS) 1902
Scandals Are 'Cuming', The (w&m
   Charles D. HICKMAN, arr. WILLIAMS)
   1891
So Was Mine (Walter HASTINGS: Will
   BINT, arr. WILLIAMS) 1889

WILLIAMS, Watkyn
Hampstead Is The Place To Ruralize
   (arr. B. HOLMANS) 1861
I've Come In Search Of A Nice Young

Man (I'm The Dark Girl Dress'd In
   Blue) 1863
Kiss In The Railway Train, The (m C. H.
   MACKNEY) 1864
Ticket Of Leave Man, The (w Tom
   FANCOURT) 1873

WILLIAMS, William
Do Your Duty Well (w Harry HUNTER)
Tam O'Shanter Hat, The (w HUNTER)
   1881

WILLS, A. E.
Fiscal Showman, The (w&m Charles
   WILLIAMS (2), arr. WILLS) 1903

WILLS, W. G. 1828–91
I'll Sing Thee Songs Of Araby (m
   Frederic CLAY); see CORE SONG-LIST
   1877

WILMOTT, Charles 1860–1955
Aloha Oe (rev. WILMOTT. orig. Queen
   LILUOKALANI) 1878
Courtship (& G. W. HUNTER:
   F. ARTHUR) 1890
In The Twi-Twi-Twilight (m Herman
   DAREWSKI) 1907
Our Society (m Fred EPLETT)
Out (m EPLETT) 1891
Philosophy (m Fred W. LEIGH) 1900
That's The Cause Of It (m George LE
   BRUNN) 1893
Theosophee (m EPLETT) 1891
What Would I Give To Be Home Again
   (m Will J. GODWIN) 1908

WILSON, Al 1868–1951
Wild Wild Women, The (m Al
   PIANTADOSI) 1917

WILSON, H. Lane° c.1864–1937
Pretty Creature, The (trad., arr.
   WILSON) 1911
Tenor And Baritone (w H. Broughton
   BLACK) 1896
Two Beggars, The (w A. VALDEMAR)
   1879

WILSON, Joe° 1841–75; all written and published on Tyneside, 1858–74
(Aa Hope Ye'll) Be Kind Te Me Dowtor (air, Die An Auld Maid)
Affected Bella
Cockney's Lament, The
Draper's Appeal, The
Flog'd In Jail!
Gallowgate Lad, The (air, Sally Grey)
Geordie, Haud The Bairn (air, The Whusslin' Thief)
Glorious Vote Be Ballot
In Memory Of The Hartley Catastrophe
Keep Yor Feet Still Geordie Hinney (air, Nelly Gray)
Lads Upon The Wear, The
Mally Dunn (m Thomas WILSON)
Maw Bonny Gyteside Lass
Maw Bonny Injineer
Me Little Wife At Hyem
Meun-Leet Flit, The
98th, The (Jack's Enlisted)
No Work
Paanshop Bleezin', The (air, XYZ)
Pork Shop Lass, The
Prepare For What's Te Cum
Row Upon The Stairs, The (air, Uncle Sam) c.1860
She's Gyen Te Place At Jarrow
Strike, The 1871
That Factory Lass
Tom Broon
Varry Canny
What Gud Can Sweerin De?

WILSON, Thomas
Mally Dunn (w Joe WILSON)

WILSON, W. d. 1875?
Cockney Tourist, The (w&m J. HARDWICK, arr. WILSON) c.1855
Oh! Wouldn't You Like To Be Me?

WIMPERIS, Arthur 1874–1953
All Down Piccadilly (& Lionel MONCKTON: MONCKTON) 1909

Band Box Girl, The (& W. DAVIDSON: Harry FRAGSON) 1907
Brighton (Take Me On The Boat To) (& Paul RUBENS: RUBENS) 1911
Charming Weather (m MONCKTON) 1909
Florrie The Flapper (m Herman FINCK) 1914
Gilbert, The Filbert (m FINCK) 1914
Half-Past Two (& Percy GREENBANK: Howard TALBOT) 1909
Here's To Love And Laughter (m RUBENS) 1911
If You Could Care (For Me) (m Herman DARWESKI) 1918
I Like London (m TALBOT) 1909
I'll Make A Man Of You (m FINCK) 1914
My Motter (m TALBOT) 1909
Only A Glass Of Champagne (m Noel GAY) 1939
Pipes Of Pan, The (m MONCKTON) 1909
Temple Bell, The (m MONCKTON) 1911
We're Really Proud Of You (m Pedro de ZULUETA) 1914
What A Happy Land Is England (m H. G. PÉLISSIER) 1904

WINCOTT, Harry 1867–1947; pseudonym of Arthur J. Walden
All Thro' Sticking To A Soldier c.1905
Can't Stop! Can't Stop!! Can't Stop!!! (arr. Alfred LAMONT) 1895
Down Fell The Pony In A Fit (& Harry LEIGHTON: John S. BAKER) 1897
Down The Dials (m Gus ELEN) 1893
'E Do Know Where He Is (m Felix DUMAS) 1894
For Me! For Me! 1895
I'm Getting Ready For My Mother-In-Law 1896
In The Rand (& LEIGHTON) 1903
Mademoiselle From Armenteers see Gitz RICE and CORE SONG-LIST c.1916
Picking All The Best Ones Out (& LEIGHTON) 1900

Right On My Doo-Dah (& LEIGHTON)
1900
Song Pirate's Lament, The (&
LEIGHTON) 1902
Take Your Umbrella With You, John!
1902
We All Went Home In A Cab (*m* George
LE BRUNN) 1892
We Put Him In A Cab And Sent Him
Home (*m* LE BRUNN) 1895
We've All Been Having A Go At It (&
LEIGHTON) 1896
When The 'Old Dun Cow' Caught Fire
1893

WINDLEY, Harry°
And The Missus Popped Up At The
Time (*m* David DAY) *c.*1888
Don't Leave Your Father, Boy (*m* James
W. DUNN) 1889
Gordon, The Hero Of Khartoum 1885
I'd Like It All Over Again (*m*
J. CLEMENTS) 1881
She Boxed My Ears With The Frying
Pan (*m* DUNN) *c.*1888
What Will The Neighbours Say? (Oh
Dear!) (*m* DUNN) 1886

WINGATE, Philip d. 1925
I Don't Want To Play In Your Yard (*m*
H. W. PETRIE) 1894
You Can't Play In Our Yard Any More (*m*
PETRIE) 1894

WINNER, Joseph E. 1837–1918; a.k.a.
R. A. Eastburn
Little Brown Jug 1867

WINNER, Septimus 1827–1902; a.k.a.
Alice HAWTHORNE
Oh Where, Oh Where, Has My Little
Dog Gone? (Der Deitcher's Dog) (air,
Lauterbach) 1864

WINTER, Banks° 1857–1936
White Wings 1870

WINTER, Charles J. d. 1943
Caretaker, The

Lost Dog, The (*w&m* Ernest A.
SEARSON, arr. WINTER) 1907

WITHER, George 1588–1667
Shall I Wasting In Despair? (set by at
least a dozen composers, incl. George
A. BARKER in 1861 and John L.
HATTON in 1869)

WODEHOUSE, P. G. (Sir Pelham)
1881–1975
Oh, Mr Chamberlain (*w&m* Jerome
KERN, *w* rev. WODEHOUSE) 1905

WOOD, Alf
Mrs Isaac Newton Moon (*m* W. FREEAR)
1896

WOOD, Arthur 1875–1953; composer of
Barwick Green Maypole, signature tune
of BBC radio's long-running drama serial
The Archers
Property Man, The (*w* Harold E.
MELVIN) 1911

WOOD, Frank° 1844–1919
Father's Whiskers 1911
They Can't Get The Better Of Me 1909

WOOD, Haydn 1882–1959
Brown Bird Singing, A (*w* Royden
BARRIE) 1922
Love's Garden Of Roses (*w* Ruth
RUTHERFORD) 1914
Oh Flower Divine (*w* Edward
TESCHEMACHER) 1914
Roses Of Picardy (*w* Fred E.
WEATHERLY) 1916

WOOD, J. (Jay) Hickory 1859–1913
Hobbies (sk.) (*m* Ernest HASTINGS)
1902
Soliloquies (mons.) 1899
You Could Hardly Notice It At All (*m*
Herman FINCK) 1903

WOOD, J. T. 1841–1902
Wait Till The Clouds Roll By (*m* H. J.
FULMER) 1881
See also Charles E. PRATT.

WOOD, Leo d. 1929
That's What God Made Mothers For
1924

WOODFORDE-FINDEN, Amy 1860–1919
Four Indian Love Lyrics (incl. Kashmiri
Song a.k.a. Pale Hands I Loved) (*w*
Laurence HOPE) 1902

WOODHOUSE, Evelyn
Eton Boating Song (W. J. CORY:
A. DRUMMOND, transcr. T. L.
MITCHELL-INNES, arr. WOODHOUSE)
1878

WOODHOUSE, J. H. d. 1906
Grass Widower, The (arr. Fred EPLETT)
1891
Sing Us One Of The Old Songs (& W. B.
KELLY) 1900

WOODVILLE, Ernie
Twiddley Bits, The (*w* J. ADAMS &
George DANCE) (see CORE SONG-
LIST) 1901

WOOLLEY, J.
Showman, The (*w* Charles LINDA)

WOOTTWELL, Tom° 1865–1941
Have An Arf O' Gin, Old Dear (*m* J. P.
HARRINGTON) 1906
Oh, Yes, We Did! 1903
Wait A Minute

WORK, Henry Clay 1832–84
Come Home, Father (Father, Dear
Father, Come Home) 1858
Grandfather's Clock, (My) 1876
Kingdom Coming (The Year Of Jubilo)
1862
Lilly Dale *c*.1853
Marching Through Georgia 1865
Oh, Daddy, Don't Go Down The Mines
Today

WRIGHT, Harry m. Nellie Gannon°
Boy Pirate, The
'E Dunno Where 'E Are *see* Jack Jones
Female Auctioneer, The

I Traced Her Little Footmarks In The
Snow 1876
Jack Jones ('E Dunno Where 'E Are) (*m*
Fred EPLETT) 1894
Lady Cricketer, The
Lady Jockey, The
Only A Few Miles Of Water (*m* J. M.
HARRISON) 1895
Our Stores Ltd (*m* EPLETT)
Recruiting Sergeant, The (*m* EPLETT)
c.1895

WRIGHT, Hugh E.° 1879–1940
Idiosyncracies 1909
Leanin' (*m* T. C. Sterndale BENNETT)
1926
What's The Use? (*m* Alan MURRAY) 1913
Wine Women And Song (*m* Wolseley
CHARLES) 1913

WRIGHT, Lawrence 1888–1964; a.k.a.
Horatio NICHOLLS and Betsy O'HOGAN
Among My Souvenirs 1927
Are There Any Little Angels Blind Like
Me? (*m* Robert DONNELLY) 1910
Are We Down-Hearted—No! (*w* Worton
DAVID) 1914
Be British! (*w* Paul PELHAM) 1912
Blue Eyes 1915
Delilah 1917
I've Never Seen A Straight Banana 1926
Wyoming 1919
Yiddisher-Irish Baby, The (& DAVID &
Fred GODFREY) 1915

WRIGHTON, W. T. 1816–80
Postman's Knock, The (*w* L. M.
THORNTON) 1855
You Need Na Come Courting O' Me (*w*
A. TRAIL) 1857

WYE, D. A. d. 1922
Little Peach In An Orchard Grew, A (&
Hubbard T. SMITH) 1889

WYE, Willie
While I Was Licking My Stamp (*m* Harry
CHAMPION)

WYNNE, J. W.
I Love But Only One—And That Is You 1907

WYNNE, Wish° 1882–1931
Ooh! 'Er! (The Slavey) 1927

XANROF, Leon 1867–1953; pseudonym of Leon Forneau
Fiacre, Le (Eng. *w* Barry GRAY) 1892
Hôtel Du No. 3, L' 1906

YEATS, W. B. 1865–1939
Down By The Salley Gardens (*m* trad., arr. Herbert HUGHES; poetry from *Crossways*, 1889) 1914

YELLEN, Jack 1892–1991
Ain't She Sweet? (*m* Milton AGER) 1927
Alabama Jubilee (*m* George L. COBB) 1915
Are You From Dixie? ('Cos I'm From Dixie Too) (*m* COBB) 1913
Happy Feet (*m* AGER) 1930
Hard-Hearted Hannah (*m* AGER) 1929
My Yiddishe Momme (*m* Lew POLLACK) 1925

YORKSTON, James
Cockles And Mussels (arr. Edmund FORMAN) 1884

YOUNG, J. Harrington *c.* 1858–1907?
Old Tattered Flag, The (*w&m* J. MACNICOLL, arr. YOUNG) 1887
My Uncle (*w* Harry SYDNEY) 1869
Take A Lesson From Me (*w&m* SYDNEY *m* adap. YOUNG)

YOUNG, Joe 1889–1939
How'Ya Gonna Keep 'Em Down On The Farm? (& Sam M. LEWIS: Walter DONALDSON) 1919
I'm Alone Because I Love You 1931
My Mammy (& LEWIS: DONALDSON) 1921
Rock-A-Bye Your Baby With A Dixie Melody (& LEWIS: Jean SCHWARTZ) 1918
Where Did Robinson Crusoe Go With Friday On Saturday Night? (& LEWIS: George W. MEYER) 1916

YOUNG, Rida Johnson 1875–1926
Ah! Sweet Mystery Of Life (*m* Victor HERBERT) 1910
I Can't Take My Eyes Off You (*m* Paul RUBENS) 1904
Mother Machree (*m* Chauncey OLCOTT & Ernest R. BALL) 1910

YOUNGE, Willie 1858–97
Linger Longer Loo (*m* Sidney JONES) 1893
Rhoda Rode A Roadster (*m* Eugene BARNETT) 1896

ZEILA
Murmuring Sea, The (*m* Wilhelm GANZ) 1859
Nightingale's Trill (*m* GANZ) 1866
Sing Birdie Sing (*m* GANZ) 1859

ZELLER, Karl 1842–98
Miller's Daughter, The (Don't Be Cross) (*w* Peter CARROLL) 1894

DATE-LIST

PRECISE dating can be impossible to ascertain. A song may not have been entered at Stationers' Hall or deposited with one of the copyright libraries until some time after its original performance. The publisher's acquisition dating is therefore an unreliable guide to a number's first appearance; a further complication is the incestuousness of the music publishing business, with mergers, take-overs, and buy-outs, and also the complexities of assignation and re-assignation.

And if a song is later included in a compilation the copyright date may be even more remote from its first airing—EMI's *Bumper Book Of Music Hall Songs* includes The Man On The Flying Trapeze with a cover copyright date of 1988, 120 years after George Leybourne and Alfred Lee wrote it to celebrate Jules Leotard's second visit to London.

Ballads offer further hazards, especially where a popular poem attracted any number of settings, only one of which survives. For example, Tennyson's *Maud* (1855) was assailed by eighteen composers; the day was won by Balfe's 1857 setting (not that the Poet Laureate cared for it much).

Examples of melody preceding lyric are Arthur C. Benson's Land Of Hope And Glory to Elgar's Pomp And Circumstance No. 1 (1902) and Fred E. Weatherly's glutinous Danny Boy (1913), forever welded, alas, to the lovely eighteenth-century melody The Londonderry Air.

Names in italic identify settings of the same text; names in brackets are either the original performers of the songs listed or have a later close association. (?) after a title indicates approximate dating only; (?) after a name indicates uncertainty of attribution. If no name is given the song was either free (non-exclusive) or not strongly identified with any particular artiste.

Not all the titles in this section are included in the Core Song-List.

13th century
Sumer Is Icumen In

16th century
Greensleeves

c.1670
Come, Lasses And Lads

c.1686
Lillibulero

c.1700
Annie Laurie

c.1720
Black-Ey'd Susan

1729
Sally In Our Alley

1740
Lass With The Delicate Air, The

c.1741
Rule Britannia (first sung by Thomas
Lowe)

c.1743
God Save The King

1759
Heart Of Oak

c.1777
Drink To Me Only With Thine Eyes

1789
Ben Backstay

1792
Marseillaise, La

1796
I Am A Friar Of Orders Grey (Wright
Bowden)

1798
Auld Lang Syne

1800
Blue Bell Of Scotland, The (Mrs Jordan)

1803
All's Well (John Braham & Charles Incledon, Patrick A. Corri & James Davis)

1805
Bay Of Biscay (John Braham)

1806
Dear (Green) Little Shamrock, The

1807
Believe Me If All Those Endearing
Young Charms

Harp That Once Through Tara's Halls,
The (Catherine Hayes)
Lesbia Hath A Beaming Eye
Minstrel Boy, The
She Is Far From The Land
'Tis The Last Rose Of Summer
(Catherine Hayes)

1810
Typitywitchet (Sam Cowell, Joseph
Grimaldi, Tom Matthews)

1811
Anchor's Weigh'd, The (John Braham)
Death Of Nelson, The (John Braham)
Lass That Loves A Sailor, The

1814
Star-Spangled Banner, The
When Thy Bosom Heaves The Sigh
(John Braham & Catherine Stephens)

1815
Erl King, The
Oft In The Stilly Night

1819
Hot Codlins (Sam Cowell, Joseph
Grimaldi, Tom Matthews)
Lo! Here The Gentle Lark (Catherine
Stephens)

1820
Wolf, The (Charles Incledon, Charles
Sloman)

1823
Home! Sweet Home! (Anna Maria Tree)

1824
Cherry Ripe (Charles Edward Horn,
John Orlando Parry, Lucy Vestris)

1825
Pilot, The

1826
Fine Old English Gentleman, The
(Henry Russell)
Hark Hark The Lark
Miss Julia (Jonathan Blewitt)

New Police, The
Who Is Sylvia?

1828
Zip Coon (Turkey In The Straw) (?)
   (Christy Minstrels, Bob Dixon & G. W.
   Farrell, D. D. Emmett, Joseph
   Sweeney)

1829
(Jump) Jim Crow (?) (John Dunn, T. D.
   Rice)

1830
Billy Barlow (?) (Sam Cowell, W. G.
   Ross, J. L. Toole)
Deep, Deep Sea, The (Charles E. Horn,
   Maria Malibran)
Love's Young Dream (?) (John Braham)
Maid Of Judah, The (Charles Sloman)
My Pretty Jane (The Bloom Is On The
   Rye) (Ben Davies, E. W. Mackney,
   Sims Reeves, Lydia Yeamans)
Spider And The Fly, The (Kate
   Castleton, Thomas Hudson, Henry
   Russell)
Steam! Steam! Steam!

1832
Love's Review (Lucy Vestris)

c.1833
Pop Goes The Weasel (Charles Sloman)

1834
All Round My Hat (parody)
Dangers Of A Patent Safety Cab, The
   (W. Rogers)
Hansom Cab Song, The
Lost Child, The (Sam Cowell)
Up The Alma's Height (Tommy Farrant,
   Emily Soldene)

1836
Kathleen Mavourneen (J. A. Cave,
   Catherine Hayes)
Old Arm Chair, The (Henry Russell)
Villikins And His Dinah (?) (see 1853)

1837
God Bless Victoria! Albion's Queen (J. A.
   Cave(?))
Oh! Woodman, Spare That Tree (Henry
   Russell)

1838
Life On The Ocean Wave, A (originally
   instrumental only)

1839
Badge, The
Nix My Dolly Pals (Mrs Keeley & Paul
   Bedford)
Rocked In The Cradle Of The Deep

1840
Ballad Of Sam Hall, The(?) (W. G.
   Ross)
Keemo Kimo (Mrs Caulfield, Mrs W. J.
   Florence, Christy Serenaders)
Mary's Ghost (Jonathan Blewitt(?))
Penny Post Act, The
Sich A Gittin' Upstairs (John Dunn,
   E. W. Mackney, T. D. Rice)

1841
Lively Flea, The (parody) (?) (Sam
   Cowell, Thomas Hudson, W. G. Ross,
   J. W. Sharp)

1842
Lord Lovel (parody) (Sam Cowell, J. W.
   Sharp)
New Income Tax, The

1843
I Dreamt That I Dwelt In Marble Halls
   (Louisa Pyne, Elizabeth Rainforth)
Song Of The Shirt, The (Henry Russell,
   Antoinette Sterling)
Then You'll Remember Me (William
   Harrison)

1844
By The Sad Sea Waves (*Bunn: Benedict*)
   (Jenny Lind)
Polkamania (J. W. Sharp)

1845
Jim Crack Corn (The Blue Tail Fly)
   (Virginia Minstrels)
Literary Dustman, The(?) (Robert Glin-
   don)
Loch Lomond(?) (Mme Patey-Whyttock)
Yes! Let Me Like A Soldier Fall (William
   Harrison)

1846
Mary Blane (Ethiopian Serenaders,
   Whitlock's Minstrels)
Our Hands Have Met But Not Our
   Hearts (Lucy Clarke, Maud Distin)

1847
Alonzo The Brave (J. B. Howe)
M'Appari Tutt'Amor (Mario)
Simon The Cellarer (Charles Santley)

1848
Ben Bolt (Sam Cowell)
Jenny Lind (J. W. Sharp)
Oh! Susanna (sundry Minstrel troupes)

1849
Queen Victoria's Visit To Ireland (J. W.
   Sharp)

1850
Camptown Races, The (sundry Minstrel
   troupes)
Excelsior!
Juanita (Christy Minstrels)
Nelly Bly (sundry Minstrel troupes)
Rose Of Tralee
Santa Lucia
To Anthea (John Hatton, Charles
   Santley)

1851
Old Folks At Home (Christy Minstrels)
Who'll Have Me? (Miss Poole)
Wi' A Hundred Pipers An' A' (R. Watkin
   Mills)

1852
Cheer, Boys, Cheer! (Henry Russell)
Massa's In De Cold, Cold Ground
   (Christy Minstrels)

Ratcatcher's Daughter, The(?) (Sam
   Cowell)

1853
Good King Wenceslas
My Old Kentucky Home (Christy
   Minstrels)
Villikins And His Dinah; *see* 1836 (Sam
   Cowell, Frederick Robson, J. L. Toole)

1854
England For The English (*Cave:
   Dagonet*) (J. A. Cave)
Hard Times Come Again No More
   (*Stephen Foster*) (Christy Minstrels)
Jeanie With The Light Brown Hair
   (sundry Minstrel troupes)

1855
Come Where My Love Lies Dreaming
   (Christy Minstrels)
Hybrias The Cretan (Signor Foli)
Listen To The Mocking Bird (sundry
   Minstrel troupes)
Old Dog Tray (My) (Christy Minstrels)
Postman's Knock, The
Village Blacksmith, The (to various
   settings) (Harry Cavendish, Joseph
   Robinson, William Scanlon (Christy
   Minstels), W. H. Weiss)
Whole Hog Or None, The (*Mackney*)
   (E. W. Mackney)

1856
Bobbin' Around (Mrs Caulfield, Sam
   Cowell, Mrs W. J. Florence)
Brindisi (*Traviata*) (Lizzie Pearce &
   Russell Grover, Marietta Piccolomini
   & C. A. Zolari)
Come Into The Garden Maud (Sims
   Reeves *et al.*)
Green Trees Whispered Low And Mild,
   The (Charlotte Sainton-Dolby)
Hen Wlad Fy Nhadau (Land Of My
   Fathers) (Signor Foli)

1857
Three Fishers Went Sailing (Louise

Kirkby Lunn, Charlotte Sainton-
Dolby, Antoinette Sterling)

1858

Come Home, Father (Alabama
Barnstormers, G. H. Chirgwin,
Horace Norman (Christy
Minstrels))

Jessie's Dream (Charlotte Russell)

1859

Bacon & Greens (Sam Cowell)

I Wish I Was In Dixie (Bryant's
Minstrels, Buckley's Serenaders)

Jingle Bells (Christy Minstrels)

Maiden's Prayer, The

Sing, Birdie, Sing (Louisa Venning)

Swiss Echo Song (*Eckert*) (Adelina Patti,
Carlotta Patti, Jenny Lind)

1860

Bacio, Il (The Kiss) (Adelina Patti,
Lucrezia Bori, Marietta Piccolomini)

Hop Light Hoo(?) (*Ware*) (E. W.
Mackney)

I'd Choose To Be A Daisy (Fred
Buckley)

Limerick Races (Sam Collins)

Tenting On The Old Camp Ground
(Hutchinson Family)

Up The Thames To Richmond (Howard
Paul)

1861

Alice, Where Art Thou?

Battle Cry Of Freedom (Union Troops'
Glee Club (Chicago))

Battle Hymn Of The Republic
(Hutchinson Family)

Hampstead Is The Place To Ruralize
(Annie Adams, Albert Steele)

John Brown's Body (Hutchinson Family)

Killarney

Murmur Of The Shell, The (Priscilla
Horton)

Perfect Cure, The (J. H. Stead)

Selina Sly (Edward Marshall, Howard
Paul)

1862

Blaydon Races (George Ridley)

Captain Jinks Of The Horse Marines
(William Lingard, Tom Maclagan,
Harry Rickards)

Dark Girl Dress'd In Blue (Harry
Clifton, Kate Harley, George
Leybourne)

Exhibition Of 1862, The (Frank Hall)

Fair Girl Dressed In Check (Alfred
Vance)

God Bless The Prince Of Wales (Sims
Reeves)

Great Exhibition, The (F. Olivier,
William Randall, J. H. Stead)

Moon Has Raised Her Lamp Above, The
(Charles Santley & William Harrison,
Ivor Foster & Herbert Cave)

No Irish Need Apply (Sam Collins, Mrs
F. R. Phillips, W. Randall)

Oot O' Wark *or* The Year '62 (Ned
Corvan)

Whole Hog Or None, The (*Westrop*)
(Charles Sloman, Marcus Wilkinson)

1863

Charming Young Widow I Met In The
Train, The (Fred Albert, William
Randall)

Cushie Butterfield(?) (George Ridley)

Dear Mother I've Come Home To Die
(Millie Lindon)

I'm The Dark Girl Dress'd In Blue (Kate
Harley)

Just Before The Battle, Mother
(Charles Bernard (Moore & Burgess
Minstrels))

Polly Perkins Of Paddington Green(?)
(Harry Clifton)

Sweet And Low (Charles Santley)

When Johnny Comes Marching Home
(G. W. 'Pony' Moore (Christy
Minstrels))

1864

Beautiful Dreamer (Christy Minstrels,
Moore & Burgess Minstrels)

Bill Stickers Beware (William Randall)

Coffee Shop At Pimlico, The (Frank Bell)

Gipsy's Warning, The (Christy Minstrels, Ernest Pike)

Isabella, The Barber's Daughter (She'd A Gingham Umbrella) (Harry Clifton)

Jemima Brown (Harry Clifton)

Jones's Musical Party (Harry Clifton, Mel B. Spurr)

Kiss In The Railway Train, The (Kate Harley)

Oh Where, Oh Where, Has My Little Dog Gone? (A. W. Young)

Sewing Machine, The (Frank Bell, Frank Hall)

Ticket Of Leave Man, The (Alfred Vance)

Tramp, Tramp, Tramp, The Boys Are Marching (Hutchinsons, Christy Minstrels)

1865

Anastatia, The Angel Of Holloway (Arthur Lloyd)

Angelina Brown (Fred French)

Bear It Like A Man(?) (Harry Clifton)

Chang The Chinese Giant (George Leybourne)

German Band, The (Alfred Vance)

I Like To Be A Swell (Arthur Lloyd)

London, Chatham And Dover, The (Jolly John Nash)

Marching Through Georgia

Merriest Girl That's Out, The (Annie Adams)

Merry, Funny Little Topper, The (Jolly John Nash)

Nice Looking Girl, The (Harriet Bowmer)

'Norrible Tale, A (Sam Cowell, J. L. Toole, Alfred Vance)

On The Sands(?) (William Randall)

Railway Belle, The (Harry Clifton)

Slap Bang, Here We Are Again (Frank Hall, Tom Maclagan, Alfred Vance)

Weeping Willer, The or The Miller's Daughter (Harry Clifton)

1866

Act On The Square, Boys (Harry Sydney, Alfred Vance)

Act On The Square (ladies' version) (Alice Dunning)

Can-Can see CORE SONG-LIST

Champagne Charlie (George Leybourne)

Champagne Charlie (ladies' version) (Louie Sherrington)

Come Back To Erin (Charlotte Sainton-Dolby)

Cruel Mary Holder (Arthur Lloyd)

Married To A Mermaid (Arthur Lloyd)

Paddle Your Own Canoe (Harry Clifton, Fred French)

Polly Crow (E. W. Mackney)

When You And I Were Young, Maggie (Christy Minstrels, Harry MacDonough)

You Naughty, Naughty Men (Nellie Cavendish, Miss F. R. Phillips)

1867

Apples Or Oranges, Bills Of The Play (Annie Adams)

Buttercup, The (George Du Maurier & Quintin Twist)

Clicquot! (Alfred Vance)

I'm A Timid Nervous Man (William Randall)

Jessie The Belle At The (Railway) Bar (Annie Adams, Henri Clark, George Leybourne, Harry Liston, Alfred Vance, George Ware, Mrs George Ware)

Little Brown Jug (James Francis (Mohawk Minstrels), Jolly John Nash, Ted Snow (Mohawk Minstrels))

Modern Swell's Diary, The (J. W. Sharp)

Mouse-Trap Man, The (George Leybourne)

Not For Joseph (Arthur Lloyd)

Pulling Hard Against The Stream (Harry Clifton)

Rollicking Rams, The (George Leybourne)

Waiting (Alexandra Dagmar)

Walking In The Zoo (Louie Sherrington, Alfred Vance)

Work, Boys, Work (Harry Clifton, Fred French)

1868

Come To Your Martha (Alfred Vance)

Day We Went To Ramsgate Oh, The (Harry Liston)

Fashionable Fred (Walter Laburnum)

Fisherman's Daughter That Lives O'er The Water, The (Nellie Power)

Flying Trapeze (Man On The), The (George Leybourne, Tony Pastor)

Husband's Boat, The (Alfred Vance)

I Couldn't Help Laughing, It Tickled Me So (Jolly John Nash)

On The Beach At Brighton (Horace Lingard)

Pull Together (Alfred Vance)

Shabby Genteel (Harry Clifton, Victor Liston)

Ten Little Nigger Boys (G. W. 'Pony' Moore)

Tommy Dodd (Sydney Barnes, Ernèe Clarke)

Up In A Balloon (George Leybourne)

Up In A Balloon (ladies' version) (Annie Adams, Alice Dunning, Nellie Power, Louie Sherrington)

Velocipede, The (New) (Fred Coyne (1))

Wait For The Turn Of The Tide (Harry Clifton)

1869

Arab's Farewell To His Favourite Steed, The (George Hodson(?))

As They Marched Through The Town (The Captain With His Whiskers) (Mrs W. J. Florence, Jenny Hill, Emma J. Nichols)

Charming Arabella (Victor Liston)

Cricketer, The (Tom Maclagan, Howard Paul)

Sweet Genevieve (Belle Cole, John McCormack, Mohawk Minstrels, Will Oakland, Peerless Quartet)

Yarn Of The Nancy Bell, The ('Bab' Ballad)

1870

Ada With The Golden Hair (G. W. 'Pony' Moore)

Brown The Tragedian (Arthur Lloyd)

Bell Goes A-Ringing For Sarah, The (Kate Santley)

Chickaleary Cove, The (Alfred Vance)

Family Man, The (Harry Clifton)

If Ever I Cease To Love (George Leybourne)

Just Touch The Harp Gently (William Leslie)

Keep Yor Feet Still Geordie Hinney(?) (Joe Wilson)

Late Lamented Jones, The (Alfred Vance)

Moet And Shandon (George Leybourne)

Mr Gorilla (Howard Paul)

My Lancashire Lass (George Leybourne)

Pal O' Mine (Alfred Vance)

Roman Fall, The (Alfred Vance)

Rosherville (James Hillier)

Sparkling Mozelle (Alfred Vance)

They All Have A Mate But Me (Sam Torr)

Tom Richard's Wedding (J. H. Stead)

White Wings (Peter Dawson, Mohawk Minstrels, Moore & Burgess Minstrels, Will Oakland, Manuel Romain, Banks Winter (Thatcher, Primrose & West Minstrels))

1871

Advertisements (Fred French)

Blind Boy, The (G. H. Chirgwin, Tom Chirgwin, Little Willie (Moore & Burgess))

Gendarmes' Duet (Edward Marshall &
   Felix Bury)
Rustic Damsel, The (Harry Liston)

1872
Dolly Varden (Alfred Vance)
Pretty Lips (Arthur Lloyd)
Ring The Bell, Watchman (Christy
   Minstrels)
Tichborne Trial (Alfred Vance)
Tiddy Fol Lol (Nellie Power)
Union Jack Of Old England, The
   (Charlie Williams)

1873
Amatory Frenchman, The (Henri Clark)
Belle Of The Ball, The (George
   Leybourne)
Covent Garden In The Morning (George
   Leybourne, Alfred Vance)
Gathering Shells By The Sea (Christy
   Minstrels)
Have You Seen The Shah? (Alfred
   Vance)
Immenseikoff (Arthur Lloyd)
It's Naughty But It's Nice (Arthur Lloyd)
Life Is Like A Game Of Cricket (Frank
   Hall)
Maid Of Athens
Nice Girl, A (Robert Soutar)
Not For Joseph (Arthur Lloyd)
Scamp, The or They Can't Hold A
   Candle To Me (G. H. Macdermott,
   Will Riley)
Silver Threads Among The Gold (sundry
   Minstrel troupes, Emily Soldene)
Speak Out Like A Man (Mrs R.
   Brennan)

1874
Czardas (*Die Fledermaus*) (Mlle C.
   Cabella, Constance Drever, Marie
   Geistinger)
Laughing Song, The (*Die Fledermaus*)
   (Miss E. Chambers, Marie Geistinger)
Life (Walter Gooch)

Mystery (Walter Gooch)
Old Union Jack, The (William Randall)

1875
Brave Captain Webb (Fred Albert)
Captain Matthew Webb (F. Jonghmans)
Close The Shutters, Willie's Dead
   (Christy Minstrels, Sydney Herbert
   (Moore & Burgess Minstrels))
Excursion Train, The(?) (Edward
   Marshall)
Flower Song, The (*Carmen*) (Italo
   Campanini)
Gold! Gold! Gold! (Hunt) (George
   Leybourne)

1876
Bradshaw's Guide (Fred Albert, Joe
   Cave)
Cheer For Plimsoll, A (Fred Albert)
Chorister, The (Antoinette Sterling)
Custom Of The Country, The (Henri
   Clark)
Don't Make A Noise Or Else You'll Wake
   The Baby (George Leybourne)
Grandfather's Clock (My) (sundry
   Minstrel troupes, John Read, Henry
   Russell)
Hildebrandt Montrose (Nellie Farren,
   Arthur Lloyd, G. H. Macdermott)
If I Was Only Long Enough (Arthur
   Roberts)
I'll Take You Home Again, Kathleen
I've Been A Good Woman To You (Jenny
   Hill)
I Won Her Heart At Billiards (Henri
   Clark)
Joconde (Charles Santley)
Joe's Birthday or Did You Ever Go To
   Hampstead In A Van? (J. W. Rowley)
Nancy Lee (Marie Compton)
Never Desert A Friend (William
   Randall)
Poor Chinee (Henri Clark)
Ring The Bell Softly, There's Crape On
   The Door (Christy Minstrels)

Rolling On The Grass (Henri Clark)

Spelling Bee (Sam Torr)

Star Of Hope (Signor Foli)

Tommy Make Room For Your Uncle (W. B. Fair, Tony Pastor)

Two Obadiahs (G. H. Macdermott, J. L. Toole)

Watching The Mill Go Round (George Leybourne)

When I Gits To Be An M.P. (William Randall)

Won't You Buy My Pretty Flowers? (George Clare (Mohawk Minstrels))

1877

Abdalla-Bulbul Ameer (revised and revived 1927, q.v.) (Frank Crumit)

Baby's Got A Tooth (J. L. Toole)

Cantineer Of The Irish Brigade, A (Marie Loftus)

Captain Cuff (George Leybourne)

Dear Old Pals (G. H. Macdermott)

Duchess Of Devonshire, The (Fred Foster)

Encore (George Leybourne)

Faint Heart Never Won Fair Lady (Arthur Roberts)

Fitz-Jones The M.P. (Alfred Vance)

For Goodness' Sake Don't Say I Told You (Arthur Lloyd)

If We Could Only See Through The Keyhole (Fred Coyne)

I Haven't Been Home This Morning (W. J. Ashcroft)

I'll Sing Thee Songs Of Araby (Sims Reeves)

In The Gloamin' (Signor Campobello)

It's Nice (Fred Coyne, Nellie Farren, John Read)

Keep It Dark (Herbert Campbell & Harry Nichols)

Lost Chord, The (Antoinette Sterling (original singer))

Macdermott's War Song (The Jingo Song) see CORE SONG-LIST (G. H. Macdermott)

Mad Butcher, The (Henri Clark)

Man In The Moon Is Looking, Love, The (George Leybourne)

Man With One Eye, The (Pat Feeney)

Naughty Johnny Morgan (Herbert Campbell)

No, No, Fathead (Arthur Roberts)

On The Strict Q.T. (G. H. Macdermott)

Quarrel In The Menagerie, The (Charlie Williams)

Riding On A Load Of Hay (Harry Birch)

Roley-Poley Over (J. W. Rowley)

Same Old Game, The (Sam Torr)

She'd A Brother In The Navy (James Francis (Mohawk Minstrels), Howard Paul)

Solid Man, The (W. J. Ashcroft)

Spelling B (Charlie Williams)

Three Weeks' Courtship (Arthur Roberts)

Turkey And The Bear, The (Fred Albert)

Up Comes Jones (Arthur Corney)

We Don't Want To Fight (Macdermott's War Song) (G. H. Macdermott)

Welsh Miners, The (Fred Albert)

What Did Your Mother Say, Johnny, My Lad? (Charles Coborn)

When The Pigs Began To Fly (Miss F. R. Phillips)

Women (Sam Redfern)

You Can't Have Too Much Of A Jolly Good Thing (Fred Albert)

You're Another (Charles Murray)

Zazel (George Leybourne)

1878

All Hands On Deck (George Lashwood)

Aloha Oe (Alma Gluck)

Awfully Awful (Kate Santley)

Bank Holiday or A Twopenny Ride On A Tramcar (Fred Coyne)

Bloomsbury Square (George Leybourne)

Carry Me Back To Old Virginny (J. A. Cave, Christy's Minstrels)

Cleopatra's Needle (Charlie Williams)

Darby And Joan (Antoinette Sterling)

Electric Light, The (Fred Coyne)

Emancipation Day (sundry Minstrel troupes)

Fizz (George Leybourne)

Here Stands A Post (Waiting For The Signal) (Bessie Bonehill, Marie Compton, W. C. Levey, Nellie Moon)

Hurrah For Beaconsfield (Fred Coyne)

I Can't Stand Mrs Green's Mother (Herbert Campbell, Little Thomas)

I Don't Want To Fight (Herbert Campbell)

I'm Determined No Longer To Stand It (Jenny Hill)

Oh, Julia! (John Read)

Oh, The Fairies! (George Leybourne)

Patrick, Mind The Baby (G. W. 'Pony' Moore)

Rolling Stone, A (Harry Sydney)

See That My Grave's Kept Green (Moore & Burgess Minstrels)

Sparkling Piper Heidsieck (George Leybourne)

Tiddle-A-Wink The Barber (John Read)

Turn Off The Gas At The Meter (G. H. Macdermott)

Twickenham Ferry (Mary Davies)

Where Was Moses When The Light Went Out? (G. H. Macdermott)

Whoa, Emma! (*Daykin*) (Bessie Bellwood(?), Kate Carney(?))

You'll All Be Wanted (Arthur Roberts)

1879

Brass (George Leybourne)

Cerulea Was Beautiful (Harry Rickards)

City Toff, The *or* Crutch And Toothpick (La-Di-Da!) (Nellie Power)

Ding Dong (Gus Leach)

Don't Run Old England Down (G. H. Macdermott)

Heavy Swell Of The Sea, The (Big) (George Leybourne)

He's Got 'Em On (T. W. Barrett)

Kerry Dance, The (Louie Sherrington, Charles Tree)

Little Miss Muffett Sat On A Tuffet (G. H. Macdermott)

Oh, Dem Golden Slippers (James Bland, Haverly's Minstrels, G. W. 'Pony' Moore (Moore & Burgess Minstrels))

Piano Girl, The (Fred Coyne)

Sailor's Farewell, The (Mr Federici)

Toothpick And Crutch (Alfred Vance)

Tuner's Oppor-Tuner-Ty, The (Fred Coyne)

1880

All On Account Of Liza (Lillian Russell)

Auntie (Janet Monach Patey)

Better Land, The(?) (Antoinette Sterling)

Bulls Won't Bellow, The (Sam Torr)

English As She Is Spoke (Charles Coborn)

Funiculi Funicula

Going To The Derby In A Donkey Cart (Edwin Boyde, Arthur Lloyd, J. W. Rowley, Alfred Vance)

Good-Bye! (*Tosti*) (Kate Cove)

I'm Getting A Big Boy Now (Herbert Campbell)

In Cellar Cool (Drinking) (Signor Foli, Robert Radford)

In The Evening By The Moonlight (James Bland)

Lounging In The Aq (George Leybourne)

Madame La Sharty (Harry Freeman, J. W. Rowley)

Myfanwy (Carmen Hill)

My Katty Kiss'em (Arthur Roberts)

Oh, Fred! Tell Them To Stop (Fred Coyne (1), George Leybourne, Tony Pastor)

Songs My Mother Taught Me (Evan Williams)

Teddington Lock (Charlotte Sainton-Dolby)

While Strolling Thru' The Park (Tom

Howard & Patsy Barret, Du Rell
Twin Bros)

Whist! The Bogie Man (*see* Hush!
The Bogie! 1890) (Christy Minstrels,
Harrigan & Hart, Mohawk
Minstrels)

Whoa, Emma! (*Lonsdale*) (Fred Coyne,
George Leybourne)

You May Pet Me As Much As You
Please

1881

Awful Little Scrub, An (Lionel Brough,
George Grossmith sen.)

Boy In The Gallery, The(?) (Marie
Lloyd, Nellie Power)

Don't Leave Your Mother When Her
Hair Turns Grey (sundry Minstrel
troupes)

Happy Eliza And Converted Jane(Sisters
Cuthburt, Sisters Jonghmans)

I'll Tell Your Mother What You've Done
(James Fawn)

I'm Living With Mother Now (Arthur
Roberts)

Lock Him Up (Harry Braham)

Lord Mayor's Coachman (W. Freeman
(Mohawk Minstrels), H. P. Matthews)

My Aesthetic Love (Alfred Vance)

Nonsense! Yes! By Jove! (George Barrett
& H. L. Shine, Robert Brough &
Harry Nicholls, Fred Stimson &
Fawcett Lomax, Herbert Campbell &
Charles Grosse)

Old Brigade, The (Norman Allin, Ian
Colquhoun, Peter Dawson, Maud
Distin, Signor Foli)

Old Rustic Bridge By The Mill, The
(C. Chivers (Mohawks), Walter
Glynne)

Old Toll-Gate, The (Arthur Lennard)

True British Swell, The (Pattie
Mortimer(?))

Wait Till The Clouds Roll By (Mohawk
Minstrels, Moore & Burgess
Minstrels)

We Are! We Are! We Are! (Arthur
Roberts)

We Won't Go Home Till Morning (James
Fawn)

What's The World A-Coming To (Harry
Braham)

1882

All Through Obliging A Lady (Arthur
Lloyd)

'Arry (Jenny Hill)

Baa Baa Baa (Jolly John Nash)

Cockles And Mussels

Curfew Shall Not Ring Tonight, The
(Mohawk Minstrels)

Father O'Flynn (Signor Foli, Plunkett
Greene, Charles Santley)

In My Fust 'Usband's Time (Herbert
Campbell)

I Say Cabby! (George Leybourne)

My Bonnie Lies Over The Ocean

Nobody Knows Who Done It (Harry
Braham)

Oh, What A Wicked Young Man You Are
(Ethel Victor)

Oh, You Little Darling (I Love You)
(Nellie L'Estrange, Kate Vaughan)

Pretty Lips (Arthur Lloyd)

(Quite A Toff In My) Newmarket Coat
(Vesta Tilley)

Remarkable Fellah!, A (Harry Braham)

Shoulder To Shoulder (Bessie Bonehill)

Signor Macstinger (Arthur Lloyd)

Those Girls At The School At The End
Of The Street (James Fawn)

Trimdown Grange Explosion (Tommy
Armstrong)

Up Went The Price (G. H. Macdermott)

What With Yours And What With Mine
(Harry Braham)

Why Part With Jumbo (The Pet Of
The Zoo)? (Fred Coyne (1),
G. H. Macdermott)

1883

Boy's Best Friend Is His Mother, A
(Brothers Bohee (Haverly's Minstrels),

J. Fuller and Harry Hunter (Mohawk
  Minstrels))
Don't Take My Children From Me
  (Hyram Travers)
Frivolity (The Leopolds)
Is That Mr Riley? (Pat Rooney)
My Nellie's Blue Eyes (Tom Costello, J.
  Fuller (Mohawk Minstrels), William
  Scanlon (Christy Minstrels))
Nobleman's Son, A (T. W. Barrett)
Only A Pansy Blossom (Mohawk
  Minstrels, Will Oakland (Moore &
  Burgess Minstrels))
She Does The Fandango All Over The
  Place (Henri Clark)
Sweet Violets (Sweeter Than All The
  Roses) (J. Fuller (Mohawks), Jenny
  Hill)
Ting, Ting, That's How The Bell Goes
  (George Leybourne)
We're Moving (James Fawn)

1884

Come Down And Open The Door, Love
  (Slade Murray)
Ghost Of Benjamin Binns, The (Harry
  Randall)
I Tell Them My Father's A Marquis
  (William Bint)
Love's Old Sweet Song (Antoinette
  Sterling, Edna Thornton)
Lucindah At The Windah (James
  Francis)
Marquis Of Camberwell Green, The
  (T. W. Barrett)
Masher King, The (Charles Godfrey)
Milly's Cigar Divan (G. H. Macdermott)
Oh! My Darling Clementine (Walter
  Howard (Mohawk Minstrels))
Only One (James Fawn)
Our Fishing Match (James Fawn)
Please Sell No More Drink To My
  Father
Pretty As A Butterfly (Richmond
  Sisters)
Skye Boat Song, The (R. Watkin Mills)

1885

Agricultural Irish Girl, The (Walter
  Munroe)
Ask A P'Liceman (James Fawn)
Boy About Town, The (Jenny Hill)
Charlie Dilke Upset The Milk (G. H.
  Macdermott)
Funny Things They Do Upon The Sly,
  The (G. W. Hunter)
He's All Behind (Marie Lloyd)
He's Going To Marry Mary Ann (Bessie
  Bellwood)
I Want To Meet A Good Young Man
  (Nellie L'Estrange)
Prince Tiptoe (Fanny Robina)
She Was! She Was!! She Was!!! (Slade
  Murray)
There's Danger On The Line (The
  Great Semaphore Song) (G. H.
  Macdermott)
They're All Very Fine And Large
  (Herbert Campbell)
This Is The House That Jerry Built, The
  (James Fawn)
What Cheer, Ria! (Bessie Bellwood,
  Nellie Farren)
You Should Go To France (Marie Lloyd)

1886

Down By The Garden Gate (G. W.
  Hunter)
Fireman In The Amateur Brigade, The
  (T. W. Barrett)
Friends Of My Youthful Days (Vesta
  Tilley)
Golden Wedding, The (Charles Godfrey)
I Did It (James Fawn)
Johnny Get Your Gun (Gus Garrick,
  Moore & Burgess Minstrels, Nellie
  Richards, Sheffer & Blakeley, Little
  Thomas (Mohawk Minstrels))
My Father's Face (Will Oliver)
Oh Jeremiah, Don't You Go To Sea
  (Marie Lloyd)
Queen Of My Heart (Hayden Coffin)
See Me Dance The Polka (Billie Barlow,

George Grossmith sen., Jolly John
  Nash)
She's The Only Girl I Love (Rosie
  Heath)
Sister Mary Walked Like That (Jolly John
  Nash)
Talkative Man From Poplar, The (The
  Merry Macs, Tennyson & O'Gorman)
That's Where The Young Man Smiles
  (Marie Lloyd)
Tablet Of Fame, The (Vesta Tilley)
Two Lovely Black Eyes (Charles Coborn)
Woman, Lovely Woman (James Fawn)

1887
Angels Without Wings (Vesta Tilley)
Comrades (Tom Costello, Helene Mora)
Down Went The Captain (Kate Royle)
Exchange And Mart (Harry Randall)
Forgive And Forget (Sam Torr)
Goodbye, Goodbye, Goodbye (George
  Leybourne(?))
His Lordship Winked At The Counsel
  (G. H. Macdermott)
Hungry Man From Clapham, The (G. W.
  Hunter)
I'll Place It In The Hands Of My Solici-
  tor (Fred Gilbert)
Killaloe (E. J. Lonnen)
Last Bus, The (James Fawn)
My Father Was Never A Marquis
  (William Bint)
Obstinate Man, An (Frederick Maccabe)
Oh! For The Jubilee! (Charles Godfrey)
Oh! The Jubilee (Charles Coborn)
Our 'Armonic Club (Albert Chevalier)
Our Empress Queen
Quite English, You Know (Alfred
  Beddoe, Henry C. Arnold, G. H.
  Macdermott)
Song That Reached My Heart, The (T.
  Campbell (Mohawks), Julian Jordan)
Star Of Bethlehem, The (Ben Davies,
  John Harrison, Michael Maybrick)
Sworn In (Fred Leslie)

Three Acres And A Cow (Arthur Lloyd)
Ti! Hi! Tiddelly Hi! (Harry Rickards)

1888
Across The Bridge (Charles Godfrey)
At My Time Of Life (Herbert Campbell)
Automatic Battery, The (Harry
  Randall)
Bald Headed Swell, The (G. W. Hunter)
Beauty's Eyes (Fraser Gange, Evan
  Williams)
Captain Called The Mate, The
  (Alexandra Dagmar, Harry Freeman,
  Arthur West)
Coster's Courtship (Albert Chevalier)
England For The English (*Bowyer:
  Baker*) (Herbert Campbell)
Hard Times Come Again No More
  (*Tabrar*) (Johnny Danvers, Harry
  Rickards)
In Olden Spain (*Le Roi d'Ys*) (Julie de
  Savigny)
Masks And Faces (Jenny Hill)
Mystery Of A Hansom Cab, The (Walter
  Munroe)
Tain't Natural (Arthur Roberts)
Where Did You Get That Hat? (J. C.
  Heffron, Millie Hylton, Joseph J.
  Sullivan)
Who Killed Cock Warren? (Harry
  Randall)
With All Her Faults I Love Her Still
  (Richard Jose, Will Oakland)
Young Men Taken In And Done For
  (Dan Leno)

1889
Don't Go Out Tonight, Dear Father
  (sundry Minstrel troupes)
Earl Of Fife, The (Walter Munroe)
Emigrant Ship, The (George Leyton)
Home Rule (Charles Collette)
I'm A Little Too Young To Know (Ada
  Reeve)
I'm A Man That's Done Wrong To My
  Parents

I'm Selling Up The 'Appy 'Appy 'Ome (Harry Champion)

It's Only A False Alarm (Great Expectations) (Harry Randall)

Johnny Jones And His Sister Sue (Letty Lind & Charles Danby, Nellie Farren & Fred Leslie)

Last Bullet, The (A Story Of Lucknow) (George Lashwood)

Little Annie Rooney (Lottie Gilson, Michael Nolan)

Little Peach In An Orchard Grew, A (Christy Minstrels, Johnny Danvers (Mohawk Minstrels), D. G. Longworth & Marie Stuart, E. J. Lonnen)

Muffin Man, The (Dan Leno)

Not At All The Silly Girl You Took Me For (George Lashwood)

Off To Philadelphia (Ian Colquhoun, Plunkett Greene)

Paris Exhibition, The (Arthur West)

Phil The Fluter's Ball (Peter Dawson, Percy French, Albert Whelan)

Polka And The Choirboy, The (Louis Bradfield, Corney Grain)

We Drew His Club Money This Morning (Pat Rafferty, J. W. Rowley)

Why Don't They Do It? (George Lashwood)

1890

Bang Goes The Bell! Ting! Ting! (Lester Barrett)

'Blige A Lady (Charles Godfrey)

Booze Is There (Sam Redfern)

Come Where The Booze Is Cheaper(?) (Charles Coborn)

Coster's Serenade, The (Albert Chevalier)

Diver, The (Norman Allin, Signor Foli, T. F. Kinniburgh)

'E Dunno Where 'E Are (Gus Elen)

Fire Escape, The (Charlie Parnell's Naughty Shape) (G. H. Macdermott)

Girls Of Today, The (Bessie Bonehill)

Hush! The Bogie (*see* Whist! The Bogie Man 1880) (E. J. Lonnen, G. H. Macdermott, Ted Snow (Mohawk Minstrels), Horace Wheatley)

Maggie Murphy's Home (Jenny Hill)

My First Cigar (Louis Bradfield, Corney Grain)

Never More (Dan Leno)

On Guard, A Story Of Balaclava (Charles Godfrey)

She May Have Seen Better Days (Rose Elliott, Bonnie Thornton, W. H. Windom)

Smiles! (*McGlennon*) (Little Tich)

Sweet Rosie O'Grady (Lil Hawthorne, Walter Munroe, Pat Rafferty)

Then You Wink The Other Eye (When The Winkle Man Goes By) (Marie Lloyd)

Wild Man Of Borneo, The (Johnny Danvers & Little Thomas, Tennyson & O'Gorman)

Wild Man Of Poplar, The (The Merry Macs, Tennyson & O'Gorman)

Wrong Man, The (Marie Lloyd)

1891

Actions Speak Louder Than Words (Marie Lloyd, Helene Mora)

'Arriet's Answer (Jenny Hill)

'Arriet's Reply (Marie Lloyd)

Bowery, The (Ada Blanche, Harry Conor)

Deathless Army, The (Thorpe Bates)

Different Styles Of Singing (Some Sang High, Some Sang Low) (George Leyton)

Every-Day Life (Charles Chaplin sen.)

Funny Without Being Vulgar (Albert Chevalier)

Good Old Annual, The (Harry Randall)

Grass Widower, The (Dan Leno)

Hearts And Flowers (US lyrics added 1899) (Anona Winn)

He Was Her Only Son (Jenny Hill)

How Dare You Come To London? (Marie Lloyd)

I'm The Bosom Friend Of Albert, Prince Of Wales

I Say (Marie Lloyd)

I Was Slapped (Marie Lloyd)

Madam Duvan (Marie Lloyd)

Man That Broke The Bank At Monte Carlo, The (Charles Coborn, Maggie Duggan, William Hooey)

Mary Was A Housemaid (Yvette Guilbert, Claire Romaine)

Miner's Dream Of Home, The (Leo Dryden)

Mischief (Marie Lloyd)

My Hat's A Brown 'Un (George Robey)

My Son, My Son, My Only Son (Charles Godfrey)

Naval Exhibition, The (George Beauchamp, Charles Osborne)

Never Introduce Your Donah To A Pal (Gus Elen)

Picture That Is Turned To The Wall, The (Andrew Mack, Julius P. Witmark)

Rowdy-Dowdy Boys, The (Millie Hylton)

Scandals Are 'Cuming', The (A Baccarat Song) (Paul Pelham)

Seventh Royal Fusiliers, The (Charles Godfrey)

Shop-Walker, The (Dan Leno)

Side By Side (Harrison) (Constance Moxon, Rose Sullivan)

Simple Pimple (George Robey)

Soldiers Of The Queen, The (Albert Christian, C. Hayden Coffin, Jay Laurier (parody?))

Ta-Ra-Ra-Boom-De-Ay (UK version) (Lottie Collins, Alice Leamar)

Ta-Ra-Ra Boom-De-Ré (orig. US version) (Mama Lou)

That Is Love (Marie Loftus)

That's Where The Trouble Begins (W. F. Moss)

That's Why The British Loved The King (Charles Coborn)

That Was Before My Time, You Know (Marie Lloyd)

Theosophee (Tom Costello)

Tin Gee-Gee, The a.k.a. The Lowther Arcade (Mel B. Spurr, Fanny Wentworth)

Trumpet Call, The (Marie Lloyd)

We All Go To Work But Father (J. C. Heffron, Leslie Reed)

Wot Cher! (Knocked 'Em In The Old Kent Road) (Albert Chevalier)

Yes You Are (Jenny Valmore)

1892

Accidents or Up To The Moon He Bunked (T. E. Dunville)

After The Ball see CORE SONG-LIST

Bois Épais (Sombre Woods) (Plunkett Greene)

Broken Melody (for cello) (Auguste Van Biene)

Daddy Wouldn't Buy Me A Bow-Wow (Arthur Roberts (parody), Vesta Victoria)

Daisy Bell (Katie Lawrence)

Fiacre, Le (Yvette Guilbert)

Following In Father's Footsteps (Vesta Tilley)

Future Mrs 'Awkins, The (Albert Chevalier)

Gal Wot Lost Her Bloke At Monte Carlo, The (Marie Lloyd)

G'arn Away! What D'Yer Take Me For? (Marie Lloyd)

Git Your 'Air Cut (George Beauchamp)

Holy City, The (Herbert Cave, Edward Lloyd, Michael Maybrick, Helene Mora)

I Haven't Been Kissed For Weeks (Arthur Williams)

I Love You Both (Lottie Gilson)

My Old Dutch (Albert Chevalier)

My Queer Old Dutch (Harry Pleon)

My Sweetheart's The Man In The
Moon (Marie Kendall, Bonnie
Thornton)
Nasty Way 'E Sez It, The (Albert
Chevalier)
Oh! Mr Porter (Marie Lloyd)
Our Little Nipper (Albert Chevalier)
Shipmates In Safety, Shipmates In
Danger (Millie Hylton)
Sweetest Story Ever Told, The (Myra
Mirella)
Tommy (from Kipling's *Barrack-Room
Ballads*) (Charles Coborn)
Twiggy Voo? (Marie Lloyd)
Two Little Girls In Blue (Lily Burnand,
Marie Kendall, James Norrie, Horace
Wheatley)
Two Sweethearts (Lester Barrett)
Whacky Whack Whack (Marie Lloyd)
What Do I Care? (Ada Reeve)
What's That For, Eh? (Johnny Jones *or* I
Know Now) (Marie Lloyd)

1893
And The Verdict Was (T. E. Dunville)
'Appy 'Ampstead (Albert Chevalier)
At Trinity Church I Met My Doom!
(Tom Costello)
Bunk-A-Doodle I Do (T. E. Dunville)
Buy Me Some Almond Rock (Marie
Lloyd)
Dandy Coloured Coon, The (Eugene
Stratton)
Down At The Farm-Yard Gate (Katie
Lawrence)
Down The Dials (Gus Elen)
Down The Road (Gus Elen)
Fatal Wedding, The (*see* Those
Wedding Bells Shall Not Ring Out,
1896)
Half-Past Nine (Charles Godfrey, Nellie
Wallace)
Happy Birthday To You (originally Good
Morning To All, 1935)
His Own Mother Wouldn't Know Him
(J. R. Rowley)

I'm One Of The Girls (Marie Kendall)
I Really Can't Stop Dancing (Little
Tich)
It's Not The Hen That Cackles The Most
(Minnie Cunningham)
Keys Of Heaven, The (Clara Butt &
Kennerley Rumford, Yvette
Guilbert, Dora Labette & Hubert
Eisdell)
King Of The Boys (Fanny Robina)
Linger Longer Loo (Yvette Guilbert,
Millie Hylton, Cissie Loftus, Ellaline
Terriss, May Yohé)
Longer You Linger, The (parody of
Linger Longer Loo) (Harry
Champion)
My Dreams (Ben Davies)
No, 'Arry, Don't Ask Me To Marry
(Marie Lloyd)
On Duty—A Tale Of The Crimea (Alf
Chester)
Oui! Tray Bong! (My Pal Jones) (Charles
Chaplin sen.)
Private Tommy Atkins (Hayden Coffin)
Same Thing (Marie Lloyd)
Sarah *or* A Donkey Cart Built For Two
(Kate Carney)
Signalman On The Line, The (F. H.
Celli)
Silly Fool! (Marie Lloyd)
Villains At The Vic (Albert Chevalier)
Volunteer Organist, The (William B.
Glenroy, Arthur Reeves)
Who'll Buy? (Albert Chevalier)

1894
And Her Golden Hair Was Hanging
Down Her Back (Lottie Gilson, Yvette
Guilbert, Seymour Hicks, Alice
Leamar, Eunice Vance)
Bandolero, The (Norman Allin, Signor
Foli)
Barmaid, The (Marie Lloyd)
Bird In The Hand, A (Marie Lloyd)
Brand New Millionaire, The (Vesta
Tilley)

Brighton (The Bowery) (R. G. Knowles)

By The Sad Sea Waves (*Barrett: Thomas*) (Lester Barrett, Vesta Tilley)

Catch 'Em Alive Oh! (Gus Elen)

Coster's Muvver, The (Gus Elen)

Curate, The (Walter Passmore)

Dancing On The Streets (UK version of Sidewalks Of New York) (Kate Carney)

Do Buy Me That Mamma Dear (Billie Barlow)

Dolly's Lament (Lydia Yeamans-Titus)

Don't Be Cross a.k.a. The Miller's Daughter (*see* Sei Nicht Bös)

Dorothy Dean (Marie Kendall)

Ghost Of Sherlock Holmes, The (H. C. Barry)

Giddy Little Girl Who Said No, The (Harry Freeman)

Hypochondriac, The (T. E. Dunville)

I Don't Want To Play In Your Yard (Jenny Clare & Madeline Majilton, Julie Mackey, The Tiny Websters)

If It Wasn't For The 'Ouses In Between (Gus Elen)

It Ain't All Lavender (Harry Randall, George Robey)

It's A Great Big Shame (Gus Elen)

La-Didily-Idily, Umti-Umti-Ay (Harry Freeman)

Looking For A Coon Like Me (Bessie Wentworth)

Man With The Bullet Proof Coat, The (Tom Woottwell)

My Brother Jack (Rose Sullivan)

No More Up At Covent Garden — Jack Jones (Alec Hurley)

Ours Is A Happy Little Home (Harry Randall)

Sanitary Inspector, The (James Fawn)

Sei Nicht Bös (The Miller's Daughter a.k.a. Don't Be Cross) (Alexander Girardi)

She Is More To Be Pitied Than Censured (Charles Falke, Harry Taft, Milner Verren)

Sidewalks Of New York (*see* Dancing On The Streets) (Lottie Gilson, Charles B. Lawlor)

So Her Sister Says (Jenny Valmore)

Spanish Senora, The (Marie Lloyd)

Sweetheart May (Vesta Tilley)

That Gorgonzola Cheese (Harry Champion)

Till Six O'Clock In The Morning (Millie Hylton)

'Tis Hard To Love And Say Farewell (The Lady Slavey) (Lily Burnand)

To Err Is Human, To Forgive Divine (Marie Loftus)

When A Fellah Has Turned Sixteen (Vesta Tilley)

Who's Coming Up In The Gallery? (Katie Lawrence)

Wot's The Good Of Hanythink? Why, Nuffink! (Albert Chevalier)

1895

Algy, The Piccadilly Johnny With The Little Glass Eye (Vesta Tilley)

Bachelors' Club, The (Vesta Tilley(?))

Band Played On, The (The Strawberry Blonde) (Tony Pastor, Lillian Russell)

Bully Song (May Irwin, Mama Lou)

Can't Stop! Can't Stop!! Can't Stop!!! (Harry Freeman)

Conundrums (T. E. Dunville)

Daddy's On The Engine (Arthur Albert)

Empty Chair, The (Charles Bignell)

Father Of The Boys (John Bull Up To Date) (Leo Dryden)

For Me! For Me! (Fred Earle)

Fresh, Fresh As The Morning (Bilton Sisters)

Gay Bohemi-ah (Maurice Farkoa)

Glorious Beer (Harry Anderson)

Her Christian Name Was Mary (Walter Kino)

In My 'Ansom (Arthur Roberts)

It's A Little Bit Of Sugar For The Bird (J. J. Dallas)

Jerusalem's Dead, The (Albert Chevalier)

Johnnie At The Gaiety (George Grossmith jun.)

Jolly Little Polly On Her Gee-Gee-Gee (Fannie Leslie)

Lamplighter, The (Little Tich)

Man At The Door, The (James Fawn)

Mary Ann's Refused Me (Dan Leno)

More Work For The Undertaker (Charles Bignell)

Mother's Advice (*Osborne*) (T. E. Dunville)

My Fiddle Is My Sweetheart (G. H. Chirgwin)

My Old Dress Suit (Corney Grain)

Near Thing (Marie Lloyd)

Never Share Your Lodgings With A Pal (Arthur Tinsley)

New Man, The (Walter Munroe)

Nineteenth Century Boys, The (Sisters Levey) (*Lamb: Peters*)

No More Fancy Balls For Me (Dan Leno)

Only A Few Miles Of Water (Nellie Gannon)

Rich Girl And The Poor Girl, The (Marie Lloyd)

Salute My Bicycle (Marie Lloyd)

Scientific Man, The (T. E. Dunville)

She's Only A Working Girl (Florrie Forde, Charles Foster)

She Was One Of The Early Birds (George Beauchamp)

Sister 'Ria (Lizzie Fletcher)

Streets Of Cairo (Bonnie Thornton)

Stroke Of The Pen, A (Lottie Elliott)

Sunshine Of Paradise Alley, The (Lottie Gilson, Sisters Levey, Julius P-Witmark)

Swallows, The (Alma Gluck)

Take Your Umbrella With You John (Harry Champion)

There'll Come A Time (Hedges Brothers & Jacobson)

There'll Come A Time Some Day (James Norrie (?))

Tricky Little Trilby (Marie Lloyd)

Waltzing Matilda (Peter Dawson)

When The Summer Comes Again (Three Pots A Shilling) (Kate Carney, Fred Mason)

Wot Cher, Polly! (Helena Dacre)

You Ain't Ashamed Of Me, Are You, Bill? (Alec Hurley, Rosie Lloyd)

You'll Have To Marry Me Now (Charles Brighton)

1896

Abide With Me (*Liddle*) (Clara Butt, Lilian Doreen)

All Coons Look Alike To Me (Emerald Sisters, Ernest Hogan, May Irwin, Eugene Stratton, Billy Williams)

All In A Row (Charles Deane)

All That Glitters Is Not Gold (*see* 1906) (James Norrie)

Amateur Whitewasher, The (Frank Seeley)

Among My Knick-Knacks (George Beauchamp)

Amorous Goldfish, The (Marie Tempest)

Chance Your Luck (Marie Lloyd)

Chon Kina (Letty Lind)

Clever, Ain't You? (George Beauchamp)

Darling Mabel (Leonard Barry)

'E Ain't Got Nuffin' To Tell (Vesta Victoria)

'E Can't Take A Roize Out Of Oi (Albert Chevalier)

Elsie From Chelsea (Seymour Hicks)

Frog Song (May Irwin)

Girl On The Ran-Dan-Dan, The (Lottie Collins, Marie Lloyd)

Great White Mother (Leo Dryden)

Hot Time In The Old Town, A (R. G.
  Knowles, Mama Lou, Josephine Sabel)
I Ain't A-Goin' To Tell (US 1893) (Alec
  Hurley)
Idler, The (Eugene Stratton)
If Only I Knew The Way (Venie Belfry)
I'm Getting Ready For My Mother-In-
  Law (Harry Champion)
In A Persian Garden (Ben Davies &
  Emma Albani & David Bispham &
  Hilda Wilson)
In The Baggage Coach Ahead (Imogene
  Comer)
I've Got The Ooperzootic (Johnny
  Danvers (Mohawk Minstrels))
I Wouldn't Leave My Little Wooden Hut
  For You (Daisy Dormer, Clarissa
  Talbot)
Lady Tom (Connie Ediss)
Like A Girl (Constance Moxon)
Love, Could I Only Tell Thee (Hayden
  Coffin)
Lucky Jim (Harry Davenport, George
  Formby)
Maid Of London, 'Ere We Part (Marie
  Lloyd)
Mister Johnson, Turn Me Loose (Daisy
  Dormer, Ben R. Harney, May Irwin)
Mother Was A Lady (Meyer Cohen,
  Lottie Gilson)
Mountains Of Mourne (John
  McCormack)
My Fiddle Was My Sweetheart (G. H.
  Chirgwin)
My Gal Is A High Born Lady (Charles
  Ernest (Haverly's Minstrels), Barney
  Fagan, Yvette Guilbert, Sisters
  Hawthorne, Clara Wieland)
Now We Shan't Be Long (Herbert
  Campbell)
Only A Jew (John Lawson)
On The Benches In The Park (R. G.
  Knowles)
Simple Little Maid In The Corner (Kitty
  Dee)
Simple Little String, A (Ellaline Terriss)

Sisters Gelatine (Belfry Sisters)
Tenor And Baritone (Ernest Pike &
  Stanley Kirkby)
Those Wedding Bells Shall Not Ring Out
  (adap. The Fatal Wedding, 1893)
  (Leonard Barrie, Gus Edwards,
  Helene Mora, Arthur Reece, William
  H. Windom)
Trixie Of Upper Tooting (George Gros-
  smith jun., Lionel Mackinder, Ada
  Reeve)
We've All Been Having A Go At It
  (Harry Champion)
While London's Fast Asleep (Marie
  Tyler)
Willow Pattern Plate, The (Sisters
  Hawthorne)
You Can't Stop A Girl From Thinking
  (Marie Lloyd)

1897

Afternoon Parade, The (Vesta Tilley)
Asleep In The Deep (Norman Allin,
  G. H. Chirgwin, Peter Dawson, Signor
  Foli)
As Your Hair Grows Whiter (Rosie
  Eaton)
'Bobbies' Of The Queen, The (Maud
  Santley)
Break The News To Mother (Norman
  Blair, Florence Chester, Ella Dean,
  Charles Foster, Alfred Hurley, Elsie
  Janis, Arthur Reece)
Down Fell The Pony In A Fit (Harry
  Champion)
Father's Gottem (Frank Seeley)
For The Week End (Vesta Tilley)
God Bless And Keep Victoria (Leo
  Dryden, Lizzie Howard)
Golden Dustman, The (Gus Elen)
I Want To Play With Little Dick (Vesta
  Victoria)
Let's Be Jubilant-Jubi-Jubi-Jubilant
  (George Beauchamp)
Little Dolly Daydream (Eugene Stratton)
Lost, Stolen Or Strayed (Ted Cowan

(parody), Millie Lindon, Sisters Lloyd)

Ma Curly-Headed Babby (Maggie Teyte)

Matinée Hat, The

May Queen Victoria Reign (Vesta Tilley)

Midnight Son, The (Vesta Tilley)

Narragansett (On The Beach At) (Dan Daly)

One Touch Of Nature Makes The Whole World Kin (Marie Loftus, Helene Mora)

Our Lodger's Such A Nice Young Man (Vesta Victoria)

Say Au Revoir But Not Goodbye (John McCormack, Julie Mackey, James Norrie)

Shall I Be An Angel, Daddy? (George D'Albert)

She Is Far From The Land (*Frank Lambert*) (John McCormack)

She Is The Belle Of New York (Harry Davenport, Frank Lawton)

Sixty Years! (Amy Curzon)

Slight Mistake On The Part Of My Valet (George Robey)

Song Of The Thrush, The (Jenny Hill, Peggy Pryde)

Sons Of The Sea (Ian Colquhoun, Arthur Reece)

Success To Her Majesty, Long May She Reign (F. V. St Clair)

Take Back Your Gold (Emma Carus, Imogene Comer, Louis W. Pritzkow (Primrose & West Minstrels), Fred Salcombe)

To Celebrate The Diamond Jubilee (Bert Radford)

Vat Ze English Call Ze— (Marie Lloyd)

Victoria's Jubilee (Harry Hunter)

What Did She Know About Railways? (Marie Lloyd, Marie Lloyd jun.)

You 'Ave To 'Ave 'Em (Harry Randall)

You Can't Punch My Ticket Again

1898

Baby On The Shore, The (George Grossmith sen.)

Bathing (Marie Lloyd)

Battle Eve, The (Hubert Eisdell & Norman Allin)

Beefeater, The (Dan Leno)

Bid Me Goodbye For Ever (All In A Day) (Vesta Victoria)

Blue Bell (Anna Driver, Haydn Quartet, Hamilton Hill)

Boy Guessed Right, The (Ellaline Terriss)

Cake Walk, The (Eugene Stratton)

Charlie On The Mash (Florrie Forde)

Ciribiribin (Lucrezia Bori)

Come Down And Open The Door (Rosie Lloyd, Sisters Wood)

Cowardy Cowardy Custard (Herbert Campbell)

'E Dunno Where 'E Are (Gus Elen)

English Speaking Race Against The World, The (Charles Godfrey)

Everything In The Garden's Lovely (Marie Lloyd)

Fallen Star, A (Albert Chevalier, Bransby Williams)

Flag Of Liberty, The (Leo Dryden)

For Old Times' Sake (Florrie Forde, Al Jolson, Millie Lindon, Harry Taylor)

Four Suits Of Cards, The (Fred J. Barnes)

Good-Bye, Dolly Gray (Tom Costello, Harry Ellis (Primrose & Dockstader's Minstrels), Hamilton Hill, Harry MacDonough, Leo Stormont)

Hanging Of Danny Deever, The (David Bispham, Stewart Gardner)

Hard To Say! (Slade Murray)

He Calls Me His Own Grace Darling (Vesta Victoria)

He's Going There Every Night (Marie Loftus)

I 'Aven't Told 'Im (Alec Hurley)

I'll Marry Him (Mrs Kelly) (Dan Leno)

I'm Not Particular (George Beauchamp)

(In) The Subbubs (George Robey)

It Don't Go Well With Scroggs (Tom Costello)

John James Murphy (Lily Marney)

Let 'Em All Come (Harry Randall)

Lily Of Laguna, The (G. H. Elliott, Eugene Stratton)

Little Bit Off The Top, A (Harry Bedford)

Lot 99 (Rose Harvey)

Man Of The Wide Wide World, The (T. E. Dunville)

Mary Ann (Pat Feeney, Tom Leamore, Jack Pleasants)

My Wife's First Husband (Nat Clifford, Ernie Mayne)

Not What 'Ria Wanted (Louis Freear)

Onaway, Awake, Beloved! (Robert Radford, Evan Williams)

O Sole Mio (Enrico Caruso, Beniamino Gigli)

Our Stores Ltd (Dan Leno)

Percy From Pimlico (Tom Leamore)

Please Will You Hold The Baby, Sir? (Percy Beaufoi)

Rosary, The (Beniamino Gigli, Alma Gluck, John Harrison, John McCormack, Charles Santley)

Sheeny Coon, The (Tom Costello)

She's Too Good For Me! (Tom Costello)

Ship I Love, The (Tom Costello)

Ship Went Down, The (Harry Rickards)

Soldiers In The Park (George Baker, Ethel Haydon, Grace Palotta, Florence Smithson)

Tatcho (Harry Randall)

There Always Will Be Fairies (F. V. St Clair)

There They Are, The Two Of Them On Their Own (Marie Lloyd)

When You Were Sweet Sixteen (Hamilton Hill, Bonnie Thornton, Julius P. Witmark)

Who Threw The Overalls In Mistress Murphy's Chowder? (Annie Hart)

Why Did I Leave My Little Back Room In Bloomsbury? (Alf Chester)

1899

Absent-Minded Beggar, The (song) (John Coates, Ian Colquhoun, Ada Reeve)

Absent-Minded Beggar, The (recitation) (Billie Burke, Mrs Brown Potter, Mrs Tree)

At The Bottom Of The Deep Blue Sea (Peter Dawson)

Bird In A Gilded Cage, A (May A. Bell, Emma Carus, Florrie Forde, Marie Kendall, James Norrie)

Bobbing Up And Down Like This (Austin Rudd)

Bravo Dublin Fusiliers (Ireland's Reply) (Leo Dryden, Pat Rafferty, Marie Tyler)

Coon Drum-Major, The (Eugene Stratton)

Could You Be True To Eyes Of Blue? (Lilian Doreen, Lottie Gilson, Hamilton Hill, J. Van R. Wheeler)

Detective Camera(?) (Dan Leno)

Eleanore (John Coates, Peter Dawson, Ruby Helder)

Everybody Wondered How He Knew (Marie Lloyd)

Girly Girly (R. G. Knowles)

Good-bye, Tilly (Rose Harvey)

Hello! Ma Baby (Marguerite Cornille, Ida Emerson & Joe Howard, Millie Legarde, Julie Mackey)

Hulloa! Hulloa! Hulloa! (Marie Lloyd)

I'll Be Your Sweetheart or Bluebells (Lil Hawthorne, Marie Kendall)

I'm Going To Get Married Today (Maggie Duggan)

I've An Inkling (Ada Reeve)

I Want To Be A Lidy (Alma Jones, Louie Freear, Hilda Trevelyan)

I Want To Be A Military Man (Louis Bradfield)

John Bull's Letter Bag (Marie Le Blanc, Marie Loftus, F. V. St Clair)

Jones's Parlour Floor (The Leonards)

Lambeth Walk, The (*Rogers*) (Alec Hurley)

Love By One Who Knows (Harry Randall)

Martha Spanks The Grand Piano (Alma Jones, Louie Freear, Hilda Trevelyan)

Moonlight Blossoms (Vesta Tilley)

Mother Tongue (Tom Costello)

My Baby May (Lily Burnand)

My Little Octoroon (Eugene Stratton)

My Wild Irish Rose (Chauncey Olcott)

No Show Tonight (Herbert Campbell)

Of Course (Marie Lloyd)

Oh! How Rude! (George Robey)

On The Banks Of The Wabash (James Norrie, Billy Rice Minstrels)

On The Margate Boat (Herbert Darnley, Charles Foster, Lillie Langtry (2), Harry Taylor)

'Ow's This For A Start? (Alec Hurley)

Parted (*Tosti*) (Peter Dawson, Edgar Granville, Hubert Eisdell)

Picture No Artist Can Paint, A (Florrie Forde)

Seaside Girls (Vesta Tilley)

Shade Of The Palm, The (Sydney Barraclough, Melville Stewart)

She'd Never Been In Pantomime Before (Arthur Roberts)

She Glories In A Thing Like That (Ada Reeve)

Tell Me Pretty Maiden (*Florodora* Sextet)

That'll Never Do For Me (Vesta Victoria)

Through The Telephone (H. C. Barry, Ernest Shand)

Trafalgar Square (Charles Deane)

What Ho, She Bumps! (*Mills & Castling*) (Charles Bignell)

What Ho, She Bumps! (*Stern: C. Collins*) (J. W. Rickaby)

Whistling Bluecoat Boy, The (Constance Moxon)

Who'll Care For The Children? (Arthur Lennard, Arthur Reece)

1900

Baby's Name Is Kitchener, The (Charles Bignell)

Baden Powell Scout, The (Tom Leamore)

Bassoon, The (W. H. Berry)

Beautiful Garden Of Roses (Hubert Eisdell, John Harrison)

Boers Have Got My Daddy, The (Tom Costello, Charles Foster, Arthur Reece)

Bravo! CIVs (City Imperial Volunteers) (Charles Bignell)

Burlington Bertie (Vesta Tilley)

Dear Old 'Bobs' (Fred Lyne, Mohawk Minstrels)

Drink! (My One Who's Had Some) (Harry Randall)

Folkestone For The Day (Marie Lloyd)

Girl In The Khaki Dress, The (Marie Lloyd)

Goo-Goo Song, The (Fanny Wentworth)

Heroes Of The Transvaal War, The (Chummie La Mara)

Hilarity (sk.) (Fred Karno Company)

Huntsman, The (Dan Leno)

I Can't Tell Why I Love You But I Do (Emma Carus, Lil Hawthorne, Julie Mackey, Harry MacDonough, Clarice Vance)

I Must Have A Day Off For That (J. R. Rowley)

It's Nice To Have A Home Of Your Own (Harry Anderson)

I Wish I'd Bought Ducks (Wilkie Bard)

Killiecrankie (Harry Lauder)

Knock The Two Rooms Into One (Ethel
   Haydon)
Lunatic Bakers, The *or* Fun In A
   Bakehouse (sk.) (Joe Boganny & Co)
Ma Blushin' Rosie (Fay Templeton)
Mafekin' Night (Albert Chevalier)
Maisie (Is A Daisy) (Rosie Boote, Gertie
   Millar)
Mrs Carter (Gus Elen)
My London Country Lane (Alec
   Hurley)
My Next Door Neighbour's Garden
   (Herbert Darnley, Gus Elen)
Nirvana (Arthur Aldridge, Ben Davies,
   Edward Lloyd, John McCormack)
Oh, The Kharki! (Ernie Mayne)
Picking All The Best Ones Out (Dan
   Crawley)
Red And The White And The Blue, The
   (Marie Lloyd)
Right On My Doo-Dah (Harry
   Champion)
Since I Came To London Town (Armand
   'Ary, Letty Lind)
Sing Us One Of The Old Songs (Millie
   Lindon)
Smoke, Smoke, Smoke (Fumed In Oak)
   (Herbert Darnley)
Stiffy The Goalkeeper (Harry Weldon)
Sweet Little Rose Of Persia (Tom
   Leamore)
Tupenny Tube, The (Kate Carney)
War Correspondent At The Front, The
   (T. E. Dunville)
Wearers Of The Little Grey Cloak, The
   (Millie Lindon)
Welcome, CIVs (Vesta Tilley)
What Do You Think Of The Irish Now?
   (Pat Rafferty)
What-Ho! There's Hair! (George
   Beauchamp, Edwin Boyde, Tom
   Costello, Will Dalton, Charles
   Deane)
What Will The Neighbours Say? (Lily
   Marney)
Whoa! Back-Pedal (T. E. Dunville)

1901
'Ackney With The 'Ouses Took Away
   (Vesta Victoria)
Bonnie Hielan' Mary (Harry Lauder)
Buying A House (Dan Leno)
Captain Reginald D'Arcy Of The Guards
   (Hetty King)
Captivating Cora (Gertie Millar)
Cheer Up, Buller! (F. V. St Clair, Harriett
   Vernon)
Coronation Day (Charles Bignell)
Early Birds (sk.) (Billy Reeves & Fred
   Karno Company)
Ev'rybody's Awfully Good To Me!
   (George Grossmith jun.)
Feminine Moods And Tenses (Marie
   Lloyd)
Girls From Bryant's And May, The (Kate
   Carney, Bella Lloyd)
Hello Central! Give Me Heaven (Byron
   G. Harlan, J. Aldrich Libbey, Baby
   Lund)
Honeysuckle And The Bee (Maud
   Courtney, Clifford Essex, Lulu Glaser,
   Ellaline Terriss)
I Love You Truly (Jessie Bartlett
   Davis)
I've Brought The Coal (J. W.
   Rickaby)
I Want Yer Ma Honey (Bert Gilbert,
   Yvette Guilbert, Alma Jones, Ellaline
   Terriss)
Jail Birds (sk.) (Fred Karno Company)
Just A-Wearyin' For You (Jessie Bartlett
   Davis)
Keep Off The Grass (Gertie Millar)
Last Of The Dandies, The (*Barnes:
   Collins*) (Lawrence Barclay(?), George
   Gray)
Leave A Little Bit For Your Tutor (Harry
   Freeman)
'Liza Johnson (Kate Carney)
Maid And The Monk, The (Ida René)
Mighty Lak' A Rose (Ada Crossley)
Millie (From Piccadilly)! (Marie
   Lloyd)

My 'Arry And Me (Kittee Rayburn)

My Flo From Pimlico (Paul Knox, Maude Mortimer)

Nice Quiet Day, A (A Postman's Holiday) (Gus Elen)

Oh, Flo! (Why Do You Go?) (Harry Dacre, Harry Taylor)

Oh! Jack, You Are A Handy Man (Katie Lawrence)

Old Dicky Bird (George Lashwood)

Our Threepenny Hop (Kate Carney)

Skylark! Skylark! (Arthur Lennard)

So I'll Never Ride Again (Frank Coyne)

Sweet Nell Of Old Drury (Bessie Bonehill)

Telegraph Boy (T. E. Dunville)

Tobermory (Harry Lauder)

Trottin' To The Fair (Plunkett Greene, Charles Santley)

Twiddley Bits, The (Alma Jones, Louie Freear, Hilda Trevelyan)

When I Marry Amelia (Henry Lytton, Fred Wright jun.)

You'll Be With Me All The While (Julie Mackey)

Young Man Who Worked At The Milk Shop (Marie Kendall)

1902

All Through A Gee-Gee-Gee (J. W. Ellison)

'Arry, 'Arry, 'Arry (Alec Hurley)

Because (Dalton Baker, Thorpe Bates, Enrico Caruso, John Harrison, John McCormack, Ernest Pike, Denham Price, Maggie Teyte)

Bella Was A Barmaid

Bill Bailey, Won't You Please Come Home? (Carroll Johnson, Victoria Monks, Fanny St Clair)

Bond Street Tea-Walk, The (Marie Lloyd)

Boys Of The Chelsea School (George Leyton)

Can London Do Without Me? (Tom E. Hughes)

Coronation Walk, The (Charles Austin)

Come Down Ma Evenin' Star (Lillian Russell)

Do They Do Those Things In London? (Marie Lloyd)

Down Where The Wurzburger Flows (*see* Riding On Top Of The Car, 1905) (Nora Bayes, Arthur Collins)

Electric Railway, The (Walter Munroe)

English Rose, The (Fanny Robina)

Girl I Want To M.A.R.R.Y., The (James Norrie)

Give Me A Ticket To Heaven (Denham Harrison, Herbert Payne)

Glow-Worm, The (Mills Brothers, May Naudain, Ellaline Terriss)

His Majesty's Guests (sk.) (Fred Kitchen & Fred Karno Company)

I Couldn't Exert Myself (George Robey)

If The Missus Wants To Go (Let Her Drown) (Phil Ray)

If You Can't Do Any Good Don't Do Any Harm (Kate Carney)

I Live In Trafalgar Square (Morny Cash)

I May Be Crazy But I Love You (Eugene Stratton)

In The Good Old Summertime (Julie Mackey, Blanche Ring, Stewart & Gillen)

It Didn't Come Off After All (Marie Lloyd)

It's All Right In The Summertime (Vesta Victoria)

Just Like The Ivy (I'll Cling To You) (Marie Kendall)

Kashmiri Song (Clara Butt, Peter Dawson, Ivor Foster, John McCormack)

Land Of Hope And Glory (Clara Butt)

Last Of The Dandies, The (*Harrington: Le Brunn*) (Millie Hylton)

Let Go Eliza (Frank Seeley)

Lighthouse Keeper, The (T. E. Dunville)

Linden Lea (John Coates, Louise Kirkby
    Lunn)
Man—By One Who Loathes 'Em (Harry
    Randall)
Miller's Daughter, The (*Rubens*)
    (Florence De Vere, Hilda Moody)
My Own Little Girl (Hayden Coffin)
Oh! The Pallis! (Arthur Rigby)
On A Sunday Afternoon (Leonard Barry,
    Florrie Forde, J. Aldrich Libbey, Baby
    Lund, Julie Mackey)
One Of The Shabby Genteel (Harry
    Bedford)
On The Day King Edward Gets His
    Crown On (Ben Albert, Harry Pleon)
O Peaceful England (Louise Kirkby
    Lunn, Henry A. Lytton, Kennerley
    Rumford)
Panama Hat, The
Pansy Faces (Irene Bentley, Leila
    McIntyre, Ellaline Terriss)
Patchwork Garden, The (Walter
    Passmore & Florence Lloyd, Paul
    Mill, Seymour Hicks)
Prehistoric Man (George Robey)
Rake's Progress, The (Ida Rene)
Ring Down The Curtain, I Can't Sing
    Tonight (J. K. Emmett, Herbert
    Payne)
Road To Ruin, The (sk.) (George Gray)
Signs (T. E. Dunville)
Sweethearts Still (James Merrylees,
    Vesta Tilley)
That Old Rocking Chair (Millie Lindon)
Under The Bamboo Tree (Marie
    Cahill)
Under The Deodar (Aileen D'Orme,
    Evie Greene, Maggie May)
Varmer Giles (George Bastow)
Walking Home With Angeline (Eily
    Helene)
Wedding March!, The (The Coster's
    Wedding) (Marie Lloyd, Marie Lloyd
    jun.)
What Is The Use Of Loving A Girl If

The Girl Don't Love You? (Sable
    Fern)
Why Can't It Always Be Christmas?
    (Julie Mackey)
Why Do The British Love Their King?
    (Medley Barrett)
W.O.M.A.N. (George Lashwood)
Yeomen Of England, The (Henry A.
    Lytton, Albert Pearce, Kennerley
    Rumford)
You Ask Me Why I Love You (Julie
    Mackey)

1903
All Through Riding On A Motor (Vesta
    Victoria)
Anona (Florrie Forde, Maidie Scott)
Are We To Part Like This? (Kate
    Carney)
Bedelia (Emma Carus, George Gros-
    smith jun., Moses Gumble, Lloyd
    Morgan, Blanche Ring)
Buying A Gun (sk.) (G. P. Huntley)
Camlachie Scout, The (Harry Lauder)
Down At The Old Bull And Bush (orig.
    Under The Anheuser Bush) (Florrie
    Forde)
Fighting Parson, The (sk.) (George
    Gray)
Fiscal Showman, The (Will Raynor)
Gold! Gold! Gold! (*Medley Barrett*)
    (Harry Clifford)
Ida, Sweet As Apple Cider (Eddie
    Leonard)
Inverary Mary (Nelson Jackson)
Is Your Mother In, Molly Malone?
    (Walter Munroe)
Little Yellow-Bird (Florence De Vere,
    Minnie Jeffs, Ellaline Terriss)
Looking For A Needle In A Haystack
    (Louis Bradfield, G. P. Huntley)
Mamie, I've A Little Canoe (Billie
    Burke, Edna May)
Midnight Son's Farewell, The (Vesta
    Tilley)

Mother O' Mine (Hayden Coffin, Ben Davies, John McCormack)

Mumps The Memory Man (T. E. Dunville)

My Cosey Corner Girl (Agnes Fraser & Henry Lytton, Edna May & George Grossmith jun., Harry MacDonough)

My Cricket Girl (Sable Fern)

Navajo a.k.a. Navaho (Peter Dawson, Louie Pounds, Ellaline Terriss)

Nevermore (Dan Leno)

Oh! The Black List (Tom Costello, Ella Dean, Charles Gardener, George Robey, J. W. Rowley, Ryder Slone, Mark Sheridan, Harry Tate)

Oh! The Coronation (Millie Hylton)

Old Man's Darling, An (*Murray & Everard*) (Vesta Victoria)

O, O, Capital O (Wilkie Bard)

Preacher And The Bear, The (Arthur Collins, Albert Whelan)

Seaside Girl, The

Seaside Holiday At Home, A (Herbert Campbell)

She'd Never Had A Lesson In Her Life (Marie Lloyd)

She Was Such A Nice Young Girl (George Bastow)

Something On His Mind (Marie Lloyd)

Sweet Adeline (*see* You're The Flower Of My Heart)

That Accounts For It (Marie Lloyd)

That's How The Little Girl Got On (Marie Lloyd)

Though All Your Friends May Leave You (Kate Carney)

(When We Were) Two Little Boys

You Do Soon Change Your Mind (Harry Ford)

You Needn't Wink—I Know (Marie Lloyd)

You're The Flower Of My Heart (Sweet Adeline) (orig. Down Home In Old New England) (George Donaldson (Symphony

Quartet), Hayden Quartet, William R. Moore (Haverly's Minstrels), Peerless Quartet, Quaker City Four, Leo Stormont)

1904

All The Little Ducks Went Quack! Quack! Quack! (Mark Sheridan)

And The Leaves Began To Fall (Marie Lloyd)

Boarding House, The (Harry Randall)

Come, Come, Caroline (Arthur Roberts)

Coster's Christening, The (Marie Lloyd)

Farewell My Little Yo-San! (Tom Costello)

Fiscal Joe (Leo Dryden)

Give My Regards To Broadway (George M. Cohan, Billy Murray)

Goodbye, My Lady Love (Ida Emerson & Joe Howard, Blanche Ring)

He's Been A Long Time Gorn (Stewart Morton)

Home-Made Motor Car, The (Medley Barrett)

I Can't Take My Eyes Off You (Constance Windom)

I Don't Seem To Want You When You're With Me (Margaret Cooper)

If I Had A Girl As Nice As You (Herbert Payne, Ernest Pike)

If You Want To Have A Row Wait Till The Sun Shines (Victoria Monks)

I Like You In Velvet (Maurice Farkoa)

I'm Going To Sing A Song (Sam Mayo)

Instinct (James Fawn)

In The Dingle Dongle Dell (Margaret Cooper)

It's A Braw Bricht Moonlicht Nicht (W. F. Frame)

It's The Poor That Help The Poor (Millie Denham, Florrie Gallimore)

Let Me Call You Daddy

Love's Gramophone (Queenie Leighton)

Mansion Of Aching Hearts, The (Florrie
  Forde)
Mattinata ('Tis The Day) (Enrico Caruso,
  John Coates, Ben Davies, Beniamino
  Gigli, John Harrison)
Mayor Of Mudcumdyke, The (George
  Robey)
Meet Me In St Louis, Louis (Nora
  Bayes, Lew Dockstader, Lottie Gilson,
  Ethel Levey, Billy Murray, Bonnie
  Thornton, Gus Williams)
Mumming Birds (orig. 'Twice Nightly')
  (Billy Reeves & Fred Karno
  Company)
My Ain Folk (Clara Butt, Maggie Teyte,
  Edna Thornton)
Naughty! Naughty! Naughty! (Marie
  Lloyd)
Oh, Dry Those Tears (Kate Cove, Edna
  Thornton)
Old Superb, The (Dalton Baker, Peter
  Dawson, Plunkett Greene, Stewart
  Gardner)
Philosophy (anon: Emmell) (Margaret
  Cooper, Maurice Farkoa)
Saftest O' The Family, The (Harry
  Lauder)
She Cost Me Seven-and-Sixpence
  (Wilkie Bard, Sam Mayo)
Stop Yer Tickling, Jock! (Harry Lauder,
  Jay Laurier)
Swimming Master, The (Dan Leno)
Swing Song (Jean Perier & Mariette
  Sully, Laurence Rea & Ruth Vincent)
Tale Of The Skirt, The (Marie Lloyd)
That's Him! (Harry Freeman)
Trifling Occurrences (Frank Lynne)
Trot Here And There (Jean Perier &
  Mariette Sully, Laurence Rea & Ruth
  Vincent)
Trumpeter, The (Arthur Aldridge, Peter
  Dawson, Ivor Foster, Plunkett Greene,
  Charles Knowles, Watkin Mills,
  Robert Radford)
When A Fellow Is Twenty-One (Hetty
  King)

Where's The Count? (Arthur Roberts)
Yankee Doodle Boy, The (George M.
  Cohan, Billy Murray)

1905
All That I Ask Of You Is Love (Frank
  Morrell, Frank Mullane, Violet
  Romaine, Bessie Wynn)
All Thro' Sticking To A Soldier(?) (Louie
  Freear, Ada Lundberg)
'Arf A Pint Of Ale (Gus Elen)
Central, Give Me Back My Dime (Joe
  Howard)
Cowslip And The Cow, The (Wilkie
  Bard)
Drake's Drum (Peter Dawson)
Everybody Works But Father (Arthur
  Collins, Lew Dockstader & His Min-
  strels, Maidie Scott)
Fou The Noo (Harry Lauder)
Give My Regards To Leicester Square
  (Victoria Monks)
Glorious Devon (Dalton Baker, Peter
  Dawson, R. Watkin Mills, Robert
  Radford, H. Lane Wilson)
How'D'Ya Like To Spoon With Me?
  (Georgia Caine & Victor Morley,
  Millie Legarde)
If I Were On The Stage (Kiss Me Again)
  (Fritzi Scheff)
If The Man In The Moon Were A Coon
  (G. H. Elliott)
If The World Were Ruled By Girls (Whit
  Cunliffe, Ada Reeve)
If Those Lips Could Only Speak (Will
  Godwin)
I'll Meet You At The Bodega (Maude
  Mortimer)
I Love A Lassie (Harry Lauder)
In The Shade Of The Old Apple Tree
  (Nora Bayes, Lillian Rosewood)
Kiss Me Again see If I Were On The
  Stage
Mary's A Grand Old Name (George
  M. Cohan, Lil Hawthorne, Fay
  Templeton)

My Gal Sal (Louise Dresser)

Next Horse I Ride On, The (Vesta Victoria)

Nobody Knows And Nobody Cares (Michael Nolan, Ernest Shand, Little Thomas)

Nurse Procter (T. E. Dunville)

Old Tin Can, The (Sam Mayo)

Put A Little Bit Away For A Rainy Day (Carlotta Levey, Ella Retford)

Red Wing (Harry MacDonough, Herbert Payne)

Riding On Top Of The Car (melody: Down Where The Wurzburger Flows, 1902) (George Lashwood)

Seaweed (Fred Earle)

She Is Ma Daisy (Harry Lauder)

Somebody's Sweetheart I Want To Be (Lillian Russell)

Thora (Joseph Cheetham, Ivor Foster, Ruby Helder, John McCormack)

Wait Till The Sun Shines, Nellie (Winona Banks, Emma Carus, Gladys Fisher, Byron G. Harlan, Harry Talley)

Watchman! What Of The Night? (Ivor Foster & Herbert Cave, John Harrison & Robert Radford)

Will You Love Me In December (As You Do In May)? (Janet Allen, American Quartet, Ernest R. Ball, Norman Blair, Haydn Quartet)

You're A Thing Of The Past Old Dear (Marie Lloyd)

1906

All That Glitters Isn't Gold (*see* 1896) (Dora Lyric)

Are We Downhearted? No! (*Robins*) (Will Edwards, Paul Mill)

At A Minute To Seven Last Night (Sam Mayo)

Au Revoir, My Little Hyacinth (E. Sidney Davies, Phyllis Dare, Ada Reeve)

Billy Muggins (Charles R. Whittle)

Bird On Nellie's Hat, The (Janet Allen, Maidie Scott, Anona Winn)

Bombay (Victoria Monks)

By The Side Of The Zuyder Zee (Maudi Darrell, Happy Fanny Fields, May Moore Duprez, Albert Pearce, Annie Purcell)

Chinaman, The (Sam Mayo)

Customs Of The Country (Marie Lloyd)

Down At The Garden Gate (Will Evans)

Federation Day (Founding song of the Variety Artistes' Federation)

Galloping Major, The (George Bastow)

Grandmamma (Gertie Millar)

How Dare You (Harry Ford)

If At First You Don't Succeed (Dora Lyric)

I Just Can't Make My Eyes Behave (Anna Held, Ada Jones)

I'm Afraid To Come Home In The Dark (May A. Bell, Della Fox, May Irwin, Hetty King, Elizabeth Murray, Ella Retford, Maidie Scott, May Vokes)

It's A Different Girl Again! (Whit Cunliffe)

It's Part Of A Policeman's Duty (Vesta Tilley)

I've Never Lost My Last Train Yet (Marie Lloyd)

I Wonder If The Girl I'm Thinking Of Is Thinking Of Me? (Maude Mortimer)

Jolly Good Luck To The Girl Who Loves A Soldier (Vesta Tilley)

Joshu-ah (Clarice Mayne)

Leader Of The Labour Party, The (George Grossmith jun.)

Mary Llewellyn (Lovedon Plass)

Merry Vagabonds, The (Foster Richardson & Ernest Pike)

My Castle In Spain (Lil Hawthorne)

My Old Pal Joe (Tom Costello)

Oh, Amelia (Vesta Victoria)

Oh, Mr Chamberlain! (Seymour Hicks)

Oh! Who Says So? (Charles Penrose)

Piano Tuner, The (George Robey)

Poor John (Ada Jones, Vesta Victoria)

Pushing Young Man, The (Sam Mayo)
Rosalie (George Grossmith jun.)
She's Proud And She's Beautiful (George Bastow)
Some Things Are Better Left Unsaid (R. G. Knowles)
Taxi Meter Car, The (Billy Williams)
That's The Reason Noo I Wear A Kilt (Harry Lauder)
Tiddley-Om-Pom (Marie Lloyd)
Too-Ra-Li-Oo-Ra-Li (Ernest Shand)
Waiting At The Church (Vesta Victoria)
Wait Till The Work Comes Round (Gus Elen)
Waltz Me Around Again, Willie (Margaret Cooper, Florrie Forde, George Grossmith jun., Blanche Ring)
We Parted On The Shore (Harry Lauder)
What A Mouth! (Harry Champion)
When Father Laid The Carpet On The Stairs (Nelson Jackson, Burt Shepard)
When She Walks (Harry Ford)
When There Isn't A Girl About (Arthur Reece, Billy Williams)
Wire In, My Lads! (George Bastow)

1907
And The Parrot Said (Daisy Jerome, Marie Lloyd)
Bailiffs, The (sk.) (Fred Kitchen)
Don't Grumble At Women Any More (Marie Lloyd)
Give Me A Cosy Parlour (Victoria Monks)
Has Anyone Seen A German Band? (Florrie Forde, Ella Retford)
Hobnailed Boots That Farver Wore, The (Billy Williams)
I Ain't Nobody In Perticuler (Alec Hurley)
I Can't Forget 'Auld Reekie' (Jessie Preston)
In The Twi-Twi-Twilight (George Lashwood)

It's No Use You Calling 'Hannah!' (Kate Carney)
I Was Shaving Myself At The Time (Bernard Russell)
John, Go And Put Your Trousers On (Billy Williams)
Johnny Morgan's Sister (Maidie Scott)
Kiss The Girl If You're Going To (Marie Kendall)
Merry Widow Waltz (Vienna 1905) (Joe Coyne & (a) Lily Elsie, (b) Constance Drever, Mizzi Gunther & Louis Treumann)
My Wife's Sister's Cat (Harry Champion)
One Of The Boys (George Formby)
On The Road To Mandalay (Peter Dawson, Lawrence Tibbett)
Parson Grey VC (sk.) (George Gray)
Pink Petty From Peter, A (Grace Leigh)
Put Me Amongst The Girls (Charles R. Whittle)
Sailing In My Balloon (Florrie Forde)
She's A Lassie From Lancashire (Florrie Forde, Ella Retford)
She's Been A Good Wife To Me (Alec Hurley)
Since I Became A Married Man (G. W. Hunter)
Sussex By The Sea
Swing Me Higher, Obadiah (Florrie Forde, Lily Lena, Mabel Thorne)
Tally-Ho (Sam Mayo)
Teddy Bears' Picnic, The (see 1930)
That Funny Little Bobtail Coat (Harry Champion)
There Are Fairies At The Bottom Of Our Garden (Dora Labette, Beatrice Lillie)
Tickle Me, Timothy, Do! (Billy Williams)
Two Little Sausages (Gertie Millar & Edmund Payne)
Vilia (Vienna 1905) (Constance Drever, Lily Elsie, Mizzi Gunther)
Waltz Song (For Tonight) (Tom Jones) (Ruth Vincent)

We All Came In The World With Nothing (Tennyson & Wallis, Billy Williams)

Won't You Come Down And Open Dat Door? (Victoria Monks)

You Splash Me And I'll Splash You (Alice Lloyd)

1908

Ayesha, My Sweet Egyptian (Evelyn Taylor)

Baden Powell's Scout (Medley Barrett)

Bang Went The Chance Of A Lifetime (George Robey)

Call Round Any Old Time (Victoria Monks)

Directoire Girl, The (Marie Lloyd)

Do You Want Any Coal? (Ella Shields)

Esau, Take Me On The Seesaw (Madge Temple)

From Poverty Street To Golden Square (Kate Carney, Florrie Forde)

Georgie Took Me Walking In The Park (Clarice Mayne)

Girls, Study Your Cookery Book (Florrie Forde)

Give Her A Vote, Papa

Good Morning, Mr Postman! (Kate Carney/Pattinson)

I Can't Help Loving A Girl Like You (Fred Godfrey)

If I Should Plant A Tiny Seed Of Love (Dora Lyric, Clarice Mayne, Maude Mortimer)

I Hear You Calling Me (Lucrezia Bori, John Coates, Charles W. Harrison, John McCormack)

I Love You Best Of All (George Ridgewell)

Is Anybody Looking For A Widow? (Vesta Victoria)

I Want To Go To Idaho (G. H. Elliott)

I Wish I Had A Girl (Al Jolson)

John! John! John! (Time's Going On) (Fred Earle)

John Willie, Come On (George Formby)

Let's All Go Down The Strand (Charles R. Whittle)

Mary From Tipperary (Ivy St Helier)

Meet Me Jenny When The Sun Goes Down (Alice Lloyd)

Mother Hasn't Spoken To Father Since (Byron G. Harlan, Vesta Victoria)

My Brudda, Sylvest' (Mabel Hite & Mike Donlin, Sam Stern)

My Girl's A Yorkshire Girl (Florrie Gallimore, Charles R. Whittle)

My Hero (New York 1909, London 1910) (Constance Drever, Olga Petrova)

My Little Deitcher Girl (Wilkie Bard)

My Moon (Margaret Cooper, Muriel George)

Now I Have To Call Him Father (Vesta Victoria)

Oh! Oh! Antonio (Edith Fink, Florrie Forde)

Oh, The Daylight Bill (R. G. Knowles)

Old-Age Pension, The (Harry Bedford)

Parker P.C. (Charles Austin)

Put Me Upon An Island Where The Girls Are Few (Wilkie Bard, Will Letters)

Rosie Had A Very Rosy Time (Marie Lloyd)

Rosie's Young Man (Eileen Douglas)

Rum-Tiddley-Um-Tum-Tay (Marie Lloyd)

She Sells Sea Shells (Wilkie Bard, Sam Mayo)

Shine On Harvest Moon (Nora Bayes & Jack Norworth, Olive Lenton)

Sue, Sue, Sue (G. H. Elliott)

Suffragette, The (Will Evans)

Take Me Out To The Ball Game (Nora Bayes, Henry Fink, Billy Murray)

Waiata Poi (Peter Dawson, Kennerley Rumford)

We Don't Want Any More Daylight (Billy Williams)

Yip-I-Addy-I-Ay (George Grossmith jun., Blanche Ring)

1909

All Down Piccadilly (Dan Rolyat)

All The Nice Girls Love A Sailor (Ship Ahoy!) (Hetty King)

Arcady Is Ever Young (Florence Smithson)

Archibald—Certainly Not! (George Robey)

Black Sheep Of The Family, The (Fred Barnes)

Boiled Beef And Carrots (Harry Champion)

By The Light Of The Silvery Moon (Al Jolson, Lillian Lorraine, Georgie Price, Ella Retford)

Casey Jones (The Two Bobs, Billy Murray, Albert Whelan)

Charming Weather (Phyllis Dare & Harry Welchman)

Come And Put Your Arms Around Me, Georgie Do (Jessie Templeton)

Corsican Maid, The (Evie Greene)

Discharged From The Force (Charles Austin)

Eriskay Love Lilt, An (Margaret Kennedy & Marjory Kennedy Fraser, Louise Kirkby Lunn)

For Months And Months And Months (Jack Norworth, Jack Smiles)

For You Alone (Enrico Caruso)

Girl In The Clogs And Shawl, The (Daisy Dormer, Charles R. Whittle)

Half-Past Two (Phyllis Dare & Harry Welchman)

Has Anybody Here Seen Kelly? (Nora Bayes, Emma Carus, Florrie Forde, Charles R. Whittle)

Hello! There, Flanagan (Florrie Forde)

Hullo! Tu-Tu (Margaret Cooper)

I Can Say 'Truly Rural' (Wilkie Bard, Lily Morris, Herbert Rule)

I Can't Reach That Top Note (Wilkie Bard, Herbert Rule)

I Do Like To Be Beside The Seaside (Mark Sheridan)

If The Wind Had Only Blown The Other Way (Maidie Scott, Bessie Wynn)

I Like London (May Kinder)

I Like Your Old French Bonnet (Daisy Dormer)

I'm Going Away (Billy Merson)

I'm Looking For Mr Wright (Madge Temple)

I'm Waiting Here For Kate (Wilkie Bard)

It's A Pity To Waste The Cake (George Lashwood)

I Used To Sigh For The Silvery Moon (G. H. Elliott, Daisy Wood)

I've Got Rings On My Fingers (Blanche Ring, Ellaline Terriss)

I Wonder Who's Kissing Her Now (Ada Reeve, Harry Woodruff)

Jimmy The Fearless (Fred Karno Co)

Love, Goodbye (Lily Elsie)

Mary's Ticket (Florrie Forde)

Meet Me Tonight In Dreamland (Reine Davies, Ernest Pike)

Molly O'Morgan (Nora Emerald, Ella Retford, Charles R. Whittle)

Moonstruck (Gertie Millar)

My Boy's A Sailorman (Daisy Dormer)

My Motter (Alfred Lester)

My Wife's Gone To The Country (Arthur Collins, Byron G. Harlan, Mabel Hite, Phil Parsons)

Nora Malone (Call Me By Phone) (Hedges Brothers & Jacobson, Herbert Payne, Blanche Ring)

Oh, Bleriot! (Harry Bedford)

Oh, I Must Go Home Tonight (Billy Williams)

Pipes Of Pan, The (Florence Smithson)

Pretty Little Girl From Nowhere, The (Edith Fink, Florrie Forde, Ella Retford)

Put On Your Old Gray Bonnet (Dolly Connolly, Hayden Quartet)

Queen Of The Cannibal Isle (Gertie Gitana)

Sadie Salome, Go Home (Fanny Brice)

Ship Ahoy! (All The Nice Girls Love A Sailor) (Hetty King)

Spaniard That Blighted My Life, The (Billy Merson (solo), also Billy Merson & (*a*) Beatrice Allen, (*b*) Dorothy Minto, (*c*) Ida Valli)

Stonecracker John (Harry Dearth)

There Are Nice Girls Everywhere (Whit Cunliffe)

They Can't Get The Better Of Me (Will Bentley, Frank Wood)

Tiddle-y-pom (The Follies)

Wait For Your Old Age Pension (Will Fieldhouse)

When Father Papered The Parlour (Billy Williams)

Where My Caravan Has Rested (Hubert Eisdell, Kennerley Rumford)

Whiffenpoof Song, The (Rudy Vallee (1936 version), The Whiffenpoofs)

With My Little Wigger-Wagger In My Hand (Fred Earle)

Yiddle On Your Fiddle Play Some Rag-Time (Fanny Brice, Sam Stern)

1910

Ah! Sweet Mystery Of Life (Orville Harrold)

By The Sea (Ernest Shand, Mark Sheridan)

Captain Ginjah, O.T. (George Bastow)

Chinatown, My Chinatown (Gwendoline Brogden, Edwin Foy, Shirley Kellogg)

Come, Josephine, In My Flying Machine (Blanche Ring, Harry Tally)

Come To The Ball (Helen Trix, Gertie Millar)

Come With Me Down Regent Street (Daisy James, Winifred Ward)

Coster Rag (Alice Lloyd)

Dance Of The Grizzly Bear, The (Fanny Brice, Vernon & Irene Castle, Sophie Tucker)

Don't Give Me Diamonds, All I Want Is You (Gertie Gitana)

Don't Go Down In The Mine, Dad (Frank Boyce, J. H. Greener)

Down By The Old Mill Stream (*Taylor*) (Frank Morrell)

Drake Goes West (Ivor Foster, Robert Radford)

Emigrant Ship, The (George Leyton)

Every Little Movement Has A Meaning Of Its Own (*Cliffe: Moore*) (Marie Lloyd)

Every Little Movement Has A Meaning Of Its Own (*Harbach: Hoschna*) (Lina Abarbanell)

Fall In And Follow Me (Whit Cunliffe, Charles R. Whittle)

Flanagan (Florrie Forde)

Ginger, You're Balmy! (Harry Champion)

Has Anybody Seen My Tiddler? (Millie Payne)

Heaven Will Protect The Working Girl (Marie Dressler)

If The Managers Only Thought The Same As Mother (Maidie Scott)

I'm Henery The Eighth, I Am! (Harry Champion)

I'm On Agen With Monaghan (Maggie Cline)

I'm Shy, Mary Ellen, I'm Shy (Jack Pleasants, Jack Smiles)

In The Shadows (instrumental)

I Put On My Coat And Went Home (George Formby)

I Want To Sing In Opera (Wilkie Bard)

I Was Standing At The Corner Of The Street (George Formby, Harry Randall)

I Wonder If You Miss Me Sometimes(?) (Lily Morris, Ella Retford)

Kiss Me, My Honey (Hetty King, Lily Morris, Maidie Scott, Malcolm Scott)

Let Me Call You Sweetheart (Maude Galbraith, Peerless Quartet)

Let's Wait And See The Pictures (Tom
    Clarke, Arthur Lennard)
Lovey Joe (Elizabeth Brice, Fanny Brice)
Macushla (John McCormack, Chauncey
    Olcott)
Mother Machree (Ernest R. Ball,
    Charles W. Harrison, John
    McCormack, Will Oakland, Chauncey
    Olcott)
My Hero (Vienna 1908, New York 1909)
    (Constance Drever, Olga Petrova)
Nature's Made A Big Mistake (Gus Elen)
Naughty Marietta (Emma Trentini)
Nursie-Nursie (Clarice Mayne)
Oh, You Beautiful Doll (American
    Ragtime Octette, Ayer & Brown, Ida
    Barr, Gene Greene, Clarice Mayne,
    Billy Murray)
One Of The Deathless Army (A
    Territorial) (Little Tich)
Perfect Day, A (David Bispham, Alma
    Gluck)
Playing The Game In The West (George
    Formby)
Put On Your Tat-Ta (Clarice Mayne)
Put Your Arms Around Me Honey (Lina
    Abarbanell, Elizabeth Murray)
Silver Bell (Gertie Gitana)
Since Poor Father Joined The Territor-
    ials (Billy Williams)
Sing! Sing! Sing! (Damerell & Rutland)
Sister To Assist 'Er, A (sk.) (Fred Emney
    & Sydney Farebrother)
Smith, Jones, Robinson And Brown (Lily
    Morris, Ella Retford, Ella Shields,
    Daisy Wood)
Some Of These Days (Shirley Kellogg,
    Ethel Levey, Ella Retford, Sophie
    Tucker)
Somewhere The Sun Is Shining (Florrie
    Forde)
Steamboat Bill (Leighton Brothers)
That's Why The British Loved The King
    (Charles Coborn)
There's Something About A Soldier
    (*Harrington: Powell*) (Florrie Forde)

Until (Ivor Foster, Maggie Teyte)
Wee Deoch-An-Doris, A (Harry
    Lauder)
We Really Had A Most Delightful
    Evening (Ernest Shand)
What D'Ye Say, Molly Molloy? (Ella
    Retford?)
When I Take My Morning Promenade
    (Marie Lloyd)

1911
Agatha Green (Margaret Cooper)
Alexander's Rag-Time Band (The Two
    Bobs, Emma Carus, Arthur Collins,
    Byron G. Harlan, Al Jolson, Ethel
    Levey, Clarice Mayne, Billy Murray,
    Ellaline Terriss, Maud Tiffany)
Any Old Iron? (Harry Champion)
Art Is Calling For Me (I Want To Be A
    Prima Donna) (Louise Bliss)
Be My Little Baby Bumble Bee
    (Elizabeth Brice & Charles King,
    Ada Jones & Billy Murray, Elizabeth
    Spencer & Walter Van Blunt)
Billy (For When I Walk) (Ada Jones,
    Madge Temple, Beth Tate)
Brighton (*Rubens*) (Connie Ediss)
Come In And Cut Yourself A Piece Of
    Cake (Jack Pleasants)
Cover It Over Quick Jemima (Harry
    Champion)
Daddy Has A Sweetheart And Mother Is
    Her Name (Lillian Lorraine)
Don't Do It Again Matilda (Harry
    Champion)
Don't Sing The Chorus (Vesta Victoria)
Don't Stop My 'Arf A Pint O' Beer (Gus
    Elen)
Everybody's Doin' It Now (Ida Barr,
    Lydia Barry, Ida Crispi & Fred Farren,
    Ida Crispi & Robert Hale, Ethel
    Levey, Ruby Raymond, Maud Tiffany)
Father's Whiskers (Frank Wood)
Floral Dance, The (Peter Dawson)
Gaby Glide, The (Gaby Deslys & Harry
    Pilcer, The Three Rascals)

Green Eye Of The Little Yellow God,
The (Milton Hayes, Bransby
Williams)

Hello! Susie Green (G. H. Elliott, Albert
Whelan)

Here's To Love And Laughter (Violet
Essex)

Here We Are Again (*Godfrey &
Williams*) (Billy Williams)

Hitchy-Koo (American Ragtime Octette,
Lew Hearn & Bonita, The Three
Rascals)

I Don't Care What Becomes Of Me
(*Mills: Scott*) (Fred Earle (?), Sam
Mayo)

I Like Your Apron And Your Bonnet
(Mabel Green, Ella Retford)

I'm Always Doing Something Silly (Jay
Laurier)

I'm Twenty-One Today (Stanley Kirkby,
Jack Pleasants, Albert Whelan)

I Want A Girl Just Like The Girl Who
Married Dear Old Dad (American
Quartet, Al Jolson, Dorothy Ward)

I Want To Be In Dixie (American
Ragtime Octette, Arthur Collins,
Byron G. Harlan, May Irwin, Jen
Latona, Ella Retford, Willie Solar,
The Three Rascals)

Jones Of The Lancers (My Word!)
(Leslie Henson)

Let's Have Free Trade Amongst The
Girls (Whit Cunliffe)

Little Grey Home In The West (Thorpe
Bates, Peter Dawson, Alma Gluck,
Charles W. Harrison, John
McCormack, Maggie Teyte)

Mary Ann She's After Me (George
Bastow)

My Beautiful Lady (Hazel Dawn)

My Boating Girl, (Floating With) (Fred
Barnes)

Photo Of The Girl I Left Behind (Billy
Merson)

Pretty Creaure, The (Louise Kirkby
Lunn)

Property Man, The (Alfred Lester)

Roamin' In The Gloamin' (Harry
Lauder)

Somewhere A Voice Is Calling (Frances
Alda, John Coates, Peter Dawson,
Hubert Eisdell, John McCormack)

Sorrento

Take A Look At Me Now (Ella Retford,
Beth Tate)

Ta-Ra-Ra Boom-De-Ré (also see Ta-
Ra-Ra-Boom-De-Ay, 1891) (José
Collins)

Temple Bell (Florence Smithson)

There'll Come A Time (Hedges Brothers
& Jacobson)

They Always Pick On Me (Ada Jones)

They're All Single By The Seaside
(Florrie Forde, Ella Retford)

Till The Sands Of The Desert Grow
Cold (Ernest R. Ball, Peter
Dawson)

We All Go The Same Way Home
(Charles R. Whittle)

What's All This Fuss About Fingerprints?
(Harry Randall)

When Our Good King George Is
Crowned

When You Live Opposite To Me (Daisy
Dormer)

Where's The Good? (Harry Ford)

Why Do They Always Pick On Me? (*see*
They Always Pick On Me)

With This Hat On (Tom Woottwell)

You Can Do A Lot Of Things At The
Seaside That You Can't Do In Town
(Mark Sheridan, Vesta Victoria)

1912

And Very Nice Too (George Robey)

Be British! (Titanic disaster) (George
D'Albert, Paul Pelham, Stanley
Kirkby)

Caretaker, The (George Robey)

Coster Girl In Paris, The (Marie Lloyd)

Danny Boy (Londonderry Air) (John
McCormack, Edna Thornton)

Does This Shop Stock Shot Socks With
Spots? (George Graves, Archie Pitt)
Fishing (sk.) (Harry Tate)
Frankie And Johnny (Frank Crumit,
Leighton Brothers, Mama Lou)
Golfing (sk.) (Harry Tate)
Hail Caledonia! (Peter Hope, Alma
Jones)
How Do You Do, Miss Ragtime? (Ethel
Levey)
I Do Like You Susie In Your Pretty Little
Sunday Clothes (Daisy Dormer)
I Love The Moon (Phyllis Dare, Maggie
Teyte)
Insurance Act, The (Yorke & Adams)
It's A Bit Of A Ruin That Cromwell
Knocked About A Bit (Marie Lloyd,
Marie Lloyd jun.)
It's A Long, Long Way To Tipperary
(Florrie Forde, Jack Judge, Maude
Mortimer)
Kangaroo Hop, The (Billy Williams)
Kitty, The Telephone Girl (Jack
Norworth)
Little Damozel, The (Lucrezia Bori,
Evangeline Florence)
Look What Percy's Picked Up In The
Park (Dolly Harmer, Vesta Victoria)
Moonlight Bay, (On) (Dolly Connolly,
Herbert Payne, Esta Stella)
Motoring(?) (sk.) (Harry Tate)
My Heart Is With You Tonight (Nellie
Wigley)
My Melancholy Baby (Tommy Lyman)
Piccadilly Trot (Marie Lloyd)
Put On Your Slippers (Marie Lloyd)
Ragtime Cowboy Joe (Daisy Dormer,
Gene Greene, Hedges Brothers &
Jacobson, The Three Rascals)
Row, Row, Row (Bonita, Daisy Jerome,
Shirley Kellogg, Lillian Lorraine)
Same As His Faither Did Before Him
(Harry Lauder)
See What Percy's Picked Up In The
Park (see Look What Percy's Picked,
etc.)

She Pushed Me Into The Parlour (Ernie
Mayne)
They All Walk The Wibbly Wobbly Walk
(Mark Sheridan)
Three Trees, The (Tom McNaughton,
Mark Sheridan, Albert Whelan)
To Cheer Him Up And Help Him On
His Way (Jack Pleasants)
Twiddly Wink (Marie Lloyd)
Vot A Game! Oi! Oi! (Arthur Aiston)
Waiting For The Robert E. Lee
(American Ragtime Octette, Peter
Barnard, The Two Bobs, Fanny Brice,
Dolly Connolly, Al Jolson)
Wakes Week (sk.) (Fred Karno
Company)
Watching The Trains Go Out (Jack
Pleasants)
When Irish Eyes Are Smiling (Ernest R.
Ball, Nora Delaney, John McCormack,
Chauncey Olcott)
When The Midnight Choo-Choo Leaves
For Alabam' (The Three Rascals)
White Dove, The (Robert Michaelis,
Lawrence Tibbett)
Who Were You With Last Night? (Mark
Sheridan)
Why Did You Make Me Care? (Manuel
Romain)
Why Do The Men Run After Me?
('Dame' Dan Crawley)
You Made Me Love You (Al Jolson,
Grace La Rue, Clarice Mayne, Ella
Retford, Florence Smithson, Willie
Solar, Lee White)

1913

All The Girls Are Lovely By The Seaside
(Harry Carlton, Harry Fragson, Ella
Retford)
Are You From Dixie? ('Cos I'm From
Dixie Too) (The Two Rascals &
Jacobson)
Ballin' The Jack (Donald Brian, Fanny
Brice, Basil Hallam & Elsie Janis,
Lillian Lorraine)

Colonel Bogey March (sundry military, brass and novelty bands)

Come On, My Baby! (Shirley Kellogg & George Robey)

Curse Of An Aching Heart, The (Joe Burns, Emma Carus, Will Oakland, Manuel Romain)

Friend O' Mine (Norman Williams)

He'd Have To Get Under (Gerald Kirby, The Three Rascals)

Hello! Hello! Who's Your Lady Friend? (Harry Fragson)

Hold Your Hand Out, Naughty Boy! (Florrie Forde, Ella Retford, Ted Yorke)

How Are Yer? (Florrie Forde)

If I Could Only Make You Care (Zigeuner Quartet)

I'll Show You Around Gay Paree (Vesta Tilley)

In The Valley Of Golden Dreams (Florrie Forde, Gertie Gitana)

I Parted My Hair In The Middle (George Formby)

I Shall Get In Such A Row When Martha Knows (Jack Pleasants)

It's Nice To Get Up In The Morning (Harry Lauder)

I've Got My Eye On You (Clarice Mayne)

I Wonder What It Feels Like To Be Poor (Tom E. Hughes)

Jere-Jeremiah (Florrie Forde, Clarice Mayne)

Love! Love!! Love!!! (Ernie Mayne)

Memphis Blues, The (W. C. Handy)

Mickey Rooney's Ragtime Band (Shaun Glenville)

Mister Bear (Norah Blaney, Margaret Cooper)

My Actor Man (Marie Lloyd)

My Otaheitee Lady (Ada Reeve)

Never Mind (Gertie Gitana, Eric Marshall, Clarice Mayne)

Now Is The Hour (Haere Ra)

P.C. Forty Nine (J. W. Rickaby)

Peg O' My Heart (José Collins, Evie Greene, Laurette Taylor)

Popsy Wopsy (Daisy Dormer, Molly McCarthy, Ella Retford, Lilian Shelley)

Roseway (Shirley Kellogg)

Shipmates O'Mine (Peter Dawson, Ivor Foster, Robert Radford, Norman Williams)

Sister Susie's Sewing Shirts For Soldiers (Harry Cove, Al Jolson, Jack Norworth)

Snookey Ookums (Harry Carlton)

Sophy (T. C. Sterndale Bennett)

Sunshine Of Your Smile, The (Norman Blair, John Coates, Olga & Elgar & Eli Hudson, John McCormack)

Take Me In A Taxi, Joe (May Moore Duprez, Vesta Victoria)

Ten Little Fingers, Ten Little Toes (Kirkby & Hudson)

That Old Sweetheart Of Mine (The Three Rascals)

That Rag-Time Suffragette (Ethel Levey)

That's An Irish Lullaby (Too-Ra-Loo-Ra-Loo-Ral) (Chauncey Olcott)

There's A Long, Long Trail A-Winding (Ernest Pike, Ada Reeve)

They Built Piccadilly For Me (Silk Hat Tony) (J. W. Rickaby)

'Tis A Story That Shall Live For Ever (Scott Expedition) (Stanley Kirkby)

Trail Of The Lonesome Pine, The (The Two Bobs, Edna Brown & James Harrison, Hedges Brothers & Jacobson, Laurel & Hardy, Molly McCarthy)

Up From Somerset (Peter Dawson, Ivor Foster, Charles Tree)

Wedding Glide, The (Shirley Kellogg, The Three Rascals)

When You're All Dressed Up And No Place To Go (Raymond Hitchcock)

While I Was Licking My Stamp (Harry Champion)

You're My Baby (Harry Cove, Lew
Hearn & Bonita)

1914

Aba Daba Honeymoon (The Two
Bobs, Jack Lee & Billy Delaney,
Elizabeth Price & Charles King,
Ruby Raymond & Fred Heider,
Ruth Roye, The Two Rascals &
Jacobson)

Algernon, Go H'On! (Florrie Forde)

Are We Downhearted? No! (*David:
Wright*) Charles Bignell, Florrie
Forde, Shaun Glenville, Harrison
Latimer)

Army Of Today's All Right, The (Vesta
Tilley)

Belgium Put The 'Kibosh' On The Kaiser
(Mark Sheridan)

Burlington Bertie From Bow (Ella
Shields)

By The Beautiful Sea (Ada Jones, Shirley
Kellogg, Bessie Wynn)

Captain Mac' (Foster Richardson)

Discoveries *see* When I Discovered
You

End Of My Old Cigar, The (Harry
Champion)

Florrie The Flapper (Elsie Janis)

From Marble Arch To Leicester Square
(Vesta Tilley)

Germans Are Coming, So They Say, The
(Harry Bedford)

Gilbert, The Filbert (Basil Hallam)

Here We Are! Here We Are!! Here We
Are Again!!! (*Knight & Lyle*) (Mark
Sheridan)

He's A Ragpicker (Jack Norworth)

I Ain't 'Arf A Lucky Kid (Kathleen
Burchell)

I Do Like A S'Nice S'Mince S'Pie (Jay
Laurier)

I Felt So Awfully Shy (Jack Pleasants)

I'll Make A Man Of You (Clara Beck,
Gwendoline Brogden)

I Want To Go Back To Michigan (Daisy

James, Beatrice Lillie, Frank Mullane,
Rae Samuels, Daisy Wood)

I Was A Good Little Girl (Till I Met You)
(Clarice Mayne, Ella Retford)

Keep The Home Fires Burning (Fred
Barnes, Stanley Kirkby, Sybil Vane)

Kiss Me Goodbye, My Little Soldier Boy
(Daisy Dormer)

Little Bit Of Heaven Fell, A (Ernest R.
Ball, Chauncey Olcott)

Lloyd Jarge (Ernest Shand)

Love's Garden Of Roses (Ben Davies)

Murders(?) (George Grossmith jun.,
Leslie Henson, Dick Henty, Louis
Rihill)

Play A Simple Melody (Elsie Baker &
Billy Murray, Sallie Fisher & Charles
King, Ethel Levey & Blanche
Tomlin)

Put On The Searchlight (Nora Delaney)

St Louis Blues, The (W. C. Handy,
Sophie Tucker)

Ten Million Germans (Lee White)

They Didn't Believe Me (Donald Brian
& Julia Sanderson, George Grossmith
jun. & (*a*) Adrienne Brune, (*b*) Haidee
De Rance, (*c*) Madge Sanders)

We're Irish And Proud Of It Too (Ella
Retford)

We're Really Proud Of You (Ellaline
Terriss)

When Angelus Is Ringing (Henri
Leoni)

When I Discovered You (Vernon &
Irene Castle, Joe Coyne & Ethel
Levey)

When You Wore A Tulip And I Wore A
Big Red Rose (Dolly Connolly, The
Two Rascals & Jacobson)

Where Are The Lads Of The Village
Tonight? (Harry Cove, George
Lashwood)

Who Paid The Rent For Mrs Rip Van
Winkle? (Sam Bernard, Al Jolson,
Marie Lloyd, Ella Retford, Sophie
Tucker)

Won't You Join The Army?

Wot Cheer, Me Old Brown Son (Harry Champion)

You Can't Get Many Pimples On A Pound Of Pickled Pork (Ernie Mayne)

Your King And Your Country (We Don't Want To Lose You) (Alice Delysia, Maggie Teyte, Edna Thornton)

1915

Alabama Jubilee (Elizabeth Murray)

At The Vicar's Fancy Ball (Ernest Shand)

Awfully Chap, The (Tom Clare)

Bolshevik, The (Ernest Hastings)

Broken Doll, A (Al Jolson, Clarice Mayne, Ida Rene)

Dance With Your Uncle Joseph (Charles R. Whittle)

Father's Got The Sack From The Water-works (Maidie Scott)

Four-And-Nine (The Two Bobs)

Good-bye, Kid! (Cicely Courtneidge)

I Ain't Got Nobody (Sophie Tucker)

I Didn't Raise My Boy To Be A Soldier (Gene Greene)

If You Can't Get A Girl In The Summer-time (Lou Lockett & Jack Waldron, Harry Tierney)

If You Want To Get On In Revue (Marie Lloyd)

I Like Your Town (Harry Bedford)

I Love A Piano (Harry Fox, Ethel Levey)

I'm Giving Up My Job To The Kaiser (Tom Costello)

I'm Glad I Took My Mother's Advice (Maidie Scott)

In These Hard Times (Whit Cunliffe)

It's Lovely To Be In Love (Clarice Mayne)

Just Try To Picture Me Back Home In Tennessee (Dainty Doris, Daisy Dormer, G. H. Elliott, Herbert Payne, Two Rascals & Jacobson)

Kitchener's Boys (Charles Tree)

Little Bit Of Cucumber, A (Harry Champion)

Little Of What You Fancy Does You Good, A (Marie Lloyd)

Memories (The Versatile Three)

Mother's Sitting Knitting Little Mittens For The Navy (Nora Bayes, Al Jolson, Jack Norworth)

Nola (lyrics added 1924) (instrumental)

Now You've Got Yer Khaki On (Marie Lloyd)

Pack Up Your Troubles In Your Old Kit-Bag (Florrie Forde, Adele Rowland)

Poor Old Cassidy (Nelson Jackson)

Rest Of The Day's Your Own, The (Jack Lane)

Road To The Isles, The (Marjory Kennedy Fraser & Margaret Kennedy)

Simpson's Stores (sk.) (Alfred Lester)

Somebody Would Shout Out 'Shop!' (Stanley Kirkby & Harry Hudson)

Somewhere In France, Dear Mother (Kate Carney)

Special Constable, The (Ernest Hastings, Nelson Jackson)

When I Leave The World Behind (Belle Baker, Gertie Gitana, Emilie Hayes, Al Jolson, Fritzi Scheff)

When The War Is Over Mother Dear (George Baker)

Which Switch Is The Switch, Miss, For Ipswich? (Jack Norworth)

1916

And The Villain Still Pursued Her (Mark Sheridan)

Another Little Drink (Alfred Lester & Violet Loraine & George Robey)

Any Time's Kissing Time (Aileen D'Orme, Violet Essex & Courtice Pounds)

Bachelor Gay, A (Thorpe Bates)

Cobbler's Song, The (Peter Dawson)

Dear Old Shepherd's Bush (Frank Lester)

Ev'ry Little While (Clarice Mayne, Lee
  White)
Green Hills O' Somerset (Margaret
  Cooper, Peter Dawson)
He's A Credit To Auld Ireland Now
  (Shaun Glenville)
I Can't Do My Bally Bottom Button Up
  (Ernie Mayne)
If You Were The Only Girl In The
  World (Violet Loraine & George
  Robey)
In Other Words (George Robey)
I Stopped, I Looked And I Listened
  (George Robey)
Jerusalem (Peter Dawson)
Kitchener! Gone But Not Forgotten
  (F. V. St Clair)
Li'l Liza Jane (Ella Retford)
Love Will Find A Way (Jose Collins)
Major-General Worthington (J. W.
  Rickaby)
Nellie Dean (Gertie Gitana)
On The Good Ship 'Yacki Hicki Doo La'
  (Billy Merson)
Paradise For Two, A (Thorpe Bates &
  Jose Collins)
Poor Butterfly (Regine Flory)
Pretty Baby (Al Jolson)
Roses Of Picardy (Joseph Cheetham,
  Peter Dawson, Hubert Eisdell, Ernest
  Pike, Florence Snmithson)
Swim, Sam, Swim! (Jay Laurier)
Take Me Back To Dear Old Blighty
  (Ouida Macdermott, Lily Morris, Ella
  Retford, Dorothy Ward, Daisy Wood)
Watching The Trains Come In (Jack
  Pleasants)
What Do You Want To Make Those Eyes
  At Me For? (Emma Carus, Walter
  Jeffries)
When Padereswki Plays (The Two Bobs)
Where Did Robinson Crusoe Go With
  Friday On Saturday Night? (Al Jolson,
  Ethel Levey)
You Can't Do Without A Bit Of Love
  (Kirkby & Hudson)

1917
Awake! (A Moving Love Song) (Joseph
  Cheetham, John Coates)
Come To The Fair (Foster Richardson,
  Herbert Thorpe)
Conscientious Objector's Lament, The
  (Alfred Lester)
Darktown Strutters' Ball, (At) The
  (Original Dixieland Jazz Band,
  Blossom Seeley, Sophie Tucker, The
  Versatile Three (Haston, Mills &
  Tuck))
Do It Again (Fred Barnes, Irene
  Bordoni)
Father Keep The Home Fire Burning
  (Maidie Scott)
For Me And My Gal (Elizabeth Brice &
  Charles King, Al Jolson, Van &
  Schenck)
Give Me The Moonlight (Fred Barnes,
  Elsie Janis, Randolph Sutton)
Good-bye-ee (Florrie Forde, Harry
  Tate, Charles R. Whittle, Daisy
  Wood)
If It's In 'John Bull' It *Is* So (Clay
  Smith)
I Had To Chalk A Cross Upon My Slate
  (Maidie Scott)
Indiana (Back Home Again In) (Original
  Dixieland Jazz Band)
Joan Of Arc (Harriett Vernon)
Let The Great Big World Keep Turning
  (Laddie Cliff & Violet Loraine)
My Meatless Day (Ernie Mayne)
Oh, It's A Lovely War (Ella Shields)
Over There (Nora Bayes, Enrico
  Caruso)
Paddy McGinty's Goat (The Two Bobs)
Peace! Peace! Peace! (Harry Champion)
Shooting Of Dan McGrew, The (Bransby
  Williams)
Smiles (*Callahan: Roberts*) (Nell
  Carrington, Clarice Mayne, Millie
  Hindon, Elsie Janis, Blossom Seeley)
Somebody's Coming To Tea (Kirkby &
  Hudson, Lee White)

They Go Wild, Simply Wild, Over Me
(George Clarke)
Tiger Rag (Original Dixieland Jazz Band)
Where The Black Eye'd Susans Grow (Al
Jolson, Beatrice Lillie)
Why Am I Always The Bridesmaid? (Lily
Morris)
Why Don't They Knight Charlie Chap-
lin? (Archie Naish)
Wild Wild Women, The (Al Lewis,
The Versatile Three (Haston, Mills
& Tuck))

1918
After You've Gone (Al Jolson, Sophie
Tucker)
All The World Will Be Jealous Of Me
(Violet Loraine, Sophie Tucker)
Everything Is Peaches Down In Georgia
(American Quartet, Al Jolson, Lee
White)
Ev'rybody Shimmies Now (Sophie
Tucker, Mae West)
Fact Is, The (George Robey)
First I Went And Won The D.C.M.
(J. W. Rickaby)
First Love—Last Love—Best Love
(George Robey & Violet Loraine,
George Robey & Clara Evelyn)
Give Me A Little Cosy Corner (Clarice
Mayne)
Good Man Is Hard To Find, A (Jack
Norworth, Sophie Tucker, Lee White)
If You Could Care (For Me) (Irene
Bordoni, Alice Delysia)
I'm Always Chasing Rainbows (Harry
Fox & The Dolly Sisters)
I'm Forever Blowing Bubbles (Fred
Barnes, Albert Campbell, Elsie Janis,
Charles Hart)
In A Monastery Garden (Peter Dawson)
Indianapolis (The Two Bobs)
I've Got The Sweetest Girl Of All (Lee
White)
K-K-K-Katy (Marie Brett & Frank
Varney, Walter Williams)

Nobody Noticed Me (Jack Pleasants)
Oh! London, Where Are Your Girls
Tonight? (Vesta Tilley)
Rock-A-Bye Your Baby With A Dixie
Melody (Al Jolson)
Russian Rag (instrumental)
Sailors Don't Care (Austin Rudd)
Smilin' Through (Jane Cowl, Walter
Glynne, John McCormack)
They All Look Alike In The Dark
(Charles Godfrey)
Till We Meet Again (Dorothy Ward)
Waggle O' The Kilt, The (Harry Lauder)
We Used To Gather At The Old Dun
Cow (Ernie Mayne)

1919
A-Be My Boy (Grock & Lily Morris,
Daisy Wood)
Alice Blue Gown (Edith Day)
Ca-bages, Ca-beans And Car-rots
(George Bass)
Don't Dilly Dally (Marie Lloyd, Marie
Lloyd jun.)
Good-Bye, Khaki! (Shirley Kellogg)
How Can A Little Girl Be Good?
(Maidie Scott)
How'Ya Gonna Keep 'Em Down On The
Farm? (Eddie Cantor, Sophie Tucker,
Dorothy Ward)
I Can't Forget The Days When I Was
Young (Marie Lloyd)
I Do Like An Egg For My Tea (Bert
Coote)
If You Look In Her Eyes (Marjorie
Gordon & Evelyn Laye)
If You're Irish Come Into The Parlour
(Shaun Glenville)
I'm A Good Girl Now (Shaun Glenville,
Marie Lloyd)
I'm Setting The Village On Fire (Billy
Merson)
Irene O'Dare (Edith Day)
Let The Rest Of The World Go By
(Ernest R. Ball, Albert Campbell,
Charles Hart)

Mademoiselle From Armenteers (Harry
Carlton, Shaun Glenville)

Night I Appeared As Macbeth, The
(Wilkie Bard)

Philomel (Maggie Teyte)

Pigtail Of Li Fang Fu, The (Bransby
Williams)

Pretty Girl Is Like A Melody, A (John
Steel)

Rose Of Washington Square (Fanny
Brice)

Sarah (Sitting In The Shoe-Shine Shop)
(Jack Hylton's Band)

Seaside Posters Round The Home, The
(Ernest Hastings)

Swanee (Laddie Cliff, Al Jolson)

Thank God For Victory (Emilie Hayes)

That Old-Fashioned Mother Of Mine
(Talbot O'Farrell)

Vicar And I Will Be There, The (Clifford
Grey)

Where Do Flies Go In The Winter
Time? (Ernie Mayne, Jack Pleasants,
Bert Weston)

Where There's A Boy There's A Girl
(Gina Palerme & Andrew
Randall)

You Ain't Heard Nothin' Yet (Al Jolson)

You Taught Me How To Love You (Clara
Beck

1920

All That I Want Is You

And He'd Say 'Oo-La-La Wee-Wee'!
(Billy Murray)

Bright Eyes (Nellie Wigley)

Come Over The Garden Wall (Dorothy
Clarke)

Ev'rybody Knows Me In My Old Brown
Hat (Harry Champion)

Fill 'Em Up (Hetty King)

Gipsy Warned Me, The (Violet
Loraine)

I Belong To Glasgow (?) (Will Fyffe)

I'll Be With You In Apple Blossom Time
(Nora Bayes)

Japanese Sandman, The (Nora Bayes,
Paul Whiteman Band)

Margie (Eddie Cantor, Original
Dixieland Jazz Band)

Mr Gallagher & Mr Shean (?) (Gallagher
& Shean)

Oh, What A Pal Was Mary (Florrie
Forde, William Thomas)

Old Soldiers Never Die

Profiteering Profiteers, The (Whit
Cunliffe)

Profiteer's Ball, The (Ernest Hastings)

Whispering (Paul Whiteman Band)

Who Put The Bricks In Brixton? (Syd
Walker, Dorothy Ward & Shaun
Glenville)

1921

April Showers (Al Jolson)

Body In The Bag, The (Kirkby &
Hudson)

Coal-Black Mammy (Marie Blanche &
Ivy St Helier, Laddie Cliff, Stanley
Holloway, Jack Hulbert)

Delaney's Donkey (Mooney &
Holbein)

Fishermen Of England, The (Thorpe
Bates, Peter Dawson)

I Get More Like A Pro Every Day (He's
A Pro) (Harry Weldon)

I Love To Go Swimmin' With Women
(Pat Rooney)

I Might Learn To Love Him Later On
(Violet Loraine)

I'm Just Wild About Harry (Lottie Gee,
Florence Mills)

Ma, He's Making Eyes At Me (Eddie
Cantor, Hilda Glyder)

My Mammy (Al Jolson)

Ours Is A Nice 'Ouse, Ours Is (Alfred
Lester)

Peggy O'Neil (Dorothy Ward)

Piccadilly (Hetty King)

Second-Hand Rose (Fanny Brice)

Sheik Of Araby, The (Fred Barnes,
Dorothy Ward)

Three O'Clock In The Morning (Paul Whiteman Band)

1922

And Yet—I Don't Know (Ernest Hastings)

Any Dirty Work Today? (George Carney)

Brown Bird Singing, A (Dora Labette, John McCormack, Stella Power)

Carolina In The Morning (Al Jolson, Dorothy Ward)

Flower, The (*Lilac Time*) (Clara Butterworth & Courtice Pounds)

How Could Red Riding Hood? (Sophie Tucker)

I'm Ninety Four This Mornin' (Will Fyffe)

It's My Bath Night Tonight (Jack Pleasants)

I Would—If I Could—But I Can't—So I Won't (Margaret Bannerman)

Kiss In The Dark, A (Edith Day)

Let's Have A Song About Rhubarb (Hal Wright)

Limehouse Blues (Teddie Gerard)

My Word You Do Look Queer (Ernest Hastings, Stanley Holloway)

Put A Bit O' Treacle On My Pudden, Mary Ann! (Harry Champion)

Toot, Toot, Tootsie! (Al Jolson)

Way Down Yonder In New Orleans (Creamer & Layton, Paul Whiteman Band)

What D'Yer Think Of That? (My Old Man's A Dustman) (Ernie Mayne)

1923

Ain' It Nice! (Daisy Dormer)

Back Answers (Robb Wilton)

In A Persian Market (Peter Dawson)

It Ain't Gonna Rain No Mo' (Wendell Hall, Norah Blaney & Gwen Farrar)

Johnnie (Sam Mayo)

Nobody Knows You When You're Down And Out (Jimmie Cox)

Only A Working Man (Lily Morris)

Out Where The Blue Begins (Florrie Forde)

She Told Me To Meet Her At The Gate (S. W. Wyndham)

Who's Sorry Now? (Original Memphis Five, Van & Schenck)

Yes, We Have No Bananas! (Eddie Cantor, Florrie Forde)

1924

California, Here I Come (Al Jolson, Dorothy Ward)

End Of The Road (Keep Right On To The End Of), The (Harry Lauder)

Nola (lyrics added to 1915 melody) (Vincent Lopez)

'Ow I 'Ate Women (A. W. Baskcomb, Hugh E. Wright)

Riley's Cowshed (George Bass)

That's What God Made Mothers For (The Two Rascals)

Turned Up (Florrie Forde, Lily Morris)

1925

Always (Gladys Clark & Henry Bergman)

Could Lloyd George Do It? (Jack Edge, Stanley Lupino)

My Yiddishe Momme (Belle Baker, Sophie Tucker)

Old Apple Tree, The (Lily Morris)

On Mother Kelly's Doorstep (Fred Barnes, Randolph Sutton)

Show Me The Way To Go Home (Ella Shields)

Ukulele Lady (Norah Blaney & Gwen Farrar)

1926

Don't Have Any More, Missus Moore (Lily Morris)

Doubles (And That Went Down) (Ernie Mayne)

I Think I'll Buy Piccadilly (J. W. Rickaby)

I've Never Seen A Straight Banana (Jack Hylton's Band)

More We Are Together, The (Jack Hylton's Band)

Viewing The Baby (Clarice Mayne)

What I Want Is A Proper Cup Of Coffee
(Ernie Mayne, Johnny Schofield)

1927
Abdul Abulbul Amir (orig. 1877, q.v.)
(Grock, Al Jolson)
Algy's Absolutely Full Of Tact (Fred
Chester)
Bless This House (Peter Dawson, Gracie
Fields, John McCormack)
I'm Going Back To Himazas (Harry
Gordon)
My Leetle Rosa (Violet Field)
Ooh! 'Er (The Slavey) (Wish Wynne)
Side By Side (Woods) (Florrie Forde)

1928
Boots (Peter Dawson)
Sonny Boy (Al Jolson)

1929
He Led Me Up The Garden (Edith
Faulkner)
I Lift Up My Finger And I Say 'Tweet
Tweet' (Stanley Lupino, Leslie Sarony)
My Mother Doesn't Know I'm On The
Stage (Billy Bennett)
Under The Bed (Nellie Wallace)

1930
Old Sam (Sam, Pick Oop Tha' Musket)
(Marriott Edgar, Stanley Holloway)
Teddy Bears' Picnic, The (Val Rosing (w.
Henry Hall's Orchestra))

1931
I'm Alone Because I Love You (Bud &
Joe Billings)
I Want To Take A Young Man In And Do
For Him (Nora Blakemore)

1932
Ain't It Grand To Be Bloomin' Well
Dead? (George Jackley, Leslie Sarony)
Did Your First Wife Ever Do That?
(Marie Kendall)
Lion And Albert, The (Marriott Edgar,
Stanley Holloway)

Underneath The Arches (Flanagan &
Allen)

1933
Heaven Will Protect An Honest Girl
(Gracie Fields)
Old Father Thames (Thorpe Bates,
Norman Blair, Peter Dawson, Roy
Henderson, Stanley Holloway)
Runcorn Ferry, The (Marriott Edgar,
Stanley Holloway)
We All Went Up Up Up The Mountain
(George Jackley, Midnight Minstrels)
When Are You Going To Lead Me To
The Altar, Walter? (Randolph Sutton)

1934
Let's All Go To The Music Hall (Variety
Artistes' Federation anthem) (Kate
Carney, Harry Claff)
Nobody Loves A Fairy When She's Forty
(Tessie O'Shea—*unlisted*)
With Her Head Tucked Underneath Her
Arm (Stanley Holloway)

1935
Brahn Boots (Stanley Holloway)
Happy Birthday To You (lyrics added to
1893 melody)
Olga Pulloffski The Beautiful Spy (Jack
Hylton's Band)
You Can't Do That There 'Ere (Jack
Payne's Band, Mrs Jack Hylton)

1936
And The Great Big Saw Came Nearer
And Nearer (Leslie Sarony)
I'll Walk Beside You (John McCormack)
I Never Cried So Much In All My Life
(Gracie Fields)
Touch Of The Master's Hand, The
(Nosmo King)

1937
Lambeth Walk, The (Gay) (Teddie St
Denis & Lupino Lane)
Walter! Walter! (Lead Me To The Altar)
(Gracie Fields)

1938

Biggest Aspidistra In The World, The
(Gracie Fields)

Knees Up, Mother Brown! (Elsie &
Doris Waters)

1939

Only A Glass Of Champagne (Evelyn
Laye)

1940

We'll Keep A Welcome (Mai Jones)

1944

Your Baby 'As Gorn Dahn The Plug-'Ole
(Elsa Lanchester)

1945

Hokey Cokey a.k.a. Cokey Cokey
(Billy Cotton & His Band, Lou
Praeger & His Orchestra (w. Paul
Rich))

Cruising Down The River (Jack Leon &
Orchestra)

1947

Maybe It's Because I'm A Londoner
(Bud Flanagan)

1952

Marrow Song, The (Oh, What A Beauty!)
(Billy Cotton & His Band)

Show Songs

SONGS were often interpolated into shows to strengthen the piece generally or at the behest of a star performer. They might be added weeks, months, or even years after a show had opened, originating in Music Hall, vaudeville, and not infrequently other shows. Revues, with their inconsequential plots, were notoriously eager to snap up the latest song or dance craze, much as pantomime still does today. The dates below therefore indicate when a song appeared in a show and not necessarily when the production opened. Only titles from the Core Song-List are included in this section. All theatres are in London unless otherwise stated.

Title of Show	Theatre	Date	Title of Song
Americans, The	Lyceum	1811	The Death Of Nelson
Arcadians, The	Shaftesbury	1909	All Down Piccadilly
			Half-Past Two (in NY int. *Girl From Montmartre*)
			My Motter
			Pipes of Pan
Artist's Model, An	Daly's	1895	Gay Bohemia
			Soldiers Of The Queen (int.)
As You Were	London Pavilion	1918	If You Could Care For Me
Back Again	Ambassadors'	1919	I Do Like An Egg For My Tea
Bang-up	Aquatic Sadler's Wells	1810	Typitywitchet
Barry of Ballymore		1910	Mother Machree (int. *Isle o' Dreams*)
Beauty Shop, The a.k.a. *Mr Manhattan*	Astor NY	1913	When You're All Dressed Up And Nowhere To Go
Belle from Bond St, The update of *The Girl from Kay's*	Shubert NY	1914	Who Paid The Rent For Mrs Rip Van Winkle? (also in *Honeymoon Express*)

Title of Show	Theatre	Date	Title of Song
Belle Of Mayfair, The	Daly's NY	1906	Why Do They Call Me A Gibson Girl? (int.)
Belle Of New York, The	Shaftesbury	1898	Conundrums (int. first UK production)
			Lucky Jim (int. first UK production)
	Casino NY	1897	Narraganset
			She Is The Belle Of New York
Belle Sauvage, La	St James's	1869	Oh Where, Oh Where, Has My Little Dog Gone? (int.)
Better 'Ole, A	Oxford	1916	What Do You Want To Make Those Eyes At Me For? (from *Follow Me*)
Big Show, The	Hippodrome	1916	Poor Butterfly
Bing Boys are Here, The	Alhambra	1916	Another Little Drink
			Dear Old Shepherd's Bush
			If You Were The Only Girl In The World
			In Other Words . . .
			I Stopped, I Looked, And I Listened
Bing Boys on Broadway, The	Alhambra	1918	First Love—Last Love—Best Love
Bing Girls are There, The	Alhambra	1917	Let The Great Big World Keep Turning
Black Crook, The	Niblo's Gardens NY	1866	You Naughty, Naughty Men
Bluebell in Fairyland	Vaudeville	1901	The Honeysuckle And The Bee (from *Prima Donna*)
			A Simple Little String (from *The Circus Girl*)
Bohemian Girl, The	Drury Lane	1843	I Dreamt That I Dwelt In Marble Halls
			Then You'll Remember Me (When Other Lips)
Bric-a-brac	Palace	1915	Chalk Farm To Camberwell Green
Brides of Venice, The	Drury Lane	1844	By The Sad Sea Waves
Buzz-Buzz	Vaudeville	1918	K-K-K-Katy

Title of Show	Theatre	Date	Title of Song
Captain Kidd	Apollo	1910	I've Got Rings On My Fingers (int. also *The Midnight Sons* and *The Yankee Girl*)
Carmen	Opéra-Comique, Paris	1875	Flower Song
	Her Majesty's	1878	
Carmen Up-to-Data	Gaiety	1890	Hush! The Bogie! (see *Mulligan Guards' Surprise*)
Cherry Girl, The	Vaudeville	1903	Little Yellow Bird
Chinese Honeymoon, A	Theatre Royal Hanley	1899	Could You Be True To Eyes Of Blue? I Want To Be A Lidy Martha Spanks The Grand Piano
	Strand	1901	Twiddley Bits, The (int.)
Chocolate Soldier, The	Lyric	1910	My Hero
Chu Chin Chow	His Majesty's	1916	Any Time's Kissing Time Cobbler's Song
Cinder-Ellen Up Too Late	Gaiety	1892	Man That Broke The Bank At Monte Carlo (int.) The Rowdy Dowdy Boys (int.) Ta-Ra-Ra-Boom-De-Ay (int.)
Circus Girl, The	Gaiety	1896	A Simple Little String (also int. *Bluebell in Fairyland*)
Clari, The Maid of Milan	Covent Garden	1823	Home! Sweet Home!
Count of Luxembourg, The	Daly's	1911	Love, Goodbye
Country Girl, A	Daly's	1902	My Own Little Girl Under The Deodar
Cox & Box	Gallery of Illustration	1867	The Buttercup
Defender, The	Herald Square NY	1902	In The Good Old Summertime
Dick Whittington	Drury Lane	1908	She Sells Sea Shells
	Grand, Islington	1891	Ta-Ra-Ra-Boom-De-Ay (int.)

Title of Show	Theatre	Date	Title of Song
Doing our Bit	Winter Garden NY	1917	The Wild Wild Women
Don Juan	Gaiety	1893	Linger Longer Loo
Dorothy	Gaiety	1886	Queen Of My Heart
Earl and the Girl, The	Casino NY	1905	How'D'Ya Like To Spoon With Me? (also int. *The Rich Mr Hoggenheimer*)
	Aldwych	1914	I Want To Go Back To Michigan (revival) (also in *5064 Gerrard*)
	Adelphi	1903	My Cosey Corner Girl (also in *The School Girl*)
	Adelphi	1902	The Patchwork Garden
Eightpence a Mile	Alhambra	1913	All The Girls Are Lovely By The Seaside
Enchantress, The	New York NY	1911	Art Is Calling For Me
English Fleet in 1342, The	Covent Garden	1803	All's Well
Everybody's Doing It	Empire	1912	Everybody's Doing It Now
Fiddle-Dee-Dee	Weber & Fields' NY	1900	Ma Blushin' Rosie
5064 Gerrard	Alhambra	1915	I Want To Go Back To Michigan (also in 1914 revival of *The Earl and the Girl*)
			Kitty, The Telephone Girl (also in *Hullo, Tango!*)
Fledermaus, Die	an der Wien Vienna	1874	Czardas
	Alhambra	1876	The Laughing Song
Florodora	Lyric	1899	I Want To Be A Military Man
			Shade Of The Palm
			Tell Me Pretty Maiden
Follow Me	Casino NY	1916	What Do You Want To Make Those Eyes At Me For? (int. *A Better 'Ole*)
Follow the Crowd orig. title *Stop! Look! Listen!* (q.v.)	Empire	1916	Where Did Robinson Crusoe Go With Friday On Saturday Night? (also in *Robinson Crusoe Jr*)
Forty-five Minutes from Broadway	New Amsterdam NY	1905	Mary's A Grand Old Name

Title of Show	Theatre	Date	Title of Song
Gaiety Girl, A	Prince of Wales's	1893	Private Tommy Atkins (also in *San Toy*)
Geisha, The	Daly's	1896	The Amorous Goldfish
Geneviève de Brabant	Bouffes-Parisiens Paris	1859	Gendarmes Duet
	Philharmonic Islington	1871	
Girl Behind the Counter, The (see *Step This Way*)	Wyndham's	1906	The Land Where The Best Man Wins
	Herald Square NY	1907	The Glow-Worm (int. NY prod.)
Girl from Dixie, The	Madison Square NY	1902	Pansy Faces (also in *Mother Goose*, Drury Lane)
Girl from Kays, The	Apollo	1902	see *Belle from Bond Street, The*
Girl from Montmartre, The	Criterion NY	1912	Half-Past Two (from *The Arcadians*)
Girl from Utah, The orig. prod.: Adelphi 1913	Knickerbocker NY	1914	Ballin' The Jack (also in *The Passing Show of 1915* and *Ziegfeld Follies of 1913*) They Didn't Believe Me (also int. *Tonight's the Night*)
Girls of Gottenburg, The	Gaiety	1907	Two Little Sausages
Grass Widow, The	Apollo Liberty NY	1917	Be My Little Baby Bumble Bee (also in *Ziegfeld Follies of 1911* and *A Winsome Widow*)
Gypsy Love	Daly's	1910	The White Dove
Heart of Paddy Whack, The		1914	A Little Bit Of Heaven Fell
Her Soldier Boy	Astor NY	1916	Pack Up Your Troubles In Your Old Kitbag (int.)
His Honor the Mayor	New York NY	1906	Waltz Me Around Again, Willie (int. *Miss Dolly Dollars* and *The New Aladdin*)
Hokey Pokey	Weber & Fields' NY	1912	Come Down Ma Evening Star (from *Twirly Whirly*)

Title of Show	Theatre	Date	Title of Song
Honeymoon Express	Winter Garden NY	1913	Waiting For The Robert E Lee (int.)
		1914	Who Paid The Rent For Mrs Rip Van Winkle? (also in *The Belle from Bond Street*)
Hullo! America	Palace	1918	Give Me The Moonlight
Hullo, London!	Empire	1910	Shine On Harvest Moon (from *Ziegfeld Follies*, 1908)
Hullo, Rag-time! 1913 revised prod.	Hippodrome London Palladium	1911	The Gaby Glide (int. *Vera Violetta*, *The Little Parisienne*, and *The Whirl of Society*)
	first edition		Hitchy-Koo (from *The Whirl of Society*) I'm Going Back To Dixie (from *She Knows Better Now*, also *The Whirl of Society*) Row, Row, Row (also in *Ziegfeld Follies of 1912*) The Spaniard That Blighted My Life (int.)
Hullo, Tango!	Hippodrome second edition	1913	By The Beautiful Sea (int.)
	first edition second edition		Get Out And Get Under Kitty The Telephone Girl (also in *5064 Gerrard*)
	first edition	1914	Sister Susie's Sewing Shirts For Soldiers
	second edition		Some Of These Days (int.)
Irene	Empire	1919	Alice Blue Gown Irene O'Dare
Isle o' Dreams	Grand Opera House NY	1913	Mother Machree (from *Barry of Ballymore*) When Irish Eyes Are Smiling
Jack Sheppard	Adelphi	1839	Nix My Dolly Pals
Jersey Lily, The	Victoria NY	1903	Bedelia (also in *The Orchid*)
Jig-Saw!	Hippodrome	1920	Swanee (also in *Sinbad*)
Jolly Bachelors, The	Broadway NY	1910	If The Managers Only

Title of Show	Theatre	Date	Title of Song
			Thought The Same As Mother
			Has Anybody Here Seen Kelly? (int.)
Keep Smiling	Alhambra	1913	You Made Me Love You
Kitty Grey	Apollo	1902	Walking Home With Angeline
Knight for a Day, A	Wallack's NY	1907	I'm Afraid To Come Home In The Dark
Lady Madcap	Prince of Wales's	1904	I Don't Seem To Want You When You're With Me
			I Like You In Velvet
Lights Up	Savoy	1939	Only A Glass Of Champagne
Lilac Time	Lyric	1922	The Flower
Lily of Killarney	Covent Garden	1862	The Moon Has Raised Her Lamp Above
Little Johnny Jones	Liberty NY	1904	Give My Regards To Broadway
London, Paris and New York	Pavilion	1921	I Might Learn To Love Him Later On
Little Parisienne, The	NY	1913	Gaby Glide, The (int. *Vera Violetta*, *Hullo, Rag-time!* and *The Whirl of Society*)
Love Birds	Apollo NY	1921	I Love To Go Swimmin' With Women (cut before opening night)
Lysistrata	Apollo Berlin	1902	The Glow-Worm
Madame Sherry	New Amsterdam NY	1910	Every Little Movement Has A Meaning Of Its Own (NB: not the Marie Lloyd song of the same title)
			Put Your Arms Around Me Honey
Maid of the Mountains, The	Daly's	1917	A Bachelor Gay
			Love Will Find A Way
			A Paradise For Two
Make it Snappy	Winter Garden NY	1923	Yes, We Have No Bananas
Maritana	Drury Lane	1845	Yes! Let Me Like A Soldier Fall

Title of Show	Theatre	Date	Title of Song
Me and my Girl	Victoria Palace	1937	The Lambeth Walk
Merry Widow, The	an der Wien Vienna Daly's	1907	The Merry Widow Waltz Vilia
Merry Widow and the Devil, The	Weber & Fields' NY	1908	Yip-I-Addy-I-Ay (int. *Our Miss Gibbs*)
Messenger Boy, The	Gaiety	1900	Maisie (Is A Daisy)
Midnight Sons, The	Broadway NY	1909	I've Got Rings On My Fingers (also int. *Captain Kidd* and *The Yankee Girl*)
Miner, The (Der Obersteiger)	Gaiety	1894	The Miller's Daughter (Don't Be Cross)
Miss Dolly Dollars	14th St NY	1906	Waltz Me Around Again, Willie (from *His Honor the Mayor*. Also int. *The New Aladdin*)
Miss Esmerelda	Gaiety	1887	Killaloe
Miss Hook of Holland	Prince of Wales's	1907	A Pink Petty From Peter
Mlle Modiste	Knickerbocker NY	1905	If I Were On The Stage (Kiss Me Again)
Monte Carlo	Avenue	1896	If I Only Knew The Way
Mother Goose	Sadler's Wells	1819	Hot Codlins
Mother Goose	Drury Lane	1902	Pansy Faces (also int. *The Girl from Dixie*)
Mousmé, The	Shaftesbury	1911	The Temple Bell
Mr Manhattan a.k.a. *The Beauty Shop*			
Mulligan Guards' Surprise, The	Theater Comique NY	1880	Whist! The Bogie Man see *Carmen Up-to-Data*
Naughty Marietta	New York NY	1910	Ah! Sweet Mystery Of life I'm Falling In Love With Someone
New Aladdin, The	Gaiety	1906	Grandmama Waltz Me Around Again, Willie (from *His Honor the Mayor*. Also int. *Miss Dolly Dollars*)
Oh, Look!	Vanderbilt NY	1918	I'm Always Chasing Rainbows
Orchid, The	Gaiety	1903	Bedelia (also in *The Jersey Lily*)

Title of Show	Theatre	Date	Title of Song
Our Miss Gibbs	Gaiety	1909	Moonstruck Yip-I-Addy-I-Ay (from *Merry Widow and the Devil*)
Parisian Model, A	Broadway NY	1906	I Just Can't Make My Eyes Behave
Passing Show, The	Palace	1914	Gilbert, The Filbert I'll Make A Man Of You
Passing Show of 1915, The	Empire	1915	Ballin' The Jack (also int. *The Girl From Utah* and *Ziegfeld Follies of 1913*)
Passing Show of 1918, The	Winter Garden NY	1918	I'm Forever Blowing Bubbles Smiles
Paul Pry	Haymarket	1824	Cherry Ripe
Peep o' Day	Lyceum	1861	Killarney
Pink Lady, The	Globe	1911	My Beautiful Lady
Pot-Pourri	Avenue	1899	Mary Was A Housemaid
Prima Donna	Herald Square NY	1901	Honeysuckle And The Bee (int. *Bluebell in Fairyland*)
Prince of Tonight, The	Princess Chicago	1909	I Wonder Who's Kissing Her Now?
Push and Go	Hippodrome	1915	Chinatown, My Chinatown (from *Up and Down Broadway*)
Quaker Girl, The	Adelphi	1910	Come To The Ball
Rich Mr Hoggenheimer, The	Wallack's NY	1906	How'D'Ya Like To Spoon With Me? (also int. *The Earl and the Girl*)
Robinson Crusoe Jr	Winter Garden NY	1916	Where Did Robinson Crusoe Go With Friday On Saturday Night? (also in *Follow the Crowd*)
Roi d'Ys, Le	Opéra-Comique Paris	1888	In Olden Spain
Rosy Rapture	Duke of York's	1915	Which Switch Is The Switch, Miss, For Ipswich?
Round the Map	Alhambra	1817	The Conscientious Objector's Lament

Title of Show	Theatre	Date	Title of Song
Runaway Girl, A	Gaiety	1898	Soldiers In The Park
Ruy Blas and the Blasé Roué	Gaiety	1889	Johnny Jones And His Sister Sue
Samples	Playhouse/ Vaudeville/Comedy	1915	Broken Doll, A
San Toy	Daly's	1899	Private Tommy Atkins (also in *A Gaiety Girl*)
School Girl, The	Prince of Wales's	1903	My Cosey Corner Girl (also in *The Earl and the Girl*)
Shameen Dhu		1913	That's An Irish Lullaby
She Knows Better Now	Plymouth, Chicago	1912	I'm Going Back To Dixie (also in *The Whirl of Society*)
Shop Girl, The	Gaiety	1894	And Her Golden Hair Was Hanging Down Her Back (int.)
Shuffle Along	63rd St Music Hall NY	1921	I'm Just Wild About Harry
Sinbad	Winter Garden NY	1920	Avalon
		1921	Mammy
		1918	Rock-A-Bye Your Baby With A Dixie Melody
		1919	Swanee (also in *Jig-Saw!*)
Some	Vaudeville	1916	Ev'ry Little While
Spanish Dollars	Covent Garden	1805	Bay Of Biscay
Spring Maid, The	Liberty NY	1910	The Three Trees
Step This Way revision of *The Girl Behind the Counter, q.v.*	Oxford	1916	
Stop! Look! Listen! see *Follow the Crowd*	Globe NY	1915	I Love A Piano
Street Singer, The	Lyric	1921	'Ow I 'Ate Women
Sunshine Girl, The	Gaiety	1911	Brighton (Take Me On The Boat To) Here's To Love And Laughter I Love The Moon
Ten Nights in a Bar-Room	National, Washington DC	1858	Come Home, Father
This and That	Comedy	1914	I Was A Good Little Girl Till I Met You

Title of Show	Theatre	Date	Title of Song
Three Little Maids	Daly's NY	1906	I Can't Take My Eyes Off You (added NY prod.)
Tillie's Nightmare	Herald Square NY	1910	Heaven Will Protect The Working Girl
Together Again	Victoria Palace	1947	Maybe It's Because I'm A Londoner
Tonight's the Night	Gaiety	1915	Murders (int.) They Didn't Believe Me (also int. *The Girl from Utah*)
Toreador, The	Gaiety	1901	Ev'rybody's Awfully Good To Me Keep Off The Grass When I Marry Amelia
Trip to Chinatown, A	Madison Square NY orig. prod.: Harlem Opera House NY	1892 1891	After The Ball Bowery, The (in UK: Brighton)
Twirly Whirly	Weber & Fields' NY	1902	Come Down Ma Evening Star (also in *Hokey Pokey*)
Up and Down Broadway	Casino NY	1910	Chinatown, My Chinatown (int. *Push and Go*)
Vera Violetta	Winter Garden NY orig. prod.: an der Wien Vienna	1911 1907	The Gaby Glide (added in NY; also int. *Hullo, Ragtime!*, *The Little Parisienne*, and *The Whirl of Society*) Ta-Ra-Ra-Boom-De-Ré (added in NY)
Véronique	Bouffes-Parisiens Paris Coronet (French) Apollo (English)	1898 1903 1904	The Swing Song Trot Here And There
Wandering Minstrel, The	Olympic	1853	Villikins And His Dinah (int.)
Watch your Step	New Amsterdam NY	1914	Play A Simple Melody (London: Empire, 1915) When I Discovered You
Whirligig	Palace	1920	The Gypsy Warned Me
Whirl of Society, The	Winter Garden NY	1912	The Gaby Glide (from *Vera Violetta*; also int. *Hullo, Ragtime!* and *The Little Parisienne*)

Title of Show	Theatre	Date	Title of Song
			Hitchy-Koo (also in *Hullo, Ragtime!*)
			How Do You Do, Miss Ragtime?
			I'm Going Back To Dixie (from *She Knows Better Now*)
Whittington & his Cat	Gaiety	1881	Nonsense! Yes! By Jove!
		1882	Oh, You Little Darling
Winsome Widow, A	Moulin Rouge NY	1912	Be My Little Baby Bumble Bee (also in *The Grass Widow* and *Ziegfeld Follies of 1911*)
World of Pleasure, A	Winter Garden NY	1916	Pretty Baby
Yankee Girl, The	Herald Square NY	1910	I've Got Rings On My Fingers (also int. *Captain Kidd* and *The Midnight Sons*)
			Nora Malone (Call Me By Phone)(int.)
Ziegfeld Follies of . . .			
1908	Jardin de Paris NY	1908	Shine On Harvest Moon (also in *Hullo, London!*)
1909	Jardin de Paris NY	1909	By The Light Of The Silvery Moon
1910	Jardin de Paris NY	1910	The Grizzly Bear, (Dance Of)
1911	Jardin de Paris NY	1911	Be My Little Baby Bumble Bee (also in *The Grass Widow* and in *A Winsome Widow*)
1912	Moulin Rouge NY	1912	Row, Row, Row (also int. *Hullo, Ragtime!*)
1913	New Amsterdam NY	1913	Ballin' The Jack (also in *The Girl from Utah* and *The Passing Show of 1915*)
			Peg O' My Heart
1919	New Amsterdam NY	1919	A Pretty Girl Is Like A Melody
1921	Globe NY	1921	Second-Hand Rose
1922	New Amsterdam NY	1922	Mr Gallagher & Mr Shean

Sources and Bibliography

—⋅◆⋅—

UNLESS otherwise stated all publishers except Oxford University Press are or were based in London.

Music Collections

Author's song sheets and albums
Bodleian Library, Music Section, Oxford
British Library, Music Department
Mander & Mitchenson Theatre Collection, Beckenham, Kent
Max Tyler
Michael Diamond
Players' Theatre Music Library
Theatre Museum, Olympia

Miscellaneous Sources

American Library, University of London
British Library, Newspaper Library, Colindale
Ealing Reference Library
EMI Archives, Hillingdon (documents)
EMI Archives, Woodford Green (music)
Green Room Club Library
National Sound Archive
Public Record Office, Kew
Theatre Museum, Covent Garden
United States Information Service Reference Center, Grosvenor Square
Westminster Music Library, Victoria
Westminster Reference Library

Published Song Collections

80 Comedy Songs, ed. Lawrence Wright (Lawrence Wright, 1960).
Allan's Illustrated Edition of Tyneside Songs (Thomas & George Allan, 1891).
Best Music Hall and Variety Songs, comp. and ed. Peter Gammond (Wolfe, 1972).
British Music Hall, The, comp. and ed. Peter Davison (Oak, 1971).
Bumper Book of Music Hall Songs, ed. Peter Foss (EMI, 1988).
Edwardian Song Book, The, ed. Michael R. Turner and Antony Miall (Methuen, 1982).

English County Songs, ed. Lucy Broadwood (Cramer, 1889).

English Song Book, ed. Harold Scott (Chapman & Hall, 1925).

Everyman's Book of British Ballads, ed. Roy Palmer (Alan Dent, 1980).

Everyman's Book of Sea Songs, ed. Richard Baker and Antony Miall (Dent, 1982).

Favorite Songs of the Nineties, ed. Robert A. Fremont (New York: Dover Publications, 1973).

Folk Songs of England, Ireland, Scotland and Wales, selected and ed. William Cole, arr. Norman Monath (Hansen, 1961).

Good Old Days Song Book, The, introduction and notes by Peter Gammond (BBC/EMI, 1980).

Great Comedy Songs (four editions; top-line and chord symbols) (EMI, 1980s).

Illustrated Victorian Song Book, The, comp. and ed. Aline Waites and Robin Hunter (Michael Joseph, 1984).

Just a Song at Twilight, ed. Michael R. Turner and Antony Miall (Michael Joseph, 1975).

Music Hall Programmes 1–4 (EMI, 1980s).

Music Hall Song Book, ed. Peter Gammond (David & Charles/EMI, 1975).

Old Songs of Skye, The, Ethel Bassin, ed. Derek Bowman (Routledge & Kegan Paul, 1977).

Parlour Song Book, The, ed. Michael R. Turner and Antony Miall (Michael Joseph, 1972).

Popular Songs of Nineteenth-Century America, comp. and ed. Richard Jackson (New York: Dover, 1976).

Read 'Em and Weep, ed. Sigmund Spaeth (Heineman, 1926).

Sixty Old Time Variety Songs (Francis, Day & Hunter, n.d.).; originally published as *News Chronicle Song Book No. 2* (1937).

Sixty Years of British Music Hall, comp. and ed. John M. Garrett (Chappell in association with Deutsch, 1976).

Soodlum's Irish Ballad Book (Oak Publications, 1982).

Tyneside Songs, arr. C. E. Catcheside-Warrington, 2 vols. (Newcastle-on-Tyne: J. G. Windows, 1927–9).

Weep Some More, My Lady, ed. Sigmund Spaeth (New York: Doubleday Page, 1927).

PERIODICALS *(all London)*

Actors by Daylight (1838).

Bat, The (1885–8).

Encore (1892–1930).

Entr'acte Almanack, The (1873–85); see also *London Entr'acte*.

Entr'acte Annual, The (1886–1907).

Era, The (1838–1939).

Era Almanac (and Annual), The (1867–1919).

Gramophone Wireless & Talking Machine News (1923–30); see also *Talking Machine News*.

Interlude (1885–6).

London Entr'acte (1869–72); see also *Entr'acte*.

Magnet, The (1866–1926).
Music Hall (Records), ed. Tony Barker (1978–84, 1998– , irregular editions).
Music Hall, The (& Theatre Review) (1889–1912).
Music Halls' Gazette (Apr.–Dec. 1868).
Musical Times & Singing Class Circular (1844–).
Musician and Music-Hall Times (May–Sept. 1862).
Performer, The (1906–57; organ of the VAF).
Performer Annual (1907–32).
Record Collector, The (1946–).
Sound Wave, The (1906–36).
Stage, The (1880–).
Stage Year Book, The (1908–28, 1949–).
Talking Machine News (1903–23); see also *Gramophone Wireless*, etc.
Times, The (1785–).
Variety Stage, The (1896–7).
Voice, The (1917–54; EMI house magazine).

BOOKS

ABBOTT, JOHN, *The Story of Francis, Day & Hunter* (FDH, 1952).
A'BECKETT, ARTHUR W., *Green Room Recollections* (Bristol: Arrowsmith, 1896).
ADELER, EDWIN, and WEST, CON, *Remember Fred Karno?* (John Long, 1939).
ALBANI, EMMA, *Forty Years of Song* (Mills & Boon, 1921).
ALLTREE, GEORGE W., *Footlight Memories* (Sampson Low, 1932).
ANDERSON, JEAN (ed.), *Late Joys at the Players' Theatre* (Boardman, 1943).
ANDREWS, CYRIL BRUYN, and ORR-EWING, J. A. (eds.), *Victorian Swansdown* (John Murray, 1935)
ASCAP Biographical Dictionary (New York: Jaques Cattell Press, 1980).
BAILEY, PETER, *Leisure and Class in Victorian England* (Routledge & Kegan Paul, 1978; repr. as University Paperback by Methuen, 1987).
—— (ed.), *Music Hall: The Business of Pleasure* (Oxford University Press, 1986).
BAKER, RICHARD ANTHONY, *Marie Lloyd Queen of the Music-Halls* (Hale, 1990).
BAKER, ROGER, *Drag: A History of Female Impersonation on the Stage* (Triton, 1968).
Baker's Biographical Dictionary of Musicians, ed. Nicholas Slonimsky (Oxford University Press, 1984).
BANKS, MORWENNA, and SWIFT, AMANDA, *The Joke's on Us* (Pandora, 1987).
BARKER, FELIX, *The House that Stoll Built* (Muller, 1957).
BARTELT, CHUCK, and GERGERON, BARBARA (comp.), *Variety Obituaries 1905–86*, 11 vols. incl. index (New York: Garland Publishing, 1987; from 1987 issued annually).
BELL, LESLIE, *Bella of Blackfriars* (Odhams, 1961).
BENNETT, BILLY, *Budget of Burlesque Monologues*, 6 vols. (Paxton, 1938).
BERRY, W. H., *Forty Years in the Limelight* (Hutchinson, 1939).
BINGHAM, MADELEINE, *Earls and Girls* (Hamish Hamilton, 1980).
Biographical Dictionary of American Music, ed. Charles Eugene Claghorn (New York: Parker Publishing, 1973).

Blackwell Encyclopedia of Musical Theatre, ed. Kurt Ganzl, 2 vols. (Oxford: Basil Blackwell, 1993).

BLOOM, KEN (ed.), *American Song*, 2 vols. (New York: Facts On File, 1985).

BLOW, SYDNEY, *The Ghost Walks on Fridays* (Heath Cranton, 1935).

——*Through Stage Doors* (W. & R. Chambers, 1958).

BOARDMAN, W. H. (Billy), *Vaudeville Days* (Jarrold's, 1935).

BOASE, FREDERICK, *Modern English Biographies*, 6 vols. (Netherton & Worth, 1892–1921; repr. Frank Cass, 1965).

BOOSEY, WILLIAM, *Fifty Years of Music* (Ernest Benn, 1931).

BOOTH, CHARLES, *Life and Labour of the People in London* (Williams & Norgate, 1889).

BOOTH, J. B., *The Days We Knew* (T. Werner Laurie, 1943).

——*Life, Laughter and Brass Hats* (T. Werner Laurie, 1939).

——*London Town* (T. Werner Laurie, 1929).

——*'Master' and Men* (T. Werner Laurie, 1926).

——*Old Pink 'Un Days* (Grant Richards, 1924).

——*Palmy Days* (Richards Press, 1957).

——*Pink Parade* (Thornton Butterworth, 1933).

——*A Pink 'Un Remembers* (T. Werner Laurie, 1937).

——(ed.), *Seventy Years of Song* (Hutchinson, 1943).

BORDMAN, GERALD, *American Musical Comedy From Adonis to Dreamgirls* (Oxford University Press, 1982).

——*American Musical Theatre* (2nd edn., Oxford University Press, 1992).

——*Concise Oxford Companion to American Theatre* (Oxford University Press, 1987).

BRATTON, J. S., *The Victorian Popular Ballad* (Macmillan, 1975).

——(ed.), *Music Hall: Performance and Style* (Oxford University Press, 1986).

Brewer's Dictionary of 20th-Century Phrase and Fable (Cassell, 1991).

Brewer's Theatre: A Phrase and Fable Dictionary (Cassell, 1994).

BRINK, CAROL R., *Harps in the Wind* (Macmillan, 1947).

BROWN, JAMES DUFF, and STRATTON, STEPHEN SAMUEL, *British Musical Biography* (Birmingham: Stratton, 1897; repr. New York: Da Capo Press, 1971).

BRYAN, GEORGE (comp.), *Stage Deaths 1850–1990*, 2 vols. (New York: Greenwood, 1991).

BUCHANAN-TAYLOR, W., *Shake the Bottle* (Heath Cranton, 1942).

——*One More Shake* (Heath Cranton, 1944)

BULLAR, GUY R., and EVANS, LEN (comp. and ed.), *The Performer: Who's Who in Variety* (The Performer, 1950).

BURKE, BILLIE, *With a Feather on my Nose* (Theatre Book Club, 1951).

BURKE, THOMAS, *English Night-Life* (Batsford, 1941).

——*Nights in Town* (Allen & Unwin, 1915).

BURNAND, SIR FRANCIS C., *Records and Reminiscences* (Methuen, 1903).

BUSBY, ROY, *British Music Hall: An Illustrated Who's Who* (Elek, 1976).

CAVE, JOSEPH A., *A Jubilee of Dramatic Life and Incident*, ed. Robert Soutar (Thomas Vernon, 1892).

CHESHIRE, D. F., *Music Hall in Britain* (David & Charles, 1974).

CHEVALIER, ALBERT, *Before I Forget* (T. Fisher Unwin, 1901).

—— and DALY, BRIAN, *A Record by Himself* (John Macqueen, 1895).

CHIRGWIN, G. H., *Chirgwin's Chirrup* (J. & J. Bennett, 1912).

CLARKE, DONALD, *The Rise and Fall of Popular Music* (Viking, 1995).

COBORN, CHARLES, *The Man Who Broke the Bank* (Hutchinson, 1927).

COCHRAN, CHARLES, *The Secrets of a Showman* (Heinemann, 1925).

COFFIN, HAYDEN, *Hayden Coffin's Book* (Alston Rivers, 1930).

COHEN-STRATYNER, BARBARA (ed.), *Popular Music 1900–19* (Detroit: Gale Research Co., 1988).

COLLINS, JOSÉ, *The Maid of the Mountains* (Hutchinson, 1932).

COOPER, MARGARET, *Myself and my Piano* (Ouseley, 1909).

COOVER, JAMES, *Music Publishing, Copyright & Piracy in Victorian England* (Mansell, 1985).

COTES, PETER, *George Robey* (Cassell, 1972).

CROXTON, ARTHUR, *Crowded Nights—and Days* (Sampson Low, 1934).

DAVENPORT, MARCIA, *Too Strong for Fantasy* (Collins, 1968).

DAVIDSON, GLADYS, *Standard Stories from the Operas* (Bodley Head, 1944).

DAVIS, JIM (ed.), *The Britannia Diaries 1863–1875* (Society for Theatre Research, 1992).

DAWSON, PETER, *Fifty Years of Song* (Hutchinson, 1951).

DE COURVILLE, ALBERT, *I Tell You* (Chapman & Hall, 1928).

DEGHY, GUY, *Paradise in the Strand* (Richards Press, 1958).

DELGADO, ALAN, *Victorian Entertainment* (Victorian & Modern History Book Club, 1972).

DICKENS, CHARLES, *Memoirs of Joseph Grimaldi*, ed. Richard Findlater (Macgibbon & Kee, 1968).

Dictionary of Catch Phrases, A, ed. Eric Partridge (Routledge & Kegan Paul, 1983).

Dictionary of Historical Slang, ed. Eric Partridge (Penguin, 1972).

Dictionary of Modern Music and Musicians, ed. A. Eaglefield-Hill (Dent, 1924).

Dictionary of National Biography

Dictionary of Popular Phrases, ed. Nigel Rees (Bloomsbury, 1990).

DISHER, M. WILLSON, *Fairs, Circuses and Music Halls* (William Collins, 1942).

—— *Romance of the Music Hall* (included in Francis, Day & Hunter's thirty-part *Music Hall Memories*, 1935–7).

—— *Victorian Song* (Phoenix House, 1955).

—— *Winkles and Champagne* (Batsford, 1938).

DOLPH, EDWARD ARTHUR, *Sounds Off!* (New York: Farrar & Rinehart, 1942).

DUNVILLE, T. E., *Autobiography of an Eccentric Comedian* (Everett, 1912).

Encyclopaedia Britannica

Encyclopedia Americana

English Theatrical Literature 1559–1900: A Bibliography, A recension of Robert W. Lowe's 1888 bibliography by James Fullerton Arnott and J. William Robinson (Society for Theatre Research, 1970).

EWEN, DAVID, *American Vaudeville, its Life and Times* (New York: Funk & Wagnall, 1940).

—— (comp. and ed.), *Popular American Composers* (New York: H. W. Wilson, 1962).

FARSON, DANIEL, *Marie Lloyd and Music Hall* (Stacey, 1972).

FELSTEAD, S. THEODORE, *Stars who Made the Halls* (Werner Laurie, 1946).

FERGUSSON, SIR LOUIS, *Old Time Music Hall Comedians* (Leicester: Gee, 1949).

FINCK, HERMAN, *My Melodious Memories* (Hutchinson, 1937).

FINDLATER, RICHARD, *Grimaldi, King of Clowns* (MacGibbon & Kee, 1955).

——and TICH, MARY, *Little Tich* (Elm Tree, 1979).

FISHER, JOHN, *Funny Way to be a Hero* (Frederick Muller, 1973).

FITZGERALD, PERCY, *Music-Hall Land* (Ward & Downey, 1890).

FITZ-GERALD, S. J. ADAIR, *Stories of Famous Songs* (John C. Nimmo, 1898).

FLANAGAN, BUD, *My Crazy Life* (Frederick Muller, 1961).

FOSTER, GEORGE, *The Spice of Life* (Hurst & Blackett, 1939).

FRASER, MARJORIE KENNEDY, *A Life of Song* (Oxford University Press, 1929).

FROW, GERALD, *Oh, Yes It Is!: A History of Pantomime* (BBC, 1985).

FULD, JAMES J., *The Book of World-Famous Music* (New York: Crown, 1966).

GALLAGHER, J. P., *Fred Karno: Master of Mirth and Tears* (R. Hale, 1971).

GAMMOND, PETER, *Oxford Companion to Popular Music* (Oxford University Press, 1991).

GANTHONY, ROBERT, *Random Recollections* (H. J. Drane, 1899).

GANZL, KURT, *The British Musical Theatre, The*, 2 vols. (Macmillan, 1986).

——and LAMB, ANDREW, *Ganzl's Book of the Musical Theatre* (Bodley Head, 1988).

GARDINER, JAMES, *Gaby Deslys: A Fatal Attraction* (Sidgwick & Jackson, 1986).

GILBERT, DOUGLAS, *American Vaudeville: Its Life & Times* (New York, McGraw-Hill, 1940).

——*Lost Chords: The Diverting Story of American Popular Songs* (New York: Cooper Square, 1970).

GLOVER, JIMMY, *Hims Ancient and Modern* (Unwin, 1926).

——*Jimmy Glover and his Friends* (Chatto, 1913).

——*Jimmy Glover—His Book* (Methuen, 1911).

GOLDMAN, HERBERT G., *Fanny Brice* (Oxford University Press, 1992).

GOOCH, BRYAN N. S., and THATCHER, DAVID S. (comp.), *Musical Settings of British Romantic Literature: A Catalogue*, 2 vols. (New York: Garland Publishing, 1982).

—— ——*Musical Settings of Early and Mid-Victorian Literature: A Catalogue* (New York: Garland Publishing, 1979).

—— ——*Musical Settings of Late Victorian and Modern British Literature: A Catalogue* (New York: Garland Publishing, 1976).

GRAIN, CORNEY, *Corney Grain by Himself* (John Murray, 1888).

Gramophone Shop Encyclopedia of Recorded Music, The (New York: Crown, 1948).

GRAVES, GEORGE, *Gaieties and Gravities* (Hutchinson, 1931).

GRAY, GEORGE, *Vagaries of a Vagabond* (Heath Cranton, 1920).

GREEN, ABEL, and LAURIE, JOE, JR., *Show Biz: From Vaude to Video* (New York: Holt, 1951).

GREEN, BENNY (ed.), *The Last Empires* (Pavilion, 1986).

GREEN, STANLEY, *Encyclopaedia of the Musical* (Cassell, 1976).

Green Room Book, The, ed. Bampton Hunt (1906) and John Parker (1907–9); continued as *Who's Who in the Theatre* (q.v.).

GREGSON, KEITH, *Corvan: A Victorian Entertainer* (Banbury: Kemble Press, 1983).

GRIEVE, AVERIL MACKENZIE, *Clara Novello 1818–1908* (Geoffrey Bles, 1955).

GROCK, *Grock: King of Clowns*, ed. Ernst Konstantin, trans. Basil Creighton (Methuen, 1957).

GROSSMITH, GEORGE, SEN., *Birthday Book* (Bristol: Arrowsmith, 1904).

——*Piano and I* (Bristol: Arrowsmith, 1910).

——*A Society Clown* (Bristol: Arrowsmith, 1888).

GROSSMITH, GEORGE, JUN., *GG* (Hutchinson, 1933).

Grove's Dictionary of Music and Musicians (sundry editions).

GUILBERT, YVETTE, and SIMPSON, HAROLD, *Yvette Guilbert* (Mills & Boon, 1910).

HADDON, ARCHIBALD, *Green Room Gossip* (Stanley Paul, 1922).

——*The Story of Music Hall* (Cecil Palmer, 1924). (NB. Little more than a pamphlet inveighing against the licensing laws. The 1935 version is much more comprehensive.)

——*The Story of Music Hall* (Fleetway, 1935).

HAILL, CATHERINE, *Fun Without Vulgarity* (Stationery Office, 1996).

——*Victorian Illustrated Musical Sheets* (HMSO, 1981).

HAMM, CHARLES, *Yesterday's Popular Song in America* (New York: Norton, 1979).

HARDING, JAMES, *Cochran* (Methuen, 1988).

——*George Robey and the Music Hall* (Hodder & Stoughton, 1990).

HARDY, PHIL, and LAING, DAVE, *Faber Companion to 20th Century Popular Music* (Faber & Faber, 1990).

HARRIS, CHARLES K., *How to Write a Popular Song* (C. K. Harris, 1906).

HARRISON, CLIFFORD, *Stray Records* (R. Bentley & Son, 1892).

HATTON, JOSEPH, *Reminiscences of J. L. Toole* (Hurst & Blackett, 1889).

HAWTREY, CHARLES, *The Truth at Last*, ed. W. Somerset Maugham (Thornton Butterworth, 1924).

HELLICAR, EILEEN, *But Who On Earth Was..?* (Newton Abbot: David & Charles, 1981); revised as *The Real McCoy* (Reader's Digest, 1982).

HENSON, LESLIE, *Yours Faithfully* (John Long, 1948).

HERBERT, MIRANDA C., and McNEIL, BARBARA (eds.), *Biography and Genealogy Master Index* (Detroit: Gale Research Co., 1980).

————*Theater, Film and Television Biographies Master Index* (Detroit: Gale Research Co., 1980).

HIBBERT, H. G., *A Playgoer's Memories* (Grant Richards, 1920).

HICKS, SEYMOUR, *Night Lights* (Cassell, 1938).

——*Seymour Hicks: Twenty-Four Years of an Actor's Life* (Alston Rivers, 1910).

HINDLEY, CHARLES, *The Life and Times of James Catnatch* (Reeves & Turner, 1878).

HOLLINGSHEAD, JOHN, *Gaiety Chronicles* (Archibald Constable, 1898).

——*Good Old Gaiety* (Gaiety, 1903).

——*My Lifetime*, 2 vols. (Sampson Low, 1895).

HONRI, PETER, *John Wilton's Music Hall* (Ian Henry, 1985).

——*Music Hall Warriors: A History of the Variety Artistes' Federation 1906–1967* (Greenwich Exchange, 1997).

——*Working the Halls* (Saxon House, 1973).

HOUSE, JACK, *Music Hall Memories* (Glasgow: Richard Drew, 1986).

HOWARD, DIANA, *London Theatres and Music Halls 1850–1950* (Library Assn., 1970).

HUGHES, RUPERT, *Music Lovers' Encyclopedia*, rev. and ed. Deems Taylor and Russell Kerr (Macdonald, 1955).

HUMPHRIES, CHARLES, and SMITH, WILLIAM C., *Music Publishing in the British Isles* (Oxford: Basil Blackwell, 1970).

HUTCHINSON, JOHN WALLACE, *The Story of the Hutchinsons*, comp. and ed. Charles E. Mann, 2 vols. (Boston: Lee & Shepard 1914).

HYMAN, ALAN, *The Gaiety Years* (Cassell, 1975).

IMESON, W. R., *Illustrated Music Titles and their Delineators* (private pub., 1912).

JACKSON, GEORGE PULLEN, *White and Negro Spirituals* (New York: J. J. Augustine, 1943).

JACOB, NAOMI, *Our Marie* (Hutchinson, 1936; repr. Bath: Chivers, 1972).

——*Me: A Chronicle about Other People* (Bath: Chivers, 1933).

JANIS, ELSIE, *So Far So Good!* (New York: E. P. Dutton, 1932).

JASEN, DAVID A., *Tin Pan Alley* (New York: Omnibus, 1988).

JOHN, CLAUDIA D., and JOHNSON, VERNON E. (comp.), *Nineteenth-Century Theatrical Memoirs* (Westport, Conn.: Greenwood Press, 1982).

KINKLE, ROGER D. (ed.), *Concise Encyclopedia of Popular Music and Jazz 1900–1950* (New Rochelle, NY: Arlington House, 1974).

KLAMKIN, MARIAN, *Old Sheet Music* (New York: Hawthorn, 1975).

KNOWLES, R. G., *A Modern Columbus* (T. Werner Laurie, 1915).

Kobbé's Complete Opera Book, ed. and rev. Earl of Harewood (Bodley Head, 1987).

KOON, HELENE WICKHAM, *Gold Rush Performers* (McFarlan & Co., 1994).

KRUMMEL, DONALD W., and SADIE, STANLEY (eds.), *Music Printing and Publishing* (Macmillan, 1980).

KUTSCH, K. J., and RIEMENS, LEO, *Concise Biographical Dictionary of Singers*, transl. and expanded Harry Earl Jones (Philadelphia: Chilton, 1969).

LAFFEY, BRUCE, *Beatrice Lillie* (Robson, 1990).

LAMB, ANDREW, *Jerome Kern in Edwardian London* (private pub., 1981).

LAUDER, SIR HARRY, *Roamin' in the Gloamin'* (Hutchinson, 1927).

LAURIE, JOE, JR., *Vaudeville: From the Honky Tonks to the Palace* (New York: Henry Holt, 1953).

LAX, ROGER, and SMITH, FRED, *The Great Song Thesaurus* (New York: Oxford University Press, 1989).

LEE, EDWARD, *Music of the People* (Barrie & Jenkins, 1970).

LEHMANN, LIZA, *The Life of Liza Lehmann* (T. Fisher Unwin, 1919).

LE ROY, GEORGE, *Music Hall Stars of the Nineties* (British Technical & General Press, 1952).

LE WHITE, JACK, and FORD, PETER, *Rings & Curtains* (Quartet Books, 1992).

LEWINE, RICHARD, and SIMON, ALFRED, *Songs of the Theater* (New York: H. W. Wilson, 1894).

LOWE, LESLIE, *Directory of Popular Music 1900–1980* (Peterson, 1986).

LUPINO, STANLEY, *From the Stocks to the Stars* (Hutchinson, 1934).

MacGEORGE, ETHEL, *The Life of Jessie Bond* (John Lane, 1930).

MacINNES, COLIN, *Sweet Saturday Night* (MacGibbon & Kee, 1967).

McKECHNIE, SAMUEL, *Popular Entertainment through the Ages* (Sampson Low, 1931).

MACKINLAY, M. STERLING, *Antoinette Sterling and Other Celebrities* (Hutchinson, 1906).

MACQUEEN-POPE, W., *Carriages at Eleven* (Hutchinson, 1947).

——*Gaiety: Theatre of Enchantment* (W. H. Allen, 1949).

——*The Melodies Linger On* (W. H. Allen, 1950).

——*Queen of the Music Halls* (Oldbourne, 1957).

MANDER, RAYMOND, and MITCHENSON, JOE, *British Music Hall* (Studio Vista, 1965; rev. edn. Gentry Books, 1974).

————*Lost Theatres of London* (Hart-Davis, 1968).

————*Revue: A Story in Pictures* (Peter Davies, 1971).

————*Victorian and Edwardian Entertainment* (Batsford 1978).

MANVELL, ROGER, *Ellen Terry* (Heinemann, 1968).

MARKS, EDWARD B., *They All Had Glamour* (New York: Julian Messner, 1944).

——*They All Sang* (New York: Viking, 1935).

MATTFELD, JULIUS (comp.), *Variety Music Cavalcade 1620–1950* (New York: Prentice-Hall, 1952).

MELLOR, GEOFF J., *The Northern Music Hall* (Newcastle: Graham, 1970).

——*They Made Us Laugh* (Littleborough, Lancs.: Kelsall, 1982).

MERSON, BILLY, *Fixing the Stoof Oop* (Hutchinson, 1926).

MILLER, RUBY, *Believe Me or Not* (John Lang, 1933).

MORELL, P., *Lillian Russell: The Era of Plush* (New York: Random House, 1940).

MORTON, RICHARD, *The Adventures of Arthur Roberts* (Arrowsmith's Bristol Library, 65 (1895)).

MORTON, WILLIAM, and NEWTON, H. CHANCE, *Sixty Years' Stage Service* (Gale & Polden, 1905).

MOZART, GEORGE, *Limelight* (Hurst & Blackett, 1938).

NASH, JOLLY JOHN, *The Merriest Man Alive* (General Publishing Co., 1891).

NATHAN, HANS, *Dan Emmett and the Rise of Early Negro Minstrelsy* (Norman: University of Oklahoma Press, 1962).

NETTEL, REGINALD, *Seven Centuries of Popular Song* (Phoenix, 1956).

New Everyman Dictionary of Music, 6th edn., ed. Eric Blom, rev. David Cummings (Everyman, 1988).

New Grove Dictionary of Jazz, ed. Barry Kernfeld, 2 vols. (Macmillan, 1988).

NEWTON, H. CHANCE, *Cues and Curtain Calls* (John Lane, 1927).

——*Idols of the Halls* (Heath Cranton, 1928; facs. repr. E. P. Publishing, 1977).

NICOLL, ALLARDYCE (ed.), *English Drama 1900–1930* (Cambridge: Cambridge University Press, 1973).

O'CONNOR, T. P. (comp. and intro.), *In the Days of my Youth* (C. Arthur Pearson, 1901).

O'DOWDA, BRENDAN, *The World of Percy French* (Blackstaff, Dundonald, 1981).

O'HARA, MARY, *A Song for Ireland* (Michael Joseph, 1982).

Oxford Companion to Music, ed. Percy V. Scholes, 10th edn., rev. John Owen Ward (Oxford University Press, 1993).

Oxford Companion to the Theatre, 3rd edn., ed. Phyllis Hartnoll (Oxford University Press, 1967).

PALMER, ROY, *A Ballad History of England* (B. T. Batsford, 1979).

PARKHURST, WINTHROP, and BEKKER, L. J. DE, *Encyclopedia of Music and Musicians* (New York: Crown, 1937).

PARKINSON, JOHN A., *Victorian Music Publishers* (Warren, Mich.: Harmonie Park Press, 1990).

PASTOR, TONY, *Tony Pastor's Irish American Song Book* (Cameron & Ferguson, 1870).

PEARL, CYRIL, *The Girl with the Swansdown Seat* (Fred. Muller, 1955).

PEARSALL, RONALD, *Edwardian Popular Music* (David & Charles, 1975).

——*Popular Music of the Twenties* (David & Charles, 1976).

——*Victorian Popular Music* (David & Charles, 1973).

——*Victorian Sheet Music Covers* (David & Charles, 1972).

PERRY, JEB H., *Variety Obits 1905–78* (Metuchen, NJ: Scarecrow, 1980).

PLANCHÉ, J. B., *Recollections and Reflections*, 2 vols. (Tinsley Bros., 1872).

PRATT, ALFRED T. CAMDEN (ed.), *People of the Period*, 2 vols. (N. Beeman, 1897).

PULLING, CHRISTOPHER, *They Were Singing* (Harrap, 1952).

RANDALL, HARRY, *Harry Randall—Old Time Comedian* (Sampson Low, 1931).

READ, JACK, *Empires, Hippodromes & Palaces* (Alderman, 1985).

REEVE, ADA, *Take it for a Fact* (Heinemann, 1954).

REEVES, J. SIMS, *My Jubilee* (London Music Publishers, 1889).

Reeves' Dictionary of Musicians, ed. Edmonstone Duncan (Reeves, 1926).

RENDLE, T. McDONALD, *Swings & Roundabouts* (Chapman & Hall, 1919).

REYNOLDS, HARRY, *Minstrel Memories* (Alston Rivers, 1928).

RITCHIE, JAMES EWING, *Days and Nights in London* (Tinsley Bros., 1880).

——*The Night Side of London* (William Teedie, 1857).

RIVIÈRE, JULES, *My Musical Life and Recollections* (Low Martson, 1893).

ROBERTS, ARTHUR, *Fifty Years of Spoof* (John Lane, 1927).

ROBEY, GEORGE, *Looking Back On Life* (Constable, 1953).

——*My Life Up Till Now* (Greening, 1908).

ROSE, CLARKSON, *Red Plush and Greasepaint* (Museum, 1964).

——*With a Twinkle in my Eye* (Museum, 1951).

RUSSELL, DAVE, *Popular Music in England 1840–1914* (Manchester: Manchester University Press, 1987).

RUSSELL, FRED, *On Ventriloquism and Kindred Arts* (Keith Prowse, 1898).

RUST, BRIAN, *My Kind of Jazz* (Elm Tree, 1990).

——(comp.), *British Music Hall on Record* (Gramophone, 1979).

——*Complete Entertainment Discography, The* (New Rochelle, NY: Arlington Gramophone Publications, 1977).

——*London Musical Shows on Record 1897–1976* (General House, 1973).

SANDERSON, MICHAEL, *From Irving to Olivier: A Social History of the Acting Profession 1880–1983* (Athlone, 1984).

SANDS, MOLLIE, *Robson of the Olympic* (Society for Theatre Research, 1979).

SANJEK, RUSSELL, *American Popular Music and its Business*, ii (1790–1909). (Oxford University Press, 1988).

SCOTT, HAROLD, *The Early Doors* (Ivor Nicholson & Watson, 1946; repr. E. P. Publishing, 1977).

SEATON, RAY, and MARTIN, ROY, *Good Morning, Boys* (Barrie & Jenkins, 1978).

SENELICK, LAURENCE, CHESHIRE, DAVID F., and SCHNEIDER, ULRICH, *British Music-Hall 1840–1923: A Bibliography and Guide to Sources* (Archon, 1981).

SHAPIRO, NAT, and POLLOCK, BRUCE (eds.), *Popular Music 1920–79*, 3 vols. (Detroit: Gale Research Co., 1985).

SHERIDAN, PAUL, *Late and Early Joys at the Players' Theatre* (Boardman, 1952).

SHORT, ERNEST, *Fifty Years of Vaudeville* (Eyre & Spottiswoode, 1946).

——and COMPTON-RICKETT, ARTHUR, *Ring up the Curtain* (H. Jenkins, 1938).

SIMPSON, HAROLD, *A Century of Ballads 1810–1910* (Mills & Boon, 1910).

SIMS, GEORGE R., *Ballads of Babylon* (J. P. Fuller, 1880).

——*Dagonet Ballads* (J. P. Fuller, 1879).

——*My Life* (Eveleigh Nash, 1917).

SITWELL, SACHEVERELL, *Morning, Noon and Night in London* (Macmillan, 1948).

SOBEL, BERNARD, *Burleycue* (New York: Farrar & Rinehart, 1931).

SOLDENE, EMILY, *My Theatrical and Musical Recollections* (Sealey Clark, 1897).

SPAETH, SIGMUND, *The Facts of Life in Popular Song* (New York: McGraw-Hill, 1934).

——*A History of Popular Music in America* (New York: Random House, 1948).

SPELL, D. and S., *Victorian Music Covers* (Levely, Adams & Mackay, 1969).

SPURR, HARRY A., *Mel B. Spurr* (A. Brown, 1905).

SPURR, MEL B., *Recitals and Monologues in Prose and Verse* (Samuel French, 1899; repr. 1920).

STEWART, HAL D., *Players' Joys* (King & Jackson, 1962).

STRATMAN, CARL J., *Britain's Theatrical Periodicals 1720–1967: A Bibliography* (New York: New York Public Library, 1972).

STUART, CHARLES DOUGLAS, and PARK, A. J., *The Variety Stage* (Fisher Unwin, 1895).

SUDWORTH, GWYNEDD, *The Great Little Tilley* (Cortney, 1984).

TERRISS, ELLALINE, *Just a Little Bit of String* (Hutchinson, 1955).

TICH, LITTLE, *A Book of Travels and Wanderings* (Greening, 1911).

TILLEY, VESTA, *Recollections of Vesta Tilley* (Hutchinson, 1934).

TIMBS, JOHN, *Club Life of London* (Bentley, 1866).

TITTERTON, W. R., *From Theatre to Music Hall* (Swift, 1912).

TOLL, ROBERT C., *Blacking Up—The Minstrel Show in Nineteenth-Century America* (New York: Oxford University Press, 1974).

TRAUBNER, RICHARD, *Operetta: A Theatrical History* (Victor Gollancz, 1984).

VARIETY PUBLISHING, *Variety Stars* (Variety Publishing Co., 1895).

VICINUS, MARTHA, *The Industrial Muse* (Croom Helm, 1974).

WALKER, WHIMSICAL, *From Sawdust to Windsor Castle* (Stanley Paul, 1922).

WALSH, COLIN (comp. and ed.), *There Goes that Song Again* (Elm Tree/EMI, 1971).

WATTERS, EUGENE, and MURTAGH, MATTHEW, *Infinite Variety: Dan Lowrey's Music Hall 1879–97* (Dublin: Gill & Macmillan, 1975).

WEARING, J. P., *American & British Theatrical Biography* (Metuchen, NJ: Scarecrow, 1979).

——(comp.), *The London Stage 1910–16* (Metuchen, NJ: Scarecrow, 1982).

WEATHERLY, FRED E., *Piano and Gown* (Putnam 1926).

WHITCOMB, IAN, *After the Ball* (Allen Lane, 1972).

——*Irving Berlin and Ragtime America* (Century, 1987).

Who's Who in Music, comp. and ed. H. Saxe Wyndham and Geoffrey L'Epine (Pitman, 1913).; ed. Sir Landon Ronald (Shaw, 1937); ed. L. G. Pine (Love & Malcomson, 1949–50).

Who's Who in the Theatre, 14 edns., 1912–67 (Pitman's). See also *Green Room Book.*

Who Was Who in America 1607–1993, 10 vols. (Chicago: Marquis, 1963).

Who Was Who in the Theatre 1912-76, 4 vols. (Detroit: Gale Publishing, 1978).

WILDER, ALEC, *American Popular Song* (Oxford University Press, 1972).

WILK, MAX, *Memory Lane 1890–1925* (New York: Studio Art, 1973).

WILLIAMS, BRANSBY, *Bransby Williams by Himself* (Hutchinson, 1954).

WILLIAMSON, DAVID (ed.), *The German Reeds and Corney Grain* (Innes, 1895).

WILLIS, FREDERICK, *101 Jubilee Road: A Book of London Yesterdays* (Phoenix House, 1948).

WILMUT, ROGER, *Kindly Leave the Stage!* (Methuen, 1985).

WILSON, A. E., *East End Entertainment* (Arthur Barker, 1954).

——*Edwardian Theatre* (Arthur Barker, 1951).

——*The Lyceum* (Dennis Yates, 1952).

WOOD, JAY HICKORY, *Dan Leno* (Methuen, 1905).

World Film Encyclopedia, The, ed. Clarence Winchester (Amalgamated Press, 1933).

WYNDHAM, HORACE, *Chorus to Coronet* (British Technical & General Press, 1951).

ZELLERS, PARKER RICHARDSON, *Tony Pastor: Dean of the Vaudeville Stage* (Ypsilanti: Eastern Michigan University Press, 1971).

ZIEGLER, PHILIP, *Diana Cooper* (Hamish Hamilton, 1981).

INDEX OF SONG AND SKETCH TITLES

Z